KIDS' SLIPS

What Young Children's Slips of the Tongue Reveal About Language Development

KIDS' SLIPS

What Young Children's Slips of the Tongue Reveal About Language Development

Jeri J. Jaeger

Department of Linguistics and
Center for Cognitive Science
University at Buffalo
The State University of New York

LAWRENCE ERLBAUM ASSOCIATES, PUBLISHERS
2005   Mahwah, New Jersey   London

Lawrence Erlbaum Associates, Inc., Publishers
10 Industrial Avenue
Mahwah, New Jersey 07430
www.erlbaum.com

Cover design by Kathryn Houghtaling Lacey

Copyrighted material used in chapter 6 by permission; Levelt, W. (1989). *Speaking: From intention to articulation*. Cambridge, MA: MIT Press.

Library of Congress Cataloging-in-Publication Data

Jaeger, Jeri J.
  Kids's slips : what young children's slips of the tongue reveal about language development / Jeri J. Jaeger.
      p. cm.

Includes bibliographical references and index.

ISBN 0-8058-3579-2 (alk. paper)
1. Language acquisition. 2. Speech errors. I. Title.
P118.J26   2004
401'.93—dc22   2004050605
                                                    CIP

Books published by Lawrence Erlbaum Associates are printed on acid-free paper, and their bindings are chosen for strength and durability.

Printed in the United States of America
10 9 8 7 6 5 4 3 2 1

Contents

Chapter 1: Kids' Slips as Evidence for Language Development

Chapter 2: Kids' Slips and Adults' Slips: General Comparison

Chapter 3: Phonetics and Phonology

Chapter 4: The Lexicon and Lexical Errors

Chapter 5: Semantic Relationships in Lexical Errors

Chapter 6: Morphology and Syntax

The adult data can be accessed at the following website:
http://linguistics.buffalo.edu/people/faculty/jaeger/adultSOT.html

Tables

Chapter 4

Chapter 5

Chapter 6

Figures and Diagrams

Preface

The seeds of this book were sown in the spring of 1986, when I was having dinner with a colleague whom I had not seen in some time. He asked me what I was working on, and I told him I was studying my daughter Anna's language acquisition longitudinally, and I was particularly interested in her slips of the tongue. He looked at me in surprise, and informed me that it was a well-known fact that children do not make slips of the tongue until they are seven years old, and that this fact was related to brain lateralization. At this point I realized I was onto something. I subsequently sent him a list of 100 of Anna's slips, made between 19 months and 3 years of age, and he wrote back that perhaps this theory about the development of lateralization in the child would have to be reconsidered.

These data were collected between 1983 when Anna made her first slip, through 1992 when Bobby turned 6. The analysis of the data and the writing of the current book occupied the next decade of my professional life. With a project this extensive, there have naturally been a very large number of people who have contributed their ideas, criticism, and enthusiasm, and thus many thanks are in order.

First, I would like to thank colleagues who have contributed some of the data from the children other than my own in this study; this includes Alicia Hoeft-Atkinson, Melissa Bowerman, and Greg Guy. Second, I would like to thank my colleagues at the University at Buffalo, past and present, who have contributed greatly to the substance of this book. Chapters 4 and 5 were originally written as a manuscript with David Wilkins, and the analysis, particularly the semantic analyses of each of the data entries, would have been impossible without his input. Jean Pierre Koenig also gave me very valuable feedback on Chapter 5. Both Robert Van Valin and Karin Michelson have read most of the book, and have given me voluminous comments on everything from commas to my theoretical analysis. Michelle Gregory showed me how to use the Latent Semantic Analysis program. Third, I am grateful to colleagues at the Max Planck Institute for Psycholinguistics in Nijmegen, where I was a visiting researcher for a month in 1996; I benefited greatly from input from Ann Cutler, Melissa Bowerman, Willem Levelt, Antje Meyer, and David Wilkins. I appreciate very much the support and input from all of these colleagues.

Next, I need to thank the members of the University at Buffalo Cross-Linguistic Slips of the Tongue Research Group, past and present. In particular, Kazuhiro Kawachi, Jennifer Cornish, and Myo Young Kim have read most of this book and given me detailed comments and insights. Other member of this group who have contributed to this project one way or another include: Elfride Aertsen, Ed Akiwumi, Osamu Amazaki, Ameyo Awuku, Wendy Baldwin, Charles Belair, Kathy Conklin, Ardis Eschenberg, Lilian Guerrero, Sun Young Hong, Sabrina Hsiao, Taeho Kim, Gabriella Kiraly, Viktoriya Lyakh, Mei Han

Low, Haesik Min, Hide Miura, Nuttanart Muansuwan, Kimio Tanihara, Michael Vitevitch, I-Ping Wan, and Sheri Wells-Jensen. I have greatly benefited from having thoughtful, intelligent, enthusiastic students who have enormously improved the clarity, consistency, and depth of this book. The editing of the data was supported by a State of New York/United University Professions Individual Development Award.

Turning closer to home, I would like to thank my parents, Chester and Eileen Jaeger, for allowing us to impose on them during our sabbatical in 1998, so that I could work on the original outline of the book. I also offer heartfelt thanks and appreciation to my husband, Robert Van Valin, for his unflagging support during this seemingly endless project.

My greatest debt of gratitude goes to my three children, Anna, Alice, and Bobby, and to the other children in this study, for allowing me to listen in on the wonders of their language acquisition process. This book is dedicated to my children.

To Anna, Alice, and Bobby

Chapter 1
Kids' Slips as Evidence for Language Development

1.1 Slips of the Tongue and Language Development

1.1.1 Prologue

On December 28, 1986, Anna, who was 4 years old at the time, her siblings, and her cousins were acting out an elaborate version of 'The Three Little Pigs' for assorted parents, aunts and uncles, and grandparents, in her grandparents' living room. One of the cousins, as the Big Bad Wolf, demanded 'Little Pig, Little Pig, let me come in!' Anna, as the Little Pig, retorted 'No! Not by the chair of my hinny hin hin!' As the other members of the cast and audience dissolved into laughter, I opened my ever-present notebook and made the following entry:

> *"12-28-86*
> OC: 'Little Pig, Little Pig, let me come in!'
> AN: 'Nó! Nòt by the [tʃèr] of my [hì.ni hìn hín]!'
> *(Reversal [tʃ] for [h], repeated. Noticed, looked embarrassed, but didn't correct because lots of people laughed at her. Context: acting out 3 little pigs with cousins at Grandma's)"*

I then soothed Anna's feelings, and the play continued.

1.1.2 Slips of the Tongue: A New Methodology for the Study of Language Development

The development of language production has been an area of intense investigation for researchers interested in both theoretical and descriptive issues in language acquisition, for both normal and abnormal language learners. The predominant methodology has been longitudinal observation of children's spontaneous speech, analyzing, for example, children's systematic substitutions and omissions in phonology (Ingram 1986), overgeneralizations in morphology (Marcus et al. 1992) and semantics (Clark 1973, 1993), and increase in complexity of syntactic frames (Brown 1973). Other researchers have performed cross-sectional experiments, asking children of various ages to manipulate linguistic units and constructions in ways which will reveal their current knowledge and abilities (Berko 1958, Menn & Bernstein Ratner 2000). One of the main purposes of this book is to add a new methodology to the study of language production: the examination of slips of the tongue made by very young children.

New? Of course slips of the tongue made by adults have been studied intensively for at least a century. Because they have been considered such a rich source of data for models of adult language representation and speech production planning, it seems obvious that an extension of this methodology to child language production could provide a wealth of new insights into exactly what a child knows about the units and processes involved in speech production at any particular time in his or her development. However, there is a major methodological drawback to the study of slips of the tongue made by young children, which becomes clear once a definition of 'slips of the tongue' is presented.

I define a slip of the tongue as a one-time error in speech production planning; that is, the speaker intends to utter a particular word, phrase, or sentence, and during the planning process something goes wrong, so that the production is at odds with the plan. It is not simply a misarticulation (e.g. stuttering or mumbling), a lack of knowledge or memory slip (where the speaker doesn't know the correct word or can't remember it at the moment), or a false start (where the speaker changes his or her mind about the propositional content of the utterance). Speakers themselves will consider the utterance to contain an error, and will often correct it immediately, sometimes with commentary on the silliness of what they have said. Extending this definition to child language, the crucial premise of the current study is that *a slip of the tongue cannot be made on a structure unless that structure has already been learned or acquired*. This is because an utterance cannot be considered to be an error *from the child's point of view*, unless the child has a standard within his or her own system by which to judge the utterance. Note that this definition of 'error' is different from one commonly used in child language studies, in which the standard by which the child's utterance is judged is the adult model (e.g. Locke 1980). Of course children produce many utterances which are different from the adult model because they haven't yet mastered the adult forms. However, if slips of the tongue made by children are to be considered the same phenomenon as adult slips, then only the child's current knowledge is relevant as a standard by which to judge the utterance.

Thus the crucial question is: *Can* you tell when a 2-year-old has made a mistake, and if so, *how*? That is, how can you tell that a 2-year-old thinks she has made an error, compared to what she had planned to say? The answer to the first question is that *you can*. The answer to the second question will become clear as this book progresses.

In this introductory chapter I will first give a brief overview of slips of the tongue (hereafter SOTs) in linguistic research, including mention of the few studies which have focussed on child data. I will then introduce a model of speech production planning which will be used as a reference model in this study. The methodology of the data collection and the subjects in this study will then be described in detail. The classification system used to categorize errors will be presented and justified, followed by a discussion of principles involved in making decisions on ambiguous cases; this section ends with a discussion of how the various types of errors relate to the speech production planning model. Finally I briefly discuss three general issues at the heart of this research: when do children begin making slips, are there individual differences in error production, and can both qualitative and quantitative comparisons be made both across the children's data and between child and adult slips?

1.1.3 Overview of SOT Research in Adults and Children

SOTs have been collected and analyzed by many researchers for different kinds of reasons. Originally they were considered a window to the subconscious, i.e. of interest as 'Freudian Slips' (Meringer & Mayer 1895, Freud 1973/1901, Yazmajian 1965). More recently they have been taken as a rich source of evidence regarding the mental representations and operations involved in speech production planning, and they have also been used to address controversial issues of linguistic structure in specific languages. Most current theories of speech production planning are based heavily on SOT data, for example Fromkin (1973a, 1983, 1988), Garrett (1975, 1980a,b, 1984, 1993), Levelt (1989, Bock & Levelt 1994), Dell (Dell & Reich 1980, 1981, Dell 1986, Dell, Juliano & Govindjee 1993), and Stemberger (1985, 1993). The actual collection and analysis of slips data probably peaked in the 1970s and 1980s, with the publication of three landmark books on this topic: Fromkin (1973b), Fromkin (1980), and Cutler (1982b). Currently there seems to be less research being conducted using this methodology, although some researchers continue to be active in this paradigm (see, for example, Harley et al. 1995, Bock 1996, Dell, Burger & Svec 1997, Gupta & Dell 1999, Harley & MacAndrew 2001, Raymond 2001).

There is probably one main reason for the ebb of SOT research, which is that most of the studies have been based on adult English. Furthermore, most of the well-known non-English corpora of slips have been collected from adult speakers of Dutch and German (Meringer & Mayer 1895, Schelvis 1985, Berg 1987a,b, Levelt 1989), and not surprisingly they have not revealed major differences from the results of studies on English. After tens of thousands of SOTs made by adult speakers of English, Dutch, and German have been collected and analyzed, some researchers have felt that there is simply not much left to be learned from this data source (Meyer 1992). For this reason, this research methodology has to some extent fallen by the wayside in recent years.

This seems like a waste of a good research methodology. The obvious way to revive it would be to expand the database to subjects other than normal adult speakers of English. Looking at data from adult speakers of other languages is of course the simplest extension, and fortunately there is an upsurge of this sort of research currently taking place, particularly by Berg and colleagues (Berg 1987a, 1991, Berg & Abd-El-Jawad 1996) and in our Cross-Linguistic Slips of the Tongue Research Group at the University at Buffalo (Kiraly 1996, Min 1996, Wells-Jensen 1999, Wan 1999, Muansuwan 2000, Kawachi 2002; see especially Wells-Jensen 1999 for a survey of cross-linguistic studies). By looking at data from non-Germanic languages it is likely that researchers may be able to refine their models of speech production planning so that they are applicable to a broader range of language structures. Furthermore, long-standing problems in the phonology, morphology, or syntax of languages other than English can be addressed in a fresh way; see, for example, Wan & Jaeger's (1998) SOT-based analysis of the representation and processing of tone in Mandarin Chinese, or our (2003) study of Mandarin vowels. For other recent examples, see Rubino (1996; Ilocano morphology), Arnaud (1999; French lexical substitutions), Hokkanen (1999; Finnish morphology), Chen (2000; Mandarin syllables), Prunet, Beland & Idrissi (2000; Semitic morphology), and Rossi (2001; French phonology), among others.

The other logical extension of previous SOT research would be to populations other than normal middle-aged monolingual adults, such as children, teenagers, the elderly, bilinguals, and subjects with abnormal language processing. Several studies have looked at the similarities between slips made by normal and aphasic adults (Stemberger 1984, Kohn & Smith 1990, Schwartz et al. 1994, Rapp & Goldrick 2000, among many others), and a recent dissertation looked at slips made by older adults (Mahoney 1997). Another interesting extension can be found in Poulisse (1999), where slips made by second language learners (young adult Dutch speakers learning English) were analyzed in terms of models of fluent vs. non-fluent speech production planning (see also Awuku 2003). On the other hand, the methodological issue raised above (that is, how can one tell a young child has produced a SOT?) has undoubtedly contributed to the paucity of SOT data on young children. However, it is clear that good SOT data from young children could provide hitherto unavailable insights into the time-course of a child's knowledge of language structures, given the basic premise that a SOT can only be made on a structure after it has been acquired. If we find, for example, that certain types of errors begin to occur at more or less the same stage in development for all children, then we can hypothesize that this is the time at which that structure is normally fully acquired.

Probably because of the compelling potential value of SOT data for studying language acquisition, a few hardy researchers have tackled this issue. One of the first was MacKay (1970) who looked at 23 spoonerisms (reversals of initial consonants) reported by Meringer (1908) to have been produced by German-speaking children, ages 3-6. MacKay compared these errors to 124 adult errors from the same corpus, and found that while there were many similarities, the differences found could be attributed to 'the child's lack of skill in integrating successive acts in the speech sequence' (1970:315). Bowerman (1978) reported on a set of verb substitution errors made by her two English-speaking daughters between the ages of 2-5, and discussed them in terms of the developing semantic system. Vihman (1981) analyzed a set of lexical substitution errors made by her son, who was learning both Estonian and English, and also looked at data from other children learning Spanish and German. Her focus was the development of the phonological structure of the lexicon. Aitchison & Straf (1982) examined 472 adult and 208 child 'malapropisms' (lexical substitution errors related by phonology only), which they solicited through an advertisement in a newspaper. They analyzed similarities and differences in phonological structure of adult vs. child errors; the exact ages of the children in the study were not provided, other than the fact that they were 'under 12'. Warren (1986) looked at (mainly lexical) SOTs made by nine English-speaking children, ages 1-3, from recorded and transcribed sessions, and compared the number of errors made by the children to those made by adults. She interpreted the fact that the children in this study made far fewer errors than the adults in terms of Freudian psychology, in that children 'are less inclined to suppress and repress ideas and impulses' (1986:309).

In the late 1980's and early 1990's there was an increase in publications regarding young children's SOTs. Smith (1990), in response to the difficulty of collecting spontaneous SOTs from children, described a 'tongue-twister' technique he developed. Reporting on the phonological errors made by the five 5-year-old children in his study, he found many similarities to adult errors, although the children in his study made many more errors than the adults. He attributed this to their immature speech production mechanisms.

The other studies which began to appear at this time were based on larger corpora of children's SOTs. The first of this set was Stemberger (1989), in which he reported on a corpus of 576 SOTs, of a broad range of types, made by his two English-speaking daughters between the ages of 1;6 (one year; six months) and 5;11. He compared these errors to errors made by adults, looking at a large number of factors derived from adult SOT research. Like MacKay, Stemberger found a majority of similarities between the child and adult data; he interpreted the differences he found within a connectionist model, in terms of the development of interrelationships among linguistic units and levels, and the maturation of processing skills. Looking at children learning Dutch, Wijnen (1988, 1990) focussed first on dysfluencies in sentence production for the evidence they provide regarding planning and representational units. In Wijnen (1992), he analyzed a collection of 250 word and sound errors collected from tape recordings of two 2-3-year-old boys, comparing these errors to the adult English errors in the London-Lund corpus (Garnham et al. 1982). As usual he found few differences between the child and adult errors, but the differences he did find he attributed to the degree of practice and automatization in children's speech production systems compared to adults. Finally, I began publishing and presenting a series of papers (Jaeger 1992a,b, 1996, 1999, to appear; Jaeger & Wilkins 1993), based on subsets of the corpus of data presented in this book, which currently numbers 1383 SOTs made by children ages 1;7-5;11, which I collected predominantly from my own three children.

Three themes seem to emerge from previous studies of children's SOTs. First, there are many similarities between child data and adult data, suggesting that children's speech production planning mechanisms develop along adult-like lines very early, possibly earlier than was hitherto thought. Second, differences between children's and adult's SOTs can be attributed both to differences in the children's linguistic representations and knowledge, and the development of their processing abilities. Therefore the study of both of these factors can benefit from children's SOT data. Third, the largest and most varied corpora of errors have been collected by parent-linguists from their own children, who were at the time the subjects of longitudinal language acquisition studies. This latter point is crucial, since intimate knowledge of a child's current grammar is a prerequisite to being able to justify the decision that a particular utterance did in fact contain a SOT for that child, particularly for very young (1-2-year-old) children. I will return to this point in §1.3.1 below. From this review of previous studies one can see that the analysis of SOTs made by very young children can provide a wealth of information about the acquisition of spoken language, and thus that the current study should add greatly to our understanding of this process.

The purpose of this book is not to assess any particular theory of language acquisition, and I assume that the data and discussion here will be relevant to researchers from various theoretical backgrounds. However, I find that the 'frames, then content' theory of MacNeilage and Davis (MacNeilage & Davis 1990, 1993, 2000; MacNeilage 1998) is extremely useful for explaining phonological, semantic, and syntactic patterns of development found in these SOTs, and thus I will be referring often to this model. Similarly, this study will not assess any particular linguistic theoretical apparatus or claims; however, it is important to use a consistent linguistic framework for discussion of the data, which I will lay out in the next section. Finally, it is not the main purpose of this book to develop a complete model of speech production planning, or to critique any model previously discussed in the literature. Nevertheless it is important to adopt a specific model in order to be able to present a unified discussion of the processing components and mechanisms involved in speech production. I will now turn to the planning model which will form the basis of much of the analysis in this study.

1.2 A Model of Speech Production Planning

The speech production planning model I will use in this book is given in Figure 1.1. It is based on the model of Garrett (1984, 1993), borrowing insights from Fromkin (1973a), Dell & Reich (1980, 1981), Dell (1986), Shattuck-Hufnagel (1983), Levelt (Levelt 1989, Bock & Levelt 1994, Levelt, Roelofs & Meyer 1999), and Caplan (1992). This model assumes that there are two basic types of elements which work together in planning an utterance. The first is a set of representations which are stored in long term memory, and contain speakers' knowledge about their language (shown inside ovals in the figure). This includes the lexicon (with semantic and formal information about each lexical entry), the morphosyntax system, and the phonological system of the language, as well as the speaker's conceptual knowledge ('semantic memory'). The second type of element is processing components, where the actual activation, selection, concatenation, and form assignment of elements from long term representations occurs (shown inside rectangles in the figure). These components perform increments of the planning task, and produce specific levels

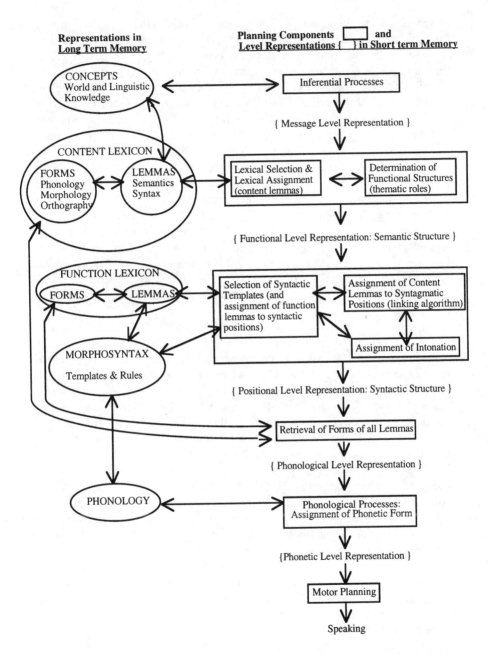

Figure 1.1: The 'Representations and Processing Components Model' of Speech Production Planning (RPC Model)

of representation in sequence. These 'level representations' (shown in curly brackets in the model) are on-line packages of information which simply move the planning process from one component to another; they are deleted as soon as they have performed their function. Some of these processing components work in sequence, and others work in parallel as indicated by their being adjacent at a particular level of the model. This model acts as a flow chart showing the order in which various operations take place during speech production planning; each of the processing components will itself have an internal structure, consisting of an interconnected network of unit types and processes which allows this particular aspect of the planning task to be performed. As I give an overview of the structure of this model, I will flesh out some aspects of the individual representations and components. I will use predominantly traditional linguistic terminology in describing the linguistic representations and units involved in the components and processes. (Psychological processes such as attention, memory, and selection per se are taken as given in this model and not further discussed.) For ease of exposition and reference, I will label this model the 'Representations and Processing Components Model', hereafter the 'RPC Model', since the distinction between representations and processing components is at the heart of this model.

The first processing component in the RPC Model is 'Inferential Processes', where the general content of the projected utterance is composed. This component works with material from conceptual representations, which includes not only general and specific world knowledge, but also the speakers' knowledge about the linguistic pragmatic conventions of their speech community (e.g. Grice's Maxims, conversational structure), the previous discourse, knowledge about the hearer(s), and the intentions of the current utterance. The output of this component is the 'Message Level Representation', which is not strictly linguistic, but contains the concepts to be conveyed.

The 'Message Level Representation' is fed into the 'Lexical Selection' component, which activates the 'Content Lexicon'; at this point candidate content lexical items which are semantically appropriate to the message are activated in the content lexicon. Specifically, the 'lemmas' (Levelt 1989, Roelofs, Meyer & Levelt 1998, Laubstein 1999) of lexical items, which contain information about the semantic and syntactic properties of the item (e.g. lexical category, verb valence), are activated. (The distinction between 'content' and 'function' words and morphemes will be discussed in detail in Chapter 4.) The 'Message Level Representation' is simultaneously fed into the 'Determination of Functional Structures' component, which, combined with information from the lemmas receiving the highest activation in the 'Lexical Selection' component, constructs the most appropriate functional frames or 'logical structures' for the utterance. Lemmas are assigned to functional slots in these frames ('Lexical Assignment'), and the resultant representation is the 'Functional Level Representation', an unordered string of semantically appropriate content lemmas, marked with their lexical category and assigned a function in the logical structure of the propositional content to be conveyed.

At this point the 'Functional Level Representation' undergoes a linear ordering in the 'Selection of Syntactic Templates' and 'Assignment of Content Lemmas to Syntagmatic Positions' components. Syntactic templates appropriate to the proposition and discourse are selected from the stored morphosyntactic representations (Van Valin & LaPolla 1997:432). These templates contain slots where particular types of function morphemes should occur, and function morphemes will be activated from the 'Function Lexicon' to fill those slots. The selection of the correct function morphemes will be governed by several things: requirements of the selected content morphemes (e.g. specific verbs require particular prepositions), requirements of the syntactic template (e.g. the passive construction requires particular verb morphology), and the tense/aspect requirements of the proposition (e.g. past perfective morphology). The 'Functional Level Representation' is linked to the selected syntactic template, following processes like the 'linking algorithms' of Van Valin & LaPolla (1997: Ch. 7), where thematic roles are assigned specific syntactic functions based on both language-specific and universal principles. Content word lemmas are then assigned to slots in the syntactic string based on their assigned functions in the 'Functional Level Representations'. During this linear ordering process, the 'Assignment of Intonational Contours' component assigns the correct intonational melody for the proposition, the syntactic frame, and the pragmatic intention of the utterance; it is specifically sensitive to the focus or information structure of the sentence, and the type of speech act. This requires a partial activation of the 'Phonology' representations, specifically elements relevant to the phonology-syntax interface.

After the lemmas of both content and function words and morphemes have been linearized, the 'Form' representations of each lemma are retrieved from the form lexicon and replace the more abstract lemmas in the linear string, for both content and function morphemes. The 'form' representation of each lexical entry is assumed to include phonological and morphological information about that word, as well as orthographic information where relevant. The morphological representations of lexical entries are taken to contain information regarding the morphological make-up of the word. Derivationally complex words, compounds, and irregularly inflected forms are assumed to be stored whole, with some information about the individual morphemes which make up the word stored in the lexical entry (see Chapters 4 and 6 for details). Regular inflectional affixes are not stored in content lexical entries, but have autonomous entries in the form lexicon and are concatenated with content morphemes during linear ordering. Phonological representations are assumed to be something like those represented in Autosegmental Phonology (or some connectionist models); i.e. there are various tiers of phonological units (or nodes), linked together by association lines, which function to some extent autonomously; prosodic structure, syllable structure, segments, and phonetic features are important parts of each phonological representation, and there is both feed-forward and feed-back among levels of representation.

In the RPC Model, the 'lemma lexicon' and the 'form lexicon' are treated as if they are two separate but related entities, similar to the 'generic 2-stage model' of Harley & Brown (1998). This distinction is supported by the psycholinguistic facts gleaned from SOT research, since each aspect of the lexicon is activated and processed at distinct points during processing, and is involved in different types of errors. An interesting issue which will recur throughout this book is just how the two subdivisions of the lexicon are linked, that is, what kinds of feed-forward and feed-backward links there are between the two aspects of the lexical representation for a single lexical entry.

The output of the 'Retrieval of Forms' component is the 'Phonological Level Representation', which consists of a string of (abstract, or partially unspecified) phonological representations in the correct linear order, with syntactic constituent structure specified, and with the general intonational melody indicated. This representation is fed into the 'Phonological Processes' component while the speaker's representation for 'Phonology', i.e. their knowledge about the phonological structures and processes of their language, is activated. In this component the phonological rules of the language assign the correct phonetic form to the more abstract phonological units in the 'form' representation, given the syntagmatic and prosodic structure of the utterance; this is done on a phrase-by-phrase basis. Productive phonological (e.g. allophonic) and morphophonemic processes take place during assignment of phonetic form. The output of this component is the 'Phonetic Level Representation', which is a fully specified phonetic representation of the utterance, and is the last element in the 'Speech Production Planning' process. This representation is sent to the 'Motor Planning' component, i.e. the motor areas of the brain, for neural motor encoding, and from there to the actual articulators, in syllable-by-syllable increments, for 'Speaking'. Errors which occur in the components from 'Inferential Processes' through 'Phonological Processes' which involve planning per se are considered SOTs; however errors which occur during speaking itself (i.e. hesitations, slurrings, etc.) or for pragmatic reasons (e.g. false starts) are not considered part of the planning process and hence are not SOTs. In §1.4.5 below, after the presentation of my SOT taxonomy, I will refer back to this model in order to link specific error types to erroneous processing in specific components of the model.

One final element of the RPC Model is the self-monitoring system (not included in Figure 1.1). I assume (with Laver 1980 and many others) that there are two distinct monitors which serve to filter out erroneous utterances, either before they are uttered or immediately after the utterance is produced. The first is an 'internal' monitor, which screens the final output of the planning mechanism for legality; that is, its role is to filter out any non-legal speech sounds, phonotactic sequences, nonsense words, or ungrammatical strings, before the utterance is produced. The existence of this internal monitor would explain why non-legal speech sounds and violations of phonotactic sequences are extremely rare in SOTs (Boomer & Laver 1973, Fromkin 1973a), and why phonological errors are likely to produce real words, at least for adults (Baars, Motley & MacKay 1975, Dell & Reich 1981); it may also explain the rarity of true phrase blends. Strong evidence for the internal monitor comes from studies by Motley and Baars (Baars, Motley & Mackay 1975, Motley 1980). In these studies, subjects were induced via the 'SLIPS' technique to produce speech errors which would result in the production of words or phrases which were slightly embarrassing or risqué. In these cases subjects would often catch themselves before they spoke the error aloud, but would blush and look embarrassed because of what they had been about to say. These studies attest to the existence of an internal monitor which scans planned output prior to speaking.

However, luckily for us, this internal monitor is far from perfect, and erroneously planned utterances can fool the monitor and be spoken aloud, producing SOTs. At this point a second monitor, the 'external' monitor, comes into play. This monitor consists of the auditory feedback loop; that is, speakers are usually listening to what they are saying, and if they hear an error (i.e. their utterance is at odds with their intention) they have the option of correcting it. One interesting question which will be addressed below is the relative efficiency of children's monitors compared to adults'.

1.3 The Current Study: Methodology

1.3.1 How Can We Tell a Child Has Made A Slip?

As discussed above, there are obvious methodological difficulties involved in detecting SOTs made by very young children, since children regularly produce utterances which differ from adult productions of the same target. In most cases these productions reflect the child's current stage of development, and are systematic substitutions or omissions of the types thoroughly documented in the acquisition literature (e.g. Ingram 1986). However, the studies cited above have shown that SOTs can be distinguished from systematic 'rules' which govern children's immature productions. In the cases where errors are collected in spontaneous settings, the researcher knows the child's current system of production thoroughly, and recognizes that a particular utterance was at odds with the usual production. The errors frequently are of a type which differ significantly from typical systematic substitutions or mutations. Furthermore, children frequently look confused and/or correct their error in the same way that adults do after making a slip. Consider the following example:

(1)   B: 'Mòmmy, mòre chéese-pùffs.' (a type of snack food)
         M: 'No, you've had enóugh.'
         B: '[ń.tÀpç]! . . . chéese-pùffs!'
               (for 'cheese-puffs' [tí.pÀpç], adult model [tʃiz.pʰʌfs]; B-28(12) 1;11)

Before discussing this example, my notational conventions need to be explicated. In errors given as examples, the 'error' units (erroneous production) are in boldface; the 'source' (source of the interference) is in boldface italics; and the 'target' (the intended production) is underlined. So, in example (1), the first [t] in 'cheese-puffs' (bold-italics) is the source of the error; the second [t] (bold) is the error itself; the [p] in the corrected utterance (underlined) is the target (i.e. intended) segment.

In the child errors, speakers are identified as follows: An=Anna, Al=Alice, B=Bobby, M=the child's mother, D=the child's father, OB=other boy, OG=other girl, OA=other adult. The notation at the end of the example should be read as follows: 1) Identification of data set and error number: AN=Anna, AL=Alice, B=Bobby, OC=other child. 2) The taxonomic class of the error (in parentheses after the error number); the classification system is given in Table 1.2 below, as well as at the beginning of the data section of this book. 3) The age of the child when the error was made, in 'years;months'; in the data section of this book the days are also given (i.e. years;months.days). Thus the error in (1) should be interpreted as follows: Bobby requests more cheese-puffs, his mother responds negatively, and then Bobby reiterates that he wants cheese-puffs, and makes an error in this utterance (which will be discussed below). The notation after the error should be read as follows: Subject: Bobby-error #28 (class 12, phonological perseverations, substitutions, consonants) age: one year; eleven months. A guide to phonetic symbols used can be found at the beginning of the data section of the book. In most cases in the text, the error will be presented in an abbreviated form, focussing only on the relevant structures; however, the full error is always given in the data section of the book. Finally, in the data section of the book I have indicated after each error where in the text this error has been discussed, if relevant. Thus in the text, if an example is repeated I will usually not indicate that it is 'repeated from above', since this information is available in the data section.

At the age at which he made the 'cheese-puffs' error, Bobby regularly realized the six adult phonemes /p,b/, /t,d/, and /k,g/ as the three voiceless unaspirated stops [p], [t], [k] respectively, and systematically differentiated the three places of articulation. Adult /f/ was realized as [p], and syllable-initial /tʃ/ as [t], while all word-final sibilants were pronounced as [ç]; all but word-final sequences of consonants were reduced to single consonants. In this example, in the first utterance Bobby pronounced 'cheese-puffs' in his usual way, [tí.pʌpç]; then when he repeated it in his second utterance, the [t] from 'cheese' [ti] was perseverated and substituted for the initial [p] in 'puffs' [pʌpç]; the child then noticed his error and corrected it to his usual pronunciation. So one can see the erroneous production flanked on both sides by the 'correct' pronunciation for this word, that is, Bobby's usual pronunciation of this word at age 1;11. The substitution of [t] for [p] was not a regular substitution for this child but represented a one-time error which violated his usual pronunciation of this word; furthermore the regular substitution of [t] for [p] is not common in early child phonology, since [p] and [t] are usually among the first segments systematically produced correctly by children. Therefore there is enough evidence to conclude that this was indeed a one-time SOT.

A few more examples will strengthen the argument.

(2)   a. OG: (looking at toothbrush; no toothpaste in view)
'Mỳ **tóothpàste** . . . mỳ tóothbrùsh.'
(substitution of 'toothpaste' for 'toothbrush'; OC-6(35) 2;0)
   b. An: (pretending to talk on the phone to "Winnie the Pooh" characters)
'Hí [tʰ ì.gɪt].'
(blend of 'Tigger' [tʰí.gɜ] and 'Piglet' [pʰí.gɪt]; AN-6(38) 1;7)
   c. Al: '**Dàddy**, mè wàtching **Dàddy** cóoking . . . nò . . . Mómmy's còoking.'
('Daddy' perseverated, substituted for 'Mommy'; AL-27(43) 2;4)
   d. B: (ready to walk to store) 'Mom, **ì wànna góing** . . . ì gòing tóo!' (blend of 'I wanna go' and 'I going too'; B-37(49) 2;1)

In (2a), the child regularly differentiated the words 'toothpaste' and 'toothbrush', but in this instance she selected the incorrect word, and then corrected herself. In (2b), Anna knew both the words 'Tigger' and 'Piglet', but during this pretend conversation she accidentally blended the two names. Alice, in error (2c), perseverated the word 'Daddy' and substituted it for 'Mommy'. Upon noticing the error she corrected herself and laughed at her mistake; she also changed the phrasal stress pattern and (very slightly) the syntax in order to emphasize the correction. Finally, in (2d), Bobby was able to correctly produce the two target syntactic structures at this time, but in this case he blended the two, correcting the utterance which he considered to be ungrammatical into one of the targets. Although this target, 'I going too', is ungrammatical by adult standards, it was a regular structure in Bobby's grammar at the time, and so was not ungrammatical by his standards.

In sum, an utterance made by a child is analyzed as containing a SOT if it includes a production which is at odds with the child's current grammar, either in terms of phonology, lexicon, morphology, or syntax. Frequently, after a SOT is made, the child looks confused, and/or corrects the utterance, which is further evidence that the child considered it an error.

On the other hand, many of the children's productions which differ from the adult model are simply a function of the child not having yet learned that linguistic structure. A systematic substitution of one phoneme for another (exemplified in example (1) above, where Bobby systematically substituted voiceless unaspirated plosives for all plosives and some fricatives), the misuse of a word, the meaning of which the child is unsure of, or the regular use of a non-adult syntactic construction are not SOTs. Similarly, fluctuations in usage while a child masters a structure are also not slips (see Stemberger 1989 for a careful discussion of this point). Consider the following examples.

(3)   a. An: 'Lóok! Álice!' (pointing at a picture of "Baby Beluga" in a book)
          M: 'Yeah, I already showed it to her yésterday.'
          An: 'Alice, come hére! Look at thís!'
          Al: 'Anna, she already showed me **tomórrow**!'
          An: (laughs) 'Yésterday!'
          Al: 'Yésterday.' (Alice, age 3;5; Anna age 5;9)
       b. Al: 'Momma, I wànted to wàtch Gène Kélly, but I jùst gòt into béd
          and **gòeded** to sléep.' (pronounced [góʷ.rəd]; age 3;5)
       c. M: 'Don't touch my túmmy.'
          Al: 'Yeah, that's **prívace**.' (pronounced [pʰ3áʲ.vəs]; age 3;3)
       d. An: (being a magician) 'And nòw I will **appèar** my assístant, rìght
          ùnder this táble.' (age 5;6)

In (3a), Alice substituted the word 'tomorrow' for 'yesterday'; however, this was
not a SOT, since she did not have the meanings of these words clearly
distinguished, and was fluctuating between the two randomly at the time. In
(3b), she produced an overregularized version of the past tense of 'go'; i.e. rather
than 'went' she added the regular past tense suffix to 'go', producing 'goed', then
double marked it by adding the suffix again, now requiring the syllabic form,
producing 'goeded'. This was an overgeneralization she was making regularly at
this time, and not a one-time SOT. In (3c), Alice had created the word 'privace',
meaning 'private', as a back-formation from 'privacy'; for a short time she
refused to pronounce it any other way. Finally, in (3d), Anna produced the verb
'appear' as if it were a causative (i.e. 'cause to appear'), which is a well-
documented type of overextension common to the early speech of many English-
speaking children (Bowerman 1974).   Such examples were carefully noted in
my journal entries as 'not a slip', and they will not be found in the corpus at the
end of this book.

    Finally, as mentioned above, there are a number of types of incomplete
utterances which are not considered SOTs per se (see Levelt 1989: Ch. 12, and
Wells-Jensen 1999:83-94 for thorough discussions of this point). These include
false starts with re-starts, where the speaker changes his/her mind about the
propositional content, lexical selection, or form of the utterance, and then plans
and speaks a new utterance before the originally planned utterance is completed.
This is illustrated in (4).

(4)   Al: 'Lòok at whàt . . . What Ànna gàve me is a fláshlight.' (age 3;8)

In this utterance, Alice started to say something like 'Lòok at whàt Ánna gàve
me', but changed her mind and re-started the utterance with a different
propositional content and syntax. Other types of utterances not counted as SOTs
include what Wells-Jensen calls 'discourse anomalies' (1999:89), where, for
example, a child uses pronouns in a confusing manner because he/she has lost
track of the discourse reference. Finally, stutterings, slurred speech, and other

motor dysfluencies are not considered SOTs as they are not caused by dysfunction of the speech production *planning* mechanism; they are rather caused by a problem in sending messages from the 'Motor Planning' component to the articulators themselves.

These are the basic principles involved in data collection; specific details regarding different types of errors and subjects will be discussed below.

1.3.2 Subjects

The majority of data analyzed in the present study were collected by me from my three children, Anna, Alice, and Bobby, when they were between the ages of 1;7-5;11. During this time period I kept diaries of all three children's language development, such that the SOTs were situated within a record of their synchronous normal productions. Further data were collected from 57 'Other' children, 29 girls and 28 boys, ages 1;10-5;11. All errors were collected by ear, in naturalistic settings; errors were recorded in a notebook immediately after they occurred, in both orthography and phonetic transcription, including information about discourse context, previous and subsequent utterances, and physical context when relevant.   Age 6 was chosen as the cut-off point for this study partly to minimize any effect of literacy, but mainly to focus on errors made by very young children as their primary linguistic abilities were developing.   Errors were collected from Other children in order to verify that the data collected from my three children were not in some sense anomalous, i.e. that such errors are produced only by children who have two linguist parents. I found no qualitative differences between the data collected from my children and the Other children; quantitative differences will be discussed in detail below. I will refer to the data collected from Anna, Alice, Bobby, and Other children as the four 'data sets' of this study.

Many of the Other errors were collected in a preschool setting, where I observed a group of 2-5-year-olds for approximately one hour, two days per week, for six weeks. Some Other errors were collected from my children's friends and cousins whose speech patterns I knew well, particularly during the age range of 3-5 years, such that their grammars were not greatly different from the adult models. Although I personally collected the great majority of errors, a few of the Other errors in my corpus were collected by my graduate students from their own children; these students were well trained in both phonetics and the study of SOTs, and their data are highly reliable. A few of the errors came from professional colleagues who collected these errors from their own children.

My corpus of child errors numbers 1,383. Table 1.1 shows the number of errors contributed to the corpus by each data set at each age, from 1 to 5 years, and the percentage of errors at each age originating from each data set. This table is to be read as follows (for example): at age 1, I collected 22 SOTs from Anna; this represents 38.5% of the age 1 errors in my corpus. Overall, Anna contributed 338 (24.5%) of the errors in the corpus. It can be seen that at each age there are very different proportions of errors contributed by each data set; I

TABLE 1.1

Number of errors in each data set at each age, and percentage of errors contributed by each data set at each age.

Age:		1	2	3	4	5	Total
Anna	N=	22	77	43	126	70	338
	%	38.5%	27%	17%	26.5%	22%	24.5%
Alice	N=	0	85	114	40	34	273
	%		30%	44.5%	8.5%	10.75%	20%
Bobby	N=	31	90	55	261	160	597
	%	54.5%	32%	21.5%	55%	50.75%	43%
Others	N=	4	30	43	46	52	175
	%	7%	11%	17%	10%	16.5%	12.5%
Total	**N=**	**57**	**282**	**255**	**473**	**316**	**1383**

will discuss this factor in more detail below.

In Table 1.1 I have divided the data by age. However, in a few cases in this study I will separate out errors made when the subjects were in the 1- or 2-word vs. 3+word (i.e. telegraphic and beyond) speech stages, rather than by strict chronological age, when this distinction is important to the issue under study. The approximate ages at which my three children were making SOTs while in each of these stages are given in Table 1.2. Anna, who was an 'expressive' language learner (see 1.5.2 below), didn't go through obvious stages; she spoke in whole phrases from the time when her earliest SOTs were recorded, including fixed phrases such as nursery rhymes, mixed with jargon babbling. Alice, who was a more 'referential' style learner, did go through a clear 1-word stage, from 1;0-1;10; however, I did not collect any errors from her during this time, and her first SOT was collected after she had entered the 2-word stage (at age 2;0). However I collected several errors from Bobby, another 'referential' learner, while he was in the 1-word and 2-word stages. My corpus also includes several errors from Other children made in these early stages. Errors made in the 1-word or 2-word stages are marked as such in the database; all errors without these designations were made when the speaker was producing utterances of 3 or more words.

1.3.3 Specific Methodological Issues Regarding Data Collection

There are three types of problems which need to be considered when collecting SOT data, particularly from children. The first one has to do with the 'pencil-and-paper' method of collection. It is frequently said (Nooteboom 1980, Cutler 1982a, Ferber 1991, Poulisse 1999, §5.2) that there is a perceptual bias which makes certain types of errors easier to detect than others; for example,

TABLE 1.2

Chronological ages for language development stages of the three main subjects, during the period when SOTs were collected.

Stage:	1-word	2-word	3+word
Anna	na	na	1;7 -->
Alice	na	2;0 -- 2;1.20	2;1.20 -->
Bobby	1;7 -- 1;8.30	1;9.0 -- 1;11.20	1;11.20 -->

word or syllable errors are said to be easier to hear than phoneme errors, and anticipations are perceived more readily than perseverations. I think it is interesting that in every naturalistic corpus I have encountered, the 'difficult-to-hear' phonological errors always outnumber other types of errors; thus it is possible that these biases are somewhat overstated (see Poulisse 1999:9 for a list of corpora in which this is true). Furthermore, in languages other than English and other Germanic languages (e.g. Thai, Mandarin, Japanese, Spanish, Hindi), anticipations and perseverations tend to be collected in equal numbers (see, for example, Wan 1999, Wells-Jensen 1999, Muansuwan 2000, Kawachi 2002), so that in languages where they are produced in equal numbers, they seem to be perceived as such. (The abundance of anticipations in Germanic languages is probably due to prosodic and information structure causes; see §3.7.3 below.)

Certainly these possible biases should cause researchers to be cautious about making definitive statements about the quantity of specific types of errors (see §1.5.3 below). However, in order to be able to make some quantitative statements in comparison to adult data, I have collected an additional set of 716 errors from adults (including teenagers; adults in the study ranged from 13-75), to use as a control corpus. Although many corpora of errors from adult speakers of English currently exist, I felt that a corpus collected by the same researcher, using the same methodology and classification system, would be the best data to use for comparison with the child data. In this case any perceptual biases attributable to the researcher would be evenly distributed across the two corpora. Furthermore, many of the adult errors in my corpus were collected from adults in the three main subjects' immediate family (including their parents, grandparents, aunts, and uncles), so they represent the target language which the children were learning. In fact, because the child data reported in this book were collected during the years of 1983-1991, the three main child subjects actually contributed most of the 'teenage' errors in the adult corpus; thus the child data are being compared to errors made by the same subjects at a later age, in several cases. Although the data I collected will be the primary source of adult data used for comparison to the child data, I will also compare the children's errors with published analyses of adult errors where appropriate.

The second type of methodological issue is the accuracy with which young children's errors can be perceived, given considerations of age, error type, and type of utterance containing the error. A further factor is how well-known the child is to the data collector. In Jaeger (1992a) I documented the guidelines I used for collecting data of different types from the various subjects, which I will reiterate here.

First, any error in a set-phrase such as a phrase from a nursery rhyme or word game, was very easy to detect for all subjects, especially since children tend to repeat these phrases many times, giving much evidence as to their normal forms. An example is given in (5). Many of the very early errors collected were in such phrases. These set-phrases become automatic very early, and so are among the earliest candidates for SOTs.

(5)   B: '[púi.ka.pùː]'   (for 'peek-a-boo' [píi.ka.pùː]; B-7(5) 1;9)

In this error, Bobby intended to produce the set-phrase 'peek-a-boo' as part of the hiding game, but erroneously anticipated the vowel [u] from the third syllable and substituted it for the vowel [i] in the first syllable.

Second, as with adult errors, word-based errors were readily noticeable, as they either consisted of one known word substituted for another known word as in (2a) above, or of two known words blended together as in (2b) above. These types of errors were also noticed by the children and self-corrected more often than any other type of error; this was equally true of data from my own children as from the Other group (see §2.4). Therefore lexical errors from Other children may be disproportionately high in my corpus, as I relied more heavily on self-correction in order to verify SOTs in Other children than in my own children.

Third, it is clear that accuracy in detecting phonological errors (i.e. errors involving features, segments, sub-syllabic units, syllables, and prosody) depends on the data collector's knowledge of a child's current phonology. I was able to collect phonological errors from my three children with confidence, as was the case with errors collected by my graduate students from their own children. Collecting phonological errors from Other children involved familiarizing myself with individual speech patterns, especially with the very young children, which I was able to do satisfactorily in the preschool setting. In fact it was usually not difficult to distinguish phonological SOTs from systematic substitutions made by Other children; this was due to a combination of my familiarity with their systems, frequent self-correction, and the fact that these errors often violate the type of phonetic relationships usually found in systematic phonological substitutions due to an immature phonology.

Fourth, the most difficult errors to collect were those which involved syntax and morphology, where the child did not correct his/her utterance. For my own children I checked uncorrected possible SOTs against journal entries documenting their current syntactic and morphological patterns, and verified that the utterance was at odds with their normal rules. For the Other children it was more difficult to verify their current syntactic and morphological systems, and so recording these errors relied to some extent on spontaneous self-correction. Again it was not as difficult to distinguish Other children's SOTs from their current immature grammars as one might expect, because such errors as phrase blends and word reversals usually result in structures which would be extremely unusual as a systematic pattern based on the child's current immature grammar (see example (2d) above). However, I did not include a potential error of any type in my corpus unless I had heard enough of the child's speech to have some verification that the utterance in question represented a deviation from the child's normal production (see also the discussion of example (26) in Chapter 3).

The third type of methodological problem is the issue of whether or not the children in the study could have become consciously aware of the focus of my data collection, and may have been intentionally producing anomalous utterances for Mom's benefit. I am often asked this question, although I find it a little odd since this is a question rarely asked of researchers collecting data from adult subjects, and it presupposes that speakers (in this case 1-5-year-old children) can intentionally create SOTs which sound natural enough to fool a seasoned researcher. (Naturally, when the children decided to pronounce the word 'spaghetti' [spə.gé.ɾi] as 'busgetti' [pə.ské.ɾi] for a few months, I did not count this as a SOT.) However, I did scan my notes for any hint that the children had any metalinguistic awareness of the phenomenon under study. Bobby seems to be the only child who was actually aware of the term 'speech error', since in two cases (at ages 4;11 and 5;1) he commented that he had 'made a speech error' after his external monitor caught the slip; one is given in (6); see also (B-429(35) 4;11).

(6)   B: (explaining why he should be first in the bathtub tonight)
             'Because I was làst [nǽst] ńight. (laughs) I màde a spéech
             èrror.' (for 'I was làst lást nìght'; B-458(1) 5;1)

In (6) Bobby anticipates the onset [n] from 'night' and substitutes it for the onset [l] in 'last'. It was quite common for the children (and adults) to comment on their own errors, either just before the repair (e.g. 'I mean') or just after it ('I should say'); this will be discussed in detail in Chapter 2. Bobby's comment on his 'speech error' is analogous to the following comment from Anna, where she uses the terminology 'mistake'.

(7)   An: (peeling apple slices; no bananas in sight)
              'I'm pèeling my **banánas**. (laughs) Oh, I made a mistáke. I sàid
              "banánas" instead of "ápples".' (AN-208(35) 4;5)

Making a comment on an error was common among the Other children as well as among adults, and so these comments are unlikely to reflect any special knowledge of the SOT phenomenon among my children. However, one contribution made by Bobby is good evidence that the children would have been unable to construct speech errors even if they had tried. One evening when Bobby was 5;7, the children's father was joking around about speech errors (to my chagrin) and engaged Bobby in the following conversation.

(8)   D: 'What's a speech error?'
       B: 'You know! Can I do one please Mom?'
       M: 'OK'
       B: 'Càke-cóffee. That's one, 'cuz it's supposed to be "cóffee-càke".'

So, at age 5;7 Bobby was consciously aware that one type of utterance that counts as a speech error is the metathesis of the two content stems in a compound. However notice that in his constructed error he carried the lexical stress with the two words when he metathesized them. In all of my naturally collected SOTs involving metathesis within a compound, the stress remained in the originally planned locations; so in a natural speech error the utterance would have been 'càke-còffee', since in this case one would expect that the compound stress would remain intact. Therefore this example shows that Bobby most likely would not have been able to intentionally construct a SOT, and if he had been trying to do it on purpose I'm quite sure I would have been able to distinguish it from a naturally occurring error. The two girls showed no signs of having any conscious awareness of the phenomenon during the study, and of course the Other children had no metalinguistic awareness of SOTs. Looking at this question from another angle, there is no evidence that metalinguistic awareness of SOTs has any affect on natural speech production one way or the other. Many of the adults in my study were very consciously and intimately aware of SOTs (in particular, myself), but produced them naturally, without intentionality or contrivance, in great abundance. Therefore metalinguistic awareness is unlikely to have had any influence on either my child or adult data, either by facilitating or inhibiting SOT production.

After collecting the data, I divided the data into the five data sets 'Anna, Alice, Bobby, Other Child, Adult'. I assigned numbers to each error consecutively according to age in each of the four child data sets. For my three children this means that their errors are numbered in the order in which they occurred. For the 'Other' data set, the different children's errors were combined into one age-ranked list (the individual children are identified only as 'male' or 'female'), and assigned consecutive numbers based on age; when the utterance included a proper name, this name was changed to protect the confidentiality of the child, unless the proper name itself was involved in the error. The adult errors were simply numbered consecutively in the order they appear in the data set; that is, the first error presented is error AD-1, and the last error in the corpus is AD-700 (see next section for why the last error is AD-700 and not AD-716). Notation used in the adult data include: AD=adult, AF=adult female, AM=adult male, TF=teen female, TM=teen male.

All errors were assigned to a specific error class according to the criteria given in the following section. When more than one error occurred in the same utterance, the errors were subscripted as (a), (b), (c); for example (only the errors are highlighted):

(9)   An: (chanting nursery rhyme)
        'Mòmmy càlled the dóctor and the **mòmmỳ** [kʰɛ́d] . . .
        Mòmmy [kʰɛ̀l.də] dóctor, and the dòctòr sáid . . .
        Mòmmy càlled the dóctor and the dòctòr sáid:
        Nò mòre mónkeys jùmpin' òn the béd!'

There are three errors in this utterance. The first is in the first line, which should have been 'Mommy called the doctor and the <u>doctor</u> said'; however, Anna substituted 'mommy' for 'doctor'; this error is listed in Class 43 as AN-26a. The second error is in the last word of the first line; Anna meant to say 'said', but the /k/ from 'called' was perseverated and substituted for the [s] in 'said', so she pronounced it *[kʰɛ́d]; this error is listed in Class 12 as AN-26b. The third error occurs in the second line, where she intended to say 'called', but the vowel from 'said' was perseverated and substituted for the vowel in 'called', producing *[kʰɛl]; this error is listed in Class 5 as AN-26c. (These classes will be explained in detail in §1.4 below.) This utterance was made at age 2;1.23 (two years, one month, 23 days). Because in some cases there were two or even three errors included under the same number, there are more errors than numbers. In the adult data there are 16 cases where a numbered utterance includes more than one error, so the highest numbered adult error is AD-700 rather than AD-716. The children's last entries are as follows: Anna, AN-330(35) 5;11.30; Alice, AL-270(38) 5;11.31; Bobby, B-588(13) 5;11.26; Other, OC-174(38) 5;11.31.

1.4 Classification System

The system used in this study for classifying errors was developed from traditional systems used for classifying adult errors in English, and makes use of the following three dimensions: 1) the linguistic component or stage involved in the error, 2) the directionality of the error, and 3) the form of the error. In the following section I will first present a discussion of these three factors, giving examples from the children's data. I will then discuss how classifications were made in ambiguous cases, indicating the decision-making procedures I used in a broad range of cases. At the end of this section I will review the RPC Model discussed in §1.2 above, showing how the various types of errors can arise given dysfunctions in specific locations in the model.

I go into minute methodological detail in this section for two reasons. First, this will allow readers to interpret the classifications I have made of the data presented in this book, and if they disagree with my classification system, they can reclassify errors according to their own systems. Second, I intend for these details to be useful to researchers wanting to utilize the SOT methodology in their own work, particularly with young children. Naturally the classification system will need some revising if the data are being collected in a language other than English, which contains different types or different proportions of linguistic units (e.g. has much more morphology; see Wells-Jensen 1999).

1.4.1 Linguistic Components Involved in Errors

Errors can occur at any stage of the speech production planning model, but they can be broadly grouped into four classes of error based on what type of linguistic unit was the locus of the misplanning. These classes are: Phonological, Lexical, Syntactic, and Propositional. Phonological errors are those which occur during the assignment of phonetic form and involve non-meaningful phonological units or prosody. Lexical errors are those which occur as lexical items are being activated and selected, and include paradigmatic lexical substitutions and blends. Syntactic errors are those which occur during the planning of the functional and linear structure of sentences, and include misplacements of lexical items and phrase blends. Finally, propositional errors are those where a speaker fluently produces an utterance which is at odds with the overall meaning he or she intended to convey.

Phonological errors are those which involve phonological units which do not carry semantic content (i.e. are not morphemes): phonetic features, segments (consonants or vowels), sub-syllabic sequences of segments (consonant clusters, rhymes, etc.), syllables, and lexical stress. The cause of an intonational error can be syntactic or pragmatic; however, because they always involve phonological (pitch) units, they are classified as phonological here, although they might be better thought of as syntactic in some cases. Because there are only 3 intonation errors in the child data and 5 in the adult data, their classification as 'phonological' vs. 'syntactic' does not have a large effect on the overall pattern of errors. The following examples are given in abbreviated form.

(10) Phonological units involved in errors

   a. Features: Al: 'I màde aʔ [áʒtʃ] . . . [áʒtʃ pʰʒà.dɛkt] . . . árt̲ pròject.' (for [áʒt pʰʒà.dʒɛkt]; feature of affrication reversed; AL-156(29) 3;8)

   b. Segments: Al: '[wàk.ʌ.bè̠ʲ bá̠ʲ.bi].' (for 'rock-a-bye-baby' [wàk.ʌ.bàʲ bé̠ʲ.bi]; vowels [aʲ] and [eʲ] reversed; AL-1(26) 2;0)

   c. Consonant clusters: Al: 'Sk̃ippy hòp, sk̲ippy hòp, [hí.pi skàp].' (for [skí.pi hàp]; [sk] and [h] reversed; AL-36(28) 2;6)

   d. Rhymes: Al: 'I was [dʒ̀ɪk] tíck̲ling hìm.' (for 'just tickling' [dʒʌst tʰík.ɬ.ɪŋ]'; rhyme [ɪk] anticipated/ substituted for rhyme [ʌst]; AL-116(6) 3;3)

   e. Syllables: B: 'Whỳ did you invìte [dè̠ʲ.brə] . . . Dàv̲id̲ an' Bár*bara* òver?' (for [dè̠ʲ.vɨd æn bár.brə]; syllable [brə] anticipated/substituted for syllable [vɨd]; B-491(11) 5;4)

f. Unclassifiable groups of segments: OG: 'Not [r̂i:s] conè! . . . Not íce-crèam cöne!'
   (for [áʲs.krìm]; see below for discussion; OC-21(34) 2;3)
g. Lexical stress: An: 'I rèally wànna **decoráte** Stràwberry's hòuse.'
   (for 'décorate'; source 'decorátion'; AN-260(32) 4;11)
h. Intonation:

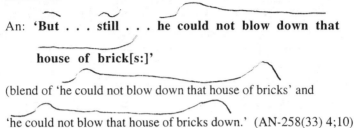

An: **'But . . . still . . . he could not blow down that**

house of brick[s:]'

(blend of 'he could not blow down that house of bricks' and

'he could not blow that house of bricks down.' (AN-258(33) 4;10)

In (10a), the feature of affrication has been reversed, causing the segments [t]-[dʒ] to be realized as [tʃ]-[d]. Segmental errors involve both consonants, as shown in (1) above, and vowels, as in (4) and in (10b) where the vowels [eʲ]-[aʲ] were reversed. In (10c), the onset consonant cluster [sk] from 'skippy' has been reversed with the onset single consonant [h]. Example (10d) shows an anticipation of the rhyme [ɪk] from 'tickling', which was substituted for the rhyme [ʌst] in 'just'. In (10e), the whole syllable [brə] from 'Barbara' was anticipated and substituted for the syllable [vəd] in 'David'. In (10f), the vowel [aʲ], and the consonants [k] and [m] have been deleted, and the [s] moved to the end of the word forming a new syllable [ris], but with the duration and pitch contour of the intended utterance; this kind of error is termed a 'telescoping', as will be explained in the next section. The error in (10g) shows a case where the lexical stress was shifted from the initial to the final syllable in 'decorate'. Finally, in (10h), the intonational pattern of the utterance reflects a blend of the word order from one of the two target phrases with the intonation from the other target.

Lexical errors involve paradigmatic substitutions and blends of meaningful lexical items. Units involved include 1) entire words, both content and function, both monomorphemic and polymorphemic; 2) content stems; and 3) inflectional and derivational affixes. Examples of substitutions involving these types of lexical items are given in (11) in abbreviated form. In Chapters 3 and 4 below I will justify treating most polymorphemic words as whole lexical items, rather than considering the error to involve specific morphemes within the words, as well as give more precise definitions of 'content' and 'function' morphemes.

(11) Lexical units involved in errors.
   a. Monomorphemic free content words: B: 'Mómmy, mòre **cóffee** . . . mòre júice!' (B-20(35) 1;10)

b. Polymorphemic free content words: OB: 'Tàke my **Súpermàn** shìrt òff.' (for 'Batman'; OC-75(35) 3;11)

c. Monomorphemic free function words:
Al: 'Hére it ìs, Mòmmy. I gòt it **fòr** my . . . òff my béd.' (AL-55(36) 2;10)

d. Polymorphemic free function words:
OB: 'Ya knòw, Móm knows hòw to dò it àll by **my** . . . hersélf.' (child started to substitute 'myself' for 'herself'; OC-84(36) 4;0)

e. Derivational affixes: B: 'My pòpsicle's in the fréez**y** . . . fréez_er_.' (B-447(37) 5;1)

f. Inflectional affixes: B: (sucking on a piece of candy)
'I've been sùck**ed** on . . . I've been sùck_ing_ on thìs for a lòng tíme.' (B-456(37) 5;1)

In example (11a), the child intends to ask for more juice, but because he sees Mommy's coffee in the environment he erroneously substitutes the word 'coffee'. In (11b) the child substitutes the compound 'Superman' for 'Batman'. The error in (11c) illustrates the substitution of an incorrect preposition, and (11d) an incorrect bimorphemic pronoun. In (11e) the child substitutes the derivational suffix {-y} (adjectival) for {-er} (instrumental), and in (11f) the inflectional suffix {-ed} (passive) is substituted for {-ing} (progressive) (I am using curly brackets to indicate the lemma of an affix).

Syntactic errors involve the syntagmatic organization of phrasal strings, and are of two basic types: the misplacement of lexical items (words and morphemes) in the syntagmatic string, and phrase blends. While the former also involve lexical units, they are classified as syntactic errors rather than lexical errors since the error is not in lexical choice but in the erroneous placement of lexical items in the linear order.

(12) Syntactic errors (see below for explanations).
a. Misplacement of content morpheme:
OG:'I'm pètting your háir.'
M: 'You are?'
OG:'Yeah, so Ì won't pét it . . . púll it.' (OC-55(43) 3;7)

b. Reversal of two free function words:
B: 'Mommy, can yóu gò with mè?'
M: 'What?'
B: 'Can Í gò with yòu?' (B-96(46) 2;7)

c. Misplacement of inflectional suffix:
B: 'I nèver líke bòat**s** rìde_ . . . bòat rìde_s_.' (*'boats ride' [boᵂt(s) raⁱd] for 'boat rides' [boᵂt raⁱd(z)]; B-397(42) 4;10)

d. Phrase blend
   M: 'Come ón; I'm trỳing to clèan this plàce úp!'
   Al: 'Ì won't lét you tò.'
   M: 'What?'
   Al: 'Ì don't . . . Ì won't lét you.' (blend of 'Ì won't lét you' and 'Ì don't wánt you tò.' AL-71(49) 2;10)

In (12a), the verb stem 'pet' has been perseverated and substituted for 'pull', leaving the inflectional suffix {-ing} behind. In (12b) the pronouns 'I' and 'you' have been reversed, although in the error each is assigned correct case. The error in (12c) is a morpheme movement: the plural {-s} has been anticipated and added to the word 'boat' instead of the intended 'ride'. Note that the morpheme is pronounced with the phonologically correct allomorph in its error position. Example (12d) is a phrase blend, where the two phrasal targets have been blended into an ungrammatical utterance (this definition will be refined below).

Propositional errors occur when the speaker has formulated and produced an utterance which encodes a proposition which is different from what he or she had intended to say. For example:

(13)   B: 'Mom, can Ì play on your compúter?'
        M: 'Wéll, "Frèsh Prínce" is gònna be òn in a fèw mìnutes.'
        B: 'Ì wànna **wátch ìt** . . . Ì mean Ì wànna plày on your compúter.'
        (B-413(50) 4;11)

Here Bobby intended to reiterate to Mom that he wanted to play on the computer, but because Mom mentioned the TV show "Fresh Prince", Bobby was thinking about watching TV and erroneously conveyed the meaning that he wanted to watch the show rather than play on the computer; he then immediately corrected his utterance to the intended content. I have very few errors of this type in both the child and adult data, partly because they are the most difficult to accurately collect, since the researcher doesn't always know what meaning the speaker actually intended to convey.

1.4.2 Directionality of Errors

The locational relationship between the target/error and source of the error is the second dimension by which errors were categorized. There are two broad parameters along which errors can be classified with regards to directionality: contextuality and the paradigmatic/syntagmatic relationship. There are also several specific categories used for labelling directionality, which will be given below.

First, errors can be divided into the broad categories 'contextual' vs. 'non-contextual'. In 'contextual' errors, the source of the error involves some linguistic unit which is actually being planned for the current discourse or has been spoken in the discourse. In 'non-contextual' errors, there is no linguistic source in the utterance context. The second broad classification is 'paradigmatic' and 'syntagmatic'. In paradigmatic errors, the target and error units are elements which are related to each other in some linguistic paradigm (e.g. both are words, both are morphemes, both are phonemes) and are competing for the same slot in a syntagmatic string. In syntagmatic errors, the target and the source of the error are being planned for different slots in the syntagmatic (linear) string, and one influences the other by, for example, anticipation or perseveration. These two parameters, 'contextuality' and 'paradigmatic vs. syntagmatic' are to some extent orthogonal, and one or the other may be more pertinent to a particular type of error.

Phonological errors are most often contextual and syntagmatic; that is, a phonological unit planned for some location in an utterance affects a like unit planned for some other location in the utterance, as in (10a-e) above. Phonological errors can be non-contextual, that is, a unit can be substituted, added, or deleted with no obvious source in the utterance; however, this type of error is very rare. An example of a non-contextual paradigmatic phonological substitution is given in (14) below; in this case the vowel [i] in 'Mickey' [mí.ki] was erroneously produced as [ɚ], but there was no [ɚ] vowel or [r] consonant which could have served as the source, produced in any other word in the utterance.

(14)   B: 'I like DèeDee on the [mì.kɚ] . . . Mìckey Móuse Clùb.'
         (for 'Mickey' [mí.ki]; no [ɚ] or [r] in context; B-241(30) 4;3)

Phonological errors can also include non-contextual additions or omissions, in cases where there is no obvious source in the utterance. In (15a), an [l] is added to the word 'food' with no obvious source; in (15b) the [r] is left out of the cluster [dʒr] for no apparent reason; the unfilled underline marks the location of the omission.

(15)   a. An: 'Whenèver I get hùngry I gèt some [fḷúd].'
              (for 'food' [fud]; AN-109(30) 3;3)
         b. OB: 'It's sòrt of fúnny that I dòn't get ànything to [dʒ_íŋk] . . .
              to drínk.'
              (for 'drink' [dʒrɪŋk]; note that the /d/ remains [dʒ] even when
              the [r] is omitted; see §3.3.5 for discussion; OC-69(30) 3;10)

Another phonological error which could be considered 'non-contextual' is the type I have called 'telescoping', where some set of segments, including at least one weight-bearing unit (vowel, rhyme, syllable) is omitted, but the utterance is produced with the same overall duration and intonation contour as the intended utterance, as illustrated in (10f) above and (29) below. The classification of telescoping errors in terms of the parameters 'paradigmatic' or 'syntagmatic' is somewhat ambiguous, although the latter is possibly more accurate because they do change the structure of the syntagmatic string. In fact, this dimension could simply be irrelevant to this type of non-contextual phonological error.

Turning to lexical errors, one can see that the errors labelled 'lexical substitution errors' in this study, such as those presented in (11) above, are paradigmatic and non-contextual by definition. In every case they involve two paradigmatically related lexical items competing for the same syntagmatic slot, and do not involve a word planned for some other location in the utterance. A second type of lexical paradigmatic error is the 'blend', when two different lexical items are planned for the same syntagmatic slot in a phrase, and their phonological forms are blended into a single word. Examples of lexical blends are given in (16), where (a) shows a content word blend, and (b) a function word blend (see also (2b) above).

(16)　a. B:　'Thàt's a grèat bìg [**fá.pa**] bèar!'
　　　　　　　(blend of 'Father' [fá.ḏ3] and 'Poppa' [pʰá.pa]; B-116(38) 2;10)
　　　b. B:　(telling what time it says on his and Alice's clocks)
　　　　　　　'Mìne is èight fòrty fíve, and [ʃɝ:] . . . hérs is èight fòrty fíve.'
　　　　　　　(blend of 'she' [ʃi] and 'hers' [hɚz]; B-363(39) 4;9)

In some lexical blends, one or both of the targets has occurred in the preceding utterance; however, both words were appropriate in the target syntagmatic slot, and even if the child corrects to one of the two targets, there is no way of knowing which word he or she actually intended to utter. Therefore these errors have been counted as paradigmatic blends rather than perseverations, although those where one or both of the targets were spoken elsewhere in the utterance are considered to be 'contextual'. For example, in (17), either word 'milk' or 'juice' would have been an appropriate utterance for the child, so this is a contextual paradigmatic blend. This example further illustrates the fact that occasionally in very early word blends there are actual blends of segments, with features from two distinct segmental targets blending into a third segment.

(17)　M:　'Do you want **mìlk** or **júice**?'
　　　　OB:'[ṇuç].' (blend of 'milk' [mɛwk] and 'juice' [tuç], with the onset consonants [m] and [t̪] blending to produce [ṇ]; OC-4(38) 1;11)

However, if one lexical item is substituted for another and both were planned for the utterance or spoken in the utterance context, this is a syntagmatic and contextual error, and is considered a 'syntactic' error in this study. Examples are given in (12a,b) above. Other researchers have reported non-contextual lexical additions or omissions (e.g. Stemberger 1989), but in my data, errors which might be classified as such are usually more simply classifiable as phrase blends. On the other hand, phrase blend errors, as in (12d), are paradigmatic errors, since they involve two competing phrases (i.e. in a paradigmatic relationship to each other) which have been blended together and inserted into the same phrasal slot. Their 'contextuality' is difficult to ascertain because they are both simultaneously being planned for the utterance, and part of each phrase is uttered; thus this will be considered an irrelevant parameter for this type of error. Finally, propositional errors are always paradigmatic since they involve two competing propositions; again the 'contextuality' parameter is irrelevant, although this type of error may involve some environmental or discourse (but not utterance) influence as in (13) above.

Naturally when a non-contextual error is made, the child may have been thinking about another word or phrasing of the proposition which was in fact the source of the error. However when such sources are not verbalized by the child, and when they are not obvious from the immediate physical or discourse context, the observer cannot report on them; for this reason such errors are classified as 'non-contextual'. One complication of the current study is the fact that the adult subjects often did verbalize the source of the error by making comments such as 'Oh, I was thinking about X' or 'I almost said X'. However, in order to keep the adult data as comparable as possible to the child data, I did not utilize these comments in my classification of the adult data for the most part, since it was usually unavailable in the child data.

The more specific divisions in terms of directionality are relevant to contextual syntagmatic errors only. In syntagmatic errors, both the target and source units are being planned for the utterance (or discourse), and one or both of these become misplaced or repeated. Both phonological and lexical units can be involved in syntagmatic errors. There are three basic types of directionality:
1) *Anticipation:* the source follows the target. Some linguistic unit planned for later in the utterance is anticipated and affects a unit planned for earlier in the utterance.
2) *Perseveration:* the target follows the source. Some linguistic unit planned for and executed earlier in the utterance perseverates and affects a unit planned for later in the utterance.
3) *Exchange:* two elements exchange positions. This can include both metathesis, where contiguous units exchange, and reversals, where non-contiguous units exchange.

Anticipations can be 'complete' or 'incomplete'. In a complete anticipation, both the error and source are spoken before the speaker corrects the utterance, as illustrated in (18).

(18)   a. An: 'I got [dʒréʹp]- *jûice*.' ([dʒ] anticipated from 'juice' [dʒus],
           substituted for [g] in grape' [greʹp]; AN-42(1) 2;4)
       b. B: 'Mommy, whèn it chéws, *it* . . . whèn I chéw, *it* húrts.'
           ('it' anticipated from second clause, substituted for 'I' in first
           clause, with change in verb agreement; B-436(41) 5;0)

In an incomplete anticipation, the error is noticed and corrected before the speaker utters the source, as illustrated in (19).

(19) a. Al: 'Nòw we have [lʌn] . . . óne ĺeft.'   ([l] from 'left' [lɛft]
           anticipated, substituted for [w] of 'one' [wʌn]; AL-153(7) 3;7)
      b. Al: (putting her feet on the kitchen table) 'My pìgs . . . my tòes are
           pígs' fèet.'   ('pig' anticipated, substituted for 'toe', stranding
           plural and possessive suffixes; AL-97(41) 3;2)

Some researchers (Shattuck-Hufnagel 1979) have argued that incomplete
anticipations should be considered a separate class from complete anticipations,
since in fact it is possible that they represent interrupted exchanges; that is, the
speaker may have planned an erroneous exchange of units, but his or her external
monitor noticed and corrected the error before the second element was uttered. So
for example, in the above utterances, Alice could have been planning to say
'Nòw we have [lʌn wèft]' and 'My pìgs are tóes' fèet.' However, there are a
number of reasons to consider these errors anticipations. First, unambiguous
(complete) anticipations are far more common than complete exchanges,
suggesting that erroneous anticipations are planned more often than exchanges in
general (see Chapter 2 for details). Second, there are many cases of incomplete
anticipations where the exchange would cause an illegal utterance, as illustrated
in (20).

(20) Al: 'I get [glʌm.pi] . . . grúmpy when I sĺeep.'   ([l] from 'sleep'
           anticipated and substituted for /r/ [ɹ] in 'grumpy'; AL-104(7) 3;3)

In this case if the /l/ and /r/ had been exchanged, the illegal cluster /sr/ would
have been produced in *'sreep'. Since planning errors rarely produce illegal
phonotactic sequences in a language, this argues against the claim that such
sequences are planned during speech production planning (although one could
make the argument that the fact that they are illegal causes the internal monitor
to spot them before they are produced).

Third, there are a number of incomplete anticipations which involve
additions or omissions, which cannot by definition be an exchange. (An actual
movement of a unit from a position planned for later in the utterance into an
earlier position is classified below as a 'movement' rather than an exchange;
such movements also occur as perseverations, and are in general quite rare.)
Fourth, in anticipations, the target and source can be several syllables away from
each other, but in exchanges they are usually only one or two syllables distant;
in many of the incompletes, the source is fairly distant from the target. Finally,
as I will argue in Chapter 3, both complete and incomplete anticipations tend to
show the same prosodic pattern, in which the source word carries the tonic
stress. Exchanges, on the other hand, show a prosodic pattern in which the tonic
syllable occurs on either the first or second element of the exchange with equal
frequency. For all of these reasons I will count incomplete anticipations as a

type of anticipation, although I will in some cases report on the complete and incomplete types separately.

Perseverations are always complete by definition, since the source must be spoken before the error. The source of a perseveration, however, can be located in three different places: 1) in an earlier portion of the same utterance by the same speaker (as shown in (21a)); 2) in a preceding utterance by a different speaker (21b); 3) in a preceding utterance by the same speaker (21c), in some cases with an utterance by a different speaker intervening (21d).

(21) a. An: 'Wìnnie-Póoh bòok. Wìnnie-*P*óoh [pʰʊk].'
        (for 'book' [pʊk]; /p/ [pʰ] perseverated from 'Pooh' [pʰu] and
        substituted for /b/ [p] of 'book'; AN-3a(12) 1;7)
      b. M: 'Whó gàve you this bòo*k*?'
        An: '[pák ʰ].' (for 'Bob' [papʰ]; /k/ from coda of adult's 'book'
        perseverated and substituted for /b/ in child's 'Bob'; becomes
        aspirated by child's rule; AN-21(12) 1;11)
      c. An: 'Whìte Ràbbit a rúnning. Àlice sèe a Whìte [ʒǽ.bɪn].'
        (for 'rabbit' [ʒǽ.bɪt]; perseveration of [n] from 'running' [ʒʌ́.nin];
        AN-22(12) 2;0)
      d. OB:'Sèe that *gù*y with a pátch on his èye?'
        M: 'Yeah.'
        OB: 'Hè's the **gúy** . . . hè's the héro.'
        ('guy' perseverated, substituted for 'hero'; OC-128(43) 5;0)

In some cases there are sources both preceding and following the target. Since it is impossible to decide which was the actual source, and since it is possible that both influenced the error, these are classed separately into the *'anticipation/perseveration'* category (A/P).

(22) a. OB:'Giràffes, [tʃɾ̥ì.kəns], *r*hinos.'
        (for 'chickens' [tʃí.kəns]; [r] in both 'giraffes' and 'rhinos' could
        be source of the addition of [r] to the onset of 'chickens'; [r]
        becomes devoiced in this environment; OC-48(21) 3;3)
      b. B: 'I don't wànt *it* for Róss! I don't wànt it Róss to drìnk *it*.'
        (addition of 'it'; source could be preceding or following 'it';
        B-87(48) 2;6)

In many cases of A/P errors, particularly phonological errors, one of the two sources is in fact the more likely source, because it has the properties most typical of unambiguous sources; e.g. it occurs in the same syllable structure location, has the same stress, has the same neighboring segments, etc. However, selecting this as the source when there were other possibilities would be in some sense circular; that is, it would involve selecting one source over another because it is a typical source, then using this evidence to support the claim that some types of sources are more common than others. Therefore I have been very conservative and for the most part have put any error into the A/P category if there are plausible sources both before and after the error, even if one is more likely than the other. For this reason I may have a higher rate of A/P errors than what is typically found in other studies.

Most *exchange* errors involve like linguistic units from similar positions in the syntagmatic string, such as two onset consonants, two stressed vowels, two stressed content words, and so forth. Thus most often these reversals involve non-contiguous units.

(23)   a. B: 'Mòmmy, I nèed [pʰin kʰǽts].' (for 'clean pants' [kʰin pʰǽts]; onset consonants [kʰ] and [pʰ] exchanged; B-40(25) 2;1)

      b. An: 'Wow, my có́lds̲ are hànd.'
          M: 'What?'
          An: 'My có́ld . . . my hànds̲ are fréezing.' (exchange of 'cold' and 'hand', with stranding of plural morpheme; correction involves new lexical item to frame same proposition; AL-46(45) 2;8)

The error presented in the prologue is also an exchange error, and will be found in the data as (AN-226(25) 4;7). Less commonly, two contiguous elements will be metathesized. In these cases the two elements are almost by definition unlike, as two identical types of linguistic units rarely abut.

(24)   a. B: 'Héy, gèt the [kʰl̩ù] . . . Kòol-Aìd bóx dòwn.'
          (for 'Kool' [kʰuɫ]; metathesis of [u] and [ɫ], with devoicing of /l/ in context of [kʰ], and develarization of /l/ as it is now in an onset; B-127(27) 3;3)

      b. An: 'I thòught I wànted some sóup, but there ány ìsn't . . . there isn't àny sòup lèft.' (metathesis of determiner 'any' and copula+negative 'isn't'; AN-157(47) 4;2)

Because the properties of metatheses are very different from non-contiguous reversals, they are usually counted and analyzed separately in this study.

1.4.3 Form of Errors

I am using the term 'form of errors' to indicate the structural relationship between the source and planned target units in the error. There are six basic forms of error: 1) substitution, 2) addition, 3) omission, 4) movement (which can be seen as a combination of an omission and either an addition or a substitution), 5) exchange (which could be considered a double substitution), and 6) blend.

In a *substitution* error, one element is completely substituted for another. There are numerous examples of substitution errors in the discussions above (e.g. examples (11) and (18-21)); substitutions can involve feature values, other phonological units, morphemes, and words.

Addition errors occur in phonological errors and syntactic errors involving words and morphemes, where an element is inserted into an incorrect location. If it is a contextual error, the source is also spoken in the correct location. For phonological errors this most often involves consonant clusters, as illustrated in (25a). A syntagmatic lexical addition is shown in (25b).

(25)   a. M: 'Whàt is thát?'
           An: 'It's a [kʰwǽm.wʌ] . . . cámera.' (for 'camera' [kʰǽm.wʌ]; AN-28(2) 2;2)
       b. An: (to Daddy) 'Wànt **me** to hèlp . . . wànt **you** to hèlp . . . wànt to hèlp *me* cólor?' (AN-89a(41) 2;11)

In (25a) the [w] from the onset of the second syllable of 'camera' is anticipated and added to the onset of the first syllable, forming the legal cluster [kʰw]. The example in (25b) involves two errors: the first is an anticipation/addition of 'me', and the second is a lexical selection error of 'you' for 'me' (AN-89b(36) 2;11).

Omission errors in my corpus mainly involve phonological omissions, and are of two types. The first is the 'assimilation' error, where a phonological unit is omitted in the context of another phonological string which also lacks that element, so that the error and source become more structurally similar, as illustrated in (26).

(26)   Al: (after discovering a hole in her tights) 'My tóe! My tóe [_tʰɪks] òut.' (for 'sticks' [stíks]; AL-122(15) 3;4)

In this error the [s] in 'sticks' is omitted in assimilation to the two preceding instances of onset /t/ in 'toe'; this is considered a perseveratory error because the two sources precede the error. Notice that the /t/ in 'sticks' aspirates when the onset /s/ is deleted, following the allophonic rules of English.

The second type of omission error is the 'dissimilation' or 'masking' error; this occurs when a segment is planned for several slots in an utterance, and one of the instances is deleted in dissimilation from the other instances. For example:

(27)   Al: 'Mỳ móvie òver. Mè [_ǽtʰ]!' (for 'mad' [mætʰ]; AL-18(15) 2;2)

Here the [m] in 'mad' is omitted in dissimilation from the preceding [m] segments, another perseveration error. In some cases it is difficult to tell whether an omission error is an assimilation or dissimilation, as both possible sources occur in the utterance.

(28)   B: 'Héy, there's sȟll *s*ome [s_í.kɚz].'
          (for 'stickers' [stí.kɚz]; B-234(15) 4;3)

In (28) the omission of the [t] in 'stickers' could be a perseveratory dissimilation from the [t] in 'still' or a perseveratory assimilation to the simple [s] onset in 'some'.

As introduced in 1.4.2 above, a *telescoping* error is a particular type of omission error in which at least one weight-bearing unit (vowel, rhyme, or syllable) is deleted, and the remaining segments are collapsed into an utterance with fewer segments but with similar duration and the same intonational pattern as the planned longer string. In these errors some of the remaining segments are lengthened in order to have enough phonetic substance to bear the intonational contour. Telescopings often result in syntagmatic word blends in which two different words which were to occur in sequence are blended into one, as shown in (29) (markers above the transcription are to be read as pitch markers).

(29)   OA: 'Ànybody wànna còme and éat?'
          OG: 'Nŏt [rǽ:ẃ] . . . nòt right nôẃ.' (OC-27(34) 2;8)

In this telescoping error, the rhyme of 'right' [aⁱt] is deleted, as well as the onset of 'now'; the onset of 'right' [r] and the rhyme of 'now' [æʷ] are collapsed into a single syllable, but the vowel is lengthened so that the erroneous string can still carry the intended intonation.

Movement errors are a combination of omission and either addition or substitution, in that one element is deleted from its originally planned location and is either added or substituted elsewhere.

(30)   a. Al: 'My [çwíp._tìk] . . . my lípstìck.'
              (for 'lipstick' [wíp.çtìk]; AL-20(3) 2;2)
          b. Al: 'Hère's Snòw-Whíte. Here's [s_ò*ʷ*.náⁱt]!'
              (for 'Snow White' [sn̥òʷ.wáⁱt]; AL-174(14) 3;9)

In (30a), the [ç] is moved from the onset of the second syllable of 'lipstick' and added to the onset of the first syllable, creating the cluster [çw]; this is an anticipatory movement. In (30b) the /n/ from the onset cluster of 'Snow' is perseverated and moved into the onset of 'White', substituting for the onset [w].

Exchange errors and *blend* errors have been discussed above in §1.4.2.

Finally, for both phonological and syntactic units, there are *multiple* errors, in which combinations of error types occur.

(31)   a. An: '[hàʷ fɚ àʲ gə.gét].'
              (for 'How could I forget?' [hàʷ kʰəd àʲ fɚ.gét]; AN-112(31) 3;5)

b. B: (choosing tokens for a board game)
   'Í wànna be grèen. Yòu **blúe bèes** . . . yòu bè̱ blúe.'
   (for 'be blue' [bì blú]; B-169(48) 3;9)

In (31a), a multiple phonological error, the syllable [fɚ] is anticipated and substituted for the syllable [kʰəd]; then the [g] from the second syllable of 'forget' is reduplicated forward, with the vowel [ə] non-contextually inserted, creating the syllable [gə]. In (31b), a multiple syntactic error, the content words 'be blue' are metathesized, as is the phrasal prosody; also the verb 'be' has had the 3rd sg. present tense suffix non-contextually added to it.

The full classification system, listed in numerical order, is given in Table 1.3 (this system is repeated at the beginning of the data section of the book, and the data are organized according to this system). Categories which are numbered with '.5', such as 'Class 6.5: Phonological anticipations (complete), additions, larger units' are those categories which contain only adult errors; some categories in the taxonomy have been indicated as 'children only' as well.

1.4.4 Making Decisions in Ambiguous Cases

Fairly often an error could be analyzed in several different ways, and therefore a set of guidelines were used for making classification judgments in ambiguous cases. The first type of unclear case is one in which an error could be either a phonological error or a lexical substitution, as illustrated in (32). (In presenting the ambiguous errors in this section, I will not mark target/source/error units in the cases where it is the identity of this unit that is in question.)

(**32**) a. B: '[**wà̱ⁱf**] it óff!' (for 'wipe' [waⁱp]; B-79(1) 2;6)
      b. An: 'Whàt would a dóg lòok lìke if it hàd a **báck** . . . um . . . if it hàd a bé̱ak, and fèathers, and a fèathery táil?'
         (for 'beak' [bik]; AN-248(35) 4;10)

In (32a), the error could either be an anticipation of the coda [f] from 'off' [af], substituting for the coda [p] in 'wipe', or it could be a paradigmatic substitution of the word 'wife' for the word 'wipe'. In (32b), the error could either be a perseveration of the vowel [æ] in 'had' which was substituted for the vowel [i] in 'beak', or it could be the substitution of the word 'back' for 'beak'.

It is well-known that phonological errors frequently produce real lexical items in the language (Fromkin 1973a, Dell & Reich 1980), particularly because such errors are more likely to fool the internal self-monitoring system. Fortunately there are several ways in which phonological and lexical errors can be differentiated. First, in lexical substitution errors the target and source words nearly always belong to the same lexical category, and often the resultant sentence is grammatical, although odd semantically. But in phonological errors, the word containing the target and the word which results from the error can

---

TABLE 1.3
Classification system for errors.

I. Phonological Errors

Class	Units, Directionality, and Type
1.	Phonological anticipations (complete), substitutions, consonants.
2.	Phonological anticipations (complete), additions, consonants.
3.	Phonological anticipations (complete), movements, consonants.
4.	Phonological anticipations (complete), omissions, consonants.
5.	Phonological anticipations (complete), substitutions, vowels.
6.	Phonological anticipations (complete), substitutions, larger units.
6.5	Phonological anticipations (complete), additions, larger units. (AO)*
7.	Phonological anticipations (incomplete), substitutions, consonants.
8.	Phonological anticipations (incomplete), additions, consonants.
9.	Phonological anticipations (incomplete), omissions, consonants.
10.	Phonological anticipations (incomplete), substitutions, vowels.
10.5	Phonological anticipations (incomplete), omissions, vowels. (AO)
11.	Phonological anticipations (incomplete), substitutions, larger units.
11.5	Phonological anticipations (incomplete), additions, larger units. (AO)
12.	Phonological perseverations, substitutions, consonants.
13.	Phonological perseverations, additions, consonants.
14.	Phonological perseverations, movements, consonants.
15.	Phonological perseverations, omissions, consonants.
16.	Phonological perseverations, substitutions, vowels.
17.	Phonological perseverations, movements, vowels. (CO)**
18.	Phonological perseverations, substitutions, larger units.
19.	Phonological perseverations, additions, larger units.
20.	Phonological A/P, substitutions, consonants.
21.	Phonological A/P, additions, consonants.
22.	Phonological A/P, omissions, consonants.
23.	Phonological A/P, substitutions, vowels.
23.5	Phonological A/P, omissions, vowels. (AO)
24.	Phonological A/P, substitutions, larger units.
25.	Phonological reversals (non-contiguous), consonants.
26.	Phonological reversals (non-contiguous), vowels.
27.	Phonological metathesis (contiguous), vowels and/or consonants.
28.	Phonological exchanges (contiguous or non-contiguous), larger units.
29.	Phonological feature errors (all types).
30.	Phonological non-contextual subst., additions, or omissions, all units.
31.	Phonological errors with multiple error types (combinations of above).
32.	Phonological errors of lexical stress.
33.	Phonological errors of intonation.
34.	Phonological telescopings of phrases.

II. Paradigmatic Lexical Errors

Class	Units, Directionality, and Type
35.	Lexical substitutions, content words.
36.	Lexical substitutions, function words.
36.5	Lexical substitutions, mixed content and function words. (AO)
37.	Lexical substitutions, affixes. (CO)
37.5	Lexical additions, affixes. (AO)
38.	Lexical blends, content words.
39.	Lexical blends, function words.
40.	Lexical blends, mixed content and function words.

III. Syntactic Errors

Class	Units, Directionality, and Type
41.	Lexical anticipations, content and function words (substitutions, additions).
42.	Lexical anticipations, affixes.
43.	Lexical perseverations, content and function words.
44.	Lexical perseverations, affixes.
45.	Lexical reversals (non-contiguous), content words.
46.	Lexical reversals (non-contiguous), function words.
46.5	Lexical reversals (non-contiguous), affixes. (AO)
47.	Lexical metathesis (contiguous), content and function words.
48.	Syntactic errors with multiple error types involving words and morphemes.
49.	Syntactic phrase blends.

IV. Propositional Errors

Class	Units, Directionality, and Type
50.	Errors of formulating the proposition.

*(AO)=errors made by adults only   **(CO)=errors made by children only

---

differ as to lexical category; thus the resultant sentence will often be not only meaningless but also ungrammatical. Second, in lexical substitution errors there is most often a semantic relationship between the target and source words, whereas in a phonological error the target word and the word erroneously produced rarely have any semantic relationship.   Third, in lexical substitution errors where there is no semantic relationship between the target and source word there is usually a fairly close phonological relationship, and the words frequently have some morphemic structure in common; however, in my data it is rare that the two sources differ by only one phoneme, and if they do there is not necessarily any phonetic similarity between the two phonemes.   In a phonological error, the target word and the erroneously produced word usually differ by only one phoneme, which are usually phonetically similar to each other. Fourth, in phonological errors there is almost always a source segment in the utterance, somewhere nearby, usually in the same syllable-structure position and in a syllable with the same stress level as the target syllable (see Chapter 3); non-contextual phonological errors are very rare. However, if one tried to analyze a lexical substitution error as a phonological error, frequently there would be no contextual source for the hypothesized phoneme substitution. Fifth, many 'real words' in the child corpus which resulted from phonological errors are in fact words which the child had not yet acquired; to be a lexical substitution error, both words must be known to the speaker. Finally, phonological and lexical errors often show different patterns of correction behavior, as will be discussed in Chapter 2. Specifically, lexical substitution errors are self-corrected more often than are phonological errors, often with an editing expression such as 'I mean'.

Using these principles, I argue that (32a) is a phonological error (anticipation/substitution of [f] for [p]) and not a lexical substitution error. First, 'wife' is a noun, but 'wipe' is a verb; they are not semantically related, and it is also unlikely that this child at this age had the word 'wife' in his active vocabulary. Secondly, the [f] and [p] both occur in codas in stressed syllables, separated by only one syllable in the utterance; furthermore, they are phonetically similar, both being voiceless labial obstruents. Finally, the resultant utterance 'wife it off' is ungrammatical and meaningless; however, the child does not correct the error. On the other hand, the error in (32b) is analyzed as a lexical substitution of 'back' for 'beak'. Although there is a possible phonological source in 'had' (a vowel with the same stress level), the target and source words 'back' and 'beak' are both common nouns and are semantically related to each other (co-partonyms, body parts), and the erroneous utterance is grammatical. Furthermore, Anna knew both the words 'back' and 'beak' at this time, and she corrects the error to the word 'beak'. Therefore there is more evidence supporting the lexical substitution analysis than the phonological analysis. In the data, when an error is highly ambiguous, it is classified into the most likely category, but there is a notation in the analysis regarding the other possible analysis or analyses.

For deciding which units were involved in phonological errors, I relied on the 'minimal movement' principle (Laubstein 1987), which states that the simplest or most conservative analysis is always chosen, involving the smallest segmental error unit. There are two basic reasons for adopting this principle. First, in previous SOT research the majority of unambiguous phonological errors have been found to involve single consonants or vowels; for this reason most researchers agree that the segment is the most prominent phonological planning unit. Therefore, if a single segment analysis is possible, it is more likely to be correct. Second, if this principle is not adopted, the researcher would be free to make different analyses on the same basic types of errors from one example to the next, which would certainly bias one's findings. So, for example, the unit of error involved in (33) could be considered to be ambiguous.

(33)   Al: '... Lìttle [ʒàʲd] Ríding Hòod ...'
         (for 'Red Riding' [ʒɛd ʒáʲ.dɪŋ]; AL-105(5) 3;3)

In this error one could argue that the whole morpheme 'ride', or the syllable [ʒaʲd], or the rhyme [aʲd], or the body [ʒaʲ], or just the vowel [aʲ] has been anticipated and substituted for elements of the intended word 'Red' [ʒɛd]. The principles distinguishing lexical from phonological errors discussed above eliminate the 'Ride' analysis, since 'red' and 'ride' belong to different lexical categories, are not semantically related, and the error produces an ungrammatical utterance. Taken as a phonological error, the 'minimal movement' principle requires that this be analyzed as a single vowel substitution error; the fact that the surrounding consonants are the same in the target word as in the source word is simply a reason why the vowel error is more likely to take place (as predicted by the 'repeated phoneme effect', Dell 1984).

Another decision-making principle is that a phonological substitution error is classified as a featural error only when there is no whole-segment source in the utterance, but there is a nearby segment which is phonetically similar to the target and which contains the feature specification erroneously produced in the error. It is classified as a 'non-contextual' error only when there is neither a whole-segment source in the utterance, nor a nearby phonetically similar segment which could allow a featural analysis. For example:

(34)   a. Al: 'I gàve him his fàvorite [pʰɛ́.ɾi]-bèar.'
            (for 'teddy' [tʰɛ́.ɾi]; AL-129(29) 3;4)
        b. B: (talking about how to open a computer game) 'You nèed to
            prèss "Màth [ræ.gɪt]" ... "Màth Rábbit" twó tìmes.'
            (for 'rabbit' [ræ.bɪt]; B-290(30) 4;5)

In (34a) there is no /p/ in the utterance which could have been the source of the error. Therefore, the labials [f] and [b] were probably the segments which influenced the target /t/ to be erroneously produced at the labial place of articulation, making this a featural error. In (34b), there is no consonant in the planned utterance spoken at the velar place of articulation which could be the source of the [g], and thus this is a non-contextual error.

There are many errors which I have classified as segmental, that one might at first think are actually featural. Consider the error in (35).

(35)   OG: 'This is [fòʷp] from my Dád.' (for 'soap' [ɕoʷp]; OC-12(1) 2;2)

In this error one could argue that it was only the labial feature of the [f] in 'from' that was anticipated and substituted for the palato-alveolar place of the target [ɕ], rather than the whole segment [f] being the substitution, since the error segment retains the fricative manner and voicelessness of the target [ç]. There are several reasons why researchers working with SOTs have consistently rejected this type of analysis. First, in the vast majority of segmental phonological errors, there is a whole segment source in the utterance. If individual features were free to substitute for each other, one would expect many more errors with no whole segment source where either a non-contextual or a featural analysis was likely (Shattuck-Hufnagel & Klatt 1979). Second, consonants are involved in errors in proportions which are correlated with frequency of occurrence of the segment, but not in any way correlated with feature frequency (Shattuck-Hufnagel & Klatt 1979). Third, errors which involve the addition or omission of a whole segment are quite common, and these have no obvious featural explanation; thus the segmental analysis can provide a more unified account of phonological errors occurring in the 'phonological processes' component of the processing model. Fromkin (1973a) has argued that features are not 'independently controlled' in speech production, and therefore are not as susceptible as segments to error. Therefore I follow a well-documented principle in classifying an error as 'featural' only if a whole-segment analysis is not possible.

A final possible ambiguity has to do with errors such as the following:

(36)   a. Al: (wanting to put her bathing suit on over her clothes)
           'I nèed to pùt it ùnder . . . òver my shírt!' (AL-77(36) 2;11)
       b. An: 'Thís is the òne I nèw gòt.' (AN-286(49) 5;4)
       c. An: 'I thòught I was lóst . . . I thòught I lóst ìt.' (AN-114(49) 3;5)

In all three cases, one might argue that there is either a lexical substitution or a phrase blend. In (36a), Alice could have accidentally selected 'under' for 'over', or she could have blended the phrases 'I nèed to pùt it [bathing suit] òver my shírt' and 'I nèed to pùt them [clothes] ùnder my báthing sùit'. In (36b), Anna could have misselected 'new' for 'just', or blended the phrases 'Thís is the nèw one I gòt' and 'Thís is the òne I jùst gòt'. Finally, in (36c) Anna could have either substituted the pronoun 'I' for 'it' (for an intended utterance 'I thought it was lost'), or could have blended the two phrases 'I thòught it was lóst' and 'I thòught I lóst it'.

Making a decision between the two classifications is very difficult, because, unlike adults, children rarely introspect about the source of the error and make it overt. In order to be consistent in my classification, I used the following basic principles. First, if the utterance was frankly ungrammatical (at odds with the child's current grammar), I considered it to be a phrase blend. This is because unambiguous phrase blends are nearly always ungrammatical, whereas in lexical substitutions, since the two words are nearly always of the same lexical category, the resultant utterance is usually grammatical. Second, there is often an odd intonation pattern in a phrase blend, showing elements of both syntactic frames, whereas the intonation in lexical substitution utterances is usually normal. Third, in some cases the utterance is grammatical, but when the child corrects the utterance, he or she corrects to a different syntactic structure rather than the other possible lexical item; such cases were analyzed to be phrase blends. Fourth, when speakers correct a lexical substitution error they often correct only the erroneous word, whereas when speakers correct a phrase blend, they nearly always repeat the entire phrase in their correction.

Using these four principles, I classified (36a) as a lexical substitution of 'under' for 'over', since the sentence 'I nèed to pùt it ùnder my shírt' is grammatical (but expresses the wrong proposition), the intonation was normal in this utterance, and the child corrects to the other lexical item without repeating the entire phrase. In a case like this, there is no evidence that the child has activated the opposing syntactic structure which would have been required by the lexical choice of 'under'. However, (36b) is classified as a phrase blend, since it is ungrammatical and the intonation reflects a blend of the two syntactic frames; this utterance was not corrected by the child. Finally, (36c) is also classified as a phrase blend; although it is grammatical and the intonation was normal, the child corrected to a different target syntactic structure, producing the entire target phrase.

It should be reiterated that when a child makes a lexical substitution, it is possible that he/she actually has two competing plans for framing the proposition. This is especially likely when the child substitutes one verb for another, as in (37).

(37)   OB:(showing adult the new pedals on his bike) 'Wànna shòw what kínd they àre? Rácing bìke!' ('show' for 'see'; OC-90(35) 4;1)

In this case the child may have misselected the verb, or may have blended two phrases, 'Wanna see what kind they are?' and 'Want me to show you what kind they are?' It could even be the case that he activated both verbs and created two functional structures, one based on 'see' and one based on 'show', and then blended the two functional structures. However, because the utterance was grammatical and had normal intonation, and the child did not resolve the utterance into a different syntactic string (the error was not corrected), the most conservative analysis is that this is a lexical substitution error. The phrase blend possibility has been noted in the data entry.

In a few cases where there were multiple possible sources for an error, but one possibility was the glaringly obvious source, I have used this most likely source in my numerical counts. In every such case I have indicated in the data entry that I counted one particular unit as the source, and explained why. Otherwise all possible sources are taken into consideration in my counts.

1.4.5 Relationship Between Error Types and Processing Model
The simplest way to discuss the relationship between the RPC Model and error types is in terms of 'what can go wrong' during speech production planning. Many of these errors can be discussed within the 'competing plans'

model of Baars and others (Baars 1980, 1992, Harley 1984). This discussion also heavily reflects arguments of Fromkin, Garrett, and Levelt, among others. Let us consider a boy who is formulating and producing an utterance in a particular discourse context in a specific setting. The first thing that can go wrong is that the child may select an incorrect proposition, i.e. formulate an incorrect 'Message Level Representation' out of the 'Inferential Processes' component. When he feeds this proposition into the speech production planning mechanism, it will encode the proposition correctly, and the utterance will be spoken with no linguistic errors, but it will simply not convey the information the child intended to convey (see example (13) above).

If the correct proposition is selected, then the child will begin activating the lemmas of appropriate lexical items from the content lexicon ('Lexical Selection'). While the most appropriate lexical items are being activated by the 'Message Level Representation', lexical items which are semantically related to them will also be activated, and will compete with the correct items. If these related items become highly activated and then erroneously selected, two things can happen. First, the erroneous item may be substituted for the correct lexical item during 'lexical assignment' to 'functional structures', and thus be planned and spoken in place of the intended word. This results in paradigmatic lexical selection errors where the target and error words are semantically related (see for example (2a), (11a,b), and (36a) above). Second, the intended and interfering words may both be selected and linked to the same slot in the functional structures; these words will be blended phonologically when their phonetic forms are retrieved because they will be associated with the same syntactic slot. These are the paradigmatic lexical blends (examples (16a) and (17)). Errors involving the misplacement or omission of words can also happen at this stage of processing, if lexical items are assigned to the wrong thematic role or given no functional assignment during the assignment of functional structures. How one can distinguish an error involving misassignment to functional structures from one involving misassignment to syntactic structures will be discussed below.

If the child has selected the correct proposition, selected the lemmas for the correct content lexical items, and correctly assigned them to functional structures, then the child will have a correct 'Functional Level Representation' to feed simultaneously into the next three processing components: 'Selection of Syntactic Templates', 'Assignment of Content Lemmas to Syntagmatic Positions', and 'Assignment of Intonation'. Several very complex things happen at this point, and so many types of errors can occur. First, syntactic templates are being selected which will appropriately frame the proposition. If there is more than one appropriate way to frame the proposition, it is possible that two frames may be selected, and the utterance may be preliminarily framed according to both competing plans. What is produced then is an ungrammatical blend of the two syntactic frames, i.e. a paradigmatic phrase blend (examples (2d), (12d)). Another possible source of phrase blends would be a situation in which two content lexical items (e.g. two verbs) have been activated but neither fully selected; syntactic structures might be constructed according to the requirements of each of the lexical items, and then a blend of the two produced; this will be discussed in detail in Chapter 6. A second type of error which can occur at this level of processing is that the correct syntactic template is selected, but activated content lexical items are misassigned to positions in the template (i.e. there is an erroneous linking between the semantic representation and the syntactic forms); this accounts for content lexical misplacements (examples (2c), (12a), (23b)). If an extra syntactic slot is erroneously planned, there may be a lexical addition (example (25a)); if a syntactic position is erroneously omitted, this will occur as a lexical omission. Third, at this level the lemmas of function words and affixes are being activated and inserted into the correct location in the syntactic frame, according to the requirements of the proposition, the content words, and the syntactic template. These function words can also be misassigned to linear slots (example (12b)). This is also the location of paradigmatic substitutions and blends of function words and morphemes, if an incorrect lemma becomes more highly or as highly activated as the intended lemma (example (16b)). Finally, a general intonational pattern is being selected at this point, in accordance with the aims of the proposition (e.g. declaration vs. question), the information structure of the sentence (e.g. new vs. old information), and any pragmatic relevance (e.g. emphatic or contrastive stress). Some intonational errors can actually be caused by a phrase blend, where the ordered lexical items of one possible phrasing are blended with the intonational structure from the other (example (10h)); others are caused by misselection of the intonational contour for this particular discourse-pragmatic situation and informational structure.

As suggested above, in order to develop a completely predictive model, one must be able to distinguish between lexical misplacement errors which occur as lexical items are being assigned to functional structures vs. those which occur when lexical items are being inserted into syntactic structures, and this is no easy task (Garrett 1993). However, it seems likely that errors of functional assignment are the more restrictive case. In such errors one would expect that the two lexical items involved (target and error words) would be semantically related content words of the same lexical category, otherwise one would be unlikely to be eligible for assignment to the function of the other (and only content words are being assigned at this point in the process). Furthermore, one would hypothesize that they would have to be words which either were being planned for the same phrase (so would be linked to the same propositional functional structure), or were being planned for identical locations in sequential phrases, such that each lemma is assigned to the correct functional location but in the wrong phrase. The following two examples, then, are good candidates for functional structure assignment errors.

(38)   a. AM: '. . . the debàte about whether there's a **bràin** in the **mìnd**.'
        (for 'a mind in the brain'; AD-638(45))

b. AM: (speaker realizes that he has accidentally interrupted a class discussion by speaking to the professor through the open doorway; he says to the class)
'Enjòy the **interrúption,** . . . I mean enjòy the <u>discússion,</u> and forgìve the ***interrúption.***' (AD-579(41))

In (38a), the speaker has activated two semantically related nouns 'mind' and 'brain', and assigned them to the wrong functions in the phrase, producing an erroneous exchange of the two words. In (38b) the speaker is planning two phrases at once, 'enjoy the discussion' and 'forgive the interruption'; he accidentally assigns the noun 'interruption' to the first rather than the second phrase. Although these two nouns are not strictly speaking semantically related, they are both nouns derived from verbs with the suffix {-ion}, so that their formal relationship may have allowed the error to fool the internal monitor. The fact that I have illustrated this type of error with adult examples is no accident, since clear cases of functional assignment errors are rare in the child data (possibly (19b) above is one example). Other syntagmatic lexical errors where lexical category is violated, where there is little semantic relationship between the two words involved, that involve addition or omission, or that involve function morphemes, are more likely to occur during morphosyntactic planning than during functional structures assignment.

One further differentiation which needs to be made is that between two types of exchanges: metathesis and reversal errors. In metathesis errors, two contiguous units exchange places, whereas in reversal errors, two non-contiguous units exchange places. Lexical reversal errors, as just discussed, can occur either by misassignment of functional structures, as in (38a), or by misassignment of lexical items to slots in syntactic structures, as in (39) below. I indicated above that in reversal errors caused by functional assignment, the two targets must have certain factors in common such as lexical category, semantics, and so on. While two targets involved in a reversal caused by syntactic slot misassignment may have less in common than in functional assignment errors, they still often are similar in terms of lexical category, semantics, phonology, and weight. So in (39), 'skim' is a verb and 'cream' is a noun in this context, although 'cream' can also be a verb; the words are both stressed content words, and they are phonetically similar (one syllable, with /k/ in the onset and /m/ in the coda). So this error was most likely made when inserting lemmas into syntactic slots, since each word is not seriously at odds with the requirements of that slot, and the two words are similar enough that this reversal was able to fool the internal monitor.

(39)   AM: 'If you **crèam** the **skìm** . . . <u>skìm</u> the <u>crèam</u> off my fólk-tùne nòvices, (etc.)' (reversal of 'skim' and 'cream'; AD-633(45))

However, metathesis is a very different kind of process. There actually seem to be several types of metathesis errors, as illustrated in (40).

(40) a. An: 'Cléan-pìper.' (for 'pipe-clèaner'; metathesis of morphemes
         'clean' and 'pipe' within the compound, with stranding of suffix
         {-er}; AN-134(47) 3;11)
      b. AF: 'You're nòt going to stànd èating úp àre you?'
         (for 'eat standing' with stranding of progressive suffix {-ing};
         AD-649(47))
      c. B: 'Mom, thèy're not éither hòme . . . thèy're not hòme éither.'
         (for 'hòme éither'; B-222(47) 4;2)
      d. An: 'I thòught I wànted some sóup, but there ány ìsn't . . . there
         isn't àny sòup lèft.' (for 'ìsn't àny'; AN-157(47) 4;2)

The error in (40a) is a metathesis of the two content morphemes within a
compound. I have four such errors: *'cándlemàke stìcker' (AN-102(47) 3;2);
*'náil-tòe' (OC-146(47) 5;5); and *'séed-gràss' (AD-645(47)), as well as the
error in (40a). It is not clear at what point in processing these errors occur; it is
possible they are lexical assignment errors, reflecting the somewhat independent
status of the content morphemes in compounds; note that in every case the
'compound stress' pattern is retained in the error. On the other hand, such errors
could occur during activation of phonological forms, or could even be a simple
phonological error, since they involve the metathesis of two contiguous
syllables. In a few errors such as (40b), the two targets were in fact from the
same lexical class, and appear to have very similar properties to the reversal
errors made during lexical insertion into syntactic frames; certainly in this case
the two verbs could have simply been assigned to the wrong slots marked for
verbs in the syntactic string. Only adults made errors of this sort. However, in
the errors such as those in (40c,d), the two words which are metathesized are
from very different lexical categories, sometimes crossing the content/function
distinction, such that the utterance produced is strikingly ungrammatical. It is
very unlikely that these types of metatheses occur due to lexical insertion into
syntax, since they cause major violations of the required lexical categories; e.g.
in (40c) a noun is inserted into an adverb slot, and in (40d), the determiner 'any'
is inserted into the copula+negative slot. In some cases the phrasal stress
remains in the originally planned location, as in (40d), but in other cases the
phrasal stress is also metathesized, as in (40c); this latter occurs most often
when the metathesis involves content words. I would like to suggest that most
metathesis errors are caused by a misordering of the actual structural slots in the
syntactic frame itself. For example, in (40c), the slots for 'noun' and 'adverb'
are metathesized, and in this case the slots themselves take the phrasal stress
properties with them. Then during lexical insertion, the lemmas are actually
inserted into the correct slots in terms of their match with the requirements of
the syntax. In this sort of error, the two target words are not expected to have

much in common, because the error is not due to the properties of the lexical items per se, but due to a misordering in the syntax in which they are inserted. The fact that children make far more lexical metathesis errors than adults do (including the interrupted metatheses counted in Class 41; see Chapter 4) supports the claim that metathesis is a misordering within syntactic structures, since children are expected to have less fixed syntactic templates than adults.

After the lemmas of all the content and function words and morphemes have been activated and ordered via syntactic templates into the correct linear order, the child activates the 'forms' of all the lemmas, which includes both phonological and morphological representations, and orthographic representations for the adults. While these forms are being activated, activation spreads to phonetically (and, I will argue below, morphologically, and rarely, orthographically) similar lexical items, and in some cases the phonetic form of a structurally related word will be misselected for insertion into the syntactic string. This results in 'malapropisms', i.e. errors in which one word is substituted for a formally similar word, where the two words have no semantic relationship. The result of the recovery of the forms of all the lexical items is the 'Phonological Level Representation', which may contain incorrectly selected lexical items, misplaced lexical items, blended syntactic structures, and so on; if so, however, the 'Phonological Processes' component will treat the input as if it is the intended string, and assign the appropriate phonetic form to it, regardless of these higher-level errors.

On the other hand, if there are no errors while lexical forms are activated, selected, and inserted into correct syntactic templates, and intonation is correctly assigned, then the child will have produced the appropriate 'Phonological Level Representation', which he can now feed into the 'Phonological Processes' component. In this component, phonetic form is assigned to the utterance, according to the phonological rules of the language and the linear arrangement of the phonetic material. All of the phonological errors, with one possible exception, take place during the assignment of phonetic form: phonological units can be moved, added, deleted, substituted, and so on during these processes (see examples in (10a-f) above, among many others). After the errors occur, productive phonological processes 'clean up' the error string in order to make sure that no rules of the phonology are violated. The one exception is errors of lexical stress, which in some cases are caused by the activation of a derivationally related word in the form lexicon, whose stress is erroneously copied onto the intended word, such as the error in (10g) above involving 'décorate/decorátion'; these errors will be discussed at length in Chapter 3. The output of the 'Phonological Processes' component is the 'Phonetic Level Representation', and at this point, speech production planning is complete.

It has often been pointed out for adult errors that there is a great deal of evidence for the independence or discreteness of the various levels and components during processing, since errors which affect one level of processing seem to not affect any other level (Fromkin 1973a, Garrett 1980b); I have hinted at this during the discussion above. For example, if a speaker activates an incorrect lemma, say the lemma for 'hot' instead of 'cold', the remainder of the system treats 'hot' as if it were the intended word. The lemma for 'hot' is assigned a functional role and is inserted into the syntagmatic string; the form for 'hot' is activated from the form lexicon; the 'Phonological Processes' component assigns the appropriate pronunciation for 'hot' rather than 'cold', and if the speaker's internal self-monitor doesn't catch it in time, the speaker utters it with no hesitation. This is also true within individual components: if a speaker deletes the [s] from the onset of the word 'stop' [stap], the 'Phonological Processes' component will cause the newly word-initial [t] to become aspirated, i.e. [tʰap] (see Chapter 3), following the allophonic rules of English. Thus there is a great deal of automaticity in this speech production planning model, and it will be very interesting to consider in the discussion below whether or not young children show evidence of the same sort of autonomous organizational structure and automaticity during language production which has been well-documented for adults.

1.5 General Issues Regarding Children's SOTs

In the chapters to follow, I will discuss in detail the types of SOTs made by children, and what these SOTs reveal about the development of language representation and processing. Three general issues will be briefly introduced here.

1.5.1 At What Age Do Children Begin Making Slips?

As presented in §1.1.2 above, a guiding principle of this study is that a child can't make an error on a construction until the child has learned that construction correctly. Any 'errors' made before this time are in fact part of the learning process and not a one-time speech production planning error, as SOTs are defined. Therefore the onset of slips depends on the age at which individual children develop various language constructions. Anna, the oldest of my three children, was an early language learner, and I collected a single telescoping slip from her at age 1;4, given in (41a) below. However, SOTs did not become common until age 1;7; her early slips were mainly phonological or lexical errors, in 1- or 2-word utterances or fixed phrases (see (41b)). Bobby, the youngest of the three, was also an early talker; he began making word blends at 1;7 (41c), and within-word syntagmatic phonological errors at 1;8 (41d), while still in the 1-word stage. I also have 4 errors made by Other children before their second birthday: one phonological perseveration (41e), one lexical substitution (41f), and two lexical blends. Alice, on the other hand, was a relatively late talker, and I collected her first slip at age 2;0 (41g), a vowel reversal. Taken together, I have 57 errors made by children before they reached their second birthday: 22 from Anna, 31 from Bobby, and 4 from Other children.

(41) a. An: (counting number of books) '[tʰuwĭ:] . . . . twŏ, thrĕe bôok.'
(for 'two, three book' [tʰŭʔ.θwĭʔ.bôk]; AN-1(34) 1;4.20)

b. An: (looking at photo album) 'Thère [pǽ.kàpʰ] . . . thère
Grándpà.' (for 'Grandpa' [kʷǽ.pà]; reversal of [p]<-->[k], plus
copy of [p] at end, with rule of word-final aspiration of
voiceless plosives, and [kʷ] delabialized; AN-2(31) 1;7.9)

c. B: (saying goodbye to Grandma who was driving away in car)
'[kâ ᶦ . . . pâ ᶦ. kô.]' (blend of 'car' [kɔ] and 'bye' [paᶦ], which
are then repeated in 'vertical construction'; 1-word stage;
B-1(40) 1;7.22)

d. B: (pointing at his bottle sitting on dishwasher) '[tá.pow].'
(for 'bottle' [pá.tow]; onsets [p]<-->[t]; 1-word stage; B-3(25)
1;8.25)

e. OA: 'Whère's the cáterpĭllar?'
OG: 'Ínna [ǽ.pĭ] . . . ápplè.'
(for 'apple' [ǽ.pòʷ], source most likely 'caterpillar'
[kʰǽ.rə.pʰĭ.lɚ]; [ɪ]-->[oʷ]; 2-word stage, 'Inna' is a single word
for 'In the'; OC-1(16) 1;10.0)

f. OB: 'Bób . . . Béckie nòse.' (pronounced: [bá: . . . bé.kiʔ nò:ʷ])
(started to say 'BobBob' [bá:.bab], his name for his grandfather;
while pointing to his grandmother Beckie's nose; 2-word stage;
OC-2(35) 1;10.22)

g. Al: '[wàk.ʌ.bèᶦ báᶦ.bi].' (for 'rock-a-bye baby' [wàk.ʌ.bàᶦ béᶦ.bi];
[aᶦ]<-->[eᶦ]; 2-word stage; AL-1(26) 2;0.2)

Stemberger (1989) also reports that his daughters produced errors during the
1-word stage (as early as 1;6). These data make it clear that SOTs can occur
during early phases of language acquisition, and that the types of errors produced
at early stages are a function of which linguistic structures have been learned
earliest. This will be a theme running throughout the analyses in this book.

1.5.2 Individual Differences

In analyzing my children's errors I noticed several differences among them
which fall into patterns best described in terms of the 'expressive-referential'
continuum (Nelson 1973, Goldfield & Snow 2001). Anna's learning style was
towards the expressive end of the scale; she never went through consistent one-
word or two-word stages, and spoke in long memorized strings very early on; she
developed syntax earlier than the other two children. Alice and Bobby tended
more towards the 'referential' style, going through clear stages, pronouncing
each word carefully, and speaking in longer phrases relatively later than Anna.
As we go through the data below it will become apparent that these learning
styles are reflected in the error patterns. Specifically, Anna's data include a
higher percentage of syntactic and function word errors than the other two. She
also produced a larger number of telescopings, which essentially consist of

skipping a rhythmic beat, as well as more multiple phonological errors, with several phonological misorderings in one phrase. Anna also corrected fewer of her errors than the other two. This is another subtext which will recur in the following pages.

1.5.3 Qualitative vs. Quantitative Analysis

One difficulty in analyzing naturalistic SOT data collected by the pen-and-paper method is the fact that one can never actually record all of the slips made by an individual subject. After collecting a large enough corpus of errors, the researcher can with confidence say 'Children of age X do make Y kinds of errors', and that Z type of error was not heard by the researcher at some particular age, (note the number of categories in the classification system above which were only pertinent to either the child or the adult database). It is much more difficult for the researcher to make quantitative statements about the data, i.e. that X type of error is made reliably more or less often than Y type of error. The absolute numbers collected can be influenced both by perceptual biases (as mentioned above), and simply by data-collection idiosyncrasies of the researcher. For example, I collected almost twice as many errors from Bobby as from Alice, but this doesn't necessarily mean that Bobby made more errors; I may have simply paid more attention to his errors than I did to Alice's. On the other hand, Bobby was an especially talkative child, so this might in fact be a real finding; there is simply no way to tell. Particularly for the Other children, the absolute numbers are only suggestive, since they are due to some extent to the fact that I didn't know the Other children as well as my own, so was very cautious in recording their errors; and, as mentioned above, lexical errors are much easier to verify with Other children than syntactic errors. Furthermore, errors collected from Other children by researchers other than myself may reflect to some extent biases of perception or interest of the other collectors. It is for this reason that I will perform no statistics of the sort designed to prove that X error type is more frequent at age Y than at age Z. Similarly, I will compare the children's data to my adult data in terms of numerical trends, but not perform statistics on these numbers. Because of the differences in the number of errors contributed by each subject, statistics comparing error types across children would also be meaningless. Finally, the potential differences in my classification procedures compared to those used for classifying adult or child errors by various other researchers would again render such statistics uninformative and potentially misleading. I will therefore simply point out in the quantitative data, patterns which hold across all subjects, and apparent developmental trends which are robustly supported by the numbers.

1.6 Summary

In this chapter I have presented a definition of 'slips of the tongue', and discussed how such slips made by children can provide evidence for our understanding of the development of language. I have documented that children do make such slips as early as age 1;7, and that there are principled ways of distinguishing slips from systematic non-adult productions. A speech production planning model, the RPC Model, was presented, and SOTs were discussed in terms of where in the model the breakdown occurred. The methodology and subjects used in this study were discussed at length. A system for classification of the SOTs was presented, along with principles for making decisions about classification in ambiguous cases. Finally, I suggested that there may be some individual differences involving the 'expressive-referential' continuum, and that qualitative analyses are more reliable than quantitative, although general quantitative trends can be discussed.

    In the next chapter I will present a general overview of the findings of my study, focussing on a comparison of the children's SOTs to adult errors, and looking at developmental changes in the types of errors and units involved in errors produced by the children.

Chapter 2
Kids' Slips and Adults' Slips: General Comparison

2.1 Overview

The focus of Chapter 1 was to demonstrate that it is possible to systematically collect SOTs from very young children, and that these slips can provide a great deal of information about the time-course of the development of both linguistic representations and language processing mechanisms. In the present chapter, I will look at general issues involving the children's SOTs, comparing the children to each other as well as to adults, on a number of dimensions. Since adult SOTs have been crucial for developing speech production planning models, it is important to document that the children's errors are similar enough to the adults' that they can be discussed in terms of the same types of models. On the other hand, if they are substantially different from adult errors, this requires a developmental explanation. Thus the following specific questions will be addressed in this chapter: Do children make all the same types of SOTs as adults, or do children and adults show qualitative differences in error types? Do children and adults make the same general proportions of errors? Do the different children in the study make the same general proportions of errors as each other? Are there any clear developmental trends in error types, in terms of structure, directionality, or units involved? Do children correct their errors as often as adults do? If there are obvious differences between child and adult SOTs in terms of these general characteristics, how can the differences be explained?

In every case I will compare the children's data to my adult corpus. In some cases I will also compare the child data to published adult studies, when those studies present figures on the specific issues under investigation. In this chapter, only general comparisons are being made; more specific comparisons will be presented in the appropriate subsequent chapter.

2.2 General Comparison to Adults

2.2.1 Children Produce Nearly All the Same Types of Errors as Adults

In Table 2.1, the numbers of errors made by the subjects in this study are presented, organized by age and by groups of categories, i.e. grouped by general units of error (phonological, lexical, syntactic, and propositional), directionality, and form type. (In this and in all future tables, the 'Adult' figures come from my corpus, unless otherwise indicated.) In general, both children and adults produced some errors in each category. It can be seen from this table that the children's errors do not differ markedly from the adults' in terms of types of errors.

However, referring back to the classification system presented in Chapter 1, Table 1.3, one can see that there are a few classes marked 'adults only' or

TABLE 2.1
Number of each type of error by age (ages 1-5 and adult); 'Lex'= content
morphemes and free function morphemes; 'Morph'=bound affixes;
'Syntactic'=lexical and morphological misplacements and phrase blends;
'Par.' = paradigmatic.

Age:	1	2	3	4	5	Total	Adult
Phonological							
Phon. Anticipations	8	69	58	104	79	318	133
Phon. Perseverations	11	43	49	79	50	232	55
Phon. A/P	2	17	24	53	33	129	38
Phon. Exchanges	7	33	19	30	15	104	45
Phon. Features	0	1	7	9	10	27	8
Non-Contextual	1	2	3	8	1	15	2
Phon. Multiple	3	12	13	8	7	43	8
Stress & Intonation	0	0	0	3	1	4	22
Telescopings	4	21	8	18	10	61	31
Total Phonological=	**36**	**198**	**181**	**312**	**206**	**933**	**342**
	63%	70%	71%	66%	65%	67.4%	48%
Lexical							
Lex. Par. Subst.	6	34	28	64	56	188	157
Morph. Par.	0	0	0	0	2	2	3
Lex. Blends	12	17	13	24	12	78	72
Total Lexical=	**18**	**51**	**41**	**88**	**70**	**268**	**232**
	32%	18%	16%	18.5%	22%	19.3%	32.3%
Syntactic							
Lex. Antic.	0	6	9	16	7	38	46
Morph. Antic.	0	3	0	4	2	9	5
Lex. Persev.	2	7	8	13	15	45	15
Morph. Persev.	0	1	3	7	2	13	6
Lex. Exchanges	0	4	5	8	5	22	17
Morph. Exch.	0	0	0	0	0	0	1
Lex. Multiple	0	3	2	4	1	10	5
Phrase Blend	1	8	6	19	7	41	44
Total Syntactic=	**3**	**32**	**33**	**71**	**39**	**178**	**139**
	5%	11.5%	13%	15%	12.5%	13%	19.3%
Propositional	0	1	0	2	1	4	3
		0.5%		0.5%	0.5%	0.3%	0.4%
Total N=	**57**	**282**	**255**	**473**	**316**	**1383**	**716**

'children only'. This indicates that there were some types of errors which were collected only from one group or the other (e.g. errors in the categories 6.5, 10.5, 11.5, and so on were made only by adults; errors in categories 17 and 37 were made only by children). For the most part, these differences shouldn't be treated too seriously, since they represent a very small proportion of the overall data and could simply be an accident of the data collection. But a closer examination of these categories may reveal some interesting differences between the children and adults in terms of representation or processing. These differences will be discussed in detail in the relevant chapters, but I will briefly review them here.

The first set of possible qualitative differences between children's and adults' errors involves morphology, and may reflect some developmental trends in the children's lexical representations for productive derivational morphemes. Examples of errors in the four relevant classes are given (in abbreviated form) in (1).

(1)   a. Al: '[kʰá.f_ tʰàʲ.mi].'
           (for 'Coffee time' [kʰá.fi tʰà'm]; AL-50(17) 2;9)
       b. B: 'My pòpsicle's ìn the [fɾí.zi] . . . [fɾí.z] . . . [ɚ].'
           (for 'freezer'; B-447(37) 5;1)
       c. AM: ' . . . is nòw the còllege advísoring cènter.'
           (for 'advising'; AD-493(37.5))
       d. AF:' . . . a wìtting and chàrmy . . . wìtty and chàrming
           conversátionalist.' (AD-644(46.5))

Class 17, perseveratory vowel movements, exemplified in (1a), is made up of three errors made by Alice at ages 2;9-3;9. All of these errors involved the movement of the single vowel [i], which was not a morpheme; in two cases it moved from the end of one word to the end of another as in (1a), and in the third case it moved from a word-internal position to a word-final position. Adults made no errors in this category. Since this type of error, i.e. movement of a single word-final segment, nearly always involved morphemes in my data, Alice may not yet have figured out which word-final [i]'s were suffixes and which were just the last phoneme in the word; note that Alice productively used the diminutive {-i} at this age. However, errors made by the children by age 5, such as the error in (1b), show that they were beginning to include information regarding the stem+derivational morphemic structure of words in lexical representations, and thus these morphemes were becoming eligible to be involved in paradigmatic errors, although errors involving derivational morphemes were rare in general (see Chapter 6). Although I had no errors of this exact type (Class 37) in my adult corpus, adults did produce two similar types of errors involving derivational morphemes. Class 37.5, exemplified in (1c), includes three affix additions made by adults; while two of these errors involved inflectional morphemes, the error in (1c) is an addition of the derivational affix {-or}. Class 46.5 included only the one derivational affix reversal given in (1d), which is similar to Bobby's affix substitution errors. These errors hint that there are some interesting developmental patterns in the children's representation of derivational morphology in lexical entries; these patterns will be discussed in detail in Chapter 6 below.

The second group of differences may suggest something about the child's developing representation for hierarchical word-internal prosodic structure. Consider these examples:

(2)   a. AF: 'I don't know whỳ they èver give [_.dʌ́łts] . . . adùlts
           amóxicìllin.' (for 'adults' [ə.dʌ́łts]; AD-107(10.5))
       b. AF: '[dʒɚ̀.nɪ.kəł] àrticle.'
           (for 'journal article' [dʒɚ̀.nəł àr.ɾɪ.kəł]; AD-32(6.5))
       c. An: '[tʃɛ̀.də.li] . . . Chèrry Cúddler.'
           (for 'Cherry Cuddler' [tʃɛ̀.ri kʰʌ́.də.lɚ]; AN-136(11) 3;11)

Classes 10.5 and 23.5, exemplified by (2a), each contain one error in which an unstressed vowel has been deleted in the context of other words which begin with this same unstressed vowel, a type of error made only by adults (see also AD-221(23.5)). Classes 6.5, 11.5, and 19, exemplified by (2b), contain a total of 10 adult errors in which a 'larger unit' (LU) containing a syllable nucleus is added to another word, anticipated or perseverated from a nearby word, causing the target word to take on the prosodic structure of the source word. There were two similar errors made by children, one given as (2c) above (which involves both substitution and addition), and another in the 'Multiple' category ([dæ̀n.sʌ.lɪŋ déⁱnt_] for 'dancing daintily'; AN-72(31) 2;9). However, the fact that this error type was more predominant in adult errors suggests a greater role for the higher-order prosodic structure of words in adult representation and planning, since the overall prosodic structure (i.e. number and structure of syllables) of neighboring words seemed to be an influence in adult errors more than children's. These errors will be discussed in detail in Chapter 3.

Third, there is one type of error which was practically non-occurring in the children's data, but which was relatively frequent in the adult data: errors of lexical stress. The only error of this type made by the children is the one given as example (10g) in Chapter 1, repeated here as (3a). However, there are 17 errors of this type in the adult corpus; two are given in (3b,c).

(3)   a. An: 'I rèally wànna decoráte Stràwberry's hòuse.'
           (for 'décorate'; source 'decorátion'; AN-260(32) 4;11)
       b. AF: 'Tàlks between ùs and Jàpanese negòtiátors . . . negótiàtors
           have (etc.)' (source 'negòtiátion'; AD-290(32))
       c. AM: 'A stùttering wórkshop will be held (etc.)'
           (for the compound 'stúttering wòrkshop'; AD-299(32))

Most of the lexical stress errors fell into two categories. In some cases, the stress followed the pattern of an incorrect derivationally related word with a different stress pattern from the intended word, as in (3a,b) (also found by Cutler 1980a). In other cases a compound was pronounced with phrasal stress (or vice versa) as in (3c); this latter type was only made by adults. It is not surprising that children produced few of the derivationally-related stress shift errors, as they knew few words of this type at the ages of data collection. Furthermore, Vogel (1999) has recently shown that English-speaking children have not yet completely internalized the compound-stress rule by age 5, and have simply entered compounds into their lexicon with the compound stress marked in the phonological representations. Thus it is unlikely that the 1-to-5-year-old children in this study would make errors involving a shift between compound and phrasal stress, since the compounds they have lexicalized are stored with fixed stress patterns. These lexical stress errors will be discussed in more detail in Chapter 3.

Finally, there was one type of error that was fairly common in the adult data but did not occur in the child data, which is not evident from the classification system. This involved lexical substitution errors in which the formal relationship between the target and error words relied to some extent on the orthographic form of the words. These most commonly, but not exclusively, occurred with proper names.

(4)   a. AF: '**K-Mart**' (for 'X-Files'; AD-433(35))
       b. AF: 'Did we shòw you our còol **St. Jòhn's W** . . . I mean <u>Mt. St.</u>
          <u>Hèlen's</u> sàlt and pépper shàkers?
          (started to say 'St. John's Wort'; AD-431(35))
       c. AM:'They're nót like **H̀B̀Ò** . . . I mean <u>ÀÒL̀</u>.' (AD-424(35))
       d. AF: 'We hàve to **ÀSAṔ** them by the ènd of the wéek . . .
          oh, <u>R̀SVṔ</u> them.' (AD-477(35))
       e. AF: (trying to think of the name of the actor in the film "The
          Producers") 'Nèro Wólfe, I mean <u>Zèro Mostél</u>.'
          ('Nero Wolfe' [nì.roʷ wʉłf] is a fictional detective; Zero Mostel
          [zì.roʷ ma.stéł] is an actor)

It can be seen that in most of these errors there is some phonological similarity between the target and source, as well as in some cases a semantic relationship ('HBO' and 'AOL' are both home-entertainment companies). However, the formal orthographic similarity is striking in every case, and in some cases is much clearer than the phonological or semantic relationship. Since all of the children in the study were pre-literate, it is not at all surprising that this is an 'adults only' type of error. It basically shows that orthography can be activated in lexical entries along with other formal properties of the words when a person is planning for speech production. (The example in (4e) was made by the author while writing this chapter, so does not appear in the data set; it was too good to pass up. Notice that the 'N' turned sideways is a 'Z', and 'W' turned upside down is 'M'.)

In sum, children and adults make nearly all the same types of errors. Those few errors made only by children may reveal the process of hypothesis testing in the setting up of morphological representations for specific words. The errors made predominantly by adults may be explained by adults having a more detailed representation of the morphological and prosodic structure of words, and the formal representation of orthography.

2.2.2 Children Make the Same General Proportion of Error Types as Adults

As shown in Table 2.1, adults in this study produced 48% phonological, 32.3% lexical, and 19.3% syntactic errors. Stemberger (1989, N=4000) found that the adults in his study made 54% phonological, 23% lexical, and 13% syntactic errors, similar to my findings. The children in my study produced a higher percentage of phonological errors than the adults (67.4%), and somewhat fewer lexical (19.3%) and syntactic errors (13%); propositional errors were .3% for children and .4% for adults. The phonological errors show an increase at ages 2-3, but a decrease at ages 4-5, possibly moving in the direction of the adult figure. This high proportion of phonological errors suggests that individual segments are the most important unit in speech production planning for very young children, certainly the unit most available for error; I will discuss this point further in Chapter 3. Lexical errors are very common at age 1 (32%). A few of these errors were made at the 1-word stage, and most at the 2-word stage. Obviously there are only a few types of error possible at this age, one being erroneous lexical choices and blends, and another being within-word phonological errors (see Chapter 1, §1.5.1). Lexical errors become fewer proportionately at ages 2-3 (due to the increase in other types of errors), and then increase to 22% at age 5, which is moving toward the adult figure of 32.3%. The most striking and obvious trend is the increase in syntactic errors. At age 1 they account for only 5% of the errors, involving one phrase blend and two lexical perseverations, one within-phrase and one across-phrases. The phrase blend and the within-phrase lexical perseveration were both made by Anna (AN-20(49) 1;11 and AN-10(43) 1;8, given as (12a) below). At 1;11, while he was in the 2-word stage, Bobby produced an utterance involving a lexical perseveration from the adult's previous utterance (B-26(43), example (12b) below). Naturally children with very little syntax will produce few phrasal errors. There is a steady increase in the percentage of syntactic errors up to age 4-5, reaching a figure similar to the 13% Stemberger found for adults, and nearing my adult figure of 19.3%. In all three areas, the child data show a general trend toward adult proportions of error types.

2.2.3 Children Make the Same General Proportion of Error Types as Each Other

Table 2.2 presents the number and overall percentages of error types made by each of the three main subjects in the child study, as well as the Other child group. It can be seen that in all four data sets, phonological errors are the most common type. In three out of the four data sets this is followed by lexical, and then syntactic errors; in Anna's case, she produced slightly more syntactic than lexical errors. Propositional errors are very rare for all subjects. There are two points to note from this table as regards the figures for the Other children. First, the figure for Other lexical errors is quite high, 32%, while the percentage of phonological errors is comparatively low, 52%. As discussed in Chapter 1, this can be explained in terms of a methodological constraint, since for children less well-known to me, it was much easier to verify that a lexical usage was incorrect than to verify that a pronunciation was at odds with the child's normal phonology. Second, lexical and syntactic errors were more commonly self-corrected than phonological errors (see §2.4 below), and since I relied to a greater extent on self-correction for verifying an error with the Other children than with my three children, this raised the percentage of both lexical and syntactic errors in this group.

In order to interpret differences in figures among my three children, it is necessary to consider the fact that I did not collect the same number of errors at each age from each child. The proportions of errors of various types made by each child may be influenced to some extent by the ages at which the bulk of their errors were collected. Table 2.3 shows the percentage of each child's errors that were collected at each age, and the median age of data collection for that child. This table is to be read as follows, for example: I collected a total of 338 errors from Anna; of these, 6.5% were collected when she was age 1, 23% at age 2, and so forth; her median error was collected when she was age 4;4 (AN-169(38) 4;4.2).

For the most part, the patterns of data collection for Anna and Bobby were similar, with a dip at age 3 and a larger number of errors at ages 4-5; however, Anna also had a substantial number of errors at age 2, giving her a slightly lower median age than Bobby (4;4 vs. 4;6). Thus some comparisons can be made between these two children's figures without too much of an age-weighted bias. On the other hand, I collected the bulk of Alice's errors at ages 2-3; her median age is approximately a year younger than the other three data sets (3;5), and her data show an effect of being collected at somewhat younger ages than for the other two children. That is, Alice shows a preponderance of phonological and lexical errors, which are the error types that tend to be made earlier; in particular, she produced a large number of lexical blends, which are characteristic of younger children. The Other children's figures show a gradual increase across the ages, reflecting the fact that it simply gets easier to recognize errors from Other children as they get older; the median age of data collected from the Other children is similar to Anna's, age 4;3.

TABLE 2.2
Number of each type of error by data set, children only; N=1383.

Subject:	Anna	Alice	Bobby	Other
Phonological				
Phon. Anticipations	73	71	146	28
Phon. Perseverations	51	45	105	31
Phon. A/P	23	25	66	15
Phon. Exchanges	37	29	35	3
Phon. Features	4	7	12	4
Non-Contextual	2	2	7	4
Phon. Multiple	20	10	12	1
Stress & Intonation	2	0	2	0
Telescoping	23	12	21	5
Total Phonological=	**235**	**201**	**406**	**91**
	69.5%	73.5%	68%	52%
Lexical				
Lex. Par. Subst.	33	21	86	48
Morph. Par.	0	0	2	0
Lex. Blends	14	21	35	8
Total Lexical=	**47**	**42**	**123**	**56**
	14%	15.5%	20.5%	32%
Syntactic				
Lex. Antic.	9	5	14	10
Morph. Antic.	1	2	6	0
Lex. Persev.	13	7	17	8
Morph. Persev.	5	3	5	0
Lex. Exchanges	9	1	8	4
Lex. Multiple	1	4	4	1
Phrase Blend	18	8	11	4
Total Syntactic=	**56**	**30**	**65**	**27**
	16.5%	11%	11%	15.5%
Propositional	0	0	3	1
			0.5%	0.5%
Total N=	**338**	**273**	**597**	**175**

TABLE 2.3
Percentage of errors from each data set which were collected at each age,
and median age of data collection for each data set; N=1383.

Age:	1	2	3	4	5	Total N	Median Age
Anna	6.5%	23%	13%	37%	20.5%	338	4;4
Alice	0	31%	42%	14.5%	12.5%	273	3;5
Bobby	5%	15%	9%	44%	27%	597	4;6
Others	2.3%	17%	24.5%	26.3%	30%	175	4;3

With these caveats in mind, several points can be made which relate to individual differences. First, as shown in Table 2.2, I collected more syntactic errors from Anna than from my other two children, accounting for 16.5% of her errors, compared to 11% for Alice and Bobby. I also collected a smaller percentage of paradigmatic lexical errors from Anna (14% compared to 15.5% for Alice and 20.5% for Bobby). In particular Anna made the largest number of phrase blends (18, which is 5.3% of her total errors, compared to 2.9% for Alice and 1.8% for Bobby). In order to make a phrase blend, the child must know at least two different syntactic templates suitable for framing the same proposition, and the child must be planning both of these whole phrases at the same time. Similarly, in order to make a syntagmatic lexical misplacement error, the child needs to be planning several words at a time, probably an entire phrase. This suggests that children who make more syntactic errors are planning longer chunks of speech in one planning unit. One might also expect there to be a trade-off between longer planning units and accuracy in producing phrase-length utterances, and this would certainly be one way of interpreting Anna's abundance of syntactic errors. Similarly, Anna contributed more telescoping errors to the corpus than the other two children (23, or 6.8% of her total errors, compared to 4.4% for Alice and 3.6% for Bobby); this again suggests planning in longer chunks but with less accuracy, since a telescoping error involves dropping out one or more rhythmic beats within a phrase, but extending the duration of the remaining segments to 'fill up' the planned intonation curve. Finally, I collected more 'multiple' phonological errors from Anna than from her siblings (20, or 5.9% of her errors, compared to 3.9% for Alice and 2.0% for Bobby), suggesting a less fixed phonological representation across phrases. These facts cannot be attributed to Anna's median age of data collection. First, both telescoping and multiple phonological errors are characteristic of younger children (they reach their highest proportion at ages 2 (7.4%) and 3 (5.1%) of overall errors respectively), but Anna's median age is 11 months older than Alice and only 2 months younger than Bobby, so age is unlikely to be the deciding factor. Second, phrase blends are more characteristic of older children, reaching their peak proportion at age 4 (4.0% of overall errors); this may explain why Anna made more phrase blends than Alice did, but it does not explain her figures in relationship to Bobby's, who made the largest percentage of age 4 errors of all the children. Thus the difference between Anna's data and the other two children is best explained by some factor other than age.

In Chapter 1 (§1.5.2) I attributed Anna's SOT behavior to her falling towards the 'expressive' end of the 'expressive-referential' continuum of learning styles. Another factor I mentioned was the fact that Anna corrected fewer of her errors than the other two children (Jaeger 1992a; see also §2.4 below). Taken altogether, these figures are consistent with the idea that children who fall more into the 'expressive' than the 'referential' learning style are more focussed on sustained interaction than on formal accuracy. These SOT data allow us now to characterize how the 'expressive' style is instantiated in speech production planning: the child plans longer phrases with less focus on phrase-internal linear accuracy (including phonological, lexical, and syntactic units), and with a less careful self-monitor. The fact that two out of the three syntactic errors I collected from age-1 children were made by Anna can be accounted for by the early emergence of a preferred learning style.

The second point regarding individual differences is that I collected a very large number of lexical selection errors from Bobby (86, or 14.4% of all his errors, compared to Anna's 9.8% and Alice's 7.7%). This is probably due to two factors. First, he tended to show more evidence of the 'referential' learning style, and thus was probably planning in shorter chunks; therefore individual lexical items were more subject to error than phrasal-sized chunks. Second, he has an older median age than any of the other children in the study, and at least in my adult study, adults tend to make more lexical substitution errors than children do. Thus this pattern could partially reflect a trend toward more lexical and fewer phonological errors as the child gets older. The fact that he produced more lexical substitution errors than Anna may reflect their 'expressive-referential' differences (since their median ages do not differ greatly); on the other hand, his higher percentage of lexical substitution errors compared to Alice may reflect their median age difference, as Bobby's median age is 13 months older than Alice's. On the other hand, Bobby's lexical substitution data bring up an interesting question. As mentioned in Chapter 1, Bobby was an exceptionally talkative child, so one possibility is that children who simply talk a lot are less careful about selection of individual lexical items than less loquacious children. This is merely speculation, but would be an interesting question to look into further. However it does strongly suggest that the designation 'expressive' is not the same thing as 'talkative', and that the two may be somewhat orthogonal to each other.

In sum, the children in the study made the same general proportion of errors as adults, and as each other. Some of the differences between children's and adult's error patterns will be explored in more detail in the remainder of this chapter. Differences among the four child data sets were attributed to differences in median age of data collection, differences along the 'expressive-referential' continuum, and differences in data collection methodology used for the Other group.

2.3 Developmental Trends

The data show a number of developmental trends in the children's slips. In this section I will discuss the overall trends in terms of directionality, error types, and linguistic unit involved in the error, and focus on the evidence such trends provide for the development of the speech production planning mechanism. The development of linguistic representations and structures per se will be the topic of the subsequent chapters. I will begin with a discussion of within-word vs. between-word phonological errors, since exploring child/adult differences in these error types will bring up several factors which will be important in explicating differences in the other three measures.

2.3.1 Developmental Trends in Within-Word vs. Between-Word Phonological Errors

Before looking at developmental trends in error types, I will first discuss developmental changes in the percentage of within-word vs. between-word phonological errors, as these two types of errors tend to have different kinds of properties. In a within-word error, the target/error and source both occur within the same word, as in the consonant anticipation/substitution error in (5a), whereas in a between-word error, the target and source(s) occur in different words, as in the A/P vowel substitution in (5b).

(5)   a. M: (pointing to a picture in a book) 'Who's thát?'
           An: [pʌm.pow]!' (for 'Dumbo' [tʌm.pow]; [t]<--[p]; AN-8(1) 1;8)
       b. B: (teasing Alice because her boyfriend got a Mohawk haircut)
           'Álice is a [móʷ.hæk] . . . a Móhawk màniæc.' (for 'Mohawk'
           [móʷ.hak]; [æ] substituted for [a], A/P; B-382(23) 4;10)

It is an interesting question whether children make more within-word phonological errors than adults do. Stemberger (1989) found this was not the case, but my data suggest that children do indeed make a larger number of within-word errors. Verifying any child/adult difference on this measure could be an important point for evaluating various hypotheses about developing representations and planning processes, as I will discuss below. However, there are a number of methodological problems involved in assessing the proportion of between- and within-word errors in the data. The first problem is that one needs to be able to unambiguously define what one means by a 'word'. Consider the following examples:

(6)   a. Al: 'Mòm, I wànt my [wáθ.kʰlàʃ].'
           (for 'washcloth' [wáʃ.kʰlàθ]; [ʃ]<--->[θ]; AL-96(25) 3;2)

b. B: '. . . I wànt my [væ.lən.kʰàⁱnz] stìc*ker*.' (for 'Valentine's
  sticker' [væ.lən.tʰàⁱnz stí.kɚ]; /t/<--/k/; B-294(1) 4;5)
c. Al: 'Yòu're gonna wàtch "[ʒà.b3 ʒǽ.dʒit]".' (for 'Roger Rabbit'
  [ʒà.dʒ3 ʒǽ.bɨt]; [dʒ]<-->[b]; AL-191(25) 3;11)
d. AF: (discussing local colleges) 'You've got ÈĊĆ and [jù.*bì*.bí] . . .
  ÙB́.' (target 'UB' [jù.bí]; syllable [bi] added, probably
  influenced by structure of 'ECC' [ìj.sì.sí]; AD-187(19))

Does one count compounds as one word, and if so, does one differentiate between lexicalized compounds such as 'washcloth' and non-lexicalized compounds such as 'Valentine's sticker'? Does one count proper names, such as 'Roger Rabbit' as one or two words? What about acronyms which are spoken either as a single word (e.g. 'NATO') or with the initials pronounced (e.g. 'UB')? And once one makes decisions on these points, how does one know that any particular child has a particular compound, name, or acronym lexicalized at any particular time? Finally, even if a compound is lexicalized, is it a phonological word? That is, is it planned for speaking as one word, or is each word within the compound planned for speaking separately. In order to come up with a rough estimate of within- vs. between-word errors, I developed the following set of criteria for making a decision about the lexical status of multi-word units which might be 'a single phonological word'. These same algorithms were applied to proper nouns as well as units in all other lexical categories.

1. In order to be considered a single phonological word, a compound needed to be spoken with compound stress, and show evidence of being lexicalized for that speaker, as in, e.g. 'washcloth' in example (6a). Evidence that a child had lexicalized a particular compound would be if a child didn't know one or both of the content stems outside this compound, as, for example, the word 'sesame', which was unknown to the children outside of the compound 'Sesame Street'. Furthermore I didn't count anything with more than two root morphemes as a compound, even if there was evidence it was lexicalized, since it is unlikely that it would be planned as a single phonological word by these children. So, for example, in the expression 'frùit róll-ùps' (a kind of fruit snack), I counted 'roll-ups' as a compound, but 'fruit' as a separate phonological word, even though this entire expression was undoubtedly lexicalized by the children (see, for example, errors B-65(1) 2;5 and AN-141(25) 4;0).

2. Two-word or multi-word units were considered phrases rather than single phonological words if they had any of the following properties: they did not have compound stress (which eliminates 'Ròger Rábbit', (6c)), they were made up of more than two root morphemes (e.g. 'fruit roll-up'), or they were probably not lexicalized (i.e made up on the spot, like example (6b), 'Válentine's stìcker'). If I knew that the speaker knew all of the content morphemes in the expression outside this potential compound, this would make it easier to classify the expression as a non-compound, since the child could have combined known words into a new phrase during planning.

3. For the younger children, who usually were only able to produce one or two words at a time with a maximum of two syllables in each word, I did not classify an expression as a phonological word if it had more than four syllables; this is because it would be unlikely that such young children could plan more than four syllables as one phonological word for speaking. So 'Teenage Mutant Ninja Turtles', while undoubtedly lexicalized as a unit for the children, was not considered a single phonological word (see B-269(7) 4;4).

4. Finally, for adult utterances, I referred to Webster's Dictionary (Neufeldt & Guralnik 1991) in unclear cases, for verification that the dictionary did or did not classify a particular expression as a compound.

5. Acronyms pronounced as one word, such as 'NATO' [néʲ.roʷ], or acronyms in which each letter us pronounced, such as 'HBO' [eʲtʃ.bi.jóʷ], were always treated as a single word; this includes the acronyms in example (6d), 'UB' and 'ECC'.

6. If these criteria gave conflicting results for some expression, I made decisions on a case-by-case basis. For example, I designated 'fruit-wrinkles' [fr̥ùt.rín.kəɬz] as a phonological word, even though it does not carry compound stress, because the children did not know the word 'wrinkles' outside this expression (e.g. AL-25(6) 2;4).

Obviously in a few cases my designation of an expression as containing one vs. more than one word will be somewhat subjective; however, I have marked in every phonological entry in the data where such designation was possible, whether the error was classified as a within-word or between-word error (or both). Compounds are indicated either by writing the word as a single orthographic form, such as 'washcloth', or by putting a hyphen in the word, such as 'picnic-basket' (AL-182(7) 3;10). Because the purpose of the present section is to compare the children's data to the adults' in my study, and I have used identical measures for categorizing both corpora in terms of within-word vs. between-word errors, the discussion below should be fairly accurate.

A second problem is that there are a number of errors with more than one potential source, where one is within-word and one is between-word, as illustrated in (7). Many of the 'A/P' errors are of this type.

(7)   a. B: 'Mom, are yòu màking [kʰǽ] . . . páncakès?'
              (for 'pancakes' [pʰǽn.kʰèʲks]; /k/ substituted for /p/, A/P;
              B-176(20) 4;0)

       b. AF: 'It complètely [kʰ]ìɬz] . . . kìlls the inféction in thrèe dáys.'
              (for 'kills' [kʰɪɬz]; [l] added to onset, A/P; AD-213(21))

In (7a) the source could be the /k/ in 'making' (between-word), or the two /k/'s in 'pancakes' (within-word). In (7b) the source could be the two /l/'s in 'completely' (between-word) or the coda /l/ in 'kills' (within-word). The question is, should these errors be counted twice, or not at all? Since one cannot be absolutely sure of the source in such errors, I decided to not count any of the A/P errors when estimating the proportion of within- vs. between-word errors.

Table 2.4, then, shows a rough count of the percentage of within-word phonological errors made by the children and adults in my study, organized by age and by general type of error. This table takes into account only contextual phonological errors (anticipations, perseverations, and exchanges, excluding telescopings), when one of three conditions held: 1) the target and single source were uniquely identifiable, as in examples (5a) and (6a-c) above; 2) there were two (or more) possible sources but they were both in words other than the error word (both between-word), as in (8a) below, where either the onset [w] from 'will' or 'wagging' could have been the source; 3) there were two possible sources, both within the error word, as in (8b) where either of the [s]'s in 'applesauce' could have been the source; example (8b) is the only instance of two within-word sources in my data.

(8)   a. Al: (reciting poem) ' . . . and their [wèɬz] . . . their tàils will be
           wàgging behind thèm.'
           (for 'tails' [tʰeɬz]; [t]<--[w]; AL-226(7) 4;6)
       b. An: 'I put [ǽ.səɬ] . . . I put ápplesàuce òn me.'
           (for 'applesauce' [ǽ.pəɬ.sàs]; [p]<--[s]; AN-123(7) 3;10)

Errors such as those in (7) above, where there is both a between-word and within-word possible source, were not counted, and no A/P errors were included in the count, nor were the 'multiple' phonological errors, since again it is very difficult to ascertain a unique source in this type of error.

Table 2.4 is to be read as follows: the rows of numbers indicate the number of errors of this type made at this age which were unambiguously either within-word or between-word errors; the rows of percentages under the numbers indicate the percent of this number which involved unambiguous within-word errors. So for example, at age 1, there were 10 contextual consonant substitution errors which were unambiguously either between-word or within-word errors. Of these, 3 (30%) were within-word errors (and thus 7 (70%) were between-word errors).

From this table, it is clear that the children did in fact make a higher percentage of within-word errors than the adults. In every category but one (vowel substitution/addition), the overall child percentage is higher than the adult figure; the total percentages show that more than a quarter of the child errors (29%) were within-word errors while only 15% of the adult errors were of this type.

Looking at the overall figures by age, it can be seen that the 1-year-olds made the largest proportion of within-word errors (46%). At age 2 the figure drops to 28%, and the figure remains at around one quarter of the errors, through age 5. This finding differs from that of Stemberger (1989) who found that, of contextual phonological errors, his children made only 8% within-word errors whereas the adults made 13% within-word errors. It is not clear what accounts for this discrepancy, but it is possible that the decisions regarding what constitutes a word were made somewhat differently in the two studies. In

TABLE 2.4

Number of phonological errors of each general type, and percentage of those errors which were unambiguous within-word phonological errors at each age.

Age:		1	2	3	4	5	Total	Adult
Consonant	N=	10	43	41	81	58	233	64
subst.	%	30%	12%	24.5%	21%	17%	19%	9%
Consonant	N=	3	19	21	32	25	100	28
additions	%	67%	31.5%	28.5%	22%	20%	26%	14%
Consonant	N=	1	16	7	8	4	36	12
move.	%	0%	44%	43%	75%	25%	47%	25%
Consonant	N=	0	10	8	14	10	42	4
omiss.	%		0%	12.5%	7%	20%	9.5%	0%
Vowel sub/	N=	4	12	21	20	8	65	31
move	%	25%	0%	19%	15%	0%	12%	16%
LU subst/	N=	1	11	9	19	16	56	40
additions	%	0%	36%	0%	10.5%	19%	16%	0%
Single seg.	N=	7	26	18	25	15	91	26
exchange	%	86%	58%	61%	84%	80%	71.5%	50%
LU exchange	N=	0	7	1	5	0	13	19
	%		43%	0%	60%		46%	10.5%
Feature	N=	0	1	6	6	8	21	7
errors	%		100%	50%	17%	50%	43%	28.5%
Totals	**N=**	**26**	**145**	**132**	**210**	**144**	**657**	**231**
	%	**46%**	**28%**	**29%**	**29%**	**26%**	**29%**	**15%**

particular, I may have been more generous than Stemberger in my analysis of what constitutes a compound. Stemberger excludes within-word errors from his phonological analyses, arguing that 'statistical properties of within-word and between-word phonological errors are notably different in adult speech' (p. 167). He also states that '[t]here are too few within-word phonological errors in child speech to make an analysis of interest' (p. 167), but this was not the case in the present study.

Given that the children in this study produced a relatively large number of phonological within-word errors, it is worth proposing an explanation for this finding. There are several different kinds of explanations which could be offered. The first is that children's phonological representations are more holistic, i.e. less fixed and structured, than adults', and thus segments are more likely to move around within children's words than within adults' words. If this were the case, then we should see some sort of correlation between a drop in within-word errors and more evidence of structure in phonological representations which would be evident in the phonological errors. Since a large drop seems to occur between age 1 (46%) and age 2 (26%), we would expect to find evidence of the children's phonological representations becoming more structured early in age 2; this is in fact what is found, as will be discussed in detail in Chapter 3 below.

A second type of explanation would be that children plan their utterances in smaller chunks of spoken language compared to adults, and therefore the potential error domain is shorter; this increases the possibility that the error will occur within a single word. If this were true, we might see fewer within-word errors as children plan longer and longer utterances, and indeed we do see a decrease in within-word errors across the age ranges. However, the figure for the 5-year-olds, 25%, is still high compared to the adult figure of 15% (or 13% in Stemberger's study), which suggests that even at age 5, children are planning smaller chunks in general than adults.

An important observation evident in Table 2.4 is that different kinds of errors are more or less likely to be within-word errors; or, conversely, within-word errors are more likely to involve specific phonological units and error types. Importantly, for the most part the same patterns of susceptibility to within-word error for different error types holds with the adults as with the children, so this must be a function of the error type and not simply age. Specifically, for all ages including adults, the exchange of individual segments (consonants or vowels) is the most common within-word error; overall the children's exchanges involve 71.5% within-word errors, and even for the adults the figure is 50%. Exchanges of LUs (i.e. 'larger units' such as syllables, clusters, rhymes) are also often within-word errors, though more often for the children; the child figure is 46%, while the adults' is a much lower 10.5%. Movements of consonants also tend to occur within words (47% children, 25% adults), and feature errors are commonly within-word (43% children, 28.5% adults). Less common is within-word errors involving single consonant additions (26% children, 14% adults) or substitutions (19% children, 9% adults). Furthermore, any error involving vowel substitution or addition is most often a between-word error (within-word figures are: 12% children, 16% adults). LU substitutions or additions are typically between-word; in my data there are more within-word errors of this type in the children's data than the adults', (16% vs. 0%), but most of the child within-word LU substitutions or additions actually involve the two stems in a compound (e.g. *[brǽŋk.dæ̀n.sɚ] for 'break-dancer' [bréʲk.dæ̀n.sɚ], B-457(6) 5;1). Finally, consonant omissions are rarely within-word errors (9.5% children, 0% adults).

There may be several different explanations for these patterns. First, we can speculate that they may be due at least in part to the amount of deformation of the phonological representation of the word that would be caused by an error involving the various units. If two consonants or vowels or even LUs are exchanged within a word, the overall structure of the word usually remains intact; the error production most often involves the same segments and prosodic structure as the intended word, but with a different linking between segments and prosodic slots than in the target. Similarly, consonant movement errors usually involve consonant clusters, so typically the structure of an overall word is deformed only slightly, with, for example, the second syllable instead of the first ending up with an onset cluster; the word retains all of the segments in the phonological lexical representation but in a slightly different order. Feature errors do not deform the prosodic structure of a word at all, but simply change the featural specifications of one or two phonemes. On the other hand, within-word substitutions or additions of larger units, particularly rhymes or syllables, can cause major deformations within a word, possibly completely altering the overall word structure; therefore they are much less likely to occur within individual words.

A second factor involves the availability of units to different kinds of error. For example, vowel substitution errors are rare within individual words. This is undoubtedly due at least in part to the fact that within a single word there is often only one fully stressed vowel, and if there are other vowels they are of less prominence. Vowels mutually involved in an error (i.e. one substituted for the other or two exchanged units) usually occur in elements with the same prosodic prominence (most often when both are stressed; see Chapter 3). Particularly in the children's words, which often contain just one or two syllables, there is typically only one vowel, or only one other vowel which is unstressed, and so there are usually not two vowels in the same word which are eligible to interact with each other. When there are, the result is usually a vowel exchange; in fact, all 8 of the children's vowel exchange errors are within-word errors. However, adults typically know longer words with more syllables and thus more vowels, and so it is not surprising that they produce slightly more within-word vowel substitution errors than the children.

This brings up the third factor. Errors which involve a change in two units rather than one (e.g. exchanges and movements) typically occur in units which are in close proximity to each other, whereas errors which only cause a change in one unit (e.g. a substitution, where the source is also produced in its originally planned location) can occur across a longer span of the utterance being planned. By definition, errors which typically occur across a shorter distance will be more likely to involve single words.

It is likely that all of these factors come into play in explaining the differences between adult and child within-word error rates, i.e. structure of phonological representations, length of planning unit, and type of error. The youngest children, with the least fixed phonological representations and the shortest planning spans, will make more within-word errors, typically involving single segments (since they haven't yet developed syllable-internal prosodic structure); exchanges in like locations in adjacent syllables in single words, or movements of a segment from one syllable to another, are a very common phonological error at early ages. As the children get older, their phonological representations become more fine-grained and fixed, and their planning spans increase. For these reasons they will have more words in a planning unit which can impinge upon each other; between-word errors will increase, and the types of errors which are more common in within-word errors will become fewer (i.e. exchanges and movements). Finally, adults' phonological representations are fully formed, and they are planning full phrases, sometimes more than one at a time, so adults will produce a majority of between-word errors; this will cause them to produce fewer exchanges and movements since these are more typical of within-word errors. In this way all three factors work together to explain the children's and adults' patterns of error. These three factors, as well as child/adult differences in within- vs. between-word error proportions, will be important in explaining the other developmental trends, to which I will now turn.

2.3.2   Developmental Trends in Directionality

It has long been reported in the literature that adults make more anticipation than perseveration phonological errors, and exchanges are less common than either (Fromkin 1973a, Nooteboom 1973, 1980). However, the studies which have made this claim have all been done with adult data from three Germanic languages: English, Dutch, and German. Recent cross-linguistic studies have shown that this finding does not hold in other languages, specifically those which do not contain a pragmatically important intonation pattern with tonic stress at the ends of phrases, such as Arabic (Abd-El-Jawad & Abu-Salim 1987), Korean (Min 1996), Mandarin (Wan 1999), Thai (Muansuwan 2000), and Spanish, Hindi, and Japanese (Wells-Jensen 1999), where anticipations and perseverations occur with approximately equal frequency. Table 2.5 shows the percentages of child phonological errors of various directionalities, compared to four adult sources; the child figures contain both between- and within-word errors. This table distinguishes completed anticipations (where the error and source are both spoken before a correction), incomplete anticipations (where the error is corrected before the source is spoken; see §1.4.2 in Chapter 1 for an argument that these are in fact anticipations), perseverations (where the source comes before the error), 'A/P' where there are potential sources both before and after the error, and exchanges, which includes both contiguous (metatheses) and non-contiguous reversals. Figures include substitutions, additions, omissions, and movements of consonants, vowels, sub-syllabic units, and syllables. (Other phonological errors such as features, multiple errors, and telescopings are not included in this count.)

The children in this study show several patterns which could be explained with reference to the factors introduced in §2.3.1: developments in phonological representations, the span of linguistic units being planned per utterance, and within- vs. between-word errors, as well as developments in self-monitoring. First, at all ages except age 1, the children produced more complete anticipations than the adults did in the two studies which separated out the completes from the incompletes (the Jaeger and the Stemberger studies). At age 1 the children produced more incompletes than completes. At ages 2-3 the children have more

TABLE 2.5

Directionality of phonological errors, by age, compared with four adult sources. Numbers are the percentages of errors in this sub-group of errors which fall into each category at this age. 'A-C'=complete anticipations; 'A-I'=incomplete anticipations; 'Pers'=perseverations; 'Exch.'='exchanges' includes both non-contiguous reversals and metatheses.

Age:	1	2	3	4	5	Total
%A-C	11	34	21.5	16	16	20.5
%A-I	18	8.5	17.5	23	29	20
%Pers.	39	26.5	32.5	30	28	30
%A/P	7	10.5	16	20	18.5	16.5
%Exch.	25	20.5	12.5	11	8.5	13
Total N=	28	162	150	267	177	784

Adult:	A1	A2	A3	A4
%A-C	13	15.5	63	75
%A-I	36	41	na	na
%Pers.	20	34	26	19.5
%A/P	14	4.5	na	na
%Exch.	17	5	11	5.5
Total N=	271	1472	386	787

A1=English adults, Jaeger corpus, between- and within-word errors.
A2=English adults, from Stemberger (1989), between-word errors only.
A3=German adults, from Nooteboom (1980), between- and within-word errors.
A4=Dutch adults, from Nooteboom (1973), between- and within-word errors.

complete than incomplete anticipations, but at age 4 the incompletes begin to outnumber the completes again; the 4-5 year-old figures of 16% for completes are similar to Stemberger's adult figure of 15.5% and my adult figure of 13.5%. Thus the children show an increase in incomplete anticipations from ages 2-5, going from 8.5% to 29%, which is beginning to approximate the adult figures of 36% (Jaeger) and 41% (Stemberger). These findings contradict Stemberger's (1989) claim that 'incompletes' do not increase with age. This 'U-shaped' pattern could be an artifact of data collection; that is, it could be due to the very few errors collected at age 1. However, a more principled explanation may be possible. This developmental pattern could indicate that when the children are in the 1-word and 2-word stages, i.e. planning utterances of only one or two words at a time, their external self-monitoring system may be very 'local' in the sense that it is checking each word as it is spoken. This may be necessary due to the children's production representations being somewhat holistic and not fully structured. At this age they could be relying heavily on their more sophisticated perception representations (Jaeger 1997) to monitor their output, in order to increase the potential success of their communication. This predicts that at age 1, most complete anticipations would be within-word errors, but incomplete anticipations would be between-word errors. This is exactly what was found, as illustrated in (9).

(9)   a. B: '[kè.wiʔ] . . . J̠èri *k*iss.' (for [tè.wiʔ kíç]; [t]<--[k]; B-6(7) 1;9)
    b. B: '[pú.ka.pừ:].' (for 'peek-a-boo' [pì.ka.pù:]; [i]<--[u]; B-7(5) 1;9)
    c. An: (commenting on the shape of a puzzle piece)
      'It's a [kʰʒ̱ǽ.kiç] (breath) *sh*àpe.'
      (for 'cracker shape' [kʰʒ̱ǽ.ki̱ʒ çe̠ʰp]; [ʒ̱]<--[ç]; AN-13(1) 1;9)

Of the five incomplete anticipations made by 1-year-olds, four were between-word, as in (9a), and of the three complete anticipations, two were within-word, as in (9b) (the other is given in (5a) above). In the third, (9c), which was a complete between-word error, the child noticed the error after producing the error word, but was too confused to correct it at that point, so in some ways this error could be called an incomplete anticipation.

However, when the children begin speaking in longer phrases at age 2, their production representations for lexical items have become more detailed. At the same time, both their planning work-space and their self-monitors need to expand to cover longer stretches, and so at ages 2 and 3 the self-monitor becomes somewhat more global, not necessarily catching errors after each word, but checking phrase-length utterances. When the children have more practice with sentence-length utterances, at ages 4-5, their self-monitors become more fine-tuned again, and at this point they begin to catch more errors immediately after they are made. Therefore, while the 1-year-olds and 4-5-year-olds would notice and correct between-word anticipations before the source was spoken (but for different reasons), the 2-3-year-olds might utter the whole phrase before the error is detected.

A second issue has to do with the proportion of exchanges produced at various ages. The hypothesis discussed with reference to complete vs. incomplete anticipations would predict that the very young children might also make a large number of exchanges since exchanges are predominantly within-word errors. This is exactly what is found in the figures in Table 2.5. The children made more complete exchanges at ages 1-2 (25% and 20.5% respectively) than at later ages, with the 5-year-old figure being 8.5%, similar to adult sources #2-4 (from 5% to 11%). At age 1, 5 out of 6 phonological exchanges were within-word, and at age 2, half the 32 exchanges were within-word. Thus the decrease in exchanges as the children get older could be due to both the development of details in their phonological production representations, and a shift in the span of their planning and self-monitor. It is often reported that adults make very few full exchanges, but this is partially due to the fact that many sources (e.g. Stemberger's in this table) only cite between-word errors, and indeed adults do make fewer between-word exchanges than children do. However, my figure of 17% for adult exchanges includes within-word and between-word figures (as, of course, do the children's figures), and many of the adult exchanges were in fact within-word errors, such as *[sɛ̀.lə.bɛ́.rəm] for 'cerebellum' (AD-232(25)) and *[mɪtʃ.mǽs] for 'mismatch' (AD-230(25)). These within-word errors are less likely to be caught by an adept adult self-monitor since they often occur in adjacent syllables, and therefore the word may be fully executed before the monitor notices the error. Thus my data suggest that adults may make more exchanges than is usually reported. Again we see a sort of U-shaped curve, with the youngest children and the adults making more exchanges than the older children. As always, this finding could be an artifact of data collection, but an explanation in the same terms as discussed above could be offered. It is likely that young children and adults make more exchange errors for different reasons: the young children are making exchange errors because their phonological representations are not fully fixed and since they are planning one or two words at a time, their domain of possible error is usually a single word. The adults are making more exchange errors because their self-monitors are not scanning word-internally but are more attuned to phrase-length or sentence-length chunks. However, the 4- and 5-year-old children both have fixed phonological representations, and are planning somewhat longer utterances than the younger children, although not as long as adults'. Therefore they are likely to make fewer within-word errors than the other groups, and are more likely to catch between-word errors in the short phrases they are planning; they thus make fewer exchanges than either group. This is simply speculation, but provides a plausible overall picture of the development of representations, processing, and monitoring.

A third telling pattern is that the 1-year-old children make more perseverations than children at other ages, and more than found in any of the adult studies. Stemberger (1989) claims that this is due to a slower decay rate for activated elements in young children compared to older speakers. This hypothesis is similar to that of Dell and colleagues (Dell, Burger & Svec 1997, Schwartz et al. 1994; see also Kawachi 2002), who suggest that a less practiced speaker (as well as a disordered speaker, i.e. aphasic) will produce fewer anticipations and more perseverations than a more fluent speaker (see also Poulisse 1999:146). They argue that this is because the more practiced speaker is planning ahead in longer chunks, thus causing previously activated items to be deactivated sooner. With less practiced speakers, "the previously activated units will have a greater influence on current encoding, and upcoming targets a lesser influence" (Schwartz et al. 1994:56). Because the adult figures in Table 2.5 are so different from each other it is not clear whether these children continue to make more perseverations than adults through age 5, but nevertheless they clearly make fewer from ages 2-5 than at age 1. Age 1 is the only age at which there are more perseverations than anticipations (with complete and incomplete anticipations combined).

While Stemberger's and Dell's explanations are plausible, I will argue in Chapter 3 below that another factor influencing the number of anticipations vs. perseverations is the age at which the children actually begin to produce syntax, since the anticipatory errors are heavily influenced by the 'tonic syllable', an element which only occurs once syntactically governed intonation is being produced. Since I take the 2-word stage to be non-syntactic (see Chapter 6), it is expected that anticipations would increase as children enter the 3+word stage, which is what is found. As mentioned above, data from several non-Germanic languages which do not have a prosodically and pragmatically prominent tonic word, typically at the end of the phrase, do not show the preponderance of anticipatory errors found in English. Therefore it is likely that there is some effect of both maturation and the structure of the language being learned which accounts for the pattern of perseveratory errors found in this and other studies.

Finally, there is a clear increase in A/P errors for the children, which is not surprising given that they are producing longer and longer utterances, with more chance of there being sources on both sides of the error; the 5-year-old figure of 18.5% is similar to my adult figure of 14%. However, both the children and adults in my study make many more A/P errors than Stemberger's adults, which is odd; this may be due to my very conservative reckoning of possible sources in utterances. It also may be due to the fact that Stemberger excludes within-word errors from his analysis, since in many A/P errors in my corpus, there is both a within-word and a between-word possible source. The other two adult sources do not include this category of error.

It is interesting to note that these directionality trends show somewhat different patterns in lexical and morphological syntagmatic errors compared to phonological errors, as shown in Table 2.6; these figures include anticipations, perseverations, exchanges, and 'multiple' errors where directionality could be unambiguously ascertained. This table shows that while the adults in my study made 57% lexical anticipations (including completes and incompletes), 21% lexical perseverations, and 22% lexical exchanges (N=82), the children produced slightly more perseverations than anticipations, with approximately the same percentage of exchanges as adults: 39% anticipations, 41% perseverations, and 25% exchanges (N=109). These differences show no obvious developmental trends during ages 1-5; even the 5-year-olds show more perseveratory lexical errors, and the rate of exchanges is fairly steady. It may be that the 'slower decay rate' posited by Stemberger and Dell has more effect on lexical items per se than on phonology, such that young children often misselect a word which has been previously spoken and not yet suppressed. On the other hand, both the children and adults produced more perseveratory than anticipatory errors with morphemes (affixes), which frequently consisted of the movement of a suffix from one word to a later word in the utterance. This most often involved verbs, and seemed

TABLE 2.6
**Directionality of syntagmatic lexical errors, children compared to adults;
N(%). "Lex"=content morphemes and free function morphemes;
"Morph"=affixes.**

	Children		Adults	
	Lex	Morph	Lex	Morph
Anticipations	39 (36%)	11 (46%)	47 (57%)	5 (38.5%)
Perseverations	45 (41%)	13 (54%)	17 (21%)	7 (54%)
Exchanges	25 (23%)	0	18 (22%)	1 (7.5%)
Total N=	**109**	**24**	**82**	**13**

to be caused by a mis-assignment of a constituent boundary, so that two contiguous words were erroneously treated as if they were the single lexical verb; the affix was then moved to the end of the erroneous unit, as illustrated in (10). This was true for both child and adult errors.

(10) a. An: 'The tòy that Àlice pláy_ wìth**ed**.'
            (for 'played with'; AN-66(44) 2;8)
      b. TF: 'Untìl the lícense rùn_ òut**s** . . . rùn**s** òut.'
            (for 'runs out'; AD-629(44))

In (10a) it appears that Anna has mis-parsed 'play-with' as the lexical verb, and has applied the past tense suffix to the preposition 'with'. Similarly in the adult error in (10b) the phrase 'run-out' is erroneously treated as the lexical verb, and the 3rd sg. present tense suffix is placed at the end of the preposition 'out'. This sort of error will be discussed in detail in Chapter 6.

In general, then, the figures for phonological errors show a gradual decrease in complete anticipations and exchanges, and a gradual increase in incomplete anticipations. A hypothesis was developed to explain these patterns, which involves the amount of structured information in phonological production representations, the size of the planning unit, and the development of the self-monitor. In phonological errors, perseverations outnumbered anticipations at age 1 only; this could be due to a slower decay rate, but could also be due to the lack of syntax with its tonic syllable which is an important cause of phonological anticipations. For lexical misplacement errors, children produce more perseverations than anticipations up through age 5, although adults produce more anticipations. But both adults and children produce a majority of affix perseverations rather than anticipations, probably due to a mis-assignment of constituent boundaries in phrases.

TABLE 2.7
Error types for phonological errors, by age, compared to two adult sources (excluding telescopings, features, or multiple errors, but including non-contextual errors). Numbers are percentages of errors in this sub-group of errors which fall into each category.

Age:	1	2	3	4	5	Total	A1	A2
%Substitions	58.5	47	52	59	63.5	56	56.5	70.5
%Additions	14	14.5	23	18	18	18	18	22
%Reversals	20.5	17.5	10	9	7	11	16	5.5
%Metathesis	3.5	2.5	2.5	2	1.5	2	0.5	na
%Omissions	0	8	6.5	9	8	8	5	2
%Movements	3.5	10.5	6	3	2	5	4	na
Total N=	29	164	153	274	178	798	273	787

A1=English adults, Jaeger corpus.
A2=Dutch adults, from Nooteboom (1973).

2.3.3 Developmental Trends in Error Type

It has also long been known (Nooteboom 1973) that in phonological errors, substitutions are much more common than any other type of error, i.e. additions, omissions, or movements (which are often not reported for adult corpora). The same pattern is found to some extent in the children's errors, as shown in Table 2.7. This table includes between- and within-word errors, as well as non-contextual errors; it excludes telescopings, feature errors, and multiple phonological errors.

This table shows the same decrease in exchanges as in Table 2.5, with metathesis separated from non-contiguous reversals to illustrate that the main decrease is in non-contiguous reversals. Substitutions are very common for the 1-year-olds (58.5%); they become less prominent at age 2 (47%) but then increase to 63.5% at age 5, showing an increase in the direction of Nooteboom's adult figure, 70.5%, and exceeding my adult figure of 56.5%. Additions increase from age 1 through age 3, and then level off at 18%, which is similar to the adult figures of 18% and 22%. Omissions do not occur at age 1, and then show a fairly steady percentage from ages 2-4 (between 6.5% and 9%); they are more frequent in general than in the adult corpora (5% or 2%). Finally, the children have a high percentage of movement errors at ages 2-3, but they nearly disappear by age 5. Nooteboom does not recognize the category 'movement', considering these errors to be an omission plus addition or substitution. However, Stemberger (1989) explicitly reports that he collected no movement errors from the adults in his study, whereas I found a small number of movement errors in my adult corpus; in general, this seems to be a type of error that is more common among very young children. The explanations given above for patterns of exchange errors are relevant to the movement errors also, since many of these early movements are in fact within-word errors, as illustrated in (11).

(11) a. B: 'Mòmmy mỳ [b_ǽŋ.klɨt] . . . blánket!' (for 'blanket' [blǽŋ.kɨt]; [l] moved from first onset to second; B-51(14) 2;4)

      b. AF: 'A [kʰ_ɨ.tʰɹ̥ik] . . . critique of thìs will (etc.)' (for 'critique' [kʰɹ̥i.tʰʲik]; [r] moved from first onset to second; AD-175(14))

An explanation for why additions and omissions increase over time may be related to the fact that in the children's (and adults') data these two types of errors most often involve consonants in onset clusters, and the very young children do not yet produce consonant clusters. Substitutions are probably the most frequent error type for several reasons (as will be discussed in detail in Chapter 3): they involve two fully activated units in target words, which are usually phonetically similar to each other and occur in the same position in syllable structures. They also most often involve units which are highly activated in the intonational phrase due to being in stressed syllables, usually including the tonic syllable (Boomer & Laver 1973). Because of their high prosodic activation and their similarity in terms of phonetic features and syllable structure position, these segments are apparently strongly interconnected as the syntagmatic string is being compiled, which makes the substitution of one for another a very likely error (Fromkin 1973a, Shattuck-Hufnagel & Klatt 1979, among many others). Furthermore, simple substitutions deform the overall prosodic shape of words less than additions, omissions, or movements, so that substitution errors would be caught less often by the internal monitor.

For errors involving lexical items, paradigmatic substitutions are by far the most common type, for children and adults alike, as shown in Table 2.8. This table includes paradigmatic substitutions, paradigmatic blends, and syntagmatic errors involving content words and free function words (excluding affixes; including the 'multiple' errors that involved only words, not affixes, in the 'syntagmatic' figures). Besides the large number of paradigmatic lexical substitutions, most of the syntagmatic errors involving whole words are also substitutions, with the children producing only four syntagmatic lexical additions, and the adults only one.

It is not surprising that lexical substitutions are more common than blends or misorderings, if we recall the level of the RPC Model at which each of these error types occurs. Lexical selection errors most commonly occur when the concepts to be expressed activate a number of semantically appropriate lemmas, and an incorrect lemma is erroneously selected; after this misselection, the system treats the error as if it were the intended lexical item, and assigns it a functional role, inserts it into the syntactic string, and activates its phonological form, which is then prepared for speaking. The other place where lexical

TABLE 2.8
Percentage of lexical errors in three form categories, by age.

Age:	1	2	3	4	5	Total	Adult
Par. Subst.	30	48.5	44	50	59	50	51
Blends	60	24.5	20	19	12.5	21	23
Syntagmatic	10	27	36	31	28.5	29	26
Total N=	**20**	**70**	**64**	**127**	**95**	**376**	**309**

selection errors can occur is during the activation of the forms of lemmas, when spreading activation can cause a word which is very similar phonologically to the intended word to be erroneously selected. These are two places where speech production planning can easily go wrong. The fact that the error involves a real word which is either semantically or phonologically (or in some cases, both) similar to the intended word, means that the internal monitor can readily be fooled into thinking a correct utterance is being planned until well after the word has been spoken (although, as will be shown below, the external monitor is very good at catching this type of error). On the other hand, a blend error occurs when two semantically related words, usually near-synonyms, are both activated but neither one is fully selected. When it comes time to insert the words into the syntactic template, the planning mechanism must activate both phonological forms and insert them into the single slot; when this hybrid is sent to the "Phonological Processes" component, it constructs a phonological blend of the two words. This is clearly a more drastic error than a substitution, in that it deforms the planned utterance more than a simple misselection of a word does. Furthermore, it often produces a form which is not a real word in the language, and thus will more often be caught by the internal monitor before it is spoken. For all these reasons, blend errors are much less common than lexical selection errors, for adults and older children as well.

Syntagmatic misorderings occur either when lexical items have been misassigned a functional role, or when they have been accidentally inserted into the wrong slot in the syntactic template. The former is somewhat rare since functional structure assignment is keyed to the lexical-semantic properties of the lemma, that is, the word's lexical category, the Aktionsart class of the verb, the mass or count status of the noun, and so on. The latter, lexical insertion errors, occur when a syntactic phrase is being planned and lemmas of both content and function words are being inserted into syntactic slots; the error will be caused when one word already selected for the utterance is inserted into an incorrect slot (usually maintaining the 'content' vs. 'function' word distinction but not always the lexical category distinction). Another possible situation would be when two phrases are being planned at once, and a word which is to take a particular slot in one of the phrases accidentally gets assigned to an analogous slot in the other phrase, often one marked for the same lexical category (e.g. both nouns). This latter error type can occur in either the functional assignment or syntactic assignment components. However, these are both fairly major deformations of the planned utterance; in errors which occur at the syntactic level, words can even be assigned to syntactic slots which require a word from a different lexical category. Therefore both of these error types are rarer than the simple misselection of a word, as they will most often be caught by the internal monitor.

There is one further explanation for the proportions of paradigmatic vs. syntagmatic lexical error types, which has to do with the number of degrees of freedom involved in performing each increment of planning. When activating an appropriate lexical item for the proposition to be conveyed, there may be a very large number of lexical items which are activated by the intended conceptual content. This competition from other lexical items makes selection of the correct one relatively difficult. On the other hand, there are many fewer slots in the syntactic templates into which lexical items need to be inserted, and thus fewer chances of making an incorrect insertion. Therefore there is less likelihood that a word will be misplaced than that a word will be misselected, as there are fewer degrees of freedom in the syntagmatic processes than in the paradigmatic ones.

Several developmental patterns are evident from Table 2.8. First, the children make a smaller percentage of paradigmatic substitutions at age 1 (30%) than at any other age; by age 2 their substitutions have nearly reached the adult percentage (48.5%; adults 51%), and stay more or less at this level for the remainder of the ages. (The dip in lexical substitution errors at age 3 will be discussed below; the high percentage of substitutions at age 5 is due in part to a large contribution from the Other children at this age, as discussed above.) Since most lexical substitution errors involve two words which are semantically related, this suggests that the semantic interrelationships within the lexicon are well-established by age 2, a point I will discuss in detail in Chapter 5. On the other hand, the children at age 1 make the largest percentage of blends of any age, 60%. At age 2 the figure is 24.5%, and this figure gradually decreases to a low of 12.5% at age 5, which is below my adult figure of 23% by nearly half. The 60% figure at age 1 suggests that at this early age the children are much less practiced in uniquely selecting a single word for production, and thus frequently allow more than one word to remain activated, which results in a blend. Since all but two of these errors occurred when the children were in the 1- or 2-word stage, the blends are not caused by the constraint of having only one slot available in a *syntactic* template (taking the 2-word stage to be non-syntactic), but instead result from the children being unable to select between two *semantically* relevant lexical items. Furthermore, many of the very early blends (and lexical selection errors) occurred when there was an environmental influence, that is, the child was looking at one object in the environment while trying to name another; this sort of 'overload' of working memory would cause the most trouble for the youngest children with the most immature working memory (see Chapter 4). Many early blends also involved some utterance influence, where one (or both) of the blended words was previously spoken in the discourse. However, by age 2 the number of blends has dropped to a figure similar to the adult level. This could be because the child simply has had more practice in selecting lexical items, but it could also show the constraining effect on the child, now in the 3+word stage, of activating and utilizing syntactic templates, since trying to insert two different lemmas into the same syntagmatic slot will be a deterrent to blends. It is not clear why the 4-5-year-olds made a smaller percentage of blends than adults. This may be a function of the adults' much larger vocabularies (particularly synonyms), allowing them more possible interfering words; also the large number of lexical substitutions from Other children at age 5 biases these numbers somewhat. (I should also note that I seem to have collected far more lexical blends than is usually reported for adults; in Stemberger's corpus of 6300 adult errors, he found that lexical substitutions outnumbered lexical blends by 3 to 1 (Stemberger 1989:168), whereas in my data the ratio is only 2 to 1.)

Looking at syntagmatic errors involving word misplacement, it can be seen that the 1-year-olds show very few such errors, which is not surprising since, as just noted, most of the children are not utilizing syntax at this age. Both errors made at age 1 were perseverations.

(12)   a. An: (pointing to pictures in a book, which included a kitty and
              cookies) 'Here's a *kìtty*-cat, dòggies, kìt . . . còokies, cáke.'
              (started to repeat 'kitty'; AN-10(43) 1;8)
        b. M: 'Come òn, let's gèt your *dìaper* òn.'
           B: (pointing at light on diaper-changing table)
              '**Dìaper** òn . . . lìght òn.'
              ('diaper' substituted for 'light'; B-26(43) 1;11)

The first of these occurred when Anna was in the 3+word stage, while she was naming, in list form, pictures in a book; she had said the word 'kitty', which she perseverated and substituted for the phonologically similar 'cookies' (both items were in view when the error was made). In (12b), Bobby was in the 2-word stage, and a word spoken by an adult perseverated in his working memory and substituted for the word he was planning. However, the percentages of syntagmatic errors rise to the adult level at age 2 and remain so throughout the subsequent age ranges. The peak in syntagmatic errors at age 3 is most likely due to the fact that the children at this age were learning many new syntactic structures; their lack of mastery of these structures would make their planning processes particularly susceptible to lexical insertion errors. This probably explains the proportional lowering of paradigmatic substitution errors. By ages 4-5 the children have had much more practice with syntax, and so both activation of syntactic templates and lexical selection and insertion are being performed with more accuracy; the age 5 figure, 28.5%, is very similar to the figure for adults, 26%.

In sum, both children and adults produce a majority of substitutions in both phonological and lexical errors. Children show an increase over time in phonological additions and omissions, probably because these error types usually involve consonant clusters, which the very young children do not produce. Likewise, children show a decrease in phonological exchanges and movements, most likely due to their phonological representations becoming more fixed over time and the length of the utterance being planned at one time increasing. Lexical blends are common at age 1, but decline sharply at age 2, due probably to more practice at lexical selection and to the onset of syntax. Syntagmatic lexical errors are rare at age 1 since there is little syntax at that age, but rise to adult levels at age 2; they peak at age 3 probably due to a focus on the acquisition of syntactic structures which may complicate lexical insertion. By age 5, the percentages for the forms of error types are very similar to adults', for both phonological and lexical errors.

2.3.4 Developmental Trends in the Linguistic Units Involved in Errors

Table 2.9 presents the percentages of errors at each age which involve specific units. These counts exclude multiple phonological or lexical errors where several different units may be involved, propositional errors (since they are rare and probably underreported), and phonological metatheses, since they may involve consonants and vowels in the same error. Errors are counted under 'LU' (syllables, rhymes, consonant clusters, etc.) if either the target or the error unit falls into this category. 'Telescopings' are technically a deletion of a 'LU', but because they have prosodic factors different from simple deletions, they are counted separately. If an error involves both a syllabic and non-syllabic liquid, it is counted in the category of the target/error and not the source (e.g. if [t]-->[r] under the influence of [ɚ], this is counted as a 'consonant' error). 'Syntactic' includes phrase blends and syntagmatic errors involving words; 'morphemes' includes both paradigmatic and syntagmatic errors where an affix is the unit of error.

The table clearly shows an increase in errors involving particular units as that type of unit becomes available to the children during language development. First, consonants and vowels maintain fairly steady error rates, showing that some segment-sized units are among the first linguistic elements learned and thus available to error; consonant errors are more frequent than vowels, as they are for adults (this will be explicated in Chapter 3). Second, paradigmatic lexical errors (substitutions and blends of words) are frequent for the youngest children, as whole words are also learned very early; the percentage decrease at later ages is simply due to an increase in other types of errors. There is a slight increase in paradigmatic lexical errors from ages 3-5, moving in the direction of the adult figures. Syntactic errors increase as children acquire more syntactic knowledge;

TABLE 2.9
Percentage of errors involving each unit type, by age.

Age:	1	2	3	4	5	Total	Adult
Consonants	43	47.5	48	47	47	47	24.5
Paradigmatic Lexical	34	19.5	17.3	19	22.5	20	33
Syntactic	6	9.5	12	12	11	11	17.5
Vowels	7.5	6.5	10	6.5	5	7	5
LUs	2	7	5.5	6	6	6	9.3
Telescoping	7.5	8	3.3	4	3	4.5	4.5
Features	0	0.5	3	2	3	2	1
Morphemes	0	1.5	1	2.5	2	2	2.3
Stress & Intonation	0	0	0	1	0.5	0.5	3
Total N=	**53**	**262**	**236**	**454**	**303**	**1308**	**700**

however, even the 5-year-old children fall short of the adult figure for syntactic errors. Errors involving phonological LUs increase as children develop more internal phonological structure, again just falling short of the adult figures. Telescoping errors are common among the younger children, suggesting less control over the linear sequencing of phonological units, in that older children are less likely to omit timing units; in this case the adult figures are similar to the older children (ages 3-5). Featural errors do not occur before age 2;10, suggesting that features are not available to the processing mechanism before about age 3. Finally, there are no errors of stress or intonation before age 4, and in general this type of error is relatively more common for adults. The details of all these patterns will be discussed in subsequent chapters.

2.4 Corrections

An important issue when looking at the development of speech production planning mechanisms is the issue of corrections. I discussed this issue in some detail in Jaeger (1992a); one conclusion I came to in that article was that there were no reliable counts for adult data in terms of how often adults notice and correct their SOTs, and thus it was difficult to say anything convincing about the child data. However, in the current study I am able to compare my child corpus to my adult corpus on this measure, and come to some fairly reliable conclusions. The aspect of the speech production planning mechanism to which corrections are most pertinent is the development of the child's external monitor.

2.4.1 Correction Types

In my data there were three basic types of responses speakers produced to SOTs, with a few sub-categories of response types. First, in some cases the speaker appeared to not have noticed the error, and continued speaking without indicating that an error had occurred; this is illustrated in example (13a), where Bobby gave no indication that he noticed his error. Such reactions are notated in my data as 'NSC', meaning 'not self-corrected'. A variation on this type of response was when a second speaker noticed and commented on the error or asked for a repair; in this case the first speaker often repaired the error after having had it brought to his or her attention. However, this is still considered 'NSC', since the speaker did not notice or correct the error until the second speaker pointed it out. This is illustrated in (13b).

(13)   a. B: 'I càn [màtʃ] a *mó*vie.'
                (for 'watch' [watʃ]; [w]<--[m]; B-103(1) 2;7; NSC)
        b. OG:'Mommy, I dòne with my *cá*ndy.'
           M: 'Dòne with your cándy?'
           OG:'No, I mèan I dòne with my ápplejùice.'
                ('candy' substituted for 'applejuice'; OC-34(35) 2;10; NSC)

The second type of reaction speakers produced after making a SOT was to give some sort of indication that they had noticed the error, but not to actually correct it. Sometimes the fact that the speaker was aware of the error was evidenced by a confused look or a hesitation as in (14a). Sometimes the speaker tried to correct the error but was unable to do so and gave up, as in (14b). And sometimes the speaker repeated the error and made fun of it but didn't overtly correct it, as in (14c). This reaction category is labelled 'N-NC', meaning 'noticed but not self-corrected'.

(14)   a. OB:'*Quíck*, [kʰw̥ìk.stɨn].' (looks confused) (for 'Kristen'
                [kʰw̥ís.tɨn]; [k] perseverated, added; OC-98(13) 4;3; N-NC)
        b. M: 'My wáshing machìne needs fìxing.'
           An: 'Well, yèsterday Bárbara càme òver and sàid hér wàshing [mi]
                . . . hér wàshing [mi.ʃʌn] . . . hér thìng she wàshes dìshes ìn
                was bròken.' (for 'machine [mə.ʃín]; [ə]<-->[i], then [ə] realized
                as [ʌ] under stress; AN-143(26) 4;0; N-NC)
        c. Al: 'I have a [sn̥ò̰ʒ] *n*éck . . . sòre [sn̥ék] . . .' (laughs, says
                wrong on purpose several times)
                (for 'sore neck' [soʒ nɛk]; first error is anticipation/addition of
                [n], second error is perseveration/addition of [s]; AL-99a(2) and
                99b(13) 3;2; N-NC)

The third type of reaction was when the speaker noticed the error and overtly corrected it, before the error was pointed out to him or her by another person. Sometimes the error was simply corrected as in (15a), but often the speaker produced some sort of editing expression such as 'I mean', 'uh', or 'rather' before (or less often, after) the correction, as in (15b) (see §2.4.2 below). Self-corrected errors sometimes also involved some commentary on the error, as in (15c), including a repetition of the error with questioning intonation before correcting it, as in (15d). These errors are designated as 'SC', meaning 'self-corrected'.

(15)   a. B: 'We chàsed the Múd-[mʌ.dʌɬ pʰàn.s] . . .
            Múd P̱ùddle M̱ònster.'
            (for 'Puddle Monster'; [pʰ]<-->[m]; B-108(25) 2;8; SC)
       b. Al: 'I wànt some mòre **cátsup** . . . I mean s̱ýrup.'
            ('catsup' substituted for 'syrup'; AL-250(35) 5;7; SC)
       c. An: (looking at TV) 'Is thìs "***Jáws***"?' (movie title)
          M: 'No.'
          An: 'Good, because I dòn't wànt to be scàred by [dʒárks]. (laughs)
             I said "jàrks" instead of "s̱hárks".'
             (lexical blend of 'Jaws' and 'sharks'; AN-213(38) 4;5; SC)
       d. AF:(talking about giving turkey giblets to the dogs)
            'We úsed to gìve the [lɪ̀:.z̃ɚd] to . . . lízard? (laughs)
            l̀iver and g̀ízzàrd to them, but (etc.)'
            (telescoping of 'liver and gizzard'; AD-341(34); SC)

Table 2.10 shows the percentage of errors at each age in each of the four main error-unit categories which fell into each of the three correction categories. There are several points which this table makes very clear. First, the children in this study corrected their errors less frequently than the adults did; the overall child percentage of self-corrections is 59%, whereas for the adults the overall average is 73%. Both adults and children produced few 'noticed-not corrected' responses (6.5% child, 8% adult overall). This leaves 34.5% errors neither noticed nor corrected by the children, whereas the adults had only 19% of their errors in this category. Furthermore, the child percentages for self-corrections increased overall as the children got older: the 1-year-olds corrected 49% of their errors; at age 2 the figure dropped to 45%, but then it rose to 55% at age 3, 67% at age 4, and took a slight drop to 63.6% at age 5. So although the overall child average is below the adult average, the children's figures are moving in the direction of the adult figure. Thus it is clear that the external self-monitor, which listens for the accuracy of the output and makes overt corrections when needed, is much more efficient in the adults than the children. This monitor clearly develops over the time span which is the focus of the current study (from 49% to 67% self-corrected), but is not up to the adult level of efficiency (73% overall) by age 5, the upper boundary of this study.

There are several patterns of error-correction rate evident in this table that are related to the type of error involved. First, propositional errors are always corrected; however, this finding is undoubtedly due to the fact that the researcher can't definitively classify an error as a propositional error unless speakers indicate that the utterance was at odds with the proposition they actually intended

TABLE 2.10

Percentage of errors in each correction category at each age, organized by four main error types: Phonological, Lexical (paradigmatic), Syntactic (syntagmatic lexical, phrase blends), and Propositional. SC=self-corrected; N-NC=noticed but not corrected; NSC= not self-corrected; N=total number of errors in this category at this age.

Age:	1	2	3	4	5	Total	Adult
Phonological							
%SC	44.5	38.5	50	62.5	59	53.5	72.5
%N-NC	5.5	8.5	6.5	7.5	6.5	7	7
%NSC	50	53	43.5	30	34.5	39.5	20.5
N=	36	198	181	312	206	933	342
Lexical							
%SC	50	63	71	76	76	71	77
%N-NC	11	8	5	6	7	7	6
%NSC	39	29	24	18	17	22	17
N=	18	51	41	88	70	268	232
Syntactic							
%SC	100	56	63.5	73.5	64	67	68
%N-NC	0	9.5	0	5.5	0	4	12
%NSC	0	34.5	36.5	21	36	29	20
N=	3	32	33	71	39	178	139
Propositional							
%SC	na	100	na	100	100	100	100
N=	0	1	0	2	1	4	3
Total							
%SC	49	45	55	67	63.6	59	73
%N-NC	7	8.5	5.5	7	5.7	6.5	8
%NSC	44	46.5	39.5	26	30.7	34.5	19
N=	57	282	255	473	316	1383	716

to convey. So this may be an artifact of the methodology. Of the three major error-unit categories, all speakers at every age corrected the lexical errors more often than errors in the other two categories, syntactic and phonological, with one exception. The 1-year-olds corrected all of their syntactic SOTs (N=3); but again, this figure is probably a methodological artifact, since the main way one can tell a 1-year-old has produced a syntactic structure at odds with their intention is the fact that they correct the utterance. The older children corrected syntactic errors with almost the same frequency as they corrected lexical errors, such that the overall figures for the children are 71% lexical and 67% syntactic self-corrections.

A possible explanation for these patterns is that the young children's external monitors are fairly global, and are focussed on whether or not they are getting across the meaning they intend to convey. Because of this, the error types which cause the greatest impediments to conveying meaning, namely incorrect lexical selection and frankly ungrammatical utterances (and of course propositional errors), are the error types most often caught by the monitor. Phonological errors, which cause a smaller deformation of the intended utterance, were often not noticed by the children's external monitors (overall 53.5% self-corrections). In fact, within-word errors, especially exchanges, were self-corrected the least often of any error type.

On the other hand, the adults seemed to correct all three classes of error with approximately the same frequency. Lexical (77%) errors were corrected the most often, probably for the same reason that children caught them most often (greatest impediment to meaning); note that the 4- and 5-year-old children corrected 76% of their lexical errors, which is equivalent to the adult figure. But syntactic and phonological errors were corrected at about the same rate as each other (phonological 72.5%, syntactic 68%). This indicates that the adults' external monitors are probably more fine-grained than the childrens' and catch both the global and the more local errors. And of course adults have simply had more practice speaking and monitoring for their errors than children have. One interesting point about adult corrections is the 12% 'noticed-not corrected' figure for syntax; many adults in this study seemed to be relying on listeners to figure out what they meant to say when they made syntactic errors, and so even when they noticed the ungrammaticality of their utterance, they didn't bother to correct it. Children, on the other hand, felt the need to correct those syntactic errors which they noticed most of the time, with only a 4% N-NC rate. But other than this one situation, the adults in this study caught and corrected their errors more often than the children, with the children's figures of self-correction gradually increasing over time.

2.4.2 The Use of Editing Expressions

In order to further compare the children's and adults' responses to errors, I looked at the editing expressions they used after making an error, and found some interesting differences related both to age and to error type. The editing expressions used by adults consisted mainly of of 'uh, um' and 'I mean'; there were a few cases of 'rather', a repetition of the error with questioning intonation before correcting it (as in (15d) above), a question such as 'Why did I say that?' or 'What did I say?' and a few other expressions ('that is', 'actually', 'oh'). The expressions used by children were somewhat more varied, and often much more elaborate than the adults'. They consisted of 'um, uh', 'I mean' as in (15b), 'Oh, I said X for Y' (or some version of this) as in (15c) and (16b) below, 'no, nah' as in (16a), repetition with question intonation before correcting, 'Oh, I made a mistake/speech error' as in (16c), and a few others ('wait', 'I should say').

(16) a. M: 'Only **bábies** need bòttles!'
Al: (looks around for her bottle) 'Mý bàby . . . nò . . . mý bòttle!'
('baby' perseverated/substituted for 'bottle'; Al-14(43) 2;2; SC)
b. An: '[kʰļú:.kʰļàk] . . . (laughs) Mommy, I said "[kʰļú:.kʰļàk]" for
"cúckoo clòck".' (for 'cuckoo clock' [kʰú.kʰu.kʰļàk]; telescoping;
AN-88(34) 2;11; SC)
c. M: 'Go tínkie befòre we gò to the stòre.'
B: 'We can bùy a báthroom. Oh! I made a spéech èrror. I mèant
we can fínd a bàthroom.' ('buy' substituted for 'find', in the
discourse context of going to the store; B-429(35) 4;11; SC)

One of the most interesting reactions the children produced following an
error was to try to 'save face' by explaining or justifying the error, as if they had
actually meant to produce that utterance. There were eight such cases in my
data, all made between 3;11 and 5;2, and all but two made by Bobby; no adults
in my study reacted this way. This type of justification occurred in all three
major correction-type categories, as illustrated in (17); see also (AN-131(43)
3:11), (B-447(37) 5;1), (B-466(29) 5;2), and (B-541(35) 5;7).

(17) a. B: (telling Mom where his imaginary 'off' switch is located)
It's behìnd my báck. Press [sták]. (pause) "Stóck"?
I said "Stóp"!' (for 'stop' [stap]; [k]-->[p]; B-422(12) 4;11; SC)
b. B: 'I'm going to sèe if there's a [sņí.dəɬ] under the còuch.'
(notices error, tries to save face; spots a bowl of cactus)
'Ya knòw what a "snéedle" is? It's a kìnd of cáctus.'
(for 'needle' [ní.dəɬ]; [s] perseverated/added; B-369(13) 4;9;
N-NC)
c. Al: 'Gèt 'em ìnto the dìrty [kʰw̥ò"z kʰļík]! (pause)
You know what "clíck" means? Quíckly!' (for 'clothes quick'
[kʰļo"z kʰw̥ɪk]; [l]<-->[w]; AL197(25) 3;11; N-NC)
d. B: (picking an olive out of Mom's salad) 'Can I hàve a? **Ómar**?'
M: 'You mean an ólive?'
B: 'Yéah. I càll it "Òmar" because it sóunds lìke "Òmar".'
('Omar' [óʷ.mar] for 'olive' [á.lɪv]; Bobby had been playing with
his friend Omar all day; B-430(35) 5;0; NSC)

In (17a), Bobby repeats the erroneous utterance, then denies he said it. In
(17b), he makes up a definition to match his erroneous production, as Alice also
does in (17c). In (17d) Bobby gives a good reason why he should call an olive
an 'Omar'. I will return to this type of reaction below, but it is interesting to
note that the two children who corrected more of their errors (see §2.4.3) and in
general exhibited the more 'referential' style of language learning, are the ones
who most often tried to 'cover up' their errors.

TABLE 2.11
Number of editing expressions of each type, by age.

Age:	1	2	3	4	5	Total	Adult
Expression							
'no, nah, not'	0	5	2	2	0	9	0
'I mean'	0	3	1	9	11	24	39
'um, uh'	0	1	0	5	1	7	69
'I said x for y'	0	1	1	9	1	12	2
save face	0	0	1	2	4	7	0
repeat?	0	0	1	3	0	4	4
'I made a SOT'	0	0	0	2	1	3	0
'rather'	0	0	0	0	0	0	3
'what/why did I...'	0	0	0	0	0	0	3
other	0	0	0	1	1	2	3
Total N=	**0**	**10**	**6**	**33**	**19**	**68**	**123**

Table 2.11 is a rough count of the use of these expressions by children and adults, organized according to age. This table shows first that the adults used the editing expressions more often than the children in general; the children used these expressions in about 7.5% of the errors which they either corrected or noticed (N=906), whereas adults use them in about 21% of such errors (N=580). There are probably (at least) three factors which are needed to explain this pattern. First, the youngest children were producing only 1- and 2-word utterances, and so adding one of these expressions would have been a major burden on their production capacities, and in fact there were no such expressions at age 1, and relatively few at ages 2 and 3. There was a fairly large increase in the number of such expressions used at age 4; this could be a function of children's abilities to plan longer and more complex utterances, although it may also be partly due to the large number of errors collected from children at age 4.

A second factor is the children's increasing knowledge of vocabulary and linguistic conventions. Most of the earliest expressions used (ages 2;0-2;4) were the simple 'no' or 'nah'; the first 'I mean' came at 2;4, and the first 'I said x for y' expression was collected from Anna, at 2:11 (16b). However, as the children got older they learned more ways of marking their errors; they also were occasionally very embarrassed by them and tried to 'cover up', as discussed above. However, even the oldest of the children produced overt editing expressions far less often than the adults in the study, and this leads to the suspicion that a third factor may be involved.

One can speculate that adults overtly mark their errors more often than children do because they are more conscious of their responsibility in accurately

TABLE 2.12
Number of errors involving specific editing expressions, by linguistic error-unit type (see text for explanation of types of editing expressions).

	Phonological	Lexical	Syntactic/Prop.	Total
Child				
'I mean'	1	20	3	24
'I said x for y'	7	5	0	12
'no, nah, not'	4	2	3	9
'um, uh'	4	2	1	7
save face	4	3	1	8
repeat?	3	1	0	4
'I made a SOT'	1	2	0	3
other	0	1	1	2
Total N=	**24**	**36**	**9**	**69**
Adult				
'um, uh'	12	48	9	69
'I mean'	2	31	6	39
repeat?	2	2	0	4
'rather'	2	0	1	3
'what/why did I...'	2	1	0	3
'I said x for y'	2	0	0	2
other	1	2	0	3
Total N=	**23**	**84**	**16**	**123**

presenting the meaning they intend to convey. Very young children are not only less adept at conversational conventions than adults, but are also used to having adults take on more than half of the responsibility for the success of the communication, to compensate for the child's lack of linguistic communicative experience. One manifestation of this is the large number of times adults asked a child for a repair after the child had produced a SOT in my corpus. Thus children may be less likely to overtly mark their errors because they are not as conscious as adults are of their communicative responsibility to the listener.

Another pattern which emerged is that different types of errors were more or less likely to elicit an overt correction marker. Table 2.12 shows the editing expressions used, organized by error-unit category; syntactic and propositional errors are collapsed into one, since these expressions were rarely used with propositional errors.

The numbers in this table show that that editing expressions were most often used while correcting lexical errors, both for the children and adults. This ties in with the point made above, that lexical errors cause the most serious problems for conveying the intended meaning. Furthermore, most instances of the expression 'I mean' occurred when the speaker was correcting a lexical substitution error in which the target and error words were semantically related, as in (15b); the expression was less common before malapropisms, where the words are related only by form, and even less common before blends, or any kind of phonological error. The hesitation marker 'uh' also seemed to most often mark a lapse in meaning. These speakers, undoubtedly unconsciously, overtly marked errors in which an unintended meaning was conveyed with the expression 'I mean' (or 'uh'), and the children began to follow this pattern as early as 2;4, although it became more common at age 4. On the other hand, the 'I said x for y' type expressions were most commonly used for phonological errors and malapropisms, where the speaker produced either a non-word or a completely anomalous real word; in this case the speaker makes reference to the erroneous form of the utterance, whereas in the case of 'I mean' the speaker draws attention to a situation where the form was appropriate but the meaning was at odds with the intention.

2.4.3   Individual Differences in Self-Correction

I have remarked several times that Anna corrected her errors less often than the other two children. The percentage of errors falling into each correction category for each of the three main subjects is shown in Table 2.13. The Other children are omitted from this count, since any individual differences would be averaged out in this count; furthermore, self-correction was relied on more heavily as verification of a SOT for the Other children, so these percentages will be relatively high due to methodology. The overall number of errors for each child in this table is slightly smaller than in previous tables, since I counted the correction status of utterances with more than one error only once in this table if there was a single correction for all parts of the error.

This table clearly shows not only that Anna corrected her errors overall less often than the other two children (SC = Anna: 48%, Alice: 55%, Bobby: 63%), but also that this was true at every age, regardless of the differences in actual numbers of errors collected from each child at each age. Furthermore, Anna had the largest percentage of 'noticed, not self-corrected' responses of the three children (Anna: 9%, Alice: 6.5%, Bobby: 5.5%). These two facts fit in with the overall picture of Anna as an 'expressive' learner, who was more interested in the interactive aspects of language than the absolute correctness of her utterances. Note also that because Alice's median age of data collection was nearly a year younger than Anna's, we would expect Alice to correct fewer of her errors than Anna; however, this was not the case, supporting the claim that it is not age but learning style that accounts for the differences between the children.

In sum, the children in this study corrected 59% of their SOTs overall, while the adults corrected 73%, showing that the adults have a more efficient external monitor than the children; it was also speculated that adults generally

TABLE 2.13

Percentages of errors in three correction categories, by subject and age. SC = self-corrected; N-NC = noticed, not self-corrected; NSC = not self-corrected.

Age:		1	2	3	4	5	Total
Anna	% SC	33	33	44	60	49	48
	% N-NC	19	7	2.5	13	7	9
	% NSC	48	60	53.5	27	44	43
	N=	21	73	43	123	70	330
Alice	% SC	na	54	50	72	59	55
	% N-NC	na	8	7	2.5	3	6.5
	% NSC	na	38	43	25.5	38	38.5
	N=	0	84	113	39	34	270
Bobby	% SC	58	40	68.4	66	70	63
	% N-NC	0	10	5.5	5	5	5.5
	% NSC	42	50	26	29	25	31.5
	N=	31	90	54	255	159	589

take more responsibility than children do for the success of their communication, and corrections facilitate this success. All subjects corrected lexical errors more often than either phonological or syntactic errors, and the 5-year-old children corrected lexical errors as often as adults did; this shows that the errors which cause the most serious deformations of the intended meaning are those which are usually noticed and corrected. The biggest difference between the child and adult figures was in the phonological errors; the children corrected only 53.5% of these errors while adults corrected 72.5%, showing that the children's external monitors were probably also more global and less fine-grained. However, all the children's correction percentages increased in the direction of the adult figures, showing development of the monitor. The adults and children in this study used a range of editing expressions to indicate overtly that they had made a mistake. However, adults tended to use 'uh' or 'I mean' most often, whereas the children used a broader range of expressions, often quite elaborate, such as 'Oh, I said x for y', and justifications of their errors. The expression 'I mean' was used most often both by adults and children to correct lexical substitution errors where the target and error words were semantically related, again reinforcing the hypothesis that this type of error was considered the biggest problem for communication. Finally, Anna, the 'expressive' learner, made fewer corrections than the other two children, who were more 'referential' learners.

2.5   Summary

The children in this study produced very similar types of errors as the adults. The very few child/adult differences were attributed to differences in the lexical representation of morphological structure, word-internal prosodic structure, and orthography in the form lexicon, and presence or absence of derivationally related words in the lexicon. In general the children produced similar proportions of error types to adults and to each other, with individual differences among the children being attributed to age of data collection and the 'expressive-referential' learning styles. Developmental trends in proportion of within-word errors, directionality of errors, formal structure of errors, units involved in errors, and self-corrections were attributed to developments in linguistic representation, the span of the speech production planning unit, and the self-monitoring system. In general, I would argue that children's SOTs are similar to adults' in most ways; therefore children's SOTs are valuable data for addressing the same kinds of issues looked at for adults, in terms of the units and structures involved in representations, and the levels and components involved in speech production planning. But more importantly, they allow us to tap into the time-course of the development of specific aspects of language, by seeing how the substance of the errors changes over time. In the next chapter I will look in detail into the development of phonological representations and processing.

Chapter 3
Phonetics and Phonology

3.1 Introduction

3.1.1 From Babbling to Phonology

In a series of important papers, Davis and MacNeilage have shown that the patterns involved in oral babbling during the first year of life can to a large extent be explained in terms of motor constraints (MacNeilage & Davis 1990, 1993, 2000, Davis & MacNeilage 1994, 1995, MacNeilage 1998, Davis, MacNeilage & Matyear 2002). The main factor is the open-close cycle of the jaw, which can be described as producing a proto-syllable. Toward the end of the first year, infants develop both more fine-grained perceptual abilities and more motor control over articulators, and this allows an expansion of the vocalizations which they are able to produce. As they repeat specific sounds and perceive the effect of this repeated motor gesture, they begin to represent specific speech sounds, consonants, and vowels, in their developing phonological system. Thus one would expect that the phonological form of early words would be organized in terms of syllables and/or segments. Yet it is often reported that first words are not represented in terms of segments, but are stored as motoric and acoustic wholes (Waterson 1971, Vihman 1981, Lindblom 1986, Locke 1986, Jusczyk 1992, Macken 1992). The purpose of this chapter is to provide evidence for the sequence of development from holistic and non-systematic lexical phonological representations, to representations which reflect a fully differentiated phonological system. This discussion will focus on the phonological development of phonetic features, segments, syllables and sub-syllabic units, as well as lexical stress and intonation. In each section of this chapter I will discuss the progression of error types involving or implicating each phonological unit, and at the end of this chapter I will present a unified sketch of the time-course of the development of the phonological system, including both lexical representations and phonological processes, which is evident in the changing patterns of phonological speech errors.

3.1.2 Overview of Development of Phonological Units

In Chapter 2, Table 2.9, I presented an overview of the age-progression of units involved in SOTs in my study. In Table 3.1 below, I present the figures for phonological errors only. These figures are slightly different from those in Table 2.9, in two ways. First, I have included metathesis errors in the numbers; this involves 10 errors where two consonants have metathesized (included under 'consonant' errors), and 7 errors where a consonant and vowel metathesized (included under 'C/V' errors); metathesis errors were excluded from Table 2.9 because they often involve both consonants and vowels. Second, I counted errors in which a syllabic and non-syllabic liquid interacted in the 'C/V' category; in Table 2.9 these are listed as either 'consonant' or 'vowel' errors,

TABLE 3.1
Number of each type of phonological unit involved in errors, by age, and percentage of phonological errors at each age involving each unit.

Age:	1	2	3	4	5	Total	Adult
Consonants	24	127	115	213	140	619	170
	73%	68.3%	68.5%	70%	70%	69.5%	51%
Vowels	4	17	23	28	15	87	36
	12%	9%	13.5%	9.5%	8%	10%	11%
Larger Units	1	19	13	26	18	77	65
	3%	10.3%	8%	8.5%	9%	8.5%	19.5%
Telescopings	4	21	8	18	10	61	31
	12%	11.3%	5%	6%	5%	7%	9%
Features	0	1	7	9	10	27	8
		0.5%	4%	3%	5%	3%	2.5%
C/V	0	1	2	7	5	15	2
		0.5%	1%	2%	2.5%	1.5%	0.5%
Stress/	0	0	0	3	1	4	22
Intonation				1%	0.5%	0.5%	6.5%
Total N=	**33**	**186**	**168**	**304**	**199**	**890**	**334**

depending on the status of the error segment (details will be given in §3.3.3 below). As in Table 2.9, 'Multiple Phonological Errors' are not included.

The most obvious point to be made from this table is that the children's early phonological errors overwhelmingly involve segments; at all ages, the percentage of errors involving individual segments is around 80%, whereas for adults the figure is 62%. This shows that at the time children begin making phonological errors, their lexical representations for words are not motoric wholes, but are clearly differentiated in terms of segments, and syllables are no longer the predominant phonological unit. How can this be explained?

I believe that the explanation lies in the fact that children do not begin making phonological SOTs until they have acquired at least 50 words. Many researchers have posited that the prerequisite for the '18-month 50-word vocabulary spurt' (however it manifests itself in an individual child) is the development of a repertoire of individual speech segments which are represented in the child's 'Phonology', independent of individual lexical items, and are used as building blocks for learning and representing the phonology of new words (Menn 1983, Ferguson 1986, Menyuk, Menn & Silber 1986, Studdert-Kennedy 1987, Lindblom 1986, 1992, Levelt, Roelofs & Meyer 1999, Menn & Stoel-Gammon 2001). It is only before this 'vocabulary spurt' that words are represented holistically. The onset of phonological errors in my three children support this hypothesis. The three children reached the 50-word mark at different

PHONETICS AND PHONOLOGY   93

ages (Anna and Bobby at about 18 months, Alice at about 23 months), and each
began making phonological slips about one month later (Anna and Bobby at 19
months, Alice at 24 months). Thus the onset of these slips is compatible with
the hypothesis that segments are the primary unit of lexical phonological
representation after the child has acquired about 50 words. (See also Ohala 1992
for an evolutionary perspective on the segment.)

However, this does not mean that the full adult phonological representation
is attained as soon as segmental SOTs begin to be produced. There is in fact
evidence that the gestalt nature of children's representations continues to some
extent as the child's phonological system is developing (see Gerken 1994 for an
overview). For example, Macken (1992) argues that the word, specifically the
word template, is the basic unit in phonology through at least age 2. Berg
(1992) similarly argues that the harmony rule evident in his daughter's early
phonology (age 2;7-2;11) can best be explained by hypothesizing that
phonological representations consist of underspecified slots which could be filled
in according to her current 'favorite' segments. Alice's metathesis rule (Jaeger
1997), where more anterior consonants were required to occur before more
posterior consonants in words, could also be explained in terms of a whole-word
prosody. Vihman (1981) studied lexical substitutions made by children between
the ages of 1-5, and found that there was somewhat more global similarity
between target and source words in the very young children (ages 1-2), compared
to a more specific phonological similarity among the older children.
Experimental studies looking into metalinguistic awareness of older children,
ages 4-6, show that larger units such as syllables and whole words tend to be
much more accessible than segments (Liberman et al. 1974, Treiman & Breaux
1982; see Derwing, Nearey & Dow 1986 for other examples). So one important
issue which could be addressed by looking at young children's SOTs is whether
or not there is any evidence that the children's slips are less well-organized in
terms of internal syllable structure than adults' slips, which would support the
hypothesis that their phonological representations and processing develop over
time by acquiring more specificity of structure. Another issue is how the
phonetic content and internal structure of segments develop over time. Further,
slips can be used to look into the genesis of phonemes, i.e. conceptual
categories, as opposed to segments per se, as well as knowledge about the
phonological processes of the language in general.

Thus, although Table 3.1 and this preliminary discussion provides a general
basis for the understanding of the development of phonological representations,
many details need to be examined before we have a full picture of this
development. I will now turn to these details, beginning with phonetic features,
followed by segments and phonemes, syllables and syllable structures, and
finally suprasegmental units.

3.2 Phonetic Features

There are two ways to assess the acquisition of phonetic features with SOT
data. The first is to look at errors which involve phonetic features rather than

segments, and see at what age these errors begin to occur; comparison can be made to adult featural errors to see if the children's developing featural organization is similar to adults'. The second is to look at segmental errors to see whether they display a kind of featural organization. It is well-known that in adult errors, one consonant is more likely to substitute for another if the two consonants differ by only one or two features (Fromkin 1973a, van den Broecke & Goldstein 1980). Vowels have been less studied than consonants, but there seems to be some phonetic consistency in vowel substitution errors, at least for some features (Shattuck-Hufnagel 1986). So whether or not the children's errors follow these same patterns will be another indication of when featural organization takes place. In this section I will first look at phonetic feature errors, and then turn to featural aspects of segmental errors.

3.2.1 Errors of Phonetic Features

As discussed in Chapter 1, there are some phonological errors which do not involve the interaction of whole segments, as no clear whole-segment source can be found for the error. On the other hand, these errors are not simply non-contextual, as there is a nearby segment which contains the feature value which seems to have influenced the change in the target segment. A child and an adult example are given in (1).

(1)   a. B: 'Èvery [pʰʌ.gɚd] . . . èvery cùpboard is líttle.' (for 'cupboard'
              [kʰʌ.bɚd]; feature of place reversed; B-567(29) 5;10)
       b. AM: 'I have a snèaki**ng** [sə.smí.ʃən] . . . suspícion.'
              (for 'suspicion' [sə.spí.ʃən]; feature of nasality and voicing A/P;
              AD-272(29))

In (1a), the feature of place was reversed between the two voiceless stop onsets, causing /k/ to be produced as /p/, and /b/ to be produced as /g/. In (1b), the positive value on the feature [nasal] was either anticipated from the /n/ in 'suspicion', or perseverated from the two nasals in 'sneaking', causing the labial /p/ to be produced as the nasal [m]; this of course also necessitated a change in voicing (and continuancy; see the feature system presented in §3.2.2 below). Since nasalized [p] is not a phoneme in English, and speech errors nearly always result in legal segments in the language (see §3.3.1 below), the speaker produced the phonetically closest legal segment in the error.

As indicated in Table 3.1 above, in my data there are 27 feature errors made by children, and 8 made by adults, all involving consonants. As can be seen from this table, I collected no feature errors at all from the children before age 2;10; the second feature error was collected at age 3;4. After age 3;4, there is a relatively steady presence of this type of error in the child data, but this type of error in general is rare throughout the child and adult data. This suggests that phonetic features are not available independently for error until the end of the third year, and in fact are not readily available for error until well into the fourth year. There are at least two possible explanations for this: one would be that the early representation of segments is holistic, i.e. that segments are stored as whole, unanalyzed units and not stored in terms of their phonetic properties in early phonological representations. Another might be that while some distinct phonetic properties are evident in segmental representations, these phonetic properties have not yet been extracted from the representations and organized into a unified feature system of the type for which there is ample evidence in adult language. It will be shown in §3.2.2 below that in fact children's consonant substitution errors are clearly governed by phonetic similarity from the earliest errors on, suggesting that the second explanation is more likely to be correct. This would lead me to hypothesize that the formal system of phonetic features is being acquired during the end of the third year and the beginning of the fourth year, and is to a large extent in place by around age 3;4. Once the system is in place, features become marginally available to error, although segmental errors remain by far the most common error type. This is also true of adult errors; as Fromkin (1973a:229) argues, only segments, not features, are 'independently controlled in speech'.

Table 3.1 also suggests that children in the 3-5-year-old range make slightly more feature errors than adults do. Although the difference is very small, one might hypothesize that when children first develop the feature system, features take on a slightly exaggerated importance in segmental representations; but for adults, since speech production is so highly automatized, the features involved in segmental representations have become more integrated and less separable. This argument was in fact made by Stemberger (1989:176) in the context of his account of consonantal substitutions; I will return to this point in §3.2.2 below.

As noted above, all of the feature errors in my corpus involved consonants; they can all be categorized as errors involving place of articulation, nasality, frication, voicing, and continuancy. (In §3.2.2 I will justify the use of these specific features.) Table 3.2 shows the number of errors involving each feature at each age; these numbers add up to more than the total number of feature errors, since several errors involved more than one feature (as, for example, error (1b) above, which involved nasality, continuancy, and voicing). This table is to be read as follows (for example): At age 3, the children produced 5 errors which involved a change in the value for the [place] feature, 2 errors involving the [fricative] feature, 2 involving [continuant], and 1 involving [nasal]. There were 7 total feature errors at age 3, with 10 total violations, so the average number of feature differences between the target and error segment at age 3 was 1.4 (out of five possible features).

The feature most commonly involved in feature errors was place of articulation, followed by frication and continuancy; nasality and voicing errors were rare. In most cases the target and error segment differed on only one or two feature values. Explanations for this pattern will be given in §3.2.2 below.

A second type of error involving features is fairly rare but nevertheless interesting. In lexical blends, where two words are phonologically blended and inserted into the same syntagmatic slot in the sentence, the division between the two target words is most commonly between two segments, usually showing a

TABLE 3.2
Number of errors involving each feature in consonant feature errors, by age, and average number of feature violations per error.

Age:	1	2	3	4	5	Total	Adult
[place]	0	1	5	7	10	23	7
[fricative]	0	1	2	1	2	6	3
[continuant]	0	0	2	2	2	6	3
[nasal]	0	0	1	2	0	3	1
[voice]	0	0	0	1	0	1	1
N of Errors=	0	1	7	9	10	27	8
Average # Feature Violations							
Per Error=	na	2	1.4	1.4	1.4	1.4	1.9

crossover at an onset/rhyme or syllable division (as will be documented below). But in a few errors, a blend of segments was produced, such that the blend contained a segment which did not occur in the representations of either target word (see also Stemberger 1983a:6). I found only three cases in the child data and one in the adult data; two are given here in (2).

(2)   a.   M: 'Do you want m**ì**lk or j**ú**ice?'
        OB: '[n̩uc̩].' (blend of 'milk' [mɛwk] and 'juice' [t̩uc̩]; OC-4(38) 1;11)
    b.   Al: 'It's rèally [sprɛ́.tʃɔ̩ɫ] . . . spécial. It's frágile.' (blend of 'special' [spɛ́.ʃɔ̩ɫ] and 'fragile' [fɹ̩ǽ.dʒɔ̩ɫ]; AL-270(38) 5;11)

In (2a), the segments [m] and [t̩] are blended, producing the dental nasal [n̩], an error involving the features [nasal], [voice], [continuant], and [place]. Similarly in (B-356(38) 4;8), a blend of 'tape' and 'kind' resulting in *'[tʰaʲm]', the segments [n] and [p] are blended to produce the labial nasal [m]. In (2b) the [ʃ] and [dʒ] in the onsets of the second syllables of the two targets combine to produce the voiceless affricate [tʃ], involving the features of [fricative], [voice], [continuant], and [place]. This is similar to the adult error (AD-520(38)), a blend of 'section' and 'chapter' producing *'[sɛ́k.tʃɚ], where the target segments [ʃ] and [t] combine into the affricate [tʃ]. The feature error made at age 1 (2a) may suggest that segments themselves are stored somewhat holistically at this age (but see §3.2.2); the errors made by the older children and adults are similar to the syntagmatic phonological errors in which features are the unit of error, and show the same set of features as found in these errors.

    In sum, children begin making errors involving (consonantal) phonetic features during the beginning of their fourth year. This suggests that features are not independently available to the processing mechanism before this time, and that late in the third year and early in the fourth year is when the phonetic feature system is being systematized in the child's representational structures.

3.2.2 Featural Similarity of Consonants Involved in Errors

Nearly every researcher who analyzes phonological SOTs has noted that two consonants are more likely to be mutually involved in an error (i.e. either one substituted for the other, or the two exchanged) if they are phonetically similar to each other (Fromkin 1973a, MacKay 1973, Nooteboom 1973, Shattuck-Hufnagel & Klatt 1979, van den Broecke & Goldstein 1980). This is an important issue to raise with reference to the child SOT data. If a pattern is found where very early errors show no clear featural similarity between targets and sources, but where featural similarity emerges as the child gets older, one could argue that segments start out being represented somewhat holistically, and then later become organized according to phonetic properties. On the other hand, if the errors seem to be sensitive to phonetic similarity from the beginning, then the second hypothesis raised in §3.2.1 above, that there is some general phonetic organization in early segments but no actual feature system as yet, will be the more likely explanation.

In Jaeger (1992b) I presented the results of a multi-dimensional scaling procedure that I performed with data from the 366 consonant substitution and exchange errors which I had collected at that time. This study was patterned after a study by van den Broecke & Goldstein (1980; hereafter V&G), which used the same procedure in analyzing adult English errors. This procedure takes all the pairings of consonants that are involved in errors, and looks at the frequency with which any two consonants interact; from these figures it creates two-dimensional plots of the relationships among the consonants. The procedure can be repeated as many times as necessary until all the dimensions needed to account for the majority of the findings are uncovered. In my study I found that there were five clear dimensions which accounted for the consonant interactions. These were: 1) place of articulation; 2) continuancy; 3) presence or absence of frication; 4) voice; and 5) nasality. Note that these features, derived by the statistical technique, are the same set as those found to be involved in the 'feature errors' discussed in §3.2.1 above.

One should not be surprised that only five features were necessary in order to account for the SOT data. As Fromkin (1973a:226-7) has pointed out, "[t]he claim that all distinctive features (as proposed by Chomsky & Halle [1968]) are identical with phonetic properties that can in principle be independently controlled in speech is not borne out by the data of speech errors. Unless 'controllable in speech' is defined in some new strange and abstract way, it would appear that whatever the needs for certain separate phonological features may be, in actual speech performance only certain of these phonological features have their counterpart as phonetic features." Similarly Stemberger (1991) argued that only fully specified features count towards 'feature similarity', based on an analysis of his corpus of speech errors. Frisch (1997), reanalyzing the same corpus of errors, found some evidence of the effect of redundant features, but acknowledged that redundant features contribute less toward featural similarity of

TABLE 3.3
Consonant features and feature specifications derived from
multidimensional scaling analysis of children's data (Jaeger 1992b).
'Place' designations are: labial, dental, alveolar, rhotic, palatal, velar,
labial-velar, and glottal.

	p	t	k	b	d	g	tʃ	dʒ	f	θ	s	ʃ
[voice]	-	-	-	+	+	+	-	+	-	-	-	-
[frication]	-	-	-	-	-	-	+	+	+	+	+	+
[place]	L	A	V	L	A	V	P	P	L	D	A	P
[continuant]	-	-	-	-	-	-	-	-	+	+	+	+
[nasal]	-	-	-	-	-	-	-	-	-	-	-	-

	h	v	ð	z	ʒ	m	n	l	r	w	j
[voice]	-	+	+	+	+	+	+	+	+	+	+
[frication]	+	+	+	+	+	-	-	-	-	-	-
[place]	G	L	D	A	P	L	A	A	R	L-V	P
[continuant]	+	+	+	+	+	+	+	+	+	+	+
[nasal]	-	-	-	-	-	+	+	-	-	-	-

segments than contrastive features. Thus, most researchers agree that only a subset of the phonetic features necessary for accounting for the phonological patterns of a language are relevant during on-line speech production planning.

In order to assess the phonetic similarity of the consonant pairs involved in the children's errors, I assigned values on each of these five features to each consonant in English which was involved in an error. The feature grid is given in Table 3.3; see Jaeger (1992b) for details of the feature value assignments, which were derived from the multidimensional scaling plots. The nasal stops [n, m] are classified as [+continuant] because they grouped with the other continuants rather than with the stops on this dimension. The nasal [ŋ] is not included in the feature grid as it was not unambiguously involved in any error in either the child or adult corpus; the fricative [ʒ] has been added to this grid (it was not included in Jaeger 1992b), as adults made several errors involving this segment, although the children did not.

A few notes about classification of early productions are in order, since the above chart represents adult phonemes of English. First, I decided that as long as no obvious distinction (i.e. perceptible to adults; see Macken & Barton 1980) was being made in the child's productions between two segments which are different phonemes for adults, these productions were encoded purely phonetically; however, as soon as there was a distinction being made, the productions were encoded categorically. For example, if all oral stops were pronounced as voiceless unaspirated, then they were all encoded phonetically as voiceless unaspirated stops; but when a distinction began being made, segments were encoded in terms of the phoneme being attempted (e.g. [pʰ] was coded as

/p/, and [p] as /b/, if this was the phonetic distinction the child was using). Similarly, when the child pronounced all instances of adult non-syllabic /r/ as [w], and all instances of /ɚ/ as [ʊ], these were coded as [w] and [ʊ] respectively. But when the child began producing slightly rhotacized versions of these phonemes, i.e. the non-syllabic [ɹ̡] and the syllabic [ɜ], then these were coded as instances of /r/ and /ɚ/ respectively, as distinct from /w/ and /ʊ/. All instances of the 'sibilant substitute' laminal-palatals [ɕ], [tɕ], and [dʑ] were coded as instances of [ʃ], [tʃ], and [dʒ] respectively, as these are the most phonetically similar segments in the mature system. Finally, the tap [ɾ] was coded as [d] in every case, since the children had no way of knowing whether the tap was underlyingly a /t/ or /d/, and it is phonetically most similar to [d], as they are both voiced. (In fact, both Anna and Alice separately developed the theory that [ɾ] was the informal pronunciation of both /t/ and /d/, and that [t] was the formal pronunciation of both /t/ and /d/, in onsets of medial unstressed syllables. Thus the informal pronunciations of 'pretty' and 'puddle' were [pʰɹ̥í.ɾi] and [pʰʌ.ɾəɫ], and their formal pronunciations were [pʰɹ̥í.ti] and [pʰʌ.təɫ]. This hypothesis lasted well into the first grade, for both girls.)

In the current study, I used the feature system developed in Jaeger (1992b) and classified the featural relationship between the consonant segments mutually involved in all the errors in both my child and adult data. This included all the consonant substitution and exchange errors, as well as non-contextual substitutions and substitutions/exchanges in 'Multiple Phonological Errors' (class 31) where target and source could be clearly identified. It did not include metathesis errors, since the physical proximity of the segments rather than their featural relationship is probably the causal factor. Furthermore, I analyzed the featural relationships between every pair of consonant phonemes in English (excluding [ŋ]), in order to calculate a figure for the average number of 'possible' feature differences, and 'possible' differences along each featural dimension. I did not take into consideration the frequency of each consonant phoneme, as V&G did, because these figures are applicable only to adult data. For the children, the frequency of various segments is constantly shifting, and thus this is an inappropriate measure to apply to the child data.

Table 3.4 presents the number of errors made by my subjects at each age in which the two consonants involved in the error differed by from 1-5 features; figures from my adult corpus are also included, as well as the 'possible' figures. Under the raw numbers are the percentages of errors in this count at this age which fell into each of the categories of 'number of features different'. At the bottom of the table is the total N out of which these percentages are calculated, and also an average number of features violated at each age. The average 'possible' number of features violated, looking at all pairs of consonants in English (excluding [ŋ]), is 2.67. This table is to be read as follows, for example: at age 1 the children produced 21 consonant substitution or exchange errors. Of these, in 15 cases the two consonants differed by only one feature value (71.5%), while 3 differed by two feature values (14%) and so on; overall the pairs of consonants differed by an average of 1.48 features at age 1 (based on

TABLE 3.4

Number and percentage of consonant substitution or exchange errors at each age, in which the target and source consonants differ by from 1-5 features.

Age:	1	2	3	4	5	Total	Adult	Possible
# Features Different								
1	15	37	44	73	58	227	59	47
	71.5%	44.5%	61%	53%	62%	55.5%	52%	18.5%
2	3	20	15	37	22	97	31	80
	14%	24%	21%	27%	23%	24%	27.5%	31.5%
3	2	21	10	24	13	70	18	84
	9.5%	25.5%	14%	17%	14%	17%	16%	33%
4	1	5	3	4	1	14	4	40
	5%	6%	4%	3%	1%	3.5%	3.5%	16%
5	0	0	0	0	0	0	1	2
							1%	1%
N=	21	83	72	138	94	408	113	253
Average # Features Different=								
	1.48	1.93	1.61	1.70	1.54	1.68	1.73	2.67

the 5-feature system).

It is evident from Table 3.4 that the largest number of errors at any age involved consonant pairs which differ by only one feature, followed by consonant pairs which differ by only two features. This is very different from the 'possible' number of feature violations, where the majority of consonant pairs differ by 2 or 3 features. At all ages except age 2, the number of errors involving consonant pairs which differ by 3 or 4 features is less than 20% of the total, and the children produced no errors in which the pair differed on all five features. The adults produced only one error which violated all 5 features, given in (3).

(3)   AF: ' . . . [tʃò°m námp.ski] . . .'
        (for 'Noam Chomsky' [nò°m tʃámp.ski]; [n]<-->[tʃ]; AD-243(25))

In this case, the fact that the two segments are in the onsets of the first and last name of a frequently mentioned person overcame the great difference in their featural make-up. At every age, the average number of feature differences is considerably less than the 'possible' average of 2.67, with the overall child figure being slightly less than the adult figure (1.68 vs. 1.73).

It is not clear whether there are any developmental trends evident in this table, but there may be a sort of U-shaped pattern. The 1-year-old children show the lowest average number of feature differences of any age, 1.48. This is probably due to the smaller number of segments in these very young children's inventories, and the fact that the segments they do know fall into phonetically similar classes: oral and nasal stops, liquids and glides, with fewer fricatives or affricates. On the other hand, these figures suggest that there is some phonetic information stored in phonological representations of segments when the earliest phonological SOTs are made, around age 1;7. The 2-year-olds, who have learned many more segments, have the highest average figure, 1.94, suggesting that even though there may be some phonetic organization at this age, there is less clear featural organization than in the older children's representations. The figures for ages 3-5 drop back down, fluctuating between 1.54 and 1.70, suggesting more influence from phonetic featural organization. Except for age 2, the children's figures are always lower than the adult average of 1.73. Stemberger (1989) also found that his children's consonantal errors were organized by phonetic features, and that the children in his study had a lower number of average feature differences than did the adults. Using a three-feature system (place, voicing, manner) and looking only at obstruents, Stemberger found that the child average was 1.21 (ages 1;8-5;11, N=148) whereas his adult average was 1.30 (N=576). He argues, as mentioned in §3.2.1, that young children's segmental representations may be more phonetically dependant than adults' since the production of words is a more automatized behavior for adults and therefore the units involved are more 'integrated' in their representations and/or processing. My data suggest that this is more true for children ages 3-5 than for the 1-2-year-olds.

Finally, the figures from my study are similar to those found by V&G for adults. In their study they also found that five features were necessary for characterizing phonetic relatedness. Four of these features were given by their multidimensional scaling: voicing, nasality, place of articulation, continuancy (which they called 'stop', i.e. oral and nasal stops and affricates vs. others). A fifth *ad hoc* feature was created, which grouped fricatives and approximants except [l], in order to uniquely distinguish all segments. They found that the adults' average for featural differences between consonant pairs involved in SOTs was 2.14; their 'random' average (calculated by taking frequency into account) was 2.44, and they found that their adult average was significantly lower than this 'random' average. Because my figures were considerably lower than 2.14, this suggests not only that my figures are also significantly lower than the 'random' average, but also that my feature system (completely derived from the scaling procedure without recourse to any *ad hoc* designations) may be a better system for capturing the actual parameters involved in consonantal similarity.

I also found that featural differences in consonant pairs which interacted in these SOTs involved the five features in different proportions; the majority of errors involved the feature [place], whereas the feature [nasal] was involved in the least number of errors. Table 3.5 gives the number and percentage of errors at each age which involved each of the five features, as well as 'possible' numbers of violations, considering all pairs of consonants in English (excluding [ŋ]).

TABLE 3.5

Number and percentage of consonant substitution or exchange errors in
which each feature was involved, by age; compared to adults and
'possible'. Percentages add up to more than 100% because many errors
involved more than one feature.

Age:	1	2	3	4	5	Total	Adult	Possible
[place]	16	62	56	99	73	306	82	209
	76%	75%	78%	72%	77.5%	75%	72.5%	82.5%
[continuant]	4	33	24	52	28	141	41	121
	19%	40%	33%	38%	30%	34.5%	36%	48%
[fricative]	4	29	16	37	19	105	31	132
	19%	35%	22%	27%	20%	26%	27.5%	52%
[voice]	6	15	9	27	12	69	23	125
	28.5%	18%	12.5%	19.5%	13%	17%	20.5%	49.5%
[nasal]	1	21	11	20	13	66	19	42
	5%	25%	15%	14.5%	14%	16%	17%	16.5%
N of Errors=	21	83	72	138	94	408	113	253

The percentages in this table add up to more than 100%, since many errors
involved more than one feature. So, for example, looking at the same 21
consonant substitution or exchange errors from Table 3.4 made by the 1-year-
olds, this table shows that 16 of these errors involved (at least) a violation of the
feature [place], which is 76% of the 21 errors; 4 errors (19%) involved a
violation of the features [continuant] and [fricative] respectively; 6 errors (28.5%)
involved a violation of [voice], and there was 1 violation of [nasal] (5% of 21).

The fact that most errors involved phonetically similar pairs of consonants
explains why in general each feature is involved in errors less often than the
'possible' percentages would predict, since this 'possible' figure would only hold
true if any two consonants were equally likely to interact as any other.
However, the pattern of involvement is very much determined by the pattern of
'possible' percentages. First, it is possible to violate [place] most often because
there are seven different feature values along this dimension, and so any two
randomly selected consonants will differ on this feature in 82.5% of the cases.
Secondly, for the features [continuant], [fricative], and [voice], about half of the
segments have the [+] value and the other half have the [-] value, so by chance
these would be involved about half the time. Finally, all but two consonants are
[-nasal], so any pair of consonants in English would differ on this feature in only
16.5% of the cases.

It seems likely, then, that the fact that [place] is the feature involved most
often in these errors is partly due to the fact that this feature is the easiest to
violate in an error; the child and adult figures range from 72%-78%, which is

only slightly less than the 82.5% expected by chance. Recall that [place] was the feature most commonly involved in featural errors, as discussed in §3.2.1 above; this frequency factor is probably at least part of the explanation. However, one could also argue that since the majority of consonantal error pairs differ on this feature, two segments which differ as to [place] but have the same values on all other features are considered to be the most phonetically similar, for both children and adults; thus such pairs of consonants are the most likely to be mutually involved in a substitution error. The features of [continuant] and [fricative] are involved at similar rates as each other (overall child: 34.5% and 26%; adult 36%, 27.5%); these are somewhat below chance (48% and 52% respectively), suggesting that a manner difference between consonants is considered a larger phonetic distinction than a place difference. Both the children and adults produced roughly half the mismatches involving [voice] as would be expected by chance (overall child: 17%, adult: 20.5%, 'possible': 49.5%), suggesting that a voicing difference is considered a rather major mismatch between two consonants, so that consonants which differ by [voice] are less likely to interact in an error. Finally, the overall figures for [nasal] are almost identical to chance: child: 16%, adult: 17%, 'possible': 16.5%. V&G found that the adults in their study produced more mismatches with the feature [voice] than with the manner features, but I did not find this with my adult data; the differences may be due to differences in our featural encoding systems.

There are no obvious differences in Table 3.5 between the child figures and adult figures, nor are there any major developmental trends. The fact that [voice] is more often involved than the two manner features at age 1 is probably due to the fact that these children were producing few fricatives, but had begun to make the voicing distinction. The large number of errors involving [nasal] at age 2 is compatible with the idea that the featural organization of segments is somewhat less clear at this age than at the older ages. However, the overall finding from this table is that the children's phonetic organization of segments is very similar to that of adults, from the earliest ages at which consonantal SOTs are produced.

3.2.3 Vowel Features

Vowels have been looked at less often than consonants in terms of their featural organization as manifested in SOTs. The major study on adult vowel SOTs is that of Shattuck-Hufnagel (1986; hereafter in this section, S-H), who analyzed a corpus of 310 adult vowel errors in terms of a five-feature system, [high, tense, low, back, round]. In this paper she provides no justification for this particular feature system or for the assignment of feature values for each vowel. S-H found that the feature [tense] had the most influence on vowel errors in that two vowels are most likely to interact in an error if they share the same value on this feature. The most readily violated feature was [back], in that pairs such as /i-u/ and /æ-ɑ/ were the most frequently involved in errors.

In order to assess the question of whether vowels are organized in terms of phonetic features as clearly as consonants are, I performed an analysis of the vowel errors in my corpus, based partially on the S-H study. However, my analysis has several innovations. First, I decided to use a four-feature system,

TABLE 3.6

Vowel feature system; 'H, M, L' = 'high, mid, low'; 'F, C, B' = 'front, central, back'.

	i	ɪ	eʲ	ɛ	æ	a	ʌ	ə	ɔ	oʷ	ʊ	u	ɚ	aʲ	oʲ	æʷ	ju
[height]	H	H	M	M	L	L	M	M	M	M	H	H	M	L	M	L	H
[place]	F	F	F	F	F	C	C	C	B	B	B	B	C	C	B	F	B
[round]	-	-	-	-	-	-	-	-	+	+	+	+	+	-	+	-	+
[tense]	+	-	+	-	-	-	+	-	-	+	-	+	+	+	+	+	+

[height, place, round, tense], where [height] has three possible values (H=high, M=mid, L=low), and [place] also has three possible values (F=front, C=central, B=back). This is because S-H's system used two height features [high, low] but only one place feature [back], which allowed more possible violations for vowels that differed in height than in backness, which could bias the results. Second, I retained S-H's feature value designations for her feature [tense II], where [a] is considered [-tense]. In fact the feature of [tense] is more of a classificatory feature than an actual phonetic parameter, since it is used to distinguish between pairs such as /i-ɪ/, and /eʲ-ɛ/, but has no consistently applicable phonetic substance (Ladefoged 2001:80-82). I will argue below that the stress value of vowels is the most important factor governing vowel pairs mutually involved in an error, and the fact that S-H found [tense] to be an important organizing factor in vowel errors is probably due to the fact that most errors involve two stressed vowels, which are usually both [+tense] almost by definition. Nevertheless I used this feature in my system, in order to be able to uniquely designate the feature values of each vowel. Finally, I assigned feature values to each vowel according to the most common pronunciation in the dialect of the subjects under study. Thus, S-H's vowel [ɑ] is pronounced as a central vowel [a] by most of my subjects, and her diphthong [au] is pronounced with a front nucleus [æʷ]. Features were assigned to diphthongs according to the properties of the nucleus vowel; [ju] and [ɚ] were both treated as vowels in this analysis, although S-H treats them separately (see arguments for treating [ɚ] as a vowel in §3.3.3 below; in my study I treated [ju] as a vowel when it interacted with another vowel in an error, but like a CV sequence when it behaved as such). My vowel feature system is given in Table 3.6.

This system has the problem that the pairs /oʷ-oʲ/ and /u-ju/ are not distinguished from each other. There was only one error in my corpus involving /oʷ-oʲ/, which I designated as being distinguished by the feature [round]; there were no errors involving /u-ju/. This system also designates /æʷ/ as [-round], which is not phonetically accurate; it distinguishes the pairs /æ-æʷ/ and /a-aʲ/ by the feature [tense], which again is phonetically questionable. However, because in my analysis this system was applied uniformly to the child data, the adult data, and 'possible' pairs of vowels in English, it does make it possible to look

TABLE 3.7

Number and percentage of vowel substitution or exchange errors at each age, in which the target and source vowels differ by from 1-4 features; compared to 'possible'.

Age:	1	2	3	4	5	Total	A1	A2	Possible
# Features Different									
1 1	6	4	8	6	25	8	129	29
17%	31.5%	15.5%	27%	31.5%	25%	21%	42%	21.5%
2 2	5	10	13	9	39	12	108	40
33%	26.5%	38.5%	43%	47.5%	39%	31.5%	35%	29.5%
3 2	7	8	7	4	28	14	66	43
33%	37%	30.5%	23%	21%	28%	37%	21%	32%
4 1	1	4	2	0	8	4	7	23
17%	5%	15.5%	7%		8%	10.5%	2%	17%
N= **6**	**19**	**26**	**30**	**19**	**100**	**38**	**310**	**135**
Average # Features Different=									
2.50	2.16	2.46	2.10	1.89	2.19	2.37	1.84	2.45

A1=English adults, Jaeger corpus
A2 =English adults, S-H (1986) corpus

for patterns of featural organization, even if the featural designations themselves have a few controversial entries.

I first counted the number of feature differences in all vowel errors in my data. These errors involve vowel substitutions and exchanges, including non-contextual errors and those errors from the 'Multiple' category where the vowel pair involved could be clearly identified. I also calculated figures for S-H's data, based on my feature system, using the figures from her chart on page 123. I then calculated chance figures from all possible pairings of vowels in English (excluding /u-ju/); as with consonants, my 'possible' figures do not take frequency into account. The results are shown in Table 3.7.

Several points can be made about this table. First, there does not seem to be as clear a featural organization in these vowel errors as there was in the consonant errors. The average feature differences at ages 1 (2.50) and 3 (2.46), as well as my adult figure (2.37), are very near the 'possible' figure of 2.45. My subjects did make fewer errors involving all four features than would be expected by chance, but their percentages for 1-3 feature errors are very close to the chance figures. Although it seems like the older children's errors are becoming more organized in terms of features, with averages of 2.10 at age 4 and 1.89 at age 5, my adult average of 2.37 out of 5 possible differences suggests that the adult vowel errors are even less organized by features than the children's errors. On the other hand, my adult figures are very different from S-H's; her data show an

TABLE 3.8

Number and percentage of vowel substitution or exchange errors in which each feature was involved, by age; compared to adults and 'possible'. Percentages add up to more than 100% because many errors involved more than one feature.

Age	1	2	3	4	5	Total	A1	A2	Possible
[place] 6	13	22	22	8	71	25	196	96
100%	68.5%	84.5%	73%	42%	71%	66%	63%	71%
[height] 3	16	19	19	13	70	23	175	93
50%	84%	73%	63%	68.5%	70%	60.5%	56.5%	69%
[round] 5	5	10	13	7	40	22	92	71
83%	26%	38.5%	43%	37%	40%	58%	30%	52.5%
[tense] 1	7	13	9	8	38	20	108	70
17%	37%	50%	30%	42%	38%	52.5%	35%	52%
N of errors=								
6	19	26	30	19	100	38	310	135

A1=English adults, Jaeger corpus
A2=English adults, S-H (1986) corpus

average of 1.84 features different (using my feature system), which is clearly less than the 'possible' figure. Since her corpus has over 8 times as many vowel errors as my adult corpus, her figure is likely to be more accurate (although the counts are not strictly comparable, for the reasons discussed above). Thus we could hypothesize that starting around age 4 the children's vowel errors begin to show some influence of phonetic featural organization, with a trend in the direction of the figure from S-H's study.

In order to see whether any of the vowel features showed a stronger influence on error organization than the others, I counted the number of errors in which each feature was involved, in my data as well as S-H's. I then counted how many violations were possible, looking at all possible pairings of vowels in English. The results are shown in Table 3.8. As in Table 3.5, the percentages add up to more than 100% because most errors involve more than one feature.

These numbers suggest that neither place nor height of the vowel are constraining factors in organizing vowel substitution errors, since the [place] and [height] features of vowels mutually involved in errors differ between target and source with a frequency near chance for all three data sets (my child and adult data, and S-H's adult data). On the other hand, [round] seems to be a somewhat constraining feature for the children as well as S-H's adults, although my adult figure is well over chance; furthermore, my child figures range from 26% to 83%, suggesting either that the influence of [round] fluctuates wildly over the years, or that this is an accident of the data. Finally, S-H's finding that [tense] is the least often violated feature in vowel errors is marginally supported in my child data, although [tense] and [round] have about the same overall status for the children. Furthermore, for the S-H data, [tense] is actually involved in errors more often than [round]. For my adults, [tense] is involved in errors at exactly the chance level.

These findings seem counterintuitive. If there are phonetic features which underlie the make-up of vowel segments, surely the [place] and [height] features would be crucial for any measure of 'phonetic similarity'. Furthermore, if linguists can't agree on the correct values on the [tense] feature for various vowels, it is unlikely that naive speakers have extracted this feature from phonological entities in some consistent way, using it as part of the organizing structure of their cognitive phonological systems. What is needed in order to assess the optimal featural organization of vowels is a much larger database of vowel errors such that a multidimensional scaling procedure can be run. Until this is done, it cannot be determined whether or not the phonetic similarity of vowels, at least as designated by the set of features under discussion, is an important factor involved in vowel errors, for either children or adults.

On the other hand, there is a factor which is not strictly featural, that I have suggested is the more important influence on vowel errors: the stress value of the vowel. It has long been noted that phonological errors usually involve units from two syllables with the same stress value, usually two stressed syllables (Boomer & Laver 1973, S-H 1986). As indicated above, this might account for the finding that the feature [tense] is the least often violated in vowel errors. In order to see whether the children in this study followed the adult pattern, I classified every vowel substitution or exchange error (including 'multiple' errors) as to the stress status of the syllables containing the target and source vowels, i.e. either both stressed, both unstressed, or a mix of the two (I only used two levels of stress: either stressed, including secondary stresses, or unstressed). I only included errors where either a single source could be identified, or where multiple sources all came from syllables with the same stress value; non-contextual and ambiguous source errors were excluded. The results are shown in Table 3.9.

It is clear from this table that the majority of both child and adult vowel errors involved two stressed vowels. For the adults, errors involving two unstressed vowels and a mix of stressed and unstressed occurred rarely, and with approximately the same frequency as each other. The children made somewhat more errors involving stressed/unstressed vowels than adults. This is probably because many of these errors involved within-word errors (six of the child and two of the adult mixed errors were within-word, as illustrated in (4)), and as discussed in §2.3.1, children make more within-word errors than adults do.

(4)   a. An: ' . . . hér wàshing [mi.ʃʌ̀n] . . . ' (for 'machine' [mə.ʃin];
          [ə]<-->[i], then [ə]-->[ʌ] under stress; AN-143(26) 4;0)
       b. TF: 'Nètscape [næ̀.vɨ.gɚ̀.rɚ]?'
          (for 'Navigator' [næ̀.vɨ.gèʲ.rɚ]; [eʲ]<--[ɚ]; AD-21(5))

TABLE 3.9
Stress of vowel pairs involved in substitution or exchange errors, by age;
between-word and within-word errors combined.

Age:	1	2	3	4	5	Total	Adult
Both Stressed	5	12	21	19	9	66 (79.5%)	30 (81%)
Both Unstressed	1	2	0	0	2	5 (6%)	4 (11%)
Stressed/Unstr.	0	2	3	6	1	12 (14.5%)	3 (8%)
Total N=	**6**	**16**	**24**	**25**	**12**	**83**	**37**

There are a number of reasons why stress is of crucial importance in vowel errors. First, stressed syllables are in general more prominent in the planning process (i.e. more highly activated), and therefore more susceptible to error (see §3.7.2 below). Second, unstressed vowels in English are typically reduced to [ə] or [ɨ], so any error involving two unstressed vowels might be simply undetectable. Indeed all the child errors and half the adult errors which I classified as involving two unstressed vowels involved two unreduced vowels; in some cases one of the vowels was actually a suffix [-i] or [-ɚ], as illustrated in (5).

(5)   B: 'Lìnda, it's vèry [wín.da].'
            (for 'windy' [wín.d(i)], source [lín.da]; B-112(16) 2;9)

Furthermore, in errors involving an unstressed reduced vowel and a stressed (unreduced) vowel, if the unstressed vowel is moved into a stressed position it must be pronounced with full vowel quality, as in (4a) above. If a stressed vowel moves into an unstressed position, it throws off the rhythmic structure of the utterance entirely, as in (6); try saying this one out loud!

(6)   B: (looking at a book) 'That's a? umbrèlla with Bíg-Bìrd ùnder it,
            èating [tʃí.koʷn], and macaròni and chéese, and bróccoli.'
            (for 'chicken' [tʃí.kən], source 'macaroni' [mæ̀.kə.ʒóʷ.ni];
            B-144(5) 3;8)

Thus, stressed vowels are more likely to be mutually involved in vowel errors, and unstressed vowels will be involved less often, across the board. This influence seems to have had a much more prominent role in vowel SOTs than did the intrinsic phonetic features of the vowels themselves, for both the children and the adults in this study.

3.2.4 Summary of Features

In sum, the earliest consonantal errors show evidence of being organized according to phonetic features, indicating that some phonetic information is represented in consonantal segmental representations from the time when phonological errors begin to occur. However, features themselves do not become available for error until late in the third year, and are not common targets of error until about 3;4, suggesting that the actual phonological feature system is being set up late in the third year and early in the fourth year. The same set of features which captures phonetic similarity in consonantal segment errors also characterizes the set of features which are involved in feature errors, namely [place, frication, voice, continuant, nasal]; this set appropriately captures relationships in both child and adult errors. The children's vowel errors, on the other hand, seem to be less clearly organized by phonetic features; this is also somewhat true of adult errors. However, the stress value of vowels is an important factor in vowel errors, due to both the organizing function of stress in speech production planning, and the effect of stress on vowel quality in English.

3.3 Segments and Phonemes

3.3.1 Allowable Segments

As discussed in §3.1.2, the children's phonological errors primarily involved individual speech segments; approximately 80% of their phonological errors (and 52% of all of their error types combined) involved segments. This is a larger percentage than for the adults in my study; of their phonological errors, 62% involved single segments (29% of their total errors). These figures indicate that the segment has a primary status in the phonological aspects of young children's speech production planning.

Furthermore, these children's SOTs show that from the onset of the errors, children have a clear representation of the allowable segment inventory of English, since their self-monitor usually does not allow them to erroneously produce any non-English segments. It is well-known that adult errors rarely result in illegal segments (Fromkin 1973a), and in my adult corpus I recorded no non-English segments. Of course when the children are very young they systematically pronounce some phonemes differently from the adult model, e.g. [ɕ] for [ʃ], and [ʒ] for [r]; if they substitute one of these segments for another, their self-monitor will allow this production since it is an acceptable part of their current phonological system. However, in my data I collected two instances of non-English segments which were not currently in the child's segment inventory, both produced by 2-year-olds making telescoping errors. Otherwise I recorded no non-English segments in my child corpus which were not currently legal in the child's system. These exceptions are given in (7), and both involve labial fricative productions; the first also involves a fricated rhotic. (Recall that the markers above vowels in telescopings are to be read as marking pitch.)

(7)   a. An: 'I'm nòt a báby, I'm a [βɼ̂ɬ].'
            (for 'big girl' [bíg gə̀ɬ]; AN-40(34) 2;4)
       b. OB: 'On the bùmpý, bùmpý rûg!'
            OG: 'On the [bββ̂ːg]!' (for 'bumpy rug' [bʌm.pí ʒʌ̂g]; OC-28(34) 2;8)

Thus the SOTs give evidence of a well-structured segment inventory as well as a filter that only allows legal segments to be produced, which is in place from the earliest errors.

3.3.2 Consonants vs. Vowels in Segmental Errors

There are two important issues involving consonant segments vs. vowel segments. The first is whether children have these two major class categories separated from the beginning of their errors, or whether this separation shows a developmental progression. The second is why there are so few vowel errors.

In adult SOTs, consonants and vowels rarely interact with each other. If this is also true in the child errors, then we can state that this major class distinction is in place at a very early age, although whether it is attributable to a phonetic distinction between the open and closed phase of the mandibular gesture (MacNeilage & Davis 1990, 1993), to the development of syllable-structure constraints, or to the acquisition of a phonological feature such as [syllabic] would need to be further explored.

There are two types of errors in my data which could be considered interactions between consonants and vowels. The first involves metathesis errors where a consonant and vowel exchange places, as illustrated in (8). The second involves interactions between the syllabic and non-syllabic liquids /l/ and /r/; this latter issue will be discussed in §3.3.3 below.

(8)   An: 'Nòw Ràffi's tàlking abòut [sn̥æ̃] . . . Sánta Clàus.'
        (for 'Santa' [sǽn.ta]; [æn]-->[n̥æ]; AN-174(27) 4;4)

Here the vowel-consonant sequence [æn] in 'Santa' is metathesized, producing the (legal) onset consonant cluster /sn/; this new sequencing causes the [n] to devoice in the environment of the voiceless [s], and the vowel to denasalize.

Such metathesis errors were very rare in both the child and adult corpus. I recorded no errors of this type at ages 1-2; at age 3 I recorded 2 such errors; 4 were made at age 4, and 1 at age 5, for a total of 7 metathesis errors involving a consonant and vowel. The adults made only one such error. It is interesting to note that in 4 of the child errors and in the one adult error (*[pʰɹoʷ.tʰɹéʲd] for 'portrayed' [pʰor.tʰɹéʲd], AD-252(27)), the consonant involved is a liquid or nasal, which are sonorous consonants that have some vowel-like properties (and can be syllabic); the other three child errors include two cases involving [z], and one case involving [dʒ]. Furthermore, in every case the metathesized segments resulted in an allowable phonotactic sequence, although syllable structure was usually altered. The children produced 17 metathesis errors total, with the other 10 involving two consonants. But in one of the consonant metathesis errors, shown in (9), a nasal moved into a syllabic position and became a syllable nucleus.

(9) B: (telling Mom names of books) 'Mommy, there's "Whàt's Wròng
          Hère in the [hɔf.n̩] . . . the Haùntẹd Hóuse?"'.'
          (for 'Haunted' [hɔ̃n.təd]; B-559(27) 5;9)

Since the metathesis errors involving consonants and vowels often produced
new consonant clusters (as in (8) above), it is not surprising that this type of
error did not occur before age 3, at which age the children began consistently
producing words with a wide range of consonant clusters. At ages 1-2, many
children are still simplifying clusters, such that these metatheses would produce
sequences outside the child's current phonology. Although C-V metathesis
errors show some interesting patterns and correlations with the development of
phonotactics, the most important point here is that they are extremely rare,
which suggests that the division between consonants and vowels is in place at an
early age. This is not surprising considering both the differences in phonetic
properties between consonants and vowels, and their differing functions in
syllables.

This leads to the next issue, which is the disparity between the number of
errors involving consonants and those involving vowels. As seen in Table 3.1,
consonant errors greatly outnumbered vowel errors at every age, for the children
as well as the adults. One possible reason for this is that there are simply more
consonants than vowels available in utterances, so that they are numerically
more likely to be involved in errors. In order to test this hypothesis, I selected
15 utterances randomly from each of the phonological error categories for each
age including adults; N=706 child utterances, N=206 adult utterances. I then
counted the number of consonants and vowels in the target utterances. Table
3.10 shows the ratio of consonants to vowels in this random sample, compared
to the ratio of consonant errors to vowel errors, at each age. The first row,
'Actual Ratio,' indicates how many consonants occurred per one vowel in the
target utterances; the second row, 'Error Ratio,' indicates the number of
consonant errors per one vowel error in my data at that age.

It can be seen that the actual ratio of consonants to vowels for the children
is around 1.57:1 from ages 1-4 (with a dip at age 2), but increases to 1.71:1 by
age 5, which is the same as the adult ratio. However, the ratio of consonant to
vowel errors greatly exceeds the actual ratio of consonants to vowels at every
age. The difference is somewhat less for the adults than for the children, which
reflects the fact that the adults made a somewhat larger percentage of vowel errors
than the children did. However, this table clearly shows that at every age, it is
not simply numbers that cause more consonant errors than vowel errors, since if
frequency of occurrence of consonants compared to vowels in utterances were the
critical factor, one would expect two consonant errors for every one vowel error,
rather than consonant errors being 5-7 times more common than vowel errors.

The most probable explanation has to do with the status of the vowel as the
nucleus of the syllable. This is not just a metaphor; the vowel is the element
without which the syllable cannot exist. Therefore it seems to be at the core of
phonological processing: it is the only segmental unit required for licensing a

TABLE 3.10
Ratio of consonants to vowels in a random sample ('Actual Ratio'), and
ratio of consonant errors to vowel errors ('Error Ratio'), by age.

Age:	1	2	3	4	5	Adult
Actual Ratio	1.57	1.37	1.56	1.59	1.71	1.71
Error Ratio	6.00	7.47	5.00	7.61	9.33	4.72

syllable node, and within syllables it serves as an anchor for the more expendable consonants. An error involving a vowel causes a greater disruption in the planned utterance than any consonantal error because it disrupts the core of the syllable (see Chapter 2, §2.3.3 for a demonstration that errors which involve larger deformations of the intented utterance are less frequent). Because of this, vowels are simply less eligible for error. There are a number of errors which amply illustrate the anchoring function of vowels; one is given in (10).

(10)   B: '[fʌ.ki tʃà̍d kʰí.tʃən] . . . Kentùcky Frïed Chïcken.'
          (for [kʰɔ̃.tʰʌ.ki fwa̍d tʃí.kən]; B-111(31) 2;9)

In this error, all vowels but the initial reduced vowel in 'Kentucky' remain intact, while the consonants move about wildly. Vowels anchor the overall prosodic structure of utterances, including the number of syllables, syllable structure, and lexical as well as phrasal stress. The fact that consonants can be added, deleted, moved, and replaced, while a vowel for the most part can only have another vowel substitute in its place, attests to the 'nuclear' importance of vowels, and is the most likely reason why vowel errors are relatively rare.

3.3.3 Syllabic and Non-Syllabic Liquids

Stemberger (1983b) and Shattuck-Hufnagel (1986) have both shown that the liquids /l/ and /r/ in English (and to some extent the nasals) have properties of both consonants and vowels, in that they can occur in both syllabic and non-syllabic form. They are unique among English phonemes in this way, although in other languages such as Mandarin, where glides are always derived from underlying vowels, the glides also show this behavior (Wan & Jaeger 2003). Stemberger uses SOT data to argue that all liquids are underlyingly consonants, and that their [syllabic] status is given by the syllable-structure position in which they occur; S-H likewise considers all syllabic liquids as underlyingly consonants, which is why she does not have the vowel [ɚ] in her vowel study.

While I find these arguments compelling from a theoretical point of view, I have found it impractical to consider syllabic /r/ as a consonant in this study, simply because it functions like a vowel in most cases. As in adult studies, my child data show the liquids having properties of both consonants and vowels, although this is much more true of /r/ in my study than /l/. This is partially due to the fact that most of the children pronounced words like 'bottle' with a vowel in the second syllable, i.e. [bá.rəɫ] 'bottle'. However, in order to look further into the status of liquids, I assessed every substitution, addition, or exchange error involving /r/, either syllabic or non-syllabic, in both the child and adult data. In each case I tabulated the status of the target, source, and error segments, in terms of whether they were vowels, consonants, or syllabic consonants. (Recall that [ɝ] is the non-pharyngealized [ɚ] vowel, and [ɹ̩] is the non-pharyngealized [r] consonant.) I found that these errors fell into the following six categories: 1) target, source, and error are all true consonants, as in (11a); 2) target, source, and error are all true vowels (11b); 3) target, source, and error are all syllabic liquids (11c); 4) target and error are syllabic liquids, but the source is a non-syllabic consonant (11d); 5) target is either a true consonant (11e) or in a consonant position in the syllable (11f), and the error is a true consonant, but the source is a vowel; 6) target and error are vowels, but the source is a consonant (11g). There were also a number of errors with multiple possible sources, as illustrated in (11h).

(11) a. B: 'Mòm, I hàve to [ɹ̩úʃ] . . . púsh the rèd bùtton.'
        (for 'push' [pʰʊʃ]; source 'red' [ɹ̩ɛd]; B-170(7) 3;10)
    b. B: 'Mòmmy, tàke mè on a [wɝk] fírst!'
        (for 'walk' [wak]; source 'first' [fɚst]; B-565(5) 5;10)
    c. An: 'In the mìddle of the [pʰéˀ.pl̩].'
        (for 'paper' [pʰéˀ.pr̩]; source 'middle' [mí.dl̩]; AN-201(12) 4;5)
    d. B: '[màr.br̩z] àre . . . màrbles àre smáll.' (for 'marbles' [már.bl̩z]; source either 'marbles' or 'are' [ar]; B-316(20) 4;6)
    e. B: 'She had a? Àlice in [rʌ́n.dɚ.lænd] . . . Àlice in Wónderlànd skìrt.' (for 'Wonderland' [wʌ́n.dɚ.lænd]; source either 'Wonderland' or 'skirt' [skɚt]; B-498(1) 5;5)
    f. An: 'Dòctor [fɹ̩à.stɹ] wènt to Glóuchester.'
        (for 'Foster' [fá.stɹ]; source either 'doctor' [dák.tɹ] or 'Glouchester' [glá.stɹ]; AN-36(21) 2;2)
    g. An: 'Thère's fíve [pʰɝ.p]. . . thère's fíve péople hère.'
        (for 'people' [pʰí.pʊl̩]; source either 'there's' [ðɛrz] or 'here' [hɪr]; AN-170(23) 4;4)
    h. Al: 'Thère's a túrtle in this [kʰɹ̩æs.rùm].'
        (for 'classroom' [kʰl̩æs.rum]; source either 'there's' [ðɛrz], 'turtle' [tʰɝ.rəɫ], or 'classroom'; AL-246(20) 5;7)

In (11a), the onset consonant [ɹ̩] is anticipated from 'red' and substituted for the onset consonant [pʰ] in 'push'. In (11b), the vowel [ɚ] is anticipated from 'first' and substituted for the vowel [a] in 'walk'. In (11c), the syllabic lateral [l̩] is perseverated and substituted for what I have written as the syllabic /r/ (r̩) (see below for explanation). In (11d), the sources are both consonants [r], but when the /r/ is substituted for the syllabic [l̩], it becomes the syllabic [r̩]. The error in

TABLE 3.11

Number of child and adult errors in which liquids behaved as
consonants, vowels, or syllabic consonants. T=target, S=source, E=error.

	Children	Adults
1. T, S, E=all consonants	60	29
2. T, S, E=all vowels	17	7
3. T, S, E=all syllabic cons.	4	2
4. T, E =syll. cons. S=cons.	3	0
5. T, E=cons. S=vowel	4	0
6. T, E=vowel S=cons.	1	0
Total N=	**89**	**38**

(11e) is a case of the vowel [ɚ] being anticipated and substituted for the consonant [w] in the onset of 'Wonderland'; because it is now in a non-syllabic slot, it becomes the consonant [r]. In (11f), the three occurrences of the vowel [3] have caused a consonant [ɜ̣] to be inserted in the second slot in the onset of 'Foster'. In (11g), the consonantal [r]s occurring before and after the target word cause the vowel [i] in 'people' to be pronounced as the vowel [ɚ]. Finally, in (11h), the substitution of the consonant [r] for the [l] in 'classroom' could have had its source in the consonantal [r]s in 'there's' or 'room', or the vowel [ɚ] in 'turtle'.

The number of each type of error is given in Table 3.11; although I only found errors in the first three categories in the adult corpus, Stemberger and Shattuck-Hufnagel found examples of all of these types in their adult corpora.

Because the consonantal liquids overwhelmingly interacted with other consonants (usually each other or [w]), and the vowel [ɚ] most often interacted with other vowels, I have chosen to use the symbol [r] (or [ɜ̣]) for the consonant and [ɚ] (or [3]) for the vowel, except in the few cases where the two syllabic liquids interacted, in which case I have written the rhotic as [ɹ̩]. The purpose of this is to simply allow me to count these errors as instances of either vowel or consonant errors, without taking a stand on any theoretical issues regarding their underlying status. However, if we assume that [r] and [ɹ̩] are consonants and [ɚ] is a vowel, then there are only five errors in my child corpus in which syllabic and non-syllabic sonorants unambiguously interact (i.e. categories 5 and 6 in Table 3.11), and no errors of this type in the adult corpus. In fact, the target and error always have the same status; it is only the source which differs in these cases. This supports the original claim that children have a clear distinction between the major classes 'consonant' vs. 'vowel'. However, the fact that the children in this study produced some errors which violated this distinction and the adults did not may suggest that the distinction is not as fixed in their phonologies as it is in adults'.

3.3.4 Phonemes and Allophones

In adult errors, when the error creates a new syntagmatic phonological sequence, segments always take on the correct phonetic form for the context in which they are spoken; that is, they show the correct allophone of the phoneme in that environment (Fromkin 1973a). It is very difficult to assess by naturalistic observation at what point in their linguistic development young children begin to group segments into conceptual categories (phonemes) with conditioned variants. However, SOT data allow us to notice the point in a child's development when allophonic variants show up in errors, because at that point the child will begin producing the same conditioned variants in new erroneous sequences that an adult would produce.

There are several cross-cutting factors involved in making this assessment. First, an analysis of 'conditioned variants' must be done in light of the child's own system. A child may not produce an adult-like form in a particular environment simply because that form is not allowed in that location in the child's phonology, as in the following examples.

(12)   a. An: 'Ápple[tàç] . . . s̲àuce.'
          (for 'applesauce' [ǽ.pow.çàç]; AN-4(30) 1;7)
      b. M: 'Whó gàve you this bòok?'
          An: '[pák^h].'
          (for 'Bob', [páp^h]; perseveration of /k/ from adult 'book' [pʊk] which Anna pronounced as [pʊk^h] at this time; AN-21(12) 1;11)

In (12a) Anna has a non-contextual substitution of [t] for [ç], possibly influenced by the stop [p] in 'apple'; but at this time (age 1;7) she was not distinguishing aspirated from unaspirated stops, so the [t] was not aspirated as it would have been if an adult had produced this error, since this syllable is stressed: *[ǽ.pəɬ.t^{h}às] (see also AL-20(3) 2;2, given as (19) below). In (12b) the [k] from Mom's word 'book' is perseverated and substituted for the [p^h] in the coda of 'Bob'. However, at this later time (1;11) Anna was now distinguishing aspirated from unaspirated stops by location in the word, with onset stops unaspirated and coda stops aspirated; so in this error she aspirated the /k/ according to her rules.

A second consideration is that within a particular word, a child may have represented a different sequence of phonemes from what an adult would represent for the same word (several examples are given below). A third factor is that a conditioned phonological alternation may be a phonetically driven automatic process vs. a learned phonological process, and this may make a difference in how that alternation develops. I will assess all three of these factors in the context of each allophonic variation to be discussed below.

In general, what the data show is that once the children's contextual variants became similar to adults' in their intended productions, the children produced the correct allophone in nearly every error where an allophone different from the target was called for. Early errors which look like 'exceptions' to these allophonic patterns are actually indications that the adult patterns were simply not yet fully incorporated into the child's phonology. These allophonic variations fell into 6 basic categories: 1) aspiration or deaspiration of stops; 2) tapping of unstressed medial alveolar stops; 3) voicing or devoicing of consonants in consonant clusters; 4) vowel nasalization or denasalization when a nasal consonant is present or absent; 5) place of articulation assimilation; and 6) velarization of the coda lateral.

First, once the children were making a distinction between 'voiced' and voiceless oral stops, and were producing aspiration in the same locations as adults (and not according to their own patterns as in (12b) above), they showed evidence that these patterns of aspiration were becoming a productive part of their phonologies. The earliest examples of this process occurred at about age 2;4 (see examples in (13) below), although for Alice the process was apparently not fully incorporated into her phonology until later (as I will discuss below). So, when an [s] was erroneously removed from the onset of an [s]-stop onset cluster, the stop became aspirated, as shown in (13a), where the [s] is moved from the onset of the first syllable to the onset of the second (also causing nasal devoicing). Conversely, when an [s] was added, the stop deaspirated, as illustrated in (13b), where the [s] is anticipated and added into the onset of the first syllable. When stops were moved from a position in which they were usually aspirated to one where they were not aspirated, or vice versa, the correct aspiration occurred, as in (13c), where the onset [k] and coda [p] are exchanged, and their aspiration adjusted accordingly.

(13)   a. An: '[_pʰú.sn̥i].' (for 'spoonie' [spú.ni]; AN-50(14) 2;5)
        b. Al: 'Whère are we gòing àfter the [spóʷst.à.fɪs]?'
            (for 'post-office' [pʰóʷst.à.fɪs]; AL-114(2) 3;3)
        c. B: 'I pèeled the [pʰéⁱk].' (for 'grape' [keⁱp]; B-50(25) 2;4)

Three apparent exceptions to these aspiration processes are given in (14). When Bobby was 4;3, he produced the error in (14a), where the [s] was moved from the beginning to the end of the word 'Stephanie' and the [t] remained unaspirated. Similarly, when Alice was 2;10, she produced two errors (14b,c) in which an /s/ was deleted before a /p/, and the /p/ remained unaspirated.

(14)   a. B: '[_té.fə.nis], I'll plày with you àfter dessért.'
            (for 'Stefanie' [sté.fə.ni]; B-243(14) 4;3)
        b. An: 'Óne tìme a spíder bìt mè rìght hére!'
            Al: 'Well, òne tìme a [_pàⁱ.dʒ] bìt mè rìght hére!'
            (for 'spider' [spáⁱ.dʒ]; AL-57(4) 2;10)
        c. Al: 'Whère's Mìster [_pák] . . . Spóck?'
            (for 'Spock' [spak]; AL-63(15) 2;10)

The error in (14a) may be a true exception, since at this time Bobby had fully learned the aspiration patterns; however, the [t] at the beginning of

'Stephanie' may be showing some influence of the [t] /d/ at the beginning of 'dessert' [tə.zɔ́t]. But Alice's two errors may have a more interesting explanation.

The error in (14b) may be a case where the [p] /b/ from 'bit' substituted for the /sp/ cluster in 'spider'. However, it may also be the case that at this age Alice was in the process of acquiring this variation, and these two errors show that it had not yet become an automatic part of her phonology. A closer look at Alice's developing phonology supports this view (see Jaeger 1997 for more details of Alice's early phonology). At age 2;0 she was producing only voiceless unaspirated stops in onsets for both the voiced and voiceless phonemes, although the voiced phonemes were sometimes fully voiced; both voiced and voiceless stops were produced as aspirated word-finally. She began making the aspirated/unaspirated stop distinction in simple onsets at age 2;1, with the voiceless phonemes always aspirated and the 'voiced' phonemes fluctuating between voiced and voiceless. Unstressed-medial-onset voiceless stops and coda voiceless stops became unaspirated. She produced only unaspirated stops after /s/ in onsets once she was able to produce consonant clusters, and there is no evidence from her SOTs as to the phoneme grouping of this stop before age 2;10, when the errors in (14b,c) were made. At age 3;1 she made the error in (15), where [s] was added to a word beginning with the voiced phoneme, which suggests that the voiceless unaspirated stops after /s/ may have not been closely linked to the voiceless aspirated stops, although there are multiple sources for this error. (See also Bobby's error (B-56(2) 2;5), which suggests that at age 2;5 he was not grouping the [k] after /s/ with the /k/ phoneme.)

(15)   Al: 'Mòmma, will yòu s̀it néar me, for I càn't [skɛ̀t] scáred?'
       (for 'get' [kɛt]; AL-95(21) 3;1)

However, starting at age 3;3, errors such as those in (16), and (13b) above, became common for Alice, showing that she now had grouped the stops after /s/ with the aspirated segments into a phonemic category, i.e. showing evidence of having acquired the phonemes /p/, /t/, and /k/.

(16)   a. M: 'Àlice, you càn't eàt còld spaghétti.'
          Al: 'I líke [skòʷɫd] . . . I líke còld spaghètti.'
             (for 'cold' [kʰoʷɫd]; AL-107(21) 3;3)
       b. Al: 'My tóe! My toé [_tʰɪks] òut!'
             (for 'sticks' [stɪks]; AL-122(15) 3;4)

In (16a), the /s/ is added to 'cold', in either anticipation or perseveration from the onset of 'spaghetti', and the /k/ deaspirates. In (16b) the /s/ is omitted from 'sticks', in assimilation to the two words which begin with a simple /t/, and the /t/ in 'sticks' becomes aspirated. After this time, all of Alice's pertinent errors show the adult-like aspiration variations. This is a particularly good example of the value of SOT data for documenting the development of phonological categories and processes. Also, it demonstrates conclusively that children begin forming these phoneme categories *before they become literate*. Therefore it is not simply spelling that causes English speakers to group the unaspirated stops after /s/ with the voiceless phonemes (see Jaeger 1980), but some pre-literate patterns young children have extracted from the input; in this case it is probably the expectation that sequences of consonants in onset clusters have the same value on the [voice] feature.

The second kind of allophonic process for which these data provide evidence is tapping. The younger children did not normally produce taps, so this process is only observed in the older children, usually age 4 and older. For these children, if a /t/ or /d/ was substituted for another medial intervocalic unstressed onset consonant (17a) or added to the onset of a medial unstressed syllable (17b), it was pronounced as a tap. Of course under these circumstances the adults always produced the tap.

(17) a. An: 'Mòmmy, [bà.ɾi] . . . Bòbby còvere*d* my mòuth with his
          hán*d*!' (for 'Bobby' [bá.bi]; [b]<--[d], then [d] becomes [ɾ];
          AN-224(7) 4;6)
      b. B: 'Wàcky cassé*tte* [pʰļèʲ.rɚ].' (for 'player' [pʰléʲ.ɚ]; [t] added,
          then becomes [ɾ]; B-562(13) 5;10)

A possible exception to this process is shown in (18), where Anna failed to produce a tap.

(18) M: 'Ànna, sì*t* dówn'
      An: 'Nó, I wànna be [sí.ti]! (laughs) I said "sìtty" instead of
      "sílly".' (for 'silly' [sí.li]; [t]-->[l]; AN-194(12) 4;5)

This error could be the perseveration of the morpheme 'sit', which she replicated exactly from her mother's utterance. But the more likely explanation for this pronunciation relates to the fact that Anna produced this utterance in a very emphatic way. As mentioned in §3.2.2, Anna had a rule at this age that medial unstressed alveolar stops were pronounced as taps in informal speech, but as [t] in formal or emphatic speech, regardless of the underlying phoneme. Thus this may not in fact have been an exception to her current rules.

The third kind of allophonic process evident in the SOTs is the voicing or devoicing of consonants in clusters. The most common example is that in adult speech, whenever a sonorant occurs as the second element in an onset cluster, it always takes on the voicing of the preceding obstruent. This is a low-level phonetic process which is almost entirely mechanical and not necessarily learned in the way that aspiration or tapping processes must be learned. However, I did find that for the very young children in this study, when they spoke words with sonorants following voiceless obstruents in clusters, the sonorants did not sound devoiced; in fact the sonorants seemed to be somewhat lengthened and voiced, as if the child was emphasizing each element of the cluster, as illustrated in (19); see also (AL-6(2) 2;1), (AN-28(2) 2;2), and (AN-34(3) 2;2) for other examples.

(19)   Al: 'My [ɕwíp._tìk] . . . my lípstìck.'
        (for 'lipstick' [wíp.ɕtìk]; AL-20(3) 2;2)

In this error the [ɕ] was anticipated from the onset of the second syllable of 'lipstick' and moved into the onset of the first syllable of 'lipstick', before the [w], but the [w] remained voiced (see also the discussion in §3.5.2 below; note also that Alice did not aspirate /t/ at this age). However, by the time the children were around 2;3, I began marking some devoicing in my notes, and after about 2;5 I marked it consistently. Thus after the children had some practice producing consonant clusters and the sonorants were produced with a more normal duration, the sonorants began to show this coarticulatory devoicing adjacent to voiceless obstruents, being at least partially devoiced in every case, as illustrated in (20).

(20)   a. B: 'Bárkley! Bárkley! I bètter fìnd [bláȝ.k̥_i]. Bárkley!'
              (for 'Barkley' [báȝ.kḷi], the dog on Sesame Street; B-67(3) 2;5)
        b. Al: 'Mommy, I wànt a [pʰȝ̊is ʌ b_ɛ́d].'
              (for 'piece of bread' [pʰis ʌ bȝɛd]; AL-47(3) 2;8)

In (20a), the devoiced [l] from the second onset of 'Barkley' is moved into the first onset next to the [b], and thus becomes voiced. In (20b) the opposite occurs, with the voiced [ȝ] moving from the onset of the last syllable into the first syllable; since it is now placed next to the voiceless [pʰ], it devoices. (I should note that the [ȝ] in this example is the consonant; however I cannot put both the devoicing and non-syllabic diacritics under the symbol.) I did not do any instrumental studies to document that this process was taking place fully in all cases; suffice it to say that after about age 2;5 I did not hear any cases which struck me as sounding 'un-English', i.e. a fully voiced sonorant consonant following a voiceless obstruent, or a voiceless sonorant after a voiced stop. (The circle under the sonorant should be read as either 'devoiced' or 'partially devoiced'.)

The fourth process is vowel nasalization or denasalization in the context of the presence or absence of a following nasal. As with devoicing of sonorants in clusters, this is a very low-level phonetic process, although there is some evidence that the nasalization of vowels before nasal consonants in the same syllable is exaggerated in English such that it is nearly phonemic, as compared to other languages such as Spanish (Solé 1992). Read (1971:18-21) looked at the representation of English phonology as manifested in preschool children's invented spellings; he found that these children almost never represent the nasal consonant with a letter when it occurs between a vowel and an oral consonant, because they perceive the nasality as simply part of the vowel: BOPY 'bumpy', MOSTR 'monster', NOOIGLID 'New England'. I found that the children in this study nasalized vowels whenever the vowel occurred before a nasal consonant, especially in the same syllable, and did not nasalize vowels in any other environment. (Again, I did not do any instrumental studies to confirm that children were actually articulating a nasal consonant in every case, and of course adults don't always produce the full nasal consonant; furthermore the nasalization may occur throughout the entire vowel, or only towards the end of it.) Note that I usually do not notate the nasalization in my data because it is entirely predictable and because the tilde interferes with the stress markers, which are always indicated in the examples.   However, in those errors in which nasalization is added or deleted because of the error and this is the focus of my discussion, I have marked it over the vowel in the text. Some examples are given in (21).

(21)   a. An: 'Tálk! Tàlk to my [pʰɾ̃in.tʰĩn] òne.'
            (for 'preténd' [pʰɾi.tʰĩn]; AN-59(2) 2;7)
        b. An: 'Nòw Ràffi's tàlking abòut [sŋæ̃] . . . Sánta Clàus.'
            (for 'Santa' [sǽn.ta]; [æ̃n]-->[ŋæ̃]; AN-174(27) 4;4)
        c. B: 'Yèah, yòur [wí_.stɔ̃n] . . . Wínston gùn.'
            (for 'Winston' [wĩn.stɔ̃n]; B-251(4) 4;4)

In (21a), the [n] is anticipated from the second coda of 'pretend' or from 'one' and added at the end of the first syllable, thus causing the vowel [i] to nasalize. In (21b), the vowel and nasal metathesize, producing the new sequence /snæ/. In this context, the nasal devoices due to the /s/, and the vowel denasalizes because it now comes after the nasal. In (21c), the nasal [n] in the coda of the first syllable of 'Winston' is omitted, in dissimilation from the other nasals which follow it, i.e. the second [n] in 'Winston' and the [n] in 'gun'. The vowel [ĩ] then denasalizes.

The fifth type of phonological process that occurred often in the data was place-of-articulation assimilation. The most commonly affected segments were nasals before plosives, but the process also involved obstruents in a few cases (see also AN-81(25) 2;10).

(22)   a. OB: '[sĩŋks] ínches . . . six ínches.'
            (for 'six inches' [sɪks ĩɲ.tʃis]; OC-88(2) 4;1)
        b. 'B: Tomòrrow, a [st̬ɛ̃ɲ.g3] . . . a stránger's gònna còme up to
            mè, and Ì'm gònna rùn awáy.'
            (for 'stranger' [st̬ɛ̃ɲ.dʒ3]; B-149(7) 3;8)
        c. M: 'Are yòu my cùte Kátie?'
            OG: 'Nó, Ì'm nót yòur [kʰ_ùt] . . . cùte Kàtie.'
            (for 'cute' [cʰjut]; OC-37(22) 3;0)

In example (22a), the palatal nasal from 'inches' is anticipated and added post-vocalically to 'six' [sɪks]; the nasal then becomes a velar in assimilation to the

[k], and causes the vowel to nasalize. In (22b), the velar [g] from 'gonna' is anticipated and substituted for the palato-alveolar [dʒ] in the second onset of 'stranger'; the [g] then causes the palatal nasal in the preceding coda to assimilate to its velar place, becoming [ŋ]. In (22c), the glide [j] is omitted from the initial position in the nucleus; the palatal [cʰ] is then realized as velar [kʰ].

The one exception to this place assimilation process in my data was produced by Bobby at age 1;10, when he was articulating each syllable relatively independently (23a; see §3.4.2). However by age 2, the children were consistently assimilating nasals to the place of articulation of following consonants, even across syllable boundaries, as illustrated in (23b).

(23) a. B: '[hǽm.kʌ.pɔ̀].'
          (for 'hamburger' [hǽm.pʌ.kɔ̀]; [p]<-->[k]; B-24(25) 1;10)
      b. Al: 'Yòu have [hǽŋ.gʌ.bɔ̀s], and yòu èating you hámburgèrs, and
            Ànna tóo!' (for 'hamburgers' [hǽm.bʌ.gɔ̀s]; [b]<-->[g], then [m]
            becomes [ŋ]; AL-29(25) 2;5)

The last allophonic process which was evident in the data is the velarization of /l/ in coda positions. The children all produced the usual substitution of [w] or a vowel such as [ʊ] for coda /l/ in their early productions, so once they began producing a true lateral in coda position it was always 'dark' (velarized). Thus when a lateral was erroneously moved into or out of the coda position in an SOT, it velarized or de-velarized, respectively.

(24) a. Al: (looking at photographs) 'Thère's Bóbby, at Séa-[lɔ̀wd] . . .
            Séa-Wòrld.' (for 'World' [wɔ̀ɫd]; AL-52(25) 2;10)
      b. B: 'Can I have twò more [mɛ́n.əɫz] . . . mélons?'
          (for 'melons' [mɛ́ɫ.ɔ̃n(z)]; B-575(25) 5;11)

In (24a) the [w] and [ɫ] exchange, causing the [l] to de-velarize as it has been moved into onset position. The example in (24b) is a particularly interesting case. The word 'melons' might be thought to be syllabified as [mɛ́.lɔ̃nz]. However, Bobby pronounced it as [mɛ́ɫ.ɔ̃nz]; the velarization of the [ɫ] shows that this is the correct syllabification. Thus, when the [n] and [ɫ] exchange, it is a clear case of a coda exchange (with the plural morpheme [z] being extrasyllabic; see §3.5.4); the fact that the vowel [ɛ] nasalized shows that the [n] is tautosyllabic with this vowel. Thus the allophonic variations discussed here can be used to correctly syllabify the children's words, which will be important in the discussion of syllable structure below.

In sum, the children's errors provide evidence regarding how and when their cognitive representations for these various phonemic categories and phonological processes develop. This is because children will produce SOTs which do not follow the adult-like patterns before they have been acquired, but will produce SOTs which show the productivity of these patterns after they have been acquired, enabling the researcher to estimate the time of acquisition. At first these productions are governed by the child's own phonological rules, but as the children develop a more adult-like phonology, the errors begin conforming to adult variants. The three low-level phonetic assimilation processes began to be evident in the children's SOTs at very early ages. The first process which occurs regularly is the nasalization of vowels before nasal consonants; this occurs without exception, as far as I can tell. Place-of-articulation assimilation occurs without exception within syllables from the earliest errors, and across syllables from about age 2. Devoicing or voicing of sonorants in consonant clusters begins to occur regularly once the children have had some practice articulating clusters fluently, around age 2;3-2;5.

On the other hand, phonological processes which are specific to English and thus must be learned follow different patterns. First, children hear coda /l/ as velarized in the input without exception, and in their earliest productions usually substitute [w] or [ʊ] for the more difficult [ɫ] in codas; (onset /l/ is often also replaced by [w], although some children, including both Alice and Anna, replace it with [j] in very early productions). Once children begin actually producing a lateral, they distinguish onset from coda /l/ phonetically by retaining the velarization on the coda /l/; therefore in SOTs this learned process is exceptionless after laterals are acquired. The various children in my study learned to pronounce the lateral at different ages (from early in the third year, through the fourth year), and therefore this process showed up in SOTs at various ages. Second, productive adult-like aspiration/deaspiration occurs in errors when the children have acquired this pattern in their normal speech; the extended example from Alice discussed above shows that she acquired this allophonic pattern at about age 3;0, but other children showed the pattern as early as 2;4. Finally, the tapping process begins to be productive when children begin consistently producing the tap, sometime around age 4. This discussion makes it clear that the SOT data presented here are a rich source of evidence about the development of phonemic categories and productive phonological processes.

3.3.5 Early Phonetically-Based Representations for Segments

It has been shown, based on evidence from children's creative spelling (Read 1971), that pre-literate children form hypotheses about the representation of various segments based on their phonetic properties; some of these hypotheses may need to be reformulated after the child becomes literate. One case of this, about which the slips data provide evidence, is the finding that children hear sequences of [coronal plosive+r], which are usually affricated in adult speech, as if there is an intentional affricate being produced. For example, the word 'troubles' was spelled by one of the children in Read's study as CHRIBLS, and so we assume it is represented as /tʃrʌ.bɫz/ in the child's lexicon; similarly this child spelled 'dragon' as JRAGIN. Evidence that the children in my study also created this analysis can be seen in the following four examples.

(25) a. OB:'It's sòrt of fúnny that I dòn't get ànything to [dʒ_íŋk] . . .
to drink.' (for 'drink' [dʒrɪŋk]; [r] deleted non-contextually, but
[dʒ] remains an affricate, in the absence of the conditioning
environment; OC-70(30) 3;10)

  b. OB:'We're [tʃɹèʲ.kɪŋ] the drúms òut.'
(for 'taking' [tʰeʲ.kɪŋ]; [r] added after /t/ in 'taking', then [tʰ]-->
[tʃ] before [r]; [r] devoices; OC-99(21) 4;3)

  c. An: 'I got [dʒréʲp]-jùice.' (for 'grape juice' [gréʲp.dʒùs]; [dʒr] is an
acceptable cluster for the child; AN-42(1) 2;4)

  d. B: 'I wànna màke those Rìce Críspy [tʰ_ìts] . . . trèats.'
(for 'treats' [tʃɹits]; Bobby at age 12;1)

In the first example, the child omitted the conditioning segment [r], but the
[dʒ] remained an affricate, showing that it is the underlying segment. In (25b),
the child added [r] after the [tʰ], causing it to be realized as [tʃ]. In (25c), the
child anticipated the segment [dʒ] and substituted it for the onset [g], giving the
sequence /dʒr/ which is a disallowed sequence in the adult phonology, but one
which was allowed for the child at that time since she phonemicized adult /dr/
sequences as /dʒr/, as in 'dream' /dʒrim/ (see also OC-17(12) 2;3, AN-124(34)
3;10, B-179(7) 4;0, B-291(20) 4;5, and B-386(13) 4;10). I found no similar
errors in the adult corpus. Finally, (25d), produced by Bobby at age 12;1 (and
thus not in the current database), shows that this phonemicization was no
longer applicable; when he dropped the [r] in 'treats', the onset /t/ reverted to the
aspirated [tʰ] allophone.

Interesting additional support for the claim that children make this early
phonetically-based analysis of /tr/ and /dr/ clusters comes from an utterance made
by a child, age 4;10, which I initially recorded as an error. I overheard this child,
whom I knew slightly, saying:

(26) OG: 'Lóok, the dòg is trỳing to [tʃɹèʲs] the cát!' (4;10)

At first I assumed this to be a case where the child's target was 'chase' [tʃeʲs],
and the [r] was a perseveratory addition from 'trying' [tʃɹáʲ.ɪŋ]. But then I asked
the child: 'Whát is the dog doing?' and she replied '[tʃɹèʲs.ɪŋ] the cát.' I asked
her 'How do you [tʃɹéʲs] something?', and she replied, in a tone of voice
suggesting her disbelief at how stupid adults can be, 'You run after it!' Thus it
became clear to me that she had lexicalized the verb 'chase' with the phonology
/tʃreʲs/, possibly from analogy to words such as 'train', 'tree' and 'try'; I
therefore did not include this utterance in my error database, because it was not in
fact an error. However, it is a fascinating bit of evidence for early child
hypotheses about phonology. These are the sorts of hypotheses, like Anna's and
Alice's tapping rule, which the child will need to reevaluate when he/she
becomes literate.

3.3.6 Summary of Segments and Phonemes

Even the children's earliest errors show evidence of being constrained by the possible phoneme inventory of English; the only non-English segments in the data occurred in errors made at age 2;4 or earlier. These errors also indicate that the distinction between [+syllabic] and [-syllabic] segments is fairly clear from an early age, with only a few metathesis errors and a few errors involving /r/ violating this distinction. As with adults, young children make far fewer errors involving vowels than consonants; I argued that this is due to the function of vowels as the 'nucleus' of the syllable, anchoring syllable structure and prosodic information, and thus being less susceptible to error.

Allophonic variation is, for the most part, as regularly honored in the children's errors as it is in the adults'; however, a few early errors which violated the usual patterns of aspiration of plosives were argued to give evidence about the age at which this alternation was learned by one of the children, Alice. Other patterns for which there is evidence include tapping, voicing and devoicing of sonorants, place-of-articulation assimilation, nasalization of vowels, and velarization of coda laterals. Finally, the children's errors provide strong evidence regarding the early phonetically-based hypotheses children typically form about the phonology of their language; specifically they show that what are phonemicized by adults as sequences of /tr/ and /dr/ are phonemicized by some children as /tʃr/ and /dʒr/. These hypotheses will be reassessed when the child becomes literate.

3.4 Syllables

3.4.1 What Is a Syllable?

Although I have demonstrated that the segment is the basic unit of speech production planning for these children, this does not mean that syllables no longer have a place in their phonologies. The earliest productions during babbling are very much syllable-governed, and thus even though the segment has gained primacy in representations and planning, it would not be contradictory to assume that some information about syllable organization is also retained in the children's phonological systems. At this point it would be useful to distinguish three functions of syllables, since these may not all have the same status for the children at all ages. First, syllables are a phonetic unit in that they are the unit of motor encoding, i.e. the unit in which commands are sent from the motor cortex of the brain to the articulators for speaking (Fujimura & Erickson 1997). This is probably true across the board, for babbling infants, young and older children, and adults, and the production patterns of intentional speech undoubtedly developed out of early babbling mechanics, as argued by Davis & MacNeilage (1994, 1995). However, this is a motor-speech fact and may not necessarily be related to the representation of syllables either in the lexicon or during phonological planning.

Second, syllables have a function in the mental representations of phonological phenomena, both in terms of the overall phonological system and in individual lexical representations. The function of syllables in the mental phonological system is both to serve as the environment for many phonological processes which occur at specific locations in syllables, and to set up the phonotactic (linear-sequencing) constraints of the system. Within individual lexical items, syllables help organize segments into a linearly and hierarchically-ordered sequence, so that lexical items can be pronounced and perceived with reference to a consistent phonological form. (I will address the third function of syllables below.)

How might we expect to see developments in these phonological functions, as reflected in the children's SOTs? Specifically, what developmental patterns would we look for in terms of processes that depend on syllable structure, knowledge about allowable phonotactic sequences, and the organization of the lexicon in terms of phonological similarity? We could hypothesize that phonological processes which are triggered by location in syllables will not be evident in children's SOTs until there is syllable-structure organization in lexical entries; this idea was inherent in the discussion of allophonic variation in the preceding section. Furthermore, as children develop the ability to produce sequences which are more complex than the CV or CVC structures which usually occur in first words, we would predict that they will show evidence of developing templates for allowable sequences of segments; this will be looked at immediately below. Finally, the adult lexicon is clearly organized to some extent by the phonological similarity of lexical items, including the syllable structure of words (Fay & Cutler 1977, Cutler & Fay 1982); chiidren's lexicons may show some development of this phonological organization.

Some developmental patterns can also be predicted in terms of the phonological representations of individual lexical items. At first a lexical entry may be stored as a set of segments with a default linear order but some flexibility as to order. These segments would be anchored to a 'phonological word' node which specifies this set of segments as a relatively fixed unit, linked to some meaningful lemma. I will give evidence for this possibility below. Then as the child's phonological representations become more complex segmentally, they may require some information as to how many syllables the form contains, and possibly information as to the syllable boundaries, in order to keep the segments organized. This could start out as a simple linear demarcation, similar to the syllable boundaries represented in phonetic transcriptions. But as both segments and syllables become more numerous in individual words, the representation will need to develop internal syllable structure organization, such as the 'onset-nucleus-coda' structure and the 'onset-rhyme' structure. Either when syllables begin to be demarcated in the linear string, or when this internal syllable structure begins to develop, the representations will necessitate some higher-order level of prosodic structure, such as the 'syllable node tier' of autosegmental phonology, in order to keep the linear order of segments organized. Eventually the representation will need something like the 'foot structure' of metrical phonology in order to keep the overall prosodic structure of the word appropriately anchored in the correct linear order to the single 'phonological word' node in the representation (Selkirk 1980, Nespor & Vogel 1986, Blevens 1995). The SOT data may provide evidence as to when this higher level of phonological organization begins to develop and is in place in representations.

The third function of syllables is that they are important units in speech processing, in both production and perception. With regard to the topic of the current study, syllables have been shown to play a crucial role in speech production planning for adults, both in terms of representations and phonological processing, in several ways. According to the processing model introduced in Chapter 1, the RPC Model, after a lemma has been selected and while its phonological form is being activated, activation will spread to entries which are phonologically similar to the target word; if some other word is extremely phonologically similar to the target word, it may be erroneously selected. This claim requires a definition of what features make two words 'phonologically similar' to each other, and having the same number of syllables, or having similar internal syllable structures, are good candidates; this hypothesis can easily be tested with SOT data, as will be done below. Furthermore, the input to the 'Phonological Processes' component of the RPC Model is a string of phonological representations of lexical items, in the correct order, with morphosyntactic information indicated. The phonological material on which this component operates seems to be something like the multi-tiered representations of autosegmental phonology, with features, segments, syllables, internal syllable structure, lexical stress, and so on, each represented in relatively autonomous tiers (Levelt 1992). As discussed above, two segments are more likely to be mutually involved in an error if they are phonetically similar to each other. But evidence from adult SOTs also shows that two segments or phonological units are more likely to be mutually involved in an error if they occur in identical syllable structure locations in their original words (MacKay 1972, Crompton 1982, Shattuck-Hufnagel 1983, Stemberger 1983a, Laubstein 1987, Anderson 1988). Finally, whole syllables can be involved in errors as the error unit, suggesting that syllable nodes may themselves be susceptible to error (Shattuck-Hufnagel 1983). Thus there is evidence that these syllabic structures are represented and utilized during phonological processing. It is my goal to look for evidence in the children's SOTs for the existence and development of overall syllable demarcation, internal syllable structure, and the syllable node tier.

In the next several sections I will assess evidence regarding the existence and development of the syllable unit per se, both in lexical entries and in phonological processing. In §3.5 and §3.6 I will explore the development of internal syllable structure in phonological processing and in lexical representation respectively; at the end of §3.6 I will summarize my findings regarding the development of syllables and syllable structure, as evident in the SOT data.

3.4.2 Syllables in Phonological Errors

As suggested in the above discussion, there are three places to look for information regarding the status of syllables in young children's phonological processing and lexical representations. One is to see whether phonological errors occur in which the syllable is the unit of error; this would suggest that syllables are part of the syntagmatic structure of the phonological material being planned for the utterance in the 'Phonological Processes' component. Second, target and error words in lexical substitution errors can be compared to see if they frequently contain the same number of syllables; if so, this would suggest that syllables are represented in lexical phonological representations, and are one factor causing two words to be 'phonologically similar'. Third, lexical blend errors can be taken as evidence for both the representation and processing of syllables. Recall that blend errors occur when two words which are both semantically appropriate for a particular proposition are fully activated, and both words are linked to a single syntactic slot. When these forms are fed into the phonological processor, it takes the two phonological forms and blends them into a single phonological word. Thus crossover points in blends suggest not only what kinds of structural information is represented in the phonological forms of the words, but also how the phonological processor deals with this input material in creating a new possible word. In this section I will discuss syllables in phonological errors; in §3.4.3 I will look at syllables in lexical substitution errors, and in §3.4.4 I will examine blends.

It is often noted that syllables themselves can be the unit of error in adult phonological SOTs, although this is a less common error unit than segments (Fromkin 1973a:229; Stemberger 1983a:22). It would be interesting to see if the very young children produce more or fewer errors involving whole syllables than the older children and adults, that is, whether the younger children have some sort of holdover influence from the predominantly syllabic organization of babbling. However, in order to be able to discuss syllables in errors, I must first make clear the principles I followed for dividing polysyllabic words into syllables in my data, not an easy task in English.

1)   Compounds were divided at the boundary between content morphemes. No other morpheme boundaries were considered in making syllabic divisions; that is, I did not use boundaries between stems and affixes as syllabification criteria (although I will argue below that inflectional affixes are in fact not fully integrated into the syllabic structure of words).

2)   Single consonants between two vowels were analyzed as the onsets of the second syllable, following the Maximal Onset Principle (MOP, sometimes called the 'Onset First Principle'; Clements & Keyser 1983, Itô 1986, Blevins 1995), except in one case. Derwing (1992) has shown that in bisyllabic words where the first syllable contains a stressed lax vowel followed by a single liquid, adult English speakers tend to consider the liquid to be the coda of the first syllable. This analysis was reflected in the childrens' errors, since liquids in this position often interacted with other codas, as the following example illustrates.

(27) An: 'Àli's wèaring púrple stripes, and Ì'm [**jèɫ**.ɪŋ **wɛ́r**.oʷ] . . . <u>yell</u>ow.'
(for 'wearing yellow' [wɛ́r.ɪŋ jɛ́ɫ.oʷ]; AN-252(28) 4;10)

In this example, the MOP would dictate the following syllabification: [wɛ̀.rɪŋ jɛ́.loʷ], in which case this error would involve the exchange of two syllable+onset units [wɛ.r]<-->[jɛ.l]. However, if both liquids are considered as codas, this is a simple syllable exchange. Although there is a possible morphological explanation for the error unit with 'wearing', there is no such possible analysis with 'yellow'. Furthermore, the fact that the [ɫ] in this position was velarized provides phonetic support for its designation as post-vocalic. (See also the discussion of example (24b) above.) For the most part, consonants were not analyzed as 'ambisyllabic', as Derwing (1992) has shown that naive adult English speakers only tend towards an ambisyllabic solution to syllable boundary assignment when single consonants are spelled with two letters, and all the child subjects in the present study were pre-literate. It would have been somewhat arbitrary on my part to assign ambisyllabicity in individual words, and so intervocalic consonants were nearly always assigned to one syllable or the other. However, in a few cases it is difficult or impossible to tell with which syllable a particular consonant is aligned in an error, and so I have posited ambisyllabic consonants in these cases; see (29b) below for an example.
3) When there were two or more consonants between vowels in polysyllabic words, several principles were relevant: phonotactic constraints of English, the MOP, allophonic variation in specific syllable positions, and divisions between morphemes in compounds. In most cases these factors all pointed to the same division, as illustrated in (28a); however when there was conflict among the cues, the MOP was considered the least important factor, as illustrated in (28b,c,d).

(28) a. B: ' . . . I want my [vǽ.lən.**kʰ**àʲnz] stì***ck***er.' (for 'valentines sticker' [vǽ.lən.tʰàʲnz stí.kɚ]; [tʰ]<--[k]; B-294(1) 4;5)
b. An: 'Nòw it sàys [**tʰ**ìk] . . . nòw it sàys <u>s</u>ìx***t***éen.'
(for 'sixteen' [sìks.tʰín]; [s]<--[tʰ]; AN-183(7) 4;4)
c. B: 'Còcoa [kʰr̥ìs.**m**iz] . . . àre ***m***y fávorite.'
(for 'Crispies' [kʰr̥ís.piz]; [p]<--[m]; B-299(1) 4;6)
d. B: 'It's nòt a [b**l**éʲs.**w**ìt].'
(for 'bracelet' [bwéʲs.lìt]; [l] and [w] exchanged; B-114(25) 2;9)

In (28a), the sequence [nk] is not allowed either in a coda (where [ŋk] would occur) or in an onset, so the syllable division between the [n] and [k] is the only one possible. This error was analyzed as involving the substitution of one single-consonant onset for another; note that the /k/ in 'sticker' is unaspirated due to being in the onset of a medial unstressed syllable, but when it occurs in the onset of the secondary-stressed syllable in 'valentines' it becomes aspirated. The sequence in (28b) of /kst/ could be syllabified as /k.st/ or /ks.t/, and the former would be preferred by the MOP; however the fact that the /t/ is aspirated and occurs at the beginning of the second morpheme in a compound indicates that the second syllabification is the correct one. Again this error involves two simple onsets. In (28c), while both [sp] and [sm] are possible onset clusters, the [s] was lengthened, as is typical in codas, and the error segment [m] was not devoiced, as it would be in an onset [sm̥] cluster; therefore the phonetics point to the target word being syllabified as [kʰr̩ís.piz] (this /p/ is not eligible for aspiration since it is in an unstressed syllable). This allows for a simple syllable-onset substitution analysis of this error. On the other hand, this same reasoning in (28d) causes a more complex analysis. If [sw] were an onset cluster, this error would involve the exchange of segments in the same onset position (i.e. the second element of an onset cluster); however because the [s] was lengthened and the [w] not devoiced, the only phonetically accurate analysis is the one given, where [s] is a coda consonant and [w] an onset: [bwéⁱs.lɪt]. Relying on the phonetic properties thus causes this error to be analyzed as a less well-structured error, as it involves units in different positions in the onset (as will be discussed in detail below). In every case the phonetic factors were taken to be more important than the consistency of syllable structure analysis, so that the syllable division decisions were not biased towards a more phonologically consistent analysis.

There are four types of phonological SOTs in which whole syllables can function as the error unit. These include substitutions, as illustrated in (29a), and exchanges (29b); adults also produced additions as in (29c) (see §6.3.1.2 for an argument that this is a phonological, not a morphological, error). Errors involving the omission of syllables are categorized as telescopings; in some cases just a syllable is deleted (29d), but in many cases both a syllable and some other units are deleted (29e).

(29)   a. B: 'That's a [dʌ.**k3**]-dè*cker* bús right there!'
             (for 'double-decker' [dʌ.bʊ.dɛ́.k3]; anticipation/substitution of
             syllable [bʊ]<--[k3]; B-52(6) 2;4)

      b. Al: 'Àlice in [**lǽnd**.dʒ . . . **wʌ̀n**].' (for 'Wónderlànd' [wʌ́n.dʒ.lænd];
              exchange of syllables [wʌn]<-->[lænd], where the [d] in the
              error is analyzed as ambisyllabic; AL-67(28) 2;10)

      c. AM: 'There are [fòr.ə̀ɫ] . . . four chór*al* gròups.'
              (for 'four choral' [for kʰór.əɫ]; anticipation/addition of syllable
              [ə̀ɫ]; AD-131(11.5))

      d. B: 'Lóok, Mòm, anòther [bí:.dʒ̀ù:s] . . . Béetlejùice.'
              (for 'Beetlejuice' [bí.rə̀ɫ.dʒùs]; deletion of syllable [rə̀ɫ];
              B-154(34) 3;8)

      e. Al: '[gǽ:.mì:].' (for 'Gramma Beckie' [gæ̀.mʌ bɛ́.kì]; deletion of
              [ʌ.bɛ.k], including a syllable; AL-5(34) 2;1)

Table 3.12 presents the number of 'LU' ('larger unit') phonological errors collected at each age, and the percentage of 'LU' errors at each age which

TABLE 3.12
Number of LU and telescoping errors, and percentage of LU and telescoping errors which involved whole syllables.

Age:	1	2	3	4	5	Total	Adult
LUs N=	1	19	13	26	18	77	65
% Syll	0	16%	0	8%	11%	10.5%	14%
Tel. N=	4	21	8	18	10	61	31
% Syll	0	28.5%	25%	33%	40%	29.5%	55%

involved syllables. It presents separately the number of telescoping errors made at each age, and the percentage of telescoping errors where at least a whole syllable was deleted (in some cases a whole syllable plus some other unit, as in (29e) above). Multiple phonological errors are excluded from this count. This table is to be read as follows (for example): at age 2 the children made 19 errors involving 'larger units', and of these, 16% (N=3) involved whole syllables.

The children at age 1 made only one LU error, a consonant cluster substitution (AN-14(11) 1;9); recall that LU errors are usually between-word errors, and nearly half of the the 1-year-old errors were within-word errors (see §2.3.1). They made 4 telescoping errors, none of which involved the deletion of whole syllables, but rather the deletion of sequences of segments; one also involved the misordering of segments. These errors will be discussed below in terms of the development of internal syllable structure. But there is no evidence from these SOTs that at age one the syllable itself is a unit of speech production planning; or at least one could say that it is not available for error, and that individual segments are more important than syllables for representation and production.

However, at age two there is an increase in the number of both LU and telescoping errors involving syllables, suggesting that the syllable is now a unit which is functioning during speech production planning. The percentage of phonological LU errors involving syllables drops to zero at age 3, and then rises during ages 4-5, to a level just below that of the adults. Similarly, there is a drop in telescoping errors involving syllables at age 3, and then a rise toward the adult level during ages 4-5. The fact that the 3-year-old errors lie outside the general developmental pattern will be seen again and again throughout this section, and will be eventually explained in terms of the development of internal syllable structure which seems to be extremely important at age 3, and which causes units other than syllables to be more salient during phonological processing for children at this age.

Another factor evident in Table 3.12 is that syllables are involved in telescopings much more often than in LU errors (substitutions, exchanges, and for the adults, additions). This is probably simply a function of the fact that telescoping errors by definition omit a syllable nucleus, and since the nucleus is tightly linked to the syllable as a whole, a salient candidate for deletion is a complete syllable. I will return to telescopings in §3.5.5 below.

Interestingly, the adults in this study made a larger percentage of phonological errors involving syllables than the children did at any age other than age 2. However, if the actual errors are examined, some telling differences in the forms of these errors are discovered. While the children's syllable errors consisted of substitution, exchange, and omission of whole syllables, the adults' errors also included addition of syllables, as exemplified in (29c) above. These addition errors could be considered a variation of the errors discussed in Chapter 2 (§2.2.1, example (2a,b)) which adults but not children produce, in which an extra rhythmic beat is added. In the adult errors, sometimes this extra beat comes in the form of a whole syllable taken from another source, as in (29c), but sometimes it is made up of syllable fragments from the source, as illustrated in Chapter 2, example (2b), and in (30a) below. In a few cases the adults produced a word blend where the prosodic structure of one word was superimposed on the segments of the other word, causing a change in number of syllables, as illustrated in (30b).

(30) a. AF: 'I hàve a [də.nàʲ.ɪŋ] . . . dÿing banána.' (for 'dying banana' [dáʲ.ɪŋ bə.nǽ.nə]; addition of [ə.n]; AD-130(11.5))
      b. AF: 'Sée, it sàys [bə.nɑ́f.n̩.ì].' (blend of 'botany' [bɑ́f.n̩.ì] and 'zoology' [zə.wá.lə.dʒì]; AD-503(38))

In (30a), the rhyme [ə] and onset [n] from the first and second syllables of 'banana' are inserted into the first syllable of 'dying', breaking it into two syllables and thus adding an extra syllabic beat to the word, causing it to take on the prosodic structure of the source 'banana'. In (30b), the error contains the number of syllables and stress pattern of 'zoology', but the segments of 'botany', some of which have had to be copied into the added syllable in order to give it pronounceable substance.

While these sorts of errors are common among adults, I found only three errors in the child data which are similar, all made by Anna.

(31) a. An: 'A dèer, dòg, dòrmouse, [dǽn.sʌ.lɪŋ déʲnt_].'
          (for 'dancing daintily' [dǽn.sɪŋ déʲn.tʌ.li]; AN-72(31) 2;9)
      b. An: '[tʃɛ̀.də.li] . . . Chèrry Cúddler.'
          (for 'Cherry Cuddler' [tʃɛ́.ri kʰʌ́.də.lɚ]]; AN-136(11) 3;11)
      c. An: 'Thrèe things are called 'chícken'. Lìke you hàve chícken pòx, and yòu can éat chìcken, and aʔ [ǽ:.mʌ̀ɬ] . . . a fèmale ánimàl, lìke a hén.'
          (for 'female' [fí.meɬ ǽ.nə.məɬ]; AN-178(34) 4;4)

In (31a), the rhyme-onset sequence [ʌ.l] was anticipated and added to the second syllable of 'dancing', causing the same changes as in the adult error in (30a) above, as well as the deletion of the final vowel [i]. In (31b), the syllable+onset sequence [də.l] from 'Cuddler' was anticipated and substituted for the [r] in 'Cherry', adding a syllable node to the word. In (31c), a very unusual sort of telescoping, Anna anticipated the segments of 'animal' and superimposed them on the syllable structure of 'female'; since there are only two syllables in 'female' one of the syllables from 'animal' had to be dropped, but the remaining vowels were lengthened, as is usual in telescopings.

I would like to suggest that these errors involving syllables can most accurately be interpreted as showing a development of the sophistication of the function of syllables. When the children are one year old, their lexical phonological representations seem to not be clearly divided into syllables. Since I have shown that the segment is an important part of representations at this age, it would follow that words may be represented as a set of segments, with a default order, but no clear hierarchical organization within the word; specifically there is no clear specification of syllable division. The word itself would be the basic 'prosodic' unit. This would be possible because most words the children are learning consist of only one or two (adult) syllables, and are often quite simplified from the adult models, involving a CV, CVC, or CVCV structure. This hypothesis is in line with claims by other researchers that the word is the basic organizing unit for early phonological representations, as discussed in §3.1 above. The function of the syllable itself at this age would be simply a motoric speech production unit, as it was during babbling.

However, at around age 2 children begin to learn words of three or more syllables, and begin to develop the ability to produce more complex sequences of segments, specifically sequences of consonants at the beginnings and ends of words as well as intervocalically. At this point the whole-word prosody begins to be inadequate for structuring phonological representations, particularly since children are now getting firm control over the linear order of segments. Thus, the syllable begins to be important in representations for clustering sequences of segments linearly, presumably organizing them around the perceptual centers of the prosodic word, the vowels. At this early stage there probably isn't a hierarchically organized 'syllable tier', but rather some sort of linear demarcation in the string of segments, such as: CVCVC$, where '$' represents syllable boundaries (this will be discussed more fully with reference to example (93) below). For this reason we begin to see clear evidence of syllables in errors made by the 2-year-old children: the earliest phonological error involving syllables was made at 2;4 (see (29a) above), and telescopings involving the deletion of syllables began at age 2;1 (AL-7(34) 2;1). These facts are related to the finding earlier in this chapter that allophonic variations sensitive to syllable boundaries (e.g. aspiration, sonorant devoicing, etc.) begin to occur early in the third year. This linearization in phonology is undoubtedly related to the development of the linearization of words, i.e. the development of syntax.

Anna's error shown above in (31a) which she made at 2;9 suggests that another aspect of structure is beginning to be developed towards the end of the third year, that is some abstract representation of the syllable as a unit of rhythm, which is independent from the segmental representation. I would argue that what is now developing is the syllable tier, with syllable nodes which organize the segments into internal syllable structures, and link with the word node. I will argue below that there is evidence for internal syllable structure beginning at around age 2;6, which supports the hypothesis that at about this age the syllable tier begins to take on this function. Then at the end of the fourth year when the whole-syllable addition error in (31b) above occurred, and the beginning of the fifth year, when the whole-word prosody telescoping error in (31c) was produced, there is evidence that foot structure is developing, such that the syllable tier itself is organized into an overall word prosody. The larger number of adult syllable node additions and prosodically based lexical blends indicates that even the 4-5-year-olds have not developed the full adult-like prosodic representations for words; however, these few errors suggest that this aspect of phonological representation is developing during ages 4-5.

Finally, these syllable-node addition errors may also be due in part to an attempt by the speaker to maintain the overall phrasal rhythm. In this case they may have something in common with the omission errors discussed by Cutler (1980c), which she attributes to the maintenance of isochronicity in the phrasal rhythm. This sort of attention to overall phrasal prosody is only possible after internal word structure is in place.

3.4.3 Syllables in Lexical Substitution Errors

As discussed in Chapter 1, there are two sources for a misselection of one lexical item for another. The first occurs when the 'Inferential Processes' activate, via concepts, the lemmas of some candidate lexical items, and a word which is semantically related to the intended word erroneously receives the higher activation and so is misselected. In Chapter 4 below I will document that this is the most common source of lexical substitution errors; an example is the substitution of *'slow' for 'fast' (OC-29(35) 2;8).

However, if the correct lemma is activated, assigned a functional role, and inserted into a syntactic string, when the phonological form of this lemma is activated its activation will spread to other words which are phonologically similar to the intended word. In this case a word with no semantic relationship to the intended word but with a close phonological relationship, i.e. a malapropism, may be erroneously spoken; this is illustrated in (32).

(32) B: 'Dàd, ya wànna sèe my **invèntion** . . . my imprèssion of a hát?'
         (B-513(35) 5;5)

In some cases the target and error words are both semantically and phonologically related.

(33) B: 'I bùmped ìnto her **hánd**. I mèan héad.' (B-293(35) 4;5)

This may suggest that some lemmas of candidate lexical items remain activated after one is selected, and one may be misselected if it also receives activation from the phonological form of the intended word. However, it is also possible that the phonological similarity is accidental, since the most common error type is one where the two words are semantically but not phonologically similar, like the 'slow/fast' error mentioned above. This will be discussed in detail in Chapters 4 and 5, where I will also make explicit my criteria for semantic and phonological relatedness.

There are several other sources of lexical intrusions which the RPC Model does not formally account for. These will be presented in detail in Chapter 4, but one important type is where something physically present in the environment is functioning as the source of the error, as illustrated in (34).

(34)   OB: (he had been admiring the new shoes he got for his birthday, but not talking about them; then he looked up and said)
'Mom, do you knòw what I'm gòing to dò with my [ʃú] I mean ámbulance?' (started to say 'shoe' or 'shoes' for 'ambulance', another birthday gift; OC-126(35) 5;0)

In cases such as this one, we expect neither a semantic nor a phonological relationship between the target and error words, although a semantic or phonological relationship might make the error more likely overall.

At issue here is the malapropisms, that is, errors which have been caused by formal similarity. The claim is that a word may be misselected because it is 'phonologically similar' to the target word, but what counts as phonologically similar can only be discovered by looking at the data. One place to look for candidate phonological phenomena to test is data from 'tip of the tongue' experiments (Brown & McNeill 1966, Harley & Brown 1998), where subjects who are trying to recall the phonological form of a word can report some aspects of that form without being able to fully activate it. These studies find that for English speakers, the first phoneme in the word, the number of syllables, the stress pattern, and the stressed vowel are the factors which subjects can recall most readily when in the 'tip of the tongue' state. This demonstrates that these aspects of the phonological form of words are represented in lexical form entries (contra theories which claim that either stress or syllable structure is assigned during phonological processing), and are the most easily accessible elements in phonological representations. This would lead us to predict that number of syllables would be an important factor involved in the phonological similarity of two lexical representations.

In order to look into this question, I selected a subset of the paradigmatic lexical substitution errors for analysis. First, I looked only at the content-word errors since there is more possibility for content word pairs to differ in number of syllables compared to function words, as the majority of function words are monosyllabic. Furthermore, function words are treated differently from content words during speech production planning, being more closely linked to syntax; thus they might not be expected to show the same kinds of form-based lexical access patterns. Second, I excluded environmentally-based errors when the erroneous word had neither a semantic nor phonological relationship to the target word, as in (34) above. However, if an environmentally-influenced lexical selection error involved a word which was semantically or phonologically related to the target, I did include this error in the count, since the semantic or phonological relationship was most likely one factor which allowed the word to be misselected.

I then analyzed each word pair (target and error) to see whether they had the same or a different number of syllables, based on the actual pronunciation of the speaker who made the error. In making this judgment, I did not include any regular inflectional suffixes as being part of the underlying phonological form of the word for subjects over the age of 2;2. The reason I excluded inflectional suffixes is that there is a good deal of evidence that regular inflectional suffixes are concatenated on-line as part of the linear assembly of a sentence, rather than being stored with stems in the lexicon (see Chapter 6). However, it was likely that the youngest children had learned some words with the inflectional suffixes incorporated into their lexical representations, i.e. not yet separated out into a distinct lexical representation. For the lexical selection errors under analysis in this section, there were only two errors which fell into this category: (B-16(35) 1;10), where 'toes' is taken to be the child's lexical representation, and (AL-13(35) 2;2), where 'crying' is considered the represented form. Excluding inflectional suffixes from underlying phonological representation for children over 2;2 and for adults affected the syllable count of only one pair of words in the child data, given in (35a). In the adult data it affected 6 pairs of words, one of which is given in (35b).

(35)   a. B: 'I wànt you to gèt me òne of those Kòol-aid **sándwìches** . . .
         I mean <u>pópsìcles</u>.' ('sandwiches' [sǽnd.wì.tʃ(əz)] for 'popsicles'
         [pʰáp.sì.kəɬ(z)]; B-133(35) 3;5)
       b. AF: 'It's got **brídges** aròund it . . . I mean <u>wálls</u>.'
         ('bridges' [brí.dʒ(əz)] for 'walls' [waɬ(z)]; AD-384(35))

In (35a) the inflected forms of the two words each have three syllables, but when the syllabic suffix is removed from 'sandwiches', the singular 'sandwich' has only two syllables, so there is a mismatch in number of syllables between the two uninflected forms 'sandwich' and 'popsicle'; two of the adult errors were of this type, where the removal of the suffix causes the two forms to have a different number of syllables. The converse is true in (35b), where after the plural suffix is removed from 'bridges', the two remaining stems 'bridge' and 'wall' have the same number of syllables; four of the adult errors were of this type.

After assessing the number of syllables in target and error words for all the lexical selection errors targeted for analysis, I then tabulated the number and percentage of cases in which the number of syllables was the same or different in the two words. I compared the number of 'same' pairs when the two words had a semantic relationship (whether they also had a phonological relationship or not)

TABLE 3.13

Percentage of content word lexical substitution errors in which the target
and error words had the same number of syllables (S#S), out of total N in
that group; errors with semantic relationship [+sem] compared to errors
with no semantic relationship but a phonological relationship [-sem];
N= number of errors in this group at this age.

Age	1	2	3	4	5	Total	Adult
[+sem] N=	5	22	15	34	37	113	102
% S#S	60%	63.5%	73%	65%	73%	68%	67.5%
[-sem] N=	0	4	5	13	5	27	37
% S#S		100%	100%	92.5%	100%	96%	76%
Overall %	**60%**	**69%**	**80%**	**72%**	**76%**	**73.5%**	**70.5%**

to the number of 'same' pairs when there was no semantic relationship, but only
a phonological relationship. If 'number of syllables' is an important factor in
causing two words to be more phonologically similar to each other, then we
would expect that the percentage of 'same' pairs will be considerably higher
among malapropisms than among semantically related pairs. The results of this
count are given in Table 3.13. These numbers are to be read as follows (for
example): at age 1, there were 5 semantically-related content word lexical
substitution errors, and of these, 60% (N=3) had the same number of syllables in
target and error word.

It can be seen from this table that, for the children age 2 and older and for
the adults, the majority of errors involved two words with the same number of
syllables, regardless of semantic relatedness. However, of the 5 lexical
substitutions made by 1-year-olds, 3 contained the same number of syllables but
2 did not, which possibly supports the 'whole word representation' hypothesis
discussed in §3.4.2. These figures are compatible with the hypothesis that after
age 1, the number of syllables becomes a more robust part of lexical
representations. In this table we see the opposite pattern regarding the 3-year-
old's behavior to the one we saw with phonological errors; in phonological
errors, the 3-year-olds showed the least influence from syllables of any age from
2 higher, but here they show the highest overall figure for same number of
syllables, 80%. Since these errors involved lexical selection rather than
phonological processing, they suggest that syllables are robustly represented in
lexical representations at age 3, but that they are less important during
phonological processing at age 3, most likely due to the fact that this is the age
when internal syllable structure shows the greatest development, as I will
demonstrate below.

Another factor evident in this table is that when there is no semantic
relationship between the target and error pair, the words are far more likely to

have the same number of syllables; the children produced only one malapropism where the target and error differed as to number of syllables (36a), for a 96% same-syllable rate, compared to 68% same-syllable rate for semantically related pairs. For the adults the malapropism same-syllable rate was 76%, compared to 67.5% for semantically related pairs. Similarly, Fay & Cutler (1977), in their study of malapropisms made by adult speakers of English, found that 87% of their malapropisms but only 75% of their semantically related errors agreed in number of syllables, and argue that this is evidence that syllables are represented lexically. These figures make it very clear that having the same number of syllables is an important factor in two words being phonologically similar, and thus the general syllable configuration of a word (i.e. information about how many syllables there are, and where syllable boundaries occur) must be stored in the phonological representation of the lexical entry, at least after age 1 (note that there were no malapropisms made at age 1). The one malapropism made by the children and the few made by adults which did not have the same number of syllables had very striking similarities in several other aspects of their phonology, and very often their morphology, as illustrated in (36).

(36)   a. An: 'Mòmmy, Bòbby pùked òut his whòle **álphabet**.'
            ('alphabet' [ǽ.fə.bɛ̀t] for 'outfit' [ǽ.fìt]; AN-237(35) 4;8)
        b. AF: 'You'll hàve to come ìn with **rècitátion** equìpment.'
            ('recitation' [rɛ̀.sə.tʰéⁱ.ʃən] for 'resuscitation' [ri.sʌ̀.sə.tʰéⁱ.ʃən];
            AD-413(35))

Further evidence for the claim that at least the number of syllables is stored in lexical representations would come from 'tip of the tongue' phenomena from the children. Although I did not systematically collect data on this point, I did note in my journal that when Anna was age 4;4, for several weeks she was confusing the words 'telescope' and 'stethoscope', as well as the words 'spectacles' and 'testicles'. Elbers (1985) documents the case of a Dutch-speaking child trying to activate the word 'dolphins' [dol.féi.nən] but mistakenly substituting the word 'soldiers' [sol.dá:.tjəs] or 'orange' [o:.rá.njə]. In each case the erroneously activated word had the same number of syllables as the target word. This is more anecdotal evidence that in English (and Dutch), 'number of syllables' is represented in phonological form representations, and is an important factor involved in phonological similarity between lexical items.

3.4.4 Syllables in Word Blends
There is a final source of evidence which could, in principle, be used to further test these hypotheses regarding syllables: word blends. As mentioned above, when two lexical items are inserted into the same slot in a syntactic frame, the phonological forms of both words are sent to the 'Phonological Processes' component for processing. Since there is only one lexical slot for these two words, the phonological processor blends the two words together. Thus if we find that the division between the two words is frequently at a

syllable boundary, this would be good evidence that syllables are part of the representations being processed by the phonological component. Developmental trends in this measure could be compared to evidence from phonological errors to further assess the hypothesis outlined above regarding the development of the function of syllables. (I should note here that it is not a relevant measure to compare the number of syllables in phonological representations for the two target words in blends; this is because they nearly always have a semantic relationship, and thus their underlying phonological similarity is less important. Furthermore there would rarely be a 'malapropism' type blend to compare the semantically related pairs against.)

Unfortunately, it is not a simple matter to assess the contribution of phonological material from each word to the uttered blend. In about one-third of the children's blends and two-thirds of the adult blends there is some phonological similarity between the two target words (see Chapter 4), and often this similarity occurs in the centers of the two words, where a juncture between the two phonological representations is likely to take place. Thus it is often extremely difficult to determine exactly where the crossover between the two words is, since the words will have some phonemes in common at possible juncture points. Consider these examples:

(37)   a. B: '. . . 'cuz my [dʒǽ.pɚ] . . . the z̲i̲p̲p̲e̲r̲ came òff my bìg
            jácket.' (blend of 'jacket' [dʒǽ.kɨt] and 'zipper' [zí.pɚ];
            B-227b(38) 4;2)
       b. An: 'Hí [tʰí.gɪt].' (blend of 'Tigger' [tʰí.gɜ] and 'Piglet' [pʰí.gɪt];
            AN-6(38) 1;7)
       c. B: 'Hí [mà.θ] . . . M̲ò̲m̲m̲a̲.' (blend of 'Momma' [má.ma] and
            '(Sa)mantha' [mǽ.θʌ]; B-8(38) 1;9)

Example (37a) is one of the few unambiguous blends: there is no phonological overlap between the two targets, so that the first syllable [dʒæ] can only have come from 'jacket', and the second syllable [pɚ] is clearly from 'zipper'. However, in (37b) the two targets overlap in terms of the vowel of the first syllable and the onset of the second, so even though this could be a syllable-division error [tʰɪ./gɪt], it could also involve the onset consonant from the first syllable of 'Tigger' joining with the remainder of the word 'Piglet' [tʰ/í.gɪt], or the first syllable and onset of the second syllable of 'Tigger' joining with the rhyme of the second syllable of 'Piglet' [tʰí.g/ɪt]. In (37c), the vowel [a] comes from 'Momma' and the fricative [θ] from 'Samantha', but which word contributed the onset [m]? Even the 'minimal movement principle' often allows more than one solution, as illustrated in (38).

(38)   An: '[réʲ.pɚ].'
            (blend of 'wrapper' [rǽ.pɚ] and 'paper' [pʰéʲ.pɚ]; AN-262(38) 5;0)

The minimal movement principle could tell us that the word 'wrapper' contributed only the onset [r] and the remainder of the word came from 'paper'; but it could just as easily say that the whole word 'wrapper' is intact except for the vowel [eʲ] from 'paper'.

There is one possibility for making principled decisions about the structure of at least some types of blends. The most common pattern in unambiguous errors is, to put it in the most general terms, that the first part of one word combines with the second part of the other word, without an interleaving of segments from the two words. This would allow us to choose the [r]+[éʲ.pɚ] analysis for (38) where the word 'wrapper' only contributes the initial [r]; similarly we would choose the [ma] from 'Momma' combined with the [θʌ] from 'Samantha' analysis of (37c). But we still wouldn't be able to decide about Tigger and Piglet, since any of the three possible analyses would satisfy the criterion 'the first part of one word and the second part of the other'. Furthermore, if we regularly used this criterion to decide ambiguous cases, it could end up giving us somewhat circular results, since making this division repeatedly would reinforce the claim that this is the correct division to make. Nevertheless it has enough support to be a valuable heuristic.

I therefore have hesitantly gone through the word blend errors and classified them into four categories: 1) the crossover point between the two target words is unambiguously at a syllable boundary, as in (37a); 2) the crossover point is most likely at a syllable boundary, as other analyses would assume a misordering of elements from the two targets, as in (37c); 3) the crossover point could be a syllable, but other analyses do not violate the 'no misorderings' principle so are equally valid, as in (37b); 4) the crossover point cannot be at a syllable boundary by any analysis, as in (38). I have only looked at errors in which at least one of the target words has more than one syllable, since if they were both monosyllabic, a crossover point at a syllable boundary would not be possible (since blends always involve the same number of syllables as one of their targets). I included both content words and function words in this analysis, since they are treated the same by the 'Phonological Processes' component. And since the actual blending of phonological material is taking place at the phonological rather than lexical level, I have used the following principle regarding morphology (see §3.5.4 below for justification): single consonant regular inflectional suffixes are treated as extrasyllabic, but all other morphology is ignored in terms of assessing syllable boundaries (except compounds). Results are given in Table 3.14; the '% Possible Syllable' figure at the bottom of the table shows the percentage of eligible errors at this age that fall into the upper three categories, that is, a syllable analysis is possible.

It is difficult to interpret these numbers since one can't know how many of the 'possible' errors actually involve syllable junctures. Furthermore, the numbers in each category are so small that it would be overinterpreting them to say too much about them.   However, the figures in this table appear to be similar to those found in Table 3.12, which looked at syllables in phonological LU and telescoping errors. There are no unambiguous blend errors at age 1 involving a crossover at a syllable boundary, and only 20% of age 1 blends could

TABLE 3.14
Number of word blend errors which may involve syllables. 'Yes' = crossover is unambiguously at a syllable boundary; 'Probably' = syllable boundary is the best but not the only analysis; 'Maybe' = syllable boundary is one of several equally good analyses; 'No' = crossover cannot be at a syllable boundary.

Age:	1	2	3	4	5	Total	Adult
Yes	0	1	0	1	2	4	8
Probably	1	3	1	3	2	10	4
Maybe	1	1	0	0	1	3	3
No	8	6	3	8	4	29	34
Total N=	**10**	**11**	**4**	**12**	**9**	**46**	**49**
% Possible Syllable Analysis							
	20%	45.5%	25%	33%	55.5%	37%	30.5%

be analyzed as involving syllables, reinforcing the claim that the syllable is not an important part of lexical representation or phonological processing at this age. Involvement of syllables rises dramatically at age 2, with 45.5% of the blends possibly involving syllables. There is a dip in involvement of syllables at age 3, and then at ages 4-5 the involvement of syllables in the blend errors rises again, to a level above the adult level. However, one salient fact that falls out from this table is that at every age except age 5, the number of errors which cannot be analyzed in terms of syllable boundaries exceeds that of all errors in which a syllable boundary analysis is possible, suggesting that there may be more important structural units involved in these errors.

It is interesting to note that many of the clear cases of syllable-boundary crossovers, for both children and adults, involved compounds, as illustrated in (39a). For the adults, syllable crossover errors also included a number of cases of single syllable words blending with multi-syllable words, as in (39b). Therefore there may be some morphological influence on such crossover points, in cases where syllable boundaries coincide with morpheme boundaries. However, this did not extend to words containing derivational affixes, since derivational affixes are usually fully integrated with the word and are not coterminal with syllable boundaries, as illustrated in (39c); I will return to this claim about the phonological status of derivational affixes in §3.5.4 below.

(39)   a. An: 'Hĕre's your [bǽθ.kʰḷḁ̀θ].' (blend of 'bathrobe' [bǽθ/.roʷb] and
        'washcloth' [wáʃ./kʰḷḁθ]; AN-65(38) 2;8)
    b. AM: 'Sòme yèars [ə.bǽk], (etc.)'
        (blend of 'ago' [ə/.góʷ] and 'back' [bæk]; AD-552(38))

c. AF: ' . . . mètal [**i.rék.ʃən**] sèt, uh <u>constrúction</u> sèt.'
(blend of 'erector' [i.rék.tɚ] and 'construction' [kʰən.stɹʌ́k.ʃən];
AD-506(38)

In (39a) Anna produced a blend of 'bathrobe' and 'washcloth' which contains one monosyllabic morpheme from each of the two compounds. In (39b), the adult blended the words 'ago' and 'back', substituting the whole word 'back' for the second syllable in 'ago'. In (39c), the adult blended 'erector', which is morphologically {erect+or} with the instrumental derivational suffix, with 'construction', which is morphologically {construct+ion} with the nominalizing suffix. However, the morphemes are not coterminal with syllable boundaries, and so although this error shows a possible crossover at a syllable boundary ([i.rék/.tɚ] with [kʰən.strʌ́k./ʃən]), this crossover was not facilitated by the morphology of the words (but perhaps shows a Freudian influence).

In general, the blend data show that syllable boundaries are one possible location where elements from two different words can be joined when their phonological forms are blended together. However, the fact that syllable junctures can only account for about a third of the blends suggests that something other than syllables may be the more important factor in phonological blends. In §3.5 I will show that this factor is the internal structure of syllables.

3.4.5 Summary of Evidence Regarding Syllables

At age 1 there is little evidence that the syllable is an important unit in either the representation of words or speech production planning, as there are no phonological errors involving whole syllables, words substituted for each other are equally likely to have the same vs. different number of syllables, and lexical blends rarely involve breaks at syllable boundaries. This supports the hypothesis that words are stored in terms of segments at this age, with the linear ordering somewhat fluid; syllables are most likely simply a mechanical part of speech production itself. However, starting at age 2, there is ample evidence that syllables have become part of both lexical representations and phonological processing. At this age the children begin to produce phonological errors involving whole syllables, lexical substitutions are more likely to have the same number of syllables, especially if the words are not semantically related, and there is an increase in blend errors with possible crossover points at syllable boundaries. This development is probably due in part to the children acquiring longer words which would be too cumbersome to store and process without some linear structure, which syllable boundaries provide. It is also due in part to children paying more attention to the linear order of linguistic units in general, as evidenced by their development of syntax and morphology at this age.

Starting at age 2 and up through age 5 the children in this study began producing malapropisms, and the target/error pairs of words in malapropisms had the same number of syllables in every case but one; semantically related pairs on the other hand only had the same number of syllables in 63-73% of the errors.

Thus it is clear that from age 2 on, the number of syllables is represented in lexical phonological representations. In Table 3.12, there appears to be a drop in phonological errors involving whole syllables at age 3; but at ages 4-5 syllables again become a stable part of phonological errors, including telescopings. Similarly at age 3, the number of blend errors where a syllable could be the crossover point decreases (Table 3.14). But the age 3 lexical substitution errors show the highest consistency in terms of number of syllables at any age (Table 3.13). I have suggested that this shows that while syllables are robustly represented in phonological lexical entries at age 3, they become less available to error during phonological processing during the 3-year-old year because other units (internal syllable structure) are taking on more importance. By ages 4-5, syllables are again becoming more involved in phonological errors and blends, suggesting that the syllable-node tier is firmly in place by this time; a few later errors of syllable addition and whole-word prosody suggest that foot structure is developing during the fifth and sixth year. However, the fact that adults make many more such errors suggests that adult-like word prosody structures are not fully in place at age 5.

3.5 Internal Syllable Structure in Phonological Errors

3.5.1 Overview

In the previous section I looked at evidence for the representation of syllables as a unit of phonological organization. In §3.5 I will address the issue of the development of internal syllable structure, focussing on phonological errors. Section 3.5.2 will deal with consonant clusters, in terms of both the acquisition of clusters and the extent to which the children's errors show knowledge of allowable English clusters. Then in §3.5.3, I will look in detail at the position of source and target/error units in phonological errors, to see whether they give evidence regarding the development of internal syllable structure; I will compare a syllable-based analysis to a whole-word-based analysis, to see if there is any evidence for the claim that young children's phonological representations are governed more by whole word shape than by syllable structure. Section 3.5.4 contains a brief digression into morphology, raising the issue of whether suffixes should be considered extrasyllabic; it also compares the 'onset/rhyme' to the 'body/coda' interpretation of phonological errors. Finally, in §3.5.5 I will look at telescoping errors as a further way of testing the findings from other phonological errors regarding internal syllable structure, particularly the onset-rhyme division. In §3.6 below I will extend this inquiry to lexical substitution errors and blends.

3.5.2 Consonant Clusters

The youngest children in the study produced words which were almost entirely of the CVCV or CVC structure, with no sequences of consonants. Once they began producing sequences, for the most part these sequences were at the ends of words and consisted of one consonant followed by [ç], which, being a substitute for sibilants, they would have heard very often at the ends of words.

In fact, all three of my children produced forms for a short period of time which were designed to avoid a word-initial /sC/ cluster, by moving the /s/ to the end of the word; so, for example, 'snake' /sneᵢk/ was produced as [neᵢkç]. However, as the children began producing consonant clusters, clusters began appearing in SOTs regularly, and with only six exceptions (to be given below) they always followed the patterns currently allowed by the child's phonology.

As an example of how SOTs illustrate the child's phonological development, consider these errors from Alice.

(40)   a.   Al: 'Stòp [tə.wi̇́] . . . té̱asing.'
            (for 'stop teasing' [tàp tí.çin]; AL-4(30) 2;0.30)
       b.   Al: 'Grándma [gwè̱ᵢv] it . . . gáve!'
            (for 'Grandma gave' [gə.wǽ.mʌ geᵢv]; AL-8(13) 2;1.27)
       c.   Al: 'My [çwíp._tὶk] . . . my lípstìck.'
            (for 'lipstick' [wíp.çtὶk]; AL-20(3) 2;2.25)
       d.   Al: 'Mommy, I wànt a [pʰʒìs ʌ b_é̱d].'
            (for 'piece of bread [pʰis ʌ bʒɛd]; AL-47(3) 2;8)

At age 2;0, Alice had an across-the-board rule of no consonant clusters in onsets, as illustrated in (40a). Obstruent-obstruent clusters were avoided by deleting one segment, as in [tap] for 'stop', but obstruent-sonorant clusters were allowed as long as they were broken up by a schwa. So in this error, Alice erroneously added a (non-contextual) [w] to the onset of 'teasing', which required the schwa to also be added. During the next month she was fluctuating between producing and not producing the schwa between elements in a cluster, and so in (40b) she produced the well-known word 'Grandma' with the schwa, but the error [gweᵢv] did not require it. During this month she also produced the forms [gə.wóç] 'gross', but [kʰwíç.ti] 'Christy', with a voiced [w]; as discussed in §3.3.4 above, when children began to produce obstruent+sonorant onset clusters, the sonorant was usually not devoiced as it would be in adult productions, and was slightly longer than an adult-like sonorant, as if the child had to exaggerate its pronunciation slightly in order to produce the cluster sequence. The word 'Christy' [kʰwíç.ti] also shows that she was beginning to allow some sequences across syllable boundaries word-medially at age 2;1. Just one month later, at age 2;2.25, she was able to produce a variety of onset clusters, as well as three-consonant sequences at syllable boundaries, as shown in (40c); sonorants were still not devoiced, however. Finally, during the second half of her third year she began producing devoiced sonorants in clusters with what sounded like adult-like durations, as illustrated in (40d). These SOTs are clearly a valuable resource for observing and verifying the progress Alice was making in the representation and production of consonant clusters, alongside her other production data.

Once the children began producing adult-like clusters, they rarely produced an error which contained a sequence not allowed in adult English, unless of course it was allowed in their current phonology. (So, for example, the [dʒr] and [tʃr] clusters discussed in §3.3.5 we̱re allowed in errors.) The following six examples are the only cases I recorded in the child data which violated the child's current consonant sequence constraints; the adults produced one such violation.

(41) a. An: '[ʃpéʲ.ʃɪp].' (for 'spaceship' [spéʲ.ʃɪp]; AN-27(1) 2;1)
      b. B: 'It's [ʃlèʲpt] ĺike a kítty càt.' (for 'shaped' [ʃeʲpt]; B-91(2) 2;7)
      c. OB:'Hè's déad, 'cùz we [skm̩íʃt] hìm . . . we squíshed hìm!' (blend of 'squished' [skw̥ɪʃt] and 'smashed' [sm̩æʃt]; OC-50(38) 3;4)
      d. B: 'We jùst cĺimbed a bìg [dl:. . .ɜ́t] pìle.' (for 'dirt' [dɜt]; B-148(21) 3;8)
      e. B: 'I don' wànna [dlù] my ĺaundry.' (for 'do' [du]; B-304(2) 4;6)
      f. OB:'Anyways, *there's* a [θjù] more wáffles lèft, and I'm nòt *that* húngry.' (for 'few' [fju]; OC-167(29) 5;9)

In (41a), Anna anticipated the [ʃ] from the onset of the second syllable in 'spaceship' and substituted it for the [s] in the first syllable, producing the illegal cluster *[ʃp]. In (41b), the [l] from 'like' is anticipated and added after the onset of 'shaped', producing *[ʃl̥] (see also AD-289(31)). In (41c), the onsets [sm̩] and [skw̥] are blended into the non-English *[skm̩] sequence. The error in (41d) shows [l] from either 'climbed' or 'pile' being inserted after the [d] in 'dirt', causing the disallowed sequence *[dl]; (41e) shows a similar case. Finally, in (41f), the place of articulation feature of [f] in 'few' is changed to interdental under the influence of 'there's' and 'that', producing the illegal sequence *[θj].

I think it is extremely interesting that the clusters in these errors all follow general allowable sequences in English, in terms of major classes: *[ʃp] follows the 'sibilant+voiceless plosive' pattern, but substitutes the palato-alveolar for the alveolar fricative. The sequences *[θj] and *[ʃl̥] follow the 'fricative+ sonorant' pattern, and [ʃl̥] is in fact allowed in some loanwords, particularly Yiddish words such as 'schlepp'. The sequence *[skm̩] follows the allowed pattern '[s]+plosive+sonorant', but this particular sequence happens not to occur in English. Similarly, *[dl] follows the 'plosive+sonorant' pattern, but it so happens that the lateral cannot occur after alveolars in English. These errors are similar to those recorded by Stemberger (1989:172) from his children, such as *'b_ock the dloor' for 'block the door'. The children in my study never produced an error such as '*[dtɔg] tag' for 'dog tag', or 'snow *[pʰnænts]' for 'snow pants', or '*[lʃeʲpt] like' for 'shaped like'; in other words, they never produced a sequence which violated major class constraints on clusters. These errors make it clear that the children are not simply memorizing the clusters they hear in the input, but are developing a more abstract schema for allowable consonant clusters, which governs their lexical entries as well as what their internal monitor will allow to occur in production.

Furthermore, the children were clearly learning different constraints for consonant clusters which occurred in syllable margins (onsets, codas) compared to those allowed across syllables word-medially, and these differences were evident as early as age 2;2. For example in the target utterance in Anna's error *'[kʰwǽm.wʌ]' for 'camera' [kʰǽm.wʌ] (AN-28(2) 2;2), she shows that the sequence [m.w] can occur across syllable boundaries, but no such sequence was ever produced in a syllable onset or coda cluster. Similarly in the target utterance in her error *'[kʰwèˈm ʌ b_ǽk.b3̍d] for 'came a blackbird' [kʰèˈm ʌ bwǽk.b3̍d] (AN-34(3) 2;2), she produces a sequence of two plosives across the syllable boundary [k.b], which again was never produced tautosyllabically. This is clear evidence for the development of syllable boundaries in lexical representations, beginning at around age 2.

Focussing in on just consonant addition and omission errors which involve consonant clusters sheds additional light on the children's acquisition of phonotactic constraints. As mentioned in Chapter 2, the majority of both addition and omission errors involved consonant clusters, most often onset clusters. This was equally true for the 2-5-year-old children in my study as for the adults; not surprisingly, the 1-year-old children did not produce errors involving clusters. For the children, 67% of their phonological addition errors (including movements) involved onset clusters, and 7% involved coda clusters (N=168); for the adults the figures were 73.5% and 10% (N=49). The children's omission errors involved onset clusters in 66% of the errors and coda clusters in 6.5% (N=62); the adult figures were 45.5% and 18% (N=11). However, again these errors nearly always resulted in allowable sequences of consonants. Other than the three addition errors given in (41) above, none of the other addition errors resulted in an illegal cluster. The additions usually consisted of adding a single consonant to another single onset or coda consonant or cluster, producing a new cluster, as exemplified in (42).

(42)   a. Al: 'I have a [sn̩ò3̍] néck . . . sòre [sn̩ɛ́k] . . . '
             (for 'sore neck' [so3̍ nɛk]; AL-99a(2) & AL-99b(13) 3;2)
       b. An: 'I'm not [ín.str̩ə._dìd].'
             (for 'interested' [ín.tr̩ə.stìd], with voicing of /t/; AN-138(3) 4;0)
       c. OB: '[sìŋks] inches' (for 'six inches' [sɪks íɲ.tʃɪs]; OC-88(2) 4;1)

In (42a), Alice produces two addition errors in trying to say 'sore neck'. First the [n] is anticipated and inserted after the [s] in 'sore', and then the [s] is perseverated and inserted before the [n] in 'neck'. But in her struggles, she never produced the illegal cluster */ns/. In (42b) Anna anticipates the [s] from the onset cluster /st/ of the third syllable of 'interested', moving it to the beginning of the /tr/ cluster in the second syllable, producing the legal sequence /str/ rather than either of the other logically possible sequences, */tsr/ or */trs/; (incidentally, the second /t/ voices to a [d] in this context). In (42c) the child anticipates the nasal from 'inches' and adds it to the coda of 'six' in the only possible place, producing (with velar assimilation) [ŋks] and not */kns/ or */ksn/.

In omission errors the same principles hold. In 2-consonant clusters, if one of the consonants is omitted the other will always be a legal onset or coda consonant by definition, since only consonants which can occur as singleton onsets or codas can be involved in clusters (in English). However, what is interesting is that in the few examples of omission from 3-consonant clusters, the remaining 2-consonant cluster is always a legal sequence, as in (43).

(43)   B: 'Í want *s*ome [_tʰ3ɪŋ] . . . strìng-chèese tóo!'
(for 'string' [st3ɪŋ]; B-135(15) 3;6)

In this error, the omission causes the legal sequence /tr/, not the illegal sequence */sr/. Taken together, the addition and omission errors further support the claim that the children are learning templates for possible consonant clusters.

There are a number of potential counterexamples to this claim, i.e. cases where segments are added to onsets or codas which would cause an illegal sequence if it had occurred in a word-initial or word-final position. However, these cases all occur word-medially, and in every case the child re-syllabifies the word to avoid the illegal cluster. For example:

(44)   An: 'Mommy, whàt does my [s_ík.tɚ] sày?'
(for 'sticker' [stí.kɚ]; AN-158(14) 4;2)

In this error Anna perseverates the [t] from the first syllable of 'sticker', and adds it after the [k] in the second syllable; however, in order to avoid the illegal */kt/ onset cluster, the [k] resyllabifies into the coda of the first syllable. This resyllabification is heard as a shortening of the vowel [ɪ], and no audible release of the [k]. There were no exceptions to this process.

So why are consonant clusters the locus of so many errors? In order to answer this question we must first look at the relative frequency of substitution, addition, and omission errors in general. Recall from §2.3.3 that substitution errors far outnumber addition and omission errors, and this was explained due to their causing a smaller deformation of the overall word structure. But it is also the case that additions far outnumber omissions, and even though the word structure is deformed in both cases, in addition errors there are no missing segments for the phonological processor to try to account for (see also Hartsuiker 2002). So omissions not only cause deformation of the prosodic structure but also cause intended segments to go missing, making them the least frequent of these types of errors. However, if a phonological unit is going to be added or deleted, why does this usually involve consonant clusters?

In §3.3.2 I argued that vowels are involved in errors less often than consonants because they are more central to the syllable, i.e. they are the nucleus around which the syllable is built. We could make a similar claim here that syllables like to have onsets and codas, but exactly how many consonants occur in the onsets or codas is not nearly as important to the syllable structure as simply having these slots filled. Therefore, consonants can be added, producing new consonant clusters, or can be deleted from clusters producing new singleton onsets or codas, without causing a change in the basic onset-nucleus-coda structure. These errors do not cause major insult to the phonological structures being planned, and therefore they escape notice of the internal monitor more often than when, for example, a zero-onset gets a consonant added, or a single-consonant onset is omitted; they are certainly less drastic than errors involving the addition or deletion of a vowel or LU.

Supporting this claim is the fact that a large number of the addition or omission errors which did not involve tautosyllabic consonant clusters per se actually involved sequences across syllable boundaries, as exemplified in (44) above (an addition error involving resyllabification), and (45) below (an omission).

(45)   OB:'Yòu have the sàme kind of [béʲ_.bàɫ] . . . básebàll as mìne.'
       (for 'baseball' [béʲs.bàɫ]; OC-109(15) 4;5)

In (45), the child deletes the coda /s/ in 'baseball', which precedes another consonant in the second syllable. Thus it appears that while the most important element in a syllable is the vowel, the least important is a consonant adjacent to another consonant, in that this slot is most frequently the locus of errors which add or delete a segment. And this seems to be as true for the children as it is for the adults. This suggests that some basic knowledge of the onset-nucleus-coda structure of syllables may be in place as early as age 2, and the function of this structural information during phonological processing is similar to that of adults. However, this does not tell us much about the internal hierarchical structure of syllables, a topic to which I will now turn.

3.5.3 Phonological Errors: Evidence for Internal Syllable Structure

It is often noted (Boomer & Laver 1973, Laubstein 1987, Poulisse 1999:13) that two elements mutually involved in a phonological SOT originate from the same locus in syllables. In order to assess the validity of this claim for the children, I did a detailed analysis of the syllable position of the target/error compared to the syllable position of the source for a subset of the phonological errors in the corpus. I looked at errors involving consonants, vowels, LUs, and features, including substitutions, additions, omissions, movements, and exchanges. I excluded from this analysis errors involving prosody (lexical stress, intonation, or telescopings), metathesis (since the segments involved are located in different syllable structure positions by definition), non-contextual errors (as there is no source), and multiple errors. The following procedure was used.

First, each multisyllabic word was divided into syllables according to the principles discussed in §3.4.2 above. Second, internal syllable structure was assigned to each syllable as illustrated in (46) below. The vowel (including offglides of diphthongs) was designated as the 'nucleus (N)'. Consonants preceding and following the nucleus were designated as members of the 'onset (O)' and 'coda (D)' respectively, and slots in complex onsets and codas were numbered from the syllable margin inward. (The sequence [ju] was treated as an onset consonant+nucleus in those errors in which it patterned this way.) The nucleus and coda together were designated as the 'rhyme (R)'. The liquids /l,r/

were coded as either a nucleus or part of the onset or coda according to the principles discussed in §3.3.3. If an error involved an onset+nucleus, but not the coda, this unit was designated as the 'body (B)'. No morpheme boundaries were considered in this assignment of structure (but see §3.5.4 below).

(46)   e.g. 'strengths'

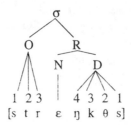

Third, all errors were classified according to the detailed taxonomy presented below. This level of detail was chosen so that these data could be compared to the findings of other corpora, both of adult English speakers and of other languages. In general, errors were included in this taxonomy if they had a single source, or in cases where there was more than one source, if all sources occurred in the same syllable-structure position. An exception to this will be given at the end of the taxonomy. Symbols used are: $=syllable boundary; C=single consonant; O=Onset; Nuc= nucleus; D=coda; R=rhyme; Syl=syllable; B=body; s=same; d=different; N=nasal; L=liquid; C̩= syllabic consonant. Since addition errors have a zero target, and omission errors have a zero error, these principles should be considered to apply to the syllable-structure slots where the zero elements occur.

$C='syllable initial single consonants': target, error, and source are syllable-initial consonants in simple onsets.
(47)   Al: 'Ràffi sìng my f àvorite [fáŋ] . . . sóng!' (for 'song' [saŋ]; the single onset consonant [f] is perseverated from either 'Raffi' [ræ.fi] or 'favorite' [féⁱv.ɟɪt], and is substituted for the single onset consonant [s] in 'song'; Al-38(12) 2;7)

Os='same onset position': target, error, and source involve consonants in the same location in syllable onsets where one or both contain complex onsets.
(48)   a. B: 'I wànt clèan [pʰlǽnts] . . . pánts.'
          (for 'pants' [pʰænts]; the [l] in onset slot #2 of 'clean' perseverates and is added into the second onset slot of 'pants', forming a new complex onset; B-64(13) 2;5)
        b. Al: 'I see [fɪn.tʰʌ.ki] Frìed Chícken.' (for 'Kentucky' [kʰɪn.tʰʌ.ki]; the [f] from the first onset slot of the complex onset /fr/ in 'Fried' is anticipated and substituted for for the single-onset consonant /k/ in onset slot #1 of 'Kentucky'; AL-176(1) 3;10)

Nuc='two nucleus positions': target and/or error and source are both syllable nuclei. (The addition error type in (49b) was exclusively produced by adults; see §2.2.1.)

(49) a. Al: 'Bàby [bʌ.wʌ́.gu] . . . Bàby Belúga òver thère.'
(for 'Beluga' [bʌ.wú.gʌ]; the two syllable nuclei [u] and [ʌ] in 'Beluga' exchange positions; AL-24(26) 2;4)

   b. AM: ' . . . is nót to [sìm.pə.li] elíminàte . . .'
(for 'simply eliminate' [sím.pli ɨ.lí.mə.nèɨt]; the vowel [ə] is anticipated from 'eliminate' and added in a position where there was no nucleus before, such that the error creates a new syllable; AD-34(6.5))

C\$='syllable final single consonants': target, error, and source are syllable-final consonants in simple codas.

(50) An: 'Are yòu gonna [brʌθ] your téeth?'
(for 'brush' [brʌʃ]; the single coda consonant [θ] from 'teeth' is anticipated and substituted for the single coda consonant [ʃ] in 'brush'; AN-92(1) 2;11)

Rs='rhyme, same unit': target, error, and source are complete rhymes.

(51) B: That [bàɨd] . . . that bùs wàs the ríde.'
(for 'bus' [bʌs]; the rhyme [aɨd] from 'ride' is anticipated and substituted for the rhyme [ʌs] in 'bus'; B-573(11) 5;11)

Syl='syllables': target and source are complete syllables (but not morphemes).

(52) B: That's a [dʌ.k3]-dècker bús right thère!' (for 'double-decker' [dʌ.bu.dɛ́.k3]; the syllable [k3] from 'decker' is anticipated and substituted for the syllable [bu] in 'double; B-52(6) 2;4)

Ds='coda, same position': target, error, and source are consonants in the same location in codas, where one or both are complex.

(53) An: 'I can't [wèɨst] . . . I can't wàit to táste it.' (for 'wait' [weɨt]; the [s] in coda slot #2 of 'taste' [tʰeɨst] is anticipated and added to coda slot #2 after the vowel but before the [t] in 'wait', causing the coda of 'wait' to become complex; AN-171(8) 4;4)

C̦='syllabic consonant': target, error, and source are all syllabic liquids (no errors involving syllabic nasals were collected). See §3.3.3 for phonetic notation of liquids.

(54) An: 'In the mìddle of the [pʰéʲ.pɬ].' (for 'paper' [pʰéʲ.pr̩]; the syllabic lateral [ɬ] is perseverated from 'middle' [mí.dɬ] and substituted for the syllabic rhotic [r̩] in 'paper' [pʰéʲ.pr̩]; AN-201(12) 4;5)

R$O='rhyme plus following onset': both target and source contain at least two syllables, and the rhyme and onset from adjacent syllables in the source are substituted for the rhyme and onset of adjacent syllables in the target (as in 55a), or a rhyme-onset sequence is added to the target, as in (55b).

(55) a. Al: 'I wànna tèll [mʌ́m.θi] sόmething.' (for 'Mommy something' [má.mi sʌ́m.θɪŋ]; the rhyme-onset sequence [ʌm.θ] from 'something' [sʌ́m.θɪŋ] is substituted for the rhyme-onset sequence [a.m] in 'Mommy' [má.mi]; AL-162(6) 3;8)

      b. AF: '[dʒɚ.nɪ.kəɫ] àrtícle.' (for 'journal' [dʒɚ.nəɫ]; the rhyme-onset sequence [ɪ.k] is anticipated from the word 'article' [ár.rɪ.kəɫ] and added in the middle of the word 'journal' [dʒɚ.nəɫ] after the segment [n], creating a new syllable, with resyllabification of segments in the target word; AD-32(6.5))

B='Body': an onset+nucleus from one syllable substitutes for some appropriate unit from another syllable (a syllable, another body, or a nucleus), where in at least one of the syllables a coda is stranded.

(56) B: 'I'll be [fɚ.rɪŋ] . . . I'll be stàrting fírst gráde.' (for 'starting first' [stár.rɪŋ fɚst]; the body [fɚ] from 'first' is anticipated and substituted for the whole syllable [star] in 'starting'; B-490(11) 5;4)

Od='onset, different position': target and/or source are consonants in different locations in complex syllable onsets as in (57a), or involve a single-consonant onset being replaced by a complex onset (or vice versa) as in (57b).

(57) a. B: 'I don't ɫike another [blὲ] . . . bɹeakfast.' (for 'breakfast' [bɹ̰ék.fəst]; the [l] from onset slot #1 in 'like' is perseverated and substituted for the [ɹ̰] in onset slot #2 in 'breakfast'; B-166(12) 3;9)

      b. M: 'Yòu have lόts of Grèat Gràndmas.' Al: 'Yèah, an' [gɹ̰àts] . . . lòts a Grèat Grándpas, tόo.' (for 'lots' [lats]; the consonant cluster [gɹ̰] substitutes for the single consonant [l] in 'lots'; AL-92(24) 3;1)

Dd='coda, different position': The target and/or source are consonants in different locations in codas where at least one coda is complex. (Note that the plural morpheme is counted as part of the coda in this error; I will return to this issue below.)

(58) An: 'Twò càrs and twò [bárɫz].' (for 'balls' [baɫz]; [r] is perseverated from coda slot #2 of 'cars' [kʰarz] and added to coda slot #3 of 'balls' [baɫz] to produce new sequence [rɫz]; AN-43(13) 2;4)

$C-C$='syllable initial and syllable final single consonants': target/error and source involve a syllable-initial single consonant and a syllable-final single consonant.

(59)   An: 'Dòn't tòuch my [mæ̀.gɪt] swórd!'
        (for 'magic' [mǽ.dʒɪk]; feature of place reversed between onset
        [dʒ] (palatal) vs. coda [k] (velar), with deaffrication of [dʒ], causing
        [dʒ]-->[g] and [k]-->[t]; AN-74(29) 2;10)

Od-Dd='onset vs. coda, different positions': target and source involve elements
from an onset and a coda, at least one of which is complex.

(60)   Al: 'It's vèry sóft. Ìsn't it [fà] . . . sòft to yóu?'
        (for 'soft' [saft]; the [f] from the complex coda of 'soft' [ft$] is
        anticipated or perseverated and substituted for the single
        consonant onset [s] of 'soft'; AL-113(20) 3;3)

V{N,L}='vowel plus a nasal or liquid': a vowel plus a nasal or liquid following
the vowel is the error/target unit or the source, stranding the remainder of the
onset and/or coda in at least one of the words.

(61)   An: '[wɪ́ŋk.bɪ̀ŋtʃ].' (for 'work-bench' [wɚ́k.bɪ̀ŋtʃ]; the sequence [ɪŋ],
        which is the nucleus and coda #2 consonant of the word 'bench'
        [bɪŋtʃ] is anticipated and substituted for the vowel [ɚ] of 'work';
        the onset and coda #1 consonants of 'bench' are not included in the
        error; AN-87(6) 2;11)

[+/-syllabic]=the target/error and source are a syllabic and a non-syllabic version
of the liquids /l,r/.

(62)   B: 'Mommy, on "[dʌ́.br̩]". . . . on "Dóuble-Dàre" làst tìme?'
        (for 'Double-Dare' [dʌ́.bl̩.dèr]; the non-syllabic consonant [r] is
        anticipated from 'Dare', and substituted for the syllabic [l̩] in
        'Double', and then becomes syllabic [r̩]; B-464(7) 5;2)

Other=other combinations of units not classifiable by the above categories.

(63)   'B: 'I wànt some ápplejuice in this "Nèw Kìds on the B*lòck*" [kʰl̩àp]
        . . . cùp.' (for 'cup' [kʰʌp]; the second onset consonant and nucleus
        [la] from 'block' [blak] is perseverated and substituted for the
        nucleus of 'cup' [ʌ]; B-186(18) 4;1)

As indicated above, the subset of phonological errors were classified
according to this system, if there was an unambiguous source or if all sources
originated from the same structure. The one exception was instances where there
were two sources which were both in onsets or both in codas, but one was
complex and the other was not. It was important to include these errors in the
count, because they represented clear cases of 'onset' or 'coda' errors. In such
cases I classified the error according to the lower-ranked classification, so as not
to bias my decision-making process towards the more structurally similar
measures. For example:

(64)   B: '[fèⁱt] for my friénd.' (for 'wait' [weⁱt]; B-415(1) 4;11)

In this error, the two possible sources are 'for' [for] and 'friend' [fɹɪnd]. If 'for' were the source, this error would be classified as '$C' since both 'for' and 'wait' have simple onsets. But if 'friend' were the source, this error would be classified as 'Os', since 'friend' has a complex onset, but the /f/ is the first element so moves into the first onset slot of 'wait'. Therefore this error was classified as 'Os', since this reflects a slight difference in onsets of target and source, whereas the '$C' classification assumes the target and source units are identical. In this case, this is undoubtedly the correct classification, since both 'wait' and 'friend' are stressed, and, as discussed in §3.7.2 below, errors usually occur between words with the same stress level. This same rationale was used to classify errors as 'Ds' rather than 'C$', and so on.

The results of this classification are given in Table 3.15, and the pattern of results in this table is quite clear. At every age the children's errors showed organization in terms of syllable structure. Overall 72% of their errors involved units in identical positions in syllables, and 14.5% involved units in analogous positions (i.e. both onsets or both codas), for a total of 86.5% errors which honor syllable structure position. These results are very similar to those found for the adults in my study: 72% same unit, 16% analogous unit, for a total of 88% honoring syllable structure. Furthermore, for both the children and adults, approximately half of the errors involving an onset and a coda were within-word errors where the onset and coda of the same syllable interacted with each other, as in (59) above; so when the errors violated syllable structure position, it was often due to the physical proximity of the two consonants involved.

Looking at this table in terms of developmental trends, one point is that the 1-year-old errors almost entirely involved single consonants or vowels. In general these errors honored syllable-structure position, although 11% of the errors involved an onset with a coda consonant (N=3). However, this cannot be taken as convincing evidence for internal hierarchical structure, since it simply shows that consonants at the beginnings of syllables, or possibly words, are more likely to interact with each other than with other consonants, and likewise consonants at the ends of syllables or words will interact with others in the same position. Vowels are more likely to substitute for vowels, for phonetic and weight reasons. In order to verify internal syllable structure, errors involving rhymes or whole consonant clusters must be found, and it can be seen that these begin to occur at age 2. In fact the first unambiguous rhyme errors started showing up at age 2;6 (see AL-32(28) 2;6), and rhyme errors were frequent after this age. Below I will look at telescoping and blend errors for more evidence regarding internal syllable structure, but these phonological errors suggest that internal syllable structure begins to be represented in phonological representations at around age 2;6. There are no clear developmental trends in this table from age 2-5, in that the percentage of phonological errors in which the target/error and source come from different syllable structure positions remains low at all ages, in the 12.5%-15.5% range.

TABLE 3.15

Syllable position of target/error and source in phonological errors, by age. See text for explanation of headings. Percentage is percent at this age of this error class.

Age:	1	2	3	4	5	Total	Adult
Identical Units							
$C	14	50	39	78	46	227	56
Os	0	28	28	43	21	120	47
Nuc	4	17	23	26	14	84	36
C$	3	9	5	14	9	40	12
Rs	0	3	4	2	3	12	9
Syll	0	2	0	1	2	5	9
Ds	0	0	0	1	3	4	3
C	0	0	0	1	3	4	2
R$O	0	1	1	1	1	4	4
B	0	0	0	0	1	1	4
N =	21	110	100	167	103	501	182
%	78%	75%	71.5%	71%	69%	72%	72%
Same Unit, Different Position							
Od	2	16	21	24	21	84	32
Dd	1	2	1	8	6	18	8
N =	3	18	22	32	27	102	40
%	11%	12.5%	15.5%	13.5%	18%	14.5%	16%
Different Units							
$C-C$	3	9	11	16	7	46	8
Od-Dd	0	4	5	10	5	24	5
V{N,L}	0	2	0	3	4	9	10
[+/- syll]	0	1	0	3	3	7	1
Other	0	2	2	4	1	9	7
N =	3	18	18	36	20	95	31
%	11%	12.5%	13%	15.5%	13%	13.5%	12%
Total N=	27	146	140	235	150	698	253

However, this brings up an important issue. If young children's phonological representations for words are more word-based than syllable-based, then we should expect that an analysis of the similarity of location based on whole-word position rather than syllable structure position would yield similar figures for consistency of location of target/error and source. Meyer (1992) in fact hypothesized that adult errors are also more word-based than syllable-based, although she presents no data to support this claim (but see Shattuck-Hufnagel 1987). However, this is a somewhat difficult calculation to make, since it is uncommon for two words mutually involved in a phonological error to have identical word shapes. In order to test this hypothesis, I performed a different categorization on a subset of the phonological errors, comparing the relative similarity of location of target/error and source in terms of word-shape vs. syllable-structure.

The subset of errors excluded all within-word errors, since the units involved in within-word errors are in different locations in the word by definition. I further excluded the feature errors, as well as the prosodic, metathesis, non-contextual, and multiple errors excluded above. This left all of the contextual between-word single consonant, single vowel, and LU substitutions, additions, omissions, movements, and exchanges. Out of these I only classified those errors which had a single unambiguous source, or more than one source each of which gave the same analysis in terms of syllable structure and in terms of wordshape. Furthermore I only analyzed errors in which I could make an unambiguous decision on both wordshape and syllable structure, as there were some errors where only one or the other was unambiguous. This seemed like the most fair set to compare, since it would be the same set of errors being compared on the two measures, and there are clear instances in these errors where wordshape is maintained but syllable-structure violated, and vice versa; examples will be given below.

I then categorized each of these errors as to whether or not the position of target/error and source units was the same or different in the words involved. Because of the difficulty of making this judgment, I was somewhat generous in my analysis. For consonant errors, target and error word position was classified as being the 'same' if both target/error and source were single consonants or consonant clusters which occurred in onsets or codas in identical positions in the words (i.e. word-initial, at the end of the first syllable, word final, etc.). Vowel and rhyme errors were counted as the same if the units were in the same syllable of the words and had the same stress; for errors where single syllable words interacted with polysyllabic words, the single syllable words were taken to be 'the same' as the first (usually stressed) syllable in the longer word. Vowel errors were considered to have the same word position if their syllables were both of the shape #CV(C), but not if one of them was #V(C), since in one case the vowel was word-second, but in the other it was word-initial. While this determination was somewhat subjective, the examples in Table 3.16 should help clarify the criteria used. Because of the findings regarding single-consonant suffixes discussed below (in §3.5.4), I treated single-consonant inflectional suffixes as extrasyllabic in analyzing codas, in both the word-based and syllable-based analysis.

All of these errors were also re-classified in terms of the similarity of syllable-structure position for the target/error and source, according to the measures discussed above, with single-consonant inflectional affixes as extrasyllabic (as will be justified in §3.5.4 below). There were three main types

TABLE 3.16
Examples of errors classified as 'Same' or 'Different' in terms of position in the whole word.

Same

1. OG: '[hù?] *h*árd!' (for 'too' [tʰu]; single onset [h] in single syllable word 'hard' anticipated and substituted for single onset [tʰ] in single syllable word 'too'; OC-16(1) 2;3)

2. B: 'I wànt my [blíg] blànket.' (second onset consonant [l] anticipated from first syllable of 'blanket', inserted into identical location in 'big'; B-54(2) 2;5)

3. Al: 'Įce, Mòmma! [áʲ_, mà.maç]!' (for 'Ice, Momma' [aʲç, ma.ma]; [ç] moved from word-final coda of first word to word-final coda of second word; AL-3(14) 2;0)

4. Al: 'Dàdd*y* fìx tápe-[kʰòʒ.di] . . . uh . . . 'còrd*er*.' (for '(re)corder' [kʰóʒ.dʒ]; unstressed word-final vowel [i] perseverated and substituted for unstressed word-final vowel [ʒ]; Al-17(16) 2;2)

5. B: 'I wànt some ápplejuice in this "Nèw Kìds on the B*lò*ck" [kʰlàp] . . . cup.' (for 'Block cup' [blak kʰʌp]; second element of the onset cluster plus the nucleus of 'block' [la] substituted for the nucleus of 'cup' [ʌ]; 'same' because they both follow a single onset consonant and precede a single coda consonant; B-186(18) 4;1)

Different

6. B: 'Yeah, [tʃèʲm] . . . sàme téac*h*ers.' ([tʃ] anticipated from onset of unstressed second syllable of 'teachers' [tʰí.tʃʒ-z], substituted for word-initial [s] in stressed word 'same'; B-571(20) 5;10)

7. B: 'I don't *l*íke another [blè] . . . I don't líke another brèakfast.' (for 'breakfast' [bʒék.fəst]; single onset [l] from 'like' is perseverated and substituted for the [ʒ] in the the second onset slot of the first syllable of 'breakfast'; B-166(12) 3;9)

8. Al: 'When i*t*'s a réd lìgh*t*, we [s_áp] . . . stóp!' ([t] in onset cluster of 'stop' [stap] is deleted in dissimilation from coda [t]'s in 'it's' and 'light'; AL-208(15) 4;2)

9. B: 'That's a? umbrèlla with Bíg-Bìrd ùnder it, èating [tʃí.koʷn], and macaròni and chéese, and bróccoli.' (for 'chicken' [tʃí.kən]; [oʷ] anticipated from medial stressed syllable in 'macaroni', and substituted for unstressed [ə] in word-final syllable in 'chicken'; B-144(5) 3;8)

10. B: 'And hè was a [bjù.tɨ.fʒ-] . . . bútterfly.' (for 'beautiful' [bjú.tɨ.fʉɫ]; rhyme [ʒ-] anticipated from middle syllable of 'butterfly', substituted for rhyme [ʉɫ] of last syllable of 'beautiful'; B-540(6) 5;7)

of errors in which the syllable-based and word-based analysis differed, all illustrated in Table 3.16. In errors such as Example 6 in this table, a single onset consonant from the middle of one word ('tea*ch*ers') is substituted for a single onset consonant at the beginning of another word ('s̲ame'); this type of error is very common, and can also involve word-initial sources with word-medial targets. In a syllable-based analysis this is classified as '$C', meaning that both units involved in the error are single consonant onsets, but in a word-based analysis this is classified as 'Different' since the source is a word-medial consonant, but the target/error is word-initial (or vice versa). The error in Example 7 is a case where the single onset consonant of one word ('*l*ike') is substituted for the second consonant in an onset ('b̲reakfast'). In a syllable-based analysis this is classified as 'Od' meaning both target and source come from onsets, but again it is classified as 'different' in a word-based analysis, since the source segment is word-initial but the target/error is word-second. On the other hand, errors involving LUs often show more word-based similarity than syllable-structure similarity, as illustrated in Example 5. In this case the error unit is the second element of the onset cluster plus the nucleus of 'b*lo*ck' [la] substituting for the nucleus of 'c*u*p' [ʌ]. On the syllable-based analysis this is classified as 'other', but on the word-based analysis it is classified as 'Same', since the error unit occurs in the same position in the word, after the first onset consonant and before the single coda consonant.

The results of this count are given in Table 3.17. In this table I have given the number of errors which are counted as involving the same 'S' vs. different 'D' position in words, compared to 'S' vs. 'D' position in syllables, by age. Errors are considered to involve the 'same' positions in syllables if the mutually involved units both occur in onsets, codas, nuclei, rhymes, or syllables (i.e. everything in the upper two-thirds of Table 3.15); they are considered different if they fall into the 'different units' classifications in Table 3.15. Errors are considered to involve the 'same' positions in words if they follow the patterns described in the upper half of Table 3.16. I have divided the 1-2-year-old errors into '1-2a' (child is in the 1- or 2-word stage) vs. '1-2b' (child is in the 3+word stage), to see if the onset of syntax has any relationship with the word vs. syllable basis of phonological errors. The results are presented in terms of errors involving single consonants, single vowels, and LUs separately.

The most obvious point of this table is that for this subset of errors, both whole-word structure and syllable structure predict the majority of error locations. Furthermore, the children's figures and the adult figures are very similar, with the younger children (ages 1-3) showing slightly more overall consistency than the older children and adults, possibly because the younger children have a smaller repertoire of word and syllable structures. However, this table also strongly suggests that syllable structure position is more important than word position overall. At every age except age 1-2a, the figure for percentage of errors which honor syllable structure is at least 10 points higher than the word-structure figures, and in fact the differences increases steadily over the years, from 7% at age 1, to 15% at age 5, which is nearly identical to the

TABLE 3.17

Number of between-word phonological errors at each age where target/error and source show same vs. different word structure relationship, compared to same vs. different syllable-structure relationship. 'SCE'= single consonant errors; 'SVE' = single vowel errors; 'FE' = feature errors; 'LUE'= larger unit errors.

Age:	1-2a		1-2b		3		4		5		Total		Adult	
Word-Based Analysis														
	S	D	S	D	S	D	S	D	S	D	S	D	S	D
SCE	9	1	58	20	52	13	84	30	53	23	256	87	81	28
SVE	3	1	12	2	15	2	12	8	6	2	48	15	23	6
LUE	0	0	11	4	11	0	19	1	14	3	55	8	44	13
N=	**12**	**2**	**81**	**26**	**78**	**15**	**115**	**39**	**73**	**28**	**359**	**110**	**148**	**47**
%	86%	14%	76%	24%	84%	16%	75%	25%	72%	28%	77%	23%	76%	24%
Syllable-Based Analysis														
	S	D	S	D	S	D	S	D	S	D	S	D	S	D
SCE	9	1	69	9	61	4	101	13	68	8	308	35	101	8
SVE	4	0	14	0	17	0	19	1	8	0	62	1	29	0
LUE	0	0	11	4	10	1	16	4	12	5	49	14	45	12
N=	**13**	**1**	**94**	**13**	**88**	**5**	**136**	**18**	**88**	**13**	**419**	**50**	**175**	**20**
%	93%	7%	88%	12%	95%	5%	88%	12%	87%	13%	89%	11%	90%	10%

adults' 14%. The discrepancy between wordshape vs. syllable structure consistency is greatest for consonant and vowel errors, but for LU errors the wordshape analysis shows slightly more consistency. And, one should not forget that these figures include only the between-word errors. If within-word errors were included in the count, then the overall percentage of phonological errors which honor wordshape location would drop considerably, while the syllable-structure figures would not be as greatly affected. For the subset of errors analyzed in Table 3.17, if within-word errors are included, the percentage of errors which honor wordshape is reduced to between 55.5-63.5% for the children (mean 57%), and 65.5% for the adults (see Jaeger (to appear) for details). Thus these figures support the claim that phonological errors are sensitive to syllable structure position rather than whole-word position.

However, there is something misleading about the figures in Table 3.17 for the children in the 1-2a age group: since there are only 14 errors in this group, a difference of one error makes a large percentage difference. A look at the actual numbers shows that in fact the wordshape numbers and syllable-structure numbers are identical with one exception; there is a single vowel error which is counted as different in terms of wordshape but the same on the syllable measure.

This means that syllable structure is not necessarily an important part of the phonological representations of words when children are in the 1- and 2-word stages, and supports the hypothesis that words may be represented and possibly processed in a somewhat more holistic way during these stages. However once children begin producing 3+word sentences, and thus the syntagmatic ordering of elements becomes crucial, the differences between the influence of wordshape and syllable structure begin to become larger, suggesting that this shift to syntagmatic processing is related to the shift to internal syllable structure organization. And the percentage of errors which honor the same internal syllable structure is the highest at age 3 (95%), again reinforcing the claim that the greatest amount of development of internal syllable structure is going on during this year.

3.5.4 Comparison to Laubstein (1987): Word vs. Morpheme; Body vs. Rhyme

In Jaeger (to appear) I present a detailed comparison of my findings to those of Laubstein (1987), who analyzed a corpus of 559 adult phonological errors in terms of syllable structure. While I will not repeat the entire analysis here, there are two important points relevant to this current discussion which I would like to summarize in this section.

First, Laubstein found a majority of errors which honored syllable structure position, with 88% of her adult errors occurring in the same syllable position. However, when she looked further into her adult errors which violated syllable structure, she found that using the word as the domain for syllable structure analysis had allowed for many of the structural mismatches. She re-analyzed her data using roots+affixes as the domain of analysis (i.e. root-final consonants were always considered codas), and found that using this measure and excluding all within-word errors, 95% of the adult errors honored syllable structure.

I similarly re-analyzed my data, but found somewhat different results. In order to perform this analysis, I looked at the same set of errors as in Table 3.15, i.e. contextual phonological errors with identifiable sources, excluding metathesis, multiple, and prosodic errors. Deciding on morpheme boundaries in the children's utterances was somewhat problematic, but I followed the following procedure (see Chapter 6 for more details). First, I placed a morpheme boundary between every root and inflectional suffix, for the children's utterances after age 2;2 and for all the adult utterances (see Chapter 6 for a definition of 'inflectional'). For the children's data, the only derivational affixes I considered in this re-analysis were {-ie/y} as a diminutive or adjectival suffix, and {-er/or} as agentive or instrumental, since these are the suffixes which showed some signs of being productive (Jaeger 1986). I made decisions about including these root+suffix boundaries in the analysis for the children, based on whether or not I thought they also knew the root without the suffix; so for example, I counted the [-i] at the end of 'Bobby' (AL-39(18) 2;7) as a suffix since the children also knew the name 'Bob', but I considered 'Bretty' (AN-135(14) 3;11) monomorphemic since the child in question was never called 'Bret'. Similarly the {-er} on 'story-teller' (B-480(8) 5;3) was considered a suffix, since Bobby knew the verb 'tell' and realized that 'tell' and 'teller' were conceptually related. But the {-er} on 'doubler' in the expression 'diaper-doubler' (B-66(2) 2;5) was not counted as a suffix, since at the age of 2;5 he knew the word 'double' only in two fixed expressions, 'diaper-doubler' and 'double-decker bus', and showed no evidence having linked the words in these expressions conceptually or lexically. For the adult errors I included a broader range of derivational affixes in the count. Because these designations were somewhat subjective, I have marked in the data section of the book all and only the affixes which were considered in this reanalysis.   (That is, if there is an affix on a targt/error/source word in the data, but the analysis of syllable structure location would be the same regardless of whether the syllable boundary were adjusted to reflect the morpheme boundary, I did not mark this affix off with parentheses in the data entry.)

After doing this assignment of structure based on root+syllable boundaries, I found 40 cases in the child data and 21 in the adult data where the word-based analysis and the root-based analysis differed from each other in terms of the syllable-structure category into which the error fell. For each error I determined whether the analysis based on the phonological word vs. that based on morphemes showed the syllable structure relationship between target/error and source to be more vs. less similar. For example:

(65) a. Al: ' . . . some [fí.r(i)] wàter.' (for 'fizzy' [fí.z(i)]; AL-194(7) 3;11)
     b. Al: ' . . . my [dǽn.ʃ(ɪŋ)] shòes. . .'
        (for 'dancing' [dǽn.s(ɪŋ)]; AL-130(1) 3;4)
     c. Al: 'I'm [tà.ʃ(ɪŋ)] the trásh òut.'
        (for 'tossing' [tʰá.s(ɪŋ)]; AL-164(1) 3;9)
     d. B: ' . . . [frǽŋ.kən.staᶦd(z)] . . . Frànkenstein̲'s Brìde.'
        (for 'Frankenstein's' [frǽŋ.kən.staᶦn(z)]; B-381(7) 4;10)

In (65a), by the word-based analysis, the onset consonant of the second syllable of 'water' [wá.rɚ] is anticipated and substituted for the onset consonant of the second syllable of 'fizzy', which is an error involving two simple onsets. However, if the root+suffix analysis is performed on 'fizz' plus the derivational suffix {-y}, as [fɪz.(i)], this becomes an error involving an onset with a coda consonant, which is a more complex relationship.   Similarly, in (65b), the word-based analysis shows this to be a simple onset substitution error, whereas the morpheme-based analysis with the participial suffix {-ing} separated from the root [dǽns.(ɪŋ) ʃuz] would be analyzed as an error involving an onset and coda. On the other hand, in (65c), the word-based analysis classifies this as the coda consonant from 'trash' [tɹǽʃ] substituting for the onset consonant of the second syllable of 'tossing', whereas the root+suffix analysis, which separates out the progressive {-ing} suffix, categorizes it as an error involving two codas, a simpler analysis: [tʰas.(ɪŋ) tɹǽʃ]. Finally, in (65d), the word-based analysis causes this error to be classified as 'Dd', since it is a single coda consonant substituting for the penultimate coda consonant in 'Frankenstein's'; however, if

TABLE 3.18
Number of errors in which the syllable structure relationship between
target/error and source are 'more similar' (M) when the root is taken as the
domain of syllabification, compared to the number of errors in which this
causes a greater difference, i.e. 'less similar' (L).

Age:	1		2		3		4		5		Total		Adult	

Derivational Morphemes

	M	L	M	L	M	L	M	L	M	L	M	L	M	L
[+syllabic]	0	0	2	1	0	3	0	3	2	4	4	11	1	3

Participial Suffixes

	M	L	M	L	M	L	M	L	M	L	M	L	M	L
[+syllabic]	0	0	0	0	0	2	0	1	0	0	0	3	1	1
[-syllabic]	0	0	0	0	0	0	0	0	0	0	0	0	1	0

Inflectional Suffixes

	M	L	M	L	M	L	M	L	M	L	M	L	M	L
[+syllabic]	0	0	1	2	2	0	2	2	1	0	6	4	4	2
[-syllabic]	0	0	2	0	2	0	3	0	5	0	12	0	8	0

the possessive suffix {-s} is treated as extrasyllabic, this is a substitution of one simple coda consonant for another. In performing this analysis I categorized the suffixes involved as being derivational, participial, or inflectional (see Chapter 6 for definitions), and as being syllabic or non-syllabic. The results of this count are shown in Table 3.18. (I included both between-word and within-word errors in this count, because I found no differences in their behavior in this analysis.)

It is apparent from this table that both the factors of morpheme type (derivational vs. inflectional) and syllabicity have some effect on which of the two analysis types yields the simpler structural relationship. For derivational morphemes, including the participial forms, the word-based analysis is usually the simpler; for the children, 83% (14 out of 18) of these errors show more structural consistency in the word-based than the morpheme-based analysis. The figures for the adults are not quite as clear: 57% (4 out of 7) are simpler in the word-based analysis. The opposite holds true of the inflectional morphemes; of 22 child errors involving inflectional suffixes, the morpheme-based analysis yields the simpler relationship in 18 (82%) cases; for the adults the figure is 86% (12 out of 14). For both children and adults, errors involving single consonant inflectional suffixes are simpler on the morpheme-based account in 100% of the cases. An analysis based purely on syllabicity doesn't account for the data as well: in the children's data 64% (18 out of 28) of the errors involving a syllabic suffix show a simpler relationship on the word-based analysis, whereas

100% of the non-syllabic suffixes show the simpler relationship with the root-based analysis. The figures are similar for adults: 50% syllabic suffixes fare better with the word-based analysis, and again 100% of the non-syllabic suffixes favor the root-based. So while both of these factors seem to affect the errors, the morpheme type analysis (derivational vs. inflectional) explains the distribution of the differences better than does the analysis in terms of pure syllabicity.

These findings fit well with the hypothesis that derived words are stored whole in the lexicon, perhaps with some information regarding their morphological make-up also in their formal representations. However, regular inflectional suffixes are not stored with individual lexical items, but are concatenated on-line with the stems in locations where the morphosyntax requires them. Because they are affiliated with the syntax of the phrase, they do not become as closely integrated with the phonological word as derivational suffixes, and therefore behave like an 'appendix' (Halle & Vergnaud 1987), i.e. extrasyllabic in the errors; this is particularly true of single-consonant morphemes, but also affects syllabic inflectional suffixes. (Laubstein also found evidence that single-consonant morphemes are extrasyllabic for adults.) This finding allows an account of several errors involving inflectional affixes which appear to be very strange on the whole-word analysis, but become extremely simple on the morphological analysis.

(66)   a. M: 'Whàt do cảts dó all dày?'
        B: 'Eàt [mǽt].'
        M: 'Eàt whát?'
        B: 'Eàt míce.' (for 'mice' [maʲs]; B-518(18) 5;5)
      b. AM: 'Later on she [tʃɔmps sảʲt.ski] and Blóomfield.'
          (for 'cites Chomsky' [saʲt(s) tʃɔmp.ski]; AD-261(28))

In the word-based analysis of (66a), the nucleus and post-vocalic obstruent [æt] of the rhyme of 'cats' [kʰæts] is perseverated and substituted for the entire rhyme of 'mice' [maʲs], causing the error to be classified as 'other'. However, if the {-s} plural morpheme in 'cats' is treated as extrasyllabic, this error is a simple rhyme substitution (assuming that the irregular plural is stored whole in the form lexicon); i.e. [kʰæt(s)] vs. [maʲs]. Similarly, in (66b), if the word 'cites' is analyzed in terms of the whole phonological word, then this error is classified as 'other' (onset+nucleus+first element of coda substitutes for a syllable); however if the inflectional 3rd sg. present tense suffix {-s} at the end of 'cite(s)' is taken as extrasyllabic, then this is a simple syllable exchange.

Thus my findings correspond with Laubstein's only for the inflectional suffixes, and most consistently for the single-consonant suffixes. If all of these single-consonant suffix errors are reanalyzed in terms of morphological boundaries, then for the children there are 12 errors which can be assigned a simpler syllable-structure analysis than shown in Table 3.15, and 8 for the adults; this includes moving some errors from the 'other' or unclassifiable into a structured classification. However, this upgrading of a few errors brings the overall total of errors which involve the same syllable position to 87% for the children, and 90% for adults, which is only marginally different from the 86.5% and 88% in Table 3.15. This is still fewer than the 95% Laubstein found for adult errors. The reason for this is not clear, but may be due in part to the fact that my data include within-word errors, which in many cases involve onsets and codas in the same word.

There are three other findings from my data relevant to the general point about the differences between wordshape analyses vs. morphological analyses of phonological errors which I will briefly mention here. First, I did not include in my count in Table 3.18, errors such as the one in (67) where a consonant is added into an onset before a suffix, causing resyllabification of former onset consonants (as discussed in §3.5.2 above).

(67)   An: 'Hè's [stáp.tɪŋ] . . . stópping.'
        (for 'stopping' [stá.p(ɪŋ)]; AN-107(13) 3;3)

I excluded this type of error because in every case the root+suffix analysis was the better one in that it avoided resyllabification, so it didn't seem to be sensitive to the status of the suffix. In my child data there are 3 such errors involving derivational suffixes and 2 inflectional; in the adult data there are one each of inflectional and derivational.

Second, although I excluded metathesis errors from this count, I found that there were several metathesis errors which attested to the extrasyllabic nature of single consonant inflectional suffixes, as illustrated in (68).

(68)   An: 'He wròte "Grámpa" òn ìt, thèn he [rì.jəɫ.zaʲd] . . .
        he rèalized that he dìdn't néed tò.'
        (for 'realized' [rí.jəɫ.aʲz(d)]; AN-238(27) 4;8)

In this error, the VC sequence [aʲz] is metathesized, stranding the past tense suffix [-d]. There were 3 such metathesis errors in the child data which stranded an inflectional suffix, and only one in which the inflectional suffix participated in the error (AL-45(27) 2;8).

Finally, there was a very interesting pattern in telescoping errors with regard to inflectional suffixes. For children younger than 3;6, the only inflectional affixes which appeared in the telescoped utterance were those which were planned for the end of the last word, as in (69a); inflectional affixes planned for the middle of the utterance were typically deleted, as in (69b). However, beginning at age 3;6, most inflectional affixes planned for a word in the middle of the telescoping got shifted to the end of the error utterance, and appeared there, as in (69c, d).

(69)   a. Al: '[fwíŋ.kòʷs].'
           (for 'fruit-wrinkles' [fwùt.wíŋ.kòʷ(s)]; AL-21(34) 2;3)
        b. B: 'I wànt my [sâ:n].' (for 'socks on' [sák(s) àn]; B-95(34) 2;7)

c. B: 'Mom, my [pʰí.dʒà:rz] . . . my P͡Js àre ùnder mỳ shírt.'
       (for 'PJs are' [pʰi.dʒeʲ(z) ar], with plural morpheme moved to
       end; B-136(34) 3;6)

d. Al: 'Mòmmy, wè [fo͡ʒ.bæ̀:ʷd] . . . wè forgòt abòut this Cìndèrella.'
       (for 'forgot about' [fo͡ʒ.gát ə.bǽʷt]; final /t/ in error is treated as
       if it is the past tense morpheme, and voices in the context of
       the vowel-final root; AL-212(34) 4;4)

It will be shown in Chapter 6 that children begin to make errors involving the shifting of inflectional suffixes from one location to another as early as age 2;2. However, this independence of inflectional suffixes doesn't show up in telescoping errors until the middle of the 4th year, possibly because this is a more complex sort of error than the simple movement of one grammatical element from one location to another.

In general these findings suggest several things. First, derivational morphemes are treated as part of the phonological word by the phonological processing component of speech production planning. This does not necessarily mean that they are not represented separately from stems in the children's phonological representations. Since there is some evidence (Jaeger 1986) that these children were using at least {-ie/y} and possibly {-er/-or} productively by age 3, there may be some information stored in the formal representation of the word which indicates that it contains more than one morpheme, but this does not affect the phonological word during planning. Second, participial forms of verbs functioning as adjectives or nouns (gerunds) behave like other derived forms in terms of the integrity of the phonological word. Again, this does not necessarily mean that all possible participial forms are stored in the lexicon, but could suggest that once a (formally) inflected form takes on a new lexical category, the inflection is no longer affiliated with the syntax and thus becomes more integrated with the root phonologically. Finally, it is very clear that for both the children and adults, inflectional suffixes are not fully incorporated into the phonological word, and thus function as extrasyllabic in phonological errors; this is particularly true of single-consonant suffixes. I will go into these arguments regarding morphology in more detail in Chapter 6.

The second way in which the children's data differ from Laubstein's (1987) adult data has to do with the status of rhymes. Laubstein found only 11 (2%) errors involving rhymes, as compared to 8 (1%) involving onset-nucleus sequences ('body'), which she argues does not show strong support for the 'reality' of the rhyme (see also Davis 1989). In my children's data (given the morphologically revised analysis, and looking only at the classifiable errors) I found 17 rhyme substitution errors and 4 errors involving the substitution of a rhyme-onset sequence (R$0), so that 21 (3%) of the children's (classifiable) phonological errors involved rhymes. In the adult data, there were 12 rhyme errors and 4 R$0 errors, which represents 6% of the adult phonological errors. On the other hand I found only 1 child error involving a body unit, and 4 body errors in the adult data. This represents less than 0.2% of the children's phonological errors, and about 1.5% of the adult phonological errors. While not overwhelming evidence for the status of the rhyme, these data certainly favor the onset-rhyme syllable structure over the body-coda structure in English. Note that Stemberger (1983a:22), looking at adult data, also found more errors involving onset-rhyme than body-coda structure (53 vs. 4); see also Treiman (1988, 1989) for experimental evidence in favor of the onset-rhyme structure in English. However, it becomes clear by looking at other sources of evidence that simple phonological errors are not the best cases to use in assessing the status of the rhyme; in fact, very strong evidence for the rhyme emerges when telescoping errors are analyzed. I will now turn to a discussion of telescopings.

3.5.5 Internal Syllable Structure in Telescoping Errors
In my child data there were 61 cases of errors in which timing units were deleted, and remaining vowels were lengthened to preserve the original intonational pattern and most of, or sometimes all of, the originally planned duration. I collected 31 such errors from adults. In order to analyze the prosodic structures involved in these errors, I assigned syllable structure to the intended utterance using the criteria outlined in §3.5.3 above (with single-consonant suffixes counted as extrasyllabic), and the error was analyzed in terms of where breaks occurred between material retained in the utterance and material deleted. I relied heavily on stress and intonation cues to decide which elements were deleted and which were retained. Errors fell into the following categories (in these examples I use diacritics to show pitch: v́=high pitch; v̂=falling pitch; v̀=low pitch, v̌=rising pitch):

0/R='onset/rhyme': the break occurs between an onset and rhyme. Usually the error deletes the rhyme from one syllable and the onset from a subsequent syllable, so that the error production contains a syllable made up of the onset from one target syllable and the rhyme from another, as in (70a). In a few cases a rhyme is deleted, and the onset from that syllable becomes the onset of a following onsetless syllable, as in (70b).

(70)   a. B: 'Thòse are thìngs that [kʰ$\hat{o}$:ʲz] wèar . . . that <u>cówbòys</u> wèar.'
                (for 'cowboys' [kʰǽ^w.bòʲz]; deletion of rhyme+onset [æ^w.b],
                resyllabification of onset [kʰ] with rhyme [oʲz]; B-196(34) 4;1)
        b. OB:'I wànt òne more [kʰú:.kʰæ̀^{w}t].' (for 'cookie out' [kʰú.kì æ̀^{w}t];
                deletion of rhyme [i], with resyllabification of onset [k] with
                following onsetless syllable [æ^{w}t]; OC-91(34) 4;1)

SYLL='syllable': the break occurs at a syllable boundary; the error deletes a whole syllable.

(71)   Al: 'The [bè:ʲ.b$\hat{ø}$] . . . the <u>bàby bêar</u>.'
                (for 'baby bear' [bèʲ.bì b$\hat{ø}$]; syllable [bi] omitted; AL-7(34) 2;1)

0/R-MO='onset/rhyme-mixed onset': the break occurs between an onset and rhyme; the rhyme of the first syllable is omitted, and its onset is combined with the entire second syllable, so that a new (allowable) complex onset is produced.

(72)   An: '[dʒrô:ʷp] . . . [dʒrô:ʷp] . . . júmp-ròpe.'
        (for 'jump rope' [dʒʌmp.ròʷp]; deletion of rhyme [ʌmp],
        combination of stranded onset [dʒ] with following syllable [roʷp],
        creating new onset cluster [dʒr], a permitted cluster for this child at
        this time; AN-124(34) 3;10)

B/D='body/coda': the break occurs between the body (onset+nucleus) of a
syllable and its coda.

(73)   AF: 'Is [ðæ̀:k.tɚ] . . . is thàt Dòctor Brázelton?' (for 'that Doctor'
        [ðæt dàk.tɚ]; deletion of coda from 'that' [t], and body from first
        syllable of 'doctor' [da]; resyllabification of body from 'that' [ðæ]
        with coda [k] from first syllable of 'doctor'; AD-325(34))

OT-ORD='other-ordered': units other than those presented above are deleted, but
the spoken form contains the remaining units in the originally planned order.

(74)   Al: '[mí.kâ:ʷ] . . . [mí.kâ:ʷ], no!' (shakes head)
        M: 'Mìckey Móuse?'
        Al: 'Yeah, Míckèy Môuse.'
        (for [mí.kì mâʷs]; deletion of rhyme+onset [i.m], and final coda
        [s], but all other elements spoken in originally planned order;
        onset [k] resyllabified with vowel [aʷ]; AL-2(34) 2;0)

OT-MIS='other-misordered': units other than those presented above are
deleted, and the spoken form contains the remaining units in a misordered
sequence.

(75)   Al: '[pʰɪ̀:k.ʃî:tʃ] . . . pìcnìc lûnch.'
        (for [pʰɪ̀k.nìk lʌntʃ]; onset and final coda consonants of 'lunch'
        combined with vowel of syllable [nɪk]; AL-103(34) 3;3)

In some cases, more than one phonological unit was involved in the
telescoping, as illustrated in (76).

(76)   An: '[tʃʊ́:.kì:].' (for 'chocolate chip cookie' [tʃà.kət tʃìp kʰʊ́.kì];
        deletion of rhyme+syllable+syllable+onset [a.kət tʃɪp kʰ],
        resyllabification of onset [tʃ] with rhyme [ʊ]; AN-30(34) 2;2)

Table 3.19 shows the results of this analysis. In those cases where more
than one unit was involved in the telescoping, the error was counted in both
categories; for example, (76) counts as one 'O/R' and one 'Syll' entry. The
percentages in the table represent the percentage of errors in which at least this
unit was involved at that age; since some errors involved more than one type of
unit, the percentages add up to more than 100%.

It is clear from this table that telescoping errors at all ages most commonly
show a division at the onset-rhyme juncture (52.5% for the children, 45%

TABLE 3.19
Break points and/or omitted units for telescoping errors; percentage of
telescoping errors in which each phonological unit was the break point.
See text for explanation of headings.

Age:	1	2	3	4	5	Total	Adult
O/R	50%	38%	50%	61%	70%	52.5%	45%
SYLL	0	28.5%	25%	33%	40%	29.5%	55%
O/R-MO	0	5%	12.5%	0	0	3%	3%
B/D	25%	5%	0	0	0	3%	6.5%
OT-ORD	25%	14%	12.5%	5.5%	0	10%	0
OT-MIS	25%	38%	12.5%	11%	10%	21%	19.5%
N=	4	21	8	18	10	61	31

adults), or at a syllable boundary (29.5% for the children, 55% for the adults).
There are only two child errors and two adult errors that could be argued to show
the body-coda structure, thus verifying that English syllables are governed by the
onset-rhyme structure. Also, the 'mixed onset' errors only begin to occur at age
2, the age at which complex onset clusters begin to appear in the children's
productions.

It might seem counterintuitive that 50% of the 1-year-old telescoping errors
show an onset-rhyme break, since the data from phonological errors discussed
above suggest that children's early word representations are somewhat holistic,
and probably don't contain even fixed demarcations of syllables, let alone
internal syllable structure. However, this figure is possibly misleading, since
there are only 4 telescoping errors made by 1-year-olds in this study, and the two
errors analyzed as 'R/O' are somewhat ambiguous, as illustrated in (77).

(77)   B: 'Nò [nô:ʷç]! . . . Nò <u>nò</u> tôast!'
             (for 'no no toast' [nòʷ nòʷ tʰôʷç]; B-18(34)-1;10)

The most principled analysis of this error is that the rhyme+onset sequence
[oʷ.tʰ] was deleted and a new syllable was formed from the onset [n] of 'no' and
the rhyme [oʷç] from 'toast'. This is the analysis which the intonation pattern
supports. But it could also be that the consonant [tʰ] was simply omitted, and
the vowel [oʷ] is a coalescence of the two vowels from the target words;
alternatively the error could involve the whole syllable [noʷ] from 'no' and the
coda [ç] from 'toast'. However, even if the 50% 'R/O' figure is correct, these
four errors also included three other types of units, including two 'Others', so
these data don't need to be interpreted as being contradictory to the hypothesis
that internal syllable structure is not in place at age 1. The figure for 'O/R' is
somewhat lower at age 2 (38%) and although the figure for errors involving

syllables has risen (from 0% to 28.5%), at age 2 there are still a number of the less well-structured errors, including 38% 'OT-MIS' errors. Taken together these figures suggest that internal syllable structure is less well represented in the 1-2-year-olds than in the children ages 3 and older. In fact the percentage of 'O/R' errors rises steadily from age 2-5, reaching a peak of 70% at age 5 which is considerably higher than that of adults (45%).

The 'Other' errors show particularly interesting patterns. The children produced a few 'other-ordered' errors at ages 1-4, with the percentage steadily dwindling, and there were no OT-ORD errors at age 5, nor did the adults produce any. It appears that as internal syllable structure becomes a more central part of the child's phonological representations, any errors which maintain the order of segments will be much more likely to break at onset/rhyme or syllable boundaries than at some random location between segments. In a few early OT-ORD within-word (compound) errors, segments were actually moved into new syllable-structure slots, as illustrated in (78).

(78)   Al: 'Mom, Ì wànt some [ǽ:.pl̩ù:s] . . . ápplèjùice.'
            (for 'applejuice' [ǽ.pəɫ.dzùs]; AL-48(34) 2;9)

In this error, the coda [ɫ] from the second syllable of 'apple' becomes part of the onset of the last syllable of the telegraphed utterance; in this environment it develarizes and devoices.

On the other hand, the 'other-misordered' errors seemed to change character over time. The largest number of these misordered errors made by the children occurred between the ages of 2;2 and 3;3 (N=9). These errors include both within-word errors (all compounds), as illustrated in (79a) below, and between-word errors, as illustrated in (79b); the 'OT-MIS' error made at 3;3 is shown in (75) above. I collected only 3 'OT-MIS' errors from children older than 3;3.

(79)   a. OG: 'Not [r̂ì:s] còne! . . . Not ice-crèam còne!'
                (for 'ice-cream' [aʲs.krim]; OC-21(34) 2;3)
        b. Al: 'My sìster's [sʌ̀:m.wʌ̂:ɫ] . . . sòmewhère êlse.'
                (for 'somewhere else' [sʌ̀m.wɛ̀ʒ êɫs]; AL-56(34) 2;10)

In the within-word error in (79a), the [ri] from the second syllable of the target 'ice-cream' is moved to the beginning of the telegraphed utterance, followed by the [s] coda from the first syllable. The between-word error given in (79b) shows both deletion and perseveration of units. In this error the rhyme of the second syllable of 'somewhere' [ɛʒ] and the last coda consonant of the word 'else' [s] are deleted (and note that this coda [s] is free to delete because it is not an inflectional morpheme); the onset [w] from 'where' is resyllabified with the partial rhyme [ɛɫ] from 'else', but the vowel [ʌ] from 'some' is perseverated and substituted for the vowel [ɛ]. This was a seriously scrambled output.

At first I was somewhat surprised at the fairly large number of 'misordered' errors in the adult data. However, on examining the data, I found that most of the misordered adult errors involved either metathesizing whole syllables as in (80a), or assigning the prosodic structure of one word to a contiguous word, as in (80b). The former type is most easily explained by arguing that two syllable nodes have metathesized within a foot, or that two feet have metathesized. The latter can be explained by invoking the whole-word prosodic structure; in this case the prosodic structure and some of the phonological material of 'assignments' has been superimposed on 'seating'. This is a kind of misordering we don't expect from the children until they have this higher level of prosodic structure in place, and indeed the only child telescoping errors which resemble these adult errors are those given in (80c), and (80d); both of these errors were made by older children.

(80) a. AF: '[dù ə.pʰéʲ.ʃʌ̀n] . . . dò pày atténtion.'
          (for [dù pʰèʲ ə.tʰɛ́n.ʃən]; syllable [tʰɛn] deleted, and syllables [pʰeʲ] and [ə] metathesized; OT-MIS; AD-313(34))

     b. AM: ' . . . confirmed [ə.síːt.mì̀nts] . . . confirmed séating assìgnments.' (for [sít.ɪŋ ə.sàʰn.mɪnts]; deletion of syllables [ɪŋ] and [saʰn], and metathesis of syllables [sit] and [ə], but could also involve imposition of prosodic structure of 'assignments' on 'seating'; OT-MIS; AD-314(34))

     c. An: ' . . . ànd aʔ [ǽː.mʌ̀ːɬ] . . . a fèmale ánìmàl . . . '
          (for [fì.mèɬ ǽ.nə̀.mə̀ɬ]; segments of 'animal' but prosody of 'female'; 'OT-ORD'; AN-178(34) 4;4)

     d. An: '[nè.vɬ] gét mè!' (for 'you'll never' [jù̀ʷɬ nè.vɚ]; feet 'you'll' and 'never' metathesized, rhyme [ɚ] and body [juʷ] deleted, [vɬ] coalesce into a new syllable, [ɬ] becomes syllabic; 'OT-MIS' AN-296(34) 5;7)

The errors in (80a) and (80d) can be illustrated schematically as in (80´).

(80´) a.

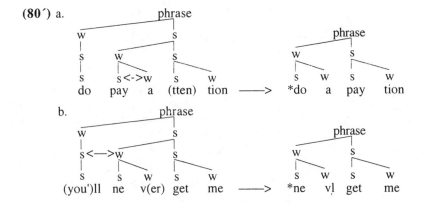

In (80´a), the two syllables 'pay a' within one foot metathesize; the syllable 'tten' is dropped, and the remaining syllables are reorganized into two feet rather than the originally planned three. Because the syllable 'pay' is now in the prosodically strongest position it takes tonic stress. In (80´b), the two feet 'you'll' and 'never' are metathesized; the coda of 'ver' and body of 'you'll' are deleted, and the remaining material coalesced into a new syllable. The four remaining syllables in their new order are organized into two trochaic feet, but because 'get' remains in the strongest prosodic slot, the tonic stress does not shift in this error utterance.

Therefore I argue that the less well-structured telescopings made by the younger children, through age 3;3, show evidence of the lack of development the syllable node tier; however the less well-structured errors made by the older children, being more like adult misordering errors involving whole syllables, feet, or whole word prosody, show evidence that the syllable node tier and foot structure is now in place.

3.5.6 Summary of Internal Syllable Structure in Phonological Errors

In the preceding section I first looked at the development of consonant clusters. Early errors give evidence regarding individual children's development of the ability to produce sequences of consonants. After the children are regularly producing clusters at around age 2, their phonological errors nearly always produce allowable English sequences of consonants. The few exceptions show that the children are learning abstract templates for allowable clusters in terms of major class features, such as '[s]+voiceless plosive+sonorant', rather than memorizing and storing individual types of possible sequences. These errors demonstrate that constraints regarding the allowable sequences of consonants within syllables is one of the earliest aspects of phonology acquired.

Next I examined segmental phonological errors for evidence of the development of internal syllable structure. In these errors, the target/error and source generally maintain syllable structure location consistency (i.e. onsets for onsets, codas for codas, etc.); for the children there was an 86.5% consistency, and for adults 88%. These figures rise slightly if single-consonant inflectional suffixes are taken to be extrasyllabic: 87% child, 90% adult. The syllable structure analysis showed more consistency than a word-based analysis for children who were producing utterances of 3+ words. However, for children in the 1- or 2-word stage, either analysis was equally good, suggesting that internal syllable structure may develop at the same time as knowledge about the linear organization of lexical items in sentences. The development of these two syntagmatic properties of language may be related to and/or influence each other.

Finally, I looked at evidence for the onset/rhyme vs. body/coda division of syllables. There was weak evidence in favor of the onset/rhyme division in segmental phonological errors, but much stronger evidence in telescopings, since most telescoping errors showed a break between onset and rhyme, (52.5% child, 44% adult) or at syllable boundaries (29.5% child, 55% adults), and very few showed the body-coda structure (3% child, 6.5% adult, a total of 4 errors). Most of the children's telescoping errors which involved misorderings of elements occurred before age 3;3, and they usually involved segments exchanging positions in the linear string. Adults' misordering errors usually involved the reordering of whole syllables, suggesting that these errors take place on the syllable node tier; the older children's misordering errors also showed evidence of this higher order of prosodic structure.

Taken altogether, the data discussed in this section provide evidence for the following scenario regarding the development of internal syllable structure. For very young children, words are stored in the lexicon as a collection of segments with a default order, but no internal structure. Once children begin to produce sequences of consonants in words, early in the third year, the possible consonant sequences follow adult English constraints, showing that children are learning abstract schema for sequences of consonants at syllable margins, and thus some indication of syllable boundaries must now be included in phonological representations. Recall from §3.4 that this is also about the time when the unit of 'syllable' begins to show up in phonological errors. Once the children begin producing utterances of 3+words, some evidence of internal syllable structure appears, in the sense that segments from like syllable structure units are most likely to be mutually involved in phonological errors. The first phonological error involving a rhyme occurred at age 2;6, indicating that internal syllable structure was in place and thus available to error beginning around this age. The misorderings in telescopings which continue into the early part of the fourth year suggest that the higher prosodic level involving syllable nodes is not available for processing by the 'Phonological Processes' component until around age 3, after which these misordering errors become far less frequent. Child 'misordered' telescoping errors become more similar to adult 'misordered' errors at ages 4 and 5, suggesting that the higher levels of prosodic structure are in place during those ages.

Thus there is a great deal of evidence from phonological errors about the development of internal syllable structure in children's phonologies. However there is another source of information on this topic, which relates to the representation of syllable structure in the lexicon; this source is paradigmatic lexical errors, to which I will now turn.

3.6 Internal Syllable Structure in Paradigmatic Lexical Errors

3.6.1 Overview

In §3.4 above, I looked at paradigmatic lexical selection errors and lexical blends for evidence about whether or not the number of syllables and basic syllable divisions were represented in lexical entries. In the current section, I will return to these same errors, but will be looking at evidence regarding internal syllable structure. As before, I will look at content word lexical selection errors only, to see if there is any evidence that hierarchical syllable structure is represented in lexical phonological forms, and if so, whether or not there are any developmental patterns evident in the data. Any evidence for the importance of internal syllable structure in explaining lexical substitution errors will argue against theories which claim that syllable structure is not represented in the lexicon of English, but is assigned during phonological processing. I will also look at the crossover points for lexical blend errors, for evidence both about the representation of internal syllable structure in phonological forms, and its importance in phonological processing. Developmental patterns will be examined to see if they are compatible with the claims about the development of syllable structure made in §3.5 above, which were based on the evidence from phonological errors.

3.6.2 Internal Syllable Structure in Lexical Substitution Errors

I argued in §3.4 that if two words have the same number of syllables, this is one factor causing the words to be phonologically similar in the lexicon and therefore may be part of the reason why one word would be misselected for another. These phonological factors were shown to be more important for malapropisms, where the target and error word have no semantic relationship, than they are for semantically related pairs.

In order to see whether internal syllable structure is also an important factor causing two lexical items to be phonologically similar to each other, I developed a measure called 'syllable structure consistency' (hereafter SSC). For each pair of target/error words with the same number of syllables, I assigned each segment to a syllable structure slot according to the principles given in example (46) above (§3.5.3; multisyllabic words were divided into syllables by the principles in §3.4.2). I then counted the number of slots in the target and error words which were filled in both words, and calculated the percentage of mutually filled slots out of the total possible slots the two words could have had in common. This is illustrated in example (81).

(81)   a. [kʰ ɪ ç] 'kiss'   b. [s l oʷ]   'slow'
        O1 N D1   O1 O2 N
         | | | | | | | |
        O1 N D1   O1   N D1 D2
        [kʰ a ʒ̩] 'car'   [f   æ   s   t] 'fast'
        3/3 = 100% consistency   2/5 = 40% consistency
        (AL-10(35) 2;2)   (OC-29(35) 2;8)

In (81a), the two words 'kiss' and 'car' both have a single onset consonant, a vowel nucleus, and a single coda consonant, so out of three possible slots all three match; this pair shows 100% SSC. However, the word 'slow' in (81b) has two onset consonants and a nucleus, whereas 'fast' has only one onset consonant, but two coda consonants. So out of five possible slots, only two match, giving a 40% consistency rating.

I selected the same subset of errors on which to perform this calculation as was described in §3.4.3. That is, I evaluated lexical substitution errors which involved content words, in which the target and source had either a semantic or phonological relationship (or both), excluding pure environmental errors. Regular inflectional suffixes were not included in the phonological analysis, for

TABLE 3.20

Average syllable structure consistency between target and error words (%SSC), content word lexical substitution errors, by age; pairs with semantic relationship (+sem) compared with pairs with no semantic relationship (-sem).

Age:	1	2	3	4	5	Total	Adult
[+sem] N=	3	14	11	22	27	77	69
%SSC	85%	76%	86.5%	76%	78.5%	78.5%	80%
[-sem] N=	0	4	5	12	5	26	28
%SSC		95%	86%	82%	91.5%	86.5%	87%
Overall %	**85%**	**80.2%**	**86.5%**	**78%**	**80.5%**	**80.5%**	**82%**

errors made by subjects older than 2;2. Table 3.20 gives the average SSC figure, by age, for errors where the target and error words have a semantic relationship, vs. those that do not (malapropisms). This table is to be read as follows (for example): at age 2, the children produced a total of 18 content word lexical substitution errors with the same number of syllables and either a semantic or phonological relationship (or both). Of these, 14 pairs had a semantic relationship, and the average SSC measure for these 14 pairs was 76%. The other 4 pairs had no semantic relationship, but had at least a phonological relationship; their average SSC measure was 95%. At age 2, the pairs of words involved in lexical substitution errors had an overall SSC average of 80.2%.

Table 3.20 shows that in general all the pairs of words involved in this subset of lexical substitution errors had fairly close SSC; at all ages, whether there was a semantic relationship or not, there was on average at least a 76% SSC between the two words. However, overall the malapropisms always showed a higher rating than the pairs with only semantic relationships (78.5% vs. 86.5%); this was true at every age except age 3 (and age 1 where there were no malapropisms produced). The adult errors also followed this same pattern (80% vs. 87%).

As far as developmental trends, there is an interesting pattern which once again shows the 3-year-olds behaving differently from children at other ages. At all ages from 2-5 (except age 3), the malapropisms showed a higher SSC percentage than the semantically related words, as we would have expected since we start to see evidence of the representation of consonant clusters at age 2;0, and the representation of hierarchical internal syllable structure around age 2;6. At age 2 there is a large difference in SSC figures between malapropisms and semantic errors, but because there were only 4 malapropisms, this figure is difficult to interpret. However, this difference shows up robustly again in the 4-5-year-olds, and also in the adult data.

What's interesting about the 3-year-olds is that they show the highest overall SSC consistency between word pairs involved in lexical substitution errors of any age, and no difference in SSC between semantically related pairs and malapropisms. (The relatively high SSC% at age 1 is most likely due to the fact that the youngest children had a very small repertoire of possible syllable structure patterns.) Recall also that the 3-year-olds produced the largest percentage of lexical substitution errors where the mutually involved words had the same number of syllables.   I have suggested that it is during age 3 that a great deal of the development of internal syllable structure is going on, and what these errors would suggest is that, as both internal syllable structure and the syllable node tier are developing, they become extremely important in organizing the phonological lexicon, and thus they heavily influence lexical selection errors regardless of whether or not the word pair has a semantic relationship. I would hypothesize that once internal syllable structure has settled into place in lexical representations, it becomes less important overall in lexical selection errors unless the word pair has only a phonological relationship, in which case it is one of the factors that can cause the malapropism to occur.

These figures suggest that internal syllable structure similarities may be one factor which promotes phonological similarity between lexical items, although perhaps not as strongly as actual number of syllables, since the same number of syllables shows a 96% rate for malapropisms overall for the children, whereas the SSC figure is 86.5%. This internal consistency effect shows up most clearly in the oldest children (age 4-5), suggesting that at least by this age internal syllable structure has been acquired as an important part of lexical phonological entries.

3.6.3   Internal Syllable Structure in Lexical Blend Errors

Finally, I examined the internal structure of lexical blend errors to see whether or not internal syllable structure contributed in any principled way to the phonological form of the blended output. In order to do so, I utilized the categories developed for telescoping errors, presented above in §3.5.5. I will briefly review them here, restating them in terms of the blending of two words; then I will introduce three new categories which a full characterization of the phonological properties of blends necessitates.

As discussed above, it is very difficult to unambiguously identify which part of a blended word derives from each of the two target words, since in most cases there are some phonological units which the two words share in common. In deciding on the classification of each error in the following taxonomy, I used the heuristic 'the first part of one word followed by the second part of the other word' as discussed in §3.4.4 above, and only considered an analysis which assumed parts of the two words were intermixed if no other analysis was available. However, if there were two or more possible analyses, none of which violated the 'no intermixing' principle, the blend was classified as 'ambiguous', since there was no principled way to decide between the possible classifications. The taxonomy used was the following (I am calling the two targets T1 and T2 for ease of exposition).

O/R='onset/rhyme': the blend crossover point is between the onset of a syllable in T1 and the rhyme of a syllable in T2, such that the two resyllabify into a new syllable.

(82)   B: (trying to get Mom to watch him twirl around in a chair) '[latʃ]!'
              (blend of T1: 'look' [lʊk] and T2: 'watch' [watʃ]; blend consists of
              the onset [l] from T1 and the rhyme [atʃ] from T2; B-310(38) 4;6)

SYLL='syllable': the crossover point occurs at a syllable boundary, such that the spoken form consists of (at least) a full syllable from T1 and a full syllable from T2.

(83)   An: 'Here's your [bǽθ.kʰl̩àθ].' (blend of T1: 'bathrobe' [bǽθ.rò^wb] and
               T2: 'washcloth' [wáʃ.kʰl̩àθ]; blend consists of the first syllable of
               T1 and the second syllable of T2; AN-65(38) 2;8)

MO='mixed onset': the blend consists of T1, with some elements from the onset of a syllable of T2 mixed into the onset of a syllable of T1, either by addition (84a) or substitution (84b).

(84)   a.   Al: 'Nòbody [sm:éʲkt] me.'
                     (blend of T1: 'spanked' [spæŋkt] and T2: 'maked' [meʲkt];
                     the [s] from the onset of T1 is added to the beginning of T2,
                     creating a complex onset [sm]; AL-78b(38) 2;11)
        b.   Al: 'You càn't fòld my pánties, becàuse they hàve to gò òut [sl̩éʲt].'
                     (blend of T1: 'straight' [st̬eʲt] and T2: 'flat' [fl̥æt]; [l] from
                     complex onset of T2 is substituted for [t̬] of complex onset of
                     T1, creating the cluster [sl̩]; AL-158(38) 3;8)

B/D='body/coda': the crossover point occurs between the body (onset+nucleus) of a syllable in T1, and the coda of a syllable in T2.

(85)   AF: 'The percèption of [st̬ɛ́tʃ] . . . stréss.' (blend of T1: 'stress' [st̬ɛs]
               and T2: 'speech' [spitʃ]; the blend consists of the body [stɛ] of T1
               and the coda [tʃ] of T2; AD-499(38))

OT-ORD='other-ordered': the crossover point occurs between units other than those presented above, but the spoken form contains the remaining units of T1+T2 in the originally planned order (with possibly some segments deleted).

(86)   Al: 'Òut in the [bɛ́.vin.ʒùm].' (blend of T1: 'bedroom' [bɛd.ʒùm] and
               T2: 'living-room' [wí.vin.ʒùm]; simplest analysis is that the blend
               contains the body [bɛ] of the first syllable of T1 followed by the
               last two syllables [vin.ʒùm] of T2, but with the coda [d] deleted
               from 'bed'; AL-26(38) 2;4)

OT-MIS='other-misordered': the spoken form contains units from both target words in a misordered or intermixed sequence.

(87)   An: (looking at a picture of a rabbit) '[pǽ.nɪtʰ].'
        (blend of T1: 'bunny' [pʌ́.ni] and T2: 'rabbit' [ɹ̪ǽ.bɪtʰ]; onset
        consonants [p] and [n] from T1 intermixed with vowels [æ] and [ɪ]
        and coda consonant [tʰ] from T2; AN-16(38) 1;10)

The three new categories necessary for characterizing the phonological
structures of blends are the following:

C/V-SUB='consonant or vowel substituted': the blend consists of all of T1,
except that either a single consonant (88a) or vowel (88b) from T2 has
substituted for a single consonant or vowel somewhere in the middle of the
otherwise intact T1. The substituted segment always occurs in the same
structural location in T1 as in T2, but not in the onset of the first syllable of
T1, since this would be considered an O/R or MO error.

(88)   a. Al: 'Is it [oʷ.ɹ̪è̞ʲ] on the déck?'
                (blend of T1: 'okay' [oʷ.kʰéʲ] and T2: 'all-right' [ɑ.ɹ̪aʲt]; blend
                consists of T1, with the consonant in the onset of the second
                syllable of T2 [ɹ̪] substituted for the consonant in the onset of
                the second syllable of T1 [kʰ]; AL-219(38) 4;5)
        b. B: 'Just [kʰóʷ.dɪŋ] . . . just jóking!' (blend of T1: 'kidding'
                [kʰɪ́.dɪŋ] and T2: 'joking' [dʒóʷ.kɪŋ]; simplest analysis is that
                the blend consists of T1, with the vowel [oʷ] from T2
                substituting for the vowel [ɪ] in T1; B-268(38) 4;4)

PROS='prosody': blend consists of either the segments from T1 organized
according to the overall prosodic structure of T2, as in (89a); or the segments
from T1 with the stress pattern of T2 which is a morphologically or semantically related word, as in (89b). This error type was produced only by adults.

(89)   a. AF: 'Sée, it sàys [bə.náɾ.n̩.ì], uh Bótanỳ.'
                (blend of T1: 'Botany' [báɾ.n̩.ì] and T2: 'Zoology'
                [zə.wá.lə.dʒì]; blend involves the segments from T1 spread
                over the prosodic structure of T2; AD-503(38))
        b. AM: 'If a pèrson's [sɚ̀.tɪ.fɨ.kʰít] . . . uh cèrtificàtion is in Spánish,
                (etc.)' (blend of T1: 'certificate' [sɚ.tʰɪ́.fɨ.kɨt] and T2:
                'certification' [sɚ̀.ɾɨ.fɨ.kʰéʲ.ʃən]; blend consists of the segments
                from T1 but lexical stress pattern of T2; AD-507(38))

AMBG='ambiguous': there is more than one possible analysis, but none of the
possible analyses violates the 'no intermixing' principle, so there is no way to
decide on the correct classification.

(90)   B: 'Thàt's a grèat bìg [fá.pa] bèar.' (blend of T1: 'Father' [fá.ḍ3] and
                T2: 'Poppa' [pʰá.pa]; could be first syllable of 'Father' plus second
                syllable of 'Poppa', or could be the onset [f] from 'Father' and the
                rhyme and second syllable [a.pa] of 'Poppa'; B-116(38) 2;10)

In most cases the 'ambiguous' errors were ambiguous between an O/R classification and a SYLL classification. In making these classificatory decisions, I counted each error as being an instance of only one category, unlike the telescoping errors which sometimes involved more than one classification. The results of this count are given in Table 3.21. Because there were so many errors which could have been classified into more than one category, the following table should be considered an estimation of the number of times different phonological units were relevant to the blend errors.

It is clear from Table 3.21 that the 'onset/rhyme' division is an important structural property of the words involved in blend errors. At every age, including adult, the percentage of errors which are best analyzed as 'O/R' errors exceeds that of any other category. The second most common crossover point is at syllable boundaries. If we assume that at least half of the ambiguous errors were either onset/rhyme or syllable errors, this means that between 65%-77% of the blend errors show evidence that one of these two structures was involved in the phonological process of blending. This suggests both that internal syllable structure (as well as syllable units) is represented in lexical entries, and that it is used by the phonological processor during assignment of phonetic form. It is also another piece of evidence that the basic internal structure of English syllables follows the onset/rhyme pattern rather than the body/coda pattern.

The developmental trends evident in this table are similar to those in Table 3.19, which presents internal syllable structure in telescoping errors. In the blends made by the 1-year-olds, there are a majority of errors which are best analyzed as having an onset/rhyme crossover point, but in many of these cases the error consists of the first segment from one word substituted for the first segment in the other, as illustrated in (91a), so these errors don't necessarily argue against a more segment-based (or more word-based) crossover. One of the 1-year-old blends analyzed as 'O/R' also includes a blend of features, (OC-4(38) 1;11). The best example of a true O/R crossover point at age 1 is given in (90b), although there is a slight ambiguity in this error since both words begin with the segment [p].

(91)   a. OG: 'Hí [dà.mi] . . . hí Mòmmy.' (blend of T1: 'Dadoo' [dǽ.du] and
        T2: 'Mommy' [má.mi]; blend consists of the onset consonant [d]
        from T1, plus the remainder of T2; OC-3(38) 1;11)

        b. B: '[pá.tʌç]' (blend of T1: 'potty' [pá.ti] and T2: 'penis' [pí.nʌç];
        blend consists of the first syllable and onset of the second
        syllable of T1, followed by the rhyme of the second syllable of
        T2; B-12(38) 1;9)

There are also several less well-structured errors at this age. At age 2 there is a drop in errors best explained in terms of the onset/rhyme structure, and an increase in errors with crossovers at syllables, showing that the syllable unit as a whole is becoming better represented than it was earlier. Again there are several less well-ordered errors. At this age, the 'mixed onset' errors start to appear, reflecting the fact that the ability to produce consonant clusters develops early in

TABLE 3.21
Crossover points for lexical blend errors; see text for description of
categories.

Age:	1	2	3	4	5	Total	Adult
O/R	7	5	9	11	4	36	25
	58.3%	29.5%	69%	46%	33.3%	46%	35%
SYLL	1	4	1	4	3	13	11
	8.3%	23.5%	8%	16.6%	25%	16.6%	15%
MO	0	1	2	1	1	5	4
		6%	15%	4%	8.3%	6.5%	5.5%
B/D	0	0	0	0	0	0	2
							3%
OT-ORD	1	2	0	0	0	3	2
	8.3%	11.5%				4%	3%
OT-MIS	1	1	1	1	0	4	1
	8.3%	6%	8%	4%		5%	1.5%
C/V-SUB	0	0	0	4	0	4	6
				16.6%		5%	8%
PROS	0	0	0	0	0	0	5
							7%
AMBG	2	4	0	3	4	13	16
	16.6%	23.5%		12.5%	33.3%	16.7%	22%
N=	12	17	13	24	12	78	72

the third year.

At ages 3-5 the percentage of onset/rhyme errors is higher than at age 2, and there are fewer misordered errors. Errors at these ages show that even though the older children's words are more phonologically complex than the younger children's, and thus there are more possibilities for blends involving seriously mixed-up productions, there is a clear preference for crossovers involving the two basic types of structures. Errors such as (92a) below, where segments in the blend show up in different locations from their original locations in the target, don't occur after age 2. The two OT-MIS errors which occured at ages 3 and 4 involve the intermixing of elements from the two words, but all segments appear in the same syllable structure slots as in the original word; the 3-year-old example is shown in (92b). However, at ages 3-5, well-organized errors like that given in (82) above are the norm (blend of 'watch' and 'look', *[latʃ]). Recall that the misordered telescoping errors were at their peak between 2;2-3;3, but were very rare in the older children, a finding analogous to the blend figures.

(92) a. M: 'Is the ̀ice cream **còld** or **hót**?'
          Al: '[**kwát**].' (blend of T1: 'cold' [kowd] and T2: 'hot' [hat]; blend
          involves the onset [k] from T1 and the coda [at] from T2, but
          the coda consonant [w] from T1 has moved into the onset of the
          error word; AL-12(38) 2;2)

      b. B: 'I còuldn't **sée** it, and I wènt ̀into the [**splìs**] . . . plàce where
          you cán sèe it, . . . (etc.)' (most likely blend of T1: 'see' [si]
          and T2: 'place' [pʰleʲs]; error contains onset [s] and nucleus [i]
          of T1, with onset /pl/ of T2 added after onset [s] of T1 forming
          new complex onset /spl/; also coda [s] of T2 is added after
          nucleus [i] of T1; B-142(38) 3;8)

Not surprisingly, there is a peak in O/R errors at age 3, reflecting the fact
that there is a great deal of focus during age 3 on the development of internal
syllable structure; the concomitant drop in errors reflecting syllable boundaries is
analogous to the lesser of importance of syllables per se during phonological
processing found for the age 3 children in phonological LU and telescoping
errors.

One particularly interesting development at age 4 is the appearance of 'C/V-
SUB' errors (see (88)). These are errors which contain the entire phonological
form from one of the targets, except that a single segment, consonant or vowel,
has been substituted from the other target into the identical prosodic position as
in T2. These errors could be interpreted to show that whole-word prosodies are
developing during ages 4-5; that is, the representations of words contain a sort of
skeleton, possibly a foot-structure organization, that anchors all the syllables to
the overall word-node in a linearly and hierarchically structured whole. Thus the
blend allows an interloper segment from one word to intervene in the sequence of
segments in the other word, as long as it fulfills the same prosodic function as
the segment it replaces. Note that the adults also made a fair number of this
type of error, but children younger than age 4 did not. Similarly, although there
are no 'prosodic' errors listed for the children in Table 3.21, the following
'ambiguous' errors could be considered examples of 'prosodic' errors.

(93) a. B: 'Mom, did yòu tell Dàd that I wènt to the [**sì.mə.tʰɛ́.ri.əm**]?
          I mean the plànetárium?'
          (blend of T1: 'cemetery' [sí.mə.tʰɛ̀.ri] and T2: 'planetarium'
          [pʰlæ̀.nə.tʰɛ́.ri.ə̀m]; simplest analysis is segments of T1, with
          stress and final syllable of 'planetarium'; B-471(38) 5;2)

      b. B: 'I'm gòing to màke an [**ɪm.pʰɚ̀.sən**] of an ìgloo.'
          (blend of T1: 'impersonation' [ɪm.pʰɚ̀.sə.néʲ.ʃən] and T2:
          'impression' [ɪm.pʰɾɛ́.ʃən]; simplest analysis is segments of T1
          fit into prosodic form of T2; B-514(38) 5;5)

The error in (93a) was counted as a syllable error, but the prosodic analysis also
explains it very well. Similarly in (93b), this could be taken as an O/R error

(with a break between the onset [n], deletion of R$O [eʲ.ʃ], resyllabification of onset [n] with rhyme [ən]), but the prosodic explanation again is very strong. If the higher-order prosodic structure being developed at this time is a kind of rhythmic organization such as foot structure, this could explain how the stress pattern from one word could be superimposed on the segments of the other word, since lexical stress in lexical entries would be linked to metrical structures (see also §3.7.1 below). Thus these 'C/V-SUB' errors and these potential 'Prosody' errors provide further evidence for the time course of the development of larger prosodic structures in the phonological word.

3.6.4 Summary of Internal Syllable Structure in Lexical Errors, and Summary of Findings Regarding Syllables

In the first part of this section I compared the internal syllable-structure consistency relationship between target and error words in content-word lexical substitution errors; the main finding was that malapropisms regularly show a stronger affinity between the structures of the two words than errors with a semantic relationship (except at age 3); this shows up most strongly in the errors made by the 4-5-year-old children, and the overall child average is similar to that of adults. In the second part of this section I looked at lexical blend errors, both content and function words combined, to see what kind of internal structure was evident in the crossover points of the phonological blends. The results were very similar to those found for telescoping errors: the 1-year-olds showed little unambiguous internal structure; starting at age 2 there are a number of whole-syllable and mixed-onset errors. The onset/rhyme division is firmly in place by age 3, and the less well-structured errors become rare after age 3. Starting at age 4, errors which reflect the overall prosodic structure of the word begin to appear.

At this point, this very detailed inquiry into the development of syllables and syllable structure is complete. I would like to return to the sketch of a theory about syllable structure development presented in §3.4.1, to see to what extent the SOT evidence is compatible with that sketch. (See Vihman, Velleman & McCune 1994 for a similar theory of the progress of phonological development.)

Most of the SOT evidence points to the conclusion that lexical entries in the 1-year-old children' lexicons, especially those children in the 1- and 2-word stages, have little if any information regarding syllables represented in the phonological forms of their entries. All the lexical substitution errors at this age are caused either by a semantic relationship between the words or some environmental influence (more on this point in Chapter 4), and thus the phonological relationships between target and error word seem to be relatively random. This is most easily explained by hypothesizing that the lexicon of the 1-year-old is organized almost entirely by semantic relationships, and very little by phonology. Words which are substituted for each other are equally likely to have the same vs. different number of syllables, and if SSC (syllable structure consistency) is high, it is undoubtedly due to the small repertoire of syllable structure types in these young children's lexicons. Two of the 11 blend errors at this age could be explained in terms of syllables, but other explanations are equally plausible. Similarly there are no whole-syllable phonological errors, nor are there whole-syllable deletions in telescopings. In phonological errors, the syllable-structure location of target and error units is usually honored, but an analysis in terms of syllable structures per se compared to a whole-word analysis shows that either of these domains can equally well explain this positional consistency. Looking at break-points in telescopings, and crossover points in blends, there is no compelling evidence for the necessity of positing either whole syllable demarcations, or internal structure. These findings are most easily interpreted by hypothesizing that early phonological lexical representations are made up of a set of appropriate consonants and vowels, linked to a phonological word node, with a default but somewhat fluid order and no internal structure; this word node guarantees a consistent relationship between this set of segments, normally in this order, with a particular meaningful lemma. The function of syllables at this age would be purely a motoric function, during speaking.

However, starting around age 2, evidence for syllables begins to appear in the SOT data, particularly for syllable boundaries which break the string of consonants and vowels into a sequence of sub-units under the word node. Looking first at lexical errors, it is found that the children begin making malapropisms at age 2;2 (see AL-13(35) 2;2), showing that the lexicon now has more phonological organization. Target and error words in malapropisms are more likely to have the same number of syllables than semantically related pairs, and also show a higher internal syllable-structure consistency rating, although this may be partly because children have a small repertoire of possible syllable structure types. Nonetheless, they do begin to produce 'mixed-onset' blend errors, since they can now produce onset clusters, and these always produce allowable sequences of segments, showing that their phonological system now represents these sequential constraints. In phonological errors, there are more LU errors involving syllables, and more telescoping errors which include the omission of whole syllables; these begin to appear around age 2;1-2;2. Errors involving consonant clusters appear at around 2;1, and usually maintain allowable sequences; this shows that there is now some linear structure or demarcation in the phonological representations, since the child now distinguishes between consonants allowed in a cluster within the same syllable, as opposed to those allowed across syllable boundaries. The few consonant cluster errors which violate legal sequences in English follow the major class patterns, suggesting that children are learning major class constraints rather than simply memorizing allowable consonant sequences. Allophonic processes begin to appear which are triggered by phonemes occurring in specific locations in syllables (e.g. aspiration, sonorant devoicing, etc.). Target and source units in phonological errors come from congruent syllable locations in the majority of cases, and the syllable-based analysis shows a higher consistency than the word-based analysis by 12%, showing that it is syllable-structure location, not whole-word location, that governs these patterns. Early errors mostly involve two onsets, two codas, or two vowels, which is consistent with syllables as a linear demarcation. However, errors involving the rhyme as the error unit begin to occur at age 2;6, showing that this hierarchical structure has now begun to be developed. Interestingly, telescoping errors with misordered sequences of segments are at their peak between 2;7-3;3, so it is likely that it is during the second half of the third year that children are developing the internal syllable structure patterns of words, and while these structures are being acquired they seem to become highly susceptible to error in telescopings. At about age 2;9, errors where rhythmic 'beats' are added in new locations begin to occur, suggesting that the syllable node per se is beginning to be developed. In fact, once internal syllable structure begins to develop, the syllable node tier must also be developing, since such a node is required to anchor each set of onset/rhyme structures, and keep each set distinct from the other. It is during the third year that the lexicon begins to be organized in terms of phonological structure as well as semantic structure, causing the form lexicon to begin to be separated out from the lemma lexicon, since each requires a different organizational structure.

Age 3 seems to be an important year in the development of phonological structures. In lexical errors, it is clear that syllables are firmly represented in lexical phonological representations, since the children at this age have the highest percentage of lexical substitution errors in which the two words have the same number of syllables, and show a clear distinction between semantically related pairs (73% same number of syllables) and malapropisms (100%). The fact that internal syllable structures have been developing during the latter half of the third year shows up in the finding that at age 3 there is the highest percentage of internal syllable structure consistency between target and error words in lexical substitution errors. This newly acquired aspect of phonological representation seems to be so important in the organization of the form lexicon at age 3, that the semantically driven lexical substitution errors show as great a consistency in number of syllables and SSC as do the malapropisms. On the other hand, the 3-year-olds' phonological errors showed the effect of internal syllable structure being a newly acquired aspect of their phonological knowledge, in that this structure seemed to have a very strong influence on phonological processing, overshadowing syllables per se in terms of importance. The 3-year-olds had the lowest percentage of phonological LU and telescoping errors involving whole syllables, and the lowest percentage of blend errors with the crossover point being at a syllable boundary. However, they had the highest percentage of onest/rhyme crossovers in blend errors, and the highest consistency of syllable structure location in between-word phonological errors (from Table 3.17) of all the ages. Similarly, the number of misordered telescoping errors dropped dramatically after age 3;3. Therefore, at age 3 it appears that although syllable nodes are in place at this time in lexical representations, the internal syllable structure of each syllable is the dominant factor during phonological processing, assigning phonetic form to the abstract phonological representations which are the input to this processing component.

During ages 4-5, there continues to be clear indication of both internal syllable structure and syllable nodes marked in lexical form entries. The percentage of lexical substitution errors in which target and error words have the same number of syllables remains high, although slightly lower than the percentage at age 3, moving in the direction of the adult figure. This is probably partly due to the fact that the 4-5-year-old children know words with a greater variety of numbers of syllables than the 3-year-olds. The lower adult figure is probably due not only to their large and varied vocabularies, but also due to the influence of morphology on adult malapropisms, a factor which can sometimes outweigh phonological similarity. Similarly the 4-5-year-olds' average SSC remains high in lexical substitution errors, although it is somewhat lower than the 3-year-olds', for possibly the same reason, i.e. greater variety of syllable structure types in their vocabulary. However, the 4-5-year-old children's lexical substitution errors show a clear distinction between semantically related word pairs and malapropisms, where the malapropisms have a consistently higher percentage of both same number of syllables and SSC. Apparently the processing mechanism is paying less attention to these factors for semantically based errors than it did during age 3, when SSC was important in all lexical substitution errors.

Errors which involve phonological processing also show patterns at age 4-5 which reflect the development of syllabic structure. In phonological LU and telescoping errors, the percentage of errors involving whole syllables rises towards adult levels, implying an increasing importance of the syllable node tier. The internal syllable structure consistency in phonological errors remains high, but the difference between the success of a syllable-based analysis compared to a word-based analysis continues to grow, reaching adult levels by age 5. This shows that the internal structure of words becomes increasingly more important than the whole wordshape during these years. In telescopings, the break-points are very well-ordered, involving mainly onset/rhyme breaks, with whole-syllable breaks also being fairly common. There was only one 'OT-ORD' error at these ages, which may be better analyzed as a prosodically-based error (see (80c) above); the few 'OT-MIS' errors made at these ages began to look more like adult misordered errors, which involve misorderings of syllables within feet, or misorderings of feet themselves (see (80d) above). Similarly, the number of blend errors which could involve syllables remains fairly high at ages 4-5, although the very high percentage at age 5 is probably due to the fact that many of these errors involved compounds. Blend crossovers nearly all involved onset/rhyme or syllable breaks, and only one misordered blend was produced. The 4-year-olds began to procude the 'C/V-SUB' type blend errors, where a single segment from one target substitutes for the analogous segment in the other target, i.e. in the identical prosodic location; this type of error requires whole-word prosodies to be in place. Thus during ages 4-5 the syllable has become more important in phonological processing than at age 3, probably due to the development of higher levels of phonological organization which are now available during phonological processing (syllable node tier, foot tier); these higher levels of organization show up clearly in telescoping and blend errors.

In sum, these data are consistent with the following hypotheses: First, the syllable as a unit of demarcation begins to become a part of children's lexical representations at around age 2;0. This linearization is necessitated by the acquisition of longer and more complex phonological forms for lexical items (especially consonant clusters), which requires some sort of internal organization in order for the child to be able to consistently perceive and produce the phonological form. It also coincides with the movement out of the 2-word stage, which is not strictly syntagmatic (i.e. there is usually no fixed word order in children's 2-word utterances), into the 3+word stage, where the linear pattern of the words and morphemes begins to be part of the message. Thus this linearization seems to appear throughout the linguistic system at approximately the same point in time, as the children's utterances become more complex and require a higher level of organization. Then, sometime during the second half of the third year, the internal syllable structure (especially the onset/rhyme structure) begins to be developed in lexical representations, and thus becomes available for error. At age 3, evidence begins to appear that there are now syllable nodes intervening between the segmental tier and the prosodic word node; these nodes are required for maintaining the internal structure of each syllable distinct from the other syllables in the word. By age 4, the evidence points to the development of foot structure, and by age 5 the children's errors implicate a phonological representation and processing system that is very nearly adult-like, although the higher-levels of phonological organization may not be as well-established in the children's representations as they are in adults'.

A schematic and probably oversimplified illustration of the progression involved in the acquisition of syllable structure supported by the SOT data is given in (94). Thus these SOT data have been able to provide evidence for a theory of the acquisition of syllable structure in English, by making use of the basic principle of this study, i.e. that a structure can only be available to an error once it has been acquired. It is hoped that the detailed analysis presented in the above three sections of this chapter will serve as a model of how SOT data can be used to probe important issues in language acquisition research.

(94) Schematic representation of the time-course of the acquisition of syllable structure.

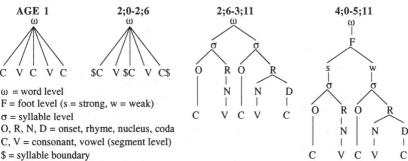

ω = word level
F = foot level (s = strong, w = weak)
σ = syllable level
O, R, N, D = onset, rhyme, nucleus, coda
C, V = consonant, vowel (segment level)
$ = syllable boundary

3.7 Stress and Intonation

In the above sections I discussed the development of phonological word prosody, looking at syllable structure and foot structure. In this section I will look at two other aspects of prosody which involve pitch and rhythm, namely lexical stress and phrasal intonation. This is a very broad area, and so my discussion will focus on four issues: 1) Is there evidence that lexical stress is stored in phonological representations in the lexicon, or that it is assigned by rule during phonological processing? 2) How does the overall phrasal rhythm set up by the strong-weak pattern of lexical stress interact with phonological errors? 3) Does the 'tonic stressed' syllable within a phrase have any predictable influence on phonological errors? 4) Do children make errors involving assignment of overall intonation patterns? In every case I will relate the results both to an overall theory of phonological development, and to the RPC Model.

3.7.1 Lexical Stress

For the past 35 years, since the publication of *The Sound Pattern of English* (Chomsky & Halle 1968), linguists have talked about lexical stress in English as if it is assigned by a rule or algorithm which can be formulated in terms of current phonological theory; this rule is said to be part of speakers' 'knowledge' about the phonology of their language. The purpose of having such a rule was, at least originally, to simplify linguistic representation in the human mind, on the assumption that the mind prefers to extract every possible regularity from stored representations and capture this regularity in an abstract system, in this case, phonological knowledge. This assumption was based on the stance that the human mind has very little storage space for representation but a great deal of space for computation (Halle & Clements 1983:2).

Even early psycholinguistic evidence disputed this finding from the cognitive point of view: 'tip of the tongue' experiments (Brown & McNeill 1966), as well as studies of malapropisms (Fay & Cutler 1977) provided strong evidence that lexical stress patterns are stored in the lexicon as part of phonological representations. Psycholinguistic experiments showed that naive speakers did not consistently shift the stress when they produce a derived neologism (Ohala 1974, Steinberg & Krohn 1975, Myerson 1976). And more recent neurolinguistic evidence supports the view that the brain prefers a balance between representation and on-line processing, depending on the complexity of the linguistic material itself (Jaeger et al. 1996:489). Since the rules, principles, algorithms, etc., designed to account for English stress have been far from simple (see especially Chomsky & Halle 1968:240, as well as Kenstowicz 1994: Ch. 10, Kager 1995, Halle 1998, and many others), this argues against them being productive. Given the complexity and for the most part non-predictability of English lexical stress patterns, the more cognitively plausible hypothesis is that stress is stored in phonological lexical entries, and that if anything, speakers extract a few general regularities regarding possible English stress patterns which they might use productively when trying to pronounce an unfamiliar word which is presented visually. The fairly complex patterns accounted for in linguistic theory could be more relevant to general issues in phonological theory such as universals of stress patterns, stress patterns in phrases, and the historical development of the phonology of English.

In fact proponents of the 'rules'-type theories have acknowledged that these rules are probably not used during processing, and that stress is in fact lexical, such that all actual surface forms are also stored in the lexicon; the 'rules' developed in linguistic theory are part of 'knowledge' but not part of processing (Halle 1973). However, this completely contradicts the original motivation for having stress rules, i.e. to minimize the amount of information which needs to be stored in lexical entries. If lexical stress is stored in lexical entries, it is unclear why speakers would need to abstract out complex and exception-ridden 'rules' of stress as part of their knowledge of phonology, such as those in Halle 1998. Nevertheless, for the sake of argument I will assume that there is a possibility that lexical stress is assigned on-line by rules, so that the SOT data can be used to contrast these two possible theories to each other, even if one may be something of a straw man.

What kinds of evidence from SOT data would be relevant to this issue? Clearly evidence from lexical substitution errors is relevant, in the same way that it was relevant to issues regarding the representation of syllables in lexical entries discussed above. If two content words are more likely to be mutually involved in a substitution error if they have the same stress pattern, and if this factor is more consistent for malapropisms than for semantically related target-error pairs, then this is strong evidence that lexical stress is marked in phonological representations and is a factor in causing two words to be phonologically similar in the lexicon. A second piece of evidence would come from blend errors involving the whole prosodic word: if blend errors occur which involve the segments from one word but the stress structure from another, this is strong support for the claim that stress is stored in the lexicon. It also tells us that stress is stored in such a way that it is associated with overall prosodic structure, but not necessarily with specific segments, or at least that it can be de-linked from those segments. A third place to look is in phonological errors: do children or adults ever make errors where a word is spoken with an incorrect stress pattern, and if so, how can this be explained? Would one want to say that the speaker has applied the rule incorrectly, or are there other more compelling explanations? Finally, telescoping errors are a valuable place to look for information about both lexical stress and phrasal stress, particularly in terms of the relationship between lexical stress and segmental aspects of a word as it is being planned for production. So in the ensuing paragraphs I will look at each of these four sources for information regarding the representation and processing of lexical stress.

First, I analyzed the content-word lexical substitution errors in which the target and error words contained the same number of syllables, since if the words had different numbers of syllables it would be difficult to decide whether or not their stress patterns were the same. I only looked at pairs with two or more syllables since lexical stress is irrelevant in one-syllable words. I used the same criteria for selecting these errors as in §3.4.3; namely, the word pair had to have either a semantic or a phonological relationship (or both), and the error could not have only an environmental cause. Because word pairs involved in function word errors are nearly always semantically related, they are not included in this count since their phonology is less relevant. I also stripped off regular inflectional suffixes (after age 2;2) in order to count syllables, as above. I then assigned primary stresses to each relevant word, and secondary stress in either compounds or four-syllable words; all other syllables were treated as unstressed, since otherwise the classification would be too fine-grained for this analysis. The following stress patterns occurred in relevant words in the children's data:

(95) Stress patterns in children's errors

2-syllable:

ó ŏ e.g.: 'Daddy' [dǽ.di]

ŏ ó e.g.: 'Eileen' [aʲ.lín]

óʼ ŏ e.g.: 'backpack' [bǽk.pʰǽk]

ò ó e.g.: 'blow-up' [blòʷ.ʌ́p]

3-syllable:

ŏ ó ŏ e.g.: 'invention' [ɪn.vɪ́ɲ.tʃɨn]

ó ŏ ŏ e.g.: 'lollipop' [lá.li.pʰàp]

ó ò ŏ e.g.: 'popsicle' [pʰáp.sì.kəɬ]

ò ŏ ó e.g.: 'rubber-band'
[rʌ̀.bɚ.bǽnd]

Besides the above, several other syllable structure patterns occurred in the adult data, including patterns with four syllables. The acronymic items such as 'HBO' and 'ASAP' were assigned stress on a case-by-case basis.

(96) Stress patterns only in adult errors

3-syllable:

ó ŏ ŏ e.g.: 'vitamin' [váʲ.rə.mən]

ŏ ŏ ó e.g.: 'recommend' [rɛ.kə.ménd]

4-syllable:

ó ŏ ò ŏ e.g.: 'orthodontist' [ór.θə.dàn.tɨst]

ò ŏ ó ŏ e.g.: 'conversation' [kʰàn.vɚ.séʲ.ʃən]

ŏ ó ŏ ŏ e.g.: 'empirical' [ɪm.pʰí.rɨ.kəɬ]

This measure may in fact be overly conservative, since by consistently distinguishing compounds from non-compounds, I end up counting the following types of word pairs as having different stress patterns: 'icing' vs. 'ice-crèam' (B-512(35) 5;5) and 'cánnibal' vs. 'cánnon-bàll' (AD-406(35)). However, because I applied this measure consistently to all words, it should provide a fair measure when word pairs with and without a semantic relationship are compared. I then counted the number of pairs of words with vs. without a semantic relationship which had the same or a different lexical stress pattern; the results are given in Table 3.22. This table is to be read as follows (for example): at age 2, there were 8 relevant lexical substitution errors (content words, same number of syllables, 2 or more syllables, etc.) with a semantic relationship between target and error word, and of these, 87.5% (i.e. 7) had the same stress pattern.

This table shows two things clearly. First, in general if two words are

TABLE 3.22
Percentage of content word lexical substitution errors in which target and
error words contain the same lexical stress pattern (% S.Str). Only pairs
with the same number of syllables, and 2 or more syllables, are included.
Error pairs with a semantic relationship [+sem] are compared to
malapropisms [-sem].

Age:	1	2	3	4	5	Total	Adult
[+sem] N=	2	8	5	10	12	37	37
% S.Str	100%	87.5%	80%	80%	67%	78.5%	70%
[-sem] N=	0	2	1	5	4	12	24
% S.Str	na	100%	100%	80%	100%	92%	96%
Overall %	**100%**	**90%**	**83%**	**80%**	**75%**	**81.5%**	**80%**

mutually involved in a lexical substitution error and fit all the other criteria
above, they are roughly 80% likely to also have the same stress pattern as each
other, regardless of their semantic relationship. This is partially due to the fact
that most of the words in the child and adult corpora followed the trochaic stress
pattern for 2-syllable words, or the [ǒ ó ǒ] pattern for 3-syllable words; thus
some of the consistency is due to frequency of stress patterns in the lexicon.
However, the more important finding is that there is a far greater likelihood that
the target and error pairs will have the same stress pattern in malapropisms than
in pairs which are semantically related. For the children, 92% of their
malapropisms (all but 1) had the same lexical stress pattern, compared to 78.5%
for semantically related pairs; similarly the adults showed a 96% same-stress rate
for malapropisms (again all but 1), but 70% for semantically related pairs. This
is similar to the figure found by Fay & Cutler (1977): 82% same stress for
semantic errors, but 98% for malapropisms. As just indicated, in the entire
corpus there were only two malapropisms with differing stress patterns, one
produced by a 4-year-old and one by an adult.

(97)   a. OG:'I nèed a **rùbber-bánd**. Nót a rùbber-bànd. Nót a rùbber-
            bànd.'
        M: 'Whát do you need?'
        OG: 'An umbrélla.' ('rubber-band' [rʌ.bɚ.bǽnd] for 'umbrella'
            [ʌm.bré.lə]; OC-112(35) 4;6)
        b. AF: (talking about an exceptionally large brassiere) 'Yòu could ùse
            it as a slíng shòt for a **cánnibal** . . . uh cánnon bàll.'
            ('cannibal' [kʰǽ.nə.bəɫ] for 'cannon-ball' [kʰǽ.nən.bàɫ];
            AD-406(35))

The error in (97a) is almost a 'tip of the tongue' error, where the child says the wrong word then struggles to access the correct one. The words 'rubber-band' and 'umbrella' just pass my criteria for phonological relatedness (see Chapter 4), but they clearly have no semantic relationship, so it must have been their phonological similarity that caused the error. The adult error in (97b) however, shows a great deal of phonological (and no semantic) similarity, and in fact it is the stress difference (plus the occurrence of the coda [n] in 'cannon') which keep these two words distinct. Thus, because the phonological forms of these two words are so similar in other respects, the malapropism could occur with a difference in lexical stress.

Clearly these errors can best be explained by assuming that lexical stress is stored in the lexicon as part of phonological form entries. Otherwise how could one explain the high level of consistency of stress patterns in malapropisms, compared to the consistently lower level in semantically related errors? One would have to argue that there is something about the consistency of the syllable structure that causes the stress rules to work the same way for both target and error words in the 'Phonological Processes' component, and since malapropisms typically have a higher degree of syllable-structure consistency, the stress rules would work the same in both target and error more often than in semantic errors. This is a much more cumbersome explanation and would need a great deal of evidence to prove; it seems unlikely that it could acount for the nearly 100% consistency of stress patterns in malapropisms. Thus the burden of proof would be on proponents of an on-line rules approach.

The second piece of evidence regarding the relationship of stress to lexical entries comes from blend errors. First, there were a few blend errors in which the target and error words contained different lexical stress patterns. In every case the erroneous utterance contained the stress pattern of one or the other of the words, intact; it was never computed differently for the erroneous utterance, by some algorithm that looks at the phonological structure of the new form to be uttered, as illustrated in (98).

(98)   a.   M: (looking at a catalogue page which has pictures of both a
                 wheelbarrow and a wagon; points to the wagon) 'What's this?'
           B: 'It's a [wɨ̂ɬ.bæ̀.gən].'   (blend of T1: 'wheelbarrow' [wɨ̂ɬ.bè.roʷ]
                 and T2: 'wagon' [wǽ.gən]; B-145(38) 3;8)
        b.   OG: '[jɛ́.stɚ.nàʲt].'   (blend of T1: 'yesterday' [jɛ́.stɚ.dèʲ] and T2:
                 'last-night' [læ̀st.náʲt]; OC-149(38) 5;6)

In (98a) the error utterance takes on the compound stress of T1: 'wheelbarrow'; although the vowel [æ] in the second syllable of the error word takes primary stress in T2, it takes secondary stress in the error. In (98b), the error takes the stress pattern of T1: 'yesterday', which means that the vowel [aʲ] in the utterance takes secondary stress, although it is the primary stressed vowel in T2: 'last-night'.

More evidence comes from the type of blend errors I called 'prosodic' in §3.5.3 above. In this type of error, one target contributes the segments of the error utterance, but the other contributes overall prosodic structure; this latter often also includes lexical stress. Example (93a) above shows the blend of T1: 'cémetèry' and T2: 'plànetárium', *[sì.mə.tʰɛ́.ri.əm], which contains the segments from T1 but the prosodic structure of T2, including lexical stress (B-471(38) 5;2). Similarly in (89b), the error *[sɚ.tɪ.fɨ.kʰít] is made up of the segments of T1 'certíficate' but the stress pattern of T2 'cèrtificátion' (AD-507(38)). Finally, in another adult error (AD-291b(38)) the segments from 'Chinése' were blended with the stress pattern of 'Mándarin' to produce *[tʃá .niz].

Although there were only 5 such errors in the adult corpus and 2 in the child corpus, these errors can be argued to show that lexical stress patterns must be stored in the lexicon, if they can be de-linked from their host word and erroneously substituted for the correct stress pattern in a different word. Otherwise one would have to argue that the stress rule operated erroneously on the phonological string created by the blend, but that this was not related to the actual stress patterns of the words involved in the blend. Thus the 'strong/weak' patterns on the rhythmic tier illustrated in example (94) above (for children age 4 and over) should be considered part of the lexical representation of the word, and not a metrical structure assigned by some rule during phonological processing. (I will return to the issue of the development of this tier below.) Something very similar to this was found in my study with I-Ping Wan regarding tone in Mandarin (Wan & Jaeger 1998). In Mandarin, lexical blends usually have a crossover point between onset and rhyme, and the tone originally linked with the rhyme spoken in the error is the tone of the blend utterance. However, there were a few cases where the blend consisted of the segments from one target word, and the tone from the other target word. Since it is indisputable that tones are represented in lexical entries in Mandarin, and the best analysis of the structure of this representation is that tones are autosegmental, and linked to segments via the syllable node, there is no reason why this same analysis shouldn't be applied to English. The difference for English would lie in the fact that the overall stress pattern (strong/weak) of the word would be linked to syllable nodes, rather than a distinct tone being assigned to each syllable.

What about errors of stress per se? Do speakers produce utterances in which a word is spoken with an incorrect lexical stress pattern, and if so, why? The reader may be surprised to learn that I collected only one error of lexical stress from the children in this study; it is given in (99a). However, I collected 16 such errors from adults, which fell into several distinct categories; examples are given in (99b-f).

(99) a. An: 'Mom, could you get some yàrn and tiè some bóws? 'Cuz I
            rèally wànna [dɛ.kə.ré t] Stràwberry's hòuse.'
         M: 'You wanna whát?'
         An: 'Décorate Stràwberry's hòuse.'
            (for 'decorate' [dé.kə.re t]; stress on final syllable instead of
            first syllable; AN-260(4;11) 32)

b. AF: 'So it gèts màrked [pʰɾá.zə.d] . . . prosódically.'
(for 'prosodically' [pʰɾə.zá.di.kḷi]; stress on first syllable instead
of second syllable; AD-294(32))

c. AM: 'A **stùttering wórkshop** will be held (etc.)' (phrasal stress for
compound stress 'stúttering wòrkshop'; AD-299(32))

d. AF: ' . . . when thèy were òne and [tʰú.jìr] . . . twò yèars óld.'
(compound stress for phrasal stress; AD-293(32))

e. AF: 'Do wè hàve a [kʰən.tʰɾǽkt] . . . a cóntract with them?'
(verb stress 'contráct' for noun stress 'cóntract' [kʰán.tʰɾæ̥kt];
AD-305(32))

f. AM: ' . . . there's the [kʰən.tʰɾǽst] of *contról* vs. nón-contròl.'
(for noun 'cóntrast' [kʰán.tʰɾæ̥st]; either wrong lexical category,
or stress anticipated from 'contról'; AD-295(32))

   The errors in (99a,b) represent the most common type of lexical stress error
(Cutler 1980a), where a morphologically complex target word is produced with
the stress pattern of another word which is derivationally related to the intended
word, i.e. one which has the same stem but different derivational affixes and
stress pattern. So in (99a), Anna produced the error *'decoráte' with stress on
the last syllable, under the influence of the word 'decorátion', which was also in
her vocabulary. (The second lexical stress error I collected from the children was
produced by Anna when she was 6 years old, and consisted of producing
*'cooperáte' with final stress, under the influence of 'cooperátion'.) In (99b),
the adult starts to produce *'prósodically' with the stress on the first syllable,
under the influence of 'prósody'.   Of the 16 adult errors, 9 involved a
morphologically related pair of words. The simplest explanation for this type of
error is that all derivationally related words are stored whole in the lexicon with
some linkage among them (semantic and morphological, as well as
phonological). When one member of the morphological family is activated, the
activation is spread to other words in the same group, so that the lexically
represented stress pattern of a related word can intrude on the intended stress
pattern of the target word. Naturally, children will make very few errors of this
type until they have developed a lexicon which contains a number of
morphologically related families of words, and these only begin to show up in
the 5-year-olds in my study.
   The second type of error is illustrated in (99c,d), in which an utterance is
spoken with compound stress when phrasal stress was intended, or vice versa.
So in (99c), a radio announcer intended to announce that a 'stúttering wòrkshop'
(a workshop about stuttering: compound stress) would be held, but instead said
that a *'stùttering wórkshop' (a workshop which stutters: phrasal stress) would
be held. In (99d) the speaker meant to talk about children when they were 'twò
yèars óld' (phrasal stress), but instead produced *'twó-yèar', and was undoubtedly
about to produce the lexical compound 'twó-yèar-òlds', i.e. children who are
two. Of the 16 adult lexical stress errors in my corpus, 4 were of this type, and

they can be explained by the speaker either misparsing the intended utterance as in (99c), or by the speaker erroneously selecting a stored lexical compound when a phrase was intended as in (99d). It may come as a surprise that the children did not produce any errors of this type, since it is well-known that English-speaking children use the process of compounding when they are very young (as early as 1;8) to produce new words for objects and concepts for which they haven't yet acquired a word (Clark 1993: Ch. 8). However, as mentioned in Chapter 2 (§2.2.1), Vogel (1999) has recently demonstrated that while children may produce compounds at early ages, they probably don't have the compound-stress rule fully learned until they are about 12 years old; before this age the children in Vogel's study were unable to utilize the distinction between compound stress and phrasal stress in a comprehension task to correctly select pictures depicting either the compound meaning or the phrasal meaning of a two-word combination (e.g. 'hót-dòg' vs. 'hòt dóg'). She suggests that one reason children may appear to have acquired the compound stress rule much earlier in their productions is that they produce novel compounds in cases where they need to distinguish among different types of some object or activity, and thus would naturally stress the distinguishing modifier which precedes the noun or verb, giving the compound stress pattern. The children in the current study also produced a number of apparent compounds which can easily be explained by this factor; for example:

(100) a An: (holding a pinecone and pretending to eat it)
            'This is a banána [kʰâ⁺n.pʰòʷn] . . . a banána pìnecòne.'
            (for 'pinecone' [pʰá⁺n.kʰòʷn]; [pʰ]<-->[kʰ]; AN-212(25) 4;5)
       b. Al: 'I'm gonna pùt my [dǽn.ʃɪŋ] shòes òn now.'
            (for 'dancing shoes' [dǽn.sɪŋ ʃùz]; [s]<--[ʃ]; AL-130(1) 3;4)

In (100a) Anna produced contrastive stress on 'banana', since this is the word which distinguishes this kind of pinecone from any other. Similarly, when Alice produced (100b), she had the compound 'schóol-shòes' in her vocabulary, and probably produced 'dáncing shòes' in contrast to other kinds of shoes.

Thus the finding that the children in this study did not make compound-stress errors while the adults produced several errors of this type supports Vogel's claims. It is most likely that when young children learn lexical items which happen to be compounds, they simply learn the compound stress pattern along with the segmental aspects of the word when they add this word to their lexicon. Since Berko (1958) has shown that even children ages 5-8 have idiosyncratic definitions for compound words which often have no relationship to the actual morphemes in the compound, it would be unlikely that the children in this study distinguished compounds from other types of words in their lexical representations as they were being acquired (but see Chapter 6, §6.4.2, where I show that compound structure may be marked in form entries). Thus compounds are entered into the lexicon with stress in place like any other word. Early novel compounds would be created with this stress pattern most likely for pragmatic reasons. Eventually the children will learn an abstract principle of the type evident in adults, which allows them to both perceive and produce compound stress correctly for novel lexical items and assign a particular meaning to this type of stress pattern. However, lexicalized compounds will continue to be stored with their correct stress patterns, in the same way that all words are stored with their stress pattern in the lexicon.

The third type of lexical stress error involved pairs of words whose lexical categories, noun vs. verb, are distinguished by stress; the error in (99e), for example, involved the pair 'cóntract' (n) and 'contráct' (v). In this case the speaker produced the verb form when she intended to produce the noun. There are 2 possible errors of this sort in my data, the other being the one in given in (99f); I will return to this error below. The simplest explanation for these errors is that the noun and verb are associated with each other in the lexicon by semantics, morphology, and phonology, and the incorrect member of the pair was selected. However, the fact that this type of error is extremely rare is consistent with the hypothesis, to be discussed in Chapter 4, that the lexicon is heavily organized by lexical category, and thus errors such as these which violate lexical category are uncommon. Again children produced no errors of this type, possibly because they knew few of the pairs of words which participate in this alternation, and also possibly because they had never noticed this morphologically relevant alternation.

The final category of lexical stress error is syntagmatic errors, where it appears that the stress from one word has been superimposed on another word in the same utterance. In my corpus there are 5 errors which look like there is some syntagmatic influence, but in four of these cases, one of the other 3 factors also occurs in the utterance. So, for example, in (99f), it could be that the erroneous stress pattern on *'contrást' is due to the misselection of the verb form of this pair: 'cóntrast' (n) vs. 'contrást' (v). But it could also be that the stress pattern from the following content word 'contról', which is phonetically very similar to the target word 'cóntrast', was anticipated and substituted for the correct stress pattern. In some cases the morphologically related word which probably caused the stress error was also planned and spoken in the same utterance, as in (101).

(101) AF: (explaining a morphologically-based lexical priming task)
'The sòurce wòrd is '[æk.tə.vè.ʃən]', when the tàrget is 'áctive'.'
(for 'activation' [æk.tə.vé.ʃən], with stress pattern of 'áctive';
AD-301(32))

In this case, the stress pattern from 'áctive' is anticipated and superimposed on 'activátion'.

These errors which appear to have a syntagmatic influence can be argued to show that the whole stress pattern of one word can be anticipated or perseverated from the source word and substituted for the stress pattern of another word during phonological processing. This reinforces the hypothesis that the lexical stress is represented on its own autosegmental tier, and under certain circumstances can be detached from its host word and can participate in phonological errors like segments do (i.e. be substituted, moved, etc.). Further evidence for this analysis comes from the one stress error I have analyzed as syntagmatic which does not involve any other influence, given in (102a). A similar child error, classified as 'multiple', is given in (102b).

(**102**) a. AM: (during a radio fund drive) 'We can màke addìtional dóllars on the **ròulette** . . . Ròlodex roulétte.' (AD-306a(32))
b. Al: 'My tèacher sàid *I cán*. My **càn I** . . . My <u>tèacher</u> sàid *I cán*.' ('I can' metathesized, substituted for 'teacher'; AL-76(48) 2;11)

In (102a), the speaker began to metathesize the two words 'roulette' [ru.lɔ́t] and 'Rolodex' [ró".lə.dɛks], but when he spoke the word 'roulette' in the syntactic slot planned for 'Rolodex', he pronounced it with the lexical stress pattern of 'Rólodex', i.e. with the stress on the first syllable. This could be interpreted to show that in this case the stress pattern became closely linked with the specific syntactic position in the utterance. In (102b), Alice either anticipated or perseverated the phrase 'I cán', and then metathesized it and inserted it into the slot for 'teacher'; in this position the phrase took on the rhythmic structure of the word 'téacher'. It is in fact the norm that when words are produced in an erroneous location in a syntagmatic string, they take on the *phrasal* (but not lexical) stress intended for that location, as in (103), where 'restaurant' takes the tonic stress intended for 'hotel', but retains its lexical stress.

(**103**) AF: 'I sùre hòpe there's a **hotèl** in the **réstaurant**.'
TF: 'A whát?'
AF: 'I mean a <u>rèstaurant</u> in the <u>hotél</u>.' (reversal of words 'restaurant' [rést.rɑnt] and 'hotel' [ho".tʰéɬ]; AD-634(45))

However, the errors given in (102) are only errors I collected where both the phrasal and lexical stress patterns remained associated with the syntagmatic slot, and were imposed on a single word or phrase which was moved into this slot erroneously.

I collected only this one syntagmatic stress error from the children (102b). However, this does not mean that children do not associate lexical and phrasal stress patterns with syntactic slots, as there is ample evidence for this linkage in their telescoping errors. One of the most important diagnostic tools for classifying an error as a telescoping (as opposed to an anticipation) is that while some rhythmic beats are missing, the overall pitch structure (and to a large extent duration) remains intact over the telescoped part of the utterance. The pitch structure derives partly from the lexical stress of the words involved (since the primary phonetic cue for stress in English is pitch), as well as overall intonation patterns. Consider the following examples:

(104) a. An: '[dʒrô:ʷp] . . . [dʒrô:ʷp] . . . júmp-ròpe.'
(for 'jump-rope' [dʒʌmp.rò"p]; AN-124(34) 3;10)

b. An: 'Aùnt [ɨ.lí:zɨ.mèʲks] . . . Aùnt Elízabeth màkes rèal gòod
hòmemade cóokies.'
(for 'Elizabeth makes' [ɨ.lí.zɨ.bəθ mèʲks]; AN-329(34) 5;11)

c. Al: 'Gìve me the [tʃǽk] . . . the chéese cràckers.'
(for 'cheese crackers' [tʃiz kʰʒæ̀.k3z]; AL-213(11) 4;4)

The first error is a telescoping: the onset from 'jump' [dʒ] and the whole word
'rope' [roʷp] are collapsed together, while the rhyme [ʌmp] from 'jump' is
omitted (this is a 'mixed onset' type error). However, the new single-syllable
utterance carries a high-to-low falling pitch on the single vowel, analogous to
the lexical high-low pitch pattern on the compound 'júmp-ròpe'. Thus in this
case the lexical stress (pitch) pattern remains, even though one of the stress-
bearing units has been deleted. Similarly, in (104b), the syllable [bəθ] is
deleted, but the lexical stress remains on the second syllable of 'Elizabeth'; it is
not shifted due to the deletion of a syllable. Neither of these could be simple
anticipations of phonological LUs. But in (104c), the utterance *[tʃæk] cannot
be a telescoping of 'cheese crackers' because the vowel [æ] takes only the phrasal
stress assigned to the word 'cheese'; if it were a telescoping, the vowel would
have to be lengthened and have a falling pitch, fulfilling the pitch requirements
of both words. Example (105) consists of constructed examples showing what
these errors would have to look like to be analyzed as the other type of error.

(105) a. *'[dʒróʷp] . . . [dʒróʷp] . . . júmp-ròpe.'
(anticipation of [roʷp], substituted for [ʌmp])

b. *'Aùnt [ɨ.lí.zɨ.meʲk] . . . Aùnt Elízabeth màkes rèal gòod
hòmemade cóokies.'
(anticipation of syllable [meʲk], substituted for syllable [bəθ])

c. *'Gìve me the [tʃæ̀:ks] . . . the chéese cràckers.'
(telescoping of 'cheese crackers' [tʃiz kʰʒæ̀.kɚz]; deletion of
rhyme+onset [iz.kʰʒ])

One further piece of evidence that (104b) is a telescoping but (105b) is not, is
that (104b) retains the 3rd sg. present suffix, which is morphologically (but not
phonologically) linked to the word 'makes'; in telescopings such morphology is
usually retained (as discussed in §3.5.4), but in phonological LU errors it is
usually stranded (i.e. the syllable [meʲk] would be anticipated and substituted for
the syllable [bəθ], leaving the suffix behind). Similarly (104c) is unlikely to be
a telescoping, because the plural morpheme does not appear in the error
utterance; the constructed telescoping example in (105c), shows the plural
morpheme as being retained. Thus these telescopings provide ample evidence
that lexical stress functions on its own autosegmental tier during phonological
processing; this is true from the earliest errors, even when segments become
intermixed from different syllables. The only cases where some of the stress-

driven pitch contour is missing are those where a long string of syllables is deleted, such as the error *'chóokìe' for 'chòcolate chìp cóokìe' (AN-30(34) 2;2); in this case there is a general high-to-low fall over the whole utterance. Overall, the pitch contours over the children's telescopings are indistinguishable from those of adults.

In sum, there is evidence from lexical substitution errors and lexical blend errors that lexical stress patterns are stored in the lexicon along with the other aspects of phonological form for each word. Two words are more likely to substitute for each other in a malapropism if they have the same stress pattern, and blends always show the lexical stress pattern of one of the two targets; the stress pattern is not computed differently for the erroneous utterance. The blends give evidence that stress patterns are linked with aspects of the segmental or syllable-structure tiers in lexical representations, but can be delinked even in a lexical error. This is because blends sometimes include the segments from one target but the stress pattern from the other, although this is mainly true of the older children and adults. Phonological errors of lexical stress usually involve two words which are derived from the same stem; however, since the children know few such pairs of words, they produced only one error of this type in my study. Adult errors of lexical stress also included compound vs. phrasal stress, and noun vs. verb stress, but the children did not show these patterns. Finally, some lexical stress errors, and all telescoping errors, show that lexical stress exists on its own autosegmental tier, and can be delinked and reassigned to other syllables during phonological processing.

The development of the actual form of the representation of stress in lexical entries is only indirectly suggested by the SOT data, but a few hypotheses can be formulated. In (93) above I presented a scenario for the development of syllable structure, and in this figure I show foot structure, which embodies lexical stress patterns in adult lexical entries, only coming into play around age 4. So what might the representation of stress be like before this age?

In very young children's speech the primary cue for stress is pitch, and it may be the case that this is the only cue. Specifically, young children produce each syllable with approximately the same duration, a fact which prompted Allen & Hawkins (1980) to suggest that for very young children, English is a syllable-timed rather than a stress-timed language. Furthermore they do not yet have the allophonic variations associated with lexical stress in their phonological systems (e.g. aspiration, tapping, vowel reduction), and since intensity is an unimportant cue for lexical stress in adult English (it is mainly used for contrastive stress, Ohala 1977), it is unlikely that young children would have developed an intensity factor for expressing syllable prominence. In Jaeger (1997) I demonstrated that Alice, at 21 months, seemed to have formed the hypothesis that English was a tone language, in that she had several pairs or triplets of words which she differentiated by pitch, and to a lesser extent, duration; for example: [tʌ́:.mʌ́:] 'Grandpa', [tʌ̄:.mʌ̄:] 'Grandma', and [tʌ́.mʌ̀] 'music'. So at least up to age 2, stress is probably represented in lexical phonological representations as a whole-word pitch pattern. Because the telescopings made by the 1-year-olds in this study maintained aspects of the pitches of the lexical items involved in the utterance, even when some vowels were deleted, it seems most likely that this prosodic pattern is linked to the word node itself rather than to vowels, for example, and thus has some autosegmental features in even the earliest representations.

However, after age 2, some of the other phonetic properties involved in adult English lexical stress begin to appear in the children's productions. As indicated in §3.3.4 above, when the children were around 2;3-2;5 the durational properties of their words began to sound more adult-like, and furthermore they began to show some evidence of allophonic variations which were linked to stress (for example, unstressed vowels became more schwa-like, medial voiceless plosives were aspirated only in onsets of stressed syllables). Thus by the age of 2;6, which I have argued above is the time that internal syllable structure begins to be developed, the children show evidence of having some sort of indication in their form lexicon of which syllables are stressed and which are unstressed. Since it is at this age that the syllable-node tier begins to develop, perhaps this information about stress is represented as a sort of feature such as [+stress] or [-stress], linked to the syllable nodes. This feature could be the basis for the eventual development of the 'strong/weak' rhythmic tier, allowing foot structure to appear, which I have argued begins to develop around age 4. While this scenario for the development of the representation of lexical stress is speculative, it is completely compatible with the SOT data, as well as the hypothesis presented above about the development of the representation of syllable structure.

3.7.2 Phrasal Rhythm

It is often noted that one of the most important functions of lexical stress, besides distinguishing one word from another, is to contribute to the overall rhythmic structure of sentences. English is often called a 'stress-timed' language since stressed syllables are said to come at relatively regular intervals in an utterance. The question I will raise here is whether or not this has any relevance to actual speech production planning, especially where the 'Phonological Processes' component is involved.

In SOT research it is a truism that two units are more likely to be mutually involved in an error if they occur in locations in the syntagmatic string with the same stress value, particularly if they are both stressed (Boomer & Laver 1973, Garrett 1975). Cutler (1980a) explains that this is because two stressed units have higher activation than unstressed units, and thus are more likely to interact with one another than two unstressed units or a stressed with an unstressed unit. In this section I will address this issue in terms of phonological errors; in Chapter 4 (§4.2.5) I will look at lexical errors in this light.

In order to see whether the children followed this same well-documented pattern, I looked at all the between-word contextual phonological anticipations, perseverations, A/Ps, and exchanges (but not 'multiple' errors) in which the target and source were uniquely identifiable, or if there was more than one source, where all sources would give the same analysis. I did not include within-word errors, since they often involve two syllables with different stress levels and so are apparently governed by a different process. I also did not include metathesis errors, since they usually occur in adjacent syllables, which almost by definition contain different stress levels. Cases in which the error involved more than one syllable, such as the rhyme of one syllable and the onset of the following syllable where the two syllables had different stress values (i.e. R$O errors), were also not included in the count. Finally, I did not include the adult errors in categories 6.5, 10.5, and 11.5, since the children did not make comparable errors (I will return to this point below).

To every syllable involved in the error, I assigned either a 'strong' or a 'weak' value, depending on its value in the rhythm of the phrase. This was a simple task since 'strong' beats were always marked in my notes when the error was originally collected. This was a somewhat different measure from that used in assigning lexical stress for looking at lexical substitution errors. First, it was binary rather than having three levels of stress, since only the syllable's status as stressed or not stressed is relevant here. Second, for this phrase-stress analysis I did mark syllables in words with 3+ syllables which carried tertiary stress as 'strong' when they were pronounced as relatively strong beats in the phrase; so for example, 'recommend' was considered to have a S-W-S pattern. Finally, I included syllabic inflectional affixes in the rhythmic structure of the phrase, whereas they were not considered in assigning lexical stress patterns to words in lexical substitution errors, since stems without inflectional affixes were taken as the unit of lexical representation. I then counted the number of errors in which target and source syllables (or both targets in the case of exchanges) were either both 'strong' or both 'weak', or involved one 'strong' and one 'weak' syllable. The results are shown in Table 3.23. In this table I have divided the 1-2-year-olds' errors into '1-2a', in this case those children in the 2-word stage when the error was made, and '1-2b', i.e. errors made by 1- or 2-year-old children in the 3+word stage.

It is clear from Table 3.23 that errors in which both the target and source syllables were stressed predominated in both the child and adult data; overall this pattern accounted for 78% of the child errors and 79.5% of the adult errors in this count, and at every age they were overwhelmingly the most common type (between 71.5-81.5%). The youngest children, i.e. 1- and 2-year olds in the 2-word stage, had the lowest percentage of errors involving units in two stressed syllables, 71.5%. This figure increased 9% for the 1-2-year-olds in the 3+word stage, so it is likely that the increase in importance of syntagmatic phrasal planning which occurs when children begin to plan utterances of three or more words accounts for the increase in importance of phrasal stress in phonological planning. Interestingly, the figure dropped somewhat for the 5-year-olds, which may be due to the fact that at this age they were learning more multi-syllabic words, and so had many more unstressed syllables available for error per phrase than the younger children. This would fit with the fact that overall the children's second most common error type involved one strong and one weak syllable, but for the adults the second most common type involved two unstressed syllables, and adults also know many multisyllabic words. In fact, if I were to add in the

TABLE 3.23

Number and percentage of unambiguous between-word phonological errors where target and source units fell into three stress categories: [+str] = both target and source units occurred in stressed syllables; [-str] = both target and source units occurred in unstressed syllables; [+/- str] = one of target/source units occurred in a stressed syllable and the other in an unstressed syllable.

Age:	1-2a	1-2b	3	4	5	Total	Adult
[+ str] %	71.5%	80.5%	77%	81.5%	73%	78%	79.5%
[-str] %	14.25%	8.5%	10%	5.5%	10%	8.5%	13%
[+/-str] %	14.25%	11%	13%	13%	17%	13.5%	7.5%
Total N=	**14**	**107**	**99**	**146**	**103**	**469**	**189**

errors from the three 'adults-only' categories, 6.5, 10.5, and 11.5, the adult figure for interaction between two unstressed syllables would be 17%, since these categories involve adding extra syllables to the target word, and in every case these syllables were unstressed. It is likely that the difference between stressed and unstressed syllables is greater both in planning and execution of speech for adults, since, as discussed in the preceding section, the phonetic cues for stress are not as robust in the children's speech as they are for adults; therefore it is not surprising that the children could violate this distinction more readily than the adults.

In §3.2.3 above I showed that the most important phonetic factor involved in explaining vowel errors was the stress level of the vowel; this factor was more important than segmental features such as height, backness, or roundness. From Table 3.23 it can be seen that the influence of phrasal stress is not just a factor in vowel errors but in all phonological errors. However, if the vowel errors are separated out from the consonant errors we find that the phrasal stress is a somewhat more important factor for vowels than for consonants. In Table 3.9, the overall figure for two stressed vowels was 79.5% for the children and 81% for adults, slightly higher than the overall averages from Table 3.23; but Table 3.9 includes both between-word and within-word errors. If we take just the between-word errors from Table 3.23, the children's figures are: two stressed syllables: 82% vowels, 77.5% consonants and LUs; two unstressed syllables: 8% vowels, 8% consonants and LUs; stressed and unstressed syllable: 10% vowels, 14% consonants and LUs, with a 90% overall 'same syllable weight' for vowels vs. 85.5% for consonants and LUs. The adults similarly show an overall 97% 'same syllable weight' for vowels vs. 92% for consonants and LUs. Thus for consonants and LUs, although the same stress level is important, other factors such as phonetic similarity and syllable structure position can outweigh the importance of syllable weight. (See Berg 1990 for a similar finding in

German.)

There may appear at first to be a contradiction in this argument, since in my illustration of the development of syllable structure in (93) above I suggested that the actual 'strong-weak' designations which are licensed by foot structure are not represented in syllable structure until age 4. However, the most likely developmental progression is that at ages 2-3, when there is evidence of the influence of the weight of syllables within the phrasal stress pattern but no clear evidence for foot structure, the 'weight' factor is given by the lexical stress, which is represented in the lexicon when the word is first learned, as discussed in the preceding section. The consistency of the weight of syllables in phonological errors would also be facilitated by the fact that function words are typically unstressed, a factor to which children are sensitive from their earliest multi-word utterances (Gerken 1994); this is one reason why function words are less susceptible to error than content words in general. As suggested above, lexical stress is probably the phonetic factor which *allows* the development of foot structure within individual lexical representations; then lexical stress along with the distinction between stressed content words and unstressed function words allows the development of phrasal rhythmic structures. I would thus predict that it would be at about age 4 that children would start showing signs of stress shifting within individual words when such shift is required by the overall rhythmic structure of the phrase, as in 'discóvered Mìssissíppi' vs. 'Mìssissìppi Ríver', where primary stress shifts to a different inherently strong syllable within the word due to phrasal rhythm (Prince 1983, Kenstowicz 1994:554-5). Testing of this prediction awaits future research.

3.7.3 Tonic Stress as an Organizer of the Syntagmatic Phonological String

In phonological phrases, there is one word which has special pragmatic prominence, typically because it is either the new information in focus in the phrase, or its meaning is being foregrounded in some pragmatically relevant way (e.g. emphasis, contrast, denial of previous statement, etc.). I will call the word which has this pragmatic prominence the 'tonic word' of the phrase. The primary-stressed syllable of the tonic word receives 'tonic stress', that is, the strongest stress in the phrase. Most typically, this syllable is marked phonetically in declarative utterances by being the highest pitched syllable in the phrase; the pitch then falls to the end of the phrase. In questions, it takes the highest pitch in the phrase except for the rising-pitch which occurs on the final word(s) of the question. Besides these pitch patterns, the tonic syllable (i.e. the syllable which takes tonic stress) is marked by an exaggeration of the other features which normally mark lexical stress: lengthening of segments, full value of vowels in the syllable, specific allophones of consonants (e.g. aspirated voiceless stops), and intensity.

Because of the special function of this prosodically marked syllable in a phrase, it would not be surprising if it played some important role in speech production planning, specifically in the planning of the phonetic properties of the utterance. (In this chapter I will focus on the role of the tonic syllable in phonological errors; in Chapter 4, §4.2.3, I will look into its role in lexical errors.) However, several different conflicting predictions are possible regarding the role of the tonic syllable in speech production planning. One possibility is that the tonic syllable would consistently be a source of errors, due to its phonetic and semantic prominence during the planning of the phrase. On the other hand, since tonic stress typically falls toward the end of a phrase in English (since this is the most common position for new information in English), one might predict that the tonic would most often be the source in anticipations, and the error in perseverations. Another possibility is that tonic syllables would rarely be produced erroneously, since the correct planning of these syllables is crucial for the information content of the utterance. Conversely, since the word containing tonic stress is usually new information and thus being planned for speaking for the first time in the discourse, it might be especially susceptible to error. We must rely on the data to sort out these various possibilities.

In order to explore this issue, I looked at all the between-word phonological errors which involved phrases of at least two words, and ascertained the involvement of the syllable with the highest prosodic prominence. I looked only at errors with a single unambiguous source, or if there was more than one source, errors in which the analysis would be the same for each source; I also excluded errors with list intonation. As usual I did not include A/P errors, metathesis errors, within-word errors, multiple errors, telescopings, or feature errors. I then classified each eligible error into one of the following categories: +T(s)=the source syllable carries tonic stress, as in (106a); +T(e)=the target/error syllable carries tonic stress, as in (106b); -T=the tonic stress falls somewhere other than either the source or target/error syllable, as in (106c); +T(b)=both the source and target/error syllables carry tonic stress in different phrases, as in (106d); +T(t1)=in an exchange, tonic stress falls on the stressed syllable of the first target word, as in (106e); +T(t2)=in an exchange, tonic stress falls on the stressed syllable of the second target word (as in 106f). There were no exchange errors where the tonic syllable fell on both the source and target/error syllable. The tonic syllable is marked in the utterances in my data (both given as examples and in the data section of the book) by the primary-stress accent marker: v́.

(106) a. Al: 'Mom, I'm èating as [kʰǽst] as I cán.'
            (for 'fast' [fæst]; +T(s); AL-66(1) 2;10)
       b. OG: 'You dòn't [déʲ] . . . you dòn't sáy that.'
            (for 'say' [seʲ]; +T(e); OC-13(12) 2;2)
       c. Al: 'Mý [bà.təm] . . . my bòttle is ìn the clóset.'
            (for 'bottle' [bá.təł]; -T; AL-60(12) 2;10)
       d. B: (telling Mom where his imaginary 'off' switch is located)
            'It's behìnd my báck. Prèss [sták].'
            (for 'stop' [stap]; +T(b); B-422(12) 4;11)
       e. Al: 'Hère's my [dú nà̀ʲ.pɚ].'
            (for 'new diaper' [nú dà̀ʲ.pɚ]; +T(t1); AL-94(25) 3;1)

f. An: 'Shòuldn't we [brʌθ] our [tʰíʃ]?'
    (for 'brush our teeth' [brʌʃ ɑr tʰiθ]; +T(t2); AN-322(25) 5;10)

I then counted the number of errors which fell into each of these categories, by age and error type (complete anticipations, incomplete anticipations, perseverations, and exchanges). In performing this count, I separated out the utterances of the 1-2-year-olds in the 2-word stage (1-2a) from those producing phrases of three or more words (1-2b), as I did in several of the counts above. The purpose of this separation was to further evaluate the issue of whether or not there is true syntax during the 2-word stage, or only after children begin forming utterances of three or more words. If there is true syntax at the 2-word stage, children in this stage should show the same tonic-syllable influence as older children and adults, where syntax is clearly in use. In order to be able to accurately interpret the figures regarding tonic syllable involvement in errors, I generated an estimate of the average number of syllables per phrase at each age by counting the syllables in all the anticipatory and perseveratory substitution error phrases. I divided this average by 2 to arrive at the percentage of utterances in which the tonic syllable could be involved in the error by chance (either as target or source, i.e. two possibilities per phrase). The results of the analysis are given in Table 3.24, with the 'chance' figures listed at the bottom of the table.

This table shows that the tonic syllable was involved in errors of all types considerably more often than would be predicted by chance at every age, with one exception. For the the 1-2-year-old children who were still in the 2-word stage, the tonic syllable was involved in errors at slightly below chance level (60% involvement, compared to 64% chance). This is compatible with the hypothesis that there is no syntactic structure in utterances during the 2-word stage, since the 'tonic' syllable is a syntactic notion, signalling pragmatic focus in conjunction with the choice of sentence structure. However once the children began systematically producing utterances of 3 or more words, the tonic syllable was involved in errors at a rate of at least twice that predicted by chance, and for adults it was involved three times as often as would be expected by chance.

The various competing hypotheses listed above about the involvement of the tonic syllable are clearly resolved by the data. First, in completed anticipations, the tonic syllable most often serves as the source of the error (overall 44.5% for the children, 45.5% adults), and less often as the target/error (10.5% children, 13.5% adults). This is not surprising given that the tonic syllable is most often at the end of a phrase in English, and thus this prosodically prominent syllable provides the material which is most often anticipated and intrudes at some earlier location in the phrase. The existence of the prosodically marked and pragmatically salient tonic syllable at the ends of phrases is undoubtedly the reason why speakers of English produce a majority of anticipatory errors, whereas speakers of languages without these factors typically produce an equal number of anticipatory and perseveratory errors (see §2.3.2).

The opposite pattern is found in perseveratory errors: the tonic syllable is most often in the target/error word (overall 46.5% children, 41% adults), and less

TABLE 3.24

Involvement of the tonic syllable in phonological errors. Anticipations, perseverations and exchanges, between-word errors only, in phrases of at least two words. 'A-C'=complete anticipations; 'A-I'=incomplete anticipations; 'PR'=perseverations; 'EX'=exchanges. 'B'= both target and source/error syllables have tonic stress; 'S'= the source syllable is the tonic; 'E'=the target/error syllable is the tonic; '-T'=the tonic syllable is not involved in the error; 'T1' or 'T2'=in exchanges, the first or second target is the tonic.

Age:	1-2a	1-2b	3	4	5	Total		Adult	
A-C B	0	0	0	0	1	1	1%	0	
S	0	21	8	11	7	47	44.5%	10	45.5%
E	0	3	4	0	4	11	10.5%	3	13.5%
-T	1	12	12	11	10	46	44%	9	41%
Total N=	1	36	24	22	22	105		22	
A-I B	0	0	0	2	0	2	2%	1	1.3%
S	1	7	7	19	17	51	47.5%	25	33.3%
E	0	4	6	9	3	22	20.5%	10	13.3%
-T	1	2	5	12	12	32	30%	39	52%
Total N=	2	13	18	42	32	107		75	
PR B	0	0	2	5	4	11	6%	1	2%
S	2	9	10	6	5	32	18%	6	14%
E	1	19	14	30	19	83	46.5%	18	41%
-T	2	10	9	22	10	53	29.5%	19	43%
Total N=	5	38	35	63	38	179		44	
EX T1	1	3	3	3	1	11	34.5%	8	27%
T2	1	6	2	2	1	12	37.5%	16	53%
-T	0	4	3	1	1	9	28%	6	20%
Total N=	2	13	8	6	3	32		30	
Grand Total=	10	100	85	133	95	423		171	
% Tonic	60%	72%	66%	65.5%	65%	67%		57%	
Chance	64%	37%	32%	28%	29%	38%		17%	

often the source (18% children, 14% adults). For exchanges, in the children's data it appears that the tonic syllable is equally likely to be either the first or second target (t1=34.5%, t2=37.5%), although in the adult data it is more often the second target than the first (t1=27%, t2=53%), so there seems to be some influence of the tonic syllable typically being at the ends of phrases in the adult exchange errors. However, the figures for complete anticipations vs. exchanges provide a strong piece of evidence regarding the status of incomplete anticipations. In §1.4.2 above I discussed some of the arguments regarding these 'incomplete' errors, which logically could be either interrupted anticipatory errors (i.e. corrected before the source was spoken) or interrupted exchanges (i.e. corrected before the second target word was spoken). The children's figures for interrupted anticipations in Table 3.24 support the hypothesis that they are actually anticipations, since as with completed anticipations, the tonic syllable is most often the source of the error in incompletes; for children the tonic is the source in 43.5% completed anticipations and 47.5% incompletes, whereas for exchanges the target and source are equally likely to contain the tonic syllable. For the adults the figure is not so clear, and in fact the second target in an exchange error was more likely to contain the tonic (53%) than was the source in a complete anticipation (45.5%). I have no clear explanation for this, and probably more data are needed to further explore this issue. At this point, all I can conclude is that while most incomplete anticipations are probably classified correctly as anticipations, a few of the errors classified as 'incomplete anticipation/substitution' could be interrupted exchanges, which is a good reason to keep them distinct from 'completed anticipations' in tables such as the one under discussion.

However, the overall finding in this section is that the tonic syllable plays a prominent role in phonological planning for children as young as 1 year old, as soon as the child begins regularly producing syntactically governed utterances of three or more words. The tonic syllable is most often the source in anticipation errors, the location of the error in perseveratory errors, and at least for the children is equally likely to be the first or second target in exchange errors.

3.7.4 Errors of Intonation

It is well known that intonation in English can perform a number of important functions (for a recent review, see Selkirk 1995). First, it serves as a pragmatic marker, indicating something about the emotional state of speakers and their attitudes towards what they are saying. Second, it can indicate what type of speech act the utterance intends to convey: declaration, question, command, and so forth. Third, within sentences it marks off phonological phrases and demarks syntactic units; it can thus be used to disambiguate various constructions. Fourth, it can mark specific types of syntactic structures, such as tag questions, fronting constructions, contrastive constructions, and so on. Because of the large variety of functions played by intonation, it is difficult to say exactly where during speech production planning an intonational error has been made. I have placed intonation assignment in the same level with the selection and compilation of syntactic structures in the RPC Model, but it is possible that intonation errors can actually arise at various locations in the planning process.

Errors of intonation seem to be very rare. This could be due at least in part to the difficulty of the hearer knowing exactly what intonational pattern the speaker intended (Cutler 1980a). However another possible reason that they are rare may be the fact that intonation is extremely closely linked either with pragmatic intentions or specific syntactic structures, so that once either the pragmatic intention or syntactic structure has been selected, there are very few possible choices for appropriate intonational patterns. I collected only 3 intonational errors from the children, all produced at ages 4 or 5, and 5 from the adults. An examination of these 8 errors shows that they do fall into some interesting patterns.

First, several of the errors could be argued to actually be phrase blends, where the erroneous utterance blends together the intended words and syntax from one target utterance, but the intonation patterns from the other.

(107) a. An: (telling the 'Three Little Pigs' story)

'But . . . still . . . he could not blow down that house of

brick[s:]. . .'

(blend of the syntax from:

'he could not blow down that house of bricks'
and the intonation from:

'he could not blow that house of bricks down';
AN-258(33) 4;10)

   b. AF: ' . . . pròbe with a relàted or unrèlated wórd as sòon as you [kʰ n̩] . . . as sòon as you cán.'
(speaker first incorrectly produced unstressed 'căn', as if she planned to say 'as sòon as you căn (sómething)'; she then produced it with full stress, [kʰǽn]; AD-307 (33))

   c. AM: (holding up a vitamin bottle)
'We're rùnning oùt of thĕse áren't we.'
(blend of: 'We're rùnning òut of thĕse vítamins, áren't wè.'
and: 'We're rùnning òut of thése, arén't wè.' AD-308(33))

In (107a), Anna produced a blend of the syntax from the utterance with the verb+ particle 'blow down' adjacent to each other, but the intonation which would have been appropriate if the particle 'down' had been moved to the end of the phrase; thus when she produced rising pitch on 'bricks', she expected to have the word 'down' after it in order to produce the phrase final falling tone. Similarly in

(107b) the adult seems to have blended the intonation of the longer phrase ('as sòon as you can (sómething)' which calls for the reduced, unstressed form of 'can', with the actual phrasing of 'as sòon as you cán', which requires the full form of 'can'. Finally, in (107c), the speaker blended the wording of the sentence which uses the stressed deictic 'thése', with the intonation of the sentence which requires the full noun (i.e. involves an unstressed 'thĕse'); the result is that the phrase 'aren't we' sounded like the item being run out of. So these errors can be explained with reference to the notion of 'phrase blend' which is easily captured by the RPC Model (see Chapter 6, §6.6.3).

Two other errors seem to show a misalignment of the intonation pattern and the intended phrasing within the utterance, but cannot be explained in terms of a phrase blend. These are given in (108).

(108) a. B: (talking to friend Mike, who was over visiting)
　　　　　　'Gùess whát, Mike? I'm gìving **you cándy, and mé**.'
　　　　　　(pauses, thinks) 'I'm gìving <u>yóu càndy, and mé</u>.'
　　　　　　(first utterance sounds like he was giving Mike 'candy and me';
　　　　　　second time, giving 'you and me' candy; B-538(33) 5;6)
　　　b. AM: 'Oh, lòts of recéipts for mè, Í sèe!'
　　　　　　(speaker meant: 'lòts of receípts for mè I sèe', with 'receipts'
　　　　　　the tonic for the whole phrase; AD-310(33))

In (108a), Bobby's intonation links the wrong lexical items together semantically; he attempts to correct the meaning, but the wording itself is still slightly ungrammatical, showing that he is trying to express a proposition for which he doesn't yet have completely appropriate syntax. In (108b), the speaker, whose job it is to collect receipts from others and enter them into a computer program, intends to merely comment that someone is giving him a large number of receipts. But with the 'tag' intonation on 'I see', it sounded like he thought there was something sneaky about the receipts, or the person handing the receipts to him.

Third, there were two adult errors which consisted of putting the phrasal stress on the wrong lexical item, specifically a function word.

(109) a. AM: (daughter leans her head on AM's shoulder at the dinner table)
　　　　　　'You're **lèaning ón** mè.'
　　　　　　(for 'You're léaning òn mè'; speaker introspected he meant the
　　　　　　second pattern; AD-309(33))
　　　b. TM: 'When Í stàrt drìving, I'm gònna drìve Dád's càr.'
　　　AF: 'Whý? He wòuldn't let **Ànna drive hís**.
　　　　　　I mean, he wòuldn't lèt <u>Ánna drìve hìs</u>.'
　　　　　　(in error, emphasis was on 'his' rather than 'Anna'; AD-311(33))

These could be caused by simple misassignment of phrasal stress in the intonational component, or could be a sort of pragmatic error, focussing on the wrong element in the phrase, which could take place in the 'Inferential Processes' component when the message is first being formulated.

Finally, there was one particularly interesting child error which involved intonation, pragmatics, and lexical selection.

(110) B: (calling to his friend David)
'[dǽːdìː] . . . I mean <u>Dávid</u>, còme ón!' (B-250b(33) 4;4)

In the first utterance, Bobby erroneously says 'Daddy' instead of 'David', but he also uses a sort of polite calling intonation which would be appropriate if he were calling for Daddy. In his correction, he uses a short, harsh, commanding intonation when he corrects to 'David', which is the pragmatically appropriate intonation to call for his same-age playmate to follow him.

It is interesting that the earliest intonation error in my corpus occurred when the speaker was 4;4. The fact that I collected no intonation errors from younger children could have several causes. The most obvious would be that younger children simply do not produce such errors, but there are other possible explanations which may relate to the development of the various functions of intonation. When children are producing one-word utterances, intonation (along with gaze, tone of voice, gestures, etc.) is the marker of the kind of speech-act the child intends to perform, and it seems extremely unlikely that a child in this stage could accidentally produce the wrong intonational pattern for the intended speech act. And even if a child did so, it would be very difficult for an adult to know the child had made an error. Similarly, when children are in the 2-word stage, the intonation serves both the speech-act function and also serves to demark the utterance phonologically; the fact that both words are spoken under the same intonation curve is the diagnostic for deciding that the child is in fact in the 2-word stage. However, intonation performs no syntactic function at this stage, as argued in the preceding section, and recognizing an error in the pragmatic intent of intonation over a two-word utterance would again be very difficult.

When children begin regularly producing utterances of three or more words, intonation begins to take on syntactic functions, but the repertoire of children this young in terms of both syntactic constructions and syntactically meaningful intonation patterns is rather small. Thus, the children have to make relatively few syntactically relevant choices about intonation, and so are unlikely to make errors, particularly errors that are discernible by an adult. It is only when children are producing a broad range of fairly complex syntactic constructions, and are regularly making syntactic choices which reflect information structures which require specific intonational patterns, that they can make errors of intonation which are obvious to an adult; at this point there really starts to be a 'right' and 'wrong' intonational pattern for specific utterances in specific contexts with specific purposes. Because the children's linguistic development had reached this point by the time they were 4 years old, I began noticing these very few erroneous intonation productions. Once the children began producing intonation errors, they showed all the same types of errors as the adults did in this corpus, except for the errors with incorrect focus (109); however, these may have been the most difficult for me to hear since I wouldn't always have known what a child meant to emphasize in an utterance.

Although intonation errors are few, they provide an especially rich source of information about how pragmatics, lexicon, syntax, and phonology all interact during speech production planning. They also provide evidence about the relationship between the development of the various functions of intonation, and how intonation is situated in speech production planning.

3.7.5 Summary of Stress and Intonation

These SOTs have provided a wealth of information regarding the representation and processing of aspects of prosody involving pitch, specifically lexical stress, phrasal rhythm, and intonational patterns. First, lexical substitution and blend errors support the claim that lexical stress is stored in lexical phonological representations in English, rather than being assigned by some sort of algorithm during phonological processing. Blend errors also show that the lexical stress pattern can be delinked from the segments of one word and substituted for the original pattern in a different word. Telescoping errors also attest to this delinking during phonological processing; when some stress-bearing units are deleted, the pitch patterns can be distributed over the remaining word or phrase. I collected only one error of lexical stress per se from any of the children, which supports the claim that lexical items are learned with their lexical stress patterns intact when the words are acquired in the first place. The one error I collected from a child was made at age 4;11, and follows the most common pattern found in adult data, which involves two derivationally related words such as 'décorate, decorátion'; in the error the stress pattern from one of the words is erroneously superimposed on the segments from the other word. I argued that this shows that morphologically related words are linked to each other in the lexicon, possibly in 'families' of words derived from the same stem; they are also semantically and phonologically related. Because young children know few multimorphemic and derivationally related words, they rarely make this type of stress error. The adults also made some errors involving compound stress vs. phrasal stress, and noun stress vs. verb stress, but these types didn't occur in the child data, indicating that these patterns may not yet have been productive for the children.

Turning to phrasal stress, one can see that the overall rhythmic properties of a phrase are extremely important in phonological planning, since any two phonological units are more likely to be mutually involved in an error if they both carry strong stress, making them more salient or highly activated during the planning, and thus more likely to interfere with one another; however this pattern is clearer once children have begun to produce utterances of 3+words. At ages 2-3 this is most likely due to lexical stress patterns, and the child's knowledge of the rhythmic properties of content vs. function words; after age 4 it also involves the metrical structure inherent in foot structure being added to lexical phonological representations, which then becomes available for assignment of phrasal rhythmic properties during phonological processing. Furthermore, the tonic-stressed syllable in any phrase is far more likely to be involved in the error than would be predicted by chance, for children in the 3+ word stage and older, and for adults, but not for children in the pre-syntactic 2-word stage. In anticipations it is most likely to be the source of the error, and in perseverations it is most often the target/error itself. Finally, intonational errors are very rare in both the child and adult data, but do not occur before children are 4 years old. These errors suggest that intonation can be linked with pragmatics, lexicon, syntax, and phonology during the speech production planning process, and that the various functions of intonation are acquired at different stages of development.

3.8   The Phonological Structure of Lexical Entries

An important general question which underlies much of the discussion in previous sections of this chapter is: Which aspects of phonological form are represented in lexical entries? Are there any differences in salience among various aspects of lexical phonological representations? Previous literature as well as data presented in this chapter suggest that number of syllables and lexical stress are salient phonological properties in lexical entries, since two words are more likely to substitute for each other, especially in a malapropism, if they have these properties in common. I also looked at a mean syllable-structure consistency measure and found that malapropisms show a higher percentage on this measure than semantically related substitution pairs. Both malapropism data (Fay & Cutler 1977, Cutler & Fay 1982) and 'tip of the tongue' studies (Brown & McNeill 1966) show that having the same initial phoneme is an important factor; one might also consider that having the same final phoneme or the same stressed vowel would contribute to similarity between words. Finally, some properties which might be hypothesized to be less salient would be such things as having the same unstressed vowels, having the same word-medial coda, or word-medial onset in an unstressed syllable. These factors are inherent in the arguments of Hurford (1981), who suggests that access to phonological forms in the lexicon is not strictly left-to-right. (See also Aitchison & Straf 1981 and Arnaud 1999 for analyses of the phonological properties involved in lexical substitution errors.)

In Table 3.25, I have presented an analysis of these phonological properties in content word paradigmatic lexical substitution errors (Class 35), by age, comparing the figures for word pairs which contain a semantic relationship (child N=113, adult N=102) to word pairs which have a phonological but not a semantic relationship (child N=27, adult N=37); word pairs with neither a semantic nor phonological relationship were not included (child N=10, adult N=5). Before presenting the table I will explain how each measurement was performed.

At the top of the table is a row of numbers that indicates the total number of errors which fell into this category at this age. The percentages in the other rows tell the percentage of this total number of errors with a positive value on this measure. So, for example, out of the 22 errors made by 2-year-olds where the target/error pair of words had a semantic relationship, 63.5% of these words also had the same number of syllables. The numbers of errors listed in the top row are the correct figures for the first 4 rows of percentages; the last 6 rows of percentages were taken from a smaller number of errors, as I will explain below.

The figures for the first row of percentages, '% Same # Syllables', comes from Table 3.13 above and report the percentages of target/error pairs of words with the same number of syllables. The second row of percentages, '% Same Init. Phon.' indicates the percentage of target/error pairs with the same word-initial phoneme, including both consonants and vowels. The third row, '% Same Str. V' indicates the percentage of pairs with the same primary-stressed vowel. The fourth row, '% Same Fin. Phon.' indicates the percentage of pairs with the same word-final phoneme, either consonant or vowel. (I have omitted regular inflectional suffixes from this phonological analysis.)

The percentages in the fifth row, 'Same Lex. Str.' come from Table 3.22 above. Every word pair where both words contain at least two syllables and the two words have the same number of syllables, was analyzed in terms of whether or not they had the same lexical stress pattern, according to the principles described in §3.7.1 above. Because this count excludes pairs with only one syllable, and multisyllabic pairs with unequal numbers of syllables, the number of errors analyzed is smaller than than in the top four rows. In the sixth row, 'Mean Syll. Str. C.' I have reiterated the figures from Table 3.20, which involve mean syllable structure consistency. In this case every word pair with the same number of syllables was analyzed in terms of the percentage of filled syllable-structure slots the two words had in common. Since only word pairs with the same number of syllables were analyzed, the N is also smaller for this row than for the top 4 rows; however, since monosyllabic word pairs were included, there are more entries in this row than in the 5th row, 'Same Lexical Stress'.

In the seventh through tenth rows I looked at measures which I did not expect to be as important for phonological similarity between word pairs; I predicted that they would have a lower overall percentage for both semantically and phonologically related pairs, and that there would be a smaller gap between the two categories in percentages. In the seventh row, 'Same On. C, Unstr' I looked at every pair of words where both members had two or more syllables, and compared the onset consonants of all the unstressed (non-word-initial) syllables to look for matches or mismatches, regardless of actual location in the word; if onsets involved clusters they could be counted twice. If one word had more syllables than the other, I allowed only as many matches or mismatches as the word with the fewer number of syllables allowed. In row 8, 'Same Unstr. Vs', I compared every word pair where both words had at least two syllables, and looked to see if any of the vowels which did not carry primary stress were identical in the two words, regardless of location in the word. If a word pair had more than one match or mismatch, each pair of vowels was counted once (i.e. there could be more than one vowel pair counted per word pair), but again I only counted as many matches or mismatches as allowed by the shorter word. In row

TABLE 3.25

Phonological properties involved in 'phonological similarity' of lexical phonological entries in content word paradigmatic lexical substitution errors. 'S'=target and error have a semantic relationship; 'P'=target and error have no semantic relationship but do have a phonological relationship (malapropisms). See text for details.

Age:	1		2		3		4		5		Total		Adult	
	S	P	S	P	S	P	S	P	S	P	S	P	S	P
N=	5	0	22	4	15	5	34	13	37	5	113	27	102	37
% Same # Syllables	60	0	63.5	100	73	100	65	92.5	73	100	68	96	67.5	76
% Same Init. Phon.	40	0	23	100	33	60	18	46	27	60	25	59	28.5	76
% Same Str. V	20	0	41	25	20	80	12	61.5	16	20	18.5	52	15	62
% Same Fin. Phon.	60	0	18	25	33	60	15	54	30.5	50	24	48	24.5	67.5
Same Lex N=	2	0	8	2	5	1	10	5	12	4	37	12	37	24
Stress %	100	0	87.5	100	80	100	80	80	67	100	78.5	92	70	96
Mean Syll N=	3	0	14	4	11	5	22	12	27	5	77	26	69	28
Str.C %	85	0	76	95	86.5	86	76	82	78.5	91.5	78.5	86.5	80	87
Same On. N=	2	0	8	1	6	1	15	4	9	5	40	11	54	40
C, Unstr.%	0	0	25.5	100	50	0	20	75	22	60	22.5	63.5	33	50
Same N=	2	0	7	3	4	1	8	5	8	5	29	14	39	39
Unstr. Vs %	50	0	28.5	67	100	0	25	40	62.5	60	45	50	46	67
Same S-2 N=	2	0	9	1	7	1	15	5	12	4	45	11	56	34
Onset %	0	0	0	0	28.5	0	7	80	17	50	11	54.5	21.5	39.5
Same S-1 N=	0	0	2	1	2	0	4	1	5	1	13	3	21	13
Coda %	0	0	100	0	0	0	25	0	40	0	38.5	0	52.5	69

9, 'Same S-2 On.', I looked at every pair of words where both words had at least two syllables, and in both words the second syllable began with a consonant onset. Out of this set, I calculated the percentage of syllable-2 consonant onsets which involved the same consonant, regardless of stress. If one onset involved a cluster and the other a single consonant which matched one member of the cluster, I counted this as one match; if both onsets contained the same 2-consonant cluster, I counted this as two matches. Finally, in row 10 'Same S-1 Coda', I looked at the first syllables of each word pair where both words contained a coda consonant and at least one of the words contained more than one syllable. These figures represent the percentage of such errors in which the coda consonants of the first syllables of the target and error words were identical.

Before trying to explicate this table, there is one caution I must make. In order to be able to completely and accurately interpret these figures, we would need to know what the 'chance' figures are for each phenomenon under study. However, this calculation is simply impossible for the child data, since in every case what would count as 'chance' would shift and change for each child at different points in time, and thus the figure would be meaningless. We might be able to calculate a figure for the adults in terms of how often any two randomly selected words would have the same number of syllables or same first phoneme, but none of the pairs of words in this study are matched randomly: they all either have a semantic relationship or a phonological relationship, and in both cases are nearly always of the same lexical category, as I will show in Chapter 4, so these factors would have to be taken into consideration when calculating 'chance'. So in the discussion below, the main comparisons will be between figures for semantic errors vs. malapropisms, but interpretation may include some estimate regarding the degrees of freedom in the phonological system for that measure. Furthermore, since there are relatively few data points in the entries for any row at any particular age, I will not try to make precise developmental claims based on this table, other than comparing the children to the adults overall. However I have included the numbers and percentages at each age to make the details of these counts explicit.

From this very complex table, then, a number of points can be made. First, comparing the data from the first four rows of the table, it appears that they are approximately rank ordered in the table according to their importance in lexical phonological representations, at least for the children. In the children's errors, words which are related phonologically are more likely to have the same number of syllables than to display any other phonological property. However, this may partly be due to the children's limited repertoire of multisyllabic words, and it can be seen that even words with a semantic relationship had the same number of syllables in 68% of the errors. For the children, the difference between semantic errors and malapropisms is 28%, but for adults, who know many more multisyllabic words than children, the difference is only 8.5%. Thus this may be a factor which carries more importance in the children's representations than the adults'.

Second, the word pairs in the children's lexical substitution errors begin with the same word-initial phoneme in 59% of the malapropisms, but in only 25% of the semantic errors, with a 34% difference. In this case there are many more possibilities for error than with numbers of syllables, and so the difference between malapropisms and semantic errors undoubtedly points to the fact that the initial phoneme is one of the most salient features in lexical phonological representations. However, it is interesting that the adults show 76% for malapropisms, and 28.5% for semantic errors, with 47.5% split. This suggests that the initial phoneme is more important in adult representations. Specifically it indicates that the entries in adult phonological lexicons are organized according to similarities among the words starting the comparison from left to right, and that the phonological lexicon is entered in this manner when being activated either by auditory input or by an already selected lexical item during speech production planning (as is argued by Fay & Cutler 1977, Cutler & Fay 1982, and predicted by the 'neighborhood' view of the phonological lexicon; Vitevitch 1997, 2002, Harley & Brown 1998). Thus the children's phonological lexicon may be slightly less organized by a 'left-to-right' structure than adults', possibly because they haven't yet been influenced by orthography and literacy.

Third, the figures for 'same stressed vowel' are slightly lower than for 'same initial phoneme': 52% of the children's malapropisms and 62% of the adults' have this vowel in common. However, in both cases there is a large split from the semantic errors, which have the same stressed vowel in only 18.5% of the child errors and 15% of the adult errors. So although having the same stressed vowel is somewhat less important than same initial segment in both the child and adult representations, it is clearly a factor which is important in the misselection of phonologically similar lexical items.

Fourth, the figures for same final phoneme are lower than the other three measures in this set for the children, whose figures for malapropisms is 48% but semantic errors 24%. For adults the figure is larger than same stressed vowel: 67.5% for malapropisms, 24.5% semantic errors. In both cases, there is a large split between semantic and non-semantic errors. One of the causes of the larger number for adults may be the fact that many word-final phonemes are in fact members of derivational suffixes, and the adults know many more words with derivational morphology (which I have argued to be stored in the lexicon as part of lexical entries) than the children do. Nevertheless, these four factors seem to play a large role in the representation of the phonology of individual words in lexical representations. Not surprisingly, these four factors, as well as the same lexical stress, are the same factors which figure prominently in explaining 'tip of the tongue' responses, and thus it appears that aspects of the phonological representation that are clearly involved in malapropisms can be thought of as having a higher resting activation level in the representation, so that they can be activated more easily than the other factors listed below, and in fact can be activated when the other factors remain inactivated.

Looking at the fifth row, it is clear that in words with more than one syllable and the same number of syllables, the lexical stress pattern is more likely to be the same in malapropisms than in semantic errors by about 20%; this was discussed at length in §3.7.1 as being an indication that lexical stress is stored in lexical entries. Mean SSC is fairly high for both malapropisms and semantic errors, with about a 10% edge to the malapropisms; thus while overall SSC may play some role in lexical representation, it is not one of the more important factors.

It is somewhat more difficult to interpret the figures in rows 7-10 of Table 3.25, since each row evaluates a different number of errors, and in some cases there are very few errors to be evaluated, even when all the children's figures are taken together. Therefore I will make only general comments. One of the reasons that I looked into what I considered to be less likely candidates for causes of phonological similarity between lexical items was to compare phonological properties which were clearly represented robustly in lexical forms, and other properties which seemed to occur randomly. However, what I actually found was that every measure I looked at showed a greater percentage of occurrence in malapropisms than in semantic errors, with one minor exception. The last row in the table shows that for the children, the coda of the first syllable (when at least one of the two words had more than one syllable) was not an indicator of phonetic similarity; but this is probably due to the fact that many of the younger children deleted codas, and the older children produced few error pairs where both members actually had a consonant in the coda position of the first syllable. But this measure shows the usual pattern in the adult errors, undoubtedly because adults know more words with complex phonological structures.

The figures in rows 7 and 8 show that having some onset consonants in unstressed syllables in common and some unstressed vowels in common is fairly unimportant; however the consistency of these latter figures is probably due in part to the fact that unstressed vowels routinely reduce to [ə] or [ɨ], although this is more common for adults than children. Having the same consonant onset in the second syllable of multisyllabic words (row 9) is less important, although the children show a rather large split between semantic errors and malapropisms. Finally, adults show a consistency of coda consonants in the first syllables of words (row 10), but children do not.

Thus I would argue that the patterns evident from these SOT errors show that both children and adults have very rich lexical phonological representations which include as the most easily accessible components the number of syllables, the first and last phonemes, the stressed vowel, and the lexical stress. The other segments and syllable structures are also represented, but at a lower level of resting activation, which is why they have less prominence both in malapropisms and 'tip of the tongue' responses. One further phonological property which might be evaluated in this light would be whether differing segments in identical locations in syllables of a target and error pair might be similar in terms of phonetic features. My impression in performing the above comparisons was that when there was a mismatch of segments in some prosodically prominent location in the target and error pairs, the two segments were often both sonorants, both nasals, both labials, and so on. However, I will leave this question to future research. Finally, it is clear that one other important factor involved in malapropisms is the morphological structure of the target and error words; this may be a separate factor but also may explain some of the phonological similarities, particularly for adult errors, as I have suggested above. This point will be taken up again in Chapter 6.

3.9 Summary and Conclusions: The Acquisition of Phonology as a 'Frames, then Content' Progression

In this chapter I have looked into a number of issues involving the development of the child's abstract mental phonological system, the development of the phonological structure of lexical representations, and the development of phonological processing for assignment of phonetic form. At the end of each section above I presented a detailed summary of the findings from the SOT data regarding the phenomenon under discussion, so in this section I would like to try to pull the various threads together into a unified picture of phonological development.

An extremely useful heuristic in which to frame this discussion is the 'Frames, then Content' developmental progression proposed by MacNeilage and Davis (1990), introduced in §3.1.1. In discussing the progression from babbling to phonology, this theory argues the following:

[A] 'Frame' for speech, in the form of a rhythmic open-close alternation of the mandible, may have evolved from cyclical ingestive events... This frame is considered to provide a universal motor base for speech acquisition, and to dominate vocal output at the babbling stage. Subsequent acquisition of speech production is considered to involve increasing ability to modulate frames by providing internal 'Content' primarily by means of independent tongue actions. A cornerstone of this framework is evidence that when infants mature into adults they possess a mode of production in which syllabic frames and segmental content elements are independently controlled. (MacNeilage 1997:311)

While this theory is presented specifically in terms of speech articulation in the above quotation, this model is useful for discussing the development of representations and processing as well.

Throughout this chapter, a developmental pattern has been evident which involves moving from a relatively course-grained, holistic representation of some phonological phenomenon, what could be called a 'frame', to a more and more fine-grained representation with more internal linear and hierarchical structure, or 'content', until the phenomenon reaches close to adult-like patterns of representation and processing. This development was evident in segments and phonetic features (especially in consonants), in syllable structure and the prosodic word, in lexical stress, and in phrasal intonational patterns.

During babbling, the 'frames' of the child's productions are certainly the open-close cycle of the mandibular gesture. As the infant begins to develop first words, the articulatory aspect of the phonological form of words may be represented as a whole-word motoric gesture, or in the case of CVCV words, possibly as a sequence of whole syllable gestures. Perceptual representations are probably also holistic, and the production and perception representations may be somewhat loosely linked together (Jaeger 1997). However, I argued in §3.1.2 that by the time children begin making SOTs at about 1;7, the representation of words, as well as the phonological processing of words for production, is largely based on individual segments, consonants and vowels. This means that during the early first-word stage, children are differentiating segments within the whole word, syllable-based frames, and when they have accumulated so many words (approximately 50) that it becomes cumbersome to represent all of this differentiated content uniquely for each word, children begin to develop an abstract phonology, or phonological system, independent of individual lexical items, which represents their knowledge about the overall phonological patterns of their language. This system of segments provides the building blocks for the acquisition of new lexical items, and thus lexical acquisition now takes off at a rapid pace.

Focussing specifically on the development of segments, the SOT data suggest the following pattern. After individual segments are differentiated from their syllabic frames, there is a major class distinction in place between consonants and vowels, which corresponds to the closed phase of the mandibular gesture (consonants) vs. the open phase (vowels). This distinction may also be influenced by the locations in words in which consonants vs. vowels most commonly occur, and possibly by other prosodic factors such as the fact that vowels carry pragmatically important pitch information. Furthermore, the mental phonological system includes constraints on what segments are allowed in the language, although children can have some idiosyncratic productions early on, and occasionally produce an error which violates even their own idiosyncratic constraints. There is some phonetic information represented in segments (at least for consonants, since two consonants are most likely to interact in an error if they are phonetically similar from the earliest errors), but there is little indication that there are phonetic features per se, represented within segments, since no errors involving features occur until the end of the third year. However, beginning about age 3;4, phonetic featural errors become relatively common (although they are always rare in comparison to segment errors, and always involve consonants), suggesting that phonetic features have been abstracted from segments, just like segments were previously abstracted from syllables, and organized into an abstract phonological featural system much like that in place in adult phonologies. So the segment itself has evolved from a holistic 'frame', to one with detailed featural 'content' related to an abstract featural system, between about 18 months and 3 years of age.

The development of syllable structure and prosodic word structure was presented in detail above, and summarized in §3.6.4, example (94). At the age at which children begin making SOTs, the frame is the whole word, with individual segments linked directly to the word-level node; there is a default order of segments, but little evidence of internal linear or hierarchical structure within the whole-word frame. In phonological errors, a comparison of the consistency of location of target and source units based on syllable structure vs. one based on word structure produced nearly identical results for the 1-year-olds. Syllables seem to be primarily a unit of motor encoding for speech at this age.

However, at about age 2;2 or so, when children begin being able to pronounce sequences of consonants, there is evidence that the word frame begins to develop a simple internal structure, in that there seem to be syllable demarcations within the word. This is because children begin to show constraints for consonant sequences within a syllable (e.g. before a vowel at the beginning of a word) which are different from those which occur across syllables. Furthermore, allophonic processes which are sensitive to syllable structure location, such as aspiration of voiceless plosives or devoicing of sonorants in clusters, begin to show up as productive processes in the children's SOTs at about age 2;3-2;4. In phonological errors, an analysis of the consistency of location of errors based on syllable structure provides a much better fit than an analysis based on whole-word shape. Children begin making malapropisms at around age 2;2, and from this point on malapropisms are more likely to occur when they involve two words with the same number of syllables. This internal structuring of the segmental representation of words is undoubtedly necessitated by the fact that children's processing capacities have developed to the point where they can represent and produce longer words with many more segments, and it would be extremely difficult to do so consistently without some internal structure within the representations. Because syllables continue to be units of motor speech organization, it is natural that phonological representations would be organized into units which map onto these long established articulatory units. Furthermore, this linearization of the representation within phonological words coincides with the onset of true syntax, when children progress from the 2-word stage into the 3+word stage, where the order of words is an intrinsic part of the message, and thus it may be part of an overall syntagmatic restructuring of the child's linguistic system.

During the second half of the third year, however, there begins to be evidence for the development of even more finely-grained content within the word-frame, that of hierarchical relationships within syllables involving the onset-rhyme-nucleus-coda structure. At around age 2;6 children begin making errors in which the rhyme itself is an error unit, and blend and telescoping errors frequently show the onset-rhyme structure in terms of crossover points and units omitted. This internal structure necessitates the addition of a syllable-node tier, which anchors individual segments into syllabic units within the word, such that blend and telescoping errors in which segments become misordered or intermixed from separate syllables become rare after age 3, and between-word phonological errors which violate syllable structure location become less common. At age 3, there is much evidence for the representation of both syllable nodes and internal syllable structure in lexical representations, since lexical substitution errors show a higher consistency between target and error words on these two factors than at any other age. However the fact that internal syllable structure is a newly acquired aspect of phonological knowledge shows up in the finding that the 3-year-olds phonological errors are heavily influenced by internal syllable structure, and show the least influence of syllables per se compared to the other ages; internal syllable structure seems to be the focus of phonological processing at this age.

By age 4 there is evidence that within the overall word-frame there is now a new level of content, the foot-level tier, which fixes the syllable nodes in a linear order, links them to intrinsic weight-bearing units 'strong/weak', and links this whole structure to the prosodic word node. At this point errors begin to occur which involve the whole word prosody, the exchange or addition of whole syllable nodes, or the exchange of feet. These types of errors are relatively common for adults, but very rare for the children before age 4. Thus it appears that by about age four, the whole-word frame which started out as a somewhat holistic unit with simple segmental content, has developed into a multi-tiered structure with content as elaborate as that of adults.

In the development of lexical stress, the SOT data again give evidence for the gradual differentiation of functions of this prosodic property, although we only get the beginnings of the picture in the current study since the oldest children in the study seem to have much to learn about phonological aspects of lexical stress. Lexical stress is originally learned as an intrinsic property of each word, and is most likely linked to the phonological word node within the representation as an overall word pitch pattern (perhaps like a tone or pitch-accent), not necessarily linked to the segments in any systematic way. The predominant phonetic property of stress at these early ages is pitch; other phonetic properties such as duration and allophonic variation will be added to the manifestation of stress as the child gets control over the production of these phenomena, starting around age 2;3. Because lexical stress is an intrinsic property of each individual word, I collected no errors involving stress from the children until age 4;11, and the error made at 4;11 was the only stress error I collected from them. Lexical stress errors made by adults involved four different types of phenomena. The most common is when the stress pattern of one multimorphemic word is superimposed on a morphologically related word with a different intrinsic stress pattern, and in fact this was the type of error made by the child at 4;11. This type of error, which could be thought of as a word blend, can only occur when children have linked a group of derivationally related words to each other in the lexicon, and children simply aren't eligible to make this sort of error until nearly age 5. Two of the other types of errors made by adults, involving compound vs. phrasal stress, and noun vs. verb derivational stress shift, were not made by the children, which suggests that these phonological processes had not reached the status of productivity in the children's phonologies by the age of 5;11. Finally, adults produced a few errors which could have been syntagmatic, that is, the lexical stress from one word planned for an utterance was superimposed on another word also planned for the same utterance. One might have expected to see such errors by the time children are around age 4-5, when they begin to produce a few whole-word prosody type errors, and when actual weight designations begin to be represented in the phonological form as part of the foot structure, but I did not hear any errors of this sort. However, it is clear that lexical stress is represented and processed on a separate tier from segments during speech production planning even for the youngest children, since the pitch patterns licensed by lexical stress are maintained in telescoping errors, even when the segments with which they would normally have been associated are deleted in the error. Thus, the SOT data only provide evidence about the first steps in the development of full phonological knowledge about lexical stress. Although apparently not eligible for error per se until some morphological influence allows this to occur, even for the youngest children lexical stress is clearly represented separately from segments in representations, and thus can be processed separately during the assignment of phonetic form, as occurs in telescoping errors. However, when children begin to learn families of morphologically related words, they may begin to notice some patterns regarding stress placement within these words; having this distinction regarding stress placement may now allow the child to produce an occasional lexical stress error involving morphologically related words. But the distinctions regarding the other functions of lexical stress (compound vs. phrasal, noun vs. verb) have not been made yet by age 5, and thus do not show up in the children's errors. It would be extremely interesting to look at SOT data from children ages 6-10, to see when these more sophisticated lexical stress error types begin to be produced.

Finally, a gradual differentiation of functions for intonation can also be seen. At first the overall pitch pattern used in producing a one-word utterance, besides reflecting lexical stress when relevant, functions to indicate the type of speech act being performed; thus the original context in which the intonation frame functions is in its overall pragmatic function. However, as the child begins to combine two words in a single utterance, the child begins to be able to use the overall pitch pattern to not only indicate the pragmatic function of the utterance, but to demarcate this particular string of speech as one meaningful unit, thus adding a second distinction of content to the use of intonation. When a child goes through the linearization process, such that the linear order in which words occur is part of the message, the combination of the overall intonation pattern and the strong-weak rhythm given by lexical stresses (and content vs. function words) becomes an important factor in phonological processing; at this age we begin to find that two phonological units are more often mutually involved in a speech error if they are both stressed, and that the tonic syllable of the phrase is involved in the error twice as often as would be expected by chance. By age 4, this phrasal metrical structure will also be a function of the foot structure which is now represented in lexical forms. The earliest intonation SOT which I collected was at age 4;4, and it involved a lexical substitution error which triggered a pragmatically incorrect intonation choice. However, as intonation begins to take on new syntactic functions, in terms of marking specific types of syntactic constructions, the children begin producing a few rare SOTs involving intonation which reflect its syntactic use, errors which are similar to those produced by adults. The first of these occurred at age 4;10 and was a phrase blend involving the intonation from one possible syntactic framing of a proposition, with the word order from the other; the second occurred at 5;6 and involved an incorrect intonational grouping of lexical items for the intended meaning. Thus the original 'frame' of intonation contours also shows a gradual differentiation into more and more sophisticated contents, as the child develops more adult-like uses of both syntax and phrasal prosody.

Thus the heuristic of 'Frames then Content' is valuable for discussing the gradual subdivisions of original holistic frames into more and more fine-grained structures which make up the content of that original frame. Inherent in this framework is the assumption that this general acquisition schema works (along with general human cognition, learning mechanisms, and input) to explain how language can be learned by human children, without the necessity of positing an innate language acquisition device which genetically designates specific linguistic material which is otherwise argued to be unlearnable (see also Bruner 1983, Macken & Ferguson 1983, Ferguson 1986, Bates & MacWhinney 1987, among many others). The discussion in this chapter regarding the developmental pathways taken by children towards the learning of phonology is completely compatible with Davis & MacNeilage's (1990) model of language acquisition.

Chapter 4
The Lexicon and Lexical Errors

4.1 Introduction

4.1.1 Overview of the Chapter

Inherent in the RPC Model is the fact that SOTs involving whole lexical items can be caused by erroneous planning at several different stages of the model. Lexical substitution errors can occur when the wrong lemma is selected during lexical selection, or the wrong phonological form is retrieved during activation of the phonological lexicon. Lexical blend errors also occur due to misselections of lemmas. Syntagmatic errors involving lexical items can occur either while assigning lemmas to functional structures or assigning lexical items to syntactic frames, or can be caused by a misordering of units within the syntactic frame.

Thus paradigmatic lexical substitution errors will most often be caused by either a semantic or phonological relationship between the target and error word, and blends will be caused by semantic similarity. But what other factors could be involved in paradigmatic lexical errors? And what causes specific lexical items to be moved or exchanged in a syntagmatic error? An examination of the errors themselves reveals a number of other factors that may be involved. First, lexical selection and assignment processes are governed by constraints on which lexical category is necessary to fulfill the functional and syntactic requirements of the utterance. Second, lexical errors are made in some sort of context, and contextual factors, such as what the speaker is looking at or thinking about may intrude, as mentioned in Chapter 3. Finally, content words and function words are activated in different phases of speech production planning, and thus errors involving words from each of these two classes of words may have very different causes.

The purpose of this chapter is twofold. First, I will catalog all the various influences which may be factors in causing errors involving whole lexical items, and rank-order them in terms of their importance. Second, I will explain these various influences and their rank-ordering both in terms of the requirements of the RPC model, and in terms of what they say about the content and organization of the lexicon. One sub-text of this discussion will be whether or not the SOT data give evidence regarding the time-course of the development of knowledge about lexical categories. That is, do the the youngest children, those in the 1- and 2-word stages, show any evidence of having information regarding lexical class represented in their lexical entries, and if not, when does this important lexico-syntactic feature manifest itself in errors?

The ideas in this chapter were originally outlined in Jaeger & Wilkins (1993), which made reference to the earlier study of lexical errors by Hotopf (1980). Recently several papers have appeared which explore some of the same ideas and have come to some of the same conclusions: Arnaud (1999) for French adults, Muansuwan (2000) for Thai adults, and Harley & MacAndrew (2001) for English adults. I will at some points refer to these other sources, as well as Hotopf (1983), Levelt (1989), and Stemberger (1989) among others, for comparisons to my findings.

4.1.2 'Lexical Errors' and 'Lexical Entries'

In Chapter 1 I defined 'lexical errors' as being paradigmatic substitutions or blends of words or morphemes; errors which involved syntagmatic shifts in lexical items were classified as 'syntactic'. However, in this chapter I am interested in making comparisons between whole words which interact with each other in errors, both paradigmatic and syntagmatic. For this reason I will use the term 'lexical errors' somewhat differently in the present chapter; 'lexical errors' are defined as errors involving whole words, specifically the kinds of errors which fall into the following 7 classes.

Class I. Paradigmatic substitutions of two content words (i.e. errors from classification category 35 in the data).

(1)   B: 'I wànna **wàtch** . . . I wànna listen to "Bàby Belúga".'
       (verb 'watch' substituted for verb 'listen to'; B-71(35) 2;6)

Class II. Paradigmatic substitutions of two function words (category 36).

(2)   B: (talking about a TV show) 'Ya knòw Claríssa? She dòesn't lìke **his** bróther. I mean hér bròther.'
       (pronoun 'his' substituted for pronoun 'her'; B-446(36) 5;1)

Class III. Paradigmatic blends of two words, content and function combined (categories 38-40). Two words, both appropriate for the utterance (although not necessarily both conveying the exact semantic content the speaker intends to convey), are both activated and blended into a single phonological form (see §1.4.2). I judged two words to be 'both appropriate' if the listener couldn't tell from the preceding utterance and from the grammaticality of the utterance which of the two words the speaker actually intended to say. In some cases two targets are activated from the lexicon and blended as in (3a); in other cases, one or both of the targets have been spoken prior to the error, but any of the targets (previously spoken or not) would be 'appropriate' according to the above definition, as in (3b). In some cases, one or both of the two target words names something immediately visible in the environment, as in (3c).

(3)   a. B: 'I'm gòing to màke an [ɪm.pʰɚ̀.sən] of an ígloo.' (blend of 'impersonation' [ɪm.pʰɚ̀.sə.néʲ.ʃən] and 'impression' [ɪm.pʰré.ʃən]; B-514(38) 5;5)
       b. D: 'I'm gonna put some **crèam** on your ówie.'
          B: '[ká.wi] . . . ówie.' (blend of 'cream' [kim] and 'owie' [ʔá.wi]; both target words appropriate; B-23(38) 1;10)

c. M: (Anna and Mom are looking at a page in a book with pictures
of both a deer and a dormouse; Mom points to dormouse)
'What's thát?'

An: 'A [díʒ.mæ^ws] . . . <u>dórmouse</u>.' (blend of 'deer' [dɪʒ] and
'dormouse' [dóʒ.mæ^ws]; AN-32(38) 2;2)

Class IV. Syntagmatic anticipations of words, content and function combined (category 41). Most syntagmatic anticipations of words are 'incomplete' anticipations, in that the error is corrected before the source is spoken. When there are one or more words or morphemes intervening between the error and the source in the target utterance, the error is taken to be an anticipation/substitution as in (4a,b) or an anticipation/addition as in (4c). However, if there are no words or morphemes intervening between the error and source in the target utterance, the error is interpreted as an interrupted metathesis, as in (4d); I will return to this point below.

(4) a. An: 'Àli put her **mòuth** over her . . . Àli put her <u>hànd</u> over her
móuth when she còughed.' ('mouth' anticipated/substituted
for 'hand'; AN-247(41) 4;10)

b. B: 'We're **gòod**<u>in</u>' . . . we're <u>dòin</u>' ***góod***.' ('good' anticipated/
substituted for 'do', stranding progressive suffix; B-545(41) 5;7)

c. B: 'Whàt is the **mòst** thing that I líke in the wòrld?'
(for 'Whàt is the thìng that I lìke móst in the wòrld?'; 'most'
anticipated/moved, added after 'the', tonic stress shifts to 'like';
B-542(41) 5;7)

d. M: (looking at a photo) 'I wònder why Gràndma lòoks so ángry?'
An: 'Màybe she dòesn't wànt her **táke?** . . . her <u>pícture</u> ***tàken***.'
(anticipation of 'taken'; sounded like she started to say 'her
táken pìcture', so probable metathesis; AN-215(41) 4;6)

Class V. Syntagmatic perseveration of words, content and function combined (category 43). In some cases a previously uttered word is substituted for a word later in the same or a subsequent utterance, and in other cases it is added. As discussed in Chapter 1 (example (21)), the source can occur in an earlier portion of the same utterance by the same speaker, in a preceding utterance by a different speaker as in (5a), or in a preceding utterance by the same speaker as in (5b), in some cases with an utterance by a different speaker intervening. These errors can be either substitutions (5a), or additions (5b).

(5) a. M: (talking about Anna to Daddy) 'She's gòne to **gèt** a bóok.'
An: 'I wànt a **gèt** . . . a <u>rèad</u> "Dúmbo"!'
('get' perseverated/substituted for 'read'; AN-39(43) 2;3)

b. B: (putting pieces into a puzzle) 'Hey, thís mìght **be** ìt. Thát
mìght **be** gò in thère.'
(perseveration/addition of 'be'; B-373(43) 4;9)

Class VI. Syntagmatic reversals of non-contiguous words, content and function combined (categories 45, 46).

(6) a. An: 'Her **rún** is n**ò**s<u>ing</u>.' (exchange of content stems 'nose' and 'run', with progressive suffix stranded; AN-57(45) 2;7)

  b. OG: (after Mom covered her with a blanket in bed)
      'You cóvered ȋt with **mè** . . . you cóvered <u>mè</u> with ȋt.'
      (exchange of function words 'me' and 'it'; OC-145(46) 5;5)

Class VII. Metathesis (category 47). Two contiguous words exchange positions.

(7) OG: (with reference to beads) 'Whàt do you néed **for thèm** . . . néed <u>them fòr</u>?' (metathesis of words 'them for', phrasal prosody remains intact; OC-107(47) 4;5)

Before presenting a count of the various types of errors made by the subjects, I need to address several points regarding the above taxonomy. The first issue which needs clarification is the actual unit under study. In previous chapters I have used the word 'word' to refer to freestanding meaningful units, in a fairly general way, and I will continue to do so in this chapter. But in fact the unit under study in this chapter is actually a specific subset of lexical entries: words and content stems, but not affixes. In Chapter 2 (§2.3.1) and Chapter 3 (§3.5.4) I discussed what I consider to constitute a 'lexical entry' in terms of the units which are represented in the lexicon, and I will be using the same constraints here, but adding information about function words (see Chapter 6 for further justification). The unit which I am calling a 'lexical entry' includes a single content or free function morpheme, more than one morpheme combined into a compound, particle verb or other lexicalized multi-word expression (such as 'in front of'; B-319(39) 4;7), or a root with any number of derivational morphemes attached; irregularly inflected forms are also assumed to be stored in the form lexicon, as a morphologically specified 'form' of the word. However, regular inflectional affixes are considered to be stored in the lexicon separate from the words they attach to and are affixed to lexical items during processing, and so the 'word' in the case of a regularly inflected form is whatever remains after all regular inflections are stripped off. Thus, in (1) above, the monomorphemic verb 'watch' and the particle verb 'listen to' are both lexical entries. In (2) the free function words 'his' and 'her' are lexical entries. In (3a), the multimorphemic words 'impression' and 'impersonation' are considered to be lexical entries, since they consist of stems plus derivational affixes; in (3c), the compound 'dormouse' is considered to be a single word. However, in (4b) and (6a), the words involved in the error are considered to be 'do, good', and 'run, nose' respectively, and the inflectional affix (the progressive {-ing}) is not considered part of these lexical entries, but is an entry on its own. Finally, there is something of a contradiction in (4d), where it looks like an inflected word 'taken' is about to be metathesized whole; I will return to this error later in this section. Thus in this chapter, the term 'word' will be used to refer to lexical entries which specify mono- and multi-morphemic content and free function words, including compounds, derived words, and multi-morphemic lexicalized units. In some errors, the actual error unit is one morpheme from a multi-morphemic word, in some cases a bound content morpheme and often a root in a compound; but the target and source units are full words. Lexical items which will not be discussed in this chapter are inflectional suffixes, and those derivational affixes which may be stored in the lexicon in their own lexical entries and used productively, such as {-er} and {un-}; these productive affixes, both inflectional and derivational, will be discussed in detail in Chapter 6.

The second issue which needs clarification is the distinction between 'content words' and 'function words', which I have used throughout my taxonomy. The definition of these terms can be somewhat controversial, and some researchers prefer the designations 'open class' and 'closed class' lexical items. However, I have chosen to use a very simple definition of 'content' vs. 'function' words, in terms of lexical categories. I use the term 'content words' to indicate common nouns, proper nouns, verbs, adjectives and adverbs. 'Function words' are everything else: pronouns, prepositions, articles, interjections, auxiliary verbs, conjunctions, and so on. I assume that content words are those whose lemmas are activated by the 'Message Level Representation', that is, the propositional content or meaning to be conveyed by the utterance. Function words are those which are either licensed by syntactic properties of the content words (i.e. prepositions required by certain verbs), or by the syntax itself. I realize that this is an oversimplification, and that there are some classes of words which have properties in common with the opposite general designation; specifically, prepositions sometimes act like content words in the errors (i.e. predicative vs. non-predicative prepositions, Bresnan 1982), and abstract adverbs and the copula may sometimes behave more like function words. Nevertheless I have used this simple definition of content vs. function words throughout this study consistently; readers who wish to evaluate the data according to a different definition are welcome to do so.

In the first two categories of error to be discussed in this chapter (i.e. Classes I & II, lexical substitution errors) I have distinguished content from function words. This is because there is almost no overlap between the two categories in lexical substitution errors: I reorded only one adult error and no child errors in which a content word and function word interact in a lexical substitution error; this one exception is given in (8).

(8)   AM: (radio commentator talking about a bombing in Africa, hadn't mentioned the FBI yet) 'If the Ù.S̀. Émbassy was tàrgeted, then **thěy**, uh, <u>the F̀B̀Í</u> will be càlled ìn.' (unstressed pronoun 'they' substituted for tonic-stressed proper noun 'the FBI'; AD-490(36.5))

This error could almost be analyzed as a pragmatic error rather than a lexical selection error; below we will see that children sometimes make blend errors involving pronouns and full nouns, due to problems in making the appropriate pragmatic choice. However, in the counts below I have counted the error in (8) as a content word error, since the target phrase 'the FBI' falls into the content category. A second reason for separating content from function words in these first two classes is that there is a fairly large number of each type for both the children and adults, and since content vs. function words tend to behave differently from each other during processing, it is important to be able to assess them separately.

However, in the other categories of error to be discussed in this chapter (Classes III-VII), I have included both content and function words in the same counts. This is because there are a few errors in all of these categories which violate the content/function distinction. Furthermore, there are relatively small numbers of errors in these classes in total; thus breaking the errors into 'content', 'function', and 'both' categories would cause a proliferation of categories with very few errors in each. So when general issues are discussed, content and function errors are collapsed in the latter 5 categories; however, the specific lexical categories involved will be looked at in detail in §4.3 below.

The final consideration that needs to be mentioned is errors involving metathesis. As indicated in Chapter 1, most metathesized productions seem to be a very different kind of processing error compared to non-contiguous reversal or substitution errors. Specifically, the two words involved are unlikely to have many features in common, since the error occurs due to syntactic factors (a metathesis of slots in the syntactic template) and not the relationship between the two words. As will be shown below, in the non-contiguous exchanges, the target and source tend to share the same lexical category, or at least are both content or both function words; they usually have the same phrasal weight, and the error usually produces a grammatical but anomalous utterance. In these errors inflectional affixes usually remain in their originally planned syntagmatic location (i.e. they are 'stranded'); phrasal stress patterns, particularly the location of tonic stress, remains intact. All of these properties are evident in (6a) above. However, in metathesis errors, the words which exchange are contiguous in the syntactic string so the erroneous production is almost by definition ungrammatical, involving words from different lexical categories which often carry different phrasal weights; I would also predict that inflected words would carry their suffixes with them in metathesized errors, although I have no examples of this. In some cases the phrasal stress pattern is maintained in metatheses (as in (7) above), but in other cases the metathesized lexical items actually carry their originally planned phrasal stress with them, as in (9).

(9)   AF: 'I'm nòt **thát ïn** bìg of a hùrry.' (for ' ïn thát'; AD-648(47))

As indicated above, a number of interrupted lexical anticipation errors contain similar properties to these metathesis errors, and so have been analyzed as interrupted metatheses. However, this is only true for the child data; I had only one instance of this type of interrupted metathesis in the adult data, *'ròulette . . . Ròlodex roulétte' (AD-306b(41)). For example, in (4d), it appears that Anna began to say 'Màybe she dòesn't wànt her **táken pìcture**' for 'picture tàken'. If this is the correct analysis, then the two lexical items involved do not derive from the same lexical category, and the utterance is ungrammatical; furthermore the inflectional suffix {-en} would have been moved with the verb stem rather than the suffix remaining in its original syntactic location; these are all characteristics of metatheses. In order to fully document these observations regarding metathesis errors, I have included them in the first table below; however, in subsequent tables and discussions regarding relationships between two lexical items involved in a lexical error, I have usually excluded both metathesis errors and the anticipatory errors which were most likely interrupted metatheses, since the relationship between the two lexical items involved is unlikely to be relevant to the error.

With these methodological issues taken care of, I will now turn to the data.

4.1.3 Quantitative Analysis and Comparison to Adults

The number of errors made in each class at each age is presented in Table 4.1, as well as the percentage of lexical errors made at each age which fell into each class. This table is to be read as follows (for example): the children at ages 1-2a made a total of 16 lexical errors; 6 of these (or 38% of 16) fell into Class I, paradigmatic content word substitutions. In this table the children's data are compared with three adult data sets. The first adult corpus is my data set; the second two were derived from figures in Hotopf (1983). The A2 figures are from data collected by Hotopf from English speaking adults, some of which were made in 'Daily Life' settings and some of which were collected from formal lectures at a psychology conference. The A3 figures are taken from the Meringer corpus of slips made by adult speakers of German (Meringer & Mayer 1875, Meringer 1908), as reported by Hotopf. I calculated these latter two sets of figures from the relevant errors listed in Table I of Hotopf (1983). (Since Hotopf did not separate out contiguous and non-contiguous lexical exchanges in his data, the figures for Class VI for the A2 and A3 corpora contain both.) Throughout this chapter I will separate out errors made by the 1-2-year-old children in the 1- and 2-word stages (1-2a) from those made by the 1-2-year-old children who were regularly producing utterances of 3 or more words (1-2b), in order to look at issues regarding the relationship between lexical development and syntactic development.

There are some general patterns to be noted from this table. First, at all ages except (1-2a), Class I contains the largest percentage of errors, and in some cases approximately half of the lexical errors under study here fell into this category. The second most common error for the children and in two of the adult corpora was lexical blends. Since these most often involve two content words, it is clear that paradigmatic content word errors are the most common type of

TABLE 4.1

Number of lexical errors in each class at each age, and percentage of that class of error at that age; child data compared to 3 adult sources. I=paradigmatic content word substitutions; II=paradigmatic function word substitutions; III=lexical blends, content & function; IV=lexical anticipations, content & function; V=lexical perseverations, content & function; VI=lexical exchanges, content & function; VII=lexical metathesis, content & function.

Age:	1-2a	1-2b	3	4	5	Total	A^1	A^2	A^3
Class									
I N=	6	26	20	51	47	150	145	233	339
%	38%	36%	32%	41%	49.5%	40.5%	47%	67%	46.5%
II N=	0	8	8	13	9	38	12	13	37
%		11%	12.7%	10.3%	9.5%	10.3%	4%	4%	5%
III N=	8	21	13	24	12	78	72	7	102
%	50%	29%	20.5%	19%	12.5%	21%	23.5%	2%	14%
IV N=	1	5	9	16	7	38	46	24	95
%	6%	7%	14%	13%	7.5%	10.3%	15%	7%	13%
V N=	1	8	8	13	15	45	15	52	77
%	6%	11%	12.7%	10.3%	16%	12%	5%	15%	10.5%
VI N=	0	3	1	3	3	10	11	18*	80*
%		4%	1.5%	2.3%	3%	2.5%	3.5%	5%	11%
VII N=	0	1	4	5	2	12	6		
%		2%	6.5%	4%	2%	3.3%	2%		
Total N=	**16**	**72**	**63**	**125**	**95**	**371**	**307**	**347**	**730**
Para=	87.5%	76.5%	65%	70.5%	71.5%	72%	74.5%	73%	65.5%
Syn=	12.5%	23.5%	35%	29.5%	28.5%	28%	25.5%	27%	34.5%

A^1 =Jaeger corpus, A^2 =Hotopf 1983 (English), A^3 =Meringer (from Hotopf 1983, German)   * These Class VI figures include both reversals and metatheses.

lexical error for all the speakers in these studies. The next two most common error types are the two syntagmatic categories of anticipations and perseverations, although different groups made these two types of errors in different proportions, as I will discuss below. Finally, paradigmatic substitutions of function words, full exchanges, and metatheses were the least common error types for all speakers.

The differences among proportions of error types evident in this table can be explained with reference to the RPC Model, and the notion of 'degrees of freedom' within different components of the model. First, when a speaker has settled on the general content of the utterance to be produced, relevant concepts are activated, and they in turn activate relevant content lexical items. In most cases there would be a large number of lexical items which could be appropriate for forming the intended proposition, thus there would be many degrees of freedom involved in making lexical selections, as discussed in Chapter 2, §2.3.3. Choosing the correct words is the least automatic part of speech production planning; Levelt (1989:28) calls it a 'controlled' activity which requires a great deal of continuing attention from the speaker. Thus this is a stage in speech production planning which is highly susceptible to error, since a large number of competing words are automatically partially activated by the concepts, and it takes a great deal of attention to select only those needed for the current utterance. Once relevant words have been selected and inserted into syntactic frames, then phonological forms are accessed from the lexicon, which is a second possible locus of lexical selection errors. In some respects there are fewer degrees of freedom at this point, since each lemma will uniquely pick out a single form from the formal lexicon (unless there is some decision to be made about register level or dialect). However, activation from the target phonological form will spread to phonologically similar forms, and one of these forms may be erroneously selected. The model would predict that there would be fewer errors caused by phonological similarity than semantic similarity for at least two reasons. First, the selection of the phonological form which is associated with a specific lemma is a highly automatic procedure which requires little attention, so there is less chance of error than when making a conceptually governed selection from an array of semantically related lemmas. Secondly, the content of the word is more important than its sounds for production; thus the internal monitor is more likely to let pass an erroneous word which means something similar to the intended word, than to be fooled by a word which sounds similar to the intended word but carries an entirely different meaning. I will elaborate on this point in §4.2.4 below.

This same explanation is relevant to blend errors, since they are caused by the activation of two competing words. However, blend errors for the most part only occur when the two words are semantically related, most often synonyms (see Chapter 5), so there is only one location in the model at which they can arise. Furthermore, in lexical selection errors one of the two competitors is fully selected, and thus when it is processed in later components, the internal monitor sees a linkage of one word to one syntactic slot and so will not necessarily interrupt the processing at this stage. Once the erroneous word has been through the phonological processing component, the internal monitor sees it as a real word in the language and again is less likely to filter it out. But in a blend error there are two words associated with one syntactic slot, which the internal monitor is likely to catch; if not, once the words are blended phonologically in the 'Phonological Processes' component, the resulting form is often not a real word, which should also set off the internal monitor. So there are both more opportunities for lexical substitution errors to occur compared to blends (i.e. both in the semantically organized lemma lexicon and in the phonological form lexicon), and more opportunities for blends to be detected by the internal monitor; thus, substitutions are found to be more common than blends in nearly every study of lexical errors, including those presented here.

Once the lemmas of content words have been correctly selected, they are then assigned functions and inserted into syntactic frames. In both of these processes there are fewer degrees of freedom which would allow errors to be made. First, in assigning functions to the content words, the functional frames licensed by the selected lexical items have very specific requirements for lexical category and semantic properties of the lemmas, and thus only if there were two lemmas with very similar semantic and morphosyntactic representations could such a misassignment occur. Similarly, once a syntactic frame is selected, each slot in the framework has constraints on lexical category which makes it more difficult for words to be misassigned to slots; the fact that in English there are a large number of words which can belong to more than one lexical category is what allows many of these errors to occur (as will be discussed below). For these reasons the syntagmatic lexical errors are less frequent than the paradigmatic content word errors.

As with phonological errors, there are more anticipation and perseveration errors than full exchanges or metatheses, undoubtedly because anticipations and perseverations involve only one erroneous unit, whereas reversals produce erroneous units in two locations, so cause a larger disruption of the planned utterance. Furthermore, I argued in Chapter 1 that the most common type of metathesis may be caused by the metathesis of structural slots in syntactic frames. Because the mental representation of syntax is most likely in the form of templates which are associated with different types of function, it is not surprising that a misordering within such a template would be extremely rare. (See also the discussion of Table 2.4 in Chapter 2.)

Finally, substitutions of function words is the least frequent error type in this set. Again we can look at this finding from the point of view of degrees of freedom. First, syntactic frames have very specific requirements for lexical categories involved in specific constructions, and in some cases there is only one function word which is licensed by this construction. So there is frequently very little choice among lexical items activated by the content word lemmas or the syntactic constructions. Secondly, there will not be as many words activated by 'semantic similarity' when making a selection of a function word; since these lexical categories are by definition 'closed class' categories, there is a finite and often very small set of other words which could possibly be activated by semantic association. This is the least true for prepositions, particularly those of location, direction, and so on (i.e. predicative prepositions, Bresnan 1982), of which there are many in the lexicon and which can be associated with each other by semantic relationships which are the same as those found in the content word lexicon (i.e. antonyms, synonyms, etc.; see Chapter 5). There is also a rather large, albeit finite, store of pronouns in English, and so it will not come as a surprise that most function word errors involve prepositions and pronouns.

However, a third reason for there being so few function word errors is that the phonological forms of these words will activate only a few other forms. It is clear from the fact that content words and function words almost never interact in lexical errors, that the content word lexicon is distinct from the function word lexicon in mental representation and processing; this factor has been assumed in the RPC Model. If this is true both in the lemma-lexicon and the form-lexicon, the only forms which will be activated by the form of a function word is other function words which are phonologically similar, which is a very small pool of possible forms. Thus there are several compelling reasons why function word errors should be the least common.

Turning now to a comparison between the child data and the adult data, it becomes evident that this may be a somewhat difficult comparison to make since there are such large differences among the three adult corpora. In particular, it is unclear why the Hotopf English corpus shows such a preponderance of Class I errors (paradigmatic content word substitutions) and so few Class III errors (blends), or why the Meringer corpus shows such a high percentage of exchanges and metatheses (Class VI). Nevertheless a few observations can be made about the child figures. First, the children in the (1-2a) group produced no function word substitutions, and in fact they produced no lexical errors involving function words except one blend involving the interjection 'bye' with the noun 'car'; clearly children at this age have not yet learned enough function words to have them figure in their errors. They produced 6 lexical substitution errors but 8 blends, and have the largest proportion of blends at any age (50%). This is undoubtedly because they have considerably less practice in making lexical decisions than the older children; the percentage of blend errors drops to 29% at age 2, and steadily decreases until it reaches a low of 12.5% at age 5. It may seem surprising that the adults in my study produced 23.5% blends (and this figure is considerably higher than those found by Hotopf, especially for the English data). More data need to be gathered to further explore this issue; if it turns out that the higher figure is accurate, we could hypothesize that this is partly due to the fact that adults have much larger lexicons than children, so have more competing words. If the lower figure turns out to be more accurate, it could be explained by the fact that adults have much more practice in making lexical decisions than children. But for now these 'explanations' remain speculation; it may turn out that in fact children and adults make approximately the same proportions of blends, but for different reasons: children blend words due to less practice in lexical selection, and adults blend words due to their large lexicon. Finally, the children in the 1-2a age range produced only two syntagmatic errors, a perseveration from a previous adult utterance and an anticipation which is given in (10); naturally they produced no exchanges, since if a child were to exchange the words in a two-word utterance, who could tell?

(10)   OG: (asking Daddy if he had used the bathroom yet)
        'P**èepee** go . . . D<u>àddy</u>, go *péepee*?'
        ('peepee' anticipated/substituted for 'Daddy'; OC-9(41) 2;0)

In (10), the child seems to have been planning two phrases at the same time, the first getting Daddy's attention, and the second asking him a question. Since all of these lexical items had been activated, one item from the second phrase was substituted into the first phrase. (See further discussion of this error in §4.2.4 and §4.3.5 below).

The first Class II error (function word substitutions) was made by a child at age 2;5 (B-59(36)) and the first blend involving a function word occurred at age 2;9 (B-113(39)). Similarly the first syntagmatic error involving a function word was produced at age 2;7 (B-96(46)). However, once the children began showing control over function words in their correct productions, they produced a higher proportion of function word errors than adults typically do (for Class II errors, 10.3% vs. 4% in the Jaeger and Hotopf studies, and 5% in Meringer), and the figures at each age are similar to the overall figure. For children the choice of function words is not as automatic as it is for adults, probably due to less practice in associating specific function words with specific syntactic constructions.

In the syntagmatic errors, there is an interesting discrepancy between the child and adult figures for Classes IV (anticipations) and V (perseverations). The table shows the children producing slightly more perseverations than anticipations (overall 12% vs. 10.3%), but this figure is somewhat misleading since over a quarter of the children's anticipatory errors (N=10) were probably interrupted metathesis errors. If these errors are excluded from the count, then it is clear that the children made many more lexical perseveratory errors than anticipations. However, the adults in my study produced many more anticipations than perseverations (15% vs. 5%), and there is only one of the adult anticipatory errors which looks like an interrupted metathesis (AD-306b (41)). Meringer's adult figures agree with mine, and Stemberger (1989:182) also found that his adults made more anticipatory lexical errors than perseveratory (62.4% vs. 13.3% of the syntagmatic lexical errors, with both complete and incomplete anticipations combined), while the children in his study made more perseverations than the adults did (child 31.3% anticipations, 21.9% perseverations). Hotopf's figures, on the other hand, look more like my child figures.

The majority of these studies suggest that children make more perseveratory lexical errors than do adults, and if this is true, it could be explained by Stemberger's (1989) claim that children have a longer decay time for previously activated elements (see §2.3.2 above), and thus are more likely to make perseveratory errors than adults are. It may also be related to Dell, Burger & Svec's (1997) claim that anticipations are characteristic of more practiced speech, in that the more practiced speaker is planning ahead in larger chunks, and suppressing the material in the previous utterances on-line at a more rapid rate than less practiced speakers. It is not obvious from Table 4.1 if there are any developmental trends in the children's percentages of perseveratory vs. anticipatory errors; however, the fact that the 5-year-olds produced twice as many perseverations as anticipations suggests that even the older children have not reached an age where they are showing the adult-like pattern.

Children's and adults' exchange and metathesis errors are both relatively rare; for the children, exchange and metathesis errors combined accounted for about 6% of their lexical errors; Jaeger adult=5.5%; Hotopf=5%, Meringer=11%, which is unusually high. However, looking at the children and adults in my study, one can see that the children made slightly more metathesis errors than adults across the board; adding in the 10 anticipation errors which are probably interrupted metatheses, this gives 6% child metathesis errors compared to 2% for the adults. This could be explained with reference to the hypothesis discussed above that children do not plan as far ahead as adults do (see §2.3.1), and so are more likely to produce errors involving units which are very close to each other, whereas lexical exchange errors can involve units which are somewhat distant in the utterance. It could also reflect a developmental trend in the children's acquisition of syntactic templates; if metatheses are due to a misordering in the syntactic template itself, this could reflect the fact that children's syntax is less fixed and thus less automatic and more error-prone than adults'.

Finally, there is an interesting overall pattern in the proportion of paradigmatic to syntagmatic errors made by the children and adults shown in Table 4.1. The Jaeger adult figures show roughly 75% paradigmatic and 25% syntagmatic errors, and the Hotopf English data has similar figures; the Meringer numbers are somewhat different in that they show 67% paradigmatic and 33% syntagmatic, which seems to be due to the large number of perseveration and exchange errors. For the children there seems to be something of a U-shaped curve. The youngest children produced the largest percentage of paradigmatic errors, 87.5%. This number drops to 76.5% at age 1-2b, and reaches a low of 65% at age 3; then it begins to rise at age 4 to 70.5% and at age 5 to 71.5%. Naturally the youngest children produced few syntagmatic errors since they were only producing utterances of one or two words. What's interesting is the peak of syntagmatic errors and trough of paradigmatic errors at age 3. One interpretation of this pattern is that the 3-year-olds are learning a great deal of syntax at this age but it has not yet become automatic, so their attention has shifted from lexical decisions to a focus on syntax during this year; note that it is the 3-year-olds who make the largest proportion of both metathesis errors and function word substitutions. However, by age 4 the children's selection of syntactic templates has become more automatic, and the templates themselves are more fixed. By ages 4-5 the children's proportion of lexical to syntagmatic errors has become very similar to the adult figures, at least those of Jaeger and Hotopf (English), and syntactically driven types of errors (metathesis and function words) are at the lowest point for the children.

This U-shaped curve is reminiscent of the pattern found in phonological errors in Chapter 3, where the 3-year-olds show the effect of working on the internal structure of phonological representations, just as they are working on the internal structure of syntactic templates at this age.

Now that the issue of the types of lexical errors produced has been explored, I will turn to a discussion of the causes of these errors.

4.2 Factors Involved in Causing Lexical Errors

In analyzing my data I find that there are 10 clearly identifiable factors needed in order to fully explain the causes of lexical errors. In this section I will present each of these factors, in decreasing order of importance. Some of these factors are those which have been discussed in previous chapters, and some will be newly introduced in this section. The 10 factors are: 1) target and error words are the same lexical category; 2) target and error words have a semantic relationship; 3) the error involves the tonic-stress position in the phrase; 4) target and error words have a phonological relationship; 5) the source word is planned for the same utterance or was spoken in a previous utterance; 6) the target and source words have the same rhythmic weight; 7) the source referent is physically present in the environment; 8) the error utterance involves a collocational phrase; 9) the error is caused by an unspoken source inherent in the discourse topic; 10) the error word refers to something which is 'on the mind' of the speaker. I will discuss the contribution of each of these factors below; at the end of this section I will look at developmental patterns relating to the relative importance of each of these factors at various ages, and those relating to the absolute number of factors involved in errors at various ages. I will also suggest one more parameter that might be necessary to fully account for all errors: 'same referent'. (In §4.3 below I will look in greater depth into the issue of lexical categories, and in Chapter 5, I will present details of semantic relationships.)

4.2.1 Lexical Category

It is well-known that in adult errors, two words mutually involved in a lexical error are usually of the same lexical category (Fromkin 1973a, Nooteboom 1973, Fay & Cutler 1977). This is partly because lexical errors are closely governed by the requirements of the functional structures and syntactic frames being planned, which themselves contain slots which can be filled only by words of a certain lexical category, as discussed in §4.1.3. above (see also Levelt 1989:182). However, this finding also supports the hypothesis that the lexicon is to some extent organized by lexical category, a hypothesis that has much support from neurolinguistic studies (Rapp & Caramazza 1998). It is quite likely that these two phenomena are related. One could argue that from the point of view of speech production planning, the most efficient organization of the lemmas in the lexicon (which contain the semantic and morphosyntactic information regarding lexical entries), would be in terms of both semantics and lexical categories. When the concepts to be conveyed in an utterance activate lemmas with the appropriate semantic content, they will preferentially activate lemmas in the appropriate lexical categories to be slotted into functional structures which are then mapped into syntactic templates; this latter mapping is also heavily determined by lexical categories. The organization of the form portion of the lexicon, on the other hand, is undoubtedly governed by the requirements of input, and so is organized in terms of the phonological properties of form representations, and to some extent their orthographic properties for literate speakers (Nooteboom 1973). I will return to this point in the discussion at the end of this section.

Assessing lexical categories in the child data poses something of a methodological problem, since the researcher cannot always tell whether the child has represented lexical category information in lexical entries by simply observing how words are used. What can be done is to assign a lexical class to each target and source based on their function in context, or in unclear cases their usual class in adult speech, and then see whether this causes the errors to fall into any particular patterns. (The exact lexical classes used will be discussed in detail in §4.3.) Following the methodology just described, I assigned lexical categories to all target and source/error words in a subset of the errors from Table 4.1, and then tabulated the number of pairs of words involved in a lexical error which belonged to the same lexical category. The results are given in Table 4.2. This count excluded metathesis errors (Class VII; child N=12, adult N=6), since two words which are metathesized are of different lexical categories almost by definition; I also excluded anticipation errors which were analyzed as interrupted metatheses (Class IV; child N=10, adult N=1). I further excluded: 7 addition errors from Classes IV and V (anticipations, perseverations), since there is only one word involved in these errors (child N=6, adult N=1); 1 Class I error from the child data where the target word is not clear (OC-144(35) 5;5); and 1 reversal error from Class VI (AN-231(45) 4;8) where the lexical category of the morphemes involved cannot be clearly assigned. Thus there are 30 fewer child errors and 8 fewer adult errors in this table than in Table 4.1. This table is to be read as follows (for example): at age 1-2b, the children made 26 errors in Class I (paradigmatic content word substitutions), and of these, 92% (N=24) involved a target and error word of the same lexical category.

According to this table, the children's lexical errors overall involved word pairs with the same lexical category in 88% of the cases, and for adults the figure is 86%. The most obvious distinction that the table illustrates is the fact that paradigmatic errors (Classes I-III) show a much higher percentage of consistency of lexical category (overall: child=92.5%, adult=94%) than do syntagmatic errors (overall: child=74%, adult=61.5%). The children in general show more consistency in every category than the adults do. However, there is an interesting dip in consistency of content word errors at age 3, which may be related to the fact mentioned above that children at age 3 are wrestling with the structures of new syntactic templates, and may have a less fixed representation for the lexical category requirements within those templates.

TABLE 4.2

Percentage of lexical errors made at each age in each class in which the target and error words came from the same lexical category; I= paradigmatic content word substitutions; II=paradigmatic function word substitutions; III=lexical blends, content & function; IV=lexical anticipations, content & function; V=lexical perseverations, content & function; VI=lexical exchanges, content & function; N=the total number of errors made at this age in this class.

Age:		1-2a	1-2b	3	4	5	Total	Adult
Class								
I	N=	6	26	20	51	46	149	145
	%	100%	92%	80%	92%	95.5%	92.5%	95%
II	N=	0	8	8	13	9	38	12
	%		87.5%	100%	100%	100%	97.5%	92%
III	N=	8	21	13	24	12	78	72
	%	87.5%	95%	92%	87.5%	91.5%	91%	92%
IV	N=	1	1	7	12	5	26	44
	%	0%	100%	86%	66.5%	60%	69%	59%
V	N=	1	8	8	11	13	41	15
	%	100%	87.5%	75%	63.5%	84.5%	78%	60%
VI	N=	0	3	1	2	3	9	11
	%		33%	0%	100%	100%	66.5%	73%
Total	**N=**	**16**	**67**	**57**	**113**	**88**	**341**	**299**
	%	87.5%	89.5%	84%	87%	92%	88%	86%

Paradigmatic Errors (Classes I-III)
Total N=	14	55	41	88	67	265	229
%	93%	93%	88%	92%	95.5%	92.5	94%

Syntagmatic Errors (Classes IV-VI)
Total N=	2	12	16	25	21	76	70
%	50%	75%	75%	68%	81%	74%	61.5%

I compared my figures to those from other studies and found that in general my figures are somewhat lower than other adult studies. For paradigmatic errors, Hotopf (1983) found 98% lexical category consistency in his English data, and Fay & Cutler (1977) found 99.5% consistency; similarly Harley & MacAndrew (2001) found 98% consistency for paradigmatic content word substitutions in English, and Arnaud (1999) found 97% consistency for paradigmatic content word substitutions in French. For syntagmatic errors Stemberger (1989) found 80% consistency. I believe that the explanation for the differences between my data and the others' lies in the very conservative measure I used for lexical categories; for example, I counted common nouns vs. proper nouns as belonging to separate categories. In fact, the two most common violations of lexical category were a proper noun/common noun interaction, as illustrated in (11a), and a noun/verb interaction where both words can function as either a noun or a verb, as illustrated in (11b).

(11)   a. OB: (playing with a set of plastic farm animals; no deer in set)
'Which òne's the **Bámbi.** (laughs) No, which òne's the báby?'
(proper noun 'Bambi' substituted for common noun 'baby';
OC-52(35) 3;4)

   b. AF: 'I thìnk there is a **sign** . . . a fórm that I **sìgn**, saying that . . .'
(verb 'sign' substituted for common noun 'form'; AD-573(41))

In (11a), although 'Bambi' is a proper noun and 'baby' is a common noun, they are both strictly speaking nouns. In (11b) both 'sign' and 'form' can be both a noun and a verb. Thus of all the errors that violate lexical category which are sent through the processor, these are the least likely to be caught by the monitor on the grounds of violation of lexical category.

However, if we look at the content/function word distinction, we see that this distinction is nearly always honored in lexical errors, both paradigmatic and syntagmatic. In paradigmatic errors there are only 2 child errors (one each at age 1 and 2, category 40) and 2 adult errors which violate this distinction, so 99% of the paradigmatic errors honor this distinction for both adults and children. In syntagmatic errors there are only 4 child errors (three at age 3, one at age 4) and 5 adult errors which violate the content/function distinction; thus 95% of the child syntagmatic lexical errors and 93% of the adult errors honor this distinction. These lexical errors support the view that content words and function words are cognitively different classes of words which are both represented and processed differently from each other.

In sum, the majority of target and error words in lexical errors honor lexical category, for both the children and the adults in this study. Paradigmatic errors honor lexical category more consistently than do syntagmatic errors, which shows that if the processing mechanism has activated two words and is planning to utilize them in an utterance, one may substitute for the other in violation of lexical category much more readily than if the two words are competing for a single slot paradigmatically. Finally, nearly all target and error words maintain the content word/function word distinction, in both paradigmatic and syntagmatic errors, supporting the view that these two classes of words are cognitively represented and processed differently from each other.

4.2.2 Semantic and Phonological Similarity

Another well-known fact is that when one word substitutes for another or two words are blended together in an error, the two words tend to have either a semantic or phonological relationship, or both (Fromkin 1973a, Fay & Cutler 1977, Hotopf 1980, 1983, among many others). Various sources differ as to their findings about which of these factors is more important. Looking at paradigmatic lexical substitution errors, Fay & Cutler found a preponderance of errors with only a phonological relationship (malapropisms): 81% of their corpus of 226 lexical substitution errors were said to be only phonologically related. Hotopf (1983) found the two to be about equal in his English data: 52% semantic errors, 48% phonological. But most studies report a preponderance of semantically related errors: Stemberger (1989) found 83% semantic pairs to 17% malapropisms; Arnaud (1999) found 67% semantically related compared to 33% phonological, and Harley & MacAndrew (2001) report 76% semantically to 24% phonologically related pairs. There may be many differences among these studies in terms of methodology, particularly how 'semantically related' and 'phonologically related' were ascertained. Furthermore, most studies so far have looked only at paradigmatic substitution errors, not blends or syntagmatic errors. Thus the question of the ratio of semantically vs. phonologically related lexical errors remains very much open.

In this section I will look at the semantic and phonological relationships among the lexical errors in my data, both paradigmatic and syntagmatic, and explicate the findings in terms of the RPC Model. I will also look for any interactions between semantics or phonology with error type, and any developmental trends in the proportions of these two influences. Naturally in order to make a consistent analysis of target and error word pairs, I must present in detail the measures I will be using to ascertain semantic and phonological relationships between word pairs.

The measurement used for determining phonological relationships between target and error words (or two targets) was derived from the findings presented at the end of Chapter 3 regarding what sorts of phonological properties are likely to be represented in phonological forms, and the rank ordering of importance of these properties derived from the data. After compiling and rank ordering the list, I developed a system for assigning points to a word pair depending on which of these factors they had in common. Table 4.3 presents the point assignment system; a pair of words was considered to be 'phonologically related' if it scored 3 or more points on this scale.

The rationale behind the scoring was as follows. First, the two factors which were found to be very consistently correlated in malapropisms but much less often correlated in semantically related errors were 'same initial phoneme' and 'same primary-stressed vowel', so these factors received 1.5 points each. Same number of syllables and same word-final phoneme were also important, but there was not as big a difference between the occurrence of these factors in malapropisms vs. semantic errors, so these factors were assigned 1 point each. If two primary stressed syllables had other phonemes in common which did not fall into any of these other categories, each was assigned 1 point; similarly, same phonemes in unstressed syllables received 0.5 point each. Finally, the

TABLE 4.3
Criteria for assigning points for phonetic similarity between target and error word, or two target words, in lexical errors. A pair is considered 'phonologically related' if it scores at least 3 points.

1. Same number of syllables=1 point.
2. Same stress pattern:
   a) if both words are stressed, but each only one syllable=0.5 points.
   b if both words have 2+ syllables and the same number of syllables, and same primary stress location=1 point.
   c) if one word is one-syllable and stressed, and the other is two-syllable and has first-syllable stress=0.5 points.
   d) if both words have 2+ syllables, but a different number of syllables, but the same general word-stress pattern=1 point (e.g. 'díctionàry' and 'líbràry').
3. Same initial phoneme=1.5 points.
4. Same final phoneme=1 point.
5. Same primary-stressed vowel=1.5 points (if only one of them occurs before /r/ or a nasal, only 1 point).
6. Other same phonemes in same position in primary-stressed syllables= 1 point each.
7. Other same phonemes in same position in non-primary-stressed syllables= 0.5 points each.
8. Same phonemes in same position in primary-stressed syllable in one word, but non-primary stressed syllable in the other word, if syllables are in same position in word=0.5 points each.
9. If a vowel is both word-initial and primary stressed, or both word-final and primary stressed=2 points total.

'same stress' measure was calculated in various ways depending on the number of syllables in the words (as explained in the table). The measure used here was somewhat more lenient than that used in Chapter 3, so that it was easier for a pair of words to be assessed has having the same stress pattern in this accounting; this was done in order to avoid too fine-grained a system which would throw out pairs with the same primary-stressed syllable location but some differences in secondary vs. tertiary stress elsewhere in the word. Example (12) illustrates how these criteria assigned a [+] or [-] value on the parameter of phonological relatedness.

(12) a. 'basket' vs. 'backpack'   same # syllables=1
          [bǽ.skɪt]   [bǽkʾ.pʰæ̀k]   same stress=1
          (AN-323(35) 5;10)   same initial phoneme=1.5
                                         same primary stressed vowel=1.5
                                         Total=5 [+phon]

       b. 'cookie' vs. 'cup'   same stress=0.5
          [kʰʊ́.ki]   [kʰʌp]   same initial phoneme=1.5
          (AN-292(35) 5;7)   Total=2 [-phon]

In §4.1.2 I discussed what unit would be considered the word to be analyzed; this includes monomorphemic words, multimorphemic words which are compounds (which were always analyzed as whole words, even if the target and error word had a stem in common), derived words, particle verbs or other lexicalized multiword expressions, and irregularly inflected forms, but excludes regular inflections. Here I need to amend this slightly: in rare cases, if a regularly inflected form interacted with an irregularly inflected form in an error, the regular affix was counted as part of the phonological form; in these cases it is noted in the entry that the count has been made this way. As in Chapter 3, I considered regular inflectional affixes to be part of the lexical phonological representations of words through age 2;2.

Chapter 5 contains a detailed presentation of the semantic analysis performed on the SOT data, and that analysis will not be repeated here. However, the classification system presented in Chapter 5 is extremely fine-grained, much more so than systems used in previous studies; for example, Hotopf (1983) used basically three categories in his analysis: coordination, antonyms, and association. As a preview to Chapter 5, I will simply list the categories I used to assign semantic relationships to target/error or target/target pairs: cohyponyms, superordinate/subordinate, co-members of a set, set-to-member or member-to-set, co-partonyms, part-for-whole or whole-for-part, binary antonyms, gradable antonyms, converses, synonyms, connotation, metonymic, causal, and 'shared criterial features' (which is a fairly loose relationship, similar to Hotopf's 'association'); personal pronoun error pairs were judged on whether or not they shared two or more features (number, case, person, gender). In assessing semantic relationships between words, I tried to take into account as much as possible the children's worldviews, and the contexts in which they interacted with the referents of words. I was very generous in assigning semantic relationships to word pairs, and thus may show a higher percentage of semantic relatedness in lexical errors than some of the studies mentioned above. The parameter of semantic relatedness will be treated as binary in this chapter; that is, a word pair either has a semantic relationship or it doesn't. However, in Chapter 5 (§5.5) I will discuss the possibility that semantic relatedness may be a somewhat more gradient feature.

Every lexical error was classified in terms of whether the word pair had a positive or negative value on these two parameters, [sem] 'related semantically' and [phon] 'related phonologically'. Thus the errors were divided into four basic types, as illustrated in (13).

(13) a. B : 'I bùmped ìnto her **hánd**. I mèan héad.'
('hand' [hænd] substituted for 'head' [hɛd]; B-293(35) 4;5)
[+phon]: phonological similarity rating of 4.
[+sem]: 'hand' and 'head' are co-partonyms, both body parts.

b. OB: 'I knòw whỳ they càll those **yèllow** lìnes . . . òrange lìnes "lánes".' ('yellow' [jɛ́.loʷ] substituted for 'orange' [orndʒ]; OC-164(35) 5;8)
[-phon]: phonological similarity rating of 0.5.
[+sem]: 'yellow' and 'orange' are co-hyponyms of color.

c. B : 'Gràndma Bèckie lìves in **Hústèd** . . . Hóuston.'
('Husted' [çjú.stɛd], the last name of a friend, for 'Houston' [çjú.stən]; B-541(35) 5;7)
[+phon]: phonological similarity rating of 7.
[-sem]: 'Husted' and 'Houston' have no semantic relationship.

d. Al: (Alice was standing on a chair watching Mom cook; Mom was using a measuring cup. Bobby tried to climb on Alice's chair)
'Gèt your ówn **cùp** . . . gèt your ówn chàir!'
('cup' [kʰʌp] substituted for 'chair' [tʃɛr]; AL-267(35) 5;11)
[-phon]: phonological similarity rating of 1.5.
[-sem]: 'cup' and 'chair' have no semantic relationship.

In errors like (13a) the target/error pair has both a phonological and semantic relationship; in (13b) there is a semantic relationship but no phonological one. The error in (13c) is a malapropism, that is, the word pair has a phonological relationship but no semantic similarity. Finally (13d) has neither a semantic nor a phonological relationship; this particular error was caused by an environmental influence.

In the discussion below I will look at the same set of errors analyzed in Table 4.2 above, that is, unambiguous substitution and blend errors, both syntagmatic and paradigmatic; the analysis excludes metathesis and addition errors, and substitution errors where the source is not clear. There are two exceptions. First, the tables below include one error which was omitted from the preceding analysis, where Anna produced *'jacking-jump' for 'jumping-jack' (AN-231(45) 4;8); in this error one cannot specify the lexical class of 'jump' and 'jack', but it is clear that they have a phonological relationship, but no semantic relationship outside this compound, so they can be included in this count. Second, the tables below exclude the following error which was included in Table 4.2.

TABLE 4.4

Number and percentage of lexical errors at each age that fell into the four categories determined by the features [sem] (word pair has a semantic relationship), and [phon] (word pair has a phonological relationship).

Age:		1-2a	1-2b	3	4	5	Total	Adult
-phon	N=	8	30	26	57	37	158	104
+sem	%	50%	44.5%	45.5%	50.5%	42%	46.5%	34.8%
+phon	N=	6	24	19	21	31	101	107
+sem	%	37.5%	36%	33.5%	18.5%	35.25%	29.5%	35.8%
+phon	N=	1	8	7	21	9	46	62
-sem	%	6.25%	12%	12%	18.5%	10.25%	13.5%	20.7%
-phon	N=	1	5	5	14	11	36	26
-sem	%	6.25%	7.5%	9%	12.5%	12.5%	10.5%	8.7%
Total N=		**16**	**67**	**57**	**113**	**88**	**341**	**299**
% +sem		87.5%	80.5%	79%	69%	77%	76%	70.5%
% +phon		44%	48%	45.5%	37%	45.5%	43%	56.5%

(14)   B: (telling about a TV show) 'There are pèople on tòp of the Èmpire
               Státe Bùilding, and they're tàlling big góops on pèople's hèads.'
               ('tall' substituted for target verb; could have been 'pour' or 'drop';
               error caused by discourse context, talking about a tall building;
               B-207(35) 4;2)

In this error, one can tell that the target was intended to be a verb, while the error word is an adjective, so the lexical category analysis can be made. However, the [phon, sem] analysis cannot be performed since the actual target word was not spoken.

The first tabulation looks at the number and percentage of errors at each age which fell into the four categories demonstrated in (13); the results are given in Table 4.4. For the children, the category into which the largest number of errors fell is [-phon, +sem], that is, word pairs that only have a semantic relationship; the overall percentage is 46.5%. Next most common was [+phon, +sem] errors, with both kinds of similarity, at 29.5%. The third most common category was [+phon, -sem], at 13.5%, and the least common were those errors with neither a semantic nor phonological relationship, at 10.5%. The overall percentage of errors where target/error words had a semantic relationship was 76%, but only

43% had a phonological relationship. This shows that for the children, having a semantic relationship was by far the more important factor in these lexical errors. Furthermore, nearly all errors (89.5%) had either one or the other. Recall that the RPC Model predicts that most lexical substitution and blend errors will be caused when lemmas which are related to the proposition are activated, and the lemma of a word which is semantically related to the intended word is more highly activated than the intended word. The second location of errors is in the activation of phonological form, where activation spreads to words which are phonologically similar to the form of the intended word. However, because there is a direct link from the selected lemma to the correct phonological form, this process is more automatic and less error-prone than the lemma selection. Thus, this model predicts not only that most errors should be caused by semantic or phonological similarity, but that semantic relationship should show more influence than phonological relationship, and this is exactly what is found.

As mentioned in §4.1.3 above, a second reason why semantically related errors are more common than phonologically related errors is that the internal monitor is paying more attention to whether or not the meaning of the sentence is being realized correctly; the actual form of the message, specifically the phonological form of words, is less important. Thus if the internal monitor detects an erroneous word which is semantically related to the intended word, it is more likely to let this word pass, since the overall meaning of the proposition may not have been drastically changed. However, if a word which is only phonologically related is planned for production, its meaning is likely to be so different from the intended meaning of the proposition that the internal monitor is more likely to catch it. Thus the phonological similarity will have to be exceedingly high in order for a phonologically related error word to be allowed to pass through by the internal monitor.

Comparing the child figures to the adult figures, we see some moderate differences. The most numerous categories for the adults were [+phon, +sem] at 36%, and [-phon, +sem] at 35%; this suggests that phonological similarity holds somewhat more weight for the adults than the children. This possibility is supported by the fact that adults produced a considerably larger percentage of [+phon, -sem] errors than the children did: child=13.5%, adult=21%. Finally, the adult percentage of errors with neither influence was very small, 8.5%. Thus the influence of semantics was somewhat less for the adults than for the children overall (child=76%, adult=70.5%), and the influence of phonology was greater for the adults (child=43%, adult=56.5%). However, in both populations the semantic relationships are more important, which is predicted by the model. I will return at the end of this chapter to the question of the interaction between phonological and semantic relationships.

Given these differences between adults and children in this study, we would expect to see the following developmental trends: the children should show a gradual decrease in the importance of semantic relationships, and a gradual increase in phonological influence, in order to move towards the adult figures.

The semantic factor is very important at age 1 (87.5%), and does gradually decrease, although it is actually at its lowest point at age 4 rather than 5. (This may be partly due to the fact that a number of the age 5 errors were contributed by Other children, and semantic errors may have been easier to detect from this group.) Nevertheless there does seem to be a mild trend in this direction. On the other hand there is no trend towards an increased importance of the phonological influence. After age 1-2a, the [+phon, -sem] category hovers around 11%, although it reaches a high of 18.5% at age 4; however, the overall [+phon] figures are between 37%-48% at all ages, with no smooth trend in any direction. There are at least two possible reasons why the children's lexicons seemed to be less structured according to phonology than the adults'. First, the more important factor when learning words for production in the first place is their meaning, so this would guide the original organization of the lexicon. But second, it is probably the case that the phonological aspects of lexical entries take on more prominence when the child becomes literate; since the orthographic representations of words becomes stored in the form lexicon, and since they are closely linked to the phonemes of the words (in English and other languages with alphabetic writing systems), this may reinforce the phonological structure of words. This is speculation; clearly errors made by English-speaking children ages 6-10 would be a very important testing ground for this hypothesis, as well as errors made by speakers of languages with non-phonological writing systems. A further possible explanation related to morphology will be given below.

Another factor which might interact with the relative influence of semantics and phonology on lexical errors is the type of error in question. That is, there may be different patterns of influence in paradigmatic errors compared to syntagmatic, or substitutions compared to blends. For that reason I tabulated the errors which fell into each [phon, sem] category, by lexical error class, for the children and adults separately. The results are given in Table 4.5. This table is to be read as follows (for example): the children made a total of 148 Class I errors; of these errors, 45.3% fell into the [-phon, +sem] category, 31% in the [+phon, +sem] category, and so forth. Overall 76.5% of the children's errors in this class showed a semantic relationship between target and error word, and 49.5% displayed a phonological relationship.

The figures in this table show that paradigmatic lexical errors (Classes I-III) for the most part demonstrate more semantic and phonological relationship between mutually involved pairs of words than do syntagmatic errors (Classes IV-VI); general figures will be given in Table 4.6 below. The class with the highest overall level of semantic relationships is Class III, the lexical blends (child=88.5%, adult=97%). This is easily explainable in the RPC Model, since blends nearly always arise when two lexical items which are both semantically appropriate for a particular utterance are selected, assigned to the same syntactic slot, and then blended into a single phonological form for speaking; thus this type of error almost requires a semantic relationship between the two words by definition. There were only 11 blend errors (9 child and 2 adult) which were

TABLE 4.5
Percentage of lexical errors which fell into the four categories determined
by the features [phon] and [sem], by lexical error class; children compared
to adults. I=paradigmatic content word substitutions; II=paradigmatic
function word substitutions; III=lexical blends, content & function;
IV=lexical anticipations, content & function; V=lexical perseverations,
content & function; VI=lexical exchanges, content & function.

Class:		-phon +sem	+phon +sem	+phon -sem	-phon -sem	N	%[+sem]	%[+phon]
I.	Child	45.25%	31%	18.25%	5.5%	148	76.25%	49.25%
	Adult	36.5%	34%	25.5%	4%	145	70.5%	59.5%
II.	Child	37%	52.5%	2.5%	8%	38	89.5%	55%
	Adult	25%	50%	0	25%	12	75%	50%
III.	Child	60.25%	28.25%	6.5%	5%	78	88.5%	34.75%
	Adult	39%	58%	3%	0	72	97%	61%
IV.	Child	31%	11.5%	19%	38.5%	26	42.5%	30.5%
	Adult	22.5%	7%	38.5%	32%	44	29.5%	45.5%
V.	Child	41.5%	22%	14.5%	22%	41	63.5%	36.5%
	Adult	27%	33%	33%	7%	15	60%	66%
VI.	Child	50%	10%	20%	20%	10	60%	30%
	Adult	55%	18%	9%	18%	11	73%	27%

classified as [-sem], and these fell into three types. The most common case (N=5) was when the speaker was actually thinking about two different propositions or two different phrases for expressing this proposition, and so the blend might be thought of as a propositional or phrase blend, as in (15a), or a syntagmatic blend as in (15b); the other three errors of this type were B-55(38) 2;5 'piece/beef', B-211(38) 4;2 'shower/cold' and AD-546(38) 'intact/ impressive'. This type also often showed an influence of the discourse context (see §4.2.8 below). The other two types of blend errors with no semantic relationship occurred with equal frequency (N=3 each). In one case the speaker has not been able to decide on the level of specificity with which to refer to some object, and blends a more general term with a more specific term, as illustrated in (15c). These errors were all made by the children; the other two were AL-224(38) 4;5 'sides/kinds' and B-356(38) 4;8 'tape/kind'. The third type involved interference from some object visible in the environment, as illustrated in (15d); the other two errors of this type were B-509(38) 5;5 'airplane/acorn' and AD-525(38) 'Van Valin/Houghtaling'.

(15) a. Al: 'Nòbody [sm:éʲkt] mè.' (looks confused)
          M: 'What?'
          Al: 'Nòbody màked me crý.' (blend of 'spanked' [spæŋkt] and 'maked' [meʲkt]; AL-78b(38) 2;11)
      b. B: 'I còuldn't sée it, and I wènt ìnto the [splìs] . . . plàce where you cán sèe it, . . . (etc.)'
              (seems to be blend of 'see' [si] and 'place' [pʰleʲs], like he started to say 'seeing place'; B-142(38) 3;8)
      c. Al: (Mom put a cassette tape of Grandpa's band into the tape deck; Alice usually referred to the tape as 'Grandpa'; Alice points to tape) 'I lóve [d̪æ̀.pa] . . . I lóve Gràndpa, Móm!'
              (blend of 'that' [d̪æt] 'Grandpa' [g̊ʒæ̃m.pa]; AL-51(40) 2;9)
      d. An: (eating popcorn while looking at her sister holding a pumpkin, on Halloween) 'Ì'm gònna gòbble ùp àll my [pʰʌmp.kʰòrn].'
              (blend of 'pumpkin' [pʰʌmp.kɪn] and 'popcorn' [pʰáp.kʰòrn]; AN-188(38) 4;5)

It is not surprising that the children in the study made the majority of blend errors in which the two target words were not semantically related, due to the fact that adults have had much more practice than children in selecting one unique propositional content to be expressed or the pragmatically appropriate level of specificity for referring to some object. Furthermore adults are less strongly influenced by environmental contaminants (see §4.2.6 below). Another difference between the child and adult figures is that while for the children only 34.75% of the blends showed a phonological relationship, the adult figure is 61%. Thus the stronger reliance on phonology for adults compared to children shows up clearly in the blend errors.

The category which comes next after blends in terms of frequency of semantic relationships is Class II, paradigmatic function word substitutions (child=89.5%, adult=75%); in fact, for the children this class is one percentage point higher than blends. Most Class II errors involved two words of the same lexical category; and for function words, words in the same lexical category (pronouns, prepositions, conjunctions, etc.) are semantically related almost by definition. Errors frequently involved two words with what one could call one semantic feature different, such as: 'you/me' (violates person; AN-89b(36) 2;11); 'what/where' (both question words, differ in object of questioning: thing vs. location; AN-120(36) 3;8); 'hi/bye' (both interjections, differ in being opening vs. closing greetings; B-164(36) 3;9); and 'before/after' (converses of relative time; B-317(36) 4;7). The adults produced 3 non-semantic Class II errors and the children produced 4, illustrated in (16). These errors can be explained either by suggesting they are a possible phrase blend, as in (16a), or result from a collocational expression as in (16b); the children also made two errors in which a pronominal determiner interacted with an article, which are not strictly semantically related, as in (16c). Four of the seven non-semantic errors (including all 3 of the adult errors) involved prepositions; since this is the largest class of 'closed class' words, and there is a greater degree of semantic variation among prepositions than among the words in other function word categories, this is not a surprising finding. This is a case where prepositions show that they have some factors in common with content word categories.

(16)   a. AF: (hairdresser, telling client how much longer she has for perm to
           set) 'You have síx more mìnutes **to** your háir like thàt.
           I mean w<u>ì</u>th your hàir like thàt.' ('to' for 'with'; possibly phrase
           blend with 'minutes to go with your hair'; AD-483(36))
       b. Al: (to Mom, talking about her friend Adam's bike)
           'I wànt to rìde his lìttle bíke.'
          OB: (not Adam; thinks Alice is talking to him)
           'It's not míne, it's my síster's.'
          Al: 'I'm tàlking **to** . . . Ádam's bìke. I'm tàlking <u>about</u> Ádam's
           bìke.' ('to' for 'about', probably due to collocation 'I'm talking
           to', frequently said to a speaker who has spoken when he has
           not been addressed; AL-206(36) 4;2)
       c. B: 'Mommy, tùrn the líght òn!'
          M: 'Where?'
          B: 'In **my** [pʰl̩] . . . in <u>the</u> pláyroom.' ('my' for 'the'; B-59(36) 2;5)

In the case of function word substitutions, the children's errors show 55% phonological similarity, and the adults' 50%. This is similar to the figures for other classes for adults, but higher than usual for the children. The explanation for this is most likely that many words within function word categories are phonologically similar (e.g. 'he, she, him, her'), and thus any two lexical items might be phonologically similar by chance.

Following the paradigmatic function word substitutions in terms of frequency of semantic similarity is the content word substitutions, Class I: child=76.25%, adult=70.5%. This is easily explained by the RPC Model; again the main difference between children and adults is that adults show 59.5% phonological similarity, while children show only 49.5%. Content word substitution errors where the target/error pair do not have a semantic relationship are most often caused by a phonological relationship (malapropisms), as well as the other factors to be discussed below: collocations, environmental influences, discourse influence, and 'on the mind'. The adult vs. child figures for the [+phon, -sem] category show that the adults made a larger percentage of malapropisms than the children did. Although this could be partially explained by a higher reliance on phonology by adults than children, as discussed above, another explanation is possible. For adults, the large majority of [+phon, -sem] Class I errors involve two words whose phonological similarity is at least in part a function of their morphological similarity, for example (all category 35): 'intuition/intonation' (AD-399), 'perception/perfection' (AD-400), 'description/ subscription' (AD-404), 'imbib(ing)/imbu(ing)' (AD-447), 'prevent/present' (AD-450), and 'functionalist/fundamentalist' (AD-464). If morphological structure is one crucial factor in the formal similarity between two lexical entries, then it is not surprising that adults make many more errors of this sort than children, since children know few of these latinate derived words as they are most often advanced vocabulary items which express somewhat abstract or complex concepts. The children produced only two errors of this sort.

(17)   a. An: (her favorite TV show "Contraption" just came on)
        'Hey, "**Colléction**" is òn!'
        M: You mean "Contráption"?'
        An: 'Yéah, "Contráption".' ('Collection' [kʰə.lɛ́k.ʃən] for
        'Contraption' [kʰən.tʰɾǽp.ʃən]; AN-60(35) 2;7)
    b. B: (acting out words in "Children's Dictionary")
        'Dàd, ya wànna sèe my **invèntion** . . . my imprèssion of a hát?'
        ('invention' [ɪn.vɪ́ɲ.tʃɪn] for 'impression' [ɪm.pʰɾɛ́.ʃɪn]; B-513(35)
        5;5)

In (17a), made when Anna was 2;7, she actually knew the word 'collection' and used it appropriately, but the word 'Contraption' was known to her only as the name of a television show, which explains the precocity of this error. However, the error in (17b) is exactly like those made by adults, where two known derived words with morphological structure in common are confused in an error. I have discussed a few other errors involving derived words in previous chapters: Anna's stress error *'decoráte' for 'décorate', based on her knowledge of 'decorátion' (AN-260(32) 4;11), and Bobby's blend errors *'cematárium' (for 'cémetery' and 'planetárium'; B-471(38) 5;2) and *'impérson' (for 'impèrsonátion' and 'impréssion'; B-514(38) 5;5). The fact that all of these errors involving morphology (other than Anna's 'Contraption' error) were made by the older children (age 4;11 and up) is an indication of when this class of word is learned by children and thus becomes available for error. The scarcity of this type of word in the children's vocabularies throughout the ages under study here, and the relationship between morphology and malapropisms in adult errors, suggests that this might be one important cause of the difference in frequency of malapropisms between adults and children. The finding that children's errors show less influence of phonology, and thus that they have less phonological organization of the lexicon, might also be a reflection of less influence of morphology on the lexicon for children. I will return to this topic in Chapter 6.
    Turning to the syntagmatic errors (Classes IV-VI), it can be seen that the

numbers in Table 4.5 drop for both semantic and phonological relationships compared to paradigmatic errors. For the children, the syntagmatic class with the highest level of semantic relationship is the perseverations, Class V (child=63.5%, adult=60%), followed by exchanges, Class VI (child=60%, adult=73%) and lastly the anticipations, Class IV (child=42.5%, adult=29.5%). Thus in general when two words are being activated for some utterance, or one has already been spoken, it is less important that the two words be semantically related for one to be substituted for the other. This is especially true of anticipations, where less than half show a semantic relationship; below I will document that there are other factors (new information, tonic stress) which are more important than semantic relatedness in anticipation errors. However, in the syntagmatic errors, again there is a large difference between the adults and children in terms of phonological relatedness. For the children, all three classes show low phonological similarity figures, but for adults there is more phonological relatedness; in particular the perseverations show a remarkable consistency of phonological form: Class IV, anticipations: child=30.5%, adult= 45.5%; Class V, perseverations: child=36.5%, adult=66%; Class VI, exchanges: child=30%, adult=27%.

Thus, for adults and children alike, a word may be anticipated and substituted for another word without much phonological or semantic relatedness; this will partially depend on lexical class, weight, and other properties to be discussed below. Two words are likely to exchange if they are semantically related, and phonological relatedness is much less important; this is more true for the adults than the children. However, this can be at least partially explained by the fact that exchanges very often take place in two adjacent content-word slots (with function word slots between them but no other content words), and any two adjacent content words in a sentence will often have a semantic relationship between them if the sentence is to make any sense. Finally, if a word has already been spoken in a discourse, it is strongly eligible to substitute for some later slot; for the children, this substitution will be most heavily influenced by a semantic relationship, but for adults the word is more likely to substitute if it is phonologically similar (or both semantically and phonologically similar) to a later target word. Possibly in a perseveration the erroneously produced word needs to be both semantically and phonologically similar for the adult's internal monitor to not notice that the same word is being planned a second time. Another contributing factor might be the fact that in adult perseverations, the source word was usually spoken by the same adult speaker in a preceding phonological phrase, whereas in the child perseverations, the source word was very often spoken by a different speaker (see Table 4.12 below). According to the RPC Model, during speech production planning, the phonological form of a word is activated after the meaningful lemma of the word is activated, and thus if the same speaker produces both the source and error, the phonological form is the most recently activated representation and therefore may have more influence on a perseveratory substitution. However, for auditory comprehension, the phonological form is activated first and the semantics second; so if a different

TABLE 4.6
Percentage of paradigmatic vs. syntagmatic lexical errors which are [+sem]
and [+phon], by age.

Age:	1-2a	1-2b	3	4	5	Total	Adult
Paradigmatic Errors							
% [+sem]	100%	82%	85.5%	76%	83.5%	82%	79%
% [+phon]	43%	51%	51%	39%	48%	46%	59.5%
N=	14	55	41	87	67	264	229
Syntagmatic Errors							
% [+sem]	0	75%	62.5%	46%	57%	56%	43%
% [+phon]	50%	33%	31%	31%	38%	34%	47%
N=	2	12	16	26	21	77	70

speaker has spoken the source word, the semantic representation will be the aspect of the word most recently activated and may then have more influence.

Interestingly, there doesn't seem to be as much influence from morphology in these syntagmatic errors, as the [+phon, -sem] adult errors involve such pairs as 'trauma/Tanya' (AD-581), 'Kinney/kitty' (AD-623) and 'after/error' (AD-625). A couple anticipation errors may involve some morphological similarity: 'interruption/discussion' (AD-579), 'assemble/address' (AD-590); however, none of the perseveratory or exchange errors clearly show this influence. Thus, the main finding here is that, as with paradigmatic errors, adults show more influence from phonology than children do; but for syntagmatic errors, this seems to be related to phonology per se, rather than including the morphological influence that was seen in paradigmatic errors. This suggests that while internal morphological structure of lexical items is an important aspect of the form of lexical entries in the lexicon, this structure is much less important during the planning of the syntagmatic string.

In order to see whether the interaction between the [+sem] and [+phon] parameters and the class of error shows some age-related trends, I recalculated the data by age; the results are given in Table 4.6. This table is to be read as follows (for example): at age 4, the children made 87 paradigmatic lexical substitutions or blends, and of these, 76% (N=66) showed a semantic relationship between the word pair involved, while 39% (N=34) showed a phonological relationship.

This table makes two things apparent. First, as indicated above, paradigmatic errors rely much more on semantic and phonological relationships than syntagmatic errors do, for both children and adults. The children's data showed overall 82% semantic relationships for paradigmatic errors vs. 56% for syntagmatic; the adults showed 79% vs. 43%. The children's paradigmatic errors contained phonological relationships in 46% of the cases, but the syntagmatic errors had 34% phonological relationships; for the adults the figures were 59.5% paradigmatic, 47% syntagmatic. The second point clearly made by the figures is that while the children's and adult's figures are not wildly different in terms of semantic relationships, they are very different in the phonological relatedness figures, with the adults showing much more effect of phonology than the children (as discussed earlier). One way to view this difference is to notice that there is a 36% difference between [+sem] and [+phon] for the children's paradigmatic errors, whereas there is only a 19.5% difference for adults. Similarly there is a 22% difference for the children's syntagmatic errors, but for the adults, phonological similarity is 4% more important than semantic similarity.

A third point to be made from this table has to do with age-related trends. In the paradigmatic category, the percent difference between the [+sem] and [+phon] figures remains relatively steady through the whole age span, ranging around 35%; the exception is age 1-2a, where the difference is 57%. Thus for lexical selection errors, there seems to be no increase in the importance of phonological influences. However, for syntagmatic errors there is a slight drop in the influence of semantics, which gradually produces a smaller difference between the [+sem] and [+phon] percentages; this difference drops from 42% at age 1-2b to 14% at age 4 and 19% at age 5. Thus the percentages for syntagmatic errors show a slight trend in the direction of the adult figures, due to a less heavy influence of semantic relatedness.

In sum, most lexical errors in this study, for both children and adults, involve two words which are either semantically or phonologically related, or both. Paradigmatic errors show a higher proportion of relatedness than do syntagmatic errors. For both children and adults, the semantic factor outranks the phonological factor. However, the main difference between children and adults is that for the adults, the phonological influence is also very high, especially in syntagmatic errors, while for the children, phonological relatedness plays a far less important role. It also appears that for adults there is an effect of morphological structure on paradigmatic errors, which is to some extent conflated with the phonological relatedness factor; this may help explain why the adults made many more malapropisms than the children did.

At this point I would like to return to the figures presented at the beginning of this section regarding the findings of other researchers as to the relative influence of semantics and phonology on lexical errors. Recall that the other studies compared paradigmatic lexical substitution errors with any semantic relationship ('semantic' errors) to those with no semantic relationship but with a phonological relationship (malapropisms); these studies vary as to whether or not they included function word substitutions in their calculations. In order to compare my findings to previous studies I selected only the paradigmatic lexical substitution errors, content and function word errors combined, which had either a semantic or phonological relationship (or both), excluding those errors which

TABLE 4.7
Comparison among 6 studies of the proportion of paradigmatic lexical
substitution errors which were related by semantics or only by phonology;
N=total number of errors in each study; C=study included content words;
F=study included function words.

	Jaeger Child	Stemberger Child	Jaeger Adult	Stemberger Adult
Semantics	84%	60%	75%	83%
Malapropisms	16%	40%	25%	17%
N=	175	45	148	649
C, F?	C&F	C&F	C&F	C&F

	Hotopf	Fay & Cutler	Arnaud	Harley & MacAndrew
Semantics	52%	19%	67%	76%
Malapropisms	48%	81%	33%	24%
N=	272	226	497	1028
C, F?	C	C&F	C	C

Stemberger (1989), Hotopf (1983), Fay & Cutler (1977), Arnaud (1999),
Harley & MacAndrew (2001)

were [-phon, -sem]. I calculated the percentages which were 'semantic' errors vs. malapropisms, and then calculated the same percentages from the various other studies, including Stemberger's (1989) child data; Table 4.7 presents the results.

As noted before, the figures vary greatly among the adult studies; however, in all but the Fay & Cutler (1977) study, semantic errors outnumber malapropisms. I have no explanation for why Fay & Cutler's proportions are so different from all other studies, other than the possibility that they may have used a very conservative measure for 'semantic relatedness', or that since their particular interest was in malapropisms they may have been listening especially for these types of errors during data collection. Hotopf's (1983) figure for malapropisms may be somewhat higher than the Jaeger or Stemberger adult figures because he did not include function words, which are rarely only phonologically related. Looking at the two child studies, there is a discrepancy between my data and Stemberger's, in that he found that the children in his study made a higher proportion of malapropisms than the adults did; however, he only collected 45 paradigmatic lexical substitution errors from his children, and he himself indicates that this makes the findings somewhat equivocal. Furthermore, he did not include any explicit discussion of his criteria for 'semantic relationship' or 'phonological relationship' in his report, and thus it is impossible to tell how these were calculated. The Arnaud (1999) and Harley &

MacAndrew (2001) figures are very similar to my adult figures, even though neither study included function words. The fact that these various studies vary so greatly in results, undoubtedly due to differences in methodology and classification systems, highlights the importance of comparing data collected by the same researcher using the same methodology and criteria for classification as 'semantic' or 'malapropisms', which is made completely explicit in the presentation of the data. Thus I argue that my findings regarding the relative proportions of semantic vs. phonological influences on lexical substitution errors are not falsified by any of these other studies.

Throughout this section I have been talking about errors which are semantically or phonologically related, without saying much about the fact that many errors are both. In fact, the interaction between the two types of relationships is quite important in the RPC Model. There are two basic questions to be asked. First, does the phonological form of two semantically related lemmas influence the possible misselection of one for the other, or is it irrelevant? The second question is whether or not target and error pairs which have no semantic relationship must have a heightened phonological relationship in order to allow a misselection. I will look into this second question first.

I suggested above that errors which are [+phon, -sem] should show a high degree of phonological relatedness in order to fool the internal monitor, since they violate the intended meaning of the utterance; however I have not yet demonstrated that this is true. What I would need to do is show that the average numerical 'phonological similarity' rating for [+phon, -sem] errors is consistently higher than the rating for error pairs which are semantically similar, whether they also have phonological similarity or not. In order to look into this issue, I calculated the average 'phonological similarity', using the numbers generated by the rules in Table 4.3 above, for errors at each age, with each combination of values on the [sem] and [phon] parameters; I calculated these numbers for paradigmatic and syntagmatic errors separately. The results are shown in Table 4.8.

Looking at general issues first, it can be seen from this table that the average phonological similarity is higher between word pairs involved in paradigmatic errors than those involved in syntagmatic errors; this was true at all ages except 1-2a, where there was basically no difference between the two. Secondly, the average phonological similarity between word pairs is higher for the adults than for the children in general; for all errors the child average is 2.5 (which is [-phon]) while for the adults it is 3.3 (which is [+phon]). Similarly, for all [+sem] word pairs, the child average is 2.3, but for adults it is 2.7; for all [+phon] word pairs, the child average is 3.8, whereas the adult average is 4.4. These figures reinforce points made above regarding the differences in phonological relatedness between syntagmatic vs. paradigmatic errors, and between children and adults. (However, it should be noted that the assignment of phonological similarity rubric is somewhat biased towards longer words; that is, it is easier to get a higher number on the similarity scale if the words have

TABLE 4.8
Average phonological similarity of pairs of words involved in
paradigmatic and syntagmatic lexical errors, by age, and by the four
categories designated by the two features [sem], [phon].

Age:	1-2a	1-2b	3	4	5	Total (N)	Adult (N)
Paradigmatic Errors							
[-phon, +sem]	1.3	1.4	1.6	1.6	1.4	1.5 (128)	1.3 (84)
[+phon, +sem]	3.9	3.5	3.6	3.6	3.9	3.7 (88)	4.0 (97)
[+phon, -sem]	na	3.6	4.3	4.7	4.0	4.2 (33)	5.6 (39)
[-phon, -sem]	na	1.5	1.3	1.3	1.3	1.4 (15)	1.4 (9)
Overall=	2.4	2.5	2.7	2.6	2.6	2.6 (264)	3.4 (229)
Syntagmatic Errors							
[-phon, +sem]	na	1.4	1.4	1.2	1.4	1.3 (30)	1.7 (20)
[+phon, +sem]	na	3.3	3.0	3.3	3.4	3.3 (13)	3.8 (10)
[+phon, -sem]	3.0	4.5	3.5	3.6	4.3	3.8 (13)	4.0 (23)
[-phon, -sem]	2.0	2.0	1.3	1.9	0.9	1.5 (21)	1.5 (17)
Overall=	2.5	2.3	1.8	2.1	2.1	2.1 (77)	2.7 (70)
All [+sem]	2.4	2.3	2.3	2.1	2.5	2.3 (259)	2.7 (211)
All [+phon]	3.8	3.6	3.7	4.0	3.9	3.8 (147)	4.4 (169)
All Errors=	**2.4**	**2.5**	**2.4**	**2.5**	**2.5**	**2.5 (341)**	**3.3 (299)**

several syllables. Thus the overall higher rating for adults may partly be due to
the fact that they know more multisyllabic words than children do. On the other
hand, this also gives the adult words more chances of being different from each
other; so perhaps the positive and negative properties of the length factor cancel
each other out.)

Regarding the specific question at hand, the most important numbers in this
table are the average phonological similarity figures for the [+phon, +sem] and
[+phon, -sem] rows. First, for the paradigmatic errors, the [+phon, -sem]
figures are higher than the [+phon, +sem] figures at every age, although at some
ages there is a very small difference. At age 1-2a there were no malapropisms,
so no comparison is possible. At age 1-2b, the [+phon, +sem] average is 3.5
whereas the [+phon, -sem] average is 3.6, only a tenth of a point different; this
difference increases at age 3 (3.6 vs. 4.3) and reaches its greatest difference at age
4 (3.6 vs. 4.7); for some odd reason it becomes less clear at age 5 (3.9 vs. 4.0).
The difference for adults is greater than that for the children at any age: 4.0 vs.
5.6. Thus my predictions are partially supported: pure malapropisms always
have a higher average phonological similarity rating than semantically related
pairs, even if those pairs also are phonologically related; the overall difference is

0.5 similarity rating points for the children compared to 1.6 points for the adults. However, to fully support the claim that it is a very close phonological relationship which allows the erroneous word to escape notice of the internal monitor, one would expect to find greater differences between the average phonological similarity of the malapropisms and the semantic errors at all ages. The adult figures are convincing (with a 1.6 point difference), but the child figures are not as strong, except at ages 3 and 4. One possible explanation for this is that for the children, many of these errors are not pure malapropisms, as they are influenced by some environmental or discourse factor, and thus some other factor is promoting the selection of the incorrect word. Compare the following two errors.

(18) a. An: (saying a rhyme, sees Bobby eating a cookie)
          'Fìve lìttle **cóokies** . . . fìve lìttle <u>mónkeys</u> bòuncin' òn the
          béd.' ('cookies' [kʰʊ́.ki(z)] for 'monkeys' [mʌ́ŋ.ki(z)];
          phonological similarity=3; AN-269(35) 5;1)
      b. B: 'Grandma Beckie lives in **Hústèd** . . . Hoúston.'
          ('Husted' [çjú.stèd] for 'Houston' [çjú.stən]; Husted is the last
          name of a friend; phonological similarity=7; B-541(35) 5;7)

In (18a) the cause of the error is the fact that a cookie is visible in the environment, and the fact that the two words 'cookie' and 'monkey' are phonologically similar (rating=3) helps allow the error to fool the planning mechanism and monitor. However, in (18b) there is no environmental or discourse cause for the error; it is a pure malapropism, and the phonological similarity is very high (rating=7). The fact that adults make far fewer errors which are influenced by external factors than the children do (as I will document below) helps explain why the adult errors show a greater gap between phonological similarity ratings of phonologically similar semantic errors vs. malapropisms.

If this explanation in terms of external factors is correct, then we would expect to find a greater difference in phonological similarity between [+phon, +sem] and [+phon, -sem] syntagmatic errors, since environmental factors are a less common influence in syntagmatic errors. And indeed, for the children as well as the adults, there is a consistent difference between the two categories at all ages. The overall difference for the children is 0.5 points (3.3 vs. 3.8), the same as for the paradigmatic errors, but the difference shows up more consistently at all ages; the difference for adults is in fact less striking: 0.2 points (3.8 vs. 4.0).

Finally, if the figures for [+phon, -sem] paradigmatic and syntagmatic errors are compared to the overall phonological similarity ratings calculated from all errors at each age (see the last row in the table), it is clear that the similarity ratings for these errors are always considerably higher than the overall average, at every age: for children the overall average is 2.5, but for phonologically governed paradigmatic errors it is 4.2, and for phonologically governed syntagmatic errors it is 3.8. For adults the figures are: overall 3.3, paradigmatic errors 5.6, and syntagmatic errors 4.0. Thus these averages support the hypothesis that errors which are caused by a phonological relationship between the word pair require a high degree of phonological similarity in order to allow the misselected word to go undetected by the internal monitor.

The second question raised above, regarding the influence of phonological form on semantically related word pairs, cannot be answered in this chapter, but the question can be formulated in more detail. I have been discussing semantically related lexical substitution errors as if the semantic relationship is the only thing that matters when a misselection is made; that is, when two semantically related lemmas are activated to fill a particular slot in an utterance, the selection of one for the other will be caused entirely by the semantic factor. There is some support for this point of view in the fact that the largest number of errors for the children involves pairs which are [-phon, +sem], that is, only semantically and not phonologically related. (For the adults, semantic errors with or without a phonological component are about equal; see Table 4.4 above.) However, there is an interesting hypothesis that could in principle be tested. I have shown that for words to be erroneously selected solely based on phonological properties, a high degree of phonological similarity is required between the two words involved (unless there is some external support for the error word). What if we found that words which are involved in [-phon, +sem] errors showed a higher degree of semantic relatedness than [+phon, +sem] pairs? This would suggest that an error word which was highly semantically related to the target word could fool the monitor without any phonological similarity, but that a word with less strong semantic similarity would need the backup of phonological similarity in order to get by the monitor and thus be uttered. Conversely, we might find that there is no interaction between the strength of semantic relationship and whether or not there is a phonological relationship between word pairs; the phonological relationship might just be accidental. It is clear that either of these findings would require different things from the model. If it were found that less strongly semantically related words need the support of a phonological relationship in order to be selected, the RPC Model would need to account for this by including multiple feed-forward and feed-back links between the semantic lexicon and the form lexicon. That is, two words whose lemmas are activated would each activate their own forms; if these two forms were phonologically similar and thus mutually related in the form lexicon, each form would feed activation back to its lemma, causing the erroneous lemma to be more likely to be selected (Dell & Reich 1981). However, if it turns out that the strength of semantic relationship shows no interaction with the presence or absence of a phonological relationship, then the model needs to demonstrate that the phonological relationship is accidental, by showing only a feed-forward link between the semantic lexicon and the form lexicon is necessary during speech production planning.

This is clearly an important issue; however, it cannot be addressed here because I have not yet discussed semantic relationships in any detail, so that a measure for 'more vs. less closely semantically related' is not available. However, I will return to this issue at the end of Chapter 5 (§5.5), and will at that point present a solution to the question of the interaction between the semantic and phonological lexicons during speech production planning.

4.2.3 Tonic Word Position

In Chapter 3 (§3.7.3) it was shown that the tonic word in a phonological phrase, that is the word with the greatest amount of prosodic prominence, was frequently involved in phonological errors. In phonological anticipatory errors the primary stressed syllable of the tonic word was most often the location of the source, in perseverations it was most often the location of the error, and in exchanges the tonic syllable occurred as the first or second target equally, at least for the children. I argued that both the prosodic and informational prominence of the tonic can contribute to its involvement in phonological errors.

There is a similar logical prediction which can be made regarding the involvement of the tonic word in lexical errors. In paradigmatic lexical substitution and blend errors, it would be expected that the tonic-stressed word would be the location of the error far more often than would be predicted by chance. This is because, as discussed in Chapter 3, the tonic word is typically the new information in focus in the phrase, and it often also contains meaning which is being foregrounded in some pragmatically relevant way, e.g. it is being emphasized, contrasted, and so on. Thus the selection of the word which will be spoken in tonic position may be especially susceptible to error because, as new information, it is being selected and planned for speaking for the first time in this discourse. The selection of a word for expressing new information will require a great deal of attention and mental resources, and this is especially true if it is also being contrasted or emphasized.

For syntagmatic lexical errors, it can be predicted that they would follow the patterns found for phonological errors: in anticipatory errors the tonic word would be the source, in perseverations it would be the error, and in exchanges either of the two words would be equally likely to be the tonic word. Overall, the tonic word should be involved in syntagmatic lexical errors at a rate greater than chance. However, for both paradigmatic and syntagmatic errors, it is likely that these predictions would hold true for content words more often than for function words, since function words are rarely the locus of tonic stress in a phrase.

In order to test these hypotheses, I first looked at all the unambiguous paradigmatic content word lexical substitution and blend errors where the error utterance contained more than one word; in the few errors which mixed content and function words, I included the error only if the target was a content word. In each case I determined whether or not the target word in the originally planned phonological phrase was intended to take tonic stress; in two-word utterances, I

TABLE 4.9

Percentage of content word paradigmatic lexical errors (substitutions and blends) in which the target word was located in tonic stress position; by age and lexical category of target word.

Age:		1-2a	1-2b	3	4	5	Total	Adult
Common	N=	3	19	16	30	24	92	110
Noun	%	100%	79%	69%	80%	71%	76%	74.5%
Proper	N=	5	9	4	8	7	33	19
Noun	%	20%	55.5%	100%	87.5%	71.5%	66.5%	68.5%
Verb	N=	0	8	7	17	13	45	33
	%		25%	28.5%	29.5%	8%	22%	30%
Adjective/	N=	0	4	4	13	12	33	37
Adverb	%		75%	100%	61.5%	33%	57.5%	57%
Total N=		**8**	**40**	**31**	**68**	**56**	**203**	**199**
% Tonic		50%	62.5%	68%	65%	48%	59.5%	63%
Chance %		53%	43%	34%	34.5%	31%	35%	35%

counted the word with the strongest stress as the tonic. As I was performing this analysis I noticed that the lexical category of the target word seemed to interact with whether or not it was the locus of tonic stress, and so in the results given in Table 4.9, I have presented the findings in terms of both age and the lexical category of the target word. This table presents the number of eligible errors at each age, and the percentage of these errors in which the target word was planned to carry tonic stress in that phonological phrase. I also calculated a 'chance' figure, by counting the number of content words in each of the phonological phrases which contained the errors analyzed in this table, and dividing by the number of phrases. The 'Chance %' figures show how often the tonic word would be expected to be involved in an error by chance; e.g. if there were 3 content words in a phonological phrase involving a lexical substitution or blend, then the tonic word would be expected to be the locus of the error by chance in 1 out of 3 cases, or 33% of the errors. This table is to be read as follows (for example): at age 1-2b the children made 19 paradigmatic content word lexical substitution or blend errors where the target was a common noun; of these 19 errors, in 15 cases (79%) the target word was the locus of tonic stress in the phonological phrase.

The first point to be made from this table is that the tonic word was the locus of the error more often than would be predicted by chance at every age except age 1-2a. The chance figure at age 1-2a is 53%, and the overall involvement of the tonic is 50%, or just at chance. At age 1-2b the tonic word was involved at 1 1/2 times the rate expected by chance (62.5% vs. 43%), and at ages 3 and older, including adults, the tonic is involved at almost twice the rate expected by chance (note that the slight drop-off in involvement of the tonic at age 5 is accompanied by a drop-off in the chance figure, meaning that there were more eligible content words per phrase at this age). The child overall figure is 59.5% tonic vs. 35% chance, and the adult overall figure is 63% tonic vs. 35% chance; the similarities between the adult and child figures are striking. Thus once children begin producing utterances of 3+words which are governed by syntactic patterns, the tonic position in the phrase begins to take on the same type of prominence in planning as it has for adults; the children reached an adult-like ratio to chance figures at age 3. These findings are similar to what was found in Chapter 3 (§3.7.3) regarding the involvement of the tonic in phonological errors.

This table also shows that my observation that different lexical categories might be involved in this pattern at different rates was correct. The involvement of the tonic word in errors was the highest for common nouns (overall child=76%, adult=74.5%), followed by proper nouns (child=66.5%, adult= 68.5%), and adjectives/adverbs (child=57.5%, adult=57%). However, target words which were verbs were rarely the site of tonic stress; the verb figures are all far below chance (overall child=22%, adult=30%). (Note the similarity between the overall child figures and the adult figures for every lexical class.) This finding regarding verbs is for the most part simply a function of the focus structure of English sentences (Lambrecht 1994). The unmarked focus structure in English is 'broad focus', with the entire predicate within focus; the default location of the tonic stress is on the right-most element of the core predicate, usually the rightmost argument of the verb, as illustrated in (19a). Since arguments of verbs are usually nouns, this means that either proper or common nouns will take the tonic stress most often by default. The more marked focus is 'narrow focus', where some specific word is in focus; this is typically used for contrastive or emphatic stress. There is a markedness hierarchy of locations for narrow-focus tonic stress (Van Valin & LaPolla 1997: Ch. 5): the most marked site would be the subject (as in (19b)), followed by the verb (particularly if transitive; (19c)), the leftmost object in a ditransitive construction (I had no examples of this, so (19d) is a constructed example), and finally the least marked site would be an adjunct to the right of the arguments of the verb; this would typically be an adverb as in (19e), or a prepositional phrase, in which case the nominal object of the preposition would take tonic stress, as in (19f). This hierarchy predicts that nouns which occur as verb or prepositional objects would most often take tonic stress, followed by adverbs, and finally verbs. Adjectives don't fit into this hierarchy per se; however, in my data for the most part when an adjective takes tonic stress it is a predicate adjective, and thus is the leftmost argument in the predicate, as in (19g). Furthermore, most of the errors involving tonic-stressed verbs occur with intransitive verbs, which are again the leftmost member of the core predicate (19h). All of these examples are taken from category (35), paradigmatic content word substitutions (recall that tonic stress in a phrase is marked with the acute accent marker: $\acute{v}$).

(19)   a. AF: 'We nèed to gèt you a **héadàche**, uh a <u>háircùt</u>.'
         (nouns 'headache' for 'haircut'; tonic-stressed word is second
         object in predicate; AD-357)

       b. AF: 'Ànna's **clóck** uh <u>wátch</u> wènt through the wàsh.'
         (nouns 'clock' for 'watch'; 'watch' is the new information,
         subject; AD-351)

       c. AM: 'Sòmetimes we stàrt **imbíbing** the chìld with màny innàte
         strúctures.' (verbs 'imbib(ing)' for 'imbu(ing)'; emphatic stress
         on verb, AD-447)

       d. (constructed example) 'I gàve **Bóbby** the bòok, uh <u>Ánna</u> I mèan.'
         (proper nouns 'Bobby' for 'Anna', contrastive stress on the
         leftmost object)

       e. OG: 'You wànt it **slów**? . . . You wànt it <u>fást</u>?' (adverbs 'slow' for
         'fast', focus of question is on adverb; OC-29 2;8)

       f. AF: (giving directions for how to get to an office in the department)
         'Jùst tùrn lèft at the **búrglar-alàrm**.'
         AM: 'You mean the <u>fíre-alàrm</u>?'
         (nouns 'búrglar-alàrm' for 'fíre-alàrm', object of preposition 'at',
         locative adjunct to predicate 'turn left'; the location of the turn
         was new information; AD-367)

       g. TF: (while turning on the car heater) 'OK I'm **hót**, I mean I'm <u>cóld</u>.'
         (adjectives 'hot' for 'cold', as predicate adjective; AD-462)

       h. AF: (asking child if his nose is bleeding)
         'Is it stìll **blów** . . . uh <u>bléeding</u> Honey?'
         (intransitive verbs 'blow(ing)' for 'bleed(ing)'; AD-435)

The sentence in (19a) demonstrates the most common tonic stress pattern, and this explains why so many nouns involved in errors were the tonic-stressed elements in the phrase. The sentence in (19b) was spoken in the following context: I was doing the wash, and discovered that Anna's watch had been in the pocket of a washed garment; I exclaimed 'Oh, no!' and someone else asked 'What's wrong?' I then planned to say 'Anna's wátch went through the wash.' In this case 'Anna's watch' was the new information, and the washing scene was the old information, so 'watch' took tonic stress. In (19c), this speaker giving a talk about language acquisition wanted to emphasize that many of the 'innate structures' linguists attribute to children may actually be ones the child has been 'imbued' with by the linguists themselves, thus the emphasis on the verb. The contrastive stress in (19d) would have been appropriate if someone had asserted that I had given the book to Alice, and I was correcting them. In (19e) the child was asking another child how fast he wanted to be pushed on a swing, so the speed referred to by the adverb was the focus of the question. In giving the directions in (19f), the speaker assumed the hearer knew he had to turn left (since a right turn would have been impossible from that location), so the new information was *where* to do so, thus putting stress on the noun in the prepositional phrase. In (19g,h) the predicate adjective and intransitive verb are the rightmost elements in their respective core predicates (excluding adjuncts), so in fact the tonic stress is falling in the default location.

Thus Table 4.9 tells us two things. First, it is the case that a word in tonic stress position is far more likely to be involved in a lexical substitution or blend error than predicted by chance, and this is as true of the children in the 3+word stage and older as it is of adults. However, the younger children in the 1- and 2-word stages show no effect of tonic stress. Second, the marked vs. unmarked location of tonic stress in English syntax makes it much more likely that nouns will occur in the tonic stress position compared to other word classes, and thus nouns show the highest rate of influence from tonic stress status in the data. I will return to this point in §4.3 below when I discuss lexical categories in more detail.

In order to look into the influence of tonic stress on syntagmatic lexical errors, I looked at all the lexical anticipation and perseveration errors (in utterances of more than one word) and noted whether tonic stress fell on the source word of the error, the target/error word, both, or neither. For exchange and metathesis errors I looked at whether the first or second target word carried tonic stress, or if neither were involved. I did not include errors with list intonation, or the within-word metathesis errors.

In doing this analysis I did not try to separate out content from function words, since there is some overlap between the two categories in syntagmatic errors; I also included metathesis errors as they sometimes involve the tonic word. However, in presenting the data I have separated out the suspected interrupted metathesis errors from the other anticipation errors since the former may pattern more like exchanges than anticipations. Furthermore, since there are comparatively few syntagmatic lexical errors in my child data, I did not try to analyze the data by age, but combined all the child data together. Finally, in order to calculate a 'chance' figure for comparison, I counted the number of content and function words in each phonological phrase involving a target word, and calculated an average number of words per phrase; I did this because these errors involve both content and function words, rather than just content words as in the discussion of paradigmatic errors presented above. I then found the percentage of times any one word would take tonic stress by chance, and doubled it, since in syntagmatic errors there are two possible chances per phrase that a word might be in tonic stress position (i.e. the source and target locations, or the two target locations in exchanges). The results are given in Table 4.10.

It can be seen that the overall percentage of syntagmatic errors involving the

TABLE 4.10
Number and percentage of syntagmatic lexical errors involving the tonic
word, either as the source, or error, both, or one of the two targets in an
exchange; children compared to adults.

		Children		Adults	
		N	%	N	%
Anticipations	source	14	52%	17	38%
	error	1	3.5%	3	7%
	both	1	3.5%	6	13%
	neither	11	41%	19	42%
Overall Tonic=		**27**	**59%**	**45**	**58%**
Interrupted	source	3	27.25%	0	
Metathesis	error	3	27.25%	1	100%
	both	0		0	
	neither	5	45.5%	0	
Overall Tonic=		**11**	**54.5%**	**1**	**100%**
Perseveration	source	11	25%	4	27%
	error	5	11.5%	6	40%
	both	9	20.5%	3	20%
	neither	19	43%	2	13%
Overall Tonic=		**44**	**57%**	**15**	**87%**
Reversals,	target (1)	5	26.3%	3	19%
Contiguous &	target (2)	5	26.3%	6	37%
Non-contig.	neither	9	47.3%	7	44%
Overall Tonic=		**19**	**52.6%**	**16**	**56%**
Total N=		**101**	**56.5%**	**77**	**63.5%**
Chance=			36%		30%

tonic word is similar to that for paradigmatic errors; child=59.5% paradigmatic,
56.5% syntagmatic; adult=63% paradigmatic, 63.5% syntagmatic. These
syntagmatic numbers are well above the chance level (child=36%, adult=30%),
making it clear that the tonic word figures heavily in syntagmatic errors. The
main difference between the adult and child figures are in the perseveration
category: for the children, the tonic is involved in 57% of the errors, but for the
adults, the figure is 87%; in fact there were only two adult perseveratory errors

which did not involve the tonic, a point I will return to below.

The second relevant factor is the location of the tonic word in the error. For phonological errors it was shown that in anticipations, the tonic is usually the source, and this is also true for these lexical errors. For the children, the (non-metathesis) anticipatory errors involve the source in 52% of the cases, and for adults it is involved in 38% of the errors. However, there is an interesting difference between the child and adult data, which is related to the length of the unit being planned for uttering. The children produced only one anticipatory error where both the source and target were tonic-stressed words, but the adults produced 6 such errors, or 13% of their anticipations. This is due to the fact that in order to produce an error where both target and source are tonic-stressed words, the speaker needs to be planning two phrases at a time. In this case the tonic-stressed word from the second phrase is anticipated and erroneously assigned to the tonic-stressed slot of the first phrase, as illustrated in (20a); this might be done either at the functional assignment level or during lexical insertion into syntax (see §1.4.5). However, for most of the children's anticipation errors, the target and source words were planned for the same phrase, and thus only the source was a tonic-stressed word, as illustrated in (20b).

(20) a. AM: (speaker realizes that he has accidentally interrupted a class discussion by speaking to the professor through the open doorway; he says to the class)
       'Enjòy the **interrúption**, . . . I mean enjòy the <u>discússion</u>, and forgìve the *interrúption*.'
       ('interruption' anticipated from tonic position of second phrase and substituted for 'discussion' in tonic position in first phrase; AD-579(41))

      b. B: 'I'm gònna gèt some **hànds** on my . . . some <u>wàter</u> on my *hánds*.' ('hands' anticipated from tonic position in phrase, substituted for 'water' in non-tonic position in same phrase; child looking at his hands while speaking; B-156(41) 3;8)

These errors reinforce the claim discussed in previous chapters that the children are in general planning shorter spans of speech than the adults are, a completely unsurprising finding.

Looking at the perseveratory errors, one can see that there is a major difference between the site of the tonic word in the lexical errors compared to the phonological errors. In phonological perseveratory errors, when the tonic-stressed syllable was involved in the error, it was usually in the target/error location (46.5% children, 41% adults). However, for the lexical errors, the tonic word is very often the source of the error. For the children the tonic word is the source in 25% of the errors, and the error in only 11.5%; furthermore *both* target/error and source fell in tonic-stressed positions in 20.5% of the children's errors (in phonological errors the 'both' figure was 6%). For the adults on the other hand, in 27% of the perseveratory errors the source is a tonic-stressed word, in 40% it is the error, and in 20% it is both. The explanation for this difference from phonological errors is that phonological perseverations usually involve units in the same phrase, for both children and adults; therefore the tonic word, which is most often at the rightmost end of the phrase, would be the location of the target in perseveratory errors. However, in lexical perseverations, the lexical item which is perseverated very often comes from a preceding phrase, sometimes spoken by the same speaker and sometimes by a different speaker. It is likely that the most strongly stressed word in a preceding utterance would be the one to perseverate and be repeated in a subsequent phrase, which would produce an error where the source is a tonic-stressed word, as illustrated in (21a); if the perseverated word is substituted for the tonic-stressed word in the second phrase, then both target/error and source would be tonic words, as illustrated in (21b).

(21)   a. M: (while putting Bobby's shoes on him)
            'These **pánts** need to be ròlled ùp.'
        B: (pulls up pant legs to show socks) 'Mòm, thése aren't just
            régular **pànts**. I mean thése aren't just régular sòcks. Thèse
            are dìfferent cólors.'
            (tonic 'pants' perseverated from Mom's utterance, substituted
            for non-tonic 'socks' in Bobby's utterance; B-553(43) 5;8)
        b. M: (Mom and Bobby had just come back from a walk)
            'Bobby, it's time for you to take a **náp**.'
        B: 'I wànna gò on anòther **náp**.'
            (tonic 'nap' perseverated from Mom's utterance, substituted for
            tonic 'walk' in Bobby's utterance; B-174(43) 3;11)

This effect is very strong for the adults, who produced only 2 errors which did not involve the tonic in either position; it was slightly less so for the children, who produced 19 errors which did not involve a tonic word. Interestingly, most of the child perseveratory errors which did not involve the tonic word involved pairs of verbs or pronouns, which typically are not the locus of focus-stress in sentences, as discussed above.

(22)   a. M: 'Bobby, I'm gònna **pìck** you úp and pùt you awáy.'
        B: 'No! Dón't **pìck** me awày . . . pùt me awày.'
            ('pick' perseverated from Mother's utterance, substituted for
            'put'; B-124(43) 3;1)
        b. M: (as we leave someone's house after dinner)
            'Well, Alice, dòn't lèave **your** brúsh.'
        Al: 'OK, Ì won't lèave **your** brúsh . . . Ì won't lèave my brúsh.'
            ('your' perseverated from Mother's utterance, substituted for
            'my'; AL-111(43) 3;3)

These perseveratory substitutions of verbs and pronouns were more influenced by semantics, phonology, and lexical category than tonic stress. Nevertheless over half the children's perseveratory errors did include the tonic-stressed word.

Finally, in the children's lexical reversals there is a similar pattern to that found for their phonological errors, in that either the first or second target is equally likely to carry the tonic stress: child t1 and t2=26.3%. This pattern did not occur in the adult phonological reversals (the tonic was most often t2), but it did occur to some extent in the adult lexical reversals (t1=19%, t2=37%). A look at the 'interrupted metathesis' figures confirms that these are indeed aborted reversals, since the first or second targets are equally likely to carry tonic stress (child t1 and t2=27.25%; the adults made only one such error).

In sum, the tonic-stressed word in a phonological phrase is more likely to be involved in paradigmatic lexical substitution or blend errors than would be predicted by chance. The explanation for this involves both the prosodic prominence of this word and the pragmatic importance of this slot in the information structure of the phrase; the fact that words of different lexical categories interact with the effect of tonic stress in different proportions can be predicted from the marked/unmarked focus structures in English syntax. Syntagmatic errors also involve the tonic-stressed word more often than chance would predict; in anticipatory errors it is most often the source, and in exchange errors it is equally likely to be the first or second target. However, in perseveratory errors, while the tonic is often the site of the error word (as in phonological errors), it is more often (for the children) the site of the source word. This is true in the cases where a tonic word from one phrase is perseverated and substituted for a word in a following phrase; often the word in the following phrase is also the site of tonic stress, such that both source and error are tonic words.

Comparing the paradigmatic with syntagmatic errors, we find that the tonic stress position has about the same effect on syntagmatic errors as on paradigmatic errors for the children in relation to chance: for paradigmatic errors, the ratio between percent tonic involvement and chance is 1.7:1, and for syntagmatic errors the ratio is 1.6:1. But for the adults, the tonic stress position has more influence on syntagmatic errors; the ratio to chance is, paradigmatic= 1.8:1, syntagmatic=2.1:1. The syntagmatic ratio may be somewhat inflated because the 'chance' figures include both content and function words, and function words are less likely to take tonic stress. But it could also be the case that paradigmatic errors are influenced primarily by the information structure status of the word which will take tonic stress, whereas at least for adults, syntagmatic errors are influenced both by these pragmatic factors and the actual prosodic structure of the phrase, in which case there would be more factors enhancing involvement of the tonic in syntagmatic errors. This fits in with the above findings that the adults in this study were more influenced by phonology in general than the children were. Finally, it is interesting to compare the effect of tonic stress on phonological vs. lexical errors. For the children, tonic stress had a more prominent effect on their phonological errors (67%) than either paradigmatic (60%) or syntagmatic (56%) lexical errors; however, the influence was reversed for the adults: phonological=57%, paradigmatic lexical=63%, syntagmatic lexical=64%. One possible explanation for this is that for adults, the information structure of the sentence plays a more prominent role in the early (propositional/semantic) stages of planning than it does for the children, so it would be more likely to affect lexical errors; this hypothesis awaits further testing. However, the most important point from this section is that tonic-stress location is another salient cause of lexical SOTs.

4.2.4 Utterance Influence

The next factor involved in lexical errors is the influence of the utterances being spoken in the discourse. While this factor is inherent in syntagmatic errors, it can also affect blend errors, since occasionally one or both of the targets have been previously spoken in the discourse, as illustrated in (23); see also error (3b) above.

(23)   B: '*Tóe* hùrts.'

     M: 'You got a? *ówie*?'

     B: '[tǽ.wi] . . . ówie.'

     (blend of 'toe' [tow] and 'owie' [ǽ.wi]; B-5(38) 1;9)

In this blend error, both targets 'toe' and 'owie' had just been spoken in the utterance, one by the child and one by the mother. This error is considered a blend rather than a perseveration of the [t] from 'toe', because both words 'toe' and 'owie' would have been appropriate in the context. In the blend data I have indicated errors which show an influence of the utterance by adding a category [+utt] to the analysis. The overall percentages of lexical errors at each age which were influenced by words spoken in the error utterance or neighboring utterances are given in Table 4.11. This table is to be read as follows (for example): at age 3, the children produced 63 lexical errors; of these, 22 were syntagmatic errors, and 2 were blend errors influenced by preceding utterances. Thus of the 63 errors, 24, or 38%, showed an influence of the utterance environment.

From this table it can be seen that the errors made by the children in this study were somewhat more influenced by neighboring utterances than the adults' errors were. First, the children produced 21 blend errors where one or both of the targets was mentioned in the preceding utterance(s), but the adults produced no blend errors which showed this influence. Second, the percentage of syntagmatic errors was slightly higher for the children (28.5% overall) compared to the adults (25.5%). Combining the blend and syntagmatic data together, the children show utterance influence in 34% of their lexical errors to the adults' 25.5%. The drop-off of utterance influence at age 5 might reflect a real trend towards the adult figures. The child/adult difference is undoubtedly due partly to the fact that adults have more practice in activating correct lexical items and inserting them

TABLE 4.11

Percentage of lexical errors which show some influence from the utterance environment, including syntagmatic errors, and blend errors influenced by the preceding utterance(s).

Age:	1-2a	1-2b	3	4	5	Total	Adult
Total Lexical Errors=	16	72	63	125	95	371	307
Syntagmatic N=	2	17	22	37	27	105	78
Blend [+utt] N=	3	5	2	10	1	21	0
% UTT	31%	30.5%	38%	37.5%	29.5%	34%	25.5%

into appropriate slots in the utterance, without the various other activated words intruding on one another. Furthermore, as discussed in §4.1.3 above, more practiced speakers are better at suppressing elements of utterances after they have been produced, so that they do not intrude as much on subsequent utterances, which is why children produce more lexical perseveration errors than adults do, as shown in Table 4.1 above (see also Stemberger 1989, Dell, Burger & Svec 1997, Kawachi 2002).

A further point of interest from these utterance-influenced errors is exactly where the source word comes from. There are several different possibilities. In anticipation errors, the source is always a word which the speaker himself or herself is planning to say, either in the same phonological phrase as illustrated in (20b) above, or in the next phonological phrase as in (20a), assuming that speakers rarely plan more than one phrase ahead. In perseverations, the source word can come from a number of different locations, as discussed in Chapter 1, example (21). The source could be a word that the speaker planned for earlier in the discourse, either in a preceding turn, during the same turn but in a preceding phonological phrase, or in the same phonological phrase as the error. However, in perseverations the source word could also come from a previous utterance made by a different speaker; in rare instances both the speaker and some other speaker could have produced preceding utterances which contributed to the error, as in (24a). In exchange errors the two targets are both planned by the speaker; they normally occur in the same phonological phrase, but can occur in adjacent phonological phrases, as in (24b); only adults made this latter type of error. Finally, in blends, one or both of the targets could have been spoken in a preceding utterance, either by the speaker who makes the blend, or usually by a different speaker; in rare instances both the same speaker and a different speaker could contribute to the blend error, as in (23 above).

(24) a. M: 'I wònder whère we could sèe a dónkey.'
          An: 'At the **zóo**?'
          M: 'I dòn't think there are any dònkeys at óur **zòo**.'
          An: 'Um . . . at fárms they have **zòos**.'
          M: 'You mean at fàrms they have <u>dónkeys</u>?'
          An: 'Yeah.' ('zoo' perseverated from both Mom's and Anna's
          utterances, substituted for 'donkey'; AN-152(43) 4;1)
      b. AM: 'Yóu know the Lìfe-Lines: Fìfty-Fífty, **phòne** the aúdience,
          and **àsk** a fríend.' (for 'ask the audience, and phone a friend';
          verbs 'ask' and 'phone' exchanged across two phonological
          phrases; AD-637(45))

Table 4.12 summarizes the location of the source of the error, by age and by
error type; this table includes all syntagmatic errors, and those blends which
showed an utterance influence. The 'exchanges' row includes both contiguous
and non-contiguous reversals. The categories of source location are: 'S-S'=same
speaker, same phonological phrase; 'S-D'=same speaker, different phonological
phrase (with or without an intervening utterance by another speaker); 'D-D'
=different speaker, different utterance; 'Both'=both the person who made the SOT
and another speaker spoke the source(s). This table is to be read as follows (for
example): at age 4, the children made 16 lexical anticipation errors, and of these,
in 12 the speaker who produced the SOT also spoke the source in the same
phonological phrase as the error ('S-S'); at age 4, 42.5% of the children's
utterance-influenced errors fell into the 'same speaker-same phonological phrase'
category.

Although the numbers in each cell in this table are small, an overall pattern
emerges which provides evidence regarding the development of the speech
production planning mechanism. First, the source of lexical anticipation errors
is consistently in the same phonological phrase as the target word for the 1-3-
year-olds; the first error which involves a source from a subsequent phrase occurs
at age 4;5, given in (25a), so this seems to be the age at which children start
showing the ability to be working on the planning of two contiguous phrases at
once. The error made at age 1-2a which seems to be an exception to this pattern
is given in (25b).

(25) a. OB: 'Know whát? Òne **dùck** . . . òne <u>dày</u> when Ì was àt my hóuse,
          my nèighbor sàw a **dùck** hàve an égg come òut of her
          stòmach.'
          ('duck' anticipated/substituted for 'day'; OC-110(41) 4;5)
      b. OG: (asking Daddy if he had used the bathroom yet)
          '**Pèepee**, go . . . Dàddy, go péepee?'
          ('peepee' anticipated/substituted for 'Daddy'; OC-9(41) 2;0)

TABLE 4.12

Location of the source of the error, by age and error type. S-S=same
speaker, same phrase; S-D=same speaker, different phrase; D-D=different
speaker, different phrase; Both=both speaker who produced the error and
another speaker spoke the source word.

Age:	1-2a	1-2b	3	4	5	Total	Adult
Anticipations							
S-S	0	5	9	12	4	30	33
S-D	1	0	0	4	3	8	13
Perseverations							
S-S	0	0	0	0	3	3	3
S-D	0	5	5	8	5	23	10
D-D	1	3	3	4	7	18	2
Both	0	0	0	1	0	1	0
Exchanges							
S-S	0	4	5	8	5	22	15
S-D	0	0	0	0	0	0	2
Blends							
S-D	0	1	1	3	0	5	0
D-D	2	4	1	7	1	15	0
Both	1	0	0	0	0	1	0
Total N=	**5**	**22**	**24**	**47**	**28**	**126**	**78**
% S-S	0	41%	58%	42.5%	43%	44%	65.5%
% S-D	20%	27%	25%	32%	28.5%	28.5%	32%
% D-D	60%	32%	17%	23.5%	28.5%	26%	2.5%
% Both	20%	0	0	2%	0	1.5%	0

As discussed in §4.1.3 above, in this latter error, the child, who was in the two-word stage at the time, seems to have been thinking about the three concepts she needed in order to ask her question; she most likely activated all the lemmas, then had trouble assembling them into the 1-word + 2-word utterances she intended. In fact, she seems to be on the verge of moving into the 3+word stage, and possibly was trying to assemble these three lemmas into a single phonological phrase. Thus it is not clear this error is really an exception, and it seems safe to hypothesize that in general children don't start planning more than one phrase at a time until well into their 5th year.

The lexical perseveration errors, on the other hand, show much interference from previous utterances; the children produced 23 errors in which a word from one of their previous utterances perseverated and was substituted for a word in (or added into) their next utterance. Adults also produced a fair number of this sort of error. The children's data also contain 18 errors in which a word spoken by a different speaker perseverated and intruded into the child's utterance; adults only produced this type of error twice. Thus these perseveration errors support the claim discussed above that children have a slower decay time for previously uttered linguistic units than adults do; however the effect of this processing phenomenon shows up much more strongly in the lexical errors than it did in the phonological errors. Evidently if a word is spoken, and so has been activated in the child's working memory, it is likely to substitute for a word in a subsequent utterance, especially if it has some other properties in common with the target word such as lexical category, phonological similarity, and so on. But the phonological material in this word per se does not linger as robustly as does the lemma, and thus individual phonological units from a spoken word do not intrude on a following utterance as often. Adults, with a faster suppression rate of previously mentioned material, show less influence from preceding utterances, which shows up in a smaller percentage of lexical perseverations than the children produce.

For the children, all lexical exchanges (both contiguous and non-contiguous) involved two words in the same phonological phrase. Adults also showed a preference for same-phrase exchanges, as they produced only two exchanges across phrases; one is given in (24b) above. Apparently full exchanges of lexical items almost require that the two words be planned for the same phonological phrase, with a few exceptions for adults.

Finally, the children produced 15 lexical blend errors in which one or more of the targets was spoken by a different speaker prior to the blend; they also produced 5 blends influenced by a prior word in one of their own utterances, and one blend which was influenced by prior utterances by both the child and another speaker. There are no blends with utterance influence in the adult data.

Looking at the percentages at the bottom of the table, it can be seen that the influence of other speakers is the greatest for the youngest children: 60% at age 1-2a and 32% at age 1-2b. This external influence is at its lowest at age 3, but then rises somewhat through ages 4-5. Nevertheless, the overall influence of other speakers on children's syntagmatic or blend errors is 26%, whereas for adults it is a negligible 2.5%, showing clearly that even the 5-year-olds have a long way to go before they are able to suppress external utterance influences while planning their own speech. In the adult errors where the source occurred in one of the speaker's own utterances, the source was located in the same phonological phrase as the error twice as often as in a different phrase (65.5% vs. 32%). But for the children, sources in their own utterances were within the same phonological phrase only half again as often as those in other phrases (43% vs. 29%), and the 'different phrase' figure is due largely to perseverations. Thus these utterance-influenced errors help us build a picture of the developing speech production planning capacities, which at first display a very short planning span and a long decay time for previously activated lexical items, producing many perseverations and much influence of other speakers, but no anticipations from later-planned phrases. These planning capacities gradually shift to a longer planning span and a rapid decay time for activated elements so that they do not intrude on later utterances as often; thus older children and adults show fewer lexical perseverations and intrusions from other speakers, and begin to show long-distance anticipations from different phrases. However, the children in this study are still too young to be showing many of these advances in their planning capacities.

4.2.5 Weight in the Phonological Phrase

Another linguistic factor which was found to influence syntagmatic errors was the weight of the word in the phrase. As discussed in Chapter 3, when the errors were collected, basic 'stressed' vs. 'unstressed' notation was included in the record of the error, so that it was possible to see whether or not in syntagmatic errors, both the target and source words had the same weight (stressed or unstressed). While this factor overlaps to a great extent with the 'content word/function word' distinction (since most content words are stressed and most function words are not), it does not overlap completely, as shown by the examples in (26).

(26)   a. B: 'We're **gòodin**' . . . we're <u>dòin</u>' *góod.*'
            (anticipation of adverb 'good', substituted for verb 'do'; both
            content words, both stressed; B-545(41) 5;7)

       b. B: (telling Mom about a movie he had been watching earlier)
            'Well, ya knòw what **th**ĕ**se** áre?   Thère are *th*ĕ*se* róbots?   And
            they gràbbed the prîncess? (etc.)'
            (intended utterance was 'ya knòw what there áre?';
            demonstrative anticipated/substituted for existential; both
            function words, both unstressed; B-352(41) 4;8)

       c. M: (buying yogurt) 'I'll get pèach for Dáddy.'
         OB: 'Yeah, **pèach** líkes . . . <u>hè</u> líkes *pèach.*'
            (anticipation of noun 'peach', substitution for pronoun 'he'; one
            content, one function word, both stressed; OC-83(41) 4;0)

       d. OG: (with reference to beads)
            'Whàt do you néed **for thèm** . . . néed <u>them fòr</u>?'
            (metathesis of pronoun 'them' with preposition 'for'; both
            function words, one stressed, one unstressed; OC-107(47) 4;5)

       e. B: (coloring a picture) 'The bèar's gònna *be* réd.   Ya knòw whý?
            'Cuz I wánt ta **bè** 'im rèd.'
         M: 'What?'
          B: 'I wánt ta <u>còlor</u> 'im rèd.'
            (verb 'be' perseverated, substituted for verb 'color'; both content
            words, one stressed, one unstressed; B-531(43) 5;6)

The examples in (26a,b) show the most common case, where two words involved in an error, even if they belong to different lexical categories, will most often be both content or both function words; the two content words will most often both be stressed and the two function words will most often both be unstressed. However, in (26c) a content word substitutes for a function word, and they are both stressed. In (26d) two function words metathesize, but one is stressed and the other unstressed; many of the stressed/unstressed errors were in fact metathesis errors. Finally, in (26e), two verbs interact, one stressed one unstressed; however, in this case one of the verbs is the copula, which in many ways acts more like a function word than a lexical verb (and most of the errors involving two content words with a stressed/unstressed relationship involved the copula as one of the verbs). Nevertheless, it is clear from these examples that the content word-function word distinction does not fully overlap with the stressed-unstressed distinction for syntagmatic errors.

I analyzed all the syntagmatic errors in the child and adult data, to find the percentages of errors where the word pair involved the same vs. different weights. I performed this analysis with and without the metathesis errors (including those in the 'interrupted anticipation' category), since most errors which violated the weight factor were metathesis errors. The results are given in Table 4.13. This table is to be read as follows (for example): at age 4 the children produced 37 syntagmatic errors; of these, 27 showed the 'strong-strong' phrasal stress pattern, 4 showed the 'weak-weak' pattern, and 6 showed the 'strong-weak' pattern, so that in 84% (N=31) of the syntagmatic errors at this age, the two words involved in the error shared the same stress level. However, if the metathesis errors are removed from the count, the percentage of error pairs which share the same weight rises to 96.5%.

The figures in this table show that most pairs of words involved in syntagmatic errors are being planned for locations with the same weight in the phonological phrase, and in fact in the majority of cases both words are being planned for strong locations. This is of course partly due to the fact that words in strong stress locations in phrases are typically content words, and content words are far more susceptible to error than function words for the various reasons discussed above. On the other hand, being planned for a stressed location in a phonological phrase makes any word more likely candidate for a syntagmatic error, as it brings this word into prominence during planning. Indeed several of the lexical errors involving function words occurred in phrases in which the function words were stressed, as illustrated in (27).

(27) a. B: 'Mommy can **yóu** gò with **mè**?'
         M: 'What?'
         B: 'Can **Í** gò with yòu?' (reversal of pronouns 'I' and 'you', with accommodation to case; first pronoun receives tonic stress, and both pronoun slots are strong positions in phrase; B-96(46) 2;7)

TABLE 4.13

Number of syntagmatic errors in which the target and source words (or locations) had the three patterns of weight: 'SS'=both occur in positions of phrasal stress or strong positions; 'WW'=both occur in unstressed or weak positions in the phrase; 'SW'=one word is in a strong position and the other a weak position; by age. Percentages shown with and without metathesis errors.

Age:	1-2a	1-2b	3	4	5	Total	Adult
SS	2	14	16	27	22	81 (77%)	73 (93.5%)
WW	0	1	4	4	3	12 (11.5%)	1 (1.5%)
SW	0	2	2	6	2	12 (11.5%)	4 (5%)
Total N=	2	17	22	37	27	105	78
% Same Weight	100%	88%	91%	84%	92.5%	88.5%	95%
% Without Metathesis	100%	100%	94%	96.5%	96%	96.5%	96%

b. AF: (talking to a student about a class assignment)
'You can tùrn it **òn** . . . you can tùrn it i̯n làter **ón**.'
(preposition 'on' anticipated, substituted for 'in', both stressed; AD-563(41))

Thus the phrasal stress of a word can be another factor which causes it to be involved in a syntagmatic error.

The reader may have noticed that I did not include lexical blends with utterance influences in this count of weight. This is because in every blend error where one or both of the target words was spoken in a preceding phrase, the source(s) and the error were all content words, nearly all of the same lexical category, with strong phrasal stress. The one exception to this was an error involving two function words; however in this case the words were also from the same lexical category, the auxiliary verbs 'do' and 'have', and both targets and the error location carried strong phrasal stress (OC-139(39) 5;2). Thus the weight factor was almost completely conflated with the lexical category factor; for this reason I did not count weight as an influence on blends because it seemed to be a redundant or fully predictable factor.

4.2.6 Environmental Influence

Occasionally a child or adult would make an error in which the referent of the error word (or in the case of blends, the referent of at least one of the target words) was physically present in the environment. These errors usually involved the common noun name for some object visible in the environment (or in a picture), but could also involve proper-noun names of individuals physically present, and in a few cases involved an auditory or tactile stimulus, such as hearing a television show or touching a body part. Harley (1984) calls these errors 'non-plan-internal', in that the intrusion comes from a source outside the actual speech production planning process. Environmental intrusions were most commonly involved in lexical substitution errors, as exemplified in (28a,b), but also affected blend errors, as in (28c), and syntagmatic errors (28d); see also (20b) above. They could not be involved in exchanges, since it would be unclear how environmental factors could cause two words to exchange positions. Almost by definition, environmental factors caused errors of content words (usually nouns) rather than function words. The one exception is that environmental factors could affect personal pronoun errors, as in (28e); a personal pronoun error was considered to have an environmental influence if an appropriate referent of the erroneous pronoun was present at the time of speaking or salient in the propositional content of the utterance.

(28)   a. B: (standing in doorway between kitchen and study, talking about where it's OK to eat; it's not OK to eat in Daddy's study; "The Simpsons" was on TV in Daddy's study)
'Thàt's "**The Símpsons**" òver thère, and thìs is the kìtchen òver hére. (pause) Oh, I mean thàt's <u>Dàddy's stúdy</u> òver thère, and thìs is the kìtchen òver hére.'
(television show "The Simpsons" was both visible and audible; substituted for 'Daddy's study'; B-300(35) 4;6)

   b. AF: 'Hey Ánna, when you clèaned the fámily ròom, did you dùst the **piáno**? I mean the <u>télevision</u>?'
(we don't own a piano, but there was piano music coming from the television when the error was made; AD-390(35))

   c. B: (pointing at a picture of Bert in "Sesame Street" book)
'[**pɜ́.ni**] . . . <u>Bért</u>.'
(blend of 'Bert' [pɜt] and 'Ernie' [ɜ́.ni]; both characters are on the page of the book Bobby is looking at; B-2(38) 1;8)

   d. Al: '**Dàddy**, mè wàtching **Dàddy** cóoking . . . nò . . . <u>Mómmy's</u> còoking.' (laughs) (Alice meant to say 'me watching Mommy cooking', but as she was looking at Daddy, she perseverated/substituted 'Daddy' for 'Mommy'; AL-27(43) 2;4)

   e. D: 'What ìs todày?'
       An: 'Todày is **my** . . . todày is <u>your</u> bírthday.' (environmental influence, since 1st person referent of 'my', i.e. the speaker, is present at the time of the utterance; AN-119(36) 3;8)

TABLE 4.14

Number of lexical errors with environmental influences, content word errors vs. personal pronoun errors, by age; and percentage of all lexical errors (excluding exchanges & interrupted metatheses) which involved an environmental influence.

Age:	1-2a	1-2b	3	4	5	Total	Adult
Total Lexical Errors=	16	68	58	117	90	349	290
Env. Infl., Content=	9	12	10	16	15	62	9
Env. Infl., Pronoun=	na	6	5	7	2	20	4
% Errors with Environmental Influence	56%	26.5%	26%	19.5%	19%	23.5%	4.5%

Table 4.14 presents a count of environmental influences in content-word errors and pronominal errors, and the percentage of all lexical errors at each age which involved an environmental influence. This table is to be read as follows (for example): at age 3 the children made 58 lexical errors (excluding exchanges and interrupted metatheses); of these there were 10 content-word errors which exhibited an environmental influence, and 5 errors involving pronouns which were influenced by environmental factors; thus at this age there were 15 environmentally influenced errors, which is 26% of 58.

It is evident from this table that the children in this study were far more influenced by environmental factors than the adults were. Over half of the errors made by the children in the 1-2a age range were influenced by environmental factors; this percentage decreased to 26.5% for the 1-2b children, and gradually decreased to 19% by age 5, but never came close to the 4.5% found in the adult errors. Thus these external influences are extremely important in the young children's errors, as visual, tactile and auditory stimuli vie for attention in the child's working memory while he or she is planning an utterance. They become less important for the older children, as the children get more control over their verbal planning and are in general less influenced by the physical here-and-now; they are more able to control the locus of their attention while they plan for speaking. However, even the 5-year-old children were influenced by environmental factors much more often than the adults, showing that the attentional factors involved in speech production planning were still far from adult levels of maturity.

On the other hand, it is interesting that nearly every word pair involved in an error influenced by environmental factors shared the same lexical category (except in those cases which involved a proper noun and common noun). Furthermore in many cases the word pair shared a semantic and/or phonological relationship (e.g. 'Daddy' for 'Mommy' (28d); 'hand' for 'head', B-293(35) 4;5). The only environmentally influenced errors in which the target and error words differed in lexical category were the following two, made by Bobby at age 4.

(29) a. B: (asking Mom to melt cheese on his hot dog for lunch)
           'I wànt you to **mílk** it . . . mélt it.'
           ('milk' [mɛɫk] substituted for 'melt' [mɛɫt]; milk visible on
           table as he spoke; B-198(35) 4;1)
      b. M: 'Bobby, why don't you brùsh your tèeth nów. Then you won't
           have to thìnk abòut it láter.'
         B: (angry, stomps into bathroom, steps on stool, and looks at sink)
           'Mòm, I wànt ta **sìnk** . . . thìnk abòut it làter!'
           ('sink' [sɪŋk] substituted for 'think' [θɪŋk]; B-331(35) 4;7)

In (29a), Bobby sees the object 'milk' and substitutes the word 'milk' for the verb 'melt'; however, Bobby knew the verb 'to milk' and so when the concept of 'milk' was activated by the visual object, the verb form was also susceptible to activation. The same argument applies to (29b); Bobby saw the object 'sink', but substituted the word 'sink' for the verb 'think'; in this case he also knew the noun and verb forms of 'sink'. And in both cases, the target and error words have a very close phonological similarity. Even in (28a) above, where 'The Simpsons' and 'Daddy's study' have nothing in common semantically, they are both proper noun phrases (the latter naming a specific location), and consist of a two-word determiner+noun phrase. Another similar environmentally influenced error is 'Rice Krispies' substituted for 'Little Mermaid' (B-392(35) 4;10); again these are two compound proper nouns. Thus even though children are more influenced by environmental factors than adults are, the word or phrase activated by the contextual object or event must have some linguistic properties in common with the intended word, such as lexical category or phonological or semantic similarity, before the erroneous word will be selected for speaking. So while the children's speech production planning mechanisms may not be as autonomous from external influences as adults' are, they still show a high degree of sophistication and control during planning, and it is still the linguistic planning which is driving the error.

4.2.7 Collocational Phrases

From their earliest speech, there are various phrases which speakers produce relatively frequently, which they may actually store as fixed phrases in the lexicon. Very young children are often said to memorize such phrases at first, and then later decompose them into their lexical units. But in some cases these phrases are used so often as children grow up, that they become re-learned as fixed phrases, and lexicalized as such. In a few of the errors in my corpora this

TABLE 4.15

Number and percentage of lexical errors which show a collocational phrase 'CP' influence, by age.

Age	1-2a	1-2b	3	4	5	Total	Adult
Total Lexical Errors=	16	72	63	125	95	371	307
CP Errors, Paradig.=	1	5	4	10	4	24	18
CP Errors, Syntagm.=	0	2	1	7	3	13	2
% CP	6%	10%	8%	13.5%	7.5%	10%	6.5%

influence was apparent; such an influence is possible in any type of lexical error, both paradigmatic as in (30a), and syntagmatic as in (30b).

(30) a. B: 'Where's Dáddy?'
      M: 'He's òut in the stúdy.'
      B: 'She's . . . he's **tùrning** òn the télephòne.'
      M: 'What?'
      B: 'He's tàlking òn the télephòne.' ('turning' substituted for 'talking'; 'turn on the X' is a collocation for the child; first error is lexical substitution of 'she's' for 'he's'; B-86b(35) 2;6)
      b. B: '**Mómmy**?! My **Mòmmy** says . . . my [tʰʌ.mɪk] sàys . . . my stòmach sàys "I'm húngry".'
      (perseveration/substitution of 'Mommy' for 'stomach'; 'My Mommy says X' is a collocation for the child; second error is phonological omission of [s] in 'stomach'; B-338a(43) 4;7)

I tabulated the number of lexical errors which I interpreted as showing a collocational phrase influence; the results are given in Table 4.15. This table is to be read as follows (for example): at age 1-2b, the children made 72 lexical errors, and of these, 5 paradigmatic and 2 syntagmatic errors showed a collocational phrase influence, which is 10% of 72.

This influence is least important at age 1-2a, where only one error shows this influence; in this error (given in 28c above) Bobby produces a blend of 'Bert and Ernie', a collocational phrase well-known to Bobby even at age 1;8 when this error occurred. The influence rises somewhat between ages 1-2b through age 4 (13.5% at age 4), but then drops off slightly. The adults show this influence in only 6.5% of their errors. Although the difference between children and adults is not great, the biggest difference occurs in the syntagmatic errors, where the adult errors only showed this influence in 2 cases. Thus for both children and adults, lexically stored collocational phrases tend to interfere with paradigmatic lexical selection more often than with lexical placement in syntactic strings; for children this influence also appears in syntagmatic errors, but is rare in adult syntagmatic errors. Overall it is a small, but nevertheless interesting, component of the causes of lexical errors.

4.2.8 Discourse Context

In a few cases, the lexical errors showed an influence not of a particular word which had just been spoken, but of words associated with the discourse topic of either the current or an immediately preceding discourse (Levelt 1989:221, Harley 1984). In some cases the intruding word had been spoken several turns before, but more often it referred to something inherent in the topic. This factor can influence paradigmatic errors only, by definition, since if the error were syntagmatic, this would mean that the error word had in fact been spoken in one of the immediately preceding phrases. Furthermore, it is mutually exclusive with the 'environmental' factor, since an influence comes either from the discourse environment or the physical environment, but not both.

(31) a. B: (talking about Anna, who is about to take a shower)
            'Dòes she wànt a [ʃóʷ] . . . cóld òne or a hót òne?'
            (blend of 'shower' [ʃǽ.wɚ] and 'cold' [kʰoʷɫd]; discourse context
            of shower event; B-211(38) 4;2)
      b. B: (in bed, talking with Dad about various colors; then says)
            'Daddy, pléase rùb my **blàck** . . . bàck.'
            (previous discourse was about colors, although color 'black' had
            not been mentioned; B-171(35) 3;11)

Table 4.16 presents the number of paradigmatic lexical errors made at each age, and the percentage of these errors which seemed to show a discourse context influence. This table is to be read a follows (for example): at age 3 the children produced 41 paradigmatic lexical errors, and of these, 2 (5%) showed the influence of the discourse topic.

While this factor influenced a small percentage of the errors, it is clear that discourse context does influence some errors, and thus is necessary for explaining some otherwise very odd substitutions and blends. It is interesting that the older children showed more effect of this factor than the younger children, possibly showing that their mental workspace has increased by age 4 or so to the point that they can keep larger conceptual domains active while planning their next utterances. This increase in the effect of discourse context may be related to the child becoming increasingly less tied to the immediate here-and-now. However, the adults showed very little effect of discourse context in their errors; in this case this is a function of their greater ability to suppress intrusions from

TABLE 4.16
Number and percentage of paradigmatic lexical errors which showed influence from the discourse context 'DC', by age.

Age	1-2a	1-2b	3	4	5	Total	Adult
Total Paradigmatic Errors=	14	55	41	88	68	266	229
N with DC=	0	2	2	14	4	22	10
% with DC=	0	3.5%	5%	16%	6%	8%	4.5%

previously activated conceptual material into the current discourse.

4.2.9 'On The Mind': Freudian Slips?

Another 'non-plan-internal' type of error (Harley 1984) is what might be called 'Freudian Slips.' Early studies of SOTs often interpreted these errors in Freudian terms (Freud 1973/1901, Yazmajian 1965, Motley 1980, Warren 1986). That is, the psychoanalytic framework assumed that when a person spoke a word different from the intended word, or made a phonological error which resulted in an unintended real word, this was caused by some repressed thought or fantasy which had surfaced unintentionally. It should be abundantly clear from the data in this book that very few errors can be interpreted in this way, since very few of them result in the speaker producing an embarrassing or offensive word (but see AD-236(25) and AD-506(38)). However, I did find a small number of paradigmatic content word substitution errors which seemed to be the result of something that the researcher knew the child had been thinking about recently, that is, something the child had 'On the Mind'. This could either be something the child had been thinking about during the day the error was made, or had been thinking about over a period of time. In some cases these errors were innocuous, in that they didn't seem to represent any particularly repressed ideas, as illustrated in (32a); however, in other cases they did represent chronic fears or strange ideas the children harbored, as in (32b,c), or things the adult speaker was worrying about, as in (32d).

(32) a. Al: (at dinner, talking about onions being 'sour')
'Mòm, do yòu like **Sárah** stùff? . . . Do yòu like <u>sóur</u> stùff?'
(substitution of 'Sarah' for 'sour'; neighbor Sarah had been visiting Alice all day, and they had been getting along fine; Sarah was gone at the time the error occurred; AL-221(35) 4;5)

b. An: 'Did Àlice gò to the dóctors' and gèt a **shárk**?'
   ('shark' substituted for 'shot'; Anna had recently seen a scene from
   the movie "Jaws" so associated sharks with fear, pain, and having
   one's skin punctured; AN-68(35) 2;9)

c. An: 'I'm gonna wèar my wàtch to béd tonìght.'
   Al: 'Nòt mé! Ì don't háve a **wìtch** . . . (quietly to self) witch . . .
   witch . . . (normal voice) Ì don't háve a wàtch.'
   ('witch' substituted for 'watch'; Alice was going through a year-
   long phase of believing herself to be a witch, after a trip to
   Disneyland, so she had witches on her mind; AL-119(35) 3;4)

d. AF: (talking about a wedding invitation)
   'We hàve to **ÀSAṔ** them by the ènd of the wéek . . .
   oh, ŔSVṔ them.' (ASAP='as soon as possible'; RSVP=respond
   to the invitation; speaker was worried about responding quickly in
   order to meet the requested deadline; AD-477(35))

Actually my favorite Freudian Slip was made by Alice when she was 6 years old, so is not included in the present corpus. Alice was waiting for me to finish something I was doing in the kitchen so I could help her with some project, and she was getting more and more impatient and irritated with me. She suddenly blurted out:

(33)   A: 'Móm, whén are you gònna be **déad**?! . . . dóne?!'
        ('dead' substituted for 'done'; Alice, age 6)

Needless to say I dropped everything to help Alice out!

The number and percentage of paradigmatic content word errors which showed this 'On the Mind' influence is given in Table 4.17. (This influence is mutually exclusive with discourse, utterance, and collocational influences.) This table is to be read as follows (for example): at age 4 the children made 51 paradigmatic content word substitutions, and of these, 4 showed the 'On the Mind' influence, which is 8% of 51. Obviously this 'OTM' factor accounted for a very small number of errors, but as with the 'Discourse Context' factor, it does account for several errors which otherwise would be impossible to explain, so must be included for completeness sake. There were very few adult errors which showed this influence (see AD-415, 464, 468, 477), which may mean that adults are better than children at focussing on the topic at hand and not letting irrelevant issues intrude in their speaking.

However, it can be seen from the examples in (32) and (33) that one property these 'OTM' errors have is that the error word is phonologically similar to the intended word in every case. This requires an explanation in terms of the RPC Model. Consider example (32a): in this error Alice meant to say 'sour', so she activated the concept of 'sour', its lemma, and then its phonological form. The phonological activation then spread to various neighbors, and the form of

TABLE 4.17

Number and percentage of Class I errors (paradigmatic content word substitutions) which showed evidence of the 'On the Mind' (OTM) factor, by age.

Age:	1-2a	1-2b	3	4	5	Total	Adult
Total Class I Errors=	6	26	20	51	47	150	145
N with OTM =	0	3	1	4	3	11	4
% with OTM=	0	11.5%	5%	8%	6.5%	7%	3%

the word 'Sarah' was activated. Then the form of the word must have fed backwards to the lemma lexicon, and since the concept/lemma for this word had been recently activated, it took little activation from the form to cause the lemma for 'Sarah' to be more highly activated than that of the intended word 'sour'. Thus the combined form/lemma activation of 'Sarah' overrode the selection of the intended word. These 'OTM' errors require the postulation of both feed forward and feed backward links between the semantic and phonological aspects of the lexicon, which are active during speech production planning.

4.2.10 Summary of Influences on Lexical Errors

In order to rank-order the importance of the various influences on these lexical errors, I calculated the percentage of errors with each influence out of the total number of lexical errors, as given in Table 4.1. The percentages in the following table will be different from many of the above tables, since most of the preceding tables are calculated out of a subset of the lexical errors. The results of these analyses are shown in Table 4.18.

This ranking may be somewhat misleading since some influences can only occur with errors from specific classes, and some are mutually exclusive. Specifically, the 'Same lexical category', [+sem] and [+phon] factors do not apply to addition errors, and are expected to be violated in metathesis errors. 'Tonic stress' can affect all types of errors. The 'Utterance' factor does not apply to paradigmatic lexical substitution errors, although it can apply to blends, and of course is inherent in all syntagmatic errors. The 'Weight' factor is not applicable to paradigmatic substitution errors, and it is redundant for blends which show some utterance influence (as argued in §4.2.5). 'Environmental' influences can affect all error types except exchanges. 'Collocational' phrases can influence all error types, and can co-occur with 'Environmental' influences. The 'Discourse' influence can only affect paradigmatic errors since it requires that the error word was not spoken immediately before the error; it is mutually exclusive with the 'Environmental' influence. Finally, the 'On the Mind'

TABLE 4.18

Percentage of lexical errors at each age which manifested each of the 'influences' discussed in this section.

Age:	1-2a	1-2b	3	4	5	Total	Adult
Same Lexical							
Category	87.5	83	78	78.5	85	81.5	85.5
[+sem]	87.5	75	71.5	62.5	71.5	70	69
Tonic Stress	37.5	50	52.5	49	44	48	57
[+phon]	44	44.5	41	33.5	42	39.5	55
Utterance	31	30.5	38	37.5	29.5	34	25.5
Weight	12.5	21	32	25	26	25	24
Environment	56	25	24	18.5	18	22.5	4
Collocational	6	10	8	13.5	7.5	10	6.5
Discourse	0	3	3	11	4	6	3
OTM	0	4	1.5	3	3	3	1
Total N=	**16**	**72**	**63**	**125**	**95**	**371**	**307**

influence was only seen to affect paradigmatic content word substitution errors, and was considered to be mutually exclusive with the 'Discourse' and 'Collocation' factors. Thus each class of error was eligible to be affected by a different number of influencing factors (as indicated in Table 4.20 below).

Nevertheless, the figures in Table 4.18 give a very clear picture of the relative importance of various factors during speech production planning. Errors are most likely to occur between two words of the same lexical category: this is required by both the conceptual planning and the syntactic planning, and so is rarely violated. Most violations of lexical category occur in metathesis errors which are, as I argued above, most likely due to an error in the structure of the syntactic frame rather than being a lexical insertion error. The overall child figures and adult figures for the lexical category factor are very similar, although the youngest children show the highest consistency; I will return to this point in §4.3 below.

The next most important factor is the semantic relationship between the two words. This is inherent in the purpose of speaking: words are selected to convey particular meanings, and their sounds are irrelevant in most contexts (other than poetry, songs, etc.). When a semantic field is activated in order to select lexical items to convey the propositional content, semantically related words are automatically activated, and this is the most common source of misselection of a word in a paradigmatic error (constrained of course by lexical category). Again the youngest children showed the strongest influence of semantics, but the overall child level is nearly identical to that of the adults.

The next most common influence is that of tonic stress; above I documented that this is due both to the pragmatic and prosodic salience of tonic stress in phrases. The children in the 1-2a age group showed no influence of tonic stress, which fits with the assumption of no syntax at this age. The 1-2b and older children showed a much higher than chance effect of this influence, although it dropped somewhat at age 5. The adults, on the other hand, showed more influence from tonic stress than the children did at any age, which was accounted for at least in part by a difference in perseveratory errors: while nearly all adult perseveratory errors involved one or two tonic-stressed words, the children had several perseveratory errors involving verbs and pronouns which were not in tonic position.

Whether or not a word pair involved in a lexical error has a phonological relationship was the next most important factor. This factor is less important than the semantic, lexical category, or tonic stress factors because it is not involved in constructing the meaning of the utterance. Between 33-44% of the children's errors exhibited this factor, but 55% of the adult errors involved a phonological relationship between the target and error words. In paradigmatic errors, adults produced more malapropisms than children, suggesting that phonology is a more important factor in the organization of the adult lexicon than it is for the child lexicon. In syntagmatic errors, the adults' perseverations seemed to be particularly influenced by phonological similarity, while the childrens' were not. This was argued to be a function of the fact that adults mainly perseverated from their own prior utterances, such that the phonological form of the word was most recently activated. However, children often perseverated from other speakers' utterances, such that the semantic representation was the most recently activated.

The next factor involved in lexical errors was whether or not both the target and the source were were planned to be spoken in the same utterance, or whether or not the source of the error had been spoken in a preceding utterance. This factor was shown to be more influential for the children than the adults, as 34% of the child errors involved utterance influences, while only 25.5% of the adult errors did. The biggest difference came in lexical blends: for the children, a previously spoken word often triggered a blend, but this did not occur in the adult errors; thus the slower decay-rate for activated words showed up in the children's blends. The fact that the utterance influence affects only about one quarter to one third of the errors reinforces the prediction of the model, that the aspect of speech production planning involving the lexicon which is most susceptible to error is the selection of words and morphemes from a group of semantically related lexical items from the same lexical category; once the correct lexical items have been selected, they are relatively likely to be inserted into the syntax in the correct location.

For syntagmatic errors, an important influencing factor is the rhythmic weight (stressed/strong vs. unstressed/weak) within the phonological phrase: two words are more likely to be mutually involved in an error if they have the same weight value, and by far the most common pattern is for two words which are both stressed to mutually interact. This factor partially, but not totally, converges with the content word/function word distinction. It affects the children and adults at about the same rate overall (child=25%, adult=24%). However, there is a clear developmental trend that reflects the children's growing utterance length, in that the 1-2a age group children showed the affect of this factor in only 12.5% of their errors overall, but its effect increases as the children get older.

The last four factors are the least important, involving influences which, to varying extents, reflect factors external to the planning of the target utterance. They affect from 22% to 3% of the children's errors, and from 6.5% to 1% of the adults'. The first of these is the 'Environmental' influence, when something that the speaker can see, hear, or feel (or, presumably, smell) intrudes in their planning, and they speak a word naming this intrusion instead of the intended word. This factor affected 22.5% of the children's errors, but only 4% of the adults', showing that adults have much more practice in allocating attention during speech production planning. In fact this factor was involved in 56% of the 1-2a children's errors; it shows a steady decrease to 18% for the 5-year-olds, moving in the direction of the adult figure. However, it was noted that in all the 'Environmental' errors, the error word had many linguistic factors in common with the intended word, particularly in terms of lexical category and form (phonological and morphological similarity), so that even the environmentally influenced errors were not random.

The second of these less common influences is 'Collocational Phrase', where a lexical item activated for speaking in the utterance is associated in the lexicon with some particular collocational phrase. The collocational phrase facilitates the misselection of another word (or words) which is inappropriate for the proposition but typical for that phrase. This influence affected the children's and adults' errors at about the same rate: child=10%, adult=6.5%. The third influence is 'Discourse', when some word which was activated by the content of either the present discourse or an immediately preceding discourse, but had not been not recently spoken aloud, intrudes on the planning process. The speaker then substitutes an unintended word which relates to the discourse, for the intended and immediately relevant word. Discourse context influenced 6% of the child errors and 3% of the adult errors.

Finally, the least important influence is what I have called 'On the Mind'; that is, there were a very few errors (child=3%, adult=1%) that were best explained in terms of an intrusion of a word which related to something the speaker had been thinking about for some period of time, either chronically (for months or years) or more recently, for example during the day in which the error was made. While these errors are few, this factor is necessarily for explaining these otherwise inexplicable substitutions. They also require that the model provide both feed-forward and feed-backward mechanisms between the semantic and formal aspects of lexical entries, which are active during speech production

TABLE 4.19
Number and percentage of errors with each number of influences,
child vs. adult, paradigmatic vs. syntagmatic (excluding
metathesis).

# Influences:	0	1	2	3	4	5	6	7	Total N
Paradigmatic									
Child N=	0	4	57	108	78	19	0	0	266
%		1.5%	21.5%	41%	29%	7%			
Adult N=	1	3	47	103	68	7	0	0	229
%	0.5%	1%	20.5%	45%	30%	3%			
Syntagmatic									
Child N=	0	3	3	22	24	30	10	1	93
%		3%	3%	24%	26%	32%	11%	1%	
Adult N=	0	1	3	15	24	24	4	1	72
%		1.5%	4%	21%	33.3%	33.3%	5.5%	1.5%	

planning. This is because although the intruding word was always phonologically related to the intended word, what kept it 'On the Mind' was the concept it was linked to.

In sum, there are a large number of factors which are available for causing a wide range of lexical errors; some of these factors are more important than others, and the rank ordering presented above is fully explained by the RPC Model of speech production planning.

So far in this section, I have discussed ten factors which may be involved in lexical errors, and have shown that they vary in influence. But another important question is: do errors usually occur when a number of these factors converge to add extra activation to an unintended word, or can errors occur equally often when only one or two of these factors are present? In order to answer this question, for each lexical error in the corpus I counted the number of influences present. (I excluded the metathesis errors from this count since the status of the relationship between words in metathesis is unclear.) Table 4.19 shows the number of errors in the child and adult lexical data which exhibited each of the possible numbers of influences, from 0 to 7; paradigmatic and syntagmatic errors are presented separately. The paradigmatic errors may in principle be affected by 6 (substitutions) to 7 (blends) factors, and the syntagmatic errors may be affected by 7 (exchanges) to 8 (anticipations or perseverations) factors.

These figures indicate that the most common situation is when three or four influences converge to cause the lexical error. For paradigmatic errors, the median number of influences for adults and children is 3; the mean for children is

3.19, and for adults the mean is 3.11. The median for syntagmatic errors for both children and adults is 4; the mean for children is 4.17 and adults, 4.16. These figures are remarkably similar, and show that overall the adults and children are working with the same kind of speech production planning mechanism and linguistic representations. Errors involving no influences or only one of these factors are extremely rare and represent special circumstances. Consider the errors in (34).

(34)   a. Al: (Mom put a cassette tape of Grandpa's band into the tape deck; Alice usually referred to the tape as 'Grandpa'; Alice points to tape) 'I lóve [ḍæ̀.pa] . . . I lóve G̲r̲à̲n̲d̲p̲a̲, Móm!'
(blend of proper noun 'Grandpa' [g̣ʒǽm.pa] and deictic pronoun 'that' [ḍæt]; AL-51(40) 2;9)

      b. AM: (radio commentator talking about a bombing in Africa, hadn't mentioned the FBI yet) 'If the Ù.S̀. Émbassy was tàrgeted, then th**ĕy**, uh, t̲h̲e̲ ̲F̂B̂Î̲ will be càlled ìn.'
(unstressed pronoun 'they' substituted for tonic-stressed proper noun 'the FBI'; AD-490(36.5))

      c. An: 'Ì g**ĕt** . . . Ì s̲h̲ŏ̲u̲l̲d̲ g**èt** mý càrds.' (anticipation of 'get', probable interrupted metathesis of 'should get'; AN-73(41) 2;9)

The error in (34a) is analyzed as having one influence, the 'Environmental' influence, since the two words involved, 'that' and 'Grandpa' are of different lexical categories, are neither semantically nor phonologically related, the tonic is not involved, and there is no utterance influence; 'Weight' is irrelevant because it is a paradigmatic error, and there are no influences from collocations, discourse, or 'On the Mind'. The error in (34b) is the only error analyzed as having no influences at all. However, these two errors have something interesting in common; in both cases the speaker intends to refer to some entity, and the error is related to choosing the pragmatically appropriate linguistic means for expressing this reference. So in (34a), Alice hasn't decided whether to refer to the tape as its usual proper name, 'Grandpa', or the deictic 'that', and blends the two. In (34b), the speaker forgets he hasn't yet introduced the FBI into the discourse, and refers to it with a definite anaphoric expression 'they', which he then corrects to the proper noun phrase 'the FBI'. So perhaps these errors actually have more influences than my analysis can account for, and in some future study a feature such as 'same referent' should be added. The error in (34c) is typical of most of the syntagmatic errors which were classed as having only one influence: these are mainly interrupted metathesis errors in the anticipation class, and the only factor they display is 'Utterance context'.

Looking at the other extreme, we see that no paradigmatic error exhibited more than 5 factors, although in principle an error could have up to 6 (substitutions) or 7 (blends) factors. An example of a paradigmatic error with 5 influences is given in (35).

(35)   Al: (getting a fork out of a drawer where there were both spoons and
                forks) 'I've gèt a [spóʒk].'
                (blend of 'spoon' [spun] and 'fork' [foʒk]; AL-146(38) 3;7)

In (35), Alice produces a blend of 'spoon' and 'fork'; the phrase 'I've get' is not
an error but her usual phrasing at this time. These two words are both common
nouns, and are semantically related as co-hyponyms (kinds of silverware);
although they are not phonologically similar (Phon=1.5) the error does occur in
the tonic position. This error shows both the environmental influence, since
spoons and forks were visible in the drawer, and the collocational influence,
since 'spoon and fork' is a common collocational phrase. Another example is
Anna's query 'Did Alice go to the doctor's and get a **shark**?', given in (32b)
above. In this error, 'shark' and 'shot' are both common nouns, and are
semantically related by 'connotation' for the child (see Chapter 5); they are
phonologically similar (Phon=4), and the target word is in the tonic-stressed
position. This error shows the 'On the Mind' influence, since Anna had been
chronically worried about sharks since seeing a scene from the movie "Jaws".

    In principle, syntagmatic errors could show 7 (exchanges) or 8 (anticipations
or substitutions) influences; however there were only two errors in the corpus
that exhibited 7 influences and none that contained all 8. One of the errors with
7 influences is given in (36); the other was given in (27b) above.

(36)   B: ('reading' story about a pizza party; there is a picture of 'pizza' on
              the page) 'Well, so mùch for a **pízza**, a **pìzza** with . . . so mùch
              for a **párty**, a **pàrty** with **pízza**.' ('pizza' [pʰít.sʌ] anticipated and
              substituted for 'party' [pʰár.ri] twice; B-361(41) 4;9)

In (36), Bobby means to 'read' a line out of a book he has memorized: "So mùch
for a párty, a pàrty with pízza", but he anticipates the word 'pizza' and
substitutes it for 'party', in both phrases. The two words 'party' and 'pizza' are
common nouns, they are phonologically similar (Phon=3.5), and they are
semantically related for the child since 'pizza' is an indispensable member of the
'party' frame for him (member/set). The error and source both occur in tonic-
stress locations, and all words involved have strong stress; there is an utterance
influence since it is an anticipation. Finally, there is also an environmental
influence since the picture Bobby was looking at showed the Ninja Turtles
dreaming about the pizza they weren't going to get because the party had been
cancelled, so that a picture of pizza was visible. In example (27b) 'You can turn
it **òn** . . . you can turn it ̲i̲n̲ later **ón**' (AD-563(41)), the words 'on' and 'in' are
both prepositions, phonologically similar (Phon=3) and semantically related (co-
members of a set of locational prepositions); they both occur in stressed
locations in the phrase, and the source word carries the tonic stress; there is an
utterance influence (anticipation). There is also a collocational influence, since

'turn it on' is a familiar collocation. These two errors were the proverbial accidents waiting to happen.

In order to complete this discussion of the influences on lexical errors, I considered two competing hypotheses regarding whether there would be age-related trends in the number of influences per error. The first hypothesis rests on the assumption that younger children plan utterances more locally than older children and adults; that is, they have fewer linguistic representations competing with each other, and are planning shorter utterances. Since the younger children have fewer degrees of freedom in their planning, there would be less chance of an error occurring, and thus one would expect that it would take more influences to cause an error. In other words, there would have to be something of a conspiracy of factors to cause an error. However, since older children and adults have a larger lexicon and more syntactic templates, it would take fewer influences to cause an error, since there would be many competing lexical items and complex syntagmatic frames activated during planning (i.e. many more degrees of freedom). The second hypothesis predicts the opposite pattern: since younger children are less practiced at speech production planning than older children, they might be more susceptible to making an error even with only one or two influences; whereas since older children and adults have much more practice at producing speech, it might take a number of influences to cause an error. Furthermore, since the older children and adults have more influences available to them, their errors would show a larger average number of influences. If in fact both of these hypotheses reflect real processes at work in the children's development, then there should not be much change in the overall percentage of influences over time. What I actually found was slightly different from either of these hypotheses.

Table 4.20 presents the average number of influences by age and category of error, for both the children and adults. In the rightmost column is the number of possible influences, and under the mean number of influences for each class considered as a whole is the percentage of possible influences reflected in the actual average. So, the mean number of influences in category I, paradigmatic lexical substitutions, was overall 3.17, which is 53% of the possible number, 6.

I think the most interesting point from this table comes from a comparison of adult to child figures for the paradigmatic errors vs. the syntagmatic errors. For the three paradigmatic classes (I-III), the adults show slightly fewer influences per error than the children do, and a slight trend downward towards the adult figures can be seen in the child data. Thus for the paradigmatic errors, hypothesis #1 seems to be the best fit: because of the large number of competing lexical items known to adults and older children, fewer influences are necessary to cause a lexical error than for young children, who have a smaller vocabulary with less competition. Hypothesis #1 also seems to hold for the syntagmatic errors in the case of the children in the 1-2a group: because of their limited repertoire of linguistic material, it takes a high number of influences to derail them and cause an error. However, for the children older than 1-2a, Hypothesis #2 seems to come into play in the syntagmatic errors (particularly

TABLE 4.20
Mean number of influences per lexical error by age and class (excluding metathesis); I=paradigmatic content word substitutions; II=paradigmatic function word substitutions; III=lexical blends, content & function; IV=lexical anticipations, content & function; V=lexical perseverations, content & function; VI=lexical exchanges, content & function. 'POSS'=possible number of influence for this category of error; %=mean # of influences is the percentage of possible influences.

Age	1-2a	1-2b	3	4	5	Total	Adult	POSS
Class								
I.	4.0	3.23	3.20	3.18	3.0	3.17	3.12	6
						(53%)	(52%)	
II.	na	2.88	3.12	3.31	3.0	3.11	2.85	6
						(52%)	(47%)	
III.	3.13	3.48	3.23	3.25	3.17	3.28	3.14	7
						(47%)	(45%)	
IV.	4.0	3.0	4.0	3.56	3.86	3.66	3.70	8
						(46%)	(46%)	
V.	5.0	4.88	5.0	4.32	4.53	4.60	4.80	8
						(57.5%)	(60%)	
VI.	na	4.33	4.0	4.0	4.3	4.20	4.18	7
						(60%)	(60%)	
N=	16	71	59	120	93	359	301	
Average=	3.63	3.48	3.57	3.38	3.37	3.44	3.33	7
						(49%)	(47.5%)	

anticipations and perseverations). In these errors the adults show a higher average number of influences compared to the children. With more practice inserting lexical items into functional and syntactic frames, the adults appear to require more influences to cause an error during this aspect of processing. The children between the ages of 1-2b and 5 show an overall rise in influences per error in the anticipations, but a slight fall for perseverations; the child and adult figures for exchanges are nearly identical. Since all subjects made more paradigmatic than syntagmatic errors, the adults have an overall lower average than the children (child=3.44, adult=3.33), and the children show an overall fall in influences per error (from 3.63 to 3.37). Because of the fact that these numbers are not amenable to statistical analysis, I cannot prove that these differences are significant, and it would take a larger database collected under conditions which allowed statistics in order to prove that these numbers reflect real trends. However, these 'influences per error' figures fit in well with the hypotheses discussed above regarding the interplay of increasing competition among lexical and syntactic representations vs. increasing processing skills, and thus can be seen as part of a viable model of the development of speech production planning.

4.3 Lexical Categories

4.3.1 Gathering Evidence on the Representation of Lexical Category

The theoretical issue to be addressed in this section is: Is there any indication that early lexical representations carry information about lexical category? This is an important question partly in its own right, but also partly because it is one piece of the puzzle regarding when syntax begins to develop. Syntax relies on the notion of lexical category; if we find evidence that children of a certain age do not show any knowledge of lexical categories per se, but that children of an older age show such knowledge unequivocally, then this would be important evidence supporting specific hypothesis regarding the onset of syntax in language acquisition.

However, as indicated in §4.2.1 above, it is difficult to assign lexical categories to words in young children's productions. In previous studies, researchers have relied on evidence gathered after the child has entered the 3+word stage, at which point phrase structure and morphology can be used to make claims about lexical category. Using descriptive methodologies, '[c]hildren's words can be identified as belonging to particular word classes only once children have begun to combine words and use them with some grammatical morphemes.' (Clark 1993:38; see also Braine 1987, Radford 1990). However, it is difficult to say anything about lexical categories during the 1- or 2-word stage; possibly the children are developing this notion at such early ages, but there is also possibly no need for such categories until the children are beginning the reorganizational process where linearization becomes crucial. Thus the SOT data could be especially useful for exploring this issue.

There is an obvious problem with the methodology, however. As linguists, we can assign a lexical class to each target, source, and error word involved in a lexical error by assessing the function of the word in context, but we can't necessarily make the assumption that this maps directly onto some knowledge the child has represented. Nevertheless we can use a two-step process to evaluate the cognitive validity for the child of lexical categories. First we can assess lexical category consistency for the very early errors compared to later errors, and see whether or not there are major differences at different ages. If early errors look fairly random as far as lexical category, but later errors maintain lexical category consistency, then we can get some idea of when lexical category becomes an important part of speech production planning. However, if consistency appears from the outset, then we go to step two of the logical process. We can hypothesize that some notion of lexical category may be developing earlier than has previously been documented, but we would need to test this hypothesis by seeing if the notion of lexical category is necessary for explaining this consistency. That is, we would need to demonstrate that the consistency cannot be completely accounted for by other factors such as the semantics of the lexical items, or by environmental factors. These are the questions I will be looking into in the following sections.

One further issue that will be addressed is the development of specific lexical categories. Looking at any changes over time regarding the actual lexical categories of words involved in errors can provide information on the development of knowledge about individual categories, based on the guiding assumption that a child can only produce a SOT that involves something which he or she has in learned previous to the error.

In the following sections, I will look only at unambiguous paradigmatic substitution and blend errors (i.e. where the lexical category of both target and error word can be ascertained), as well as unambiguous syntagmatic substitution errors (anticipations, perseverations, and exchanges); I will exclude additions, metathesis errors, and interrupted anticipations which are most likely metatheses. Thus this section will focus on the same sub-set of errors presented in Table 4.2 above (child N=341; adult N=299). I will address the two research questions in the opposite order from which they were discussed in this introduction: I will look at lexical category consistency and actual categories involved in errors first, and then focus in on the children in the 1- and 2-word stages.

4.3.2 Lexical Category Consistency

Table 4.2 above presented the percentage of each class of lexical errors at each age in which the target and source words fell into the identical lexical categories. Table 4.21 below gives the details regarding the lexical categories involved in these errors, by age. The top section of the table shows the lexical categories involved in errors in which all the mutually involved words came from identical lexical classes (i.e. all common nouns, all verbs, etc.); the section is organized in descending order of frequency of involvement of the various classes. The middle section of this table gives the details of errors which involve words from different lexical categories, but which honor the content word/function word distinction. Finally, the bottom section of the table presents the cases in which lexical errors involved words from different lexical categories which crossed the content word/function word boundary; e.g. where a common noun interacted with an interjection or a pronoun. This table is to be read as follows (for example): of the 16 lexical errors made at age 1-2a, 8 involved two common nouns, and 6 involved two proper nouns; thus 14 of these 16 errors (or 87.5%) involved two words which belonged to the same lexical category.

As discussed in §4.2.1 above, the majority of the children's errors involved two words from the same lexical category, as did the adult's errors; the overall percentage for children was 88%, and for adults, 86.5%. The majority of errors, for both children and adults, involved two common nouns, verbs, proper nouns, pronouns, or adjectives (I will discuss specific lexical categories in detail below).

TABLE 4.21
Number of lexical errors involving each lexical category, by age.

Age:	1-2a	1-2b	3	4	5	Total	Adult
Same Lexical Category							
Com. Noun	8	25	18	37	30	118	139
Verb	0	9	9	19	15	52	40
Prop. Noun	6	11	4	7	11	39	21
Pronoun	0	5	9	11	8	33	10
Adjective	0	4	3	10	8	25	29
Adverb	0	2	1	5	4	12	11
Preposition	0	2	1	5	1	9	8
Determiner	0	1	1	1	1	4	0
Interjection	0	0	1	2	0	3	1
Auxiliary V.	0	1	0	0	2	3	0
Numeral	0	0	0	1	0	1	0
Question Wd.	0	0	1	0	0	1	0
Conjunction	0	0	0	0	1	1	0
Total N=	**14**	**60**	**48**	**98**	**81**	**301**	**259**
	87.5%	89.5%	84%	87%	92%	88%	86.5%
Different, Both Content or Both Function Words							
CN-PropN	0	1	4	6	3	14	9
CN-Verb	0	2	1	3	0	6	9
CN-Adj.	0	2	1	1	1	5	3
Dem.-Exist.	0	1	0	1	0	2	0
Adj.-Verb	0	0	0	1	1	2	5
PropN-Verb	1	0	0	0	0	1	0
Adj.-PropN	0	0	0	1	0	1	1
Adj.-Adv.	0	0	0	1	0	1	2
Adj.-Num.	0	0	0	0	1	1	0
Verb-Adv.	0	0	0	0	1	1	2
Total N=	**1**	**6**	**6**	**14**	**7**	**34**	**31**
	6.25%	9%	11%	12%	8%	10%	10.5%
Different, Content with Function Word (blends/syntagmatic)							
CN-Interj.	1	0	1	0	0	2	0
PropN-Pro.	0	1	0	0	0	1	1
Verb-Prep.	0	0	1	0	0	1	1
Adv.-Det.	0	0	1	0	0	1	0
CN-Pronoun	0	0	0	1	0	1	0
Other	0	0	0	0	0	0	7
Total N=	**1**	**1**	**3**	**1**	**0**	**6**	**9**
	6.25%	1.5%	5%	1%		2%	3%
Grand Total=	**16**	**67**	**57**	**113**	**88**	**341**	**299**

As mentioned in §4.2.1, the most common violation of lexical category involved a common noun with a proper noun (see example (11a) above, 'Bambi/baby'), or a noun with a verb where both words could actually belong to either lexical category; see (11b) which involves the pair of words 'form/sign' and (29), which involves 'milk/melt' and 'sink/think'. In some cases where the error pair consists of a proper noun and common noun, the two words refer to the same entity, as illustrated in (37), where both targets of this blend, the proper noun 'Johnny' and the common noun 'leopard', referred to Alice's favorite stuffed animal.

(37)   Al: 'I wànt my [lá.ni].'
       (blend of 'leopard' [lέ.p3d] and 'Johnny' [dʒá.ni], both referring to
       toy leopard named Johnny; AL-217(38) 4;5)

This error is similar to those given in (34a,b), and supports the claim that perhaps another category, 'same referent', is necessary to fully characterize the causes of lexical errors.

Very few errors violated the content word/function word distinction, and those which did didn't fall into any particular patterns; only one of the adult errors involved the same lexical categories as those in the child errors (the adult error is given in (38c)). Most of these errors exhibited several other influences besides lexical category, as in (38a), and the majority were syntagmatic errors, as illustrated in (38b,c).

(38)   a. B: (saying 'goodbye' to Grandma who was driving away in car)
          '[kâʲ . . . pâʲ. kɔ̂.]'
          (blend of 'car' [kɔ] and 'bye' [paʲ], which are then repeated in
          'vertical construction'; child in 1-word stage; B-1(40) 1;7)
       b. B: 'Which táble òn they àre . . . òn?'
          (exchange of copula verb 'are' [ar] and preposition 'on' [an];
          B-159(46) 3;8)
       c. AF: 'She's betwèening . . . she's decìding betwèen ùs and
          Stánford.' (anticipation of preposition 'between', substitution
          for verb stem 'decide', with stranding of progressive suffix;
          possibly phrase blend with 'It's between us and Stanford';
          AD-566(41))

In (38a), the first SOT which I collected from Bobby, he was watching his Grandmother drive away in her car; he knew two words which were appropriate for this context, the interjection 'bye' (which may also have been verb-like for him at the time) and the common noun 'car'. Because he was in the one-word stage, an error-free production would have consisted of his producing one or the other of these two words. However he had trouble uniquely selecting one word, and his error was a blend of the two, which he corrected by then repeating each intended target in a 'vertical construction', i.e. two contiguous one-word utterances which express different elements of the scene being commented on. This error was influenced both by [+sem] (since 'car' and 'bye' had a metonymic relationship for the child), and environmental factors, as he could see the car being driven away. The error in (38b) is a reversal of the preposition 'on' and the copula verb 'are', with a partial correction. The two words involved are in the same utterance, have the same weight, and are phonologically similar (Phon=3.5), so there are three influences causing this error. Furthermore, this is another example where the copula shows an affiliation with function words. In (38c) the speaker anticipates a preposition 'between', and substitutes it for a verb 'decide'; the preposition then takes the verbal inflection. The error is influenced by the two words being planned for the same utterance, having the same weight, and the semantic relationship between the words 'decide between' (metonymic). Thus these rare content word/function word category violations have other explanations for their occurrence.

From Table 4.21 it appears that there are no major discrepancies between the errors made by the children in the 1- and 2-word stages and the older children in terms of lexical category consistency; all but two of the 16 lexical errors made at this age honor lexical category. With just this information, there would be no reason to claim that the youngest children do not represent lexical category information in their lexical representations, since there is ample evidence from morphology and linear sequencing that the older children do have clear lexical category representations. Thus we will need to go to step two in the process of assessing this hypothesis, that is, seeing if there is some other explanation for this consistency in the very young children; this will be the topic of §4.3.5 below.

4.3.3 Specific Lexical Categories

Table 4.21 makes it clear that specific lexical categories are involved in lexical errors at varying rates, and that there are some similarities and some differences between children and adults in terms of lexical categories. In order to focus in on this issue, I counted the number of words involved in the lexical errors under consideration here which fell into each lexical category. For errors where the pair of words belonged to the same category (e.g. both target and error words were verbs), I counted two points for that category; for errors where the pair of words belonged to different categories, I counted one point for each category. Thus the number of words counted is twice the number of errors (child N=682, adult N=598). The results are given in Table 4.22; this table shows the percentage of words in the lexical errors which belonged to each lexical category, by age. This table is to be read as follows (for example): at age 4, there were 226 words involved in the lexical errors counted in this table (as target, source, or error); of these, 37.5% (N=85) were common nouns.

This table shows that at age 1, nearly all words involved in lexical errors were nouns, with two exceptions. At age 2, the percentage of nouns involved in

TABLE 4.22

Percentage of words in lexical errors in each lexical category, by age.

Age:	1-2a	1-2b	3	4	5	Total	Adult
Com. Noun	53	41	38	37.5	36.5	38.5	50
Verb	3	15	17.5	18.5	18	17	16.5
Prop. Noun	41	18	10.5	9	14.5	14	9
Adjective	0	7.5	6	10.5	11	9	11.5
Adverb	0	3	2.5	5	5	4	5
Numeral	0	0	0	1	0.5	0.5	0
% Content							
Words	**97**	**84.5**	**74.5**	**81.5**	**85.5**	**83**	**92**
Pronoun	0	8	16	10	9	10	3.5
Preposition	0	3	2.5	4.5	1	3	3.5
Determiner	0	1.5	2.5	1	1	1	0
Interjection	3	0	2.5	2	0	1	0.5
Auxiliary	0	1.5	0	0	2.5	1	0.5
Demonstr.	0	0.75	0	0.5	0	0.3	0
Existential	0	0.75	0	0.5	0	0.3	0
Question Wd.	0	0	2	0	0	0.3	0
Conjunction	0	0	0	0	1	0.3	0
% Function							
Words	**3**	**15.5**	**25.5**	**18.5**	**14.5**	**17**	**8**
Total N=	**32**	**134**	**114**	**226**	**176**	**682**	**598**

errors drops somewhat, especially proper nouns, while verb, adjective, and adverb errors begin to occur, as well as some function word errors, particularly pronouns and prepositions. At age 3 the involvement of content words is at its lowest, 74.5%, and function words account for a quarter of the errors. Nevertheless, errors involving verbs particularly continue to rise in number. At age 4, content word errors begin to become more numerous again, particularly due to increases in verb and adjective errors. By age 5, content word errors have risen to 85.5%, on their way to the adult 92% figure.

These figures suggest an interesting developmental progression. As children become more familiar with each category, it becomes available for error: first nouns, then verbs, then adjectives and pronouns, and so on. This progression follows the usual order of acquisition of these various lexical categories (Bates et al. 1994). Then as the children become more practiced with that type of lexical category, the number of errors begins to depend more on the size of the lexical class. For function words, errors begin to dwindle, since the children have essentially learned and practiced all the forms in each category; this seems to also be true of proper nouns, since the set of proper nouns commonly used by a particular child is finite. However for content words, especially verbs and adjectives, the children's vocabularies continue to expand, and the errors in these categories remain high. Nevertheless, the children continue to make proportionately more function word errors (child=17%, adult=8%) and fewer content word errors (child=83%, adult=92%) than the adults do, showing that this progression will need to continue as the children get older in order to reach adult-like levels. Similarly, Hotopf (1983) found that the adults in his (English) study produced only 4% function word errors.

This U-shaped curve which reaches a peak/trough at age 3 may remind the reader of the figures in Table 4.1 above. In that case we saw that the percentage of the children's syntagmatic errors reached a peak at age 3, and their paradigmatic errors were at a low point at age 3. I argued that since the 3-year-olds were learning a great deal of syntax at this age, and it had not yet become automatic, this would explain a proportional increase in syntagmatic errors. This would also predict an increase in function word errors at age 3, since the development of function words is necessitated by syntactic development (and vice versa), causing their use at this age to be less automatic and more error-prone. By age 4 the children's selection of syntactic templates and the function words necessitated by specific templates has become more automatic, and thus the focus of attention returns to the selection of content words; for this reason paradigmatic errors increase. Furthermore, paradigmatic errors involve content words far more often than they involve function words by definition, and thus these two factors work together to explain the U-shaped curve in terms of lexical categories involved in errors found in Table 4.22.

Another important issue is the relative frequency of errors from the different lexical categories per se. Table 4.22 shows that errors involving common nouns greatly outnumber errors involving all other lexical categories. For the very young children, proper nouns are the second most frequently involved lexical category, but verbs become more numerous at age 3 and continue to outnumber proper nouns in errors for the older children and the adults. Adjective errors are the next most common, followed by pronoun errors for the children, and adverb errors for the adults.

The various proportions of errors involving different lexical categories could have a number of different explanations. The differences between frequency of errors involving content words vs. function words was discussed in detail in §4.1.3. above, and won't be repeated here. Looking just at the content words, one could argue that the frequency of occurrence of words from the various classes in these errors could be simply a function of the possibility of occurrence in sentences of each lexical class. In a simple sentence, for example, there is a slot for one verb, but potentially 3 or more nouns. The occurrence of adjectives, which are usually optional, is to a large extent dependent on how many nouns occur. Adverbs are always optional. So to some extent, based on pure numbers of occurrence (and thus availability to error), we would expect nouns to outnumber verbs, which would in turn outnumber adjectives and adverbs, and this is what is found. In order to see if pure numbers of available words could account for the proportions of errors involving different content word categories, I created an estimate of the proportion of words from different lexical categories which occur in random utterances, in the following way. For all the Class I and Class III errors for the children, I counted the number of common nouns, proper nouns, verbs, adjectives, and adverbs in the target utterances spoken by the children. I only counted utterances that contained either one word or a whole clause, not lists or fragments of utterances, and in particular I did not include correction fragments. This count involved 210 child utterances, and I take this to be an accurate random sampling of the occurrence of content words in the children's utterances at the various ages. For the adults I counted only the Class I errors, following the same procedure, which involved 130 utterances; again I assume this to be an accurate random sample of the adult utterances. I calculated the percentage of words in this sample which fell into each of the five content word categories. I then took only the child and adult errors in which the involved words fell into these 5 content word categories, and calculated the percentages of errors out of this set at each age which involved each lexical category. The results are given in Table 4.23.

This table shows that the frequency of occurrence of errors involving words from different content word categories can be explained in terms of their possibility of occurrence in random utterances for some lexical categories, but not for others. For the children age 1-2b and older, the common noun errors occurred at between twice and 1 1/2 times as often as would be predicted by chance, while the verb errors occurred at roughly half the rate that would be predicted by chance. On the other hand, proper noun errors occurred at slightly above chance level at most ages (except age 3-4 where they were at or slightly below chance), while adjective and adverb errors occurred at about chance levels at all ages. Hotopf 1980 also calculated a 'chance' figure and found that verbs occurred in his two corpora at a much lower rate, and nouns at a higher rate, than would be predicted by chance.

The most striking fact from this table is that for the children ages 1-2b and older and adults, verbs are actually more numerous than common nouns in the random sample. A little thought shows that this should be no surprise: first, in many utterances the arguments of the verb are pronouns rather than common nouns; second, there are a number of imperative utterances which do not require a subject noun; third, in many cases an utterance will involve several verbs in sequence, such as the child's 'I *wanna call* you' (AN-47(35) 2;4) or the adult's 'And that *means* you have to *use* a hot-pad to *get* it out' (AD-352(35)); note that there is only one common noun, 'hot-pad', in these two sentences combined (I counted 'have to' as a modal, and not a lexical verb). Thus the fact that verbs are involved in errors at about half the rate of nouns cannot be accounted for by

TABLE 4.23

Percentage of words in a random sample of utterances ('R') which fell into each of the five content-word lexical categories: common noun 'CN', verb, proper noun 'PN', adjective 'ADJ', adverb 'ADV', vs. the actual percentage of words involved in errors from this same set of categories ('E'), by age. All numbers in the table are percentages.

Age:	1-2a		1-2b		3		4		5		Adult	
	R	E	R	E	R	E	R	E	R	E	R	E
CN	50	55	29.5	49	31	51	30	46.5	27.5	43	34	54.7
Verb	15	3	43.5	17	40.5	23.5	38	23	39	21.5	40	18
PN	30	42	15.5	21	14.5	14	15.5	11.5	13	17	5.5	9.7
ADJ	0	0	7	9	9	8	12.5	13	15.5	12.5	11	12.7
ADV	0	0	4.5	4	5	3.5	4	6	5	6	9.5	5

frequency of occurrence in random utterances. So why are verb errors relatively rare and noun errors so common?

The rarity of verb errors has been noted by a few other investigators. For example, errors involving two verbs constitute only 3% of Hotopf's (1980) English content-word substitution corpus, and 9% of the German corpus; similarly verbs constitute 9% of Fromkin's (1973a) content-word substitution errors. Harley & MacAndrew (2001) found that nouns outnumbered verbs 4.8 to 1 in their semantically related paradigmatic lexical substitution errors, and 3 to 1 in their malapropisms.

Other researchers have reported a higher rate of verb errors than is usually found. In Fay & Cutler (1977), verbs constitute approximately 32% of the errors in their corpus, but since these are all malapropisms, the data are not strictly comparable. Similarly, Bowerman (1978) found a majority of verb errors and very few common noun errors in her corpus collected from her daughters between ages 2-5, a finding which is at odds with most other studies.

My figures fall in between the extremes; overall 17% of the children's lexical errors involved verbs, and 16.5% of the adults'. In order to compare my figures to those studies which looked only at paradigmatic substitutions, I calculated the percentages of verbs involved in Class I errors in my corpus. For the children the figure is 22% and adults, 16%. These figures are higher than the Hotopf, Fromkin, and Harley & MacAndrew figures, but they are still much lower than the 'chance' figure, indicating that in my study as in most others, verbs are involved in errors at a rate that cannot be predicted by their frequency of occurrence in sentences.

If we accept as true the claim that verb errors occur considerably less often than would be predicted by chance, this fact may remind the reader of the discussion of consonant and vowel errors in Chapter 3. In that chapter I argued that vowels are more central to the syllable than consonants, in that the vowel is the only required element in a syllable, and functions as the core anchor for the peripheral consonants. A similar argument could be made for verbs. Verbs are the core of a proposition and a clause, and thus the selection of the appropriate verb may be the central decision needed to be made in planning an utterance (Hotopf 1980:103, Bock & Levelt 1994:968). Misselection of a verb causes greatest disruption of the intended meaning of a proposition, and so should be caught by the internal monitor more often than errors involving other lexical categories. Therefore one would expect that verbs would be misselected less often than other word classes due to their centrality in the proposition, and verb misselections would be detected more often.

A second consideration is the effect of tonic stress in phonological phrases, as discussed in §4.2.3 above. Tonic stress was argued to enhance the likelihood that a word would be involved in an error, and tonic stress is far more likely to fall on a noun in English than on any other word class. Related to this is the fact that tonic stress most often signals new information, and new information, because it is being selected and planned for speaking for the first time in the discourse, is the most error-prone location in the planning frame. This again would heighten the susceptibility of nouns to error and lessen the susceptibility of verbs. It is likely that some combination of these two factors (the 'verb-centeredness' of planning and the prominence of the tonic-stress location) conspires to cause the relative overabundance of common noun errors and scarcity of verb errors, in relationship to chance.

One final point about verbs is that the children in the corpus produced proportionately more verb errors than the adults did. This is not true of the 1-2a children, who produced only one error in which one of the two words was a verb (and the other a proper noun; see (25b) above). However, a look at the numbers in Table 4.23 reveals that the age 1-2b children produced 17% verb errors (of these content-word errors); at age 3 the figure is 23.5%, at ages 4-5 it begins to drop a bit (23%, 21.5%); however, at age 5 it is still higher than the adult figure of 18%. Wijnan (1992) also found that the Dutch-speaking children in his study made proportionately more verb errors than did the adults. One explanation for the higher rate of verb errors among the children may be the often noted principle that 'verbs are harder'; that is, it takes children many years to firmly represent in their lexical entries the complex information regarding the semantic and argument structures appropriate to each verb (Bowerman 1978, Clark 1993:4). Thus verbs may be more susceptible to error in the child productions due to more immature lexical representations, as well as perhaps their having less practice in selecting a verb with the appropriate semantic/syntactic features for expressing a particular state of affairs. The children's speech production planning may in fact be less verb-oriented and more noun-oriented than the adults', particularly for the youngest children. As the children get older and their lexical representations for verbs become more fine-tuned, they begin to show

TABLE 4.24
Percentage of words in each lexical category, by 3 basic classes of lexical errors; children vs. adults.

	Class I & II		Class III		Classes IV-VI	
	Child	Adult	Child	Adult	Child	Adult
Common Noun	33	53	51	42.5	40	53
Verb	17.5	15	16	16	16.5	21
Proper Noun	14	10.5	13.5	9	13	5
Adjective	10.5	10	8	16.5	6	9
Adverb	3.5	4	4	10.5	4.5	1.5
Numeral	1	0	0	0	0	0
% Content Words	**79.5**	**92.5**	**92.5**	**94.5**	**80**	**89.5**
Pronoun	12	3.5	2	3	14	4
Preposition	4	4	1	0.5	2	5
Determiner	1.5	0	0	0	2	0
Interjection	1	0	2	1.5	0.7	0
Auxiliary V.	0.5	0	2.5	0.5	0	1.5
Demonstrative	0.25	0	0	0	0.7	0
Existential	0.25	0	0	0	0.7	0
Question Wd.	0.5	0	0	0	0	0
Conjunction	0.5	0	0	0	0	0
% Function Words	**20.5**	**7.5**	**7.5**	**5.5**	**20**	**10.5**
Total N=	**374**	**314**	**156**	**144**	**152**	**140**

proportions of noun vs. verb errors more similar to the those of the adults; this trend may be showing up in the 4-5-year-olds in this study.

4.3.4 Lexical Category vs. Error Class

One final point to be made in this section is that the proportion of errors involving various lexical categories is to some extent dependent on the class of error. This is demonstrated in Table 4.24, which shows the percentages of words in each lexical category which were involved in the three main categories of lexical errors: paradigmatic substitutions (Classes I-II), blends (Class III), and syntagmatic errors (Classes IV-VI), comparing the children to adults.

First, there is a difference between children and adults in the relative occurrence of content vs. function words in the three groups of error classes. For the children, in both paradigmatic substitution and syntagmatic errors, content words outnumber function words by about 80% to 20%, but for blends the ratio is 92.5% to 7.5%. On the other hand, for the adults the content words constitute around 90% of the errors in all three error class groups. In particular, the children made many pronoun errors in the paradigmatic substitutions and syntagmatic errors, but the adults made very few, and this seems to account for a great deal of the differences between children and adults; since pronouns are rarely involved in blends, there is no major child/adult difference in the blend errors. In the blend errors, the adults show many more adjective, and adverb errors than the children, but the same proportion of verb errors and fewer noun errors. As I will show in Chapter 5, blend errors typically involve synonyms; the children apparently knew fewer pairs of adjectives and adverbs which were in a relationship of synonymy, but knew many synonymous noun and verb pairs, which may be part of the reason why their percentages of content/function word errors were similar to adults' only in the blend category; see §5.3.4 for further discussion of the relationship between lexical category and semantics.

4.3.5 Lexical Categories at the 1-Word and 2-Word Stages?

The issue raised at the beginning of §4.3 was whether or not children in the 1-word or 2-word stages (the 1-2a children) show any evidence of representing abstract information regarding the lexical category of words in their lexical representations. I suggested a two-step process for assessing this question, and have already presented evidence from the first step: I looked to see if there were any differences in lexical category consistency between the two words mutually involved in lexical errors at these early ages, compared to later ages. In my corpus I have 16 lexical errors made by children in the 1-2a stages, and of these, 14, or 87.5%, involved two words of the same lexical category; this figure is very similar to the figures found at all other ages (which range from 84%-92%, see Table 4.21), and is not much different from the overall average for the children of 88%. Thus there is no discontinuity between the 1-2a children and the older children in terms of lexical category consistency of word pairs involved in lexical errors.

The second step, then, is to see whether or not the concept of abstract lexical category is necessary for explaining these early lexical errors, or whether they are fully explainable in terms of other factors. In Table 4.25 I have collated the relevant information regarding these 16 errors so that they can be examined as a group. (In this section I have given ages in years;months.days so that the fine-grained details of the analysis are available.) One can see that all of the errors in this table were either made by Bobby, or by one of the 'Other' children. This is because Anna never went through clear 1-word or 2-word stages, as explained in Chapter 1 (Table 1.2), so all of her early errors were classified as belonging to the (1-2b) age group. I did not collect any errors from Alice during her 1-word stage, nor any lexical errors during her 2-word stage; all 6 errors I collected from Alice during her 2-word stage were phonological.

Looking first at the paradigmatic errors, it can be seen that within the 6 lexical substitution errors, there are 3 involving 2 common nouns and 3

TABLE 4.25
**Pertinent facts regarding the 16 lexical errors made by children in the
1-word or 2-word stage.**

E #	Age	Word Pair	Class	Lexical Category	PHON/SEM	ENV	Other?
One-Word Stage							
B-1	1;7.22	car/bye	III	CN/interj.	[-phon, +sem]	[+env]	no
B-2	1;8.24	Bert/Ernie	III	PNx2	[-phon, +sem]	[+env]	coll.
Two-Word Stage							
B-5	1;9.1	toe/owie	III	CNx2	[-phon, +sem]	[-env]	utt.
B-8	1;9.6	Mommy/'Mantha	III	PNx2	[+phon, +sem]	[-env]	no
B-9	1;9.7	Daddy/Mommy	I	PNx2	[+phon, +sem]	[-env]	no
B-12	1;9.25	potty/penis	III	CNx2	[+phon, +sem]	[+env]	no
B-16	1;10.1	penis/toes	I	CNx2	[-phon, +sem]	[+env]	no
B-20	1;10.7	coffee/juice	I	CNx2	[-phon, +sem]	[+env]	no
B-23	1;10.9	cream/owie	III	CNx2	[-phon, +sem]	[-env]	utt.
OC-2	1;10.22	BobBob/Beckie	I	PNx2	[+phon, +sem]	[+env]	no
OC-3	1;11.0	Mommy/Dadoo	III	PNx2	[-phon, +sem]	[+env]	no
B-26	1;11.6	diaper/light	V	CNx2	[-phon, -sem]	[+env]	utt.
OC-4	1;11.15	milk/juice	III	CNx2	[-phon, +sem]	[-env]	utt.
OC-6	2;0.7	toothpaste/ toothbrush	I	CNx2	[+phon, +sem]	[-env]	no
OC-7	2;0.7	Daddy/Mommy	I	PNx2	[+phon, +sem]	[+env]	no
OC-9	2;0.14	peepee/Daddy	IV	PN/verb	[+phon, -sem]	[-env]	no

involving 2 proper nouns; all 6 errors show a strong semantic relationship between the target and error word, in 4 pairs the words are phonologically similar, and 4 errors were partially caused by environmental influences. Similar consistencies are found in the 8 blend errors: 4 involve two common nouns and 3 involve 2 proper nouns; the earliest error, made in the 1-word stage, involves a common noun with an interjection. All 8 blend errors show a semantic relationship between the target pairs although only two are phonologically similar; 4 were influenced by environmental factors, 1 by a collocational phrase, and in 3 errors one or both of the target words were spoken prior to the error. What do all these consistencies mean in terms of lexical category?

I think it would be very difficult to argue that the notion of 'noun' or 'verb' would be necessary to explain these errors. In every error, there was a strong conceptual relationship between the two words involved in the error; that is, the referents of these two words were closely related in the children's experiences and thus in their conceptual-semantic mental organization (as will be discussed in

Chapter 5). In every case we can imagine that the child had activated the concept and the lemma for the appropriate referent, and activation had spread to the other closely related concept and lemma; in many cases, the incorrect word was supported either by something in the environment or by the fact that one of the two words had just been spoken. These two situations are illustrated in (39).

(39) a. B: (holding up his bottle to Mom, requesting more juice, but
              looking at Mom's coffee) 'Mómmy, mòre cóffee?'
          M: 'Thàt's mý còffee.'
          B: 'Mòre júice!' ('coffee' substituted for 'juice'; referent of error
              word visible; B-20(35) 1;10.7)
      b. M: 'Do you want *mìlk* or *júice*?'
          OB:'[ɲuç]' (blend of 'milk' [mɛwk] and 'juice' [ţuç], with feature
              blend of [m] and [ţ]; both targets spoken in preceding utterance;
              OC-4(38) 1;11.15)

In (39a), Bobby intended to request more juice, but saw Mom's coffee; he had a conceptual relationship between various kinds of drinks that people in the household frequently drink, and so both the lemmas for 'juice' and 'coffee' were activated, and he accidentally selected the incorrect word, under the influence of the visual stimulus. In (39b), the Mother asked her son if he wanted 'milk' or 'juice'; both these words had thus been activated in his working memory, and his response was a blend of the two words, including a feature blend. Crucially, the words which name the two activated concepts in both cases, ('juice/coffee' and 'milk/juice') are common nouns *because* the referents are non-animate, generic entities, which is what common nouns are used to refer to, but the concept of 'common noun' is not necessary to explain these misselections. Thus these errors support the view that the young child's lexicon is organized by concepts such as 'food', 'people, 'activities', 'toys', and so on (Clark 1993:30-31); this conceptual organization, along with the external influences of environment, utterance, and collocation, can be argued to fully explain these errors without necessitating some abstract notion of lexical category. In fact, the 1-2a children showed the highest influence of the 'environmental' factor of any age group (see Table 4.14).

There are only three paradigmatic errors made by the 1-2a children in which there is no external influence (environmental, utterance, or collocational); in each of these, two words with an extremely close conceptual relationship are involved: B-8 'Mommy/'Mantha', B-9 'Daddy/Mommy', and OC-6 'toothbrush/ toothpaste'. In B-8, Bobby accidentally calls his mother by a blend of 'Mommy' and the name of his Nanny; obviously the names of his two primary female caregivers are closely conceptually linked, and 'Daddy' and 'Mommy' also have this close conceptual relationship. 'Toothpaste' and 'toothbrush' are not only conceptually linked in the 'tooth brushing' actional frame, but are also compounds with the first meaningful element in common. These words are so closely conceptually linked that the concepts of 'proper noun' or 'common noun' would seem to be redundant.

One might point out that in all the paradigmatic errors involving two-word utterances, the children did not produce an 'ungrammatical' utterance, as they would have if they had substituted a word from a different lexical category, which may argue for some syntactic structure. This is true, but it is also the case that in these errors the *semantic* relationship between the intended word and the other word in the utterance is never changed by the insertion of the erroneous word. For example, 'more juice' and 'more coffee' both consist of a word requesting an action plus the object of that action; similarly 'Beckie nose' and 'BobBob nose' both consist of a possessor and possessed; 'powder toes' and 'powder penis' both consist of an entity and its location; and so on. Thus this consistency can be explained in terms of those semantic relationships commonly considered to be the primary structures during the two-word stage (Brown 1973: 193-8), without necessitating support from syntax or lexical categories.

The two syntagmatic errors made at this stage are given in (40); (40b) was discussed in detail in §4.2.4 above.

(40)   a. M: (Mom lifts Bobby up and puts him on the changing table; Bobby always requested that the light be turned on over the changing table as part of the diaper changing routine)
'Come òn, let's gèt your **diaper** òn.'
       B: (pointing at light over changing table)
'**Diaper** òn . . . light òn.'
('diaper' perseverated, substituted for 'light'; B-26(43) 1;11.6)
       b. OG:(asking Daddy if he had used the bathroom yet)
'**Pèepee**, go . . . Dàddy, go **péepee**?'
('peepee' anticipated, substituted for 'Daddy'; OC-9(41) 2;0.14)

In the first error, 'diaper' and 'light' are both common nouns, referring to visible objects; while the words themselves have no semantic relationship per se, the concepts are metonymically related for the child in the context of the diaper-changing event. Furthermore, Mother had just said not only the word 'diaper', but the whole phrase 'diaper on', which Bobby repeats, and then corrects to his intended 'light on'. Thus the conceptual relationship, environmental context, and utterance context entirely explain this error. In (40b), the child substitutes a verb '(go) peepee' for a proper noun 'Daddy'; as I argued above, this child was about to go into the 3+word stage, and had probably activated all three words relevant to the utterance, then had problems sequencing them. This error that violates lexical category is in fact a useful test of when lexical categories begin to be developed, since the child realized she had sequenced the words incorrectly for the proposition she was trying to express. This is the earliest lexical error in my corpus which involved an anticipation from the child's own utterance, and seems to show a crossover point into the stage of speech production which requires syntax.

If the notion of lexical category is unnecessary for explaining the above errors, the next question is: what sort of error would be considered evidence that such categories have now been developed. The best evidence would be an error in which the target and source words had nothing in common except lexical category and there were no external factors which could explain the error; second best would be if the two words only had lexical category and form in common, since the form similarity is usually not enough to cause an error unless the two words have lexical category in common also. There are no lexical errors in my child corpus with neither a phonological nor semantic relationship between the two mutually involved words that do not have any external or utterance cause; however there are of course a number of [+phon, -sem] pairs, i.e. malapropisms. The earliest [+phon, -sem] lexical error in my corpus where the two words are from the same lexical category is given in (41).

(41)   Al: (holding fingers to lips) 'Mè **crỳing** Dàddy sléeping.'
              (looks confused)
         M: 'You mean you're quíet?
         Al: 'Yéah!' ('crying' substituted for 'quiet'; AL-13(35) 2;2.11)

In this error, Alice means to say 'Mè quìet Dàddy sléeping', meaning 'I'm being quiet because Daddy is sleeping'. She substitutes the word 'crying', clearly a verb containing the progressive suffix, for the intended 'quiet' which for her functioned as a verb at this time (i.e. 'to be quiet'). The two words are phonologically similar (Phon=5), but not semantically related (although it is possible that there is a sort of oppositional relationship between the two words, since 'crying' entails making noise). Nevertheless this looks like the first malapropism in my corpus, and was produced when Alice had been in the 3+word stage for about three weeks (she went into the 3+word stage around 2;1.20). The second malapropism in my corpus also involved two verbs, and was produced by Bobby at age 2;6 ('turning' for 'talking', B-86b(35) 2;6.21), but at this age, there is no doubt that lexical categories are in place in the children's representations and processing. So it would be good to find some further evidence that Alice's malapropism at age 2;2 coincided with the time that the lexico-syntactic categories of words were beginning to be represented. Fortunately such evidence exists. Consider the following errors:

(42)   a. M: 'Let me rinse off your bóttle. It's all stícky.'
             Al: 'Mỳ **stìck** . . . mỳ <u>bòttle</u> *stícky*. Mý àpple-jùice.
                  Mỳ stìcky bóttle.' (anticipation of 'sticky', probably interrupted metathesis; AL-9(41) 2;2.5)

b. Al: 'Búbble-gùm. Twó bùbbleS- . . . gùm_. Twó bùbble-gùms.'
(plural suffix {-s} anticipated from 'gum', added to 'bubble';
AL-11(42) 2;2.5)

c. M: 'Only *bábies* need bòttles!'
Al: (looks around for her bottle, and says) 'Mý bàby . . . nò . . .
mý bòttle!' ('baby' perseverated, substituted for 'bottle',
stranding plural suffix in Mom's utterance; AL-14(43) 2;2.12)

The error in (42a) shows that Alice was working on word order at this time; now that she was producing strings of 3 or more words she was careful to get the words in the order she intended. I suspect that she intended 'Mỳ bòttle sticky' to agree that her bottle was indeed sticky, but 'Mỳ sticky bóttle' asserted that this sticky bottle belonged to her; the different word orders now mean different things. In (42b), made on the same day as (42a) she showed that she was working on the placement of inflectional affixes, and thus that these affixes were beginning to take on autonomous status; in this case she accidentally placed the plural suffix {-s} in the middle of the compound 'bubble-gum' instead of at the end, then corrected its placement. In (42c), made a few days later, she perseverated only the uninflected content morpheme 'baby' from her mother's utterance, leaving the plural morpheme behind, showing that these inflectional categories were becoming associated with syntactic slots rather than lexical items during the linearization processes. Therefore there is evidence from an array of different types of errors made at this age that Alice was beginning to develop the constellation of properties which are required by linearization all during the same two-week period; that is, the systematization of word order, inflectional morphology, and lexical categories.

In sum, although there was a great deal of lexical category consistency between word pairs involved in lexical errors made by the children in the 1-word and 2-word stages, it was shown that this consistency can be entirely accounted for by relationships among conceptual categories, as well as environmental, utterance, and collocational influences. A focussed look at Alice's errors at age 2;2 showed that her earliest lexical error which honored lexical category but exhibited no semantic relationship occurred a few weeks after she began to consistently produce 3+word utterances, and her other errors at this time showed that she was working on setting up syntactic frames and linking inflectional morphology to syntagmatic slots in these frames. Therefore the earliest clear evidence for lexical category representation in these errors coincides with evidence that syntax is being developed, so that lexical categories are now necessary. These findings, combined with the finding that neither tonic stress position nor phrasal weight show any major influences on the children's errors in the 1-2a stage, support the claim that there is no syntax before the 3+word stage begins.

4.4 Summary and Conclusions

The purpose of this chapter was to look at errors involving whole lexical items, for the information they provide regarding the development of the lexicon as well as the development of the speech production planning mechanism. In §4.1 I defined the type of errors to be examined (paradigmatic substitutions and blends, syntagmatic anticipations, perseverations, and exchanges, including substitutions and additions); I clarified the notion of 'lexical item' and the distinction between content and function words. I then provided an overview of the numbers each of these types of errors made by age, and interpreted the relative frequency of different types of errors in terms of the RPC Model of speech production planning; specifically, this model predicts that paradigmatic errors will outnumber syntagmatic errors, and substitutions will outnumber blends, and this is indeed what was found. Furthermore, paradigmatic substitution errors involving content words far outnumbered function word errors, which is also predicted by the model. There were also some interesting developmental patterns; the children produced more function word errors than the adults did due to less practice and thus less automaticity in selecting function words; they also produced more perseverations than adults, due to a slower decay time of previously activated words, especially when spoken by a different speaker. Adults, on the other hand, produced far more anticipatory lexical errors, showing that they tend to be planning ahead in longer chunks than the children, and suppressing previously uttered material more rapidly. Finally, there was a U-shaped curve in the children's ratio of paradigmatic to syntagmatic errors; at age 3 the children produced the largest proportion of syntagmatic errors as well as function word errors, showing that this is an age at which there is a great deal of work going on in developing syntactic templates.

In §4.2 I looked at 10 factors which I found to be relevant in causing lexical errors. These factors, in order of importance, were: same lexical category, semantic relationship, tonic-stress position, phonological relationship, utterance influence, same phrasal weight, environmental influence, collocational phrase, discourse topic, and being 'On the mind'; it was suggested that an 11th factor might need to be added to the list, namely 'same referential target'. Each of these factors was introduced and examined in terms of its effect on lexical errors; patterns of effect were discussed in terms of the RPC Model as well as the development of attentional and processing abilities. One point that this examination made clear is that this model has been developed to account for 'plan-internal' errors, i.e. errors where the influence comes from somewhere within the structures being planned for this specific utterance. This would include interrelationships among words in the lexicon: same lexical category, semantic and phonological relationships, as well as possibly the spreading of lexical activation to collocational phrases associated with the lemmas being activated. It would also include prosodic factors (tonic syllable and phrasal weight), as well as the fact that both words are being planned for the current utterance, or one of the involved words has just been spoken such that it is currently activated in the lexicon. It could be said to account for 'discourse' influences since a range of concepts, not all spoken aloud, will be activated by a discourse topic, and if one topic is finished and a new topic introduced, some of these concepts may remain activated; however, such a factor is only implicit and not explicit in the model. This model however does not overtly account for the factors of environmental intrusions, ideas which are 'On the Mind', or errors which involve different ways of referring to the same referent. For environmental intrusions the model needs some explicit mention of attentional factors and the possibility that attention can be diverted by some 'plan-external' sensory input; similarly, lexical selection can be waylaid by a recurring thought that the speaker is having, the word for which is formally similar to a word being planned for speaking (such as 'shark' for 'shot', as in (32b) above). Finally, the model obviously lacks any overt mention of the myriad of pragmatic factors which must be taken into account when any utterance is being planned, and certainly a complete model would add on an entire pragmatics component; in terms of these data, this would be required to explain those errors which seemed to be caused by the speaker not being able to uniquely decide on a pragmatically appropriate level or specificity of reference. Thus while most of these lexical errors can be fully explained by the RPC Model, they also suggest some missing components and refinements that a full model would need to adopt.

The effects of these 10 causality factors were examined for developmental trends (see Table 4.18). One major difference between the children and adults was that the adult errors showed much more influence of phonology than the child errors; I suggested that the childrens' early errors rely heavily on semantic relationships, and that the phonological (and probably morphological) organization of the lexicon is less important for the children than for the adults. The prosodic factor of tonic-stress location was more important for adults than children, possibly due to its importance in the pragmatic aspects of information structure and focus in sentences. On the other hand, the children were much more affected than the adults were by the other influences such as the fact that a word had been recently spoken in an utterance, collocational, discourse, and 'On the Mind' factors, and especially environmental distractors. This can be explained by the immaturity of the young children's attentional mechanisms, and the fact that much of speech production planning is less automatic for the children than for the adults, so that extraneous intrusions are more likely to occur.

It was found that for both children and adults, most errors involved 3 or 4 influences; it was rare for an error to only exhibit one or two influences, or have more than 5 or 6. However, the adults showed fewer influences-per-error than the children for paradigmatic errors, probably because their larger vocabularies make these lexical selection errors more likely to occur with fewer causal factors influencing the misselection. On the other hand, the children showed fewer influences-per-error than the adults for syntagmatic errors; the fact that they have had far less practice than adults in fluently organizing lexical items into syntactic strings probably causes such misordering errors to occur with fewer causal influences.

The specific lexical categories involved in lexical errors, as well as lexical category consistency, was examined in detail in §4.3. The adults and children in the study both showed a high level of lexical category consistency in target/error pairs of words, and showed the same general proportion of errors involving different lexical categories, the biggest difference being that the children made many more proper noun and pronoun errors than adults. The relative scarcity of errors involving verbs was argued to be a function of the centrality of verb choice to utterance planning, as well as the tonic-stress factor which favors common nouns; since verbs occurred with the same approximate frequency as common nouns in target utterances (for all but the youngest children), this difference between noun vs. verb errors is not simply a matter of numbers of possible targets. However, since children produced somewhat more verb errors than adults, it may be that the children have less dense semantic representations for verbs (i.e. fewer criterial features), and thus the choice of the correct lexical item is less automatic for them. It was also found that the adults produced approximately 90% content word errors and 10% function word errors regardless of the type of error; the children, however, produced 80% content word to 20% function word errors in the substitution errors, both paradigmatic and syntagmatic, and only reached the adult proportions in the blend errors, where function words rarely occurred. Thus the children's less mature control over the selection of function words shows up in these two categories of error.

Finally, I examined the errors made by children in the 1-word and 2-word stages of development in detail, and argued that while their errors showed a clear lexical category consistency, other factors could completely account for these errors without positing that these very young children had abstract lexical categories represented in the lexicon. Specifically, the two words involved in the error always had a very close conceptual-semantic relationship, and in most cases there were several other factors involved in supporting the error, including environmental, utterance, and collocational influences. The first malapropism in my corpus occurred at age 2;2, and I argued that this is the age when there begins to be some evidence in my data for the abstract notion of 'lexical category'.

Inherent in a great deal of this chapter is some notion of 'semantic relatedness' between lexical items. It is now time to make explicit what kinds of relationships I found to hold in the children's lexical errors, and ask questions regarding the development of these semantic networks of interrelatedness. These are the issues which I will take up in Chapter 5.

Chapter 5
Semantic Relationships in Lexical Errors

5.1 Introduction

A great deal of current linguistic research has focussed on the semantic content of lexical representations in the adult lexicon. Language acquisition researchers have likewise been interested in the question of how semantic representations develop, looking into the issues of the types of information represented at various ages, and how representations change over time (see Jaeger & Wilkins 1993 for an earlier version of this chapter). Furthermore, the structural relationships among lexical entries has been at issue: while it is clear that in the adult lexicon, lexical entries are related to other entries by semantic factors, the development of semantic relationships in the lexicon has not been definitively tracked.

Evidence for the semantic organization of the adult lexicon comes from many sources, including SOTs, aphasia, priming experiments, word association tasks, and so forth, in which the effects of semantic relatedness of words account for patterns of behavior. However, it is more difficult to ascertain whether or not very young children's lexicons have this internal organization, and not all researchers agree on this point. Early lexical representations are considered by some researchers to contain mainly conceptual, functional, and phonological information, but actual lexical-semantic relationships in the lexicon among individual words is thought to develop only after age 5 (Nelson 1985: Ch. 6). One main source of evidence for this claim is the fact that in word association tests, young children give responses which are primarily conceptually related (e.g. 'dark-moon') or syntagmatically related (e.g. 'dark-night') to the probe word, rather than giving the paradigmatically or 'logically' related responses which adults tend to give (e.g. 'dark-light') (Brown & Berko 1960). However, other researchers have argued that semantic relationships are inherent in the earliest lexicons, and that the reason paradigmatic responses in word-association tasks show an increase around age 5 is linked to the child's entering school, since such paradigmatic responses are typical in education-related activities. In this vein, Entwisle (1966) has shown that there is no sudden shift from syntagmatic to paradigmatic responses in word association tasks at age 5; rather there is a gradual shift beginning at age 5 and culminating around age 7, which reflects not only the effects of education per se, but also the lexical categories of individual words, the conditions under which the task is administered, and even the socioeconomic status of the child. Bowerman (1978:980) has strongly argued that the child's lexicon is primarily organized according to semantics from the start, and that the metalinguistic task of word association simply does not tap the actual organization of the child's lexicon.

Inherent in the claim that there is a developmental shift from a more conceptually based semantic organization of words to a more lexically based organization is the hypothesis that these two aspects of semantics, i.e.

conceptual semantics and lexical semantics, are distinct systems in the adult mind. According to this type of hypothesis, 'conceptual semantic' knowledge is manifested in the structures of concepts, and as such it is not necessarily linguistic, although it undoubtedly develops its structure under the influence of the categories embodied in the words of the language spoken by the individual. On the other hand, the lemmas in the lexicon, which are formal linguistic units, contain semantic information relevant to the meaning and function of that particular word; lemmas are associated with relevant concepts, and they are also associated with other lemmas which share relevant linguistic features with them (and of course they are associated with the appropriate form representation). This is the position held by Levelt (1989: Ch. 6, 1992) among many others. Levelt argues that lexical errors can be caused either by the activation of two closely related concepts which then each activate their individual lemmas, or by the activation of one concept which activates an appropriate lemma, and then activation spreads from this lemma to another semantically related lemma in the lexicon. He diagrams these two possibilities as follows:

(1) Conceptual and lexical relationships in lexical errors (adapted from Levelt 1989, Figure 6.6)

a. Conceptual Intrusion   b. Associative Intrusion

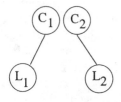

Levelt suggests that for adults, most lexical blend errors are caused by 'conceptual intrusion'; that is the same or very similar concepts are activated, and the concepts activate competing lemmas from the lemma lexicon. However, for lexical substitution errors, he suggests that they predominantly occur when the concept to be expressed activates an appropriate lemma, but then activation from this lemma feeds to another lemma in the lexicon which has lexical-semantic links to the intended lemma. In this latter case, if the appropriate concept for the second lemma is activated, it is mainly due to feedback from the activated lemma. In Levelt, Roelofs & Meyer (1999), the authors present a great deal of psycholinguistic evidence for the separation of concepts and lemmas in representation and processing (see also Laubstein 1999, Roelofs, Meyer & Levelt 1998). This distinction has also been built in to the RPC Model being used in the present study.

However, it is not the case that all semanticists work with this distinction. There are some semantic theories, such as Cognitive Semantics, which assume that there is a single semantic system: concepts and words are governed by the same semantic system, and concepts are directly linked to individual lexemes with no intervening lemma level (e.g. Talmy 2000).

What difference would it make to adopt either of these positions when looking at children's lexical substitution and blend errors? On the Cognitive Semantics view, in order to demonstrate that the child's lexicon is organized semantically, one would need to show that word pairs involved in lexical selection or blend errors have conceptual-semantic relationships with each other, of the same types found in adult errors. As we go through the data below it will become abundantly clear that the children's lexical errors show conceptual relationships from the very beginning (i.e. age 1;7), and thus from a Cognitive Semantic point of view, the claim that children's lexicons are not organized by semantics until around the age of 5 will receive no support from these data.

The position which assumes that there is a lemma level of lexical representation which cannot be conflated with the conceptual underpinnings of word meanings will be somewhat more difficult to test. In order to show that the child has distinguished the lemma level from the concepts (i.e. there is now a lexical semantics distinct from conceptual semantics), one would have to demonstrate that a particular error is not necessarily explained fully in terms of the concepts involved, but that a better explanation entails semantic featural knowledge of the kind represented in lemmas in the adult lexicon. In this case I would only be able to claim that children's lexicons are organized by semantics (assuming that this requires a lexical-semantic organization) when they begin to produce errors which cannot be fully explained in terms of conceptual or environmental effects.

An example may clarify the distinction I am making. If a child of 1;10 were to say 'Mommy' when she meant to say 'Daddy', one could argue that the concept of 'Mommy' necessarily activates the concept of 'Daddy' for this child since the two entities usually occur together in the child's world, have a similar functional role, etc., and thus that the two lemmas would not require a formal link in the lexicon in order to cause this error. Thus this error could be fully explained in terms of conceptual activation, as illustrated in (1a) above. On the other hand, if a child of 2 were to say 'down' when he meant to say 'up', one could argue that the concept of 'upness' would not necessarily activate the concept 'downness' when the child was constructing a proposition regarding an activity which involved only 'upness' (for example, 'Pick me up'). In fact, the concept of 'downness' would be antithetical to the proposition being planned, to the point where it might interfere with the proposition being expressed if it were activated. Thus an error involving the substitution of 'down' for 'up' is better explained by lexical semantics, that is, assuming that it was an actual link between lemmas in the lexicon which caused this error (in this case the lexical-semantic relationship of 'antonym'); this is the scenario depicted in (1b) above. In looking at the data below, it will become clear that there is evidence for such lemma-based errors beginning at age 2;6, and these errors look no different from adult errors of the same sorts which are taken to demonstrate semantic links in the lexicon for adults. Thus, if one takes the point of view that lemmas are distinct from concepts, one also does not need to wait until age 5 to find evidence for the semantic organization of the lexicon; however, the evidence shows that the onset of such organization comes not with the very first errors but at around age 2;6. In the remainder of this chapter I will assume the point of view which distinguishes concepts from lexical semantics, partially because there is much psycholinguistic evidence to support it (Levelt, Roelofs & Meyer 1999), and partly because it poses the more difficult challenge in terms of demonstrating that child lexicons are organized by semantics. However, proponents of the Cognitive Semantics theory will have no trouble interpreting the data below in terms of conceptual-semantic relationships.

The two main issues to be addressed in this chapter are: 1) whether there is any developmental progression in the effect of semantics in lexical substitution and blend errors, which would require an explanation in terms of the development of semantic representations and relationships in the lexicon, and 2) whether or not it is possible to discern a shift from purely conceptually motivated semantic relationships to lexical-semantic links in the lexicon. In the discussion below I will argue that lexical semantic relationships develop out of conceptual semantic relationships, and that these SOTs provide evidence for the point at which lexical-semantic relationships begin to be active in children's lexicons. A third issue stems from the fact that there are very few SOT studies which focus on semantic relationships per se, and in those studies of which I am aware (Hotopf 1980, Levelt 1989, Wijnen 1992, Arnaud 1999, Harley & MacAndrew 2001), very general taxonomies of semantic relatedness are used, which typically involve from 3-5 categories. Thus the third goal of this chapter is to develop a more detailed taxonomy of semantic relationships between target/error word pairs (or target/target in blends), in order to make very specific comparisons between the children's and adults' patterns of error. This will allow me to address a fourth set of questions, namely, what kinds of semantic relationships occur in the children's earliest errors, do the types of semantic relationships apparent in children's lexical SOTs change over time, and if so, what does this reveal about the development of the semantic organization of the lexicon?

This chapter is organized as follows. After a brief discussion of the general rationale behind the classificatory system to be used here, the taxonomy of semantic relationships will be presented, with relevant examples. The methodology for assigning a particular semantic relationship category to a particular target/error or target/target pair will be explained in detail. The results of the semantic analysis will be presented and discussed in terms of comparisons among the various children's data sets, and comparisons across age, error types, and lexical categories. The results will also be compared to the results of several other SOT studies. The next section will look at the relationship between phonological and semantic similarity during processing. Finally, I will address the issue of the age at which there is evidence that lexical-semantic links in the lexicon have been developed.

5.2 Semantic Relations

5.2.1 Frame Semantics as a Basis for the Taxonomy

It is difficult to know exactly what a particular word 'means' to a particular individual, and this is especially true if the individual is 2 years old. The approach to semantic meaning and semantic relatedness I will take in this chapter is a combination of the Frame Semantics theory of Fillmore (1975, 1978, 1982; see also Lakoff 1987, Langacker 1990, Talmy 2000), which is inherently cognitive-semantically focussed, and more traditional theories such as that found in Lyons (1968, 1977), which is a more lexical-semantically based approach. For my purposes the two approaches are not seriously at odds with each other, in the sense that they both use more or less the same terminology to label semantic relations, although they may use different criteria for making those designations. In the taxonomy below, I have used all the traditional labels for semantic relationships, but have also added a few non-traditional categories which are supported by the Frame Semantics approach. Another reason I am using Frame Semantics here is because it has many factors in common with the 'Frames, then Content' theory of MacNeilage & Davis (1990), which was introduced in Chapter 3, and thus will allow for a unified treatment of the acquisition of various components of linguistic structure.

Fillmore (1978) explained the concept of a 'frame' as follows:

> A 'frame' . . . is a lexical set whose members index portions or aspects of some conceptual or actional whole. The items in a frame, in other words, are only understandable to somebody who has (conceptual) access to the underlying schema onto which the parts of the frame fit. . . . Within the set of words linked together in a 'frame' can be found many that form paradigms, contrast sets, taxonomies, and the rest; but all of them require, for their semantic specification, a prior detailing of the nature of the associated conceptual schema. (Fillmore 1978:165)

Note that the Frame Semantics theory is applicable to words in all lexical categories, since all content words including proper nouns, as well as all function words, can be said to be related to specific aspects of conceptual or actional wholes. Thus this framework allows me to use a unified taxonomic system for classifying the relationships between all the word pairs involved in lexical errors, regardless of lexical category.

Looking at child lexical errors from this point of view, we would say that two words are semantically related if they index different aspects of some scene or actional whole that are linked together in a particular way for that child, i.e. because of the child's experiences with the entities and scenes to which the words are linked. As Fillmore points out, these conceptual-semantic relationships can usually also be expressed in terms of lexical-semantic categories such as 'synonyms', 'antonyms', 'co-hyponyms', and so forth. What I will argue below is that in very young children's lexicons, the words are linked to each other solely via their conceptual relationships; however eventually their lemmas will also become linked to each other in the lexicon due to their meaning relationships per se, that is by lexical-semantic features. (Here, and throughout this chapter, I use the term 'features' in a fairly general way, to indicate any semantic properties which may be represented in lexical entries and may be involved in organizing the lemma lexicon. I do not mean the use of the term 'feature' to imply any particular theoretically relevant set of semantic features, or any specific formal semantic feature theory.)

But how can one know what a child thinks a word means? Very early vocabularies tend to include words for frequently encountered objects, persons, and actions, and be somewhat general in their meanings (Clark 1973, 1979, 1993, Griffiths 1986, among many others). So for example, when a 20-month-old utters the word 'juice' she may mean 'that is juice', 'I want more juice', 'you give me some juice', 'that's my juice', or any number of other messages. Fillmore (1975) also addresses the developmental issue:

> . . . in meaning acquisition, first one has labels for whole scenes, then one has labels for parts of particular familiar scenes, and finally one has both a repertory of labels for schematic or abstract scenes and a repertory of labels for entities or actions perceived independently of the scenes in which they were first encountered. (Fillmore 1975:127)

This description is similar to the 'Frames, then Content' theory of MacNeilage and Davis, which suggests that the child learns the larger chunk first, and then fills in the details. In this case the child learns words for whole scenes (whether they correspond to the analogous adult word or not, e.g. the child's word 'apple' could correspond to the adult word 'fruit'), and then eventually learns words for the individual properties of the scene. Fillmore's description of the acquisition of meaning highlights the fact that the meaning of a particular word, as well as the relationship between that word and the scenes to which it is anchored, may be constantly shifting as the child matures.

Fortunately this does not make the assessment of children's word meanings, or semantic relationships among words, impossible. The parent-linguist who is closely observing her child can make a reasonable assumption about what she thinks a word means to her child at any particular point in time, based on a number of factors such as the child's current vocabulary and word usage, the child's recent and habitual experiences, and the circumstances in which the word is being used in a specific utterance. She can then feel confident in assessing the semantic relationship between a pair of words, given her analysis of the meaning of each individual word. Further analysis of any particular error can suggest whether this relationship is mainly conceptual, or whether it may also contain a lexical link. Consider the following example:

(2)   B: (pointing at a picture of Bert in "Sesame Street" book)
            '[pɜ́.ni] . . . Bért.' (blend of 'Bert' [bɜt] and 'Ernie' [ʔɜ́.ni]; child
            did not know word 'Bernie'; B-2(38) 1;8)

There are a number of reasons for feeling confident that there is a conceptual-semantic association between the words 'Bert' and 'Ernie' for this child. First, the child watches the television show "Sesame Street" regularly, listens to "Sesame Street" audio tapes, and looks at "Sesame Street" books, and is well aware that Bert and Ernie are distinct members of the "Sesame Street" world, along with Cookie Monster, Oscar, Big Bird, and so on. Second, Bert and Ernie are closely paired members on "Sesame Street"; they are roommates, they wear similar clothes, and when you see or hear one you expect to see or hear the other. Third, the fact that they occur together so often and are spoken about as a pair results in there being a fairly fixed collocational phrase 'Bert and Ernie', as opposed to *'Ernie and Bert'. Finally, although they are friends, they are also used to show opposing and contrasting characteristics. Even their appearance is contrastive: Ernie is round and cheerful and his shirt contains horizontal stripes; and Bert is thin and serious and his shirt contains vertical stripes. Whether just one or all of these factors triggered the blend, there seems to be enough information to support the conceptual foundations of the association, and thus to claim that there is a conceptual-semantic relationship between the two words. However, it is not necessarily the case that one needs to assume lexical-semantic links between the lemmas of these two words to explain this blend, and such links would be unlikely at age 1;8. I analyze this error as following the pattern shown in (1a) above, where two related concepts cause two distinct lemmas to be activated; in this case the two lemmas activated their appropriate forms, and the two forms were blended into a single phonological word.

Conceptual-semantic relationships can be of a broad variety of types, and different criteria may be necessary for making decisions about the type of relationship found between any two semantically related words, as well as deciding whether or not there is evidence for lexical-semantic relationships. A few more examples will make this clearer.

(3)   a. An: 'Did Àlice gò to the dóctor's and gèt a **shárk**?'
                ('shark' substituted for 'shot'; AN-68(35) 2;9)
       b. B: ('reading' story about a Ninja Turtles pizza party)
                'Well, so mùch for a **pízza**, a **pìzza** with . . . so mùch for a
                párty, a pàrty with pízza.'
                ('pizza' anticipated/substituted for 'party' twice; B-361(41) 4;9)

  c. Al: (she had hurt her foot on the slide, and wanted to sit with her
          foot up on a pillow; she says to her babysitter)
          'Can yòu get a **blànket** for my fóot?'
     OA: 'A blánket?'
     Al: 'No, a p<u>í</u>llow.'
          ('blanket' substituted for 'pillow'; AL-229(35) 4;6)

In example (3a), Anna, at age 2;9 had recently seen a scene from the movie
"Jaws", which involves sharks, and she was somewhat fixated on sharks and
their relationship to fear and pain, particularly their ability to pierce the skin.
When asking about Alice's trip to the doctor's office, where Alice indeed had
gotten a shot, Anna erroneously substituted the word 'shark' for 'shot'. These
two words were clearly associated with each other in Anna's mind, due to both
being linked with concepts of fear and pain, as well as the shared physical
similarity of needles and sharks' teeth; they were also semantically associated
with each other due to the negative connotations of the words themselves. It is
unlikely that most adults would have a lexical connection between the words
'shark' and 'shot', but in Anna's case these were both perpetual fears of hers, and
so I can confidently claim that these words had at least a conceptual-semantic
relationship for Anna. (The two words are also both nouns and phonologically
similar to each other, which probably facilitated the error's occurrence.) This
error is analyzed as having a 'connotational' relationship in the taxonomy.
    In (3b), Bobby was 'reading' a story in which the Teenage Mutant Ninja
Turtles were supposed to have a pizza party, but somehow the pizza went
missing, so the Turtles were bemoaning the fact that the party would not
happen. At this time in Bobby's life (age 4;9), every party that he had ever
attended (that he could remember) involved pizza; this was a given at parties for
him, and thus the words 'pizza' and 'party' were semantically related for Bobby
in the context of the 'party' scene. Furthermore the collocation 'pizza party' was
one with which Bobby was familiar, and so the words were syntagmatically
linked to each other, as well as conceptually linked. Adults may or may not
have a lexical connection between the words 'party' and 'pizza', but for Bobby
(and perhaps every 4-year-old American boy) there was at least a conceptual-
semantic link, and possibly also a lexical-semantic link between these two
words. Again these words are phonologically similar and they are both nouns;
their relationship is classed as 'member to set', since 'pizza' was an
indispensable member of the 'party' set for Bobby.
    Finally, in (3c), Alice, at age 4;6, substituted the word 'blanket' for
'pillow'. These two words belong to the same frame which indexes items
typically found on a bed and used for resting and sleeping, and Alice encountered
them together on a regular basis. This error is analyzed as involving co-
members of a non-taxonomic set; however, because blankets and pillows are
often physically contiguous, this is also an example of metonymic association.
There is no doubt that these two words were conceptual-semantically related for

Alice. However, in this case there is also strong evidence for the lexical-semantic link, given the propositional content of the utterance itself. In making this error, Alice activated the concept of 'pillow' since this was the concept involved in the intended utterance; however it is not necessarily the case that the concept of 'pillow' will always activate the concept of 'blanket'. In this particular situation Alice was proposing a non-canonical use of a pillow, i.e. to put under her injured foot, and so the concepts of 'bed' and 'sleeping', which might lead to 'blanket', were unlikely to have been activated. Furthermore, there was no bed with blankets and pillows in view, so there was no environmental influence. What is most likely is that the concept of 'pillow' activated the lemma for 'pillow'; activation of the 'pillow' lemma spread to other lemmas related to it by semantic features, which in this case included the co-member of a set/metonym 'blanket'. Another possible influence is that she may have associated pillows with heads, and blankets with body parts below the head, including feet, and this association, whether lexical or conceptual, may have also affected the error. Nevertheless, since most adults, at least in cultures in which blankets and pillows are used, would have a lexical-semantic association between 'pillow' and 'blanket', if an adult were to produce this error it would be analyzed as involving spreading activation from one lemma to another in the lexicon due to shared semantic features, as illustrated in (1b) above (Levelt 1989:219). I see no reason to treat Alice's error any differently.

In the taxonomy below, I have used primarily conceptual-semantic criteria for making decisions about the specific semantic relationships holding in word-pairs involved in lexical errors. The question of whether or not there are also lexical-semantic relationships will be put on hold until the final section of this chapter, at which point I will argue for an age at which such lexical-semantic organization becomes evident in errors. The criteria I used for deciding that two words involved in a lexical SOT were semantically related included the following: First, each of the two words in the slip had to be recognized as being a stable part of the child's vocabulary, i.e. being used with a consistent meaning, prior to the time of the slip (see Bowerman 1978). In this way the child's understanding and use of the words independently of the slip could be assessed. Second, the concepts evoked by the two words were considered to be habitually associated with one another for the child, independently of the particularized environmental and linguistic context of the slip utterance. Third, what is shared by the two words had to go beyond their particular part-of-speech categories, or their morphological properties. In one sense almost all of the words involved in lexical SOTs could be considered semantically similar because both words overwhelmingly belong to the same part-of-speech category (as was discussed in Chapter 4), and often shared morphology (as will be discussed in Chapter 6). However, to be considered semantically similar within the context of this chapter, more than this basic information had to be shared. Thus in the error *'He's **tùrning** òn the télephone', corrected to 'He's tàlking òn the télephone' (B-86b(35) 2;6), although the error and target word are both verbs with progressive marking and refer to activities, they are not considered semantically related for this child, since the verbs 'talk' and 'turn' have no inherent semantic relationship. For each word pair which I determined had some kind of semantic relationship for the child by the above criteria, I decided on a specific classification for that word pair based both on the general meaning of the words, and on my knowledge of the individual child's experiences with and usage of that word, to the best of my ability. In the data section of the book I have made explicit the rationale behind my categorization of semantic relationships in every case where the child's idiosyncratic meanings or experiences seem to have led to a categorization which is different from what might be expected for a typical adult.

In the taxonomy of semantic relations to be detailed below, then, the point of view of Frame Semantics and the methodological principles presented above are the starting points for making the best determination of whether or not a particular pair of words is semantically related for a particular child at a particular point in time, and what type of relationship the child sees as holding between the two words.

5.2.2 Classification of Semantic Relations

As discussed above, Fillmore (1978, 1982) has shown that most of the traditional categories of semantic relatedness remain valid in a Frame Semantics approach, although the interpretation of a particular pair of words as having a particular relationship may be arrived at through different reasoning. Thus, like many researchers in this field I will rely on the classificatory framework discussed in Lyons (1968, Ch. 10), but I will augment this with notions from prototype theory, frame semantics, and cognitive semantics, following Fillmore (1978, 1982). The schema for classification is given below; only those classes are presented which are needed to explain the semantic relationships in the children's data, and which allow for comparison with my adult data and that of other researchers. I will first present the definitions used in classifying the children's errors, and then give a brief discussion of the decision-making rationale for unclear cases. These same classificatory principles were used for determining semantic relationship categories in the adult errors.

Taxonomic Classifications: A *semantic taxonomy* is a semantic network founded on the relation 'is a kind of'. So, for example, an 'apple' is a kind of 'fruit', and thus these two words are in a taxonomic relationship; namely, 'fruit' is the *superordinate* and 'apple' is one of its *subordinates* or *hyponyms* in this taxonomy. 'Apple' and 'orange' are *co-hyponyms*, since they are both subordinates of the same superordinate. The taxonomic associations which are found in the data are the following.

co-hyponyms - members of a taxonomy that share the same superordinate.

(4)   B: 'I wànna **wàtch** . . . I wànna l̀isten to "Bàby Belúga".'
              ('watch' substituted for 'listen to'; "Baby Beluga" is an audio tape;
              co-hyponyms: kinds of perception; B-71(35) 2;6)

In labelling two words as co-hyponyms, I do not mean to imply that the child actually knows the superordinate word; i.e. in example (4), calling 'watch' and 'listen to' co-hyponyms does not entail that the child knows the word 'perception'. Rather, I assume that the child conceptualizes 'watch' and 'listen to' as two modes or instances of the same kind of event or activity, being 'kinds of' ways of experiencing external input.

superordinate/subordinate - use of a superordinate notion for a hyponym, as shown in example (5a), a subordinate hyponym for a superordinate, as in (5b), or a blend of a superordinate and a subordinate word, as in (5c); only the adults produced the 'subordinate for superordinate' type of error. Since in blend errors one cannot tell the directionality of the influence, these three types of errors have been grouped into a single category in the counts below. In the children's errors, the superordinates were usually fairly general in the sense of being somewhat distant from the subordinates; for example, the children produced blends of pronouns or deictics with more specific nouns, and substitutions of very general verbs such as 'do' and 'have' for more specific verbs such as 'show' and 'wear' (as was also found by Bowerman 1978).

(5)   a. B: 'Mom, I wànna **dó** . . . I wànna shów you sòmething.'
                   ('do' substituted for 'show'; superordinate for subordinate:
                   'showing' is a kind of 'doing'; B-403(35) 4;11)
          b. AF: (noticing that it looks like it's going to rain) 'I thìnk Rìck
                   pròbably bètter pùt the **lí́d** ùp on his cár, I mean the tóp ùp.'
                   ('lid' substituted for 'top'; subordinate for superordinate, since a
                   'lid' is a kind of 'top'; AD-376(35))
          c. B: 'I wànna plày with a bíg [**wèg**].'
                   (blend of 'one' [wʌn] and 'egg' [ɛg]; superordinate/subordinate:
                   'one' is a general way to refer to 'egg'; B-80(38) 2;6)

Errors such as that in (5a), where a very general superordinate is substituted for a more specific subordinate, may look at first to be something other than a true speech error, perhaps a false start. However, I will argue in §5.4 below that such utterances are in fact speech errors, caused by the same factors as the blend in (5c), which is indisputably a SOT.

Non-Taxonomic Sets: Words may be grouped together because they index entities which furnish or make up a prototypical scene. Non-taxonomic sets involve words for a collection of objects or activities which taken together make up this scene, but are not physically integral. Thus 'pillow' and 'blanket' in example (3c) above belong to the non-taxonomic set of things typically found on a bed and used for resting and sleeping; they are physically distinct, i.e. separable from each other, and thus do not entail a physical whole (in contrast with the 'part/whole' category to be presented next). I didn't consider 'blanket' and 'pillow' to have a taxonomic relationship for the child as I doubted that the child had some superordinate concept which links the target and error semantically, such as the concept of 'bedclothes'. The relations in this domain parallel those of taxonomic sets, as follows.

co-members of a set - members that share affiliation in a set by virtue of furnishing distinct portions of the same scene, as shown in (6) below, as well as in example (2) above, involving 'Bert/ Ernie', and example (3c) 'blanket/pillow'.
(6)   AN: (pretending to talk on the telephone to "Winnie the Pooh" characters)
       'Hí [tʰǐ.gɪt].' (blend of 'Tigger' [tʰí.gɜ] and 'Piglet' [pʰí.gɪt];
       co-members of the set of characters from "Winnie the Pooh";
       AN-6(38) 1;7)

This relationship is common among proper nouns, and tends to be a more concrete relationship in general than that of co-hyponym. This is because the 'set' which the 'members' make up is typically also a concrete entity (e.g. 'things you find on a bed'), whereas for co-hyponyms, the superordinate is often somewhat abstract (e.g. 'perception'). Also, co-members of a set by definition are encountered together as a group, whereas co-hyponyms often occur in a more paradigmatic relationship; for example, at a meal a child might get an apple, an orange, or a banana, but would not necessarily encounter all three co-hyponymous fruits at the same time. Again this suggests that in general, co-member of a set is a more concrete relationship than co-hyponym.

set-to-member or _member-to-set_ - substitution of the word naming a whole scene for the word for a member of the set of things that fill out that scene as in (7a), or vice versa as in (3b) above ('party/pizza'), or a blend of the two, as in (7b). As with the 'superordinate/subordinate' category, I have combined these three possible interactions of set and member words into a single category.
(7)   a. M: (Anna and Mom looking at picture book, discussing donkeys)
          'I wònder whère we could sèe a dónkey.'
       An: 'At the zóo?'
       M: 'I dòn't think there are any dònkeys at óur zòo.'
       An: 'Um . . . at fárms they have zòos.'
       M: 'You mean at fàrms they have dónkeys?'
       An: 'Yeah.' ('zoo' perseverated and substituted for 'donkey', and
          made plural as appropriate for the sentential context; set-to-
          member, since 'zoo' is the whole scene or set, and 'donkey' is a
          member of the set of individual entities that makes up a 'zoo';
          AN-152(43) 4;1)

b. AF: 'I've gòt to get [rɛ́st].' (blend of 'ready' [rɛ́.ɾi] and 'dressed'
[drɛst]; set/member, since getting dressed is one of the
activities that makes up the set of things called 'getting ready'
to go out somewhere; AD-538(38))

Partonomic Classifications: A *semantic partonomy* is a semantic network
founded on the notion 'is part of'. Parts may form a whole which itself is a part
of a larger whole and so on. In this case the various parts are physically
integrated into the larger whole, and each component is (normally) necessary for
making up the whole, unlike members of a set. The associations identified in
these data are the following.

<u>co-partonyms</u> - words which label parts of the same whole.
(8)   OG:'Lòok what hàppened to my [fɪ̃ŋ] . . . to my thúmb.'
        (child started to substitute 'finger' for 'thumb'; co-partonyms:
        'finger' and 'thumb' are both 'part of' the hand, physically
        integrated into a single whole; OC-97(35) 4;3)

<u>part-for-whole</u> or <u>whole-for-part</u> - use of a word for the whole in place of a
part as in (9a), or use of a word for a part in place of the whole as in (9b), a
blend of the two as in (9c), or a reversal of the two, as in (9d). As with the
superordinate/subordinate and set/member errors above, I grouped whole-for-part
and part-for-whole errors together in my counts. Only the adults produced part-
for-whole errors, which is similar to the fact that only the adults produced
subordinate-for-superordinate errors.
(9)   a. OB: 'I hùrt my lég . . . thigh.' ('leg' substituted for 'thigh'; whole for
           part: the 'thigh' is part of the 'leg'; OC-127(35) 5;0)
        b. AM: (while feeling an avocado to see if it is ripe enough)
           'Oh boy, I thìnk it's tìme for màking àvocádo . . . for màking
           guàcamóle.' ('avocado' substituted for 'guacamole'; part for
           whole, since 'avocado' is one ingredient that makes up
           'guacamole'; AD-359(35))
        c. B: 'Yeah, 'cuz my [dʒæ̀.pɚ] . . . the zipper came òff my bìg
           jácket.' (blend of 'jacket' and 'zipper'; whole and part
           blended: a zipper is part of a jacket; B-227b(38) 4;2)
        d. OG: (reporting on trip to an equine museum)
           'And wè saw the dèad hòrse of a bónes.'
           (reversal of 'dead horse' with 'bones'; part/whole exchange,
           since 'bones' are part of the 'dead horse'; OC-116(45) 4;7)

From these examples one can see that the notion of 'physically integrated' can
be somewhat different depending on the substances involved. For example,
thighs are 'a part of' the leg in a different sense than avocado is 'a part of'

guacamole; in the former, the thigh is one section of the leg, but in the latter, the avocado is mashed up and fully integrated with the spices and other ingredients which make up the avocado dip, guacamole. Similarly I have labelled the adult error involving 'mind/brain' as a part/whole relationship (the 'mind' is part of the 'brain'; AD-638(45)), envisioning this as something like the 'avocado/guacamole' example (i.e. not a particular section of the whole but fully integrated into it); but certainly this classification depends on one's particular concept of the mind, and the mind/brain relationship.

Contrastive Relations: As Lyons (1977:271) has discussed in detail, " . . . binary opposition is one of the most important principles governing the structure of languages; and the most evident manifestation of this principle, as far as the vocabulary is concerned, is antonymy. But lexical opposites . . . are of several different kinds; and it is a moot point just how many dichotomous relations should be held to fall within the scope of 'antonymy'. " I find the following contrastive relations in my data.

binary antonyms - a relation in which the ability to perceive one property or quality in an entity or event absolutely entails the absence of another property or quality in that same entity or event. These opposed properties do not admit of degrees, and exist in the same dimension or frame of relevance. Traditionally, the negation of one form's meaning entails the other form's meaning.

(10)   M: (after finishing a jigsaw puzzle with Bobby)
            'You can tàke it **apàrt** and pùt it bàck in the bóx if you wànt.'
        B: 'Nò, I wànna lèave it **apárt**.'
        M: 'You wànna lèave it togéther?'
        B: 'Yeah.' ('apart' perseverated from previous utterance and
            substituted for 'together'; 'together' and 'apart' are binary antonyms
            of cohesion, since if a puzzle is 'not together' it is 'apart' and vice
            versa; B-92(43) 2;7)

gradable antonyms - a relation between two notions that mark the two ends (poles) of a perceived continuum that has intermediate points. Traditionally, the negation of the word relating to one pole does not entail the meaning of the word referring to the opposite pole; instead it can indicate a point in between.

(11)   OG:'You wànt it **slów**? . . . You wànt it fást?'
            ('slow' substituted for 'fast'; gradable antonyms of speed: if
            something is 'not slow' it is not necessarily 'fast'; OC-29(35) 2;8)

converses - When two forms describe essentially the same conceptual relation between two entities (X & Y) and the only distinction appears to involve the thematic order of presentation of those entities (i.e. one word requires a focus on X before Y, while the other requires an ordering of Y before X), then the two forms are said to be converses of one another. Traditionally, converses are described as an implicational relation such that, for example, 'If X is above Y, then Y is below X'.

(12) B: 'When I'm sixtéen, you can **lèarn** me . . . you can [tʰə̀n] me . . .
         you can <u>tèach</u> me hòw to týpe.'
         ('learn' substituted for 'teach', then the two words are blended;
         converses: in this situation, if mother is 'teaching' Bobby to type,
         Bobby is 'learning' how to type; B-326a(35) and B-326b(38) 4;7)

<u>opposed</u> - This relation presents a vaguer notion of contrast which crosscuts other classes, particularly the classes of co-hyponyms and co-members of a set. The entities referred to by two words may not be opposites in the strict sense, but they may be seen as constituting a pair whose members are thought of as 'contrasting with', or having features which make them 'opposed to' one another. Thus, while 'Daddy' and 'Mommy' not really opposites or antonyms with respect to one another, they do reside on opposite sides of a binary opposition having to do with gender; they are also co-members of the set of family members, and are the adult caretakers (i.e. the named parents). While mainly adjectives, adverbs and prepositions fall into the 'Contrastive Relations' categories, proper nouns, common nouns, and verbs which are not strictly contrastive often show an 'opposed' relationship. Proper nouns show an especially high number of 'opposed' but not 'contrastive' pairings, including 'Bert' vs. 'Ernie', 'Mommy' vs. 'Daddy', 'Anna' vs. 'Alice', and 'Beckie' vs. 'Eileen' (the grandmothers of the three main subjects).

(13) a. B: (thinking of ways to keep warm, wrapping scarf around hands
              while talking) 'I could wràp my scàrf aròund my **féet**.'
          M: 'Your féet?'
          B: 'My <u>hánds</u>!' ('foot' substituted for 'hand', both common nouns,
              in a syntactic location marked for plural; co-partonyms (body
              parts), as well as opposed, since hands and feet are the upper
              and lower ends of the paired limbs, arms vs. legs, and are
              physically similar to each other; B-285(35) 4;5)
      b. Al: (hears a dog barking next door) 'I **sàw** . . . I <u>hèard</u> a púppy!'
              ('see' substituted for 'hear', both verbs, in a syntactic location
              marked for past tense; co-hyponyms of perception, as well as
              opposed, as 'seeing' and 'hearing' are often thought of as the
              two poles of perceptual input; AL-184(35) 3;10)
      c. B: 'Dad, can you pùt some more **chòc** . . . <u>stràwberry</u> mílk in
              hère?' (started to substitute 'chocolate' for 'strawberry', both
              adjectives in this context; co-hyponyms (kinds of flavorings for
              milk), as well as opposed, since these were the only two
              flavorings he used in milk, and he regularly had to choose
              between them; B-215(35) 4;2)

In order to get an accurate picture of the number of errors that included some sort of oppositional relationship, I included in this count of 'opposed', both the error pairs with 'Contrastive Relations' (i.e. binary antonyms, gradable antonyms, and converses) and the error pairs which primarily manifested another relationship (co-hyponyms, co-members of a set, etc.) but in addition had an 'opposed' pairing. Naturally pairs of words that are in a synonymous relationship, or in what I will call 'subsumative' below (i.e. superordinate/subordinate, whole/part, set/member) cannot also be 'opposed', since in both cases the words refer to essentially the same entity or state of affairs. The reasons for including the 'opposed' factor are twofold: first, I found that the adults and children in my study differed markedly on the number of 'opposed' pairs in their errors, and this difference requires an explanation. Second, the inclusion of this factor will turn out to be crucial for comparing my results to the results of other studies of semantic relationships in lexical errors, as will be seen in §5.4 below.

Relations of Synonymy: In this schema, <u>synonyms</u> refer broadly to two words which are essentially referentially or propositionally equivalent, even though they may have various types of more fine-grained differences.

(14) a. OG: (child is hanging by her knees from a bar, Mom has set child's pants on floor under her, but she can't reach them, so she says to Mom)
        '**Brìng** me the pánts. <u>Gét</u> me the pànts, I should sày.'
        (substitution of 'bring' for 'get'; synonyms: activities of transporting objects to someone, but from different perspectives in terms of the speaker, hearer, and location of the pants; OC-124(35) 5;0)

     b. M: 'Do you wànt your **búnny** cùp?'
        Al: 'Yeah, me [ʒʌ.ni] . . . <u>rábbit</u> cùp.' (blend of 'rabbit' and 'bunny'; synonyms: both names for the same animal, but 'bunny' somewhat more informal, 'rabbit' more formal, so stylistic variants; AL-16(38) 2;2)

     c. OB: 'It's tíme to [pʰ ìn] ùp! It's tíme to <u>clèan</u> ùp!'
        (blend of 'clean (up)' and 'pick (up)'; synonyms: activities of tidying up or making things more neat and clean; 'clean up' may have a somewhat broader range of application and can involve such things as washing, sweeping, etc., whereas 'pick up' has a narrower range, referring to putting objects away which are untidily strewn about; however in this case they both referred equally to straightening the crafts area in the preschool; OB-74(38) 3;11)

Arnaud (1999:238) defines these relationships as having 'denotational identity but different patterns of linguistic behavior', for example, different selectional restrictions. Not surprisingly, the 'synonymous' relationship occurred most frequently in blend errors; in substitution errors I have qualified this designation to indicate that they are typically 'quasi-synonyms', as will be discussed in detail below.

Associated Relations: The relations discussed above correspond fairly closely with the basic traditionally-recognized categories. Here I present some other kinds of relations which were also identified in the data. In general, these other associations may be considered, from a lexical-semantic point of view, as more vague, more distant, and less structured relations; but from a conceptual point of view, they are as important for understanding the nature and range of mechanisms of semantic association involved in blends and substitutions.

metonymic - This labels a relation between two words which refer to things that tend to be either spatially contiguous, often by virtue of a functional relation, as in example (15a), or which refer to notions which tend to appear together when discussing a particular scene, as in example (15b). Metonymic relationships were especially common in lexical pairs involved in syntagmatic errors.

(15) a. An: (telling what her imaginary baby is going to eat)
        'Gònna drìnk [bù?] . . . mìlk in my **bóobie**.'
        ('boobie' anticipated/substituted for 'milk'; metonyms: both
        functionally and physically related, as milk is contained in
        'boobies' (breasts); AN-24(41) 2;0)
      b. OG: (telling what her favorite gift would be from Disneyland)
        ' . . . could pròbably be a T̂-shirt with Mìnnie Móuse òn it.
        Or with **Dìsney** Dúck.' (hesitated, looked confused)
        (target is 'Daisy Duck'; 'Disney' substituted for 'Daisy'; 'Disney'
        and 'Daisy' metonymically related as they are usually
        discussed together as part of the Disneyland or Disney cartoon
        scenes; OC-137(35) 5;2)

connotation - Two words related strongly by connotation can be substituted for each other, such as the 'shark/shot' error given in (3a) above. Another type of connotational error occurs when the word for a connotation which is associated with or entailed by a particular notion may enter into a substitution or blend with the word for that notion, as exemplified in (16). Only the children produced errors with this type of semantic relationship.

(16) a. Al: (hugging Anna after she hurt her toe)
        'I'm gìving her a lìttle **lúllaby**.'
        M: 'You're whát?'
        Al: 'I'm gìving her a lìttle lóve.' ('lullaby' substituted for 'love';
        connotational connection between 'lullaby' and 'love', since
        'lullaby' is associated with mother's love, nurturing, caring for
        child; AL-109(35) 3;3)

b. Al: (talking about a new delicate plate)
'It's really [sprɛ.tʃəł] . . . spécial. It's frágile.' (blend of
'special' and 'fragile'; connotational connection, since if
something is 'fragile' it is treated as 'special', i.e. it entails that
it is 'special'; AL-270(38) 5;11)

causal - Two words may refer to concepts that are associated by a link of
causality.

(17)   a. B: 'I hìt . . . I hùrt Hànna and Ahmád.' ('hit' for 'hurt'; he hadn't
hit them but hurt them some other way; 'hit' causes 'hurt';
B-74(35) 2;6)

b. B: (coloring a picture) 'The bèar's gònna *be* réd. Ya knòw whý?
'Cùz I wánt ta bè 'im rèd.'
M: 'What?'
B: 'I wánt ta còlor 'im rèd.' ('be' perseverated, substituted for
'color'; causal relationship, since to 'color' the bear is to cause
him to 'be red'; B-531(43) 5;6)

shared criterial features - This is a residual class of items which are
semantically associated but do not fall neatly into any of the other classes. Pairs
of words assigned to this category can be associated by physical, conceptual, or
functional features.

(18)   a. OA: 'Téll me the nàmes of those Nìnja Túrtles agàin.'
B: 'Nò, nòt yét . . . nòt agáin.' ('yet' substituted for 'again'; 'yet'
and 'again' share the criterial features of indicating temporality;
also opposed; B-193(35) 4;1)

b. M: 'Lòok at all the bìrds *flý*ing abóve us!'
An: 'Àre they thís flỳ?' (holding arms above head)
M: 'What?'
An: 'Àre they thís hìgh?'
('fly' perseverated and substituted for 'high'; 'high' and 'fly' are
related by the criterial feature of 'upness'; AN-279(43) 5;2)

Function Word Distinctions: For errors involving prepositions, interjections,
impersonal pronouns, and auxiliaries, the semantic relationships between the
word pairs all fell into one of the categories given above, as illustrated in (19).

(19)   a. B: (refusing to get dressed in the morning) 'I wànna stày in my
PJs Mom; **befòre** . . . àfter lúnch I'll get drèssed.'
('before' substituted for 'after', both prepositions; converses of
relative time; B-317(36) 4;7)

    b. B: (asked Mom a question, told her what to answer, then asked the same question again; after Mom answered 'correctly', Bobby gushed) '[gra:ʲt]!'
(blend of interjections 'great' [greʲt] and 'right' [raʲt]; synonyms of affirmation; B-365(39) 4;9)

    c. An: 'Thìs is my éye thìng. If **èveryone** . . . if ànyone wànts to pláy wìth it, thèy cán.' ('everyone' substituted for 'anyone', both impersonal pronouns; shared criterial features, indefinite reference; opposed (opposite polarity); AN-117(36) 3;7)

    d. B: (getting diaper changed) 'I [mʌ.stʌ] chánge it.'
(blend of modals 'must' and 'hafta'; synonyms of obligation; B-113(39) 2;9)

However, the personal pronouns present a different situation, since the dimensions of opposition for personal pronouns involve case, person, number, and, in the case of third person pronouns, gender, and thus cannot be classified by the system given above. While 'case' strictly speaking is a syntactic feature, it did occasionally happen that case was violated in a lexical selection error; 'case' is certainly marked as a syntactically relevant property in lemmas, and therefore I assumed it to be one factor affecting the confusability of two lemmas. Two personal pronouns were analyzed as being semantically similar if they shared two or more of these features. In fact it turned out that in all errors involving two personal pronouns, the target/error pronouns shared at least two of these factors, i.e. there were no errors involving, for example, 'I' with 'them'; therefore all personal pronoun errors were considered semantically related.

(20)   a. An: 'Whìch màn did **you** . . . whìch màn did <u>he</u> fìx your báck?'
(pronoun 'you' for 'he'; semantically similar because they share the features of number and case, but differ on person; AN-80(36) 2;10)

    b. Al: 'My Mòm thìnks he's sòrta cúte. But Í thìnk **shè's** . . . <u>hè's</u> réal cùte.' (pronoun 'she' substituted for 'he'; semantically similar because they share features of case, number, and person, but differ on gender; AL-207(36) 4;2)

In all the counts below, I have grouped the semantic relationships into several sub-groupings, which are slightly different from the groupings in which the relationships were just introduced. The first group I have called 'coordinate' relationships, which includes co-hyponyms, co-members of a set, and co-partonyms; in these three semantic categories, the two words represent elements of a scene which have equivalent status in that scene and are of the same level of specificity; e.g. 'apple' and 'orange' are both 'basic level' terms which furnish equivalent portions of the 'fruit' scene. The second group I will call 'subsumative' relationships, and includes superordinate/subordinate, set/member,

---

TABLE 5.1
Classification system for categorizing semantic relationships between target and error words in lexical substitution errors, and the two target words in lexical blend errors.

Coordinate Relations
    Co-Hyponyms
    Co-Members of a Set
    Co-Partonyms

Subsumative Relations
    Superordinate/Subordinate
    Set/Member
    Whole/Part

Contrastive Relations
    Binary Antonyms
    Gradable Antonyms
    Converses

Synonyms

Associated Relationships
    Metonyms
    Connotation
    Causal
    Shared Criterial Features

Personal Pronouns

Opposed
    (crosscuts other categories)

---

and whole/part relationships. In these cases, the element of the scene referred to by one of the words subsumes the other, such that one is subordinate to, or a part of, or a member of the other, and they differ as to level of specificity. The third grouping is the contrastive set, including binary antonyms, gradable antonyms, and converses. The fourth group includes all the variations on synonymous relationships under one heading (i.e. true synonyms and quasi-synonyms). The fifth group includes those relationships which are associated, or more loosely connected from a lexical-semantic point of view, i.e. metonyms, connotation, causal, and shared criterial features. Personal pronouns are listed separately from all other categories. I organized the results of my study into these groupings partially because these sub-divisions fell out of the data when it was being analyzed, i.e. it became apparent that these were the important divisions for explaining patterns of behavior. Furthermore, these sub-divisions map fairly well onto categories used by other researchers in looking at semantic errors, and thus they will be useful in making comparisons to other studies.

Table 5.1 presents the classification system of semantic relationships to be used in the remainder of this chapter, organized by the sub-headings just introduced.

5.2.3 Procedure for Classification

It was quite common that a pair of words could have been classified in several different ways. In order to be able to count the number of errors involving each semantic classification, I assigned each error pair to what I considered to be the most specific classification which I felt confident about; i.e., I assigned it to the classification which showed the 'closest' semantic relationship. My hierarchy for overall semantic 'closeness' is presented and justified in §5.5 below: basically coordinates, synonyms, and contrastives are considered the closest semantic relationship types, followed by subsumatives, and then the three associated types: metonyms, connotation, and causal; the category of shared criterial features is considered the most loosely related category. Within the general class of coordinates, error pairs could fall into more than one of these categories, and so I have considered co-hyponym to be a closer relationship than either co-member of a set or co-partonym. Sub-classifications within the general categories of subsumatives and contrastives are mutually exclusive (e.g. a target/error pair can't be both binary antonyms and converses); within the associated set, if an error could be classed as both shared criterial features and one of the other categories, shared criterial features was considered the less close relationship. Occasionally in the data I have mentioned other classifications which were less specific but which were also appropriate for some particular word pair, but I did not count these less specific relationships into the tables. (In the data there is always an indication of cases where the pair falls into the 'opposed' sub-classification.) The following examples illustrate how two of the errors which were amenable to multiple classification were classified.

(21) a. B: (looking in his backpack for his lunchbox)
              'Is my **báck** . . . is my <u>lúnchbox</u> in hère?'
              (started to substitute 'backpack' for 'lunchbox'; B-445(35) 5;1)
      b. Al: (pointing to a picture of herself putting on shoes and socks)
              'That's mè pùtting on my [ʃáks].'
              (blend of 'shoes' and 'socks'; AL-98(38) 3;2)

In (21a), the two words 'backpack' and 'lunchbox' are metonymically related for Bobby, since his lunchbox is usually physically located in his backpack. They are also co-members of the set of things he takes to school, and they have shared criterial features since they are both containers one opens and puts things into. But they are also co-hyponyms for the child, that is they are both 'kinds of school containers', and since this is the most specific classification, this is how the error was classified. In (21b), 'shoes' and 'socks' are metonymic for Alice since they are worn in physically contiguous locations; they are also co-members of the set of things worn on the feet. But their most specific classification is co-hyponyms, that is 'kinds of clothing (specifically worn on feet)'. Furthermore, since 'shoes and socks' is a common collocation and thus these two items are usually thought of as an opposed pair, this error is also classified as 'opposed'.

5.3 Results

All lexical errors in which the word pair involved was analyzed as having a semantic relationship were included in the counts to be reported in this section. The specific types of errors examined include the following: 1) paradigmatic lexical substitution errors involving both content and function words (Classes 35, 36, 36.5); 2) paradigmatic lexical blend errors involving both content and function words (Classes 38, 39, 40); 3) syntagmatic lexical substitution errors, including anticipations, perseverations, and reversals of content and function words (Classes 41, 43, 45, 46), excluding metathesis, interrupted metathesis, and multiple errors. I will present the results here first in terms of data set, then age, then error type, and finally by lexical category. In §5.4 I will compare my results to those of other studies of both adult and child lexical errors.

5.3.1 Semantic Relationships by Data Set

Table 5.2 shows the number of semantically related lexical errors which displayed each type of semantic relationship, organized by data set. At the bottom of this table, after the total number of errors in each column is given, there is a line labelled 'opposed'. This represents the number of errors for each data set which contained the 'opposed' feature, including all the contrastive errors as well as those which were tabulated under one of the other categories, but also had an 'oppositional' meaning, as discussed in the preceding section. So, for example, Bobby produced 32 errors labelled as 'opposed'; of these, 9 were of the 'contrastive' types (antonyms, converses), and the other 23 were classified as some other basic semantic relationship category, but also contained an oppositional component. The percentage of 'opposed' errors was calculated from the total number of errors in this table, minus the 'personal pronoun' errors, since personal pronouns were not considered eligible for participation in this opposition. So, Bobby's 32 'opposed' errors are 32% of 99 (total 111 minus the 12 pronoun errors).

From Table 5.2 it is evident that there were no overwhelming differences among the various subjects in the study. For all data sets, the largest percentage of errors fell into the coordinate group, with co-hyponyms being the most numerous type of relationship, followed by co-members of a set. For the children overall, the coordinate group represented 39% of the errors, and for the adults, 33.5%. (Differences between the child and adult data will be discussed in §5.3.2 below.) The associated category is the next most frequent in all data sets (overall 25% for the children, 28% for the adults), with shared criterial features and metonyms being the most common of these classes. For the children, synonyms (11%) and personal pronoun errors (12%) were of medium frequency, whereas subsumative (6%) and contrastive (7%) errors were the least frequent categories in most data sets. For the adults, synonyms were very frequent (21.5%), but the other three categories showed low numbers: personal pronouns (3%), subsumatives (9%), and contrastives (5%).

There seem to be some individual differences among the three main subjects

TABLE 5.2
Number of lexical errors with each type of semantic relationship, and percentage of each major division of semantic relationships; by data set. (Percentage of 'opposed' pairs calculated from total, excluding personal pronoun numbers.)

Data Set :	Anna	Alice	Bobby	Other	Total	Adult
Coordinates						
Co-Hyponyms	9	10	33	13	65	53
Co-Memb. Set	4	3	13	9	29	12
Co-Partonyms	2	0	3	3	8	5
N=	**15**	**13**	**49**	**25**	**102**	**70**
	31%	33.5%	44%	41%	39%	33.5%
Subsumatives						
Superord./Subord.	0	1	5	2	8	9
Set/Member	1	0	1	0	2	3
Whole/Part	1	0	1	3	5	7
N=	**2**	**1**	**7**	**5**	**15**	**19**
	4%	2.5%	6%	8%	6%	9%
Contrastives						
Binary Antonyms	0	2	2	1	5	5
Gradable Antonyms	0	2	4	3	9	2
Converses	1	0	3	0	4	4
N=	**1**	**4**	**9**	**4**	**18**	**11**
	2%	10%	8%	6.5%	7%	5%
Synonyms	**7**	**7**	**11**	**4**	**29**	**45**
	15%	18%	10%	6.5%	11%	21.5%
Associated						
Metonyms	6	7	6	3	22	16
Connotation	1	2	2	0	5	0
Causal	0	0	3	1	4	2
Shared Criterial Feat.	9	1	12	11	33	39
N=	**16**	**10**	**23**	**15**	**64**	**57**
	33%	26%	21%	25%	25%	28%
Personal Pronouns	**7**	**4**	**12**	**8**	**31**	**7**
	15%	10%	11%	13%	12%	3%
Total N=	**48**	**39**	**111**	**61**	**259**	**209**
'opposed'	4	9	32	9	54	26
	10%	26%	32%	17%	24%	13%

which may be due to their differences along the 'referential/expressive' dimension. The expressive child, Anna, has the largest percentage of more loosely related associated errors (33%) and personal pronoun errors (15%), whereas the more referential children, Alice and Bobby, show lower percentages of the less closely related errors (26% and 21%) and personal pronoun errors (10% and 11%). On the other hand, Anna produced the fewest 'opposed' errors (10%) compared to Bobby (32%) and Alice (26%); this dimension seems to be more important in organizing the referential children's lexicons. Nevertheless, there is enough general consistency among the four child data sets that it is likely these figures represent a true difference in relative frequency among semantic relationship types; thus we can feel confident about grouping the four data sets into a single pool, to look at the contribution of other factors such as age and lexical category to the pattern of semantic relationships in the errors.

5.3.2 Semantic Relationships by Age

Table 5.3 presents the same set of data as Table 5.2, but in this case the errors are organized by age. I have divided the 1-2-year-old data into the 1-2a (1-word and 2-word stages) and 1-2b (3+word) categories, to see if the semantic relationships involved in these errors shift when the children begin producing syntactically structured utterances.

Overall, the children's figures are similar to the adults' at every age except 1-2a. At all ages, coordinate semantic relationships are the most common types; the overall figure for the children is 39%, and for the adults, 33.5%. At every age except 1-2a this is due to a preponderance of co-hyponym errors, but at age 1-2a the most frequent type is co-members of a set. At all ages the associated errors are the next most frequent (25% overall for the children, 28% for the adults). For the younger children this is due to metonymic errors being quite frequent, but by age 3 the shared criterial feature errors become more common, and they are very frequent for the children ages 4-5, and in adult errors. There are no subsumative errors at age 1-2a; the first error of this type occurred at age 2;6 (see (5c) above, discussed below). Subsumative errors continue to be comparatively rare at all ages; the adults produced a slightly larger percentage of this type overall than did the children (child 6%, adult 9%). The 1-2a children produced no errors with the contrastive relationship. These began to be produced at age 2;2; however the earliest contrastive errors involved influence from the previous utterances. Pure contrastive errors with no utterance or environmental influences begin to occur around age 2;8; contrastive errors continued to be infrequent throughout the age span, but the children produced slightly more of this type of error overall than did the adults (child 7%, adult 5%).

The 1-2a children produced no errors involving synonyms. Note that this was not a function of age but of linguistic stage, since Anna produced synonym errors at age 1;10 (blend of 'rabbit/ bunny', AN-16(38) 1;10), and Bobby at 1;11 (blend of 'Bobby/Robert', B-30(38) 1;11), when they were both in the 3+word stage. The children's rate of synonym errors was at its highest at ages 1-2b and 3, and then declined somewhat towards age 5. Overall the child synonym rate

TABLE 5.3
Number of lexical errors with each type of semantic relationship, and percentage of each major division of semantic relationships; by age. (Percentage of 'opposed' pairs calculated from total, excluding personal pronoun numbers.)

Age:	1-2a	1-2b	3	4	5	Total	Adult
Coordinates							
Co-Hyponyms	2	14	13	20	16	65	53
Co-Memb. Set	7	8	2	3	9	29	12
Co-Partonyms	1	0	0	6	1	8	5
N=	**10**	**22**	**15**	**29**	**26**	**102**	**70**
	71.5%	41%	33.3%	37%	38%	39%	33.5%
Subsumatives							
Superord./Subord.	0	1	4	2	1	8	9
Set/Member	0	0	0	2	0	2	3
Whole/Part	0	0	0	3	2	5	7
N=	**0**	**1**	**4**	**7**	**3**	**15**	**19**
		2%	9%	9%	4.5%	6%	9%
Contrastives							
Binary Antonyms	0	2	1	2	0	5	5
Gradable Antonyms	0	3	1	5	0	9	2
Converses	0	0	0	3	1	4	4
N=	**0**	**5**	**2**	**10**	**1**	**18**	**11**
		9%	4.4%	13%	1.5%	7%	5%
Synonyms	**0**	**9**	**6**	**8**	**6**	**29**	**45**
		17%	13.3%	10%	9%	11%	21.5%
Associated							
Metonyms	4	8	4	1	5	22	16
Connotation	0	2	1	1	1	5	0
Causal	0	1	0	1	2	4	2
Shared Criterial Feat.	0	1	5	10	17	33	39
N=	**4**	**12**	**10**	**13**	**25**	**64**	**57**
	28.5%	22%	22%	17%	37%	25%	28%
Personal Pronouns	**0**	**5**	**8**	**11**	**7**	**31**	**7**
		9%	18%	14%	10%	12%	3%
Total N=	**14**	**54**	**45**	**78**	**68**	**259**	**209**
'opposed'	4	11	9	22	8	54	26
	28.5%	22.5%	24.5%	33%	13%	24%	13%

was half that of the adult rate (child 11%, adult 21.5%). The children also produced no personal pronoun errors at age 1-2a; they produced a few at 1-2b, and then the rate increased at age 3 and remained moderately common throughout the age span, dropping slightly at age 5. Overall the children produced many more personal pronoun errors than did the adults (child 12%, adult 3%). Finally, the children produced a fairly high rate of opposed errors (24% overall), which was nearly twice the percentage of the adults (13%); again the child rate dropped off considerably at age 5.

These data provide a rich source of evidence regarding the child's developing knowledge about semantic relationships. At age 1-2a, the children have a fairly small vocabulary, which consists mostly of concrete content words which they use to label the most clearly evident entities and actions involved in the basic scenes which they encounter in their lives. Therefore the simplest lexical substitution or blend errors involve words which label two distinct elements of a scene which are of equivalent specificity (i.e. one does not subsume the other), and which are either two of the same kind of entity, i.e. coordinates, or are usually found together in that scene, i.e. metonyms. The fact that the children's errors at this point involve extremely concrete associations between concepts is shown by their large number of errors involving co-members of a set, such as 'Bert/Ernie', 'Mommy/Daddy', 'toothpaste/toothbrush' (rather than co-hyponyms, which can have a slightly more abstract relationship to each other because they are not necessarily found together in a typical scene, but are the same 'kinds of' things). Furthermore, most of the errors at this age were supported either by some influence from the preceding utterance, as illustrated in (22a), by the physical environment as in (22b), or by a common linguistic collocation, as in the 'Bert/Ernie' blend, where the phrase 'Bert and Ernie' was very common for the child (see example (2) above; B-2(38) 1;8).

(22)   a. B: '*Tóe* hùrts.'
            M: 'You gòt a? *ówie?*'
            B: '[tǽ.wi] . . . ówie.'
                (blend of 'toe' and 'owie', both appropriate in the context;
                metonyms: 'owie' (a sore or cut) is located on the 'toe'; both
                targets spoken in preceding utterances; B-5(38) 1;9)
        b. B: (on toilet, looks down) '[pá.tʌç]'
                (blend of 'potty' and 'penis'; both referents visible; metonyms:
                'penis' is source of urination, 'potty' is goal; B-12(38) 1;9)

Thus the errors at age 1-2a show very concrete semantic relationships based on the child's conceptual knowledge of particular scenes which are common in everyday life.

Several things change during the 1-2b age range. From the growing diversity of semantic relationships involved in these errors, it is apparent that the children are now able to do a more fine-grained analysis of the scenes or frames they encounter in their lives, and have developed a richer vocabulary for expressing more elements of the scenes. This includes beginning to acquire more than one word that can refer to the same entity or state of affairs; this allows them to make errors involving synonyms, as well as facilitating the subsumative errors, since they may now have a more general and more specific word for the same referent. The earliest errors involving synonyms were the blend errors discussed above that involved 'rabbit/bunny' (AN-16(38) 1;10 and AL-16(38) 2;2, given in (14b) above), and 'Robert/Bobby' (B-30(38) 1;11). The earliest lexical substitution errors involving synonyms were made early in the second year: 'talk (to)/call' AN-47(35) 2;4), and 'open/blow up' (AN-55(35) 2;7); these errors will be discussed in §5.3.3 and §5.4 below as actually being 'quasi-synonyms'. The earliest superordinate/subordinate error was the blend of 'egg' (subordinate) and 'one' (superordinate) (B-80(38) 2;6), given as (5c) above.

Also during the 1-2b stage, children learned more words relating to qualities of objects and events, and thus added adjectives and adverbs to their vocabularies. Since contrastive relations are very common for adjectives and adverbs, the children began producing more contrastive errors during this stage. The earliest contrastive error was a blend of the adjectives 'cold/hot' (Al-12(38), 2;2); however, as mentioned above, the earliest contrastive errors usually involved some environmental or utterance influence. Pure contrastive errors with no external influences became common around age 2;8, for example the substitution of the adverb 'slow' for 'fast' given in (11) above (OC-29(35) 2;8).

As the children learned a broader vocabulary for referencing more details of a scene, as well as gaining a more detailed understanding of the elements and relationships within scenes, they developed a wider range of associated types of relationships among words. While metonymic relationships were the only associated types found in the 1-2a age range, the 1-2b children produced all four types of associated relationships, even though metonyms continued to predominate. The earliest causal error occurred at age 2;6, involving 'hit/hurt' (B-74(35) 2;6, (17a) above); the earliest connotation error was Bobby's substitution of 'scary' for 'owie' (B-94(35) 2;7), and the earliest shared criterial features error involved 'always/already' at age 2;7 (B-90(35) 2;7).

Finally, the 1-2b children were learning more function words to express relationships among entities in the frames, and thus they began to produce more errors involving function words. The earliest semantically related function word errors were substitution errors involving pronouns ('she/he', honors person, number and case; B-86a(36) 2;6), and prepositions ('for/off', binary antonyms of source/goal; AL-55(36) 2;10). The earliest semantically related function word blend occurred at age 2;9, and was a blend of the auxiliaries 'must' and 'hafta' (synonyms of obligation; B-113(39) 2;9, (19d) above).

The figures for the children ages 3-5 are quite similar across the age ranges. The coordinate errors continued to make up 33.3%-38% of the relationships in lexical errors, with co-hyponyms predominating at every age; co-members of a set were less common than co-hyponyms, and co-partonyms were uncommon at all ages. The subsumative errors remained scarce (4.5%-9%). Contrastive errors show a somewhat odd pattern; they were relatively common at age 4 (13%), but then dropped off substantially at age 5 (1.5%); this is probably due to limitations of the data, but could reflect a real trend towards the adult lower figures. The percentage of errors involving synonyms tapered off slightly over the three years (from 13.3%-9%), which is again somewhat odd since the adults produced twice the percentage of errors involving synonyms as the children, so it would have been expected that synonym errors would increase. Errors involving associated relationships were quite common (17%-37%), but errors involving shared criterial features became more frequent than metonyms at age 3, and continued to be more frequent at ages 4-5, moving in the direction of adults' very frequent number of shared criterial feature errors.   Clearly as children's vocabularies increased, the possibility of having one word cause the activation of a variety of other words with only a loose semantic relationship increased greatly.

Finally, the adult figures reflect their very sophisticated understanding of the various scenes in their world, and the elaborate vocabulary they have for talking about those scenes. They produced a smaller percentage of coordinates than the children did (33.5% adult, 39% child); their coordinate errors predominately involved co-hyponyms, which, as mentioned above, is a relatively more abstract relationship than co-members of a set, a relationship which is more common in the child than the adult errors. The adults produced relatively more subsumative errors, as they undoubtedly have a greater understanding of taxonomic relationships than the children, and know that entities can be referred to with a variety of levels of specificity. They produced slightly fewer contrastive errors than the children; an explanation will be given below in the context of 'opposed' errors. They produced a much higher percentage of synonym errors than the children, reflecting the fact that they have many more words with overlapping meanings eligible for misselection. The adults also produced a higher percentage of associated errors, which were predominately the shared criterial feature type, again attesting to their greater vocabulary and greater range of possible semantic associations. Finally, the adults produced very few personal pronoun errors, which is not surprising given the many years of practice that adults have had in accurately selecting pronouns from this relatively small, closed set of words.

One interesting difference between the adults and children is that the children produced many more 'opposed' errors than the adults; this included both pairs with a contrastive relationship (antonyms, converses), and those with some other relationship where the two referents are seen to be an oppositional pair. As mentioned above, these oppositional pairs were very common in proper noun errors (e.g. 'Bert/Ernie', 'Mommy/Daddy', 'Beckie/Eileen', 'BobBob/Beckie', 'Longs/Luckys', 'Todd/Copper'), but also occurred in many other lexical categories: common nouns 'feet/hands', 'husband/wife', 'shoes/socks'; verbs 'see/hear', 'eat/drink', 'write/read'; adjectives 'chocolate/strawberry', 'hungry/thirsty'; adverbs 'yet/again', 'yet/always'. One possible explanation for the frequency of such oppositions in the child errors could be that such oppositions are very important for the children in terms of setting up an organization within the lexicon, or perhaps within their worlds. In a very general sense, one of the first tasks the child faces in making sense out of the world is to learn to make distinctions between objects and events which they encounter in their environments. Putting this into a Jakobsonian framework (Jakobson 1941/ 1986), one could argue that the child is predisposed to make binary distinctions between objects, events, or percepts which are very similar to each other and differ in only one feature (see also the Lyons 1977 quote in §5.2.2 above). Perhaps for the child, selecting pairs of very similar objects to focus on and then making a distinction between the two is an important developmental phenomenon, given the child's limited attentional capabilities (J-P. Koenig, p.c.)

As seen in the lexical errors, at first the entities referred to with 'opposed' pairs of words are functionally, conceptually, or environmentally related to each other in some sort of oppositional pair (like 'Bert/Ernie' who are functionally and physically related in the "Sesame Street" scene), and in many cases these terms are also spoken together in very frequent collocations: 'Bert and Ernie', 'Mommy and Daddy', 'shoes and socks', 'husband and wife'. Eventually oppositions are set up between entities which are usually not found together in the same scene, but whose relationship is more abstract, such as 'Beckie/Eileen', the children's two grandmothers, who are rarely encountered together but who are co-hyponyms, related by the abstract concept of 'grandmother'; or 'Longs/Luckys', two stores that the children frequently went to, but which were not physically contiguous, so they were co-hyponyms of 'kinds of stores' and opposed because they were the two main stores regularly frequented. Thus it seems that the children's early very concrete oppositional pairs of concepts allowed these pairs of words to become associated with each other in the lexicon in an oppositional relationship, and then this type of relationship was used later on to help organize more abstract relationships into orderly pairs of words. And, as pointed out in §5.3.1 above, this organizing principle was more important for the two referential children than for the expressive child, since Anna produced a much lower rate of 'opposed' errors than either Alice or Bobby. The fact that 'opposed' pairs reached their peak at age 4, and began to drop off at age 5 suggests that the 5-year-olds are being somewhat freed up from this oppositional heuristic which seems very strong at earlier ages. This may seem contradictory to the claim that children in word association tasks rarely answer with an antonym, while this is a very common response for adults. But this simply highlights the fact that the skills needed to perform the metalinguistic task of word association do not necessarily tap into the fundamental organization of the child's lexicon.

In sum, the types of semantic relationships involved in the children's errors begin as a very few, simple, conceptually-based relationships (co-members of a set, metonyms), most often supported by some environmental or utterance influence, and very often involving an oppositional pair of words referring to a pair of entities which are salient in the child's world. However, even at age 1-2b, the types of semantic relationships begin to expand, as the children are able to identify and understand more elements of the scenes in their environment, and develop more lexical frames for talking about the entities, actions, qualities, and relationships in these scenes. They begin to realize that individual entities can be referred to in more than one way, and they begin to build somewhat abstract relationships among entities, such as 'banana is a kind of fruit'. From ages 3-5 the overall figures for relative proportions of different types of relationships are similar between the children and adults, except that the adults continue to produce more errors involving synonyms, subsumatives, and shared criterial features than the children, due to their more elaborate and fine-grained vocabularies.

5.3.3 Semantic Relationships by Error Type

I have suggested above that different kinds of semantic relationships might be more likely to occur in different types of lexical errors, given the locus of this error during processing. In order to test this hypothesis I counted the number of error pairs with each type of semantic relationship in four categories separately, using the same numbering system for the error types as given in Chapter 4: I=paradigmatic content word substitutions; II=paradigmatic function word substitutions; III=word blends (content+function combined); IV-VI=syntagmatic substitutions (anticipations, perseverations, and exchanges). I omitted metathesis errors (including interrupted metatheses), and multiple errors. The results are given in Table 5.4.

This table makes it very clear that indeed the semantic relationships between error pairs follow different patterns depending on the type of error. There also seem to be a few differences between the adult and child patterns, although overall they are very similar.

In lexical substitution errors involving content words, the largest percentage of errors for both the children and adults involve the coordinate types (61% child, 51% adult), followed by the associated types (24% child, 27% adult). The other three types of relationships, subsumative, contrastive, and synonyms, all fall in the lower percentages for both children and adults (from 3.5%-9%). This shows that when a speaker is planning an utterance and has begun to activate the set of lexical items relevant to the concepts in the proposition, this activation is most likely to spread to other lexical items which are related to the target lexical items by sharing a number of semantic features and sharing values on these features (e.g. both are [+animate, +human]), and also being at the same level of specificity as required by the discourse-pragmatic context. Thus the speaker's task is to choose among competing co-hyponyms, co-members of a set, words with shared criterial features, etc. in order to be able to accurately frame the intended proposition. Contrastives are less likely to be activated because their meanings are at odds with the intended proposition, as illustrated in (23). Most

TABLE 5.4

Number of lexical errors with each type of semantic relationship, and percentage of each major division of semantic relationships; by error class (see text). Child 'C' compared to Adult 'A' figures.

Class:	I		II		III		IV-VI	
	C	A	C	A	C	A	C	A
Coordinate								
Co-Hyponyms	44	40	0	0	17	10	4	3
Co-Memb. Set	19	8	1	0	5	2	4	2
Co-Partonyms	6	4	0	0	1	1	1	0
N=	**69**	**52**	**1**	**0**	**23**	**13**	**9**	**5**
	61%	51%	3%		33.3%	19%	21%	17%
Subsumative								
Superord./Subord.	4	4	0	0	3	4	1	1
Set/Member	0	2	0	0	0	1	2	0
Whole/Part	2	3	0	0	1	2	2	2
N=	**6**	**9**	**0**	**0**	**4**	**7**	**5**	**3**
	5.5%	9%			6%	10%	11.5%	10.5%
Contrastive								
Binary Ant.	1	0	2	4	0	0	2	1
Gradable Ant.	4	1	1	0	1	1	3	0
Converses	2	4	1	0	1	0	0	0
N=	**7**	**5**	**4**	**4**	**2**	**1**	**5**	**1**
	6%	5%	11.5%	44.5%	3%	1.5%	11.5%	3.5%
Synonyms	**4**	**8**	**1**	**0**	**23**	**37**	**1**	**0**
	3.5%	8%	3%		33.3%	53.5%	2.3%	
Associated								
Metonyms	5	6	0	0	8	0	9	10
Connotation	4	0	0	0	1	0	0	0
Causal	3	1	0	0	0	0	1	1
SCF	15	21	8	0	7	11	3	7
N=	**27**	**28**	**8**	**0**	**16**	**11**	**13**	**18**
	24%	27%	23.5%		23%	16%	30.3%	62%
Personal Pronoun	**0**	**0**	**20**	**5**	**1**	**0**	**10**	**2**
			59%	55.5%	1.4%		23.3%	7%
Total N=	**113**	**102**	**34**	**9**	**69**	**69**	**43**	**29**
'opposed'	34	17	6	4	7	4	7	1
	30%	17%	43%	100%	10%	6%	21%	4%

contrastive errors involved either adjectives or adverbs, since this is the type of lexical item that is most likely to have an antonym or converse in the lexicon (lexical categories will be discussed in detail in §5.3.4 below). Several contrastive errors also involved some sort of environmental or discourse influence, as in (23b).

(23)   a.   OB: (child is getting into bed with his socks on, which is unusual)
               'I dòn't néed còvers; my fèet are **cóld** . . . my fèet are <u>àlready</u>
               <u>wárm</u>.' ('cold' for 'warm', with 'already' added into correction;
               OC-77(35) 3;11)
       b.   OG: (explaining a cartoon in which a pup jumps down onto an
               object which is rising up) 'The pùp jùmped on tòp of the òne
               that came **dówn** . . . <u>úp</u>.' ('down' for 'up; OC-118(35) 4;9)

In (23a), the child substitutes the adjective 'cold' for 'warm'; this could almost be argued to be a propositional rather than a lexical error. In (23b) the adverb 'down' is substituted for 'up'; this was probably facilitated by the fact that in the scene being described, the pup is jumping down while the object rises up.

True synonymic lexical substitution errors would be nearly impossible to detect, since if a speaker substituted one synonym for another, the hearer would have no way of knowing that the speaker did not intend the spoken word, unless a correction was made (see Levelt 1989:220 for a similar point). For the most part, the substitution errors which I have analyzed as involving synonyms in fact involve two words which refer to the same entity, action, or quality, except that each is relevant to a different set of selectional restrictions. For the children, most synonym lexical substitution errors involved verbs, whereas the adult synonymic errors mainly involved nouns and adjectives.

(24)   a.   An: (handing Mom a balloon) '**Ópen** thìs.' (looks confused)
               M: 'Do whát?'
               An: '<u>Blòw</u> it <u>úp</u>!' ('open' for 'blow up'; AN-55(35) 2;7)
       b.   AM: (asking about avocados) 'Wère they **dóne** enòugh?'
               ('done' for 'ripe'; AD-459(35))

In (24a), the child asks Mom to 'open' her balloon; but she realizes that when referring to an outward expansion 'opening up' type event involving balloons, the correct verb is 'blow up' rather than 'open', which would be more appropriate for books, presents, etc. Similarly, in (24b), the adult asks if the avocados are 'done'; however, when referring to reaching maturity or readiness in the context of avocados, 'ripe' is the correct word. 'Done' would be more appropriate for food being cooked, for example. So, in all the lexical substitution errors classified as 'synonyms', in fact the words typically stand in a quasi-synonymous relationship which violates some requirement of selectional restrictions. It is not surprising that occasionally during speech production planning, such quasi-synonymic words are activated in the lexicon in the wrong context, due to their sharing of criterial semantic features. I will present a more detailed discussion of synonyms and quasi-synonyms in §5.4 below.

Finally, errors of the subsumative type are rare in paradigmatic lexical substitution errors, probably because they, by definition, violate the specificity with which the speaker intends to refer to the entity or action involved. Furthermore, as with synonyms, it is difficult to tell when a speaker has accidentally substituted a more general for a more specific term, because if the more general term conveys the proposition in a meaningful way, the hearer would not necessarily know that this was not the intended word; this is particularly true for superordinate/subordinate pairs. The errors which I have placed into this category were most typically ones where the speakers corrected from the more general term to the more specific one, particularly when they sensed that the general term, while not incorrect, would not convey the intended content. This type of error occurred only with nouns and verbs.

(25)   a. OG: 'Mommy, I wànt some **cér** . . . I wànt some Lífe.'
          (began to substitute 'cereal' for 'Life', which is a kind of cereal;
          OC-54(35) 3;6)
       b. B: (after bath, handing Mom a towel)
          'Còuld you **pùt** me . . . wràp me úp in thìs?'
          ('put' for 'wrap'; 'wrap' is a kind of 'putting'; B-147(35) 3;8)
       c. AM: 'This was clèarly a schóol-àge **chìld** . . . a schóol-àge gìrl.'
          ('child' for 'girl'; a 'girl' is a kind of 'child'; AD-375(35))

In (25a), the child wants a specific type of cereal, so amends her request to indicate the subordinate 'Life'; otherwise she might not have received the cereal she wanted. In (25b), Bobby uses the generic 'put', and then corrects to the more specific 'wrap', appropriate for towels; this error could also have been a phrase blend with 'put this towel on/around me'. In (25c), the adult had some reason to want to specify the gender of the child he was talking about, so corrected from the superordinate 'child' to the more specific 'girl'. I will also discuss subsumatives in more detail in §5.4.

In general, then, paradigmatic content word substitution errors most typically involved two lexical items with a coordinate or associated semantic relationship, at the same level of specificity, as these are the most likely to be activated during the compilation of the basic set of words to be used in the proposition. The adult and child errors follow the same general patterns.

In contrast, the adults and children show somewhat different patterns in the semantic relationships involved in paradigmatic function word substitutions. Both the child and adult errors in this category involved contrastive relationships in greater proportions than for content word substitutions; but the children also produced a number of shared criterial features pairs, which the adults did not. Furthermore, the children produced 20 substitution errors involving pronouns, to the adults' 5. In fact there are only 9 adult errors total in Category II, compared to 34 child errors, once again attesting to the greater control adults have over function words in general. Specifically, adults are much better at selecting the appropriate pronouns on-line, given the demands of the discourse-pragmatic context and the identity of the entities to be referred to pronominally.

For both adults and children, the error pairs involved in contrastive relationships in Class II were almost entirely prepositions, as illustrated in (26).

(26)   a. Al: 'Hére it ìs Mòmmy. I gòt it **fòr** my . . . **òff** my béd.'
         ('for' for 'off', binary antonyms in terms of goal vs. source;
         AL-55(36) 2;10)
        b. B: 'I wànna stày in my P̂Js Mòm; **befòre** . . . àfter lúnch I'll get
         drèssed.'
         ('before' for 'after', converses of relative time; B-317(36) 4;7)
        c. AF: 'Kitty, I'm gònna stép on yòu if yòu kèep gètting **behínd** mè,
         uh in frónt of mè.' ('behind' for 'in front of', binary antonyms of
         location relative to speaker; AD-482(36))

In Chapter 4 (§4.1.2) I mentioned that prepositions sometimes show properties of content words, and this is a case in point. These prepositions participate in the same types of contrastive relationships that are typical of adjectives and adverbs, and some prepositions are homophonous with adverbs (e.g. 'behind', 'down'); they are also more numerous than most other 'closed class' words. Prepositions are also closely linked to nouns and verbs, in that the selectional restrictions of particular nouns and verbs will require specific prepositions to occur in phrases being constructed based on these nouns or verbs. So while I have analyzed prepositions as function words in this study, and have claimed that function words are closely linked to syntax, this is obviously an oversimplification in the case of prepositions, and the semantic relationships between prepositions which are involved in SOTs attest to their more concrete lexical properties.

The one type of relationship which occurs in the children's paradigmatic function word errors which does not occur in the adults' is error pairs with shared criterial features. This type of semantic relationship occurred in child errors involving a wide range of function word types, including impersonal pronouns ('everyone/anyone', AN-117(36) 3;7), question words ('what/where', AN-120(36) 3;8), interjections ('hi/thanks', AN-175(36) 4;4), modals ('should/could', OC-154(36) 5;7), and prepositions ('by/with', OC-143(36) 5;4). This type of error suggests that the children's representations for these function words may not be as detailed as the adults', so that misselection due to vague resemblances are more likely. Another possible explanation is that the children's syntactic templates are less specific in terms of which function words are required for some construction. Either way, the fact that there were no adult errors of this type shows that with practice, these looser relationships have less of an effect on lexical selection of function words.

In paradigmatic lexical blend errors, the most common semantic relationship for the adults was synonyms; for the children, synonyms were as frequent as coordinates. The frequency of synonyms is what is expected, given the definition of lexical blends: if two lexical items are competing for the same slot in the utterance, then the most likely situation will be that the two words will convey nearly the same meaning. And in the case of blends, the synonyms are most often true synonyms, with in some cases only a difference in formality level; there are fewer of the quasi-synonyms which were found in lexical substitution errors. This includes word pairs from nearly every lexical category: common nouns such as 'bunny/rabbit' (AN-16(38) 1;10 and AL-16(38) 2;2); proper nouns, 'Father/Poppa' (B-116(38) 2;10); verbs, 'like/want' (AL-93(38) 3;1 and B-150(38) 3;8); adjectives, 'darling/adorable' (AN-325(38) 5;11); adverbs, 'straight/flat' (Al-158(38) 3;8); auxiliary verbs, 'must/hafta' (B-113(39) 2;9); prepositions, 'before/in front of' (B-319(39) 4;7); and interjections, 'great/ right' (B-365(39) 4;9).

Other types of semantic relationships were for the most part less common in blends, although the adults showed more of a preponderance of synonyms than did the children (33.3% child, 53.5% adult). For the children, relationships of coordination were as common as synonyms (33.3%), but for the adults less so (19%). This may be due to the adults' larger vocabularies, having more synonyms to choose from, or it may be due to the children having less practice in uniquely selecting among lexical entries which have close semantic ties (e.g. co-hyponyms) although only one of the words is in fact appropriate for the proposition being formulated. Similarly, the children produced a fairly large number of errors involving metonymic relationships and shared criterial features, which were less common for the adults. The metonymic errors were often facilitated by the fact that one or both of the targets had been spoken in a preceding utterance; recall that these are classified as blends rather than as syntagmatic errors because either of the two words involved in the blend would have been appropriate and grammatical in the error utterance.

(27)   D: 'I'm gonna put some *crèam* on your *ówie*.'
       B: '[**ká.wi**] . . . ówie.' (blend of 'cream' [kim] and 'owie' [ʔá.wi],
          metonyms: the cream is on the owie; B-23(38) 1;10)

Metonymic relationships were very common in syntagmatic errors in general, for reasons which will be discussed below.

For both children and adults, contrastive relationships were very rare in lexical blends. Logically, it should be rare by definition that a speaker would activate a word and its opposite, and then would not be able to uniquely select one of them, given that the contrastive word would be directly at odds with the intention of the proposition. The child contrastive blends involved one error where the two target words 'cold' and 'hot' had both been spoken in the preceding utterance (AL-12(38) 2;2), and one blend of the converses 'teach/learn' (B-326b(38) 4;7); the adults also produced one blend of 'cold/hot' (AD-541(38)).

The blend errors involving subsumative relationships are particularly interesting. As with the substitution errors, they usually involved the speaker activating two words relevant to the same entity or action with different levels of specificity, and then not being able to uniquely select one or the other of the candidates. All of the child errors of this sort involved nouns, but the adult errors involved nouns, verbs, and adjectives.

(28)   a. Al: 'I wànt my [lá.ni].' (blend of 'leopard' and 'Johnny', the name
          of her toy leopard; AL-217(38) 4;5)
       b. AM: 'We should gò out to Tárget, and [gàʲ] òne of those bíg ònes.'
          (blend of 'get' and 'buy'; AD-533(38))
       c. AF: 'I've gòt to get [rést].'
          (blend of 'ready' and 'dressed'; AD-538(38))

In (28a) Alice blended the superordinate common noun 'leopard', with the subordinate proper name for her particular stuffed leopard, 'Johnny'. This is akin to Alice's earlier error where she blended the proper name 'Grandpa' with the deictic pronoun 'that' to refer to a tape of Grandpa's band (AL-51(40) 2;9); while 'that' and 'Grandpa' are not strictly speaking semantically related, the error was most likely caused by Alice not being able to resolve the level of specificity with which she wanted to refer to the tape. The adults produced no blend errors of this sort involving pronouns, although they did produce one substitution of 'they' for 'the FBI' (AD-490(36.5)). In (28b), the adult introspected that he was thinking of the verbs 'get', the superordinate, and 'buy', the subordinate, since 'buying' is a specific kind of 'getting'. In (28c), the adult speaker was thinking about getting 'ready' to go out (adjective); one member of the set of things involved in getting 'ready' is getting 'dressed', so this was counted as a 'set/member' error. It is interesting that the adults produced a slightly larger proportion of this type of subsumative error than did the children; this was also true in the lexical substitution errors. This is most likely due to their larger vocabularies and more sophisticated knowledge of taxonomic, set/member, and whole/part type relationships, but it also shows that even adults can slip up when trying to resolve the level of specificity appropriate for the discourse-pragmatic context when referring to a particular entity.

The final category, syntagmatic errors (Classes IV, V, VI) show much more variety of semantic relationships than any other type of error. This is undoubtedly due to the fact that any two words planned for the same utterance, or planned for a subsequent utterance following the source utterance, could be in pretty much any possible semantic relationship with each other. The only exception to this is that it is unlikely that two synonyms would be planned for the same utterance, as this would make the utterance redundant; and indeed, the children produced one such error involving 'pick up/put away' (B-124(43) 3;1) and the adults none. The most common semantic relationships in syntagmatic errors were the associated types, particularly metonyms. This is not surprising since two entities typically found in a contiguous relationship in a scene, or functionally related in a particular scene, are quite likely to be activated together in an utterance discussing that scene. Metonymic relationships in syntagmatic lexical errors occurred in anticipations, perseverations, and exchanges, and almost exclusively involved nouns.

(29)   a. An: (telling what her imaginary baby is going to eat)
       'Gònna drìnk [bù?] . . . mìlk in my *bóobie*.'
       ('boobie' anticipated/substituted for 'milk'; AN-24(41) 2;0)
   b. Al: 'I'm the kíd lìon: *Róar*! And Mòmmy's the Mómmy *ròar* . . .
       the Mómmy lìon.' ('roar' perseverated/substituted for 'lion';
       AL-134(43) 3;4)
   c. AF: 'You nèed a new **cán** for that lìd. I mean a líd for that càn.'
       ('lid' and 'can' exchanged; AD-635(45))

In (29a) Anna anticipates the noun 'boobie' (a baby word for 'breast') and substitutes it for 'milk'; these are metonymically related since milk is located in the breast. In (29b) Alice produces the interjection 'Roar', which is metonymically related to lions by being the noise lions make; she then perseverates 'roar' and substitutes it for the noun 'lion', the source of the noise. In (29c) the adult exchanges the two nouns 'lid' and 'can'; because 'lids' are located on top of 'cans', this is a metonymic relationship.

Although associated relationships are the most common, there are many syntagmatic lexical errors involving coordinates, and a substantial number of subsumatives and contrastives also. Again it is not surprising that words linked by any of these relationships could be planned for the same utterance or discourse, as they could easily index different aspects of the same scene or different functional components of a scene which are relevant to the current utterance.

(30)   a. An: 'Àli put her **mòuth** over her . . . Àli put her hànd over her
       móuth when she còughed.' ('hand' anticipated/substituted for
       'mouth', co-partonyms; AN-247(41) 4;10)
   b. OB: (watching a cowboy show on TV; says to Mom)
       'Sèe that *gùy* with a pátch on his èye?'
   M: 'Yeah.'
   OB: 'Hè's the **gúy** . . . hè's the héro.'
       ('guy' perseverated/substituted for 'hero', superordinate/
       subordinate; OC-128 (43) 5;0)

    c. B: 'Mom, do wè have any óld bològna?'
       M: 'No, you'll hàve to òpen some **ném**. But that's OḰ, that's a
            góod snàck.'
       B: (runs into kitchen, says to Nanny) 'Sèe, I tóld ya we dòn't hàve
           any **nèw** . . . we dòn't hàve any <u>òld</u> bològna.'
           ('new' perseverated substituted for 'old', gradable antonyms;
           B-407(43) 4;11)

In (30a), Anna anticipates 'mouth' and substitutes it for 'hand'; these are co-partonyms, i.e. both parts of the human body. In (30b), the speaker perseverates the word 'guy' and substitutes it for 'hero'; this is a superordinate substituting for a subordinate, since a 'hero' is a kind of 'guy'. Bobby, in (30c) perseverates the word 'new' from Mom's utterance, and substitutes it for its antonym 'old', in his utterance. I think it is interesting that all the syntagmatic lexical errors involving contrastive pairs of words (antonyms, converses) were perseveration errors like that in (30c), where the word which contrasts with the target word was spoken either in a preceding utterance or in an earlier part of the same utterance. In most cases the speaker intended to contrast something in his/her utterance with something which had just been said, but instead perseverated the opposing word from the previous discourse and substituted it for the intended contrast.

In sum, this section has shown that there is a correlation between different types of errors and different kinds of semantic relationships involved in the errors, and that these patterns can be explained with reference to the location in processing at which the error occurs. In general the children in this study followed the same types of patterns as adults: paradigmatic lexical substitutions of content words most often involved coordinate and associated relationships, whereas function word errors (not involving pronouns) often involved contrastive relationships; lexical blends most often involved synonyms, and syntagmatic errors involved a broad variety of error types, but metonyms were particularly frequent. The children differed from the adults in that they produced more errors involving personal pronouns and word pairs with the shared criterial features designation in their function word errors, and fewer synonym pairs in blends. This was explained in terms of the children having had less practice with the meaning and usage of function words, and the adults having a larger content vocabulary and thus more possible synonyms to choose from.

5.3.4 Semantic Relationships in Lexical Classes

In the preceding section I mentioned that various semantic relationships were more common in errors involving words of particular lexical classes. In this section I will examine this phenomenon in detail. Tables 5.5 and 5.6 present the number of errors in which the pairs of words involved fell into each of the semantic relationship categories, by lexical category; Table 5.5 gives the child figures, and Table 5.6 the adult figures. I only included in this count cases

TABLE 5.5

Semantic relationships of pairs of words involved in lexical substitution errors (paradigmatic and syntagmatic) and lexical blends, by lexical category; children only. In each pair, both words belong to the same lexical category. CN=common noun; PN=proper noun, V=verb, Adj=adjective, Adv=adverb, Prep=preposition, OF=other function words.

	CN	PN	V	Adj	Adv	Prep	OF	Total
Coordinates								
Co-Hyponyms	36	8	9	11	1	0	0	65
Co-Memb. Set	6	19	2	0	0	0	1	28
Co-Partonyms	7	0	0	0	1	0	0	8
N=	**49**	**27**	**11**	**11**	**2**	**0**	**1**	**101**
	54.5%	87%	30%	48%	16.7%		9%	48%
Subsumatives								
Super./Subord.	3	0	3	0	0	0	0	6
Set/Member	2	0	0	0	0	0	0	2
Whole/Part	5	0	0	0	0	0	0	5
N=	**10**	**0**	**3**	**0**	**0**	**0**	**0**	**13**
	11%		8%					6%
Contrastives								
Binary Ant.	0	0	0	2	0	3	0	5
Gradable Ant.	0	0	0	4	4	1	0	9
Converses	0	0	2	1	0	1	0	4
N=	**0**	**0**	**2**	**7**	**4**	**5**	**0**	**18**
			5.5%	30.4%	33.3%	62.5%		8.5%
Synonyms	**7**	**2**	**12**	**1**	**2**	**1**	**3**	**28**
	8%	6.5%	32.5%	4.3%	16.7%	12.5%	27%	13%
Associated								
Metonyms	15	1	0	0	0	0	0	16
Connotation	2	0	0	1	0	0	0	3
Causal	0	0	4	0	0	0	0	4
SCF	7	1	5	3	4	2	7	29
N=	**24**	**2**	**9**	**4**	**4**	**2**	**7**	**52**
	26.5%	6.5%	24%	17.3%	33.3%	25%	64%	24.5%
Total N=	**90**	**31**	**37**	**23**	**12**	**8**	**11**	**212**
'opposed'	8	12	11	9	7	5	2	53
	9%	39%	30%	39%	58.3%	62.5%	18%	25%

TABLE 5.6

Semantic relationships of pairs of words involved in lexical substitution errors (paradigmatic and syntagmatic) and lexical blends, by lexical category; adults only. In each pair, both words belong to the same lexical category. CN=common noun; PN=proper noun, V=verb, Adj=adjective, Adv=adverb, Prep=preposition, OF=other function words.

	CN	PN	V	Adj	Adv	Prep	OF	Total
Coordinates								
Co-Hyponyms	31	8	6	5	1	0	0	51
Co-Memb. Set	8	3	0	0	0	1	0	12
Co-Partonyms	5	0	0	0	0	0	0	5
N=	**44**	**11**	**6**	**5**	**1**	**1**	**0**	**68**
	43%	78.5%	21.5%	24%	9%	20%		37%
Subsumatives								
Super./Subord.	3	1	4	0	0	0	0	8
Set/Member	2	0	0	1	0	0	0	3
Whole/Part	6	0	0	0	0	0	0	6
N=	**11**	**1**	**4**	**1**	**0**	**0**	**0**	**17**
	11%	7%	14.5%	5%				9%
Contrastives								
Binary Ant.	0	0	1	0	0	4	0	5
Gradable Ant.	0	0	0	2	0	0	0	2
Converses	0	0	1	1	2	0	0	4
N=	**0**	**0**	**2**	**3**	**2**	**4**	**0**	**11**
			7%	14%	18%	80%		6%
Synonyms	**18**	**0**	**9**	**8**	**6**	**0**	**3**	**44**
	17.5%		32%	38%	55%		75%	24%
Associated								
Metonyms	8	0	2	1	0	0	0	11
Connotation	0	0	0	0	0	0	0	0
Causal	1	0	1	0	0	0	0	2
SCF	20	2	4	3	2	0	1	32
N=	**29**	**2**	**7**	**4**	**2**	**0**	**1**	**45**
	28.5%	14.5%	25%	19%	18%		25%	24%
Total N=	**102**	**14**	**28**	**21**	**11**	**5**	**4**	**185**
'opposed'	6	6	3	4	3	4	0	26
	6%	43%	11%	19%	27%	80%		14%

where both words involved in the error were from the same lexical category; I omitted the 16 child errors and 17 adult errors in which the two words belonged to different lexical categories. I also excluded the 'personal pronoun' errors, as their semantic relationships are not pertinent to any other lexical category.

Looking at Tables 5.5 and 5.6 together, some patterns emerge. Similar patterns between the child and adult figures are probably due to the types of semantic relationships most common to specific lexical categories; e.g. antonyms are more common in adverbs and adjectives than in nouns in the lexicon in general. On the other hand, differences between the child and adult figures seem to be due to differences in vocabulary, as I will detail below.

For common nouns, both child and adult errors show more influence of coordinate and associated semantic relationships, with the largest category being co-hyponyms; these types are followed by subsumatives and synonyms for the children, and the reverse for the adults. There were no common noun errors which were classified as contrastives. The adult errors contained nearly twice the number of synonymous pairs as the children, for reasons discussed above, i.e. their larger vocabularies allow for more possible synonyms. Most of the subsumative errors for both children and adults involved common nouns, as this is the lexical category most likely to index entities which are involved in taxonomic, set/member or whole/part relationships.

Proper nouns were overwhelmingly involved in coordinate relationships, with a few associated pairs and 2 synonym blends in the child data: 'Bobby/ Robert' (B-30(38) 1;11), and 'Father/ Poppa' (B-116(38) 2;10). For the children, the most common relationship was co-members of a set, involving persons who come in pairs, such as 'Bert/Ernie', 'Mommy/Daddy', 'Anna/ Alice', and so forth. For the adults, co-hyponyms were more common, and the proper nouns included not just persons but also places such as 'L.A./New York' (AD-428(35)), and 'Connecticut/Kentucky' (AD-423 (35)); holidays such as 'Christmas/Easter' (AD-421(35)); names of companies such as 'HBO/AOL' (AD-424(35)); and days of the week such as 'Wednesday/Thursday' (AD-425(35)). Thus for the adults a larger range of semantic relationships was possible in proper nouns. Again note that the relationships expressed by the children are in general more concrete than those expressed by adults, since, as opposed to co-members of a set and co-partonyms, co-hyponyms require the knowledge of some sort of superordinate category such as 'major cities on opposite coasts of the USA', 'entertainment companies', and 'days of the week'.

Perhaps surprisingly, the most common semantic relationship among verbs for both the children and adults was synonyms. This may suggest that in early vocabularies, expanded choices for referring to the same activity may begin to occur at a younger age than choices for referring to other types of referents. It could also indicate that it is more difficult for children to learn the detailed criterial features required for individual verbs than for some other lexical categories, such that quasi-synonyms can more easily intrude (Clark 1993:4; see also §4.3.3 in Chapter 4). However, since this is the one case in which the children produced as many synonyms as the adults did, it is likely that the children do have more synonymic choices for verbs than for other lexical categories. This may be due to the fact that some very basic verbal vocabulary which is highly salient to young children allows for synonyms, e.g. 'like/want' (AI-93(38) 3;1 and B-150(38), 3;8), 'pick (up)/clean (up)' (OC-74(38) 3;11), 'joking/kidding' (B-268(38) 4;4), 'close/shut' (AN-192(38) 4;5), and 'look/watch' (B-310(38) 4;6), among many others.

Coordinate and associated relationships are the next most common semantic relationships for verbs. Nearly all the causally related error pairs involved verbs: 'hit/hurt' (B-74(35) 2;6 and B-554(35) 5;8), 'show/see' (OC-90(35) 4;1), and 'open/let(in)' (AD-572(41)). The only exception was the following adult error involving common nouns, where 'fire' causes 'heat'.

(31)   AF: 'Chrìs must have tùrned the **fìre** òn in his óffice.'
         ('fire' for 'heat'; AD-396(35))

After common nouns, subsumative relationships were most common in verbs, and in every case involved a very generic superordinate verb interacting with a much more specific subordinate term. This type of error was produced by the children and adults alike.

(32)   a. B: 'Mom, I wànna **dó** . . . I wànna <u>shów</u> yòu sòmething.'
              ('do' for 'show'; B-403(35) 4;11)
         b. AF: 'When I was trying to **màke** . . . <u>dràw</u> a distínction betwèen
              (etc.)' ('make' for 'draw'; AD-441(35))

In (32a), to 'show' is a kind of 'doing'; and in (32b), to 'draw' is a more specific kind of 'making' in this context; I will return to these errors in §5.4 below, and justify the analysis of these utterances as speech errors rather than false starts.

Finally, contrastive relationships were rare among verbs; in the child data the only such pair was the converses 'teach/learn' (B-326a(35) and 326b(38) 4;7), and the adults produced one converse pair 'introduce/intrude' (AD-437(35)) and one quasi-antonymic pair 'pull/put' (AD-614(43)). There were many pairs of verbs that were counted as 'opposed', e.g. 'see/hear', 'read/write', and so forth, but these weren't considered to be contrastive in the formal sense.

The child and adult adjective and adverb pairs involved in lexical errors followed similar patterns. For the children, contrastive relationships were very common in both, whereas for the adults, synonymic relationships were more common. For both, coordinate and associated relationships were also common, although not in the same proportions, and subsumative relationships did not occur. The reason contrastive relationships were so common for the children is that most of their adjective or adverb errors involved very concrete, very frequent lexical items which occur in well-established antonymic pairs, such as 'cold/hot'

(B-311(35) 4;6 and Al-12(38) 2;2), 'dark/light' (B-378a(43) 4;10), 'new/old' (B-407(43) 4;11), 'apart/together' (B-276(35) 4;5 and B-92(43) 2;7), 'down/up' (OC-118(35) 4;9), and so forth. However, a look at the synonyms which adults produced in adjective/adverb errors shows why the children did not produce many of this type of error, as they typically involved sophisticated, morphologically complex vocabulary with fine-grained details of meaning which the children would simply not yet have learned; for example, 'substantial/substantive' (AD-296b(35)), 'old/ancient' (AD-542(38)), 'exactly/precisely' (AD-549(38)), and 'dramatically/drastically' (AD-550(38)). Thus the differences between the children's and adults' adjective/adverb error types can be attributed to differences in the sophistication and size of their vocabularies.

On the other hand, errors involving prepositions were most often of the contrastive type, for both adults and children. This includes both the more concrete prepositions such as 'over/under' (gradable antonyms, AL-77(36) 2;11), and the prepositions more closely linked to grammatical constructions such as 'for/from' (binary antonyms, AD-479(36)). A few other semantic categories also occurred in prepositional errors but in no particular pattern. The 'other function word' errors most often involved quasi-synonyms or shared criterial features, since the concepts referred to with auxiliary verbs, wh-question words, deictics, and so forth do not typically enter into coordinate, contrastive, or subsumative semantic relations with other similar words.

Errors in which the target and source word, or two targets, belonged to different lexical categories were excluded from the counts in Tables 5.5 and 5.6. However, it is interesting to note that these errors most often involved the more loosely related associated relationships. This follows from the fact that if two words are of different lexical categories, they are unlikely to be antonyms, synonyms, co-hyponyms, and so forth. For the children, 12 of the 16 errors mismatched for lexical category (75%) involved associated relationships, including 6 cases of metonyms, 2 connotational, and 4 shared criterial features. In the 17 adult mismatched errors, 12 were of the associated type, including 5 metonyms and 7 shared criterial features. These often occurred in syntagmatic errors, where the semantic relationship between the two words was relatively distant.

(33) a. M: 'Lòok at all the bìrds *flỳing* abóve us!'
        An: 'Àre they thís **flỳ**?' (holding arms above head)
        M: 'What?'
        An: 'Àre they thís hìgh?' ('fly' perseverated/substituted for 'high', shared criterial features; AN-279(43) 5;2)
      b. AM: 'If you **crèam** the **skìm** . . . skìm the crèam off my fólk-tùne nòvices, (etc.)'
        (exchange of 'skim' and 'cream', metonyms; AD-633(45))

In (33a), Anna perseverates the verb 'fly' from Mother's utterance, and substitutes it for the adjective 'high'. These two words are analyzed as having shared criterial features relating to 'upness', but the relationship is fairly loose. In (33b), the verb 'skim' and the noun 'cream' are exchanged. These two words are related metonymically, in the sense that 'to skim' is an action functionally related to 'cream'; this error could have been facilitated by the fact that 'cream' can also be a verb, although not in this context. In general, then, error pairs which honor lexical category are more likely to have a closer semantic relationship than error pairs which violate lexical category.

The 'opposed' figures at the bottom of these two tables show interesting patterns in relation to the various lexical categories. For the children and adults, prepositions have the highest percentage of 'opposed' pairs in these SOTs, due to the fact that the majority of preposition errors are of the contrastive type. Furthermore, for both children and adults, 'opposed' pairs are relatively infrequent among common nouns; as mentioned above, common nouns rarely enter into true antonymic relationships with each other, and so the pairs analyzed as 'opposed' are pairs which have some other primary relationship but are typically seen to be in some sort of oppositional relationship with each other, such as 'feet/hands' which are co-partonyms (body parts), but also opposed in being the terminal appendages on the upper body vs. lower body (B-285(35) 4;5); other examples are 'question/answer' (co-hyponyms; B-406(35) 4;11), 'husband/wife' (co-members of a set; B-544(35) 5;7), 'spoon/fork' (co-hyponyms; Al-146(38) 3;7), and 'shoes/socks' (co-hyponyms; AL-98(38) 3;2 and B-347(38) 4;8). But in general most common nouns in these error pairs did not enter into opposed relationships.

On the other hand, proper nouns, adverbs, and adjectives all had a fairly high rate of 'opposed' pairs for both the children and adults. For adjectives and adverbs this is due to the fact that words in these lexical categories are often involved in true antonymic or converse relationships, as discussed above. For the proper nouns, there were many cases in both the child and adult data where the two words involved index either a pair of people who are seen to be in a binary relationship, such as 'Bert/Ernie', 'Mommy/Daddy', 'Anna/Alice', 'Todd/Copper', or a pair of locations which can be seen as involved in a contrastive relationship such as 'L.A./New York' (two major cities on opposite coasts, also perhaps opposed in cultural focus). Therefore the 'opposed' relationship was common in the proper noun errors.

Finally, the children produced a number of 'opposed' verb errors, whereas these were less common in the adult errors. In the child errors there were many verb substitutions which involved a pair of co-hyponyms which are commonly thought of as referring to an opposing pair of activities; this includes many very basic vocabulary words which these young children would have as staples in their lexicons, such as 'see/hear' (involved in 4 errors: AL-43(35) 2;8; AL-184(35) 3;10; B-218(35) 4;2; B-521(35) 5;5)), 'watch/listen to' (B-71(35) 2;6), 'write/read' (AN-277(35) 5;2), 'eat/drink' (B-261(35) 4;4), and 'hide/find' (B-552(35) 5;8). However, the adult verb errors often involved fairly complex vocabulary which is less likely to participte in a simple binary opposition, causing them to have fewer 'opposed' pairs of verbs.

In sum, word pairs from the various lexical categories were more likely to be involved in specific types of semantic relationships in these errors, depending to a large extent on what sorts of relationships are available for this lexical category (see also Hotopf 1980 for a similar argument). Differences between the child and adult data in terms of behavior of lexical classes were explained as being a function of vocabulary that is learned earlier vs. later in the various lexical classes. For both children and adults, common nouns most often participate in coordinate or associated relationships, and do not often show 'opposed' relationships. Proper nouns are most often co-members of a set for the children, whose errors most often involve words referring to pairs of people; for adults, whose proper nouns can refer to a broader set of entities (people, places, holidays, etc.), most error pairs are co-hyponyms. The semantic relationships involved in verb errors are very similar between the children and adults, with synonyms being the most common, followed by coordinates and associated pairs; however, the children show a number of oppositional relationships in verbs whereas the adults do not. For adjectives and adverbs, the children show a high percentage of contrastives, since their vocabulary in these two categories depends mostly on very concrete, basic words which often occur in pairs. On the other hand the adults have a number of synonym pairs in these categories, due to their more sophisticated and fine-grained lexicons. Prepositions are most often contrastives for both children and adults, since this is a very common type of semantic relationship found in prepositions in general, both early- and late-learned. Finally, 'other function word' error pairs are typically either synonyms, or, particularly for the children, show the shared criterial features relationship, suggesting that the details of the meanings of some of these words may not be fully worked out by the children. In general, then, the children seem to be well on their way to developing the same types of semantic relationships among words in different lexical categories as the adults demonstrate in these SOTs. Once the children have acquired a larger and more detailed lexicon, patterns of semantic relationships in their lexical errors which are due to the constraints of the various lexical categories will undoubtedly become more like the adult patterns.

5.4 Comparison to Other Studies

There are actually very few studies of lexical substitution errors that look at the semantic relationships in such errors in any detail. In this section I will review the findings of several studies, comparing and contrasting their results with mine, and looking to see whether they shed any light on the acquisition issues.

Hotopf (1980) reports on a corpus of 224 'semantic slips' and 104 lexical blends, taken from his own corpus of adult English slips, and the Meringer corpora of adult German slips (Meringer & Mayer 1895, Meringer 1908). The 'semantic slips' are defined as plan-internal substitution errors involving two open-class words which are at least semantically related, although other factors such as phonology, collocation, or environment may also influence the error; his semantic slips include both paradigmatic and syntagmatic substitutions. His blends are defined in the same way they are defined in the current study, but his data are restricted to content words.

Hotopf classifies the semantic substitution errors into the following three types of semantic relationships (1980:98). In 31.2% of these errors, the error and target word stand in 'complementary, antonymous or converse relationships', such as 'early/late' and 'husband/wife'. Another 44.6% are 'co-hyponyms', in the sense of being immediately dominated by the same superordinate word; examples are 'red/black', 'breakfast/lunch', and 'foot/finger'. The remaining 24.2% of the errors also stand in an approximately hyponymous relationship, but with a more distant superordinate, for example 'Saturday/January' and 'thermometer/clock.' He notes that in substitutions, the words involved are never synonyms; likewise he finds only one case of a superordinate/subordinate error, which was *Obst* 'fruit' for *Äpfel* 'apples'.

A different pattern of semantic relationship holds for blends, where 10.5% of the errors are either co-hyponyms or opposites, but 89.5% are approximate synonyms, such as **uberstaunt*, from *uberrascht* 'surprised' and *erstaunt* 'astonished'. He suggests that plan-internal blends most often occur due to two coexisting intentions for the words to be spoken in the utterance; the fact that they could both be meaningfully inserted into the same syntagmatic slot predisposes them to be synonymous. This is in accord with the analysis of blends in the current study,

Levelt (1989: Ch. 6) agrees that lexical substitution errors made by adults most often involve the relationships of 'antonym' and 'co-hyponym', followed by 'more remote co-hyponyms', and that most blends involve the relationship 'synonym'; however, he does not give any numbers regarding the proportion of these various categories in his data. He makes a point about the lack of superordinate and synonymic errors in substitutions which is similar to that given in §5.3.3 above, i.e. that this may be due to the fact that either the target or the error word would be appropriate in the context of the utterance and that therefore a listener would not necessarily recognize it as an error. Hotopf also makes this suggestion, but prefers an argument based on types of semantic relationships available for error in different lexical categories.

Wijnen (1992) looked at the issue of semantic relationships both in his Dutch child language corpus, and in the 'London-Lund' English adult corpus (Garnham et al., 1982). The children in his study produced 35 paradigmatic lexical substitution errors with at least a semantic relationship, and the adult data contained 47 such errors, including both open- and closed-class errors. He classifies the 'conceptual relationships' between target and error words into the following categories: coordination, synonymy, antonymy, associative, and other. Although he gives examples of each type, he does not define these relationships or justify the inclusion of particular error pairs in one category or another. From the examples and text it becomes evident that 'coordination' refers to co-hyponyms (e.g. 'Protestants/Catholics', 'blue/yellow'; note that I am giving the English translation of his Dutch examples); 'synonyms' include such pairs as 'no/not'; 'antonyms' include 'come/go'; 'associatively related' pairs seem to be distant co-hyponyms or metonyms such as 'throw away/break', 'advertisements/applicants', and 'crane/chimney'. 'Other' relationships are usually collocational, such as 'engineering degree' for 'engineering job'. Wijnen found a larger proportion of coordinate errors than did Hotopf (72.5% child, 71.5% adult), very few synonyms or antonyms, which he groups into a single class (13% children, 3% adult), and a similar percentage of the less close relationships, associated and 'other', as that found by Hotopf (14.5% child, 25.5% adult).

Arnaud (1999) discusses the semantic relationships involved in the French adult lexical errors in his corpus using similar terms to the preceding studies (substitutions, N=332, blends, N=23). He argues that most word pairs involved in substitution errors are 'category coordinates' and 'antonyms'. 'Category coordinates' include either close relationships such as co-hyponyms or co-partonyms ('rabbit/chicken', 'direction indicator/rear-view mirror'; I am giving English translations of the French), or more distant relationships such as 'napkin/necktie' (which may have also been influenced by phonology: *serviette/cravate*). 'Antonyms' involve both clear-cut cases such as 'cold/hot', 'theoretical/practical', and less clear cases which he calls 'discourse opposites', such as 'metro (subway)/taxi' which are opposed in terms of being alternate forms of ground transportation in the city. Arnaud agrees with the two earlier studies that word blend errors most often involve synonyms, whereas synonyms and superordinates/subordinates do not occur in lexical substitution errors. Unfortunately Arnaud does not present any figures indicating the percentage of his errors involved in each type of semantic relationship, so his data cannot be compared quantitatively with the other studies. However, one interesting point he makes (1999:274) is that often his blend errors involve two words which are quasi-synonyms, but differ greatly in their level of formality, such as '*voiture/bagnole*', a formal vs. informal way to refer to a car, and '*copier/pomper*', a neutral vs. slang way to refer to someone who cheats; this was also found in my study, to a somewhat lesser degree (e.g. 'Father/Poppa' B-116(38) 2;10; 'fix/repair' AD-532(38)).

Finally, Harley & MacAndrew (2001), hereafter H&M, divide the semantic relationships found in the lexical substitution errors in their adult English study into two broad classes: 'sharing of semantic features' and 'associative errors'. The shared-feature errors are further subdivided into synonyms, antonyms, superordinates, subordinates (e.g. cat/animal), and coordinates (e.g. cat/dog). Associative errors are said to involve looser relationships such as that between 'dog/bone' (which would be classified as metonymic in my system). In their 784 semantically related substitution errors, there were 483 (61.5%) 'shared semantic features' types, excluding antonyms, 106 antonyms (20.4%), and 141 associative pairs (18%); because coordinates, subsumatives, and synonyms were

TABLE 5.7
Percentage of lexical substitution errors which fell into each semantic relationship type, comparing 4 studies. See text for references and languages.

	Jaeger Child	Wijnen Child	Jaeger Adult	Hotopf Adult	Wijnen Adult	H&M Adult
Coordinate	49%	72.5%	43%	44.6%	71.5%	61.5%*
Subsumative	7%	0	9%	0	0	*
Contrastive	10%	13%**	7.5%	31.2%	3%**	20.5%
('Opposed')	(29.5%)		(16.5%)			
Synonyms	4%	**	6%	0	**	*
Associated	30%	14.5%	34.5%	24.2%	25.5%	18%
Total N=	**160**	**35**	**133**	**224**	**47**	**784**

*= Harley & MacAndrew's 'coordinate' figures include subsumatives and synonyms.
**=Wijnen's 'contrastive' figure includes both antonyms and synonyms.

grouped into the same category in this study, it is impossible to know what proportion of this 61.5% 'shared semantic features' fell into each category.

In order to make a general quantitative comparison across the various studies, I attempted to equate as closely as possible the categories used by each study, and calculate the percentage of errors which fell into each class. In this case I looked only at lexical substitution errors, excluding blends, since blends were not analyzed in all studies. The figures given in Table 5.7 must be considered as a very rough comparison, since some studies but not others included function words, and some studies but not others included both paradigmatic and syntagmatic errors. In my data I have included both paradigmatic and syntagmatic errors, and have included all function word errors except those involving personal pronouns, which do not enter into the same types of semantic relationships as do other lexical classes. I have indicated in the table where two or more of my categories are collapsed into a single category in other studies; I have inserted my 'opposed' category below 'contrastive' for comparison. H&M's two categories 'associative' and 'other' are collapsed into my 'associated' category in this table.

In all four studies, the coordinate-type relationships are the most common. For the Jaeger and the Hotopf studies, the figures are 43%-49%. The H&M figure may be higher (61.5%) because this category includes not only coordinates, but also subsumatives and synonyms; however, these latter two types of relationships are rare in substitution errors, and are unlikely to have contributed many data points. The reason for the very high figures in the Wijnen data is unclear, but since Wijnen had a much smaller database than the other three studies, these figures are probably somewhat less reliable. In all studies except Hotopf, the next most common type is associated (14.5%-34.5%); for Hotopf the next most common was contrastive; I will return to this issue below. Again, Wijnen's data are somewhat out of step with the others, particularly his adult 'contrastive' figure of 3%.

While there are some general similarities among the studies, there are three noteworthy differences between previous studies and the current data, namely my finding of a handful of subsumative and synonym word pairs in paradigmatic lexical substitutions, and the fact that I have far fewer contrastives than the two larger studies. I will address each of these three issues in turn.

As discussed in §5.3.3 above, the claim that speakers don't produce subsumative type errors, particularly in paradigmatic lexical substitutions, has been argued to be a function of the fact that typically both the higher-level term (superordinate, set, whole) and the lower-level term (subordinate, member, part) would have the same reference, and so would be propositionally equivalent. This would mean that substituting one for the other would result in an utterance with the same truth value, and the researcher would not necessarily recognize it as an error. This is true in some of the cases in my data involving nouns (N=5), where the higher-level term is spoken erroneously and then corrected to the lower-level term, such that the only way the listener would know this was an error was due to the correction.

(34)   a. OB:'I hùrt my lég . . . thigh.'
       (whole 'leg' substituted for part 'thigh'; OC-127(35) 5;0)
       b. OG: 'Mommy, I wànt some cér . . . I wànt some Life.'
       (began to substitute superordinate 'cereal' for subordinate 'Life';
       OC-54(35) 3;6)

In (34a), the child did indeed hurt his leg, since 'thigh' is part of a 'leg', and in (34b) the child did want some cereal, specifically the brand name 'Life'. The other paradigmatic lexical substitution errors of this type were 'arm' for 'wrist' (OC-125(35) 5;0), 'child' for 'girl' (AD-375(35)), and 'supper' for 'dessert' (AD-395(35)). One could make the argument that these errors are something like a 'false start', where the speaker changed his/her mind about the level of specificity with which to refer to the object or event in question, given the discourse situation. Specifically, Grice's maxim of quantity may have come into play in the speaker deciding that he/she hadn't given enough information by using the superordinate. For example, in the 'cereal/Life' case, if the child hadn't corrected to the subordinate, Mother's next question would have undoubtedly been 'What kind of cereal?'.

However, in all the other paradigmatic substitution errors involving a subsumative relationship (N=10), this sort of equivalency did not hold. In several errors, both child and adult, a verb which was more general and inappropriate to the specific situation being expressed was substituted for the more specific verb; an example is given in (35).

(35)   B: 'Mom, I wànna **dó** . . . I wànna <u>shów</u> yòu sòmething.'
        (superordinate 'do' substituted for subordinate 'show';
        B-403(35) 4;11)

While 'do' is certainly a superordinate to 'show' in terms of meaning, the sentences 'I want to do something' or *'I want to do you something' are clearly not propositionally equivalent to the target, and the latter is even ungrammatical. Other examples are: 'have' for 'wear' (B-143(35) 3;8), 'put' for 'wrap' (B-147(35) 3;8), and 'make' for 'draw' (AD-441(35)). These are the kinds of errors discussed in Bowerman (1978), to which I will return below; they are very clear cases of subsumative errors.

With noun errors, the opposite pattern was found: most often a speaker produced a subordinate/member/part which was not only too specific for the intended propositional content but also inaccurate, and corrected to the word indicating the more general or larger entity; these errors were all produced by adults.

(36)   AF: (talking about finding a specific book)
        'It's èasy to find in the **díctionary**, uh **encyclopédia**, uh <u>líbrary</u>.'
        (AD-371a,b(35))

'Dictionary' and 'encyclopedia' are members of the set of things which make up a 'library', and in this case the lower-level terms were not appropriate for the intended proposition.   The other such errors involved part-for-whole substitutions: 'avocado' for 'guacamole' (AD-359(35)) and 'gate' for 'fence' (AD-388(35)). Finally, there were two very interesting adult errors in which an incorrect subordinate term was substituted for one of its co-hyponyms, and then corrected to the superordinate.

(37)   a. M: 'Did you brìng alòng some móney so you can bùy some tréats?'
            TF: 'Yeah, twènty búcks. But I'm nòt gònna **pày** áll of ìt . . .
            I'm nòt gònna <u>úse</u> àll of ìt, I mèan.'   (AD-440(35))
        b. AF: (noticing that it looks like it's going to rain)
            'I thìnk Rìck pròbably bètter pùt the **líd** ùp on his càr, I mèan
            the <u>tóp</u> ùp.'   (AD-376(35))

In (37a), the speaker erroneously used the verb 'pay', and then corrected to the superordinate 'use', whereas the correct subordinate would have been 'spend', a co-hyponym with the error word 'pay'; in this case 'use' was also propositionally accurate (along with 'spend'). In (37b), the error word was 'lid', which is a kind of 'top' but not a word appropriately used to indicate the top of a convertible car. In this case the speaker could have either corrected to the superordinate 'top' or the co-hyponym 'roof', either of which would have been equally appropriate in this utterance.

The fact that there are 15 cases of paradigmatic lexical substitution errors in my data best analyzed as involving a subsumative relationship is strong evidence that in fact such semantic relationships can and do hold between word pairs involved in substitutions. Furthermore they appear to be true lexical substitution errors; only a few of them are potential 'false starts'. The adult errors show some patterns which do not occur in the child errors, in particular correcting from part/member to whole/set, and producing the wrong subordinate, correcting to the appropriate superordinate; this may show that adults have a more elaborated network of connections in the lexicon in the vertical dimension than do the children.

It is also the case that there were several blend and syntagmatic errors in my corpus best explained in terms of subsumative relationships. Blends most often involved a very near superordinate/set/whole with its subordinate/member/part: 'leopard/Johnny' (a toy 'leopard' named 'Johnny'; Al-217(38) 4;5), 'zipper/jacket' (where 'zipper' is a part of a 'jacket'; B-227b(38) 4;2), 'speech/stress' (where 'stress' is a part of what makes up 'speech'; AD-499 (38)), 'section/chapter' (where a 'chapter' is a kind of 'section'; AD-520(38)), 'Chinese/Mandarin' (where 'Mandarin' is a kind of 'Chinese'; AD-291b(38)), 'stuck/stitched' (where to 'stitch' something together is a kind of 'sticking' it together; AD-527(38)), 'cheese/Wheatables' (where 'cheese' is one ingredient in the cracker 'Wheatables'; AD-553(38)), and 'ready/dressed' (where getting 'dressed' is one member of the set of things involved in getting 'ready'; AD-538 (38)). However, a few errors involved a more distant superordinate: 'one/egg' (B-80(38) 2;6), 'things/ trees' (B-146(38) 3;8), and 'get/buy' (AD-533(38)). Besides these 11 blends, there were 8 syntagmatic errors involving subsumative relationships, all of which involved two concrete nouns both planned for the same utterance: 'pizza/party' ('pizza' is part of the set of things that make up a party; B-361(41) 4;9), 'zoo/donkey' (where 'donkey' is a member of the set of things which make up a 'zoo'; AN-152(43) 4;1), 'CAT/C' (where the letter 'C' is a part of the spelling of the word 'CAT'; AN-193(43) 4;5), 'guy/hero' (where a 'hero' is a kind of 'guy'; OC-128(43) 5;0), 'bones/dead horse' (where the 'bones' are part of the whole 'dead horse'; OC-116(45) 4;7), 'paper/conference' (where a 'paper' is one part of the whole 'conference'; AD-571(41)), 'language/English' (where 'English' is a kind of 'language'; AD-612(43)), and 'brain/mind' (where the 'mind' is arguably part of the 'brain' (see the discussion of example (9) above); AD-638(45)).

In the blend errors, it is clear that the speaker activated two words related by a subsumative type relationship, and did not fully select either, creating a phonological blend of the two. Similarly in the syntagmatic errors there is no doubt that the speaker activated two lexical items in a higher-level to lower-level relationship, and was planning both of them for speaking in the utterance, when one was substituted for the other; in a few cases the intruding word came from a preceding utterance by the same or different speaker, but this also means that both words were activated. Importantly, if the cases of blends and syntagmatic errors show unambiguously that two lexical items in a subsumative relationship can be activated during processing and can interact with each other in an error, there is no reason to believe that this phenomenon could not also occur in lexical substitution errors. Thus I argue that, contrary to what is frequently reported, paradigmatic lexical substitution errors can occur with word pairs which are in a superordinate/subordinate, whole/part, or set/member relationship, and that these errors reflect the same lexical activation and processing mechanisms as those involved in similar blend or syntagmatic errors. Furthermore, children and adults alike produce such errors, although they are relatively uncommon for both (child N=15, adult N=19).

The second difference between my study and previous studies is that I recorded lexical substitution errors which I claim involve synonyms. Most researchers find synonyms to be common in lexical blend errors, and my data show similar findings. However, as discussed in §5.3.3, synonyms are said not to occur in lexical substitution errors, since if one true synonym were substituted for another, the two utterances would be for all intents and purposes synonymous, and thus a listener would not detect the error, as in the constructed pair of sentences 'I want my bunny cup' and 'I want my rabbit cup' (see AL-16(38) 2;2 for a blend of 'bunny/rabbit'). This is obviously true, and so in the cases where I have analyzed the relationship between a word pair involved in a lexical substitution error as being synonyms, the relationship is really quasi-synonyms, as defined in §5.3.3: the words refer generally to the same entity or activity or state of affairs, but typically have different selectional restriction or scope requirements. If one accepts this definition of quasi-synonym, then in fact target and error pairs in paradigmatic lexical substitution errors can be (quasi-) synonyms. In my data I analyzed 5 child and 8 adult errors of this type as involving synonyms.

The largest group of synonyms was cases where the two words refer to the same entity, action, or quality, but in different semantic domains, i.e. with different selectional restrictions.

(38)   a. An: (handing Mom a balloon) 'Ópen thìs.' (looks confused)
        M: 'Do whát?'
        An: 'Blòw it úp.' ('open' for 'blow up'; AN-55(35) 2;7)
     b. AF: (child got some bathroom cleanser on her feet)
        'Rìnse your féet òff, becàuse you'll blèach hóles, uh pátches in
        the rùg.' ('holes' for 'patches'; AD-394(35))
     c. AF: 'Boy, that tíre looks smàll, uh lów I mèan.'
        ('small' for 'low'; AD-460(35))

In (38a), 'open' and 'blow up' both refer to the same event, i.e. causing something to expand outwards, but only 'blow up' is appropriate in the context of balloons. There was also one adult error which was very similar to this: the phone was ringing and the adult asked 'Shàll I ópen now? . . . uh, pìck ùp the phóne?' (AD-442(35)). This error was classified as involving shared criterial features, i.e. doing an action which causes something to become operational or functional, because I considered the relationship between 'open' and 'pick up' in the context of telephones to be somewhat less close than 'open' and 'blow up' in the context of balloons; however one could certainly make the argument that this adult error also involves quasi-synonyms.

In (38b), 'holes' and 'patches' are both gaps in the middle of some larger surface; however, the speaker corrects from 'holes' to 'patches' in the context of bleached-out locations on the rug, since for her, 'holes' requires that the gap penetrate through the material, rather than just changing the quality of the surface. In (38c), both 'small' and 'low' are adjectives referring to less physical size or extent; however, the idiom for tires which need air is 'low' rather than 'small'. The two other synonymic errors in this category also involved adjectives: 'higher' for 'taller' (talking about a person's stature; AD-458(35)), and 'done' for 'ripe' (talking about an avocado; AD-459(35)).

In two other quasi-synonymous errors, the target and error words differed from each other in taking different perspectives on the same event: 'bring' vs. 'get' (in the context of Mom picking up an article of clothing and bringing it to the child; OC-124(35) 5;0), and 'students' vs. 'children' (a school principal speaking to a parent group, referring to the children as *'your students'; the persons in question are 'students' from the principal's perspective, but 'children' from the parents'; AD-348a(35)). Three other errors involved very close synonyms, with one being of slightly larger scope than the other: 'talk (to)' vs. 'call (on the phone)' (AN-47(35) 2;4), 'which ever' vs. 'which other', where the latter implies more of a negative polarity than the former (AL-268(36) 5;11), and 'retirement home' vs. 'rest home', where to the speaker these terms refer to the same type of entity, except that the former requires that the person living there has actually retired from a job (AD-369b(35)).

The last set of quasi-synonyms involved a pair of words which derive from the same root, where only one was syntactically or semantically appropriate for the phrase: 'three' vs. 'third' (OC-133(35) 5;0), 'substantial' vs. 'substantive' (AD-296b (35)), and 'man' vs. 'men's' (AD-297b(35)); the latter two also involved lexical stress errors.

I have argued for a particular definition of quasi-synonym which I think accurately captures the types of relationships exemplified in the preceding section, and if this is accepted, then the category of quasi-synonym needs to be added to the list of types of semantic relationships which can occur in paradigmatic lexical selection errors. A good reason for including this category is that it would be difficult, and perhaps misleading, to classify these errors into one of the other categories of semantic relatedness. For example, one could classify 'talk to' and 'call' as co-hyponyms (kinds of events of speaking), but it seems to me that this misses the fact that 'talking to' someone on the telephone and 'calling' someone on the telephone (assuming that person answers) are essentially the same event. Likewise 'holes/patches' (kinds of gaps?) are much more similar in terms of the physical phenomenon they refer to than clear co-hyponyms such as 'apples' and 'oranges' (kinds of fruit); and 'higher/taller' refer to the identical physical property (greater distance in a vertical direction), except that 'higher' is used for entities which are not necessarily anchored (a high cloud), and 'taller' is used for anchored entities (a tall tree). Therefore I believe that the quasi-synonym designation is more accurate than, for example, a co-hyponym designation for these word pairs, and is in fact a very useful way of explaining this class of word pairs which can be involved in lexical selection errors. Again, both the children and adults produced errors best described as quasi-synonyms, although this category was not frequent in either age group. The analogy to blends holds here too: if speakers can activate synonyms and blend them into an erroneous single word, there is no reason to assume that they will not also activate quasi-synonyms, and then misselect the less accurate of the pair, substituting it for the more felicitous word.

Finally, in Table 5.7 it can be seen that my figures for 'contrastive' relationships (antonyms and converses) are much lower than those for the Hotopf (1980) or H&M (2001) studies; Hotopf found 31.2% 'antonyms', and H&M reported 20.5%, whereas my figures are: child=10%, adult=7.5%. However the reason for this becomes obvious when one examines the examples of antonymous relationships given in the Hotopf and H&M studies. In my classification system, I only labelled a word pair as being in a contrastive relationship if the words were binary antonyms (i.e. the presence of one entails the absence of the other), gradable antonyms (i.e. the words mark the endpoints of a continuum), or converses (thematic differences in perspective on the same phenomenon). However, as indicated in the Lyons (1977) quotation given above, there are many different viewpoints on what should be analyzed as 'antonymy', and both Hotopf and H&M used a broader definition than I did. For example, Hotopf (1980:98) gives 'husband/wife' as an example of an antonymous relationship, but I counted this as an example of co-members of a set (of spouses; see B-544(35) 5;7). Similarly, H&M (2001:410) distinguish three types of antonym: complementary pairs such as 'alive/dead', gradable pairs such as 'hot/cold', and relational pairs such as 'teacher/pupil'; many of the pairs in their latter category were not considered contrastives in the present study. However, all of these were labelled as 'opposed' in my study, and I have given the 'opposed' figures in Table 5.7 under the contrastive figures; these numbers are much more similar to the figures of other studies: child=29.5% 'opposed', adult=16.5% 'opposed'. Therefore this turns out not to be a real difference between my study and previous reports, but is rather a difference in how certain types of semantic relationships were classified in different systems.

In sum, there are some striking similarities between the proportions of different types of semantic relationships I found in my data, and other studies which have previously looked at such relationships in lexical substitution errors. All studies find that coordinate relationships are the most common, followed typically by associated, with a fair number of contrastive (or 'opposed') error pairs. All studies also find that lexical blends involve largely word pairs in a synonymous relationship. The fact that my child data follow very similar patterns to the adult data suggests that the interrelationships among lemmas in the child lexicon are organized by very similar semantic principles to those manifested in the adult lexicon, and that this organization occurs at a very early age (see §5.6 below). On the other hand, my errors included a number of target/error pairs in a subsumative relationship, which are typically reported not to occur. Similarly I argued for the category of quasi-synonyms in paradigmatic lexical substitution errors, contra other researchers who argue that synonyms do not occur in such errors. Therefore my data partially reinforce and partially expand on previous studies of semantic relationships in lexical errors.

One final study relevant to the current discussion is that of Bowerman (1978). In this study, Bowerman collected verb substitution errors made by her daughters and a few other children, ages 2;1-6;1. She focussed specifically on the verbs 'put, give, make, let', and found that after her subjects had been using these verbs correctly for some time, they would occasionally substitute one for another from this set, which she argued could be seen as similar to adult SOTs. She uses these substitutions to argue against the claim that children's lexicons are not organized semantically until much later. Her explanation for this type of error is reminiscent of the 'U-shaped curve' explanation commonly given for such phenomena as the acquisition of regular and irregular morphology; it is also similar to the 'Frames, then Content' hypothesis, as well as Fillmore's (1975) Frame Semantics account quoted in §5.2.1 above.

> [A]lthough children initially may have a general conceptual understanding of the kinds of contexts in which particular words are appropriate, they have not yet isolated those aspects of the contexts that are of particular linguistic significance--that serve as semantic features or "lexical organizers" (Carey's [1978] term) across a number of words in the same lexical domain. According to this account, an important facet of early semantic development is the child's gradual abstraction of those elements of the meanings of individual words--for example "cause" and "change of location"--that serve to structure lexical domains taken as a whole. (Bowerman 1978:983)

On this account, the children's initial correct usage of these verbs is due to their having a somewhat immature representation for the meaning of the words, and also due to not yet having abstracted out the crucial semantic features of each verb which will eventually be part of its lexical representation. Once the child begins extracting these features, verbs which share some features will be occasionally substituted for each other because they are now linked semantically in the lexicon. One could argue that the words serve initially as 'frames' in the MacNeilage & Davis (1990) sense, i.e. they are a relatively unanalyzed chunk of meaning; once the featural analysis begins to occur, the 'content' of each lexical entry becomes more detailed and fully specified, to the point where lexical links based on semantic relationships are possible. It is these links which are argued to cause (semantic) lexical substitution errors in adults, and, as I will argue in §5.6 below, they are also evident in all but the very youngest children's lexical SOTs.

In order to compare my study to Bowerman's, I scanned my SOT data for similar errors, as well as my notes on each of my children, to see whether or not they produced errors following these same patterns. In fact I found several differences between my data and Bowerman's. First, I did find a few lexical substitution errors involving these or similar relatively generic verbs (child N=7, adult N=3); but in every case the speaker self-corrected, showing that he/she was aware that the verb was spoken in error. In Bowerman's corpus, one key feature of the data was that the verb substitutions were never corrected by the child, indicating that at the point of speaking, the child may have been somewhat ambivalent about the exact meaning of the word and showed no immediate awareness that the word would have been an error from the adult point of view. The analogous child errors in my corpus involved mainly the superordinate/ subordinate type word pairs discussed in detail above, such as 'have/wear', 'put/wrap', 'do/show'; they also involve other relationships such as quasi-synonyms 'get/bring' and shared criterial features 'be/get'; the adult errors also involved superordinate/subordinate relationships: 'use/pay', 'make/draw', 'get/ talk about', although this latter was analyzed as not having a semantic relationship per se.

A second difference was that I did not find that my children overextended this specific set of verbs in the recurrent pattern evident in Bowerman's study. The most common recurrent overextensions made by my children were the patterns involving causatives and prepositions which are very well-documented in other studies (Bowerman 1974, Maratsos et al. 1987; see Clark 2003: Ch. 9 for an overview).

(39)   a. An: (explaining how she avoided getting water in her eyes in the shower) 'I jùst stàyed them shút.' (for 'kept'; 3;5.14)
        b. An: 'Mòmmy's màking súpper to mè.' (for 'for'; 3;4.13)

I did not count these utterances as SOTs, since the child was regularly producing such overextensions during this time period. I found only one utterance, made by Bobby, involving an overextension of 'put' which I did not count as a SOT, since he did not self-correct; in my notes I indicated that he appeared to be ambivalent about the use of 'put' at this point in time. This one example fits very well with Bowerman's data.

(40)   B: (describing a picture of one of the Ninja Turtles with a gag over
his mouth)
'It's a thìng that **pùts** òver your móuth, so you càn't tálk.' (4;4.7)

On the other hand, I collected one child phrase blend involving the verb 'put',
which looks very much like Bowerman's data, the difference being that the child
corrected this error to a grammatical phrase.

(41)   B: 'Lèt me sèe the bòx of the créam that **pùts** . . . that <u>you pùt</u> on my
hànds. The kìnd that <u>gòes</u> on my hánds.' (blend of 'that goes on
my hands' and 'that you put on my hands'; B-303(49) 4;6)

However, the fact that my data are somewhat different from Bowerman's
does not negate her findings by any means. It is possible that individual
differences in strategies used to sort out verb meaning may have led to differences
among her subjects and mine. On the other hand, it is possible that my children
made more utterances of this type than I was aware of, and for some reason I
failed to record them. (As an aside, I have had a number of well-respected child
language researchers, upon hearing me give a presentation on this research,
inform me that 'My child never made slips of the tongue'. I frankly don't
believe it, but since SOTs sound so normal, most listeners simply mentally
undo them when they hear them, do not include them in journal entries, and
eliminate them from transcripts.) However, since I was very careful in my
documentation of my children's language development, I believe the 'individual
differences' argument is stronger. But even if I didn't collect many of this same
type of error, the explanation given by Bowerman for a child's initial correct
usage and subsequent erroneous production of a verb fits extremely well with the
hypotheses being developed in this chapter. Specifically, a child's first use of
words is somewhat holistic and does not contain a fine-grained semantic
representation; as this representation develops, lexical links between words begin
to develop based on semantic features, such that misselection of one word for
another is facilitated by these lexical links. The fact that adults also produce
some of these same kinds of errors, even though they typically correct them, is a
strong argument that the lexical semantic links which are developing in young
children continue to be the factors which organize the lemma lexicon in
adulthood. I will return to these points in §5.6 below.

5.5 Semantic vs. Phonological Relationships in Processing
In Chapter 4 (§4.2.2, Table 4.8) I discussed the possibility of some trade-off
between phonological relationships and semantic relationships between lexical
items involved in substitution or blend errors. Specifically, I suggested that if
one word is substituted for another or two words are blended, and the pair has a
semantic relationship, then the phonological relationship will not be as
important and the overall 'phonological similarity' score will be lower in

general. On the other hand, if the mutually involved pair of words has no semantic relationship but does have a phonological relationship, then the phonological relationship needs to be stronger in order to cause the error, and thus the overall 'phonological similarity' score will be higher for malapropisms than for semantic errors. I found this to be true for both the children and adults in the study, although the differences were clearer for the adults compared to the children, and also more convincing for paradigmatic than syntagmatic errors. I argued from these figures that in order for one word to be substituted for or blended with another on purely phonological grounds, a high degree of phonological similarity is necessary in order to fool the monitor and allow a semantically anomalous word to be produced.

In that chapter I also raised the question of whether or not the reverse was true: that is, if a pair of words involved in an error has a semantic but not a phonological relationship, does the semantic similarity have to be closer than if the pair has both a semantic and phonological relationship? I indicated that at that point in the book I was unable to investigate this question because it was premature to lay out criteria for what counts as a 'closer' or 'looser' semantic relationship. I am now in a position to be able to address this issue.

The theoretical issues involved, discussed in §4.2.2, have to do with the links between the lemma and form lexicon, and the relevance of feed-forward and feed-back mechanisms between them. One possibility is that if the error word has a high degree of semantic similarity to the target word, it can fool the monitor and be erroneously spoken, regardless of any phonological similarity. However, if the semantic relationship is less close, then it might need some backup from phonological similarity in order to be misselected. This would require that there be multiple feed-forward and feed-backward links between the two lexicons, for the following reasons. When the two semantically related lemmas are activated, they each activate their own forms from the form lexicon; if the words have a very close semantic relationship, this form similarity might be irrelevant, but if the semantic relationship is less close, the similarity in form might feed back to the lemma lexicon and make it more likely that the incorrect lemma would be selected. On the other hand, it might be the case that the only factor causing the error is the semantic similarity, and thus any phonological similarity would simply be an accident; this would require only a feed-forward mechanism from the lemma to the form lexicon. Some support for the latter hypothesis, at least for the children, comes from the fact that the majority of the children's [+sem] lexical errors do not show a phonological relationship between the word pair, although in the adult data the number of [+phon, +sem] and [-phon, +sem] pairs is about equal. Some examples are given in (42).

(42)   a. B: 'Anna, ya dón't wànna gò up on **Màrs** . . . on <u>Vènus</u>. It's so hót!' ('Mars' [marz] for 'Venus' [vi.nəs], co-hyponyms; phonological similarity: .05; B-420(35) 4;11)

b. B: 'I **hìt** mys: . . . I <u>hùrt</u> mysèlf twíce.'
        ('hit' [hɪt] for 'hurt' [hɚt], causal; phonological similarity: 4;
        B-554(35) 5;8)

c. B: 'Gràndma Bèckie lìves in **Hústèd** . . . Hoúston.' ('Husted'
        [çjú.stәd] for 'Houston' [çjú.stәn], no semantic relationship;
        phonological similarity: 7; B-541(35) 5;7)

In (42a), the proper nouns 'Mars' and 'Venus' have the very close semantic relationship of being co-hyponyms (kinds of planets) but very little phonological similarity. In (42b), the words 'hit' and 'hurt' are related by the less strong connection of 'causality', but they have a higher phonological similarity rating. Finally in (42c), there is no semantic relationship between the proper nouns 'Husted' and 'Houston', but a very high phonological similarity. Do these three examples represent the norm?

In order to test this hypothesis, I rank-ordered the types of semantic relationships found in the SOT data in terms of their 'closeness'. In most analyses of the tightness of various semantic relationships, data from word association experiments are used to justify the rankings; a classic example is Clark (1970). Based on word association data, antonymic relationships are considered the closest since they are the most commonly produced association responses, followed by coordinates such as co-hyponyms, then superordinate/ subordinate relationships, and then synonyms and associated type relationships such as metonyms. Clark (1970) explains this ranking in terms of the number of features which differ between target and response (which can include a feature change, addition, or omission), selectional feature realizations, and idiomatic expressions.

However, it should be clear at this point that the requirements of the word-association task (i.e. say the first word that comes into your mind when you hear the target word) are very different from the lexical activation properties which are involved in SOTs. The former is a metalinguistic task where the subject is presented with a random target word devoid of any conceptual or discourse context, and normally responds with a semantically related word. Very often the subject activates a word which occurs in an oppositional pair with the target word; the two words are also often linked in a collocational phrase. In other cases the subject produces a co-hyponymic word, i.e. a word at the same level of taxonomic specificity with a shared superordinate. In this context it makes sense that speakers often produce words with a contrastive or coordinate relationship to the target word, but rarely produce synonyms. However, in SOTs the speaker is activating a set of concepts relevant to the proposition being formulated, and then a set of lemmas which appropriately formulate these concepts, and thus lemmas which are synonyms or quasi-synonyms are highly likely to be activated by the same concepts. Lemmas in a coordinate relationship are also likely to be activated, as they are very closely related (in Clark's terms, they differ by only one or a few features from the intended lemma), and are of the same level of (taxonomic) specificity; their meanings will not clearly conflict with the intended meaning. Contrastives can be argued to be a very close semantic relationship for the same reasons (only one feature different, same level of taxonomic specificity), but they are less likely to be activated and misselected in SOTs than coordinates because their meanings are the opposite of those required by the proposition. Superordinates or subordinates are less likely to interfere because they will not necessarily encode the concept at the level of specificity appropriate for the discourse. 'Syntagmatic' or 'functional' type relationships such as metonyms and causality may occur fairly often in SOTs because the concepts for the related words may be related in terms of the scene to be expressed, although this does not necessarily mean that the lemmas themselves are closely linked in the lexicon. This is why metonymic relationships are so common in syntagmatic errors: the concepts are often spoken about in the same utterance, and thus the two distinct lemmas are activated by different concepts. Connotation can also be seen as a fairly weak lexical relationship, since the connotational features of the lemmas of most words are not criterial features, central to their definition, so that two words which are related primarily by connotation will differ in many other features. Finally, the shared criterial features category contains the loosest set of relationships by definition (i.e. links which don't fall into any of the better-defined categories); these words will have some criterial features in common but many other features will differ. However, such misselections will be common in SOTs since there is such a large range of possibility of relationships that may fall into this category.

Using this rationale, I divided the semantic relationship types into four categories, which I have ranked from closest to loosest; in this system I am using the metaphor of 'vertical' distance as indicating the superordinate/ subordinate type relationships, and 'horizontal' distance as indicating semantic relationships at the same taxonomic level.

1) Most closely related: co-hyponyms, co-members of a set, co-partonyms, antonyms, converses, synonyms. These can be seen as word pairs with most of their semantic features in common, but with different values on one or a few features. They are one conceptual step distant from each other in the horizontal direction, i.e. they are of the same level of (taxonomic) specificity. For synonyms, the distinction is typically either in formality level, or selectional restrictions.

2) Second: superordinate/subordinate, set/member, whole/part. These are also very closely related, with many semantic features in common, but one step apart in the vertical direction, so that they are different levels of specificity. In the 'feature' terminology, one could say that superordinate/set/whole lemmas lack features that the subordinate/member/part lemmas contain, whereas the latter contain features missing in the former; thus they differ not by feature changes but by feature additions/omissions (Clark 1970).

3) Third: metonymic, causal, connotation. Metonymic and causal are more syntagmatic than paradigmatic relationships, such that while the concepts may

be closely related, the lemmas themselves are not necessarily closely linked in the lexicon, and will differ by many features. Likewise word pairs linked mainly by connotation will usually differ in many other criterial features. Lemmas which are involved in these types of relationships are often of the same level of specificity, however.

4) Least closely related: shared criterial features. By definition this is the loosest type of relationship, as it can involve word pairs related by only a few features, although they must be criterial. The words can be at the same or differing levels of specificity, and can share a range of types of relationships in terms of which features they have in common (i.e. shape, size, effect, texture, function, and so forth).

In order to get some external validation of this rank ordering, I turned to the 'Latent Semantic Analysis (LSA)' program (http://lsa.colorado.edu; Landaur & Dumais 1997), which contains an estimate of the 'similarity' of word pairs in English (and other languages), based on their probability of occurring near one another in texts. (The actual measure used is the cosine of the angle between vectors in a multidimensional space, which estimates the semantic space of the vocabulary of the language in question.) I selected the 'General Reading up to 1st Year College' topic space (the most general database), and did a term-to-term search for the 'similarity rating' of a subset of the content word pairs involved in lexical substitution and blend errors in my adult data; this excluded proper nouns, and baby words such as 'owie'. I did not run the calculations on the child data, since the database (written texts from elementary school up through college) would be an inappropriate base for comparison to the child vocabulary. The average similarity ratings for word pairs in each of my main headings tended to follow the same pattern as the one I have given above, in terms of closeness of relationships. Coordinates had an average similarity rating of 41.02 and the rating for contrastives was 49.11; these were the two highest ranked categories. Subsumatives had a somewhat lower rating of 37.64, and metonyms/ connotation/causal had a similarity rating of 21.2 (I used the children's connotational errors in this count, since the adults did not make this kind of error). So these four categories were rank ordered by the LSA program in the same order as in my ranking above.

Oddly, my synonyms had a somewhat lower rating than one would expect, 32.55; I'm not sure how to interpret this, but I believe it may be due in part to the fact that my data come from natural conversations, and many of the synonyms in my data are words which would occur infrequently in written (educational) texts. For example, the pairs 'kitty/cat' and 'dope/drug' both have similarity ratings of .09 in the LSA, which is clearly counterintuitive. (Note that this lower ranking was not due to the quasi-synonyms involved in my lexical substitution errors; the LSA assigned the quasi-synonyms approximately the same average 'semantic similarity' ranking as it did the true synonyms which occurred in blends.) Because the relationship of synonym is such a close one in the context of lexical selection during speech production planning, I have decided

TABLE 5.8

Mean 'semantic relatedness' value for semantically related pairs of words involved in lexical errors, on a 4-point scale; by error type and age; [+phon]=the error pair also has a phonological relationship; [-phon]=the error pair does not have a phonological relationship.

Age:	1-2a	1-2b	3	4	5	Total (N)	Adult (N)
Paradigmatic Substitutions							
[+phon]	4.00	3.18	2.81	3.40	3.17	3.20 (54)	3.08 (52)
[-phon]	4.00	3.83	3.63	3.26	2.78	3.26 (72)	3.30 (54)
Paradigmatic Blends							
[+phon]	3.00	4.00	4.00	4.00	2.17	3.41 (22)	3.30 (44)
[-phon]	3.00	3.44	3.70	3.38	2.80	3.35 (46)	3.64 (25)
Syntagmatic Substitutions							
[+phon]	na	3.33	3.33	2.00	3.00	3.00 (13)	3.76 (9)
[-phon]	na	2.40	1.50	3.67	2.75	2.95 (20)	2.28 (18)

to leave it in the most closely related group in my ranking. Finally, the wordpairs with shared criterial features, which I expected to be the most loosely related set, had a fairly high average similarity rating, 31.8. However, there was a large amount of variation in similarity ratings among pairs in this set, from .02 to .64, and so these numbers reflect the variability of types of relationships which fell into this heading; because of this tremendous variability, I decided to leave shared criterial features in the lowest rank.

Using these four criteria, then, I calculated the mean 'semantic relatedness' figures for the lexical errors, depending on whether or not the word pair was analyzed as being phonologically similar (i.e. ranking 3 or more on the rating scale given in Chapter 4). I assigned 4 points to errors with the semantic relationships listed as 'most closely related' (coordinates, converses, synonyms), 3 points to the second ranked (subsumatives), 2 points for the looser relationships (metonym, causal, connotation), and 1 point for shared criterial features; thus the highest mean 'semantic relatedness' figure possible would be '4', and the lowest '1'. I calculated these means for the paradigmatic substitutions, paradigmatic blends, and syntagmatic errors separately, at each age, with content and function words combined. The results are given in Table 5.8. In order for the data to support the hypothesis that closer semantic relationships do not require support from phonological similarity, the mean semantic relatedness figure in the [-phon] rows should always be higher than the figure in the [+phon] rows.

These figures suggest that in the children's errors, there is no trade-off between semantic and phonological relatedness, as the average semantic relatedness in the [-phon] pairs is not consistently higher than in the [+phon] pairs. In the paradigmatic substitution errors, this pattern is followed at ages 1-2b and 3, but not at any other age; the overall difference, 3.20 vs. 3.26, is very small (.06 points). And for the paradigmatic blends and syntagmatic substitutions, the figure for the [-phon] pairs is slightly less than that for the the [+phon] pairs, directly contradicting the hypothesis. Therefore for the children it appears that the semantic relationship is the most important factor causing these lexical substitution or blend errors, and that any phonological similarity is simply an accident, or at least does not contribute greatly to causing the error. Thus it is not surprising that the majority of child lexical substitution/blend errors involve word pairs which do not also have a phonological relationship.

However, the adult data may tell a different story. For the adult paradigmatic substitution errors, the mean semantic relatedness of the [-phon] pairs is closer than for the [+phon] pairs, 3.30 vs. 3.08 (a difference of .22 points). Similarly, for the paradigmatic blends the [-phon] mean is 3.64, but for the [+phon] pairs the mean is 3.30 (a difference of .34 points). In the absence of formal statistics, I cannot definitively state that the phonological relationship in word pairs has an effect on lexical selection errors. However, compared to the child figures, it appears that for the adults, the phonological relatedness of a word pair can boost the possibility that one word will be misselected for another when the pair has a less close semantic relationship. This in fact fits with the findings in Chapter 4, that adult lexical SOTs are more strongly affected by phonological relationships than are child lexical SOTs, suggesting that the phonological relationships in the lexicon become more robust at a later age than do semantic relationships. On the other hand, the adult figures for syntagmatic errors do not follow this same pattern, and in fact the [-phon] errors have a considerably lower mean semantic relationship than the [+phon] pairs. This is undoubtedly at least partially due to the fact that when two words are activated and are being planned for the same utterance, one can substitute for the other with little semantic or phonological similarity, since both words are already activated. On the other hand, since the adults showed more influence of phonetic relatedness in syntagmatic errors than did the children (especially anticipations; see Table 4.5), it may be that the phonological relationship was the more important factor in some cases and the semantic relationship less important or possibly irrelevant (although the lexical category of the two words is certainly always influential).

From these figures the following pattern emerges. For the children, semantically based lexical errors are caused primarily by the semantic relationship between the two mutually involved words; whether the words also have a formal relationship is less important and perhaps irrelevant to the error. This suggests that the feed-forward from the lemma lexicon to the form lexicon is the primarily active channel for the children during lexical selection, such that there is little influence of formal similarity feeding back to the lemma lexicon to influence the misselection of a less strongly semantically related word. However, if the two words involved in the error have no semantic relationship and only a phonological relationship, then the phonological relationship is typically very close, closer than what is usually found in error pairs which are [+phon, +sem] (as demonstrated in Chapter 4). So for the children, the links among phonologically similar lexical items in the form lexicon are more active during speech production planning than the feed-backwards links between the form to the lemma lexicon. (Clearly these links from form to lemma lexicon must exist for speech perception, but whether the same form lexicon is used in both production and perception is a different issue, well beyond the scope of this book.) But for the adults, the formal relationship between two words can influence paradigmatic lexical substitution or blend errors, such that when the two candidate words have a less close semantic relationship, the fact of formal similarity can tip the balance in favor of the error occurring. This means that for the adults, the feed-back lines from the form lexicon to the lemma lexicon are also active during speech production planning. Besides the feed-back mechanism being more effective in adults, this may also be due to the adult monitoring mechanism having more practice, in that it might not allow an error to pass through the filter if the semantic distance from the intended target was too great; but if the words were also formally related this might make the similarity close enough that the monitor could miss the error. However, in syntagmatic errors, just the fact that both words have been planned for the current utterance seems to be more important than either the semantic or phonological factors, such that this interplay disappears.

5.6 The Onset of Lexical Semantic Relationships

In the first section of this chapter I introduced the distinction between 'conceptual semantics', i.e. relationships among the concepts to which words refer, and 'lexical semantics', a link between lemmas in the lexicon based on having semantic properties in common. I suggested that lexical substitution errors could arise from either type of semantic relationship, as well as non-plan-internal factors. So, in one type of error, two closely linked concepts might be activated during 'inferential processes', i.e. the planning of the meaning of the intended utterance; both lemmas may be activated, and then the incorrect lemma selected and planned for speaking (as illustrated in example (1a) above). As discussed at length in Chapter 4, errors can also be influenced by environmental factors (e.g. the intruding referent being present visually), discourse factors (one of the intruding words being part of a previous discourse topic), or 'on the mind' (OTM) factors (the intruding word being something the speaker has been recently or chronically thinking about). When an error arises from any of these causes, one does not need to posit semantic connections in the lexicon per se in order to explain the error; the conceptual relationships and/or non-plan-internal factors may be enough to explain the substitution.

However, in errors in which the activation of the concept of the target word does not necessarily entail the activation of the concept of the error word, the most likely explanation is that the semantic links between the two lemmas in the lexicon have caused the error. In these cases, the target concept has activated the target lemma, and activation has spread from this lemma to other lemmas which share semantic properties, and thus are in the various types of relationships with the target word discussed above: co-hyponyms, metonyms, antonyms, etc. (as illustrated in the diagram in (1b) at the beginning of this chapter).

In adult lexical substitution errors, the latter process is assumed to be the norm (Levelt 1989: Ch. 6), although certainly conceptual relationships and non-plan-internal interferences can come into play. For adults, these lexical links are very well-documented, not by SOT data alone but also by word association tasks, priming experiments, and other psycholinguistic tasks. The evidence from word association is particularly clear, since there is no context, environmental or discourse or conceptual, during the presentation of the stimulus word, so that responses most often consist of the closest lexically linked word. As discussed in §5.1, because children's responses in word association tasks are documented to be very different from adults', some researchers have argued that the child's lexicon is not organized by these same semantic features as the adults' until the child has reached the age of 5 or so. If this is true, then we would expect that most of the lexical substitution errors in the current study, particularly those made by the younger subjects, would be analyzable entirely in terms of conceptual, environmental, discourse, or OTM factors, and there would be no need to posit semantic links in the lemma lexicon. On the other hand, if lexical semantic relationships are set up at an earlier age than the word association data would predict, then we should begin to see errors which reflect this semantic organization of the lemma lexicon at a much earlier date, as Bowerman (1978) would predict. What do the data tell us?

In Table 5.9 I have listed all of the paradigmatic lexical substitution errors from my corpus made by the 1- and 2-year-old children. (I have not looked at the blend errors here since they typically involve synonyms or very close co-hyponyms, which could be argued even for adults to be caused by conceptual overlap; see Levelt (1989:215). Also I have excluded syntagmatic substitutions since they always involve an influence other than semantics, namely the fact that both words were planned for the utterance or discourse.) In the first column is listed the error number; the second column is the child's age, and the third column reports the target and error words in the error. The fourth column indicates the semantic relationship analyzed as holding between the two words; word pairs with no semantic relationship are marked as [-sem]. The right-hand column indicates other factors which may have influenced the error, including phonological similarity [+phon], environmental influences [+env], discourse [+disc], collocational [+colloc], or 'On the Mind' [+OTM] influences, and whether or not these words are taken to represent oppositional pairs.

The first thing apparent from this table is that most early errors, particularly

TABLE 5.9

Paradigmatic lexical substitution errors made during ages 1-2; [+environ]= environmental influence; [+phon]=word pair has a phonological relationship.

Error #	Age	Word Pair	Semantic Rel.	Other Influences
AN-9	1;8	box/tub	[-sem]	[+env, +colloc]
B-9	1;9	Mommy/Daddy	co-members of a set	[+phon, +opp]
AN-15	1;9	hot/hard	co-hyponyms	[+phon]
B-16	1;10	penis/toes	co-partonyms	[+env]
B-20	1;10	coffee/juice	co-hyponyms	[+env]
OC-2	1;10	BobBob/Beckie	co-members of a set	[+env, +phon, +opp]
OC-6	2;0	toothpaste/ toothbrush	co-members of a set	[+phon], shared stem
OC-7	2;0	Daddy/Mommy	co-members of a set	[+env, +phon, +opp]
B-42	2;2	Mommy/Alice	co-members of a set	[+env]
AL-10	2;2	kiss/car	[-sem]	[+phon, +OTM]
AL-13	2;2	crying/quiet	[-sem]	[+phon], possibly [+opp]
AN-45	2;4	Daddy/Anna	co-members of a set	[+phon, +OTM]
AN-47	2;4	talk (to)/call	synonyms	[+phon]
B-58	2;5	candy/quesadilla	co-hyponyms	[+phon, +disc]
B-71	2;6	watch/listen to	co-hyponyms	[+opp]
OC-23	2;6	Todd/Copper	co-members of a set	[+env, +opp]
B-74	2;6	hit/hurt	causal	[+phon]
B-77	2;6	green/yellow	co-hyponyms	
B-78	2;6	Daddy/Anna	co-members of a set	[+phon]
B-83	2;6	floor/table	metonyms	[+env]
B-84	2;6	Puss in Boots/ Mother Goose	co-hyponyms	[+phon]
B-86b	2;6	turning/talking	[-sem]	[+phon, +colloc]
B-90	2;7	always/already	shared crit. features	[+phon, +opp]
B-94	2;7	scary/owie	connotation	[+phon]
B-98	2;7	cake/soup	co-hyponyms	(spoken in restaurant)
AN-55	2;7	open/blow up	quasi-synonyms	
AN-60	2;7	Collection/ Contraption	[-sem]	[+phon]
OC-29	2;8	slow/fast	gradable antonyms	
OC-30	2;8	watermelon/egg	co-hyponyms	[+env]
AL-43	2;8	see/hear	co-hyponyms	[+opp]
AN-68	2;9	shark/shot	connotation	[+phon, +OTM]
OC-34	2;10	candy/applejuice	co-hyponyms	

those up through age 2;5 (N=14, of which 11 are [+sem]), involve two very concrete words, most often nouns (including proper nouns), with a few cases of adjective and verb pairs. One subset of errors involves two proper nouns which refer to important people commonly encountered together in the child's life, such as 'Mommy/Daddy', 'Daddy/Anna', 'Mommy/Alice', and 'BobBob/Beckie' (the child's grandparents); these were all analyzed as 'co-members of a set', and the 'Mommy/Daddy' and 'BobBob/Beckie' cases further analyzed as [+opposed]. In these cases there is undoubtedly a strong conceptual relationship between the two entities, and thus it is not necessary to claim a lexical link between these words to explain the errors. One pair, 'talk (to)/call' was analyzed as involving a synonymous relationship, and in this case again it could be argued that the shared conceptual features of the events to which these two words refer would be sufficient to cause the error, without positing a lexical link.

Another subset of errors involves word pairs where the referent of the error word was physically present in the environment; 5 of the 11 [+sem] errors made during this time period (through age 2;5) showed an environmental influence (e.g. 'penis/toes', 'coffee/juice', as well as 3 of the proper noun errors). The two non-plan-internal factors of 'discourse' and 'OTM' each affected one [+sem] error. Thus, of the 11 [+sem] errors made before age 2;6, all but one either involve the proper name co-members of a set, or show some non-plan-internal influence, or both. While many target/error pairs were phonologically similar, most pairs also showed the influence of some other factor; since a phonological relationship would be lexical by definition, it is possible that the phonological similarity was irrelevant to the error at this age. Only one error, 'hot/hard' had only a phonological influence beside the semantic relationship; I will return to this error below.

It is interesting to note that the 3 [-sem] errors produced during this time period also show the same sorts of influences. The first error involving 'box/tub' was caused by environmental and collocational factors, since Anna was holding the 'box' when she meant to say 'tub', and 'in the box' was a frequent collocation for her. While the two words were not considered to be semantically related, the two objects have some physical properties in common, being roughly the same shape, and both being containers which can hold water. Alice's substitution of 'kiss' for 'car' was influenced by the fact that she had just kissed her mother and was still thinking about it when she attempted to name the 'car', so this was classified as 'OTM'. The verb substitution of 'crying' for 'quiet', while not classified as reflecting a semantic relationship between the two words, may have been influenced by the oppositional meanings of the two words in the specific context of the utterance, i.e. if one is 'crying' one is not '(being) quiet', and therefore one might wake up Daddy. Therefore the errors which were not analyzed as involving a semantic relationship between the word pair require the same types of conceptual, environmental, or OTM explanations as the [+sem] errors.

However, at age 2;6 something begins to change. In B-71, Bobby declared that he wanted to '**watch** . . . listen to' an audio tape. In this case the concept of 'listening to' an audio tape does not necessarily activate the concept of 'watching' something; furthermore there were no other influences on this error, i.e. no phonological similarity, and no environmental, discourse, or 'OTM' support (although this semantic relationship can be seen as 'opposed'). This appears to be the first error which requires that a lexical link between the lemmas of 'watch' and 'listen to' be posited, i.e. they are related as co-hyponyms of perception typically found in the domain of entertainment media (audio tapes, TVs, radio, etc.). Several other errors at this age show the same type of lexical-semantic relationship. In B-77 (2;6) Bobby asks for the 'green' nipple, and corrects to the 'yellow' one, when there was no green nipple in view; 'yellow' and 'green' are co-hyponyms of color, but there is no reason why the activation of the concept 'yellow' would automatically activate the concept of 'green'. Anna, at age 2;7 (AN-55) produces the quasi-synonyms 'open' and 'blow-up' in the context of handing Mother a balloon; presumably the lemma of the appropriate word 'blow-up' was activated, and then activation spread to other lemmas with the semantic properties 'action involving expanding something outward', and the erroneous lemma was misselected. Alice's substitution of 'see' for 'hear' (AL-43(2;8)) is similar to Bobby's 'watch/listen to' error. And in particular, the error involving the gradable antonyms 'slow/fast' (OC-29, 2;8) is a very clear case of lexical semantic links; if one activates the concept 'fast', it does not necessarily activate the opposing concept 'slow', since 'slow' would be by definition completely contradictory to the proposition being planned. Antonyms are taken to be the paradigm case of lexical semantic relationships in adult lexicons, and there is no reason to believe that child lexicons are radically different from adults' on this measure.

Similarly, there are several errors beginning at age 2;6 which involve both a semantic and a phonological relationship, but no other influence. So in B-74 Bobby declares that he '**hit** . . . hurt' his two friends; however, he had not hit them, but hurt them in some other way. The concepts of 'hit/hurt' may have been fairly closely related in Bobby's mind, but it is not necessarily the case that activating the concept of 'hurt' would automatically activate the concept 'hit', since there are many different activities which could cause 'hurt'. But it is the case that if he had activated the target lemma 'hurt', it is likely that activation would have spread to words linked by causality to the target word, and 'hit' would be one of the most closely lexically related lemmas to 'hurt'. If both lemmas were activated, and then the form lexicon were accessed and both forms activated, the fact that they are phonetically similar would make it more likely that if the error form 'hit' were misselected for 'hurt', the error would not be detected by the internal monitor. Thus these errors with semantic and phonological relationships but no other influences and no necessary activation of one concept from the other, suggest that lexical links are beginning to be developed in both the lemma and the form lexicon. Other pairs of this sort include B-84 'Puss in Boots/Mother Goose', and B-94 'scary/owie'. I showed in

§5.5 above that semantic relationships are more important than phonological relationships in the children's lexical substitution errors. However, the fact that malapropisms, such as Anna's error involving the substitution of 'Collection' for 'Contraption' (AN-60, 2;7), begin to occur at this age shows that links in the form lexicon are also beginning to develop at this time.

The one very early error which appears to be similar to these [+sem, +phon] errors is given in (43).

(43)   An: (Mom was helping Anna put some tight shoes on; she pushed too
            hard and it hurt Anna's foot) 'Is tòo **hót**.' (looks confused)
        M: 'Too hót?'
        An: 'Is tòo hárd.' ('hot' [hatʰ] for 'hard' [ha:ʒtʰ]; AN-15(35) 1;9.20)

It is possible that this was actually a phonological error, where the /r/ was omitted from 'hard'. However, since both words 'hot' and 'hard' were known to Anna at the time, and they are both adjectives, describing unpleasant physical sensations, it is more likely to be a lexical substitution error. As far as the causes of the error, it is unlikely that the concept of 'hard' would activate the concept of 'hot'; but I would be uncomfortable arguing that at age 1;9, the child has semantic links in the lexicon between the lemmas of these two words, and/or that there were lexical links in the form lexicon between the two phonetically similar words at this age. What is more likely is that Anna activated the more general concept of 'physical sensations which cause pain', and from there activated the wrong lemma, among the set of words which would be selected by this superordinate concept; the fact that the two words sound similar to each other would make this misselection less likely to be caught by the internal monitor. However, the external monitor caught it immediately, as Anna looked confused after producing the erroneous utterance; after Mom's prompt, Anna was able to activate and produce the intended word 'hard'.

Another thing begins to happen at age 2;6 which is of interest to the current question. With the exception of the one synonym 'talk (to)/call', all of the [+sem] errors made from 1;8-2;5 involve error pairs in a coordinate relationship: co-members of a set=6, co-hyponyms=3, co-partonyms=1. However, beginning at age 2;6, the semantic relationships begin to expand, and from 2;6-2;10 they include causality, metonyms, shared criterial features, connotation, quasi-synonyms, and gradable antonyms.

The lexical substitution errors made by children from ages 3-5 continue to show these patterns, including many 'pure' semantic errors (i.e. with no other influences), and involving a broad range of semantic relationships. The paradigmatic lexical substitution errors of the children at these ages are essentially indistinguishable from errors made by adults, with a few exceptions noted above in this chapter and in Chapter 4. Specifically, children continue to be more affected by environmental influences than adults, probably due to less mature attention systems (see §4.2.6), and children are more affected by 'opposed' relationships; this sort of binary opposition of entities seems to be a very important factor for them in organizing their conceptual and linguistic spaces (see §5.3.2).

So what is happening at age 2;6? As discussed previously, most researchers agree that early word meanings are somewhat holistic and are very closely linked to concrete contexts, scenes, action schema, and so forth (see the Fillmore 1975 citation in §5.2.1 above, and the Bowerman 1978 citation in §5.4; see also Clark 2003:138ff for a recent review.) However, the child begins to gradually abstract the semantic features relevant across lexical items in the same semantic domain, and these features begin to be an organizational factor in the lemma lexicon, linking lexical items to each other. That is, as knowledge about the internal meaning structures of individual lexical items gradually develops, the lexicon gradually becomes organized not only by conceptual structures, but also by lexical semantic properties of the words in the lexicon. While most researchers would agree with some version of the above scenario, the age at which this lexical restructuring (in Bowerman's terms) takes place is controversial.

I would like to argue that my data indicate that the extraction and systematization of semantic features is probably going on during the first half of the third year, and that by age 2;6, enough lexical semantic structure has taken hold of the lemma lexicon that the words' meanings are beginning to be freed up from the constraints of specific, concrete contexts. This is because at age 2;6, the children begin to produce SOTs where the target and error words are less closely linked conceptually, such that the activation of one concept does not necessarily imply the activation of the other. Furthermore these errors occur without any influence from external factors such as environment, previous discourse, or ideas which are on the speaker's mind. However, these word pairs have clear semantic relationships which it is likely have begun to be marked in the lexicon, and spreading activation from one lemma to another is the simplest explanation for these errors. Similarly, a broad range of semantic relationships begin to emerge in SOTs at age 2;6, such that these errors are no longer constrained by the very concrete linkings inherent in coordinate relationships. The knowledge developing about the internal structure of the meaning of individual words necessitates the positing of a variety of different types of semantic features; this in turn leads to a variety of lexical semantic relationships between lemmas, such as metonyms, causality, connotation, and the more general shared criterial features. This finding may be related to the finding in Chapter 4, that there is no need to posit the notion of 'lexical category' in the children's early lexical slips; since lexical category is one of the aspects of linguistic knowledge represented in lemmas, the appearance of evidence for lexical categories in the middle of the third year reinforces the claim that this is the time during which lemmas are coming to be crucial in the representation of lexical knowledge. While the children's paradigmatic lexical substitution errors continue to show a few differences from adults', the types of semantic relationships evident in these errors are extremely similar to those produced by adults. If the hypothesis is accepted that adult semantic paradigmatic lexical substitutions are caused primarily by spreading activation in the lemma lexicon caused by shared lexical-semantic features (Levelt 1989:219, Levelt, Roelofs & Meyer 1999), then I see no reason to analyze the children's errors any differently, after about age 2;6. Naturally, conceptual semantics continues to be influential in the planning and execution of speech, as it does in adult speech; however, after about 2;6 it is no longer the sole semantic organizing system affecting the children's speech production planning.

If, on the other hand, the distinction between conceptual and lexical semantics is rejected, then there is evidence that the child's lexicon is organized by semantics from the earliest errors (age 1;7), since nearly all word pairs in early lexical substitution and blend errors have a conceptual-semantic relationship.

5.7 Summary and Conclusions

In the first section of this chapter I introduced the distinction between 'conceptual semantics' and 'lexical semantics', which defines a major controversy surrounding the organization of the lexicon. I briefly discussed the 'frame semantics' theory of Fillmore (1974, 1978, 1982), which served as a starting point for the taxonomy of semantic relationships, which I presented in detail in §5.2. In §5.3 I looked at the frequency of various types of semantic relationships in the lexical SOTs, from the perspective of four parameters. First, I found that there were very few differences in proportions of different semantic relationships types across the four child data sets. A few differences were found between Anna and my other two children, which I attributed to the 'expressive/referential' parameter.   Specifically, Anna, the more 'expressive' child produced more loosely related errors than Bobby and Alice, the more 'referential' children, whereas the latter two children produced more 'opposed' errors; the binary 'opposed' semantic relationship seemed to be more important in the organization of the referential children's lexicons. Second, I found that there were changes over time in the types and proportions of semantic relationships evident in the children's errors; I attributed this to their growing ability to identify and understand more elements of the scenes salient in their worlds, and to develop a more fine-grained semantic representation of individual words. The children ages 3-5 produced very similar proportions of different semantic relationships in their errors as the adults; however, in general the adult errors reflected a more sophisticated understanding of hierarchical relationships among lexical items, and a more elaborate vocabulary.

Third, I compared the semantic relationships involved in different types of errors: paradigmatic substitutions, blends, and syntagmatic substitutions. Coordinate and associated relationships were most common in paradigmatic substitution errors; synonyms and coordinates were most common in blends; and the syntagmatic substitutions displayed a broad range of relationship types, with the more loosely related associated types predominating. The child data were very similar to the adults, except for the adults producing more synonyms in blends, undoubtedly due to their larger vocabularies. These patterns were explicated in terms of the RPC speech production planning model, given that different factors come into play during planning at the points at which each type of error is made. Fourth, I looked at the interplay of semantic relationships and lexical category. I argued that differences in proportions of semantic relationships can be shown to be a function of the types of relationships available to the vocabulary in that category; differences between child and adult errors were attributed to vocabulary which is learned early vs. learned late.

In §5.4 I compared the results of my study to several other studies of semantic SOTs. While my results were very similar in many respects to other studies in terms of proportion of types of semantic relationships, I argued that my data show that both quasi-synonyms and subsumatives occur in lexical substitution errors, contra the other studies. I also discussed Bowerman's (1978) study of her children's verb errors involving 'put, give, make, and let', and agreed with her analysis of the causes of such errors, in terms of the development of the semantic featural organization of the lexicon.

In §5.5 I looked at the issue of the interplay between semantic and phonological relationships in the lexicon. I found that for adults, the word pairs involved in lexical SOTs with a very close semantic relationship tended to have a looser phonological relationship, but word pairs with a less close semantic relationship tended to have more phonological properties in common. Thus, for adults, phonological similarity can serve as an enhancing factor for SOTs when the semantic relationship might not be strong enough to cause the misselection. On the other hand, for the children there was very little if any interaction of phonological relatedness with semantic relatedness; the data appear to show that the semantic relationship is the most important factor in the children's SOTs, and any phonological relationship in semantic SOTs is much less important, if not irrelevant, suggesting that feedback channels from the form lexicon to the lemma lexicon are not as important during speech production planning for the children compared to the adults.

The issue discussed in §5.6 was that raised in the introduction, i.e. whether or not there is any evidence that the child's lexicon is organized by semantics, and if so, is it possible to discern a shift from purely conceptual-semantic relationships to the emergence of lexical-semantic links among lemmas in the lexicon. A detailed analysis of the paradigmatic lexical substitution errors made at ages 1-2 showed that before age 2;6, errors could be entirely accounted for by close conceptual relationships, supported by concrete 'oppositional' pairings, environmental influences, and other non-plan-internal influences. However, beginning at age 2;6, the children began to produce errors which could not as easily be accounted for purely on conceptual grounds, and which showed no external influences. Furthermore, the types of semantic relationships evident in errors began to expand at this age, to include most of the same types as produced by adults. Thus I argued that these errors show strong evidence that the lemma lexicon begins to be organized by lexical semantics at around age 2;6.

The overall picture that emerges from these errors is the following: at ages 1;7 through 2;5, children produce lexical SOTs which show semantic relationships between the target and error words, or two targets. However, in non-environmentally influenced errors, the errors are largely governed by associations of the two words with specific concrete scenes and concepts, and the links between the two words are conceptual-semantic links. Most early errors involve common or proper nouns, and relatively simple coordinate relationships; word meaning is most likely fairly global and linked to concrete contexts at this age. However, during the first half of the third year, children are becoming more sophisticated about analyzing the scenes they encounter in their lives, and extracting more fine-grained properties from these scenes. This allows them to begin to develop a broader vocabulary to talk about entities, events, and qualities involved in these scenes, which requires the acquisition of words in a wider range of lexical categories: verbs, adjectives, adverbs, and function words. At the same time the internal meaning structure of each individual word begins to become more detailed, and the child begins to notice that particular features of meaning are relevant to many different words. At this point, around age 2;6, the children begin to produce SOTs in which the relationship between the word pair reflects these lexical semantic features; they are somewhat more abstracted from their concepts, and do not require any environmental support. Simultaneously the types of semantic relationships evident in errors begin to expand; this is due partially to a richer inventory of possible semantic features which can figure into relationships, and partly due to adding new lexical classes into the vocabulary, since various lexical categories are likely to enter into semantic relationship types in different proportions. The latest arriving semantic relationships to show up in the children's errors were the subsumatives, which require not only horizontal links in the lexicon at the same taxonomic level, but also vertical hierarchical links across levels; there was only one such error before the age of 3;6.

This view of the developing lexicon is similar to that presented by many other researchers, as discussed throughout this chapter; specifically, it reflects the scenarios described by Fillmore (1975:127) and Bowerman (1978:983), and fits easily into the 'Frames, then Content' heuristic of MacNeilage & Davis (1990). Although the latter was developed to account for phonological development, it can be seen that the same general developmental progression occurs in the acquisition of semantics, showing that this is a general principle of language acquisition. What the study of SOTs has added to this discourse is a clear picture of when semantic relationships of various types begin to develop in the lexicon, and what types of semantic relationships are relevant to lexical organization. This methodology provides a way to tap the child's unconscious knowledge about word meanings and lexical semantic relationships, and as such gives a much more accurate view of the developing lexicon than methodologies such as word association tasks which require metalinguistic behavior on the child's part (as pointed out by Bowerman (1978)). The main finding of this study is that the child's lexicon is organized by conceptual-semantic relationships as early as 1;7, and lexical-semantic relationships begin to be relevant to the organization of the child's lexicon at a very early age, most likely around age 2;6.

Chapter 6
Morphology and Syntax

6.1   Introduction

In the preceding chapters I have frequently discussed issues which are pertinent to the representation and processing of morphology and syntax, and the development of these aspects of language structure. The purpose of the present chapter is to look in more detail into a set of specific questions regarding the development of the representation and processing of morphology and syntax, which will partially be related to previously discussed issues but will also involve new questions. At the end of the chapter I will summarize the aspects of morphosyntax about which SOT data provide developmental evidence.

6.2   The Morphological Structure of Lexical Entries

In previous chapters I have taken a very specific stance regarding the morphological make-up of lexical entries, and the relationship between inflectional morphology and syntax in English. Specifically, I have argued that in English, multi-morphemic words, including derived forms, compounds, and particle verbs, are stored in the lexicon as single entries, but regularly inflected forms are not. Rather, the inflectional affixes themselves are stored as individual lexical entries, and stems+affixes are concatenated on-line during processing. During speech production planning, inflectional morphology is closely related to syntactic frames rather than lexical items. On the other hand, irregularly inflected forms are stored in the form lexicon, linked with the forms of their stems. This model is similar to the models called 'dual-route' in the literature (see Pinker 1991, Pinker & Prince 1988, 1991), and fits with the 'stages' type processing models, such as those of Fromkin (1973a), Garrett (1980a, 1993), Levelt (1989, Bock & Levelt 1994), and the RPC Model introduced in Chapter 1. Naturally the details of the composition of lexical entries may differ depending on the morphological structure of the language; see, for example, Hokkanen (1999) on Finnish, or Prunet, Beland & Idrissi (2000) on Semitic languages.

These claims regarding the units of lexical entry are very controversial, and have been so for decades (Jackendoff 1975, Aronoff 1976, Miller 1978). Many prominent hypotheses regarding the make-up of the lexicon which differ from the present stance are readily available in the literature (Frauenfelder & Schreuder 1991, Waksler 1999). Other hypotheses include the possibility that all morphemes of a language are stored in the lexicon, and concatenated on-line during processing (Taft & Forster 1975, Taft 1994). At the other extreme is the hypothesis that all possible words in a language are stored in the lexicon (Butterworth 1983a, 1989, Dell & O'Seaghda 1992, Stemberger 1994). A large body of psycholinguistic evidence regarding these issues exists in the literature (see, for example, papers in Marslen-Wilson 1989 and Sandra & Taft 1994; also Bauer 2001: Ch. 4).

There is also some neurolinguistic evidence pertinent to the regular/irregular issue. A number of neuroimaging studies have been done looking at brain areas activated during the processing of regular vs. irregular verbs or nouns, in English and German (Jaeger et al. 1996, Indefrey et al. 1997, Ullman, Bergida & O'Craven 1997, Beretta et al., 2003; see Jaeger 2003 for a review). Although the details of the studies differ, all studies so far have found that partially different and partially overlapping cortical areas are activated by the two types of processing; no study has found identical cortical activation for regular and irregular forms. For example, in our PET study of regular vs. irregular verb processing (Jaeger et al. 1996), we found cortical activation for the regular verbs which was compatible with the hypothesis that the stem+suffix forms were being concatenated on-line during processing, specifically pre-frontal cortex activation. However, for the irregular forms there was activation in temporal lobe cortex usually associated with auditory memory, suggesting that these forms were being activated from the 'form' lexicon. Again these studies are compatible to a large extent with the 'dual-route' representation and processing mechanisms cited above.

In the present chapter I will add to this body of research by assessing the three competing hypotheses introduced above regarding the representation of morphology in the lexicon, and the concomitant processing of morphology during speech production planning. Specifically, I will look at the following four questions, both in general and in terms of development:

1) How is morphology represented in the lexicon? There are two sub-parts to this question. First, what is the unit of the lexical entry? Are all morphemes represented in the lexicon individually? Are there some multimorphemic words represented as single lexical entries? Or are all the possible words in the language stored as individual lexical entries? Second, if multimorphemic words are stored, do they carry some information in their form entry about their morphological composition?

2) How is morphology processed during speech production planning? Are some affixes more closely related to content stems, while others are linked to syntagmatic slots in the syntactic frame? Is allomorphy completely productive and always honored? During planning, do errors allow for incorrect case assignment or agreement, or are illegal case assignment and agreement always 'cleaned up' in the utterance containing the error?

3) In what order are bound morphemes learned? Do the children's errors follow patterns predicted by previous research, specifically Brown's 14 morphemes (Brown 1973:274)?

4) Are the answers to the above questions different depending on whether the focus is on derivational vs. inflectional morphology? Regular vs. irregular? Productive vs. non-productive?

Before being able to tackle these questions it is important to define some terms. First of all, I am using the term 'morphology' rather loosely in this chapter to primarily indicate bound morphemes, usually affixes, as well as processes such as internal modification or compounding. In some cases I will use the term 'stem' to mean content morphemes to which affixes can be attached. I will use the term 'clitic' to mean free function morphemes which can be cliticized to content words in contracted forms. I will use the notation of curly brackets to indicate the lemma of a morpheme; so for example {-ing} indicates the present participle suffix.

An important distinction in this chapter will be that of 'inflectional' vs. 'derivational' morphology. This distinction has been the subject of much debate in the literature, and the division is far from clear-cut (Stump 1998, Beard 1998). However, it does seem to be a very important factor in the findings to be discussed below, and so I will present a working definition here. I define a 'derivational' affix or process as one which creates a new word. This can include cases which change the lexical category of the stem, such as *sing*(V)--> *sing+er*(N) where the agentive suffix {-er} has changed the verb to a noun. It can also include cases where the lexical category has not been changed, but the meaning of the stem has been altered significantly, for example *tie*(V)--> *un+tie*(V), where the prefix {un-} has changed the meaning of the stem to its opposite. Compounding is considered a derivational process, as it produces a new lexical item; similarly 'zero derivation', where e.g. a noun such as *hand* is used as a verb, is also a derivational process.

On the other hand, 'inflectional' affixes or processes are those which allow the basic meaning of the stem to remain intact, and add grammatical or relational meaning to the utterance. The inflectional morphemes in English will be defined as the set shown in (1), following Quirk & Greenbaum (1973). All other affixes will be considered derivational in this study.

(1)

Abstract Form	Name of Inflected Form	Allomorphs	Irregular Forms?
{-s}	plural (N)	[-s, -z, -əz]	yes (few)
{-s}	possessive	[-s, -z, -əz]	no
{-ing}	present participle (V)	[-ɪŋ] ([-ən, -in])	no
{-s}	3rd person singular present tense (V)	[-s, -z, -əz]	yes (few)
{-ed}	past tense (V)	[-t, -d, -əd]	yes (many)
{-ed/-en}	past participle (V)	[-t, -d, -əd] or [-ən]	yes (see below)
{-er}	comparative (adj)	[-ɚ]	some suppletive
{-est}	superlative (adj)	[ɨst]	some suppletive

A few clarifications of this list are in order.

1) The present participle formed with {-ing} has two functions. First, it combines with the auxiliary 'be' to produce the progressive aspect, as in 'be singing'. Second, present participles can be used as gerunds (nouns) such as 'the singing of the birds', as adjectives such as 'the running boy', and as adverbs such

as 'raving mad'. Because it is the function of the suffix rather than its form which will usually be of more importance in the following discussion, I will distinguish between these two functions of the present participle by referring to {-ing} as the 'progressive suffix' when it functions in progressive verb phrases, but referring to forms with this suffix which function as a lexical category other than verbs as 'present participials'. Although present participials superficially contain an inflectional suffix, they are actually derived from inflected verbs by zero derivation. The present participle, whatever its function, has one basic allomorph, [-ɪŋ], but in casual speech it is often pronounced as [-ən] or [-ɨn], and, in the dialect of many of the subjects in this study, [-ɪn].

2)   The past participle has three functions. First, in combination with the auxiliary 'have' it forms the perfect aspect, as in 'has eaten'; I will refer to this suffix when it performs this function as the 'perfect'. Second, in combination with the auxiliary 'be' it forms the passive voice, as in 'was eaten'; this will be referred to as the 'passive' suffix. Third, like the present participle, the past participle can be used as an adjective, as in 'the broken cup', which I will refer to as 'past participials'; these are also considered to be derived from verbs by zero derivation. In this chapter I am treating both the /-en/ and /-ed/ forms of the past participle suffix as being regular, since both are very common and it is quite unlikely that the children considered either of these forms to be irregular, due to their frequency. Only past participle forms with stem changes ('had bought', 'was bought') or the zero allomorph ('had hit', 'got hit') are considered irregular.

3)   The designation of the comparative and superlative as inflectional is probably the most controversial among the above forms (Stump 1998:31), but since these affixes do not change lexical category and could be said to add relational meaning, they are classed as inflectional here (but see below).

4)   I will refer to the 3rd person singular present tense marker as '3sg' throughout this chapter, for the sake of simplicity.

The traditional structural relationship between inflectional and derivational processes is that all derivational processes must be complete before inflectional affixes are added. Thus in English, derivational suffixes occur between the content root and any inflectional suffix, and no further suffixes can occur to the right of an inflectional suffix. Also in English, all inflectional affixes are suffixes, whereas derivational affixes include both prefixes and suffixes.

A second distinction which will figure in the discussion below is that between affixes which are 'productive' and 'non-productive' (Cutler 1980b, Baayen 1994, Aronoff & Anshen 1998, Bauer 2001). A full discussion of this term is well beyond the scope of this book, but a working definition would be as follows: an affix will be considered 'productive' if it can be freely affixed to members of an appropriate lexical category and result in acceptable words. All regular inflectional affixes are productive by definition because they must be affixed to the majority of the members of the appropriate word class (usually either nouns or verbs, or in the case of the possessive, the last element in a modifying nominal), although there are some exceptions (e.g. mass nouns normally don't take the plural suffix). The comparative and superlative are productive only for stems of one or two syllables, with some exceptions; longer stems take the *more* and *most* forms.   However, most derivational affixes in English are not fully productive. The most productive would be those with very transparent meaning, which do not cause any distortion in the phonology of the stem; in general this would be the 'Stratum II' affixes in Lexical Phonology (Kiparsky 1982, Goldsmith 1990: Ch. 5). In the data below, the derivational affixes which show some productivity are: the diminutive {-ie} which occurs in words such as *owie, blankie,* and so on; the adjectival {-y} in words such as *witty, scary*; and the agentive or instrumental {-er} or {-or} as in *singer, advisor,* or *heater.*   However, suffixes such as the nominalizer {-ity} which causes a shift in the vowel (e.g. *sane* [seʰn] vs. *sanity* [sǽ.nɨ.ti]) and others which shift stress (e.g. *apply* [ə.pʰlá͡ʲ] vs. *application* [æ̀.plə.kʰé͡ʲ.ʃən] are fairly unproductive, in that speakers do not freely form new words with these suffixes; in general these would be the 'Stratum I' affixes. Some prefixes such as {un-} and {re-} are relatively productive in that they can be affixed to new stems with fairly transparent meaning and no distortion of the stem phonology. However, they can only be meaningfully affixed to stems which fall in a fairly narrow range of semantic meanings; e.g. {un-}, in its meaning of 'to reverse an action' can most felicitously be prefixed to verbs of fastening such as 'untie, unglue'. It should be clear from this discussion that the notion of productivity is a relative and gradient one, and the purpose of presenting it here is to see to what extent this factor is necessary for explaining the pattern of errors to be discussed below.

I will now turn to an examination of the data, looking at the issues raised above regarding the morphological structure of lexical representations, and the on-line processing of morphology.

6.3 Errors Involving Morphology

There are two types of error where individual bound morphemes function separately from stems. In the first type, the affix or bound morpheme is the unit of error per se, in that it is added or substituted in an erroneous location. Although these are predominantly syntagmatic errors involving morpheme movement, morphemes can also be added or substituted paradigmatically, and so both types of errors will be discussed here, in §6.3.1.   The second type of error involving affixes is strandings, where a stem moves, leaving an affix behind; these will be discussed in §6.3.2. In §6.3.3 I will compare the age-based order in which various affixes are involved in the errors in my corpus, to the order of acquisition of English morphemes discussed by Brown (1973), to see whether or not the two are compatible. Finally, in §6.3.4. I will look at issues involving 'accommodation', that is, allomorphy and agreement in syntagmatic errors. Throughout this section, I will relate the data to the various issues raised above regarding the structure of lexical entries, and the processing of morphology.

6.3.1 Morpheme-Unit Errors
6.3.1.1 Types of Errors, and Lexical Categories Involved
There are two types of error where an affix is the actual unit of error, which I will call morpheme-unit errors. One involves syntagmatic errors in which an affix moves and is either added to a new location, as in (2a), or substituted for another morpheme in a different location, as in (2b); this can include anticipations, perseverations, or exchanges (classes 42, 44, 46.5).

(2)   a. An: 'It**s** mèan__ you gò to schóol.'
           (for 'it means' [ɪt min(z)]; 3sg {-s} anticipated/moved from
           'means', added to 'it' [ɪt(s)]; AN-69(42) 2;9)

       b. AF: 'Creàt**ing** wríte . . . creàt*ive* wrít*ing*.'
           (present participial suffix {-ing} anticipated and substituted for
           derivational adjectival suffix {-ive}; AD-607(42))

The second type of morpheme-unit error is paradigmatic errors where an incorrect affix is either substituted non-contextually for the target affix, as in (3a) below (class 37), or added non-contextually as in (3b) (class 37.5).

(3)   a. B: (sucking on a piece of candy) 'I've been sùck**ed** on . . . I've
           been sùck*ing* on thìs for a lòng tíme.' (perfect {-ed} [-t],
           substituted for progressive {-ing}; B-456(37) 5;1)

       b. AF: 'He gèts a fùll còurs**ing** redúction.' (for 'course'; progressive
           {-ing} added non-contextually; AD-492(37.5))

Table 6.1 presents the number of errors of each type at each age from my data. In this table, the one adult 'exchange' error is counted as a substitution. 'Multiple' errors are counted more than once when there is more than one morpheme error in the utterance; 'multiple' errors can fall into any of the above categories (i.e. paradigmatic or syntagmatic, additions or substitutions). I only counted four 'multiple' errors (class 48) into this table, as they were the only ones where I could clearly identify the morphemes involved; they are AL-69, B-169, AL-214, and AD-651.

It can be seen from this table that this type of error is somewhat rare, both for the children and adults; however, a few patterns emerge. First, syntagmatic morphological errors are more common than paradigmatic (83% for children, 82.5% adults), and additions are more common than substitutions (79% for children, 70.5% adults). The most common morpheme unit error occurs when a suffix is moved from one location and added to a new location (as in (2a)), for both children and adults. The one difference between children and adults is in the paradigmatic errors: the children produced two pure paradigmatic substitutions at age 5 (illustrated in (3a) above), and the other three paradigmatic errors were part

TABLE 6.1
Number of affix errors of each type: syntagmatic (Syn) vs. paradigmatic (Par); substitutions (Sub) vs. additions (Add); by age.

Age:	1-2a	1-2b	3	4	5	Total	Adult
Syn/Sub	0	1	0	1	0	2	5
Syn/Add	0	4	3	11	4	22	9
Par/Sub	0	1	0	1	2	4	0
Par/Add	0	0	1	0	0	1	3
Total N=	0	6	4	13	6	29	17

of complex 'Multiple' errors in which affixes were substituted or added non-contextually (see examples in (8), (14b), and (19b) below). However, the three adult paradigmatic errors were all of the single non-contextual addition type shown in (3b) above. So, even though these numbers are small, the adult paradigmatic errors look somewhat more well-organized than the children's.

In order to test the hypothesis that inflectional and derivational affixes behave differently from each other in morpheme-unit errors, I assigned a lexical status to each morpheme involved in these errors as follows: inflectional, participial, (other) derivational, copula or auxiliary clitic, and 'other' (see, for example, (14a) below which involves the pronoun 'them'). I have included the contractible copula and auxiliary in this count because they function as clitics in the same manner as the inflectional possessive marker, and in fact have the same phonological form as the possessive, as well as the regular plural and 3sg suffixes. In the majority of substitution errors the two affixes involved belonged to the same category (i.e. one inflectional affix substituting for another), but in a few cases the target and source morphemes were of different lexical categories. Therefore I have counted the number of tokens of morphemes from each category which were involved in the substitution errors listed in Table 6.1; the results are given in Table 6.2, organized by age and whether or not the error involved a substitution or an addition. (Because I counted tokens, there are twice as many substitution errors in this table as in Table 6.1.) Since no errors of this type occurred at age 1-2a, this column is eliminated.

This table makes it clear that inflectional affixes were involved in morpheme errors more often than any other type of morpheme counted in this table. Overall, inflectional affixes made up 71.5% (25 out of 35) of the morphemes involved in the children's errors and 54.5% (12 out of 22) of the adults', whereas derivational affixes (participial and other derivational combined) made up 17% of the children's errors (6/35) and 36.5% (8/22) of the adults'. In fact, all four of the age 1-2b derivational/participial errors, which make up 4 of the 6 derivational child errors, came from the same 'Multiple' error, *'That's a scar**in'** look**ed** witch' for 'scar<u>y</u> look<u>in</u>' witch' (AL-69(48) 2;10); this error will

TABLE 6.2
Number of affixes of the four categories: inflectional, derivational,
copula/auxiliary, and other, which occurred in affix errors, by age;
comparing substitutions to additions.

Age:	1-2	3	4	5	Total	Adult
Substitutions						
Inflectional	0	0	3	2	5	3
Participial	3	0	0	0	3	3
Derivational	1	0	0	2	3	2
Other	0	0	1	0	1	2
Additions						
Inflectional	4	3	10	3	20	9
Participial	0	0	0	0	0	0
Derivational	0	0	0	0	0	3
Cop/Aux	0	1	1	1	3	0
Total N=	8	4	15	8	35	22

be discussed at length below (example (14a)). While a wide variety of inflectional affixes were involved in these errors (as will be discussed in §6.3.3 below), most of the 14 derivational errors either involved participial forms (N=6), or the four suffixes mentioned above as being candidates for being 'productive', namely the adjectival {-y} or diminutive {-ie} (both [-i]), or the agentive/instrumental {–er/-or} (both [-ɚ]). All the child 'derivational' errors involved these suffixes, as did 3 of the 5 adult errors. Some examples are given in (4); see also example (2b) above.

(**4**)   a. B: 'My pòpsicle's in the fréez**y** . . . fréez<u>er</u>. Mòm, what's pópsìcle mèan? It mìght mèan that it's rèal cóld, and it's fréezing.' (adjectival suffix {-y} substituted non-contextually for instrumental {-er}; B-447(37) 5;1)

   b. AF: 'The sèemingly ìnsecure proféssor is àctually a wìtt**ing** and chàrm**y** . . . wìtt<u>y</u> and chàrm<u>ing</u> conversátionalist.' (exchange of adjectival suffix {-y} and participial {-ing}; AD-644(46.5))

Another point that can be made from Table 6.2 is that derivational affixes were most typically involved in substitution errors, whereas addition errors, particularly those involving the movement of some morpheme, most often involved inflectional suffixes (see examples in (11) below). None of the children's addition errors involved derivational affixes. The adults produced one paradigmatic addition error involving a derivational affix (see (7b) below), and two syntagmatic additions. One of these syntagmatic additions was the only error involving a prefix in my corpus, given in (5) below; all other morpheme errors involved suffixes.

(5)   AF: 'It would be **en**hàrder to . . . hàrder to **en**còde in the fírst plàce.'
        (derivational prefix {en-} anticipated and added to 'harder';
        AD-611(42))

Finally, it is interesting to note that all the copula/auxiliary clitic errors were made by the children, and were syntagmatic movement/additions, as illustrated in (6).

(6)   An: 'The òne that_ rèading'**s** the bóok! . . . The òne that'**s** rèading the
        bóok!' (for 'that's' [ðæt(s)]; contracted auxiliary [-s] perseverated/
        moved from 'that', added to 'reading' [ri.dɪŋ(z)]; AN-240(44) 4;9)

These clitic errors were indistinguishable from inflectional suffix syntagmatic additions (e.g. (2a) above and (11a) below), and since there is no doubt that the copula/auxiliary is an independent morpheme and affiliated with the syntax, this is good evidence that the inflectional suffixes are also more closely affiliated with the syntax than the lexical item they are affixed to, at the time these errors occur.

Before discussing these errors in terms of the RPC Model, and looking at any developmental trends, it is crucial to demonstrate that these are in fact errors involving morphemes, and not simply phonological errors or errors of lexical substitution. In the next section I will explore this issue in depth.

6.3.1.2 Morphological, Phonological, or Lexical?

As just suggested, the reader might be wondering if these errors which I have called morpheme-unit errors could in fact be either phonological or lexical errors. So, for example, the error in (5) might be considered to be similar to the other adult errors in which a syllable is added to the target word (classes 6.5, 11.5, 19), and not actually involve the morpheme {en-}. Likewise the error in (3a) above might be a simple substitution of the word 'sucked' for 'sucking'. This is an important issue, because proponents of the 'full listing' theory of the lexicon might want to make such an argument. On the other hand, proponents of the 'all morphemes' theory of lexical representation might want to claim that many of the errors I have classified as phonological are actually morphological. I will therefore look into this question in some detail, organizing my discussion in terms of the four basic classes of error: paradigmatic additions, paradigmatic substitutions, syntagmatic additions, and syntagmatic substitutions.

The adults made 3 paradigmatic addition errors, and the children made one. One adult error is given in (3b) above (*'full coursing reduction' for 'full course reduction'), and the other two are given in (7a,b). Two errors which involved the addition of a syllable node but which were classified as phonological rather than morphological are given in (7c,d). (I will discuss the child error below.)

(7)   a. AF: 'The màin cláim was that fèatures [hæ̀.dəd] to be bínary.'
          (for 'had'; addition of past tense suffix [-əd]; AD-491(37.5))

       b. AM: ' . . . is nòw the còllege advísoring cènter.'
          (for 'advising'; addition of agentive {-or}; AD-493(37.5))

       c. AF: 'Here's [æ̀.nə.məz] cínnamon tòast.'
          (for 'Anna's' [ǽ.nə(z)]; addition of [ə.m] or [mə]; AD-33(6.5))

       d. AF: 'You've got ÈĆĆ and [jù.bì.bí].'
          (for 'UB' [jù.bí]; perseveration/addition of syllable [bi], but also influenced by prosodic structure of 'ECC'; AD-187(19))

In all of the 'LU/addition' errors considered 'phonological', there was some phonological unit in the utterance which served as the source of the error. (That is, I collected no non-contextual phonological errors from either the adults or children which involved the addition of a whole syllable or syllable node.) The addition usually included both some segmental material from another source, such as the [ə.m] in 'cinnamon' in (7c), as well as a whole-word prosodic structure which seemed to be superimposed on the target word from another source, as in both (7c,d). In (7c) the word 'Anna's' takes on the prosodic structure of 'cinnamon', and in (7d) the word 'UB' takes on the structure of 'ECC'. However, in the three morpheme addition errors, there is no phonological source in the utterance for the addition. In example (3b) it appears that an erroneous slot for the progressive morpheme has been added to the syntactic string. In (7a), the past tense marker has been doubled, causing the speaker to produce both the irregular past tense of 'have' as 'had', plus add the regular suffix [-əd]. In (7b) the speaker added the derivational suffix {-or}; this may possibly be a blend of 'advisor' and 'advising' (although in all other blends, the error word has the same number of syllables as one of the two target words), or the error may have been influenced by the collocation 'college advisor'. In any case there is much evidence that these errors involve morphemes rather than simply phonological material. Furthermore, they are unlikely to be lexical substitutions. First, the words *hadded and *advisoring do not exist in English. While the word 'coursing' may exist in some vocabularies (e.g. 'the blood was coursing through his veins'), it would be a very odd lexical substitution in this location, since the slot requires a noun, not an inflected verb.

The child non-contextual addition of a suffix was part of a 'Multiple' error which also included a metathesis:

(8)   B: 'Í wànna be grèen. Yòu **blúe bèes** . . . you bè blúe.'
        (metathesis of 'be blue', with addition of {-s} suffix to 'be' [bi(z)];
        B-169(48) 3;9)

In this error, what appears to be the 3sg suffix was non-contextually added to the verb 'be'. Again, I have no other non-contextual additions of single coda consonants; all the non-contextual consonant additions in my corpus involve onsets, so this is most likely a suffix addition.

Contrary to the argument that that these errors are phonological, there is evidence that some of the errors I have called 'phonological' might in fact have some morphological influence. Consider the following two adult addition errors.

(9)   a. AM: 'There are [fòr.əɫ] . . . fòur chór*al* gròups.'
            (for 'four choral' [for kʰór.əɫ]; syllable [əɫ] anticipated/added to
            'four'; AD-131(11.5))
       b. AF: 'If you fìnd that the lògical [**ri**.strʌk.ʃɚ] . . . lògical strùcture
            requìres anòther àrgument, . . .' (for 'structure requires';
            syllable [ri] anticipated/added to 'structure'; AD-133(11.5))

In (9a), one could argue that the syllable [əɫ] is actually a derivational suffix (cf. 'choral', 'chorus'), and it has been anticipated and added erroneously to the word 'four'. Similarly in (9b) one could argue that the syllable [ri] is actually a prefix (cf. 'require', 'inquire') which has been anticipated and added. I have classified these errors as phonological for two reasons; first, it is not clear that all speakers consider these two syllables to be affixes of any sort, and I was conservative in my designation of such errors as involving affixes. Second, there is a whole word source in the utterance which not only contributed the segmental material but also the prosodic word structure of the error word: thus *[fór.əɫ] has segments from and the prosodic form of 'choral' [kʰór.əɫ], and *[ri.strúk.ʃɚ] has segments from and the prosodic form of 'requires' [ri.kʰwáj.ɚz]. Conversely, the error in (5) does not show this pattern: *enharder [ɛn.hár.dɚ] has only the prefix from of the source 'encode' [ɛn.kʰóʷd], but not its prosodic form, so there less evidence in favor of the phonological analysis.

One way of interpreting these phonological errors that may involve a syllable/morpheme unit is to posit that derived multimorphemic words are stored whole in the lexicon, with some information in their form representations regarding their morphological make-up. If this were the case, then this could cause phonological LUs which actually make up a morpheme to be more susceptible to error than meaningless strings of phonemes. (This is in fact what was found in an elicited slips experiment by Melinger 2000; see also Pillon 1998.) This would cause some errors to be somewhat ambiguous in terms of whether they involve syllables or derivational morphemes, as in (9) above. I will return to this suggestion below.

The second type of error to look at in terms of the question of phonology vs. morphology vs. lexicon is the paradigmatic morpheme substitution errors. The children made four such errors and the adults none. Two of the children's errors were simple substitutions: one is the error given in (3a) above ('sucked/sucking'), involving the inflectional suffixes {-ed [-t]} and {-ing}; the other is the error given in (4a) above ('freezy/freezer'), involving the derivational suffixes {-y} and {-er}. In order to argue that these are phonological, sources in the utterance would need to be found for the phonological form of the error, since there are no comparable non-contextual phonological errors in my data (i.e. non-contextual substitution of LUs). In the first case we would have to argue that the onset [t] in the last word in the utterance, 'time' [tʰaɪm], was anticipated and substituted for the rhyme [-ɪŋ] in 'sucking', an extremely unlikely analysis. In the second case, it would be the first vowel [i] in 'freezer' which perseverated and substituted for the second vowel; however, as shown in Chapter 2 (Table 2.4), unambiguous within-word errors involving vowels are very rare. Furthermore, it is unlikely that these are lexical substitution errors; *freezy is not an English word, and if (3a) were a substitution of 'sucked' for 'sucking', it would be the only lexical substitution error in the entire corpus where one inflected form of a verb was erroneously substituted for another. (There is one blend error that involves 'does/doing' (AN-253b(38) 4;10), but this was part of a phrase blend.) The fact that Bobby was sensitive to the morphological structure of words at the time of these errors is shown by his reaction in the first error: he goes on to discuss the etymology of the word 'popsicle', using a third form of the stem 'freeze', namely 'freezing'. Thus the analysis that these are morphological substitution errors receives the most support.

The other two child paradigmatic substitutions occurred as part of a complex 'Multiple' error; one is given in (10), and the other will be discussed in (14).

(10)   Al: 'Mòmmy, my féver**ed** gòe**s** . . . my féver gòe_d_ awày.'
([fi.v3(d) goʷ(z)] for [fi.v3 goʷ(d)]; past {-ed} anticipated/moved from 'goed', added to 'fever'; then 'go' gets 3sg {-s} to replace past tense; AL-214(48) 4;4)

In this error, it appears that the marker for the past tense {-ed}, which should have been planned to follow the verb 'go', has been anticipated/moved, and added to the noun 'fever' (a syntagmatic addition error). However, when the tense marker moved away from the verb, it seemed to leave behind some indication that the verb needed to be inflected for tense, and so the 3sg marker was non-contextually substituted for the originally planned suffix after the verb 'go'. This type of substitution has no analog in any phonological error, and is most easily explained as a shuffling of inflectional suffixes; there is certainly no phonological source for the [-z] on 'goes' in the utterance, and the only syntagmatic source for the [-d] on 'fevered' is the past tense suffix on 'goed'.

A very different type of error from the paradigmatic additions or substitutions is syntagmatic errors involving the movement and addition of suffixes, where the error unit is either a single consonant or a whole syllable. These morpheme-movement errors involved both between-word and within-word errors, as illustrated in (11); only the children produced within-word errors of this sort. All of the child movement/addition errors, and all but 2 of the adult movement/addition errors, involved inflectional suffixes.

(11) a. Al: 'In "Slèeping Béauty", the bàd wìtch's wìsh rèally còme__
         trúeS.' (for 'comes true'; 3sg moved from 'comes', added to
         'true' in collocation 'come true'; AL-179(44) 3;10)

     b. AM: ' . . . he was dòuble__ bácking.' (for 'dòubling báck';
         progressive {-ing} moved from 'doubling', added to 'back' in
         collocation 'double back'; AD-630(44))

     c. Al: 'Mom, this [wìgZ.əɬ__] mè aróund.' (for 'wiggles' [wɪ.gəɬ(z)];
         3sg {-s} anticipated from end of 'wiggles', added word-
         internally, as if 'wig' were the stem; AL-62 (42) 2;10)

These errors very often involved collocational phrases or lexicalized particle verbs or compounds, where the affix was placed on the wrong member of the phrase or the wrong morpheme; I will return to this point below. It is obvious that these cannot be lexical substitution errors since in some cases they result in non-words (e.g. *trues, *wiggsle), and in many cases one would need to argue that there was a double substitution of lexical items in the same utterance (e.g. 'double' for 'doubling', and 'backing' for 'back'), which is extremely unlikely.

   As just noted, these syntagmatic addition errors all involved suffixes (except for the one adult prefix error given in (5)), and usually involved single coda consonants. However, in my corpus the vast majority of phonological errors consisting of the movement and addition of a single consonant affected syllable onsets; most typically, a consonant is added to a single onset consonant causing it to become a cluster. (This onset preference is also true of addition errors where there is no movement, i.e. where the error segment is copied, not moved, from the source; see §3.5.2.) An example of this type of error is given in (12).

(12) An: 'It's a [kʰḷǽ.səɬ pʰ__èʲ] . . . cástle plàyhouse.'
         (for 'castle playhouse' [kʰǽ.səɬ pʰḷéʲ.hæ̀ʷs]; [l] moved from first
         syllable onset of 'playhouse', added to first syllable onset of
         'castle'; AN-301(3) 5;7)

   However, there were very few phonological movement/addition errors which involved codas, either between- or within-word. There was only one such between-word error which resembled the suffix movement errors in that it involved movement of a coda consonant which was then added to a different syllable as a coda; this error is given in (13a). There were a few other consonant movement errors where a coda consonant moved to an internal slot in another word, as in (13b); these could be said to resemble (11c) above.

(13)   a. Al: 'Íce, Mòmma! [áʲ_ mà.maç]!'
           ([ç] moved from 'ice' [aʲç], added to 'Momma'; AL-3(14) 2;0)
       b. Al: '[ɔ:.moʷ_ ímpsti].' (for 'almost empty' [ɔ:.moʷs ímp.ti]; [s] moved from end of 'almost' and added between [pt] of 'empty'; syllable boundary unclear in error; could be [ímp.sti] or [ímps.ti]; AL-42(14) 2;7)

When Alice made the first of these errors she was in the 2-word stage and had no productive morphology; however, this error may be evidence that she was beginning to notice the coda sibilants and form a hypothesis about the possibility that they were meaningful units on their own. The error in (13b) is a case where a non-suffix coda [s] is moved into the middle of the following word, in a location where it could be a syllable-final consonant. The syllable boundary is not clear in the error, although by the Maximal Onset Principle, the syllabification should be [ímp.sti], so that the [s] is actually in an onset. In this case there is no question of this being anything but phonological, since there is no possible morphological meaning for the [s] in either of its locations; however, this error could reflect the fact that children in these early stages may be still testing hypotheses regarding the morphological status of coda [s]. After age 2, all errors involving the movement/addition of coda material involved unambiguous suffixes, which strongly supports the claim that these suffix movement errors are morphological and not phonological errors.

The most complex case for arguing that these errors are morphological rather than phonological involves the syntagmatic substitution of an affix. These are rather rare, as shown in Table 6.1 above; the children produced 2 and the adults 5. They also involve all the cases in the data in which an affix from one lexical category substituted for an affix from a different lexical category (e.g. derivational for inflectional). Therefore it might be the case that some of these are in fact not morphological but are phonological errors.

The children's errors of this sort are actually quite straightforward; they are given in (14).

(14)   a. Al: 'Sòmebody mùst of tàke__ áll of 'èn . . . tàken áll of 'èm.'
           (perfect suffix [-ən] moved from 'taken' [tʰéʲ.k(ən)], substituted for contracted form of 'them' [əm]; AL-232(44) 4;7)
       b. Al: 'That's a [skɛ̀.ʒən lʊ́.kɨd] wítch, Mom!'
           (for 'scary lookin' [skɛ́.ʒ(i) lʊ́.k(ən)]; participial {-ing [-ən]} moved from 'looking', substuted for derivational {-y} on 'scary'; then 'look' gets past participle [-ɨd] to replace moved morpheme; AL-69(48) 2;10)

In (14a), Alice moves the perfect suffix [-ən] from the verb 'taken', and substitutes it for the contracted form of the pronoun 'them' [əm]. In the 'Multiple' error in (14b), the participial {-ing [-ən]} is anticipated from 'lookin', and substituted for the derivational suffix {-y} on 'scary'. However, similar to the error in (10) above, it appears that a slot for a suffix remains after the stem 'look', and therefore the past participle suffix is substituted for the intended present participle (this is the other child paradigmatic substitution error).

I would argue that these errors are morphological, for several reasons. First, it is clear they are not lexical as they all result in non-words. Second, in both of these errors a syllable moves from one location to replace a syllable in a different location, and I have no unambiguous phonological errors involving syllable movement/substitution, from any of the children or adults (all the syllable substitution errors involve copies of syllables, not relocation). Furthermore, most LU errors involve onsets, or phonological material in the interior of the word, and very few involve the final coda of a word, where suffix errors would occur. The fact that in (14a) the suffix {-en} substitutes for the word {'em} may be partly due to their phonological similarity, but the unit involved seems to be two independent morphemes. And, as in (10), there is no syntagmatic source for the [-ɨd] which appears on 'looked', so it is most likely to be a suffix substitution (although in this error it produces an incorrect past participle form for the verb 'look'). Therefore all the evidence points to these being errors of morphology rather than phonology.

One of the reasons these errors may be so rare is that in substitution errors which looked like they might involve a suffix, I only counted them as morphological when both the target and the source were possible suffixes. When one might have been a suffix but the other was clearly not, I counted these as phonological, as illustrated in (15). (Note that neither of these is a movement error, and most unambiguous affix errors involve movement.)

(15) a. Al: ' . . . yòu got your [pʰík.kən] . . . your pícture tàken, right?'
        (for 'picture taken' [pʰík.tʃɜ téʲ.kən]; [ən] substituted for [tʃɜ];
        source of [k] in error is unclear, so it is notated as ambisyllabic;
        AL-228(11) 4;6)

      b. B: 'Gràndpa, I gòt my [sl̥íŋ.kəɬ] . . . I gòt my slínky tàngled ùp.'
        (for 'slinky tangled' [sl̥íŋ.ki tʰǽŋ.gəɬ(d)]; [əɬ] substituted for [i];
        B-359(11) 4;9)

In (15a), the passive suffix {-en} was anticipated from 'taken', and substituted for the syllable [tʃɚ]; since this latter is not a suffix, I counted this as a pure phonological error. Similarly, in (15b), the rhyme [əɬ] was substituted for what might be considered the derivational adjectival suffix {-y}; however since the [əɬ] is not a morpheme, this was considered phonological. Note also that the past tense on 'tangled' was excluded from this LU substitution error; this type of error was discussed in §3.5.4 above, and shows that while the past tense suffix was functioning as extrasyllabic in the error, the two rhymes were behaving as if they were integral parts of the phonology of the two words 'slinky' and 'tangle'.

Adult syntagmatic morpheme substitution errors mostly consisted of movement errors where a suffix moved from one location and substituted for another in another location, and errors of this sort that were purely phonological (i.e. movement/substitutions of an LU which cannot be construed as a morpheme) did not occur. However, there were a few possible parallels in phonological errors: consider the following pairs of errors.

(16) a. AF: 'Creàt**ing** wríte . . . creàti̲ve̲ wrít*ing*.'
       ('creating' [kʰɹi.éʲ.ɾ(ɪŋ)] for 'creative' [kʰɹi.éʲ.ɾ(ɨv)]; source
       'writing' [ráʲ.ɾ(ɪŋ)]; participle {-ing} anticipated, substituted for
       derivational {-ive}; AD-607(42))
    b. AM: 'That's just the òld Vàn [vèʲ.li] . . . Vàn Vàli̲n̲ fàmil*y*
       tradítion.' (for 'Van Valin' [væn.véʲ.lɪn], source 'family'
       [fǽm.li]; [i] substituted for [ɪn]; AD-121(11))
    c. AF: ' . . . a wìtt**ing** and chàrm*y* . . . wìtt̲y̲ and chàrmi̲n̲g̲
       conversátionalist.' ('witting' [wi̇.ɾ(ɪŋ)] and 'charmy' [tʃár.m(i)]
       for 'witty' [wi̇.ɾ(i)] and 'charming' [tʃár.m(ɪŋ)]; reversal of
       derivational suffix{-i} with participle {-ing}; AD-644(46.5))
    d. AF: (mentioning two cartoon characters)
       '[lǽm.boʷ] and [dʌ́m.bɚt] . . . Làmbe̲r̲t̲ and Dúmbo̲.'
       (for 'Lambert' [lǽm.bɚt] and 'Dumbo' [dʌ́m.boʷ]; reversal of
       rhymes [ɚt] and [oʷ]; AD-270(28))

In (16a,b) it appears that a rhyme has been anticipated and substituted for a preceding rhyme. In (16a) the two syllables involved happen to be the derivational adjectival suffix {-ive} and the participial nominalizer {-ing}; in (13b) they involve the phonological material [-i] from 'family' and [-ɪn] from 'Van Valin', neither of which is a morpheme in its own right. Similarly, in (16c,d) two rhymes exchange. In (16c) they are two derivational affixes, the adjectival {-i} from 'witty' and the participial adjectival {-ing} from 'charming'. In (16d) they are the rhyme [ɚt] from 'Lambert' and the rhyme [oʷ] from 'Dumbo', again neither of which are morphemes. In both of these cases, there is no way to tell the difference between the error pairs in a formal sense. Thus it may be the case that some of these syntagmatic substitution errors are in fact phonological rather than morphological, particularly those involving derivational affixes. In this case one could again argue that if morphological structure is marked in lexical representations for derived words, then a syllable which is actually a morpheme might be more susceptible to phonological error than a syllable which has no particular status (Pillon 1998, Melinger 2000).

In sum, there is a great deal of evidence that the errors which I have claimed to involve a single affix as their error unit are in fact morphological rather than phonological. This is very clear for the paradigmatic substitution errors and the syntagmatic addition errors, which mostly involve inflectional affixes. For paradigmatic addition errors I have argued that I may have been overly conservative, and that some of the errors which I have classified as phonological may in fact reflect some morphological knowledge. For syntagmatic substitution errors, in a few cases these errors are indistinguishable from phonological LU syntagmatic substitutions, particularly in cases involving derivational affixes.

Most of these errors also cannot be lexical. First, the majority of these 'morphology' errors result in non-words. In the few cases where the error results in a real word, it is usually a different lexical category from the intended word, which is rare for lexical substitution errors (see §1.4.4, and Chapter 4). In some cases a lexical explanation would require positing a double lexical substitution where each substituted word just happened to have the intended morphology for that syntagmatic slot, e.g. *'double backing' for 'doubling back' (AD-630(44)). Finally, if the single case where one inflected word substituted for another with the same stem were considered a lexical substitution error, this would be the only case of its kind in the corpus. Therefore the morphological analysis gives a more consistent and plausible interpretation of the data than either the phonological or lexical analysis.

6.3.1.3 Morphology and Speech Production Planning

In the above sections I have presented the following findings. First, errors in which affixes are the unit of error were fairly rare in both the child and adult data. The most common error of this type involved the movement of a suffix from one location to another in the syntagmatic string; syntagmatic substitutions, and paradigmatic errors, both substitutions and additions, were less common. Most errors involved inflectional suffixes, and this was especially true of the movement/addition errors. There was much support for the claim that all of these errors are in fact morphological and neither phonological nor lexical, although a few syntagmatic substitution errors involving derivational affixes may be argued to be simply phonological. The next question to be asked is how these errors can be explained in terms of the planning model.

In order to look into this issue, some of the questions raised in the introductory section of this chapter need to be revisited. From these data, it appears that inflectional and derivational affixes behaved differently in the morpheme errors, in that inflectional errors were much more common and usually involved syntagmatic movement, while derivational errors were far less common and usually involved substitution. The derivational suffixes most often involved in errors were those which are relatively productive, and therefore probably have lexical entries of their own, as well as being stored in lexical entries with appropriate stems. The hypothesis which best fits with these facts is that derived words are stored in the lexicon, but with some information marked in their form representation regarding their morphological make-up. However, regularly inflected words are not stored in the lexicon as lexical entries, but inflectional affixes are stored as their own lexical entries; during processing they are closely linked to the syntax and concatenated with stems on line. This would cause affix movement errors to occur much more often with inflectional affixes because they would be associated with syntagmatic slots whose order could be erroneously planned. Derivational affixes could also be available for these types of movement error, but this would occur much less often since they are more fully integrated with their stem. Let us now see how these morpheme errors would be explained in terms of speech production planning.

Many speech production planning models, particularly of the 'stage' type, assume that inflectional morphology has a special affinity with syntactic planning; this is true of the RPC Model as well as models of Fromkin (1973a), Garrett (1980b, 1988, 1993), and Bock & Levelt (1994); (see Stemberger 1985, 1998 for a different view). This hypothesis is certainly supported by the syntagmatic errors in my corpus. The simplest explanation, for at least the inflectional suffix errors, is that the error involves the movement of the abstract marker for that morpheme to an incorrect location in the syntactic string, while the syntactic string is being planned. There are several pieces of evidence for this. First, inflectional movement errors very often involve two-morpheme expressions such as verb+particle constructions or compounds; in these cases the error seems to lie in mis-parsing the string and placing the affix in an incorrect location. This was illustrated in (11) above; further examples are given in (17).

(17)   a. Al: 'Búbble-gùm. Twó bùbbleS- . . . gùm__. Twó bùbble-gùm<u>s</u>.'
          (plural {-s} anticipated/moved from the end of 'gums', added to
          'bubble'; AL-11(42) 2;2)

       b. TF: 'Shè spènds wéeks lòok__ fór**ing** . . . lòok*ing* fórward to
          thèse còncerts.' (progressive {-ing} perseverated/moved from
          'looking', substituted for second stem {ward} in compound
          'forward'; AD-627(44))

In (17a), Alice has misplaced the plural marker by putting it into the middle of what at the age of 2;2 was just beginning to become a lexicalized compound, 'bubble-gum'; however, at this time it may have been phonologically a two-word phrase and therefore susceptible to misplacement of the plural. In (17b), a very unusual error in which an inflectional affix is substituted for the second stem in a compound, the teen has apparently been fooled by the collocation 'look for', and the progressive suffix has erroneously moved to the end of this two-word phrase.

A second piece of evidence for the claim that what has actually moved is the abstract morpheme marker comes from the three errors involving the contracted copula or auxiliary 'be'. An example of the auxiliary was given in (6) above; (18) shows an error involving the copula.

(18)   B: 'Dòn't you knòw that ònly óne of's 'em__ . . . óne of 'em's hàrd?'
        (for 'one of 'em's'; cliticized copula 'is' [-z] anticipated/moved from
        pronoun 'them', added to preposition 'of'; B-583(42) 5;11)

These errors don't seem to be as sensitive to phrasal boundaries as the
inflectional errors, but they do show a shift in location of the cliticized copula or
auxiliary one word to the left or right.   As mentioned above, it is not
controversial that the copula or auxiliary placement is a function of the syntactic
string being planned, and therefore these shifts must involve misorderings of the
syntactic markers for the function morphemes.   Since inflectional suffix
movement errors are indistinguishable in structure from the clitic copula and
auxiliary movement errors, this is very strong evidence for the close relationship
between inflectional morphology and syntax.
      A third piece of evidence comes from errors such as those in (19), which
would be very difficult to explain otherwise.

(19)   a. Al: 'You còuld have gèt__ your tòen òut of the wáy.' (for 'gotten
           your toe'; 'toen' pronounced [tʰóʷ.ən]; AL-186(44) 3;10)

        b. Al: 'Mòmmy, my févered gòes . . . my féver gòed awày.'
           ([fí.v3(d) goʷ(z)] for [fí.v3 goʷ(d)]; AL-214(48) 4;4)

        c. An: 'Well, if hè wànna pláys . . . if hè wànts ta pláy, he cán.'
           (for 'wants ta play' [wʌnt(s) tə pʰleʲ]; 3sg {-s} perseverated/
           moved from 'wants', added to 'play' [pʰle̥ʲ(z)]; AN-282(44) 5;3)

In (19a), it appears that the abstract marker for the perfect {-en} has been
erroneously moved from the slot after the verb {get} to the slot after the noun
{toe}.   Because the verb is now not associated with any suffix, when it is
planned for speaking in the phonological component it is planned in its stem
form [gɛt].   It is not produced as the phonological form [gat] which is what
would have been left behind if this were simply an error where the rhyme from
the second syllable of the phonological word [gá.tən] had been moved and added
to the word [tʰoʷ].   Further, the neologism {toe}+{perfect} is pronounced with
one of the two regular allomorphs, [-ən].   The error in (19b) was discussed above
as a case where the marker for the past tense {-ed} has been moved to the slot
after the noun {fever}; the neologism {fever}+{past} is then pronounced with the
correct regular allomorph of the past tense morpheme, in this case the [-d] since
'fever' ends in a voiced liquid.   However, when the tense marker moved, it
seemed to leave behind some abstract marker indicating that the verb needed to be
inflected for tense, and so the 3sg marker was inserted after the verb {go}; this
form was then produced with the correct allomorphy for the sequence {go}+
{3sg}, i.e. [goʷ(z)].   In (19c), the 3sg suffix is moved from the end of 'want' and
added to 'play'; however, without the suffix on 'want', the sequence 'want to' is
pronounced in its contracted form 'wanna' [wʌ́.nʌ].   These sorts of errors are best

explained by arguing that they involve erroneous placement of slots for function affixes within the syntactic string, either by moving the slot or copying it. When the forms of affixes and content words are inserted into the string and then sent to the phonological component, the resultant syntagmatic sequences of morphemes are planned for speaking as if this were the intended string. (The regularity of allomorphy will be discussed in more detail in §6.3.4.1 below.)

What about paradigmatic errors? In the (very rare) substitution errors, one could argue either that the incorrect abstract marker has been selected for the correct location in the syntagmatic string, or the incorrect suffix has been activated from the lexicon. With only two simple (i.e. not 'Multiple') errors of this type it is difficult to decide between these possibilities. In the case of the 'sucked/sucking' error (number 3a above) it seems equally likely that either the abstract marker for the passive/past tense morphemes or the lemmas of these two morphemes was the locus of the error. However, in the case of the 'freezy/freezer' error (4a), the lexical explanation seems more likely. The suffixes {-y} and {-er} are highly productive morphemes, and Bobby knew them both and used them productively at age 5 when this error was made. Therefore it is likely that they were both stored in his lexicon as separate lexical entries; it is also likely that his lexical entry for 'freezer' had some morphological structure marked in the form entry, i.e. that this word consisted of a stem plus suffix. When he activated the lexical item 'freezer', perhaps the suffix {-er} caused some activation to spread to the suffix {-y} which was then erroneously selected and substituted for the target. While this is a lot of theorizing over a single example, it certainly is a more plausible argument than to claim that the derivational suffix {-er} was linked to the syntax in the originally planned string, and the incorrect abstract marker for the {-y} suffix was erroneously substituted for {-er} in the syntactic string.

The three adult paradigmatic suffix addition errors were discussed in some detail in §6.3.1.2 above (examples (3b) and (7)). It was argued that two of them (*hadded, *coursing) were caused by the planning of an extra inflectional slot in the syntax, and the third (*advisoring) may have been caused by a lexical blend of two derived words 'advisor' and 'advising' (since the speaker was a college professor, this noun is surely lexicalized for her), and influenced by the collocation 'college advisor.' Again we see distinct explanations for the inflectional vs. derivational errors.

Finally, for some of the adult syntagmatic affix substitution errors (examples in (16)), these may in fact be phonologically based, as discussed in §6.3.1.2 above. This is particularly true of errors involving derivational affixes, where the possibility that the morphological structure is marked in the lexical entry makes syllables (or rhymes) which are morphemes more susceptible to phonological error than other LUs of sound.

6.3.1.4 Developmental Patterns in Morpheme-Unit Errors
The final question for this section is whether or not there are any

developmental patterns evident in these errors in which affixes are the error unit. The figures in Table 6.1 show that I did not collect any errors where affixes were the error unit when the children were in the 1-word and 2-word stages. This may be partly due to the fact that the very young children didn't produce many words with inflectional morphology in these stages. However even when they did speak words with inflections, the words were most likely fixed forms, with the affixes not analyzed out from the stems. The three earliest errors I collected which involved the movement of coda consonants were the following; (AN-7(8) 1;7) may also be an example of a coda /s/ moving from one location to another, but since the error was interrupted it is ambiguous.

(20) a. M: 'Àrms úp!'
          B: '[àm_ ʌ́ç].' (for 'arms up' [amç ʌp]; [ç] moved from 'arms', substituted for [p] in 'up'; 2-word stage; B-13(14) 1;9.25)
      b. B: '[çún ʔàç].' (for 'shoes on' [çuç ʔan]; codas [ç] and [n] exchanged; 2-word stage; B-25(25) 1;11.6)
      c. Al: 'Íçe, Mòmma! [áʲ_, mà.maç]!' (for 'ice, Momma' [aʲç, má.ma]; [ç] perseverated from 'ice', added to end of 'momma'; 2-word stage; AL-3(14) 2;0.14)

In (20a), Bobby moved the coda [ç] from 'arms', and substituted it for the coda [p] in 'up'. However, I did not classify this error as a morpheme error because at age 1;9 Bobby knew the word 'arms' as an unanalyzed chunk had shown no signs of factoring out the plural suffix. Also recall that true suffix errors usually involve addition, not substitution. Similarly, in (20b) Bobby exchanged the codas from 'shoes' and 'on', but there was no indication that he thought of these two consonants as having any different status from each other. However, in (20c), Alice is just on the verge of beginning to analyze out suffixes, and it appears she is unclear as to which instances of coda [ç] constitute suffixes. So in this case the coda [ç] in 'ice' which is not a suffix, behaves as one in the error, in that it is moved from the end of the first word and added to the end of the second. The first error to clearly involve an actual suffix is the one given in (17a) above, repeated here:

(21)   Al: 'Búbble-gùm. Twó bùbbleS- . . . gùm_. Twó bùbble-gùms̲.' (plural {-s} anticipated/moved from the end of 'gums', added to 'bubble'; AL-11(42) 2;2.5)

At this age, Alice was beginning to use the plural morpheme productively, and she was also beginning to produce utterances of three or more words.

From these errors I would argue that there is a close connection between the time when inflectional movement errors begin to occur and the onset of telegraphic speech. Specifically, it may be the case that it is necessary for the child to have analyzed out inflectional affixes and begun to have stored them in independent lexical entries before syntactic templates where word and affix order is fixed in a specific pattern can begin to be developed. This is not necessarily a new finding (Brown 1973, Peters 1995), but it does receive independent support from the speech error data.

After the age of 2;2, affix errors continue to occur on a regular basis, as shown in Table 6.1. Since I have very few errors of this type I can't say much about the drop-off of these errors at age 3 in my data, and their upsurge at age 4; but qualitatively I can say that they do occur throughout the age range of my study. Two types of errors that occurred in the children's data but not the adult data suggest, however, that the exact identification of affixes and their placements continues to develop during this time period. The first type is the within-word error where it appears that an affix has been moved into the middle of a word. The children produced four such errors, all anticipations (class 42): *wiggzle for 'wiggles' (2;10), *opsen for 'opens' (4;1), *hiccsup for 'hiccups' (4;1), and *opten for 'opened' (5;4). (Alice's error *dectorated for 'decorated' (AL-220(2) 4;6) may also be an addition of the past tense morpheme in the middle of the word, although I have classified it as phonological.) These could be phonological errors rather than morphological, but they do have some properties in common with morpheme movement errors. In the case of 'hiccups', it could be that the child was unclear about the compound make-up, and placed the plural in the middle of the compound. The other three cases may suggest problems with word boundaries and affix placement, and the fact that this type of error continued into age 5 implies that children at this age are continuing to work on solidifying their knowledge of word boundaries.

The second type of error which only the children made was discussed briefly in Chapter 2, §2.2.1. At ages 2-3, Alice made three vowel movement errors (class 17) one of which involved a word-final vowel [i] moving to a new location to form a new syllable (22a), and two of which involved the movement of a word-internal [i] to the end of the word ((22b) and Al-102(17) 3;3).

(22)   a.   Al: '[kʰá.f__ tʰàʲ.mi].'
            M: 'What?'
            Al: 'Cóffee tìme.'
                (for 'coffee time' [kʰá.fi tʰaʲm]; [i] moved from 'coffee', added at
                end of 'time', with resyllabification; AL-50(17) 2;9)
       b.   Al: '[gʌ.m__ -bὲ.ʒiz].' (for 'Gummi-Bears' [gʌ.mi-bὲʒ(z)]; [i]
                moved from 'Gummi', added at end of 'Bears' but before plural
                inflection; AL-171(17) 3;9)

Because the single vowel [-i] can be a derivational suffix (diminutive or adjectival), it is likely that the reason this was the only vowel which participated in these addition errors is because Alice had not yet figured out which of these word-final [i]'s were affixes and which were simply phonological syllables. This caused this vowel to be susceptible to movement errors whereas other word-final vowels were not. (Note that the error in (22b) moves the [i] between the original coda of the word 'Bears' but before the plural suffix, exactly the location where a derivational affix should go; however, since Alice didn't know that 'gum' and 'Gummi' had any relationship, this is clearly a phonological error.) Therefore these errors support the claim that children between the ages of 2;2 and at least 5;4 (when the *'opten' error was made) are actively involved in sorting out the morpheme and lexical boundaries in their language.

One final developmental point is that the adults in this study made a greater proportion of errors involving derivational affixes than the children did, particularly the non-participial forms; the children produced errors involving 6 derivational affixes, half of them participials, while the adults produced 8 such errors, with only 3 participials. The most likely explanation for this is that adults simply know more derived words than children, particularly those with latinate origins, since these are typically more formal, learned vocabulary. Also, adults may have more information about morphological structure stored in their form lexicons, partly due to literacy. This explanation was given in Chapter 3 for the paucity of child lexical stress errors, and will be discussed again below in the context of malapropisms.

In sum, the focus of §6.3.1 has been errors in which an affix is the error unit. We have seen that these errors most commonly involve inflectional affixes, specifically the movement and addition of a suffix. These errors have been shown to be morphological rather than phonological or lexical, and their occurrence has been discussed in terms of the RPC Model of speech production planning. Finally, some developmental trends have been discussed: affix errors do not occur until the onset of telegraphic speech, and thus they coincide with the beginnings of syntax. When they do begin to occur, they show the same patterns as adult errors, particularly in terms of the link between morphology and syntax. Children but not adults produce errors which show that they are still developing fixed representations for word boundaries, knowledge of specific suffixes, and suffix placement. Finally, children produce fewer errors than adults involving derivational affixes, probably due to their limited vocabularies.

In this section I have made a great deal out of a fairly small number of errors, and actually it may be more realistic to consider the summary above as a list of hypotheses to test rather than a list of conclusions. Fortunately there are a number of other types of errors which provide more data pertinent to these same issues, so that we can look for a convergence of evidence to strengthen the conclusions. I will now turn to a discussion of 'stranding' errors, which will shed more light on the issue of the relationship between morphology and syntax.

6.3.2 Strandings
6.3.2.1 Types of Errors and Lexical Categories

There are three types of errors which can be said to involve the 'stranding' of a morpheme; the first two are syntagmatic and the third involves phrase blends.

In the first case, one content word substitutes for another in the syntagmatic string, and the affix which was planned for the slot following the target content word affixes itself to the error word, as illustrated in (23).

(23) a. Al: 'Wow, my **cólds** are **hànd**.'
         (for 'my hands are cold'; content words 'hand' and 'cold'
         exchanged, plural {-s} stranded; AL-46(45) 2;8)
      b. AF: (looking at various electric shavers in a catalog)
         'That lòoks like it's **hòlder** . . . **èasier** to **hóld**.'
         (content word 'hold' anticipated, substituted for 'easy', then
         takes comparative {-er} suffix; AD-600(41))

In the second type of stranding error, a content word which was planned in one location in the utterance to co-occur with an affix, loses that affix when also spoken in an erroneous position.

(24) OG: 'I'm **pètting** your háir.'
      M: 'You áre?'
      OG: 'Yeah, so Ì won't **pét** it . . . **púll** it.'
         (content word 'pet' perseverated, substituted for 'pull', leaving
         progressive {-ing} behind; OC-55(43) 3;7)

In some cases a content word movement can cause the content word to take on a new affix which is appropriate for the erroneous syntagmatic slot, as well as to lose the originally planned affix, as shown in (25).

(25) AM: 'I **wòrked** in a . . . I grèw ùp in a **wórking** clàss nèighborhood.'
         ('work' anticipated and substituted for 'grow up', stranding
         participle {-ing}, but taking on the past tense marker appropriate
         for the new syntagmatic slot; note that 'work' takes the regular
         past tense, but 'grew' is irregular; AD-595(41))

The third type of error which can involve stranding is phrase blends, where an unaffixed word from one of the two target phrases is linked to a location in the other target phrase which is associated with an affix. In this case the erroneously spoken word takes the affix .

(26) B: 'Lèt me sèe the bòx of the créam that **pùts** . . . that you pùt on my
         hànds. The kìnd that gòes on my hánds.'
         (blend of T1: 'that goes' and T2: 'that you put'; B-303(49) 4;6)

In this error the verb 'put' from the second target phrase (T2) is mislinked to the verb slot planned for the first target phrase, and is spoken with the 3sg inflection planned for T1 'goes'.

TABLE 6.3

Number of morphemes in the four categories: inflectional, derivational, contractible copula, and compounding, involved in stranding errors, by age.

Age:	1-2a	1-2b	3	4	5	Total	Adult
Inflectional	0	4	2	4	8	18 (64%)	22 (67%)
Derivational	0	0	2	1	0	3 (11%)	5 (15%)
Copula	0	0	0	0	1	1 (3.5%)	1 (3%)
Compound	0	0	2	4	0	6 (21.5%)	5 (15%)
Total N=	**0**	**4**	**6**	**9**	**9**	**28**	**33**

Finally, I have included in the count of 'stranding' errors, instances where one morpheme moves out of a compound and 'strands' the remainder of the compound, as shown in (27), as a comparison to the errors which strand affixes.

(27) a. B: 'We párked in sòme of . . . in front of sòmebody.'
       ('some' anticipated from compound 'somebody', substituted for 'front' in phrase 'in front of'; B-357(41) 4;8)
     b. An: 'Cándlemàke-stìcker.'
       (for 'Cándlestìck-màker'; stems 'make' and 'stick' metathesized, stranding remainder of the first compound 'candle', and the {-er} agentive suffix; AN-102(47) 3;2)

I have excluded from the present analysis paradigmatic errors such as the substitution of 'turning' for 'talking' (B-86b(35) 2;6). In §6.4.2.2 below I will argue that these errors consist in substituting one stem for another (in this case 'turn' for 'talk'), stranding the inflectional suffix, i.e. that the suffix is not part of the substitution error. However, in the current section I will only look at syntagmatic errors and phrase blends in this light, pending justification of this analysis for the paradigmatic errors.

In order to look again at the question of whether inflectional and derivational affixes behave similarly in these types of errors, I assigned a classification to every affix involved in a stranding: inflectional, derivational (including participial forms), contractible copula (there were no contractible auxiliary errors), or one element of a compound. The results, shown in Table 6.3, are given in terms of tokens in each category, by age. Some errors contributed to more than one category; for example, error (25) above is counted once in 'inflectional' for the past tense, and once in 'derivational' for the participial {–ing}. The error in (27b) was counted in both the derivational category for the {-er} suffix, and in the compound category.

Again it is found that errors involving inflectional affixes greatly outnumbered those from any other class. As usual, the derivational affixes involved in these stranding errors included mainly participial forms (child N=1, adult N=3), or the instrumental/agentive {-er} (child N=2, adult N=1). All of the child derivational errors were produced as part of exchanges of content stems within compounds; I will return to this point in §6.3.2.3. The adults produced the same number of errors involving derivational affixes as those involving one content morpheme from a compound, but the children produced twice as many errors involving shifts out of compounds as those involving derivational affixes. These stranding figures are quite similar to those of morpheme-unit errors (see Table 6.2), and lend support to the view that derivational affixes are closely linked with their stems in the lexicon and during processing (similar to the stems in a compound), but inflectional affixes have a strong affinity with their syntactic location. The following minimal pair illustrates this difference:

(28)   a. Al: 'Thèy got a pìcture of a giráffe.'
            M: 'Whó dòes?'
            Al: '*Grámma*! Shè líkes **Gràmma**s . . . giràffes.'
            ('Gramma' substituted for 'giraffe', plural suffix stranded;
            AL-144(43) 3;6)

        b. B: **Gràmma**, thìs is hís **Gràmma** . . . no wait, thìs is hís
            gràbber.' ('Gramma' substituted for 'grabber', a kind of toy;
            B-263(43) 4;4)

In (28a) the single morpheme 'Gramma' was perseverated and substituted for the morpheme 'giraffe', but the plural suffix planned for the noun+plural slot in the phrase remained in its originally planned location, causing 'Gramma' to be spoken in its plural form. Crucially, the word 'Gramma' did not substitute for the whole inflected form 'giraffes'. However, in (28b), the single morpheme 'Gramma' was perseverated and substituted for the word 'grabber', which contains the stem+derivational affix sequence {grab}+{er, instrumental}. Here the suffix {-er} was not stranded; it remained affiliated with the lexical item 'grabber' rather than the syntagmatic slot.

6.3.2.2 Exceptions to Strandings?

An important finding is that in my data, stranding occurred with inflectional affixes in nearly every case where it was possible. From Table 6.3 it can be seen that the children produced 18 inflectional stranding errors and the adults 22. However, there were 6 exceptions in my study, where a stranding could have occurred but didn't (child N=4, adult N=2). Five of these exceptions involved exchanges (or possibly interrupted exchanges) of two lexical items; the sixth occurred in a phrase blend. But all six of them involved a very specific class of lexical items, and all involved the plural suffix. Examples are given in (29).

(29)   a.   B: 'I'm gònna gèt some **hànds** on my . . . some <u>wàter</u> on my **hánds.**'
(anticipation/substitution of 'hands' for 'water' (possibly interrupted exchange), plural not stranded; B-156(41) 3;8)

b.   An: 'Thère's **cráckers on the crùmbs**. (pause) Thère's <u>cràcker crùmbs on the flòor</u>.' (blend of T1: 'thère's cráckers on the flòor' and T2: 'thère's crácker crùmbs on the flòor'; AN-186(49) 4;5)

c.   AM: (speaker giving a talk about the mental life of various animals) ' . . . the mèntal **còws** of **l̃ife.**'
('life' and 'cows' exchanged, plural not stranded; AD-640(45))

The children produced three exchanges of the sort in (29a) where the plural suffix remained with the originally planned target, and in every case the lexical item which kept the plural referred to body parts which are normally thought of in pairs or groups; besides the 'hands' error in (29a) they also produced non-stranding errors with 'bones' (OC-116(45) 4;7) and 'arms' (AN-312(48) 5;9, where the plural is added to 'long' but also retained on 'arms'). Furthermore, in (29a) there may have been some effect of the fact that 'water' is a mass noun, so even though it is not formally plural it is semantically plural. In the phrase blend in (29b), Anna has mislinked the word 'crumbs' from T2 into the singular noun slot planned for 'floor' in T1, but 'crumbs' carries its plural marker with it; again 'crumbs' is something canonically discussed in the plural. In (29c), the adult has exchanged the words 'life' and 'cows', where the latter retains the plural suffix.

The fact that the children sometimes lexicalized particular nouns as plural is illustrated in the following phonological errors.

(30)   a.   B: 'I'm nòt gètting my [pʰǽɲtʃ] . . . my pánt<u>s</u> **chà**nged!'
(for 'pants' [pʰænt(s)]; [tʃ] from onset of 'changed' anticipated/ substituted for coda cluster [ts] in 'pants', which includes the plural morpheme; B-107(11) 2;8)

b.   B: 'I gòtta chànge [pʰí.zèⁱdʒ].' (for 'PJs' [pʰí.dʒèⁱ(z)]; onset [dʒ] and coda [z], which is the plural morpheme, exchanged in second syllable; B-242(25) 4;3)

In (30a), the coda cluster [ts], which contains the plural suffix [-s] is treated as if it is a simple consonant cluster, and the single phoneme /tʃ/ is substituted for the cluster [ts], showing that this word 'pants' was probably lexicalized as plural, as it is for most English speakers (i.e. as a *plurale tantum*; Corbett 2000:172). In (30b), the onset and coda consonants from the second syllable of 'PJs' are exchanged; the coda consonant happens to be the plural suffix, but it is treated like an integral part of the syllable; this shows that it is probably lexicalized with the stem, since single-consonant inflectional suffixes are usually extrasyllabic in phonological errors (see §3.5.4 above).

The adults produced two errors of this sort where the noun which kept its plural is something usually thought about in groups, including the 'cows' error in (29c), and the exchange *"gèt these **béd** to **kìds**' where 'kids' are usually spoken of in the plural (AD-641(45)). (While writing this chapter, I overheard Alice, now a teen, remark about her brother: 'He has a lot of **hánds** on his **tìme** . . . **tíme** on his **hànds**.' In this case the word 'hands' is clearly lexicalized as part of this idiomatic expression.)   The 'cows' error was also probably enhanced by the fact that if the plural had remained in its originally planned location, the erroneous string {life}+{plural} would have required a morphophonemic adjustment of the stem to produce [laᶤvz], since 'life' has an irregular plural.

As just discussed, the main exceptions to strandings were cases where two words exchanged, and one whose referent is typically talked about in pairs or groups carried its plural morpheme with it. However even these lexical items can strand their plural suffix, as shown in (23a) above, *'my **colds** are **hand**'; these cases show that both 'hand' and 'hands' are probably stored in the lexicon (see also Stemberger & MacWhinney 1988). A couple more 'PJs' errors will further demonstrate this point.

(31)   a. B: 'I'm hàving a [pʰéᶨ.dʒì] . . . a P̲J̲ pàrty todày.' (for 'PJ' [pʰí.dʒèʲ], vowels [i]<-->[eʲ] reversed; B-435(26) 5;0)

   b. B: 'Mom, my [pʰí.dʒà:rz] . . . my P̲J̲s àre ùnder mỳ shìrt.'
         (telescoping of 'PJs are' [pʰí.dʒèʲ(z) àr], with plural suffix moved to end; B-136(34) 3;6)

In (31a), the word 'PJ' occurs without the plural suffix, in the phrase 'PJ party'; so this indicates that the singular 'PJ' is also stored in the lexicon. In (31b), the phrase 'PJs are' is telescoped, but here the plural suffix acts like an independent inflectional suffix, moving to the end of the telescoped phrase (see §3.5.4). This may be best interpreted as showing that in the form representation of the lexical word 'PJs' /pi.dʒeʲz/, there is some indication that the final segment in this word is a separate morpheme; this would be analogous to what I have argued for derived words, i.e. that the form representation carries some information about morphological structure.

Stemberger (1989) reported similar findings in his study of child and adult SOTs. Stemberger recorded 9 child and 135 adult 'stranding and accommodation' errors involving the stranding of inflectional affixes or pronoun accommodation (he doesn't separate out the two categories in his report). In his data, the children and adults produced the identical proportions of strandings/ accommodations in errors where they were possible, 89% for both children and adults. He notes that '[t]he main inflectional category that is exceptional to stranding and accommodation in adult speech is plurality (9 of 15 exceptions)' (1989:171); the one child exception also involved plurality. In Stemberger

(1985:162) he gives examples from adults such as *'I presume you could get **light** in poorer **pictures**' (for 'pictures in poorer light'), which also shows the mass noun vs. plural count noun exchanges I have discussed above. So this type of exception seems to be the most common. In my data the children produced a lower percentage of inflectional strandings than did the adults (children, 17 out of 21 possible=81%; adults, 23 out of 25 possible=92%), but these numbers are close enough to Stemberger's to be interpreted as a similar result. Thus Stemberger's study supports the findings of the current study, that both children and adults will most often strand inflectional suffixes in content morpheme movement errors, again highlighting the close relationship between inflectional affixes and syntax, for both children and adults.

However, this is another situation in which inflectional and derivational affixes behave differently from each other, as there are a number instances such as those in (32) where a derivational affix is not stranded (see also (28b) above); this can include both participial and non-participial forms.

(32)   a. AF: 'Èverybody make sùre your drápes are còld . . . clòsed, so your róoms won't get còld.' ('cold' anticipated, substituted for participial 'closed'; AD-576(41))

   b. AF: (talking about what to do if we hadn't ordered enough pizza) 'Well if nót, we hàve anòther fròzen òne in the óven.' ('oven' substituted for derived 'freezer'; AD-383(35))

In (32a) one could imagine that the past participle suffix from the adjective 'closed' could have remained in the planned location, producing a novel form something like *'colded' or *'colden', but in fact the monomorphemic adjective 'cold' was simply substituted for the derived word 'closed'. Similarly in (32b) the speaker did not produce a novel form such as *'ovener', but merely substituted the monomorphemic word 'oven' for 'freezer'. This type of error will be discussed in some detail in §6.4.2.1 below, but in the present section I need only point out that this lack of stranding with derivational affixes is the norm rather than the exception.

6.3.2.3   Strandings in Planning

These findings fit in a very simple way into the RPC Model of speech production planning. When the syntactic template is selected and in the planning stage, abstract markers for inflectional affixes are associated with specific locations in the syntactic string. If a content morpheme is erroneously inserted into a slot planned for the stem preceding an affix, the abstract marker for that affix will affiliate itself with whatever stem happens to be inserted into this slot (as in (23) above). Similarly, if a stem is planned for a slot which is associated with an inflectional affix, and then is perseverated or anticipated and erroneously inserted into a different unaffixed slot, it will not carry with it the affix planned for the target location (as in (24)). The few exceptions involve exchange errors where the default meaning for one of the lexical items is plural, and in these cases the stem may take the plural suffix with it.

The only derivational stranding errors in the child data are three errors involving the reversal of two stems in a compound: *'jack<u>ing</u> jump' for 'jumping jack' where {-ing} is a participial adjectival suffix (AN-231(45) 4;8); *'candle<u>make</u> stick<u>er</u>' (given in (27b) above, AN-102(47) 3;2), where {-er} is the agentive suffix; and 'clean pip<u>er</u>' for 'pipe <u>cleaner</u>' with instrumental {-er} stranded (AN-134(47) 3;11). It's not clear to me exactly where in the model these errors take place, but they are very different types of errors from the usual inflectional strandings, as they involve word-internal morpheme shifts.

An interesting derivational affix stranding error made by an adult is given in (33).

(33)   AF: 'Instrùct<u>ion</u> of . . . perm̀ission of *instrùct<u>or</u>* is álways OK̀.'
('instruct' [ɪn.stɹʌ́kt] anticipated and substituted for 'permit' [pʰɚ.mít], with stranding of derivational suffixes {-ion} and {-or}, and morphophonemic changes; AD-591(41))

In this error one could argue that the stem {instruct} was anticipated and substituted for the stem {permit}, leaving the agentive suffix {-or} stranded. The new sequence of {instruct}+{ion, nominalizer} requires the /t/-->[ʃ] phonological change in the stem to produce [ɪn.stɹʌ́k.ʃən] (compare to 'instructor' [ɪn.stɹʌ́k.tɚ]), just as {permit}+{ion} requires the same shift, i.e. [pʰɚ.mí.ʃən]. However one could also argue that since the two target words 'permission' and 'instructor' have both been planned for the utterance, some activation has spread from the word 'instructor' to the derivationally related word 'instruction'; since this word is formally similar to the planned word 'permission', it is misselected. That is, one could argue that this is actually a lexical selection error. A similar example is an error I made while working on this chapter: ' . . . I can clàrif<u>y</u>, uh, I can idè<u>ntify</u> prètty *cléar*ly.' In this error, one could argue that I anticipated the stem {clear} from the word 'clearly' [kʰlír.li], stranding the derivational suffix {-ly}, and substituted it for the stem {ident} in 'identify'. The new sequence {clear}+{ify} required a shift in the vowel of the stem, to produce [kʰlé.rə.faʲ]. However, it could also be that the planned word 'clearly' activated other related derived words in the lexicon including 'clarify', which then was misselected for the intended 'identify', due in part to having a morpheme in common with the target word. So unlike the morpheme-unit errors discussed in §6.3.1, some of these stranding errors which involve derivational morphology could actually be lexical substitution errors. Whatever the correct explanation, it seems that these errors involving derivational affixes are qualitatively different from those involving inflectional affixes.

Several stranding errors involving irregular morphology lend further support to the processing model. Some examples are given in (34).

(34) a. AM: (talking about a dog who jumped up to eat from lying down,
           and one of her legs went numb) 'So she gòbbled her **fóot** down
           . . . she gòbbled her fóod down, hòlding òne of her **féet** in the
           àir.' (stem 'foot' [fʊt] anticipated from second phrase,
           substituted for 'food' [fud] in first phrase; source is plural 'feet'
           [fit]; AD-588(41))
      b. AF: 'He's **drìven** hòw you constráin it, but nòt whàt's **drívi**ng it.'
           (for 'given' [gí.vən]; anticipation of stem 'drive' [draʲv] from
           inflected 'driving', substituted for stem 'give' [gɪv]; AD-589(41))

The best explanation for (34a) is that at the time of the error, the word 'feet' was
still represented as {foot(irregular)}+{plural}, so that the stem {foot} was
anticipated and substituted for 'food', due in part to phonological similarities of
the underlying forms [fʊt] and [fud]. In the corrected utterance, the sequence
{foot(irregular)}+{plural} makes contact with the lexicon to activate the irregular
form [fit]. In (34b), the stem 'drive' [draʲv] from the sequence {drive}+
{progressive} is anticipated and substituted for the stem 'give' [gɪv] in the
sequence {give}+{perfect}. However, since 'drive' has an irregular perfect form,
the spoken form of {drive(irregular)}+{perfect} reflects the required vowel change,
and therefore the vowel in the error is different from that in the source: [draʲv]
vs. [drí.v(ən)]. These errors can only be easily explained if one assumes that the
inflectional markers are linked to syntactic slots, and that irregular forms are
stored in the lexicon and accessed when the syntagmatic string requires them.

These stranding errors may have reminded the reader of the discussion in
Chapter 3 of the 'extrasyllabicity' of inflectional suffixes, particularly those
which contain a single consonant (see §3.5.4, Table 3.18, and examples in (65)).
In Chapter 3 I showed that phonological errors showed greater consistency
between the syllable location of the target and source units if single-consonant
inflectional suffixes were considered extrasyllabic, that is, not integrated with the
phonological structure of the syllable. Syllabic inflectional suffixes were less
well integrated with the phonological word when they occurred as actual verb
forms (progressive, past, perfect, passive), but were more integrated when they
derived a participial adjective. Derivational affixes were most often fully
integrated in the phonological word. These phonological errors further support
the hypothesis that there is a difference between the representation and processing
of inflectional vs. derivational affixes, since even the very productive derivational
affixes {-er}, {-or}, {-y}, {-ie} behave most of the time as if they are integrated
into the phonological word. This is most easily explained if we posit that
inflectional affixes are affiliated with the syntactic structure and thus not fully
integrated with the phonological word even during assignment of phonetic form,
whereas derivational affixes are more fully integrated with the phonological
word, probably because they are stored together with the stems in the lexicon. I
do not, however, mean to suggest that all participial forms of verbs which can
function as adjectives or nouns are stored in the lexicon, although it is likely

that some high-frequency participial forms are (such as 'broken', and 'closed'). I would hypothesize that for novel participial forms, the inflectional suffix is affixed to the stem during processing. But since the word produced by this affixation is associated with a single slot in the syntax marked for 'noun' or 'adjective', and thus the affix is no longer functioning to mark tense or aspect in the phrase, the suffix becomes disassociated from the syntax and more fully integrated with the phonological word.

6.3.2.4 Developmental Patterns in Strandings

The last question to be asked regarding stranding errors is whether or not there are any developmental trends evident from these data presented in Table 6.3. As with the morpheme-unit errors, it was found that the children in the 1-word and 2-word stages produced no stranding errors, supporting the hypothesis that the separation of inflectional affixes from stems and their independent representation and processing coincides with the onset of syntax. The earliest stranding errors occurred at age 2;2 and were of the type where the source word was inflected, but then was perseverated and substituted in a later slot without its inflection, as illustrated in (35a). Stranding errors involving exchanges began to occur at age 2;7 (35b) (see also (23a) above, *'my **colds** are **hand**'), and stranding errors where a non-inflected word was moved into a slot marked for an inflection began to occur at age 3;6 (the earliest was AL-144, shown in (28a) above, *'**grammas**' for 'giraffes').

(35)   a.   An: (chanting a nursery rhyme)
            'Thrèe lìttle ***mónkeys*** jùmpin' òn the béd,
            Mòmmy càlled the **mónkey**, and the **mònkèy** . . . Mòmmỳ . . .
            Mómmy?' (perseveration/substitution of 'monkey' for
            'Mommy', leaving plural behind; AN-29(43) 2;2)
       b.   An: 'Her **rún** is **nòsing**.'
            (for 'Her nóse is rùnning'; 'nose' and 'run' exchanged',
            progressive suffix stranded; AN-57(45) 2;7)

The number of stranding errors in my child data increased slightly as the children got older, ranging from 4 at age 1-2b to 9 at ages 4 and 5. The adults in this study made relatively more stranding errors than the children. This is most likely a function of their producing phrases with more complex verbal morphology than that produced by the children; as will be seen in §6.3.3 below, adults produced a particularly large number of errors involving perfect or passive morphology, which was not the case with the children. If this is the correct explanation, then the increase in stranding errors as the children got older may show a trend towards more complex verbal morphology in the older children.

To complete this section, I have combined the figures from §6.3.1, morpheme-unit errors, with the stranding figures, looking specifically at

TABLE 6.4
Number of affixes in the three categories: inflectional (including copula/aux), participial derivational, and other derivational, involved in 'morpheme' errors; by age.

Age:	1-2b	3	4	5	Total	Adult
Inflectional	8	6	18	15	47 (84%)	35 (73%)
Particip. Deriv.	3	0	1	0	4 (7%)	6 (12.5%)
Derivational	1	2	0	2	5 (9%)	7 (14.5%)
Total N=	**12**	**8**	**19**	**17**	**56**	**48**

inflectional vs. derivational affixes; these figures are given in Table 6.4. In this table I have included contractible copula/auxiliary errors under 'inflectional' (since they are all grammatical morphemes), separated out participial derivations from other derivational affixes, and eliminated the 'other' and 'compound' categories. This table highlights the difference between the behavior of inflectional affixes and derivational affixes in morpheme-based errors or strandings, lending further support to the hypotheses regarding the relationship between inflectional morphology and syntax being developed in this chapter. It also shows that the adults in this study made proportionately more errors involving derivational morphology than the children did; this is probably due in part to their knowing more derived words, and also representing more information about morphological structure in the form lexicon.

6.3.3 Order of Acquisition of Morphemes

As is well-known, in *A First Language,* Roger Brown (1973) studied the development of morphology in three English speaking children and found that they all acquired a set of 14 specific morphemes in a nearly identical order; this finding was further confirmed with a larger number of children by de Villiers & de Villiers (1973). In order to see whether or not the morpheme-unit and stranding errors in my data reflect this same order of acquisition, I counted the number of times each affix was involved in an error, at each age (i.e. number of tokens). The results are given in Table 6.5. In this table I have only included affixes or clitics. In Brown's original list (1973:274) he included the prepositions 'in/on' (#2/3 on his list) and the non-contracted forms of the copula (#7), and auxiliary (#12), and articles (#8), but in my study, errors involving these forms are counted as lexical errors rather than morphological. The 'irregular 3rd sg. present' (#11) category does not occur in the table as I had no errors clearly involving this morpheme. I have added to this table the categories 'past participle', 'comparative', and 'irregular plural' which do not occur in Brown's original list but were involved in my errors. Since what is at issue here

TABLE 6.5
Number of each type of morpheme involved in morpheme-unit or
stranding errors, by age; compared to Brown's 14 morphemes.

Brown's Number	Age:	1-2b	3	4	5	Total	Adult
Inflectional							
1. progressive		2	1	3	3	9	10
4. regular plural		4	1	7	4	16	12
9. regular past tense		1	0	1	2	4	2
10. 3rd sg. present		2	2	3	1	8	2
na. past participle		1	1	1	1	4	10
13. contr. copula		0	1	0	2	3	1
6. posessive		0	0	2	1	3	0
14. contr. auxiliary		0	0	1	0	1	0
5. irregular past tense		0	0	0	1	1	0
na. comparative		0	0	0	0	0	2
na. irreg. plural		0	0	0	0	0	1
Total N =		**10**	**6**	**18**	**15**	**49**	**40**
Derivational							
diminutive/adj {-y, -ie}		1	0	0	1	2	2
agent/instrument {-er,-or}		0	2	0	1	3	2
other		0	0	0	0	0	3
Total N=		**1**	**2**	**0**	**2**	**5**	**7**

is the use of these specific suffixes in any function, I have included under Brown's designation of 'progressive,' any use of the {-ing} suffix, whether it be a progressive or a participial form (noun, adjective or adverb). Similarly, any use of the {-en/ed} suffix, perfect, passive or participial, is counted under 'past participle'. I have also added derivational affixes at the bottom of the list for comparison. (If a suffix was involved in a multiple error, where it was both moved to a new location and had another suffix substituted in the old location, I only included it once in this table; e.g. in *'scar**in**' look**ed** witch' (AL-69(48) 2;10) I only counted the {ing [-ən]} suffix once.)

The figures in this table are compatible with the order of acquisition found by Brown for most of the relevant morphemes. The children made errors involving Brown's morphemes #1, 4, 9, and 10 at age 1-2b, when in the telegraphic speech stage; however they also made one error involving the perfect suffix at this age. At age 3 they added the contractible copula, #13, and at age 4 the contractible auxiliary, #14. Two morphemes are out of order: #6, possessive, which was involved only in three errors at ages 4 and 5, and #5, irregular past tense, which was only involved in one 5-year-old phrase blend (AN-313(49) 5;9). The adults made errors involving the comparative and the irregular plural forms, which are not part of Brown's set; children did not make morpheme errors involving these forms. For both children and adults, errors involving the earlier learned morphemes tend to be more frequent than errors involving later learned morphemes. Thus, these data from early child SOTs are shown to reflect to a large extent the order of acquisition of these morphemes found in longitudinal observational studies, a convergence of findings which supports the accuracy of the SOT results.

6.3.4 Accommodation

One of the strongest arguments for the on-line productivity of various morphological processes is the fact that when morphemes find themselves in new locations or affixed to new stems in errors, the morphemes nearly always accommodate in form to the erroneous syntagmatic string (see Fromkin 1973a, Garrett 1980b, Stemberger & Lewis 1986, Berg 1987b, among many others). This accommodation takes various forms, including the speaker producing the correct allomorph of a morpheme with several phonologically conditioned allomorphs or regular vs. irregular forms, the speaker changing the verb to agree with the erroneous subject, changes in pronoun case due to erroneous placement of pronouns, and appropriate determiner-noun sequences. I will discuss all of these factors in this section, as well as look at the few cases where accommodation does not occur.

6.3.4.1 Allomorphy and Regularity of Inflectional Morphemes

In my data, when an inflectional suffix with more than one allomorph occurred on a new stem in an error, the suffix was always spoken with the correct allomorph for the new stem, regardless of the allomorph required for the target stem. This phenomenon occurred in syntagmatic errors as illustrated in (36a), in paradigmatic substitutions as illustrated in (36b), in word blends (36c), and in phrase blends, as in (36d). (I will justify this analysis of the paradigmatic errors in §6.4.2.2 below.)

(36) a. An: 'The tòy that Àlice pláy__ wìth**ed**.' (for 'played' [ple^{j}(d)]; past tense {-ed} erroneously moved from verb 'play', added to end of 'with' producing [wɪθ(t)]; AN-66(44) 2;8)

  b. B: 'I wànt you to gèt me òne of those Kòol-aid sándwìch<u>es</u> . . . I mean pópsìcles.'
('sandwich' substituted for 'popsicle', taking on plural marker: [pʰáp.sì.kəɬ(z)] vs. [sǽnd.wì.tʃ(əz)]; B-133(35) 3;5)

  c. Al: 'That's mè pùtting on my [ʃáks].'
(blend of 'shoes' [ʃu(z)] and 'socks' [sak(s)]; plural allomorph is appropriate for consonant which ended up in the coda of the blend, i.e. voiceless; AL-98(38) 3;2)

TABLE 6.6
Number of errors in which regular inflectional suffixes accommodated to an erroneous stem by changing to a different allomorph; by type of suffix and by age.

Age:	1-2a	1-2b	3	4	5	Total	Adult
Reg. Plural	0	0	4	6	2	12	13
Reg. Past	0	1	0	0	1	2	3
3rd Sg. Pres.	0	1	0	2	1	4	3
Past Partic.	0	0	0	0	0	0	2
Aux.	0	0	0	2	0	2	0
Total N=	**0**	**2**	**4**	**10**	**4**	**20**	**21**

   d. B: 'Lèt me sèe the bòx of the créam that pùts . . . that you pùt on
          my hànds. The kìnd that gòes on my hánds.'
          (phrase blend of 'that goes on my hands' vs. 'that you put on
          my hands'; 'put' takes the 3sg suffix intended for 'goes': 'puts'
          [pʰʊt(s)] vs. 'goes' [goʷ(z)]; B-303(49) 4;6)

In my data there were 20 child errors and 21 adult errors which involved regular allomorphy; that is, in both the target and error utterances a regular inflectional affix (or the contractible auxiliary) occurs, and the error word requires a different allomorph from the target word. The number of such errors involving each affix are given in Table 6.6. As usual I am counting both the /-en/ and /–ed/ allomorphs of the perfect suffix as 'regular'; also any neologisms, such as *'withed' in (36a) are considered 'regular' by default. No errors of this sort occurred when the children were in the 1-word or 2-word stages; the earliest error which showed allomorphic accommodation was that given in (36a) above, at age 2;8. Stemberger (1989:172) also collected one error from one of his child subjects showing allomorphic accommodation: *'We better put the hood_ ups' for 'hoods up' ('hoods' [hʊd(z)] vs. *'ups' [ʌp(s)]); he does not report the age of the child who made this error, but does report that accommodation occurred.

   Errors involving irregular morphology also showed this kind of accommodation, in that if an irregular noun or verb was erroneously substituted for a regular noun or verb (or vice versa), the error word was spoken with the correct form for its regular/irregular status.

(37) a. B: 'I could wràp my scàrf aròund my féet.'
         M: 'Your féet?'
         B: 'My hánds!' (irregular 'foot' substituted for regular 'hand', both
             spoken with correct plural morphology; B-285(35) 4;5)

b. TF: 'In our Énglish clàss todày, we **gòt** . . . we tàlked abòut the
   dìfference betwèen the Clàssical and Romántic pèriods.'
   (irregular 'get' substituted for regular 'talk', both with correct
   past tense morphology; AD-454(35)

There were 5 child errors and 9 adult errors which showed this regular/irregular
alternation in inflected forms (see the adult 'foot/food' error in (34a) above).
Besides the error involving the plural suffix in (37a), one of the child errors
involved the 3sg inflection, when a blend of 'lives' (regular) and 'is' (irregular)
was produced (B-515(38) 5;5). The other three child errors were paradigmatic
substitutions made by 4-year-olds, involving two irregular verbs (or deverbal
adjectives), one of which was being regularized by the child at the time of the
error: 'seen/heared' (B-218(35) 4;2); 'broken/bended' (OC-103(35) 4;4); and
'ate/drinked' (B-261(35) 4;4).

Furthermore there were 5 child errors and 1 adult error involving inflected
nouns or verbs where both the target and error word were irregular; in all of these
cases the correct surface form of the word was produced in the error, as illustrated
in (38).

(38)   a. Al: (hears a dog barking next door) 'I **sàw** . . . I hèard a púppy!'
           ('see' substituted for 'hear', both irregular past tense;
           AL-184(35) 3;10)
        b. B: (talking about a game)
           'And the shàrk attàcks your **féet** . . . físh.'
           ('foot' substituted for 'fish', both irregular plural; B-192(35) 4;1)

On the other hand, there were two errors, one child and one adult, that
seemed to be exceptions to inflectional morphology accommodation. These
errors are given in (39); (39a) is repeated from (14b) above where it was
discussed in some detail.

(39)   a. Al: 'That's a [skè.ʒən lù.kɪd] wítch, Mòm!'
           (for 'scary looking' [skɛ́.ʒi lú.kən]; AL-69(48) 2;10)
        b. AF: 'Well, you shòuld have gòtt**en** úp and tùrn**en** it ófft.'
           (for 'turned it off' [tʰɚ-n(d) ɪt áf]; error was [tʰɚ-.nən ɪt áft];
           AD-651(48))

In (39a), Alice has anticipated the present participial suffix {-ing [-ən]} from the
word 'looking' and substituted it for the derivational {-y} on 'scary'. However,
she seems to have recognized that there needed to be some sort of suffix on the
stem {look} and has added the past participle suffix in this slot. The problem is
that the past participle form of the verb {look} should be 'looked' [lʊk(t)];
although she has produced the form with the oral stop rather than the nasal stop

(i.e. [-ən]), she produces the full syllable allomorph [-ɨd] rather than the single consonant allomorph [-t] which is correct for the verb {look}. My guess is that this was done for rhythmic purposes, since the target word 'looking' has two syllables, but 'looked' has only one; so she maintained the phrasal rhythm by producing 'look+ed' as two syllables. This error was made at age 2;10, and there were no other exceptions in errors made by the older children. The error in (39b) was made by an adult, and seems to be based on the actual surface forms of the suffixes involved rather than their more abstract forms. The stem {get} takes the perfect suffix {-en}, but the perfect of {turn} is [tʰɚn(d)]. In this error it looks like the actual phonological form of the perfect suffix [-ən] was perseverated from the word 'gotten' and substituted for the correct form of the perfect suffix on the word 'turned', producing the illegal form *'turnen' [tʰɝ.nən]; the perfect suffix from 'turned' [-d] is then perseverated and added to the word 'off'. Now that this suffix is adjacent to a voiceless fricative, it is produced as the voiceless allomorph [-t], in *offt [af(t)]. So this is a sort of chain reaction that involves bumping the surface forms of the two verbal suffixes one verb or particle to the right. These sorts of errors are very rare; they show that the actual phonetic forms of affixes can be moved around in errors, but this sort of lack of accommodation is by far the exception rather than the rule.

In general, then, these accommodation errors fit well with the RPC Model that shows lexical substitution, blend, misplacement, and phrase blend errors occurring before the actual phonological forms of lexical entries are activated. When inflected forms of stems are to be computed, it is the lemmas of the stem plus inflectional affix which are concatenated and used to address the form lexicon. If the stem is marked as irregular (as I will argue for in §6.4.2.4 below), then the correct irregular form is accessed from the form lexicon. If the stem is regular, then the form of the unaffixed stem will be activated, and then the affix in the stem+affix sequence will be assigned the correct phonologically conditioned allomorph during the assignment of phonetic form. Malapropisms of course take place when the form lexicon is being addressed; again in this case if an incorrect form entry is activated, its correctly inflected form will be computed by the remainder of the system, as if it were the intended form.

6.3.4.2   Agreement in Verbs and Pronouns

In my data there were three child errors in which an erroneous pronoun was substituted in the subject slot of a sentence, requiring a change in the verb agreement morphology. In all three cases this change was correctly made. One example is given in (40); the other two examples are (AL-157(41) 3;8) and (B-436(41) 5;0), both involving 'I/it'. There were no analogous errors involving full nouns, and I did not collect any examples of this sort from the adults.

(40)   B :   'Robb has G.I. Jóe, but I ònly hàve . . . he ònly hàs the cár.'
       ('I' substituted for 'he'; B-425(36) 4;11)

In this error, the pronoun 'I' was substituted for 'he', causing a change in the verb from 'have' to 'has'. Another example where there seemed to be some verb accommodation may in fact have been a false start.

(41) B: (looking for strawberry milk powder)
           'Where àre **the** . . . where is that pówder?'
           ('the' substituted for 'that', with change in copula; B-137(36) 3;7)

In this error Bobby seems to have erroneously planned for a plural noun, producing the plural form of the copula 'are'; he then corrected to singular, producing 'is' before the singular determiner 'that'.

Another type of accommodation occurred in a few errors where a pronoun was perseverated or anticipated and substituted for another pronoun. In every error but one in which the target pronoun would have had the incorrect case for the new location, the pronoun shifted to the correct case. This type of error was also rare. I collected only two from the children and one from the adults; see also (AL-190(48) 3;11) 'me/my', and (AD-488(36)) 'I/me/you'.

(42) B: 'Mommy, can **yóu** gò with **mè**?'
      M: 'What?'
      B: 'Can Í gò with yòu?'
           (exchange of 'I' and 'you', with shift in case; B-96(46) 2;7)

In (42), Bobby is asking if he can go with his mother on an outing, but reverses the first person and second person pronouns. Now that the first person is in the object slot, it takes the object form 'me' rather than the subject form 'I'. The one possible exception to this case accommodation is the following error:

(43) Al: (wanting to watch the video she rented)
            'Bòbby wàtched **hims**, . . . his, so nòw I can wàtch míne.'
            ('him' [hɪm] misselected, substituted for 'his' [hɪz], but then 'him' is marked as possessive; AL-266(36) 5;11)

This is an interesting case in which the incorrect object pronoun 'him' was selected and substituted for the possessive 'his'. However it appears that the abstract marker for possession was not deleted when this substitution was made, and possibly the lemma {him} was treated as if it were a noun of some sort. Thus the sequence {him+POSS} was sent to the form lexicon for activation of phonological form; then the forms [hɪm+s, possessive] were sent to the phonological component for compilation, and the phonological processor selected the correct allomorph of the possessive suffix for a stem ending in a voiced sonorant, namely [z]. The final phonological output was [hɪmz]. So although a pronoun with the incorrect case was selected, the processor accommodated for the error by treating the erroneous pronoun as if it were a correctly selected noun and inflecting it accordingly.

Again both the verb agreement and pronoun case errors support the model in which these lexical substitution and misplacement errors occur before the form representations are accessed. Subsequent components then clean up any possible surface violations of agreement or case marking.

6.3.4.3   Articles and Other Determiners

In a number of errors, determiners find themselves next to new or altered nouns, and some accommodation may be necessary. In this section I will first talk about allomorphic variation of the definite and indefinite articles, and then look at accommodation of determiners to changes in three factors: mass vs. count nouns, number, and proper vs. common nouns.

I did not consistently record the pronunciation of the definite article, which is usually [ðə] before nouns (or adjectives) beginning in consonants, and [ði] before vowels, so I will not be able to discuss this variation in any detail. There were only a few errors for which this would have been pertinent, such as AD-579(41) involving 'the [ði] interruption' and 'the [ðə] discussion', and B-379(31) 4;10, in which the adjective 'original' was produced with some phonological changes, causing it to begin with a consonant: 'the [ði] original' vs. 'the [ðə] *[rə.ní.dʒə.nəɬ]'.

For the speakers in this study, the indefinite article is usually pronounced [ʌ] before consonant-initial nouns (or adjectives), and [ʌʔ], [ʌn], or [æn] before vowel-initial words. In my corpus I recorded 8 errors in which a shift in the form of the indefinite article was required. These included 2 child phonological errors in which the consonant/vowel status of the onset of the word following the article was shifted, illustrated in (44a); (see also AN-178(34) 4;4). There were two child and two adult paradigmatic lexical substitutions which required this change, as in (44b) (also B-94(35) 2;7, AD-421(35), and AD-378(35)). There was one child blend (44c) and one child syntagmatic error (44d) which required this shift.

(44)   a. B: 'I'll gìve ya [ʌʔ __ ínt].'
                 (for 'a hint' [ʌ hɪnt]; [h] deleted non-contextually; [ʌʔ] allomorph of indefinite article selected; B-375(30) 4;9)
        b. OG: 'I nèed a **rùbber-bánd**. Nót a rùbber-bànd. Nót a rùbber-bànd.'
             M: 'Whát do you need?'
             OG: 'An umbrélla.' ('rubber-band' substituted for 'umbrella', causing shift from [ʌ] to [æn]; OC-112(35) 4;6)
        c. Al: 'I wànt a [**græʔ.pəɬ**].'
                 (blend of 'grape' and 'apple'; because the onset of the blend is the consonant [g], the [ʌ] allomorph of the indefinite article is chosen; AL-227(38) 4;6)

d. M: 'How 'bout an **àpple**, òrange, or banána?'
   OB:'Uh, [ʌʔ **ǽp**] . . . a banána.'
      ('apple' perseverated, substituted for 'banana', requiring the [ʌʔ]
      allomorph of the indefinite article, which is pronounced as [ʌ]
      before 'banana'; OC-129(43) 5;0)

In every case where this shift in the form of the indefinite article was required, it occurred without exception. The earliest error showing this alternation was made at 2;7, involving 'a scary' vs. 'aʔ owie' (B-94(35)).

In the vast majority of errors in which one noun was substituted for another, whether paradigmatically or syntagmatically, any determiner which was planned to proceed the target noun was also appropriate for the error noun. This was usually because such factors as mass/count, or proper/common were identical between the target and error words; that is, the words were both mass or both count, or both proper or both common (see also 6.4.2.4 below). However, it was also the case that in most errors where one of these factors differed between the two words, the determiner was one that was grammatical with either class, as illustrated in (45).

(**45**) a. OB: (I had just given him a piece of candy)
            'Thànk you fòr the **cóokie**.' ('cookie', a count noun, substituted
            for 'candy', a mass noun; OC-36(35) 3;0)
       b. B: 'I'm gònna gèt some **hànds** on my . . . some <u>wàter</u> on my
            hánds.' ('hands', plural count noun, anticipated, substituted
            for 'water', mass noun; B-156(41) 3;8)

In (45a) the count noun 'cookie' was substituted for the mass noun 'candy', but since both can take the definite article 'the', this did not require any accommodation. In (45b) the plural count noun 'hands' was anticipated and substituted for the mass noun 'water'. Although the phrase 'some hands' doesn't make any sense in this context, it is not ungrammatical; imagine a mother saying to her children just before dinner: 'I see some hands that need washing.' So in most cases no accommodation of determiners was necessary.

However I think it is extremely interesting that when a determiner+noun sequence which was ungrammatical was produced by an error, I recorded no cases where the determiner actually did accommodate. This means that the one area of morphosyntax which did not get cleaned up by later processing components was lexical substitution errors where the relationship between the determiner and noun was ungrammatical. In my data there are 4 such cases involving the mass/count distinction (1 child, 3 adult); 2 cases involving number (1 child, 1 adult); and 1 child error involving the proper/common distinction. Examples are given in (46).

(46) a. OG: (showing Mom a toothbrush) 'Mom, thìs is a **tóothpàste** . . .
          a tóothbrùsh.' ('toothpaste', a mass noun, substituted for
          'toothbrush' a count noun, producing illegal sequence
          *a toothpaste; OC-87(35) 4;1)

      b. AF: 'Hère's some **quèsadílla**, I mean guàcamóle.'
          ('quesadilla', a count noun, substituted for 'guacamole', a mass
          noun, producing illegal sequence *some quesadilla;
          AD-379(35))

      c. OG: 'And wè saw the **dèad hòrse** of a **bónes**.'
          (phrase 'dead horse', singular, exchanged with 'bones', plural,
          producing illegal sequence *a bones; OC-116(45) 4;7)

      d. An: '**Mòmmy** càlled the dóctor and the **Mòmmỳ** sáid. . .'
          (proper noun 'Mommy' substituted for common noun 'doctor',
          producing illegal sequence *the Mommy; AN-26a(43) 2;1)

The other adult errors similar to (46b) also involved the food domain: *'making
avocado' for 'making guacamole' (AD-359(35)), and *'a **juice** of' for 'a glass
of' (AD-570(41)). The adult error which involved an exchange similar to (42c)
was *'let's get these **bed** to **kids**' (AD-641(45)), with the illegal sequence
*'these bed', given that 'bed' is singular. The two cases involving number,
recall, are those rare instances where a lexical item seems to be represented as
both singular and plural, so that when it is shifted to a new location it takes its
plurality with it.

Although there were only 7 errors in my data which showed this non-
accommodation phenomena, there were none that showed a different determiner
being produced in the error utterance because it was required by the semantics of
the error noun. In a couple cases, nouns moved carrying their original
determiner with them (e.g. *'**my head**'s over **the water**' for 'the water's over
my head', B-578(45) 5;11), but there was never an actual replacement of a
determiner caused by a noun substitution. It appears that the semantic/syntactic
requirements of the originally planned noun determine the functional structure of
the noun phrase; then when an erroneous noun is inserted into the noun slot, the
functional structure is not affected by the new noun. This fits nicely with the
claim by Levelt (Levelt 1989:196-7, Bock & Levelt 1994:975) that grammatical
properties such as mass/count, proper/common, and in a few cases plurality are
part of the lemma of a lexical entry, which is the element involved in setting up
functional structures. As mentioned above, in most lexical substitution errors
involving nouns, both target and error noun had the same value on these
parameters, and this would cause determiner violations to be rare. However,
because the functional structure of noun phrases is set at a very early stage of
processing, this appears to be one kind of agreement-type error which is allowed
to slip through the internal monitor and be produced on the surface occasionally.
Since there were only three child errors of this sort (all given in (46)), no
developmental interpretations can be made; but it should be noted that there were

no child exceptions to this pattern at any age.

The cases in which accommodation did not occur in my data are very similar to the type of error which Berg (1987b) also found did not show accommodation in German. In his data he found that when a noun with a different gender from the target was erroneously substituted, the articles did not adapt to the gender of the error word. An example is given in (47); I have presented this example from Berg (1987b:285, example (18a)) in my formatting.

(47) 'Der **Christa** und die **Helmut** . . .
the (nom. masc.) Christa and the (nom. fem.) Helmut . . .
der <u>Helmut</u> und die <u>Christa</u>.'
('Helmut' (masculine) and 'Christa' (feminine) exchanged)

In this error the articles do not accommodate to the gender of the noun when the nouns exchange. Berg argues that in general, if the error itself is in a function morpheme (such as a pronoun or article), then accommodation will occur (e.g. case accommodation in pronouns). But if the error occurs in a content morpheme, the function morpheme will not accommodate to it, unless it is a rule-governed allomorphic alternation triggered by phonological forms, such as the indefinite article accommodation seen in English. He argues that the explanation for this lies in different degrees of activation of the articles and nouns during the serial planning of the string of words: at the time during planning when it would need to accommodate to a noun which was different from the one originally planned, the article is not activated highly enough to allow it to accommodate. This connectionist type explanation is somewhat at odds with the explanation given above, but in fact it can be interpreted in terms of a 'stages model'. Marx (1999), also looking at gender violations in articles in German, proposes a two-stage model of lexical retrieval and speech production. He points out that information about gender is part of the lemma representation of German, analogous to the 'mass/count' distinction in English. When lemmas are activated early in the speech production planning process, this information is required for setting up functional structures. However, this information is not utilized in later stages of processing (perhaps because it has become less highly activated), allowing gender agreement violations to occur. This explanation is completely in line with the RPC Model, which would expect that gender information would be part of the lemma representations, and thus violations at a later stage would be similar to those found for the mass/count distinction in English.

On the other hand, it was found in §6.3.4.2 above that verbs will shift their agreement features to accommodate to person and number in errors involving pronominal subjects, and surely person and number are part of the grammatical information stored in the lemmas of pronouns. The difference is that in the case of verb agreement, the verb is assigned the correct agreement markings during the assignment of syntactic form, not during the construction of functional structures. Furthermore, the accommodation of a verb to a new subject requires the selection of a different suffix or allomorph, but for the noun-determiner case, it means selection of an entirely different lexical item (i.e. re-accessing the lexicon), which causes much more strain on the processing mechanism. Therefore it is not surprising that verbs accommodate to person and number of erroneous subjects, whereas determiners do not accommodate to incorrectly selected nouns.

6.3.5 Conclusions

In the preceding three sections I have focussed on errors in which individual affixes function separately from the larger lexical item, either by moving to a new location, by allowing a stem to move away from the affix, stranding that affix in its syntagmatic position, or by allowing an erroneous stem to substitute for the correct stem associated with some affix. The findings from these types of errors strongly support the hypothesis that inflectional and derivational affixes behave differently from each other in both representation and processing, although highly productive derivational affixes can have some behavior in common with inflectional affixes. The processing model implicated by these findings has been discussed in detail. Furthermore it has repeatedly been found that children in the 1-word and 2-word stages do not make the types of morphological errors discussed in this section; such errors become fairly common as soon as children enter the 3+word stage. However, these findings are only part of the picture. In order to further verify the claims regarding the morphological make-up of lexical entries, lexical substitution and blend errors need to be examined, to see whether or not this same view of morphological structure in the lexicon is supported by these paradigmatic errors. I will now turn to an examination of the morphological structure of target and error words in lexical substitutions and the two targets in blend errors.

6.4 Morphological Structure in Lexical Substitution and Blend Errors

I have suggested in this and earlier chapters that two words may be more likely to substitute for each other in either paradigmatic or syntagmatic substitution errors, or blend together in blend errors, if they have some 'form' in common. This means that they have some structure represented in their lexical entries which may cause them to be formally similar to each other, and thus are more likely to be erroneously selected without the internal monitor catching the error. In Chapter 3 I discussed the formal phonological relationships between lexical items involved in these errors, and found that there also seemed to be some morphological structure involved. In the present section I will look at the following questions:

1) Are two lexical items more likely to be mutually involved in an error if they have the same morphological structure (i.e. both derived, same number of morphemes, etc.)? Do different types of errors (paradigmatic/syntagmatic, substitutions/blends) show different patterns of morphological relatedness?

2) Are all the various types of morphological structures (i.e. derivational or inflectional affixes, compounds, particle verbs) involved in these errors in the same way? What about the regular/irregular status of nouns and verbs?
3) Do the answers to these questions differ if the mutually involved pair of words has a semantic relationship vs. no semantic relationship?
4) Are there differences in these patterns between the children and the adults?

6.4.1   Methodology

In order to determine the involvement of morphological structure in lexical errors, I assigned morphological structure to all target and error words in content-word paradigmatic substitutions and blends, and content-word syntagmatic substitutions. I excluded the function word errors from these counts since they typically do not include any of the types of morphology under consideration in this chapter. Although I have argued above that stems are probably not stored in the lexicon with any regular inflectional morphology affixed to them, for the sake of testing this hypothesis I have analyzed substitutions which involve inflected forms as if the inflection was part of the formal morphological representation of the word; for example, 'dogs' was counted as a two-morpheme word involving a stem and inflectional affix. I have also treated regular and irregular forms alike; that is, I have counted a word such as 'feet', the irregular plural of 'foot', as a 2-morpheme word involving a stem and inflectional morpheme. The methodology used to determine what counts as a compound was explained in Chapter 2 (§2.3.1). A verb was counted as a 'particle verb', i.e. lexicalized with a verb stem plus particle, if the particle was required in the logical form of the verb to specify the correct functional frame; particle verbs found in these errors were: child: 'talk to, listen to, hear of, blow up, wrap up, pick up, put away, spit up'; adult: 'burn down, pick up'. Verbs in their stem forms were considered monomorphemic; zero-inflected past tense forms such as 'hit' were counted as two morphemes.

The most difficult aspect of making the designation of morphological structure was to decide what should count as a morpheme, since the analysis of words by a linguist undoubtedly produces many more morphemes than either children or non-linguist adults are aware of. However, in order to be as consistent as possible, I referred to Webster's Dictionary (Neufeldt & Guralnik 1991) for a basic morphological analysis of all the words in question, and marked nearly every morpheme possible regardless of my opinion about its transparency to the children or non-linguist adults. There were a couple exceptions to this, two of which involved the suffix [-i]. First, I did not count any words with either the diminutive or adjectival use of [-i] as having a suffix before age 2, since there is little evidence that children of this age had any recognition of this affix; however, there is evidence that they do become aware of [-i] as a suffix during the third year (Jaeger 1986) so starting with age 2 I counted it as a derivational morpheme. Second, the words 'Mommy' and 'Daddy' were always counted as monomorphemic, since the children never used any other forms for referring to their parents. Third, I did not count extremely obscure forms such as the word 'Mutant' in the phrase 'Teenage Mutant Ninja Turtles' as having internal morphological structure. Nevertheless, this methodology caused me to claim multimorphemic status for many words which were probably monomorphemic for these speakers. I chose to err in this direction, however, in order to be consistent and to fully test the hypothesis that morphology may be marked in the lexicon and affect underlying similarity of words, regardless of whether or not speakers are fully aware of the morphological structure of words. If no real consistency in the morphological structure of target and error words is found, it may be a real finding, but may also be due to the fact that I have assigned too much underlying structure to the words. (I have indicated the morphological status assigned to each word in the data section of the book, so that readers will be able to interpret the numbers below accordingly.)

For paradigmatic substitutions and blends, I only analyzed errors which were semantically and/or phonologically related, since those which were [-phon, -sem] were usually environmentally influenced, and thus the morphological make-up of the words involved was unlikely to be an influential factor in the error. (So in the data, no morphological analysis is presented in the entries of these errors.) I also only included errors in which both the target and source, or the two targets, were unambiguous (i.e. I excluded those errors where the source was not obvious and was not actually spoken). I omitted 4 adult content-word blends which involved words from different lexical categories, because the morphological structure was too difficult to ascertain. For syntagmatic substitutions I did not include any of the metathesis errors, both full metathesis and the potential metathesis errors listed as anticipations, since these types of errors are usually not affected by the formal similarity of the words involved but are caused by a sequencing error in the syntactic string, as discussed at length in previous chapters. I also did not include errors involving strandings; I only looked at errors where the whole source substituted for the whole target word. However, I did include [-phon, -sem] pairs from syntagmatic errors, since if two words are activated to be produced in the same utterance, any morphological similarity between the two might be a factor in their interaction, regardless of their semantic or phonological relationship.

For all words involved in these errors I noted not only how many morphemes there were in the word but also exactly what those morphemes were; I also noted any irregular forms. I then tabulated how many of the target/error pairs fell into the various categories to be introduced in the next section, in particular, how many word pairs contained identical vs. different morphological structure. I will now turn to that analysis.

6.4.2 Morphological Relatedness of Words Involved in Lexical Errors
6.4.2.1 General Comparison

In Table 6.7 below I present figures showing the number of errors in my data with each type of morphological relationship between target and source (or the two targets in blends), by age. Before presenting this table, however, I will explain all the headings and give some examples. The first set of headings, under the word 'same', indicates cases where the target and source words had the same morphological structure as each other; the headings are to be read as follows: 'mono X2'=both words are monomorphemic; '2-infl X2'=both words are bimorphemic, involving a monomorphemic stem and an inflectional affix; '2-cmpd X2'=both words are two-stem compounds, where each stem is monomorphemic; '2-deriv X2'=both words are bimorphemic, involving a stem and a derivational affix; '2-PV X2'=both words are bi-morphemic particle verbs; 3-same=both words have 3 morphemes with the same structure as each other; 4-same=both words have 4 morphemes with the same structure as each other. Examples of each of these relationships are given in (48); in these examples the '+' sign is to be read as a morpheme boundary.

(48) a. mono X2:   'hot' for 'hard'; two monomorphemic words (AN-15(35) 1;9)

   b. 2-infl X2:   'turn+ing' for 'talk+ing'; two monomorphemic stems each with an inflectional suffix, in this case {-ing} progressive (B-86b(35) 2;6)

   c. 2-cmpd X2:   'tooth+brush' for 'paint+brush'; two two-stem compounds (AN-100(35) 3;2)

   d. 2-deriv X2:   'Collect+ion' for 'Contrap+tion'; two stems, both with a derivational suffix, in this case {-(t)ion} nominalizer (AN-60(35) 2;7)

   e. 2-PV X2:   blend of 'clean up' and 'pick up'; two verbs with stem and particle 'up' (OC-74(38) 3;11)

   f. 3-same: 'lolli+pop+s' for 'pop+sicle+s'; two two-stem compounds both with plural suffix {-s} (OC-82(35) 4;0)

   g. 4-same: 'pre+suppos+(i)tion+s' for 'pre+requis+ite+s'; derivational prefix, stem, derivational suffix, plural suffix (AD-356(35))

In the second set of headings in Table 6.7 I have listed relationships between word pairs where the two words have different morphological structure from each other. The headings are to be interpreted as follows: 'mono vs. infl'=one monomorphemic word interacts with a word made up of a stem+inflectional affix; 'mono vs. cmpd'=a monomorphemic word interacts with a compound (with from 2-4 stems); 'mono vs. deriv'=a monomorphemic word interacts with a derived word; 'mono vs. PV'=a monomorphemic word interacts with a particle verb; '2-different'=two bimorphemic words with different morphological make-up from each other interact; '2 vs. 3/4'=a bimorphemic word interacts with a word that has three or four morphemes, with different morphological structure; '3-different'=two 3-morpheme words interact, which have different morphological structure from each other; '3 vs. 4'=a 3-morpheme word interacts with a 4-morpheme word. Examples are given in (49).

(49) a. mono vs. infl: 'quiet', monomorphemic, substituted by 'cry+ing', stem+{-ing} progressive (AL-13(35) 2;2)

b. mono vs. cmpd: 'candy', monomorphemic, substituted for 'apple+juice', compound (OC-34(35) 2;10)

c. mono vs. deriv: blend of 'jacket', monomorphemic, and 'zipp+er', stem+{-er} instrumental (B-227b(38) 4;2)

d. mono vs. PV: 'watch', monomorphemic, substituted for 'listen+to' particle verb (B-71(35) 2;6)

e. 2-different: 'comput+er', stem+{-er}instrumental, substituted for 'xerox+machine', compound (AD-374(35))

f. 2 vs. 3/4:   'pretzel+s', stem+plural, for 'fruit+wrinkle+s', compound+plural (B-454(35) 5;1)

g. 3-different: blend of 'dumm+ie+s', stem+{-ie}(diminutive)+plural, with 'dodo+head+s' compound+plural (AN-169(38) 4;4)

h. 3 vs. 4:   blend of 'im+press+ion', 3 morphemes: {im-} 'in' prefix+stem+{-ion} nominalizer suffix, with 'im+person+at+ion', 4 morphemes: {im-} 'in' prefix+ stem+{-ate} verbalizer suffix+{tion} nominalizer suffix; all affixes derivational (B-514(38) 5;5)

The numbers of pairs of words which fell into each of these categories are given in Table 6.7.

Several things are clear from this table. First, for all subjects at all ages, there are more errors where the mutually involved words have the same morphological structure than errors where they have different structure. Overall, in 84% of the children's errors, the morphological structure of the two words was the same; for the adults the figure is 76.5%. The most common case is when two monomorphemic words interact in an error, undoubtedly due to the frequency of monomorphemic words in English. But even if the monomorphemic words are omitted from the count, 58% of the child errors and 57.5% of the adult errors show the same morphological structure between target and error words. It would be difficult to calculate a 'chance' figure for morphological structure, which would have to take into consideration all possible morphological structures of English words plus the frequency of each type; nevertheless it seems intuitively extremely unlikely that nearly 60% of these errors for both children and adults would involve words with the same morphological structure purely by chance. These figures suggest that morphological similarity could be an important factor in causing two words to interact in lexical errors.

TABLE 6.7

Number of pairs of words in lexical errors with each morphological relationship (see text for explanation of headings), by age.

Age:	1-2a	1-2b	3	4	5	Total	Adult
Same							
mono X2	13	33	25	48	34	153	109
2-infl X2	0	4	6	14	11	35	24
2-cmpd X2	1	1	2	2	3	9	13
2-deriv X2	0	2	1	2	0	5	18
2-PV X2	0	0	2	0	0	2	0
3-same	0	0	0	3	1	4	17
4-same	0	0	0	0	0	0	7
Total =	**14**	**40**	**36**	**69**	**49**	**208**	**188**
	93%	80%	92%	84%	79%	84%	76.5%
Different							
mono vs. infl	1	1	1	1	0	4	4
mono vs. cmpd	0	3	1	6	5	15	13
mono vs. deriv	0	1	0	2	2	5	14
mono vs. PV	0	3	0	0	1	4	1
2-different	0	0	0	2	2	4	3
2 vs. 3/4	0	2	1	1	2	6	16
3-different	0	0	0	1	0	1	2
3 vs. 4	0	0	0	0	1	1	5
Total =	**1**	**10**	**3**	**13**	**13**	**40**	**58**
	7%	20%	8%	16%	21%	16%	23.5%
Total N =	**15**	**50**	**39**	**82**	**62**	**248**	**246**

Overall the adults and children show similar patterns of morphological relationships. For word pairs where the structure is the same, the most common interaction involves two monomorphemic words, followed by monomorphemic words with a single inflectional affix; pairs with other morphemic structures are less common, although more so for the children, as I will discuss below; child N=20, adult N=55. Among word pairs where the morphological structures are different, monomorphemes interacting with compounds are the most common type for the children, whereas for adults, monomorphemic words interacting with compounds or derived words are both common. For both children and adults, bimorphemic words interacting with words of three or four morphemes are also common among the word pairs with differing morphological structure.

The other fact which is evident from this table is that there are some age-related trends. The youngest children show the most morphological consistency in these errors (93% at age 1-2a). The percentage of errors involving word pairs with the same morphological structure drops to 80% at age 1-2b, rises to 92% at age 3, then steadily drops to 79% at age 5, moving in the direction of the adult figure (76.5%). These figures can best be explained in terms of the types of words the children knew at different ages, and the amount of morphology represented in lexical representations. The large majority of early errors involved monomorphemic words; since the very young children didn't know many multimorphemic words, they had many fewer chances of substituting one word for another which had different morphological structures. The dip in morphological consistency at age 1-2b was probably due to the fact that many of the words involved in errors which I analyzed as being multimorphemic were in fact unanalyzed wholes in the children's lexicons. So some of the 'mono vs. infl' or 'mono vs. deriv' errors at age 1-2b probably involved two monomorphemic words as far as the children were concerned. As the children got older, they learned more derivational morphology and acquired more lexicalized compounds, and this caused them to have more candidates for lexical errors which differed in morphological structure; they may also have been representing more morphological structure in lexical entries. The figures from this table show in particular that errors involving derived words were much more common among the adults than the children. I will have more to say about the details of the adult-child differences below.

Finally, one might wonder if paradigmatic and syntagmatic errors behave differently from each other in terms of morphological consistency. In order to check on this possibility, I calculated the percentage of errors from Table 6.7 which had the same morphological structure, for syntagmatic and paradigmatic errors separately. For the children, the percentage of 'same' morphological structure was nearly identical: paradigmatic=84%, syntagmatic=83.5%. There was more difference for the adults: paradigmatic=75%, syntagmatic=82%. This may seem counterintuitive in that one might have predicted that the form of the target and error words would be more important in paradigmatic than syntagmatic errors. But these adult figures fit well with the finding in Chapter 4 (see Table 4.6) that phonological representations show more influence in adult syntagmatic errors than in child syntagmatic errors, and apparently this is also true of the influence of morphology on syntagmatic errors. The low figure for the adult paradigmatic errors is probably due in part to the fact that paradigmatic errors are more heavily influenced by semantics than by form, and that, as mentioned above, adults simply know many more words with varied morphological structure than children do.

6.4.2.2 Behavior of Different Types of Morphemes

An important point which provides data for the issue of the relationship between inflectional morphology and syntax is the fact that in these errors, whenever one inflected form was substituted for or blended with another inflected form, the target and error words nearly always contained the identical inflectional morpheme. This was true for all of the adult (N=24) and all but one of the child (N=35) bi-morphemic inflectional errors, as well as all of the errors involving 3-same, 4-same, or different morphological structure where both words contain an inflectional affix: child N=7, adult N=16. Examples are given in (50).

(50) a. OB: 'I don't lìke the **núts** . . . I don't lìke the s<u>é</u>eds.'
          ('nut(s)' substituted for 'seed(s)', both with plural suffix;
          OC-80(35) 4;0)
      b. AM: ' . . . whose chùrch bùilding has **dĩed** . . . has bùrned dówn.'
          ('die(d)' substituted for 'burn(ed) down', both inflected for the
          perfect; AD-438(35))
      c. Al: 'My pìgs . . . my t<u>ò</u>es are **pígs'** fèet.' ('pig(s)' substituted for
          'toe(s)'; morphology ambiguous (see below); AL-97(41) 3;2)
      d. M: 'Why dòesn't she jùst kèep her éyes shùt?'
          An: 'Thàt's what she [**dúz**] . . . thàt's what she's d<u>ó</u>in', Mom!'
          (blend of 'does' [dʌz] and 'doin' [dú.wɪn] as part of phrase
          blend; AN-253b(38) 4;10)

The error in (50a) represents the most common case, where one monomorphemic word substitutes for another, but both the target and error word take the same inflectional suffix since it is required by the syntactic frame appropriate for the proposition being expressed (in this case, this noun slot must be plural). In (50b), a monomorphemic verb 'die' is substituted for a particle verb 'burn down', but both target and error are inflected with the perfect morpheme, which is again appropriate for the syntactic frame encoding this proposition. The anticipation/substitution of 'pigs' for 'toes' in (50c) is ambiguous in that the source 'pigs' is inflected for the possessive, but the target 'toes' is plural; since the phonological form of these two morphemes is identical, there is no way to tell which morpheme is spoken on the error word 'pigs'; this type of ambiguity is rare (child N=2, see also B-248(43) 4;4; adult N=1, AD-431(35)).

The single exception to this pattern is given in (50d), and paradoxically it makes the case even stronger. This error is actually a phrase blend of the two phrases 'That's what she's doin'' and 'That's what she does'. The lexical blend *[duz] was a blend of 'does' and 'doin'' (the informal pronunciation of 'doing'), two forms of the same verb stem 'do' with different inflections; 'does' contains the 3sg marker, while 'doing' contains the progressive. However, this blend of two inflected forms with different inflections was caused by a blend of two different syntactic frames, and thus once again we find support for the claim that inflectional affixes are closely linked to the syntax.

Turning to the errors involving word pairs with different morphological make-up, it can be seen from Table 6.7 that roughly half of these involve monomorphemic words interacting with compounds, derived words, and particle verbs (child N=24, 60%, adult N=28, 48%); however, monomorphemic words interacting with inflected words are rare (child N=4, adult N=4). Some examples of errors involving these mismatches were given in (49) above; these examples illustrate a monomorpheme/inflected word pair 'crying/quiet' (49a), a monomorpheme/compound pair 'candy/applejuice' (49b), a monomorpheme/derived pair 'jacket/zipper' (49c), and a monomorpheme/particle verb pair 'watch/listen to' (49d). Other error pairs which have mismatched numbers of morphemes or the same number of morphemes with different structures most often involved derived words, compounds, and particle verbs; for example the derived/compound pair 'computer/xerox machine' (49e), and two derived words with different numbers of morphemes 'impression/impersonation' (49h). If the inflectional affixes are stripped from these errors, we find that what remains usually continues to fall into the above categories: monomorpheme/compound 'pretzel(s)/fruit wrinkle(s)' (49f), derived word/compound 'dummie(s)/dodohead(s)' (49g), and so forth. There were 3 child errors and 1 adult error of this latter type (i.e. mismatched numbers of morphemes or mismatched structures) which involved the interaction of inflected with non-inflected forms.

In order to fully examine the types of morphological structure in word pairs which interacted in the lexical errors, I reorganized the figures from Table 6.7 in terms of what types of morphemes occurred in the lexical items, regardless of the number of morphemes in each word. In this count I have excluded the 12 errors (child N=7, adult N=5) in which an inflected form interacted with a non-inflected form (which I will discuss in detail below); for both children and adults, these exceptions constituted a very small percentage of the errors being analyzed here (child: 7/247=2.8%; adult 5/246=2%). I have also stripped off all the inflectional suffixes from the words involved in this count where both words had the same inflection (including those like (50c) above, which are somewhat ambiguous, but both involve an inflectional suffix). The results are given in Table 6.8.

It can be seen from this table that for the children and adults, monomorphemic words, compounds, derived words, and particle verbs freely substitute for each other in the errors. The fact that it is more common for the two words mutually involved in an error to have identical morphological structure supports the hypothesis that some information about morphological structure is represented in the form lexicon for each lexical entry, and this is one factor which would make it more likely that one word could be substituted for another and not have the error caught by the internal monitor. On the other hand, the fact that words of all these various morphological structures can substitute for each other in errors supports the claim that these are the units involved in lexical representation; specifically, derived words are not concatenated on-line as inflected words are. There are some differences between the adult and child figures which I will return to below.

In many of the errors involving two compounds, derived words or particle verbs, the target and source word or two target words did in fact have some morphemes in common. For the compounds and particle verbs, this was in

TABLE 6.8

Morphological structure of words involved in lexical substitution or blend errors, excluding inflections, regardless of number of morphemes per word.

	Child	Adult
2 Monomorphemic Words	188 (78%)	133 (55%)
2 Compounds	11 (4.5%)	19 (8%)
2 Derived Words	8 (4%)	49 (20.5%)
2 Particle Verbs	3 (1%)	0
Mono vs Compound	17 (7%)	15 (6%)
Mono vs Derived	5 (2%)	15 (6%)
Mono vs PV	5 (2%)	2 (1%)
Derived vs. Compound	4 (1.5%)	8 (3.5%)
Total N=	**241**	**241**

every case transparently due to the semantic relationship between the two words, as in the 'toothbrush/paintbrush' error in (48c), the 'lollipop/popsicle' error in (48f), and the 'clean up/pick up' error in (48e).

Similarly, in about 70% of the 48 adult errors involving two derived words and in all 9 of the child errors involving two derived words, the two words have some derivational affix in common, as illustrated in the 'Collection/ Contraption' error in (48d), and the 'impression/impersonation' error in (49h). One might want to argue that this makes the derivational errors similar to the inflectional errors, since something about the requirements of the syntax may have dictated that this affix should occur in this slot; i.e. the slot might be marked for an abstract noun, and thus the {-(t)ion} suffix is required. However, three facts argue against this. First, even if the proposition required an abstract noun, and the syntactic slot were marked as such, there are many different derivational affixes which could perform the same function (e.g. {-(t)ion}, {-ity}, {-ness}, {-al}, {-ate}); the actual affix is never dictated by the syntax as inflectional affixes are. It makes more sense to argue that if two words are represented in the lexicon with the same derivational suffix, then they would be candidates for being misselected for each other because they would be of the same lexical category by definition, since the derivational suffixes determine lexical category, and they would have some form in common. Second, in 30% of the adult errors involving two derived words, the two words did not contain the same derivational affix, whereas in inflected pairs the two words always contained the same inflectional affix; although there were a few ambiguous cases, in these errors the suffix pronounced in the error word was homophonous between the target and source suffix, and so certainly could have been the suffix intended for that slot in the syntax. Third, the derivational affix which the word pair had in common was a prefix rather than a suffix in 30% of the adult cases and 20% of the child cases; it would be very difficult to argue that prefixes (which do not determine lexical category) could be assigned by the syntax. Therefore I think the fact of mutually involved derivational affixes does not show that derivational morphology behaves like inflectional morphology in these errors. On the other hand it does give very strong support to the claim that such morphology is represented as part of the form lexical entry of the word, and is part of what causes formal similarity between the two words. One would hardly want to argue that the following pairs of words were mutually involved in lexical errors with no influence from the morphology: child errors: 'invention/impression', 'cemetery/planetarium', 'impression/impersonation', and possibly 'hungry/thirsty'; adult errors: 'insane/incredible', 'intuition/intonation', 'perception/perfection', 'imbibe/imbue', 'functionalist/fundamentalist', 'revolution/resolution', 'impressionable/influential', and many more.

Another important point is that present or past participles which are functioning as something other than a verb (i.e. are derived by zero derivation from verb forms), freely interact with compounds, other derived words, and particle verbs, as illustrated in (51).

(51)   a. Al: (in living-room, telling adult where some toy is)
            'Oùt in the [bɛ́.vin.ʒ̀ùm].'
        OA:'Where?'
        Al: 'In the bédròom.' (blend of 'bedroom' [béd.ʒ̀ùm] and 'living-room' [wí.v(in).ʒ̀ùm]; AL-26(38) 2;4)
    b. AF: 'Èverybody make sùre your drápes are còld . . . clòsed, so your róoms won't get còld.' (anticipation/substitution of 'cold' [kʰoʷɫd] for 'closed' [kʰloʷz(d)]; AD-576(41))

In (51a), 'bedroom' is a compound made up of two stems; 'living-room' is a compound made up of the stem 'live' plus the present participle suffix {-ing} which produces the noun 'living', and is then compounded with 'room'. This error was counted as '2 vs. 3/4' because 'bedroom' has two morphemes, and 'living-room' three, but 'living-room' was not counted in the 'inflectional' count because the {-ing} is behaving as a derivational affix here; importantly, the two compounds 'bedroom' and 'living-room' are free to substitute for each other, showing that each is a unitary lexical entry. (In Table 6.8 above, this type of error is counted into the 'derived vs. compound' category; child N=1, adult N=4.) Similarly, in (51b) the word 'cold' is a monomorphemic adjective, and 'closed' consists of the stem 'close' with the past participle suffix {-ed}, which produces the adjectival form 'closed'. This error was counted as 'mono vs. deriv', and reinforces the claim that monomorphemic and derived words freely interact.

However, in order to complete the argument that inflected words behave differently from other types of words, I need to be able to account for the exceptions. As presented above, in my data the children and adults each produced 4 errors where monomorphemic words interacted with inflected forms. Furthermore there were 3 child and 1 adult multimorphemic errors which involved inflected with non-inflected forms, for a total of 12 exceptions. These exceptions fell into a few non-surprising categories. Four of these exceptions were the syntagmatic exchange or movement errors discussed in 6.3.2.2 above where a singular noun exchanged with a plural noun which took its plural inflection with it. These involved the word pairs 'hands/water' counted as 'mono vs. infl' (B-156(41) 3;8), 'cows/life' counted as 'mono vs. infl' (AD-640(45)), 'kids/bed' counted as 'mono vs. infl' (AD-641(45)), and 'bones/dead horse' counted as '2-different' (OC-116(45) 4;7). I argued above that in each case the referent of the noun was something prototypically discussed in groups, and thus it is likely that the plural form is lexicalized. Three further exceptional errors also fell into the category of lexicalized plurals, including the following two child errors.

(52)   a. B: (poured powder on his toes while touching penis)
                'Pòwder **pénis** . . . pòwder tóes.'
                ('penis' [pí.nʌɕ] for 'toes' [toᵂɕ]; B-16(35) 1;10)
      b. B: 'I wànt **Pùss in** . . . I wànt Mòther Góose tàpe.'
                ('Puss in Boots' for 'Mother Goose'; B-84(35) 2;6)

In (52a) it is extremely unlikely that Bobby, at age 1 year 10 months, knew that the form 'toes' carried a plural morpheme; although this was classified as 'mono vs. infl' it is far more likely that this was the substitution of one monomorphemic word for another, as far as Bobby was concerned. In (52b), Bobby had lexicalized the proper name 'Puss in Boots' (the title character in a fairy story) with the plural suffix included. Although this was counted as '2 vs. 4', the plural morpheme is in fact part of the lexical entry. The other example of this type was a blend of 'McDonald's' and 'Burger King' (OC-174(38) 5;11), which was classified as '2-different', but is really a blend of a monomorphemic word 'McDonald's' which is lexicalized with the possessive, and a compound 'Burger King'. These errors are similar to the adult substitution of 'K-Mart' for 'X-Files' (AD-433(35)), since 'X-Files' is lexicalized as plural; however, this error was not counted into the above tables, since it is [-sem, -phon]. Thus many of these errors which look on the surface like exceptions to the principle that inflected forms do not interact with non-inflected forms are in fact not exceptions, since in these cases the inflectional suffixes are part of the lexical entry, rather than being part of the morphosyntax.

Another of the children's exceptions has something in common with (52a) in that it was made by a very young child.

(53)   Al: (holding fingers to lips) 'Mè **crỳing** Dàddy sléeping.'
           (looks confused)
       M: 'You mean you're qúiet?'
       Al: 'Yéah!' ('crying' [kʰ3áʲ.in] for 'quiet' [kʰwáʲ.ʌt]; AL-13(35) 2;2)

In this error Alice, at age 2;2, substituted the verb 'crying' which has the
progressive suffix, for the monomorphemic 'quiet', which she used as a verb at
that time. Although the progressive suffix is usually one of the first inflections
learned by children learning English (see Brown's (1973) 14 morphemes above),
it is not clear that Alice had necessarily separated out this morpheme from all her
verb stems yet at this age. The first errors where {-ing} behaved as a separate
unit from the stem occurred at ages 2;7 (AN-57(45)) and 2;10 (AL-69(48)).
Certainly 'crying' was a very frequent word for Alice at age 2;2, and thus it may
be the case that it was lexicalized as a single lexical entry at this age;
presumably by the second half of the third year such forms are no longer
necessary in the lexicon and are concatenated on-line in a productive manner.

   Of the other 4 exceptions, only one was made by a child; it is given in
(54a); (54b) is a similar adult error.

(54)   a. OB1: (making a huge pile of cheese on his plate)
                  'I have a mòuntain of **trées.**'
           OB2: 'What?'
           OB1: 'I have a mòuntain of <u>chéese</u>.'
                  ('trees' [tʃɻi(z)] substituted for 'cheese' [tʃiz]; OC-108(35) 4;5)
       b. AF: 'She's ùsing mòre [**mor.fîmz**] . . . uh morphólogy.'
               (blend of 'morphemes' [mór.fim(z)] and 'morphology'
               [mor.fá.lə.dʒi]; AD-508(38))

In (54a), the child substitutes 'trees' for 'cheese'; this may have been partly due
to phonological similarity, and partly due to a semantic association between
trees and mountains. This error was counted as 'mono vs. infl'. However, since
the target word 'cheese' is a mass noun, and 'tree' is a count noun, the word
'trees' may have been produced as plural in order to make semantic sense in the
utterance (*'mountain of tree'). Similarly, in (54b) the adult blends
'morphemes' with 'morphology', taking the segments of the former but the
stress pattern of the latter; this was counted as '3-different'. Again, if the
speaker had produced the singular 'morpheme' in the slot after 'more', the
utterance *'more morpheme' would have been ungrammatical, since 'more'
requires either a mass noun or a plural count noun. So in both of these cases the
semantic requirements of the preceding modifiers may have caused the speaker to
produce a plural in substitution for or blend with a mass noun. The other 2
exceptions, made by adults, were 'man/men's' (AD-297b(35)), and 'top/highest'
(AD-543(38)). The 'man/men's' error was part of a larger compound-stress error
and thus is more complex than a simple lexical substitution; this and the

'morphemes/morphology' error both involve different forms of the same stem. The 'top/highest' error shows the ambiguous status of the superlative suffix as inflectional, since in this case it acts like part of the lexical form. It can be seen from this discussion that each of these exceptions requires an idiosyncratic explanation, and seems to be caused by some other factor overriding the usual status of inflectional affixes.

As interesting as the exceptions are, however, it is clear that there are many more cases where inflected words only interact with other inflected words carrying the same inflection. Because half the exceptions involved words lexicalized as plural or possessive, and several occurred at such early ages that the the child probably hadn't yet separated the affix from the stem, these exceptions do not serve to greatly weaken the main argument of this section: inflected words behave differently from other types of multimorphemic words, showing that they are not usually lexicalized in inflected form.

As briefly mentioned above, there is an important difference between the child and adult errors evident in Table 6.8. With the inflectional morphology stripped off (and excluding the 'exceptions'), 78% of the children's errors involved two monomorphemic words, 9.5% involved two morphologically complex words with the same structure, and 12.5% involved two morphologically complex words with different structures. On the other hand, only 55% of the adult errors involved two monomorphemic words, 28.5% involved two morphologically complex words with the same structure, and 16.5% involved morphologically complex words with different structures. These numbers suggest that adults represent more information about morphology in lexical entries, so that morphological similarity plays a larger role in adult errors than in child errors; hence the adult errors involving multimorphemic words showed more morphological consistency than did the children's.

In particular, as suggested above, the children knew fewer latinate type words with derivational morphology than the adults; very few such words occurred in the child errors, whereas they were quite frequent in the adult errors. Only 7% of the child errors involved at least one derived word, whereas 30% of the adult errors involved at least one derived word. It may be the case that until children begin learning a number of multimorphemic words with derivational affixes, they have no reason to begin marking such structure in their lexical entries, and thus such structure has less effect on their errors than for adults. I will return to this point in the section on malapropisms below.

On the other hand, the children produced numerous errors involving compounds; 13.3% of the child errors reported in Table 6.8 involved at least one compound, which is not much different from the adult figure of 17%. This is not surprising, given that compounding is well-known to be the earliest word-formation strategy used by children learning English, preceding derivation by many years (Berko 1958, Derwing & Baker 1986, Clark 1993: Ch. 8). Interestingly, the children produced slightly more errors involving particle verbs than did adults, although such errors were quite rare for both groups (child: 3%;

adult: 1%). Since these words involve a combination of two content stems rather than a stem with a suffix, they have more in common with compounds than with derived words, and thus the children seemed to have acquired them early.

The strongest case for the claim that morphological structure is represented in lexical form entries would come from showing that malapropisms, which are lexical substitution errors based purely on form, show more morphological consistency than semantic-based errors. Developmental claims would also be strengthened if the adults show more of this effect than the children. I will now turn to this issue.

6.4.2.3 Morphological Structure in Malapropisms

In order to compare the morphological similarity of words involved in malapropisms to that of word pairs involved in semantically-driven lexical substitution errors, I tabulated the number of [+sem] vs. [-sem, +phon] pairs of words which had the same vs. different morphological structure. Table 6.9 presents these figures by age. In this table I only looked at errors from Class 35, paradigmatic substitution of content words, since this is the class of words in which classic malapropisms occur. This table is to be read as follows, for example: at age 1-2b the children produced 21 content word substitution errors which were classified as showing a semantic relationship between the target and error words (regardless of whether or not they had a phonological relationship). Of these, 71.5% (N=15) word pairs had the same morphological structure, whereas 28.5% (N=6) word pairs had differing morphological structures.

This table shows that at almost every age, there was a larger percentage of pairs of malapropisms which showed the same morphological structure than pairs of semantically related words with the same morphological structure; the exception is age 4, where the two figures are the same. For the children, the overall 'same' average for the semantically related pairs was 84%, but for malapropisms it was 89% (there were only 3 child malapropisms which did not have the same morphological structure). Similarly, for the adults the semantically related pairs also showed morphological identity in 74.5% of the errors, but the malapropisms showed it in 81% of the errors.

Because the figures in Table 6.9 include errors involving monomorphemic words as well as multimorphemic words, they suggest that one of the factors involved in lexical substitution errors may be having the same number of morphemes in the target and error words. However, in order to look at the effect of internal morphological structure per se, I recalculated the figures with all the monomorphemic pairs (including monomorphemes with the same inflectional suffix) removed. Table 6.10 presents this count.

In this table the difference between the children and adults in terms of morphological representation becomes clear. For the children, malapropisms were more likely to have consistent morphological structure than semantically related substitutions (50% vs. 42%). However, the children made very few

TABLE 6.9
Percentage of errors at each age with the same (SM) vs. different (DM) morphological structure, organized by [+sem] vs. [-sem, +phon] pairs.

Age:		1-2a	1-2b	3	4	5	Total	Adult
[+sem]	SM	83%	71.5%	93%	85%	86.5%	84%	74.5%
	DM	17%	28.5%	7%	15%	13.5%	16%	25.5%
N=		6	21	15	34	37	113	102
[-sem	SM	na	75%	100%	84.5%	100%	89%	81%
+phon]	DM		25%	0	15.5%	0	11%	19%
N=		0	4	5	13	5	27	37

TABLE 6.10
Percentage of errors at each age with the same (SM) vs. different (DM) morphological structure, organized by [+sem] vs. [-sem, +phon] pairs. Only errors involving at least one word with more than one morpheme included.

Age:		1-2a	1-2b	3	4	5	Total	Adult
[+sem]	SM	50%	14%	75%	54.5%	28.5%	42%	48%
	DM	50%	86%	25%	45.5%	71.5%	58%	52%
N=		2	7	4	11	7	31	50
[-sem	SM	na	50%	na	33%	100%	50%	75%
+phon]	DM		50%		67%	0	50%	25%
N=			2		3	1	6	28

malapropisms involving more than one morpheme (N=6), and only half of these maintained morphological consistency. Most of the children's malapropisms involved monomorphemic words with very similar phonological structure (as discussed in Chapter 3; e.g. 'Sarah/sour' (AL-221(35) 4;5), 'zucchini/bikini' (B-308(35) 4;6), 'Houston/Husted' (B-541(35) 5;7)); the morphological structure seemed much less important. Only in a few errors, mainly made by the 5-year-old children, do we see morphological similarity in word pairs which is of the same type as that found in adult errors (e.g. substitution of 'invention' for 'impression' (B-513(35) 5;5); blend of 'impression' and 'impersonation' (B-514(38) 5;5)). On the other hand, the adult figures in Table 6.10 show that of lexical substitution errors involving words with more than one morpheme, the semantically related pairs have identical morphological structure in only 48% of the errors, but the malapropisms do so in 75% of the errors. Clearly morphology is represented in the form lexicon for the adults, and it influences their lexical selection errors, especially when the error is based on form and not semantics. Thus this reinforces the suggestion made above that the children not only knew fewer morphologically complex words than the adults, but they also seemed to not represent much morphological structure in lexical entries, at least before the age of 5. Their form lexicons and thus their malapropisms seemed to be based much more heavily on phonology than morphology. Since morphological structure is such an important factor in adult malapropisms, the fact that children know few multimorphemic words and probably represent less morphological structure in the lexicon seems to be at least part of the explanation for why children produce fewer form-based lexical substitution errors than adults do in general.

This finding ties in with a fact discussed at some length in Chapter 3 above (§3.7.1) regarding lexical stress. I showed in that section that the most common type of lexical stress error made by adults was shifting the stress on a derivationally complex word to match the stress pattern of a derivationally related word, such as *'irrègulárly' for 'irrégularly' under the influence of 'irrègulárity' (AD-298(32)). These errors support the hypothesis that derived words which share a stem are stored in the lexicon in 'families' of derivationally related words, and that members of these derivationally related families can intrude on others during processing. Since the children in this study made exactly one error of this type (*'decoráte' for 'décorate', under the influence of 'decorátion' (AN-260(32) 4;11)), this fits well with the claim of less importance for morphological structure in the child lexicons. It stands to reason that if children know very few words of this type, they don't yet have the data or the motivation to set up internal morphological structure in the lexicon, and this lack of structure shows up clearly in the differences between adult and child errors, both lexical and prosodic.

6.4.2.4 Regular vs. Irregular Morphology; Mass vs. Count; Transitivity

A final question to be asked is whether there are any other morphological properties marked in lexical representations which could contribute to explaining the pattern of lexical substitution and blend errors. Candidates would include 1) the mass/count status of a common noun or the transitivity of a verb, which would be marked in the lemma of a lexical entry, and 2) the regular/irregular status of a noun or verb, which may be marked in the form lexicon as part of the morphology entry. I will discuss each of these in turn, focussing first on nouns, and then on verbs.

It is uncontroversial that mass/count status must be encoded in the lemmas of common nouns, as this status is crucial for selecting appropriate syntactic templates in which the noun will occur. For this reason one might expect that the mass/count status of nouns would always be honored in lexical substitution or blend errors, since a noun of the correct mass/count status would be required by the syntax. However, there are two factors which make this not quite so clear. First, there are many determiners which can take either a mass or count noun, and in such cases a mass noun could be substituted for a count noun or vice versa without causing an ungrammatical utterance, such as 'my cup' (count) vs. 'my juice' (mass). Second, it was shown in §6.3.4.3 above that when violations of the mass/count distinction occur in lexical substitution errors, determiners do not accommodate to the new noun, so that the requirements of the syntax can in fact be ignored in some errors. Therefore, in order to claim that the mass/count status of a noun could come into play when nouns are being misselected in lexical substitution or blend errors, two things would need to be found. First, two common nouns mutually involved in an error would be of the same mass/count status in percentages which were above chance; this would indicate that having the same value on this feature would be one factor involved in causing two words to be similar enough to allow one to be misselected for the other (or the two blended). Second, there would be fewer violations of this distinction in word pairs which were semantically related, since the semantic meanings of the words would be closely related to their mass/count status in the lemma, and thus the similarity of lemma would be the causal factor for the misselection; conversely, word pairs mutually involved in a lexical error which were related only by form would allow this distinction to be violated more often, since the mass/count information is not part of the form entry.

In order to determine whether a noun was being used as a mass or count noun in a particular utterance (since some nouns can be used both ways), I used simple frame tests. If the sequences 'a/an ____' and 'six ____+{plural}' were grammatical, the noun was classified as a count noun (e.g. 'a seed, six seeds'). If the sequence 'some ____' without a plural marker was grammatical with a noun, and the noun could not occur in the frame 'six ____' without a classifier, and the noun could not normally be pluralized, then the noun was classified as a mass noun (e.g. 'some juice', *'six juices', 'six cups of juice'). An intermediate class of nouns occurred in the adult data; these were abstract 'singularia tantum' nouns such as 'perfection', 'decompression', which were clearly not count nouns (*'a perfection'), but didn't fully pass the 'mass' tests (?'some perfection'); (see Corbett 2000:173). Because these had more in common with mass than count nouns, I classified them as such in the count, in order to avoid a proliferation of categories; crucially, both the mass and abstract nouns could occur in the frame '____ is X' in the singular form, without an article; e.g. 'intuition is important', 'milk is good', *'toy is good'.

In this count I looked at both paradigmatic and syntagmatic lexical substitution and blend errors where both the target and source, or both targets, were common nouns (excluding metatheses and multiple errors). I separated pairs with a semantic relationship from those did not involve a semantic relationship; the latter included both [+phon, -sem] pairs and [-phon, -sem] pairs,

TABLE 6.11

Number of lexical substitution or blend errors involving two common nouns, where the nouns were both count, both mass, or count vs. mass, by age; [+sem]=the word pair has a semantic relationship; [-sem]=the word pair does not have a semantic relationship.

Age:	1-2a	1-2b	3	4	5	Total	Adult
[+sem]							
2 Count	3	15	9	22	19	68	80
2 Mass	2	4	0	3	3	12	12
Count/Mass	2	2	2	1	2	9	9
Total N=	**7**	**21**	**11**	**26**	**24**	**89**	**101**
% same	71.5%	90.5%	82%	96%	92%	90%	91%
[-sem]							
2 Count	1	3	6	7	5	22	26
2 Mass	0	0	0	2	0	2	5
Count/Mass	0	1	1	2	1	5	6
Total N=	**1**	**4**	**7**	**11**	**6**	**29**	**37**
% Same	100%	75%	86%	82%	83%	83%	84%
Overall % Same							
	75%	88%	83%	92%	90%	88%	89%

since in either case it would not be the similarity of the lemma which was crucial to the error. The results are given in Table 6.11.

This table shows that in my data, the most frequent type of error involving two common nouns occurred when two count nouns interacted with each other, followed by two mass (including *singularia tantum*) nouns, and finally a mass with a count noun. Overall for the children, the error pairs honored the mass/count distinction in 88% of the cases, and for adults the figure was 89%. This cannot simply be due to chance. In these errors there were roughly 80% count noun tokens and 20% mass/abstract noun tokens; if we take this to be a plausible estimate of the relative proportion of count vs. mass nouns in the corpus, then the probability of choosing two nouns of the same type at random would be approximately 68% ((0.8 x 0.8)+(0.2 x 0.2)=.68), and 88% is far above this figure. While this finding is undoubtedly due in part to the requirements of the syntax, the fact that the distinction can in many cases be violated in an error without producing an ungrammatical utterance argues that there must also be some influence of the count/mass status represented lemmas. Therefore in both the child and adult errors, the lexical status of common nouns as mass or count was one factor which caused two words to be treated as similar to each other and therefore eligible for misselection.

Another important point from this table is that for both the children and adults, error pairs with a semantic relationship were usually more sensitive to the mass/count distinction than error pairs with no semantic relationship. Overall for the children the consistency on this measure was 90% for [+sem] pairs but 83% for [-sem] pairs; similarly for the adults the [+sem] pairs showed 91% consistency, but the [-sem] pairs only 84% consistency. This supports the claim that this feature is closely linked to semantic factors in lemmas.

Finally, the child figures were nearly identical to the adult figures, at every age. However, the lowest consistency on the mass/count measure was found with the 1-2a children, at only 75% overall consistency. While the numbers at this age are low, this could suggest that the mass/count distinction is only beginning to be represented in lemmas at this age, i.e. when the children are in the 1-2-word stages, which seems logical since they are not yet attempting to use determiners with nouns. However, when the children go into the 3+word stage, their consistency on the mass/count feature matches that of adults, showing that once this stage begins, the co-occurrence restrictions between common nouns and determiners are beginning to be part of the child's morphosyntactic knowledge, and thus coded in the lemmas of nouns.

A second factor which could be involved in lexical errors involving count nouns is whether the nouns take a regular or irregular plural. The larger issue is whether or not there is any evidence that the formal lexical entries of nouns and verbs are marked for their regular or irregular status. I have argued above (§6.2) that there is neurolinguistic evidence that regular vs. irregular inflected forms are processed differently from each other, with regular forms being concatenated on-line and irregular forms stored in the form lexicon. However, this raises the question of how the processing mechanism knows that a particular stem takes a regular or irregular inflection. In the dual mechanism theory mentioned in §6.2 above, proposed by Pinker and colleagues (Pinker 1991, Pinker & Prince 1988, 1991), when a speaker intends to produce the past tense form of a verb, first the phonological form of the stem is activated. It is then fed into the regular rule mechanism and the associative memory system in parallel. If it finds an associated irregular past tense form in the lexicon, it sends an inhibitory signal to the regular rule mechanism; the irregular past tense form is then activated and planned for speaking. However, if it does not find an associated irregular past tense form, then the regular rule is followed and the suffixed form planned for speaking (see also Plunkett 1995, Pinker 1999:130-1). In Jaeger et al. (1996) we raised several problems with this processing theory. First, there are some verb pairs which are homophones, but one member of the pair is regular and the other irregular; this includes the famous case of 'fly', which is irregular in its basic uses (e.g. 'The bird flew away'), but regular in the baseball idiom 'fly out' (i.e. 'The batter flied out to center field'; see Kim et al. 1991, 1994). Thus the assignment of regular vs. irregular past tense cannot be based solely on phonological properties of the stem. Second, this processing mechanism is somewhat cumbersome, causing the speaker to partially plan both a regular and irregular form during on-line processing for each verb to be spoken. We suggested (Jaeger et al. 1996: footnote 15) that possibly the stems which take irregular past tense forms have some sort of marker in their lexical entries which indicates their irregular status. In this case verbs without this marker would automatically be processed with the regular rule, whereas the activation of the irregular form in the lexicon would be initiated when the 'irregular' marker was encountered. This would complicate lexical entries by requiring an additional piece of morphological information to be stored in some lexical entries, but would make processing more efficient, and would allow for a very simple explanation as to why regular past tense forms can be computed much more rapidly than irregular forms (Jaeger et al. 1996:477).

How would such a theory show up in speech errors? What I would predict is that if the regular/irregular status of a stem were marked in its lexical entry, words with the same value on this feature would be considered more formally similar to each other and thus would be more likely to be substituted for each other or blended together. This effect would be particularly strong in malapropisms, where it is the formal relationship between the two words which causes the error. On the other hand, I would expect there to be a greater effect of the regular/irregular factor with verbs than nouns, since there are so few commonly used irregular nouns in English, but the most frequent verbs in English are for the most part irregular (Bloch 1947, Pinker 1999: Ch. 5).

In order to see whether morphological regularity had any status in the lexicon evident in these errors, I first looked at every error involving the substitution of one common count noun for another, or a blend of two common count nouns; I will return to verbs below. (Note that since I considered all of the *singularia tantum* nouns as 'mass', they are not included in this count; however, if they were inflected with the plural, they would all be regular, e.g. 'intuitions'.) I assigned each noun 'regular' or 'irregular' status depending on how it forms its plural, regardless of whether it appeared as singular or plural in the error, since the theory being tested is whether or not the regularity status is part of the lexical form entry. I classified a noun as 'irregular' if the plural was formed by a vowel change as in 'foot/feet', 'mouse/mice'; or it took a zero plural as in 'deer/deer', 'fish/fish'; or there was some consonant change when the regular suffix was added, as in 'wife/wives'; or if the plural involved an irregular suffix, as in 'child/children' (which also shows a vowel change). If a word took an irregular plural in the adult model, but the child was regularizing the plural during the time period when the error was made, I counted that noun as regular for the child. Some examples are given in (55).

(55)   a. Al: 'Mòmma, can Ì put my **bèd** right . . . my <u>hèad</u> right hére?'
        ('bed' substituted for 'head', both regular; AL-192(35) 3;11)
     b. B: 'And the shàrk attàcks your **féet** . . . <u>físh</u>.'
        ('feet' substituted for 'fish', both irregular; B-192(35) 4;1)

   c. B: 'I màde a [fʒɪʃ].'
          (blend of 'frog', regular, and 'fish', irregular; B-76(38) 2;6)
   d. An: 'Àli put her **mòuth** over her . . . Àli put her <u>hànd</u> over her
          móuth when she còughed.'
          ('mouth', irregular for adult but regular for child, anticipated/
          substituted for 'hand', regular; AN-247(41) 4;10)

In this tabulation I included both paradigmatic and syntagmatic lexical substitution errors, and paradigmatic blends, excluding metatheses and multiple errors. I separated the errors into two categories: those where the word pair had a semantic relationship, and those where the pair had a phonological but not semantic relationship. I did not include pairs where there was neither a semantic nor phonological relationship, as these were unlikely to be influenced by formal markings in the lexicon; I will return to this type of error briefly below. Because these pairs were excluded, there are 8 fewer child errors and 7 fewer adult errors in this count. Table 6.12 gives the number of errors involving two regular count nouns, two irregular count nouns, and an irregular/regular count noun pair.

Because the total number of errors in this table is very small, any interpretation of these figures should be taken as purely suggestive, and subject to future research. However, this table shows that the vast majority of errors involving two count nouns honored the regular/irregular status. This may be at least partially due to the very small number of irregular nouns in the corpus, and indeed in English in general. For both the children and adults, approximately 96% of these errors involved regular tokens, and 4% irregular; the only irregular nouns which occurred in these errors were: child: 'deer, dormouse, foot, fish', N=6 tokens; adult: 'child, leaf, knife, species', N=6 tokens. The probability of two nouns having the same regularity status by chance in these errors would be roughly 92%, which is only slightly less than the overall child figure of 96.5% or the overall adult figure of 94%.

However, that being said, it is still very interesting to note that all of the child violations of the regular/irregular distinction, and all but one of the adult violations, involve a semantically related pair of nouns, as illustrated in (56a). Thus all but one of the [+phon, -sem] pairs had the same regularity status; the exception is given in (56b). Because all errors made by the children in the 1-2a age range involved two regular nouns, these patterns do not begin showing up until the children entered the 3+word stage (1-2b).

(**56**) a. B: 'I could wràp my scàrf aròund my **féet**.'
         M: 'Your féet?'
         B: 'My <u>hánds</u>!'
         ('feet', irregular, substituted for 'hands', regular; B-285(35) 4;5)

TABLE 6.12
Number of lexical substitution or blend errors involving two common
count nouns, where the stems were both regular, both irregular, or regular
vs. irregular in forming the plural, by age; [+sem]=the word pair has a
semantic relationship; [-sem]=the word pair has only a phonological
relationship.

Age:	1-2a	1-2b	3	4	5	Total	Adult
[+sem]							
2 Regular	3	13	9	21	18	64	75
2 Irregular	0	1	0	0	0	1	0
Reg/Irreg	0	1	0	1	1	3	5
Total N=	**3**	**15**	**9**	**22**	**19**	**68**	**80**
% Same	100%	93%	100%	95.5%	95%	95.5%	94%
[-sem]							
2 Regular	0	1	4	5	3	13	18
2 Irregular	0	0	0	1	0	1	0
Reg/Irreg	0	0	0	0	0	0	1
Total N=	**0**	**1**	**4**	**6**	**3**	**14**	**19**
% Same		100%	100%	100%	100%	100%	95%
Overall % Same							
	100%	94%	100%	96.5%	95.5%	96.5%	94%

b. AF:'. . . mèntal **spécies** . . . (laughs) mèntal <u>spáces</u>.'
('species' [spí.siz], irregular, substituted for 'spaces' [speʲ.s(əz)],
regular; AD-407(35))

In (56b), the word 'species' has an irregular (zero) plural, whereas 'spaces' takes
the regular suffix. This is the one case where it looks like the phonological
relationship between the two plural forms was so great that it facilitated the
error. Otherwise, the regular/irregular distinction was only violated in errors in
which it was the semantic, not the formal relationship that caused the error.
Furthermore, three of the adult [-phon, -sem] errors also violated the
regular/irregular feature, suggesting that without a lexical relationship between
the word pair, this feature is irrelevant. These errors were syntagmatic
substitutions involving the pairs 'story/house' (AD-596(41)), 'child/hand' (AD-
598(41)), and 'cow/life' (AD-640(45)). The fact that nearly all noun error pairs
which were related by form also had regularity in common, whereas all but one
of the violations of regularity involved either semantically related pairs or pairs
which were not related in the lexicon, suggests that the feature of regularity is

marked as part of the morphological information about a lexical entry in the form lexicon.

Turning now to verbs, the property analogous to the mass/count distinction for nouns would be the transitivity distinction for verbs, which would be expected to be marked in the lemmas of lexical entries. Unlike with nouns, where a particular NP can be grammatical with either a mass or count noun, substituting a verb of a different transitivity nearly always results in an ungrammatical utterance. Thus we would expect that the requirements of the syntax would make such violations extremely rare. However, if it were the case that two verbs were more likely to be mutually involved in a lexical substitution or blend error because they are marked for the same valence in the lexicon, i.e. they are similar in their lemma properties, then it would be expected that word pairs related by semantics would show this consistency more often than pairs with no semantic relationship; this difference was found for the mass/count feature for nouns, and we would predict it would also hold true for verb valence.

In order to test this hypothesis, I looked at all the verb substitution errors (paradigmatic and syntagmatic) and verb blend errors, excluding metatheses and multiple errors; I also excluded errors which involved different versions of the same stem, or where the target word was not actually spoken in the error so was unclear. Each verb involved in an error was assigned to one of three categories from the following very simple 3-way taxonomy: 'intransitive' verbs were those which did not require an NP object; 'transitive' required at least one NP object; and 'linking' verbs required a predicate nominal, predicate adjective, or predicate locative; the only 'linking' verbs in the corpus were the copula 'be' and the verb 'get' as in 'get dirty'. For verbs which could fall into more than one category, I categorized each token in terms of its function in the error phrase. I counted the number of verb pairs involved in these errors which fell into the categories given in Table 6.13, separating the pairs with a semantic relationship from those without such a relationship. Since there were relatively few errors of these types, I have not divided the child data by age; however I should note that no verb errors were made by children in the 1-2a stage.

The figures in Table 6.13 indicate that that the majority of errors involved two verbs with the same transitivity, as expected; the overall percentages for 'same transitivity' are higher even than those for the mass/count distinction in nouns, probably due to the fact mentioned above that a violation of transitivity always causes an ungrammatical utterance. In order to compare these figures to what would be expected by chance, I calculated a rough estimate of 'chance' by looking at the verbs in a random set of error utterances, selected from the phonological error corpus. I selected the first 100 verbs from the children's utterances in Class 12, and the first 100 verbs in the adults' utterances from Classes 12-21, and counted the number of tokens which fell into each of these three categories. (Since there were relatively fewer verb errors than noun errors, I didn't feel there were enough data to use the number of verbs in each category in the errors per se as an estimate of chance.) I found that for both the children and

TABLE 6.13

Number of lexical substitution or blend errors involving two verbs, where the verbs were both transitive, both intransitive, both linking, or had different valences; [+]=the word pair has a semantic relationship; [-]=the word pair does not have a semantic relationship.

	Child		Adult	
	+	-	+	-
Both Transitive	29	10	21	11
Both Intransitive	3	3	6	1
Both Linking	2	0	0	0
Trans/Intransitive	0	2	1	0
Trans/Linking	1	0	0	0
Total N=	**35**	**15**	**28**	**12**
% Same Transitivity	97%	87%	96.5%	100%
Overall % Same	94%		97.5%	

adults, the verbs in this random sample were about 60% transitive, 20% intransitive, and 20% linking, which means that the probability of two verbs selected at random having the same transitivity is .44; obviously verb errors honored transitivity at a much higher rate.

The children's and adults' figures differed only marginally. The child errors were slightly less well-organized by transitivity than the adults', as the children had 3 violations (6%) and the adults only one (2.5%). The child violations were: 'sleep/have' (B-349(35) 4;8), 'let/sit' (OC-115(41) 4;7), and 'be/color' (B-531(43) 5;6), all made by 4-5-year-olds; the adult violation is given in (57) below. Also, the children made several errors involving linking verbs, but the adults made none; clearly the use of the copula and other linking verbs is so over-practiced for adults that errors with these verbs would be extremely rare. And for both children and adults, errors involving linking verbs occurred at a rate much under the 20% that would be predicted by chance.

As far as the prediction that semantically related pairs would be more consistent than pairs without such a relationship, it is difficult to say much since there were only four violations in the data altogether. For the children, there is a higher percentage of consistency on this feature for the [+sem] pairs than the [-sem] pairs, as predicted. But the single adult error involved a semantically related pair of verbs.

(57)   AF: ' . . . that mày have **introdúced** . . . intrúded in the sèntence.'
        (AD-437(35))

In this error, 'introduce' is transitive and 'intrude' is intransitive; they are analyzed as semantically related since they are converses; i.e. if something has been 'introduced' into the sentence, then it has 'intruded'. However, it is possible that the speaker was actually thinking of both these phrasings of the proposition, and blended the two, so that this may be a phrase blend rather than a lexical substitution error. In any event, the fact that violations of transitivity are extremely rare regardless of the relationship between the two words is probably due to both the requirements of the syntax, and the fact that the internal monitor is watching out for blatantly ungrammatical utterances, so that such a violation would usually be detected before the sentence is spoken. In some future study it would be very interesting to look at the Aktionsart categories of verbs mutually involved in errors, to see if this factor is preserved as faithfully as transitivity is.

The issue of the regularity status of verb pairs involved in errors should prove to be somewhat more interesting than it was for nouns, since there are a considerable number of high-frequency irregular verbs in English. In order to do this analysis, I assigned 'regular' or 'irregular' status to every verb involved in these errors, based solely on whether or not the verb forms its past tense with the {-ed} suffix and no other stem changes. Verbs which involve stem changes (with or without the suffix), or which take zero past tense forms were considered irregular. As with the noun count, this designation was made regardless of the actual form in which the verb occurred in the error, since the regular/irregular status would occur in the form lexicon, where it would influence the erroneous word choice. Some examples are given in (58).

(58) a. Al: 'I [**wáʲk**] sòme . . . I <u>wánt</u> sòme.'
(blend of 'want' and 'like', both regular; AL-93(38) 3;1)
b. Al: 'I wànna **sèe** that sóund . . . I wànna <u>hèar</u> that sóund.'
('see' substituted for 'hear', both irregular; AL-43(35) 2;8)
c. Al: 'Còuld you **pùt** me . . . <u>wràp</u> me úp in thìs?'
('put', irregular, substituted for 'wrap', regular; B-147(35) 3;8)
d. B: 'Have you èver **sèen** . . . have you èver <u>hèared of</u> "Dúdes"?'
('seen', irregular, substituted for 'heared of' [hɪrd ʌv], regularized; B-218(35) 4:2)

In (58a) both verbs are regular, and in (58b) both are irregular; in (58c) there is one regular and one irregular verb. In (58d), Bobby produces the correct perfect form of 'see' as 'seen'; however he produces the perfect of 'hear' as [hɪrd] rather than [hɚd], which is a regularized form. Since Bobby is treating this as a regular verb in this error, I have counted the error as involving one regular and one irregular verb. This phenomenon only occurred in three errors; the other two are (AL-78b(38) 2;11), a blend of 'spanked' and 'maked' where the latter is treated as regular, and (B-218(35) 4;4), where the regularized 'drinked' is substituted for irregular 'ate'.

TABLE 6.14

Number of lexical substitution or blend errors involving two verbs, where
the verbs were both regular, both irregular, or regular vs. irregular in
forming the past tense; [+sem]=the word pair has a semantic relationship;
[-sem]=the word pair has only a phonological relationship.

Age:	1-2a	1-2b	3	4	5	Total	Adult
[+sem]							
2 Regular	0	2	5	3	2	12	16
2 Irregular	0	2	2	0	7	11	3
Reg/Irreg	0	1	2	7	2	12	9
Total N=	**0**	**5**	**9**	**10**	**11**	**35**	**28**
% Same		80%	78%	30%	82%	66%	68%
[-sem]							
2 Regular	0	2	0	1	0	3	6
2 Irregular	0	0	0	2	1	3	1
Reg/Irreg	0	0	0	0	0	0	1
Total N=	**0**	**2**	**0**	**3**	**1**	**6**	**8**
% Same		100%		100%	100%	100%	87.5%
Overall % Same							
	na	86%	78%	46%	83%	71%	72%

As with the nouns, I divided the errors into pairs of verbs which had a
semantic relationship vs. those with only a phonological relationship; I excluded
the pairs with neither, since they do not have any influence of form, by
definition. I included both paradigmatic and syntagmatic substitutions and
blends, excluding metatheses and multiple errors; as with the transitivity count, I
excluded errors which involved different versions of the same stem, or where the
target word was unclear. The results of this count are given in Table 6.14;
although the numbers are small, I have presented them by age, in order to show
that the pattern which emerges occurs at all ages.

The regularity status of verbs is not honored as consistently as the
transitive/intransitive status, but nevertheless it is honored in 71% of the child
errors and 72% of the adult. To see if this could be due to chance, I again made a
count of the regularity status of the verbs in a random set of utterances taken
from the child's phonological errors, as I did for the 'transitivity' counts; I
looked at 109 verb tokens each for the children and adults. However, I excluded
the 'linking' verbs from this count since they are extremely numerous and are all
irregular, but they rarely participate in errors. I felt that including the linking
verbs in this count would skew it towards 'irregular' verbs in a way that was out
of proportion to the types of verbs involved in the errors. I found that 62.5% of

the children's verb tokens in this random count were irregular, and 37.5% regular, so that the probability that any two verbs would have the same regularity status by chance would be .53. The adult verb tokens were 54% irregular vs. 46% regular, with the chance 'same regularity' probability being .50. Therefore the 71% and 72% 'same regularity' figures found in the data were considerably above chance, suggesting that regularity status is one factor involved in lexical similarity of word pairs. The fact that the children's verb usage involved a larger proportion of irregular verbs than the adults' explains why the children made many more errors involving irregular verbs than did the adults. This is not surprising since many of the most basic verbs in English come from the Germanic vocabulary and are irregular, and these are among the verbs children learn first (e.g. do, see, hear, say, have, get, bring, etc.). However, the adults produced many errors with more abstract, latinate verbs such as 'require/recommend', 'exchange/explain', and so forth, and verbs in this class all take the regular past tense form. Furthermore, adults have much more experience with the more frequent irregular verbs than do children, so would be less likely to misselect them. So this difference is easily explained by differences in vocabulary and expertise between the children and adults.

Very strong evidence that regularity is marked in the form lexicon comes from the fact that none of the child [+phon, -sem] error pairs, and only one of the adult pairs (59a), violated this distinction. However, violations in [+sem] pairs were numerous for both the children and adults, as in (58c,d) above. This pattern shows up as early as the 1-2b age bracket; the earliest [+sem] pair which violated regularity was made at age 2;7 (59b). Furthermore, many of the [-phon, -sem] pairs which had no influence from the form violated regularity; (59c) is an example.

(59) a. AF: 'Thàt's whỳ you dòn't **thròw** . . . <u>clòse</u> your èyes and **thrów** thìngs.' ('throw', irregular, anticipated/substituted for 'close', regular; AD-575(41))

 b. An: (handing Mom a balloon) '**Ópen** thìs.' (looks confused)
    M: 'Do whát?'
    An: '<u>Blòw</u> it <u>úp!</u>' ('open', regular, substituted for 'blow (up)', irregular; AN-55(35) 2;7)

 c. B: 'We're gònna pláy, and **eàt** móv? . . . <u>wàtch</u> móvies, and **èat** pópcorn.' ('eat', irregular, anticipated/substituted for 'watch', regular; B-414(41) 4;11)

In (59a), the adult, chiding a child for throwing something which hit someone, anticipates the irregular verb 'throw' from the second clause and substitutes it for the regular verb 'close'. This was the only case in my data where two words related by form but not meaning violated the regularity distinction. However, while 'throw' and 'close' are phonologically similar by my criteria, the fact that they were both activated and planned for analogous verb slots in adjacent phrases was probably more important than the formal relationship between the two lexical items in causing the error. In (59b), Anna substitutes the regular verb 'open' for the semantically related irregular verb 'blow up'. In (59c), the two verbs 'eat' and 'watch' have neither a semantic nor phonological relationship, and this error pair violates regularity; other similar examples include 'have/talk (to)' (OC-141a(35) 5;3); 'sew/tell' (AN-264(41) 5;0); 'get/talk (about)' (AD–454(35)), and 'work/grow (up)' (AD-595(41)). Altogether these errors suggest that when the form of the verb is an important causal factor in the error, the regularity status of the target and error words is usually identical; if the form is not the most relevant factor, regularity is easily violated. And the fact that this pattern shows up in the errors of the children in the 1-2b age range suggests that regularity is marked in the lexicon for verbs at about the same time it seems to be marked for nouns, i.e. once the child has entered the 3+word stage.

One final interesting fact which is not evident from Table 6.14 is that the majority of both child and adult blend errors involved regular verbs (child 70%, adult 73%); for the children, the bulk of errors involving irregular verbs were paradigmatic lexical substitution errors. One possible explanation for this is that blend errors very often involve synonyms or near-synonyms, and perhaps very frequent, basic, irregular verbs are less likely to be involved in synonymous relationships with other verbs. However, the less frequent regular verbs which are more numerous in type, may provide many more variations in meaning to choose from, and therefore it is more likely that near-synonyms will exist in regular verbs (for example: child errors involving 'want/like', 'look/watch', 'squish/smash'; adult errors involving 'flail/thrash', 'test/check', 'end/finish'; see also §5.3.4 above). Furthermore if these regular verbs are less frequent, it may be more difficult to make a definitive selection of one verb, in which case two verbs may become activated and blended together in the error utterance. This explanation is pure speculation, but it seems like an interesting proposal to be followed up in future research.

In this section I have looked at whether the mass/count or regularity status of nouns, or the transitivity or regularity status of verbs, can influence the pattern of lexical substitution and blend errors. I found evidence that both the mass/count and transitivity features are involved in lemma similarity, so that errors involving two semantically related words usually also honor these distinctions. This is hardly a surprising finding, as it is uncontroversial that these properties are represented in the lemmas of nouns and verbs, and are important for creating appropriate functional structures during speech production planning. More controversial is the finding that the regularity status of nouns and verbs can influence lexical errors, particularly when the word pair involved in the error has a formal rather than a semantic relationship. Because the regularity status in error pairs related by form functions in an extremely similar manner to the mass/count or transitivity status in error pairs related by semantics, this is strong evidence that regularity status is also marked in lexical entries.

Furthermore, these influences are as important in the children's errors as they are in the adults', showing that these factors are marked in lexical entries at a very early age.

6.5 Morphology: Summary and Discussion

In §6.2 above I discussed various controversies regarding the representation and processing of morphology.   In §6.3 I discussed errors involving morphology, i.e. where a morpheme is either the unit of error, or where morphemes become stranded when content words move.   I also looked at morphological accommodation. In §6.4 I examined the role of morphology in lexical substitution and blend errors, both paradigmatic and syntagmatic. In this section I will summarize these findings, and discuss them in terms of acquisition issues.

To a large extent these errors supported the general view of morphology presented at the beginning of the chapter. Morphological errors predominantly involved inflectional affixes, and this was particularly true of errors where a morpheme moved from one location and was added in a new location. Similarly, stranding errors most often involved inflectional affixes, and for the most part whenever an error occurred in which stranding of an inflectional affix was possible, the stranding did take place. The few exceptions involved common nouns typically lexicalized as plural (e.g. 'hands'), and proper nouns lexicalized with plural or possessive morphology ('MacDonald's', 'X-Files'). When morphemes found themselves in new locations in errors, they always accommodated to the requirements of the erroneous location; this included cases where the speaker produced correct allomorphs of the inflectional affixes and the indefinite article, verb agreement, and pronoun case in the error utterance. However, if a lexical substitution necessitated a change in determiner due to violation of number or the mass/count distinction, these errors usually did not show accommodation. In lexical errors, two words were more likely to substitute for or blend with each other if they had the same morphological structure; this was especially true of adult malapropisms. In word pairs with different morphological structure, monomorphemic words, compounds, derived words and particle verbs interacted with each other freely, but inflected words nearly always interacted with other words carrying the same inflection. The exceptions again were words lexicalized as plural. Finally, in lexical substitution or blend errors, if two nouns or two verbs mutually involved in the error had a semantic relationship with each other, then they were also highly likely to have the same value on the mass/count or transitivity features; on the other hand, if the two nouns or two verbs were related by phonological and/or morphological form, they nearly always had the same value on the regularity feature.

These findings were interpreted in terms of the RPC processing model, which assumes that inflectional morphology is closely linked to syntax. Although the data don't necessarily require the stages-type model adopted here, I find this type of model to be the most straightforward fit (but see Stemberger

1998 for a connectionist approach). For the purposes of the present study, the most important question is whether or not these SOT data give us a clear picture of how morphological representation and processing develops.

In my data there were no errors involving morphology made by children in the 1-word or 2-word stages. Errors such as those in (20) which appear at first glance to involve suffixes were demonstrated to be movement-substitution errors of what was treated by the child as a coda consonant, not a meaningful morpheme (e.g. 'arms up'-->*'arm_ us'). The earliest morpheme-unit and stranding errors which clearly involved morphemes occurred at age 2;2 (see example (21) above, 'bubble gums'-->*'bubbles gum_'), when the children were producing utterances of three or more words with stable word order, as well as producing an increasing number of free function words. I argued above that there is a close relationship between the time when children begin to produce these errors and the onset of telegraphic speech. During children's early lexical development they learn many inflected words as unanalyzed wholes, but during the second half of the second year they have accumulated enough words that they can start seeing regular patterns in the latter portion of words which consistently link up with grammatical meanings, in the ways discussed in detail by Slobin (1985) and Peters (1995), among others. At this point, around age 2, children have begun to associate such markers with locations in syntagmatic strings, which may facilitate the stabilization of morpheme order in utterances, and thus facilitate the setting up of syntactic templates. The fact that the children continued to make errors that showed a misanalysis of morphological structure (e.g. the movement of a false suffix, see examples (20) and (22) above), but adults never made such errors, shows that the process of analyzing out bound grammatical elements from stems continues at least into the 6th year. It is obvious that during these years a great deal of syntactic development is taking place also, and thus these two aspects of development appear be very closely related. This will be the topic of the subsequent sections of this chapter.

Differences were found between adults and children in terms of the numbers of morpheme unit and stranding errors made. The children in this study made more morpheme-movement errors than did the adults, probably as a function of the process of stabilizing morpheme location in the syntactic string. However, the adults produced more stranding errors than the children. I showed above that this is due to the adults producing utterances with more morphologically complex syntax, particularly in terms of perfect and passive constructions. Thus the adults had more opportunities to strand inflectional morphemes in errors because they used more inflectional morphology in their utterances.

In terms of the actual morphemes involved in errors, it was shown that the various morphemes were involved in errors in a developmental order which reflected to a large extent that predicted by Brown's 14 morphemes (Brown 1973), indicating that these morphemes were being analyzed out from words and taking on independent status in the predicted order. Once the children began using inflectional affixes regularly, their errors always reflected the correct allomorphic productions. The earliest error that clearly showed allomorphic accommodation was produced at age 2;8 (see (36a) above, 'play[d] with'--> *'play_ with[t]'), but there were no exceptions to this finding; earlier errors simply did not require accommodation. Similarly, errors involving inflected forms always accommodated to the regular/irregular status of the stem spoken in the error utterance (see (37a) above involving 'feet' vs. 'hands', which occurred at age 4;5). When an error placed a noun after the indefinite article which required a different allomorph of the article, the correct allomorph was spoken; the earliest instance of this was recorded at age 2;7 ('a scary' vs. 'a? owie', B-94(35)). If an erroneous subject was placed before a verb which required a different agreement marker from the target subject, the verb accommodated in its agreement to the new subject; the earliest recorded instance of this phenomenon was at age 3;8 ('I like it'-->*'it likes it', AL-157(41)). Finally, if a pronoun was shifted into a location where it was required to take on a new case, the case was always appropriately assigned; the earliest error I collected of this type was at age 2;7 (see example (42) above, involving 'I' vs. 'me'). Errors which required accommodation of either allomorphy or agreement were relatively infrequent for both the children and adults in the study. However, the fact that there were no exceptions to accommodation in errors of the types discussed above, for either children or adults, shows that these morphological processes were robustly productive for the children, and that the children's mechanisms for processing morphology on-line were very similar to the adults'; this finding is most evident beginning at about age 2;7, when errors of this kind begin to show up regularly in the children's data. On the other hand, when one noun substituted for another which required changes in the actual selection of determiner, these changes did not occur (see examples in (46)); this was equally true in adult and child errors, and again points to the similarity of the adult and child processing mechanisms.

Turning to the paradigmatic lexical substitution and blend errors, some evidence is apparent for both the acquisition of different types of morphologically complex words in the lexicon, and the representation of morphological structure in lexical entries. The youngest children (age 1-2a) produced mainly errors involving monomorphemic word pairs. In the one lexical substitution error involving an inflectional affix made when a child was in the 2-word stage ('penis' for 'toes', see (52a) above), there was no evidence that the word 'toes' was anything but a monomorpheme for this child, stored as a single unanalyzed whole in the lexicon. Errors involving compounds began to occur quite early, the first being collected from a child at 2;0 who was in the 2-word stage (OC-6(35), involving 'toothpaste/toothbrush'). Errors in which one inflected word substituted for another with the same inflection began to occur at age 2;6 (B-74(35), involving 'hit/hurt'), a few months after morpheme-unit errors began to occur (at around 2;2). After the children began making errors involving multimorphemic words, compounds were the most frequently involved type; however, the adults produced many more errors involving derived words than did the children. And in malapropisms, i.e. lexical substitution errors caused entirely by form, the adults showed a high degree of influence from morphological (structural) similarity of target and source, whereas the children did not.

I argued from this that since children know fewer multimorphemic words than adults, especially derived words, they have less reason to parse out internal morphological structures and represent them in lexical entries. (Again this reflects a difference between inflectional and derivational morphology, since children do actively separate out inflectional morphemes from stems and store them in separate representations starting at around age 2.) Thus since children have less morphological structure represented in lexical entries, such structure is less important in influencing lexical substitution and blend errors than for adults. Since morphological similarity seems to be extremely influential in adult malapropisms, but not child lexical substitution errors, this may be one reason why children produce fewer such form-based substitutions than adults do.

Finally, the errors produced by the children in the 1-2b age range and older reflect the morphosemantic properties of mass/count in nouns and transitivity in verbs; because these factors are crucial for producing grammatical utterances, they seem to be marked in the lemmas of lexical entries as soon as children begin to enter the 3+word stage. Similarly, the pattern of children's errors involving regular vs. irregular nouns and verbs is identical to that of adults' starting at age 1-2b; thus children seem to be starting to mark this important distinction in their form lexicons during their third year. And, more generally, it would be difficult to explain this pattern of errors if regularity were not marked in the form lexicon, as hypothesized by Jaeger et al. (1996).

These SOTs made by young children have provided a great deal of information about the development of morphology, both in terms of representations and processing. One theme running through the present section has been that the developmental patterns in the acquisition of morphology depend to some extent on the development of syntax. In the following section, the focus will be on the relevance of SOTs to issues in the acquisition of syntax.

6.6   Syntax

6.6.1   Introduction

In the preceding chapters I have frequently discussed the various aspects of syntactic processing and development about which the SOT data provide evidence. In the remainder of this chapter I will focus in on two topics relevant to syntactic development. The first has to do with whether or not the SOT data necessitate the positing of syntactic knowledge for children in the 2-word stage. Various pieces of evidence regarding this question have been discussed throughout the preceding chapters, and they will be brought together here into a coherent statement. The second question has to do with the analysis of phrase blends. Looking at phrase blends from the 'competing plans' point of view, I will present a syntactic analysis of the types of phrase blends which were produced by the subjects in my study, and specifically look for patterns of development implicated by the types of phrase blends made at different ages. At the end of this section I will briefly summarize what the SOT data reveal about the development of the representations and processing utilized in constructing syntactically well-structured sentences.

6.6.2   Syntax in the 2-Word Stage?

Previous studies using observational data from longitudinal studies have demonstrated conclusively that when English-speaking children begin producing utterances of 3+ words, they show evidence of some syntactic knowledge. This knowledge includes appropriate word orders to express specific meanings, knowledge of lexical categories and their syntactic function, and some knowledge of hierarchical structure (Brown 1973, Garman 1979, Peters 1986, 1995, Valian 1986, Ihns & Leonard 1988, Gleitman & Gillette 1995, among many others). There has been somewhat more controversy about whether or not it makes sense to talk about 'syntax' in the 1-word and 2-word stages (Bloom 1973, Brown 1973, Bowerman 1976, Braine 1976, Scollon 1976, Peters 1986, 1995). Many researchers would agree that while infants may comprehend some aspects of grammar during the 1-word and 2-word stages (Gerken & McIntosh 1993, Hirsh-Pasek & Golinkoff 1996), their productions during these stages are mainly guided by semantics and pragmatics, and show little evidence of syntactic structure (see Peters 1986 for a review of these issues).

Data from the present study support this latter view, i.e. that the transition from the 2-word stage to the 3+word stage involves a transition from juxtaposition of words to indicate semantic relationships, to producing linearly and hierarchically structured sentences. Evidence for this claim comes from a number of findings which have been presented in earlier chapters, and will be reviewed here.

First, the children in this study produced only two errors which were of the 'syntactic' type while in the 2-word stage, and none in the 1-word stage. (Recall that I am using the term 'syntactic' to refer to errors involving lexical or morphological misplacements and phrase blends; see Chapter 2, Table 2.1.) These two errors were discussed extensively in Chapter 4, and are presented again in (60).

(60)   a.   M: (Mom lifts Bobby up and puts him on the changing table; Bobby always requested that the light be turned on over the changing table as part of the diaper changing routine)
'Come òn, let's gèt your *díaper* òn.'
B: (pointing at light over changing table)
'**Díaper** òn . . . l̆ight òn.'
('diaper' perseverated, substituted for 'light'; B-26(43) 1;11.6)

b. OG: (asking Daddy if he had used the bathroom yet)
'**Pèepee**, go . . . Dàddy, go *péepee*?'
('peepee' anticipated, substituted for 'Daddy'; OC-9(41) 2;0.14)

In (60a), the word 'diaper' is perseverated from the adult utterance and substituted for 'light' in Bobby's 2-word utterance. It is true that Bobby substituted the word 'diaper' for 'light', not for 'on' (i.e. he didn't produce something like *'light diaper'. However, in this case he was planning the sequence 'light on'; he had just heard the sequence 'diaper on', and substituted the word he had just heard spoken before the word 'on' in the slot before 'on' in his own utterance. This doesn't necessarily require syntax as much as it does word recognition, and the semantic knowledge that the words 'diaper' and 'light' both refer to objects which can be 'on'. In (60b), the child seems to be planning two possible utterances at the same time, 'Daddy' and 'go peepee?'; she anticipates the second word from the second utterance, erroneously producing it first. This child was just on the verge of going into the telegraphic speech stage, and therefore she may have been attempting to plan larger chunks than she was able to utter fluently at the time. Neither of these two errors make a strong case for positing syntax in the 2-word stage. Furthermore, I collected only these 2 syntactic errors from children in the 2-word stage, but I collected 33 such errors from children in the 1-2b stage, which makes a strong case for syntax being available at the later stage. Note that this is not simply a function of age. When Anna was still a 1-year-old, but was producing telegraphic utterances, I collected the following 2 syntactic errors from her. (The accent marks above the words are to be read as pitch markers here; I have put pitch rather than stress marks here in order to emphasize the phrasal intonation patterns in these errors.)

(61)   a. An: (pointing to pictures in a book, which included a kitty and
            cookies) 'Here's a *kìtty*-cát, dòggíes, kìt . . . còokíes, câke.'
            (started to substitute 'kitty' or 'kitties' for 'cookies'; AN-10(43)
            1;8.15)
        b. An: (pretending to read a book aloud)
            '**Whàt ìs Bèrt háppèn, Běr** . . . Bêrt, whàt háppèn?'
            (blend of 'Whàt ìs Bèrt dóing?' and 'Whàt háppèn, Běrt?',
            AN-20(49) 1;11.13)

In (61a) Anna perseverates a word from her own utterance, and begins to substitute it for a word later in the utterance. Although this error is environmentally supported (i.e. both referents are visible), and the latter part of the sentence is a list rather than a syntactically complex structure, it still shows that she has planned a well-formed sentence including the copula, indefinite article, and several noun objects spoken in sequence, which requires syntax. In (61b), when Anna 'read' this particular page aloud there was a range of appropriate sentences she could say; she had not memorized what was actually on the page. In this error she apparently started to plan two different sentences, both appropriate for the context, which involved the different framings of the event required by the words 'doing' and 'happened'; in her production she didn't fully select either target but blended the two targets. She then corrected to a third possibility, different from either of the two targets. Although she may have memorized certain sentences which were appropriate to say when she encountered this particular page in this book, notice that the blend itself shows internal structure in that it crosses over from one phrase to the other at the site of the verb (see §6.6.3 below for a more thorough discussion of blends). Thus it is clear that she had some syntactic knowledge at the time. As discussed earlier, Anna was an expressive talker and was more daring in exploring different types of syntax at an earlier age than any of the other children in the study. There is a larger percentage of syntactic errors in Anna's data than in the other three data sets, as was discussed in Chapter 2 (Table 2.2).

However, when the children began to regularly produce utterances of 3+words, they all began to produce syntactic errors with some frequency. Lexical anticipation and perseveration errors were the most common, starting at age 2;0. Unambiguous phrase blends were produced from age 2;1 on. Other syntactic errors involving lexical exchanges and multiple errors began to be frequent around age 2;7; since these errors involved more than one element of the planned phrase, they did not occur in the earlier stages of telegraphic speech.

Related to these findings about syntactic errors is the fact that function word errors (involving free function words such as pronouns, prepositions, and determiners) were not produced by the children in the 1-2-word stages.

(62) Earliest age for lexical errors involving content vs. function words

	Content words	Function words
Lexical substitutions:	1;8	2;5
Lexical blends:	1;7	2;9
Lexical misplacement:	1;8	2;6

All of the first function word errors in each category occurred when the speaker was fully into the telegraphic speech stage. The only marginal exception was the error Bobby made at age 1;7.22, when in the 1-word stage, where he blended the noun 'car' with the interjection 'bye' (B-1(40) 1;7). In this case it's not clear that the distinction 'content' vs. 'function' makes any sense, since his word 'bye' was used as a part of an action scheme or routine, and so was actually more like a verb in his usage. Combined with the data on the onset of syntactic errors, these figures suggest that while children are developing syntactic frames during the early part of their third year, they do not have enough experience or facility with function words to allow them to be involved in errors independently until about halfway through this year. Since the correct use of function words is heavily dependent on syntax (and vice versa), the fact that there were no function word errors in the 1-word and 2-word stages again points to a lack of syntax during these stages.

A third factor is the fact that the children made no errors involving morphology before they were producing sentences of 3+ words, as discussed in §6.3.2.4 above. The earliest errors which involved the movement of an affix occurred at age 2;2. Stranding errors where the child copied only the stem from an inflected form in a previous utterance and spoke it without the inflection began to occur at age 2;2. Strandings where the child moved a stem from within his or her own utterance, leaving an inflection behind, began to occur at age 2;7. Again, since the development of morphology and syntax are closely intertwined, the fact of no morpheme errors before the telegraphic speech stage supports the claim of no syntax at this stage.

In Chapter 4 (§4.3.5) I discussed lexical errors made by children in the 1-word and 2-word stages, looking at a fourth factor: whether or not these errors necessitate the positing of knowledge of lexical categories such as 'noun, verb'. Such designations would be required in order to posit that the child was using syntax, since syntactic frames are set up with reference to such categories. I argued extensively in that section that all of the errors made by the children in these early stages can be completely explained with reference to semantics, environmental influences, and utterance influences. The first errors which absolutely require the assumption of lexical category are malapropisms in which lexical category is identical, but there are no semantic, environmental, or utterance influences. The earliest malapropism was produced at age 2;2, by a child producing a 4-word utterance.

In Chapters 3 and 4 I looked at the influence of 'tonic stress' in phrases on the location of errors. In §3.7.3 I showed that in phonological errors made by speakers from the 3+word stage on, the syllable carrying the tonic phrasal accent was more likely to be involved in the error than would be expected by chance. However, for 2-word error utterances made by the children in the 2-word stage, the most heavily stressed syllable in the phrase (which I designated as the 'tonic' for the sake of doing this count) was involved in the error at exactly chance. In comparison, children in the 1-2b age range showed involvement of the tonic syllable at twice the percentage expected by chance. Similarly, in §4.2.3 I found that for most speakers, lexical substitution, blend and misplacement errors involved the word which took tonic phrasal stress far more often than predicted by chance. For the 1-2a age group, the figures were at chance; but for the children in the 1-2b age range and above, the tonic was involve at 1 1/2 times the chance level. In both cases it appears that the children in the 2-word stage were not using intonation to express any syntactic organization, and the tonic syllable or word had no structural status during speech production planning. Instead these young children were using intonation for primarily pragmatic purposes, expressing either speech acts or attentional focus.

Finally, in §6.4.2.4 above I showed that the syntactically relevant property of the mass/count distinction on nouns began to show adult-like patterns in terms of its effect on lexical substitution and blend errors at age 1-2b; however, the errors at age 1-2a showed less influence of this factor.   In verb errors, transitivity showed adult-like influence at ages 1-2b; however, I am not able to say whether or not this pattern would show up in the 1-2a errors since in my corpus there were no lexical errors involving verbs made by the children in the 1-word or 2-word stages. I would predict that transitivity would not be a relevant property of verbs before the 3+word stage began.

In sum, the various types of errors discussed in this section support the conclusion that there is no syntax during the 1-word or 2-word stages. However, when children begin to produce utterances of three or more words, there is ample evidence from these errors that the children are beginning to develop knowledge about syntax; I would characterize this knowledge as a store of syntactic templates which carry information about word/morpheme order and internal hierarchical structure. Lexical entries are also beginning to include information about lexical category and morphosemantically relevant categories in their lemmas. Inflectional morphology begins to be stripped away from stems and represented separately; after about 2;2 these affixes begin to be involved in errors independently. Function words get into the processing act as independent entities around age 2;5. Intonation over the phrase begins to take on syntactic functions, both in terms of information structure (new/old information) and syntactic category of the utterance (declarative, imperative, etc.). Syntax and morphology continue to be developed over the next many months. The peak in both syntactic and function word errors took place at age 3 in my data, as reported in Chapter 4 (§4.1.3 and §4.3.3). I argued there that it is at age 3 that children are learning a great deal of syntax and the function words required by increasingly complex syntactic frames, and thus at this age these two factors are especially error-prone. By age 4 the children's selection of syntactic templates and the selection of function words required by these templates has become more automated and practiced, and thus the focus of attention can return to selecting appropriate content words. Starting at age 4 and on through the adult errors, lexical selection errors, particularly involving content words, were proportionately more common than syntagmatic errors. However, morpheme errors increased during ages 4-5; this is undoubtedly because during these ages the children were working on acquiring more complex tense/aspect combinations which require more complex inflectional morphology, and thus there were more possibilities for error. Therefore the SOT data discussed in this and previous chapters give a convincing negative answer to the question of whether or not there is syntax in the 2-word stage, as well as providing a clear sketch of the overall development of syntax, morphology, and lexical categories, and their interactions with each other.

6.6.3 Phrase Blends
6.6.3.1 Introduction
I will now turn to an examination of a specific type of syntactic error, phrase blends. As discussed in Chapter 1, a phrase blend is an error which

occurs when the speaker has planned two distinct utterances with different syntactic constructions, and then has blended the two into a single utterance. In §1.4.4 (see example (3b)) I discussed in detail the diagnostics used for distinguishing phrase blends from paradigmatic lexical errors, which I will review here. First, in phrase blends, typically the utterance is frankly ungrammatical and the error phrase has an unusual intonation pattern, whereas in lexical substitution errors the error phrase is usually grammatical and the intonation normal. Furthermore, phrase blend errors cannot be explained in terms of simple shifts, additions, or omissions of lexical items planned for the utterance. Finally, in lexical substitution errors the speaker typically hesitates after the incorrect word, then corrects that word and continues with the remainder of the utterance; in phrase blends the speaker typically produces the entire erroneous phrase, and then in the correction, repeats one or both of the target phrases in its entirety.

Early studies which looked at this type of error attributed the ungrammatical productions to errors in performing transformations from deep to surface structure; this was said to involve applying a rule incorrectly, failing to apply an obligatory rule, applying a rule when it should not apply, and applying only part of a rule (Fay 1980a,b). However Stemberger (1982) showed that phrase blend errors (as well as lexical and morphological shifts) could be accounted for without transformations, by assuming that the semantic constraints of lexical items chosen to express the proposition could directly activate appropriate phrase structures from the speaker's 'Syntax Component'. Activation of the intended phrase structure could spread to semantically related phrase structures, which could cause incorrect phrase structures to be partially activated. If they are not suppressed by selection of the intended phrase structure, then the two structures can interfere with each other in planning, and be planned simultaneously as a blend. Stemberger accounts for this process with an interactive activation model which does not require transformations or deep structure.

A follow-up experiment testing the 'transformation' vs. 'competing plans' hypotheses, was performed by Chen & Baars (1992), in which subjects memorized two short, related phrases such as 'Can I turn off this light?' and 'Can I turn this off?' The phrases were all based on actual errors from Fay's (1980a) corpus. Subjects then saw each of the sentences displayed briefly on a screen and were instructed to either repeat that sentence, or to speak the other sentence memorized in conjunction with the sentence they had just seen. Speakers frequently produced errors which contained elements of both of the target sentences, and these errors were of exactly the types that both Fay and Stemberger had discussed in their previous papers. Thus Chen & Baars showed experimentally that competing plans will cause phrasal errors, and discussed their results in terms of the 'competing plans hypothesis' (Baars 1980, 1992).

In this study I concur with Stemberger and Chen & Baars that phrase blends are caused when the speaker is planning two different ways of phrasing the target proposition, and the two are blended together. However, I have distinguished two different properties of such blends which I believe need to be discussed separately. The first is what caused the speaker to plan two distinct syntactic representations for the utterance; that is, what happened during the activation of concepts, lemmas, and syntactic frames that caused the speaker to plan more than one utterance. This issue will be discussed in §6.6.3.2 below. The second issue is the actual structure of the blend; that is, how did elements from the semantic or syntactic representations from one of the planned utterances become associated with the structure of the other planned utterance. This issue will be discussed in §6.6.3.3. In both cases, developmental trends in the causes or structures of blends will be the focus of the discussion.

For the purposes of talking about the structures involved in these errors, I will frame the discussion in terms of syntactic 'templates' rather than 'phrase structures' or 'transformations'. As discussed in Chapter 1, the RPC Model assumes that the 'Morphosyntax' component in long term memory contains representations for a number of syntactic templates which are specific to different kinds of functional structures, speech acts, etc., and which are the representation units selected during the planning of the syntagmatic string. The 'Functional Level Representation: Semantic Structures', which is the output of the activation of lemmas and assignment of functional structure components, are linked to these syntactic templates according to the linking algorithms of the language (see Van Valin & LaPolla, 1997: Ch. 7). I make these assumptions because they are the simplest possible assumptions which fully account for both the causes of and the structures involved in the phrase blend errors to be discussed below.

6.6.3.2 The Causes of Phrase Blends

In my study I found that all the phrase blends produced by both the adults and children could be categorized into the following five types, in terms of the planning factors which caused the speakers to activate and plan two distinct structures.

Type 1: Lexical Selection. The speaker has activated two different content words which are both relevant to the proposition to be expressed (or in some cases, two different propositions which are both relevant to the state of affairs the speaker plans to talk about). The content words are not morphologically related to each other, and do not express an opposition. The speaker has then planned the different functional structures required by each of the two content words, and activated the syntactic structures appropriate to the planned 'Semantic Structures'. The two phrases are then blended in ways which will be discussed in §6.6.3.3 below. For example:

(63) a. M: 'Come ón, I'm trỳing to clèan this plàce úp!'
         Al: 'Ì won't léṭ you tò.'
         M: 'What?'
         Al: 'Ì don't . . . Ì won't lét you.' (blend of 'Ì won't lét yòu' and
             'Ì don't wánt you tò'; AL-71(49) 2;10)
      b. An: 'Mommy, sìt dòwn thìs médiately!' (blend of 'sìt dòwn thìs
             mínute' and 'sìt dòwn immédiately'; AN-140(49) 4;0)

In (63a), Alice has activated the lemmas for the verbs 'let' and 'want', which
would be involved in two different ways of framing the same proposition. She
then constructs the syntactic structures appropriate for the requirements of these
two different verbs, activating the function lemmas appropriate to each phrasing:
'won't' and 'don't . . . to'.   Finally she blends them into an ungrammatical
utterance. Fortunately, she indicated what her competing plans were in the repair
she produced.   In (63b), Anna activates the lemmas for the two synonymous
ways of framing the concept of immediacy, 'this minute' and 'immediately', and
produces a phrase blend which includes a partial word blend (*'thìs médiately',
with the intonation of 'thìs mínute, and omitting the first syllable of
'immédiately'). This type of phrase blend is very 'local', in that it involves the
activation of individual lexical items appropriate for the propositional content,
and may occur with fairly simple syntactic constructions. Type 1 phrase blends
are also very cognitively or semantically based, in that the error occurs in
choosing words to express the proposition rather than in constructing the
syntactic frame.

Type 2: Opposite Perspectives. In this type of error, two phrases are being
planned which involve content words which frame the proposition from one
perspective and its opposite perspective. This includes such oppositions as
active vs. stative/passive, source vs. goal, positive vs. negative, cause vs.
effect/result, etc. Type 2 errors will usually involve a change in a content word,
but sometimes will involve different variants of the same content word.

(64) a. An: 'Momma, lòok what Ì got at swímming lèssons: a scrápe.
             Ìt's blóod. (pause) Ìt's bléeding. It gòts blóod òn it.'
             (blend of 'Ìt's bléeding', active, vs. 'It gòts blóod òn it', stative;
             AN-155(49) 4;2)
      b. TF: (wondering why her cat is having digestion problems)
             'Àll we've been èating him . . . fèeding him is Kítty-Òs.'
             (blend of 'Àll we've been fèeding him', cause, with 'Àll he's
             been èating', result; AD-674(49))

In (64a), Anna has blended an active way of talking about her scrape, 'It's
bleeding', with a stative way, 'It gots blood on it', producing the ungrammatical
*'It's blood'.   In this case the content words were the same, but function
morphemes were different in the two framings. In (64b), the teen was thinking

about what she has been 'feeding' her cat (cause), and what the cat has been 'eating' (result), and she blended phrases based on these two different lexical items which frame opposite perspectives. Note that this was classed as a phrase blend rather than a lexical substitution error since the phrase *'all we've been eating him' is ungrammatical. Type 2 errors could also be considered to be quite 'local' and semantic in that they can involve lexical selection (e.g. 'feed' vs. 'eat'). When they involve different structures which frame the proposition from opposite perspectives they are still syntactically 'local' in that they involve individual phrases.

Type 3. Expanded vs. Contracted Phrase. Some blends involve competing syntactic frames with a truncated and expanded version of the same phrasal constituent. If both the truncated and expanded versions of the same phrasal constituent are grammatical and express the same proposition, the speaker may end up producing a blended phrase with some elements of each. Usually this involves simply adding or deleting some content words, but sometimes it necessitates changes in function words or morphemes due to the new syntagmatic string.

(65)   a.   M: (reading book) ' "Í'm not àngry." '
             An: '**He lóoks like àngry.**' (looks confused)
             M: 'He lóoks like he's àngry.'
             An: 'Yeah, <u>he lóoks like he's àngry.</u>'
             (blend of 'He lóoks like he's àngry' and 'He lóoks àngry'; AN-173(49) 4;4)
       b.   AF: 'Pick a few things òff the lìst **for sènd to** . . . <u>for mè to sènd to</u> Grándma's.' (blend of 'òff the lìst to sènd to' vs. 'òff the lìst, for mè to sènd to'; AD-683(49))

In (65a) Anna has produced a hybrid of 'he looks angry' and 'he looks like he's angry', which includes the verb 'like' but not the required 'he's'. In (65b), the adult has blended the phrase 'for me to send', overtly mentioning the agent, with the agentless 'to send', resulting in the erroneous preposition-verb sequence *'for send'. Because the two wordings of this phrase require different intonational patterns in the preceding phrase, the error utterance has the correct intonation for the first target sentence, but not for the target that involves the word 'for'. Type 3 errors involve the structure of single synonymous phrases, which can be either expanded or contracted; in that respect they are 'local' syntactically, but more 'global' lexically than Type 1 or 2 errors as they involve not the substitution of lexical items, but the addition, omission, or movement of lexical items.

Type 4. Internal Phrase Structures. This type of blend involves competing sentences with different syntactic structures within some specific constituent (e.g. argument phrase, complement), where the structures are roughly synonymous. This type of error often causes changes in the morphosyntactic structure of the verb phrase, although it is not restricted to verbs. The two target phrases usually involve the same content stem but in two different morphological forms.

(66)   a. Al: 'Mommy, we gòt to sàw the [f î:n] . . . we sàw the fíre èngine tòday.' (blend of 'we gòt to sèe' and 'we sàw', with telescoping of 'fire engine'; AL-209a(49) 4;2)

   b. AF: 'Thìs is the búsy I've . . . thìs is the búsiest I've èver sèen our stréet.' (blend of 'the búsiest' with 'as búsy as'; AD-686(49))

In (66a), Alice has blended two synonymous framings of the verb phrase 'we got to see X' and 'we saw X', one of which involves the infinitive form and the other the past tense form of the verb 'see'. In (66b), the adult has blended the predicate phrases 'the busiest' and 'as busy as', with the adjective 'busy' in its stem form in one case and inflected for the superlative in the other. Type 4 errors, although they involve the internal structure of individual phrases and therefore are syntactically 'local', usually require that the child has a firm grasp on morphology, and has more than one possible way of expressing, for example, tense and aspect in a verb phrase. So these errors require a more advanced morphosyntactic knowledge than Types 1-3.

Type 5.   External Phrase Shifts. In this type of error there are competing sentences with more than one phrase, where alternative orderings of one or more of the phrases are grammatical. In the blend, there is some confusion about the ordering of the two phrases, and elements can be misordered, deleted, or added; however, the actual lexical items being planned for each phrase are not changed (e.g. a misordered adverbial phrase, dative shift, etc.).

(67)   a. Al: (discussing a rattle that a friend had given her)
      'When Ì was a báby, **she gáve me ìt to mé.**' (blend of 'she gáve me ìt' and 'she gàve it to mé'; AL-168(49) 3;9)

   b. AF: 'Which **is thínk I whàt** . . . whàt I thínk you mèant to sày.' (blend of 'which is whàt I thínk you mèant to sày' and 'which I thínk is whàt you mèant to sày'; AD-693(49))

In (67a), Alice has mixed up the two possible orders of the direct and indirect object: 'me ìt' and 'it to mé', ending up with some elements of each: *'me ìt to mé'. In (67b), the speaker has problems with the placement of the phrase 'I think' with reference to the copula 'is' and the complementizer 'what'; rather than 'is whàt I thínk' or 'I thínk is whàt' she produces *'is thínk I whàt', with 'I' and 'is' exchanged, and the intonational pattern appropriate for the second pattern. Type 5 errors require that the child be able to plan and produce syntactic constructions which involve several phrases, and have the knowledge that these phrases can occur in different orders. So these could be considered to be syntactically 'global'.

TABLE 6.15

Number of each type of phrase blend cause at each age. Type 1: Lexical
Selection; Type 2: Opposite Perspective; Type 3: Expanded vs. Contracted
Phrase; Type 4: Internal Phrase Structures; Type 5: External Phrase
Shifts.

Age:	1;11 2;5	2;6- 2;11	3	4	5	Total	Adult
Type 1	2	2	0	3	3	10 (24%)	14 (32%)
Type 2	1	1	3	4	2	11 (27%)	9 (20.5%)
Type 3	1	1	0	4	1	7 (17%)	7 (16%)
Type 4	0	1	2	7	1	11 (27%)	8 (18%)
Type 5	0	0	1	1	0	2 (5%)	6 (13.5%)
Total N=	4	5	6	19	7	41	44

All of the phrase blend errors made by the children and adults were
categorized into one of these five types. Table 6.15 presents a count of the
numbers of each type of phrase blend made at each age. Since there were no
phrase blend errors made at age 1-2a, I have divided the 1-2b age group into two
6-month periods in this table.

This table shows that there were some developmental trends in the types of
errors made by the children. Type 1 errors were produced by the youngest
children, and continued to be produced throughout the age range (with an odd
absence at age 3); they were among the most numerous errors for the children
(along with Types 2 and 4), and were the most numerous for adults. The earliest
phrase blend was that made by Anna at age 1;11, discussed in detail in §6.6.2
above (example (61b), repeated here as (68a)); Bobby's earliest phrase blend is
given in (68b).

(68)   a. An: (pretending to read a book aloud)
              'Whàt ìs Bèrt háppèn, Bĕr . . . Bêrt, whàt háppèn?'
              (blend of 'Whàt ìs Bèrt dôing?' and 'Whàt háppèn, Bĕrt?'
              AN-20(49) 1;11)
        b. B: (ready to walk to store)
              'Mom, Ì wànna góing . . . Ì gòing tóo!'
              (blend of 'Ì wànna gó' and 'Ì gòing tóo'; B-37(49) 2;1)

I have classified (68a) as a Type 1 error, since there is competition between the
lexical items 'happened' and 'doing', around which the two different syntactic
structures are built. One could make an argument that this should be a Type 2

error, since there is an oppositional quality about 'What happened (to Bert)' and 'What is Bert doing?' However, I think it is unlikely that Anna really thought of 'happened' and 'doing' as lexically oppositional at age 1;11. One could also argue that these errors didn't revolve around lexical choice, since the phrases may have been somewhat collocational wholes for her at the time. But, as I pointed out above, there is evidence of syntactic structure in this error, since the crossover point between the two phrases comes at a constituent boundary, i.e. just before the verb. I will return to this point below. However, Bobby's error in (68b) is an unambiguous Type 1 error, since he has clearly activated the verbs 'want' and 'go', and framed two different constructions based on these lexical choices: 'wanna go' and 'going too'. I would argue that these lexically based phrase blend errors could be considered the 'simplest' type, since they are produced by the youngest children and involve the most 'local' planning, i.e. single lexical choices. Furthermore they would be expected to be the most numerous for adults since there are many more degrees of freedom in selecting lexical items than there are in choosing perspectives, internal phrase structures, or external phrase structures, and this is what was found.

The younger 2-year-olds also produced errors of Type 2 and 3; these errors involved what could again be seen as frequent collocations for the children, specifically 'get my teeth brushed' vs. 'brush my teeth' (B-49(49) 2;3), and 'I am' vs. 'I'm in here', in answer to 'who's there?' (B-68(49) 2;5). But these errors show that even in the first half of the third year, the children are learning to make choices about perspectives from which to frame their utterances, and between longer and shorter versions of synonymous syntactic constructions. This also shows that they have developed in their syntax component, a storehouse of syntactic templates which can compete with each other during planning. The older 2-year-olds also produced one Type 4 error, which involved a blend of two verb phrases, 'be quiet' and 'being quiet' (AN-78(49) 2;10), with different types of morphology. The 2-year-old children did not make any errors of Type 5; the first Type 5 error was made by Alice at age 3;9 (given in (67a) above), and this type of error was the most rare for the children. This is undoubtedly because the younger children had not yet developed multi-phrasal syntactic templates, particularly those in which there was some freedom of movement of the phrases within the sentence. Furthermore, this type of blend was also the most rare for the adults, most likely because there are far fewer syntactic constructions in English that allow for this type of phrase movement within sentences than the constructions involved in the other types of phrase blends (i.e. internal phrasal constructions).

It is clear that these phrase blend errors are most easily explained in terms of the 'competing plans hypothesis', and that the competing plans which cause the errors can occur at several stages of the planning model. Competition will occur at different levels of planning for children of different ages. First, some Type 1 errors seem to be caused by the speaker not having firmly decided between two propositional contents which would both be appropriate for the speaker to express in the current context. A good example is (68a) above, where Anna has not fully selected between the propositional contents 'What happened, Bert?' and 'What is Bert doing?' An adult example is (AD-667(49)), where the adult blends 'Bobby has a headache' and 'Bobby needs a Tylenol', to produce *'Bobby needs a headache'. However, most of both the child and adult Type 1 errors involved true lexical selection competition rather than propositional competition.

Other Type 1 errors and some Type 2 errors involve activating more lemmas than necessary, and having the activated lemmas compete for the privilege of setting up the functional structure which will then determine the syntax of the utterance. This is something that will effect the errors of very young children, since they have a fairly large storehouse of lexical entries at the time they begin producing blends. A good example is Bobby's error in (68b), where he has activated 'want', 'go', and 'too', which he cannot combine easily into a single phrase at age 2;1. Still other Type 2 errors involve knowing that one can frame the same general proposition from more than one point of view, and having the opposing syntactic structures stored in the 'Morphosyntax' representations component in long term memory. This type of error begins to be produced at age 2;3 with relatively fixed phrases (e.g. Bobby's 'teeth brush' blend, B-49(49) 2;3), but by age 3 it shows more productivity. Type 3 errors occur when the speaker has in his or her store of syntactic templates, more than one possible template for expressing the same content, one of which is a truncated version of the other. This type of error begins to be produced at age 2;5 (B-68(49) 2;5), showing that children have by this age begun to store such competing syntactic structures.

Type 4 errors also involve competing phrase-internal structures, but very often they involve the selection of one type of tense/aspect marking over another. Thus in order to be able to produce this type of error in abundance, the child would have to now have represented different ways of framing the same basic verbal meaning, but with the tense/aspect structures (including modals, auxiliaries, and inflectional morphology) appropriate for the particular function of the sentence in the discourse.

I think it is interesting that the 4-year-olds produced the largest number of Type 4 errors in my study. This probably ties in with the findings discussed above that the 4-year-olds produced more morphological errors than children at any other age. Since Type 4 errors involve phrase-internal structure, and often involve two phrases with the same stem but with different inflectional properties, it is likely that this is the age at which the children are developing the kind of morphosyntactic knowledge necessary for producing this type of error frequently.

Finally, Type 5 errors involve competition between multi-phrasal syntactic structures in which the same propositional content can be framed with some of the phrases occurring in differing orders. The actual order in which the phrases occur in fluent speaking is usually a function of discourse demands, that is, packaging information for the most coherent discourse flow, or performing the appropriate pragmatic function. This requires even more knowledge of discourse/pragmatics than the Type 4 errors, which is probably why it is the latest error type to appear in my data. The competition in this case is not only among syntactic structures, but also among different approaches to the framing of the proposition for discourse.

It can be seen, then, that these phrase blend errors reflect the development of the locus of attention in planning, as well as the development of the structures and knowledge necessary for planning. Early errors occur during local planning, based on semantic and propositional competition. Then the children begin making errors based on selection of competing syntactic templates for individual phrases. The latest errors to emerge involve global syntactic planning in multi-phrasal sentences, and require input from overall discourse planning. Simple lexically based errors (Type 1) continue to be the most common among adults since there are more possibilities of making errors of lexical selection than of selection of syntactic templates; however, the adults produce phrase blends of the other four types with roughly equal frequency.

6.6.3.3 The Structure of Phrase Blends

In the previous section I discussed causes of phrase blends in terms of the duplication during speech production planning which would have caused the speaker to plan two distinct syntactic structures. In the present section I will look at these same errors from a different point of view: the structure of the error per se. During processing, after the two syntactic representations have been constructed but neither has been fully selected, some erroneous planning occurs in which elements from the two distinct representations are joined into a single representation; form representations associated with the activated lemmas are inserted into this erroneous string, creating the erroneous 'Positional Level Representation: Syntactic Structure', which is then sent on to later components for further processing. The notion of 'syntactic template' will be crucial in my discussion of the structures of phrase blend errors.

From my data it appears that there are three possible ways the two syntactic constructions can be formally blended. The first type occurs when two syntactic templates are selected and two target strings are planned, but the lemma of one word from one of the two targets is erroneously linked to a location in the other target which is tagged for the same lexical category. In the following examples I have referred to the two targets as T1 and T2.

(69) a. M: 'Lòok what Í fòund: your nècklace we gòt at Lássen.'
         An: 'Oh yéah! Ì wànt to wèar it thís dày. **I thòught I was lóst . . .**
              I thòught I lóst ìt.'
         T1: 'I thòught it was lóst.' vs. T2: 'I thòught I lóst ìt.'
         (AN-114(49) 3;5)

b. AF: (some of her hair caught in hearer's car door)
'Well, you'll háve a bùnch of hàir **to remínd me** . . . to
remémber me bỳ.'
T1: 'to remémber me bỳ' vs. T2: 'to rèmind you of mé'
(AD-670(49))

In (69a) the pronoun 'I' from T2 is erroneously linked with the location marked
for 'pronoun' in T1, substituting for the target 'it' in the spoken phrase. In
(69b), the verb 'remind' from T2 is erroneously linked with the 'verb' slot in
T2, substituting for 'remember' in the erroneous utterance. This type of
mislinking error is characterized by having the entire T1 spoken intact, including
its planned syntactic structure and intonation pattern, but with one word from the
other target inserted into a location marked for the same lexical category in T1.
Furthermore, if some morphology has been planned for that specific slot in T1,
the mislinked word from T2 will be spoken with that morphology in the error
utterance, as in (70).

(70)   B: 'Lèt me sèe the bòx of the créam that **pùts** . . .
            that you pùt on my hánds. The kìnd that gòes on my hánds.'
            T1: 'the kìnd that gòe(s) on my hánds' vs.
            T2: 'the kìnd that you pùt on my hánds' (B-303(49) 4;6)

In this error the verb 'put' from T2 is mislinked to the verb slot in T1, taking
the 3sg suffix {-s} planned as part of the T1 template. This type of mislinking
error would be expected to be associated most often with blends with causality
Types 1 and 2, since they revolve around competing lexical items.
    The second type of blend of the forms of the two targets occurs when the
speaker selects two syntactic templates and plans each of the target strings; the
speaker then begins to produce one of the targets, but at some point in either the
syntactic planning or while sending the utterance to the next set of components
for further planning, the speaker shifts from the syntactic structure of one of the
targets to that of the other. In such cases the crossover location typically occurs
at either a like constituent boundary or at a point in the string where both targets
have the same lexical item. In the following example, I have put a slash mark
'/' at the locations in the two targets where the crossover takes place.

(71)   Al: 'When Ì was a báby, she **gáve me ìt to mé**.'
            T1: 'she gáve me ìt/' vs. T2: 'she gàve it /to mé' (AL-168(49) 3;9)

In this error, Alice produced the phrase 'she gáve me ìt' from T1, then at the
location where both target phrases contained the word 'it', she shifted over to the
structure of T2 'to mé'. Note that the intonation pattern also shifts from T1 to
T2, giving two tonic stresses in the error phrase. These crossover type errors

can be seen to be analogous to the word blend errors in which an onset from one word and a coda from another are blended into a new form. In this case rather than the syllable structure being the crucial factor, it is the template structure which provides the location where the two phrases can be broken up. These errors are also somewhat akin to either intentional code-switching productions in bilingual speakers, or bilingual errors where the speaker unintentionally shifts from one syntactic system to another in the middle of an utterance (Myers-Scotton & Jake 2001, Awuku 2003). This error structure would be expected to be most often associated with blends with causality Types 3 and 5, since these involve competing syntactic templates with different placement of specific constituents.

The third type of structural property involved in blends occurs when two more-or-less synonymous but syntactically different templates have been selected, two phrases have been planned, and structural elements of the two syntactic templates are blended, so that when lexical items are inserted into the string, the resultant string violates the morphosyntactic requirements of both of the two templates. This most typically involves producing an utterance with incorrect morphology on a content word, and sometimes involves deleting a function word or two; it is usually associated with Type 4 errors.

(72) a. AF: 'Thìs is **the búsy** I've . . . thìs is <u>the búsiest</u> I've èver sèen our stréet.'
            T1: 'Thìs is the búsiest I've èver sèen our stréet.' vs.
            T2: 'This is as búsy as I've èver sèen our stréet.' (AD-686(49))
      b. B: 'Ì **want gètting** a páper plàte.
            T1: 'Ì am gètting' vs. T2: 'I wànt to gèt' (B-160(49) 3;8)

In (72a) the syntactic representations for the two phrases 'the busiest I've' and 'as busy as I've' are blended, causing the speaker to plan the frame 'the __ I've' from T1, but with the uninflected slot for 'busy' from T2. In (72b), the syntactic representations for the phrases 'I am getting' and 'I want to get' are blended; the speaker produces the verb 'want' from T2, which requires the 'to X' complement, but with the progressive form of the verb 'getting' appropriate to T1; also the verb 'want' is unstressed, as would be appropriate for the 'I am getting' frame. These errors cannot be a simple lexical mislinking because typically the lemma which one would have to argue was mislinked is in fact the same lexical item in both of the two targets (i.e. both 'busy' in (72a), and both 'get' in (72b)).

A final possibility would be that the speaker could produce an error with some combination of these structural errors, such as in (73).

(73) a. AF: 'I have nó idèa **whère to gò thís gòes**.'
            T1: 'I have nó idèa whère to pùt thís.'
            T2: 'I have nó idèa where thís gòes.' (AD-672(49))

b. B: 'Mom, Ì wànna góing . . . Ì gòing tóo!'
    T1: 'Ì wànna gó!'
    T2: 'Ì gòing tóo!' (B-37(49) 2;1)

In (73a), first the verb 'go' from T2 has been mislinked to the uninflected verb slot in T1 being planned for 'put', producing 'go'; second, there is a crossover from T1 to T2 at the word 'this', so that the word 'goes' from T2 is added onto the completed syntactic frame of T1, producing 'this gòes', with the intonation pattern of T2. In (73b), the basic frame 'Ì wànna gó', with the lexical item 'wanna' and the intonation pattern of this phrasing, is produced in the error; however, the slot for the progressive inflectional suffix {-ing} from T2 is added to the verb slot of T1, producing the ungrammatical *'Ì wànna góing'. This could also be though of as a crossover, with the deletion of 'too', except that the intonation of T1 occurs on the word 'go', not the intonation planned for 'going' in T2. Again this cannot be a simple mislinking error since the stem 'go' is identical in both targets.

In order to see whether there were any developmental trends in the production of these different types of phrase-blend structures, I analyzed each phrase blend in terms of its structural category. I used the following criteria:
1) **Mislinking**: T1 is spoken intact in terms of syntactic frame and intonation; one word from T2 is linked to a slot in T1 of the same lexical category; the word from T2 substituted for the word from T1 does not have the same stem.
2) **Crossover**: The first portion of T1 is spoken intact, usually with its own intonation; at some constituent boundary or where the two targets share a common word, the utterance crosses over to to T2, finishing with both the remaining syntax/lexical items and intonation pattern of T2.
3) **Internal Phrase Blend (IPB)**: Nearly synonymous phrases planned for T1 and T2 with different morphosyntactic requirements are blended; the planned phrases typically involve the same content stem in both but with different morphological requirements, so that the error will usually include a content word in an incorrect morphological form.
4) **Mixed**: Usually some combination of the above, often with words either omitted or repeated erroneously.

There were a number of cases where more than one analysis was possible, as illustrated in (74).

(74) An: 'No, I'm tòo finished . . . I'm jùst finished.'
    T1: 'I'm tòo fúll.' vs. T2: 'I'm jùst finished.' (AN-62(49) 2;8)

The error in (74) could be a linking error, where the adverb 'too' from T1 is mislinked into the adverb slot for 'just' in T2; this could be justified since 'too' and 'just' are of the same lexical category, they derive from distinct stems, and the intonation of T1 is intact. On the other hand it could be a crossover error, where 'I'm too' comes from T1 and 'finished' from T2, with the crossover

TABLE 6.16

Number of each type of phrase blend structure at each age. 'Mislink'=
mislinking of elements; 'X-over'=crossover between two structures; 'IPB'=
internal phrase blend; 'Mixed'=other structural relationships.

Age:	1;11-2;5	2;6-2;11	3	4	5	Total	Adult
Mislink	1	1	1	3	3	9 (25%)	21 (52.5%)
X-over	1	2	1	5	1	10 (28%)	7 (17.5%)
IPB	0	1	2	6	2	11 (30.5%)	8 (20%)
Mixed	2	0	0	3	1	6 (16.5%)	4 (10%)
Total N=	**4**	**4**	**4**	**17**	**7**	**36**	**40**

occurring between the adverb-adjective constituents. Since the intonation of the two targets is identical, intonation doesn't allow us to distinguish between the two analyses. In the counts below I have not included any of these ambiguous errors; I have also not included any blends where the speaker interrupted the utterance before committing him/herself to the syntax of the rightmost portion of the error, since in these cases the full structure of the error utterance is unclear. This eliminated 5 child errors and 4 adult errors.

The results of this analysis, by age, is presented in Table 6.16. Again, since there were no phrase blend errors made by children in the 1-2a age range, I divided the 1-2b age range into younger vs. older children, in order to see whether there were any developmental trends during this time period.

The youngest children made only 4 unambiguous phrase blends; the first was a crossover error (at age 1;11), the next two were the less well-organized mixed types, and the fourth, at age 2;5 was a linking error. In the second half of this age range, the IPB-type error was added; the earliest of this type was at age 2;10 (AN-78(49) 2;10). The 3-year-olds made all the more structured types of errors; the 4-5-year-olds and adults made some errors of each type. However, the IPB types become more numerous for the 4-year-olds, and the mixed types were a smaller percentage of their overall errors for the 4-5-year-olds than for the early 1-2b children. The children overall produced relatively equal numbers of the three structured types of blends, and fewer of the mixed type; the adults, on the other hand, produced a majority of mislinking structures, and relatively fewer of the other types. How can these patterns be explained?

First, the crossover type pattern was the earliest one produced. This involves activating the templates for two syntactic structures, and then simply splicing the two together somewhere in the middle of the structures. Anna's crossover at 1;11 ((68a) above) split right before the verb, and most of the crossovers, even for the youngest children, occurred at some constituent boundary. However, when a child is producing utterances of only 3-4 words, pretty much any location could be considered a constituent boundary, so this doesn't necessarily require that the child has started to represent constituent structure in his/her templates. In fact it might be the case that the very young children's templates are somewhat more general and have less internal structure than the templates of the older children and adults, so that a very early crossover error would be caused by the child simply switching from one syntactic construction to the other in the middle of the utterance, most often where the two phrases had a lexical item in common. Thus it is not surprising that this type of error could be produced by the youngest children. However, as the children got older and their phrases became longer and more complex, the crossover point was always at a well-defined constituent boundary; these cases probably reflect the fact that their templates were becoming more fine-grained and detailed. Similarly, the fact that 50% of the youngest children's blends were of the mixed type suggests that the very young children's templates were still somewhat less well structured than the older children's; this percentage is considerably less in the older children's and adults' data.

The second structure type to appear in these blends is lexical mislinking. This type of error involves the speaker planning two phrases with similar structures, and then mislinking one word from one of the structures into the other, at a slot marked for the appropriate lexical category. This is a very 'local' error, as it involves only one word from the competing target phrase, and in fact it distorts the intended utterance less than the other types: the syntax remains the same but the utterance is now ungrammatical because of lexical properties of the erroneously inserted word. This error type requires at least knowledge about lexical categories, and also that syntactic templates have such categories marked in the correct linear location. The fact that the children began making this type of error at age 2;5 (B-68(49) 2;5) fits in with the fact that their lexical substitution errors honored lexical category consistently at this age, and that they had been producing fixed word order phrases consistently for several months preceding this first error.

The third type to appear is the internal phrase blend (IPB). This did not appear in my data until age 2;10, and the earliest of this type involved a fixed phrase 'be quiet' (AN-78(49) 2;10). Errors of this type involving more productive syntax did not begin to occur until age 3;9, as in Alice's blend of 'this is where' vs. 'this is going to be' (AL-141(49) 3;9). This is clearly a more complex error type, as it requires that the child have competing templates for two different ways of framing the same constituent, usually with different morphological requirements as well as word orders. So this error type involves more complex knowledge of internal phrasal syntax than the other two, and thus it is not surprising that the younger children did not produce this type of error.

The adults showed a very different pattern overall from the children. The children produced roughly equivalent numbers of the three main types of error structure, with somewhat fewer of the mixed type. However, over half the adults' errors were of the mislinking type, with smaller percentages of the crossover and IPB types, and very few mixed errors. This is most likely due to two factors, involving the development of syntactic representations and the maturation of the planning mechanisms. First, as young children learn and store syntactic templates, their templates may at first be somewhat less fine-grained and less robustly fixed in memory than adults', and therefore blend errors which distort the template structure may be more common. However, adults have a finite store of templates which are both internally well-structured and detailed, and also rigidly fixed in long-term memory. Due to long practice in selecting and implementing these templates, the templates themselves are less likely to be eligible for blending during processing. Second, the adults' self-monitors are more practiced than the children's, and the mislinking type error is the one which distorts the intended syntax the least amount. Therefore this is the error type which is most likely to fool the monitor and make its way into speech. One might hypothesize that this predominance of mislinking errors in adults is due to the fact that they most often co-occur with errors of the Type 1 or Type 2 causality factors, which both involve individual lexical items, and these two causality types make up 52.5% of the adult errors. However, it is also the case that Types 1 and 2 causality types make up 51% of the children's errors, but mislinking only makes up 25% of their structural types. So this is not simply a matter of possibility of error, but can be best explained in terms of the children's less fixed syntactic template representations, as well as the adults having more practice in producing a variety of syntactic constructions, and monitoring their intended output.

6.6.4 Summary of Syntax

I began this section by arguing that the SOT evidence comes down against the claim that there is any syntax during the 2-word stage. Children in this stage produce no clear 'syntactic' errors, no errors involving function words, and no errors involving morphology. There is no clear evidence that they have the notion of 'lexical category' at this age, and no evidence that the morphosemantic categories of transitivity of verbs or mass/count status of nouns have any influence on errors. Finally, there is no influence of phrasal tonic stress on either phonological or lexical errors. However, once children begin consistently producing utterances involving 3+ words, all of these factors begin to appear: syntactic errors, errors involving free function words and bound morphemes, clear evidence of lexical categories, influence of tonic stress, and so forth. Thus these errors lend strong support to the hypothesis that moving from the 2-word to the 3+word stage marks the onset of true syntactic structures.

Once the children enter the 3+word stage, they begin making phrase blends, of the types discussed at length above. The earliest phrase blends are very 'local' in that they are driven by competing lexical choices which cause children to plan different functional structures to express the same proposition; the differing functional structures require different syntax. In form these early blends most often involve either the insertion of a single lexical item from one target into the other, or a crossover in the middle of the two intended targets, both of which require only simple syntactic structures and notions of lexical category. Starting around age 2;5, the children begin to produce more complex phrase blends, which involve competing internal phrase structures, but this type of error does not occur in productive phrases until age 3;6. This shows that in the first half of the 4th year, children are beginning to set up templates which allow them to express the same content with different syntactic constructions, which typically involve differing morphology. Finally, at around age 3;9, the children begin producing blends involving external phrase organization; that is, they are planning a multiphrasal utterance in which there is some flexibility as to the order in which the various phrases come, and the error involves producing a hybrid of two possible phrasal orders.

This progression is reminiscent of the discussion of 'Frames, then Content' in Chapter 3, in the context of phonological development, which was expanded in Chapter 5 to include semantic development. In early child syntax, the immature templates are the first 'frames', which may be somewhat holistic but at least contain linearly ordered slots for words of specific lexical categories and slots for some basic inflectional morphology such as plural. There may be no need for hierarchical constituent structure, as long as utterances are relatively short, perhaps 3-5 words. However, as the children's knowledge of syntax increases, and their working space for planning speech expands, they begin to represent more 'content' in their syntactic frames than previously. As their understanding of discourse requirements develops, they will need to have more than one template which can express the same basic type of information, but in ways that would be appropriate in different discourse contexts; this typically depends on filling in more morphological 'content' in their syntactic frames. When they begin to combine different templates into multi-phrasal utterances, they may at first simply juxtapose individual phrases; but eventually they need to fill in the appropriate content which indicates various juncture types between phrases or clauses (e.g. relative pronouns, 'that' complements, etc.). The more complex their templates become and the longer their utterances become, particularly when they become multi-clausal, the more necessary it becomes for them to be able to represent hierarchical constituent structure in their syntactic constructions. The children's phrase blend errors show all the same types of syntactic structures as the adults' by the time they are about 3;9, showing that their frames now have content that is similar to that of an adult.

In this discussion I have talked about syntactic development in terms of the development of syntactic templates; this discussion also presupposes linking algorithms that link semantic/functional structures to syntactic structures during speech production planning. This template-based theory is a natural fit with the 'competing plans' hypothesis, in that what is planned is two competing phrases based on competing templates or combinations of templates. However, as I indicated in §6.6.3.1, early discussions of phrase blends were framed in terms of syntactic 'transformations', or more simply 'rules' being applied erroneously during planning. One might be able to construct a rule-based explanation for the phrase blends which involve either the internal structure of two competing phrases, or which involve the placement of moveable phrases within a multi-phrasal utterance. However, it is difficult to imagine a rule-based explanation for a crossover blend, where the speaker shifts from one syntactic structure to a different one, in the middle of the phrase. Similarly, it is unclear how a rule-based theory would explain how a single lexical item in the planned utterance could be displaced by a different lexical item of the same category, producing an ungrammatical structure (recall that simple lexical substitution errors are nearly always grammatical). One of the strongest pieces of evidence for the competing plans explanation is that speakers usually correct blend errors by producing at least one, and often both, of the grammatical phrases which had been in competition, making overt what those plans were. Because the competing plans hypothesis offers the most straightforward processing explanation for phrase blends, and the template-based syntactic approach can be matched to the competing plans processing theory in a very simple and elegant manner, these SOT data lend support the cognitive status of such template-based syntactic theories.

6.7 Conclusions and Epilogue

In writing this book, I have had two main purposes. The first purpose has been to explore the value of looking at young children's SOTs for the evidence they provide regarding the development of linguistic representations and speech production planning. These SOT data have been found to be extremely useful for looking at questions regarding the development of phonetics, phonology, the lexicon, semantics, morphology, and syntax. Naturally there are many more questions than those discussed in this book to which these data could provide answers. The value of including all of the child data here is that other researchers can use the raw data to look into the remaining questions on their own, or can reanalyze the data according to their various individual approaches.

The second main purpose of this book has been to lay out the methodology of the SOT approach to studying child language in detail, so that other researchers may have a model for pursuing such studies in the future. In particular, it would be enormously useful to have such studies performed on languages other than English, with distinct typological systems, where one would expect different patterns of SOT behavior. Cross-linguistic studies using this methodology would certainly provide a great deal of insight into what is universal and what is language specific in the development of the representation and processing of language.

At the time of this writing, Anna and Alice are in college, and Bobby is in high school; he is now called 'Bob'. Anna went on to become an acting major, in spite of her early trauma with "The Three Little Pigs". Alice is studying modern European history, and Bob looks like he's heading toward philosophy. None of them is interested in becoming a linguist, although in a way they all three already are linguists, in spite of themselves. They frequently report to me SOTs which they hear their friends and teachers say, and they are all three extraordinarily sensitive to language. They seem to have recovered from the trauma of having had their mother collect data from them as young children, although I occasionally hear one of them tell a friend: 'When I was a kid, every time I made a mistake my mother wrote it down, and then told everyone about it!' So in the spirit of never ceasing to be in awe of my children's language development, I will leave the reader with one last slip. When Anna was about 7, she had seen a picture of the painting "The Mona Lisa", and had apparently mis-analyzed the word 'Mona' as 'Moaning'. We were not aware of this until one day she opened an art book, and upon seeing a reproduction of this painting, exclaimed 'Look Mom! "The Whining Lisa"!'

References

Abd-El-Jawad, H. & Abu-Salim, I. (1987) Slips of the tongue in Arabic and their theoretical implications. *Language Sciences, 9,* 145-171.

Aitchison, J. & Straf, M. (1982) Lexical storage and retrieval: A developing skill? In A. Cutler (Ed.), pp. 197-241.

Allen, G. & Hawkins, S. (1980) Phonological rhythm: Definition and development. In G. Yeni-Komshian, J. Kavanaugh, & C. Ferguson (Eds.), pp. 227-256.

Anderson, J. (1988) More on slips and syllable structure. *Phonology, 5,* 157-159.

Arnaud, P. (1999) Target-error resemblance in French word substitution speech errors and the mental lexicon. *Applied Psycholinguistics, 20,* 269-287.

Aronoff, M. (1976) Word formation in generative grammar. *Linguistic Inquiry Monograph One.* Cambridge, MA: MIT Press.

Aronoff, M. & Anshen, F. (1998) Morphology and the lexicon: Lexicalization and productivity. In A. Spencer & A. Zwicky (Eds.), pp. 237-247.

Awuku, A. (2003) Bilingual slips of the tongue: Evidence for multilingual speech production planning. Unpublished ms., University at Buffalo.

Baars, B. (1980) A competing plans hypothesis: An heuristic viewpoint on the causes of errors in speech. In H. Dechert & M. Raupach (Eds.), pp. 39-49.

Baars, B. (1992a) A dozen competing-plans techniques for inducing predictable slips in speech and action. In B. Baars (Ed.), pp. 129-150.

Baars, B. (Ed.) (1992b) *Experimental slips and human error: Exploring the architecture of volition.* New York: Plenum.

Baars, B., Motley, M. & MacKay, D. (1975) Output editing for lexical status from artificially elicited slips of the tongue. *Journal of Verbal Learning and Verbal Behavior, 14,* 382-391.

Baayen, R. (1994) Productivity in language production. In D. Sandra & M. Taft (Eds.), pp. 447-469.

Bates, E., Marchman, V., Thal, D., Fenson, L., Dale, P., Reznick, S., Reilly, J., & Hartung, J. (1994) Developmental and stylistic variation in the composition of early vocabulary. *Journal of Child Language, 21,* 85-123.

Bates, E. & MacWhinney, B. (1987) Competition, variation, and language learning. In B. MacWhinney (Ed.), pp. 157-193.

Bauer, L. (2001) *Morphological productivity.* Cambridge, UK: Cambridge University Press.

Beard, R. (1998) Derivation. In A. Spencer & A. Zwicky (Eds.), pp. 44-65.

Beretta, A., Campbell, C., Carr, T., Huang, J., Schmitt, L., Christianson, K., & Cao, Y. (2003) An ER-fMRI investigation of morphological inflection in German reveals that the brain makes a distinction between regular and irregular forms. *Brain and Language, 85*, 67-92.

Berg, T. (1987a) *A cross-linguistic comparison of slips of the tongue.* Bloomington, IN: Indiana University Press.

Berg, T. (1987b) The case against accomodation: Evidence from German speech error data. *Journal of Memory & Language, 26,* 277-299.

Berg, T. (1990) The differential sensitivity of consonants and vowels to stress. *Language Sciences, 12,* 65-84.

Berg, T. (1991) Phonological processing in a syllable-timed language with pre-final stress: Evidence from Spanish speech error data. *Language and Cognitive Processes, 6,* 265-301.

Berg, T. (1992) Phonological harmony as a processing problem. *Journal of Child Language, 19,* 225-257.

Berg, T. & Abd-El-Jawad, H. (1996) The unfolding of suprasegmental representations: A cross-linguistic perspective. *Journal of Linguistics, 32,* 291-324.

Berko, J. (1958) The child's learning of English morphology. *Word, 14,* 150-177.

Berko Gleason, J. (Ed.) (2001) *The development of language,* 5th Edition. Boston: Allyn & Bacon.

Blanken, G., Dittmann, J., Grimm, H., Marshall, J., & Wallesch, C-W. (Eds.) (1993) *Linguistic disorders and pathologies: An international handbook.* Berlin: Walter de Gruyter.

Blevins, J. (1995) The syllable in phonological theory. In J. Goldsmith (Ed.), pp. 206-244.

Bloch, B. (1947) English verb inflection. *Language, 23,* 399-418.

Bloom, L. (1973) *One word at a time.* The Hague: Mouton.

Bock, K. (1996) Language production: Methods and methodologies. *Psychonmic Bulletin and Review, 3,* 395-421.

Bock, K. & Levelt, W. (1994) Language production: Grammatical encoding. In M. Gernsbacher (Ed.), pp. 945-984.

Boomer, D. & Laver, J. (1973) Slips of the tongue. In V. Fromkin (Ed.), pp. 120-131.

Bowerman, M. (1974) Learning the structure of causative verbs: A study in the relationship of cognitive, semantic, and syntactic development. *Papers & Reports on Child Language Development (Stanford University), 8,* 142-178.

Bowerman, M. (1976) Semantic factors in the acquisition of rules for word use and sentence construction. In E. Morehead & A. Morehead (Eds.), *Normal and deficient child language.* Baltimore, MD: University Park Press, pp. 99-179.

Bowerman, M. (1978) Systematizing semantic knowledge: Changes over time in the child's organizaiton of word meaning. *Child Development, 49,* 977-987.

Braine, M. (1976) Children's first word combinations. *Monographs of the Society for Research in Child Development, 41,* serial no. 164.

Braine, M. (1987) What is learned in acquiring word classes--A step toward an acquisition theory. In B. MacWhinney (Ed.), pp. 65-87.

Bresnan, J. (1982) Control and complementation. In J. Bresnan (Ed.) *The mental representation of grammatical relations.* Cambridge, MA: MIT Press, pp. 282-390.

Brown, R. (1973) *A first language: The early stages.* Cambridge, MA: Harvard University Press.

Brown, R. & Berko, J. (1960) Word association and the acquisition of grammar. *Child Development, 31,* 1-14.

Brown, R. & McNeill, D. (1966) The "tip of the tongue" phenomenon. *Journal of Verbal Learning and Verbal Behavior, 5,* 325-337.

Bruner, J. (1983) *Child's talk: Learning to use language.* New York: W.W. Norton & Co.

Butterworth, B. (1983a) Lexical representation. In B. Butterworth (Ed.), pp. 257-294.

Butterworth, B. (1983b) *Language production, Volume 2: Development, writing and other language processes.* London: Academic Press.

Butterworth, B. (1989) Lexical access in speech production. In W. Marslen-Wilson (Ed.), pp. 108-135.

Caplan, D. (1992) *Language: Structure, processing, and disorders.* Cambridge, MA: MIT Press.

Carey, S. (1978) The child as word learner. In M. Halle, J. Bresnan, & G. Miller (Eds.), pp. 264-293.

Chen, J. (2000) Syllable errors from naturalistic slips of the tongue in Mandrin Chinese. *Psychologia, 43,* 15-26.

Chen, J. & Baars, B. (1992) General and specific factors in "transformational errors"; An experimental study. In B. Baars (Ed.), pp. 217-233.

Chomsky, N. & Halle, M. (1968) *The sound pattern of English.* New York: Harper and Row.

Clark, E. (1973) What's in a word? On the child's acquisition of semantics in his first language. In T. Moore (Ed.) *Cognitive development and the acquisition of language.* New York: Academic Press, pp. 65-110.

Clark, E. (1979) Building a vocabulary: Words for objects, actions, and relations. In P. Fletcher & M. Garman (Eds.), pp. 149-160.

Clark, E. (1993) *The lexicon in acquisition.* Cambridge, UK: Cambridge University Press.

Clark, E. (2003) *First language acquisition.* Cambridge, UK: Cambridge University Press.

Clark, H. (1970) Word associations and linguistic theory. In J. Lyons (Ed.), *New horizons in linguistics.* Middlesex, England: Penguin Books, pp. 271-286.

Clements, G. & Keyser, S. (1983) *CV phonology: A generative theory of the syllable.* Cambridge, MA: MIT Press.

Corbett, G. (2000) *Number.* Cambridge, UK: Cambridge University Press.

Crompton, A. (1982) Syllables and segments in speech production. In A. Cutler (Ed.), pp. 109-162.

Cutler, A. (1980a) Errors of stress and intonation. In V. Fromkin (Ed.), pp. 67-79.

Cutler, A. (1980b) Productivity in word formation. In J. Kreiman & A. Ojeda (Eds.), *Proceedings of the 6th Annual Meeting of the Chicago Linguistics Society,* pp. 45-51.

Cutler, A. (1980c) Syllable omission errors and isochrony. In H. Dechert & M. Raupach (Eds.), pp. 183-190.

Cutler, A. (1982a) The reliability of speech error data. In A. Cutler (Ed.), pp. 7-28.

Cutler, A. (1982b) *Slips of the tongue and language production,* The Hague: Mouton.

Cutler, A. & Fay, D. (1982) One mental lexicon, phonologically arranged: Comments on Hurford's comments. *Linguistic Inquiry, 13,* 107-113.

Davis, B. & MacNeilage, P. (1994) Organization of babbling: A case study. *Language and Speech, 37,* 341-355.

Davis, B. & MacNeilage, P. (1995) The articulatory basis of babbling. *Journal of Speech and Hearing Research, 38,* 1199-1211.

Davis, B., MacNeilage, P., & Matyear, C. (2002) Acquisition of serial complexity in speech production: A comparison of phonetic and phonlogical approaches to first word production. *Phonetica, 59,* 75-107.

Davis, S. (1989) On a non-argument for the rhyme. *Journal of Linguistics, 25,* 211-217.

Dechert, H. & Raupach, M. (1980) *Temporal variables in speech.* The Hague: Mouton.

Dell, G. (1984) Representation of serial order in speech: Evidence from the repeated phoneme effect in speech errors. *Journal of Experimental Psychology: Learning, Memory and Cognition, 10,* 222-233.

Dell, G. (1986) A spreading activation theory of retrieval in sentence production. *Psychological Review, 93,* 283-321.

Dell, G., Burger, L., & Svec, W. (1997) Language production and serial order: A functional analysis and a model. *Psychological Review, 104,* 123-147.

Dell, G., Juliano, C., & Govindjee, A. (1993) Structure and content in language production: A theory of frame constraints in phonological speech errors. *Cognitive Science, 17,* 149-195.

Dell, G. & O'Seaghdha, P. (1992) Stages of lexical access in language production. *Cognition, 42,* 287-314.

Dell, G. & Reich, P. (1980) Towards a unified model of slips of the tongue. In V. Fromkin (Ed.), pp. 273-286.

Dell, G. & Reich, P. (1981) Stages in sentence production: An analysis of speech error data. *Journal of Verbal Learning and Verbal Behavior, 20,* 611-629.

Derwing, B. (1992) A 'pause-break' task for eliciting syllable boundary judgments from literate and illiterate speakers: Preliminary results for five diverse languages. *Language and Speech, 35,* 219-235.

Derwing, B. & Baker, W. (1986) Assessing morphological development. In P. Fletcher & M. Garman (Eds.), pp. 326-338.

Derwing, B., Nearey, T., & Dow, M. (1986) On the phoneme as the unit of the 'second articulation'. *Phonology Yearbook, 3,* 45-69.

de Villiers, J. & de Villiers, A. (1973) A cross-sectional study of the acquisition of grammatical morphemes in child speech. *Journal of Psycholinguistic Research, 2,* 267-278.

Elbers, L. (1985) A tip-of-the-tongue experience at age two? *Journal of Child Language, 12,* 353-365.

Entwisle, D. (1966) Form class and children's word associations. *Journal of Verbal Learning and Verbal Behavior, 5,* 558-565.

Fay, D. (1980a) Performing transformations. In R. Cole (Ed.), *Perception and production of fluent speech.* Hillsdale, NJ: Lawrence Erlbaum Associates, pp. 441-468.

Fay, D. (1980b) Transformational errors. In V. Fromkin (Ed.), pp. 111-122.

Fay, D. & Cutler, A. (1977) Malapropisms and the structure of the mental lexicon. *Linguistic Inquiry, 8,* 505-520.

Ferber, R. (1991) Slip of the tongue or slip of the ear? On the perception and transcription of naturalistic slips of the tongue. *Journal of Psycholinguistic Research, 20,* 105-122.

Ferguson, C. (1986) Discovering sound units and constructing sound systems: It's child's play. In J. Perkell & D. Klatt (Eds.), pp. 36-51.

Ferguson, C., Menn, L., & Stoel-Gammon, C. (Eds.) (1992) *Phonological development: Models, research, implications.* Timonium, MD: York Press.

Fillmore, C. (1975) An alternative to checklist theories of meaning. In C. Cogen et al. (Eds.), *Proceedings of the First Annual Meeting of the Berkeley Linguistics Society.* Berkeley Linguistics Society, pp. 123-131.

Fillmore, C. (1978) On the organization of semantic information in the lexicon. In D. Farkas, W. Jacobsen, & K. Todrys (Eds.), *Papers from the Parasession on the Lexicon.* Chicago Linguistic Society, pp. 148-173.

Fillmore, C. (1982) Frame semantics. In Linguistics Society of Korea (Ed.), *Linguistics in the morning calm.* Seoul: Hanshin, pp. 111-138.

Fletcher, P. & Garman, M. (Eds.) (1979) *Language acquisition: Studies in first language development,* 1st Edition. Cambridge, UK: Cambridge University Press.

Fletcher, P. & Garman, M. (Eds.) (1986) *Language acquisition: Studies in first language development,* 2nd Edition. Cambridge, UK: Cambridge University Press.

Fletcher, P. & MacWhinney, B. (Eds.) (1995) *The handbook of child language.* Oxford: Blackwell.

Frauenfelder, U. & Schreuder, R. (1991) Constraining psycholinguistic models of morphological processing and representation: The role of productivity. In G. Booij & J. van Marle (Eds.), *Yearbook of Morphology.* Dordrecht: Kluwer, pp. 165-183.

Freud, S. (1973/1901) Slips of the tongue. In V. Fromkin (Ed.), pp. 46-81. (Reprinted from *Psychopathology of everyday life,* 1901, tr. A. Brill.)

Frisch, S. (1997) Against underspecification in speech errors. *Studies in the Linguistic Sciences, 27,* 79-97.

Fromkin, V. (1973a) On the non-anomalous nature of anomalous utterances. In V. Fromkin (Ed.), pp. 215-242.

Fromkin, V. (Ed.) (1973b) *Speech errors as linguistic evidence.* The Hague: Mouton.

Fromkin, V. (Ed.) (1980) *Errors in linguistic performance: Slips of the tongue, ear, pen, and hand.* New York: Academic Press.

Fromkin, V. (1983) Aspects of a model of speech production: Evidence from speech errors. In M. van den Broecke et al. (Eds.), *Sound structures.* Publications in Language Sciences, pp. 105-112.

Fromkin, V. (1988) Grammatical aspects of speech errors. In F. Newmeyer (Ed.), *Linguistics: The Cambridge survey, V. II: Linguistic theory: Extensions and implications.* Cambridge, UK: Cambridge University Press, pp. 117-138.

Fujimura, O. & Erickson, D. (1997) Acoustic phonetics. In. W. Hardcastle & J. Laver (Eds.), pp. 65-115.

Garman, M. (1979) Early grammatical development. In P. Fletcher & M. Garman (Eds.), pp. 177-208.

Garnham, A., Shillcock, R., Brown, G., Mill, A., & Cutler, A. (1982) Slips of the tongue in the London-Lund corpus of spontaneous conversation. In A. Cutler (Ed.), pp. 251-263.

Garrett, M. (1975) The analysis of sentence production. In G. Bower (Ed.), *Psychology of learning and motivation: Volume 9.* New York: Academic Press, pp. 133-177.

Garrett, M. (1980a) Levels of processing in sentence production. In B. Butterworth (Ed.), *Language production I: Speech and talk.* London: Academic Press, pp. 177-220.

Garrett, M. (1980b) The limits of accommodation: Arguments for independent processing levels in sentence production. In V. Fromkin (Ed.), pp. 263-271.

Garrett, M. (1984) The organization of processing structure for language production. In D. Caplan, A. LeCours, & A. Smith (Eds.), *Biological persepectives on language.* Cambridge, MA: MIT Press, pp. 172-193.

Garrett, M. (1988) Processes in language production. In F. Newmeyer (Ed.), *Linguistics: The Cambridge survey: III. Language: Psychological and biological aspects.* Cambridge, UK: Cambridge University Press, pp. 69-96.

Garrett, M. (1993) Errors and their relevance for models of language production. In G. Blanken et al. (Eds.), pp. 72-92.

Gerken, L. (1994) Child phonology: Past research, present questions, future directions. In M. Gernsbacher (Ed.), pp. 781-820.

Gerken, L. & McIntosh, B. (1993) Interplay of function morphemes and prosody in early language. *Developmental Psychology, 29,* 448-457.

Gernsbacher, M. (Ed.) (1994) *Handbook of psycholinguistics.* San Diego, CA: Academic Press.

Gleitman, L. & Gillette, J. (1995) The role of syntax in verb learning. In P. Fletcher & B. MacWhinney (Eds.), pp. 413-427.

Goldfield, B. & Snow, C. (2001) Individual differences: Implications for the study of language acquisition. In J. Berko Gleason (Ed.), pp. 315-346.

Goldsmith, J. (1990) *Autosegmental and metrical phonology.* Oxford: Blackwell.

Goldsmith, J. (1995) *The handbook of phonological theory.* Oxford: Blackwell.

Griffiths, P. (1986) Early vocabulary. In P. Fletcher & M. Garman (Eds.), pp. 279-306.

Gupta, P. & Dell, G. (1999) The emergence of language from serial order and procedural memory. In B. MacWhinney (Ed.), *The emergence of language.* Mahwah, NJ: Lawrence Erlbaum Associates, pp. 447-481.

Halle, M. (1973) Prolegomena to a theory of word formation. *Linguistic Inquiry, 4,* 3-16.

Halle, M. (1998) The stress of English words. *Linguistic Inquiry, 29,* 539-568.

Halle, M., Bresnan, J., & Miller. G. (Eds.) *Linguistic theory and psychological reality.* Cambridge, MA: MIT Press.

Halle, M. & Clements, G. (1983) *Problem book in phonology.* Cambridge, MA: MIT Press.

Halle, M. & Vergnaud, J-R. (1987) *An essay on stress.* Cambridge, MA: MIT Press.

Hardcastle, W. & Laver, J. (Eds.) (1997) *The handbook of phonetic sciences.* Oxford: Blackwell.

Harley, T. (1984) A critique of top-down independent levels models of speech production: Evidence from non-plan-internal speech errors. *Cognitive Science, 8,* 191-219.

Harley, T. & Brown, H. (1998) What causes a tip-of-the-tongue state? Evidence for lexical neighbourhood effects in speech production. *British Journal of Psychology, 89,* 151-174.

Harley, T., Jones, G., Dunbar, G., & MacAndrew, S. (1995) From meaning to sound: Serial order from parallel systems. *Language and Cognitive Processes, 10,* 383-386.

Harley, T. & MacAndrew, S. (2001) Constraints upon word substitution speech errors. *Journal of psycholinguistic research, 30,* 395-418.

Hartsuiker, R. (2002) The addition bias in Dutch and Spanish phonological errors: The role of structural context. *Language and Cognitive Processes, 17,* 61-96.

Hirsh-Pasek, K. & Golinkoff, R. (1996) *The origins of grammar: Evidence from early language comprehension.* Cambridge, MA: MIT Press.

Hokkanen, T. (1999) One or more: Psycholinguistic evidence for divergence of numerosity and grammatical number assignment. *Brain and Language, 68,* 151-157.

Hotopf, W. (1980) Semantic similarity as a factor in whole-word slips of the tongue. In V. Fromkin (Ed.), pp. 97-109.

Hotopf, W. (1983) Lexical slips of the pen and tongue: What they tell us about language production. In B. Butterworth (Ed.), pp. 147-199.

Hurford, J. (1981) Malapropisms, left-to-right listing, and lexicalism. *Linguistic Inquiry, 12,* 419-423.

Ihns, M. & Leonard, L. (1988) Syntactic categories in early child language: Some additional data. *Journal of Child Language, 15,* 673-678.

Indefrey, P., Brown, C., Hagoort, P., Herzog, H., Sach, M., & Seitz, R. (1997) A PET study of cerebral activation patterns induced by verb inflection. *NeuroImage, 5,* S548.

Ingram, D. (1986) Phonological development: Production. In P. Fletcher &
    M. Garman (Eds), pp. 223-239.
Itô, J. (1986) *Syllable theory in prosodic phonology.* Doctoral dissertation,
    University of Massachusetts, Amherst. New York: Garland Press, 1988.
Jackendoff, R. (1975) Morphological and semantic regularities in the lexicon.
    Language, 51, 639-671.
Jaeger, J. (1980) Testing the psychological reality of phonemes. *Language
    and Speech, 23*, 233-253.
Jaeger, J. (1986) On the acquisition of abstract representations for English
    vowels. *Phonology Yearbook, 3*, 71-97.
Jaeger, J. (1992a) Not by the chair of my hinny hin hin: Some general
    properties of slips of the tongue in young children. *Journal of Child
    Language, 19*, 335-366.
Jaeger, J. (1992b) Phonetic features in young children's slips of the tongue.
    Language and Speech, 35, 189-205.
Jaeger, J. (1996) The development of syllable structure: Evidence from slips of
    the tongue. Paper presented at the Linguistic Society of America Annual
    Meeting, January.
Jaeger, J. (1997) How to say 'Grandma': The problem of developing
    phonological representations. *First Language, 17*, 1-29.
Jaeger, J. (1999) Early slips of the tongue and children's developing
    phonology. Paper presented at the 8th International Congress for the
    Study of Child Language, San Sebastian, Spain.
Jaeger, J. (2003) Commentary on A. Beretta et al. 'An ER-fMRI investigation
    of morphological inflection in German reveals that the brain makes a
    distinction between regular and irregular forms'. *Brain and Language,
    85*, 524-526.
Jaeger, J. (to appear) The acquisition of syllable structure: Evidence from slips
    of the tongue. To appear in a festschrift for Bruce Derwing.
Jaeger, J., Lockwood, A., Kemmerer, D., Van Valin, R., Murphy, B., &
    Khalak, H. (1996) A Positron Emission Tomographic study of regular
    and irregular verb morphology in English. *Language, 72*, 451-497.
Jaeger, J. & Wilkins, D. (1993) Some lexical and semantic properties of young
    children's slips of the tongue. Unpublished ms., University at Buffalo
    (SUNY).
Jakobson, R. (1941/1986) *Child language, aphasia, and language universals.*
    A. Keiler (Trans.); The Hague: Mouton.
Jusczyk, P. (1992) Developing phonological categories from the speech signal.
    In C. Ferguson, L. Menn, & C. Stoel-Gammon (Eds.), pp. 17-64.
Kager, R. (1995) The metrical theory of word stress. In J. Goldsmith (Ed.),
    367-402.

Kawachi, K. (2002) Practice effects on speech production planning: Evidence from slips of the tongue in spontaneous vs. preplanned speech in Japanese. *Journal of Psycholinguistic Research, 31,* 363-390.

Kenstowicz, M. (1994) *Phonology in generative grammar.* Cambridge, MA: Blackwell.

Kim, J., Marcus, G., Pinker, S., Hollander, M., & Coppola, M. (1994) Sensitivity of children's inflection to morphological structure. *Journal of Child Language, 21,* 173-209.

Kim, J., Pinker, S., Prince, A. & Prasada, S. (1991) Why no mere mortal has ever flown out to center field. *Cognitive Science, 15,* 173-218.

Kiparsky, P. 1982. From cyclic phonology to lexical phonology. In H. van der Hulst & N. Smith (eds.), *The structure of phonological representations,* Volume 1. Dordrecht: Foris, pp. 131-175.

Kiraly, G. (1996) *Hungarian slips on the icy slopes of language.* Unpublished honors thesis, University at Buffalo (SUNY).

Kohn, S. & Smith, K. (1990) Between-word speech errors in conduction aphasia. *Cognitive Neuropsychology, 7,* 133-156.

Ladefoged, P. (2001) *A course in phonetics,* 4th Edition. Orlando, FL: Harcourt Brace Jovanovich.

Lakoff, G. (1987) *Women, fire and dangerous things: What categories reveal about the mind.* Chicago: University of Chicago Press.

Lambrecht, K. (1994) *Information structure and sentence form.* Cambridge, UK: Cambridge University Press.

Landaur, T. & Dumais, S. (1997) A solution to Plato's problem: The Latent Semantic Analysis theory of the acquisition, induction, and representation of knowledge. *Psychological Review, 104,* 211-240.

Langacker, R. (1990) *Concept, image and symbol: The cognitive basis of grammar.* Berlin: Mouton De Gruyter.

Laubstein, A. (1987) Syllable structure: The speech error evidence. *Canadian Journal of Linguistics, 32,* 339-363.

Laubstein, A. (1999) Lemmas and lexemes: The evidence from blends. *Brain and Language, 68,* 135-143.

Laver, J. (1980) Slips of the tongue as neuromuscular evidence for a model of speech production. In H. Dechert & M. Raupach (Eds.), pp. 23-26.

Levelt, W. (1989) *Speaking: From intention to articulation.* Cambridge, MA: MIT Press.

Levelt, W. (1992) Accessing words in speech production: Stages, processes, representations. *Cognition, 42,* 1-22.

Levelt, W., Roelofs, A., & Meyer, A. (1999) A theory of lexical access in speech production. *Behavioral and Brain Sciences, 22,* 1-75.

Liberman, I., Shankweiler, D., Fischer, F., & Carter, B. (1974) Explicit syllable and phoneme segmentation of the young child. *Journal of Experimental Child Psychology, 18*, 201-212.

Lindblom, B. (1986) On the origin and purpose of discreetness and invariance in sound patterns. In J. Perkell & D. Klatt (Eds.), pp. 493-510.

Lindblom, B. (1992) Phonological units as adaptive emergents of lexical development. In C. Ferguson, L. Menn, & C. Stoel-Gammon (Eds.), pp. 131-163.

Locke, J. (1980) The prediction of child speech errors: Implications for a theory of acquisition. In G. Yeni-Komshian, J. Kavanaugh, & C. Ferguson (Eds.), pp. 193-210.

Locke, J. (1986) Speech perception and the emergent lexicon: An ethological approach. In P. Fletcher & M. Garman (Eds.), pp. 240-250.

Lyons, J. (1968) *Introduction to theoretical linguistics.* Cambridge, UK: Cambridge University Press.

Lyons, J. (1977) *Semantics (Vols. 1-2).* Cambridge, UK: Cambridge University Press.

MacKay, D. (1970) Spoonerisms of children. *Neuropsychologia, 8,* 315-22.

MacKay, D. (1972) The structure of words and syllables: Evidence from errors in speech. *Cognitive Psychology, 3,* 210-227.

MacKay, D. (1973) Spoonerisms: The structure of errors in the serial order of speech. In: V. Fromkin (Ed.), pp. 164-194.

Macken, M. (1992) Where's phonology? In C. Ferguson, L. Menn, & C. Stoel-Gammon (Eds.), pp. 249-269.

Macken, M. & Barton, D. (1980) The acquisition of the voicing contrast in English: A study of voice onset time in initial stop consonants. *Journal of Child Language, 7,* 41-75.

Macken, M. & Ferguson, C. (1983) Cognitive aspects of phonological development. In K. Nelson (Ed.), *Children's language*, Volume 4. Hillsdale, NJ: Lawrence Erlbaum Associates, pp. 225-282.

MacNeilage, P. (1997) Acquisition of speech. In W. Hardcastle & J. Laver (Eds.), pp. 301-332.

MacNeilage, P. (1998) The frame/content theory of the evolution of speech production. *Behavioral and Brain Sciences, 21,* 499-546.

MacNeilage, P. & Davis, B. (1990) Acquisition of speech production: Frames, then content. In M. Jeannerod (Ed.), *Attention and performance XIII: Motor representation and control.* Hillsdale, NJ: Lawrence Erlbaum Associates, pp. 453-476.

MacNeilage, P. & Davis, B. (1993) Motor explanations of babbling and early speech patterns. In B. de Boysson-Bardies, S. de Schonen, P. Jusczyk, P. MacNeilage & J. Morton (Eds.), *Developmental neurocognition: Speech and face processing in the first year of life.* Dordrecht: Kluwer.

MacNeilage, P. & Davis, B. (2000) Deriving speech from nonspeech: A view from ontogeny. *Phonetica, 57,* 284-296.

MacWhinney, B. (Ed.) (1987) *Mechanisms of language acquisition.* Hillsdale, NJ: Lawrence Erlbaum Associates.

Mahoney, P. (1997) Language production, speech errors, and aging. *Dissertation Abstracts International: Section B: The Sciences & Engineering, 58,* 2148.

Maratsos, M., Gudeman, R., Poldi, G., & DeHart, G. (1987) A study in novel word learning: The productivity of the causative. In B. MacWhinney (Ed.), pp. 89-113.

Marcus, G., Pinker, S., Ullman, M., Hollander, M., Rosen, T., & Xu, F. (1992) Overregularization in language acquisition. *Monographs of the Society for Research in Child Development, 57* (4, Serial No. 228).

Marslen-Wilson, W. (Ed.) (1989) *Lexical representation and process.* Cambridge, MA: MIT Press.

Marx, E. (1999) Gender processing in speech production: Evidence from German speech errors. *Journal of Psycholinguistic Research, 28,* 601-621.

Melinger, A. (2000) *Morphological complexity in English prefixed words: An experimental investigation.* University at Buffalo (SUNY), PhD. Dissertation (*Dissertation Abstracts International A,* 2001, 61, 12, June, 4752-A).

Menn, L. (1983) Develpment of articulatory, phonetic, and phonological capabilities. In B. Butterworth (Ed.), pp. 3-50.

Menn, L. & Bernstein Ratner, N. (2000) *Methods for Studying Language Production.* Mahwah, NJ: Lawrence Erlbaum Associates.

Menn, L. & Stoel-Gammon, C. (2001) Phonological development: Learning sounds and sound patterns. In J. Berko Gleason (Ed.), pp. 70-124.

Menyuk, P., Menn, L., & Silber, R. (1986) Early strategies for the perception and production of words and sounds. In P. Fletcher & M. Garman (Eds.), pp. 198-222.

Meringer, R. (1908) *Aus dem Leben der Sprache.* Berlin: Behrs Verlag.

Meringer, R. & Mayer, K. (1895) *Versprechen und Verlesen: Eine Psychologisch-Linguistische Studie.* Stuttgart: Goschensche Verlagsbuchhandlung.

Meyer, A. (1992) Investigation of phonological encoding through speech error analyses: Achievements, limitations, and alternatives. *Cognition, 42,* 181-211.

Miller, G. (1978) Semantic relations among words. In M. Halle, J. Bresnan, & G. Miller (Eds.), pp. 60-118.

Min, H. (1996) Syllabification in Korean: Evidence from speech errors. Unpublished ms., University at Buffalo (SUNY).

Motley, M. (1980) Verification of 'Freudian slips' and semantic prearticulatory editing via laboratory-induced spoonerisms. In: V. Fromkin (Ed.), pp. 133-147.

Muansuwan, N. (2000) Lexical errors in Thai slips of the tongue. Unpublished ms., University at Buffalo (SUNY).

Myers-Scotton, C. & Jake, J. (2001) Explaining aspects of code-switching and their implications. In J. Nichol (Ed.), *One mind, two languages: Bilingual language processing.* Oxford: Blackwell, pp. 84-116.

Myerson, R. (1976) Children's knowledge of selected aspects of 'Sound Pattern of English'. In R. Campbell & P. Smith (Eds.) *Recent advances in the psychology of language: Formal and experimental approaches.* New York: Plenum Press, pp. 377-402.

Nelson, K. (1973) Structure and strategy in learning to talk. *Monographs of the Society for Research in Child Development, 38.*

Nelson, K. (1985) *Making sense: The acquisition of shared meaning.* New York: Academic Press.

Nespor, M. & Vogel, I. (1986) *Prosodic phonology.* Dordrecht, Holland: Foris Publications.

Neufeldt, V. & Guralnik, D. (Eds.) (1991) *Webster's New World Dictionary of American English,* 3rd College Edition. New York: Prentice Hall.

Nooteboom, S. (1973) The tongue slips into patterns. In V. Fromkin (Ed.), pp. 144-156.

Nooteboom, S. (1980) Speaking and unspeaking: Detection and correction of phonological and lexical errors in spontaneous speech. In V. Fromkin (Ed.), pp. 87-96.

Ohala, J. (1974) Experimental historical phonology. In J. Anderson & C. Jones (Eds.), *Historical linguistics, Volume 2.* Amsterdam: North-Holland, pp. 353-389.

Ohala, J. (1977) The physiology of stress. In L. Hyman (ed.), *Studies in stress and accent (Southern California Occasional Papers in Linguistics, #4)*; Los Angeles: University of Southern California), pp. 145-168.

Ohala, J. (1992) The segment: Primitive or derived? In G. Docherty & D. Ladd (Eds.), *Papers in laboratory phonology II: Gesture, segment, prosody.* Cambridge, UK: Cambridge University Press, pp. 166-183.

Perkell J. & Klatt, D. (Eds.) (1986) *Invariance and variability in speech processes.* Hillsdale, NJ: Lawrence Erlbaum Associates.

Peters, A. (1986) Early syntax. In P. Fletcher & M. Garman (Eds.), pp. 307-325.

Peters, A. (1995) Strategies in the acquisition of syntax. In P. Fletcher & B. MacWhinney (Eds.), pp. 462-482.

Pillon, A. (1998) Morpheme units in speech production: Evidence from laboratory-induced verbal slips. *Language and Cognitive Processes, 13,* 465-498.

Pinker, S. (1991) Rules of language. *Science, 253,* 530-35.

Pinker, S. (1999) *Words and rules: The ingredients of language.* New York: Basic Books.

Pinker, S. & Prince, A. (1988) On language and connectionism: Analysis of a parallel distributed processing model of language acquisition. *Cognition, 28,* 73-193.

Pinker, S. & Prince, A. (1991) Regular and irregular morphology and the psychological status of rules of grammar. *Berkeley Linguistics Society, 17,* 230-51.

Plunkett, K. (1995) Connectionist approaches to language acquisition. In P. Fletcher & B. MacWhinney (Eds.), pp. 36-72.

Poulisse, N. (1999) *Slips of the tongue: Speech errors in first and second language production. (Studies in Bilingualism 20).* Amsterdam: John Benjamins.

Prince, A. (1983) Relating to the grid. *Linguistic Inquiry, 14,* 19-100.

Prunet, J-F., Beland, R., & Idrissi, A. (2000) The mental representation of Semitic words. *Linguistic Inquiry, 31,* 609-648.

Quirk, R. & Greenbaum, S. (1973) *A concise grammar of contemporary English.* New York: Harcourt Brace Jovanovich, Inc.

Radford, A. (1990) *Syntactic theory and the acquisition of English syntax: The nature of early child grammars of English.* Oxford: Blackwell.

Rapp, B. & Caramazza, A. (1998) Lexical deficits. In M. Sarno (Ed.), *Acquired aphasia,* 3rd Edition. San Diego, CA: Academic Press, pp. 187-227.

Rapp, B. & Goldrick, M. (2000) Discreteness and interactivity in spoken word production. *Psychological Review, 107,* 460-499.

Raymond, W. (2001) Toward a theory of grammatical encoding in speech production: Evidence from speech errors. *Dissertation Abstracts International, A: The Humanities and Social Sciences, 61,* 2687A.

Read, C. (1971) Pre-school children's knowledge of English phonology. *Harvard Educational Review, 41,* 1-34.

Roelofs, A., Meyer, A., & Levelt, W. (1998) A case for the lemma/lexeme distinction in models of speaking: Comment on Caramazza and Miozzo (1997). *Cognition, 69,* 219-230.

Rossi, M. (2001) The phonological processes of speech production in light of slips of the tongue. *Revue Parole, 17-19,* 139-168.

Rubino, C. (1996) Morphological integrity in Ilocano: A corpus-based study of the production of polymorphemic words in a polysynthetic language. *Studies in Language, 20,* 633-666.

Sandra, D. & Taft, M. (Eds.) (1994) *Morphological structure, lexical representation and lexical access.* Hillsdale, NJ: Lawrence Erlbaum Associates.

Schelvis, M. (1985) The collection, categorization, storage, and retrieval of spontaneous speech error material at the Institue of Phonetics, Utrecht. *Progress Report of the Institute of Phonetics at the University at Utrecht, 10,* 3-14.

Schwartz, M., Saffran, E., Bloch, D., & Dell, G. (1994) Disordered speech production in aphasic and normal speakers. *Brain and Language, 47,* 52-88.

Scollon, R. (1976) *Conversations with a one year old.* Honolulu: University of Hawaii Press.

Selkirk, E. (1980) The role of prosodic categories in English word stress. *Linguistic Inquiry, 11,* 563-605.

Selkirk, E. (1995) Sentence prosody: Intonation, stress and phrasing. In J. Goldsmith (Ed.), pp. 551-569.

Shattuck-Hufnagel, S. (1979) Speech errors as evidence for a serial-ordering mechanism in sentence production. In W. Cooper & E. Wales (Eds.), *Sentence processing.* Hillsdale, NJ: Lawrence Erlbaum Associates, pp. 295-342.

Shattuck-Huffnagel, S. (1983) Sublexical units and suprasegmental structure in speech production planning. In P. MacNeilage (Ed.), *The production of speech.* New York: Springer-Verlag, pp. 109-136.

Shattuck-Huffnagel, S. (1986) The representation of phonological information during speech production planning: Evidence from vowel errors in spontaneous speech. *Phonology Yearbook, 3,* 117-149.

Shattuck-Hufnagel, S. (1987) The role of word-onset consonants in speech production planning: New evidence from speech error patterns. In E. Keller & M. Gopnik (Eds.), *Motor and sensory processes of language.* Hillsdale, NJ: Lawrence Erlbaum Associates, pp. 17-51.

Shattuck-Hufnagel, S. & Klatt, D. (1979) The limited use of distincive features and markedness in speech production. *Journal of Verbal Learning and Verbal Behavior, 18,* 41-55.

Slobin, D. (1985) Crosslinguistic evidence for the language-making capacity. In D. Slobin (Ed.), *The crosslinguistic study of language acquisition. Vol 2, Theoretical issues.* Hillsdale, NJ: Lawrence Erlbaum Associates, pp. 1157-1249.

Smith, B. (1990) Elicitation of slips of the tongue from young children: A new method and preliminary observations. *Applied Psycholinguistics, 11,* 131-144.

Solé, M-J. (1992) Phonetic and phonological processes: The case of nasalization. *Language and Speech, 35,* 29-43.

Spencer, A. & Zwicky, A. (1998) *The handbook of morphology*. Oxford: Blackwell.

Steinberg, D. & Krohn, R. (1975) The psychological validity of Chomsky and Halle's Vowel Shift Rule. In E. Koerner (Ed.), *The transformational-generative paradigm and modern linguistic theory*. Amsterdam: John Benjamins, pp. 233-259.

Stemberger, J. (1982) Syntactic errors in speech. *Journal of Psycholinguistic Research, 11*, 313-345.

Stemberger, J. (1983a) *Speech errors and theoretical phonology: A review*. Indiana University Linguistics Club.

Stemberger, J. (1983b) The nature of /r/ and /l/ in English: Evidence from speech errors. *Journal of Phonetics, 11*, 139-147.

Stemberger, J. (1984) Structural errors in normal and agrammatic speech. *Cognitive Neuropsychology, 1*, 281-343.

Stemberger, J. (1985) An interactive activation model of language production. In A. Ellis (Ed.), *Progress in the psychology of language*. London: Lawrence Erlbaum Associates, pp. 143-186.

Stemberger, J. (1989) Speech errors in early child language production. *Journal of Memory and Language, 28*, 164-188.

Stemberger, J. (1991) Apparent anti-frequenty effects in language production: The addition bias and phonological underspecification. *Journal of Memory and Language, 30*, 161-185.

Stemberger, J. (1993) Spontaneous and evoked slips of the tongue. In G. Blanken et al. (Eds.), pp. 53-65.

Stemberger, J. (1994) Rule-less morphology and the phonology-lexicon interface. In S. Lima, R. Corrigan, & G. Iverson (Eds.), *The reality of linguistic rules*. Amsterdam: John Benjamins, pp. 147-169.

Stemberger, J. (1998) Morphology in language production with special reference to connectionism. In A. Spencer & A. Zwicky (Eds.), pp. 428-452.

Stemberger, J. & Lewis, M. (1986) Reduplication in Ewe: Morphological accommodation to phonological errors. *Phonology Yearbook, 3*, 151-160.

Stemberger, J. & MacWhinney, B. (1988) Are inflected forms stored in the lexicon? In M. Hammond & M. Noonan (Eds.), *Theoretical morphology*. San Diego, CA: Academic Press, pp. 101-116.

Studdert-Kennedy, M. (1987) The phoneme as a perceptuomotor structure. In A. Allport, D. MacKay, W. Printz, & E. Scheerer (Eds.), *Language, perception and production*. New York: Academic Press, pp. 67-84.

Stump, G. (1998) Inflection. In A. Spencer & A. Zwicky (Eds.), pp. 13-43.

Taft, M. (1994) Interactive-activation as a framework for understanding morphological processing. In D. Sandra & M. Taft (Eds.), pp. 271-294.

Taft, M. & Forster, K. (1975) Lexical storage and retrieval of prefixed words. *Journal of Verbal Learning and Verbal Behavior, 14*, 638-647.

Talmy, L. (2000) *Toward a cognitive semantics*. Cambridge, MA: MIT Press.

Treiman, R. (1988) Distributional constaints and syllable structure in English. *Journal of Phonetics, 16*, 221-229.

Treiman, R. (1989) The internal structure of the syllable. In G. Carlson & M. Tannenhaus (Eds.), *Linguistic structure in language processing*. Dordrecht: Kluwer, pp. 27-52.

Treiman, R. & Breaux, A. (1982) Common phoneme and overall similarity relations among spoken syllables: Their use by children and adults. *Journal of Psycholinguistic Research, 11*, 569-598.

Ullman, M., Bergida, R., & O'Craven, K. (1997) Distinct fMRI activation patterns for regular and irregular past tense. *NeuroImage, 5*, S549.

Valian, V. (1986) Syntactic categories in the speech of young children. *Developmental Psychology, 22*, 562-579.

van den Broecke, M. & Goldstein, L. (1980) Consonant features in speech errors. In: V. Fromkin (Ed.), pp. 47-65.

Van Valin, R. & LaPolla, R. (1997) *Syntax: Structure, meaning, and function*. Cambridge, UK: Cambridge University Press.

Vihman, M. (1981) Phonology and the development of the lexicon: Evidence from children's errors. *Journal of Child Language, 8*, 239-264.

Vihman, M., Velleman, S., & McCune, L. (1994) How abstract is child phonology? Toward an integraion of linguistic and psychological approaches. In M. Yavas (Ed.), *First and second language phonology*. San Diego, CA: Singular Press, pp. 9-44.

Vitevitch, M. (1997) The neighborhood characteristics of malapropisms. *Language and Speech, 40*, 211-228.

Vitevitch, M. (2002) The influence of phonological similarity neighborhoods on speech production. *Journal of Experimental Psychology: Learning, Memory, and Cognition, 28*, 735-747.

Vogel, I. (1999) Children's acquisition of stress in English. Paper presented at the 8th International Congress for the Study of Child Language, San Sebastian, Spain.

Waksler, R. (1999) Cross-linguistic evidence for morphological representation in the mental lexicon. *Brain & Language, 68*, 68-74.

Wan, I-P. (1999) *Mandarin phonology: Evidence from speech errors*. PhD. Dissertation, University at Buffalo (SUNY). (*Dissertation Abstracts International, A: The Humanities & Social Sciences*, 2000, 60, 8, Feb, 2899-A)

Wan, I-P. & Jaeger, J. (1998) Speech errors and the representation of tone in Mandarin Chinese. *Phonology, 15*, 417-461.

Wan, I-P. & Jaeger, J. (2003) The phonological representation of Taiwan Mandarin vowels: A psycholinguistic study. *Journal of East Asian Linguistics, 12,* 205-257.

Warren, H. (1986) Slips of the tongue in very young children. *Journal of Psycholinguistic Research, 15,* 309-344.

Waterson, N. (1971) Child phonology: A prosodic view. *Journal of Linguistics, 7,* 179-211.

Wells-Jensen, S. (1999) *Cognitive correlates of linguistic complexity: A cross-linguistic comparison of errors in speech.* PhD. Dissertation, University at Buffalo (SUNY). (*Dissertation Abstracts International, A: The Humanities & Social Sciences,* 2000, 60, 8, Feb, 2899-A 2900-A)

Wells-Jensen, S. (2003) The "Parallel Impromptu Narrations Corpus": Collection and analysis of cross-linguistic slips of the tongue. In D. Coleman, W. Sullivan, & A. Lommel (Eds.), *Linguistic Association of Canada and the United States Forum, 29,* pp. 359-364.

Wijnen, F. (1988) Spontaneous word fragmentations in children: Evidence for the syllable as a unit in speech production. *Journal of Phonetics, 16,* 187-202.

Wijnen, F. (1990) The development of sentence planning. *Journal of Child Language, 17,* 651-675.

Wijnen, F. (1992) Incidental word and sound errors in young speakers. *Journal of Memory and Language, 31,* 734-55.

Yazmajian, R. (1965) Slips of the tongue. *Psychoanalytic Quarterly, 34,* 413-419.

Yeni-Komshian, G., Kavanaugh, J., & Ferguson, C. (Eds.) (1980) *Child phonology, Volume 1: Production.* New York: Academic Press.

KIDS' SLIPS

CHILD DATA

The adult data can be accessed at the following website:

**http://linguistics.buffalo.edu/people/faculty/jaeger/adultSOT.
html**

Notes On The Data

I. Organization

These data are organized according to the classification system given in Chapter 1, Table 1.3. Each section is headed by its class number and title, and the sections are grouped into the four basic error-unit types, Phonological, Lexical, Syntactic, and Propositional. Within each class the errors are presented in chronological order, with data from all four data sets intermixed. A dashed line within each class of errors indicates the change from one age to the next (e.g. from the 1-year-olds' errors to the 2-year-olds' errors).

II. General Format

In each error there is a standard format for presentation; however, some aspects of this format differ according to error type. I will first give the general conventions for the data presentation, and then go into the details of specific types of error.

Each error is presented in three columns. The first column indicates the data set and the number of the error within this set: AN=Anna, AL=Alice, B=Bobby, OC=Other Child. AN-1=the first error collected from Anna. Errors are numbered chronologically and separately within each of the four data sets.

The second column tells the age of the child when he/she made this error, in 'years;months.days'. For example, 1;7.20=one year;seven months.20 days. In a few cases I didn't know the exact number of days for one of the 'Other' children, so I recorded it as '0'.

The third column presents the error. Each speaker is indicated by a prefix as follows: An=Anna, Al=Alice, B=Bobby, OG=Other Girl, OB=Other Boy, M=the child's mother, D=the child's father, OA=other adult, not one of the parents.

Following the indicator of the first speaker, there will sometimes be background information about the context of the utterance in parentheses; then the first utterance is given. After the error utterance there will sometimes be information about how the child reacted to his/her own error, in parentheses.

In all errors except telescoping and intonational errors, the accent marks in the utterances indicate phrasal stress; the grave accent 'v̀' indicates a strong but not tonic syllable, and the acute accent 'v́' indicates the tonic syllable in the phrase; occasionally a vowel will be marked as unstressed 'v̆' when this is important to the error. In telescoping and intonation errors, the marks above the vowels indicate pitch: 'v́'=high pitch, 'v̀'=low pitch, 'v̂'=falling pitch, 'v̌'=rising pitch. In the phonetic transcriptions given in parentheses under the error, the accent marks indicate lexical stress, not phrasal stress: 'v́'=primary stress; 'v̀'=secondary or tertiary stress; 'v'=unstressed.

Conventions for the presentation of the error utterance, and the material following the utterance, will be given by error type.

III. Format for Phonological Errors (Classes 1-34)

A. Format of Errors

1. *Substitution:* the word containing the error is written in phonetic transcription, and the error (the phonological unit(s) spoken in error) is indicated with boldface. The source(s) (i.e. other material in the utterance which caused the substitution) is indicated with boldface italics. The target (i.e. the intended phonological unit(s)) is underlined, if it is also spoken by the speaker who made the error.

2. *Addition:* same as for substitutions, except that the whole intended target word is underlined.

3. *Omission:* same as for substitutions, except that the location of the omitted phonological unit is marked with a boldface underline.

4. *Movement:* location of moved target phonological unit marked with boldface underline, location of substituted or added material boldfaced; targets in corrections underlined.

5. *Exchange:* both errors are boldfaced, and both targets are underlined.

B. Material Following the Error

1. First is the intended pronunciation of the target word in phonetic transcription, and the source in phonetic transcription if necessary (i.e. if not completely clear from the spelling). In the phonetic transcription of the target (and sources), the accent marks indicate lexical stress, not phrasal stress, as mentioned above. If a suffix has been analyzed as extrasyllabic (see §3.5.4), it has been marked off with parentheses in the phonetic transcription, as: 'cats' [kʰæt(s)].

2. Second, a description of the error itself, indicating what phonetic units were involved, and what the directionality of the error was: x<--y indicates an anticipation; y-->x indicates a perseveration, and x<-->y an exchange; other pertinent facts are indicated in prose (e.g. '/t/ deaspirates', or 'target most likely y but could also be z', or definitions of unclear words). In telescoping errors, there is an indication of the type of crossover involved (see §3.5.5).

3. Third, if the child was in the 1-word or 2-word stage, this is indicated next. In all other errors the child was in the 3+word stage.

4. Fourth is an indication of whether this error is being counted as a between-word error (B), a within-word error (W), or is ambiguous between the two (B/W). If it is a between-word error and has an unambiguous source, then there is an indication of whether or not the tonic syllable of the phrase was involved in the error, and if so, what its location was: '-T'=tonic not involved; +T(s)=source arose from tonic syllable; +T(e)=error was in tonic syllable; +T(b)=both target and error involved tonic syllables; +T(t1), +T(2) in an exchange, the first or second target was in the tonic syllable. If the error was spoken as part of a list intonation sequence, this is indicated here.

5. Fifth is the indication of the correction status of the error: SC=self-corrected; N-NC=noticed, not self-corrected; NSC=not self-corrected.

6. Sixth, if the error is subscripted, indicating that there was more than one error involved in this utterance, the classification status of the other error(s) is indicated; e.g. after error AN-3a(12) 1;7, there is the notation '3b=Class 16'.

7. Seventh, if this error is discussed in the text, the page number of its location in the text is indicated.

IV. Format for Lexical Errors (Classes 35-40)
A. Whole Word Substitutions
1. The erroneously produced word is boldfaced; the target is underlined if spoken by the same speaker. There are no sources since these are paradigmatic (non-contextual) substitutions.

2. The material in parentheses immediately following the error is arranged as follows:

a) First, the target word and error word are given in phonetic transcription; accent marks indicate lexical stress. Inflectional suffixes assumed to not be part of the lexical entry of content words are in parentheses (see Chapter 6). Any pertinent phonetic or contextual notes follow.

b) Second, if the child is in the 1-word or 2-word stages, this is indicated next; all other errors were made in the 3+word stage.

c) Third, if there is no semantic relationship between the target and error words, the notation [-sem] comes next.

d) Fourth is an indication of the correction status of the error (see explanation for phonological errors).

e) Fifth, if the error is subscripted, indicating that there was more than one error involved in this utterance, the classification status of the other error(s) is indicated.

f) Sixth, if this error is discussed in the text, its location in the text is indicated by page number.

3. The material following the parenthetic information is organized as follows:

a) First, on the left-hand margin is the indicator 'Phon' followed by a number; this number is the 'phonological similarity' rating of the target and error words, calculated based on the criteria in Table 4.3. Following this number is the indication of whether or not the tonic word was involved, where relevant. See the explanation of notation for phonological errors.

b) Second is the notation 'Lex/Morph'. Following this is an indication of the lexical category of the target and error words; if they both belong to the same category the notation 'X2' is used, e.g. 'Common noun X2' means both words involved are common nouns. Then in some cases there is an indication of the subcategorization of the lexical items; for nouns this includes whether they are count ('C') or mass ('M'), regular ('R') or irregular ('I') in their plural formation, and whether they are singular ('S') or plural ('P') in the error. So for example, the designation 'both CIS' means that the target and error words were two count nouns, both which take irregular plurals, but which occur in the singular form in this error. For verbs the factors indicated include transitivity, regularity, and the form of the verb in the error, e.g. 'transitive, regular, progressive'. Following this lexical information is an indication of how the error was classified in terms of morphological structure; for the morphological structure classification system, see §6.4.2, examples (48) and (49) in Chapter 6. If the error is [-phon, -sem], no morphological analysis is presented.

c) Third, if the target and error words have a semantic relationship, the next line is headed 'Sem:', and is followed by the semantic relationship class of the pair (see Chapter 5), with explanatory notes.

d) Fourth, if there are other factors involved in the relationship between the target and error words, the last line will be headed 'Other', and details given; this includes 'Environmental', 'Collocation', 'Discourse context', and 'On the mind' (see Chapter 4).

e) In a few cases the target word was not spoken and it was impossible to know exactly what the child meant to say. In these cases the 'Phon', 'Sem', or 'Lex/morph' analyses may not be performed.

B. Word Blends

1. The format of word blend errors is the same as that for lexical substitutions, except that the blend is always given in phonetic transcription. Also, possible sources in preceding utterances are in bold/italics.

2. The material following the error, in parentheses, is the same as for substitutions, except that it is the two target words which are given in phonetic transcription. If there is a possible source in a preceding utterance, the notation [+utt] is indicated before the correction status.

3. The material after the parenthesis is the same for blend errors as for substitutions.

C. Morpheme (affix) Substitution Errors follow the same format as phonological errors, but with an indication of which morphemes were involved in the parenthetical material after the error. Error morphemes are printed in larger type than the remainder of the entry.

V. Format for Syntactic and Propositional Errors (Classes 41-50)
A. Syntagmatic Whole Word Errors

1. In lexical anticipations and perseverations, the error word is given in boldface in its erroneous location; if it is also spoken in the correct location it is treated as a source and given in boldface italics. If the error is a substitution, if the target word is spoken in the correct location (either previously or in a correction), it is underlined. In lexical exchanges, both words are bolded when in their erroneous location, and underlined if corrected. In some cases the error production is written in phonetic transcription, if this is needed to clarify what was actually spoken. If the error utterance involves the stranding of a suffix, this suffix is underlined to show it was part of the target.

2. The material in parentheses after the error follows the same format as for paradigmatic lexical substitution errors, with one addition: if an anticipatory error is being analyzed as an interrupted metathesis, it will say so at this point.

3. The material after the parenthetical information is the same as for paradigmatic lexical substitution errors, only when the error involved a substitution or reversal (i.e. not an addition or metathesis) and both target and source words were identifiable.

4. For interrupted or full metathesis errors, the 'Phon:' analysis indicates whether or not the tonic was involved, but does not include a phonological similarity rating, since phonological similarity is usually irrelevant in such errors. Furthermore, semantic, lexical, and morphological analyses are not presented as these are likewise irrelevant. In metathesis errors, the accent marks in the parenthetical material after the error indicate phrasal stress, not lexical stress, since one relevant factor in a metathesis is whether or not the words involved keep their phrasal stress pattern.

B. Syntagmatic Affix Errors

1. The affix which has been moved to a new location is printed in boldface, in larger type than the remainder of the utterance. The location from which it has been moved is indicated with boldface underline. If corrected, the affix in its correct location is underlined.

2. The material in parentheses is the same as for paradigmatic lexical substitution errors, but with a discussion of which affixes are involved. Also, any allomorphic variation in the error is specified in the parenthetical material.

C.   Syntagmatic Multiple Errors

1. The error utterance is presented using the notational devices described above, on a case-by-case basis: error in boldface, source bold/italics, target underlined, bold/underline in locations from where elements have been moved, etc.

2.   The material in parentheses presents the target in phonetic transcription, then discusses the various movements, additions, substitutions, etc. which were involved in each error on an individual basis.

D. Phrase Blends

1.   The entire phrase in which the erroneous blending occurs is in boldface. If the error is completely or partially corrected, the corrected utterance is underlined, as it contains one or both of the target utterances.

2. Following the error there will be some parenthetical information, which will differ depending on the properties of each error; for example, if a word blend has occurred as part of the error this will be mentioned here. If the error is subscripted, the class of the other error will be noted. Next will follow the correction status of the error. Finally, if the error is discussed in the text, the page number(s) will be given.

3. After the parenthetical information, the two target utterances are given, as T1 and T2. Where appropriate, there is a slash mark '/' in the middle of each target, indicating where the crossover between the two phrases took place.

4. Following the two targets is the designation 'Type X', indicating which causation type this error falls into (see §6.6.3.2).

5. Finally, there is the designation 'Form', with the indication of the structural properties of the blended utterance (see § 6.6.3.3).

E. Propositional Errors

1. The portion of the utterance which seems to be at odds with the speaker's intention is in boldface, and corrections to the errors are underlined.

2. The material in parenthesis after the error explains why this was classified as a propositional error. Following the explanation is the correction status, and page numbers of any mention in the text.

VI. Phonetic Notes

A. Consonants

1. In general, all the phonetic symbols used for consonants in this study have their International Phonetic Alphabet values, with the following clarifications.

2. The symbols [ç, z, tç, dz] are used to indicate a laminal pre-palatal fricative or affricate, which the children produced before they could produce any of the alveolar or palato-alveolar sibilant fricatives or affricates; in the text I sometimes refer to these as 'sibilant substitutes'.

3. The symbol [r] is used to represent the American English rhotic approximant, rather than using the IPA symbol [ɹ], for typographical ease; the errors never involved the apical trill indicated in IPA by the symbol [r]. The symbol [ɜ] is used to indicate the children's early substitution for non-syllabic [r]; the [ɜ] was typically a central approximant with some lip-rounding and an apical constriction, but no pharyngealization. Most of the children alternated between [w] and [ɜ] as their substitutions for [r] for some time. The children also produced the usual substitution of either [w] or [j] for [l] in early speech.

4. Diacritics are used with their IPA values: [pʰ]=aspirated, [ṽ]= nasalized, [l̥]=devoiced or partially devoiced, [ɫ]=velarized, [n̩]=syllabic. Because nasalization of vowels is completely predictable (it always occurs before a tautosyllabic nasal consonant), it is usually not marked in the data, unless it is actually added or deleted as part of the error process. Devoicing or partial devoicing of sonorants after voiceless obstruents was also highly predictable after age 2;3 (see §3.3.4). I did mark this devoicing in the data, with the exception of the liquid [ɜ], where the devoicing marker interferes with the 'non-syllabic' diacritic; in all consonant clusters involving a voiceless obstruent followed by [ɜ], the sonorant should be taken as fully or partially devoiced.

5. The main three child subjects in this study (and some of the 'other'

children) spoke a dialect in which word-final voiced obstruent phonemes were very often pronounced as devoiced, with the preceding vowel lengthened. In my data I have usually written these obstruents as the voiced phoneme, but in some cases when it functioned as voiceless in the error, I transcribed it as the voiceless segment. This is not an inconsistency in my rendering of the children's productions, but an attempt to be phonetically accurate when the voicing status of a word-final obstruent was crucial to the error.

B. Vowels

1. I am using the following values for vowels in this study (R=round; U=unround)

	Front		Central		Back	
	R	U	R	U	R	U
High		i		ɨ	u	ɯ
Lower-High		ɪ			ʊ	
Mid	ø	eʲ	ɚ	ə	oʷ	
Lower-Mid		ɛ		ʌ	ɔ	
Low		æ		a	ɑ	

2. Other diphthongs include [æʷ] or [aʷ], [aʲ] or [ɑʲ], and [oʲ] or [ɔʲ]. The sequence [ju] sometimes behaved as a vowel nucleus, and sometimes as a CV sequence, so was assigned structure on a case-by-case basis.

3. The vowels [ə] and [ɨ] normally occur as an unstressed mid or high vowel, respectively. However, in the three main subjects' dialect (Californian), sometimes [ɨ] (or [ɯ]) could occur in a stressed location, such as in the word 'good' [gɨd]. These children also did not have the distinction between [ɪ] and [ɛ] before nasals; in this position [ɛ] is neutralized to [ɪ] as in 'pen' [pʰɪn]. Furthermore, they did not have the vowel [ɔ], which was usually realized as [a] or sometimes [ɑ]; e.g. both 'cot' and 'caught' are pronounced [kʰat]. However, some of the 'Other' children made these distinctions.

4. The vowel [3] is the non-pharyngealized early substitution for the vowel [ɚ] as in 'bird' [bɚd] or [b3d]. The vowel [ɚ] was considered a bona fide vowel rather than a syllabic consonant in most cases, except for the few rare errors where it interacted with another syllabic consonant such as [ɫ̩]; see §3.3.3 for details.

5. I did not systematically mark vowel length in the children's utterances, because it was impossible to accurately record nuances of vowel length by ear. In many cases where, for example, a word final consonant was omitted or became voiced in an error, it is most likely the case that the children lengthened the vowel; however, this will not be noted in most errors. I did systematically note vowel lengthening in telescoping errors.

TABLE OF CONTENTS OF ERROR TYPES

II. Paradigmatic Lexical Errors

III. Syntactic Errors

IV. Propositional Errors

I. Phonological Errors

1. Phonological anticipations (complete), substitutions, consonants.

AN-8   1;8.7   M: (pointing to picture in book) 'Who's thát?'
                     An: '[pʌ́m.pow]!'
                     (for 'Dumbo' [tʌ́m.pow]; [t]<--[p]; W; NSC; p. 61)

AN-13   1;9.2   M: (Anna putting pieces in puzzle) 'What shape is thát?'
                     An: 'It's crácker!'
                     M: (didn't understand) 'What?'
                     An: 'It's a [kʰʒǽ.kɨç] (breath) *sh*àpe.'
                     (for 'cracker shape' [kʰʒǽ.kɨʒ çeʲp]; [ʒ]<--[ç]; B; -T; N-NC;
                     p.70)

OC-8   2;0.14   OG: '[ʒɛ́.çi wɛ̀.çi] . . . réad̲y Wèsley?'
                     (for 'ready Wesley' [ʒɛ́.di wɛ́.çi]; [d]<--[ç]; 2-word stage; B;
                     -T; SC)

AN-27   2;1.25   An: '[ʃpéʲ.ʃɪp].'
                     (for 'spaceship' [spéʲ.ʃɪp]; [s]<--[ʃ], producing illegal
                     sequence */ʃp/; W; NSC; p. 144)

OC-12   2;2.0   OG: 'This is [fòʷp] *f*rom my Dád.'
                     (for 'soap from' [çoʷp fwʌm]; [ç]<--[f]; B; -T; NSC; p. 38)

B-45   2;2.16   B: 'I wànt [ǽ.pə.nʲùç] ì*n* it.'
                     (for 'want applejuice in it' [wʌ̃ʔ ǽ.pə.dzùç ɪnʲ ɪt]; [dẓ]<--[nʲ];
                     B; -T; NSC)

OC-16   2;3.0   OG: '[hù? *h*áʒd]!'
                     OA: 'Is it tòo hárd?'
                     OG: 'Yéah!'
                     (for 'too hard' [tʰu? haʒd]; [tʰ]<--[h]; B; +T(s); NSC; p. 155)

AN-37   2;3.26   An: 'Mòmmy's [tʃ í.*tʃ*ɨn].'
                     (for 'teachin' (informal) [tʰí.tʃ(ɨn)]; [tʰ]<--[tʃ]; W; NSC)

AN-41   2;4.20   M: 'You're talking like a báby all of a sudden.'
                     An: ' 'Càuse I'm nòt a [gì.doʷ] báby, I'm a bíg gìrl.'
                     (for 'little' [lí.doʷ]; [l]<--[g]; B; T?; NSC)

AN-42   2;4.20   An: 'I got [dʒré͡p]-júice. Thìnk you'd wànna drínk?'
(for 'grape-juice' [gré͡p.dʒùs]; note that [dʒr] is an
acceptable cluster in her phonology; [g]<--[dʒ]; W; NSC;
p. 28, 123)

AN-46a   2;4.25   An: 'Óne dày . . . [mʌ̃:] mórnìng, (etc.).'
(for 'one morning' [wʌ̃:.mór.nĩŋ]; [w]<--[m]; B; +T(s); NSC;
AN-46b=Class 12)

B-61   2;5.14   B: 'One, twò, thrèe, fòur, [sà͡v], sìx, sèven èight níne.'
(counting objects; for 'five' [fa͡v]; [f]<--[s]; B; list
intonation; NSC)

B-65   2;5.19   B: 'Thòse are [flùt] róll-ups.'
(for 'fruit' [fwut]; [w]<--[l], not devoiced at this age; B;
+T(s); NSC; p. 62)

B-79   2;6.15   B: '[wà͡f] it óff!'
(for 'wipe it off' [wà͡p ɪt áf]; [p]<--[f]; B; +T(s); NSC; p. 34)

AN-54   2;7.12   An: 'Thìs is a [pʰl̩̀.ti] cólor.'
(for 'pretty color' [pʰɾí.ti kʰʌ́.lɚ]; [r]<--[l]; B; -T; NSC)

B-103   2;7.21   B: 'I càn [màtʃ] a móvie.'
(for 'watch' [watʃ]; [w]<--[m]; B; +T(s); NSC; p. 81)

B-105   2;7.30   B: '[mán.sk3 s], gò awáy!'
(for 'monsters go' [mán.st3 s koʷ]; [t]<--[k]; B; -T; NSC)

B-118   2;10.13   B: 'Mom, whère'd my [vá͡.tʌ.gʌn] . . . gò?'
(for 'vitamin go' [vá͡.tʌ.mʌn goʷ]; [m]<--[g]; B; -T; N-NC)

AL-66   2;10.20   Al: 'Mom, I'm eàting as [kʰæst] as I cán.'
(for 'fast' [fæst]; [f]<--[kʰ]; B; +T(s); NSC; p. 200)

AN-91   2;11.17   An: (showing Mom a surprise in a bag)
'Mommy, wànna lòok in hére, and sèe what [ɪ̆z íz]?'
(for 'it is' [ɪt ɪz]; [t]<--[z]; could also be anticipation of
whole word 'is'; B; +T(s); NSC)

AL-81   2;11.18   Al: '[ho:.wé͡ hoʷ.zè͡].'
(for 'No way, José' [no:.wé͡ hoʷ.zè͡], an expression meaning
'emphatically no'; [n]<--[h]; B; -T; NSC)

AN-92   2;11.20   An: 'Are yòu gonna [brʌθ] your téeth?'
(for 'brush your teeth' [brʌʃ jɚ tʰiθ]; [θ]<--[ʃ]; B; +T(s) NSC; p. 149)

AL-83   2;11.25   Al: 'There's one more book: "Snòw Whìte an' the [mè.fi] Dwárfs . . . Mèssy Dwárfs".'
(for 'Messy Dwarfs' [mé.s(i) dworfs]; [s]<--[f]; B; +T(s); SC)

AN-101   3;2.9   An: 'I àte [ʃʌm] shrímp.'
(for 'some shrimp' [sʌm ʃɹɪmp]; [s]<--[ʃ]; B; +T(s); NSC)

AN-104   3;2.13   An: 'Once upòn a tíme thère lìved thrèe lìttle pígs. And the thrèe lìttle [bígs] had a bìg bàd wólf in the hòuse.'
(for 'pigs' [pʰɪgs]; [pʰ]<--[b]; possibly anticipation of whole word 'big'; B; +T(e); NSC)

OC-44   3;3.5   OB: '[wàf] òut for my búilding.'
(for 'watch' [watʃ]; [tʃ]<--[f]; B; -T; NSC)

AL-120   3;4.10   Al: 'After I sày [búd.bàʲ], I will sày gòodbỳe to yòu tóo.'
(for 'good-bye' [gùd.báʲ] but with emphatic stress on the first syllable; [g]<--[b]; W; NSC)

AL-130   3;4.18   Al: 'I'm gonna pùt my [dǽn.ʃɪŋ] shòes òn now.'
(for 'dancing shoes' [dǽn.s(ɪŋ) ʃuz]]; [s]<--[ʃ]; B; -T; NSC; p. 159, 191)

B-130   3;5.21   B: 'Ya knòw where [bléʰn]-Blàster is?'
M: 'Where?'
B: 'At Lóngs.'
(for 'Brain-Blaster' [bʒéʰn.blæ̀.stɚ]; [ʒ]<-[l]; 'Brain-Blaster' is a toy, 'Longs' is a drug store; W; NSC)

B-153   3;8.16   B: 'Wè don't háve Gòofy [mɪm] . . . gymnàstics'.
(for 'gymnastics' [dʒɪm.nǽ.stɪks]; [dʒ]<--[m]; W; SC)

AL-164   3;9.0   Al: (sing-song) 'I'm [tʰà.ʃɪŋ] the trásh òut; I'm tòssing the trásh òut.'
(for 'tossing' [tʰá.s(ɪŋ)], source 'trash' [tʰʒæ̀ʃ]; [s]<--[ʃ]; B; +T(s); SC; p. 159)

OC-67   3;10.0   OG: (suggesting a kind of box for burying a dead bird)
'A bòx that [ʃæ̀d] shóes.'
(for 'had shoes' [hæd ʃuz]; [h]<--[ʃ]; B; +T(s); NSC)

AL-176 3;10.5   Al: 'I see [fɪn.tʰʌ.ki] Fríed Chícken.'
(for 'Kentucky Fried' [kʰɪn.tʰʌ.ki fʒà̯d]; [kʰ]<--[f]; B; -T;
NSC; p. 148)

OC-78   4;0.0   OB:'[fl̩à.stɪd] Flákes.'
(for 'Frosted Flakes' [fr̩à.stɪd fl̩éˑks]; [r]<--[l]; B, although
possibly a compound; +T(s); NSC)

AL-200 4;0.6   Al: (identifying Sesame Street characters in a picture)
'Thìs one's [pʰʒ̀è.ɾi]-Dáwn, and thìs one's Bètty-
Lóu.'
(for 'Prairie' [pʰʒ̀éˑ.ʒi]; source probably 'Betty' [bé.ɾi],
although the [d] in 'Dawn' is a possible source; [ʒ̀]<--[ɾ] /d/;
B/W; NSC)

AN-148 4;1.22 An: 'Prètty [bléˑs.l̩t] Àl̩ice . . Prètty brácelet.'
(for 'bracelet' [bréˑs.lɪt]; [r]<--[l]; B/W; SC)

B-200   4;1.27 B: (explaining why he doesn't wear underpants with
pajamas) 'I [bèt] my bóttom aìr oùt.'
(for 'let' [lɛt]; [l]<--[b]; B; +T(s); NSC)

AN-162 4;2.23 An: (telling long silly story) 'The [ʃʌnz] not shíning.'
M: 'The whát?'
An: 'The s̩ùn's not shíning.'
(for 'sun's' [sʌnz]; [s]<--[ʃ]; B; +T(s); NSC)

AN-165b 4;3.28 An: ' . . . and hìg rùs . . . [hìg] rùg. . . hìs̩ rùg is réd.'
(for 'his rug' [hɪz rʌg]; [z]<--[g]; B; -T; SC; 165a=Class 25)

OC-100 4;4.0   OB: 'Dòwn thère's the [dʌ́n.ʃən] she's ìn.'
(for 'dungeon she's' [dʌ́n.dʒən ʃiz]; [dʒ]<--[ʃ]; B; -T; NSC)

B-254   4;4.7   B: 'I don't líke it when Dàddy [hèˑks] me hóme.'
(for 'takes' [tʰéˑks]; [tʰ]<--[h]; B; -T; NSC)

B-294   4;5.29   B: 'I wànna tèll 'em I wànt my [væ.lən.kʰàⁱnz] stìcker.'
M: 'Your what?'
B: 'My Válentine's stìcker.'
(for 'Valentine's sticker' [væ.lən.tʰàⁱnz stí.k(ɚ)]; [tʰ]<--[k],
then [k] --> [kʰ]; B; -T; NSC; p. 62, 128)

B-296   4;6.5   B: 'They're [kʰàⁱ.dɨn] the clués?'
(for 'hidin' (informal) [háⁱ.dɨn]; [h]<--[kʰ]; B; +T(s); NSC)

B-299   4;6.9   B: 'Còcoa [kʰr̥ìs.miz] . . . àre my fávorite.'
(for 'Crispies' [kʰr̥ís.p(i)z]; [p]<--[m]; B; -T; N-NC; p. 128)

B-322   4;7.4   B: 'Spèedy [gan.ʃà.ləs] ènchiládas.'
(for 'Gonzales enchiladas' [gan.zá.ləs ìn.ʃə.lá.dəz]; [z]<--[ʃ];
B; -T; NSC)

B-332   4;7.16   B: (telling Mom how he acts like some cartoon character)
'I [làk] alóng, and I hàve the híccups, so I jùmp úp!'
(for 'walk along' [wak ə.láŋ]; [w]<--[l]; B; +T(s); NSC)

B-358   4;9.3   B: 'I hùrt my [lìf] on the phóne.'
(for 'lip' [lɪp], source 'phone' [foʷn]; [p]<--[f]; B; +T(s); NSC)

B-360   4;9.10   B: 'Yóu gèt the [pʰìz.oʷz] . . . pìllows.'
(for 'pillows' [pʰíɫ.oʷz]; [l]<--[z]; W; SC)

B-366   4;9.17   B: 'And [spr̥ìn.tɚ] . . . was a lìttle rát.'
(for 'Splinter' [splín.tɚ]; [l]<--[r] or [ɚ]; B/W; N-NC)

B-394   4;10.25   B: 'I wànt some [zɨ.zɔ́ᵻt].'
(for 'dessert' [dɨ.zɔ́ᵻt]; [d]<--[z]; W; NSC)

B-415   4;11.11   M: 'Whàt are you gònna dó nòw?'
B: '[fèⁱt] for my fríend.'
(for 'wait' [weⁱt]; [w]<--[f]; B; T?; NSC; p. 152)

OC-135 5;1.17   OB: '[ɪn.stèr] of a cár, we gòt a nèw ván.'
(for 'instead' [ɪn.stéd]; [d]<--[r]; B; +T(s); NSC)

B-458   5;1.25   B: (explaining why he should be first in the bathtub tonight) 'Because I was làst [nǽst] n̂ight. (laughs) I màde a spéech èrror.'
(for 'last night' [læst naɪt]; [l]<--[n]; B; +T(e); N-NC; p. 19)

AN-281 5;2.16   An: 'Mom, thìs pàrt is [mèɪdʒ] of spónge.'
(for 'made' [meɪd], source 'sponge' [spʌndʒ]; [d]<--[dʒ]; B; +T(s); NSC)

B-498   5;5.1   B: 'She had a? Àlice in [rʌn.dɚ.lænd] . . . Àlice in Wónderlànd skìrt.'
(for 'Wonderland skirt' [wʌn.dɚ.lænd skɚt]; [w]<--[ɚ], then [ɚ] becomes non-syllabic; if [ɚ] in 'skirt' is source, this is Class 7, interrupted; B/W; SC; p. 113)

B-506   5;5.24   B: (he's 'reading' his dictionary) 'I'm [dʌ.nə] d̂ò the néxt one.'
(for 'gonna' [gʌ.nə]; [g]<--[d]; B; -T; NSC)

AN-299 5;7.19   An: 'Î know what hàppened to the [ʃɛr]; I'll shów you.'
(for 'chair' [tʃɛr], source 'show' [ʃoʷ]; [tʃ]<--[ʃ]; B; +T(b); NSC)

OC-160 5;8.0   OG: 'My túmmy's fùll.'
D: 'OK, Î'll èat your cóokie.'
OG: 'No, nòt from the cóokie, from the [tʃàt] cĥócolate.'
(for 'hot chocolate' [hàt tʃák.lɪt]; [h]<--[tʃ]; B; +T(s); NSC)

B-551   5;8.4   B: (showing Mom that his marker didn't show through the page) 'Do you sèe any [lɛ́.loʷ]? . . . yéllow?'
(for 'yellow' [jɛ́.loʷ]; [j]<--[l]; W; SC)

AN-307 5;8.11   An: 'Mommy, àren't you gònna [wàk] our àcrobátics?'
(for 'watch' [watʃ], source 'acrobatics' [æ̀.kr̥ə.bǽ.rɪks]; [tʃ]<--[k]; B; -T; NSC)

AN-314 5;9.12   An: 'Mòmma, [kʰɛ̀.rʌ] cùt . . . Sàrah cùt her háir.'
(for 'Sarah cut' [sɛ́.rʌ kʰʌt]; [s]<--[kʰ]; B; -T; SC)

B-561   5;10.5   B: (telling what a sign should say) 'It would say "Spèed [lì.nɪt] Thìrty Óne". '
(for 'limit' [lí.mɪt], source 'one' [wʌn]; [m]<--[n]; B; +T(s); NSC)

AL-259 5;10.9 Al: (Grandpa was teasing her, asking where her pigtails
went) 'Thìs is the [hèˑm] *h*àir as *h*àd the pígtails!'
(for 'same' [seˑm]; [s]<--[h]; B; -T; NSC)

2. Phonological anticipations (complete), additions, consonants.

AL-6 2;1.12 Al: '[wáˑç.kʰwìm] . . . íce-crèam.'
(for 'ice-cream' [áˑç.kʰwìm]; [w] anticipated from 'cream',
added as onset of 'ice'; 2-word stage; W; SC; p. 119)

AN-28 2;2.3 M: 'Whàt is thát?'
An: 'It's a [kʰwǽm.wʌ] . . . cámera.'
(for 'camera' [kʰǽm.wʌ]; [w] anticipated from second
syllable of 'camera', added into onset of first syllable; W;
SC; p. 32, 119, 145)

B-46 2;2.25 B: 'I [sìt] *s*ome móre.'
(for 'eat' [it]; [s] anticipated from 'some', added as onset of
'eat'; B; -T; NSC)

B-54 2;5.3 B: 'I wànt my [blíg] b*l*ànket.' (hesitates)
(for 'big' [bɪg]; [l] anticipated from 'blanket', added to onset
of 'big'; B; +T(e); N-NC; p. 155)

B-56 2;5.10 B: 'The [kw̥ḛ̀ʒ.kw̥ò"] and the líon!'
(for 'scarecrow' [kḛ́ʒ.kw̥ò"]; [w̥] anticipated from second
syllable of 'scarecrow', added to onset of first syllable; note
that Bobby still produced /r/ as [w] in consonant clusters,
but as [ʒ] when a single consonant; W; NSC; p. 117)

B-66 2;5.27 B: '[dáˑ.pḷ3]-Dòub*l*er . . . Díaper-Dòubler.'
(for 'Diaper-Doubler' [dáˑ.p3.dʌ.bl3]; [l] anticipated from
onset of second syllable of 'Doubler' added into onset of
second syllable of 'Diaper; {-er} not a derivational
morpheme, since he didn't know the word 'double'; W; SC;
p. 159)

B-73 2;6.9 B: 'Thìs [gà̰ʒm] *g*òes ìn hére.'
(for: 'arm' [a̰ʒm]; [g] anticipated from 'goes', added as
onset of 'arm'; B; -T; NSC)

B-91   2;7.2   M: (doing a puzzle) 'Look, thìs one's shàped like a
                  kíttycàt.'
                  B: 'A kíttycàt! It's [ʃʃè¦pt] ʰike a kíttycàt!'
                  (for 'shaped' [ʃe¦pt]; [l] anticipated from 'like', added into
                  onset of 'shaped', producing illegal sequence */ʃl/; B; -T;
                  N-NC; p. 144)

AL-40   2;7.16   Al: (pretending to eat a truck) 'Thàt's a [jʌmp.ti] trúck.'
                  (for 'yummy' [jʌ.m(i)]; [t] anticipated from onset of 'truck',
                  added as onset of second syllable of 'yummy',
                  resyllabification of [m], epenthetic [p]; B; +T(s); NSC)

AN-59   2;7.27   An: 'Tálk! Tàlk to my [pʰr̥ĩn.tʰín] òne.'
                  M: 'Talk to your what?'
                  An: 'My preténd òne.'
                  (for 'pretend' [pʰr̥i.tʰín]; [n] anticipated from either the
                  second syllable in 'pretend' or 'one' added into coda of first
                  syllable of 'pretend', causing vowel to nasalize; B/W;
                  NSC; p. 120)

AN-61   2;7.29   An: '[kʰòʷ.kʰéʲ].'
                  (for 'OK' [òʷ.kʰéʲ]; [kʰ] anticipated from second syllable of
                  'OK', added as onset of first syllable; W; NSC)

B-110   2;9.1   B: 'Can you [stèɬ] me a stóry?' (looks confused)
                  (for 'tell' [tʰeɬ]; [s] anticipated from 'story', added to 'tell',
                  /t/ deaspirated; B; +T(s); N-NC)

AN-99   3;0.28   An: 'Mòmmy, would yòu [tʰàʲk] this ʰike a bów, plèase?'
                  (for 'tie' [tʰaʲ]; [k] anticipated from 'like', added as coda of
                  'tie'; B; -T; NSC)

B-125   3;2.20   M: 'What kind of céreal do you want?'
                  B: '[kʰlóȝn]flàkes.'
                  (for 'cornflakes' [kʰóȝn.flèʲks]; [l] anticipated from 'flakes',
                  added into onset of 'corn'; W; NSC)

AL-99a   3;2.24   Al: 'I have a [sn̥òȝ] néck . . . sòre snéck . . .'
                  (laughs, says wrong on purpose several times.)
                  (for 'sore neck' [soȝ nɛk]; [n] anticipated from 'neck, added
                  into onset of 'sore'; B; +T(s); N-NC; 99b=Class 13; p. 81,
                  145)

AL-114 3;3.26   Al: 'Whère are we gòing àfter the [spóʷst.à.fɪs]?'
(for 'post-office' [pʰóʷst.à.fɪs]; [s] anticipated from one of
the two codas within the word 'post-office', added into the
onset of the first syllable, /p/ deaspirated; W; NSC; p. 116)

AL-115 3;3.27   Al: 'Mòm, càn you [ðóʷ.pən] *th*ìs . . . Can you ópen thìs?'
(for 'open' [óʷ.pən]; [ð] anticipated from 'this', added as
onset of 'open'; B; +T(e); SC)

B-157 3;8.18   B: 'But I don't wánna gò to [spèʲ.k3z] *S*quàre!'
(for 'Baker's Square' [pèʲ.k3z skw̥ɛ́ʒ], the name of a
restaurant; [s] anticipated from onset of 'Square', added to
onset of 'Baker's'; B; -T; NSC)

OC-60 3;9.0   OG: 'You bètter wàtch òut for [spòʲ.zən] *s*píders, 'cuz thèy
can *s*tíng!'
(for 'poison' [pʰóʲ.zən]; [s] anticipated from either 'spiders'
or 'sting', added to onset of 'poison', /p/ deaspirated; B;
+T(s); NSC)

AL-167 3;9.2   Al: 'I hàd to pùt 'em in the [stèⁱm] *st*áck.'
(for 'same stack' [seⁱm stæk]; [t] anticipated from 'stack',
added to onset of 'same'; could also be perseveration from
'to' or 'put', but this is less likely than the [st] cluster in
'stack'; B; +T(s); NSC)

B-167 3;9.8   B: 'They [stèɫ] it at a móvie *s*tòre.'
(for 'sell' [sɛɫ]; [t] anticipated from 'store', added to onset
of 'sell'; could also be anticipation of /t/s in 'it at', but less
likely than the [st] cluster in 'store'; B; -T; NSC)

AL-203 4;0.20   Al: (singing) 'Rùbber [dʌk.li] I'm àwfu*ll*y fònd of yóu.'
(for 'Ducky' [dʌ́.ki]; [l] anticipated from 'awfully' [á.fʊ.l(i)],
added into onset of second syllable of 'Ducky', causing
resyllabification; B; -T; NSC)

B-185 4;1.6   B: 'Daddy, àfter I gèt out of the túb, I wànt to dò some
[hórm.wɚk]!'
(for 'homework' [hóʷm.wɚk]; [ɚ] anticipated from second
syllable of 'homework', added after vowel in first syllable,
becomes non-syllabic and replaces offglide, vowel denasalizes; source could also be 'after', but less likely; W;
NSC)

OC-88   4;1.7   OB: (measuring how high water is in a jar)
                    '[sĩŋks] ínches . . . <u>sìx</u> ínches.'
                    (for 'six inches' [sɪks ín.tʃɪs]; nasal anticipated from
                    'inches', added after vowel in 'six', then assimilates to [k],
                    preceding vowel is nasalized; B; +T(s); SC; p. 120, 145)

B-220   4;2.16   B: 'Nòw [maⁱm] fóur! . . . Nòw <u>I'm</u> foúr.'
                    (for 'I'm' [aⁱm]; [m] anticipated from coda of 'I'm' added as
                    onset; W; SC)

B-284   4;5.15   B: (telling about a Nintendo game) 'They're in Sùper
                    Màrio the [ʌ.rí.dʒəɫ . . . nəɫ] òne, (etc.)'
                    (for 'original' [ʌ.rí.dʒə.nəɫ]; [ɫ] anticipated from coda of
                    last syllable of 'original', added as coda to third syllable;
                    {-əl} not a suffix, since he didn't know 'origin'; W; N-NC)

AN-202   4;5.21   An: 'I've gòt to [ri.r] . . . <u>eráse</u> this.'
                    (for 'erase' [i.réⁱs]; [r] anticipated from second syllable of
                    'erase', added to onset of first syllable; W; SC)

AN-205   4;5.23   An: 'The òne in my [mǽg.zə.zín].'
                    (for 'magazine' [mǽ.gə.zín]; [z] anticipated from onset of
                    last syllable of 'magazine', added to onset of second
                    syllable, causing resyllabification; W; NSC)

B-304   4;6.14   B: (singing song from "Weird Al Yankovic" video)
                    'I don' wànna [dlù] my *l*aúndry.'
                    (for 'do' [du]; [l] anticipated from 'laundry', added to onset
                    of 'do' producing illegal cluster */dl/; B; +T(s); NSC;
                    p. 144)

B-305   4;6.15   B: (telling what he was for Halloween)
                    'I was the [déɫ.vəɫ].'
                    (for 'devil' [dέ.vəɫ]; [ɫ] anticipated from second syllable of
                    'devil', added into coda of first syllable; W; NSC)

AN-222   4;6.18   An: (tests soup, sees it has cooled down)
                    'It's jùst [f̬ɹ̀àⁱt] *f*or mè to éat.'
                    (for 'right' [raⁱt]; [f] anticipated from 'for', added to onset of
                    'right', causing [r] to devoice; B; -T; NSC)

AL-220 4;6.20   Al: 'I àlready [dék.to.ʒèʲ.təd] ìt!'
(for 'decorated' [dɛ́.ko.ʒèʲ.t(əd)]; [t] anticipated from either
the third syllable of 'decorated' or the coda of 'it', added to
onset of second syllable of 'decorated', causing
resyllabification; could also be addition of past tense
morpheme in the middle of the word, in which case it
should be syllabified [dɛ́kt.o.ʒèʲt.(əd)]; B/W; NSC;
p. 406)

AL-235 4;9.18   Al: 'A [stè.kənd] stòry . . . a sècond stòry stóre.'
(for 'second' [sɛ́.kənd]; [t] anticipated from either 'story' or
'store', added to onset of 'second'; B; T?; SC)

B-462 5;2.0   B: ('reading' alphabet book)
'Bíg [lèm], líttle M̀.'
(for 'M' [ɛm]; [l] anticipated from 'little', added as onset of
'M'; B; +T(s); NSC)

B-488 5;4.7   B: 'I don't hàve my [blíg] blånket. I just have thís one.'
(for 'big' [bɪg]; [l] anticipated from 'blanket', added to onset
of 'big'; B; +T(e); NSC)

B-510 5;5.24   B: (discussing flowers)
'When [jè.vɚ] you sméll one, you snéeze.'
(for 'ever' [ɛ́.vɚ]; [j] anticipated from 'you', added to onset
of 'ever'; B; -T; NSC)

B-511 5;5.24   B: (pointing to pictures of children with these colors of
hair) 'It can [bli] òrange, blåck, brówn.'
(for 'be' [bi]; [l] anticipated from 'black', added to onset of
'be'; B; list intonation; NSC)

AN-321 5;10.1   An: 'This is [sʌ́.mɚ.skàlt] schòol.'
(for 'somersault school' [sʌ́.mɚ.sàlt skùl]; [k] anticipated
from 'school', added to onset of 'somersault'; B; -T; NSC)

OC-171 5;10.24   OB: (while walking into a store)
'There mìght be [stɛ́.sə.mi]-Strèet stùff hère.'
(for 'Sesame-Street' [sɛ́.sə.mi.strìt]; [t] anticipated from
onset of 'street' or 'stuff', added to onset of 'Sesame';
source could also be 'might', but less likely than [st]
clusters; B/W; NSC)

3. Phonological anticipations (complete), movements, consonants.

AN-34 2;2.19 An: (reciting nursery rhyme)
'. . . when dòwn [kʰwè⸍m] a [b__ǽk.b3̌d] . . .'
(for 'came a blackbird' [kʰe⸍m a bwǽk.b3̌d]; [w] moved from
initial cluster in 'blackbird', added to form cluster in 'came';
B; +T(s); NSC; p. 119, 145)

AL-20 2;2.25 Al: 'My [çwíp.__tìk] . . . my lípstìck.'
(for 'lipstick' [wíp.çtìk]; [ç] moved from onset of second
syllable, added to onset of first syllable; W; SC; p. 33,
115, 119, 143)

AN-51 2;5.28 An: 'Óh, Ì should gèt that [bɚ.ni] and __ért thìng.'
(for 'Ernie and Bert' [ɚ.ni æn bɚt]; [b] moved from onset of
'Bert', added as onset of 'Ernie'; B; +T(s); NSC)

B-67 2;5.30 B: (pretending to call the dog on Sesame Street):
'Bárkley! Bárkley! I bètter fìnd [blá3̰.k__i]. Bárkley!'
(for 'Barkley' [bá3̰.kḷi]; [l] moved from second syllable
onset of 'Barkley' and added into first syllable onset,
voiced; W; NSC; p. 119)

B-102 2;7.19 B: 'I can [bè⸍k] the [__wídʒ].'
M: 'What?'
B: 'I can màke the brídge.'
(for 'make the bridge' [mè⸍k dʌ bwídʒ]; [b] moved from
onset of 'bridge', substituted for [m] in 'make'; B; +T(s);
NSC)

AL-47 2;8.20 Al: 'Mòmmy, I wànt a [pʰ3̰is ʌ b__έd].'
M: 'What?'
Al: 'I wànt a pìece of bréad.'
(for 'piece of bread' [pʰis ʌ b3̰έd]; [3̰] moved from onset of
'bread', added to onset of 'piece', devoiced; B; +T(s); NSC;
p. 119, 143)

AL-58 2;10.16 Al: 'Sésame-Strèet! I líke [sè.stə.mi.s__3̰ìt]!'
(for 'Sesame-Street' [sé.sə.mi.st3̰ìt]; [t] moved from onset
of 'Street', added to onset of 'Sesame'; W; NSC)

AN-82   2;10.22   An: '[ò^w.pən wì.li __á^jd].'
(for 'open really wide', [ó^w.pən rí.li wa^jd]; [w] moved from onset of 'wide', substituted for onset [r] in 'really'; B; +T(s); NSC)

B-140   3;7.30   B: 'I'll [p^hrɨ.stènd a^j __t^hɨɬ] have diápers.'
(for 'pretend I still' [p^hrɨ.t^hɛ́nd a^j stɨɬ]; [s] moved from onset of 'still', added to onset of 'pretend', /t/ in 'still' aspirates, /t/ in 'pretend' deaspirates; B; -T; NSC)

AN-138   4;0.17   An: 'I'm not [ín.stɹə.__dìd].'
(for 'interested' [ín.tɹə.st(ɨd)]; [s] moved from onset of last syllable, added into onset of second syllable; note voicing of /t/ intervocalically; W; NSC; p. 145)

B-228   4;2.28   B: 'Mòmmy, are yòu gonna [rɔ̃__m] . . . wàrm up my pásta?'
(for 'warm' [wɔrm]; [r] moved from middle of 'warm' to beginning, substituted for [w], vowel becomes nasalized; W; SC)

B-256   4;4.7   B: 'Just càll the Poóch-[p^hṛa.t^h__ò^wɬ].'
(for 'Pooch-Patrol' [p^hútʃ.p^ha.t^hṛò^wɬ]; [r] moved from second syllable of 'Patrol', added to onset of first; W; NSC)

AN-214   4;6.0   An: '[brʌ.kɪŋ b__áŋ.ko].' (looks embarassed, laughs)
(for 'bùcking brónco' [bʌ.kɪŋ bráŋ.ko], here treated as two separate phonological words but possibly a compound; [r] moved from first syllable onset of 'bronco', added to first syllable onset of 'bucking'; B; +T(s); N-NC)

B-441   5;0.30   B: 'Mom, Lìttle [blò^j b__ú] . . . Lìttle Bòy Blúe, blòwed his hórn.'
(for 'Boy Blue' [bo^j blu]; [l] moved from onset of 'blue', added to onset of 'boy'; B; +T(s); SC)

B-444   5;1.3   B: 'Guess whát? Làst time I got ùp befòre the rèst of my [fḷǽm.__i], and I wàtched "Dàrk Wìng Dúck".'
(for 'family' [fǽm.li]; movement of [l] from onset of second syllable, added to onset of first syllable of word; 'last time' means 'yesterday' here; W; N-NC)

AN-301 5;7.19   An: 'It's a [kʰ]ǽ.sə˩ pʰ__èʲ] . . . cástle plàyhouse.'
(for 'castle playhouse' [kʰǽ.sə˩ pʰ]éʲ.hæ̀ʷs]; [l] moved from
first syllable onset of 'playhouse', added to first syllable
onset of 'castle'; B; +T(e); SC; p. 397)

AL-262 5;10.27   Al: (Daddy being funny, naming body parts; says
something about 'arm pits and nose pits')
'[nóʷt pʰì__s]? I ònly have nóstrils.'
(for 'nose pits' [noʷz pʰɪt(s)]; [t] moved from 'pits',
substituted for [z] in 'nose'; B; +T(e); NSC)

4. Phonological anticipations (complete), omissions, consonants.

B-33   2;0.16   B: (pointing at picture of Alice and Anna)
'[æ̀.lə__ ǽ.nə].'
(for 'Alice, Anna' [ǽ.ləç ǽ.nə]; [ç] omitted from second
syllable coda of 'Alice', assimilation to codaless [ə] in
'Anna'; B; list intonation; NSC)

B-60   2;5.13   B: (pointing at pictures of himself and his sisters)
'[__à.bi], Á.lice, Á.nna!'
(for 'Bobby' [bá.bi]; [b] omitted from onset of 'Bobby',
assimilation to onsetless first syllables of 'Alice' and
'Anna'; B; list intonation; NSC)

OC-25   2;8.0   OG: 'This [báʲ__] is stùck.'
(for 'bike' [baʲk]; [k] omitted from coda of 'bike',
dissimilation from coda [k] of 'stuck' [stʌk]; B; +T(e); NSC)

AL-57   2;10.14   An: 'Óne tìme a spíder bìt mè rìght hére!'
Al: 'Well, òne tìme a [__pà ʲ.d3 pìt] mè rìght hére!'
(for 'spider' [spáʲ.d3]; [s] omitted from first syllable onset of
'spider', in assimilation to single-consonant onset /b/ [p] in
'bit'; /p/ in 'spider' not aspirated, so could be a substitution
of /b/ [p] from 'bit' for [sp]; B; -T; NSC; p. 116)

AL-178 3;10.6   Al: 'He's rìght out thère where the [s__íŋ]-sèt ìs.'
(for 'swing-set' [swíŋ.sèt]; [w] omitted from first syllable of
'swing-set', assimilation to single onset [s] of second
syllable; could also be dissimilation from preceding [w] in
'where' [wɛ3], but less likely; W; NSC)

AN-128 3;10.27   An: 'Mòmmy, I'm gètting [b__úm] st̺àws . . . br̺óom
stràws.'
(for 'broom' [brum]; [r] omitted from onset of 'broom',
dissimilation from /r/ in onset of 'straws'; B; +T(e); SC)

B-231   4;3.1   B: (telling Mom what he wants for lunch)
'[ʃá__k]-Pàsta . . . Shár̺k-Pàsta.'
(for 'Shark-Pasta' [ʃár̺k.pʰà.stə]; [r] omitted from coda
cluster of 'Shark', assimilation to nucleus [a] in first
syllable of 'Pasta'; W; SC)

B-236   4;3.9   B: (reciting line of Halloween poem after Dad read it)
'[g__ì.nɪŋ] gò.blins fîghting dúels.'
M: 'Whát kind of gòblins?'
B: 'Grínning!'
(for 'grinning' [grí.nɪŋ]; [r] omitted from onset of 'grinning',
assimilation to single-consonant onset of first syllable of
'goblins'; B; -T; NSC)

B-251   4;4.3   B: (telling a neighbor boy what he had left at our house)
'Yèah, yòur [wí__.stə̃n] . . . Wínston gùn.'
(for 'Winston gun' [wĩn.stə̃n gʌ̃n]; [n] omitted from first
syllable of 'Winston', dissimilation from coda [n] in second
syllable of 'Winston' or from 'gun'; the vowel [ɪ] gets
de-nasalized when nasal is dropped; B/W; SC; p. 120)

B-451   5;1.17   B: (driving by Chenz and Bina's house)
'[tʃèn __] an' Bína.'
(for 'Cenz an' (informal form of 'and') [tʃɛnz æn]; [z]
omitted from coda of 'Cenz', assimilation to single nasal
coda [n] of 'an'; B; -T; NSC)

5. Phonological anticipations (complete), substitutions, vowels.

B-7   1;9.5   B: '[pú.ka.pʉ̀:].'
(for 'peek-a-boo' [pí.ka.pù:]; [i]<--[u]; 2-word stage; W;
NSC; p. 18, 70)

AN-26c 2;1.23   An: (chanting nursery rhyme)
                  'Mòmmy càlled the dóctor and the mòmmỳ [kʰέd] . . .
                  Mòmmy [kʰèl.də] dóctor, and the dòctòr sáid,
                  Mòmmy càlled the dóctor and the dòctòr sáid:
                  Nò mòre mónkeys jùmpin' òn the béd.'
                  (for 'called the' [kʰál.də], source 'said' [sɛd], or 'bed' [bɛd]
                  but less likely; [a]<--[ɛ]; B; +T(s); SC; 26a=Class 43,
                  26b=Class 12; p. 21)

B-85   2;6.21   B: 'I blow mỳ [nùs] tóo Mommy.'
                  (for 'nose' [noʷs], source 'too' [tʰu]; [oʷ]<--[u]; B; +T(s);
                  NSC)

AL-44   2;8.20   Al: (pointing to page in coloring book)
                  'I wànt [stǽmps] òn hère.'
                  M: 'You mean stámps?'
                  Al: 'Yeah.'
                  (for 'stamps' [stæmps], source 'on' [an]; [æ]<--[a]; B; +T(e);
                  NSC)

AL-65   2;10.19   Al: 'Mòmma, thère's a wìcked wìtch, and [d̪ǽwz] . . .
                  her hóuse.'
                  (for 'there's' [d̪ɛwz]; source 'house' [hæws]; [ɛ]<--[æ]; B;
                  +T(s); N-NC)

AL-105 3;3.13   Al: 'Mommy, when wé got Lìttle [ʒàʲd] Rìding Hòod, the
                  wólf came, (etc.)'
                  (for 'Red Riding' [ʒɛd ʒáʲ.dɪŋ]; [ɛ]<--[aʲ]; could be
                  anticipation of morpheme 'ride'; B; -T; NSC; p. 38)

AL-145 3;7.1   Al: 'I lìke [bɔ́g]-Bìrd.'
                  (for 'Big-Bird' [bíg.bɔ̀d]; [ɪ]<--[ɔ]; W; NSC)

OC-56   3;8.0   OG: 'Tòm, when yòu go hóme, [jɚ] hàve to bríng yóurs
                  hòme.'
                  (for 'you' [ju], source 'yours' [jɚz]; [u]<--[ɚ]; could also be
                  lexical selection error 'your'; B; -T; NSC)

B-144   3;8.4   B: (looking at book) 'That's a? umbrèlla with Bíg-Bìrd
ùnder it, èating [tʃí.koʷn], and macarǒni and cheése,
and bróccoli.'
(for 'chicken' [tʃí.kən]; source 'macaroni' [mæ̀.kə.ʒóʷ.ni];
[ə]<-[oʷ]; B; list intonation; NSC; p. 108, 155)

AL-155 3;8.4   Al: (wearing witch costume) 'I will [tʰȁk] it ǒff when I
fínish . . . I will tàke it òff when I fínish.'
(for 'take it off' [tʰeʲk ɪt af]; [eʲ]<--[a]; B; -T; SC)

B-173   3;11.13 B: 'Mom, whàt's the tràshcan [mèʲns] . . . náme?'
(for 'man's name' [mænz neʲm]; [æ]<-[eʲ]; B; +T(s); N-NC)

B-195   4;1.16   B: 'Mòmmy, I'm [mæ̀.kɪŋ] a tràp dòorway for Álice, on
the flóor.'
(for 'making' [méʲ.kɪŋ], source either 'trap' [tʰɹæp] or 'Alice'
[ǽ.ləs]; [eʲ]<--[æ]; B; T?; NSC)

AL-210 4;2.27   Al: 'Yòu do thóse, and Ì'll [dì] thése.'
(for 'do these' [du ðiz]]; [u]<--[i]; B; +T(s); NSC)

AN-207 4;5.26   An: 'Thèy have [pʰáʲ.ǹ.pə+] ìn them.'
M: 'They have whát?'
An: 'Píneapple.'
(for 'pineapple in them' [pʰáʲ.næ̀.pə+ ɪn ðɪm]; [æ]<--[ɪ]; B;
-T; NSC)

AL-233 4;9.13   Al: 'I had [gʒéʲ.ɪŋ]-pàɪns, and thòse gro͟w͟ing-pàins hùrt
tòo múch.'
(for 'growing-pains' [gʒóʷ.ɪŋ.pʰèʲnz]; [oʷ]<--[eʲ]; compound,
since she didn't use these words outside the compound; W;
NSC)

B-438   5;0.29   B: (telling a friend how to build with plastic blocks)
'[sə.pʰʊ̀.stə] pùt it like thís.'
(for 'supposed-to put' [sə.pʰóʷ.stə pʰʊt]; [oʷ]<-[ʊ]; B; -T;
NSC)

B-528   5;6.4   B: 'My [bís.kɚts] are bùrnin'.'
(for 'biscuts are burnin' (burning) [bís.kəts ɚ bɚ́.nɪn];
[ə]<--[ɚ]; B; -T; NSC)

B-565   5;10.15   B: 'Mòmmy, tàke mè on a [wɚ̀k] fírst!'
(for 'walk first' [wak fɚst]; [a]<--[ɚ]; B; +T(s); NSC; p. 113)

6. Phonological anticipations (complete), substitutions, larger units.

AN-23   2;0.14   An: (reciting nursery rhyme) 'I said [nɔ̀r] mòre mónkeys!'
(for 'no more', [noʷ mɔr]; rhymes [oʷ]<--[ɔr]; B; -T; NSC)

AL-25   2;4.8   Al: 'Mè wànt a [fĩnt]-wrínkles.' (for 'fruit-wrinkles',
[fwùt.wíŋ.kɘɫz]; [wu]<--[ĩŋ], with place assimilation; 'a' is
filler function word; W; NSC; p. 63)

B-52   2;4.17   B: 'That's a [dʌ.k3]-dècker bús right thère!'
(for 'double-decker' [dʌ.bʊ.dɛ́.k(3)]; syllables [bʊ]<--[k3];
compound, because he doesn't otherwise use the word
'decker'; W; NSC; p. 129, 149)

AN-64   2;8.12   An: 'Àlice Eiléen, mỳ [kʰw̥ì.dow] Quéen.'
(for 'little queen', [lì.dow kʰwín]; onsets [l]<--[kʰw̥]; B;
+T(s); NSC)

AN-87   2;11.0   An: '[wíŋk.bɪ̃ntʃ].'
(for 'workbench', [wɚk.bɪ̃ntʃ]; [ɚ]<--[ɪ̃ŋ], with place
assimilation; W; NSC; p. 151)

AL-82   2;11.18   Al: 'Mom, òpen my [fʒĩnt-ʒíŋ.kɘɫz].'
M: 'Your whát?'
Al: 'Frùit-wrínkles.'
(for 'fruit-wrinkles' [fʒùt.ʒíŋ.kɘɫz]; [u]<--[ĩŋ], with place
assimilation; W; NSC)

AL-116   3;3.27   M: (Alice teasing Bobby) 'Alice, lèave him alóne.'
Al: 'I was [dʒɪk] tíckling hìm.' (hesitated, looked
sheepish)
(for 'just tickling' [dʒʌst tʰík.ɫ.ɪŋ]; rhymes [ʌst]<--[ɪk]; B;
+T(s); N-NC; p. 22)

AL-125   3;4.13   Al: (picking out a video to watch) 'Anna, do yóu wànt to
wàtch the [tʰʌ̀ŋ.kɪŋ] . . . pùnkin one fìrst?'
(for 'talking punkin (pumpkin)' [tʰá.k(ɪŋ) pʰʌ́ŋ.kɪn]; rhymes
[a]<--[ʌŋ]; B; -T; N-NC)

AL-162 3;8.28   Al: 'I wànna tèll [mʌ́m.θi] sòmethïng.'
                  (for 'mommy something' [má.mi sʌ́m.θɪŋ]; [a.m]<--[ʌm.θ];
                  B; +T(e);NSC; p. 150)

AL-185 3;10.23   Al: 'Whỳ is [ʒ̣ì.kɪŋ] rúnnïng?'
                  (for 'Ricky running' [ʒ̣í.ki ʒ̣ʌ́.n(ɪŋ)]; [i]<--[ɪŋ], but could be
                  morphological; B; -T; NSC)

B-258   4;4.9   B: (telling Mom something that happened at the mall)
                  'And the mónster said: "Yòu're going to [fò⅃] the
                  fún!" '
                  (for 'spoil' [spo⅃]; onsets [sp]<--[f]; B; +T(s); NSC)

AN-189 4;5.4   An: 'We're [dʒʌk] gonna chèck out what Dáddy's dòin.'
                  (for 'just' [dʒʌst]; codas [st]<--[k]; B; -T; NSC)

B-457   5;1.24   B: 'He looks like a grèat [brǽŋk]-dä̀ncer.'
                  (for 'break-dancer' [bréʲk.dæ̀n.sɚ], [eʲ]<--[æn], with place
                  assimilation; W; NSC; p. 66)

B-540   5;7.2   B: (telling the end of a story)
                  'And hè was a [bjù.ɾɨ.fɚ] . . . bútterfly.'
                  (for 'beautiful butterfly' [bjú.ɾɨ.fʊ⅃ bʌ́.ɾɚ.fḷaʲ]; rhymes
                  [ʊl]<--[ɚ]; B; -T; p. 155)

7. Phonological anticipations (incomplete), substitutions, consonants.

B-6   1;9.3   B: (after giving his Mom a kiss) '[kè.wiʔ] . . . Jèri ḱiss.'
                  (for 'Jeri kiss' [tè.wiʔ kíç]; [t]<--[k]; 2-word stage; B; +T(s);
                  SC; p. 70)

AL-23   2;4.2   Al: 'A blùe [pʰá.wi] . . . no . . . [w̲á.wi.pʰàp].'
                  (for 'lollipop' [wá.wi.pʰàp]; [w]<--[pʰ]; W; SC)

B-57   2;5.10   B: (telling Mom what he saw at the zoo)
                  'I [nì] the . . . I s̲ee the (s)nákes!'
                  (for 'see' [si]; source is 'snakes' [neʲks], i.e. usually
                  pronounced without [s]; [s]<--[n]; B; +T(s); SC)

B-99   2;7.12   B: 'I hàfta wèar my [dǽn] . . . sándals.'
(for 'sandals' [sǽn.dəɫs]; [s]<--[d]; W; SC)

B-106   2;8.7   B: '[mèʲk] . . . wàke úp Mǐss.'
(for 'wake' [weʲk]; [w]<--[m]; B; +T(s); SC)

AN-79   2;10.11   An: 'Mommy, "[rì.stɚ] . . . Mìster Rògers'
Néighborhood"!'
(for 'mister' [mí.stɚ]; source most likely 'Rogers', but
possibly also the vowels [ɚ]; [m]<--[r]; B; -T; SC)

B-117   2;10.11   B: 'I have òne [mǽ] . . . páckage Mòm.'
(for 'package' [pʰǽ.kɪdʒ]; [pʰ]<--[m]; B; +T(e); SC)

AN-86   2;10.27   An: 'I don't know hów you [lèʲ] . . . hów you say 'ʔòt'. '
(for 'say' [seʲ]; [s]<--[l]; B; -T; SC)

AL-79   2;11.17   Al: 'Mòm, lèt's gò to a [skò̰ʒ] . . . stòre where a hàve
cóffee.'
(for 'store' [sto̰ʒ]; 'a' is filler function word; [t]<--[k]; B;
+T(s); SC)

AL-85   3;0.7   Al: 'That's her nó . . . tóenàil.'
(for 'toenail' [tʰóʷ.neɫ]; [tʰ]<--[n]; W; SC)

OC-45   3;3.5   OB: (naming pictures in book)
'[hì.toʷ] . . . hìppopótamus.'
(for 'hippopotamus' [hì.poʷ.pʰá.tə.məs]; [p]<--[t]; W; SC)

OC-46   3;3.5   OB: (naming pictures in book)
'[pʰɪks] . . . nah . . . sìx pénguins.'
(for 'six' [sɪks]; [s]<--[pʰ]; B; +T(s); SC, with 'nah' as if
saying 'no' to self)

AL-104   3;3.11   Al: 'I get [glʌ́m.pi] . . . grúmpy whèn I sɫeep.'
(for 'grumpy' [gʒʌ́m.pi]; [ʒ̰]<--[l]; B; +T(e); SC; p. 29)

AL-127   3;4.16   Al: (trying to fold up a blanket) 'Mòmmy, could yòu
please [hòʷ] me . . . shòw me hòw ta dó thìs? I càn't
dò it ríght.'
(for 'show' [ʃoʷ], source 'how' [hæʷ]; [h]<--[ʃ]; B; -T; SC)

AL-132 3;4.19   Al: 'I [skɪɫ] . . . st̬ill c̈an't f̈ind skúnk̇ie.'
(for 'still' [stɪɫ]; [t]<--[k]; B; T?; SC)

AL-149 3;7.13   Al: 'Mòmmy, I [pʰàɫd] . . . I c̥àlled the trùck "P̈óopie
Bràin". '
(for 'called' [kʰaɫd]; [kʰ]<--[pʰ]; B; +T(s); SC)

AL-153 3;7.19   Al: 'Nòw we have [lʌn] . . . óne l̇èft.'
(for 'one left' [wʌn lɛft]; [w]<--[l]; B; +T(e); SC; p. 29)

OC-57   3;8.0   OA: 'Whò's thís?' (pointing to photo)
OG: '[kʰ]l̥ìs] . . . Chr̥istian and Ál̇ice.'
(for 'Christian' [kʰr̥ís.tʃən] and 'Alice' [ǽ.lɨs]; [r]<--[l]; B; -T;
SC)

B-149   3;8.15   B: (talking about what to do if accosted by a stranger)
'Tomòrrow, a [st̬ʒéʲŋ.g3] . . . a stránger's g̈ònna còme
up to mè, and Ȉ'm gònna rùn awáy.'
(for 'stranger' [st̬ʒéʲn.dʒ(3)], source 'gonna' [gʌ́.nʌ];
[dʒ]<--[g], with place assimilation of nasal; B; -T; SC;
p. 120)

AL-161 3;8.28   Al: 'Thìs is my [wæ̀] . . . m̬àgic ẅánd.'
(for 'magic wand' [mǽ.dʒɪk wand]; [m]<--[w]; B; +T(s); SC)

AL-169 3;9.4   Al: (singing) 'Whèn you [wìs:ʔ . . . ʃ:] upòn a sẗár, (etc.)'
(for 'wish' [wɪʃ]; [ʃ]<--[s]; B; +T(s); SC immediately after
error segment)

AN-123 3;10.1   An: 'I put [ǽ.sə̀ɫ] . . . I put ápp̥le̥sàu̇ce ȍn me.'
(for 'applesauce' [ǽ.pəɫ.sàs]; [p]<--[s]; W; SC; p. 64)

B-170   3;10.5   B: 'Mòm, I hàve to [ʒúʃ] . . . púsh the r̥èd bùtton.'
(for 'push' [pʰʊʃ]; source 'red' [ʒ̥ɛd]; [pʰ]<--[ʒ̥]; B; +T(e); SC;
p. 113)

AL-182 3;10.20   Al: 'Look at the [pʰís] . . . pìc̥nic-bàṡket.'
(for 'picnic-basket' [pʰík.nɪk.bæ̀s.kɨt]; [k]<--[s]; W; SC;
p. 63)

AL-194 3;11.14   Al: 'Can I tàste some [fí.ri] . . . fízzy-wàter?'
(for 'fizzy-water' [fí.z(i).wà.rɚ]; [z]<--[ɾ] /t/; source could
also be 'taste', but less likely since 'water' has a tap in
the same prosodic position; W; SC; p. 159)

B-179 4;0.20   B: 'He lìves [ə.tʃràs] . . . he lives acròss the streét.'
(for 'across' [ə.kʰrás], source 'street' [stʃrit]; [kʰ]<-[tʃ]; B;
+T(s); SC; p. 123)

OC-85 4;1.0   OG: (explaining why she didn't want to see "Jurassic Park"
movie) 'Becàuse the dìnosaurs get òut of their [tʃéʲ]
. . . cáges, and chàse èveryone aróund!'
(for 'cages' [kʰéʲ.dʒis]; [kʰ]<--[tʃ]; B; +T(e) SC)

B-188 4;1.9   B: (very excited after hearing thunder)
'I hèard a [sʌn] . . . a thúnderstòrm!'
(for 'thunderstorm' [θʌn.dɚ.stòrm]; [θ]<--[s]; W; SC)

B-190 4;1.14   B: 'The dràin is too smàll for [pʰíg] . . . bíg pèople to
go dòwn.'
(for 'big' [bɪg]; [b]<-[pʰ], as first /p/ in 'people' is most
likely source; B; +T(e); SC)

AN-150 4;1.24   An: 'Mòmma, does thìs got [sé.rə] . . . does thìs got
célery in it?'
(for 'celery' [sé.lə.ri]; [l]<--[r]; W; SC)

AN-154 4;1.29   An: 'I wànna [màˀt] . . . I wànna wríte sòmething on my
árm.'
(for 'write' [raˀt]; [r]<--[m]; B; T?; SC)

B-206 4;2.0   B: (after being told to pick up his room so it would look
nice) 'I don't wánt it to [lùs . . . k] nìce.'
(for 'look' [lʊk]; [k]<--[s]; B; -T; SC immediately after
erroneous segment)

B-212 4;2.6   B: (discussing Anna taking a shower)
'Dòes she wànt a [kʰàt] . . . hòt or cóld òne?'
(for 'hot' [hat]; [h]<--[kʰ]; B; +T(s); SC)

B-221 4;2.18   B: 'Nò, nò, nó! I càn't [fèˀnt] . . . pàint my fáce.'
(for 'paint' [pʰeˀnt]; [pʰ]<--[f]; B; +T(s); SC)

AN-161 4;2;21   An: '[pʰæm] . . . [pʰæm] . . .' (gives up)
(target: 'shampoo' [ʃæm.pʰúː]; [ʃ]<--[pʰ]; W; N-NC)

B-223   4;2.23   B: 'Nòw can I [pʰàɫ] . . . càll Páulie again?'
(for 'call' [kʰaɫ]; [kʰ]<--[pʰ]; B; +T(s); SC)

AN-183 4;4.27   An: (discussing a series of books)
'Nòw it sàys [tʰìk] . . . nòw it sàys sìxtéen.'
(for 'sixteen' [sìks.tʰín]; [s]<--[tʰ]; could be perseveration
from 'it', but unlikely; W; SC; p. 128)

B-269   4;4.30   B: '[nìn.eⁱdʒ] . . . Tèenage Mùtant Nìnja Túrtles!'
(for 'teenage' [tʰìn.eⁱdʒ]; [tʰ]<--[n], but if the second [n] in
'Teenage' is the source, this is Class 1; B/W; SC; p. 63)

B-273   4;5.0   B: (telling what kinds of things one uses an electric mixer
to prepare) ' . . . but nòt the [pʰlù.bɛ.ri] mìx . . . nòt
the blùeberry mìx or the páncake mìx.'
(for 'blueberry' [blú.bɛ.ri]; [b]<--[pʰ]; B; +T(s); SC)

B-283   4;5.12   B: (being silly while stirring ice cream)
'I'm swìrling it to anòther [mə] . . . diménsion.'
(for 'dimension' [də.mín.tʃʌn]; [d]<--[m]; W; SC)

AL-218 4;5.12   Al: (looking in "Disney Magazine")
'I'll shòw you where I [pʰæ͏ʷnd] . . . I fòund Pèe Wee
Hérman.'
(for 'found' [fæ͏ʷnd]; [pʰ]<--[f]; B; -T; SC)

AN-197 4;5.12   An: 'Mòm, remèmber when Gràndpa Chét sàid "No [fígz]
. . . no pígs' fèet for dìnner."?'
(for 'pigs' ' [pʰɪgz]; [pʰ]<--[f]; B, but 'pigs' feet' could be a
compound; +T(e); SC)

AL-222 4;5.21   Al: 'I [hòʷm] I can fìnd . . . I hòpe I can fìnd my
hómewòrk bòok.'
(for 'hope' [hoʷp]; [p]<--[m]; source could also be 'my', but
less likely; B; +T(s); SC)

AL-226 4;6.3   Al: (reciting poem) 'Lèave them alòne and thèy'll come
hóme, and their [wèɫz] . . . their tàils will be
wàgging behìnd thèm.'
(for 'tails' [tʰeɫz]; [tʰ]<--[w]; B; -T; SC; p. 64)

B-306   4;6.15   B: ' 'Cuz they didn't [ì.vəs] . . . èven sée ùs.'
(for 'even see us' [í.vən si ʌs]; [n]<--[s]; B; T?; SC)

AN-224 4;6.26   An: 'Mòmmy, [bà.ri] . . . Bòbby còvered my mòuth with
his hánd!'
(for 'Bobby' [bá.bi]; [b]<--[d], then becomes a tap; B; T?;
SC; p. 118)

B-313   4;6.27   B: ('reading' what the hen says in a book)
' "Hàve a nice [béʲ] . . . dáy, bák bák bák".'
(for 'day' [deʲ]; [d]<--[b]; B; +T(b); SC)

B-324   4;7.7   B: 'I think they're [mèʲ.sɪŋ] . . . màking quèsadíllas at
schòol todày.'
(for 'making' [méʲ.k(ɪŋ)], source most likely 'quesadillas'
[kʰèʲ.sə.dí.jəz]; [k]<--[s]; B; -T; SC)

B-325   4;7.8   B: 'Evèry dày the [kʰɚ.r̩z] . . . Tùrtles còme òut of the
sèwer.'
(for 'Turtles' [tʰɚ.r̩z]; [tʰ]<--[kʰ]; B; -T; SC)

B-334   4;7.16   B: 'Mom, can you open the [sì.mə.tɨn] . . . Cìnnamon
Tòast Crúnch?'
(for 'Cinnamon' [sí.mə.nɨn]; note that his usual
pronunciation has metathesis of nasals; [n]<--[tʰ], then
deaspirated; B, but 'Cinnamon Toast' could be a
compound; -T; SC)

AN-229 4;7.19   An: '[blèʲ] . . . Bràve Hèart Líon.'
(for 'brave' [breʲv]; [r]<--[l]; B; +T(s); SC)

B-339   4;7.19   B: (pointing to a picture of a building with an eyeball
over the doorway)
'Sèe that éyeball right there? Thàt's why it's [tʰàɫd]
. . . that's why it's càlled the "Téchnodròme".'
(for 'called' [kʰaɫd]; [tʰ]<--[kʰ]; B; +T(s); SC)

B-364   4;9.15   B: (telling Mom the name of a book)
' "The Vèry Hùngry [kʰǽ.lə] . . . Cáterpìllar".'
(for 'caterpillar' [kʰǽ.rə.pʰì.lɚ]; [r] /t/ <--[l]; W; SC)

AN-244 4;9.25   An: ('reading' book) 'So Mìckey sàid "Whàt's the fúss?
                 Ì get mìlk the [wí.ki] . . . the Míckey wày".'
                 (for 'Mickey' [mí.ki]; [m]<--[w]; could be perseveration
                 from 'what', but less likely; B; +T(e); SC)

B-381   4;10.12 B: 'I wanna see [fræ̀ŋ.kən.staⁱdz] . . . Frànkenstein's
                 Brìde.'
                 (for 'Frankenstein's Bride' [fræ̀ŋ.kən.staⁱn(z) braⁱd];
                 [n]<--[d]; B; +T(s); SC; p. 159)

B-388   4;10.20 B: 'Mòm, lóok! I gòt a sáilbòat. And a [ʃí] . . .
                 séashèll.'
                 (for 'seashell' [sí.ʃèɫ]; [s]<--[ʃ]; W; SC)

AL-236 4;10.23 Al: (looking at pictures of swimming pools) 'There's a
                 déep one that hàs a [bàʲ] . . . dìving bòard.'
                 (for 'diving-board' [dáʲ.vɪŋ.bo̰d]; [d]<--[b]; W; SC)

B-398   4;11.0   B: 'I knòw lóts of thìngs that [spàrt] . . . stàrt with "B̀". '
                 (for 'start' [start]; source 'B' [pi]; [t]<--[p]; B; -T; SC)

B-427   4;11.25 B: (makes wierd sound)
                 'Càn [gʌ.líʔ] . . . càn gori̲llas dò thàt?'
                 (for 'gorillas' [gʌ.rí.ləz]; [r]<--[l]; W; SC)

OC-131 5;0.10   OB: 'Well, I had a [gri̋] . . . a dréam about a Chìnese
                 gìrl.'
                 (for 'dream' [drím]; [d]<--[g]; B; +T(e); SC)

B-431   5;0.12   B: (telling Mom what's on TV)
                 'This is "Fàmily [dʌ́.br̩] . . . Doúble-Dàre". It just
                 stárted.'
                 (for 'Double-Dare' [dʌ́.bɫ.dèr]; [ɫ]<--[r], then [r] becomes
                 syllabic; W; SC)

B-434   5;0.20   B: 'I wànna stày hòme and [kʰà] . . . wàtch cartoóns.'
                 (for 'watch' [watʃ]; [w]<--[kʰ]; B; -T; SC)

B-440   5;0.29   B: (talking about a Batman toy)
                 'This [dʒù] . . . this shòots the Jòker's fáce òff there.'
                 (for 'shoots' [ʃuts]; [ʃ]<--[dʒ]; B; -T; SC)

B-464   5;2.1   B: 'Mòmmy, on "[dʌ́.br̩]" . . . on "Dóuble-Dàre" làst
                     tìme?'
                     (for 'Double-Dare' [dʌ́.bɫ.dèr]; [ɫ]<--[r], then [r] becomes
                     syllabic; W; SC; p. 151)

B-467   5;2.5   B: (talking about driving)
                     'Do you [skà] . . . sṭòp qúickly on thìs?'
                     (for 'stop quickly' [stap kʰẉɪ́k.li]; [t]<--[kʰ], then [k]
                     deaspirates; most likely source is first /k/ in 'quickly'; B;
                     +T(s); SC)

B-470   5;2.8   B: 'Whỳ did you bè a cóllege [pʰɚ.sὲ] . . . profѐssor?'
                     (for 'professor' [pʰɚ.fέ.sɚ]; [f]<--[s]; W; SC)

B-474   5;3.10   B: 'Snàcks rìght [ǽf.tɫ̩] . . . rìght àfter spécials.'
                     (for 'after specials' [ǽf.tr̩ spέ.ʃɫ̩(z)]; [r]<--[ɫ]; B; -T; SC)

AN-285 5;4.5   An: (talking about whether or not dogs can talk) 'But they
                     [tʰǽnt] . . . but they c̲àn't t̲àlk t̲o pèople lìke ús.'
                     (for 'can't' [kʰænt]; 'but' is [bʌʔ]; if the source is the coda /t/
                     in 'can't', then this is Class 1; [kʰ]<--[tʰ]; B/W; -T; SC)

B-494   5;4.22   B: 'Can Ì have some [sẉɪtʃ] . . . Swìss ch̲éese plèase?'
                     (for 'Swiss' [sẉɪs]; [s]<-[tʃ]; B; +T(s); SC)

B-500   5;5.8   B: (telling what kind of cereal he wanted, with emphatic
                     stress) 'Sùgar [fḷá:] . . . Fŕósted Fl̲àkes.'
                     (for 'Frosted Flakes' [fɹás.təd flḙˡks]; [r]<--[l]; B, but
                     possibly a compound; +T(e); SC)

B-503   5;5.24   B: '[wèr] . . . wѐl̲l̲, thѐre's this bág, and (etc.). . .'
                     (for 'well there's' [wɛɫ ðɛr(z)]; [ɫ]<--[r]; B; -T; SC)

B-507   5;5.24   B: 'Nìce [dʒù.k] . . . jùic̲y stéak̲!'
                     (for 'juicy steak' [dʒú.s(i) steˡk]; [s]<--[k]; B; +T(s); SC)

B-539   5;6.27   B: 'The [bɪ̀ɫ] . . . the bìg gúl̲p I hàd.'
                     (for 'big gulp' [bɪg gʌ́ɫp]; [g]<--[l]; B; +T(s); SC)

AN-290 5;6.30   An: '[sìŋk] . . . [sìŋk] . . . th̲ìnk of s̲òmebody éls̲e.'
                     (for 'think' [θɪŋk]; [θ]<--[s]; B; T?; SC)

B-547   5;7.9   B: 'But I hàve to [skæ̀n] . . . stànd guárd.'
(for 'stand guard' [stæn kard]; [t]<--[k]; B; +T(s); SC)

OC-156   5;7.14   OB: (watching a TV show)
'Tinà's sistèr's [fǽt] . . . hát fèll òff.'
(for 'hat' [hæt]; [h]<--[f]; B; +T(e); SC)

AN-316   5;9.21   An: (telling what she wants for breakfast)
'Jùst a pìece of [tʰí.n] . . . cìnnamon-tòast.'
(for 'cinnamon-toast' [sí.nə.mən.tʰòᵂst]; [s]<--[tʰ]; source
could also be 'jusť or 'toasť, but less likely; W; SC)

AL-264   5;11.1   Al: 'Mommy, Ì want this [ræ̀st] . . . làst róll for my
dìnner.'
(for 'last' [læst]; [l]<--[r]; source most likely 'roll'; B; +T(s);
SC)

AN-326   5;11.15   An: 'Mòmma, [bàⁱks] . . . Mìke's got a B́ig-Whèel!'
(for 'Mike's' [maⁱks]; [m]<--[b]; 'Big-Wheel' is a kind of
bike; B; +T(s); SC)

AN-327   5;11.18   An: 'Jèan Stàpleton is the [mèr] . . . Fàiry Gòdmòther in
Cìnderélla.'
(for 'fairy' [fé.ri gád.mλ.ðɚ]; [f]<--[m]; B; -T; SC)

B-579   5;11.19   B: (watching a cartoon which he had seen before)
'I lóve this pàrt. He's nòt rèally [sẃip] . . .
slḛepẁàlking.'
(for 'sleepwalking' [slíp.wà.kɪŋ]; [l]<--[w], then [w]
devoices; W; SC)

B-585   5;11.25   B: (talking about some cookies) 'They're càlled [sàk] . . .
chòcolate sándwiches, but they're rèally Óreos.'
(for 'chocolate' [tʃák.lɪt]; [tʃ]<--[s]; B; +T(s); SC)

8. Phonological anticipations (incomplete), additions, consonants.

AN-7   1;7.20   M: 'Is that a smáll hòuse?'
An: '[máʷç h. . .]' (gets confused, stops)
(for 'small house' [maʷ haʷç]; [ç] anticipated from coda of
'house' added as coda of 'small'; B; +T(e); N-NC; p. 405)

B-27   1;11.12   An: 'Càn yòu sày "Álice" ?'
B: '[læ] . . . Álice.' (for 'Alice' [ǽ.lɛs]; [l] anticipated
from onset of second syllable of 'Alice,' added as onset of
first, possibly metathesis; 2-word stage; W; SC)

B-82   2;6.19   B: 'Daddy, I càn't [flàˀnd] . . . I càn't fìnd my plᴀ́ne.'
(for 'find' [faˀnd]; [l] anticipated from onset of 'plane' added
into onset of 'find'; B; +T(s); SC)

B-101   2;7.19   B: 'Mommy, what's thís? A [pʰléʲ.p3] . . . a páper-cl ìp?'
(for 'paper-clip' [pʰéʲ.p3.kʰlìp]; [l] anticipated from onset of
'clip', added to onset of 'paper; W; SC)

OC-53   3;5.18   OG: (coming into the kitchen where her mother was
making sandwiches with bread; reporting on child's
activity in the bedroom)
'I'm dòing it in the [bréd] . . . in the bédròom.'
(for 'bedroom' [béd.rùm]; [r] anticipated from onset of
'room', added to onset of 'bed'; could also be lexical
selection error 'bread'; W; SC)

OC-68   3;10.0   OG: 'Mòmmy, I hàve [sə.nʌ̀] . . . anòther surpríse for
yòu.'
(for 'another' [ə.nʌ́.ðɜ]; [s] anticipated from onset of
'surprise', added as onset of 'another'; B; -T; SC)

AL-183   3;10.22   Al: 'Hère's my [blǽθ] . . . báth slìppers.'
(for 'bath' [bæθ]; [l] anticipated from onset of 'slippers',
added to onset of 'bath'; B; +T(e); SC)

AN-153   4;1.29   An: 'Mòmma, Kàtie's a [skíd] . . . Mòmma, Kàtie's a . . .
Kàtie's . . . Kàtie's a kíd-scòut.'
(for 'kid-scout' [kʰíd.skæ̀ʷt]; [s] anticipated from 'scout',
added to onset of 'kid', causing /k/ to become deaspirated;
W; SC, after several tries)

B-232   4;3.3   B: 'Mom, when thìs is óver, you can tùrn the [pʰḷéⁱdʒ] . . .
tùrn the páge, and rèad the lúllabìes.'
(for 'page' [pʰeⁱdʒ]; [l] anticipated most likely from onset of
'lullabies', but also second onset is possible source, added
to onset of 'page', devoiced; B; +T(b) probably; SC)

AN-171 4;4.2   An: (anticipating eating a cupcake)
'I can't [wèⁱst] . . . I can't wàit to táste it.'
(for 'wait' [weⁱt]; [s] anticipated from coda of 'taste', added
to coda of 'wait'; B; +T(s); SC; p. 149)

B-289   4;5.24   B: (explaining a commercial) 'It's nòt "Kày Bèe [stó:]
. . . Tóy Stòres", it's "Pláymàtes".'
(for 'toy stores' [tʰóⁱ stòrz]; [s] anticipated from 'Stores',
added to onset of 'Toy' causing the /t/ to deaspirate; source
could also be 'its', but less likely; B; +T(e); SC)

B-292   4;5.27   B: '[stú] . . . twó stòries will cheèr me ùp.'
(for 'two' [tʰu]; [s] anticipated from 'stories', added to onset
of 'two' causing /t/ to deaspirate; B; +T(e); SC)

AN-221 4;6.18   An: 'I'm gòing to tèll you [stú] . . . twó stòries.'
(for 'two' [tʰu]; [s] anticipated from 'stories', added to onset
of 'two' causing /t/ to deaspirate; B; +T(e); SC)

B-333   4;7.16   B: 'Lèt's [sṇàⁱn] ùp . . . sìgn ùp to brìng a snáck,
plèase!?'
(for 'sign' [saⁱn]; [n] anticipated, most likely from onset of
'snack', although coda from 'sign' is possible, added to
onset of 'sign', devoiced; B/W; SC)

B-384   4;10.16 B: (being silly at the table, to the tune of "Here Comes
the Bride") 'Plèase [pʰṛǽs] . . . pàss the brí́de.'
(for 'pass' [pʰæs]; [r] anticipated from onset of 'bride', added
into onset of 'pass', devoiced; B; +T(s); SC)

AN-259 4;11.13 An: 'Ali, [gàs] . . . Òscar's gréen!'
(for 'Oscar's' [ás.kɚz]; [g] anticipated from onset of 'green',
added as onset of 'Oscar'; B; +T(s); SC)

B-424   4;11.17   B: (telling about a dream he had)
'And we [θɾàt] . . . thòught tròlls wɛre rɛál!'
(for 'thought' [θat]; [r] anticipated, added to onset of
'thought'; most likely source is the onset of 'trolls', but the
onset of 'real' and the vowel in 'were' are possible sources;
B; T?; SC)

B-433   5;0.19   B: (telling about how to set up StringRacer toy with door
knob) 'You hàve to [tʰàⁱp] it . . . tìe it tò my knób.'
(for 'tie' [tʰaʲ]; source 'knob' [na:p]; [p] anticipated from
coda of 'knob', added as coda of 'tie'; B; +T(s); SC)

AN-275 5;2.1   An: (explaining TV previews)
'Mòmma, they [ʃòr] which ònes . . . they shòw which
ònes are gònna bè òn néxt.'
(for 'show' [ʃoʷ], source 'are' [ar]; [r] added, replaces
offglide [w]; B; -T; SC)

B-473   5;3.0   B: 'Mommy, I nèed my [bɪɫg] . . . my Bíg-Whèeler.'
(for 'Big-Wheeler' [bíg.wì.l(ɚ)]; [l] added to coda,
velarizes; W; SC)

B-480   5;3.25   B: (telling Mom about a television show)
'It was "Bùgs Bùnny a [stór.li] . . . a stórytèller"?
And (etc.).'
(for 'storyteller' [stó.ri.tʰɛ̀.l(ɚ)]; [l] anticipated from fourth
syllable of 'storyteller', added as onset in second syllable,
causing the [r] to resyllabify with the preceding syllable;
W; SC; p. 159)

B-543a 5;7.3   B: 'We [sl̥à] . . . we sàw a rèal squírrel . . . snaíl, I
mean.'
(for 'saw' [sa]; [l] anticipated from coda of 'real' or
'squirrel', added to onset of 'saw', devoiced; B; T?;
SC; 543b=Class35)

AN-309 5;8.23   An: ' . . . so wè had to [dʒràk] . . . dràw Jáck.'
(for 'draw Jack' [dʒra dʒæk]; [k] anticipated from coda of
'Jack', added as coda of 'draw'; not telescoping, from
intonation; B; +T(s); SC)

B-560   5;10.3   B: 'I rèally dó wànt Sùper-[skò"] . . . Sùper-Sòaker Twò
Thòusand, fòr my bírthday!' ('Super-Soaker 2000' is a
large squirt gun)
(for 'soaker' [sóʷ.k(ɚ)]; [k] anticipated from onset of second
syllable of 'Soaker', added into onset of first syllable; W;
SC)

B-563   5;10.6   B: (telling what people put into Super-Soakers)
' . . . or [fḷèᵏk] . . . fàke blóod!'
(for 'fake blood' [feᵏk blʌd]; [l] anticipated from onset of
'blood', added to onset of 'fake', devoiced; B; +T(s); SC)

AL-265 5;11.14   Al: (talking about Cinderella's sister) 'She thìnks she
lòoks so [ɛ́.glə] . . . élegant, that the prìnce should
márry her!'
(for 'elegant' [ɛ́.lə.gənt]; [g] anticipated from third syllable
of 'elegant', added to onset of second syllable; W; SC)

9. Phonological anticipations (incomplete), omissions, consonants.

AN-71   2;9.20   An: 'Dàddy, I [b__àt] . . . I br̥òught thrée mòvies.'
(for 'brought' [brat]; [r] omitted from onset of 'brought',
dissimilation from onset [r] in 'three'; could also be lexical
selection error; B; +T(s); SC)

AL-195 3;11.16   Al: 'Watch out for [s__ l̥ìn.t3s] . . . splìnters when you
sléep on it.'
(for 'splinters' [splín.t3z]; [p] omitted from onset cluster of
'splinters', assimilation to onset [sl̥] cluster in 'sleep'; B;
+T(s); SC; 3-44a)

AL-204 4;1.25   Al: 'You knòw the [__ȝ̊ɪ̀ntʃ] . . . the Grìnch is rèal mád!'
(for 'Grinch is real' [gȝ̊ɪntʃ ɪs ȝ̊ɨɫ]; [g] omitted from onset
cluster in 'Grinch', assimilation to single [r] onset of 'real';
B; -T; SC)

AN-198 4;5.15   An: 'Mòmmy, tàke mý pìcture.'
M: 'OK, what do you want to be dóing?'
An: 'Just stànding hère plàying with my [s__ìt] . . . my
Swèet Sécrets.'
(for 'Sweet Secrets' (a kind of doll) [swìt sí.kríts]; [w]
omitted from onset cluster of 'Sweet', most likely in
assimilation to the single [s] onset of 'Secrets'; could also
be dissimilation from 'with', but less likely; B, but
'Sweet Secrets' may be a compound; +T(s); SC)

OC-150 5;6.7   OG: (discussing casting of "The Wizard of Oz")
'Whò's the [s__ér] . . . whò's the scárecròw?'
(for 'scarecrow' [skér.kʰɹòʷ]; [k] omitted in onset of first
syllable of 'scarecrow', dissimilation from [k] in onset of
second syllable; W; SC)

AN-303 5;7.28   An: 'Daddy, I gèt ta [s__ìp] . . . I gèt ta slèep on Álice's
sìde tonìght.'
(for 'sleep' [slip]; [l] omitted from onset cluster of 'sleep',
either dissimilation from [l] in 'Alice', or assimilation to
single [s] onset in 'side'; B; -T; SC)

AL-258 5;9.30   Al: (after getting down from the roof where she and her
cousins had been watching fireworks)
'Mom, we were stàndin' on tòp of Sèan and [g__éʲ.g]
. . . Sèan and Grégory's bèdroom.'
(for 'Gregory' [gréʲ.gə.ri]; [r] omitted from onset of first
syllable of 'Gregory', either assimilation to the single [g]
onset of the second syllable, or dissimilation from the [r] in
'bedroom'; B/W, +T(e); SC)

10. Phonological anticipations (incomplete), substitutions, vowels.

B-22   1;10.9   B: '[wʌ.pi] . . . Rùbber Dúcky.'
(for 'Rubber Ducky' [wʌ.pɜ tʌ.ki], pointing to picture;
[ɜ]<--[i]; 2-word stage; 'Rubber Ducky' lexicalized as one
word, but probably planned for speaking as two at this age;
B; -T; SC)

AL-70   2;10.25   Al: 'Mòmmy, I [ló▪] . . . I lı̇́ke càsserȯle.'
(for 'like casserole' [laʲk kʰǽ.sə.ʒȯ▪]; [aʲ]<--[o▪], could also
be substitution for rhyme [aʲk] in 'like'; B; +T(e); SC)

AL-142 3;6.22   Al: 'Can I have a [pʰı̇́] . . . pó̱psı̀cle?'
(for 'popsicle' [pʰáp.sì.kəɫ]; [a]<--[ı]; W; SC)

AL-147 3;7.11   Al: 'Ì'll hàve a [g̠ʒ̠áp] . . . grápe pȯpsìcle.'
(for 'grape popsicle' [g̠ʒ̠eʲp pʰáp.sì.kəɫ]; [eʲ]<--[a]; B; +T(e);
SC)

B-158   3;8.17   B: 'Look, I tòok the [ǽ▪s] . . . ı̇ce ȯut.'
(for 'ice out' [aʲs ǽ▪t]; [aʲ]<--[æ▪]; B; +T(e); SC)

OC-69   3;10.0   OB: (several children are mixing tofu and peanut butter;
OB is excitedly telling others that they are going to
eat it on crackers.) 'We're nót gònna èat it òff [ɔr] . . .
we're nót gònna èat it òff o̱u̱r fórks!'
(for 'our forks' [ar fɔrks]; [a]<--[ɔ]; B; +T(s); SC)

AL-193 3;11.13 Al: 'Look, I [tʰ ̀ıtʃt] . . . I tòu̱ched my tòothbrush to the
cé̱ı̇ling.'
(for 'touched' [tʰʌtʃt], source 'ceiling' [sı́.lıŋ]; [ʌ]<--[i]; B;
+T(s); SC)

OC-79   4;0.0   OG: 'Ì'm gonna hàve some [ı̇s] . . . ı̇ce-crèam.'
(for 'ice-cream' [áʲs.kʰr̥ı̀m], [aʲ]<--[i]; W; SC)

AL-198 4;0.4   Al: 'Yóu know, the [pʰʎ.ni] . . . the póny pu̇zzle.'
(for 'pony puzzle' [pʰó▪.ni pʰʎ.zəɫ]; [o▪]<--[ʌ]; B; +T(e); SC)

AL-211 4;4.8   Al: 'They made a [ʒ̠ó▪] . . . they made a ráinbȯw for hìm
to rìde on.'
(for 'rainbow' [ʒ̠éʲn.bò▪]; [eʲ]<--[o▪], possibly substitution for
rhyme [eʲn], but not telescoping, by intonation; W; SC)

B-341   4;7.24   B: 'Mom, since today's a [stȯ▪] . . . stày hóme day,
. . . (etc.).'
(for 'stay home' [steʲ hõ▪m]; [eʲ]<--[o▪], with denasalization;
B; +T(s); SC)

B-408   4;11.7   B: 'I'll [bà] . . . I'll bè at the pótty.'
                        (for 'be' [bi], source 'potty' [pʰá.ɾi]; [i]<--[a]; B; +T(s); SC)

B-432   5;0.12   B: (after seeing an advertisement on TV)
                        'Mòm, will yòu gèt us [tʰù.nɚ] . . . Tùna̠ Hélper?'
                        (for 'Tuna Helper' [tʰú.nʌ hé⬩.pɚ]; [ʌ]<--[ɚ]; B; -T; SC)

AN-271   5;1.28   An: 'Mom, is Sàn-[di.jó".g] . . . [é̠ʲ.gò"] clòse to Téxas?'
                        (for 'San-Diego' [sæ̀n.di.jéʲ.gò"]; [eʲ]<--[o"]; B/W; SC in
                        mid-word)

B-530   5;6.11   B: 'I [mì? b] . . . I mìght bè Dònnátello for next
                        Hàllowéen.'
                        (for 'might be' [maʲ? bi]; [aʲ]<--[i]; B; T?; SC)

AL-254   5;9.5   Al: 'Mom, lòok at that [ʃ ì.nì] . . . shìny grèen cár!'
                        (for 'shiny green' [ʃáʲ.ni grin]; [aʲ]<--[i]; B/W; SC)

OC-168   5;9.21   OB: 'I lóve [pʰì.p] . . . pèpperòni pìzza.'
                        (for 'pepperoni' [pʰɛ̀.pə.ró".ni]; [ɛ]<--[i]; B/W; SC)

AN-324   5;11.9   An: 'I knòw èvery [ɪ̀st] . . . èvery làst trìck in the tráde.'
                        (for 'last' [læst]; [æ]<--[ɪ]; B; -T; SC)

11. Phonological anticipations (incomplete), substitutions, larger units.

AN-14   1;9.2   D: (Dad and Anna are reading a picture book about
                        colors.) 'What's thís color?' (pointing to green)
                   An: 'It [fʒʌ] . . . c̠òlor fróg.'
                   D: 'It's the còlor of a fróg.'
                        (for 'color frog' [kʰʌ́.ʌ́ʒ fʒá:k]; onsets [kʰ]<--[fʒ]; B; +T(s);
                        SC; p. 130)

AL-41   2;7.23   Al: 'Knock knock.'
                   M: 'Who's there?'
                   Al: 'Mìnnie Móuse.'
                   M: 'Whàt's Mìnnie Móuse dòing?'
                   Al: '[fàʲ.ən] . . . just tr̠ỳin a f́ind us.'
                        (for 'tryin' [tʰʒaʲ.ən]; 'just' added in correction; onsets
                        [tʰʒ] <--[f]; B; +T(s); SC)

B-107   2;8.13   B: 'I'm nòt gètting my [pʰǽɲtʃ] . . . my pánts *chà*nged!'
(for 'pants' [pʰænt(s)]; [ts]<--[tʃ], causing nasal place
assimilation; B; +T(e); SC; p. 411)

AN-136 3;11.25   An: '[tʃɛ̀.**də.**li] . . . Chè<u>rr</u>y Cú**ddl**er.'
(for 'Cherry Cuddler' [tʃɛ̀.ri kʰʌ.də.lɚ], name of doll;
syllable [də] from 'Cuddler' anticipated, added to
'Cherry'; also onset [l] from 'Cuddler' anticipated,
substituted for [r] in 'Cherry': [r]<--[də.l]; B; -T; SC; p. 54,
131)

AN-139 4;0.17   An: 'You'll wìn a [**pʰ**ṛæ̀.b] . . . a . . . ' (gives up)
(for 'a fabulous prize' [fǽ.bjə.ləs pʰṛaʲz]; onsets [f]<--[pʰṛ];
B; +T(s); N-NC)

AL-205 4;2.5   Al: 'I wànt [g̊ʒòʒ] . . . <u>m</u>òre *gr*ápes.'
(for 'more' [moʒ], source 'grapes' [g̊ʒeʲps]; onsets
[m]<--[g̊ʒ]; B; +T(s); SC)

B-216   4;2.14   B: 'Mom, this is bíg [stì] . . . <u>k</u>ìds' *st*ùff.'
(for 'kids' ' [kʰɪdz]; onsets [kʰ]<--[st]; B; -T; SC)

AL-213 4;4.13   Al: 'Gìve me the [tʃǽk] . . . the chée<u>se</u> cr**à**ck<u>e</u>rs.'
(for 'cheese crackers' [tʃiz kʰʒǽ.k3z]; [iz]<--[æ.k]; B, but
could be compound; +T(e); SC; p. 194)

B-288   4;5.20   B: 'Ícecrèam, thàt's my [stèʲv.r:] . . . <u>f</u>àvorite *st*úff.'
(for 'favorite' [féʲv.rət]; onsets [f]<--[st]; B; +T(s); SC)

AL-225 4;5.29   Al: (naming popsicle flavors)
'Thìs one is [ʃà.b] . . . Strà<u>w</u>berry **Sh**órtkook.'
(for 'Strawberry' [stʒá.bɛ̀.ʒi]; onsets [stʒ]<--[ʃ]; B; +T(s);
SC)

AL-228 4;6.16   Al: 'You're nèxt to the kítchen, and yòu got your [pʰík.kən]
. . . your pic<u>ture</u> tàk**en**, rìght?'
(for 'picture taken' [pʰík.tʃʒ tʰéʲ.kən]; [tʃʒ]<--[(k)ʔən];
unclear which syllable is the source of the [k], so it is
notated as ambisyllabic; B; -T; SC; p. 399)

AN-232 4;8.4   An: 'Our [stàr] . . . our c̲àr's st̀arting to drìve awáy.'
(for 'car' [kʰar]; onsets [kʰ]<--[st]; B; -T; SC)

B-359 4;9.10 B: 'Gràndpa, I gòt my [sl̥íŋ.kəɬ] . . . I gòt my slínky̲
tàngle̲d ùp.'
(for 'slinky tangled' [sl̥íŋ.ki tʰǽŋ.gəɬ(d)]; rhymes [i]<--[əɬ];
B; -T; SC; p. 399)

OC-123 4;11.9 OA: 'Whèn's your bírthday?'
OB: 'Septèmber [fʌ.ni] . . . t̀wenty-th̲ird.'
(for 'twenty-third' [tʰwʌ̀.ni.f ɜ̃d]; child regularly substitutes
[f] for [θ]; onsets [tʰw̥]<--[f]; W; +T(s); SC)

OC-132 5;0.14 OB: 'Wè [spàt] . . . wè gòt sp̲ider wèbs in thère.'
(for 'got' [gat]; onsets [g]<--[sp]; B; +T(s); SC)

B-490 5;4.15 B: 'I'll be [fɚ.ɾɪŋ] . . . I'll be st̀arting f ìrst gráde!'
(for 'starting first' [stár.ɾ(ɪŋ) fɚst]; body [fɚ] anticipated/
substituted for syllable [star]; B; -T; SC; p. 150)

B-491 5;4.18 B: 'Whỳ did you invìte [dèʲ.brə] . . . Dàvi̲d an' Bár**bara**
òver?'
(for 'David an' Barbara' [dèʲ.vɨd æn bár.brə]; syllables
[vɨd]<--[brə]; B; -T; SC; p. 22)

B-499 5;5.4   B: (telling Mom what tape he wanted to listen to)
'Yés, yés! "Sèsame-[kʰɹ̀it] . . . Str̲èet **Chr̲**ístmas"!'
(for 'Street Christmas' [strit kʰɹís.mʌs]; onsets [st]<--[kʰ]; B;
+T(s); SC)

B-516 5;5.24 B: (Bobby had written out a 'menu', and insisted that
Mom cook only what was on that menu, then changed
his mind) 'You dòn't hàve to màke what I hàve on
[mɪ̆n] . . . my̆ m**é**nu.'
(for 'my menu' [maʲ mín.ju]; rhymes [aʲ]<--[ɪn]; B; +T(s);
SC)

AN-305 5;7.30 An: 'I lìke [dʒèɬ] . . . Gène K**é**lly.'
(for 'Gene Kelly' [dʒìn kʰé.li]; [in]<--[ɛ.l], then [l]-->[ɬ]; B;
+T(s); SC)

B-564   5;10.6   B: (telling what kind of punch he wanted)
'I'm hàving the Grèat [du] . . . Bluedíni fírst.'
(for 'Bluedini' [blu.dí.ni]; onsets [bl]<--[d]; W; SC)

B-573   5;11.6   B: (at the zoo, explaining that there is only one ride, the
bus ride we had already taken)
'That [bà^{j}d] . . . that bùs wàs the ríde.'
(for 'bus' [bʌs]; rhymes [ʌs]<--[a^{j}d]; B; +T(s); SC; p. 149)

B-576   5;11.10   B: 'Know what would happen if bèes think vènus flý-tràps
are flówers? Then the vènus [tʰ$\underset{\circ}{r}$à^{j}] . . . flỳ-tràps will
èat the bées.'
(for 'fly-traps' [fl$\underset{\circ}{}$á^{j}.tʰ$\underset{\circ}{r}$æps]; onsets [fl$\underset{\circ}{}$]<--[tʰ$\underset{\circ}{r}$]; W; could be
A/P; SC)

B-580   5;11.20   B: (while landing in Chicago airport)
'I don't knòw if it [ʃ ò^{w}z] in . . . snòws in Chicágo.'
(for 'snows' [sn̥o^{w}z]; source 'Chicago' [ʃə.kʰá.go^{w}]; onsets
[sn̥]<--[ʃ]; B; -T; SC)

12. Phonological perseverations, substitutions, consonants.

AN-3a   1;7.15   An: (chanting name of book she wanted to read)
'Wìnnie-Póoh bòok. Wìnnie-Póoh [pʰʊk].
Wìnnie-Póoh bick.'
(for 'Pooh book' [pʰu pʊk]; [pʰ] /p/-->[p] /b/; B; +T(s); NSC;
3b=Class 16; p. 130)

AN-11   1;8.15   An: (singing a song which she made up)
'Ùp in the ský, dòwn in the ský, ùp in **th**e [st̪áʲ].'
(for 'the sky' [t̪ə skaʲ]; [t̪]-->[k]; B; +T(e); NSC)

B-14   1;9.27   D: 'Bobby, hère's a bóttle.'
B: (holding up a book for Daddy to read):
'[pút̪ʰ] . . . bóok.'
(for 'book' [pʊkʰ], source 'bottle' [bá.ɾəɫ]; /t/ [ɾ]-->[k], then
aspirated by Bobby's rules; 2-word stage; B; SC)

B-17   1;10.1   B: '[t̪íθʔ, tʌ́ç].'
(for 'teeth, brush' [tiθʔ, pʌç]; [t]-->[p]; 2-word stage, but two
one-word utterances; B; NSC)

B-19   1;10.5   B: (while getting ready to brush his teeth): '[t̪úθʔ.tʌ̀ç].'
(for 'toothbrush' [t̪úθʔ.pʌ̀ç]; [t]-->[p]; 2-word stage, one-word
utterance; W; NSC)

AN-21   1;11.13 M: 'Whó gàve you this bòok?'
An: '[pákʰ].'
(for 'Bob' [papʰ], perseveration from 'book' [bʊk]; [k]-->[pʰ],
then aspirated by Anna's rule; B; NSC; p. 30, 115)

B-28   1;11.14 B: 'Mòmmy, mòre chéese-pùffs.'
M: 'No, you've had enóugh.'
B: '[t̪í.tʌ̀pç]! . . . chéese-pùffs!'
(for 'cheese-puffs' [t̪í.pʌ̀pç], a type of snack food; [t]-->[p];
2-word stage; W; SC; p. 11)

OC-5   2;0.2   OG: 'Níght-night **D**àdoo. Níght-night [dè] . . . Wèsley.'
(for 'Wesley' [wé.si]; [d]-->[w]; 2-word stage; B; -T; SC)

AN-22   2;0.13   An: 'Whìte Ràbbit a rúnning.
Àlice sèe a Whìte [ʒǽ.bɪn].'
(for 'rabbit' [ʒǽ.bɪt]; source 'running' [ʒʌ́.n(in)] with the
coda nasal the most likely source; [n]-->[t]; B; -T; NSC;
p. 30)

OC-11   2;0.29   OG: (notices her brother, whom she calls 'Dadoo', has the
gum she wanted)   'Dádoo [dʌm], Dádoo gùm.'
(for 'gum' [gʌm]; [d]-->[g]; 2-word stage; B; +T(s); SC)

AN-26b 2;1.23   An: (chanting nursery rhyme)
'Mòmmy càlled the dóctor, and the Mòmmỳ [kʰɛ́d]
. . . Mòmmy càlled the dóctor and the dòctòr said'
(for 'said', [sɛd], source probably 'called' [kʰawd] not
'doctor' [dak̚.t3]; [kʰ]-->[s]; B; +T(e); SC; 26a=Class 43,
26c=Class 5; see 26a for full utterance; p. 21)

OC-13   2;2.0   OG: 'You dòn't [déʲ] . . . you dòn't say that.'
(for 'don't say' [dõʔ seʲ]; [d]-->[s]; B; +T(e); SC; p. 200)

B-43   2;2.4   B: 'Mòmmy gèt me Chéetos, [tɕiz].' (looks surprised)
M: 'No.'
B: 'Gèt me Chéetos, plèase.'
(for 'please' [pʰiz]; [tɕ]-->[pʰ]; B; +T(s); N-NC)

OC-17   2;3.0   OG: 'Lòok at the giráffe. Mònkey's húgging the [grǽf].'
(for 'giraffe' [dʒrǽf], source 'hugging' [hʌ́.g(in)]; [g]-->[dʒ];
B; -T; NSC; p. 123)

OC-18   2;3.0   OB: '[kʰ in ʌp kʰàˈm] . . . ' (looks confused)
(for 'clean up time' [kʰin ʌp tʰaˈm]; [kʰ]-->[tʰ]; B; +T(s);
N-NC)

AN-46b 2;4.25   An: (telling story) 'Óne dày, mù mórning, the Smúrf
[mòʷk] ùp.'
(for 'woke' [woʷk]; [m]-->[w]; B; +T(s); NSC; 46b=Class 1)

AL-38   2;7.5   Al: (as Mom puts on Raffi tape)
'Ràffi sìng my f àvorite [fáŋ] . . . sóng!'
(for 'song' [saŋ]; [f]-->[s]; B; +T(e); SC; p. 148)

B-97   2;7.7   B: 'Bè cáreful, bè [bɛ́ʒ.fʉɬ].' (looks confused)
(for 'careful' [kʰɛ́ʒ.fʉɬ]; [b]-->[kʰ]; B; +T(e); N-NC)

AN-77   2;10.9   An: 'Mòmmy, wànna *h*èar my [hé¦ps]?'
(for 'tapes' [tʰe¦ps]; [h]-->[tʰ]; B; +T(e); NSC)

AL-60   2;10.19   Al: 'Mom, can I have some ápple-juice?'
M: 'What happened to your bóttle?
Al: '*M*y [bà.təm] . . . my bòttḷe is ìn the clóset.'
(for 'bottle' [bá.təɫ]; [m]-->[ɫ]; could also be lexical
selection error, 'bottom', but unlikely, since 'bottle' had just
been spoken by Mom; B; -T; SC; p. 200)

AL-84   2;11.28   Al: 'So I crìed and crìed and críed, for that dùmb spìder
*b*ít [bì] . . . bít mè.'
(for 'me' [mi]; [b]-->[m]; 'for' means 'because' here; B;
+T(s); SC)

OC-35   3;0.0   OA: 'Whò wants to gò on a wálk?'
Al: 'Í dò.'
OG: 'Ì *d*ò [d́ú] . . . I dò t́óo!'
(for 'too' [tʰu]; [d]-->[tʰ], but could be repetition of whole
word; B; +T(e); SC)

OC-41   3;2.24   OG: (naming colors on Mom's t-shirt)
'Yèllow, blàck, bròwn, blàck, bròwn, b*l*àck, [blàʷn]
. . . ' (looks confused)
(for 'brown' [braʷn]; [l]-->[r]; B; list intonation; N-NC)

AL-100   3;3.0   Al: (chanting, sing-song)
'I tóld you, I tóld you; Í'm gòing to [tʰǽn.sɪŋ] clàss.'
(for 'dancing' [dǽn.sɪŋ]; [tʰ]-->[d]; could also be from 'to'
but less likely; B; +T(b); NSC)

OC-49   3;4.0   OB: 'Dón't say you càn't *t*àke òff your [tʰùz], yòu cán!'
(for 'shoes' [ʃuz]; [tʰ]-->[ʃ]; source could also be final /t/s in
'don't' and 'can't', but less likely than initial aspirated /t/ in
'take'; B; -T; NSC)

AN-111   3;5.0   M: 'What are you pláying?'
An: '[kʰǽ.rə.pʰì.rɚs].'
(for 'caterpillars' [kʰǽ.rə.pʰì.lɚs]; [r] /t/ -->[l]; W; NSC)

AL-135 3;5.15   Al: 'Whèn the blùe òne wàves her màgic wánd, the
                   wìcked [ì.və̃n] fàiry còmes òut of the wáll.'
                   (for 'evil' [í.vəɫ]; [n]-->[ɫ], with vowel nasalization; B; T?;
                   NSC)

B-132   3;5.30   B: 'I wànted to èat a whòle Swìss [tʃíːtʃ] . . . chéeṣe.'
                   (for 'cheese' [tʃiːs]; [tʃ]-->[s]; W; SC)

AL-148 3;7.11   D: 'Alice, you've got your pánties on bàckwards.'
                   Al: 'I l íke 'em this [lèʲ].'
                   (for 'way' [weʲ]; [l]-->[w]; B; +T(s); NSC)

AN-115 3;7.24   An: (singing "Rudolph, the Red-Nosed Reindeer")
                   'Thèy nèver [nèt] pòor Rúdolph, (etc.).'
                   (for 'let' [lɛt]; [n]-->[l]; B; -T; NSC)

B-155   3;8.16   B: 'I don't wànna gó to the [gʒèʲd] . . . I don't wànna gó
                   to the paràde.'
                   (for 'parade' [pʰʒeʲd]; [g]-->[pʰ]; B; +T(s); SC)

B-163a 3;8.29   B: 'If a bèe stìngs me on the fóot, Ì'll be [bǽ] . . .
                   Ì'll be má . . . Ì'll be ṣád.'
                   (for 'sad' [sæd]; [b]-->[s]; could also be lexical selection
                   error, 'bad'; B; +T(e); SC; 163b=Class 35)

AL-166 3;9.1   Al: 'He ís brùshing. I sée [hìz].'
                   (for 'him' [hɪm]; [z]-->[m]; could also be lexical selection
                   error, 'his' for 'him'; B; +T(s); NSC)

B-166   3;9.4   B: (complaining that his class was going out for a second
                   breakfast) 'I don't ƒíke another [blè] . . . I don't líke
                   another brèakfast.'
                   (for 'breakfast' [bʒék.fəst]; [l]-->[ʒ]; B; +T(s); SC; p. 150,
                   155)

OC-72   3;10.18   OB: (putting on his best shirt)
                   'Thìs is my ƒáncy [fɚ̀] . . . my fáncy shìrt.'
                   (for 'shirt' [ʃɚt]; [f]-->[ʃ]; emphatic stress on 'fancy', not
                   compound; B; +T(s); SC)

AL-189 3;11.6   Al: 'Nòt nów, anóther [nèʲ] . . . anóther dày.'
                   (for 'day' [dèʲ]; [n]-->[d]; B; T?; SC)

B-204 4;1.30 B: 'Mom, *l*óok! A? [ǽ.*l* ɨ.lèʲ.ɾɚ] . . . álligàtor.'
(for 'alligator' [ǽ.lɨ.gèʲ.ɾɚ]; [l]-->[g]; B/W; SC)

B-209 4;2.5 B: 'À*l*ice *l*èt me [lúz] hèrs.'
(for 'use' [juz]; [l]-->[j]; B; +T(e); NSC)

B-213 4;2.7 An: 'Bòbby, wrìte *m*ý nà*m*e.'
B: 'OK! Hòw do you [sm̥ɛ́ɫ] it?' (looks embarassed)
(for 'spell' [spɛɫ]; [m]-->[p], then devoices; B; +T(b)
probably; N-NC)

OC-94 4;2.20 OG: ' . . . to *C*orrína's [kʰàʷs] . . . Corrína' h̲òuse.'
(for 'house' [haʷs]; [kʰ]-->[h]; B; -T; SC)

AN-160 4;2.21 An: 'It was a strànge [*k*ʰ̥ɹ̥í.cjɚ].'
(for 'creature' [kʰɹ̥í.tʃjɚ]; [kʰ]-->[tʃ], but deaspirates when
unstressed and becomes palatalized to [c] before [j]; W;
NSC)

B-245 4;3.29 M: 'What kind of cereal do you want, Còrn Chèx or Kíx?'
B: 'I saì*d* [kʰíts] . . . Kíx̲!'
(for 'Kix' [kʰɪks], source 'said' [sɛːt]; [t]-->[k]; [s] on 'Kix'
acting like plural suffix; B; +T(e); SC)

B-246 4;3.29 B: (trying to get out of wearing extra clothes)
'I wòn't *f*rèeze no [fɛ́.li]-bùttons!'
(notices error, laughs; for 'belly' [bɛ́.li]; [f]-->[b]; B; +T(e);
N-NC)

B-253 4;4.6 B: 'My nàme is Ròbert Chèster *V*àn-[*v*éʲ.vɪn] . . .
Vàn-Válin.'
(for 'Van-Valin' [væ̀n.véʲ.lɪn]; [v]-->[l]; W; SC)

B-265 4;4.18 B: (talking about a video) 'It was ònly Jór*d*an's,
and he lè*tt*e*d* them [bá.roʷ] it!'
(for 'borrow' [bá.roʷ]; source most likely tap in 'letted'
[lɛ́.ɾ(əd)]; source could also be /d/ in 'Jordan' or coda of
'letted'; [ɾ]-->[r]; B; +T(e); NSC)

AN-177 4;4.24 An: 'Mommy hòw doe*s* my [sárp] . . . hòw does my
s̲hárpener wòrk?'
(for 'does my sharpener' [dʌːs maʲ ʃár.pə.nɚ]; [s]-->[ʃ]; B;
+T(e); SC̀)

B-274   4;5.1   B: 'Mòm, can wè have a *t*ápe-[tʰæns]?'
(for 'tape-dance' [tʰéˑp.dæns], i.e. dance to music from the
tape deck; [tʰ]-->[d]; W; NSC)

AN-190 4;5.4   An: 'I have tèn bábies and they'*r*e c*r*ý́ing.
They'*r*e àll c*r*ỳing at [rʌns].'
(for 'once' [wʌns]; [r]-->[w]; B; +T(e) and possibly (s); NSC)

AN-194 4;5.5   M: 'Anna, sì*t* dówn!'
An: 'Nó, I wànna be [síˑti]! (notices error, laughs) I said
"sìtty" instead of "s*í*lly".'
(for 'silly' [síˑli]; [t]-->[l], note she didn't flap /t/; could also
be perseveration of morpheme 'sit'; B; -T; SC with
commentary; p. 118)

AN-196 4;5.10   An: (after drawing around her sister's foot)
'I did one of Ali's *f*óot. Thàt's why I tòok òff her
[fæn] . . . her pánts.'
(for 'pants' [pʰænts]; [f]-->[pʰ]; B; +T(e) and possibly (s);
SC)

AN-201 4;5.19   An: 'In the mìddl*e* of the [pʰéˑ.pɫ].'
(for 'paper' [pʰéˑ.pr]; [ɫ]-->[r]; B; -T; NSC; p. 113, 149)

AN-220 4;6.18   An: (setting up a story) 'We'll sèe how the stòry will
[*b*i.b ín], OK?'
(for 'begin' [bi.gín]; [b]-->[g]; W; NSC)

B-312   4;6.21   B: (having just finished supper)
'I get [*d*i.dɚt] . . . dessért.'
(for 'dessert' [di.zɚt]; [d]-->[z]; W; SC)

B-327   4;7.8   B: (telling Mom which crayons to use)
'Mommy, you gòtta hàve your "*C*òlor By The
[kʰʌm.bɚz]" . . . "Còlor By The Números".'
(for 'numbers' [nʌm.bɚz]; [kʰ]-->[n]; B; +T(e); SC)

B-337   4;7.18   B: (with friend John, tying scarves around their shoulders, one of which has a picture of Dick Tracy on it)
'Lèt's wèar thèse like cápes.
Mom, will you [kʰàʲ] . . . t̪ie my Dìck Tràcy on Jóhn?'
(for 'tie' [tʰaʲ]; note that 'Dick Tracy' is [dì?.t̪ʃɾé̪ʲ.si]; [kʰ]-->[tʰ]; B; +T(s); SC)

AN-234 4;8.5   An: 'Alice, did you t̪àke [tʰæ̀ʷn] our dóor?'
(for 'down' [dæ̀ʷn]; [tʰ]-->[d]; B; [-T]; NSC)

B-345   4;8.6   B: (telling Mom what to say)
'Mom, you shòut "Hurráy". '
M: (teasing) 'Shòut hurráy.'
B: 'Mòmmy, you sáy "[ʃɚ] . . . Hurrày"!'
(for 'hurray' [hɚ.réʲ]; [ʃ]-->[h]; B; -T; SC)

B-351   4;8.13   B: 'Lèt's [pʰʊ́.si.pʰʊ̀t].'
(for 'pussyfoot' [pʰʊ́.si.fʊ̀t], a silly way to walk; [pʰ]-->[f]; W; NSC)

B-354   4;8.20   M: 'What kind of céreal do you want?'
B: 'Fròsted [fɾé̥ʲks] . . . Fl̪ákes.'
(for 'flakes' [fl̥eʲks]; [r]-->[l]; B; +T(e); SC)

B-370   4;9.18   B: 'I lóve màshed [mə.tʰèʲ.roʷs] . . . màshed pot̪àtoes.'
(for 'mashed potatoes' [mæʃt pʰə.tʰéʲ.roʷs]; [m]-->[pʰ]; B; -T; SC)

B-378b 4;10.8   B: 'Mom, dàrk [grìm] is . . . um . . . l̀ight grèen is yéllow.'
(for 'green' [grin]; [m]-->[n]; B; -T; SC; 378a=Class 43)

B-384   4;10.17 B: (picking out which toy to take into the bathtub)
'Ràphaél wòn't get [rʌ̀.f] . . . rùsty.'
(for 'rusty' [rʌ́.st(i)], source 'Raphael' [ræ̀.fi.jél̪]; [f]-->[s]; B; -T; SC)

AN-254 4;10.21 An: 'The C̀àt in the [kʰæt]. (laughs) I said "The Càt in the Cát"!'
(for 'hat' [hæt]; [kʰ]-->[h]; could be perseveration of whole word; B; +T(e); SC with comments)

AN-256 4;10.23   An: 'Mòmma, tàke off my [kʰéˑm]-tàg. Káme-tàg?
I said "káme-tàg" for "náme-tàg". '
(for 'name' [neˑm]; [kʰ]-->[n]; B; +T(e); SC)

B-402   4;11.3   B: 'We wàtched [tʃàr] . . . [tʃàr] . . . Chàrlotte's Wéb.'
(for 'Charlotte's' [ʃár.lɨts], source 'watched' [watʃ(t)];
[tʃ]-->[ʃ]; B; -T; SC, with difficulty)

B-405   4;11.5   B: 'Thìs is what Róbin dòes. Thìs is what [wá.bɨn]
dòes.'
(for 'Robin' [rá.bɨn]; source 'what' [wʌt]; [w]-->[r]; B;
+T(e); NSC)

B-409   4;11.8   M: (reading "Seaworld ABCs" book)
'Q̇ is for Quèen Tríggerfish.'
B: 'I lóve Quèen [tʰw̜ì.gɚ.fìʃ].'
(for 'triggerfish' [tʰɾí.gɚ.fìʃ], source 'Queen' [kʰw̜in];
[w]-->[r]; B; -T; NSC)

B-421   4;11.16   M: (Bobby, Alice, and Mom are running to neighbors' to
play) 'Àlice, dòn't rùn ahéad of Bòbby.'
B: (to Mom) 'We'll gèt there quíck if we [wʌn].'
(for 'run' [rʌn]; [w]-->[r]; not racing, so no interference from
'won'; B; T?; NSC)

B-422   4;11.17   B: (telling Mom where his imaginary 'off' switch is
located) 'It's behìnd my báck. Prèss [sták]. (pause)
"Stock?" I said "Stóp". '
(for 'stop' [stap]; [k]-->[p]; B; +T(b); SC with comments,
saving face; p. 85, 200)

B-426   4;11.25   B: (looking out airplane window) 'Ì can sèe [év.ri.sìŋ].'
(for 'everything' [év.ri.θìŋ]; [s]-->[θ]; B; -T; NSC)

AN-266 5;1.20   Al: 'A dùck just bíte me.'
An: (to Mother) 'A [dʒʌk] bìt her?'
(for 'duck' [dʌk]; perseveration of [dʒ] from preceding
utterance; probably not telescoping of 'duck just' since
didn't have duration of two words; [dʒ]-->[d]; B; +T(e);
NSC)

AN-268 5;1.26   An: (singing song) 'Mý Lìttle [mòʷ.ni] ànd fríends.'
(for 'Pony' [pʰóʷ.ni]; [m]-->[pʰ]; B; -T; NSC)

B-472   5;2.29   B: 'Knòw what Íwould do? Màke a [sm̥óʷ] . . .
snówbàll.'
(for 'snowball' [sn̥óʷ.bàɬ]; [m]-->[n], then devoiced; B;
+T(e); SC)

B-476   5;3.19   M: 'How did Daddy fíx it?'
B: 'Easy. He glùed aʟʟ the pàrts that're [blòʷ.kɨn] . . .
bròken togéther.'
(for 'broken' [bróʷ.kɨn]; [l]-->[r]; B; -T; SC)

B-479   5;3.21   Al: 'Màybe todáy is a bàke sàle.'
B: '[tʰə.mèʲ] . . . todày hás to bè a bàke sàle.'
(for 'today' [tʰə.déʲ]; [m]-->[d]; B; -T; SC)

B-481   5;3.26   D: 'What's he gonna dó?'
B: 'He's gonna búdge.'
D: 'What does "búdge" mean?'
B: '[bìnz] "fáll"; he's gònna fáll.'
(for 'means' [minz]; [b]-->[m]; B; +T(s); NSC)

B-489   5;4.10   B: (looking at new game)
'Is it Dádʼs [dèʲm] . . . gàme?'
(for 'game' [geʲm]; [d]-->[g]; B; +T(s); SC)

AL-240 5;5.20   Al: 'Iťs stàrting to be [stɹ̥íŋ].'
(for 'spring' [spɹ̥ɪŋ]; [t]-->[p], most likely souce one of the
onset [t]'s; B; +T(e); NSC)

B-504   5;5.24   B: 'Jánuary, Fébruary, Márch, Ápril, Máy, Júne, Julý,
Aúgust, [fɛp] . . . Septémber, (etc.)'
(for 'September' [sɛp.tʰɛ́m.bɚ]; [f]-->[s]; possibly non-
contextual, but 'February' is likely source since both have
vowel [ɛ] followed by bilabial stop in error syllable; B; list
intonation; SC)

B-505   5;5.24   B: (defining 'baby')
'And you're [jì] . . . lìttle, and tìny, and rèal cúte.'
(for 'little' [lí.rɬ]; [j]-->[l]; B; list intonation; SC)

B-517   5;5.25   B: (holding up video tape)
                 'Thìs one isn't èven [ɾi.ɹǽ^wnd].'
                 (for 'rewound' [ɹi.wǽ^wnd]; [ɹ]-->[w]; W; NSC)

B-520   5;5.30   B: 'Gràpes are a [gàˌnd] of frúit.'
                 (for 'kind' [kʰaˌnd]; [g]-->[kʰ]; B; -T; NSC)

B-532   5;6.16   B: (showing Mom the sticker he got for writing in his
                 journal at school)
                 'Stìcker for my joúrnal! [stí.kɬ] . . . stícker!'
                 (for 'sticker' [stí.kɹ̩]; [ɬ]-->[ɹ]; B; -T; SC)

OC-152 5;6.24   OA: 'Can I help you tie your shóe?'
                 OG: 'Yeah. It's hàrd for mè to [ʃáʲ] . . . t̪ie.'
                 (for 'tie' [tʰaʲ]; [ʃ]-->[tʰ]; B; +T(b); SC)

AL-243 5;7.13   Al: (saying the names of singers on TV) 'Shàron,
                 [lò.wən], and Brám . . . Shàron, Lòi̱s, and Brám.'
                 (for 'Lois' [ló.wəs]; [n]-->[s]; B; list intonation; SC)

AL-244 5;7.15   Al: (sees a group of movie stars on TV, spots Jerry Lewis,
                 who played a professor in a movie she had recently
                 seen) 'Òne of those gùys plàys that [pʰɚ.fɛ́ˊfɚ].'
                 (looks confused)
                 (for 'professor' [pʰɚ.fé.sɚ]; [f]-->[s]; W; N-NC)

AL-252 5;7.24   Al: 'Mom, Cèlia's còmin' óver todày. Ròund [tʰɹ̥éɬv]?'
                 M: 'Yeah, round twélve.'
                 (for 'twelve' [tʰwɛɬv]; [ɹ]-->[w], devoices; B; +T(e); NSC)

OC-159 5;7.29   OG: (drawing a picture of her father) 'Oops, my Dàd's
                 mòustache is bláck, but Ì pùt it [blǽ^wn].'
                 (for 'brown' [bɹǽ^wn]; [l]-->[ɹ]; B; +T(b); NSC)

B-550   5;8.2   B: ('reading' book title) ' "Trìck or Trèat [hæ̀.lə.ɾín]".'
                 (for 'Halloween' [hæ̀.lə.wín]; [ɹ]-->[w]; B; +T(e); NSC)

AN-306 5;8.5   M: (looking at pictures of vehicles in a book)
                 'How would yóu lìke to tràvel?'
                 An: 'Í'd like to tràvel on the [dʌ́mp.tʰɹ̥ʌp].'
                 (for 'dump-truck' [dʌ́mp.tʰɹ̥ʌk]; [p]-->[k]; W; NSC)

OC-163 5;8.10   OB: 'I knéw you hàd Tèenage Mùtant Nìnja Tùrt*l*es Frùit
                         Wrínk*l*es, 'cuz I sàw some [ræ.p*l̩*z] . . . I sàw some
                         wráppe*r̩*s of thèm dòwnstáirs.'
                         (for 'wrappers' [ræ.p*r̩*(z)]; [*ɫ*]-->[*r̩*]; B; -T; SC)

AN-315 5;9.15   An: (making up a birthday story) 'Once there was a gírl,
                        and thàt *d*ày was her bírthd*à*y. And she ràn [ə.dè*ʲ*]
                        . . . and she ràn a__wày to óur hòuse. The end.'
                        (for 'away' [ə.wé*ʲ*]; [d]-->[w]; B; -T; SC)

AN-319 5;10.0   An: 'Mom, ya knòw what *M*onròe's dòing to *m*y [mɛ́g]?
                        He's lícking it.' ('Monroe' is a dog)
                        (for 'leg' [lɛg]; [m]-->[l]; B; +T(e); NSC)

B-569   5;10.21   B: 'You *t*òok awày my [t*ʰ*í.dʒè*ʲ*z] . . . PJs.'
                        (for 'PJs' [p*ʰ*í.dʒè*ʲ*z]; [t*ʰ*]-->[p*ʰ*]; B; +T(e); SC)

B-570   5;10.23   B: (in department store)
                        'I'm gònna gò in the jéwelry [*s*èk.sən] . . . sect__ion.'
                        (for 'section' [sék.ʃən]; [s]-->[ʃ]; W; SC)

13. Phonological perseverations, additions, consonants.

AN-17   1;10.12   An: '[*p*ʰák*ʰ*.p*ʰ*òrn].'
                        (for 'popcorn', [p*ʰ*á:.k*ʰ*òrn]; [p*ʰ*] perseverated from onset of
                        first syllable of 'popcorn', added before vowel in second
                        syllable, causing [k*ʰ*] to be resyllabified; W; NSC)

AL-8   2;1.27   M: 'Anna, get your feet off Alice's stóol!'
                   Al: 'Grándma [gwè*ʲ*v] it . . . gáve!'
                        (for 'Grandma gave it' [gə.wǽ.mʌ ge*ʲ*v ɪt], i.e. 'Grandma
                        gave it to me'; [w] perseverated from onset of 'Grandma',
                        added into onset of 'gave', in functionally identical
                        position; B; +T(s); SC; p. 143)

AN-43   2;4.20   An: (naming pictures) 'Twò càr*s* and twò [bárɫz].'
                   M: 'Balls?'
                   An: 'Yeah.'
                        (for 'balls' [baɫz]; [r] perseverated from coda of 'cars'
                        [k*ʰ*arz], added into coda of 'balls', postvocalically; B; +T(e);
                        NSC; p. 150)

B-64   2;5.16   B: 'I wànt clèan [pʰḷǽnts] . . . pánts.'
(for 'pants' [pʰænts]; [l] perseverated from onset of 'clean',
added into onset of 'pants'; B; +T(e); SC; p. 148)

B-75   2;6.11   M: 'Do you want your blúe jacket?'
B: 'No, my gréen [dʒʒ̣ǽ.kɪt].'
(for 'jacket' [dʒǽ.kɪt]; [ʒ] perseverated from onset of
'green', added into onset of 'jacket'; B; +T(s); NSC)

B-104   2;7.27   B: 'I want "Snòw Whìte and the [sṇè.vən] Dwárfs". '
(for 'seven' [sɛ́.vən]; [n] added into onset of 'seven', several
possible sources; B; -T; NSC)

AN-94   2;11.21   An: 'Are you gònna do anòther one about
[sṇɛ́.sə.mi]-Strèet?'
(for 'Sesame' [sɛ́.sə.mi]; [n] added into onset of 'Sesame',
several possible sources; B; +T(e); NSC)

AL-99b 3;2.24   Al: 'I have a snòre néck . . . sòre [sṇɛ́k] . . .
(laughs, says wrong on purpose several times)
(for 'sore neck' [soʒ̣ nɛk]; [s] is perseverated from onset of
'sore', added to onset of 'neck', causing [n] to devoice; B;
+T(e); N-NC; 99a=Class 2; p. 81, 145)

AN-107 3;3.6   An: 'Hè's [stáp.tɪŋ] . . . stópping.'
(for 'stopping' [stá.pɪŋ]; [t] perseverated from first onset of
'stopping', added as onset of second syllable, causing the
[p] to resyllabify; W; SC; p. 162)

AL-112 3;3.26   M: 'Who did we see nursing at Grándma's?'
Al: 'Cásey, my friénd.'
M: 'Your cóusin.'
Al: 'Friénd [kʰʒ̣ʌ.zənd].'
(for 'friend cousin' [fʒ̣ɪnd kʰʌ.zənd]; [ʒ] perseverated from
onset of 'friend', added into onset of 'cousin'; 'cousin'
normally pronounced with final [d]; B; +T(s); NSC)

AL-117 3;3.29   Al: 'You're a bóy, and you have blàck háir.'
D: 'I dó? Do áll boys have blàck hàir?'
Al: 'Yeah, áll [blòʲz] . . . áll bòys.'
(for 'boys' [boʲz]; [l] added into onset of 'boys', multiple
possible sources; B; +T(s) probably; SC)

AL-143 3;6.25   Al: 'This is not *b*lùe, this is [*b*wá⸍t] . . . white.'
(for 'white' [wa⸍t]; [b] perseverated from 'blue', added into
onset of 'white' added; note that [bw] is an acceptable
cluster for her, as a possible realization of /br/; B; +T(e);
SC)

AL-159 3;8.25   Al: 'S̹trétch-[spǽnts].'
(for 'stretch-pants' [st̬ɛ́tʃ.pʰǽnts]; [s] perseverated from
onset of 'Stretch', added into onset of 'pants', causing the
/p/ to deaspiarate; source could also be plural [-s] on
'pants', but less likely; W; NSC)

AL-180 3;10.10   OA: 'What's that?'
Al: 'It's a [spáʲ.ʒət]-shìp.'
OA: 'A whát?'
Al: 'A pírate-shìp!'
(for 'pirate' [pʰáʲ.ʒət]; [s] perseverated from coda of 'It's'
[ɪts], added to onset of 'pirate', causing the /p/ to
deaspirate; B; +T(e); NSC)

AN-126 3;10.11   An: 'Mommy, thìs thing fèll òff this twı́ce. Twó [tʰw̥à⸍mz]
. . . twó times.'
(for 'times' [tʰa⸍mz]; [w] perseverated from onset of 'twice',
added into onset of 'times'; B; +T(s); SC)

B-172   3;11.13   B: (someone had just called Bobby a "Roadrunner", a kind
of bird) 'I'm not a [ʒóʷd̲.ʒʌn.d̲ʒ], I'm a fást rùnner.'
(for 'roadrunner' [ʒóʷd.ʒʌ.n(ʒ)]; [d] perseverated from coda
of first syllable of 'roadrunner', added as coda of last
syllable, causing [n] to resyllabify, nasalizing vowel; W;
NSC)

AL-201 4;0.11   M: 'Why don't you go s̹ìt by Dàddy and wàtch TV́?'
Al: 'I háte to [sw̥àtʃ] the nèws.'
(for 'watch' [watʃ]; [s] perseverated from 'sit', added to
onset of 'watch', causing [w] to devoice; possibly blend of
'sit' and 'watch'; B; -T; NSC)

AL-202 4;0.18   Al: 'We shòulda b*r*àng [b̬ʒíbz]!'
(for 'bibs' [bɪbz]; [ʒ] perseverated from 'brang' (which is her
normal pronunciation for 'brought'), added into onset of
'bibs'; B; +T(e); NSC)

OC-98 4;3.19   OB: '*Qui̇́ck*, [kʰwi̇̀k.stɨn].' (looks confused)
(for 'Kristen' [kʰwi̇́s.tɨn]; [k] perseverated, added after
vowel in first syllable of 'Kristen', causing [s] to
resyllabify; could be perseveration of morpheme 'quick'
[kʰwɪk]; B/W; +T(s); N-NC; p. 81)

AN-168 4;4.1   An: (saying her interpretation of the sub-title of a Sesame-
Street book, which was actually "Starring the Number
Six") 'Sta̋rting in the nùmber [stí] . . . si̋x.'
(for 'six' [sɪks]; [t] perseverated from onset of 'starting'
[stár.rɪŋ], added into onset of 'six'; B; +T(e); SC)

B-259 4;4.11   An: 'Whàt's the sècret pássword?'
B: 'Um, [sti̇̀n.eʲdʒ] Mùtant Ni̇̀nja Túrtles?'
An: 'No!'
(for 'Teenage' [tʰʲín.eʲdʒ]; [s] added, /t/ deaspirated; B; T?;
NSC)

AN-184 4;4.29   An 'It's the pàrt where you pùt your stòmach in a clówn
[kʰl̥à] . . . in a clówn còstume.'
(for 'clown costume' [kʰl̥æʷn kʰás.tum]; [l] perseverated
from onset of 'clown', added into onset of 'costume'; B;
+T(s); SC)

AN-185 4;5.1   An: 'He sàved the fèmale [fl̥áks] . . . the fèmale fóx.'
(for 'fox' [faks]; [l] perseverated from coda of 'female'
[fi.meɫ], added to onset of 'fox', becoming develarized and
devoiced; B; +T(e); SC)

B-323 4;7.5   B: (explaining that while the "Peter Rabbit" book belongs
to Anna, he keeps it in his room.)
'I just bórrow that [brùk].'
(for 'book' [bʊk]; [r] perseverated from onset of second
syllable of 'borrow' [bá.roʷ], added into onset of 'book'; B;
-T; NSC)

B-369 4;9.18   B: 'I'm going to sèe if there's a [sn̥í.dəɫ] under the
còuch.' (notices error, tries to save face; spots a bowl
of cactus) 'Ya knòw what a "snéedle" is? It's a ki̇̀nd of
cáctus.'
(for 'needle' [ní.dəɫ]; [s] perseverated from onset of 'see',
added to onset of 'needle', devoicing [n]; B; +T(e); N-NC
with comments; p. 85)

B-372 4;9.19   B: 'This'll keep S*t*rètch-Ghòs*t* [stè*ʲ*f].'
(for 'safe' [se*ʲ*f]; [t] perseverated from one of the /st/
clusters in 'Stretch Ghost', added into onset of 'safe'; B; -T;
NSC)

B-386 4;10.17   B: 'Mom, I lóve g*r*ìlled [t∫ɻ̥ìz] . . . chèese.'
(for 'grilled cheese' [grɨd t∫iz]; [r] perseverated from onset
of 'grilled', added into onset of 'cheese'; [t∫ɻ̥] is a
permissible initial consonant cluster in his speech; B; -T;
SC; p. 123)

B-412 4;11.9   B: (explaining where his brain is located)
'My bràin is ìn my [fɻ̥é*ʲ*s].'
(for 'face' [fe*ʲ*s]; [r] perseverated from onset of 'brain',
added to onset of 'face', causing [r] to devoice; B; +T(e);
NSC)

B-418 4;11.16   B: (telling about a hole at minature-golf course)
'It*'s* lìke a *s*óccer [nèst] . . . nèt.'
(for 'net' [nɛt]; [s] perseverated, added into coda of 'net';
could also be lexical selection error, 'nest'; B; +T(s)
probably; SC)

AN-263 5;0.18   An: 'We can s*t*íll [stì] a lòt of pìnk.'
(for 'still see' [stɨ si]; [t] perseverated from onset cluster of
'still', added into onset of 'see'; source could also be /t/ in
'lot of' [lá.rəv], but less likely than [st] cluster; B; +T(s);
NSC)

B-439 5;0.29   B: (telling about Batman)
'And the*n* he spìn*s* aróu*n*d, and the*n* he gets
[dìz.ni] . . . dìzzy and dìzzy and dízzy.'
(for 'dizzy' [dí.zi]; [n] added as onset of second syllable of
'dizzy', causing [z] to resyllabify, multiple possible sources
(but 'and' an unlikely source); no 'Disney' in context, but
could be a malapropism; B; T?; SC)

B-450 5;1.15   B: 'He lèft in the mìddle of "The Prìnce and the
[pʰɾá.pɚ]".'
(for 'Pauper' [pʰá.pɚ]; [r] perseverated from onset cluster of
'Prince', added into onset of 'Pauper'; B; +T(e); NSC)

B-459   5;1.28   B: 'Móm, will yòu gèt me my s*l* ípper-[s|àks] . . .
                        sòcks?'
                        (for 'slipper-socks' [s|í.pɚ.sàks]; [l] added, source most
                        likely onset cluster in 'slipper', not coda of 'will'; W; SC)

B-487   5;4.7   M: (Bobby is sick, so Mom is getting him to drink fluids)
                        'How ya cómin'? Ya drínkin' any of this?'
                    B: 'Yeah, I *t*òok a [stíp] . . . a sip.'
                        (for 'sip' [sɪp]; /t/ perseverated from 'took', added to onset
                        of 'sip', deaspirated; B; +T(e); SC)

B-502   5;5.15   M: (helping Bobby on with snowpants) 'Óther fòot!'
                    B: (showing Mom his foot was stuck in the lining)
                        'Mom, my [frʊts] not all the way óut, sée?'
                        (for 'foot's' [fʊts], source 'other' [ʌ.ðɚ]; syllabic [ɚ]
                        perseverated, added to onset of 'foot', becomes non-
                        syllabic [r], devoiced; B; -T; NSC)

B-522   5;5.30   Al: (looking at picture of human heart in book)
                        'A heárt! A heárt!'
                    B: 'Thàt's what it lòoks like in you*r* [bár.di] . . .
                        your bódy.'
                        (for 'body' [bá.di]; source most likely [hart] rather than
                        'your' [jɚ]; [r] perseverated from coda of 'heart', added into
                        coda of 'body'; B; +T(b); SC)

OC-166   5;9.2   OB: (chanting, after getting OK from Mom for friend to
                        stay for lunch) 'Dàvid èats óver! *D*àvi*d* [dɨts] óver.'
                        (for 'David eats' [déʲ.vɨd its]; clear extra [d] added,
                        perseverated from 'David'; B; T?; NSC)

AN-320   5;10.1   An: (telling how to play a game in the pool that involves
                        singing a specific song)
                        '*W*e càn't júmp, *w*e just s*w*̥ìm aròund in the póol,
                        and *w*e [sw̥íŋ] . . . we síng it.'
                        (for 'sing' [sɪŋ]; [w] added to onset of 'sing', devoiced,
                        multiple possible sources; B; +T(e); SC)

B-562   5;10.6   B: (telling what you can get with Kool-Aid points)
                        'Wàcky cassé*tt*e [pʰ|èʲ.rɚ].'
                        (for 'cassette player', [kʰə.sét pʰ|éʲ.ɚ]; [t] perseverated from
                        coda of 'cassette', added as onset of second syllable of
                        'player', then [t]-->[r]; B; +T(s); NSC; p. 118)

B-588   5;11.26   D: (distributing waffles)
'Do you want bluéberry or règular?
B: 'I wànt [blóʷθ] . . . bóth.'
(for 'both' [boʷθ]; [l] added to onset of 'both'; B; +T(e),
probably also (s); B; SC)

14. Phonological perseverations, movements, consonants.

B-13   1;9.25   M: 'Àrms úp!'
B: '[àm__ ʌç].'
(for 'arms up' [amç ʌp]; [ç] moved from coda of 'arms',
substituted for coda [p] of 'up'; not a morphological error,
since Bobby didn't know 'arm' as a separate word from
'arms'; 2-word stage; B; +T(e); NSC; p. 405, 458)

AL-3   2;0.14   Al: 'Íce, Mòmma! [áʲ__, mà.maç]!'
(for 'ice, Momma' [aʲç, má.ma]; [ç] moved from coda of
'ice', added as coda of second syllable of 'Momma'; 2-word
stage; B; +T(s); NSC; p. 155, 398, 405)

AN-31   2;2.15   An: 'Mòmma, mỳ [__ʌ.mi tʰèʲks].'
(for 'tummy aches', [tʰʌ.mi eʲks]; [tʰ] moved from onset of
'tummy', added as onset of 'aches'; B; +T(s); NSC)

AN-35   2;2;29   An: (telling part of "Dumbo" story)
'. . . and whèn that bòy [ʃǽ__.dəw] . . . whèn that
bòy shóuted "Whàt a clùmsy élephant", . . . '
(for 'shouted' [ʃǽw.dəd]; [w] moved from coda of first
syllable of 'shouted', and substituted for coda of second
syllable; W; SC)

B-51   2;4.8   B: 'Mòmmy mỳ [b__ǽŋ.kḷit] . . . blánket!'
(for 'blanket' [blǽŋ.kit]; [l] moved from initial consonant
cluster, added to onset of second syllable in same word,
devoiced; W; SC; p. 75)

AN-50   2;5.14   An: '[__pʰú.sn̥i].'
(for 'spoonie' [spú.ni], diminutive of 'spoon'; [s] moved
from onset of first syllable of 'spoonie', added to onset of
second syllable, with aspiration of initial /p/, and
devoicing of [n]; W; NSC; p. 116)

OC-22 2;5.22   OG: '[__è.wə.mi æn dʒéʲ.mi] . . . J̰eremy an' Ámy.'
(for 'Jeremy an' Amy' [dʒɛ́.wə.mi æn éʲ.mi]; [dʒ] moved
from onset of 'Jeremy', added as onset of 'Amy'; B; +T(e);
SC)

AL-42 2;7.24   Al: (holding up a handcream bottle) 'Lòok at thís!'
M: 'Yeah, it's àlmost émpty.'
Al: '[ɔ́:.moʷ__ ímpsti].'
(for 'almost empty' [ɔ́:.moʷs ímp.ti]; [s] moved from coda
of 'almost' and added between [pt] of 'empty'; syllable
boundary unclear in error, could be [ímp.sti] or [ímps.ti],
but MOP favors former; B; T?; NSC; p. 398)

AL-49 2;9.11   Al: 'I'm [pʰ__i.tʰʒ̰ìn.dɪŋ] thìs is a thíng.'
(for 'pretending' [pʰʒ̰i.tʰín.dɪŋ]; [ʒ̰] moved from onset
consonant cluster of first syllable of 'pretending', added to
onset of second syllable; W; NSC)

B-123 3;1.16   B: (naming a picture in a book): '[__ɛ́.ʒ̰ɪk] . . . cárrot.'
(for 'carrot' [kʰɛ́.ʒ̰ɪt]; [kʰ] moved from onset of first syllable
of 'carrot', substituted for coda [t] of second syllable,
deaspirated; W; SC)

B-131 3;5.28   B: 'I'll [sè:ʲ__ ʌf] my móney.'
(for 'save up' [se:ʲf ʌp]; [f] moved from coda of 'save',
substituted for [p] in coda of 'up'; B; -T; NSC)

AL-174 3;9.18   Al: 'Hère's Sn̰ow-Whíte! Hère's [s__ò̰ʷ.náʲt]!'
(for 'Snow-White' [sn̰ò̰ʷ.wáʲt]; [n] moved from onset of
'Snow', substituted for onset [w] in 'white', voiced; W;
NSC; p. 33)

AN-125 3;10.9   An: '[à.lə __àʲ méʲgs] . . . àlla m̰y̰ éggs.'
(for 'Alla (all of) my eggs' [á.lə maʲ eʲgs]; [m] moved from
onset of 'my', added as onset of 'eggs'; B; +T(e); SC)

AN-129 3;10.28 An: 'Hère's the whole fàmily [__ə.gɛ́:ðɚ tʰə.gìn].'
(for 'together again' [tʰə.gɛ́:ðɚ ə.gín]; [tʰ] moved from
onset of first syllable of 'together', added as onset of first
syllable of 'again'; B; -T; NSC)

AN-135 3;11.22   An: '[__ré.bi].'
(for 'Bretty', child's name, [bré.ɾi]; [b] moved from onset
of first syllable of 'Bretty', substituted for [ɾ] in onset of
second syllable; W; NSC; p. 158)

AN-158 4;2.13   An: 'Mommy, whàt does my [s__ík.tɚ] sày?'
M: 'Your what?'
An: 'Stícker!'
(for 'sticker' [stí.kɚ]; [t] moved from onset cluster of first
syllable of 'sticker', added to onset of second syllable,
causing [k] to be resyllabified; W; NSC; p. 146)

B-243   4;3.28   B: '[__té.fə.nis], I'll plày with you àfter dessért.'
(for 'Stephanie' [sté.fə.ni]; [s] moved from onset of first
syllable of 'Stephanie', added as coda of last syllable;
initial [t] did not become aspirated, possibly in assimilation to the [t] /d/ in 'dessert' [tɨ.zɚt]; W; NSC; p. 116)

B-244   4;3.28   B: (pretending to eat 'nothing')
'I spìt my 'nòthing' on your clèan [f__óɾɫ].'
(for 'floor' [fḷor]; [ḷ] moved from initial cluster of 'floor',
added at end of word, voiced and velarized; W; NSC)

AN-228 4;7.9   An: (in restaurant, watching colors change on a beer sign)
'Now the tòp is gonna turn rèd because the rèd part is
on the tóp, and the [b__ù pʰḷàrt] . . . the blùe pàrt is
on the bóttom.'
(for 'blue part' [blu pʰart]; [l] moved from onset of 'blue',
added into onset of 'part', devoiced; B; -T; SC)

15. Phonological perseverations, omissions, consonants.

AL-18   2;2.24   Al: '*M*y̌ *m*óvie òver. *M*è [__ǽtʰ]!'
M: 'What?'
Al: 'Mè mád!'
(for 'mad' [mǽtʰ]; [m] omitted from onset of 'mad',
dissimilation from preceding [m]'s; B; +T(e), possibly also
(s); NSC; p. 32)

B-88   2;6.26   B: 'I wànt my grápes.'
M: 'You wanna sáve 'em?'
B: 'I wànna sàve my [g__éʲps].' (looks confused)
(for 'grapes' [g̰ʒeʲps]; [ʒ] omitted from onset cluster of
'grapes', probably assimilation to C[eʲ] in 'save'; B; +T(e);
N-NC)

B-109   2;8.20   B: (riding in car, he suddenly realizes where we are)
'Móm! Dòwntown [__éʲ.vəs].'
M: 'What?'
B: 'Dòwntown D̲ávis.'
(for 'Davis' [déʲ.vəs]; [d] omitted from onset of 'Davis',
dissimilation from onset [d] in 'downtown'; B; +T(e); NSC)

AL-63   2;10.19   Al: 'Whère's Mìster [__pák] . . . Spóck?
(for 'Mister Spock' [mí.st3 spak]; [s] omitted from onset
cluster of 'Spock', dissimilation from preceding [s]; note
that /p/ doesn't aspirate; B; +T(e); SC; p. 116)

AL-72   2;10;25   Al: 'Ì can sèe my cláy [kʰ__æ̀s].'
(target 'class' [kʰḷæs]; [l] omitted from onset cluster of
'class', dissimilation from [l] in 'clay'; B; +T(s); NSC)

AL-122   3;4.11   Al: (after discovering a hole in her tights)
'My tóe! My tóe [__tʰìks] òut.'
(for 'sticks' [stɪks]; [s] omitted from onset cluster of 'sticks',
assimilation to single [t] onset of 'toe', although could be
dissimilation from coda /s/ in 'sticks'; /t/ aspirates; B;
+T(s); NSC; p. 32, 117)

B-135   3;6.9   B: 'Í want s̲ome [__tʰ3ìŋ] . . . s̲tring-chèese tóo!'
(for 'string' [st3íŋ]; [s] omitted from onset cluster of 'string',
dissimilation from preceding [s], though could be assimilation to onset [tʰ] in 'too'; /t/ aspirates; B; -T; SC; p. 146)

B-162   3;8.29   B: (being silly) 'That means you ìron your cómb; and
you ìron your vácuum [kʰ__ì] . . . cl̲èaner.'
(for 'vacuum cleaner' [vǽ.kjum kʰḷ̀ì.nɚ]; [l] omitted from
onset cluster of 'cleaner', most likely assimilation to single
[kʰ] onset in 'comb'; 'vacuum cleaner' may be a lexical
compound, but probably too complex phonetically to be a
single phonological word; B; T?, but (s) if 'comb' is source;
SC)

AL-172 3;9.7   Al: 'I'm a níce girl! I'm shàring my bíg blúe
[b__ǽŋ.kɪt].'
(for 'blanket' [blǽŋ.kɪt]; [l] omitted from onset cluster of
'blanket'; could be assimilation to single [b] onset in 'big'
or dissimilation from [l] in 'blue'; B; +T(e); NSC)

AN-127 3;10.24   An: 'Mommy, Naòmi's gònna sày us a [__tʰó.ri].'
(for 'story' [stó.ri]; [s] omitted from onset cluster in 'story',
dissimilation from preceding [s]'s; /t/ aspirates; B; +T(e);
NSC)

AN-142 4;0.19   An: 'I'm allèrgic to [__lǽ.sɪs] . . . glásses.'
(for 'glasses' [glǽ.sɪs]; [g] omitted from onset cluster of
'glasses', assimilation to single [l] onset in second syllable
of 'allergic' [ə.lɚ.dʒɪk]; B; +T(e); SC)

AL-208 4;2.7   Al: 'When it's a réd lìght, we [s__áp] . . . stóp!'
(for 'stop' [stap]; [t] omitted from onset cluster of 'stop',
dissimilation from preceding [t]'s; B; +T(e); SC; p. 155)

B-234   4;3.5   B: 'Héy, there's stíll some [s__í.kɚz].'
(for 'stickers' [stí.kɚz]; [t] omitted from onset cluster of
'stickers', could be assimilation to single [s] onset of 'some'
or dissimilation from [t] in 'still'; B; +T(e); NSC; p. 33)

B-252   4;4.4   B: (while we are looking for a parking spot) 'I don't sèe
a spót. (pause) Thére's a [__pʰàt] . . . spòt!'
(for 'spot' [spat]; [s] omitted from onset cluster of 'spot',
dissimilation from preceding [s]'s; /p/ aspirates; B; T?; SC)

OC-109 4;5.12   OB: 'Know whát Tim? Yòu have the sàme kind of
[béʲ__.bàɫ] . . . básebàll as mìne.'
(for 'baseball' [béʲs.baɫ]; [s] omitted from coda of first
syllable of 'baseball', dissimilation from [s] in 'same'; B;
+T(e); SC; p. 147)

B-282   4;5.12   B: (explaining a game)
'Whoèver gòbbles ùp all the [mà__.b] . . . whoèver
gòbbles ùp àll the màrbles wíns.'
(for 'marbles' [már.bəɫz]; [r] omitted from coda of first
syllable of 'marbles', assimilation to [a.b] sequence of
'gobbles' [gá.bəɫz]; B; -T; SC)

AN-211 4;5.28   M: 'Are you still wét?'
An: 'Yés, Ĭ'm [__tʰɨɬ] . . . Ĭ'm stìll wèt.'
(for 'still' [stɪɬ]; [s] omitted from onset cluster of 'still',
dissimilation from [s] in 'yes'; /t/ aspirates; B; -T; SC)

B-309 4;6.20   B: (writing the letter 'B' on blackboard)
'Mom, lòok at my bìg [__i:] . . . um [bí].'
(for 'B' [bi]; [b] omitted from onset of 'B', dissimilation
from [b] in 'big'; not confusion about which letter he was
writing; B; +T(e); SC)

B-328 4;7.8   B: 'Móm, lòok how bìg my [__ʌ.s] . . . múscles àre.'
(for 'muscles' [mʌ.səɬz]; [m] omitted from onset of
'muscles', dissimilation from preceding [m]'s; B; +T(e); SC)

B-400 4;11.3   B: (singing silly rhyme he made up) 'Mìster Cléan,
Mìster [kʰ__in] . . . Cléan, hè èats béans.'
(for 'clean' [kʰlin]; [l] omitted from onset cluster of 'Clean',
dissimilation from [l] in preceding 'Clean'; B; +T(b); SC)

AL-237 5;0.13   Al: 'Thìs pàrt is kìnda [__kʰɛ́.ri].'
M: 'Kinda what?'
Al: 'Kìnda scáry.'
(for 'scary' [skɛ́.ri]; [s] omitted from onset cluster of 'scary',
assimilation to single [k] onset of 'kinda'; /k/ aspirates; B;
+T(e); NSC)

AN-278 5;2.6   An: 'I have to lèt my bág drỳ, becàuse the [__lí] . . .
the glítter is wèt.'
(for 'glitter' [glí.rɚ]; [g] omitted from onset cluster of
'glitter', could be assimilation to single [l] onset of 'let', or
dissimilation from [g] in 'bag'; B; +T(e); SC)

B-475 5;3.17   B: 'Thère's a Stèphanie in Mr. Blaír's [kʰ__æs] . . .
clàss.'
(for 'class' [kʰlæs]; [l] omitted from onset cluster of 'class',
dissimilation from [l] in 'Blair'; B; +T(s); SC)

OC-161 5;8.5   OG: '[bí:.kʰ__ɚ᷆d].'
(for 'Big-Bird' [bík.bɚ᷆d]; [b] omitted from onset of second
syllable of 'Big-Bird', dissimilation from [b] in onset of
first syllable; then [k] is resyllabified as onset of second
syllable, aspirated; W; NSC)

OC-162 5;8.9   OB: 'Can I have some [__ó".də]?'
(for 'soda' [só".də]; [s] omitted from onset of 'soda',
dissimilation from onset [s] in 'some'; B; +T(e); NSC)

B-556 5;8.27   D: (joking about washing his hair in beer) 'How are we
gonna get bèer to come out of the shówer?'
B: 'Easy! It'll jùst go dòwn the [__ré¹n] . . . go dòwn
the dráin.'
(for 'drain' [dre¹n]; [d] omitted from onset cluster of 'drain',
dissimilation from [d] in 'down'; note that Bobby
misunderstands what Dad means: he interprets 'come out
of the shower' as 'leave the bathtub', rather than 'come out
of the shower head'; B; +T(e); SC)

AL-269 5;11.30   Al: 'I'm fúll. I have a small [__tʰʌ.mɪk].'
D: 'You have a small tomach?'
Al: 'I have a smàll stómach.'
(for 'stomach' [stʌ.mɪk]; [s] omitted from onset cluster of
'stomach', dissimilation from [s] in 'small'; /t/ aspirates; not
blend, as she rarely says 'tummy'; B; +T(e); NSC)

16. Phonological perseverations, substitutions, vowels.

AN-3b 1;7.15   An: (chanting name of book she wanted to read)
'Wìnnie-Póoh bòok. Wìnnie-Póoh pòok.
Wìnnie-Póoh [pɪk].'
(for 'book' [pʊk], source 'Winnie' [wí.ni]; [ɪ]-->[ʊ]; B; -T;
NSC; 3a=Class 12)

OC-1 1;10.0   OA: 'Whère's the cáterpìllar?'
OG: 'Ínna [æ.pɪ̀] . . . ápplè.'
(for 'apple' [æ.pò"], source most likely 'caterpillar'
[kʰǽ.ɾə.pʰì.lə˞]; [ɪ]-->[o"]; 2-word stage, 'Inna' is a single
word for 'In the'; B; -T; SC; p. 47)

B-39 2;1.26   B: 'Yòu lìe dówn [wàʲθ] mè.'
(for 'with' [wɪθ], source 'lie' [laʲ]; [aʲ]-->[ɪ]; B; -T; NSC)

AL-17 2;2.22   Al: 'Dàddy fìx tápe-[kʰò̰ʒ.di] . . . uh . . . 'corder.'
(for '(re)corder' [kʰó̰ʒ.dʒ], source 'Daddy' [dǽ.di]; [i]-->[ʒ];
B; -T; SC; p. 155)

OC-19   2;3.0   OG: 'Stèp in the [pʰέ.dəw].'
                    (for 'puddle' [pʰʌ.dəw], source 'step' [stɛp]; [ɛ]-->[ʌ]; B;
                    +T(e); NSC)

B-53   2;5.1   B: 'Bĭg bòys w̌ant a [bĭ.dəɫ].'
                    (for 'bottle' [bá.dəɫ], source 'big' [bɪg]; [ɪ]-->[a]; B; +T(e);
                    NSC)

AL-34   2;6.11   Al: 'The ȍrange brùsh is [ó.̌nəz] . . . (laughs) . . .
                    Ánna's!'
                    (for 'Anna's' [ǽ.nəz], source 'orange' [oʷ.ɪndʒ]; [oʷ]-->[æ]; B;
                    +T(e); SC)

B-112   2;9.14   B: 'Lìnda, it's vèry [wín.da] . . . w̌indy.'
                    (for 'windy' [wín.di], source 'Linda' [lín.da]; [a]-->[i]; B; -T;
                    SC; p. 108)

AL-87   3;0.9   Al: 'Mom, thìs thíng fàlled òff.'
                    M: 'ÓK, I'll gȍ gèt the glúe.'
                    Al: 'Then just [glȍʷ] it . . . glṳe it back ón.'
                    (for 'glue' [glu], source either 'OK' [ó.̌keʲ] or 'go' [goʷ],
                    which is more likely; [oʷ]-->[u]; 'falled' is normal for her;
                    B; -T; SC)

OC-42   3;3.0   OA: (talking to OB1) 'Did you do your fair share of clέan
                    up today?'
                    OB2: 'Í did mý fàir [ʃ̌iː] . . . shàre.'
                    (for 'share' [ʃɛr], source 'clean' [kʰlin]; [i]-->[ɛ]; B; +T(s);
                    SC)

B-126   3;3.5   B: 'I wànt you to gȅt me a frùit [ʒɛ́ɫ]-ùp.'
                    (for 'roll-up' [ʒóʷɫ.ʌp], source 'get' [gɛt]; [ɛ]-->[oʷ]; B; +T(e);
                    NSC)

AL-123   3;4.11   Al: 'I ȍpended this [óʷp].'
                    M: 'What?'
                    Al: 'I òpened this úp!'
                    (for 'up' [ʌp]; [oʷ]-->[ʌ]; notice that after Mom's prompt she
                    not only corrects speech error, but also gets correct
                    pronunciation of past tense on verb: 'opended' [óʷ.pən.dəd]
                    vs. 'opened' [óʷ.pənd]; B; +T(e); NSC)

B-139   3;7.26   B: 'Is '*B*' for 'blúe'?'
                   M: 'Yeah.'
                   B: 'I'll find a [blí] . . . [blí] . . . I said "[blì]" for "blúe". '
                   (for 'blue' [blu], source 'B' [bi]; [i]-->[u]; B; +T(e); SC)

B-161   3;8.21   B: (telling Mom about the 'pants' [pʰǽnts] he was
                      wearing; then, next sentence is)
                   'I have bòots on with nò [sǽ:] . . . nò sócks.'
                   (for 'socks' [saks]; probably perseveration from 'pants',
                   although could be a word blend of 'socks/pants'; [æ]-->[a];
                   B; +T(b); SC)

OC-64   3;9.0   OG: 'I plàyed Mìster [wí?] . . . I plàyed Mìster Rógers.'
                   (for 'Mister Rogers' [mí.st3 wá.dʒ3z]; [ɪ]-->[a]; B; +T(e);
                   SC)

AL-181   3;10.11   Al: 'Have you èver hèard of a grèen cát?
                   M: 'No.'
                   Al: 'Í [hɜ̀v] . . . Í hàve.'
                   (for 'have' [hæv], source 'heard' [h3d]; [3]-->[æ]; B; -T;
                   NSC)

OC-81   4;0.0   D: 'What cólor are they, Jim?'
                   OB:'Blùe and [rúd].'
                   (for 'red' [rɛd], source 'blue' [blu]; [u]-->[ɛ]; B; +T(e); NSC)

B-180   4;0.22   D: (talking about fruit he bought) ' . . . óranges.'
                   B: (changing the subject) 'Lòok at [óʲ.ləs].'
                   (for 'Alice' [ǽ.ləs]; [o] perseverated from 'oranges'
                   [órŋ.dʒɨz], substituted for [æ]; epenthetic [j] probably due to
                   palatal [ɲ] in 'oranges'; B; +T(b); NSC)

OC-89   4;1.7   OB: 'Nów can I rìde it [ʌ.gàn] . . . agàin?'
                   (for 'again' [ʌ.gén]; source 'now' [naʷ], but only the vowel
                   nucleus, not the offglide, is substituted; [a]-->[ɛ]; B; +T(s);
                   SC)

B-239   4;3.12   M: 'What did you do with that stícker bòok?'
                   B: 'That stícker [bɚk]? (thinks) It's ìn your róom.'
                   (for 'book' [bʊk], source 'sticker' [stí.kɚ]; [ɚ]-->[ʊ]; B; -T;
                   NSC)

B-247   4;3.29   B: (explaining some game he's just making up)
'If ànyone pìcks 'cóokie', it'll be cóokie tìme.
But dòn't [pʰɒ̀k] . . . pǐck thís òne.'
(for 'pick' [pʰɪk], source 'cookie' [kʰʊ́.ki]; [ʊ]-->[ɪ]; B; +T(s);
SC)

B-264   4;4.16   B: 'I'm góod at sètting [tʰɛ̀.bəɬs] . . .
I'm góod at sètting tàbles.'
(for 'tables' [tʰéʲ.bəɬz], source 'setting' [sɛ́.rɪŋ]; [ɛ]-->[eʲ]; B;
-T; SC)

OC-111 4;6.0   OA: 'Sùe pàinted some pǐctures.'
OG: 'She dìdn't paìnt [pʰʌ́k.tʃ] . . . pǐctures.'
(for 'pictures' [pʰík.tʃɚz], source 'some' [sʌm]; could also
be blend of 'some' and 'pictures; [ʌ]-->[ɪ]; B; +T(e); SC)

B-297   4;6.5   B: 'It's rǒot beer [sú.rʌ] . . . sóda.'
(for 'soda' [sóʷ.rʌ], source 'root' [rut]; [u]-->[oʷ]; B; +T(e);
SC)

AN-225 4;6.26   M: 'What dréss do you wànt?'
An: (pointing) 'Thàt, with a [ʃʊ́t] òver it . . . shǐrt òver it.'
(for 'shirt' [ʃɚt], sources 'do you' [du ju]; [u]-->[ɚ]; B; +T(e);
SC)

B-395   4;10.30 B: (explaining a Teenage Mutant Ninja Turtle toy)
'You pùt the wèapons in his shéll, and you ǒpen his
shèll [óʷp] . . . úp, and (etc.)'
(for 'up' [ʌp], source 'open' [óʷ.pən]; [oʷ]-->[ʌ]; B; +T(e);
SC)

B-417   4;11.12 B: ' "Ooooo, Ooooo." Thàt's what a dóve [dùz] . . .
dòes.'
(for 'does' [dʌz], dove sound is [u: u:]; [u]-->[ʌ]; could also
be misselection of verb form 'do' [du]; B; T?; SC)

B-469   5;2.7   M: 'You guys can play until it's time for Anna to go.'
B: 'Tò her [pʰár.rɚ]?'
M: 'What?'
B: 'Tò her párty?'
(for 'party' [pʰár.ri], source most likely 'her' [hɚ], or [r] in
'party'; [ɚ] (or [r]) -->[i]; B/W, T?; NSC)

AN-288 5;5.17   An: 'You know what Bóbby did? He crìed his [hǎ↓d] . . .
                    he crìed his héad off.'
                    (for 'head' [hɛd], source 'cried' [kʰɹḁɪd]; [aɪ]-->[ɛ]; B; +T(e);
                    SC)

OC-172 5;11.6   OG: 'Sàlly, Péter; Pèter, [sǽ.lɚ] . . . (laughs) Sálly!'
                    (for 'Sally' [sǽ.li], source 'Peter' [pʰí.ɹɚ]; [ɚ]-->[i]; B; -T;
                    SC)

17. Phonological perseverations, movements, vowels.

AL-50 2;9.13   Al: '[kʰá.f__ tʰà ʲ.mi].'
                   M: 'What?'
                   Al: 'Cóffee tìme.'
                   (for 'coffee time' [kʰá.fi tʰaɪm]; [i] moved from end of
                   'coffee' and added to end of 'time', with resyllabification;
                   B; -T; NSC; p. 53, 406)

AL-102 3;3.9   M: 'What do you want for bréakfast, Alice?'
                   Al: '[sì.ʒ̲__ə.li] . . . [sì] . . . (6 more times, can't get
                       untangled; finally takes deep breath) cèreal, èggs,
                       and tóast.'
                   (for 'cereal' [sí.ʒi.ə+]; [i] moved from nucleus of second
                   syllable to end of word, with resyllabification; could be
                   analyzed as exchange of larger units; W; SC with struggle;
                   p. 53, 406)

AL-171 3;9.7   Al: '[ɡʌ́.m__.bè.ʒiz].'
                   (for Gummi-Bears' [ɡʌ́.mi.bèʒ(z)]; [i] moved from end of
                   first word and added to end of second word, but before
                   plural morpheme; she didn't know 'gum' was related to
                   'Gummi', so not morphological, although she did know the
                   word 'berries'; W; NSC; p. 53, 406)

18. Phonological perseverations, substitutions, larger units.

OC-14 2;2.0   OB: (describing a picture of Micky Mouse playing
                       baseball) 'Mìckey Mòuse [mì.kən] báseball.'
                   (target 'playin' ' (playing), [pʰéʲ.ən], source 'Mickey'
                   [mí.ki]; [mɪ.k]-->[pʰeʲ], as if 'mick' was a verb stem; B; -T;
                   NSC)

B-63   2;5.16   B: 'I want cl̀ean [kʰl̥ǽnts] . . . clèan pánts.'
                  (for 'pants' [pʰænts], source 'clean' [kʰl̥in]; onsets [kʰl]-->[pʰ];
                  B; +T(e); SC)

AL-39   2;7.14   Al: 'Yùkky [bʌ́.k] . . . Bóbby fòod!'
                   (for 'Bobby' [bá.b(i)], source 'yukky' [jʌ́.k(i)]; [ʌ.k]-->[a.b];
                   B; +T(e); SC; p. 158)

OC-47   3;3.5   OB: 'Gràndma's trỳin' ta gèt me awày from the [fá.daʳ],
                       but the spìder's trỳin' ta gét me!'
                  (for 'spider' [θpa.daʳ], source 'from' [fr̥ʌm]; onsets [f]-->[θp];
                  B; +T(e); NSC)

OC-71   3;10.17   OB: (talking to his Grandmother on the phone)
                        'Gràmma, I got nèw Scòoby Doo [grǽn] . . . I got
                        nèw Scòoby Dòo pánties.'
                    (for 'panties' [pʰǽn.tiz], source 'Gramma' [grǽ.mə]; onsets
                    [gr]-->[pʰ]; B; +T(e); SC)

AL-188   3;11.2   Al: 'I want Bòbby's [bá.ti] . . . bóttle.'
                    (for 'bottle' [bá.təɫ], source 'Bobby's' [bá.bi(z)]; rhymes
                    [i]-->[əɫ], minus posessive suffix; B; -T; SC)

AN-132   3;11.16   An: 'Todày we were wàtching a [kʰaʳ] . . . a cartóon.'
                     (for 'cartoon' [kʰar.tʰún], source 'were' [waʳ]; [aʳ]--->[ar]; B;
                     -T; SC)

B-186   4;1.8   B: 'I wànt some ápplejuice in this "Nèw Kìds on the
                      Blòck" [kʰl̥àp] . . . cùp.'
                  (for 'cup' [kʰʌp], source 'Block' [blak]; [la]-->[ʌ]; B; -T; SC;
                  p. 151, 155)

B-189   4;1.11   B: (singing) 'The Rìght [d̪ʌ́f].'
                   (for 'Stuff' [stʌf], source 'the' [d̪ʌ]; not just omission of [s],
                   since [d] was voiced and dentalized; onsets [d̪]-->[st]; B;
                   +T(e); NSC)

B-237   4;3.9   B: (looking through book) 'Where is that stòry on the lòst
                      cárd? I'm [fár.ɾɪŋ] . . . I'm fínding ìt.'
                  (for 'finding' [fá.ʰn.dɪŋ], source 'card' [kʰard]; V{N,L}
                  [ar]-->[aʰn], then [d]-->[ɾ]; B; +T(b); SC)

B-287   4;5.20   B: (pulling his dirty socks out of his boots)
'The s*ock*s are in the [báks]. (notices error, laughs)
I said "[báks]".'
(for 'boots' [but(s)]; rhymes [ak]-->[ut], minus plural suffix;
B; +T(e); N-NC)

B-295   4;6.4   B: 'Does Anna have a smóck?'
M: 'Yeah. It's in her *cl*óset.'
B: 'Well, Ì have [kʰ]à] . . . sm̥òcks at afternóon schòol.'
(for 'smocks' [sm̥aks], source 'closet' [kʰlá.zɨt]; onsets
[kʰl]-->[sm̥]; or possibly he started to perseverate the
whole word 'closet'; B; +T(s); SC)

AL-231 4;6.22 Al: 'Momma, where's one of those [sɜ́ f.bɜ̀dz] . . .
Where's one of those súrfboards?'
(for 'surfboards' [sɜ́f.bò̰dz]; [ɜ]-->[o̰]; W; SC)

AN-284 5;4.3   M: 'What do you want to drínk, *apple*jùice?'
An: 'Mom, wè sàw Slèeping Bèauty on a?
[æ̀.pə].tʰá̩z.mɨnt].' (looks confused)
(for 'advertisement' [æ̀d.vɚ.tʰá̩z.mɨnt], source 'apple'
[ǽ.pə]]; [pə]]-->[d.vɚ]; it is possible that the whole
morpheme 'apple' is perseverated, but since 'adver' is not a
morpheme, better to analyze this as a phonological error;
B; -T; N-NC)

B-518   5;5.30 M: 'Whàt do cà̀ts dó all dày?'
B: 'Eàt [mǽt].'
M: 'Eàt whát?'
B: 'Eàt míce.'
(for 'mice' [maɪs], source 'cats' [kʰæt(s)]; rhymes [æt]-->[aɪs],
minus the plural suffix on 'cats'; B; +T(e); NSC; p. 161)

AL-253 5;8.1   An: 'Alice, you *sm*éll bad.
Al: 'Yeah, I [sm̥ár.rəd] . . . fárted.'
(for 'farted' [fár.rəd], source 'smell' [sm̥ɛ]]; onsets
[sm]-->[f]; B; +T(b); SC)

OC-173 5;11.30 OG: 'It's òut of [ǽʷ.rɚ].'
(for 'order' [ór.rɚ], source 'out' [ǽʷt]; [ǽʷ]-->[or]; B; +T(e);
NSC)

19. Phonological perseverations, additions, larger units.

B-201   4;1.27   B: (telling Daddy that Mommy said it was OK)
'Ì càn have a *gl*àss of Kóol-[**gl**è ͯd].'
(for 'Kool-Aid' [kʰúɬ.è ͯd], source 'glass' [glæs]; [gl]
perseverated from 'glass', added as onset to second
syllable of 'Kool-Aid'; B; -T; NSC)

20. Phonological A/P, subsitutions, consonants.

B-10   1;9.11   M: 'You wànna rèad a *b*óok?'
B: '[pìtʰ] . . . <u>rèad</u> *b*óok.'
(for 'read book' [witʰ pʊkʰ]; [p] substituted for [w]; 2-word
stage; B; SC)

AN-25   2;0.27   An: (reciting her version of poem)
'*P*átty-càke, *p*átty-[**pʰ**è ͯk] . . . no. . . [**pʰ**è ͯk] . . .
Pátty-<u>c</u>àke, pátty-<u>c</u>àke, *P*ízzà Mán.'
(for 'patty-cake' [pʰǽ.ti.kʰè ͯk]; [pʰ] substituted for [kʰ];
either perseveration from 'patty' or interrupted anticipation
of 'Pizza'; B/W; SC)

B-35   2;1.1   M: 'You wànna gò *b*ùck náked?'
B: '[bòʷ] . . . *b*ùck náked.'
(for 'go' [goʷ]; [b] substituted for [g]; B; N-NC)

B-38   2;1.16   M: 'Bobby, your bìb's fùll of jé*ll*y.'
B: 'My bìb's fu*ll* a [lέ] . . . jé*ll*y?'
(for 'jelly' [dʒέ.li]; [l] substituted for [dʒ]; B/W; SC)

OC-15   2;2.0   OG: (singing "Wheels on the Bus")
'The drìver o*n* the [nʌs] says móve òn bàck.'
(for 'bus' [bʌs]; [n] substituted for [b]; B; NSC)

AL-28   2;5.2   Al: (saying rhyme)
'*P*átty-[**pʰ**è ͯk], *p*átty-<u>c</u>àke, bàkèr's mán.'
(for 'cake' [kʰe ͯk]; [pʰ] substituted for [kʰ], probably
perseveration from same phrase; B/W; NSC)

AL-64   2;10.20   Al: 'Mòm, can wè go to the [gȝòʷ.kȝi] stòre . . . can wè
                      go to the gròcery stòre and bùy some Bónkers?'
                      (for 'grocery' [gȝóʷ.sȝi]; [k] substituted for [s]; probably
                      anticipation from 'Bonkers' [báŋ.k3z] candy; B; SC)

B-120   2;10.28   B: 'I'll tèll [lù] . . . yòu I wànt a pópsicle. Can I have
                      a pópsicle?'
                      (for 'you' [ju]; [l] substituted for [j]; 'tell' means 'ask' B;
                      SC)

AL-74   2;11.0   M: 'You càn't have Bònkers after bréakfast, only after
                      lúnch.'
                      Al: 'Mòmmy [lì] . . . thìs ís lúnch!'
                      (for 'this' [dɪs]; [l] substituted for [d]; B; SC)

AL-113 3;3.26   Al: 'It's vèry sóft. Ìsn't it [fà] . . . sòft to yóu?'
                      (for 'soft' [saft]; [f] substituted for [s]; B/W; SC; p. 151)

AL-126 3;4.13   M: 'How 'bout some chèrry jéllo?'
                      Al: '[tʃè.li] . . . chèrry jéllo? Yéah!'
                      (for 'cherry' [tʃé.ȝi]; [l] substituted for [ȝ]; B; SC)

AL-138 3;6.3   D: 'Why don't you put the sáusage in it?'
                      Al: 'Yeah, [sá.tʃɪ] . . . sáusage!'
                      (for 'sausage' [sá.sɪtʃ]; [tʃ] substituted for [s]; B/W; SC)

AL-139 3;6.5   D: 'What do you want for bréakfast? How 'bout
                      páncakes?'
                      Al: 'Hòw 'bòut [kʰǽn] . . . hòw 'bòut páncàkes?'
                      (for 'pancakes' [pʰǽn.kʰèⁱks]; [kʰ] substituted for [pʰ]; B/W;
                      SC)

AN-121 3;8.13   M: 'Ánna, come eat lúnch.'
                      An: 'Nó, I don't wánt [nʌm] lùnch.'
                      (for 'some' [sʌm]; [n] substituted for [s]; could also be blend
                      of 'some' and 'no', since more stressed than would expect
                      for 'some'; B; NSC)

AL-160 3;8.25   Al: 'It tùrns òut to bè a [béⁱn.bòʷ] . . . ráinbòw.'
                      (for 'rainbow' [ȝéⁱn.bòʷ]; [b] substituted for [ȝ]; B/W; SC)

AN-130 3;11.7   M: (doing an alphabet puzzle) 'We're still mìssing the
                      " *f* ".'
                 An: (working on a puzzle of a person) 'And we're still
                      [mì.fɪŋ] . . . mìssing on mé, thìs and the *f*áce!'
                      (for 'missing' [mí.s(ɪŋ)]; 'f' is [ɛf]; [f] substituted for [s];
                      B; SC)

B-175   4;0.3   B: (playing with neighbor boy) 'Mommy, could yòu *g*et
                     my [ɡóʷ.stɚ], so hè can plày *Gh*óstbùsters wìth me?'
                 M: 'Get your ghóster?'
                 B: 'My ṛóaster!'
                    (for 'roaster' [róʷ.stɚ], a toy gun; [ɡ] substituted for [r]; B;
                    NSC)

B-176   4;0.5   B: 'Mom, are yòu màk*ing* [kʰǽ] . . . ṗáncàk*es*?'
                    (for 'pancakes' [pʰǽn.kʰèⁱks]; /k/ substituted for [pʰ]; B/W;
                    SC; p. 63)

OC-92   4;2.0   OG: '*M*ỳ [mèⁱ*m*] . . . mỳ ṇàme is *M*égan, and I'*m*
                      fóur.'
                     (for 'name' [neⁱm]; [m] substituted for [n]; B/W; SC)

B-229   4;2.28   B: 'Mom, *l*òok at his [blẻʲ] . . . ḅráce*l*et.'
                    (for 'bracelet' [bréʲs.lɨt]; [l] substituted for [r]; B/W; SC)

AN-163 4;2.29   An: 'Áli, we bòth *g*òt the sáme, 'cuz we [ɡòʷθ] . . . we
                     ḅòth *g*òt pínk.'
                     (for 'both' [boʷθ]; [ɡ] substituted for [b]; B; SC)

AN-164 4;3.14   An: (after drawing picture for Mom) 'You *w*ànt me to
                     [wèʲk] . . . you wànt me to ṃàke *o*ne for Dáddy?'
                     (for 'make' [meʲk]; 'one' is [wʌn]; [w] substituted for [m]; B;
                     SC)

B-255   4;4.7   B: (finding a hiding place in Mom's study, behind the
                     door) 'Thàt'*s* a [grèʲs] . . . grèaṭ plàce to híde.'
                    (for 'great' [greʲt]; [s] substituted for [t]; most likely
                    anticipation from 'place', as it has the same adjacent vowel
                    and stress; B; SC)

AN-181 4;4.26   M: (getting kids dressed for Halloween; Anna's costume
                      was a ghost)
                      'Nó, you càn't wèar Alìce's clówn còstume.'
                  An: 'Yéah, *be*càuse I'm [bù] *b*íg.' (looks confused)
                      (for 'too big' [tʰu bɪg]; [b] substituted for [tʰ]; could also be
                      lexical selection error 'boo', in Halloween context; B;
                      N-NC)

B-272   4;4.30   B: 'Mom, tà*ke* it apárt, then [pʰʊk] it bà*ck* togéther
                      agàin, OK?'
                      (for 'put' [pʰʊt]; [k] substituted for [t]; B; NSC)

AN-195 4;5.7   An: 'We *c*án't get the chì*ck*en [kʰa] . . . the chìcken
                      p*o*x, '*c*uz we alrèady hád 'em.'
                      (for 'pox' [pʰaks]; /k/ substituted for [pʰ]; B/W; SC)

B-279   4;5.8   M: 'Alice, yòu're the Trásh *Q*uèen.'
                  B: 'Í'm the [kʰɹ̥æ̀ʃ] . . . Í'm the Tràsh *K*íng.
                      (for 'trash' [tʰɹ̥æʃ]; [kʰ] substituted for [tʰ]; B; SC)

AN-199 4;5.16   An: 'Mom, Àli's gonna lèt me *p*ùt the [pʰéʲp] . . .
                      pùt the t̯ápe on.'
                      (for 'tape' [tʰeʲp]; /p/ substituted for [tʰ]; B/W; SC)

B-291   4;5.27   B: (while watching a commercial) 'Hérshey's *d*rìnks!
                      I lóve [dʒɚ.ʃiz] *d*rìnks, but you háte 'em.'
                      (for 'Hershey's drinks' [hɚ.ʃiz dʒrɪŋks]; [dʒ] substituted for
                      [h]; B; NSC; p. 123)

OC-114 4;6.15   OB: (talking about Nintendo game with 'giant dinosaurs',
                      which he said several times, then)
                      '. . . becàuse [dʒɛ] . . . t̲h̲ere's nò such thìng in the
                      wórld as *g*ìant dìnosaurs.'
                      (for 'there's' [ðɛ̰ʒ̰ θ]; [dʒ] substituted for [ð]; B; SC)

B-316   4;6.31   B: ('reading' "Big and Small" book)
                      '[màr.brz] à*re*. . . màrb̲les àre smáll.'
                      (for 'marbles are' [már.bɬz ar]; non-syllabic (r) substituted
                      for [ɬ], becomes syllabic; B/W; SC; p. 113)

B-321   4;7.4   B: (talking about kinds of TV dinners) 'Nèxt time gèt
me [skì.di] . . . um. . . Spèedy Gonzáles.'
(for 'Speedy' [spí.di]; sources 'get' [kɛt] and 'Gonzales'
[kan.sá.ləs]; [k] substituted for [p], or possibly feature
error; B; SC)

B-329   4;7.9   B: (singing) 'La Cùcaràchá! La [kʰù.tʃə.rà:.tʃá]!'
(for 'Cucaracha' [kʰù.kə.rà:.tʃá]'; [tʃ] substituted for [kʰ];
B/W; NSC)

AN-235 4;8.7   An: (bottom of piggy bank fell inside)
'Momma, the thìng that kèeps the mòney in my lìttle
[tʰæ̀ŋk] has gòtten ín hère.'
(for 'bank' [bæŋk]; /t/ substituted for [b]; B; NSC)

AN-243 4;9.23 An: (wearing rainbow sunglasses) 'Thèse are my sécret
shàdes. Thèse are càlled [ʃ ík] . . . sécret shàdes.'
(for 'secret' [sí.kɹ̩t]; [ʃ] substituted for [s]; B; SC)

B-376   4;10.7   B: (was just told to drink water, not soda)
'I háte wàter! I [wéʰt] . . . I háte wàter.'
(for 'hate' [heʰt]; [w] substituted for [h]; B; SC)

B-377   4;10.8   B: 'Hè's [hòʷ] hót . . . hè's sò hót I càn't hóld hìm.'
(for 'so' [soʷ]; [h] substituted for [s]; B; SC)

B-383   4;10.13 B: (telling Mom what street a friend lives on) 'It's the
sàme plàce where [bɨɬ] . . . where Bén lìves.'
(for 'Ben' [bĩn]; [ɬ] substituted for [n], vowel denasalizes;
not lexical selection error since he doesn't know any kids
named 'Bill'; B; SC)

AN-250 4;10.14 An: (Mom is reading a story to her; at a certain point in
the story she expects Mom to say 'fascinating', but
Mom forgets) 'Momma, you dìdn't sày
[sǽ.sʌ.nèʲ.tɪŋ].' (grins, realizes error)
M: 'Sáscinàting.' (imitating her)
An: 'No! Fáscinating!'
(for 'fascinating' [fǽ.sʌ.nèʲ.tɪŋ]; [s] substituted for [f]; B/W;
N-NC)

B-393   4;10.24   B: (Anna had spilled water on the kitchen floor, and was
supposed to have wiped it up)
'Anna, you didn't get all the méss. There's some
wáter there. I [stéps] òn . . . sòme wàter.'
(for 'stepped' [stɛpt]; [s] substituted for [t]; could also be
morpheme selection error, present for past tense; B/W;
N-NC)

B-428   4;11.30   B: 'Wátermèlon! I lóve [mà.rɚ] . . . wàtermèlon.'
(for 'watermelon' [wá.rɚ.mè.lən]; [m] substituted for [w];
B/W; SC)

AN-272 5;1.28   An: (some guests are napping in the study)
'Mòm, I wànna slèep with thém! I wànna [sw̥ip]
w̥ith thém!'
(for 'sleep' [sl̥ip]; [w] substituted for [l]; B; NSC)

B-461   5;2.0   B: (naming pictures) '[kʰ ɪ̀.kɨn], kàngaróo.'
(for 'kitten' [kʰí.tɨn]; [k] substituted for [t]; B/W; NSC)

AL-239 5;5.13   Al: 'Í líke chòcolate and [və.lí] . . . vanílla.'
(for 'vanilla' [və.ní.lə]; [l] substituted for [n]; B/W; SC)

B-508   5;5.24   B: 'Mom, Dàd might want áll the Tèrminator tòys.
[tʰɚ] his . . . for his nèxt bìrthday I'm gònna gìve
him áll the Tèrminators.'
(for 'for' [fɚ]; [tʰ] substituted for [f]; B; SC)

B-519   5;5.30   B: (explaining dictionary words) 'A drèss is sòmething
gírls [rèr], lìke thís.' (points to Alice's nightgown)
(for 'wear' [wɛr]; [r] substituted for [w]; B/W; NSC)

B-524   5;5.30   B: 'I knòw what a? [áʲ.nʌn] . . . I knòw whàt a?
ísland ìs.'
(for 'island' [áʲ.lʌn]; [n] substituted for [l]; B/W; SC)

B-535   5;6.20   An: 'When you bùy a snáck, you gìve mòney to Màple-
                   Eást.'
                   B: 'Fróm [mè'.s . . . pʌɫ]-Eàst.' ('Maple-East' is their
                      elementary school)
                   (for 'maple' [méʲ.pʌɫ]; [s] substituted for [p], although it
                   could have been an addition; not clear why he
                   thought 'from' was the correct preposition; B/W; SC)

B-536   5;6.22   B: 'I'm gonna skì dòwn the hìghest [nǽʷn.tən].'
                   (for 'mountain' [mǽʷn.tən]; [n] substituted for [m]; B/W;
                   NSC)

AN-294   5;7.8   An: 'I wànt my pìnk tèddy-[pʰɛ̀r] pánties.'
                   (for 'teddy-bear' [tʰɛ́.ɾi.bèr]; [pʰ] substituted for [b]; B;
                   NSC)

AL-245   5;7.17   Al: (wearing her Christmas ring) 'Yòu could wèar your
                       [ré.ɾɪŋ] rìng, so wè could mátch!'
                   (for 'wedding' [wɛ́.ɾɪŋ]; [r] substituted for [w]; B; NSC)

AN-300   5;7.19   An: 'Grándpa's name is Ròbert, and Dáddy's name is
                       Ròbert, and Bóbby's name is [rà.rɚt].'
                   (for 'Robert' [rá.bɚt]; possibly A or P of /t/, then flapping;
                   could also be tap from 'Daddy' [dǽ.ɾi]; [ɾ] substituted for
                   [b]; B/W; NSC)

AL-246   5;7.19   Al: 'Thère's a túrtle in this [kʰɾæ̀s.rùm].'
                   (for 'classroom' [kʰlǽs.rùm]; [r] substituted for [l]; B/W;
                   NSC; p. 113)

AL-247   5;7.20   Al: (showing Mom how big the gob of shampoo was she
                       got in her eye) 'I gòt one [dɪ́g] bìg . . . thìs big.'
                   (for 'this' [d̪ɪs]; [g] substituted for [s]; B; SC)

B-549   5;7.23   B: 'Dàvid ràn [ə.réʲ] . . . ràn awáy from mè.'
                   (for 'away' [ə.wéʲ]; [r] substituted for [w]; B; SC)

AN-308   5;8.15   M: (offering her a quesadilla) 'Do you want a whóle one?'
                   An: 'Yes, a whóle òne. A [lóʷɫ] òne.'
                   (for 'whole' [hoʷɫ]; [ɫ] substituted for [h], develarized; B/W;
                   NSC)

AL-257 5;9.27   Al: 'Even póo*l* [wà.lɚ] . . . even póol wàter màkes you
clèan, sórt òf.'
(for 'water' [wá.rɚ]; /l/ substituted for [r] /t/; B; SC)

OC-170 5;10.13   OG: '*M*y [mèst] *m*è*m*ory of kìndergarten is rèading
bóoks.'
(for 'best' [bɛst]; [m] substituted for [b]; B/W; NSC)

B-571   5;10.24   D: 'Are thère the sàme téa*ch*ers at sùmmer càmp as làst
sùmmer?'
B: 'Yeah, [tʃè'm] . . . s̲àme téa*ch*ers.'
(for 'same teachers' [se'm tʰi.tʃ(ɚ)(z)]; [tʃ] substituted for [s];
B; SC; p. 155)

B-572   5;11.4   B: 'Yèah, thàt'*s* where the [á.si.jəns] . . . s̀it*s*.'
(for 'audience' [á.di.jəns]; [s] substituted for [d]; B/W;
N-NC)

B-577   5;11.10   D: (joking about where we stayed in the Grand Canyon)
'We slèp*t* under a *t*áble, dídn't wè.'
B: 'No, we [stèp*t*] in a béd! . . . We s̲l̲èpt in a béd!'
(for 'slept' [s̲lɛpt]; [t] substituted for [l]; B/W; SC)

B-587   5;11.25   B: (looking for the house number of a house we had
stopped at)
'Doe*s* thìs *s*ay [sén] . . . t̲én *s*omeplàce?'
(for 'ten' [tʰɛn]; [s] substituted for [tʰ]; B; SC)

21. Phonological A/P, additions, consonants.

B-4   1;8.29   M: 'Who's thát?' (pointing to picture of Cookie Monster in
book)
B: 'Cóokie.' (then sees Oscar, points) '[ká.*k*3]'
(for 'Oscar' [á.k3]; [k] added to onset of 'Oscar'; source
'Cookie' is [kú.ki]; 1-word stage; B/W; NSC)

AN-36   2;2.29   An: (saying nursery rhyme)
'Dòc*tor* [f3à.st3] wènt to Glóuchest*er*.'
(for 'Foster' [fá.st3]; [3] added to onset; sources are the
vowel [3]; 'Glouchester' is pronounced [glá.st3]; B/W; NSC;
p. 113)

B-70   2;6.2   B: 'I want some cráckers; I want some [tʃ₃́iz]
cràckers.'
(for 'cheese' [tʃiz]; source 'crackers' [kʰ₃ǽ.k₃s]; [₃] added to
onset; source either consonant [₃] or vowel [₃]; B/W; NSC)

OC-26   2;8.0   OG: 'Are thèse pópcòrns?   Are thèse [pʰárp.kʰòrns]?'
(for 'popcorns' [pʰáp.kʰòrns]; [r] added into coda of 'pop';
B/W; NSC)

AL-95   3;1.18   Al: 'Mòmma, will yòu sìt néar me, for I càn't [skèt]
scáred?'
(for 'get scared' [kɛt skɛ₃d]; [s] added into onset, most
likely anticipation of [sk] cluster; 'for' means 'so that'; B;
NSC; p. 117)

OC-48   3;3.15   OB: (telling what's in his zoo)
'Giràffes, [tʃ̢ì.kəns], rhínos.'
(for 'chickens' [tʃí.kəns]; [r] added into onset; [tʃ̢r̥] is a
permissible initial cluster for this child; 'giraffes' is
[dʒræfs], so this is more likely a perseveration; B; NSC;
p. 30)

AL-107   3;3.16   M: 'Àlice, you càn't eàt còld spaghétti.'
Al: 'I líke [skò̀ʷɬd] . . . I líke còld spaghètti.'
(for 'cold' [kʰoʷɬd]; [s] added to onset, /k/ deaspirated; B;
SC; p. 117)

AL-121   3;4.11   An: 'I lóve the tòy-stòre.'
Al: 'I háte the [stòʲ] . . . tòy-stòre.'
(for 'toy-store' [tʰóʲ.stòr]; [s] added onto onset, /t/
deaspirated; B/W; SC)

B-134   3;6.4   M: 'We're having bèef and ríce, your fávorite!'
B: 'Mỳ fávorite?   It's [nóʷ.b₃ə.diz] fàvorite!'
(for 'nobody's' [nóʷ.bə.diz]; source 'favorite' [féʲv.₃ət];
[₃] added into onset; B; NSC)

OC-58   3;8.0   OG: (playing with Sesame Street phone; she dials Oscar,
Oscar says) 'Háve a ròtten dáy.'
OG: '[rá] . . . Óscar, hàve a ròtten dáy!'
(for 'Oscar' [á.skɚ]; [r] added as onset; B/W; SC)

OC-59   3;8.0   OB: (sticking objects into playdough: straws, toothpicks, beans, etc.) 'Want me to get some stráw?'
OG: 'Yès, [sḷ̀ì.təɬ] stráw!'
(for 'little' [lí.təɬ]; [s] added to onset, [l] devoiced; B; NSC)

AL-154   3;8.1   M: 'What kind of frúit do you wànt, Alice? There's gràpes, and pèars, and stráwberries.'
Al: '[spɛ́ʒ̀:s] . . . péars.'
(for 'pears' [pʰɛʒ̀:s]; [s] added to onset, /p/ deaspirated; B/W; SC)

B-148   3;8.12   B: 'Mòmma, guèss whát? We jùst clìmbed a bìg [dl: . . . ɜ́t] pìle.'
(for 'dirt' [d3t]; [l] added into onset, producing illegal cluster */dl/; B; N-NC; p. 144)

B-151   3;8.14   B: 'Our plàyschòol dòes wáter pèts at [spḷ̀èʲ] . . . plàyschóol.'
(for 'playschool' [pʰḷ̀éʲ.skù̀ɬ]; [s] added to onset, /p/ deaspirated; B/W; SC)

OC-66   3;9.10   OG: 'I'm nòt going to èat those [pʰŏ̀ʷz:] . . . pŏtàtoes at áll.'
(for 'potatoes' [pʰoʷ.tʰéʲ.toʷz]; [z] added to coda; could also be substitution for [t] or movement of the plural morpheme [z]; not telescoping, by stress; B/W; SC)

AL-175   3;10.0   An: 'Whìch fàmily?'
Al: 'Thís [fḷ̀æ̀m.ḷi].'
An: 'Flámily?' (laughs to tease Alice)
(for 'family' [fǽm.li]; [l] added into onset, devoiced; B/W; NSC)

AL-177   3;10.5   Al: 'I tòok mìne [tʰàf] with the twéezers.'
(for 'off' [af]; [tʰ] added as onset; B; NSC)

AN-145   4;1.13   An: (reading Dr. Seuss book)
'Ì can rèad in píckle [kʰḷ̀ʌ̀.lɚ] . . . píckle còlor tóo!'
(for 'pickle color' [pʰí.kəɬ kʰʌ́.lɚ]; [l] added into onset, devoiced and develarized; B/W; SC)

B-197   4;1.22   B: 'My *l* ìps are còvered with [tʰúθ.pʰļèⁱst] sḽobber.'
(for 'toothpaste' [tʰúθ.pʰèⁱst]; [l] added into onset; B/W;
NSC)

B-219   4;2.16   B: 'I wàɲt to gìve hiɱ ɱy [pʰĩŋk] . . . picture of
Dònɲie Wálberg.'
(for 'picture' [pʰík.ʃɚ]; nasal added into coda, assimilates
to velar place of [k], vowel nasalizes; B; SC)

OC-99   4;3.26   OB1: (getting drums off piano)
'We're tàking the drúms òut.'
OB2: 'What?'
OB1: 'We're [tʃɾèⁱ.kɪŋ] the drúms òut.'
(for 'taking' [tʰéⁱ.kɪŋ]; [r] added into onset, devoices;
[tʰ]-->[tʃ] before [r]; B; NSC; p. 123)

B-277   4;5.7   B: 'Whòever wànts me to [ʃòr] them a stó*r*y, with
bóoks, *r*àise their hánd.'
(for 'show' [ʃoʷ]; [r] added to coda, replaces offglide; B;
NSC)

B-280   4;5.8   B: (picking some grapes off stem)
'Thèn I'm gònna dò *s*ome [fæst], jú*c*y ònes.'
(for 'fat' [fæt]; [s] added into coda; possibly lexical
substitution of 'fast' for 'fat'; B; NSC)

B-298   4;6.9   D: (talking about gas station)
' . . . but thàt was their cásh prìces.'
B: (misunderstood) 'Cásh prìzes?
Whàt àre [kʰɾǽʃ] prìzes?'
(for 'cash' [kʰǽʃ]; [r] added into onset; B; N-NC)

B-318   4;7.0   B: 'Hìs [stʌ́ŋ] . . . his tóngue is sticking òut.'
(for 'tongue' [tʰʌ́ŋ]; [s] added to onset, /t/ deaspirates; B;
SC)

B-330   4;7.9   B: (handing out crayons)
'Here's mý còḽor, and here's yóur [kʰļʌ́] . . . còḽor.'
(for 'color' [kʰʌ́.lɚ]; [l] added into onset, devoiced; B/W;
SC)

B-336   4;7.18   B: (to a friend) 'Ì'll bè *s*úperbòy, and yòu [sp̀ì] . . . yòu
                        bè̲ *s*úpermàn.'
                        (for 'be' [pi]; [s] added to onset; B; SC)

AL-234   4;9.13   Al: 'I thìn*k* I [sk̀ì] . . . sèe̲ S*k*ipper.' ('Skipper' is a doll)
                        (for 'see' [si]; [k] added into onset; B; SC)

B-389   4;10.21   M: 'In*s*tèad of plàying háᵑgmàn, lèt'*s* plày *S*quíggle.'
                    B: 'Hòw do you [sp̯l̯é̯ʲ] *S*q̀ùiggle?'
                        (for 'play' [pʰle̯ʲ]; [s] added to onset, /p/ deaspirated; B;
                        NSC)

B-416   4;11.12   B: 'I nèed to tèll Álice something, if I could b*r*ìng òne of
                        he*r* [brúks] in hè*r*e.'
                        (for 'books' [bʊks]; [r] added into onset; 'tell' means 'ask';
                        B; NSC)

B-448   5;1.14   B: 'Mommy, the gìr*l*s a*r*e wàtching thei*r* [ʃór]
                        downstàir*s*, and I wanna wàtch my móvie!'
                        (for 'show' [ʃoʷ]; [r] added to coda, replaces offglide; B;
                        NSC)

B-484   5;4.3   B: (talking about what kind of vitamins he gets)
                        'Do I have óne with èx*t*ra [st̀i], or *t*wó?'
                        (for 'extra C' [ék.stɾʌ si]; [t] added to onset of 'C'; B; NSC)

B-493   5;4.20   B: 'Bìl*l*s S*l*ipper Sòx! Gò Bíl*l*s! Gò [blɪ́ɫs]!'
                        ('Bills' is a football team)
                        (for 'Bills' [bɪɫs]; [l] added to onset; B/W; NSC)

B-527   5;6.3   B: 'It's trácing [pʰɾ̀è̯ʲ.pɚ] . . . pàp̯er.'
                        (for 'paper' [pʰé̯ʲ.pɚ]; [r] added to onset; B/W; SC)

B-546   5;7.7   B: (Dad says it's a bad day to call a friend)
                        'Mòm sàid I could cál*l* Jòhn [pʰl̯àɫ].'
                        (for 'Paul' [pʰaɫ]; [l] added to onset, devoiced and
                        develarized; B/W; NSC)

AN-310 5;8.25   M: 'What do you want for dessért?'
An: 'A chòcolate hèart and a [báɾŋ.kɚ].'
(Bonker' is a kind of fruit candy)
(for 'Bonker' [báŋ.kɚ]; [r] added post-vocalically,
nasalized; B/W; NSC)

22. Phonological A/P, omissions, consonants.

AL-31   2;5.21   Al: 'I a lìttle sìster an' yòu a bìg [__íɕ.t3].'
(for 'sister' [ɕíɕ.t3]; onset [ɕ] omitted, dissimilation; B/W;
NSC)

B-89   2;7.1   M: (putting makeup on the children)
'Anyone want eyébrows?'
B: 'Í want [àʲ.b__æwz] . . . èyebrows.'
(for 'eyebrows' [áʲ.bwæwz]; onset [w] omitted,
dissimilation; B/W; SC)

AL-61   2;10.19   Al: 'Mòm, I líke [g__æs] . . . glàss bòttles.'
(for 'glass' [glæs]; onset [l] omitted, dissimilation; B; SC)

OC-37   3;0.1   M: 'Are yòu my cùte Kátie?'
OG: 'Nó, Ì'm nót yòur [kʰ__ùt] . . . cute Kàtie.'
(for 'cute' [cʰjut]; second element of onset [j] omitted, [kʰ]
becomes depalatalized; assimilation to 'Katie' or
dissimilation from 'your'; B; SC; p. 120)

B-182   4;0.29   B: 'Mommy, did thìs only còst [sìk__] dóllars . . . sìx
dóllars?'
(for 'six' [sɪks]; coda [s] omitted, dissimilation; B; SC)

B-187   4;1.9   M: 'Whàt's he dóing, cámping?'
B: 'Yéah, he's [kʰǽ__.pɪŋ] . . . cámping.'
(for 'camping' [kʰǽm.pɪŋ]; coda [m] omitted, dissimilation
from other nasals, vowel denasalizes; B/W; SC)

B-301   4;6.12   B: (nagging Mom about when he can eat his Kit Kat bar)
'Befòre or áfter; [bi.__jòr] . . . befòre or áfter.'
(for 'before' [bi.fór]; onset [f] omitted, dissimilation; [j]
epenthetically inserted between [i] and [o]; B; SC)

B-314   4;6.30   B: (singing a commercial)
                       'Gìve me a *br*éak, gìve me a [__ré'k].
                       *Br*èak me òff a pìece of thàt Kít Kàt *B*àr.'
                       (for 'break' [bre'k]; onset [b] omitted, dissimilation; B;
                       NSC)

B-338b 4;7.18   B: 'Mommy?! My Mòmmy *s*àys . . . my [__tʰʌ.mɪk]
                       *s*àys . . . my s̲tòmach sàys "I'm húngry".'
                       (for 'stomach' [stʌ.mɪk]; onset [s] omitted, dissimilation,
                       causing /t/ to become aspirated; B; SC; 338a=Class 43)

B-344   4;8.5   B: 'Hè*r*e's my bóok [ò^w__.dɚ] . . . ò̲r̲de*r*.'
                       (for 'order' [ór.dɚ]; coda [r] omitted, dissimilation; note
                       that offglide [^w] appears when [r] is omitted; B/W; SC)

OC-120 4;9.21   OB: 'Mommy, I'*ll* [sp__ìt] . . . I'll spl̥ìt the pì*l*e in hálf.'
                       (for 'split' [spl̥ɪt]; onset [l] omitted, dissimilation; B; SC)

B-390   4;10.20   B: 'Mom, *l*èt's [pʰ__è^j] . . . pl̥ày some schóo*l*.'
                       (for 'play' [pʰl̥e^j]; onset [l] omitted, dissimilation; B; SC)

B-526   5;6.2   B: (turns on the TV, then exclaims)
                       'Oh, my gósh, my fávorite! "The Inc*r*èdible [ʃ__ìŋk]
                       . . . Sh̲r̲ìnking T*úr*tles"!'
                       (for 'shrinking' [ʃr̥íŋ.kɪŋ]; onset [r] omitted, dissimilation;
                       B; SC)

B-574   5;11.6   B: 'I'*m* [kʰæ̂^w__.tɪn] . . . I'm còu̲n̲ti*ng* hòw *m*any
                       cárs go bỳ.'
                       (for 'counting' [kʰæ̂^wn.tɪn]; coda [n] omitted; either
                       dissimilation due to other nasals in utterance, or
                       assimilation to non-nasal vowel in 'how'; B/W; SC)

B-586   5;11.25   B: 'Lè*t* my [s__ʌ́] . . . s̲tómach *s*è*tt*le.'
                       (for 'stomach' [stʌ.mɪk]; onset [t] omitted, dissimilation
                       from /t/s or assimilation to single onset /s/ in 'settle'; B;
                       SC)

23. Phonological A/P, substitutions, vowels.

OC-10   2;0.29   M: 'Did you pàint with your hánd?'
OG: '[pʰæ̀] . . . pàint hánd.'
(for 'paint hand' [pʰeʰnt hænd]; [æ] substituted for [eʲ];
2-word stage; B; SC)

OC-20   2;3.0   OG: 'Ì gòt ángry! [à gà] . . . Ì gòt ángry!'
(for 'I got' [aʲ gat]; [a] substituted for [aʲ]; B; SC)

AL-140 3;6.7   Al: 'I wànna wàtch "[dʒàk] an' the Béanstàlk" agàin.'
(for 'Jack' [dʒæk]; [a] substituted for [æ]; B; NSC)

AN-170 4;4.2   An: 'Thère's fĩve [pʰɚ̀.p] . . . thère's fĩve péople hère.'
(for 'people' [pʰí.puɫ]; consonantal /r/ substituted for vocalic
[i], realized as [ɚ]; B; SC; p. 113)

OC-121 4;10.0   OB: 'Do yòu knòw what tóday is? Tòday is túrkey dày,
so I hàve to tèll a [dʒɚ̀k] about um . . . jòke about
túrkey.'
(for 'joke' [dʒoʷk]; [ɚ] substituted for [oʷ]; B; SC)

B-382   4;10.12   B: (teasing Alice because her boyfriend got a Mohawk
haircut)
'Àlice is a [móʷ.hæk] . . . a Móhawk màniac.'
(for 'Mohawk' [móʷ.hak]; [æ] substituted for [a]; B; SC;
p. 61)

AN-255 4;10.22   M: 'Why don't you mix up some blue and yellow and
make a gréen one?'
Al: 'Mòm, thàt's a [grít] idèa!'
(for 'great' [greʲt]; [i] substituted for [eʲ]; B; NSC)

B-401   4;11.3   B: (reciting Sesame Street poem) 'Ì like flówers, Ì lìke
dírt, but mòst [ɚ̀v] áll, Ì lìke Bért.'
(for 'of' [ʌv]; [ɚ] substituted for [ʌ]; B; NSC)

AN-297 5;7.18   An: (talking about "The Cat In The Hat")
'You knòw what thèy could dó? They could tàke
out the [fóʃ], and pùt it in the físhbowl, and splàt the
wàter on his héad.'
(for 'fish' [fɪʃ]; [ʊ] substituted for [ɪ]; B; NSC)

24. Phonological A/P, substitutions, larger units.

B-81   2;6.18   B: 'Thòse are blúe.'
M: 'Uh huh, rèal dárk blùe.'
B: '[blíɫ] dàrk blùe!'
(for 'real', [ȝɪɫ]; onset [bl] substituted for [ȝ]; B; NSC)

AL-92   3;1.3   M: 'Yòu have lóts of Grèat Gràndmas.'
Al: 'Yèah, an' [gȝàts] . . . lòts a Grèat Grándpas, tóo.'
(for 'lots a great' [lats ʌ gȝeʼt]; onset [gȝ] substituted for [l];
'a' is 'of'; B; SC; p. 150)

AL-124   3;4.12   Al: 'You can wàtch [tʃáȝ.tʃȝèk] . . . Stár-Trèk.'
(for 'Star-Trek' [stáȝ.tʃȝèk]; onset [tʃ] substituted for [st];
B/W; SC)

B-238   4;3.10   B: (pretending a plate of crackers is intestines) 'I'll èat
my [ɪn.tʰ ín.stɪns] . . . intéstìnes for dínmèr.'
(for 'intestines' [ɪn.té.stìns]; rhyme [ɪn] substituted for [ɛ];
B/W; SC)

AN-245 4;10.2   An: (pulling her washcloth from under her knees in the tub)
'Mómma! It was ùnder my knées, and nòbody pút it
[ʌ.mɚ] . . . nòbody pút it ùnder my knèes, it was jùst
thére!'
(for 'under' [ʌn.dɚ]; [m] substituted for [n.d]; possibly
ambisyllabic [ʌm.mɚ]; B; SC)

B-581   5;11.20   B: 'Ïm on Amèrican [áʲ.làⁱnz].'
(for 'Airlines' [ér.làⁱnz]; [aʲ] substituted for [ɛr]; B/W; NSC)

AN-328 5;11.25   An: 'Like if Kélly can't còme? Or Samántha [kʰʌmpt]
còme?'
(for 'can't' [kʰæn(t)]; [ʌm] substituted for [æn], with
epenthetic [p]; B; NSC)

25. Phonological reversals (non-contiguous), consonants.

B-3   1;8.25   B: (pointing at his bottle sitting on dishwasher)
'[tá.pow].'
(for 'bottle' [pá.tow]; onsets [p]<--->[t]; 1-word stage; W;
NSC; p. 47)

AN-12   1;8.15   An: '[pí.kʌ.pʰù].'
(for 'peek-a-boo' [pʰí.kʌ.pù]; onsets /p/ [pʰ]<--->/b/ [p]; W;
NSC)

B-21   1;10.7   B: '[pí.pa.kù].'
(for 'peek-a-boo' [pí.ka.pù]; onsets [k]<--->[p]; 2-word stage;
W; NSC)

B-24   1;10.29   B: '[hǽm.kʌ.pɔ̀].'
(for 'hamburger' [hǽm.pʌ.kɔ̀]; onsets [p]<--->[k]; 2-word
stage; W; NSC; p. 121)

B-25   1;11.6   B: '[çún ʔàç].'
(for 'shoes on' [çuç ʔan]; codas [ç]<--->[n]; 'shoes'
monomorphemic at this age; 2-word stage; B; +T(t1); NSC;
p. 405)

B-29   1;11.23   B: 'Ápple-jùice, Bòbby's cúp. Ápple-jùice, Bòbby's
[pʌkʰ].'
(for 'cup' [kʌpʰ]; onset /k/<--->coda /p/; note that he only
aspirates voiceless plosives word finally; voiced and
voiceless plosives are not distinguished word-initially; W;
NSC)

B-32   2;0.5   B: '[sà.ma.k] . . . Sàcraménto.'
(for 'Sacramento' [sà.ka.mín.to]; onsets [k]<--->[m]; W; SC)

B-40   2;1.28   B: 'Mòmmy, I nèed [pʰin kʰǽts].'
(for 'clean pants' [kʰin pʰæts]; onsets [kʰ]<--->[pʰ]; B; +T(t2);
NSC; p. 31)

B-48   2;3.5   B: 'I wànna [bʌt maʲ ʃ íç].'
(for 'brush my teeth' [bʌʃ maʲ tʰiç]; coda [ʃ]<-->onset [tʰ],
then [tʰ] deaspirates word-finally; B; +T(t2); NSC)

AL-22   2;4.2   Al: '[gè wi ḍóʷ]'
(for 'There we go' [ḍɛ wi goʷ]; [ḍ]<-->[g]; B; +T(t2); NSC)

B-50   2;4.5   An: 'Lóok, Mòm, I pèeled the grápe.'
B: 'I pèeled the [pʰéʲk].'
(for 'grape' [keʲp]; onset [k]<-->coda [p], then [p] aspirates;
W; NSC; p. 116)

AN-48   2;5.3   An: (to Alice) 'Hí, [fr̥ì.di pʰéʲs].'
(for 'Pretty Face' [pʰr̥í.di feʲs]; onsets [pʰ]<-->[f]; B; +T(t1);
NSC)

AN-49   2;5.3   An: '[sí.tʰèt].'
(for 'tea-set' [tʰí.sèt]; onsets [tʰ]<-->[s]; W; NSC)

AL-29   2;5.9   Al: 'I want hámburgèrs. Yòu have [hǽŋ.gʌ.b3̀s], and yòu
eàting you hámburgèrs and Ànna tóo!'
(for 'hamburgers' [hǽm.bʌ.g3̀s]; onsets [b]<-->[g], then [m]
assimilates to the velar place of [g]; W; NSC; p. 121)

AN-52   2;5.30   An: '[spèk.tor dʒǽ.gʌt].'
(for '(In)spector Gadget' [spèk.tor gǽ.dʒʌt]; onsets
[g]<-->[dʒ]; W; NSC)

AL-33   2;6.6   Al: (picking tokens for a game) 'I wànt a bè a [wé.joʷ].'
(i.e. 'I want to be the yellow (one)'; for 'yellow' [jé.woʷ];
onsets [j]<-->[w]; 'a' is filler function word; W; NSC)

AN-53   2;6.20   An: '[mǽ.kɪtʃ].'
(for 'magic' [mǽ.dʒɪk]; onset [dʒ]<-->coda [k] and word-
final devoicing of [dʒ]; W; NSC)

B-93   2;7.2   B: 'I [jàʲk lɛ́ʔ] . . . yéllow.'
(for 'like yellow' [laʲk jé.loʷ]; onsets [l]<-->[j]; B; +T(t2);
partially SC)

B-108   2;8.13   B: 'We chàsed the Múd-[mʌ̀.dʌɬ pʰan.s] . . . Múd-P̲ùddle Mònster.'
(for 'Mud-Puddle Monster' [mʌ́d.pʰʌ̀.dʌɬ mán.st3]; onsets [pʰ]<-->[m]; B; -T; SC; p. 82)

B-114   2;9.23   B: 'It's nòt a [bléʲs.wìt].'
(for 'bracelet' [bwés.lìt]; onset sonorants [w]<-->[l]; W; NSC; p. 128)

AN-76   2;10.6   An: 'Mòmmy, whỳ did you tùrn the [wàt há.dɚ] òn?'
(for 'hot water', [hat wá.dɚ]; onsets [h]<-->[w]; B; +T(t2); NSC)

AL-52   2;10.7   Al: (looking at photographs)
'Thère's Bóbby, at Séa-[l3̀wd] . . . Séa-W̲òrl̲d.'
(for 'world' [w3ɬd]; onset [w]<-->coda [ɬ], [l] develarizes; W; SC; p. 121)

B-119   2;10.19   OB:'Whò ya gonna cáll?'
B: '[bò̀ʷst.gʌ́.st3s] . . . G̲hòst-B̲ústers!'
(for 'Ghost-Busters' [góʷst.bʌ̀.st3s]; onsets [g]<-->[b]; but said with chant intonation, not compound stress, in this error; W; SC)

AN-81   2;10.21   An: 'She tòoch (s)ome ṕickers . . . she tòo̲k̲ some ṕictures
[ʃi: tʰʊ̀.tʃ:ʌm   pʰí.kɚz] . . . [ʃi: tʰʊ̀k sʌm pʰí.tʃɚz]
of me.
(reversal of [k]<-->[tʃ]; then complete assimilation of [s] to [tʃ]; B; +T(t2); SC; p. 120)

AL-75   2;11.3   Al: 'I lìke a yéllow [kʰʌ̀.fɪn mʌ̀ps].'
(looks surprised, giggles)
(for 'muffin cups' [mʌ́.fɪn kʰʌps]; onsets [m]<-->[kʰ]; 'a' is filler function word; B; -T; N-NC)

AL-91   3;0.26   Al: 'It was a [wàŋ lèʲ] dówn.'
(for 'long way' [laŋ weʲ]; onsets [l]<-->[w]; B; -T; NSC)

AL-94   3;1.13   Al: 'Hère's my [dú nà^j.pɚ].' (looks confused)
M: 'Your what?'
Al: 'My néw dìaper.'
(for 'new diaper' [nu dá^j.pɚ]; onsets [n]<-->[d]; B; +T(t1);
N-NC; p. 200)

AL-96   3;2.10   Al: 'Mòm, I wànt my [wáθ.kʰ]àʃ].'
M: 'What?'
Al: 'My wáshclòth.'
(for 'washcloth' [wáʃ.kʰ]àθ]; codas [ʃ]<-->[θ]; W; NSC;
p. 61)

AL-101 3;3.7   Al: 'I háte [blà.ko^w.ʒi].'
M: 'What?'
Al: 'I háte bròccoli.'
(for 'broccoli' [bʒá.ko^w.li]; onsets [ʒ]<-->[l]: W; NSC)

AL-108 3;3.24   M: 'Look, Alice. Hère's a càrd from Mària-Eléna.'
Al: '[ma.lì:.ɛ.ʒé^j.nə]?'
(for 'Maria-Elena' [ma.ʒì:.ɛ.lé^j.nə]; adult pronunciation
[ma.rì:.ɛ.lé^j.nə] onsets [ʒ]<-->[l]; W; NSC)

AL-110 3;3.25   Al: 'I wànt some [sí.li.òw] . . . I wànt some céreàl.'
(for 'cereal' [sí.ʒi.òɫ]; onset [ʒ]<-->coda [ɫ], but [ʒ] realized
as [w] word finally, [ɫ] develarized; W; SC)

AL-118 3;4.3   An: 'Look! Thèse are Whéat-Thìns.'
Al: 'I don't [wá^jk lìt]-Thìns.' (looks embarassed)
(for 'like Wheat' [la^jk wit]; onsets [l]<-->[w]; B; +T(t1);
N-NC)

AL-128 3;4.16   Al: 'I'm [blà^jt æn ʒ́.wi].'
(for 'bright and early' [bʒa^jt æn ʒ́.li]; onsets [ʒ]<-->[l], then
[ʒ] realized as [w] after the vowel [3]; B; +T(t2); NSC)

AN-113 3;5.7   An: '[ʃʌn.sà^jn].'
(for 'sunshine' [sʌn.ʃà^jn]; onsets [s]<-->[ʃ]; W; NSC)

AL-165 3;9.0   Al: 'Nów could I hàve some [dɨ.tʰʒ́s]?'
(for 'dessert' [dɨ.sʒ́t]; onset [s]<-->coda [t], which then
aspirates; W; NSC)

B-165   3;9.3   B: 'The [ʃʌn] is [sàʲ.nɪŋ] . . . the sún is sh̀ining.'
(for 'sun is shining' [sʌn ɪz ʃáʲ.nɪŋ]; onsets [s]<-->[ʃ]; B;
+T(t1); SC)

AL-191 3;11.7 Al: 'Yòu're gonna wàtch "[ʒà.b3 ʒǽ.dʒɨt]".'
(for 'Roger Rabbit' [ʒá.dʒ3 ʒǽ.bɨt]; onsets [dʒ]<-->[b]; B; -T;
NSC; p. 62)

AL-197 3;11.19 Al: 'Gèt 'em ìnto the dìrty [kʰw̥òʷz kʰḷík]! (pause)
You know what 'clíck' means? Quíckly!'
(for 'clothes quick' [kʰḷoʷz kʰw̥ɪk]; second member of onset
clusters [l]<-->[w]; B; +T(t2); N-NC, saving face after
noticed error; p. 85)

AN-141 4;0.18 An: 'I'm lìcking my frùit [lóʷr]-ùp.'
M: 'Your frùit whát?'
An: 'Róll-ùp!'
(for 'roll' [roʷɫ]; onset [r]<-->coda [ɫ], which then
develarizes; W; NSC; p. 62)

AN-144 4;0.27 An: (getting into bathtub) 'Oúch, my tóes!'
M: 'Oh, becàuse you have cúts on your tòes?'
An: 'No, becàuse the [há.rɚz wàt].' (looks confused)
M: 'The háter's wàt?' (laughs)
An: 'No! The hót . . . the hót . . . ' (gives up)
(for 'wáter's hòt' [wá.rɚz hat]; onsets [w]<-->[h]; B; +T(t1);
N-NC)

B-181   4;0.29 B: 'Nó! I'm nót [kʰə.rà.pə.wèʲ.tɪŋ]. I'm jùst pláying!'
(for 'cooperating' [kʰə.wá.pə.rèʲ.tɪŋ]; onsets [w]<-->[r]; W;
NSC)

AN-144 4;1.19 An: '[di.lí.siʃ].'
(for 'delicious' [di.lí.ʃɨs]; onset [ʃ]<-->coda [s]; W; NSC)

AN-151 4;1.27 An: 'Mòmmy, yòu don't lìke [pʰɚ.sè.f] . . . Profèssor
Cóldhart.'
(for 'professor' [pʰɚ.fé.sɚ]; onsets [f]<-->[s]; W; SC)

B-202   4;1.27 B: '[pʰʊd ju kʰʊt] this . . . pùt this in some hòt wáter?'
(for 'could you put' [kʰʊd ju pʰʊt]; [kʰ]<-->[pʰ]; B; -T;
partially SC)

B-235   4;3.7   B: 'Can Ì have anòther [wɔ́.rɔ̀ɫ] . . . rólḷ?'
(for 'roll' [rɔ́.wɔ̀ɫ], 2 syllables; onsets [r]<-->[w]; W; SC)

B-242   4;3.25   B: 'I gòtta chànge [pʰí.zè↓dʒ].'
(for 'PJs' [pʰí.dʒè↓z], i.e. 'pajamas'; the plural morpheme/
coda [z] exchanges with onset phoneme [dʒ]; W; NSC;
p. 411)

AN-165a 4;3.28   An: (looking at a book about kindergarten kids sleeping on
rugs) 'Hís rùg is blùe, and hís rùg is bròwn, and [híg
rʌ̀s] . . . híg rùg . . . (very slowly) his̱ rùg is réd!'
(for 'his rug' [hɪz rʌg]; codas [z]<-->[g], then [s] devoiced;
B; +T(t1); SC; 165b=Class 1)

B-271   4;4.30   B: (identifying pictures in Bert book)
'Pìgeon, pìgeon, [pʰí.nɪdʒ] . . . pígeon!'
(for 'pigeon' [pʰí.dʒɪn]; onset [dʒ]<-->coda [n]; W; SC)

AN-203 4;5.21   An: '[sí.mə.nən]-tòast.'
(for 'cinnamon' [sí.nə.mən]; onsets [n]<-->[m]; W; NSC)

AN-212 4;5.29   An: (holding pine cone and pretending to eat it)
'Thìs is a banána [kʰà↓n.pʰòʷn] . . . a banána pìnecòne.'
(for 'pinecone' [pʰá↓n.kʰòʷn]; onsets [pʰ]<-->[kʰ]; W; SC;
p. 191)

AN-217 4;6.1   An: '[rʌ̃.mòʷ] is my fríend dòg.'
M: 'Who?'
An: 'Monróe!'
(for 'Monroe' [mʌ̃n.róʷ]; onsets [m]<-->[r], then complete
assimilation of [n] to [m]; W; NSC)

OC-113 4;6.4   OB: 'I wànt to plày in the [bǽnd.sàks] . . . sánd-bòx.'
(for 'sand-box' [sǽnd.bàks]; onsets [s]<-->[b]; W; SC)

AN-219 4;6.5   An: 'Like the òne in my [mæ̀.zə.gín] . . . my màgazíne?'
(for 'magazine' [mæ̀.gə.zín]; onsets [g]<-->[z]; W; SC)

AN-226 4;7.1   An: (acting out the "Three Little Pigs" story)
'Nó! Nòt by the [tʃɛr] of my [hɪ̀.ni hɪ̀n hín].'
(looks surprised, too embarassed to correct)
(for 'hair of my chinny chin chin' [hɛr ʌv maʲ tʃí.ni tʃɪn
tʃɪn]; onsets [h]<-->[tʃ], repeated; B; +T(t2); N-NC;
p. 1, 31)

B-350   4;8.13   B: 'Lèt's [pʰʊ́.ɾi.fʊ̀s].'
(for 'pussyfoot' [pʰʊ́.si.fʊ̀t], a funny way to walk; onset
[s]<-->coda [t], then /t/ becomes tap medially; W; NSC)

AN-241 4;9.21   D: 'Alright, Anna, I'm màkin' yòu a húge pàncake.'
An: 'A hùge [kʰǽm.pʰèʲk]? . . . páncàke?'
(for 'pancake' [pʰǽŋ.kʰèʲk]; onsets [pʰ]<-->[kʰ], then nasal
assimilates to place; W; SC)

AN-274 5;2.1   An: 'Hèy, you're plàyin' [kʰǽ.ɾi.pʰèʲk].'
(looks embarassed, knows it's wrong)
(for 'patty-cake' [pʰǽ.ɾi.kʰèʲk]; onsets [pʰ]<-->[kʰ]; W; N-NC)

B-468   5;2.7   B: '[tʰɚ.nə.mèʲ] . . . Términàtor.'
(for 'Terminator' [tʰɚ.mə.nèʲ.ɾɚ]; onsets [m]<-->[n]; W; SC)

B-478   5;3.19   B: 'Mòm, ya wànna plày [dá.nə . . . mòʷz]?'
(for 'Dominoes' [dá.mə.nòʷz]; onsets [m]<-->[n]; W; N-NC)

B-482   5;3.26   B: (naming a picture in a book about insects)
'[kʰátʃ.ròʷk] . . . cóckroàch!'
(for 'cockroach' [kʰák.ròʷtʃ]; codas [k]<-->[tʃ]; W; SC)

AL-242 5;7.1   M: 'Alice, do you want hóney tòast, jélly tòast, or
cínnamon tòast?'
Al: '[tʰɛ́.li dʒòʷst].'
M: 'Huh?'
Al: 'Jélly tòast.'
(for 'jelly toast' [dʒɛ́.li tʰoʷst]; onsets [dʒ]<-->[tʰ]; B, but
possibly a compound; +T(t1); NSC)

AN-293 5;7.5   An: '[bá.ɾɚ foɬ] sàle! Bóttle foɾ sàle!'
(for 'bottle for' [bá.ɾəɬ for]; codas [ɬ]<-->[r], then [ər]-->[ɚ];
B; -T; SC)

AN-311 5;8.25   An: 'I àte móst of my [kʰæ̀.dʒɪb].'
(for 'cabbage' [kʰǽ.bɪdʒ]; onset [b]<-->coda [dʒ]; W; NSC)

B-557 5;9.23   B: 'Hòney [nə.v] . . . Hòney V̠anílla.'
(for 'vanilla' [və.ní.lə]; onsets [v]<-->[n]; W; SC)

AN-322 5;10.20   An: 'Shòuldn't we [brʌθ] our [tʰíʃ]?' (looks embarassed)
M: 'What?'
An: (deep breath) 'Shòuldn't we [brʌθ] . . . brùs̠h our
téet̠h?'
(for 'brush our teeth' [brʌʃ ar tʰiθ]; codas [ʃ]<-->[θ]; B;
+T(t2); first time N-NC, second time SC; p. 201)

B-575 5;11.7   B: 'Can I have twò more [mɛ́n.ə̀łz] . . . mélo̠ns?'
(for 'melons' [mɛ́ł.ɔ̃n(z)]; codas [ł]<-->[n], minus plural
suffix, causing vowels to reverse nasalization; W; SC;
p. 121)

26. Phonological reversals (non-contiguous), vowels.

AL-1 2;0.2   Al: '[wàk.ʌ.bè̀ʲ bá̀ʲ.bi].'
(for 'rock-a-bye baby' [wàk.ʌ.bàʲ béʲ.bi]; [aʲ]<-->[eʲ]; 2-word
stage; B; +T(t2); NSC; p. 22, 47)

B-34 2;0.18   B: '[ì.n3ç̀ʔ] . . . È̠rnie's fíngers.'
(for 'Ernie's fingers' [ɜ̃.nìç? fí.n3ç]; [3]<-->[i]; W; SC)

AL-24 2;4.7   Al: 'Bàby [bʌ.wʌ́.gu] . . . Bàby Belúg̠a òver thère.'
(for 'Beluga' [bʌ.wú.gʌ]; [u]<-->[ʌ]; W; SC; p. 149)

AN-122 3;9.23   An: '[pʰju.fɚ̀m]'
(for 'perfume', [pʰɚ̀.fjúm]; [ɚ]<-->[ju]; could be classified as
'LU' if [j] is considered an onset glide rather than part of
the vowel; W; NSC)

AN-143 4;0.24   M: 'My wáshing machìne needs fíxing.'
An: 'Well, yèsterday Bárbara càme òver and sàid hér
wàshing [mi] . . . hér wàshing [mi.ʃʌn] . . . hér thìng
she wàshes dìshes ìn was bròken.'
(for 'machine' [mə.ʃin]; [ə]<-->[i], then [ə] -->[ʌ] under
stress; Barbara is her·babysitter; W; N-NC; p. 81, 107)

AN-167 4;4.1   An: 'I'm Súperwòman! [sɚ̀.pu] . . . ' (laughs, says it
                wrong on purpose a couple times, doesn't correct)
                (for 'Superwoman' [sú.pɚ.wʊ̀.mɪn]; [u]<-->[ɚ]; W; N-NC)

B-435   5;0.24 B: 'Mòm, I'm hàving a [pʰéʲ.dʒì] . . . a P̌J pàrty todày.'
                (for 'PJ' [pʰí.dʒèʲ], i.e. 'pajamas'; [i]<-->[eʲ]; W; SC; p. 412)

B-495   5;4.27 B: (telling joke) 'What's blàck and whìte and rèd all
                óver? A sùnburned [zʌ́.bri] . . . zébra.'
                (for 'zebra' [zí.brʌ]; [i]<-->[ʌ]; W; SC)

27. Phonological metathesis (contiguous), vowels and/or consonants.

AN-18   1;10.16 An: '[æks].'
                 (for 'ask' [æsk]; coda cluster [s]<-->[k]; W; NSC)

B-41   2;1.29 B: '[dæt fi:.glʊt].'.
                (for 'that feels good' [dæt fɪɫ gʊt]; coda [ɫ]<-->onset [g],
                resyllabified as onset cluster; [i] lengthens in open
                syllable; B; NSC)

AL-19   2;2.24 Al: 'Mòmmy mè bróke thìs. Yòu [físk] ìt.'
                (for 'fix' [fiks]; coda cluster [k]<-->[s]; W; NSC)

AN-63   2;8.1   An: 'I càn't sèe with [kʰɾʌ́ts] in my èyes.'
                (for 'crust' [kʰɾʌst]; coda cluster [s]<-->[t]; W; NSC)

AL-45   2;8.20 Al: 'I wànt [kʰʌ́p.kʰèʲs] . . . [kʰʌ́p.kʰèʲsk] . . . [kʰʌ́p.kʰèʲk̲]
                . . . [s] . . . [ks].'
                (for 'cupcakes' [kʰʌ́p.kʰèʲk(s)]; coda cluster [k]<-->[s], where
                [-s] is the plural suffix; W; SC with difficulty; p. 162)

AL-88   3;0.16 Al: 'Yeah, lìttle chòcolate [sprín.kḷə] . . . sprínkles.'
                (for 'sprinkles' [sprín.kəɫ(z)]; rhyme [ə]<-->[ɫ], minus plural
                suffix, then [ɫ] develarizes and devoices as it is now in
                onset cluster /kl/; W; SC)

AN-98 3;0.22   An: '[ǽs.kɪ.dìnt].'
                (for 'accident' [ǽk.sɪ.dìnt]; coda [k]<-->onset [s] across
                syllable boundary, although syllabification could be
                [ǽks.ɪ.dìnt] in which case error involves coda cluster; W;
                NSC)

AL-106 3;3.14 Al: 'It was jùst a? [ǽs.kʌ.dìnt] . . . ìt was a? áccident.'
                (for 'accident' [ǽk.sʌ.dìnt]; [k]<-->[s], see previous error;
                W; SC)

B-127 3;3.24   B: 'Héy, gèt the [kʰḷù] . . . Kòol-Àid bóx dòwn.'
                (for 'Kool' [kʰuɫ]; rhyme [u]<-->[ɫ], then [ɫ] develarizes and
                devoices in onset cluster /kl/; W; SC; p. 31)

B-240 4;3.23   B: (changing his mind about which cup he wants)
                'I don't wánt that cùp! I dìdn't [ǽks:] . . . [ǽks:]. . .
                ásk fòr it!'
                (for 'ask' [æsk]; coda cluster [s]<-->[k]; W; SC with
                difficulty)

AN-172 4;4.7   An: (chanting; 'Kaiser' is our medical plan; she is spelling
                'ALICE') 'Càll Kàiser for A L I C E. Càll Kàiser for
                A L I C E. Càll [kʰà ͡ɪ.ɚz] . . . [kʰà ͡ɪ.ɚz]? I said
                "[kʰá ͡ɪ.ɚz]"! (laughs) Càll Káiser!'
                (for 'Kaiser' [kʰá ͡ɪ.zɚ]; onset [z]<-->nucleus [ɚ]; W; SC with
                commentary)

AN-174 4;4.8   An: 'Nòw Ràffi's tàlking abòut [sņǽ] . . . Sánta Clàus.'
                (for 'Santa' [sǽn.ta]; rhyme [æ]<-->[n], then [n] devoices in
                onset cluster /sn/, vowel denasalizes; W; SC; p. 110, 120)

AN-180 4;4.26 An: 'Mòmmy, mỳ [θ6rt] hùrts.'
                (for 'throat' [θṛoʷt]; second element of onset [ṛ]<-->nucleus
                [oʷ], [r] replaces [ʷ] as offglide, voices; W; NSC)

AN-238 4;8.25 An: 'He wròte "Grámpa" òn ìt, thèn he [rì.jəɫ.za ͡ɪd] . . .
                he rèalìzed that he dìdn't néed tò.'
                (for 'realized' [rí.jəɫ.a ͡ɪz(d)]; rhyme [a ͡ɪ]<-->[z], minus past
                tense suffix; W; SC; p. 162)

B-452 5;1.17   B: 'Is wáter [ìn.**dʒɚʔ**] . . . ènergy?'
(for 'energy' [í.nɚ.dʒi]; nucleus [ɚ]<-->onset [dʒ] across
syllable boundary, then word resyllabified; W; SC)

B-559 5;9.27   B: (telling Mom names of books)
'Mommy, there's "Whàt's Wròng Hère in the [hɔ̀t̚.ņ]
. . . the Hàunted Hóuse?". '
(for 'haunted' [hɔ́n.t(əd)]; coda [n]<-->onset [t] across
syllable boundary, then [n] becomes syllabic, past tense
suffix is deleted, [t̚] has no audible release, vowel is
denasalized; W; SC; p. 111)

AL-263 5;10.30 Al: 'There's òne [bà**sk**] . . . there's òne bò**x** I càn't réach.'
(for 'box' [baks]; [k]<-->[s]; W; SC)

28. Phonological exchanges (contiguous or non-contiguous), larger units.

AL-32 2;6.3   Al: '[ʌ̀ŋ.**ki** bí**r.ʌ**w].'
(for 'Uncle Billy', [ʌ́ŋ.kʌw bí.wi]; rhymes [ʌw]<-->[i];
unclear where tap comes from, unless it is reflex of /l/
before [ʌ]; B; -T; NSC; p. 152)

AL-36 2;6.23 Al: (skipping to the store)
'**Skí**ppy **h**òp, **skí**ppy **h**òp, [**hí**.pi **sk**àp].'
(for 'skippy hop' [skí.pi hap]; onsets [sk]<-->[h]; B; +T(t1);
NSC; p. 22)

AN-67 2;9.1   An: 'Dòn't put the pìllow on my [pʰ**ís**.əɬ pʰ**ʌ̀z**.əz].'
(for 'puzzle pieces' [pʰʌ́z.əɬ pʰís.əz]; rhymes [ʌz]<-->[is]; B;
+T(t1); NSC)

OC-32 2;9.17 OB:(naming a picture of Wiley Coyote)
'[kʰa.**jí**.joʷt] . . . Cóyote.'
(for 'coyote' [kʰa.jóʷt.i]; syllables [joʷt]<-->[i], with
epenthetic [j] to break up vowel cluster; W; SC)

B-115 2;9.24 B: 'Gìvè me my [**stá**p.t**ʃ**ìks].'
(for 'chopsticks' [tʃáp.stìks]; onsets [tʃ]<-->[st]; W; NSC)

AL-59   2;10.19   Al: 'Bòbby's thròwin' [tʃí.ʒi.æ̀ts.ò̀ʷ] . . . àt my síster.'
(for 'Cheerios at' [tʃí.ʒi.ò̀ʷ(z) æt]; nucleus [oʷ]<-->syllable
[æt], but stranding plural morpheme [-z], which then
becomes devoiced next to [t]; B; -T; partially SC)

AL-67   2;10.21   Al: 'Àlice in [lǽnd.dʒ . . . wʌ̀n].'
(for 'Wonderland' [wʌ́n.dʒ.læ̀nd]; syllables [wʌn]<-->[lænd],
where [d] in error is ambisyllabic; W; N-NC; p. 129)

AL-90   3;0.26   Al: (telling Mom what a video tape is not.)
'It's nót "[kʰʒ̀è.v3 nà̀ʲ] Wòlf".'
(for 'Never Cry' [né.v3 kʰʒ̀aʲ]; onsets [n]<-->[kʰʒ̀]; B; -T;
NSC)

AN-191 4;5.4   An: 'Nòw we hàve to [fè̀ʲnt.pʰè̀ʲst] mý (pause) fàce and
Áli's fàce.'
(for 'face-paint' [féʲs.pʰè̀ʲnt]; codas [s]<-->[nt], with retention
of final [t] in 'paint', possibly because 'faint' and 'paste'
are real words; W; N-NC)

B-380   4;10.12   B: 'It's nòt my Shòw-'n'-[tʰéʲ dè̀ɫ].'
(for ('Show-'n'-)Tell day' [tʰɛ̀ɫ deʲ]; rhymes [ɛɫ]<-->[eʲ]; B;
+T(t1); NSC)

AN-251 4;10.18   An: 'Tòday I gòt a [stí.bì̀ŋ], bùt I dìdn't èven crý.'
M: 'You gòt a whát?'
An: 'A [stí] . . . a bée-stì̀ng.'
(for 'bee-sting', [bí.stìŋ]; onsets [b]<-->[st]; W; NSC the
first time, SC the second time)

AN-252 4;10.18   An: (excitedly discussing the dresses they are wearing)
'Àli's wèaring púrple strìpes, and Ì'm [jè̀ɫ.ɪŋ wér.oʷ]
. . . yèllow.'
(for 'wearing yellow' [wèr.ɪŋ jéɫ.oʷ]; syllables
[wer]<-->[jel]; B; +T(t2); partially SC; p. 128)

OC-122 4;11.0   OG: 'Whàt [ʃúɫ.skù̀z] are hèrs?'
OA: 'What?'
OG: 'Whàt [ʃúl] . . . schóol-shòes are hèrs?'
(for 'school-shoes' [skúɫ.ʃùz]; onsets [sk]<-->[ʃ]; W; NSC the
first time, SC the second time)

29. Phonological feature errors (all types)

AN-74 2;10.4   An: 'Dòn't tòuch my [mæ̀.gɪt] swórd!'
(for 'magic' [mǽ.dʒɪk]; feature of place reversed (palatal
vs. velar), with deaffrication of [dʒ], causing [dʒ]-->[g] and
[k]-->[t]; W; NSC; p. 151)

AL-129 3;4.17   Al: 'I gàve him his fàvorite [pʰɛ́.ɾi]-bèar.'
M: 'What?
Al: 'I gàve him his fàvorite t̪éddy-bèar.'
(for 'teddy' [tʰɛ́.ɾi]; anticipation of labial place of [b],
possibly also perseveration from [f], causing [tʰ]-->[pʰ]; W;
NSC; p. 38)

AL-136 3;5.17   M: 'Look at the dòuble-dècker bús.'
Al: 'The [dʌ̀.gɫ] . . . dòuble-dècker bús!'
(for 'double decker' [dʌ̀.bɫ.dɛ́.k(3)]; anticipation of velarity
of [k], causing [b]-->[g]; W; SC)

AL-137 3;5.20   Al: 'It dóes [pʰèʲst] . . . it dóes t̪àste bàd.'
(for 'taste' [tʰeʲst]; anticipation of labial place of [b],
causing [tʰ]-->[pʰ]; B; -T; SC)

AL-152 3;7.19   Al: 'Hè's a [mǽŋk]- . . . bánk-ròbber.'
(for 'bank' [bæŋk]; anticipation of nasality of [ŋ], causing
[b]-->[m]; W; SC)

AL-156 3;8.7   Al: 'I màde a? [á̰tʃ] . . . [á̰tʃ pʰʒ̰à.dɛkt] . . . árt pròject.'
(for 'art project' [a̰t pʰʒ̰á.dʒɛkt]; feature of affrication
reversed, causing [t]-->[tʃ] and [dʒ]-->[d]; B; +T(t1); SC;
p. 22)

OC-62 3;9.1   OB: 'He thrèw a [sm̥ó̰ʷ] . . . a sn̥ówbàll àt 'im.'
(for 'snowball' [sn̥ó̰ʷ.bàɫ]; probably anticipation of labial
place from [oʷ.b], though could just be anticipation of [m]
from ' 'im' ('him') [m̥]; [n]-->[m]; B/W; SC)

OC-63 3;9.2   OB: 'Did you èver hèar of the wìcked wìtch?'
OG: 'Yóu're the [wì.ʃəd] . . . wìcked wìtch!'
(for 'wicked' [wí.kəd]; A/P influence of place and frication
of [tʃ] in 'witch'; causes [k]-->[ʃ]; could be substitution of
just the fricative part of the affricate [tʃ]; B; T?; SC)

AL-199 4;0.5   Al: 'Mommy, I'm clèaning [ʒʌ.gʒ] . . . Rùbber-
Dúckie.'
(for 'rubber' [ʒʌ.bʒ]; A/P of velar place, causing [b]-->[g];
'Rubber-Duckie' probably one word at this age; B/W; SC)

B-194 4;1.16   B: (yelling at Dad)
'Whère are [sn̥ǽ] . . . stámps, Dàddy?'
(for 'stamps' [stæmps]; anticipation of nasality of [m],
causing [t]-->[n], then [n̥] devoices in onset cluster /sn/; W;
SC)

B-275 4;5.1   B: 'Í knòw whàt you're tàlking abòut. You're [pʰà.kɪŋ]
abòut bàd T.V́. shòws.'
(for 'talking' [tʰá.kɪŋ]; A/P of labial place, causing
[tʰ]-->[pʰ]; B; T?; NSC)

AN-187 4;5.3   An: 'I'm clòsing this dóor so èverything will be
[gárk].'
(for 'dark' [dark]; A/P of velar place, causing [d]-->[g];
B/W; NSC)

B-307 4;6.15   B: (chanting, as Mom gets brown box of popsicles out of
freezer) 'Bròwn bóx! Bròwn [dáks]! Bròwn bóx!'
(for 'box' [baks]; most likely perseveration of alveolar
place from contiguous [n], causing [b]-->[d]; could also be
influence from [s] in 'box'; B; +T(e); NSC)

B-335 4;7.17   B: (putting together plastic cake toy)
'It's gònna [mì] . . . it's gònna bè a bírthday càke.'
(for 'be' [bi]; perseveration of nasality of [n], causing
[b]-->[m]; B; -T; SC)

B-342 4;7.28   B: (picking mushrooms off of his pizza)
'Thère's a [mʌθ.] . . . [ʃ.rùm]. I háte mùshròoms.'
(for 'mushroom' [mʌʃ.rùm]; inter-dental place perseverated
from 'there's' [ðɛrz], causing [ʃ]-->[θ]; B; +T(e); SC in the
middle of the word)

B-343   4;8.2   B: (helping Mom set the table)
'Mom, I'll do the nàpkins ánd the sìlverwàre.
I'll dò the [mæ̀p] . . . n̪àpkins fírst.'
(for 'napkins' [nǽp.kɪns]; A/P of labial place from /p/,
causing [n]-->[m]; could also be perseveration of [m]'s in
'Mom', but less likely; B/W; SC in middle of the word)

OC-117 4;9.0   OB: '[dàd dártʃ].'
(for 'Dodge Dart' [dadʒ dart], a kind of car; reversal of
affrication feature, causing [dʒ]-->[d] and [t] -->[tʃ]; B, but
possibly a compound; NSC)

B-460   5;2.0   B: ('reading' Dr. Seuss) 'Fòur flùffy [fɛ́.vɚz] on a
Fìffer Fèffer Féff.'
(for 'feathers' [fɛ́.ðɚz]; A/P of labio-dental place of /f/,
causing [ð]-->[v]; source 'fluffy' is [fl̩ʌ́.f(i)]; B/W; NSC)

B-466   5;2.4   M: (helping Bobby put his shoes on)
'Óther fòot, óther fòot!'
B: '[ʌ́.vɚ θʊ̀t]. (laughs) It's òne of my jókes.'
(for 'other foot' [ʌ́.ðɚ fʊt]; reversal of place of articulation,
causing [ð]-->[v] and [f]-->[θ]; B; -T; N-NC, but makes joke
about it to save face; p. 85)

AN-280 5;2.13   An: 'Mom, this mòrning in Súnday-[stʉ̀ɬ]? Èveryone
got to wàsh clóthes.'
(for 'Sunday-School' [sʌ́n.deʲ.skʉ̀ɬ]; perseveration of
alveolar place, causing [k]-->[t]; most likely from within
compound: W; NSC)

B-477   5;3.19   B: (wanting to go to the neighbors' house)
'I can gò to [tʃɛ̀ndʒ] 'n . . . Cènz 'n Bína's.'
(for 'Cenz' [tʃɛ̀nz]; perseveration of palato-alveolar place
and affricate manner of [tʃ], causing [z]-->[dʒ]; W; SC)

B-525   5;6.0   B: (telling a joke)
'Whỳ dìd the [stʌ̀ŋk] . . . sk̠ùnk cròss the róad?'
(for 'skunk' [skʌ̀ŋk]; A/P of alveolar place from other stops,
causing [k]-->[t]; not lexical substitution of 'stunk', even
though skunks 'stink', because he doesn't know 'stunk' as
past participle of 'stink'; he says 'stinked'; B; T?; SC)

AL-241 5;6.12   Al: 'Thìs is where I *k*èep all my árt [pʰrà.gɛ] . . .
pròjects.'
(for 'projects' [pʰrá.dʒɛkts]; A/P of velar place, with
deaffrication, causing [dʒ]-->[g]; B/W; SC in middle of
word)

AN-295 5;7.12   An: (watching game show where teams search rooms for
treasure) 'Gùess whát? The rèd tèam gòt fóur ròoms
to [ʃɚ *tʃ*].'
(for 'search' [sɚtʃ]; anticipation of palatal place of [tʃ],
causing [s]-->[ʃ], or could be anticipation of just fricative
part of [tʃ]; W; NSC)

OC-167 5;9.20   OB: (explaining why he didn't finish his breakfast)
'Anyways, *th*ere's a [θjù] more wáffles lèft, and I'm
nòt *th*at húngry.'
(for 'few' [fju]; A/P of inter-dental place, causing [f]-->[θ];
B; -T; NSC; p. 144)

B-558   5;9.23   B: (explaining what happens if one misbehaves)
'Tàke [pʰríg.lı.dʒəz].'
(for 'privileges' [pʰrív.lı.dʒəz]; perseveration of velar place
and stop manner from the [k] in 'take', causing [v]-->[g];
possibly just non-contextual; B; +T(e) NSC)

B-567   5;10.18   B: 'Èvery [pʰʌ.gɚd] . . . èvery cùpboard is líttle.'
(for 'cupboard' [kʰʌ.bɚd]; place of articulation reversed
(labial vs. velar), causing [kʰ]-->[pʰ] and [b]-->[g]; W; SC;
p. 94)

30. Phonological non-contextual substitutions, additions, or omissions, all units.

AN-4   1;7.15   An: 'Ápple[tàç] . . . s̲àuce.'
(for 'applesauce' [ǽ.pow.çàç]; [t] substituted for [ç], no [t] in
context; could be influence of stop manner of [p]; SC;
p. 115)

AL-4   2;0.30   Al: 'Stòp [tə.wí] . . . téasing!'
(for 'stop teasing' [tap tí.çin]; [w] added, no [w] in context;
schwa inserted to break up cluster, her rule at the time;
2-word stage; SC; p. 143)

AL-30   2;5.10   Al: 'Yóu hàve bìg bòobies, and Dàddy dón't hàve bìg
bòobies. Ònly [dʒú] . . . yóu.'
(for 'you' [ju]; [dʒ] substituted for [j], no [dʒ] in context; SC)

OC-43   3;3.0   OG: 'I wànt a bìg [tʃǽ.k3].'
(for 'cracker' [kʰ3ǽ.k3]; [tʃ] substituted for [kʰ3], no [tʃ] in
context; NSC)

AN-109 3;3.9   An: 'Whenèver I get hùngry I gèt some [fļúd].'
M: '[fļud]?'
An: 'Food!'
(for 'food' [fud]; addition of [l], no [l] in context; NSC;
p. 26)

OC-70   3;10.5 OB: 'It's sòrt of fúnny that I dòn't get ànything to [dʒ__íŋk]
. . . to drínk.'
(for 'drink' [dʒrɪŋk]; omission of [r] for no obvious reason;
note that the /d/ remains [dʒ] for the child when the [r] is
omitted; SC; p. 26, 123)

OC-93   4;2.0   OG: 'I wànt some móre! Even anóther mòre [bèʲ] . . .
bìscuit.'
(for 'biscuit' [bí.skət]; [eʲ] substituted for [ɪ], no [eʲ] in
context; possibly started to say the name of some other
food such as 'bacon'; SC)

B-241   4;3.23 B: 'I like DèeDee on the [mì.kɚ] . . . Mìckey Móuse
Clùb.'
(for 'Mickey' [mí.ki]; [ɚ] substituted for [i], no [ɚ] or [r] in
context; SC; p. 26)

OC-105 4;4.11 OG: 'My bòo-boo's gòne on my [lí], on my knée.'
(for 'knee' [ni]; 'boo-boo' is child word for injury such as a
cut or bruise; [l] substituted for [n], no [l] in context;
possibly a blend with 'leg'; SC)

B-262b 4;4.14   B: (on Christmas Eve) 'We're nòt opening áll our
                      prèsents tonight, ònly [**dú**] . . . twó, fóur.'
                      (for 'two' [tʰu]; [d] substituted for [tʰ], no [d] in context; SC;
                      262a=Class 35, i.e. 'two' was lexical error since he meant
                      'four')

B-267   4;4.22   B: (explaining what a toy is called) 'Thàt's a Fíre
                      Blàster. Dàd, thàt's a Fíre [b__æ̀st] . . . Blàster.'
                      (for 'Blaster' [blǽ.stɚ]; [l] omitted for no obvious reason;
                      SC)

B-290   4;5.25   B: (talking about how to open a computer game)
                      'You nèed to prèss "Màth [rǽ.gɪt]". . . "Màth Rábbit"
                      twó tìmes.'
                      (for 'rabbit' [rǽ.bɪt]; [g] substituted for [b], no other velars
                      in utterance; SC; p. 38)

B-371   4;9.19   B: (playing with Ghostbusters figure)
                      'Mom, nòw he's flýin', 'cuz he'll gèt ùp in [tʰɪks] . . .
                      s̱ìx séconds.'
                      (for 'six' [sɪks]; [tʰ] substituted for [s]; various possibilities
                      for source: note that 'get up' is [gɛ.ɾʌp], but this could be
                      the source; could also be blend of 'ten' and 'six', or
                      influence of various stops in phrase; SC)

B-375   4;9.25   B: 'Ī'll gìve ya a? [__ínt].'
                      (for 'hint' [hɪnt]; [h] omitted, indefinite article realized as
                      [ʌʔ]; NSC; p. 424)

B-455   5;1.20   B: 'Thàt's what they dò ta [gì] . . . ta ḇè a wréstler.'
                      (for 'be' [bi]; [g] substituted for [b], no other velars in
                      utterance; SC)

31. Phonological errors with multiple error types (combinations of above).

AN-2   1;7.9   An: (looking at photo album)
                       'Thère [**pǽ.kàpʰ**] . . . thère Gránḏpà.'
                       (for 'Grandpa' [kʷǽ.pà]; reversal of [p]<-->[k], plus copy of
                       [p] at end, with rule of word-final aspiration of voiceless
                       plosives, and [kʷ] delabialized; SC; p. 47)

B-15   1;9.29   B: '[ná ͥ] dìaper . . . nó nó dìaper.'
                  (for 'no no diaper' [noʷ noʷ dá ͥ.pʊ]; [oʷ]<--[a ͥ] anticipation/
                  substitution, and syllable 'no' deleted; 2-word stage;
                  possibly a telescoping; SC)

B-31   1;11.25   M: 'Thère's Bòbby's ápplejùice.'
                  B: '[__à.pidz á.pow.dẓ̀ùç] . . . B̲ò̲b̲b̲y̲'s̲ ápplejùice.'
                  (for 'Bobby's applejuice' [pá.piç ǽ.pow.dzùç]; omission of
                  [p], anticipation/substitution of [dz] for [ç]; perseveration/
                  substitution of [a] for [æ]; SC)

B-36   2;1.9   B: '[kʰɚ̀.na lú.dʌɬ].'
                  (for 'curley noodle' [kʰɚ̀.li nú.dʌɬ], a kind of soup; onsets
                  [n]<-->[l], and non-contextual substitution of [a] for [i];
                  NSC)

B-44   2;2.11   D: 'Hèy Bóbby, whàt's your náme?'
                  B: '[bà.t3] . . . Ròbert Chèster Vàn Válin.'
                  (for 'Robert' [ʒ̣á.b3t]; [b] anticipated, substituted for [ʒ̣]; [t]
                  and [3] metathesized; could also be blend of 'Bobby'
                  [bá.bi] and 'Robert'; SC)

AL-15   2;2.18   Al: '[hǽ.pʊ.ʔà:ç] . . . s̲àuce . . . ápples̲àuce.'
                  (for 'applesauce' [ǽ.pʊ.çàç]; non-contextual addition of [h]
                  to 'apple', deletion of onset [ç] on 'sauce', insertion of [ʔ]
                  to break up vowel sequence; SC)

B-62   2;5.16   B: (as Mom takes him into bedroom to change his
                       diapers) 'I wànt [kʰ__ìn kʰǽnts] . . . c̲lèan p̲ánts.'
                  (for 'clean pants' [kʰl̀in pʰǽnts]; [l] omitted non-contextually
                  in onset cluster, and onset [kʰ] perseverated/substituted for
                  [pʰ]; SC)

AN-56   2;7.21   An: '[mè ͥ__ ʔən dʒá ͥ.kow].'
                  (for 'Jane and Michael' [dʒe ͥn ʔən má ͥ.kow], characters in
                  "Mary Poppins"; reversal of onset [dʒ]<-->[m]; omission of
                  [n] at end of 'Jane'; NSC)

AN-58   2;7.24   An: 'Yòu're [lǽ.wɪŋ] . . . yélling!'
                  (for 'yelling' [jéw.lɪŋ]; movement of onset [l] from second
                  syllable, substituted for [j] in first syllable; non-contextual
                  substitution of [æ] for [ɛ]; resyllabification of [w]; SC)

B-111   2;9.11   B: '[fʌ.ki tʃàɪd kʰí.tʃən] . . . Kentùcky Frìed Chícken!'
(for 'Kentucky Fried Chicken' [kʰə́.tʰʌ́.ki fwàɪd tʃí.kən];
multiple errors: first syllable deleted, and most onset
consonants shifted; SC; p. 112)

AN-72   2;9.26   An: ('reading' from a book) 'A dèer, dòg, dòrmouse,
[dæ̀n.sʌ.lɪŋ déɪnt__].'
(for 'dancing daintily' [dǽn.sɪŋ déɪn.tʌ.li]; anticipation/
movement with addition of sequence [ʌ.l] from 'daintily' to
'dancing'; omission of vowel [i] at end of 'daintily'; NSC;
p. 54, 131)

AL-53   2;10.7   Al: '[mæ̀.li.wú:].'
(for 'Mary Lou', usually [mè.ʒ̰i.lú:]; anticipation/
substitution of [l] for [ʒ̰]; non-contextual substitutions of
vowel [æ] for [ɛ] and consonant [w] for [l]; N-NC)

AL-68   2;10.21   M: 'Ali, you want some lùnch like Bóbby?'
Al: 'Yeah, [bʌ.bǽ.m] . . . banánas, and thát thìng, and
thát thìng.' (pointing to things on Bobby's plate)
(for 'bananas' [bʌ.nǽ.nʌz]; [b] perseverated/substituted for
first [n]; second [n] takes labial place of articulation from
preceding [b]'s; SC in the middle of the word)

AN-85   2;10.27   An: '[pʰáɪ.ɚ kʰɾæ̀t] . . . [pʰɾáɪ.ɚ kʰæ̀k.təs].'
(too confused to correct)
(for 'choir practice' [kʰwáɪ.ɚ pʰɾæ̀k.təs]; multiple errors,
including [pʰ]<-->[kʰ]; N-NC)

AL-80   2;11.18   M: (handing Alice a book) 'Is thís the one you want?'
Al: 'Yeah! Thìs [wì.tʃə__.wìtʃ] . . . thìs wìcked wìtch.'
(for 'wicked witch' [wí.kəd wɪtʃ]; [tʃ] anticipated/substituted
for [k]; coda [d] deleted; SC)

AN-95   3;0.11   An: '[bè.li.blú]'
(for 'Betty-Lou' [bè.ɾi.lú]; anticipation/substitution of onset
[l] for [ɾ]; perseveration/addition of onset [b] before [l];
NSC)

AL-86   3;0.9   Al: 'Mòmmy, thóse pόisonous àpple is [lò^w.ʒi] . . .
                 <u>reàlly</u> rúbber.'
                 (for 'really' [ʒí.li]; reversal of [l]<-->[ʒ]; perseveration/
                 substitution of [o^w] for [ɪ]; 'those' is her normal substitution
                 for 'this'; SC)

AN-97   3;0.22   An: (wants to drink from cup without the usual lid)
                 'I wànt to drìnk it wìth the [tʰáf ʌp].'
                 (for 'top off' [tʰap af]; reversal of [p]<-->[f]; also, [ʌ]
                 substituted for [a] possibly perseveration from 'the' [ðʌ];
                 NSC)

OC-38   3;2.0   OG: '[fúf.gàɫ].'
                 (for 'goofball' [gúf.bàɫ]; [f] substitutes for [g] in word onset,
                 [g] substitutes for [b] in second syllable onset; possibly
                 onset [g] and [b] reverse, then [b]-->[f]; NSC)

AN-105 3;2.15   An: 'Mmmmmm, those [sm̥ǽ.wɚz f__èɫ] góod!'
                 (for 'flowers smell' [fl̥ǽ.wɚz sm̥eɫ]; reversal of [sm̥] and
                 [fl̥], with deletion of [l]; NSC)

AN-110 3;4.1   An: '[hà.zi ən ʔé.ri__].'
                 (for 'Ozzie 'n' Harriet' [ʔá.zi ən hé.ri.ət]; reversal of onset
                 [h] and [ʔ]; deletion of final syllable from 'Harriet'; NSC)

AN-112 3;5.0   An: '[hà^w fɚ à^j gə.gét].'
                 (for 'How could I forget?' [ha^w kʰəd a^j fɚ.gét]; multiple
                 errors, including syllable [fɚ] anticipated and substituted
                 for [kʰəd]; NSC; p. 33)

AL-150 3;7.15   Al: 'Momma, I'm gònna bè the wítch in The [wà.dʒ3d] of
                 Óz . . . The Wìzard of Óz.'
                 (for 'wizard' [wí.z3d]; [a] anticipated from 'Oz' [az],
                 substituted for [ɪ]; palato-alveolar affricate persevered from
                 'witch', substituted for [z], but retains voicing of [z]; SC)

B-138   3;7.16   B: (coloring a picture of Batman) 'Mommy, I hàven't
                 [fì.ʃən__] Bátman yèt, so I'm gonna gò get drèssed
                 and thén fìnish Bàtman.'
                 (for 'finished' [fí.n̈iʃt]; reversal of [ʃ] and [n]; lowering of
                 unstressed vowel, deletion of [t]; [ən] could be
                 perseveration from 'haven't', or it could be incorrect
                 selection of past participle morpheme; NSC)

AL-163 3;9.0   Al: 'Thìs is my [pʰ**óʷ**n.kʰ**æ̀**n].'
                 M: 'Your whát?'
                 Al: 'Pĭne-cône.'
                 (for 'pine-cone' [pʰáⁱn.kʰòʷn]; vowels reversed, [aʲ] fronts to
                 [æ]; NSC)

AL-173 3;9.12   Al: '**J**áe**g**er, thàt's your [jéⁱ**ŋg**].'
                 (for 'name' [neⁱm], source 'Jaeger' [jéʲ.g3]; onset [j]
                 perseverated/substituted for [n], [g] perseverated/added to
                 coda, then [m]-->[ŋ] before [g]; N-NC)

AN-133 3;11.20 An: 'It's so [dí.**k**] . . . [**k**ʰí.kə.fʊ̀ɫ].' (looks confused)
                 (for 'difficult' [dí.fə.kʰʊ̀ɫt]; first error is anticipation/
                 substitution of [k] for [f]; second error is anticipation/
                 substitution of [k] for [d], reversal of [f] with [k]; N-NC)

AN-137 3;11.27 An: 'I gòt a [**g**ù brʊ̀k] . . . I gòt a nèw bòok from
                 Grándma.'
                 (for 'new book' [nu bʊk]; A/P substitution of onset [g] for
                 [n]; anticipation/addition of onset [r] from 'Grandma'; SC)

AN-149 4;1.22   An: 'Mommy, ya knòw whát? I got to [pʰ **ɪk** ʌ **t**ʰák] . . .
                 p**è**t a **c**óckatòo.'
                 (for 'pet a cockatoo' [pʰɛt ʌ kʰá.kə.tʰù]; reversal of coda [t]
                 and onset [kʰ], with reversal of aspiration; non-contextual
                 substitution of vowel [ɪ] for [ɛ]; SC)

B-205   4;2.0   B: 'Mòm, whò plàys [**mì**.k__ɚ ʔǽ.nəs]?'
                 (for 'Rick Moranis' [rɪk mɚ.rǽ.nəs]; movement of [m] from
                 'Moranis', substituted for [r] in 'Rick'; resyllabification,
                 with loss of onset [r] in 'Moranis', insertion of [ʔ] between
                 vowels; NSC)

B-302   4;6.14   B: (telling Mom name of book) ' "Mòther Góose"!
                 "[mʌ.**g**ɚ **d**ús]"! . . . "Mòther Góose"!'
                 (for 'Mother Goose' [mʌ.ðɚ gús]; reversal of onsets [g] and
                 [ð], then stopping of [ð]-->[d̪]; SC)

AN-206 4;5.26   An: 'I'm [**br**ĩn.tʰì**n**.dĩn] that my **b**èdroom is our hóuse.'
                 (for 'pretending' [pʰɹi.tʰín.din]; onset [b] anticipated/
                 substituted for [pʰ]; causing [r] to voice; [n] anticipated
                 from coda of second or third syllable in 'pretending', added
                 to coda of first syllable, causing vowel to nasalize; NSC)

AN-227 4;7.8   An: (telling a story) 'And thèn the Pùrple Píeman pùts
pìzza in a bìg clóud [__ʃ ì:m] . . . machìne, and (etc.)'
(for 'machine' [mə.ʃín]; onset [m] perseverated/moved/
substituted for coda [n], [ə] deleted and [i] lengthened;
possibly interrupted reversal of [ʃi] and [mə] or complex
telescoping; SC)

AN-230 4;7.29   An: '[rʌ__ nàʲt] . . . rìght nòw you're òlder than Dáddy.'
(for 'right now' [raʲt næʷ]; perseveration/movement with
substitution of ryhme [aʲt] for [æʷ]; non-contextual vowel
[ʌ] inserted; SC)

AN-239 4;9.5   An: 'Does that [meʲks ju s:ní:v].'
M: 'What?'
An: 'Does thàt make you snéeze?'
(for 'make you sneeze' [meʲk ju sn̥í:z]; addition of [s] on
'make', possibly morpheme addition; non-contextual
substitution of [v] for [z] in 'sneeze'; lengthening of onset
[s] in 'sneeze', voicing of [n]; NSC)

B-379   4;10.8   B: 'I lóve the [rə.nì.dʒə.nəɫ] "Blòb". '
("The Blob" is a movie)
(for 'original' [ə.rí.dʒə.nəɫ]; onset [r] anticipated, added to
beginning of word; onset [n] anticipated/substituted for [r];
N-NC; p. 424)

AN-267 5;1.23   An: 'Momma, I wànna lìe dówn, 'cuz I have a?
[ʌp.sɛp s__ʌ́.mɪk].'
(for 'upset stomach' [ʌ́p.sɛt stʌ́.mɪk]; coda [p] perseverated/
substituted for [t]; [t] in 'stomach' omitted non-contextually;
N-NC)

AL-238 5;5.13   Al: 'Whàt if òne of these púzzle [pʰˤì.pəɫ] . . . púzzle
pìeces gòt wárped?'
(for 'pieces' [pʰˤì.səz]; onset [p] A/P substituted for [s]; [l]
persevered from coda of second syllable of 'puzzle',
substituted for [z]; could be lexical substitution error,
'people' for 'pieces'; SC)

B-534   5;6.18   M: (tells Bobby to be quiet in church)
'Whát did I just sày?'
B: 'I hàf*ta* be as [kʰwàⁱt.sʌ] *às a* móuse.'
(for 'quiet' [kʰwáⁱ.jət]; [t] added to coda of first syllable,
syllable [sʌ] substituted for [jət], multiple possible sources
for each error; NSC)

AN-289   5;6.30   An: 'We'll gèt a lìttle tóy that lòoks like a [hǽn.də.bɚ̀]
. . . a hámburger or sòmething, but ìt'll rèally bè a
róbot!'
(for 'hamburger' [hǽm.bə.gɚ̀]; non-contextual change in
place feature for [m.b] cluster, substitution of onset [b] for
[g]; SC)

AN-291   5;7.0   An: 'Have you [fɪn__] my [pʰǽʷd] yet?' (looks confused)
M: 'What?'
An: 'Have you fòund my pád yet?'
(for 'found my pad' [fæʷnd maʲ pʰæd]; non-contextual
omission of [d] on 'found'; perseveration/substitution of
vowel [æʷ] in 'found' for [æ] in 'pad', or possibly addition of
offglide; non-contexual substitution of [ɪ] for vowel [æʷ] in
'found'; N-NC)

AL-260   5;10.16   Al: 'I wànt my [pʰèʲs ʌv pʰέ.pɚ].'
(for 'piece of paper' [pʰis ʌv pʰéʲ.pɚ]; [eʲ] anticipated/
substituted for [i] in 'piece'; non-contextual substitution of
[ε] for [eʲ] in 'paper'; NSC)

B-568   5;10.20   B: 'This is [pʰɚ̀.flə__.k__i] (hesitates) blúe.'
(for 'perfectly' [pʰɚ̀.fəkt.li]; onset [l] anticipated/moved/
added to onset of second syllable, voiced; [t] omitted from
coda of first syllable, and [k] resyllabified; N-NC)

32. Phonological errors of lexical stress.

AN-260   4;11.14   An: 'Mom, could you get some yàrn and tìe some bóws?
'Cuz I rèally wànna [dε.kə.réⁱt] Stràwberry's hòuse.'
M: 'You wanna whát?'
An: 'Décorate Stràwberry's hòuse.'
(for 'decorate' [dέ.kə.reⁱt]; stress on final syllable instead of
first syllable; probable influence from 'decorátion'
[dε.kə.réⁱ.ʃən], which she knew: see AN-159(34) 4;2;
NSC; p. 23, 54, 189, 248, 444)

33. Phonological errors of intonation.

B-250b 4;4.3   B: (calling to his friend David)
'[dǽ:.dì:] . . . I mean <u>Dávid</u>, còme ón!'
(says 'Daddy' nicely, politely. Then says 'David' short,
harsh, like command; pragmatics of intonation changed
due to lexical selection error; SC; B-250a=Class 35;
p. 206)

AN-258 4;10.22 An: (telling "Three Little Pigs" story')

'But. . . still. . . he could not blow down that house

of brick[s:] . . .'

(blend of the syntax of:

'he could not blow down that house of bricks'

and the intonation of:

'he could not blow that house of bricks down'
N-NC; p. 23, 204)

B-538   5;6.24   B: (talking to friend Mike, who was over visiting)
'Gùess whát, Mìke? I'm gìving **you cándy, and mé**.'
(pauses, thinks) 'I'm gìving <u>yóu càndy, and mé</u>.'
(first time it sounded like he was giving Mike 'candy and
me'; second time, giving 'you and me' candy; SC; p. 205)

34. *Phonological telescopings of phrases.*

(Diacritics are used as pitch markers: ˇ=rising pitch; ^=falling pitch; ´=high pitch; `=low pitch)

AN-1   1;4.20   An: (counting number of books)
'[tʰuwǐ:] . . . . twǒ, thrěe bôok.'
(for 'two, three book' [tʰǔʔ θwǐʔ bûk]; syntagmatic blend, ordered: deletion of coda+first onset consonant [ʔ.θ], resyllabification of body [tʰu] with rhyme [wi] to form one syllable; fixed phrase; SC; p. 47)

AN-5   1;7.15   M: (looking at book) 'Who's thát?'
An: '[ɜ̌:.bì] . . . Érnie Bèrt.'
(for 'Ernie Bert' [ɜ̌.nǐʔ bɜ̀t]; syntagmatic blend, misordered: deletion of onset [n] and coda [ʔ] and rhyme [ɜt], metathesis and resyllabification of [i.b]; SC)

B-11   1;9.23   B: 'Bíb òn! [pâ:n]! Bíb òn!'
(for 'bib on' [píp ʔàn]; deletion of rhyme+onset [íp.ʔ], resyllabification of onset [p] with rhyme [an]; 2-word stage; SC)

B-18   1;10.5   D: 'Bòbby, I gòt your tòast and céreal rèady.'
B: 'Nò [nô:ʷɕ]! . . . Nò nò tôast!'
(for 'no no toast' [nòʷ nòʷ tʰôʷɕ]; deletion of rhyme+onset [òʷ.tʰ], by stress, resyllabification of onset [n] with rhyme [ôʷɕ]; 2-word stage; SC; p. 165)

AL-2   2;0.7   Al: '[mí.kâ:ʷ . . . mí.kâ:ʷ], no!' (shakes head)
M: 'Mìckey Móuse?'
Al: 'Yeah, Míckèy Môuse.'
(for 'Mickey Mouse' [mí.kì mâʷs]; syntagmatic blend, ordered: deletion of rhyme+onset [i.m] and coda [s], resyllabification of onset [k] with nucleus [aʷ]; 2-word stage; N-NC; p. 165)

AL-5   2;1.5   Al: '[gǽ:.mì:].'
(for 'Gramma Beckie' [gæ̀.mʌ bɛ́.kì]; deletion of rhyme+syllable+onset [ʌ.bɛ.k], resyllabification of onset [m] with rhyme [i], overall prosody of word 'Beckie'; 2-word stage; NSC; p. 129)

AL-7   2;1.23   Al: (watching baby bears on TV)
'The [bè:ʲ.bɵ̀:] . . . the <u>baby bear</u>.'
(for 'baby bear', [bèʲ.bì bɵ̀]; deletion of syllable [bi] by
stress; [ɵ] was part of her current vowel system; SC;
p. 132, 164)

AN-30   2;2.5   An: '[tʃʊ́:.kì:].'
(for 'chocolate chip cookie' [tʃà.kət tʃìp kʰʊ́.kì]; deletion of
rhyme+syllable+syllable+onset [a.kət.tʃɪp.kʰ],
resyllabification of onset [tʃ] with rhyme [ʊ]; NSC; p. 165,
195)

B-47   2;2.25   B: 'We're hàving <u>còokies and bròwnìes</u> for dìnner. We're
hàving [bʊ́.kìz] for dìnner.' (looks confused)
M: 'What?'
B: 'We're hàving bròwnìes.'
(for 'cookies and brownies' [kʰʊ̀.kìz an bwæ̀ʷ.nìz];
syntagmatic blend, misordered, single onset consonant of
'brownies' substituted for single onset consonant of
'cookies', remainder of 'brownies' deleted; possibly
paradigmatic blend; N-NC)

AL-21   2;3.5   Al: '[fwíŋ.kò̀ʷs].'
(for 'fruit-wrinkles' [fwùt.wíŋ.kò̀ʷs]; deletion of
rhyme+onset [ut.w], resyllabificaiton of onset [fw] with
coda [ɪŋ]; NSC; p. 162)

OC-21   2;3.10   OA: 'This is an íce-crèam còne.'
OG: 'Not [rì:s] còne! . . . Not íce-crèam còne!'
(for 'ice-cream' [áʲs.krìm]; syntagmatic blend, misordered:
[ri] from second syllable moved to front of word, followed
by coda [s] from first syllable, all other segments deleted;
SC; p. 23, 167)

AN-38   2;3.26   An: 'He [fwèw] on his fâce.'
(for 'fell flat' [fèw fwæ̀t]; syntagmatic blend, misordered;
onset [fw] from second word combined with rhyme [ɛw] of
first word; NSC)

AN-40   2;4.20   An: 'I'm nòt a báby, I'm a [βɽ̂:ɬ].'
(for 'big girl' [bíg gɚ̀ɬ]; deletion of rhyme+onset [ɪg.g],
coalescence of [b+ɚ] with non-English segments [βɽ]
resulting; NSC; p. 109)

AN-44   2;4.20   An: 'Sometimes I èat my éggs, and [sò:ʷté:ʲ.tòʷz], and
                    sòme péas, and sòme múshrooms, and èat my lûnch.'
                    (for 'some potatoes' [sʌm pʰòʷ.téʲ.tòʷz]; deletion of
                    rhyme+onset [ʌm.pʰ]; NSC)

B-69   2;6.2   B: (pointing to elementary school where Anna is)
                    '[ǽ:.nǽʷ] there . . . Ánna's òut thère.'
                    (for 'Anna's out' [ǽ.nʌs ǽʷt]; syntagmatic blend, ordered,
                    deletion of rhyme [ʌs] from 'Anna's' and coda [t] from 'out',
                    resyllabification of onset [n] with nucleus [ǽʷ]; SC)

AL-37   2;7.1   Al: 'I wànt [fʒíŋ.kʌ̀w] . . . I wànt frùit-wrínklès.'
                    (for [fʒùt.ʒ íŋ.kʌ̀ws]; deletion of rhyme+onset [ut.ʒ],
                    resyllabification of onset [fʒ] with rhyme [ıŋ]; error
                    interrupted and corrected before speaking the plural [-s];
                    SC)

B-95   2;7.7   B: 'I wànt my [sâ:n].'
                    M: 'Your what?'
                    B: 'I wànt my sócks òn.'
                    (for 'socks on' [sáks àn]; deletion of rhyme [aks],
                    resyllabification of onset [s] with rhyme [an] (could also be
                    gemination of vowel [a]); NSC; p. 162)

B-100   2;7.17   B: 'Can yòu sìng the [sḷǎ:ŋ]?'
                    M: 'What?'
                    B: 'Can yòu sìng the flỳing sóng?'
                    (for 'flying song' [fḷà ̀.íŋ sáŋ]; syntagmatic blend,
                    misordered; second onset consonant [l] of 'flying' inserted
                    into onset of 'song', remainder of 'flying' deleted; NSC)

OC-27   2;8.0   OA: 'Snáck is rèady! Ànybody wànna còme and éat?'
                    OB: 'Nòt ríght nôẃ!'
                    OG: 'Nǒt [rǽ:ẃ] . . . nòt ríght nôẃ!'
                    (for 'right now' [rá ̍t nǽẃ]; deletion of rhyme+onset [a ̍t.n],
                    resyllabification of onset [r] with rhyme [æw]; SC; p. 33)

OC-28   2;8.0   OB: 'On the bùmpý, bùmpý rûg!'
                    OG: 'On the [bβʌ̂:g]!' (looks confused)
                    (for 'bumpy rúg' [bʌm.pí ʒʌ̀g]; deletion of rhyme+syllable
                    [ʌm.pi], coalescence of [bʒ] resulting in non-English
                    segment [β]; N-NC; p. 109)

AL-48   2;9.8   Al: 'Mom, Ì wànt some [ǽ:.p̩l̩ù:s] . . . ápplèjùice.'
                   (for 'applejuice' [ǽ.pə̆ɫ.dzùs]; syntagmatic blend, ordered;
                   deletion of vowel [ə] and onset [dz], causing
                   resyllabification of /pl/ as an onset with the coda [us]; SC;
                   p. 167)

AL-56   2;10.11   OA: 'Where's your sìster?'
                   Al: 'My sìster's [sʌ̀:m.wʌ̂:ɫ] . . . sòmewhère êlse.'
                   (for 'somewhere else' [sʌm.wɛ̀ʒ êɫs]; syntagmatic blend,
                   misordered: deletion of rhyme [ɛʒ], resyllabification of
                   onset [w] with rhyme [ɛɫ], but perseveration/substitution
                   of vowel, [ʌ]-->[ɛ], deletion of coda [s]; SC; p. 167)

AN-88   2;11.13   An: '[kʰl̩ú:.kʰl̩àk] . . . (laughs) Mommy, I said
                   "[kʰl̩ú:.kʰl̩àk]" for cúckoo clòck.'
                   (for 'cuckoo clock' [kʰu.kʰu.kʰl̩àk]; syntagmatic blend,
                   misordered; omission of syllable [kʰu], with anticipation/
                   addition of [l] from 'clock'; SC; p. 85)

AN-90   2;11.15   An: '[kʰl̩ú:.kʰl̩à:k].'
                   (for 'cuckoo clock'; see above; NSC)

AN-93   2;11.21   An: 'Mòmmy, I'm nòt the [blá:ŋk.stɚ] àny mòre.'
                   (for 'block monster' [blák màn.stɚ], a monster who throws
                   blocks; syntagmatic blend, misordered; deletion of body
                   [ma], movement of nasal [n] before [k], assimilation to [k];
                   NSC)

AL-103 3;3.11   M: (reading) 'I will hàve a pìcnìc lûnch tòdày.'
                   Al: (smiles, excitedly) '[pʰ ì:k.l ì:tʃ]!'
                   M: 'What?'
                   Al: 'Pìcnìc lûnch!'
                   (for 'picnic lunch' [pʰìk.nìk lʌ̀ntʃ]; syntagmatic blend,
                   misordered; onset and final coda consonants of 'lunch'
                   combined with vowel of [nɪk]; NSC; p. 165)

B-128   3;5.16   B: 'Dàddy, you [rì̃:.b3] . . . you remèmber those gènies in
                   Aláddain? Well, you áre one. And I lóve Gènies!'
                   (for 'remember' [ri.mĩm.b3]; syntagmatic blend, ordered;
                   deletion of rhyme+onset/coda consonants [i-m/m], but
                   vowel [ĩ] retains nasalization from [m] context;
                   resyllabification of onset [r] with nucleus [ĩ]; SC)

B-129   3;5.16   B: 'I lèft my Bàtman shìrt at Grándma's, so I'm gònna
                 drive my [έk.tò".mi̊ɬ] . . . éctòmòbìle and gét ìt.'
                 (for 'ectomobile' [έk.tò".mò".bi̊ɬ], a Ghostbusters toy;
                 deletion of rhyme+onset [o".b], resyllabification of onset
                 [m] with rhyme [i̊ɬ]; SC)

B-136   3;6.15   B: 'Mom, my [pʰi.dʒà:rz] . . . my P̲J̲s̲ ̲à̲r̲e̲ ùnder mỳ shìrt.'
                 (for 'PJs are' [pʰi.dʒèʲ(z) àr]; deletion of rhyme [eʲ],
                 resyllabification of onset [dʒ] with rhyme [ar], movement
                 of plural morpheme to end of phonological word; SC;
                 p. 163, 412)

AL-151 3;7.17   Al: 'Thìs is [lèf.tʰò".dʌ] Í can drìnk.'
                 (for 'leftover soda' [lèf.to".v3 sò".dʌ]; deletion of rhyme+
                 syllable+onset [o".v3.s], with resyllabification of onset /t/
                 with rhyme [o"], becomes aspirated under stress; NSC)

B-154   3;8.16   B: 'Lóok, Mòm, anòther [bi̊:.dʒù:s] . . . B̲é̲e̲t̲l̲e̲j̲ù̲i̲c̲e̲.'
                 (for 'Beetlejuice' [bi̊.ɾəɬ.dʒùs]; deletion of syllable [ɾəɬ];
                 SC; p. 129)

OC-61   3;9.0   OG: 'Thère was a spíder in hère a fèw [mi̊.nə.gò"z].'
                 (for 'minutes ago' [mi̊.nɨt(s) ə.gò"]; deletion of rhyme [ɨt],
                 resyllabification of onset [n] with rhyme [ə], and
                 movement of plural morpheme to end of resultant form;
                 note that plural morpheme voices when it occurs after
                 vowel; NSC)

AN-124 3;10.5   An: '[dʒrô:"p] . . . [dʒrô:"p] . . . j̲ú̲m̲p̲-̲r̲ò̲p̲e̲.'
                 (for 'jump rope' [dʒʌmp.rò"p]; deletion of rhyme [ʌmp],
                 resyllabification of onset [dʒ] with syllable [ro"p] creating
                 new onset cluster [dʒr]; SC; p. 123, 165, 194)

B-196   4;1.18   B: 'Thòse are thìngs that [kʰô:ʲz] wèar . . . that c̲ó̲w̲b̲ò̲y̲s̲
                 wèar.'
                 (for 'cowboys' [kʰǽ".bòʲz]; deletion of rhyme+onset [æ".b],
                 resyllabification of onset [kʰ] with rhyme [oʲz]; SC; p. 164)

OC-91 4;1.18   OB: (asking Mom to get a cookie out for him to decorate)
                  'I want òne mòre [kʰʊ́:.kʰæ̀ʷt].' (looks confused)
                  (for 'cookie out' [kʰʊ́.kì æ̀ʷt]; deletion of vowel [i], with
                  resyllabification of onset [k] with rhyme/syllable [æ̀ʷt];
                  N-NC; p. 164)

AN-159 4;2.16   An: 'Hère's some [də̀.réʲ] . . . (breath) dècòrátiòn.'
                  (for 'decoration' [dè.kə̀.réʲ.ʃʌn]; deletion of rhyme+onset
                  [ɛ.k], resyllabification of onset [d] with vowel [ə]; error
                  interrupted before end of word; SC)

AL-209b 4;2.16   Al: 'Mommy, we gòt to sàw the [f îːn] . . .
                  we sàw the fíre èngìne todày.'
                  (for 'fire engine' [fáʲʒ ìɲ.dʒìn]; deletion of rhyme+
                  syllable+onset [aʲʒ.ɪɲ.dʒ], resyllabification of onset [f] with
                  rhyme [ɪn]; SC; 209a=Class 49; p. 470)

B-224 4;2.25   B: 'Òne [mîːr] . . . òne mòre yêar!'
                  (for 'more year' [mòr jîr]; deletion of rhyme+onset [or.j],
                  resyllabification of onset [m] with rhyme [ɪr]; SC)

B-230 4;2.30   B: 'Could you còme into the bàsement [nǎːʲ] . . . nǒw . . .
                  rìght nǒw?'
                  (for 'right now?' [ràʲt næ̌ʷ]; syntagmatic blend, misordered;
                  onset [n] from 'now' resyllabified with nucleus [aʲ] of 'right',
                  all other units deleted; SC)

AN-166 4;4.0   An: '[jǽː.dì].'
                  (for 'Yéah, Dàddy' [jɛ́: dæ̀.dì]; deletion of rhyme+onset
                  [ɛ.d], resyllabification of onset [j] with rhyme [æ]; NSC)

AL-212 4;4.8   Al: 'Mòmmy, wè [foʒ.bæ̀ːʷd] . . . wè forgòt abòut thís
                  Cìnderèlla.'
                  (for 'forgot about' [foʒ.gàr ə.bæ̀ʷt]; deletion of syllables
                  [gar.ə]; [t] at the end of the phrase acts like the past tense
                  marker and voices; SC; p. 163)

AN-178 4;4.24   An: 'Thrèe things are called 'chícken'. Lìke you hàve
                  chícken pòx, and yòu can éat chìcken, ànd aʔ [ǽː.mʌ̀ɬ]
                  . . . a fèmale ánìmàl, lìke a hén.'
                  (for 'female animal' [fî.mè́ɬ ǽ.nə̀.mə̀ɬ]; syntagmatic blend,
                  ordered, syllable structure of 'female' with segments of
                  'animal, note change in indefinite article; SC; p. 131, 168,
                  424)

AN-179 4;4.24   An: 'My spóts are àll gòne, so I'm dòne with [ðĭ:.kən] . . .
the chìcken pòx forévèr!'
(for 'the chicken' [ðə tʃĭ.kən]; deletion of rhyme+onset
[ə.tʃ], resyllabification of onset [ð] with rhyme [ɪ]; SC)

AN-182 4;4.27   An: 'Mòm, have yòu seen pèrsons [lĕ:ʲgz]?'
M: 'What?'
An: 'Have yòu seen pèrsons làay ĕggs?' (making a joke)
(for 'lay eggs' [lèʲ ʔĕʲgz]; deletion of rhyme+onset [eʲ.ʔ], by
stress; resyllabification of onset [l] with stressed rhyme
[eʲgz]; NSC)

AN-200 4;5.18   An: '[tʃà:k.lĕ:łk].'
(for 'chocolate milk' [tʃàk.lɨt mɛ́łk]; deletion of
rhyme+onset [ɨt.m], resyllabification of onset [l] with
rhyme [ɛłk]; NSC)

AN-210 4;5.27   An: 'I wànna ask Bàrbara if Chrísty [kʰʌ̀:d] òver . . .
if Chrísty còuld còme òver for dínnèr.'
(for 'could come' [kʰʊ̀d kʰʌm]; syntagmatic blend,
misordered; onset and coda of 'could' with vowel of 'come';
or body of 'come' with coda of 'could'; SC)

AL-230 4;6.18   Al: '[bá:.bàʲ] . . . Bóbbỳ, Ì héard you!'
(for 'Bobby I' [bá.bì àʲ]; deletion of rhyme [i],
resyllabification of onset [b] with vowel (syllable/rhyme)
[aʲ]; SC)

AN-233 4;8.5   An: (making 'car' noise with cup)
'Our cár's stàrting to drìve awày.'
M: 'Whát? Dìd you sée it?'
An: 'No, I héard it. (laughs) My [kʰʌ́:.pʰ ɪ̀ŋ] . . .
my cúp's màking the sòund.'
(for 'cup's making' [kʰʌ́p(s) mèʲk.(ɪŋ)]; deletion of auxillary
[-s] plus syllable (morpheme) [meʲk]; resyllabification of
coda [p] as onset (aspirated), with rhyme (morpheme) [-ɪŋ];
SC)

AN-236 4;8.8   An: (being funny, playing around with pronouns)
'Mòm, I càll [gî:z] . . . I càll gìrls 'hê'. '
(for 'girls he' [gɚ̀ł(z) hî]; omission of rhyme+syllable
[ɚł.hi] and movement of plural morpheme to end of
resultant form; SC)

B-362 4;9.12 B: '. . . remember when [dà.na.séz] . . . when
Dònnatèllo sáys "Ya snòoze, ya lóse!"?'
(for 'Donnatello says' [dà.nə.tʰὲ.loʷ séz]; deletion of
syllables [tʰɛ.loʷ]; SC)

AN-246 4;10.5 M: 'Time to start thinking about what you want for
bréakfast.'
An: '[pʰǽːn.fə᷋] . . . páncàkes fòr my brèakfast.'
(for 'pancakes for' [pʰǽn.kʰè᷆ks fə᷋]; deletion of syllable
(and plural morpheme) [kʰeʲk(s)]; SC)

B-443 5;1.3 B: (telling Mom which night is kids' night at Pizza Hut)
'[tʰûːʷz.nà᷆ʲt] . . . túesdày nìght is kìds' nìght at Pìzza
Hùt.'
(for 'tuesday night' [tʰúʷz.dè᷆ʲ nà᷆ʲt]; deletion of syllable
[deʲ]; SC)

B-465 5;2.1 B: 'Thère's this [vɪ̆ː.nə᷆᷈] . . . thère's this vĭnégár? And it's
rĕd?'
(for 'vinegar' [vɪ̆.nə᷈.gə᷆᷈]; deletion of rhyme+onset [ə.g],
resyllabification of onset [n] with rhyme [ə᷈]; SC)

AN-287 5;4.17 An: (talking about an imaginary Halloween party)
'Thèn I'm gòing to tàke off my [hǽ̂ːsk] . . . tàke off
my hàt ànd mâsk, and sày "It's ònly Ánna". '
(for 'hat and mask' [hǽt ǽn mǽsk]; deletion of rhyme+
syllable+onset [æt-æn-m], by stress; resyllabification of
onset [h] with rhyme [æsk]; SC)

B-496 5;4.29 B: 'I lóve [mə.nàː.pə.lə᷈ː]. (looks confused) I have a
Monòpoly Júnior gàme.'
(for 'Monopoly Junior' [mə.nà.pə.li dʒjùɲ.jə᷆᷈]; deletion of
rhyme+syllable+onset [i.dʒjuɲ.j]; resyllabification of onset
[l] with rhyme [ə᷈]; N-NC)

B-497 5;5.1 B: 'I don't wànt the [dík.ʃə.nìː] . . . díctionàry.'
(for 'dictionary' [dík.ʃə.nὲ.ri]; deletion of rhyme+onset [ɛ.r];
resyllabification of onset [n] with rhyme [i]; SC)

B-533 5;6.17 B: '[gɪ̀ːtʃ] . . . gùess whìch cùp has the pénny insìde of it?'
(for 'guess which' [gès wìtʃ]; deletion of rhyme+onset
[ɛs.w]; resyllabification of onset [g] with rhyme [ɪtʃ]; SC)

B-548   5;7.12   B: 'I lóve the [mʌ̀ː.rə̵] . . . the mùd pùddle.'
(for 'mud puddle' [mʌd pʰʌ.rə̵]; deletion of rhyme+onset
[ʌd.pʰ]; resyllabification of onset [m] with rhyme [ʌ]; could
also be coda+syllable [d.pʰʌ]; SC)

AN-296 5;7.13   An: '[nɛ̀.v̵] gét mè!'
(for 'You'll never' [jùʷ̵ nɛ̀.vɚ]; syntagmatic blend,
misordered; feet [juʷ̵] and [nɛ.vɚ] metathesized, body
[juʷ] and rhyme [ɚ] deleted, [v̵] coalesced into one
syllable, [̵] becomes syllabic; NSC; p. 168)

B-582   5;11.21   B: (telling what kind of jello we were making)
'[pʰáːʲ.nʌ̀ː̵] . . . píneàpple bèrry blùe jèllo.'
(for 'pineapple' [pʰáʲ.næ̀.pə̵]; deletion of rhyme+onset
[æ.p]; resyllabification of onset [n] with rhyme [ə̵], then
vowel becomes [ʌ] under stress; SC)

AN-329 5;11.30   An: 'Ali, ya know whát?   Aùnt [ɨ.lí̇ː.zɨ.mè̇ʲks] . . . Aunt
Elízabeth màkes rèal gòod hòmemade cóokies, dóesn't
shè Mòm?'
(for 'Elizabeth makes' [ɨ.lí.zɨ.bəθ mè̇ʲk(s)]; deletion of
syllable [bəθ]; possibly phrase blend with 'Aunt Liz
makes'; SC; p. 194)

II. Paradigmatic Lexical Errors

35. Lexical substitutions, content words.

AN-9   1;8.7   M: (Anna is in bathtub, playing with nesting boxes; there
                        is no water in the boxes) 'What is thát?'
                 An: 'It is wàter in the **bóx**.'
                 M: 'There's wáter in the bòx?'
                 An: 'Yeah.' (pause; looks confused)
                 M: 'You mean the túb?'
                 An: 'YEAH!'
('box' [paks] for 'tub' [tʰʌb]; [-sem]; NSC; p. 376)
Phon: 1.5, +T.
Lex: Common noun X2, both CRS. (Note: because this error is
[-phon, -sem], the morphological analysis is not relevant.)
Other: Environmental, child sees both box and tub while speaking.
Other: Collocation, 'in the box'.
(Note: while analyzed as [-sem], could be shared criterial features:
similar shape, both able to hold water)

B-9   1;9.7   B: (pointing at chair where Mom usually sits)
                        '**Dàddy** sít.' (looks embarassed)
                        '**Mómmy**.' (correcting himself)
                 M: 'Whát, hòney?'
                 B: 'Mómmy sìt.'
('Daddy' [tǽ.ti] for 'Mommy' [má.mi]; only Mommy visible at the
time, so no environmental influence; 2-word stage; SC; p. 302,
303, 376)
Phon: 3, -T.   Lex/Morph: Proper noun X2; mono X2.
Sem: Co-members of a set (parents); (also possibly co-hyponyms
'parents', but unlikely at this age; also metonyms); opposed.

AN-15   1;9.20   An: (Mom was helping Anna put some tight shoes on; she
                        pushed too hard and it hurt Anna's foot)
                        'Is tòo **hót**.' (looks confused)
                 M: 'Too hót?'
                 An: 'Is tòo **hárd**.'
('hot' [hatʰ] for 'hard' [ha:ʐtʰ]; N-NC; p. 376, 379, 431)
Phon: 5, +T.   Lex/Morph: Adjective X2; mono X2.
Sem: Co-hyponyms (physical sensations which cause pain).

B-16   1;10.1   B: (poured powder on his toes while he was touching his penis) 'Pòwder **pénis** . . . Pòwder tóes.'
('penis' [pí.nʌç] for 'toes' [toʷç]; 2-word stage; SC; p. 135, 302, 376, 439, 459)
Phon: 1.5, +T.   Lex/Morph: Common noun X2, both CR; one singular, one morphologically plural ('toes' probably lexicalized as plural); mono vs. 2-infl.
Sem: Co-partonyms (body parts; also perceived physical similarity).
Other: Environmental, touching one body part, while talking about the other.

B-20   1;10.7   B: (holding up his bottle to Mom, requesting more juice, but looking at Mom's coffee) 'Mómmy, mòre **cóffee?**'
M: 'Thàt's mý còffee.'
B: 'Mòre júice!'
('coffee' [ká.fi] for 'juice' [tuç]; 2-word stage; NSC; p. 23, 302, 303, 376)
Phon: 0.5, +T.
Lex/Morph: Common noun X2, both mass; mono X2.
Sem: Co-hyponyms (kinds of drinks).
Other: Environmental, looking at coffee while requesting juice.

OC-2   1;10.22   OB: '**Bób** . . . Béckie nòse.'
[bá: . . . bé.kiʔ nò:ʷ]
(started to say 'BobBob' [bá:.bab], his name for his grandfather; while pointing to his grandmother Beckie's nose; both grandparents in room; 2-word stage; SC; p. 47, 302, 338, 376, 377)
Phon: 3.5, +T.   Lex/Morph: Proper noun X2; mono X2.
Sem: Co-members of set (grandparents); opposed.
Other: Environmental, both grandparents visible.

OC-6   2;0.7   OG: (looking at toothbrush; no toothpaste in view)
'Mỳ **tóothpàste** . . . mỳ tóothbrùsh.'
('toothpaste' [tʰúf.pʰèⁱç] for 'toothbrush [tʰúf.bʌ̀ç]; 2-word stage; SC; p. 13, 302, 303, 376, 459)
Phon: 7, +T.
Lex/Morph: Common noun X2; mass vs. CRS; 2-cmpd X2.
Sem: Co-members of a set (items involved in brushing teeth; also metonyms).

OC-7   2;0.7   OG: (handing toy to Mom, but looking at Dad)
                 'Hére-go **Dàddy** . . . hére-go M̀ommy.'
('Daddy' [dǽ.di] for 'Mommy' [má.mi]; 2-word stage, 'here go'
considered one word; SC; p. 302, 376)
Phon: 3, -T.   Lex/Morph: Proper noun X2; mono X2.
Sem: Co-members of a set (parents); opposed.
Other: Environmental, looking at Daddy while talking to Mommy.

B-42   2;2.2   B: (asks Alice to give him one of the sponges in the tub,
                     and she does) 'Thánk you **Mà** . . . thánk you A̱lice.'
(started to say 'Mommy' [má.mi] for 'Alice' [ǽ.lʌç]; SC; p. 376)
Phon: 2, -T.   Lex/Morph: Proper noun X2; mono X2.
Sem: Co-members of set (immediate family members).
Other: Environmental, Mom was in the room bathing them.

AL-10   2;2.5   Al: (gives Mom a kiss when Mom picks her up, then
                      points to the car) 'Mý **kìss** . . . mý càr.'
('kiss' [kʰɪç] for 'car' [kʰa̰]; [-sem]; SC; p. 171, 376)
Phon: 3, -T.   Lex/Morph: Verb vs. common noun; mono X2.
Other: 'On the mind', thinking about having just kissed Mom.

AL-13   2;2.11   Al: (holding fingers to lips)
                       'Mè **crỳing** Dàddy sléeping.' (looks confused)
                   M: 'You mean you're qúiet?'
                   Al: 'Yéah!'
(for 'I'm being quiet because Daddy's sleeping', which would
normally be 'Mè qùiet Dàddy sléeping.' This was clear from
context; 'crying' [kʰʒá̰ʲ.(in)] for 'quiet' [kʰwáʲ.ʌt]; [-sem] but see note;
N-NC; p. 135, 180, 305, 376, 432, 436, 440)
Phon: 5, -T.   Lex/Morph: Verb X2 ('quiet' used as a verb),
both intransitive, regular (?); one with progressive suffix {-ing};
mono vs. 2-infl. (Semantic note: could argue that for the child these
were opposed: crying=making noise vs. being quiet).

AN-45   2;4.23   An: (Anna tells her Daddy that it's time to get up, then
                    reports to Mom) '**My Dáddy** say, I mean <u>Ánna</u> say:
                    "It's tìme to get úp".'
                    M: 'And whàt did your Dáddy sày?'
                    An: ' "Fíne." '
('(My) Daddy' (maʲ) [dǽ.di] for 'Anna' [ǽ.nʌ]; deletes determiner
'my' in correction; SC; p. 376)
Phon: 3.5, +T.
Lex/Morph: Proper noun X2 (one in a noun phrase); mono X2.
Sem: Co-members of a set (immediate family members).
Other: 'On the mind', thinking about having just spoken to her
father. (Note: possibly wrong proposition)

AN-47   2;4.27   An: 'I wànna **tàlk** . . . I wànna <u>càll</u> yóu!'
('talk' [tʰak] for 'call' [kʰaɬ], probably started to say phrase 'talk to';
SC; p. 297, 337, 363, 376)
Phon: 3, -T.   Lex/Morph: Verb X2, both transitive, regular,
infinitives; mono vs. 2-PV.
Sem: Synonyms (in terms of telephone; broad vs. narrow scope).

B-58   2;5.12   B: (pointing at the quesadilla he was having for lunch)
                   'Whàt is thát, my **cándy**?'
('candy' [kʰǽn.di] for 'quesadilla' [kʰè.sʌ.dí.jʌ]; NSC; p. 376)
Phon: 3.5, +T.
Lex/Morph: Common noun X2, mass vs. CRS; mono X2.
Sem: Co-hyponyms (kinds of food).
Other: Discourse context, Alice had just been talking about various
kinds of candy, but hadn't said the word 'candy'.

B-71   2;6.2   B: 'I wànna **wàtch** . . . I wànna <u>lìsten to</u> "Bàby Belúga".'
('watch' [wátʃ] for 'listen to' [lí.sʌn tʰu]; "Baby Beluga" is an audio
tape; SC; p. 222, 321, 354, 376, 378, 432, 436)
Phon: 0.5, -T.   Lex/Morph: Verb X2, both transitive, regular,
infinitives; mono vs. 2-PV.
Sem: Co-hyponyms (kinds of perception); opposed.

OC-23   2;6.7   OG: (looking at a book, "The Fox and the Hound", in which
                    'Todd' and 'Copper' are the main characters)
                    'Where's Cópper?' (turns page, sees both on page)
                    'Hére's [tʰɔ́] . . . Còpper.'
('Todd' [tʰɔd] for 'Copper' [kʰɔ́.p3]; SC; p. 338, 354, 376)
Phon: 2, -T.   Lex/Morph: Proper noun X2; mono X2.
Sem: Co-members of a set (main characters in book); opposed.
Other: Environmental, both characters visible on page.

B-74   2;6.11   B: 'I hĭt . . . I hùrt Hànna and Ahmád.'
('hit' [hɪt] for 'hurt' [h3t]; explaining why he got in trouble in school;
he hadn't hit them, but hurt them some other way; SC; p. 328, 337,
352, 376, 378, 459)
Phon: 4, -T.   Lex/Morph: Verb X2, both transitive, irregular,
zero past tense; 2-infl X2.
Sem: Causal (hitting causes hurt).

B-77   2;6.12   B: 'I wànt the yéllow tòp.' (meaning nipple of bottle)
              M: (holding one up) 'Is thĭs the right one?'
              B: 'Uh huh, the **gréen** tòp . . . the yéllow tòp.'
('green' [g̰ɜin] for 'yellow' [jé.loʷ]; there were no green nipples; SC;
p. 376, 378)
Phon: 0.5, +T.   Lex/Morph: Adjective X2; mono X2.
Sem: Co-hyponyms (kinds of color).

B-78   2;6.13   B: (talking to Anna) 'Hére I àm, **Dàd:** . . . Ànna.'
('Daddy' [dǽ.di] for 'Anna' [ǽ.nʌ]; when noticed error, lengthened [d]
in 'Daddy'; SC; p. 376)
Phon: 3.5, -T.   Lex/Morph: Proper noun X2; mono X2.
Sem: Co-members of set (immediate family members).

B-83   2;6.21   M: (giving Bobby his ice cream)
              'OK, gèt ùp in your hĭgh chàir.'
              B: 'I wànna gèt it òn the **flóor** . . . òn the táble I mèan.'
('floor' [f̬lo̰ɜ] for 'table' [tʰéʲ.bʌɬ]; i.e. he wanted to eat it sitting in a
chair pulled up to the table, not in his high chair; SC; p. 376)
Phon: 0.5, +T.
Lex/Morph: Common noun X2, both CRS; mono X2.
Sem: Metonyms (physically contiguous in dining room, table sits on
floor; also shared criterial features, physical similarities: large flat
surfaces).
Other: Environmental, floor and table both visible.

B-84   2;6.21   B: 'I wànt **Pùss in** . . . I wànt Mòther Góose tàpe.'
('Puss in Boots' [pʰʊ̀s.ɪn.bút(s)] for 'Mòther Góose' [mʌ̀.d̰ɜ.gús]; they
are two different audio tapes; SC; p. 376, 378, 439)
Phon: 4.5, +T.   Lex/Morph: Proper noun X2 (functioning as
nominal modifiers); 2 (2-cmpd) vs. 4 (3-cmpd+infl).
Sem: Co-hyponyms (kinds of audio tapes; literally, 'Puss in Boots' is
a fairy story, and 'Mother Goose' is a fictional character who
oversees nursery rhymes, but in this case he uses these names to
refer to the tapes).

B-86b   2;6.21   B: 'Where's Dáddy?'
                   M: 'He's òut in the stúdy.'
                   B: 'She's . . . he's **tùrning** òn the télephòne.'
                   M: 'What?'
                   B: 'He's <u>tàlking</u> òn the télephòne.'
('turning' [tʰɔ́n.(ɪn)] for 'talking' [tʰák.(ɪn)]; [-sem]; NSC; 86a=Class
36; p. 277, 305, 319, 376, 409, 431)
Phon: 3, -T.   Lex/Morph: Verb X2, both intransitive,
regular, progressive; 2-infl X2.
Other: Collocational, turn on the X.

B-90   2;7.2   D: 'Bobby, whèn are you gònna g̊o on the pótty?'
                 B: 'I **àlways** díd!'
                 D: 'You álways did?'
                 B: 'I <u>àlready</u> díd.'
('always' [ɑ́ɫ.wɪz] for 'already' [ɑ́ɫ.ʒɛ.di]; NSC; p. 337, 376)
Phon: 4, -T.   Lex/Morph: Adverb X2; mono X2.
Sem: Shared criterial features (quasi-antonyms of temporality);
opposed.

B-94   2;7.4   B: 'Lóok, Mòmmy. I gòt a **scáry** òn my fòot.'
                 M: 'What?'
                 B: 'I gòt aʔ <u>ówie</u> òn my fòot.'
('scary' [skɛ́.ʒi] for 'owie' [ǽ.wi], a child word for a cut or sore; note
shift in form of article; NSC; p. 337, 376, 378, 424, 425, 459)
Phon: 3, +T.
Lex/Morph: Adjective vs. common noun; 2-deriv X2 (both with
suffix {-ie/y}, although probably not analyzed out of these forms).
Sem: Connotation (negative association, being scared and being
hurt).

B-98   2;7.14   B: (in restaurant, Mom was giving him spoonfuls of her
                      soup; no cake visible)
                   'Can Ì get òne a your **cáke** agàin?'
('cake' [kʰeʲk] for 'soup' [sup]; meant a bite of soup; 'a' is filler
function word; NSC; p. 376)
Phon: 1.5, +T.
Lex/Morph: Common noun X2, both mass; mono X2.
Sem: Co-hyponyms (kinds of food).

AN-55   2;7.14   An: (handing Mom a balloon) 'Ópen thìs.'
                      (looks confused)
                      M: 'Do whát?'
                      An: '<u>Blòw</u> it úp!'
('open X' [ó".pʌn] for 'blow X up' [blo" ʌp]; N-NC; p. 337, 342, 362, 376, 378, 455)
Phon: 2, +T.   Lex/Morph: Verb X2, both transitive, regular/ irregular, imperative; mono vs. 2-PV.
Sem: Synonyms (cause to expand out; different selectional restrictions).

AN-60   2;7.27   An: (her favorite TV show "Contraption" just came on)
                      'Hey, "**Colléction**" is òn!'
                      M: 'You mean "Contráption"?'
                      An: 'Yéah, "<u>Contráption</u>".'
('Collection' [kʰə.lék.ʃən] for 'Contraption' [kʰən.tʰr̥ǽp.ʃən]; [-sem]; NSC; p. 248, 376, 379, 431, 437)
Phon: 5.5, +T.   Lex/Morph: Proper noun X2 (both used in proper noun slot here; however, 'collection' only known to the child as a common noun, 'Contraption' as a proper noun); 2-deriv X2 (both with prefix {con-}, nominal suffix {-ion}).

OC-29   2;8.0   OG: (asking another child how she wanted to be pushed on the swing) 'You wànt it **slów**? . . . You wànt it <u>fást</u>?'
('slow' [slo"] for 'fast' [fæst]; SC; p. 133, 171, 260, 324, 337, 376, 378)
Phon: 1.5, +T   Lex/Morph: Adverb X2; mono X2.
Sem: Gradable antonyms (of speed); opposed.

OC-30   2:8.0   OG: (watching Mom eat watermelon, but talking about eggs) 'I líke [**wà**] . . . I líke <u>ègg</u>.'
(started to say 'watermelon' [wá.dʒ.mè.lʌn] for 'egg' [eʲg]; SC; p. 376)
Phon: 0.5, -T.
Lex/Morph: Common noun X2, both mass; mono vs. 2-cmpd.
Sem: Co-hyponyms (kinds of food).
Other: Environment, looking at watermelon.

AL-43   2;8.5   Al: (watching Daddy pour fizzy water)
                      'I wànna **sèe** that sóund . . . I wànna <u>hèar</u> that sóund.'
('see' [si] for 'hear' [hɪ3]; SC; p. 354, 376, 378, 453)
Phon: 1.5, -T.
Lex/Morph: Verb X2, both transitive, irregular, infinitive; mono X2.
Sem: Cohyponyms (kinds of perception); opposed.

AN-68   2;9.12   An: 'Did Àlice gò to the dóctor's and gèt a **shárk**?'
('shark' [ʃark] for 'shot' [ʃat]; Anna had recently seen a scene from the
movie "Jaws" so associated sharks with fear and pain; N-NC; p. 280,
287, 308, 317, 376)
Phon: 4, +T.
Lex/Morph: Common noun X2, both CRS; mono X2.
Sem: Connotation (very negative emotions, two events related to
skin being punctured by sharp point, evoking pain and fear; also
shared criterial features, physical similarities between needle and
teeth).
Other: 'On the mind', thinking about the movie "Jaws".

OC-34   2;10.18   OG: 'Mommy, I dòne with my **cándy**.'
M: 'Dòne with your cándy?
OG: 'No, I mèan I dòne with my **ápplejùice**.'
('candy' [kʰǽn.di] for 'applejuice' [ǽ.pʌɫ.dʒùs]; NSC; p. 81, 376, 432,
436)
Phon: 2.5, +T.
Lex/Morph: Common noun X2, both mass; mono vs. 2-cmpd.
Sem: Co-hyponyms (kinds of sweet snack food).

OC-36   3;0.0   OB: (I had given him a piece of candy, and his mother told
him to say thank you to me)
'Thànk you fòr the **cóokie**.'
('cookie' [kʰʊ́.ki] for 'candy' [kʰǽn.di]; NSC; p. 425)
Phon: 4.5, +T.
Lex/Morph: Common noun X2, mass vs. CRS; mono X2.
Sem: Co-hyponyms (kinds of sweet snack food).

B-122   3;1.9   B: 'Whère's [ǽ.nʌ . . . lʌs]? Whère's Álice?'
('Anna' [ǽ.nʌ] for 'Alice' [ǽ.lʌs]; partially SC in mid-word)
Phon: 4.5, +T.   Lex/Morph: Proper noun X2; mono X2.
Sem: Co-members of a set (sisters); opposed.

OC-39   3:2.0   OG: (talking about Santa Claus while watching her dad
make sauce) 'Sánta **Sàuce**.'
('sauce' [sas] for 'Claus' [kʰl̩az]; [-sem]; NSC)
Phon: 3, T?
Lex/Morph: Common noun, mass vs. proper noun; mono X2.
Other: Environmental, watching Dad make sauce.

AN-100   3;2.3   An: 'Mòmmy dòn't hòld my **tóothbrùsh** . . . dòn't hòld my
                         páintbrùsh.'
                     (while painting; 'toothbrush' [tʰúθ.brʌʃ] for 'paintbrush' [pʰéⁱnt.brʌʃ];
                     SC; p. 431, 437)
                     Phon: 4.5, +T.
                     Lex/Morph: Common noun X2, both CRS; 2-cmpd X2.
                     Sem: Co-hyponyms (kinds of brushes).

AL-109   3;3.25   Al: (hugging Anna after she hurt her toe)
                         'I'm gìving her a lìttle **lúllaby**.'
                     M: 'You're whát?'
                     Al: 'I'm gìving her a lìttle <u>lóve</u>.'
                     ('lullaby' [lʎ.lʌ.baʲ] for 'love' [lʌv]; NSC; p. 327)
                     Phon: 3.5, +T.
                     Lex/Morph: Common noun X2, mass vs. CRS; mono X2.
                     Sem: Connotation (positive emotions; lullabies associated with
                     Mother's love).

OC-52   3;4.0   OB: (playing with a set of plastic farm animals; no deer in
                         set.) 'Whìch òne's the **Bámbi**? (laughs) No, whìch
                         òne's the <u>báby</u>?'
                     ('Bambi' [bǽm.bi] for 'baby' [béʲ.bi]; SC; p. 237, 293)
                     Phon: 5, +T.
                     Lex/Morph: Proper noun vs. common noun, CRS; mono X2.
                     Sem: Shared criterial features ('Bambi' is the name of a particular
                     'baby' deer).
                     Other: Environment, as I suspect one of the toy animals reminded
                     him of Bambi; there was a llama in the set which looked like a
                     deer.

AL-119   3;4.8   An: 'I'm gonna wèar my wàtch to béd tonìght.'
                     Al: 'Nòt mé! I don't háve a **wìtch** . . . (quietly to self)
                         witch . . . witch . . . (normal voice) I don't háve a
                         <u>wàtch</u>.'
                     ('witch' [wɪtʃ] for 'watch' [watʃ]; [-sem]; SC after some thought;
                     p. 280)
                     Phon: 4.5, -T.
                     Lex/Morph: Common noun X2, both CRS; mono X2.
                     Other: 'On the mind', Alice was going through a year-long phase of
                     believing herself to be a witch, after a trip to Disneyland.

B-133   3;5.31   B: 'I wànt you to gèt me òne of those Kòol-aid
sándwìches . . . I mean <u>pópsìcles</u>.'
('sandwiches' [sǽnd.wì.tʃ(əz)] for 'popsicles' [pʰáp.sì.kəɫ(z)]; SC;
p. 135, 419)
Phon: 1.5, +T.   Lex/Morph: Common noun X2, both CRP;
2 (2-infl) vs. 3 (2-cmpd+infl).
Sem: Co-hyponyms (kinds of food).

OC-54   3;6.2   OG: 'Mommy, I wànt some [**sí.r**] . . . I wànt some <u>Lífe</u>.'
('cereal' [sí.ri.əɫ] for 'Life' [laⁱf], a kind of cereal; SC; p. 343, 359)
Phon: 0.5, +T.
Lex/Morph: Proper noun vs. common noun; mono X2.
Sem: Superordinate ('Life' is a kind of 'cereal').

AN-118 3;7.30   An: (explaining why she's folding up a picture she just
drew) ' 'Cùz it's a cárd. For Gràndma [aʲ.l] . . .
for Gràndma <u>Béckie</u>.'
(started to say 'Eileen' [aʲ.lín] for 'Beckie' [bɛ́.ki], her two
grandmothers; SC; p. 325, 338, 339)
Phon: 2, +T.   Lex/Morph: Proper noun X2; mono X2.
Sem: Co-hyponyms (names of grandmothers); opposed.
(Note: not co-members of a set, since they rarely occurred in the
same scene, so child had to have abstract category of 'grandmothers')

B-141   3;8.3   B: 'Ì want "Tèenage **Móvie**" . . . Ì want "Tèenage <u>Mútant</u>
Nìnja Tùrtles" tòday.'
('movie' [mú.vi] for 'mutant' [mjú.ʔn̩t]; [-sem]; SC; p. 430)
Phon: 4.5, +T.   Lex/Morph: Common noun X2 (child only
knows 'mutant' as a noun), both CRS; monoX2.
Other: Discourse context, talking about which movie he wanted to
watch.

B-143   3;8.3   M: 'Bobby, put your pánts back on.'
B: 'No! My gìrlfriend said bòys don't **hàve** . . . don't <u>wèar</u>
pánts.'
('have' [hæv] for 'wear' [wɛr]; not clear who his 'girlfriend' is; 'have'
is stressed, so he didn't start to say 'haveta'; SC; p. 360)
Phon: 1.5, -T.
Lex/Morph: Verb X2, both transitive, irregular, stem form;
mono X2.
Sem: Superordinate (to 'wear' is a kind of 'having').

B-147   3;8.5   B: (after bath, handing Mom a towel)
'Coùld you pùt me . . . wràp me úp in thìs?'
('put (on)' [pʰʊt] for 'wrap (up)' [ræp]; possibly phrase blend with 'put
this on/around me'; SC; p. 343, 360, 453)
Phon: 1.5, -T.   Lex/Morph: Verb X2, both transitive,
regular/irregular, stem form; 2-PV X2.
Sem: Superordinate (to 'wrap' is a kind of 'putting').

B-163b   3;8.29   B: 'If a bèe stìngs me òn the fóot, I'll be [bǽ] . . . I'll be
[mǽ] . . . I'll be sád.'
('mad' [mæd] for 'sad' [sæd]; SC; 163a=Class 12)
Phon: 4, +T.   Lex/Morph: Adjective X2; mono X2.
Sem: Co-hyponyms (kinds of negative emotion).

AL-184   3;10.21   Al: (hears a dog barking next door)
'I sàw . . . I hèard a púppy!'
('saw' [sa:] for 'heard' [h3d]; SC; p. 325, 354, 421)
Phon: 1.5, -T.
Lex/Morph: Verb X2, both transitive, irregular, past tense; 2-infl X2.
Sem: Co-hyponyms (kinds of perception); opposed.

B-171   3;11.6   B: (in bed, talking with Dad about various colors; then
says) 'Daddy, pléase rùb my blàck . . . bàck.'
('black' [blæk] for 'back' [bæk]; probably lexical substitution error,
but could also be phonological perseveration of [l] from 'please';
[-sem]; SC; p. 278)
Phon: 5.5, -T.
Lex/Morph: Adjective vs. common noun; mono X2.
Other: Discourse context, topic of 'colors', although word 'black' had
not been mentioned.

OC-75   3;11.7   OB: (wearing a Batman shirt, says to Mom)
'Takè my Súpermàn shìrt òff.'
('Superman' [sú.pɚ.mæ̀n] for 'Batman' [bǽt.mæ̀n]; NSC; p. 24)
Phon: 3, +T.   Lex/Morph: Proper noun X2; 2-cmpd X2.
Sem: Co-hyponyms (kinds of superheros).

AL-192   3;11.8   Al: (lying on Mom's bed) 'Mòmma, can Ì put my bèd
rìght . . . my hèad rìght hére?'
('bed' [bɛd] for 'head' [hɛd]; [-sem]; SC; p. 448)
Phon: 4, -T.
Lex/Morph: Common noun X2, both CRS; mono X2.
Other: Environmental, lying on bed while speaking.

AL-196 3;11.18 Al: (carrying her canvas bookbag)
'I gòt some **bágs** in hère.'
M: 'You got some bágs in there?'
Al: '<u>Bóoks</u>! I gòt some <u>bóoks</u> in thère!'
('bags' [bæg(z)] for 'books' [buk(s)]; NSC)
Phon: 3, +T.   Lex/Morph: Common noun X2, both CRP; 2-infl X2.
Sem: Metonymic (books are found in bookbags).
Other: Environmental, carrying bookbag while speaking.

OC-77 3;11.26 OB: (child is getting into bed with his socks on, which is
unusual) 'I dòn't néed còvers; my fèet are **cóld** . . . my
fèet are àlready <u>wárm</u>.'
('cold' [kʰoʷɫd] for 'warm' [wɔrm]; 'already' added when error
corrected, possibly phrase blend with 'my feet aren't cold'; SC;
p. 342)
Phon: 2.5, +T.   Lex/Morph: Adjective X2; mono X2.
Sem: Gradable antonyms (adjectives of temperature); opposed.

OC-80 4;0.0 OB: (picking seeds out of watermelon)
'I don't lìke the **núts** . . . I don't lìke the <u>séeds</u>.'
('nuts' [nʌt(s)] for 'seeds' [sid(z)]; SC; p. 435)
Phon: 1.5, +T. Lex/Morph: Common noun X2, both CRP; 2-infl X2.
Sem: Shared criterial features (physical similarity: small, oval, part
of food).

OC-82 4;0.10 OB: 'Daddy, knòw what we're hàving for dessért?
Spècial **lólli** . . . spècial <u>pópsìcles</u>!'
('lollipops' [lá.li.pʰàp(s)] for 'popsicles' [pʰáp.sì.kəɫ(z)]; SC; p. 431,
437)
Phon: 3.5, +T.   Lex/Morph: Common noun X2, both CRP; 3-same.
Sem: Co-hyponyms (kinds of sweet dessert foods you lick).

OC-86 4;1.0 OB: 'I'm **dùcking** . . . I'm <u>dìpping</u> my cràckers ìnto my
sóup.'
('ducking' [dʌ́k.(ɪŋ)] for 'dipping' [díp.(ɪŋ)]; SC)
Phon: 3, -T.
Lex/Morph: Verb X2, transitive, regular, progressive; 2-infl X2.
Sem: Shared criterial features (downward motion, possibly quasi-
synonyms).
Other: Discourse context; earlier OB had been talking about going
on 'duck walk', i.e. a walk to see the ducks at the duck pond.
(Note: while 'duck' in the discourse context is a noun, 'ducking' and
'dipping' were both verbs known to the child, so this was counted as
two verbs)

OC-87   4;1.2   OG: (showing Mom a toothbrush in its package; no
                        toothpaste in sight)
                        'Mom, thìs is a **tóothpàste** . . . a tóothbrùsh.'
('toothpaste' [tʰúθ.pʰèⁱst] for 'toothbrush' [tʰúθ.b̥ʒʌʃ]; SC; p. 426)
Phon: 6,+T.   Lex/Morph: Common noun X2, CRS vs. mass
('a toothpaste' is ungrammatical); 2-cmpd X2.
Sem: Co-members of a set (set of items required for teeth-brushing
activity); also metonyms.

OC-90   4;1.7   OB: (showing adult the new pedals on his bike)
                        'Wànna **shòw** what kínd they àre? Rácing bìke!'
('show' [ʃoʷ] for 'see' [si]; could also be phrase blend with 'Want me
to show you what kind they are?'; NSC; p. 40, 352)
Phon: 1.5, -T.   Lex/Morph: Verb X2, intransitive, regular/
irregular, infinitive; mono X2.
Sem: Causal (to 'show' is to cause to 'see'); opposed.

B-191   4;1.15   B: 'Mòm, Dàd took àll the **ápplejùice**.'
                        M: 'Whát kind?'
                        B: 'Órange-jùice.'
('applejuice' [ǽ.pəɫ.dʒùs] for 'orange-juice' [órndʒ.dʒùs]; since Dad
only drinks orange juice, Mom knew Bobby must have made a
mistake; NSC)
Phon: 3, +T.
Lex/Morph: Common noun X2, both mass; 2-cmpd X2.
Sem: Co-hyponyms (kinds of fruit drinks); opposed (since these were
the only two fruit juices drunk by family members at breakfast).
Other: Environmental, there were both applejuice and orange-juice
on the table, visible.

B-192   4;1.15   B: (telling about a board game called "Shark Attack")
                        'And the shàrk attàcks your **féet** . . . físh.'
('feet' [fit] for 'fish' [fɪʃ]; [-sem]; SC; p. 421, 448)
Phon: 3, +T.
Lex/Morph: Common noun X2, both CIP; 2-infl X2.
Other: 'On the mind', sharks attacking body parts.

B-193   4;1.16   OA: 'Téll me the nàmes of those Nìnja Túrtles agàin.'
                        B: 'Nò, nòt **yét** . . . nòt agáin.'
('yet' [jɛt] for 'again' [ə.gín]; SC; p. 328)
Phon: 0.5, +T.   Lex/Morph: Adverb X2; mono X2.
Sem: Shared criterial features (temporality); opposed (quasi-
antonyms).
Other: Collocation, 'not yet'.

B-198   4;1.23   B: (asking Mom to melt cheese on his hot dog for lunch)
'I wànt you to **mílk** it . . . mélt it.'
('milk' [mɛɫk] for 'melt' [mɛɫt]; [-sem]; SC; p. 276, 293)
Phon: 6.5, +T.
Lex/Morph: Verb X2, both transitive, regular, infinitive; mono X2.
(Note: 'milk' is also a common noun, but he knew the verb 'to milk',
and it is used as a verb in the error)
Other: Environmental, milk visible on the table as he spoke.

B-207   4;2.2   B: (telling about a TV show)
'There are pèople on tòp of the Èmpire Státe Bùilding,
and they're **tàll**ing big góops on pèople's hèads.'
('tall' [tʰaɫ], most likely for 'pour' or 'drop', probably because of the
context of the Empire State Building; includes progressive suffix
which would have been correct on a verb, but not on 'tall'; most
likely [-sem]; NSC; p. 242)
Phon: ?, -T.   Lex: Adjective vs. verb.
Other: Discourse context, talking about a tall building.

B-215   4;2.12   B: 'Dad, can you pùt some more **chòc** . . . stràwberry mílk
in hère?'
(began to say 'chocolate' [tʃá.kl̩t] for 'strawberry' [strá.bè.ri]; SC;
p. 325)
Phon: 2.5, -T.   Lex/Morph: Adjective X2; mono vs. 2-cmpd.
Sem: Co-hyponyms (kinds of flavors for milk); opposed (since these
were the only two flavorings he used in milk, and he regularly had
to choose between them).

B-218   4;2.15   B: 'Have you èver **sèen** . . . have you èver hèared of
"Dúdes"?'
('seen' [sin] for 'heared of' [hírd.ʌv]; 'Dudes' was a TV show he had
just made up; this was Bobby's normal pronunciation for 'heard'; SC;
p. 354, 421, 453)
Phon: 1.5, -T.   Lex/Morph: Verb X2, transitive, irregular (one
regularized), past participle; 2 (2-infl) vs. 3 (2-PV+infl).
Sem: Co-hyponyms (kinds of perception); opposed.

B-226   4;2.26   B: (eating "Shark Bites" fruit snacks, discussing
                           Halloween)
                    'I gòt my òwn **shárk** . . . I mean <u>Drácula</u> tèeth.'
('shark' [ʃark] for 'Dracula' [dræ.kju.lə]; SC)
Phon: 1.5, +T.   Lex/Morph: Proper noun vs. common noun,
(functioning as nominal modifiers); mono X2.
Sem: Connotation (negative emotion, fear, blood, pain, etc.); also
shared criterial features, fear-inducing teeth.
Other: Environmental, eating snack with picture of shark on
package.

OC-97   4;3.11   OG: 'Lòok what hàppened to my [**fíŋ**] . . . to my <u>thúmb</u>.'
(started to say 'finger' [fíŋ.gɚ] for 'thumb' [θʌm]; SC; p. 323)
Phon: 0.5, +T.   Lex/Morph: Common noun X2, CRS; mono X2.
Sem: Co-partonyms (parts of the hand); possibly opposed.
Other: Environmental, both fingers and thumb visible.

B-250a   4;4.3   B: (calling to his same-age friend David)
                    '**Dáddỳ** . . . I mean <u>Dávid</u>! Còme ón!'
(says 'Daddy' [dǽ:.dì:] nicely, politely, with calling intonation.
Then says 'David' [déʲ.vəd] short, harsh, like command, so both
lexical and intonational error; SC; 250b=Class 33; p. 206)
Phon: 3.5, +T.   Lex/Morph: Proper noun X2; mono X2.
Sem: Co-members of a set (males commonly encountered at home).

OC-103   4;4.5   OG: 'Móm, lòok up thére.'
                    M: 'Whàt's up thére?'
                    OG: 'A **bròken**, a <u>bènded</u>, a náil that got bènt.'
('broken' [bróʷ.kən] for 'bended' [bén.dɨd] (regularized), then
rephrased grammatically; SC; p. 421)
Phon: 4, -T.
Lex/Morph: Adjective X2 (from past participle of verb); 2-deriv X2.
Sem: Co-hyponyms (kinds of physical damage).

B-261   4;4.14   B: 'I've **àte** out of my lé . . . I've <u>drìnked</u> out of my
                           léaking cùp when I was twó.'
('ate' [eʲt] for 'drinked' [drɪŋk(t)]; SC; p. 354, 421, 453)
Phon: 1.5, -T.
Lex/Morph: Verb X2, both intransitive; two past tense forms, one
irregular produced correctly 'ate', one overregularized irregular
'drinked'; auxiliary 'I've' used incorrectly, since 'when I was two'
can't co-occur with perfective aspect; 2-infl X2.
Sem: Co-hyponyms of (kinds of ingestion); opposed.

B-262a 4;4.14   B: (on Christmas Eve) 'We're nòt òpening áll our
                          prèsents tonìght, ònly [dú] . . . **twó** . . . <u>fóur</u>.'
        (meant 'four' [for], not 'two' [tʰu]; SC; 262b=Class 30)
        Phon: 1.5, +T.   Lex/Morph: Numeral X2; mono X2.
        Sem: Co-hyponyms (numbers).

B-276   4;5.2   B: (there is a jigsaw puzzle on the kitchen table which
                          Bobby had assembled; Alice is about to take it apart)
                          'Dón't tàke it **togèth** . . . dón't tàke it <u>apàrt</u>!'
        ('together' [tʰə.gé.ðɚ] for 'apart' [ə.pʰárt]; SC; p. 353)
        Phon: 1.5, -T.   Lex/Morph: Adjective X2; mono X2.
        Sem: Binary antonyms (of cohesion); opposed.

OC-108 4;5.5   OB1: (making a huge pile of cheese on his plate)
                          'I have a mòuntain of **trées**.'
                OB2: 'What?'
                OB1: 'I have a mòuntain of <u>chéese</u> .'
        ('trees' [tʃɹ̥í(z)] for 'cheese' [tʃiz]; could be non-contextual
        phonological addition of [r], but child possibly associated 'mountain'
        with 'trees'; [-sem]; NSC; p. 440)
        Phon: 4.5, +T.
        Lex/Morph: Common noun X2, mass vs. CRP; mono vs. 2-infl.

B-278   4;5.8   B: (talking about new popsicles, and what color they are;
                          none were blue, however) 'Daddy, you sàid I could
                          hàve òne of the **blùe** ones àfter dínner.'
        ('blue' [blu] for 'new' [nu]; he meant 'new', as there was no
        contrastive stress; [-sem]; NSC)
        Phon: 3.5, -T.   Lex/Morph: Adjective X2; mono X2.
        Other: Discourse context, talking about colors of popsicles.

B-285   4;5.16   B: (thinking of ways to keep warm, wrapping scarf around
                          hands while talking)
                          'I could wràp my scàrf aròund my **féet**.'
                 M: 'Your féet?'
                 B: 'My <u>hánds</u>!'
        ('feet' [fit] for 'hands' [hænd(z)]; NSC; p. 325, 354, 420, 449, 459)
        Phon: 1.5, +T.
        Lex/Morph: Common noun X2, CRP vs. CIP; 2-infl X2.
        Sem: Co-partonyms (parts of body); opposed.

B-286   4;5.20   B: 'Mom?'
                   M: 'Yeah?'
                   B: 'I'm [hǽ] . . . thírsty.'
(started to say 'hungry' [hʌ́ŋ.gri] for 'thirsty' [θɚ́.sti]; SC; p. 438)
Phon: 3, +T.
Lex/Morph: Adjective X2; formally 2-deriv X2, both with {-y}
suffix.
Sem: Co-hyponyms (of digestive sensations); opposed.

AL-221   4;5.21   Al: (at dinner, talking about onions being 'sour') 'Mòm, do
                   yòu like **Sárah** stùff? . . . Do yòu like sóur stùff?'
('Sarah' [sɛ́.ʒʌ] for 'sour' [sǽ.w3]; [-sem]; SC; p. 279, 443)
Phon: 4, +T.   Lex/Morph: Proper noun (functioning as
modifer in error) vs. adjective; mono X2.
Other: 'On the mind', Alice's neighbor Sarah had been visiting most
of the day, but was gone at the time the error occurred. They had
been getting along fine, so she didn't think of Sarah as 'sour'.

AN-204   4;5.23   An: 'Mommy, I won't cút mysèlf, I'm **éasy** . . . I'm cáreful.'
('easy' [í.zi] for 'careful' [kʰér.fʊɫ]; possibly phrase blend with 'it's
easy'; SC)
Phon: 2, +T.   Lex/Morph: Adjective X2; mono vs. 2-cmpd.
Sem: Shared criterial features (cautiousness, as in 'take it easy',
'easy now').

AN-208   4;5.27   An: (peeling apple slices; no bananas in sight)
                   'I'm pèeling my **banánas**. (laughs) Oh, I made a
                   mistáke. I sàid "banánas" instèad of "ápples".'
('bananas' [bə.nǽ.nə(z)] for 'apples' [ǽ.pəɫ(z)]; SC with comments;
p. 19)
Phon: 2.5, +T.
Lex/Morph: Common noun X2, both CRP; 2-infl X2.
Sem: Co-hyponyms (kinds of fruit).
Other: Collocational, 'peel' occurs in collocations with bananas more
often than apples.

B-293   4;5.28   B: (crying, fighting with Anna)
                   M: 'Whàt háppened?'
                   B: 'I bùmped ìnto her **hánd**. I mèan héad.'
('hand' [hænd] for 'head' [hɛd]; SC; p. 133, 241, 276)
Phon: 4, +T.
Lex/Morph: Common noun X2, both CRS; mono X2.
Sem: Co-partonyms (body parts).
Other: Environmental, Anna's head and hand both in view.

OC-112 4;6.0   OG: 'I nèed a **rùbber-bánd**. Nót a rùbber-bànd. Nót a rùbber-bànd.'

M: 'Whát do you need?'

OG: 'An <u>umbrélla</u>.'

('rubber band' [rʌ.bɚ.bǽnd] for 'umbrella' [ʌm.bré.lə]; [-sem]; SC with prompting; almost a 'tip of the tongue' error; p. 187, 424)

Phon: 3, ₊T.   Lex/Morph: Common noun X2, both CRS; mono vs. 2-cmpd; note article shift from 'a' to 'an'.

B-300   4;6.9   B: (standing in the doorway between the kitchen and Daddy's study, explaining that it's OK to eat in the kitchen but not in the study; "The Simpsons" was on TV in the study) 'Thàt's **"The Símpsons"** òver thère, and thìs is the kìtchen òver hére. (pause) Oh, I mean thàt's <u>Dàddy's stúdy</u> òver thère, and thìs is the kìtchen òver hére.'

('The Simpsons' [ðʌ símp.sən(z)] for 'Daddy's study' [dǽ.di(z) stʌ́.di]; [-sem]; SC; p. 274, 276)

Phon: 2, +T.

Lex: Proper noun X2, both phrases; (inflectional morphemes are part of fixed phrases; not counted into 'morphology' counts).

Other: Environmental, looking at "The Simpsons" on TV.

AL-229 4;6.16   Al: (she had hurt her foot on the slide, and wanted to sit with her foot up on a pillow; she says to her babysitter) 'Can yòu get a **blànket** for my fóot?'

OA: 'A blanket?'

Al: 'No, a <u>píllow</u>.'

('blanket' [blǽŋ.kɪt] for 'pillow' [pʰí.loʷ]: NSC; p. 318)

Phon: 2, -T.

Lex/Morph: Common noun X2, both CRS; mono X2.

Sem: Co-members of set (bedclothes); also metonyms.

B-308   4;6.19   B: (Anna and Alice drew a picture of Mr. Spock from "Star Trek" wearing a bikini bathing suit; Bobby tells Mom that it is a picture of) 'Mr. Spòck in a **zucchíni**!' (looks confused, laughs; then repeats several times erroneously on purpose)

('zucchini' [zu.kʰí.ni] for 'bikini' [bə.kʰí.ni]; [-sem]; N-NC; p. 443)

Phon: 6, +T.

Lex/Morph: Common noun X2, both CRS; mono X2.

B-311 4;6.20 B: (pointing to faucet handle)
'Thère's the 'Č' for 'Hót' . . . 'Cóld'. '
('hot' [hat] for 'cold' [kʰoʷɬd]; SC; p. 352-3)
Phon: 1.5, +T.   Lex/Morph: Adjective X2; mono X2.
Sem: Gradable antonyms (temperature); opposed.
Other: Environmental, both 'hot' and 'cold' faucets visible.

AN-223 4;6.25 An: 'Mòm, if Bòbby **wàkes-úp** . . . if Bòbby spìts-úp, lòok
what's ón hìm! His spít ràg!'
('wakes up' [wèᵏk(s).ʌp] for 'spits up' [spìt(s).ʌp]; [-sem]; SC)
Phon: 4.5, +T.   Lex/Morph: Verb X2, both intransitive, regular
3rd sg. present tense (irregular in the past); 3-same (PV+infl).
Other: Collocation, 'wake up' is a common phrase for this child.

B-326a 4;7.8 B: (Bobby had just been telling Mom that she could teach
him to drive when he turned 16; then he saw Mom
typing) 'When I'm sixtéen, you can **lèarn** me . . . you
can [tʰə̀n] me . . . you can tèach me hòw to týpe.'
('learn' [lɚn] for 'teach' [titʃ]; SC; B-326b=Class 38; p. 325, 352)
Phon: 1.5, -T.   Lex/Morph: Verb X2, both transitive, regular/
irregular, stem form; mono X2.
Sem: Converses (of the education process); opposed.
Other: Discourse context, teaching and learning.

B-331 4;7.14 M: 'Bobby, why don't you brùsh your tèeth nów. Then
you won't have to thìnk abòut it láter.'
B: (angry, stomps into bathroom, steps on stool, and
looks at sink)
'Mòm, I wánt ta **sìnk** . . . thìnk abòut it làter!'
('sink' [sɪŋk] for 'think' [θɪŋk]; [-sem]; NSC; p. 276, 293)
Phon: 5, -T.   Lex/Morph: Verb vs. common noun; mono X2.
Other: Environmental, looking at sink while speaking.

B-349 4;8.13 B: (talking to Anna about getting ready for bed)
'Anna, ya knòw what I wànted to **slèep** . . . ya knòw
what I wànted to hàve for pajámas? My Bílls shìrt.'
('sleep' [sl̥ip] for 'have' [hæv]; possibly phrase blend with 'to sleep
in'; 'Bills' is the local football team; [-sem]; SC; p. 452)
Phon: 1.5, -T.
Lex: Verb X2, transitive/intransitive, both irregular, infinitive.
Other: Discourse context, talking about going to bed.

AN-237 4;8.25   An: 'Mòmmy, Bòbby pùked òut his whòle **álphabet!**'
                          (looks embarassed)
                  M: 'What?'
                  An: 'Bòbby pùked òut his whòle <u>óutfit</u>.'
('alphabet' [ǽ^w.fə.bèt] for 'outfit' [ǽ^w.fìt]; to 'puke out an outfit' is to
vomit thoroughly on it so that the outfit is no longer wearable
without washing; [-sem]; N-NC; p. 137)
Phon: 5.5, +T.
Lex/Morph: Common noun X2, both CRS; mono X2.

OC-118 4;9.0   OG: (explaining what happened in a cartoon) 'The pùp
                          jùmped on tòp of the òne that came **dówn** . . . **úp**.'
('down' [dǽ^{w}n] for 'up' [ʌp]; SC; p. 342, 353)
Phon: 1.5, +T.   Lex/Morph: Adverb X2; mono X2.
Sem: Gradable antonyms (vertical motion or direction); opposed.
Other: Discourse, in the cartoon the pup jumped down onto an object
which was moving upward.

B-368   4;9.18   B: (on the way to get a haircut, explaining reward
                          system) 'They gìve the ònes that are hàving
                          páper-cùts búbble gùm.'
                  M: 'Páper-cùts?'
                  B: 'Háir-cùts!'
('paper-cuts' [p^{h}éⁱ.pɚ.k^{h}ʌt(s)] for 'hair-cuts' [hɛ́r.k^{h}ʌt(s)]; NSC)
Phon: 3, +T.
Lex/Morph: Common noun X2, both CRP; 3-same (2-cmpd+infl).
Sem: Shared criterial features (both involve cutting things on the
body; also, Bobby was somewhat afraid of haircuts, so some
negative connotation in common).

OC-119 4;9.21   OB: (child had been in the bathroom at Grandma's, had
                          looked out the window and had seen Bobby in the
                          backyard pool; child comes into Grandma's kitchen,
                          where OA is)
                  OA: 'Do yòu know where Bóbby ìs?'
                  OB: 'I jùst sàw him in the **báthroom**. I mean in the <u>póol</u>.'
('bathroom' [bǽθ.rùm] for 'pool' [p^{h}úɫ]; clearly meaning to express
where Bobby was, not where child was when he saw Bobby; SC)
Phon: 1, +T.
Lex/Morph: Common noun X2, both CRS; mono vs. 2-cmpd.
Sem: Co-partonyms (both salient parts of Grandma's home).
Other: 'On the mind', he had just come from the bathroom.

AN-242 4;9.22   An: 'They're in òuter **páste**.' (laughs) Mom, I said "páste"
for "<u>spáce</u>".'
('paste' [pʰeⁱst] for 'space' [speⁱs]; possibly phonological, but fairly
complex for a phonological error; [-sem]; SC)
Phon: 5, +T.   Lex/Morph: Common noun X2, both mass;
mono X2 (although 'outer-space' may be a compound for her).

AN-248 4;10.6   An: 'Whàt would a dóg lòok lìke if it hàd a **báck** . . . um
. . . if it hàd a <u>béak</u>, and féathers, and a fèathery táil?'
M: 'Ì don't knów; whát?'
An: 'A bírd-chàsing dòg.' (laughs at her joke)
('back' [bæk] for 'beak' [bik]; possibly a phonological perseveration
of the vowel [æ] from 'had'; SC; p. 34)
Phon: 4.5, list intonation.
Lex/Morph: Common noun X2, both CRS; mono X2.
Sem: Co-partonyms (body parts).

B-392 4;10.24   B: (telling Mom about the movie "The Little Mermaid",
looking at TV; commercial for Rice Krispies, a kind of
cereal, comes on TV) 'Ya knòw why I lìke **Rìce
Kríspies**?   I mèan, ya knòw why I lìke "<u>Lìttle
Mérmaid</u>"?   Because (etc.)'
('Rice Krispies' [ràⁱs.kʰrís.pìz] for 'Little Mermaid' [lì.ɾɛɫ.mɚ.mèⁱd];
[-sem]; SC; p. 276)
Phon: 1, +T.
Lex: Proper noun X2; (both compounds, one formally plural).
Other: Environmental, Rice Krispies ad on TV.

B-396 4;10.30   B: (trying to get Mom to give him back a toy she had just
taken away from him at the breakfast table) 'I'll èat
àll my [sʌ́] . . . <u>bréakfast</u> if you'll gìve me it báck.'
(started to say 'supper' [sʌ́.pɚ] for 'breakfast' [brék.fəst]; SC)
Phon: 2, +T.   Lex/Morph: Common noun X2, both mass; mono X2.
Sem: Co-hyponyms (kinds of meals).

B-399 4;11.2   B: 'Mom, can I have pàrt of my **Snéakers**? . . . <u>Sníckers</u>?
. . . Sníckers Bàr?'
('Sneakers' [sn̩í.kɚz] for 'Snickers' [sn̩í.kɚz]; [-sem]; SC)
Phon: 6.5, +T.   Lex/Morph: Proper noun X2; 2-infl X2
(although only formally plural; also child not aware that either of
these words has derivational affix {-er}).
Other: 'On the mind', Bobby had been at a friend's house all day,
playing with a dog named 'Sneakers'. He was now at home; the
friend had given him a Snickers candy bar, and he was asking Mom
if he could eat it now.

B-403   4;11.4   B: 'Mom, I wànna **dó** . . . I wànna <u>shów</u> yòu sòmething.'
('do' [du] for 'show' [ʃoʷ]; SC; p. 321, 352, 360)
Phon: 1.5, +T.   Lex/Morph: Verb X2, both transitive, regular/
irregular, infinitive; mono X2.
Sem: Superordinate ('show' is a kind of 'doing').

B-406   4;11.5   B: (Mom had told him if he wanted to eat in the
                basement on a school day the answer is always "no";
                five minutes later he asked Mom)
            'Whỳ is the **quèstion** àlways "nó"?'
('question' [kʰwɛ̥s.tʃən] for 'answer' [æn.sɚ]; NSC; p. 354)
Phon: 2.5, -T.
Lex/Morph: Common noun X2, both CRS; mono X2.
Sem: Co-hyponyms (parts of the 'asking' speech act); opposed.

B-411   4;11.9   B: (reporting on what he did at a birthday party)
            'I skìpped the **pízza** . . . I skìpped the <u>càke and íce
            crèam</u>, and I plàyed Ninténdo.'
('pizza' [pʰít.sʌ] for 'cake and ice cream' [kʰèⁱk.n.áⁱs.kʰrìm], both of
which were at the party; SC)
Phon: 0.5, +T.
Lex/Morph: Common noun X2, both mass; mono vs. 4-cmpd.
Sem: Co-hyponyms (kinds of food you eat at a birthday party);
opposed (since these two things are the main units of food found at
all birthday parties he was familiar with).
Other: Discourse context, talking about food at party.

B-420   4;11.16   B: (explaining to Anna what he and Daddy had been
                discussing about the planets)
            'Anna, ya dón't wànna gò up on **Màrs** . . . on <u>Vènus</u>.
            It's so hót!'
('Mars' [marz] for 'Venus' [ví.nəs]; SC; p. 368)
Phon: 0.5, -T.   Lex/Morph: Proper noun X2; mono X2.
Sem: Co-hyponyms (kinds of planets).
Other: Discourse context, talking about various planets.

B-423   4;11.17   B: (telling about a long dream he had)
            'No, wè were at Gràndma [**bé**] . . . Gràndma <u>Eiléen's</u>.'
('Beckie's' [bé.ki(z)] for 'Eileen's' [aʲ.lín(z)]; SC; p. 325, 338, 339)
Phon: 2, +T.
Lex/Morph: Proper noun X2, both possessive; 2-infl X2.
Sem: Co-hyponyms (his two grandmothers); opposed.

B-429   4;11.30   M: 'Go tínkie befòre we gò to the stòre.'
                    B: 'We can **bùy** a báthroom. Oh! I made a spéech èrror.
                    I mèant we can f́ind a bàthroom.'
('buy' [baʲ] for 'find' [faʲnd]; [-sem]; SC with comments; p. 19, 85)
Phon: 3, -T.   Lex/Morph: Verb X2, both transitive, irregular,
stem form; mono X2.
Other: Discourse context (going to store to buy something).

OC-124   5;0.0   OG: (child is hanging by knees from a bar, Mom has set
                     child's pants on floor under her, but she can't reach
                     them, so she says to Mom)
                     '**Brìng** me the pánts. Ǵet me the pànts, I should sày.'
('bring' [brɪŋ] for 'get' [gɛt]; SC; p. 326, 363)
Phon: 1.5, -T.   Lex/Morph: Verb X2, both transitive, irregular,
imperative; mono X2.
Sem: Synonyms (activities of transporting objects to someone, but
from different perspectives).

OC-125   5;0.0   OB: 'But the spàce sàucer gòes on his **árm** . . .
                     on his wrı́st.'
('arm' [arm] for 'wrist' [rɪst]; SC; p. 359)
Phon: 1.5, +T.
Lex/Morph: Common noun X2, both CRS; mono X2.
Sem: Whole for part ('wrist' is part of 'arm').

OC-126   5;0.0   OB: (he had been admiring the new shoes he got for his
                     birthday, but not talking about them; then he looked
                     up and said) 'Mom, do you knòw what I'm gòing to dò
                     with my [ʃú] I mean ámbulance?'
(started to say 'shoe' or 'shoes' [ʃu(z)] for 'ambulance' [æm.bjə.ləns],
another birthday gift; [-sem]; SC; p. 134)
Phon: 0.5, +T.   Lex: Common noun X2, both count, regular;
one singular, the other unclear.
Other: Environmental, looking at shoes just before speaking.
(Note: while not semantically related, the shoes and ambulance
were circumstantially related by virtue of being two of his birthday
presents, so possibly 'on the mind'.)

OC-127   5;0.2   OB: 'I hùrt my **lég** . . . thı́gh.'
('leg' [lɛg] for 'thigh' [θaʲ]; SC; p. 323, 359)
Phon: 1.5, +T.
Lex/Morph: Common noun X2, both CRS; mono X2.
Sem: Whole for part ('thigh' is part of 'leg').
Other: Environment, looking down at leg.

B-430   5;0.4   B: (picking an olive out of Mom's salad)
                       'Can I háve a? **Ómar**?'
                  M: 'You mean an ólive?'
                  B: 'Yéah. I càll it "Ómar" because it sóunds lìke
                       "Òmar".'

('Omar' [ó".mar] for 'olive' [á.lɪv]; first time was obviously a
mistake, and his 'analysis' was face-saving; [-sem]; NSC; p. 85)
Phon: 2, but since child introspects that they sound alike, counted as
[+phon]; note that they have 100% syllable structure consistency; +T.
Lex/Morph: Proper noun vs. common noun; mono X2.
Other: 'On the mind', he had been playing with friend named Omar
all day.

OC-133 5;0.19   OB: 'Chrìs is getting rèady for **thrèe** . . . thìrd gráde.'
('three' [θr̩i] for 'third' [θɚd]; SC; p. 363)
Phon: 3.5, -T.   Lex/Morph: Numeral vs. adjective (cardinal vs.
ordinal number); mono X2.
Sem: Synonyms (identical semantic base, the number 3).

B-442   5;1.1   B: (to Dad) '**Móm**, tòday in schóol, . . . I mean Dád,
                       tòday in schóol, . . .'
('Mom' [mam] for 'Dad' [dæd]; SC)
Phon: 1.5, +T.   Lex/Morph: Proper noun X2; mono X2.
Sem: Co-members of a set (parents); opposed.
Other: Environmental, Mom was in room at time of utterance.

B-445   5;1.4   B: (looking in his backpack for his lunchbox)
                       'Is my **báck** . . . is my lúnchbox in hère?'
(started to substitute 'backpack' [bǽk.pʰæk] for 'lunchbox'
[lʌ́ntʃ.bàks]; SC; p. 331)
Phon: 2.5, +T.
Lex/Morph: Common noun X2, both CRS; 2-cmpd X2.
Sem: Co-hyponyms (kinds of child's daily containers for school); also
metonyms (the lunchbox is inside the backpack).
Other: Environmental, looking in backpack while speaking.

B-454   5;1.20   B: 'Dàd, for dèssert Mòm gàve me dìnosaur **prétzels** . . .
                       I mean dìnosaur frùit-wrínkles.'
('pretzels' [pʰrét.zəɬ(z)] for 'fruit-wrinkles' [frùt.ríŋ.kəɬ(z)]; SC;
p. 434, 436)
Phon: 2.5, +T.   Lex/Morph: Common noun X2, both CRP;
2 (2-infl) vs. 3 (2-cmpd+infl).
Sem: Co-hyponyms (snack foods).
Other: Environmental, he was eating pretzels at the time of
speaking, reporting on an earlier event.

AN-269 5;1.28   An: (saying a rhyme, sees Bobby eating a cookie)
'Fìve lìttle **cóokies** . . . fìve lìttle <u>mónkeys</u> bòuncin' òn the béd.'
('cookies' [kʰʊ́.ki(z)] for 'monkeys' [mʌ́ŋ.ki(z)]; [-sem]; SC; p. 255)
Phon: 3, +T.   Lex/Morph: Common noun X2, both CRP; 2-infl X2.
Other: Environmental, sees Bobby eating cookie while speaking.

AN-270 5;1.28   An: (talking to Alice, while both are under a table)
'You're thàt much **hígher** . . . you're thàt much <u>lówer</u> than the tàble.'
('higher' [háʲ.j(ɚ)] for 'lower' [lóʷ.w(ɚ)]; SC)
Phon: 3, +T.   Lex/Morph: Adjective X2; 2-infl X2 (both with comparative suffix {-er}).
Sem: Converses (of height dimension); opposed.

B-463 5;2.0   B: ('reading' book, which has yellow creatures on page)
'Bìg V́, **yéllow** V́ . . . líttle V̀.'
('yellow' [jé.loʷ] for 'little' [lí.rəɫ]; [-sem]; SC)
Phon: 2.5, +T.   Lex: Adjective X2.
Other: Environmental, looking at yellow creatures in book.

AN-277 5;2.2   An: (showing Mom a book) 'Mòmmy, I **wròte** this . . . I <u>rèad</u> this àll to mysélf while yòu were nùrsing Bóbby.'
('wrote' [roʷt] for 'read' [rɛd]; SC; p. 354)
Phon: 3, -T.
Lex/Morph: Verb X2, both transitive, irregular, past; 2-infl X2.
Sem: Co-hyponyms (actions involved in literacy scene); opposed.

OC-136 5;2.3   OB: (wanting to play with Ghosbuster figures Winston and Ray; has been looking also for Peter, but can't find him; says to Dad) 'Daddy, could you brìng me **Pèter** and Ráy? . . . <u>Wínston</u> and Ràry?'
('Peter' [pʰí.rɚ] for 'Winston' [wín.stən]; SC)
Phon: 2, -T.   Lex/Morph: Proper noun X2; mono X2.
Sem: Co-members of a set (the Ghostbusters).
Other: 'On the mind', had been looking for Peter figure.

OC-137 5;2.19   OG: (telling what her favorite gift would be from
                     Disneyland) '. . . could pròbably be a T̂-shirt with
                     Mìnnie Móuse òn it. Or with **Dìsney** Dúck.'
                     (hesitated, looked confused)
('Disney' [díz.ni] for 'Daisy' [déʲ.zi]; N-NC; p. 327)
Phon: 5, -T.   Lex/Morph: Proper noun X2; mono X2
(although 'Daisy Duck' is a compound).
Sem: Metonymic (Daisy Duck and Walt Disney discussed as part of
Disneyland or Disney cartoon scenes).
Other: Discourse context, talking about Disneyland (see also OC
138(43)).

OC-140 5;2.26   OB: 'Hey, yòu should còme sèe my Chrístmas trèe!
                     It's àll còvered with **bútter** . . . oh . . . I mèan sóap.'
                     (i.e. soap flakes that look like snow)
('butter' [bʌ.ɾɚ] for 'soap' [soʷp]; SC)
Phon: 0.5, +T.
Lex/Morph: Common noun X2, both mass; mono X2.
Sem: Shared criterial features (physical similarity of soap flakes and
butter).

OC-141a 5;3.0   OG: 'Can I **hàve** . . . can I invìte . . . can I tàlk to Aníta?
                     I was gonna say "Can I háve Anìta".'
('have' [hæv] for 'talk to' [tʰák tu]; [-sem]; SC: p. 456)
Phon: 0.5, -T.
Lex: Verb X2, both transitive, regular/irregular, stem form.
Other: Collocation, 'Can I have X (over)' (see also next entry).

OC-141b 5;3.0   OG: 'Can I hàve . . . can I **invìte** . . . can I tàlk to Aníta?
                     I was gonna say "Can I háve Anìta".'
('invite' [ɪn.váʲt] for 'talk to' [tʰák tu]; SC)
Phon: 1, -T.   Lex/Morph: Verb X2, both transitive, regular,
stem form; mono vs. 2-PV.
Sem: Shared criterial features (activities involving getting together
with her friend, i.e. inviting her over, calling her up; possibly
even 'have over', from 141a).

OC-142 5;4.0   OG: (asking Dad to put his legs apart so she can swing
                    through them) 'Put your **whèels** . . . uh, lègs rèal wíde.'
('wheels' [wiɫ(z)] for 'legs' [lɛg(z)]; SC)
Phon: 1.5, -T.
Lex/Morph: Common noun X2, CRP; 2-infl X2.
Sem: Shared criterial features (perceived physical and functional
similarity between legs and wheels: binary lower appendages,
allowing locomotion).

B-485   5;4.4   B: (Mom is drying Bobby off after a shower)
'I thòught you díd my àrmpits yèt. (pause, thinks)
I thòught you díd my àrmpits alrèady.'
('yet' [jɛt] for 'already' [aɫ.rɛ́.di]; SC)
Phon: 1.5, -T.   Lex/Morph: Adverb X2; mono X2.
Sem: Shared criterial features (time relative to speaking); opposed.

B-486   5;4.5   B: (talking about being allowed to participate in "Show-
and-Tell", which comes once a week) 'I hàve to be
góod todày, because yès . . . làst-wèek I was bád.'
(started to say 'yesterday' [jɛ́s.tɚ.dèʲ] for 'last-week' [lèst.wík]; SC)
Phon: 0.5, -T.   Lex/Morph: Adverb X2; 2-cmpd X2.
Sem: Co-hyponyms (past times).

OC-144 5;5.0   OG: (Mom opens door to room on which child has hung a
sign 'Do Not Disturb'; OG points to the sign and says)
'You líed!'
(then breaks off, knowing it's the wrong word, but
doesn't try to correct. Probably meant 'cheated' or
'broke the rule'; however, no full analysis is possible)
('lied' [laʲd]; N-NC; p. 235)
Phon: +T.
Lex: Probably Verb X2, one intransitive, regular, past tense.

B-512   5;5.24   B: (discussing "Children's Dictionary" entry about icing)
'Ícing is whàt you pùt òn a chòcolate cáke. And
chócolate ìce-crèam . . . ̀icing is my fávorite!'
('ice-cream' [áʲs.kʰr̩ìm] for 'icing' [áʲ.sɪŋ]; SC; p. 186)
Phon: 4, -T.   Lex/Morph: Common noun X2, both mass;
2- different (2-cmpd vs. 2-deriv).
Sem: Co-hyponyms (kinds of sweet creamy desserts); also
metonymic (cake and ice cream eaten together).
Other: Collocation, 'chocolate ice cream'.

B-513   5;5.24   B: (acting out words in "Children's Dictionary") 'Dàd, ya
wànna sèe my invèntion . . . my imprèssion of a hát?'
('invention' [ɪn.vín.tʃɪn] for 'impression' [ɪm.pʰré.ʃɪn]; he knows the
meanings of both words; [-sem]; p. 133, 248, 438, 443)
Phon: 5, -T.
Lex/Morph: Common noun X2, CRS; 3-same (both with
derivational prefix {iN-}+stem+derivational suffix {-ion}).

B-521   5;5.30   B: (putting a pillow on his head which has a picture of a
                         cat on it; he was doing 'impersonations', some of
                         which were verbal and some visual)
                         'Wànna **hèar** my . . . wànna s<u>è̀e</u> my àct of a cát-hàt?'
('hear' [hɪr] for 'see' [si]; SC; p. 354)
Phon: 1.5, -T.   Lex/Morph: Verb X2, both transitive, irregular,
infinitive form; mono X2.
Sem: Co-hyponyms (kinds of perception); opposed.

OC-148 5;6.0   OG: (telling a story about what she does at bedtime)
                       'I **wàsh** my . . . I <u>brùsh</u> my téeth, and I (etc.) . . . '
('wash' [waʃ] for 'brush' [brʌʃ]; did not say 'wash' as part of story; SC)
Phon: 2.5, -T.   Lex/Morph: Verb X2, both transitive, regular,
present tense; mono X2.
Sem: Co-members of a set (sub-parts of 'getting ready for bed'
frame).
Other: Discourse context, talking about getting ready for bed.

OC-153 5;7.0   OG: (Mom has just told OG to go to bed because it's late)
                       'Hòw **òld** ís it?'
                M: 'How óld is it?'
                OG: (laughs)
('old' [oʷɫd] for 'late' [leɫt]; NSC)
Phon: 1.5, -T.   Lex/Morph: Adjective X2; mono X2.
Sem: Shared criterial features (largest extent of time domain,
negative connotation).

B-541   5;7.2   B: 'Gràndma Bèckie lìves in **Hústèd** . . . <u>Hoúston</u>. Dàd,
                        "Hùsted" and "Hoùston" sóund àlike.'
('Husted' [çjú.stèd] for 'Houston' [çjú.stən]; 'Husted' is the last name
of one of Alice's friends; [-sem]; SC; p. 85, 241, 255, 369, 443)
Phon: 7, +T.   Lex/Morph: Proper noun X2; mono X2.

OC-155 5;7.2   OB: 'Daddy, my hèad's **bĕing** . . . <u>gĕtting</u> hót.'
('being' [bí.(ɪŋ)] for 'getting' [gɛ́ɾ.(ɪŋ)]; SC)
Phon: 1.5, -T.
Lex/Morph: Verb X2, copular, irregular, progressive; 2-infl X2.
Sem: Shared criterial features (states of experiencing, becoming).

B-543b   5;7.3   B: 'Wè slaw . . . wè saw a rèal **squirrel** . . . <u>snáil</u> I
                      mean.'
('squirrel' [skwɔ́.əɫ] for 'snail' [sn̥éʲ.əɫ]; SC; 543a=Class 8)
Phon: 5, +T.
Lex/Morph: Common noun X2, CRS; mono X2.
Sem: Co-hyponyms (small, outdoor, non-domestic but benign
animals).

B-544   5;7.3   Al: (to Nanny, whom Bobby wanted to marry)
                      'Yòu're my bìg síster.'
                      B: 'Yòu're my bìg **húsband**! . . . (quietly, embarassed)
                      Wífe.'
('husband' [hʌ́z.bənd] for 'wife' [wáʲf]; SC; p. 354, 364)
Phon: 0.5, +T.
Lex/Morph: Common noun X2, both CS, regular/irregular; mono X2.
Sem: Co-members of set (spouses); opposed.

AN-292   5;7.4   An: (Bobby is in his highchair eating a cookie, which he
                      throws on the floor)
                      'Bòbby thrèw his **cúp** on the flòor.'
                      M: 'His cúp? He dìdn't háve a cùp.'
                      An: 'I mèan his <u>cóokie</u>.'
('cup' [kʰʌp] for 'cookie' [kʰʊ́.ki]; NSC; p. 240)
Phon: 2, +T.
Lex/Morph: Common noun X2, both CRS; mono X2.
Sem: Metonyms (items found together in eating frame).
Other: Environmental, there were cups on a nearby table.

OC-157   5;7.15   OB: (naming colors of Christmas balls hanging on a
                      garland; none of the balls were red) 'Yèllow, blùe,
                      [**rè?**] . . . <u>grèen</u>, blúe.'
(started to substitute 'red' [rɛd] for 'green' [grin]; SC)
Phon: 2.5, list intonation.   Lex/Morph: Adjective X2; mono X2.
Sem: Co-hyponyms (kinds of color).

AL-250   5;7.23   Al: (eating pancakes) 'I wànt some mòre **cátsup** . . .
                      I mean <u>sýrup</u>.'
('catsup' [kʰǽ.tʃəp] for 'syrup' [sɔ́.əp]; SC; p. 82)
Phon: 3.5, +T.
Lex/Morph: Common noun X2, both mass; mono X2.
Sem: Co-hyponyms (kinds of food-sauces/condiments from squeeze
bottles).

B-552   5;8.9   B: (after hiding Easter eggs for Alice) 'Alice, you hàve to
                 hìde . . . you hàve to f̱ı̱ṉḏ àll the éggs.'
('hide' [haɪd] for 'find' [faʲnd]; SC; p. 354)
Phon: 4, -T.
Lex/Morph: Verb X2, both transitive, irregular, infinitive; mono X2.
Sem: Co-members of set (actional subparts of Easter frame; also
partially converses, since to 'hide' is to cause not to find, however to
'find' doesn't entail that something has been 'hidden'); opposed.

B-554   5;8.18   B: (after twisting foot, then scraping it)
                 'I hìt mys: . . . I ẖùṟṯ mysèlf twíce.'
('hit' [hɪt] for 'hurt' [hɚt]; he hadn't actually 'hit' himself; SC; p. 352,
369)
Phon: 4, -T.   Lex/Morph: Verb X2 both transitive, irregular,
past tense; 2-infl X2 (zero past tense).
Sem: Causal (hit causes hurt).

OC-164   5;8.25   OB: 'I knòw whỳ they càll those yèllow lìnes . . . òrange
                 lìnes "lánes". Becàuse so that càrs dòn't cràsh ìnto
                 óther càrs.'
('yellow' [jέ.loʷ] for 'orange' [orndʒ]; SC; p. 241)
Phon: 0.5, -T.   Lex/Morph: Adjective X2; mono X2.
Sem: Co-hyponyms (kinds of color).

OC-165   5;8.26   M: 'Fìnd your ráincoat.'
                 OB: 'It's in the cár . . . it's in the w̱ágoṉ.'
('car' [kʰar] for 'wagon' [wǽ.gən]; he had left his raincoat in his toy
wagon; SC)
Phon: 0.5, +T.
Lex/Morph: Common noun X2, both CRS; mono X2.
Sem: Co-hyponyms (kinds of vehicles).

B-555   5;8.27   B: (he had just called John Paul, who couldn't play)
                 'Mòmmy, can Ì càll Jòhn P . . . Ḏáviḏ?'
(started to say 'John Paul' [dʒàn.pʰáɫ] for 'David' [déʲ.vɪd], who live
next door to each other down the street from Bobby; SC)
Phon: 1, +T.   Lex/Morph: Proper noun X2; mono vs. 2-cmpd.
Sem: Co-members of a set (male friends on block that he plays
with).
Other: 'On the mind', thinking about John Paul, to whom he had just
spoken.

AL-256 5;9.19   Aɬ: (talking about when she used to say "weeping
boobies" for "Sleeping Beauty")
'I ùsed to sày that when I was fòur years óld,
and dìdn't be àble to sèe my Ŕ's.'
('see' [si] for 'say' [seʲ]; may be phonological perseveration of [i]
from 'be', but unlikely since 'be' is unstressed; [-sem], but see below;
NSC)
Phon: 3, -T.
Lex/Morph: Verb X2, both transitive, irregular, infinitive; mono X2.
(Note: not strictly related semantically, but possibly related
metonymically in literacy scene, i.e. seeing and saying letters)

AN-318 5;10.0   OG: 'Did you brìng your Bárbies?'
An: 'Nò, I lòst . . . I forgòt to brìng thèm.'
('lost' [last] for 'forgot' [fɚ.gát]; SC)
Phon: 3, -T.
Lex/Morph: Verb X2, both transitive, irregular, past tense; 2-infl X2.
Sem: Co-hyponyms (kinds of events of absence of things).

B-566 5;10.18   B: (after returning to Buffalo from a trip to Davis,
California, where he used to live) 'I'm gonna èither
mòve to Dávis, or stày in Búffalo todày . . . hère.'
('today' [tʰə.déʲ] for 'here' [hɪr]; SC)
Phon: 0.0, -T.   Lex/Morph: Adverb X2; mono X2 (unlikely he
treated 'today' as a compound).
Sem: Shared criterial features (deictic center).

AN-323 5;10.24   An: 'I wànna pùt my snàck in my lìttle pìnk básket.'
(she meant 'backpack'; no basket in sight)
('basket' [bǽ.skɨt] for 'backpack' [bǽk.pʰæk]; NSC; p. 240)
Phon: 5, +T.   Lex/Morph: Common noun X2, both CRS;
mono vs. 2-cmpd.
Sem: Co-hyponyms (kinds of containers in which child can carry
objects).

AL-261 5;10.24   Aɬ: (to Mommy) 'Mòmmy, gùess whát?'
B: 'Whát?'
Aɬ: (to Bobby) 'I was tàlking to [bá] . . . Mómmy!'
(started to say 'Bobby' [bá.bi] for 'Mommy' [má.mi]; SC)
Phon: 4.5; +T.
Lex/Morph: Proper noun X2; mono X2.
Sem: Co-members of a set (immediate family members).
Other: Environmental, Bobby in sight during utterance.

B-584   5;11.23   B: 'Mommy, yòu get to stày up **lóuder** than mè.'
                   M: 'What?'
                   B: 'Yòu get to stày up lónger than mè.'
('louder' [lǽ^w.d(ɚ)] for 'longer' [láŋ.g(ɚ)]; NSC)
Phon: 4.5, +T.   Lex/Morph: Adjective X2; 2-infl X2 (both with
comparative suffix {-er}).
Sem: Shared criterial features (fullest extent of domain).

AL-267   5;11.26   Al: (Alice was standing on a chair watching Mom cook;
                    Mom was using a measuring cup. Bobby tried to
                    climb on Alice's chair)
                    'Gèt your ówn **cùp** . . . gèt your ówn chàir!'
('cup' [kʰʌp] for 'chair' [tʃɛr]; [-sem]; SC; p. 241)
Phon: 1.5, -T.   Lex: Common noun X2, both CRS.
Other: Environmental, Alice looking at cup.

AN-330   5;11.30   An: (looking at a picture of the Seven Dwarfs with their
                    hats off) 'They àll tòok their **héad**s òff.'
                    (looks surprised, then laughs)
('heads' [hɛd(z)] for 'hats' [hæt(s)]; N-NC)
Phon: 3, +T.   Lex/Morph: Common noun X2, both CRP; 2-infl X2.
Sem: Metonymic ('hats' are found on 'heads').
Other: Environmental, both hats and heads are visible in the picture.

36. Lexical substitutions, function words.

B-59   2;5.12   B: 'Mommy, tùrn the líght òn!'
                  M: 'Whére?'
                  B: 'In **my** [pʰ]̥] . . . in the pláyroom. The lìght is óff.'
('my' [maʲ] for 'the' [ðʌ]; [-sem]; SC; p. 232, 247)
Phon: 1.5, -T.   Lex: Determiner X2 (possessive pronoun vs.
definite article; both definite).
Other: Environment, self.

B-86a   2;6.21   B: 'Whère's Dáddy?'
                   M: 'He's òut in the stúdy.'
                   B: '**She's** . . . he's tùrning òn the télephòne.'
                   M: 'Whát?'
                   B: 'He's tàlking òn the télephòne.'
('she's' [ʃi(z)] for 'he's' [hi(z)], stranding auxiliary, SC; 86b=Class 35;
p. 337)
Phon: 3.5, -T.   Lex: Personal pronoun X2.
Sem: Honors person, number, case (3rd sg, subject); violates gender.
Other: Environment, female (Mom) is addressee.

AN-70   2;9.14   An: 'Thère was a báby crỳing ìn **my** . . . thère was my
sìster crỳing ìn <u>her</u> róom.'
('my' [maʲ] for 'her' [hɚ]; also 'a baby' for 'my sister', probably
stylistic change so not counted as SOT; SC)
Phon: 1.5, -T.   Lex: Personal pronoun X2.
Sem: Honors number, case (singular, possessive); violates person.
Other: Environment, self.

AN-75   2;10.6   An: (pulling sticker out of barette box)
'**Thĭs** was . . . <u>thĕre</u> was a stícker in thère.'
('this' [ðɪs] for 'there' [ðɛr]; not deictic, since unstressed; [-sem], but
see below; SC)
Phon: 3, -T.   Lex: Demonstrative vs. existential.
Other: Environment, deictic. (Not semantically related, but deictic
meaning of 'there' seems to have intruded: opposed, this/there)

AL-55   2;10.7   Al: (looking for her bottle; finds it, shows Mom)
'Hére it ìs, Mòmmy. I gòt it **fòr** my . . . <u>òff</u> my béd.'
('for' [foʒ] for 'off' [af]; SC; p. 24, 337, 344)
Phon: 2, -T.   Lex: Preposition X2.
Sem: Binary antonyms (goal/source; 'for' signifies a goal in
expressions such as 'she headed for home' or 'he ran for cover');
opposed.
Other: Collocation, 'get something for someone'.

AN-80   2;10.12   An: 'Whìch màn did **you** . . . whìch màn did <u>he</u> fìx your
báck?'
('you' [ju] for 'he' [hi]; could be anticipation of 'you' from 'your',
though pronunciation is quite different; resumptive pronoun normal
for this child at this time; SC; p. 329)
Phon: 1.5, -T.   Lex: Personal pronoun X2.
Sem: Honors number, case (singular, subject); violates person.
Other: Environment, addressee is 'you'.

AL-77   2;11.5   Al: (wanting to put her bathing suit on over her clothes)
'I nèed to pùt it **ùnder** . . . <u>òver</u> my shírt!'
('under' [ʌn.d3] for 'over' [óʷ.v3]; SC; p. 39, 353)
Phon: 3, -T.   Lex: Preposition X2.
Sem: Gradable antonyms (location); opposed.

AN-89b 2;11.15 An: (to Daddy) 'Wànt me to hèlp . . . wànt **you** to hèlp
                . . . wànt to hèlp <u>me</u> cólor?'
                ('you' [ju] for 'me' [mi]; SC; 89a=Class 41; p. 264)
                Phon: 1.5, -T.   Lex: Personal pronoun X2.
                Sem: Honors number, case (singular, object); violates person.
                Other: Environment, addressee is 'you'.

AN-108 3;3.7   An: 'Òne of **hĕrs** . . . òne of <u>hĕr</u> róses is gònna òpen.'
                ('hers' [hɚz] for 'her' [hɚ]; could be anticipation of plural morpheme
                or segment [z] from 'roses' [róʷ.z(əz)], or phrase blend with 'one of
                hérs is'; SC)
                Phon: 4.5, -T.   Lex: Personal pronoun X2.
                Sem: Honors person, number and gender (3rd singular, feminine);
                violates case.

B-137 3;7.5   B: (looking for strawberry milk powder)
                   'Where àre **the** . . . where ìs <u>that</u> pówder?'
                ('the' [ðə] for 'that' [ðæt], with number agreement change on copula;
                SC; p. 423)
                Phon: 3, -T.
                Lex: Determiner X2 (definite article vs. demonstrative).
                Sem: Shared criterial features (definite reference).

AN-117 3;7.24   An: (holding a toy up to her eye)
                   'Thìs is my éye thìng. If **èveryone** . . . if <u>ànyone</u> wànts
                   to pláy wìth it, thèy cán.'
                ('everyone' [év.ri.wʌn] for 'anyone' [í.ni.wʌn]; SC; p. 329, 344)
                Phon: 4.5, -T.   Lex: Impersonal pronoun X2.
                Sem: Shared criterial features, indefinite reference; opposed
                (opposite polarity).

AN-119 3;8.5   D: 'What ís todày?'
                   An: 'Todày is **my** . . . todày is <u>your</u> bírthday.'
                ('my' [maʲ] for 'your' [jɚ]; SC; p. 274)
                Phon: 1.5, -T.   Lex: Personal pronoun X2.
                Sem: Honors case (possessive, used as modifiers), number
                (singular); violates person.
                Other: Environment, self.

AN-120 3;8.5   An: (parents talking about going shopping at several
                    different stores)
                    'Whàt are we . . . whère are we gòing fírst?'
          ('what' [wʌt] for 'where' [wɛr]; SC; p. 246, 344)
          Phon: 3, -T.   Lex: Question words.
          Sem: Shared criterial features (question words).

B-164   3;9.0   B: (saying goodbye to friend on phone) 'Hi . . . bye.'
          ('hi' [haʲ] for 'bye' [baʲ]; SC; p. 246)
          Phon: 3.5.   Lex: Interjection X2.
          Sem: Co-members of set (greetings); opposed.

AL-187 3;10.27 Al: 'We gòt some púdding òn the . . . fròm the stòre.'
          ('on' [an] for 'from' [f₃ʌm]; SC)
          Phon: 1.5, -T.   Lex: Preposition X2.
          Sem: Binary antonyms (source vs. goal); opposed.

OC-73   3;11.0   OA: 'Do yòu want pízza sàuce on yòurs?'
                    OB: 'Nòt mé . . . nòt mìne.'
          ('me' [mi] for 'mine' [maʲn]; SC)
          Phon: 3, +T.   Lex: Personal pronoun X2.
          Sem: Honors person, number (1st. sg.); violates case (subj. vs. poss).
          Other: Collocation, 'not me!'

OC-84   4;0.19   OB: (boy wants Dad to help Mom shampoo his hair,
                    though he knows she can do it herself; says to Dad)
                    'Ya knòw, Móm knows hòw to dò it àll by my . . .
                    hersélf.'
          (started to say 'myself' [maʲ.sɛ̷lf] for 'herself' [hɚ.sɛ̷lf]; SC; p. 24)
          Phon: 5.5, +T.   Lex: Personal pronoun X2.
          Sem: Honors number, case (singular, reflexive); violates person (and
          gender).
          Other: Environment, self.

AL-206 4;2.5   Al: (to Mom, talking about her friend Adam's bike)
                    'I wànt to rìde his lìttle bíke.'
                    OB: (not Adam; thinks Alice is talking to him about a
                    different bike) 'It's not mìne, it's my sìster's.'
                    Al: 'I'm tàlking to . . . Ádam's bìke. I'm tàlking about
                    Ádam's bìke.' (last sentence soft, embarassed)
          ('to' [tʰu] for 'about' [ə.bæ̃t]; [-sem]; SC; p. 247)
          Phon: 0.5, -T.   Lex: Preposition X2.
          Other: Collocation, 'I'm talking to X', frequently said to a speaker
          who has spoken when he has not been addressed.

AL-207 4;2.5   Al: 'My Mòm thìnks he's sòrta cúte. But Í thìnk she's . . .
hè's réal cùte.'
('she's' [ʃi(z)] for 'he's' [hi(z)], stranding copula; SC; p. 329)
Phon: 3.5, -T.   Lex: Personal pronoun X2.
Sem: Honors person, number and case (3rd singular, subject);
violates gender.
Other: Environment, discussing 'Mom', female; also Mom is present.

B-210   4;2.6   B: 'You wanna búy it to mè?'
M: 'What?'
B: 'You wanna búy it for mè?'
('to' [tʰu] for 'for' [for]; possibly phrase blend of 'buy it for me' and
'give it to me'; NSC)
Phon: 1.5, -T.   Lex: Preposition X2.
Sem: Shared criterial features (goal-hood).

OC-95   4;3.0   OB1: (to OB2, playing in OB2's room, talking about OB2's
little brother 'Les') 'Could yóu get Lès out òf your
ròom? 'Cause she . . . 'cause he's bóthering ùs.'
('she' [ʃi] for 'he' [hi], stranding auxiliary; SC)
Phon: 3.5, -T.   Lex: Personal pronoun X2.
Sem: Honors person, number, and case (3rd singular, subject);
violates gender.

OC-101 4;4.0   OA: 'Hére ya gò Jùstin.'
OB: 'I mèan . . . you mèan Jónathan.' (correcting adult;
OB is named 'Jonathan'; 'Justin' is OB's brother)
('I' [aʲ] for 'you' [ju]; SC)
Phon: 1.5, -T.   Lex: Personal pronoun X2.
Sem: Honors number, case (singular, subject); violates person.
Other: Collocation, 'I mean';
Other: Environment, self.

B-249   4;4.2   B: 'Mom, tálk like Sànta Gìrl.'
M: 'What does Santa Girl sóund like?'
B: 'He sòunds lìke . . . she sòunds lìke Míckey.'
('he' [hi] for 'she' [ʃi]; SC)
Phon: 3.5, -T.   Lex: Personal pronoun X2.
Sem: Honors person, number, case (3rd singular, subject); violates
gender.
Other: Discourse context, 'he/Mickey/Santa' male.

AN-175 4;4.11   M: (handing Anna a cup of juice; Anna is jumping around, distracted) 'Hére, Hòn.'

An: '**Hí**, Mòm.' (looks surprised) 'I said "Hí, Mòm" instead of "Thánks, Mòm".'

('hi' [haʲ] for 'thanks' [θæŋks]; SC; p. 344)
Phon: 1.5, +T.   Lex: Interjection X2.
Sem: Shared criterial features (automatic social formulae for being nice); could be considered wrong proposition.

B-260   4;4.14   B: (on Christmas Eve)
'Daddy, did you know that tònight we're gonna òpen sòme of **your** . . . sòme of <u>our</u> présents?'

('your' [jɚ] for 'our' [ar]; SC)
Phon: 3 (counting [ɚ]/[r] as the same final), -T.
Lex: Personal pronoun X2.
Sem: Honors case (possessive pronouns used as modifiers); violates person and number (although morphologically 'your' can be plural; also, both speaker and addressee are male, so doesn't violate gender).
Other: Environment, addressee is 'you'.

B-317   4;7.0   B: (refusing to get dressed in the morning)
'I wànna stày in my PJs Mòm; **befòre** . . . <u>àfter</u> lúnch I'll get drèssed.'

('before' [bɪ.fór] for 'after' [æf.tɚ]; SC; p. 246, 328, 344)
Phon: 2.5, -T.   Lex: Preposition X2.
Sem: Converses (relative time); opposed.

B-346   4;8.7   B: (telling the story of a movie in which a woman gets amnesia) ' . . . and she dòesn't knòw **his** húsband . . . <u>her</u> húsband àny mòre.'

('his' [hɪz] for 'her' [hɚ]; SC)
Phon: 3, -T.   Lex: Personal pronoun X2.
Sem: Honors case (possessive pronouns used as modifiers), person and number (3rd singular), violates gender.
Other: Discourse context, 'his/husband' male.

B-353   4;8.18   B: (looking for Dad in Dad's office building, asks an adult) 'Whère's **your** Dád? . . . Whère's <u>mý</u> Dàd?'

('your' [jɚ] for 'my' [maʲ]; emphasizes correction; SC)
Phon: 1.5, -T.   Lex: Personal pronoun X2.
Sem: Honors case (possessive pronouns used as modifiers), number (singular); violates person.
Other: Environment, addressee is 'your'.

B-425 4;11.18 B: (explaining to Mom why it's OK to play with GI Joe
toys at Robb's house since his toys aren't violent;
Bobby knows Mom doesn't approve of GI Joe toys)
'Ròbb has G.I. Jóe, but I ònly hàve . . . he ònly hàs
the cár.'
('I' [aʲ] for 'he' [hi]; note shift in agreement of verb; SC; p. 422)
Phon: 1.5, -T.   Lex: Personal pronoun X2.
Sem: Honors number, gender and case (singular, masculine,
subject); violates person.
Other: Environment, self.

AN-265 5;1.5   An: (holding a locket) 'Thìs is a lìttle pícture fràme. And
thèn you . . . whèn you wànt to sèe the pícture, you
òpen it úp.'
('then' [ðɪn] for 'when' [wɪn]; possibly phonological A/P from 'this'
and 'the'; SC)
Phon: 4, -T.   Lex: Conjunction X2 (temporal particles).
Sem: Shared criterial features (temporal placement).

B-446 5;1.7   B: (talking about a TV show) 'Ya knòw Clarìssa?
She dòesn't lìke his bróther. I mean hér bròther.'
('his' [hɪz] for 'her' [hɚ]; correction emphasized; SC; p. 222)
Phon: 3, -T.   Lex: Personal pronoun X2.
Sem: Honors number, person and case (3rd singular, possessive
modifiers); violates gender.
Other: Discourse context, 'his/brother' male.

AN-283 5;3.15   An: (opened a fruit roll-up packet by herself)
'Mòmmy, I dìd it bỳ hersélf.'
M: 'You whát?'
An: 'I dìd it bỳ mysélf.'
('herself' [hɚ.sɛɬf] for 'myself' [maʲ.sɛɬf]; NSC)
Phon: 5.5, +T.   Lex: Personal pronoun X2.
Sem: Honors number, gender and case (singular feminine,
reflexive), violates person.

OC-143 5;4.0   M: 'But Bènnie can't wálk.'
OG: 'Yéah he can. He can dò like thís, by . . .
with Jùlie hòlding his hánds.'
('by' [baʲ] for 'with' [wɪθ]; SC; p. 344)
Phon: 1.5, -T.   Lex: Preposition X2.
Sem: Shared criterial features (manner, facilitation of action).

B-523   5;5.30   B: (pretending to be an insect, pinching Mom)
'Thàt's just a . . . thàt's just my hánd.'
('a' [ʌ] for 'my' [maʲ]; [-sem]; SC)
Phon: 1.5, -T.
Lex: Determiner X2 (indefinite article vs. possessive pronoun).

B-529   5;6.4   B: (telling Anna that she may not go out to lunch with
Dad and himself)
'Ánna! He sàid just yòu . . . just mè and hím!'
('you' [ju] for 'me' [mi]; 'me and him' his usual expression; SC)
Phon: 1.5, -T.   Lex: Personal pronoun X2.
Sem: Honors and number and case (singular, object); violates
person.
Other: Environment, addressee is 'you'.

OC-154 5;7.0   OG: (explaining why she should have been more careful
around a fragile object)
' . . . because I shòuld have hìt it and bróke it.
I mèan I cóuld have hìt it and bròke it.'
('should' [ʃʊd] for 'could' [kʰʊd]; 'broke' is her usual pronunciation for
'broken'; SC; p. 344)
Phon: 4, -T.   Lex: Auxiliary verb X2.
Sem: Shared criterial features (modality).

AL-266 5;11.16 Al: (wanting to watch the video she rented) 'Bòbby
wàtched hîms, . . . hís, so nòw I can wàtch míne!'
('him' [hɪm] misselected, substituted for 'his' [hɪz], but possessive
{-s} suffixed=[hɪm(z)]; SC; p. 423)
Phon: 4.5, +T.   Lex: Personal pronoun X2.
Sem: Honors person, number, gender (3rd singular, masculine),
violates case.

AL-268 5;11.30 Al: (handing Mom some rubber bands)
'Mòm, when you wànt a rùbber bánd, tàke which òther
. . . tàke which èver you wánt.'
('other' [ʌ.ðɚ] for 'ever' [ɛ́.vɚ]; SC; p. 363)
Phon: 3, -T.   Lex: Impersonal pronoun X2.
Sem: Synonyms, singular impersonal reference.

37. Lexical substitutions, affixes.

B-447   5;1.12   B: 'My pòpsicle's in the [fɹ̥í.zi] . . . [fɹ̥íz] . . . [ɚ].
Mòm, whàt's 'pópsìcle' mèan? It mìght mèan that it's
rèal cóld, and it's fréezing.'
('freezy' [fɹ̥í.z(i)] for 'freezer' [fɹ̥í.z(ɚ)]; adjectival {-y} substituted for
instrumental {-er}; could just be vowel perseveration from first
syllable of 'freezer', but the child shows he is thinking about
morphological relatedness with his comments; SC with difficulty;
p. 24, 53, 85, 392, 396, 404)

B-456   5;1.24   B: (sucking on a piece of candy) 'I've been sùcked on
. . . I've been sùcking on thìs for a lòng tíme.'
('suck-ed' [sʌk(t)] for 'suck-ing' [sʌ́.k(ɪŋ)], perfect suffix for
progressive suffix; SC; p. 24, 390, 396)

38. Lexical blends, content words.

AN-6   1;7.20   An: (pretending to talk on the phone to "Winnie the Pooh"
characters) 'Hí [tʰɪ́.gɪt].'
(blend of 'Tigger' [tʰɪ́.g3] and 'Piglet' [pʰɪ́.gɪt]; N-NC; p. 13, 138,
322)
Phon: 4, -T.   Lex/Morph: Proper noun X2; mono X2.
Sem: Co-members of a set ("Winnie the Pooh" characters).

B-2   1;8.24   B: (pointing at picture of Bert in Sesame Street book):
'[pɜ́.ni] . . . Bért.'
(blend of 'Bert' [pɜt] and 'Ernie' [ʔɜ́.ni]; child didn't know word
'Bernie' so not lexical substitution; 1-word stage; SC; p. 274, 277,
302, 317)
Phon: 2.   Lex/Morph: Proper noun X2; mono X2.
Sem: Co-members of a set (characters on Sesame Street); opposed.
Other: Environment, both characters are on the page the child is
looking at.
Other: Collocation, 'Bert and Ernie'.

B-5   1;9.1   B: '*Tóe* hùrts.' (pronounced: [tów ʔɔ̀tɕ])
                 M: 'You got a? *ówie*?'
                 B: '[tǽ.wi] . . . ówie .'
        (blend of 'toe' [tow] and 'owie' [ǽ.wi], a baby term for sore or cut;
        2-word stage; [+utt]; SC; p. 266, 302, 336)
        Phon: 0.5.   Lex/Morph: Common noun X2, both CRS; mono X2
        (he didn't know 'owie' had the diminutive suffix at this age).
        Sem: Metonymic ('owie' is located on 'toe').

B-8   1;9.6   B: (to Mom) 'Hí [mà.θ] . . . Mòmma.'
        (blend of 'Momma' [má.ma] and '(Sa)mantha' [mǽ.θʌ]; Samantha
        was his babysitter, but was not present at time of error; 2-word
        stage; SC; p. 138, 302, 303)
        Phon: 3.5, -T.   Lex/Morph: Proper noun X2; mono X2.
        Sem: Co-members of a set (female adult caregivers in home).

B-12   1;9.25   B: (on toilet, looks down) '[pá.tʌɕ]'
        (blend of 'potty' [pá.ti] (toilet) and 'penis' [pí.nʌɕ]; 2-word stage;
        NSC; p. 176, 302, 336)
        Phon: 3.5.   Lex/Morph: Common noun X2, both CRS; mono X2.
        Sem: Metonymic (source and goal of urination).
        Other: Environment, said while on toilet, so both referents visible.

AN-16   1;10.0   M: (showing Anna a picture of a rabbit) 'Whàt's thís?'
                 An: '[pǽ.nɪtʰ].'
        (blend of 'bunny' [pʌ́.ni] and 'rabbit' [ɹǽ.bɪtʰ]; NSC; p. 175, 334,
        337, 345)
        Phon: 2.   Lex/Morph: Common noun X2, both CRS; mono X2.
        Sem: Synonyms (stylistic variants).

B-23   1;10.9   D: 'I'm gonna put some *crèam* on your *ówie*.'
                 B: '[ká.wi] . . . ówie.'
        (blend of 'cream' [kim] and 'owie' [ʔá.wi]; 2-word stage; [+utt]; SC;
        p. 222, 302, 345)
        Phon: 1.   Lex/Morph: Common noun X2, mass vs. CRS; mono X2.
        Sem: Metonymic ('cream' is located on 'owie').

OC-3   1;11.0   OG: (looks at brother whom she calls 'Dadoo', then looks
                     at Mother, says) 'Hí [dà.mi] . . . hí Mòmmy.'
        (blend of 'Dadoo' [dǽ.du] and 'Mommy' [má.mi]; 2-word stage; SC;
        p. 176, 302)
        Phon: 2, -T.   Lex/Morph: Proper noun X2; mono X2.
        Sem: Co-members of a set (immediate family members).
        Other: Environment, both referents are in the room.

AN-19   1;11.11   M: 'What are you drínking?'
                  An: '[wa'ç].'
                  M: 'Ice?'
                  An: 'Ice. Water, ice.'
(blend of 'water' [wá.t3] and 'ice' [a'ç]; NSC)
Phon: 0.5.   Lex/Morph: Common noun X2, both mass; mono X2.
Sem: Metonymic (water and ice typically occur together in glass).
Other: Environment, both referents visible.

OC-4   1;11.15   M: 'Do you want *mìlk* or *júice*?'
                  OB: '[ṇuç]'
(blend of 'milk' [mɛwk] and 'juice' [ṭuç]; also phonetic feature
blend, [m]+[ṭ]=[ṇ]; 2-word stage; [+utt]; NSC; p. 27, 96, 176, 302,
303)
Phon: 1.5.   Lex/Morph: Common noun X2, both mass; mono X2.
Sem: Co-hyponyms (kinds of drink).

B-30   1;11.23   OA: (babysitter, trying to teach him to say his full name)
                  'What's your náme, *Bòbby*?'
                  B: '[pá.pi.j3t]'
(blend of 'Bobby' [pá.pi] and 'Robert' [wá.p3t]; [+utt]; NSC; p. 334,
337, 351)
Phon: 4.   Lex/Morph: Proper noun X2; mono X2.
Sem: Synonyms (stylistic variants of child's own name).

AL-12   2;2.8   M: 'Is the ìce cream *còld* or *hót*?'
                  Al: '[kwát] . . . cóld!'
(blend of 'cold' [kowd] and 'hot' [hat]; [+utt]; SC; p. 178, 337, 346,
352-3)
Phon: 1.5.   Lex/Morph: Adjective X2; mono X2.
Sem: Gradable antonyms (of temperature); opposed.
Other: Collocation, 'hot and cold'.

AN-32   2;2.19   M: (Anna and Mom are looking at a page in a book with
                  pictures of both a deer and a dormouse) 'What's thát?'
                  (pointing to dormouse)
                  An: 'A [dɪʒ.mæʷs] . . . dórmouse.'
(blend of 'deer' [dɪʒ] and 'dormouse' [dóʒ.mæʷs]; SC; p. 223)
Phon: 3, +T.
Lex/Morph: Common noun X2, both CIS; mono vs. 2-cmpd.
Sem: Co-hyponyms (kinds of animals).
Other: Environment, both animals visible on page.

AL-16   2;2.22   M: 'Do you wànt your **búnny** cùp?'
              Al: 'Yeah, me [ʒʌ.ni] . . . rábbit cùp.'
(blend of 'rabbit' [ʒæ.bɪt] and 'bunny' [bʌ.ni]; [+utt]; SC; p. 326, 337, 345, 362)
Phon: 2, +T.   Lex/Morph: Common noun X2, both CRS; mono X2.
Sem: Synonyms (stylistic variants).

AL-26   2;4.18   Al: (in living-room, telling adult where some toy is)
              'Oùt in the [**bé.vin.ʒ̣ùm**].'
              OA: 'Where?'
              Al: 'In the bédròom.'
(blend of 'bedroom' [béd.ʒ̣ùm] and 'living-room' [wí.vin.ʒ̣ùm]; NSC; p. 174, 438)
Phon: 3, +T.   Lex/Morph: Common noun X2, both CRS; 2 (2-cmpd) vs. 3 (2-cmpd+deriv).
Sem: Co-hyponyms (kinds of rooms).
Other: Environment, she was in living room at time of speaking.

B-55   2;5.8   B: 'I wànt some túrkey.'
             M: 'It's nòt túrkey, it's **béef**. You wànt a **píece**?'
             B: '[pʰif]?'
(blend of 'piece' [pʰis] and 'beef' [bif]; [-sem]; [+utt]; NSC; p. 245)
Phon: 3.
Lex/Morph: Common noun X2, mass vs. CRS; mono X2.

B-72   2;6.4   B: 'After I gò to [láŋ.kìs] . . . after I gò to Lóngs fìrst, I gònna gò to the grócery stòre.'
(blend of 'Longs' [laŋs] and 'Luckys' [lʌ.kis], a drug store and a grocery store; SC)
Phon: 3, +T.   Lex/Morph: Proper noun X2; 2-infl X2 (both treated as possessive, and clearly lexicalized as possessive).
Sem: Co-hyponyms (kinds of store); opposed (these were the two main stores the child was familiar with).
Other: Discourse context, going to the store.

B-76   2;6.12   B: (drawing with chalk on the driveway; says to self)
             'Thàt's a **fróg**.' (then says to Mom) 'I màde a [fʒɪʃ].'
             M: 'A what?'
             B: 'A físh.' (as if he changed his mind about what he'd drawn)
(blend of 'frog' [fʒag] and 'fish' [fɪʃ]; [+utt]; NSC; p. 449)
Phon: 3, +T.   Lex/Morph: Common noun X2, both count, regular/irregular, singular; mono X2.
Sem: Co-hyponyms (kinds of small water-dwelling animals).

AL-35   2;6.13   Al: (looking for raisins, but sees bowl of grapes)
'I wànt anòther [g̰ʒé͡.zən].'
(blend of 'grape' [g̰ʒe͡ip] and raisin [ʒé͡ʲ.zən]; NSC)
Phon: 3, +T.
Lex/Morph: Common noun X2, both CRS; mono X2.
Sem: Co-hyponyms (kinds of snacking fruit).
Other: Environment, bowl of grapes visible.

B-80   2;6.15   B: 'I wànna plày with a bíg [wèg].'
(blend of 'one' [wʌn] and 'egg' [ɛg]; could also be perseveration of
[w] from 'wanna' and 'with'; NSC; p. 321, 337, 361)
Phon: 1.5, -T.   Lex/Morph: Common noun X2, both CRS (one
concrete and one abstract); mono X2.
Sem: Superordinate/subordinate ('one' is a general way to refer to
'egg').
Other: Collocation, 'bíg òne' (stress pattern sounded like this, rather
than 'bìg égg').

AN-65   2;8.19   An: (wrapping towel around self, treating it like bathrobe)
'Hère's your [bǽθ.kʰḷàθ].'
(blend of 'bathrobe' [bǽθ.rò͡ʷb] and 'washcloth' [wáʃ.kʰḷàθ]; NSC;
p. 140, 174)
Phon: 2, +T.   Lex/Morph: Common noun X2, both CRS,
since child regularized plural of 'cloth'; 2-cmpd X2.
Sem: Comembers of a set (bath-related items).

OC-31   2;9.0   OG: 'I gòt a [tʰó̰ʒ] . . . I gòt a tápe that sàys thàt.'
(blend of 'tape' [tʰe͡ip] and 'story' [stó.ʒi]; SC)
Phon: 0.5, +T.
Lex/Morph: Common noun X2, both CRS; mono X2.
Sem: Metonyms (these 'tapes' are associated with books with the
same 'story').

AL-54   2;10.7   Al: 'My [tʰʌ́.li] . . . my túmmy is dìrty.'
(blend of 'tummy' [tʰʌ́.mi] and 'belly' [bɛ́.li]; in next sentence, began
talking about 'belly button'; SC)
Phon: 3, +T.   Lex/Morph: Common noun X2, both CRS; mono X2.
Sem: Synonyms (stylistic variants).

B-116   2;10.7   B: 'Thàt's a grèat bìg [fá.pa] bèar!'
(blend of 'Father' [fá.ḓʒ] and 'Poppa' [pʰá.pa]; NSC; p. 27, 175, 345,
351, 357)
Phon: 3.5, +T.
Lex/Morph: Proper noun X2 (functioning as modifiers); mono X2.
Sem: Synonyms (stylistic variants).

AL-73   2;10.28   Al: 'Can you réad thìs [wɪŋ] . . . thìs <u>thing</u>?'
(blend of 'one' [wʌn] and 'thing' [fɪŋ]; clearly started to say 'one', by
stress pattern; SC)
Phon: 1.5, -T.
Lex/Morph: Common noun X2, both CRS; mono X2.
Sem: Synonyms (both general levels of referential specificity).

AL-78b   2;11.9   Al: 'Nòbody [sm:éʲkt] mè.' (looks confused)
            M: 'What?'
            Al: 'Nòbody <u>màked</u> me crý.'
(blend of 'spanked' [spæŋk(t)] and 'maked' [meʲk(t)]; [-sem]; N-NC;
also phrase blend of 'nòbody spánked me' and 'nòbody màked me
crý', AL-78a=Class 49; p. 174, 246, 453)
Phon: 3, +T.   Lex/Morph: Verb X2, both transitive, regular
past (for child, as 'maked' was normal' for her); 2-infl X2.

AL-89   3;0.25   Al: 'Mommy, 'Àlice' and 'àpplejuice' stàrt with the sàme
            [léʲ:] . . . the sàme <u>náme</u>.'
(blend of 'letter' [lé.t3] and 'name' [neʲm]; she used 'name' to refer to
'sound'; could just be perseveration of [l] from 'Alice' or 'apple'; SC)
Phon: 0.5, +T.
Lex/Morph: Common noun X2, both CRS; mono X2.
Sem: Metonymic (a 'letter' is functionally paired with its 'name', i.e.
sound).

AL-93   3;1.6   Al: 'I [wáʲk] sòme . . . I <u>wánt</u> sòme.'
(blend of 'want' [wʌnt] and 'like' [laʲk]; SC; p. 345, 352, 453)
Phon: 1.5, +T.
Lex/Morph: Verb X2, both transitive, regular, 1st singular present
form; mono X2.
Sem: Synonyms (activities of desiring).

AL-98   3;2.17   Al: (pointing to a picture of herself putting on shoes and
            socks) 'That's mè pùtting on my [ʃáks].'
(blend of 'shoes' [ʃu(z)] and 'socks' [sak(s)]; N-NC; p. 331, 354, 419)
Phon: 1.5, +T.
Lex/Morph: Common noun X2, both CRP (formally, although both
are probably represented in the lexicon in plural form); 2-infl X2.
Sem: Co-hyponyms (clothing worn on feet); also metonymic;
opposed.
Other: Environment, both shoes and socks visible in photo.
Other: Collocation, 'shoes and socks'.

OC-50   3;4.0   OB: (looking at a bug he had just smashed)
                        'Hè's déad, 'cùz wè [**skm̥íʃt**] hìm . . .
                        we squíshed hìm!'
(blend of 'squished' [skwɪʃ(t)] and 'smashed' [sm̥æʃ(t)], producing
illegal cluster *[skm̥]; SC; p. 144)
Phon: 4, +T.
Lex/Morph: Verb X2, both transitive, regular, past; 2-infl X2.
Sem: Synonyms (activities of destroying by flattening).

AL-133   3;4.25   M: 'What do you want, the one with the **kìtty** or the
                        búnny?'
                     Al: '[**bʌ́.ri**].'
                     M: 'What?'
                     Al: 'The búnny òn ìt.'
(blend of 'bunny' [bʌ́.ni] and 'kitty' [kʰʌ́.ri]; [+utt]; NSC)
Phon: 3.   Lex/Morph: Common noun X2, both CRS; mono X2.
Sem: Co-hyponyms (kinds of small, furry, cute animals).

AL-146   3;7.5   Al: (getting a fork out of a drawer where there were both
                        spoons and forks) 'I've gèt a [**spóȝk**].'
                     An: 'She said "spork".' (laughs)
                     Al: 'Fork!'
(blend of 'spoon' [spun] and 'fork' [foȝk]; she didn't know the word
'spork'; 'I've get' was normal for her at this age; NSC; p. 287, 354)
Phon: 1.5, +T.
Lex/Morph: Common noun X2, both CRS; mono X2.
Sem: Co-hyponyms (kinds of silverware); opposed.
Other: Environment, both spoons and forks visible.
Other: Collocation, 'spoon and fork'.

B-142   3;8.3   B: 'I còuldn't **sée** it, and I wènt ìnto the [**splìs**] . . .
                        plàce where you cán sèe it, (etc.) . . . '
(seems to be blend of 'see' [si] and 'place' [pʰleʲs], like he started to
say 'seeing place'; possibly phonological, but more complex than
most phonological substitution errors; possibly phrase blend; [+utt];
[-sem]; SC; p. 178, 246)
Phon: 1.5, -T.   Lex: Verb vs. common noun.

B-145   3;8.4   M: (looking at catalogue page which has pictures of both a
wheelbarrow and a wagon; points to the wagon)
'What's thís?'
B: 'It's a [wʰɬ.bæ̀.gən].' (looks confused)
(blend of 'wheelbarrow' [wɬ.bɛ̀.roʷ] and 'wagon' [wǽ.gən]; N-NC;
p. 188)
Phon: 2.5, +T.
Lex/Morph: Common noun X2, both CRS; mono vs. 2-cmpd.
Sem: Co-hyponyms (kinds of small, manually moved transport).
Other: Environment, both wagons and wheelbarrows visible on page.

B-146   3;8.5   B: (pointing up at some trees)
'There's bées in the [çɪ̀z] . . . [çɪ̀z] . . . thìngs up thère.'
(blend of 'things' [çɪŋ(z)] and 'trees' [tʃʒi(z)], although possible some
influence from 'bees'; SC; p. 361)
Phon: 1.5, -T.
Lex/Morph: Common noun X2, both CRP; 2-infl X2.
Sem: Superordinate/subordinate ('thing' is superordinate for 'tree').

B-150   3;8.15   B: 'No, I ònly [lʌ̀nt] some béans.'
(blend of 'like' [laʲk] and 'want' [wʌnt]; usually he says 'like' in this
construction; NSC; p. 345, 352)
Phon: 1.5, -T.   Lex/Morph: Verb X2, both transitive, regular,
1st singular present; mono X2.
Sem: Synonyms (activities of desiring).

AL-158   3;8.22   Al: 'You càn't fòld my pánties, becàuse they hàve to gò
òut [slɛ́ʲt].'
M: 'Whát?'
Al: 'They hàve to gò out stráight.'
(blend of 'straight' [stʒeʲt] and 'flat' [fḷæt]; NSC; p. 174, 345)
Phon: 2.5, +T.   Lex/Morph: Adverb X2; mono X2.
Sem: Synonyms (horizontal, thin dimension).

AL-170   3;9.6   Al: 'Mommy, I'm [tʰʌ́ŋ.gʒi].'
M: 'Whát?'
Al: 'I'm húngry.'
(blend of 'tired' [tʰáʲ.ɜd] and 'hungry' [hʌ́ŋ.gʒi]; NSC)
Phon: 2, +T.   Lex/Morph: Adjective X2; 2-deriv X2 (one
with adjectival {-i} and one with participial {-ed}).
Sem: Co-hyponyms (kinds of ways to feel physically uncomfortable).
Other: Collocation, 'tired and hungry'.

OC-74   3;11.0   OB: (chanting)
      'It's time to [pʰɪn] ùp! It's time to clèan ùp!'
(blend of 'pick up' [pʰɪk ʌp] and 'clean up' [kʰlin ʌp]; SC; p. 326, 352, 431, 437)
Phon: 1.5, -T.
Lex/Morph: Verb X2, both intransitive, regular, infinitive; 2-PV X2.
Sem: Synonyms (activities of tidying up).

B-177   4;0.15   B: 'Mommy, I àlready góed [pʰɪŋ.ki] . . . tinkie.'
(blend of '(go) pee pee' [pʰi.pʰi] and '(go) tinkie' [tʰɪŋ.ki], both children's words for urination; SC)
Phon: 3, -T.   Lex/Morph: Verb X2, both intransitive, (regularized irregular past 'goed'); 2-different (2-cmpd vs. 2-deriv: 'tinkie', derived from 'tinkle').
Sem: Synonyms (activity of urination).
Other: Collocations, 'go peepee/go tinkie'.

B-208   4;2.5   B: 'Mom, can I tàke a [pʰáʲ] . . . piece?'
(blend of 'piece' [pʰis] and 'bite' [baⁱt]; SC)
Phon: 1.5, +T.
Lex/Morph: Common noun X2, both CRS; mono X2.
Sem: Shared criterial feature (small portions separated from larger food item).
Other: Collocation, 'take a bite'.

B-211   4;2.6   B: (talking about Anna, who is about to take a shower)
      'Dòes she wànt a [ʃóʷ] . . . cóld òne or a hót òne?'
(blend of 'shower' [ʃǽ.wɚ] and 'cold' [kʰoʷɫd]; could be perseveration from 'she'; [-sem] but see note; SC; p. 245, 278)
Phon: 0.5, +T.   Lex: Common noun vs. adjective.
Other: Discourse context, shower event; (possibly some metonymic relationship since water temperature is often discussed in the 'shower' scene).

B-214   4;2.7   B: (Bobby is trying to decide what kind of cereal he
              wants for breakfast; Anna is discussing Corn Chex in
              the background) 'I wànt [tʃɪks].'
(blend of 'Chex' [tʃɛks] and 'Kix' [kʰɪks], two brand names of cereal; [+utt]; NSC)
Phon: 3.5, +T.   Lex/Morph: Proper noun X2; mono X2
(although there is a plural sense to the meaning).
Sem: Co-hyponyms (kinds of cereal).

B-227b 4;2.28 D: 'I fixed the *zípper*.'
M: 'Oh, on his *jácket*?'
B: 'Yeah, 'cuz my [dʒæ̀.pɚ] . . . the z̀ipper came òff my
bìg *jácket*.'
(blend of 'jacket' [dʒǽ.kɨt] and 'zipper' [zí.pɚ]; [+utt]; SC; 227a=
Class 41; p. 138, 323, 361, 432, 436)
Phon: 2, -T.   Lex/Morph: Common noun X2, both CRS;
mono vs. 2-deriv ({-er}).
Sem: Whole/part (a 'zipper' is part of a 'jacket').

AN-169 4;4.2 An: 'You s̀illy [dʌ́m.dò̀ʷz] . . . you s̀illy dódohèads!'
(blend of 'dummies' [dʌ́m.i(z)] and 'dodoheads' [dóʷ.doʷ.hɛ̀d(z)]; SC;
p. 432, 436)
Phon: 2.5, +T.   Lex/Morph: Common noun X2, both CRP;
3-different (2-deriv{-ie}+infl vs. 2-cmpd+infl).
Sem: Synonyms (derogatory names to call someone).

B-268 4;4.26 B: 'Just [kʰóʷ.dɪŋ] . . . just jóking!'
(blend of 'kidding' [kʰí.d(ɪŋ)] and 'joking' [dʒó.k(ɪŋ)]; SC; p. 175,
352)
Phon: 1.5, +T.   Lex/Morph: Verb X2, both intransitive,
regular, progressive; 2-infl X2.
Sem: Synonyms (speech acts of jesting/teasing).

B-270 4;4.30 B: 'I'm making a spàce *shìp* and a spàce *shúttle*.
Sée Mom? My spáce [ʃʌ̀.pəɫ] . . . shùttle.'
(probably blend of 'shuttle' [ʃʌ́.rəɫ] and 'ship' [ʃɪp], although it could
be a phonological perseveration of [p] from 'space'; [+utt]; SC)
Phon: 2, -T.
Lex/Morph: Common noun X2, both CRS; mono X2.
Sem: Co-hyponyms (kinds of space vehicles).
Other: Environment, drawing pictures of both vehicles.

AN-188 4;5.4 An: (eating popcorn while looking at her sister holding a
pumpkin, on Halloween)
'I'm gònna gòbble ùp àll my [pʰʌ́mp.kʰòrn].'
(noticed, laughed)
(blend of [pʰʌ́mp.kɪn] and 'pópcòrn' [pʰáp.kʰòrn]; [-sem], as she didn't
consider 'pumpkin' to be food; N-NC; p. 246)
Phon: 6, +T.   Lex/Morph: Common noun X2, both mass in
this context; mono vs. 2-cmpd.
Other: Environment, looking at pumpkin.

AN-192 4;5.4   M: 'Just **shữt** the dóor.'
　　　　　　　　An: 'Yeah, [kʰḷʌ̀t] . . . <u>clòse</u> the dóor.'
(blend of 'close' [kʰloʷz] and 'shut' [ʃʌt]; [+utt]; SC; p. 352)
Phon: 1.5, -T.　　　　Lex/Morph: Verb X2, both transitive,
regular/irregular, imperative; mono X2.
Sem: Synonyms (same action).
Other: Collocation, 'shut the door'.

AL-217 4;5.10   Al: 'I wànt my [**lá.ni**].'
(blend of 'leopard' [lέ.p3d] and Johnny' [dʒá.ni]; toy leopard named
Johnny; NSC; p. 293, 346, 361)
Phon: 2, +T.
Lex/Morph: Proper noun vs. common noun, same referent; mono X2.
Sem: Superordinate/subordinate ('Johnny' is a specific name for the
toy 'leopard').

AL-219 4;5.15   Al: (wanting to go barefoot) 'Is it [**oʷ.ʒὲʲ**] on the déck?'
(blend of 'okay' [oʷ.kʰέʲ] and 'all-right' [ɑ.ʒá̰ɨt]; NSC; p. 175)
Phon: 2, -T.
Lex/Morph: Adverb X2; mono X2 (or possibly compounds).
Sem: Synonyms (of affirmation).

AL-224 4;5.28   Al: (looking at cookie with different 'kinds' of faces on
　　　　　　　　　　each 'side') 'I'm gònna lòok at bóth [**skà**ʲ] . . . <u>kìnds</u>.'
(blend of 'sides' [saⁱd(z)] and 'kinds' [kʰaⁱn(z)]; [-sem]; SC; p. 245)
Phon: 4, -T.
Lex/Morph: Common noun X2, both CRP; 2-infl X2.
Other: Discourse context, two sides a salient property of this type of
cookie.

AN-213 4;5.30   An: (looking at TV) 'Is thìs "**Jáws**"?'
　　　　　　　　　　M: 'No.'
　　　　　　　　　　An: 'Góod, because I dòn't wànt to be scàred by [**dʒárks**].
　　　　　　　　　　　　(laughs) I said "jàrks" instead of "<u>shárks</u>".'
(blend of 'Jaws' [dʒɑ(z)] and 'sharks' [ʃark(s)]; [+utt]; SC; p. 82)
Phon: 1.5, +T.
Lex/Morph: Proper noun vs. common noun; 2 infl X2 (both with
plural morpheme {-s}, although lexicalized in the case of "Jaws").
Sem: Metonymic (the film "Jaws" involves sharks, thus the
association; also negative connotation).

AN-218 4;6.3   M: 'What color thréad do you want: grèen, *yèllow*, or
                       réd?'
                 An: '[jéd] . . . réd.'
(blend of 'yellow' [jé.loʷ] and 'red' [rɛd]; [+utt]; SC)
Phon: 2.
Lex/Morph: Adjective X2; mono X2.
Sem: Co-hyponyms (kinds of color).

AL-227 4;6.5   M: 'If you want a snáck, you can have some chèese or
                       some *grápe*s.'
                 Al: 'I wànt a [grǽ.pəɫ].' (looks confused)
(blend of 'grape' [greⁱp] and 'apple' [ǽ.pəɫ]; what she wanted was an
apple; [+utt]; N-NC; p. 424)
Phon: 1, +T.
Lex/Morph: Common noun X2, both CRS
(although 'grapes' is plural in adult utterance); mono X2.
Sem: Co-hyponyms (kinds of fruit).

B-310   4;6.20   B: (trying to get Mom to watch him twirl around in a
                      chair) '[látʃ]!'
(blend of 'look' [lʊk] and 'watch' [watʃ]; NSC; p. 174, 352)
Phon: 1.5.
Lex/Morph: Verb X2, both transitive, regular, imperative; mono X2.
Sem: Synonyms (activities of vision).

B-326b 4;7.8   B: (he had just been saying that I could teach him to
                      drive when he turned 16. Then he saw me typing, and
                      added) 'When I'm sixtéen, you can *lèarn* me . . . you
                      can [tʰɚn] me . . . you can tèach me how to týpe!'
(blend of 'teach' [tʰitʃ] and 'learn' [lɚn]; [+utt]; SC; 326a=Class 35;
p. 325, 346, 352)
Phon: 1.5, -T.
Lex/Morph: Verb X2, both transitive, regular/irregular, stem form;
mono X2.
Sem: Converses (learn vs. teach); opposed.
Other: Discourse context, teaching and learning various things.

B-347   4;8.12   M: (coming into room where Bobby was getting dressed)
'Did you get your **shòes** and **sócks** on?'
B: (pointing to socks he was putting on at the moment)
'[ʃáks] . . . sócks.'
(blend of 'shoes' [ʃuz] and 'socks' [saks]; [+utt]; SC; p. 354)
Phon: 1.5.
Lex/Morph: Common noun X2, both CRP (formally, although both
are probably represented in the lexicon in plural form); 2-infl X2.
Sem: Co-hyponyms (clothing worn on feet); also metonymic;
opposed.
Other: Environment, both shoes and socks visible.
Other: Collocation, 'shoes and socks'.

B-356   4;8.22   B: (struggling with one kind of roll of tape, takes a
different kind out of drawer) 'How 'bout this [tʰàⁱm]
. . . how 'bout this tàpe?'
(blend of 'tape' [tʰeⁱp] and 'kind' [kʰaⁱn], with feature blend:
[n]+[p]=[m]; [-sem]; SC; p. 96, 245)
Phon: 1.5, -T.   Lex: Common noun X2, mass vs. CRS.
Other: Collocation, 'this kind'.

AN-253b 4;10.19 M: 'Whỳ doèsn't she jùst kèep her éyes shùt?'
An: 'Thàt's what she [dúz] . . . thàt's what she's dóin',
Mom!'
(blend of 'does' [dʌz] and 'doin' ' (doing) [dú.w(ɪn)]; possibly some
influence from Mom's utterance 'doesn't' [dʌz.ṇt], so [+utt]; SC;
253a=Class 49; p. 396, 435)
Phon: 2, +T.
Lex/Morph: Verb X2, same stem; one 3rd singular present tense,
one progressive (due to phrase blend); 2-infl X2.
Sem: Shared criterial features (same lexical base 'do').

AN-261 5;0.2   An: 'Yóu're in a [hʌ̀ʃ]!'
(blend of 'hurry' [hɚ.ri] and 'rush' [rʌʃ]; NSC)
Phon: 0.5, -T.
Lex/Morph: Common noun X2, both CRS (deverbal); mono X2.
Sem: Synonyms (states of needing to act quickly).
Other: Collocations, 'in a hurry/in a rush'.

AN-262   5;0.17   An: (talking about the paper wrapper on food)
'. . . [réʲ.pɚ].'
(blend of 'wrapper' [ræ.pɚ] and 'paper' [pʰéʲ.pɚ]; NSC; p. 138)
Phon: 3.5, +T.
Lex/Morph: Common noun X2, mass vs. CRS; mono vs. 2-deriv
([-ɚ] is a nominalizing suffix on 'wrapper' but not on 'paper').
Sem: Shared criterial features (food 'wrappers' are typically made of
'paper').

B-471   5;2.14   B: 'Mom, did yòu tell Dàd that I wènt to the
[sì.mə.tʰɛ́.ri.əm]? I mean plànetárium?'
(blend of 'cemetery' [sí.mə.tʰɛ̀.ri] and 'planetarium'
[pʰļæ̀.nə.tʰɛ́.ri.əm]; SC; p. 178, 189, 248, 438)
Phon: 3, +T.
Lex/Morph: Common noun X2, both CRS; 2 (2-deriv) vs. 3 (3-deriv).
Sem: Shared criterial features (public locations one can visit; formal
connotation).

B-509   5;5.24   B: (looking in "Children's Dictionary"; page has entries
and pictures for 'acorn' and 'airplane')
'An [èr.korn] . . . àcorn is a kìnd of a nút.'
(blend of 'airplane' [ɛ́r.pļeʰn] and 'acorn' [éʲ.korn]; [-sem]; SC; p. 246)
Phon: 3, -T.
Lex/Morph: Common noun X2, both CRS; mono vs. 2-cmpd.
Other: Environment, both referents visible on page.

B-514   5;5.24   B: (doing impressions of things in "Children's Dictionary")
'Ì'm gòing to màke an [ɪm.pʰɚ̀.sən] of an ígloo.'
(blend of 'impersonation' [ɪm.pʰɚ̀.sə.néʲ.ʃən] and 'impression'
[ɪm.pʰré.ʃən]; he knew both of these words; NSC; p. 178, 222, 248,
432, 436, 437, 438, 443)
Phon: 6, -T; could be analyzed as segments from one target, but
prosodic structure from the other.
Lex/Morph: Common noun X2, both CRS; 3 (3-deriv) vs. 4 (4-deriv),
both with prefix {im-}, suffix {-ion}.
Sem: Synonyms (activities of mimicking or portraying something
else).

B-515   5;5.24   B: (discussing entry in "Children's Dictionary")
'A pàlace is where a qùeen and kíng [ǰɪvz] . . . lives.'
(sounded like blend of 'is' [ɪz] and 'lives' [lɪv(z)], with transitional
[j]; SC; p. 421)
Phon: 3.5, -T.   Lex/Morph: Verb X2, both linking,
regular/irregular, 3rd singular present tense; 2-infl X2.
Sem: Shared criterial features (be at a place).

OC-149 5;6.0   OG: '[jɛ́.stɚ.nàⁱt].' (laughs when realizes error)
(blend of 'yesterday' [jɛ́.stɚ.dèʲ] and 'last night' [lǽst.náⁱt]; N-NC;
p. 188)
Phon: 1.   Lex/Morph: Adverbs (temporal); 2-cmpd X2.
Sem: Co-partonyms (parts of preceding day).

AL-249 5;7.22   Al: (talking about a box of fruit snacks) 'No, they're the
[sàⁱn] . . . they're the <u>same</u> as we úsed to gèt.'
(blend of 'same' [seⁱm] and 'kind' [kʰaⁱn]; SC)
Phon: 1.5, -T.
Lex/Morph: Adjective vs. common noun; mono X2.
Sem: Shared criterial features (designation of a particular type).
Other: Collocations, 'they're the same' and 'they're the kind'

AN-325 5;11.14 An: 'Ya know when I was śick, and dĭdn't go to schóol?
They màde this cùte, [ə.dàr.lɪŋ] lĭttle búnny? And I
dĭdn't get to máke òne.'
(blend of 'adorable' [ə.dór.ə.bɬ] and 'darling' [dár.lɪŋ]; NSC; p. 345)
Phon: 3, -T.
Lex/Morph: Adjective X2; mono ('darling' was mono for this child)
vs. 2-deriv ({-able}).
Sem: Synonyms (affectionate terms to describe cuddly, loveable
entities).

AL-270 5;11.31 Al: (talking about new delicate plate)
'It's rèally [sprɛ́.tʃɚɬ] . . . <u>spécial</u>. It's <u>frágile</u>.'
(blend of 'special' [spɛ́.ʃɚɬ] and 'fragile' [fɹǽ.dʒɚɬ], also feature
blend: [ʃ]+[dʒ]=[tʃ]; SC, mentioning both words; p. 96, 328).
Phon: 3.5, +T.   Lex/Morph: Adjective X2; mono X2.
Sem: Connotation (something which is 'fragile' entails or is treated
as 'special').

OC-174 5;11.31 OB: (family trying to decide between going to McDonald's
or Burger King for dinner)
'I wànt to gò to [mɪk.bɚ́.gɚ.kʰ ɪ̀ŋ].'
(blend of 'McDonald's' [mɪk.dá.nɚɬ(z)] and 'Burger King'
[bɚ́.gɚ.kʰɪ̀ŋ]; NSC; p. 439)
Phon: 1, +T.
Lex/Morph: Proper noun X2; 2-different (2-infl vs. 2-cmpd, although
both are lexicalized in these forms).
Sem: Co-hyponyms (kinds of fast food restaurants).
Other: Discourse context, discussion of where to eat.

39. Lexical blends, function words.

B-113 2;9.15 B: (getting diaper changed) 'I [**mʌ̀.stʌ**] chánge it.'
(blend of 'must' [mʌst] and 'hafta' (have to) [hǽf.tʌ]; NSC; p. 232, 329, 337, 345)
Phon: 1, -T. Lex: Auxiliary verbs (modals) X2.
Sem: Synonyms (obligation).

B-319 4;7.2 B: (explaining the spelling of "Splinter", a "Ninja Turtles" character) 'Ŝ is [**bi.fr̥ʌ̀nt ʌv**] Ǹ in "Splínter". '
M: 'Whát?'
B: 'Ŝ is <u>in frònt of</u> Ǹ in "Splínter".'
(blend of 'before' [bi.fór] and 'in front of' [ɪn fr̥ʌ́nt ʌv]; NSC; p. 224, 345)
Phon: 2, -T. Lex: Preposition X2.
Sem: Synonyms (location in relation to another object, prior).

B-363 4;9.14 B: (telling what time it says on his and Alice's clocks) 'Mîne is eìght fòrty fîve, and [**ʃɚ́:**] . . . <u>hérs</u> is èight fòrty fîve.'
(blend of 'she' [ʃi] and 'hers' [hɚz]; SC; p. 27)
Phon: 1.5, +T. Lex: Personal pronoun X2.
Sem: Honors person, number and gender (3rd singular, feminine); violates case.

B-365 4;9.15 B: (asked Mom a question, told her what to answer, then asked the same question again; after Mom answered 'correctly', Bobby gushed) '[**gra:ⁱt**]!' (looked confused)
(blend of 'great' [greⁱt] and 'right' [raⁱt], his two usual responses; N-NC; p. 329, 345)
Phon: 3.5. Lex: Interjection X2.
Sem: Synonyms (affirmation).

OC-139 5;2.24 D: 'How 'bout a péar? You ***dìd***n't ***hàve*** òne of thóse yèt.'
OB: 'Yés I [**hìd**].' (looks confused)
(sounded like blend of 'have' [hæv] and 'did' [dɪd]; possibly just perseveration of [h] from Dad's utterance; [+utt]; N-NC; p. 273)
Phon: 1.5, -T. Lex: Auxiliary verb X2.
Sem: Shared criterial features (completion of activity in the past).

40.   *Lexical blends, mixed content and function words.*

B-1   1;7.22   B: (saying 'Goodbye' to Grandma who was driving away
                          in car) '[kâ^j . . . pâ^j.   kɔ̂.]'
           (blend of 'car' [kɔ] and 'bye' [pa^j], which are then repeated in
           'vertical construction'; 1-word stage; SC; p. 47, 293, 302, 463)
           Phon: 1.5.
           Lex/Morph: Interjection vs. common noun; mono X2.
           Sem: Metonymic ('car' and 'bye' functionally related in leavetaking
           scene).
           Other: Environment, car visible, driving away.

AL-51   2;9.22   Al: (Mom put a cassette tape of Grandpa's band into the
                          tape deck; Alice usually referred to the tape as as
                          'Grandpa'; Alice points to tape)
                          'I lóve [d̪ǽ.pa] . . . I lóve Gràndpa, Móm!'
           (blend of 'that' [d̪æt] and 'Grandpa' [g̣ʒǽm.pa]; [-sem]; SC; p. 246,
           286, 346)
           Phon: 2, -T.
           Lex: Proper noun vs. demonstrative (deictic pronoun), same referent.
           Other: Environment, looking at tape, pointing (deictic).

III. Syntactic Errors

41. Lexical anticipations, content and function words (substitutions, additions).

OC-9   2;0.14   OG: (asking Daddy if he had used the bathroom yet)
'P**è**epee, go . . . D**à**ddy, go *péepee?*'
('peepee' [pʰí.pʰi] anticipated, substituted for 'Daddy' [dǽ.di]; 2-word
stage; [-sem]; SC; p. 232, 268, 302, 304, 462)
Phon: 3, +T(s).   Lex/Morph: Proper noun vs. verb; mono X2.

AN-24   2;0.14   An: (telling what her imaginary baby is going to eat)
'G**ò**nna dr**ì**nk [b**ù**?] . . . m**ì**lk in my *bóobie.*'
('boobie' [bú.bi], baby word for 'breast', anticipated, substituted for
'milk' [mɪɫk];   SC; p. 327, 347)
Phon: 0.5, +T(s).   Lex/Morph: Common noun X2, mass vs. CRS;
mono+2-deriv ('boob+{-i}').
Sem: Metonymic (milk is contained in boobies).

AL-9   2;2.5   M: 'Let me rinse off your b**ó**ttle. It's all st**i**cky.'
Al: 'M**ỳ** st**ì**ck . . . m**ỳ** b**ò**ttle *sticky.* M**ý** **à**pple-j**ù**ice. M**ỳ**
st**ì**cky b**ó**ttle.'
(probable interrupted metathesis of 'bottle' [bá.toʷ] with 'sticky'
[tí.ki]; SC, and repeated with variations; p. 305)
Phon: +T(t2).

AN-33   2;2.19   M: 'What's that?'
An: 'He's a c**ú**p . . . C**ó**okie-M**ò**nster *cùp.*'
(probable interrupted metathesis of 'Cookie-Monster' [kʰú.ki mã̀.sɚ]
with 'cup' [kʰʌp], although she could have started to say 'He's a cup-
monster'; 'he' is not an error, as she was using 'he' for generic 3rd sg.
pronoun; SC)
Phon: +T(t1).

AN-73   2;9.29   An: 'Ì g**ε**t . . . Ì sh**ŏ**uld g**è**t m**ý** c**à**rds.'
(probable interrupted metathesis of 'should' [ʃɪd] with 'get' [gɛt]; SC;
p. 286)
Phon: -T.

AN-89a 2;11.15   An: (to Daddy) 'Wànt **me** to hèlp . . . wànt you to hèlp. . .
          wànt to hèlp *me* cólor?'
      ('me' anticipated, added to phrase 'want to help'; SC; AN-89b=Class
      36; p. 32)
      Phon: -T.
      Other: Collocation, 'want me to . . .?'

B-121   3;0.12   B: (telling what movie he wanted to watch)
          'I wànna "**Chìp 'n'** " . . .
          I wànna watch "**Chìp 'n'** Dále" when I gèt hòme.'
      (probable interrupted metathesis of 'watch' [watʃ] with 'Chip 'n'
      [tʃíp.n̩]; could be phrase blend with 'I want Chip 'n' Dale'; SC)
      Phon: +T(t2).

AL-97   3;2.14   Al: (putting her feet on the kitchen table)
          'My pìgs . . . my tòes are *pígs'* fèet. And I háte to
          èat pìgs' fèet.'
      ('pig' [pʰɪg] anticipated, substituted for 'toe' [tʰoʷ]; plural/possessive
      stranded; [-sem]; SC; p. 29, 435)
      Phon: 1.5, +T(s).   Lex/Morph: Common noun X2, both CR;
      source possessive, error plural; 2-infl X2.

OC-51   3;4.0   OB: (asking another child if she is imitating him on an art
          project) 'Are yòu making **mìne** . . . yòurs like *míne?*'
      ('mine' [maˑn] anticipated, substituted for 'yours' [jɚz]; SC)
      Phon: 1.5, +T(s).   Lex: Personal pronouns X2.
      Sem: Honors case (possessive), number (singular); violates person.
      Other: Environment, self.

AL-131   3;4.18   M: 'I hèar a chícken.'
          Al: 'I hèar **tòo** chì? . . . I hèar ă chìcken *tóo!*'
      ('too' [tʰu] anticipated, substituted for 'a' [ʌ]; [-sem]; SC)
      Phon: 1.5, +T(s).   Lex: Determiner (indefinite article) vs. adverb.

AN-116   3;7.24   An: 'Thàt's hòw you flàsh the **éye** in your . . . thàt's hòw
          you flàsh the lìght in your *èye.*'
      ('eye' [aˑ] anticipated, substituted for 'light' [laˑt]; [-sem]; SC)
      Phon: 3, +T(e).
      Lex/Morph: Common noun X2, both CRS in this context; mono X2.
      Other: Environment, looking at Mom's eye when she made the error.

AL-157 3;8.9   An: 'Alice, yòu don't lìke the stéw that I màke?'
                 Al: 'Yeah, **it** líkes *it* . . . I̲ lìke it.'
('it' [ɪt] anticipated, substituted for 'I' [aʲ], with verb agreement shift;
SC; p. 422, 459)
Phon: 1.5, -T.   Lex: Personal pronoun X2.
Sem: Honors case (subject), number (singular); violates person.

B-152   3;8.14   M: 'Whén are you gònna gìve me a kìss?'
                 B: (kisses Mom, then says) 'Tomórrow I'm gonna gìve **a**
                     kiss . . . gìve y̲o̲u̲ *a kìss* agáin.'
(anticipation of NP 'a kiss', but with unstressed intonation of 'you';
probable metathesis of 'you' with 'a kiss' [ju ʌ kʰɪs], or phrase blend
with 'give a kiss to you'; SC)
Phon: -T.
Other: Collocation 'give a kiss to . . .'

B-156   3;8.16   B: 'I'm gònna gèt some **hànds** on my . . . some w̲à̲t̲e̲r̲ on
                    my **hánds**.'
('hands' [hænd(z)] anticipated, substituted for 'water' [wá.ɾɚ]; note
that 'hands' carries plural morpheme with it; [-sem]; SC; p. 263, 411,
425, 439)
Phon: 0.5, +T(s).
Lex/Morph: Common noun X2, mass vs. CRP; mono vs. infl.
Other: Environment, child looking at his hands.

OC-76   3;11.24 OB: (his Daddy is sick and is using OB's cup)
                     'Dàddy got **my** . . . got h̲i̲s̲ gèrms on *my* cúp.'
('my' [maʲ] anticipated, substituted for 'his' [hɪz]; SC)
Phon: 1.5, -T.   Lex: Personal pronoun X2.
Sem: Honors case (possessive modifier), number and gender
(singular, masculine); violates person.
Other: Environment, self.

OC-83   4;0.18   M: (buying yogurt) 'I'll get pèach for Dáddy.'
                 OB: 'Yeah, **pèach** líkes . . . h̲è̲ líkes **pèach**.'
('peach' [pʰitʃ] anticipated, substituted for 'he' [hi], although it could
be A/P; also possible phrase blend with something like 'Peach is his
favorite'; [-sem]; SC; p. 271)
Phon: 3, -T.   Lex: Common noun vs. pronoun.

B-227a 4;2.28   D: 'I fixed the zípper.'
     M: 'Oh, on his jácket?'
     B: 'Yeah, 'cuz **my** [dʒæ̀.pɚ] . . . the zìpper came òff **my** bìg jácket.'
(anticipation of phrase 'my jacket', with 'my' [maʲ] substituted for 'the' [d̥ʌ] and blend of 'zipper/jacket'; B-227b=Class 38; [-sem]; SC)
Phon: 1.5, -T.
Lex: Determiner X2 (possessive pronoun vs. definite article), both definite.
Other: Environment, self.

OC-96 4;3.9   M: 'Your sócks are ìnside-òut.'
     OG: 'Do they belóng **òut-** . . . ìnside-**òut**?'
(sounded like she started to say 'òutside-ín'; 'out' [aʷt] anticipated, substituted for stem 'in' [ɪn] in 'inside'; could be A/P; SC)
Phon: 1.5, -T.
Lex: Preposition X2 (one is part of a compound).
Sem: Binary antonyms (of location), opposed.

OC-102 4;4.2   OB: 'Go **wáy** . . . go thát **wày**, and gèt Nìcholas and Chrístopher.'
(probable interrupted metathesis of 'that' [ðæt] with 'way' [weʲ]; SC)
Phon: +T(t1).

OC-104 4;4.9   OB: (a different child had told an adult his own age, but said the wrong age; OB said to the adult, referring to the other child) 'Í knòw how **hè** . . . Í knòw how òld **he** ìs, and hè's jùst kídding.'
(probable interrupted metathesis of 'old' [oʷɫd] with 'he' [hi]; SC)
Phon: -T.

OC-110 4;5.12   OB: 'Know whát? Òne **dùck** . . . òne dày when Ì was àt my hóuse, my nèighbor sàw a **dùck** hàve an égg come òut of her stòmach.'
('duck' [dʌk] anticipated, substituted for 'day' [deʲ]; [-sem]; SC; p. 268)
Phon: 3, -T.
Lex/Morph: Common noun X2, both CRS; mono X2.

AN-215 4;6.0   M: (looking at a photo) 'I wònder why Gràndma lòoks so
                        ángry?'
                   An: 'Màybe she dòesn't wànt her **táke?** . . . her p̆icture
                        tàken.'
(anticipation of 'taken'; sounded like she started to say 'her táken
p̀icture', which would make this an interrupted metathesis of 'picture'
[pʰík.tʃɚ] with 'taken' [tʰéⁱ.k(ən)]; SC; p. 223, 227)
Phon: +T(t1).
Other: Collocation, 'to take one's picture'; possibly phrase blend with
this phrase.

OC-115 4;7.0   OG: (discussing an unfriendly classmate)
                        'She won't even sĭt me . . .
                        lèt me **sĭt** nèxt to her dùring réading t̀ime.'
('sit' [sɪt] anticipated, substituted for 'let' [lɛt]; possible phrase blend
with 'she won't even sit next to me'; [-sem]; SC; p. 452)
Phon: 2.5, -T.
Lex/Morph: Verb X2, transitive vs. intransitive, both irregular, stem
form; mono X2.

B-352 4;8.15   B: (telling Mom about a movie he had been watching
                        earlier) 'Well, ya knòw what **thĕse** áre? Thère are
                        thĕse róbots? And they gràbbed the pr̆incess? (etc.)'
('these' [d̪iz] anticipated, substituted for 'there' [d̪ɛr], as his intended
utterance was 'ya know what there are?', i.e. existential, not deictic,
since he wasn't watching the movie when he made the utterance;
also the lack of stress on 'these' implies he meant the existential;
NSC; p. 271)
Phon: 3, -T.
Lex: Demonstrative vs. existential.
Sem: Shared criterial features (deixis, location in space or
existence).

B-357 4;8.27   B: 'We párked in sòme of . . . in frònt of sòmebody.'
(stem 'some' [sʌm] from 'somebody' anticipated, substituted for
'front' [fɹʌnt]; [-sem]; SC; p. 409)
Phon: 3, -T.
Lex: Adverb vs. adjective (one is part of a compound).

B-361   4;9.11   B: ('reading' story about the Ninja Turtles, whose pizza
                         party has been cancelled; there is a picture of pizza on
                         the page) 'Well, so mùch for a pízza, a pìzza with . . .
                         so mùch for a párty, a pàrty with pízza.'
('pizza' [pʰít.sʌ] anticipated, substituted for 'party' [pʰár.ɾi] in both
'party' slots; SC; p. 287, 317, 361)
Phon: 3.5, +T(b).
Lex/Morph: Common noun X2, both CRS in this context; mono X2.
Sem: Member/set ('pizza' is an indispensible member of 'party'
scene for this child).
Other: Environment, picture of pizza visible.

B-367   4;9.17   B: (pointing to rings on a stacking toy in a picture book,
                         naming the color of each as he points to it; the top,
                         smallest ring is red, then the color order is yellow,
                         green, and the largest on the bottom is blue)
                         'Rèd, blùe . . . I mean . . . Rèd, yèllow, grèen, and
                         blúe.'
(substitution of 'blue' [blu] for 'yellow' [jɛ́.loʷ]; either anticipated, or
a simple lexical selection error; SC)
Phon: 0.5, +T(s) (note that even though this is list intonation, 'blue'
takes the tonic in the list because it is the largest, most salient, and
last of the rings).
Lex/Morph: Adjective X2; mono X2.
Sem: Co-hyponyms (kinds of color).
Other: Environment, the blue ring was visible and the most salient
ring.

B-374   4;9.21   B: 'Anna, can I plèase òne of . . . can I plèase hăve òne
                         of those béach bàlls?'
(anticipation of phrase 'one of'; possibly a metathesis, or an
omission of the word 'have', or a phrase blend with 'can I hàve òne
of'; SC)
Phon: -T.

AN-247 4;10.5   An: 'Àli put her mòuth over her . . . Àli put her hànd over
                         her móuth when she còughed.'
('mouth' [mæʷθ] anticipated, substituted for 'hand' [hænd]; SC;
p. 223, 347, 449)
Phon: 1.5, +T(s).
Lex/Morph: Common noun X2, both CRS (child regularized plural of
mouth); mono X2.
Sem: Co-partonyms ('mouth' and 'hand' are parts of the body).

B-414   4;11.10   B: (telling Mom about a party he wants to have)
'We're gònna pláy, and eàt móv? . . . wàtch móvies,
and èat pópcòrn.'
('eat' [it] anticipated, substituted for 'watch' [watʃ]; [-sem]; SC;
p. 455)
Phon: 1.5, -T.   Lex/Morph: Verb X2, both transitive, regular/
irregular, infinitive; mono X2.

B-419   4;11.16   B: 'Hòw do you sqùare . . . hòw do you tie a squáre
knòt?'
('square' [skwɛr] anticipated, substituted for 'tie' [tʰaʲ]; 'squre-knot' is
possibly a compound; [-sem]; SC)
Phon: 1.5, +T(s).   Lex/Morph: Verb vs. common noun (possibly
part of a compound); mono X2.

AN-264   5;0.20   An: (wanting to make a skirt) 'You just sèw me . . .
you just tèll me how to dó it, and I'll séw it.'
('sew' [soʷ] anticipated, substituted for 'tell' [tʰɛɫ]; possible influence
from 'show', which is semantically appropriate in this slot; [-sem];
SC; p. 456)
Phon: 1.5, +T(s).   Lex/Morph: Verb X2, both transitive, regular/
irregular, imperative; mono X2.

B-436   5;0.25   B: (Bobby had a sore in his mouth) 'Mommy, whèn it
chéws, it . . . whèn I chéw, it húrts.'
('it' [ɪt] anticipated, substituted for 'I' [aʲ], with verb agreement shift;
SC; p. 28, 422)
Phon: 1.5, -T.   Lex: Personal pronoun X2.
Sem: Honors case (subject), number (singular); violates person,
gender.

AN-273   5;1.30   An: 'Mom, can wè tàke a [nɛ?] . . . can wè tàke a wàlk
with Naómi àfter dìnner?'
('Naomi' [ne.jóʷ.mi] anticipated, substituted for 'walk' [wak]; Naomi
is over visiting; possibly phrase blend with 'take Naomi on a walk;
[-sem]; SC)
Phon: 0, +T(s).
Lex/Morph: Proper noun vs. common noun; mono X2.
Other: Environment, Naomi was visible when child was speaking.

B-542   5;7.3   B: 'Whàt is the **mòst** thing that I líke in the wòrld?'
(for 'Whàt is the thìng that I lìke móst in the wòrld?'; movement/
addition of 'most', with tonic stress shifting to 'like'; possibly phrase
blend with 'What is the best thing that I like in the world'; NSC;
p. 223)
Phon: +T(s).

B-545   5;7.5   B: 'We're **gòodin'** . . . we're <u>dòin'</u> **góod.**'
('good' [gʊd] anticipated, substituted for 'do' [du], stranding
progressive suffix; [-sem]; SC; p. 223, 271)
Phon: 1.5, +T(s).
Lex: Verb vs. adverb (i.e. 'good' as a manner adverb).

AL-248   5;7.19   Al: 'Hòw do you **Jà?** . . . hòw do you <u>plày</u> "**Jácks**"?'
(probable interrupted metathesis of 'play Jacks'; 'Jacks' is a game;
SC)
Phon: +T(t2).

OC-158   5;7.27   OB: 'Mom, when I get bàck from tàking **Jèsse** . . . from
tàking <u>Aàron</u> to **Jésse<u>'s</u>** hòuse, can I pàint my Brío
tràck?'
('Jesse' [dʒé.si] anticipated, substituted for 'Aaron' [ɛ́.rʌn], stranding
possessive suffix; Aaron is OB's big brother, and Jesse is Aaron's
best friend; 'Brio' is a kind of wooden toy train set; SC)
Phon: 3.5, +T(s).   Lex: Proper noun X2.
Sem: Co-members of set (older boys, closely affiliated with child);
opposed.

42. Lexical anticipations, affixes.

AL-11   2;2.5   Al: 'Búbble-gùm. Twó bùbble**s**- . . . gùm__. Twó
bùbble-gùm<u>s</u>.'
(for 'bubble-gums' [bʌ́.bəɫ gʌm(z)]; plural suffix {-s} anticipated/
moved from 'gums', added to 'bubble'; SC; p. 306, 402, 405, 458)

AN-69   2;9.16   An: 'Mòm, whàt are you dóing?'
M: 'I'm wòrking on a tést rìght nòw. Do yòu know whàt a
tést ìs?'
An: 'It**s** mèan__ you gò to schóol.'
(for 'it means' [ɪt min(z)]; 3rd sg. present tense suffix {-s}
anticipated/moved from 'means', added to pronoun 'it' [ɪt(s)];
devoiced after [t]; NSC; p. 390)

AL-62   2;10.19   Al: 'Mom, this [wɪgz.əɬ__] mè aróund.'
(for 'wiggles' [wɪ́.gəɬ(z)]; 3rd sg. present tense suffix {-s}
anticipated/moved from end of word to middle, as if 'wig' were the
stem; NSC; p. 379, 406)

B-183   4;1.0   B: ' . . . and whèn she [óʷpS.ən__] ìt . . . whèn she ópens
ìt, (etc.)'
(for 'opens' [óʷ.pən(z)]; 3rd sg. present tense suffix {-s} anticipated/
moved from end of word to middle, as if 'op' were the stem;
devoiced after [p]; SC; p. 406)

B-203   4;1.28   B: 'I rèally hàve the [híkS.ʌp__] . . . híccups todày.'
(for 'hiccups' [hík.ʌp(s)]; plural suffix {-s} anticipated/
moved from end of word to middle, as if 'hic' were the
stem; SC; p. 406)

B-281   4;5.10   B: (telling Mom about TV show)
' . . . Mrs. Pènnypacker tùrned into Lìttle Rèd RìdingS
Hòod__ . . . um . . . Grándmòther!'
(for 'Riding Hood's' [rá.dɪŋ hʊd(z)]; possessive suffix {-s}
anticipated/moved from 'Hood's', added to 'Riding'; N-NC)

B-397   4;10.30   B: (complaining about a boat ride he was forced to take)
'I nèver líke bòatS rìde__ . . . bòat rìdes.'
(for 'boat rides' [boʷt ra͡id(z)]; plural suffix {-s} anticipated/moved
from 'rides', added to 'boat' [boʷt(s)]; devoiced after [t]; 'bóat-rìdes'
possibly a compound; SC; p. 24)

B-492   5;4.20   B: (reporting what he did on Christmas Day)
'I wènt downstàirs and [òʷpt.ən__] our présents.'
(for 'opened' [óʷ.pən(d)]; past tense marker {-ed} anticipated/moved
from end of 'opened' into middle of word, as if 'op' were the stem,
then devoiced next to [p]; NSC; p. 406)

B-583   5;11.23   B: (talking about computer games) 'Dòn't you knòw that
ònly óne ofS 'em__ . . . óne of 'em's hàrd?'
(for 'one of 'em's' (i.e. them is) [wʌn ʌv əm(z)]; contracted copula
{-s} anticipated/moved from 'em's', added to 'of'; SC; p. 403)

43. Lexical perseverations, content and function words (substitutions, additions).

AN-10   1;8.15   An: (pointing to pictures in a book, which included a kitty and cookies)
'Here's a *kìtty*-cat, dòggies, kìt . . . còokies, cáke.'
(started to substitute 'kitty' [kʰí.ti], perseverated from own utterance, for 'cookies' [kʰú.ki(z)]; possibly would have said 'kitties' [kʰí.ti(z)]; [-sem]; SC; p. 56, 78, 462)
Phon: 4.5; list intonation.
Lex: Common noun X2, both CR; singular/plural unclear.
Other: Environment, kitties visible on page.

B-26   1;11.6   M: (Mom lifts Bobby up and puts him on the changing table; Bobby always requested that the light be turned on over the changing table as part of the diaper changing routine)
'Come òn, let's gèt your *díaper* òn.'
B: (pointing at light over changing table)
'Díaper òn . . . líght òn.'
('diaper' [táʲ.pʊ] perseverated, substituted for 'light' [wáᵗt]; [-sem];
2-word stage; SC; p. 56, 78, 302, 304, 461)
Phon: 2, +T(b).
Lex/Morph: Common noun X2, both CRS; mono X2.
(Note: while not semantically related, 'diaper' and 'light' were related for this child in the context of the diaper-changing event, since he always requested that the light be turned on when the event began)
Other: Environment, both diaper and light visible.

AN-26a 2;1.23   An: (chanting a nursery rhyme)
'*Mòmmy* càlled the dóctor and the *Mòmmỳ* [kʰέd]
. . . Mòmmy [kʰὲl.də] dóctor and the dòctòr sáid,
Mòmmy càlled the dóctor and the dòctòr sáid:
Nò mòre mónkeys jùmpin' òn the béd!'
('Mommy' [má.mi] perseverated, substituted for 'doctor' [dák.t3]; SC;
AN- 26b=Class 12; AN-26c=Class 5; p. 21, 426)
Phon: 3.5, -T.
Lex/Morph: Proper noun vs. common noun; mono X2.
Sem: Co-members a of set (adults who care for child).
Other: Environment, child's Mommy is visible at time of utterance.

AN-29 2;2.3 An: (chanting nursery rhyme)
'Thrèe lìttle **mónkeys** jùmpin' òn the béd,
Mòmmy càlled the **mónkey**, ànd the **mònkèy** . . .
Mòmmỳ . . . Mómmy?'
M: 'What?'
An: (goes on to tell Mom something else, forgets poem)
(for 'Mòmmy càlled the dóctor, and the dòctòr sáid'; 'monkey'
[mʌ́ŋ.ki] perseverated, substituted for 'doctor' [dák.t3] twice; plural
stranded; [-sem]; N-NC; p. 416)
Phon: 2.5, +T(b).
Lex: Common noun X2, both CR; source plural, error singular.

AL-14 2;2.12 M: 'Only **bábies** need bòttles!'
Al: (looks around for her bottle, and says)
'Mý **bàby** . . . nò . . . mý bòttle!'
('baby' [béʲ.bi] perseverated, substituted for 'bottle' [bá.toʷ]; plural
stranded; SC; p. 85, 306)
Phon: 3.5, +T(s).
Lex: Common noun X2, both CR; source plural, error singular.
Sem: Metonymic (babies and bottles are typically spatially
contiguous).

AN-39 2;3.26 M: (talking about Anna to Daddy)
'She's gòne to **gèt** a bóok.'
An: 'I wànt a **gèt** . . . a rèad "Dúmbo"!'
('get' [gɛt] perseverated, substituted for 'read' [ʒid]; 'a' is filler
function morpheme; [-sem]; SC; p. 223)
Phon: 1.5, -T.
Lex/Morph: Verb X2, both transitive, irregular, infinitive; mono X2.

AL-27 2;4.23 Al: '**Dàddy**, mè wàtching **Dàddy** cóoking . . . nò . . .
Mómmy's còoking.' (laughs)
('Daddy' [dǽ.di] perseverated, substituted for 'Mommy' [má.mi]; SC;
p. 13, 274, 276)
Phon: 3, -T.   Lex/Morph: Proper noun X2; mono X2.
Sem: Co-members of a set (parents); opposed.
Other: Environment, both parents visible.

OC-24 2;6.19 OB: 'Thìs is a **píll** bòx. Open the **pìll** . . . bòx líd.'
('pill' [pʰil] perseverated, substituted for 'box' [baks]; SC)
Phon: 1.5, +T(s).
Lex/Morph: Common noun X2, both CRS; mono X2.
Sem: Metonymic (in the context of pill box, the pills are in the box).

B-92   2;7.2   M: (after finishing a jigsaw puzzle with Bobby)
'You can tàke it **apàrt** and pùt it bàck in the bóx if you wànt.'
B: 'Nò, I wànna lèave it **apárt**.'
M: 'You wànna lèave it togéther?'
B: 'Yéah.'
('apart' [ə.pʰárt] perseverated, substituted for 'together' [tʰʊ.gɛ́.ðɔ̃3], NSC; p. 324, 353)
Phon: 1, +T(e).   Lex/Morph: Adjective X2; mono X2.
Sem: Binary antonyms (cohesion), opposed.

B-124   3;1.25   M: 'Bobby, I'm gònna **pìck** you úp and pùt you awáy.'
B: 'No! Dón't **pìck** me awày . . . pùt me awày.
I'm gonna pùt away yóu!'
('pick' [pʰɪk] perseverated, substituted for 'put' [pʰʊt], SC; p. 264, 347)
Phon: 3, -T.   Lex/Morph: Verb X2, both transitive, regular/ irregular, infinitive; mono X2 (although both are lexicalized as particle verbs: 'pick up' and 'put away').
Sem: Synonyms (activities of cleaning up, since Mom was joking about 'cleaning up' Bobby; also possibly co-partonyms of 'cleaning up' scene).

AN-106   3;3.1   An: (playing with baby doll; says to Mom)
'Nòw **Bàby** wànts to trỳ to tálk. Would yòu get [béʲ.b] . . . would yòu get Álice to tàlk to hèr?'
('Baby' [béʲ.bi] perseverated, substituted for 'Alice' [ǽ.lʌs]; Alice was 1;11; SC)
Phon: 2, +T(e).   Lex/Morph: Proper noun X2; mono X2.
Sem: Shared criterial features (both Alice and doll are 'babies' in different contexts).
Other: Environment, 'Baby' is visible.

AL-111   3;3.25   M: (as we leave someone's house after dinner)
'Well, Alice, dòn't lèave **your** brúsh.'
Al: 'OK, Ì won't lèave **your** brúsh . . . Ì won't lèave my brúsh.'
('your' [j3] perseverated, substituted for 'my' [maʲ]; SC; p. 264)
Phon: 1.5, -T.   Lex: Personal pronouns X2.
Sem: Honors case (possessive modifiers), number (singular); violates person.
Other: Environment, addressee is 'your'.

AL-134   3;4.26   Al: 'I'm the kíd lìon: **Róar**! And Mòmmy's the Mómmy
                       ròar . . . the Mómmy lìon.'
('roar' [ɹoɹ] perseverated, substituted for 'lion' [láj.ʌn]; SC; p. 347)
Phon: 0.5, +T(s).   Lex/Morph: Interjection (animal noise) vs.
common noun (although 'roar' can be a noun); mono X2.
Sem: Metonymic (animal and its sound).

AL-144   3;6.28   Al: 'Thèy got a pìcture of a giráffe.'
                     M: 'Whó dòes?'
                     Al: '**Grámma**! She líkes **Gràmma**s . . . giràffes.'
('Gramma' [gɹæ.ma] perseverated, substitued for 'giraffe' [dʒɹ.ɹæf];
plural stranded; SC; p. 410, 416)
Phon: 3, +T(s).   Lex: Proper noun vs. common noun.
Sem: Metonymic (Gramma has large collection of giraffe statues
and artifacts, and so Alice associates Gramma with giraffes).

OC-55   3;7.15   OG: 'I'm **pèt**ting your háir.'
                    M: 'You are?'
                    OG: 'Yeah, so Ì won't pét it . . . púll it. So Ì won't púll it.'
('pet' [pʰɛt] perseverated, substituted for 'pull' [pʰʊɫ]; progressive
stranded; SC; p. 24, 408)
Phon: 3, +T(e).
Lex: Verb X2, transitive, regular; source progressive, error stem.
Sem: Co-hyponyms (activities of touching with the hand).

AN-131   3;11.7   An: 'Daddy, I'm rèady to gó. Í have **my** shòes on, and Áli
                       has **my** shòes on.'
                     M: 'Áli has your shòes on?'
                     An: 'No, I said **hér** shòes òn!' (laughs)
('my' [maj] perseverated, substituted for 'her' [hɚ]; NSC; p. 85)
Phon: 1.5, -T.   Lex: Personal pronoun X2.
Sem: Honors case (possessive modifier), number and gender
(singular feminine); violates person.
Other: Environment, self.

B-174   3;11.24   M: (Mom and Bobby had just come back from a walk)
                       'Bobby, it's time for you to take a **náp**.'
                     B: 'I wànna gò on anòther **náp**.'
(he meant 'walk'; substitute 'nap' [næp] for 'walk' [wak]; [-sem];
NSC; p. 264)
Phon: 1.5, +T(b).
Lex/Morph: Common noun X2, CRS (both deverbal); mono X2.

AN-147a 4;1.21   An: 'Sòmetimes I gèt to eàt pòpcorn at **Bárbara**'s hòuse,
and nòw I gèt to èat **Bàrbara** . . . I èat to gèt . . .
I gèt to eàt p<u>òpcorn</u> hére!'
('Barbara' [bár.brʌ] perseverated, substituted for 'popcorn'
[pʰáp.kʰorn]; possessive stranded; [-sem]; SC; AN-147b=Class 45)
Phon: 3.5, +T(s).   Lex: Proper noun vs. common noun.

AN-152 4;1.27   M: (Anna and Mom looking at a picture book, discussing
donkeys) 'I wònder whère we could sèe a dónkey.'
An: 'At the **zóo**?'
M: 'I dòn't think there are any dònkeys at óur **zòo**.'
An: 'Um . . . at fárms they have z<u>òos</u>.'
M: 'You mean at fàrms they have d<u>ónkeys</u>?'
An: 'Yeah.'
('zoos' [zu] perseverated, substitued for 'donkey' [dáŋ.ki]; plural
stranded; NSC; p. 268, 322, 361)
Phon: 0.5, +T(s).
Lex: Common noun X2, both CR; source singular, error plural.
Sem: Set/member (a 'zoo' is made up of a set of animals, including
'donkeys' sometimes).

B-248   4;4.0   D: (commenting on Bobby's hair, after Bobby wore a cap
all day) 'Bòb, your hàir **lòok**s góod tonìght.'
B: 'Yeah, my **lòok**<u>'s</u> . . . my h<u>àir's</u> stìcking úp tonìght.'
('looks' [lʊk(s)] perseverated, substituted for 'hair's' [hɛr(z)]; [-sem];
SC; p. 435)
Phon: 1.5, -T.
Lex/Morph: Verb vs. common noun; 2-infl X2; note that both end in
{-s}, but one is the 3rd sg. present tense suffix, and the other is
the contracted auxiliary 'be'; probably just stems 'look' and 'hair'
were involved.

B-263   4;4.15   B: '**Gràmma,** thìs is hís **Gràmma** . . . no wait, thìs is hís
gr<u>àbber</u>, and (etc.)'
('Gramma' [grǽ.ma] perseverated, substituted for 'grabber' [grǽ.bɚ];
a 'grabber' is a kind of toy; [-sem]; SC; p. 410)
Phon: 6, -T.
Lex/Morph: Proper noun vs. common noun; mono vs. 2-deriv
(instrumental {-er}).
Other: Environment, child is speaking to Gramma, who is visible.

AN-176 4;4.22   M: (Anna is playing with a cookie)
                     'Are you gonna éat it, or just pláy **with** it?'
                 An: 'Eát **with** ìt.'
                 M: 'Whát did you sày?'
                 An: 'I said "Eát with ìt".' (grins)
                 M: 'Whàt did you méan?'
                 An: 'Eát ìt!'
('with' perseverated and added betwen 'eat' and 'it'; NSC)
Phon: -T.
Other: Collocation, 'eat with X.'

AN-193 4;5.5   An: (writing as she talks)
                     'You can wrìte '**Cát**' with a '**Càt**' or a 'Ḱ'.'
('cat' [kʰæt] perseverated, substituted for letter 'C' [si]; NSC; p. 361)
Phon: 1.5, +T(s).
Lex/Morph: Common noun X2, both CRS; mono X2.
Sem: Whole/part (letter 'C' is part of the spelling of 'CAT').

B-338a 4;7.18   B: '**Mómmy**?! My **Mòmmy** sàys . . . my [tʰʌ.mɪk] sàys
                     . . . my <u>stòmach</u> sàys "I'm húngry".'
('Mommy' [má.mi] perseverated, substituted for 'stomach' [stʌ.mɪk];
[-sem]; SC; B-338b=Class 22; p. 277)
Phon: 2.5, +T(s).
Lex/Morph: Proper noun vs. common noun; mono X2.
Other: Environment, Mommy visible.
Other: Collocation, 'My Mommy says X'.

B-340 4;7.22   M: (asking Bobby if he brought anything for "Show and
                     Tell Day") 'Did yòu bring ànything to **shów**?'
                 B: 'Nò, it's nòt my **shów**. (pause) It's nòt my <u>dáy</u>.'
('show' [ʃoʷ] perseverated, substituted for 'day' [deʲ]; [-sem]; SC)
Phon: 1.5, +T(b).
Lex/Morph: Common noun X2, both CRS; (although 'show' is a verb
in the source utterance, it is a noun in the error); mono X2.
Other: Collocation, "Show and Tell Day".

B-373 4;9.19   B: (putting pieces into a puzzle)
                     'Hey, thís mìght **be** ìt. Thát mìght **be** gò in thère.'
('be' perseverated, added between 'might' and 'go'; could be phrase
blend; NSC; p. 223)
Phon: -T.
Other: Collocation, 'that might be X.'

B-378a 4;10.8   B: (discussing relationships among colors, had just told
                    Mom what **dárk** blue and líght blue were) 'Mom,
                    dàrk grèem is . . . um . . . l̲i̲g̲h̲t̲ grèen is yéllow.'
        ('dark' [dark] perseverated, substituted for 'light' [laⁱt]; SC; B-378b=
        Class 12; p. 353)
        Phon: 1.5, -T.   Lex/Morph: Adverb X2; mono X2.
        Sem: Gradable antonyms (intensity of color); opposed.

B-387   4;10.19 B: (telling Mom about yo-yo toy) 'And you pùsh it
                    dówn, and it còmes **dówn** . . . it còmes b̲à̲c̲k̲ úp.'
        ('down' [dæʷn] perseverated, substituted for '(back) up' [ʌp], with
        'back' added in correction; SC)
        Phon: 1.5, +T(b).   Lex/Morph: Adverb X2; mono vs. 2-cmpd.
        Sem: Gradable antonyms (vertical motion); opposed.

B-404   4;11.4   B: (to Mom) 'Yòu sàid "Did you brush **your** téeth?",
                    and I wènt in thère and I brùshed **your** . . . m̲y̲ téeth.'
        ('your' [jɚ] perseverated, substitued for 'my' [maʲ]; SC)
        Phon: 1.5, -T.   Lex: Personal pronoun X2.
        Sem: Honors case (poss. mod.), number (singular); violates person.
        Other: Environment, addressee is 'your'.

B-407   4;11.6   B: 'Mom, do wè have any óld bològna?'
                    M: 'No, you'll hàve to òpen some **néw**.
                        But that's OḰ, that's a góod snàck.'
                    B: (runs into kitchen, says to Nanny) 'Sèe, I tóld ya we
                        dòn't hàve any **nèw** . . . we dòn't hàve any ò̲l̲d̲
                        bològna.'
        (because he's not supposed to open a new package if there is still
        some left in an old, i.e. opened, package; 'new' [nu] perseverated,
        substituted for 'old' [oʷɫd]; SC; p. 348, 353)
        Phon: 1.5, +T(s).   Lex/Morph: Adjective X2; mono X2.
        Sem: Gradable antonyms (age); opposed.

OC-128 5;0.2   OB: (watching a cowboy show on TV; says to Mom)
                    'Sèe that **gùy** with a pátch on his èye?'
                    M: 'Yéah.'
                    OB: 'Hè's the **gúy** . . . hè's the h̲é̲r̲o̲.'
        ('guy' [gaʲ] perseverated, substituted for 'hero' [hí.roʷ]; SC; p. 30,
        347, 361)
        Phon: 0.5, +T(e).
        Lex/Morph: Common noun X2, both CRS; mono X2.
        Sem: Superordinate (a 'hero' is a kind of 'guy').

OC-129 5;0.3   M: 'How 'bout an **àpple**, òrange, or banána?
OB: 'Uh, a? [ǽp] . . . a <u>banána</u>.'
(started to substitute 'apple' [ǽ.pəɬ], perseverated from Mom's
utterance, for 'banana' [bə.nǽ.nə]; SC; p. 425)
Phon: 3, +T(b).
Lex/Morph: Common noun X2, both CRS; mono X2.
Sem: Co-hyponyms (kind of fruit).

OC-130 5;0.7   OB: (crying)
M: 'What's wróng?
OB: 'You didn't lèt **me** kíss **me**.'
M: 'I didn't whát?'
OB: 'Lèt me kíss <u>you</u>.'
('me' [mi] perseverated, substituted for 'you' [ju]; NSC)
Phon: 1.5, -T.
Lex: Personal pronoun X2.
Sem: Honors case (object), number (singular); violates person.
Other: Environment, self.

OC-134 5;0.19   OB: (after finishing a drawing of MegaMan, a superhero)
'Instèad of wrìting "*MégaMàn*" in the mìddle, I'm
gònna pùt "**Méga**" . . . I'm gònna pùt "<u>Séan</u>", 'cuz Ì
dráwed ìt.'
(started to substitute 'MegaMan' [mé.gə.mæ̀n], perseverated from
previous phrase for 'Sean' [ʃɔn], the child's name; [-sem]; SC)
Phon: 1, +T(b).
Lex/Morph: Proper noun X2; mono vs. 2-cmpd.
Other: Environment, looking at drawing of MegaMan.

B-437 5;0.27   B: 'Móm, this mòrning when I **wàtch**<u>ed</u> Inspèctor Gádget
when I rìght got úp, **wátch**! . . . <u>Gùess whát</u>!'
('watch' [wátʃ] perseverated, substituted for 'guess what' [gɛs wʌ́t];
past tense stranded; 'right' was not an error, as he was using it to
mean 'just' or 'first'; [-sem]; SC)
Phon: 1, +T(e).
Lex: Verb X2; both transitive, regular; source past tense, error
imperative.

B-453   5;1.20   B: (telling about a Nintendo game)
'And thère's this *dóg*? He càtches àll the **dógs** . . .
he càtches àll the <u>dúcks</u>.'

('dogs' [dag] perseverated, substituted for 'duck' [dʌk]; plural
stranded; SC)
Phon: 3, +T(b).
Lex: Common noun X2; both CR; source singular, error plural.
Sem: Co-members of a set (the set of of animals in this Nintendo
game; possibly also co-hyponyms, kinds of animals, but in this
context the words refer to elements of the Nintendo scene).

AN-276   5;2.2   M: 'Hey, you three kids, why don't you go in your room
and watch for Bàrbara out the wíndow. You can plày
with your **Bárbies** whìle you're wàiting.'
An: 'Nó!' (sees other two going into rooms) Àli and
Bàrbie . . . Àli and <u>Bòbby</u> will be the ònly ònes ín
thère!'

('Barbie' [bár.bi] perseverated, substituted for 'Bobby' [bá.bi]; plural
stranded; [-sem]; SC)
Phon: 6.5, +T(s).
Lex: Proper noun X2; source is plural, target and error are singular.

AN-279   5;2.12   M: 'Lòok at all the bìrds *flýing* abóve us!'
An: 'Àre they thís **flỳ**?' (holding arms above head)
M: 'What?'
An: 'Àre they thís <u>hìgh</u>?'

('fly' [f̥laʲ] perseverated, substituted for 'high' [haʲ]; progressive
stranded; NSC; p. 328, 353)
Phon: 3.5, -T.
Lex: Adjective vs. verb; source is progressive, target/error
uninflected.
Sem: Shared criterial features (upness).
Other: Collocation 'to fly high'.

OC-138   5;2.19   OG: (telling what her favorite gift would be from
Disneyland) 'Or còuld be a **pròb**? . . . could <u>pròbably</u>
be a T̂-shirt with Mìnnie Móuse òn it.'

('probably' moved from correct syntagmatic slot after 'could', added
to position after 'be a'; could also be a phrase blend; SC)
Phon: -T.
Other: Collocation, 'could be X'.

OC-151 5;6.10   An: 'I'm màking a **quìlt** squàre for Bàby Cásey.'
                  OG: 'How óld is Bàby [kʰw̥ɪ̥t̪.ti] . . . Bàby <u>Càsey</u>?'
('quilt' [kʰwɪ̥t̪t] perseverated, substituted for 'Casey' [kʰeⁱ.si], but
retaining the [i]; could be considered a stranding, except that the [-i]
on 'Casey' is not a suffix; possibly just phonological; [-sem]; SC)
Phon: 3.5, -T.
Lex: Proper noun vs. common noun.

B-531   5;6.11   B: (coloring a picture) 'The bèar's gònna **be** réd.
                      Ya knòw whý? 'Cùz I wánt ta **bè** 'im rèd.'
                  M: 'What?'
                  B: 'I wánt ta <u>còlor</u> 'im rèd.'
('be' [bi] perseverated, substituted for 'color' [kʰʌ.lɚ]; he was not
overgeneralizing 'be' this way in his normal speech, although this
could have been a phrase blend with 'I wánt him to bè rèd'; NSC;
p. 271, 328, 452)
Phon: 0.5, -T.
Lex/Morph: Verb X2, copula/transitive, irregular/regular, infinitive;
mono X2.
Sem: Causal (to 'color' the bear is to cause him to 'be red').

AL-251 5;7.28   M: 'Alice, dòn't jùmp aroùnd with **fóod** in your mòuth;
                      yòu could chóke.'
                  Al: (pointing to her mouth)
                      'I dòn't have ànything in my **fóod**.'
('food' [fud] perseverated, substituted for 'mouth' [mæʷθ]; NSC)
Phon: 1.5, +T(b).
Lex/Morph: Common noun X2, mass vs. CRS (child regularized
plural of 'mouth'); mono X2.
Sem: Metonymic (food commonly located in mouth).

B-553   5;8.13   M: (while putting Bobby's shoes on him)
                      'These **pánts** need to be ròlled ùp.'
                  B: (pulls up pant legs to show socks)
                      'Mòm, thése aren't just régular **pànts**. I mean thése
                      aren't just régular <u>sòcks</u>. Thèse are dìfferent cólors.'
('pants' [pʰænts] perseverated, substituted for 'socks' [saks]; SC;
p. 264)
Phon: 2.5, +T(s)
Lex/Morph: Common noun X2, CRP; 2-infl X2.
Sem: Co-hyponyms (kind of clothing, worn on lower part of body).
Other: Environment, both pants and socks visible.

Al-255 5;9.14   Al: (just discovered that the person who played Pinocchio
in a film she had seen was PeeWee Herman)
'*Pinòcchio* really díd be plàyed by **Pinòcchio**.'
('Pinocchio' [pʰə.nóʷ.ki.jòʷ] perseverated, substituted for 'PeeWee
Herman' [pʰíi.wi hɚ.mən]; [-sem]; NSC)
Phon: 3, -T.   Lex/Morph: Proper noun X2, mono vs. 2-cmpd,
assuming 'PeeWee' is one word.
(Note: could make a case that these two are metonymically related
in the context of this actor playing this character)

AN-317 5;9.27   An: (to Mom) 'Smèll my bándaid.'
M: 'It smèlls *like* a bándaid.'
An: 'It smells gróss!' (to Alice) 'Smèll **like** my bándaid
. . . smèll my bándaid.'
Al: 'It smèlls like a bándaid.'
('like' perseverated, added after 'smell'; SC)
Phon: -T.   Other: Collocation, 'smell like X'

44. Lexical perseverations, affixes.

AN-66 2;8.24   An: 'Do yòu know whère the thíng wènt?'
M: 'Whát thìng?'
An: 'The tòy that Àlice pláy__ wìth**ed**.'
(for 'played with' [pʰle(d) wɪθ]; past tense suffix {-ed} perseverated/
moved from 'played', added to 'with' [wɪθ(t)], devoiced after [θ];
NSC; p. 73, 419, 459)

AN-96 3;0.13   An: 'Ì got a bòok that__ jùst lìke'**s** Aústen's.'
(for 'that's just like' [ðæt(s) dʒʌst laɪk]; contracted copula {-'s}
perseverated/moved from 'that's', added to 'like' [laɪk(s)]; NSC)

AL-179 3;10.9   Al: 'In "Slèeping Béauty", the bàd wìtch's wìsh rèally
còme__ trúe**s**.'
(for 'comes true' [kʰʌm(z) tʰru]; 3rd sg. present tense {-s}
perseverated/moved from 'comes', added to 'true' [tʰru(z)]; NSC;
p. 397)

AL-186 3;10.25   Al: 'You còuld have gèt__ your tòen òut of the wáy.'
(for 'gotten your toe' [gá.t(ən) jɚ tʰoʷ]; perfect suffix {-en}
perseverated/moved from 'gotten', added to 'toe' and pronounced
[tʰó.w(ən)]; 'got' then reverts to stem 'get' [gɛt]; NSC; p. 403)

B-178   4;0.16   B: (wanting to go to the toy store)
'Dàddy, can wè go to Tòy__ R̀s . . . Tòy<u>s</u> R̀ Ús?'
(for 'Toys R Us' [tʰoⁱ(z) ar ʌs]; plural suffix {-s} perseverated/moved
from 'Toys', added to 'R' [ar(z)]; SC)

B-184   4;1.0   B: 'I wànna wèar my "Néw Kìd__" còats.'
(for 'New Kids coat' [nu kʰɪd(z) kʰoʷt], which is odd since he didn't
have one; plural suffix {-s} perseverated/moved from 'Kids', added
to 'coat' [kʰowt(s)], devoiced after [t]; 'New Kids (On The Block)' is
the name of a rock band; NSC)

B-233   4;3.4   B: (chanting nursery rhyme)
'Nò mòre mónkèy<i>s</i> jùmpin' òn the béd.
Òne lìttle mónkèys . . . Òne lìttle <u>mónkèy</u> jùmpin' òn
the béd.'
(plural suffix {-s} from 'monkeys' [mʌŋ.ki(z)] perseverated from first
sentence, added to 'monkey' in second sentence; SC)

AL-232 4;7.27   Al: 'Sòmebody mùst of tàke__ áll of 'èn . . .
tàk<u>en</u> áll of '<u>èm</u>.'
(for 'taken all of 'em' [tʰéⁱ.k(ən) ał əv əm]; perfect suffix {-en}
perseverated/moved from 'taken', substituted for abbreviated form of
'them' [əm]; possibly just phonological; SC; p. 398)

AN-240 4;9.15   An: (answering 'who is different' on "Sesame Street")
'The òne that__ reàding's the bóok! . . .
The òne that'<u>s</u> reàding the bóok!'
(for 'that's reading' [ðæt(s) rí.dɪŋ]; contracted auxiliary {-'s}
perseverated/moved from 'that's', added to 'reading' [rí.dɪŋ(z)],
voiced after [ŋ]; SC; p. 393)

AN-249 4;10.13 M: (sees Anna picking Bobby up) 'Ànna, pùt him dówn.'
An: 'I jùst was tàke__ cári**ng** of hìm.'
(for 'taking care' [tʰéⁱ.k(ɪŋ) kʰɛr]; progressive {-ing} perseverated/
moved from 'taking', added to 'care' [kʰɛ́.r(ɪŋ)]; SC)

B-391   4;10.22   B: (getting food out of cupboard when not supposed to be)

M: 'Whàt are you thínk*ing*?!'

B: 'I'm húngr**ing**!'

(for 'hungry' [hʌŋ.gri]; progressive {-ing} perseverated from 'thinking' [θíŋ.k(ɪŋ)], added to 'hungry', producing [hʌŋ.grɪŋ], with [-i] deleted; could be substitution of {-ing} for {-i}, but 'hungry' was probably monomorphemic for him; possibly just phonological; NSC)

AN-282   5;3.3   An: 'Well, if hè wànna pláy**s** . . . if hè wànt**s** ta pláy, he cán.'

(for 'wants to play' [wʌnt(s) tə pʰle͜ʲ]; 3rd sg. present tense {-s} perseverated/moved from 'wants', added to 'play' [pʰle͜ʲ(z)], voiced after vowel; when suffix is omitted from 'wants', the resulting sequence 'want__ to' is produced as the contracted form 'wanna' [wʌ́.nə]; SC; p. 403)

B-483   5;3.30   B: (talking about dinner) 'That means that I rèally rèally rèally one hùndred tìme**s** lóve**s** ìt!'

(plural {-s} from 'times' [tʰaˈm(z)] perseverated and added to 'love' [lʌv(z)]; could just be phonological, or selection of wrong form of verb, i.e. 3rd sg. present tense 'loves'; NSC)

45. Lexical reversals (non-contiguous), content words.

AN-57   2;7.22   An: 'Her **rún** is nòs*ing*.'

(for 'Her nóse is rùnning'; reversal of 'nose' [no͜ʷz] with 'run' [rʌn]; progressive suffix stranded; NSC; p. 224, 416, 440)

Phon: 1.5, +T(t1).   Lex: Verb vs. common noun.

Sem: Metonymic (functional relationship between 'nose' and 'run', in this particular sense).

AL-46   2;8.20   Al: 'Wow, my **cóld**s are **hànd**.'

M: 'What?'

Al: 'My **cóld** . . . my hànds are fréezing.'

(for 'my hands are cold'; reversal of 'hand' [hænd] with 'cold' [kʰo͜ʷld], with stranding of plural {-s}, producing 'colds' [kʰo͜ʷld(z)]; note change in phrasal prosody when 'freezing' is selected instead of 'cold' in repair; NSC; p. 31, 408, 412, 416)

Phon: 2.5, +T(t1).   Lex: Adjective vs. common noun.

Sem: Metonymic (functional relationship between body part and sensation).

AN-147b 4;1.21   An: 'Sòmetimes I gèt to eàt pòpcorn at Bárbara's hòuse,
                 and nòw I gèt to eat Bàrbara . . . I **èat** to **gèt** . . . I g<u>èt</u>
                 to e<u>àt</u> pòpcorn hére!'
          (for 'get to eat'; reversal of 'eat' [it] and 'get' [gɛt]; [-sem]; SC;
          AN-147a=Class 43)
          Phon: 2.5, -T.
          Lex/Morph: Verb X2, transitive, irregular, stem/infinitive form;
          mono X2.

OC-116 4;7.0   OG: (reporting on a trip to an equine museum)
                     'And wè saw the **dèad hòrse** of a **bónes**.'
                 D: 'You saw the bònes of a dèad hórse?'
                 OG: 'Yeah.'
          (reversal of 'dead horse' [dɛd hɔrs] with 'bones' [boʷn(z)]; plural suffix
          moves with lexical item 'bones', so ungrammatical with indefinite
          article 'a'; NSC; p. 323, 361, 411, 426, 439)
          Phon: 0.5, +T(t2).
          Lex/Morph: Common noun X2, CRS phrase vs. CRP; 2-different
          (2-infl vs. 2-cmpd).
          Sem: Whole/part (bones are part of the dead horse).

AN-231 4;8.0   An: 'Lóok, Mòm! A dòuble **jáck**<u>ing</u>-**jùmp**.'
                     (looks confused)
                 M: 'A júmping-jàck?'
                 An: 'Yeah.'
          (reversal of 'jump' [dʒʌmp] with 'jack' [dʒæk], stranding present
          participle suffix {-ing}; a 'jumping jack' is a kind of exercise
          movement; [-sem]; N-NC; p. 235, 241, 414)
          Phon: 3, +T(t1).
          Lex: Reversal of two content morphemes within compound noun.

B-537 5;6.24   B: (telling friend about video he rented)
                     'We gòt "The **Hàt** in the **Càt** Comes Báck". '
          (reversal of 'cat' [kʰæt] with 'hat' [hæt]; could also be phonological
          reversal of [h] and [kʰ]; NSC)
          Phon: 4, -T.
          Lex/Morph: Common noun X2, both CRS; in this context they are
          sub-parts of a proper noun phrase "The Cat in The Hat"; mono X2.
          Sem: Metonymic (in the story, the Cat is always wearing the Hat).

B-578   5;11.19   B: 'I can gò in the déep pàrt where **my hèad's** òver **the wáter**; wànna sée mè?'
M: 'You mean the wàter's òver your héad?'
B: 'Yeah.'
(reversal of NPs 'the water' with 'my head', with stranding of contracted copula {-'s}; [-sem]; NSC; p. 426)
Phon: 0.5, +T(t2).
Lex: Common noun (phrases) X2, mass vs. CRS.

46. Lexical reversals (non-contiguous), function words.

B-96   2;7.7   B: 'Mommy can **yóu** gò with **mè**?'
M: 'What?'
B: 'Can Í gò with yòu?'
(reversal of 1sg and 2sg pronouns 'I' [aʲ] vs. 'you' [ju], but with correct subject/object forms, such that 'I' becomes 'me' [mi]; NSC; p. 24, 232, 272, 423, 459)
Phon: 1.5, +T(t1).   Lex: Personal pronoun X2.
Sem: Honors number (singular), violates person, case.

B-159   3;8.17   B: 'Which táble **òn** they **àre** . . . òn?'
(reversal of 'are' [ar] and 'on' [an]; [-sem]; partially SC by reiterating 'on' at the end; p. 293)
Phon: 3.5, -T.   Lex: Preposition vs. verb (copula).

OC-145   5;5.0   OG: (after Mom covered her with a blanket in bed)
'You cóvered ìt with **mè** . . . you cóvered mè with ìt.'
(reversal of 'me' [mi] and 'it' [it]; SC; p. 224)
Phon: 1.5, -T.   Lex: Personal pronoun X2.
Sem: Honors case (object), number (singular); violates person.

47. Lexical metathesis (contiguous), content and function words.

AN-84   2;10.26   An: 'We got something for dessért. Knòw what is . . .
is ìt . . . it. . .'
M: 'Knòw what it ís?'
An: 'Knòw what it ís? Íce crèam!'
(metathesis of 'it is' [ɪt íz]; phrasal prosody remains intact; N-NC)
Phon: +T(t2).   Other: Collocation, 'What is X?'

AN-102 3;2.12   An: (reciting nursery rhyme) 'Cándlemàke-stìcker.'
(for 'cándlestìck màker' [kʰǽn.dəɫ.stìk.mèʲ.kɚ]; metathesis of two
content morphemes within compound, stranding agentive suffix
{-er}; compound stress remains intact; NSC; p. 44, 409, 414)

AN-103 3;2.13   An: (holding up something for Mom to see)
M: 'What is it?'
An: 'It's a **strìng pìnk**.'
M: 'A pìnk . . . you mean a pìece of thréad?'
An: 'Yeah.'
(metathesis of 'pink string' [pʰìŋk strín]; phrasal prosody moves with
words; NSC)
Phon: +T(t1).

B-168 3;9.24   B: (looking at sidewalk)
'I **sàw jùst** . . . I jùst sàw póopòo.'
(metathesis of 'just saw' [dʒʌ̀st sà:]; SC)
Phon: -T.

AN-134 3;11.21 An: '**Cléan-pìper**.'
(for 'pìpe-clèaner' [pʰáʲp.kʰḷ̀i.nɚ]; metathesis of content morphemes
within compound, stranding instrumental suffix {-er}; compound
stress remains intact; NSC; p. 44, 414)

AN-157 4;2.6   An: 'I thòught I wànted some sóup, but there **ány ìsn't** . . .
there ìsn't àny sòup lèft.'
(metathesis of 'isn't any' [íz.n̩t ìn.i]; phrasal prosody remains intact;
SC; p. 31, 44)
Phon: +T(t1).

B-217 4;2.14   B: 'How óld **I àm**? . . . How óld am Ì?'
(metathesis of 'am I' [ɪm àʲ]; phrasal prosody remains intact; SC)
Phon: -T.
Other: Collocation, '(That's) how old I am'.

B-222 4;2.23   B: 'Mom, thèy're not **éither hòme** . . . thèy're not hòme
éither.'
(metathesis of 'home either' [hòᵂm i.ðɚ]; phrasal prosody moves
with words; SC; p. 44)
Phon: +T(t2).

OC-107 4;5.0   OG: (with reference to beads)
　　　　　　　　　'What do you néed **for thèm** . . . néed them fòr?'
(metathesis of 'them for' [ðɛm fòr]; phrasal prosody remains intact;
SC; p. 224, 271)
Phon: -T.

B-320 4;7.3   B: (finding the page in his sticker book he was looking
　　　　　　　　　for) 'Hére ìs **it** . . . hére it ìs.'
(metathesis of 'it is' [ɪt ìz]; phrasal prosody moves with words; SC)
Phon: -T.
Other: Collocation, 'Here is X'

OC-146 5;5.0   OG: 'I have a bròken **náil-tòe** . . . oh, I mean tóe-nàil.'
(metathesis of two content morphemes in compound 'toe-nail';
compound stress remains intact; SC; p. 44)

AN-302 5;7.26   An: (talking about being on another planet) 'Even if we
　　　　　　　　　júmped, there would **nò bè** grávity to hòld us dòwn.'
(for 'be no' [bì nò*]; possibly phrase blend with 'not be', but more
likely she would contract to 'wouldn't'; NSC)
Phon: -T.

48. Syntactic errors with multiple error types involving words and morphemes.

B-87   2;6.24   B: (refused to take his bottle, so Mom said she would
　　　　　　　　　give it to Ross, his toy leopard) 'I don't wànt **it** for
　　　　　　　　　Róss! I don't wànt **it** Róss to drìnk **it**.'
(A/P addition of 'it'; NSC; possibly a phrase blend; p. 30)

AL-69 2;10.21 Al: 'That's a [skɛ̀.ʒən lʊ́.kɪd] wìtch, Mòm!'
(for 'scary lookin'' [skɛ́.ʒ(i) lʊ́.k(ən)]; present participal suffix {-ing}
[-ən] moved from 'looking', substituted for derivational {-y} on
'scary'; then 'look' gets past participle pronounced as [-ɪd] to replace
moved morpheme, possibly to maintain phrasal rhythm; NSC;
p. 390, 391, 398, 418, 421, 440)

AL-76 2;11.3   Al: 'I gòt some mòre tóys. My t̲è̲a̲c̲h̲e̲r̲ sàid *I cán*. My
            càn I . . . my tèacher sàid *I cán*.'
    (A/P substitution of 'I can' for 'teacher' [tʰi.tʃɜ], then metathesis of
    these two words; phrasal prosody moves with words, although note
    also that 'cán I' [kʰæ.naʲ] has the same stress pattern as 'téacher';
    SC; p. 193)

B-169 3;9.28   B: (choosing tokens for a board game)
            'Í wànna be grèen. Yòu **blúe bèes** . . . yòu b̲è̲ b̲l̲ú̲e̲.'
    (metathesis of 'be blue' [bì blú], with what appears to be the 3rd sg.
    present tense suffix added non-contextually to 'be' producing [bi(z)];
    phrasal prosody moves with words; SC; p. 34, 390, 395)

AL-190 3;11.6   Al: 'Héy, you guỳs. Could you pléase get **your wày òut
            of mè**!'
    (for 'could you pléase get òut of my wày' or 'get yoursèlves òut of
    my wày'; multiple lexical movements; possibly phrase blend; note
    accommodation of pronoun to correct case: 'me' vs. 'my'; NSC;
    p. 423)

B-225 4;2.25   B: (talking about a timer that was set) 'Whén **it bèep**?
            . . . Whén **it** . . . whén i̲s̲ i̲t̲ g̲ò̲i̲n̲g̲ t̲o̲ bèep?'
    (anticipation of 'beep', omission of 'is' and 'going to'; possibly phrase
    blend or telescoping, but too complex to clearly classify; SC)

OC-106 4;4.14   OB: 'Còme ón, lèt__ gò [tʰus: ʔnǽk] . . . lèt'̲s̲ gò to s̲n̲á̲c̲k̲.'
    ([s] for 'us' in 'let's' [lɛt(s)] deleted, possibly moved to end of 'to'; [s]
    from begining of 'snack' also moved to end of 'to', causing geminate
    [s]; glottal stop inserted into first onset slot of 'snack'; SC)

AL-214 4;4.19   Al: 'Mòmmy, my féver**ed** gòe**s** . . . my féver g̲ò̲e̲d̲ awày.'
    ([fi.v3(d) gòʷ(z)] for [fi.v3 gòʷ(d)]; anticipation/movement of past
    tense suffix from 'goed', added to 'fever', then 3rd sg. present tense
    suffix substituted for originally planned suffix on 'go'; 'goed' was
    normal for her at this time; SC; p. 390, 396, 403)

B-410 4;11.9   M: 'Whỳ don't you gò sèe if Chrís can plày.'
            B: '**He díd Chrìs**.'
            M: 'What?'
            B: 'Chrìs díd còme òver.' (Chris was in front yard)
    (possibly phrase blend with 'He did come over'; NSC)

AN-312 5;9.6   An: (talking about a character in a movie whose arms get
                   pulled until they are very long)
                   'He's the gùy that gèts his **lóngs àrms**.'
(probably for 'He's the guy that gets his árms lòng', but 'arm' and
long' are exchanged, and both get plural marking; NSC; p. 411)

49. *Syntactic phrase blends.*

AN-20 1;11.13   An: (pretenting to read a book aloud)
                     '**Whàt is Bèrt háppèn**, Bĕr . . . Bêrt, whàt háppèn?'
                     [wʌt ìz bɔ̃t hæ.pìn, bɔ̃ . . . bɔ̂, wʌt hæ.pìn]
                     (diacritics are pitch markers in this example)
                   T1: 'Whàt is Bèrt/ dóìng.' vs. T2: 'Whàt /háppèn, Bĕrt?'
                   (SC to third phrasing, 'Bêrt, whàt háppèn?; p. 56, 462, 471, 473,
                   478)
                   Type 1, competing lexical choices: 'doing' vs. 'happen(ed)' (possibly
                   'perspectives', Type 2).
                   Form: crossover, with intonation of T1 switching to T2.

B-37   2;1.13   B: (ready to walk to store)
                    'Mom, **Ì wànna góing** . . . Ì gòing tóo!'
                T1: 'Ì wànna/ gó!' vs. T2: 'Ì /gòing tóo!' (SC; p. 13. 471, 473, 477)
                Type 1, competing lexical choices: 'wanna go' vs. 'going too'.
                Form: mixed, crossover with deletion of 'too', intonation of T1.

B-49   2;3.10   B: 'Ì wànna **gèt my brúsh tèeth**.'
                M: 'What?'
                B: 'Ì wànna brùsh my téeth.'
                T1: 'Ì wànna gèt my téeth brùshed.' vs. T2: 'Ì wànna brùsh my
                téeth.' (NSC; p. 472, 473)
                Type 2, competing perspectives: passive 'get my teeth brushed' vs.
                active 'brush my teeth'.
                Form: mixed, syntactic and intonational form of T1 minus participle
                suffix on second verb 'brushed'; verb 'brush' and noun 'teeth' appear
                in T2 order.

B-68   2;5.31   M: 'Who's thére?'
           B: 'Ì'm ám! . . . Í àm.'
T1: 'Ì'm hére.' vs. T2: 'Í àm.' (SC; p. 472, 473, 479)
Type 3, competing expanded/contracted synonymous phrases, 'I (am)
here' vs. 'I am'.
Form: mislinking of predicate, 'am' for 'here'.

AN-62   2;8.0   M: 'Anna, did you èat your hám?'
           An: 'No, I'm tòo fínished . . . I'm jùst fínished.'
T1: 'Ì'm tòo/ fúll.' vs. T2: 'Ì'm jùst /fínished.' (SC; p. 477)
Type 1, competing lexical choices: 'just finished' vs. 'too full',
possibly competing perspectives, 'I'm finished' because 'I'm too full'.
Form: ambiguous, either mislinking of adverb, 'too' for 'just', or
crossover.

AN-78   2;10.10   An: (tells someone to 'Be quiet!', then says)
           'Yòu're not nóisy, yòu're jùst bè qúiet . . . yòu're jùst
           bèing qúiet.'
T1: 'yòu're jùst bèing qúiet.' vs. T2: 'Bè qúiet!' (possible
perseveration from her previous utterance; SC; p. 472, 478, 479)
Type 4, competing internal phrase organization: 'being quiet' vs. 'be
quiet'.
Form: internal phrase blend (be/being).

AL-71   2;10.25   M: 'Come ón; I'm trỳing to clèan this plàce úp!'
           Al: 'Ì won't lét you tò.'
           M: 'What?'
           Al: 'Ì don't . . . Ì won't lét you.'
T1: 'Ì won't lét/ you.' vs. T2: 'Ì don't wánt /you tò.'
(NSC; p. 25, 468)
Type 1, competing lexical choices: '(won't) let' vs. '(don't) want'.
Form: crossover.

AN-83   2;10.25   An: 'Daddy, would yoù please wìpe me mỳ nóse?
           Would yòu please wìpe me òn the nóse?'
T1: 'wìpe me/ òn the nóse?' vs. T2: 'wìpe /mỳ nóse?' (SC)
Type 3: competing expanded/contracted version of phrase 'wipe (my)
nose' and 'wipe (me) on the nose'.
Form: crossover.

AL-78a 2;11.9   Al: 'Nòbody [**sm:éʲkt**] **mè**.' (looks confused)
M: 'What?'
Al: 'Nòbody <u>màked me crý</u>.'
T1: 'Nòbody spánked me.' vs. T2: 'Nòbody màked me crý.'
(includes lexical blend of 'maked' and 'spanked'; AL-78b=(38);
N-NC; p. 246)
Type 2: competing perspectives: cause/effect, being 'spanked'
'makes' one cry.
Form: mislinking of verbs, 'maked' for 'spanked'.

OC-40   3;2.0   OG: (putting rubber bands over nails in a board to make a
design) 'Could **pùt** . . . could <u>thìs be hére</u>?'
T1: 'Could thìs be hére?' vs. T2: 'Could Ì pùt this hére?' (SC)
Type 2, competing perspectives: to 'put' is to cause to 'be at'.
Form: unclear, since error utterance was interrupted.

AN-114 3;5.21   M: 'Lòok what Í fòund: your nècklace we gòt at Lássen.'
An: 'Oh yéah! Ì wànt to wèar it thís dày. **I thòught I was
lóst** . . . <u>I thòught I lóst ìt</u>.'
T1: 'I thòught it was lóst.' vs. T2: 'I thòught I lóst ìt.'
(note that 'this day' was her usual way of saying 'today'; SC; p. 39,
474)
Type 2, competing perspectives: active vs. passive, 'I lost it' vs. 'It
was lost'.
Form: mislinking of pronoun, 'I' for 'it'.

AL-141 3;6.18   Al: 'Thìs is **gòing to where Bóbby's stàck**. (pause)
<u>Thìs is where Bóbby's stàck ìs</u>.'
T1: 'Thìs is gòing to be Bóbby's stàck.' vs. 'Thìs is where Bóbby's
stàck ìs.' (SC, p. 479)
Type 4, competing internal structures: 'going to be X' vs. 'where
X is'.
Form: internal phrase blend (be/is).

B-160   3;8.19   B: 'Ì **want gètting** a páper plàte.'
T1: 'Ì am gètting' vs. T2: 'I wànt to gèt' (NSC; p. 476)
Type 4, competing internal structures: 'am getting' and 'want to get'.
Form: internal phrase blend (getting/get).

OC-65 3;9.4 OG: 'But ǐf it còmes the ráin clòuds, we'll stày in hére.'
T1: ' ìf the ráin clòuds còme' vs. T2: ' ìf it ráins' (probably; targets unclear; NSC)
Type 2: competing perspectives; if 'the rain clouds come' then this causes 'it rains'.
Form: unclear, since actual targets unclear.

AL-168 3;9.4 Al: (discussing a rattle that a friend had given her)
'When ǐ was a báby, she gáve me ìt to mé.'
T1: 'she gáve me ìt/.' vs. T2: 'she gàve it /to mé.' (NSC; p. 470, 472, 475)
Type 5, competing external phrasal organization: placement of dative.
Form: crossover.

AN-140 4;0.17 An: 'Mòmmy, sìt dòwn thìs médiately.'
T1: 'sìt dòwn thìs/ mínute.' vs. T2: 'sìt dòwn im/médiately.'
(includes partial word-blend; NSC; p. 468)
Type 1, competing lexical choices: 'this minute' vs. 'immediately'.
Form: crossover.

AN-155 4;2.2 An: 'Momma, lòok what ǐ got at swímming lèssons: a scrápe. ǐt's blóod. (pause) ǐt's bléeding. It gòts blóod òn it.'
T1: 'ǐt's bléeding.' vs. T2: 'ǐt gòts blóod òn it.' ('it gots' is her usual phrasing; SC; p. 468)
Type 2, competing perspectives: active 'it's bleeding' vs. stative 'it gots blood on it'.
Form: internal phrase blend (blood/bleeding).

AN-156 4;2.4 An: (angry at Mom for taking the remote from her)
'You just tòok it [tʰu.wèʲ] . . . you just tòok it [tʰu.wèʲ] . . . (three more times; stops, takes deep breath) You jùst took it awày from mè to be méan.'
T1: 'You just tòok it tò/ be méan.'
T2: 'You just tòok it a/wày from mè to be méan.' (SC with much difficulty)
Type 3, competing expanded/contracted synonymous phrases, 'took it away from me' vs. 'took it'.
Form: crossover, with partial word blend.

AL-209a 4;2.16   Al: 'Mommy, **we gòt to sàw the [fî:n]** . . . <u>we sàw the fíre</u>
<u>èngine todày.</u>'
T1: 'We gòt to sèe the fíre èngine.' vs. T2: 'We sàw the fíre èngine'
(with a telescoping in 'fire engine'; AL-209b=(34); SC; p. 470)
Type 4, competing internal phrasal org.: 'got to see' vs. 'saw'.
Form: internal phrase blend (see/saw)

AN-173 4;4.7   M: (reading book) ' "Í'm not àngry!" '
An: **He lóoks like àngry.'** (looks confused)
M: 'He lóoks like he's àngry.'
An: 'Yeah, <u>he lóoks like he's àngry.</u>'
T1: 'He lóoks like/ he's àngry.' vs. T2: 'He lóoks /àngry.' (N-NC;
p. 469)
Type 3, competing expanded/contracted synonymous phrases: 'looks
angry' and 'looks like (he's) angry'.
Form: crossover.

B-257 4;4.7   B: 'I was gòing to shòot Shrèdder with some sléeping gàs.
Shhhhhh. **Hè's sléep.** (pause) <u>Hè's asléep.</u>'
T1: 'Hè's asléep.' vs. T2: 'He's sléeping.' (SC)
Type 4, competing internal phrasal organization: 'is asleep' vs. 'is
sleeping'.
Form: internal phrase blend, 'He's' and uninflected predicate slot
from T1, stem 'sleep' from T2 (sleep/asleep).

B-266 4;4.18   B: (Mom pouring milk in B's cereal)
'Mom, I dòn't have [ə] **vèry [nʌf]** mílk.'
M: 'What?'
B: 'I dòn't have <u>enòugh</u> mílk.'
T1: 'I dòn't have enòugh mílk.' vs. 'I dòn't have vèry mùch mílk.'
(NSC)
Type 1, competing lexical choices: 'enough' and 'very much'.
Form: mixed, 'very' inserted into the middle of the word 'enough'
[ə.nʌf].

AL-215 4;4.23   Al: **Nów how mùch it got scràmbled!** (pause)
<u>Lòok how mùch it got scrámbled!</u>'
T1: 'Nów/ (sèe/lòok at) how mùch it got scràmbled.' (unclear) vs.
T2: 'Lòok /how mùch it got scrámbled.' (SC)
Type 4, competing internal phrase organization: with different
lexical choices ('now') and different intonation, indicating different
pragmatic focus.
Form: unclear; possibly crossover, retaining intonation of T1.

AL-216 4;4.29   Al: (Mom told Alice she thought a piece was missing to Alice's puzzle and thought it might be in the wrong box; Alice looks through pieces in a different box and finds it) 'Yòu were ríght; there wás one **in mìssing** . . . there wás one <u>in thère</u>.'
T1: 'There wás one in/ thère.' vs. T2: 'There wás one /mìssing.' (SC)
Type 2, competing perspectives: negative 'missing' vs. positive 'in there'.
Form: crossover.

AN-186 4;5.2   An: 'Thère's **cráckers on the crùmbs.** (pause) Thère's <u>crácker crùmbs on the flòor</u>.'
T1: 'cráckers on the flòor.' vs. T2: 'crácker crùmbs on the flòor.' (SC; p. 411)
Type 3, competing expanded/contracted synonymous phrases 'crackers' vs. 'cracker crumbs'.
Form: mislinking of noun, 'crumb' for 'floor', but retains plural marking from T2.

AL-223 4;5.23   Al: 'Lóok, Mòmmy, flówers! I **could sáw** . . . I <u>sáw them</u>.'
T1: 'I could sée them.' vs. T2: 'I sáw them.' (SC)
Type 4, competing internal phrasal org.: 'I sáw' vs. 'I could sée'.
Form: internal phrase blend (see/saw).

AN-209 4;5.27   An: (Anna and Bobby waiting for video tape to rewind; Bobby is only 3 months old, so Anna is speaking for him) ' "Whèn is mine . . . móvie is còming back òn?", Bobby says.'
T1: 'Whèn is my móvie còming back òn?' vs. T2: 'Whèn is míne còming back òn?' (tries to correct, but still ungrammatical; N-NC)
Type 3, competing expanded/contracted synonymous phrases: 'my móvie' and 'míne'.
Form: mixed, internal phrase blend (my/mine), with repetition of 'is'.

AN-216 4;6.0   M: 'Lóok, hère's your núrsery rhỳme bòok.'
An: 'Yeah, **thàt was I lóoking fòr**.'
T1: 'thàt was what I was lóoking fòr.' vs.
T2: 'thàt's what I was lóoking fòr.' (NSC)
Type 4, competing internal phrasal organization: 'thàt's what Ì was' and 'thàt was what Ì was'.
Form: mixed, internal phrase blend (is/was) but 'what' and second 'was' omitted.

B-303   4;6.14   B: Lèt me sèe the bòx of the créam that **pùt**s . . . that
                        you pùt on my hànds. The kìnd that gòes on my
                        hánds.'

T1: 'that gòes on my hánds.' vs. T2: 'that you pùt on my hànds.'
(SC; p. 367, 408, 420, 475)

Type 2, competing perspectives: to 'put' something somewhere is to
'cause it to go' there.

Form: mislinking of verb, 'put' for 'go', but 3rd sg. present tense
marker remains in originally planned syntactic slot.

B-315   4;6.30   B: (putting away toys; doesn't want Daddy to help)
                        Ì'm gòing to dò thàt. Stóp! Ì'm **gòing thàt!** Ì'm dòing
                        thàt!'

T1: 'Ì'm dòing thàt.' vs. T2: 'Ì'm gòing to dò thàt.' (SC)

Type 4, competing internal phrasal organization: 'doing' and 'going
to do'.

Form: internal phrase blend (do/doing).

B-348   4;8.13   B: 'Ì wànt **ta some slèep in clòthes.'**

T1: 'Ì wànt to slèep in some clóthes.' or 'I wànt to hàve some sléep-
in clòthes.' vs. T2: 'Ì wànt some clòthes to slèep ìn.' or 'some
slèeping clòthes.' (targets unclear; NSC)

Type 5, competing external phrasal organization, placement of 'to
sleep in' (probably).

Form: unclear, but 'sleep in' in the error did not have compound
intonation.

B-355   4;8.21   B: (picking out shirt to go with pants)
                        'Mom, thát will **bè look gòod!'**

T1: 'thát will bè/ gòod.' vs. T2: 'thát will /lòok gòod.' (NSC)

Type 1, competing lexical choices: 'be' vs. 'look'.

Form: crossover, with deletion of phrasal stress on 'look'.

AN-253a 4;10.19 M: 'Whỳ dòesn't she jùst kèep her éyes shùt?'
                        An: 'Thàt's what **she [dúz]** . . . thàt's what she's dóin',
                        Mòm!'

T1: 'thàt's what she dóes.' vs. T2: 'thàt's what she's dóin' (doing).'
(SC; with word blend of 'does' [dʌz] and 'doin' [dú.wın]; AN-
253b=(38); p. 396, 435)

Type 4, competing internal phrasal organization: 'she does' vs. 'she's
doin'.

Form: internal phrase blend (does/doing).

AN-257 4;10.23   An: 'Momma, I wànt **you to shów** . . . I wànt <u>to shów you</u>
         sòmething.'
         T1: 'I wànt you to sée sòmething.' vs. T2: 'I wànt to shów you
         sòmething.' (SC)
         Type 2, competing perspectives: cause 'show' vs. result 'see'.
         Form: mislinking of verb, 'show' for 'see'.

B-449 5;1.14   B: (telling Mom about someone on his bus; Mom asked if
         the person lived in a certain house)
         'Yeah, **thát's gùy** . . . <u>thát gùy.</u>'
         T1: 'thát's the gùy.' vs. T2: 'thát gùy.' (SC)
         Type 4, competing internal phrasal organization: 'that guy' vs. 'that's
         the guy'.
         Form: internal phrase blend (that's/that).

AN-286 5;4.5   An: 'Thís is the **òne I nèw gòt**.'
         T1: 'Thís is the òne I jùst gòt.' vs. T2: 'Thís is the nèw one I gòt.'
         (NSC; p. 39)
         Type 1, competing lexical choices: 'new' vs. 'just'.
         Form: mislinking of modifiers, 'new' for 'just'.

OC-147 5;5.11   D: (a string broke on OB's toy, but it was easy to fix; Dad
         said jokingly) 'Oh nó, hòw are we gònna fíx ìt?'
         OB: 'It's **cínch**, it's <u>símple</u>, Dàddy.'
         T1: 'It's/ símple.' vs. T2: 'It's a /cínch.' (SC)
         Type 1, competing lexical choices: the idiom 'a cinch' vs. 'simple'.
         Form: crossover.

AN-298 5;7.19   An: 'Lóok! Ì have a **tòngue** . . . <u>cùt</u> tóo.'
         T1: 'Ì have a cùt tóo.' vs. T2: 'Ì have a cùt on my tòngue tóo'. (SC)
         Type 3, competing expanded/contracted synonymous phrases: 'cut'
         vs. 'cut on my tongue'.
         Form: mislinking of noun, 'tongue' for 'cut'.

AN-304 5;7.30   M: (sees Anna blowing air into a toy)
                     'Whàt are you dóing, Anna?'
                 An: '**I nèed blòwing úp.**'
                 M: 'What?'
                 An: 'I nèed to blòw it úp.'
T1: 'I nèed/ to blòw it úp.' vs. T2: 'It nèeds /blòwing úp.' (NSC)
Type 2, competing perspectives: active 'to blow it up' vs. stative
'blowing up'.
Form: internal phrase blend (blow/blowing), but could be crossover.

AN-313 5;9.10   M: 'Where did you fínd it?'
                 An: 'It **was just fàll** . . . ìt was just òn the gróund.'
T1: 'It was just/ òn the gróund.' vs. T2: 'It just /fèll on the gróund.'
(she didn't use the construction 'it was fallen' at the time; SC;
p. 419)
Type 2, competing perspectives: causal 'fell' vs. result '(be) on the
ground'.
Form: mixed, crossover, but with verb losing past tense morphology.

OC-169 5;10.0   OG: 'Bìting is **jùst as éating** . . . the sàme thìng as éating.'
T1: 'Biting is just like eating.' vs. T2: 'Bìting is the sàme thìng as
éating.' (SC)
Type 1, competing lexical choices: 'just like' vs. 'the same thing as'.
Form: mislinking of preposition, 'as' for 'like'.

50. *Errors of formulating the proposition.*

OC-33 2;10.9   OG: (telling her Mom that her Dad had gone to get her
                     another dress, since the first one he had gotten her was
                     torn) 'I gonna gèt . . . my Dàddy gonna gèt me
                     anòther dréss.'
(started to express that the wrong person went to get the dress; SC)

B-199 4;1.27   B: (had been playing at Dave's house, came home
                    bringing Dave, rang our doorbell, opened our door, and
                    announced) 'Dáve's hòme! . . . Dáve càme òver!'
(wrong proposition: 'come over' vs. 'be home'; SC)

B-413   4;11.10   B: 'Mom, can Ì play on your compúter?'
M: 'Wéll, "Frèsh Prínce" is gònna be òn in a fèw minutes.'
B: 'Ì wànna **wátch** ìt . . . Ì mean Ì wànna **plày on your compúter.**'
(intonation of first part indicated that what he meant was that he still wanted to play on the computer, even though a TV show he liked was on; wrong proposition; SC; p. 25)

B-501   5;5.12   M: (Bobby was carrying a purse)
'Is thàt your púrse, Bòbby?'
B: 'Nò, it's **my** . . . Ánna's.'
(as if he was going to deny 'purse' at first, then denied 'your'; 'my' for 'Anna's', but as part of wrong proposition; SC)

Author Index